W9-BYI-614

CONTENTS

LIST OF MAPS

ABOUT THE AUTHORS

Ron Emmons taught English in Africa and the Americas before moving to Thailand, where he now works as a freelance writer/photographer. He is the author and photographer of *Portrait of Thailand* and *Walks Along the Thames Path* (New Holland, UK), as well as writer of *Spiral Guide to the Dominican Republic* (Automobile Association, UK). Ron has also made major contributions to several other guide books, such as *Top Ten Bangkok* (Dorling Kindersley, UK), the *Rough Guide to Vietnam* and *National Geographic Traveler Vietnam.*

Jennifer Eveland spent part of her childhood in Singapore, has studied in Hong Kong, lived for a spell in Bangkok, and has traveled extensively throughout East and Southeast Asia. In addition to *Frommer's Singapore & Malaysia*, she has authored previous editions of *Frommer's Thailand.* In 1999 she returned to Singapore, where she has been based as a full-time freelance writer. She writes regularly for *The International Herald Tribune* and contributes travel, finance, and lifestyle stories to numerous local and international magazines, newspapers, and books.

Jen Lin-Liu is the author of *Serve the People: A Stir-Fried Journey Through China* (Houghton Mifflin) and the founder of the Beijing cooking school Black Sesame Kitchen. She was raised in southern California, graduated from Columbia University, and has lived in China since 2000, when she was awarded a Fulbright fellowship to study in Beijing. She has also written for *Newsweek, the New York Times, the Wall Street Journal, Travel + Leisure, Saveur,* and *Food & Wine.*

Daniel White is a British writer who has been published in major magazines and newspapers in Europe and Asia. He has written for publications such as the UK's *Guardian, Observer, Maxim,* and *Marie Claire.* He has also worked on guidebooks and political commentaries as both a writer and editor, and was editor-in-chief of the now defunct Absolute Phuket magazine in Thailand. He has traveled the corners of Southeast Asia by motorcycle and is currently working on a website project chronicling his trips on two wheels. Previously based in London and Paris, he has been based in Bangkok since 2002.

HOW TO CONTACT US

In researching this book, we discovered many wonderful places—hotels, restaurants, shops, and more. We're sure you'll find others. Please tell us about them, so we can share the information with your fellow travelers in upcoming editions. If you were disappointed with a recommendation, we'd love to know that, too. Please write to:

Frommer's Southeast Asia, 7th Edition
Wiley Publishing, Inc. • 111 River St. • Hoboken, NJ 07030-5774
frommersfeedback@wiley.com

ADVISORY & DISCLAIMER

Travel information can change quickly and unexpectedly, and we strongly advise you to confirm important details locally before traveling, including information on visas, health and safety, traffic and transport, accommodation, shopping and eating out. We also encourage you to stay alert while traveling and to remain aware of your surroundings. Avoid civil disturbances, and keep a close eye on cameras, purses, wallets and other valuables.

While we have endeavored to ensure that the information contained within this guide is accurate and up-to-date at the time of publication, we make no representations or warranties with respect to the accuracy or completeness of the contents of this work and specifically disclaim all warranties, including without limitation warranties of fitness for a particular purpose. We accept no responsibility or liability for any inaccuracy or errors or omissions, or for any inconvenience, loss, damage, costs or expenses of any nature whatsoever incurred or suffered by anyone as a result of any advice or information contained in this guide.

The inclusion of a company, organization or Website in this guide as a service provider and/or potential source of further information does not mean that we endorse them or the information they provide. Be aware that information provided through some Websites may be unreliable and can change without notice. Neither the publisher or author shall be liable for any damages arising herefrom.

FROMMER'S STAR RATINGS, ICONS & ABBREVIATIONS

Every hotel, restaurant, and attraction listing in this guide has been ranked for quality, value, service, amenities, and special features using a **star-rating system.** In country, state, and regional guides, we also rate towns and regions to help you narrow down your choices and budget your time accordingly. Hotels and restaurants are rated on a scale of zero (recommended) to three stars (exceptional). Attractions, shopping, nightlife, towns, and regions are rated according to the following scale: zero stars (recommended), one star (highly recommended), two stars (very highly recommended), and three stars (must-see).

In addition to the star-rating system, we also use **eight feature icons** that point you to the great deals, in-the-know advice, and unique experiences that separate travelers from tourists. Throughout the book, look for:

special finds—those places only insiders know about

fun facts—details that make travelers more informed and their trips more fun

kids—best bets for kids and advice for the whole family

special moments—those experiences that memories are made of

overrated—places or experiences not worth your time or money

insider tips—great ways to save time and money

great values—where to get the best deals

warning—traveler's advisories are usually in effect

The following **abbreviations** are used for credit cards:

AE	American Express	DISC	Discover	V	Visa
DC	Diners Club	MC	MasterCard		

FROMMERS.COM

Frommer's travel resources don't end with this guide. Frommer's website, **www.frommers. com**, has travel information on more than 4,000 destinations. We update features regularly, giving you access to the most current trip-planning information and the best airfare, lodging, and car-rental bargains. You can also listen to podcasts, connect with other Frommers. com members through our active-reader forums, share your travel photos, read blogs from guidebook editors and fellow travelers, and much more.

THE BEST OF SOUTHEAST ASIA

Southeast Asia offers a glimpse of the extraordinary, an explosion of colors, sounds, smells, textures, and life that will send you home with a wider vision of the human experience. In this chapter, we share our picks of the region's unrivaled highlights.

THE most UNFORGETTABLE TRAVEL EXPERIENCES

- **Making Merit** (Thailand & Laos): For centuries, the *sangha*, or monkhood, has lived off the donations of food and money from the community. The tradition continues to this day: Every morning, monks walk the streets around their temple not just to receive their daily food, but also to allow the giver to make merit. By giving food in this lifetime, Buddhists believe that they will not go hungry in the next lifetime. If you are interested in making merit this way, talk to your hotel's concierge. See chapters 3 and 4.

- **Staying in a Hill-Tribe Village near the China Border** (Laos): They still ask visitors, "Why do you come here, anyway?" in villages along the Nam Ha River in northern Laos. Thanks to the folks who run the Nam Ha Ecotourism Project, these vast tracts of pristine jungle won't be overrun by tourists anytime soon. Jungle trekking or river kayaking takes you through lush jungle terrain where you're likely to see monkeys and exotic birds. You'll arrive in villages where kayaks are still an oddity, and spend fun evenings around the fire communicating by charades or stick figures in a notebook. It's not about the villages being "pristine"; it's about the fact that your visit is part of a cultural exchange. See chapter 4.

- **Participating in a Baci Ceremony** (Laos): The Baci is a touching Lao ceremony used to say welcome or farewell and to honor achievements. Participants sit in a circle and receive group blessings, after which there is traditional dancing and *lao lao*, rice wine. It's a chance for the ultrafriendly Lao people to express their hospitality to you, their honored guest. See chapter 4.

o **Sailing the South China Sea** (Vietnam): Opportunities for watersports and sailing are many as you travel along Vietnam's coast. Most resorts have boats for rent, and Nha Trang is a good bet, as is Mui Ne Beach near Phan Thiet, which is becoming a very popular kite-surfing and windsurfing spot. See chapter 5.

o **Waiting for the Magic Hour at Angkor Wat** (Cambodia): You'll want to plan your day around it, and temple aficionados all have their favorite spots; but whether from a hillside overlooking a glowing temple facade or from the heights of the main temple itself, with the horizon framed by the famed ancient towers, be sure to see an Angkor sunset. Sunrise is equally worth the early-morning ride. See chapter 6.

o **Sipping a Singapore Sling in the Long Bar at the Raffles Hotel** (Singapore): Ah, the Long Bar, home of the Singapore Sling. Sheltered by long timber shutters that close out the tropical sun, the air cooled by lazy punkahs (and air-conditioning), you can sit back in an old rattan chair and have a saronged waitress serve you sticky alcoholic creations while you toss back a few dainty crab cakes. It's fun to imagine the days when Somerset Maugham, Rudyard Kipling, or Charlie Chaplin would be sitting at the bar. Come in the afternoon, before the tourist rush. See chapter 7.

o **Walking the Streets of Georgetown** (Penang, Malaysia): Evidence of former British colonization and early Chinese, Indian, and Arab immigration is apparent in many major cities in Malaysia, but Penang has a special charm. In some ways, the city still operates the way it did half a century ago. Life hums in these streets, and for anyone who has witnessed the homogenization of Singapore or the modernization of Kuala Lumpur, Penang is a charming reminder of what life might have been like in these old outposts. See chapter 8.

o **Sunsets at Hindu Temples** (Bali): The beauty of Bali's coastline is unmatched at two particular temples, both within easy reach where most tourists stay, in the south. At Uluwatu, a cliffside temple is decorated with mischievous monkeys while at Tanah Lot the crowds come at sunset to watch the sun dip under the Indian Ocean. Both are must-sees, even if you're not on your honeymoon. See chapter 9.

THE best TOWNS & VILLAGES

o **Chiang Saen** (Thailand): Crumbling 11th-century temples take you back to the birthplace of the Lanna Kingdom, one of Thailand's wealthiest and most influential. The nearby **Golden Triangle,** a notorious trade point for the international opium industry, has a state-of-the-art opium museum and riverside views of Laos, Thailand, and Myanmar. See chapter 3.

o **Luang Prabang** (Laos): This town, proclaimed a World Heritage Site by UNESCO for its glorious Buddhist temples, is also a charming retreat. Shady lanes are lined with French-style country homes that have been restored and converted to house cafes, galleries, shops, and some quaint guesthouses. The sunset over the Mekong is the perfect end to a day spent in Luang Prabang. See chapter 4.

o **Hoi An** (Vietnam): The small size of Hoi An belies its importance to Vietnam; it was once a major trading port, with canals leading right up to merchants' quarters for easy delivery of goods. The canals are now peaceful streets, but little else has changed. Almost every building in central Hoi An is a historic Vietnamese-, Japanese-, and Chinese-influenced residence or meeting hall. See chapter 5.

o **Battambang** (Cambodia): Until recently Battambang was often considered an undiscovered gem among those who ventured further afield than Siem Riep, Phnom Penh, and Sihanoukville. At present, Battambang is in that precarious period of grace where the town is free of tourist influx, but the comforts and facilities you might want to make it a comfortable stay are all in place. In the surrounding countryside are temples, Angkorian ruins, and rich scenery. This is the "rice bowl" of Cambodia, and if you are here when the paddies are green and the sun is shining, you'll witness a quintessential vision of Cambodian rural life. See chapter 6.

o **Ubud** (Bali): This is the cultural heart of Bali, bursting with art and greenery and some of the best food on the island—and recently made more famous with the movie *Eat, Pray, Love*. Even though it's dependent on tourism and is far from a typical Balinese village, you still get a sense of a real town, with real life going on around you. Ubud is the richest region in Bali for art production, and because of its central location, the town is the perfect base for exploring the rest of the island. See chapter 9.

THE best BEACHES

o **Chaweng Beach** (Ko Samui, Thailand): Chaweng is real fun in the sun, though it can get crowded in high season (Dec–Jan). The beach itself is gorgeous, with bungalows nestled in the trees just beyond the sand. Behind the beach lies a small town full of life, from wonderful Thai and seafood eateries to shopping and wild nightlife options. See chapter 3.

o **Mai Khao Beach** (Phuket, Thailand): Look to your right—nobody. Look to your left—nobody. Just 17km (11 miles) of deserted beachfront, the longest beach on Phuket, with only a handful of resorts dotting its shores. Not a place to come if you want to party, though, since the only excitement occurs during March, when hundreds of baby sea turtles are released into the ocean. See chapter 3.

o **Mui Ne Beach** (Phan Thiet, Vietnam): Just a few hours from Ho Chi Minh City (Saigon), Mui Ne is the latest getaway in Vietnam. Oceanside development is in full swing here, and there are some great boutique resorts along the golden sands of Mui Ne Beach. Golfers will enjoy the spectacular SeaLinks golf course (the first links course in Vietnam), the seafood here is good, and the nearby town of Phan Thiet itself is an interesting little fishing port worth a wander. There are some great day trips to enormous remote dunes and smaller fishing villages. See chapter 5.

o **Tanjung Rhu** (Langkawi, Malaysia): This huge, secluded cove has one of the longest stretches of private beach ever. Wide with soft sand, the beach has cooling shady spots provided by palm trees overhead, and beautiful deep-blue waters for good swimming. Best of all, there's only one resort here (and the beach is kept picture-perfect), so you won't have to elbow for space or suffer jet skis. See chapter 8.

o **Lombok** (off the coast of Bali, Indonesia): The pure white-sand beaches of Lombok, with clear aqua-blue water lapping against them, are sometimes so private that you can have one all to yourself. And Lombok is just a short hop from neighboring Bali. See chapter 9.

THE best OUTDOOR ADVENTURES

o **Exploring Phang Nga Bay** (Thailand): From the island of Phuket, sea-canoe operators guide visitors through caves to lagoons hidden deep inside the craggy island rocks of Phang-Nga Bay. Outside, the islands thrust up to the sky, their jagged edges laced with scattered trees. Lie flat in your canoe to slip through the small cave openings, inside which you'll find magnificent chambers believed to have once hidden pirate operations. See chapter 3.

o **Caving & Kayaking in Vang Vieng** (Laos): Countless caves and caverns are hidden in the magnificent mountains surrounding Vang Vieng, a small village along the Nam Song River. Some of them are well known and some are barely on the map. Kayak tours on the Nam Song include some fun caves that you'll swim into; you can test your mettle on natural mudslides. Spend your days exploring and evenings talking about it over drinks in this laid-back little backpacker town. See chapter 4.

o **Sea Kayaking in Halong Bay** (Vietnam): The more than 3,000 arresting limestone karst formations rising out of Halong Bay's peaceful blue-green waters provide a perfect place for paddling. Moving among them, you'll pass in and among intriguing grottoes and caverns. Nights are spent on the deck of a mother ship. See chapter 5.

o **Trekking to Hill-Tribe Villages in Sapa** (Vietnam): Dressed in elaborate costumes of leggings, tunics, and headdresses, Hmong and Yao people (among other groups) gather to sell their weavings, fine dyed clothing, or crude but intricate metalwork in the central market. Markets at nearby Bac Ha and Can Cau are even more colorful. A trip to Sapa means that the hill tribes come to you, but don't limit your trip to the town; be sure to get off into the countryside and trek in the shadow of Fansipan, the highest mountain in Vietnam. Among lush terraced rice fields, you can visit many villages on even the shortest trek and experience different hill-tribe traditions and cultures. See chapter 5.

o **Jungle Trekking in Taman Negara** (Malaysia): With suitable options for all budgets, levels of comfort, and desired adventure, Malaysia's largest national park opens the wonders of primary rainforest and the creatures that dwell in it to everyone. From the canopy, walk high atop the forest on night watches for nocturnal life. This adventure is as stunning as it is informative. See chapter 8.

o **Wreck and Wall Diving** (Bali): Bali offers two fascinating dive areas that are unmatched in the region. At Tulamben, you can float around the USS *Liberty*, which sank during World War II, and Menjangan, on the north coast, boasts beautiful wall diving and coral. You're likely to see turtles and possibly even whale sharks, fish the size of school buses. See chapter 9.

THE best RELIGIOUS & HISTORICAL SITES

o **Grand Palace & Wat Phra Kaeo** (Bangkok, Thailand): These two places are number one on every travel itinerary to Bangkok, and rightly so. The palace is indeed grand, with a mixture of traditional Thai and European Victorian architecture. Wat Phra Kaeo, the royal temple that houses Thailand's revered and mysterious Emerald Buddha, is a small city in itself. See chapter 3.

o **Ayutthaya** (north of Bangkok, Thailand): This was the thriving capital of Siam that the first Europeans saw when they visited amazing Thailand. Ruling a rich and powerful kingdom of more than a million inhabitants, the monarchy supported the arts, especially literature. As the city grew, international trade was encouraged. Today, all that remains are brick remnants of a grand palace and many temples that were destroyed during an earthquake and sacked during the Burmese invasion. It's best to hire a guide who can walk you through. See chapter 3.

- **Sukhothai** (central Thailand): Founded in the 13th century, Sukhothai ("Dawn of Happiness") was the capital of the first unified state in what is today Thailand. Its borders grew to include parts of Burma to the west and extended as far as Luang Prabang to the east. Now a UNESCO World Heritage Site, the Sukhothai Historical Park encompasses the ruins of the former royal palace as well as more than 20 temples. Best enjoyed from the seat of a bicycle and in combination with a trip to nearby Sri Satchanalai. See chapter 3.

- **Wat Xieng Thong** (Luang Prabang, Laos): The glittering Xieng Thong, built in 1560, sits grandly on a peninsula jutting into the Mekong River. The facades of two of its buildings are covered by glittering glass mosaics; another building contains an ornate chariot with the heads of seven dragons and the remains of a king. This temple was spared any damage during the sacking of the city in 1887 by Chinese marauders. This was because their leader, Deo Van Tri, had studied here as a monk in his early life. The peace lives on. See chapter 4.

- **Plain of Jars** (Xieng Khouang, Laos): How did hundreds of huge stone urns, some measuring 2.7m tall (8¾ ft.), come to be placed on a few meadows in northern Laos? No one really knows, and that's what's fun here. The most prevalent explanation is that the urns were made by prehistoric peoples in the area about 2,000 years ago to be used as sarcophagi, but there's lots of room for conjecture. See chapter 4.

- **Citadel** (Hue, Vietnam): Containing the Imperial City and Forbidden Purple City, this atmospheric walled compound features some impressive remnants of Vietnam's former capital. Don't miss the Thai Hoa Palace or the Mieu Temple with its Nine Dynastic Urns, and allow time for a trip up the Perfume River to the royal mausoleums. See chapter 5.

- **Cao Dai Holy See Temple** (Tay Ninh, northwest of Ho Chi Minh City, Vietnam): This is the spiritual home base of the Cao Dai religion, a faith characterized by philosophical inclusion and influence gathered from all beliefs, including the world's great scientists and humanitarians. Its headquarters is like a fantasyland of colored mosaic and elaborate painting. Followers are dressed in colorful robes during the picturesque daily services. It's quite unique. See chapter 5.

- **Angkor Wat** (Cambodia): One of the world's man-made wonders, Angkor Wat is the Disneyland of temples in Asia. This ancient city was known to the Western world only in myth until it was rediscovered and hacked free of jungle overgrowth in the late 1800s. The magnificent temples are arrayed over a 97-sq.-km (37-sq.-mile) compound that dates from the rise and fall of the mighty Angkor civilization (A.D. 802–1295). See chapter 6.

- **Thian Hock Keng Temple** (Singapore): One of Singapore's oldest Chinese temples, it is a fascinating testimony to Chinese Buddhism combined with traditional Confucian beliefs and natural Taoist principles. See chapter 7.

- **Jamek Mosque** (Kuala Lumpur, Malaysia): Built at the central point of the city, this is one of the oldest mosques in Kuala Lumpur. It is the heart of Malay Islam. See chapter 8.

- **Jalan Tokong** (Melaka, Malaysia): This street, in the historic heart of the city, has a Malay mosque, a Chinese temple, and a Hindu temple living peacefully side by side—the perfect example of how the many foreign religions that came to Southeast Asia shaped its communities and learned to coexist in harmony. See chapter 8.

- **Uluwatu** (Bali): This dramatic cliffside temple overlooks the crashing waves of Bali's southern beaches. See chapter 9.

○ **Besakih Temple** (Bali): Built in homage to Gunung Agung, the island's feisty, smoke-belching creator, the Besakih Temple does justice to the awe and grandeur of the Balinese creation myths surrounding the volcano. The spires of individual family shrines and temples are something like Chinese pagodas, and the place is always abuzz with local worshipers. You're likely to get pulled into a ceremony here. See chapter 9.

THE best MUSEUMS

○ **National Museum** (Bangkok, Thailand): From prehistory to recent events, this museum—the former palace of the brother of King Rama I—gives an excellent overview of Thai history and culture through the ages. See chapter 3.

○ **War Remnants Museum** (Ho Chi Minh City, Vietnam): Of the many museums in Vietnam dedicated to the country's war-torn past, this is the hardest hitting. It's impossible to look at the weaponry, stark photography of war scenes, and mock-ups of prisons without being deeply moved. See chapter 5.

○ **Cham Museum** (Danang, Vietnam): This open-air colonial structure houses the largest collection of Cham sculpture in the world. Not only are relics of this ancient Hindu-inspired culture rare, but the religious artwork itself—more than 300 pieces of sandstone—is also voluptuous, captivating, and intense. See chapter 5.

○ **National Museum** (Phnom Penh, Cambodia): Don't miss this repository for the statues and relief sculpture that have been recovered from the Angkor temples and other ancient sites throughout Cambodia. See chapter 6.

○ **Tuol Sleng, Museum of Genocide** (Phnom Penh, Cambodia): Be warned that a visit here can be distressing, but also important if you want to understand modern Cambodia. From 1975 to 1979, Tuol Sleng was Cambodia's most important interrogation facility, at a time when the entire country had been turned into one vast concentration camp. It is a chilling reminder of what human beings can be capable of. See chapter 6.

○ **Peranakan Museum** (Singapore): This brand-new display is the only museum in the world solely devoted to Peranakan culture, a subculture of intermarriage that is unique to Southeast Asia. See chapter 7.

THE best FESTIVALS & CELEBRATIONS

○ **Songkran** (Thailand): Every year in spring, Thais welcome the traditional new year. Because Songkran falls in the middle of the hottest season in an already hot country, how do you think people celebrate? Every Thai heads out into the streets with water guns and buckets of ice water—plus handfuls of talcum powder, just to add to the mess—and spends the next 3 days soaking one another—and *you*. Foreigners are especially favorite targets. See chapter 3.

○ **Dragon Boat Races** (Laos): Celebrating the end of Buddhist Lent, dragon boat races are held in every riverside town in Laos (and that's most towns, really). See chapter 4.

○ **That Luang Festival** (Vientiane, Laos): In early November, thousands of Buddhist followers from all over the country, and even a few neighboring countries, converge on the spectacular That Luang temple in Vientiane. See chapter 4.

- **Chinese New Year** (Singapore): If you're in Southeast Asia around the end of January or the beginning of February, hop up to Hong Kong or down to Singapore for the festivities. See chapter 7.
- **Tet** (Vietnam): Vietnam's version of Chinese New Year in late January or early February is largely a family affair, though you'll see colorful parades and catch everyone in high spirits. See chapter 5.
- **Thaipusam** (Singapore & Malaysia): Around the end of January and the beginning of February, Hindus celebrate Thaipusam. Men give thanks for prayers answered by carrying *kavadi,* huge steel racks attached to their bodies with skewers piercing the skin. See chapters 7 and 8.

THE best RESORTS & LUXURY HOTELS

- **The Mandarin Oriental, Bangkok** (Bangkok, Thailand): The original address in Thailand, the Mandarin Oriental has seen modernization detract from its charms of yesterday, but there's still an aura of grandeur here. See p. 51.
- **JW Marriott Phuket Resort & Spa** (Phuket, Thailand): One of the most relaxing resorts in Thailand, the JW Marriott is set on a secluded 17km (11-mile) stretch of white-sand beach far from the debauchery and din of Patong. An ideal getaway. See p. 133.
- **Four Seasons Resort Chiang Mai** (Chiang Mai, Thailand): Set in the hills of the Mae Rim Valley north of Chiang Mai, luxurious Lanna-style pavilions overlook working terraced rice paddies. Each suite has its own *sala* (covered porch or gazebo) from which to admire the grounds and surrounding hills. See p. 159.
- **La Résidence Phou Vao** (Luang Prabang, Laos): Lording it over the town in boutique luxury, the gardens and large suites of the Phou Vao (formerly the Pansea) are comfortable, and the atmosphere is done to a T. This is typical of other Orient Express properties in the region. See p. 215.
- **Settha Palace Hotel** (Vientiane, Laos): Once the address of note for visitors to the French colony, the Settha Palace only recently returned from obscurity and is now one of the finest hotels in the region. It's a nice marriage of colonial elegance and modern comfort. See p. 198.
- **Sofitel Metropole Hanoi** (Hanoi, Vietnam): The history of the Metropole, one of the country's premier grande dames, tells the history of the last tumultuous century in Vietnam. Though everything is luxurious and comfortable and you're in a prime downtown location, you'll certainly feel like you've walked into old Indochina. See p. 256.
- **Six Senses Ninh Van Bay** (Nha Trang, Vietnam): Earth-toned private villas are secreted away in a secluded cove near Nha Trang that can be reached only by boat. Set into the forested beach or rocky coast, and each with a private pool, Six Senses' villas set a high benchmark by which to measure Vietnam's luxury getaways. See p. 312.
- **Sofitel Dalat Palace** (Dalat, Vietnam): It's real old-world opulence in the king's former palace in Vietnam's central highlands. Private spaces are decorated in a cool colonial baroque style, while service is, in short, kingly. See p. 322.
- **The Nam Hai** (Hoi An, Vietnam): The first glimpse of the infinity pools disappearing into the ocean horizon will leave you breathless. This stylish resort, perched on

a stretch of private beach, is an absolute must for those seeking a romantic getaway or a pampered, luxurious vacation. See p. 296.

- **Caravelle** (Ho Chi Minh City, Vietnam): A former haunt of wartime correspondents, the Caravelle has been revamped several times and now offers the most comfortable and convenient base in the heart of this bustling city. See p. 339.

- **Amansara** (Siem Reap, Cambodia): If there's one place to splurge on a jaunt through Southeast Asia, this is the one. Built around former King Sihanouk's private guesthouse, the Amansara is flawless in detail and service, making it a perfect base of operations for exploring the temples of Angkor. See p. 391.

- **Raffles Hotel** (Singapore): For old-world opulence, Raffles is second to none. This is a pure fantasy of the days when tigers still lurked around the perimeters. See p. 429.

- **Shangri-La Hotel** (Singapore): The Shang is a meticulously landscaped tropical oasis, with lush garden views from every angle. Three individual wings give you a choice of accommodations styles: urban contemporary, natural resort, and Asian opulence. See p. 441.

- **Hilton Kuala Lumpur** (Kuala Lumpur, Malaysia): The rooms feel like suites, decorated in slickety-slick contempo style with the latest entertainment and IT built in—even in the bathrooms. See p. 527.

- **Four Seasons Langkawi** (Langkawi, Malaysia): This resort is an exotic Moorish paradise on the most gorgeous beach in Malaysia. Rooms and public areas drip with the ambience of the *Arabian Nights*. Three words: To. Die. For. See p. 559.

- **Four Seasons Resort at Jimbaran Bay** (Jimbaran, Bali): With its individual bungalows and plunge pools overlooking the blue sea and its famous Four Seasons pampering, this is one of the great hotels in the world. See p. 599.

- **COMO Shambhala** (Ubud, Bali): This resort is so self-confident that it calls itself "The Estate"—and it's a title that's well earned. With 41 hectares (100 acres) of sculpted grounds and wild jungle, top-notch detox and wellness programs steered by qualified specialists, and elegant rooms with antique touches, you may never want to leave. See p. 607.

- **Alila Villas Soori** (Tabanan, Bali): Up the coast from busy and crowded Seminyak, these pristine villas sit on a black-sand beach framed by palm trees. Private plunge pools, movies and music on demand via Apple TV, and delicious yet healthful food make this a must if you're willing to splurge. See p. 591.

THE best HOTEL BARGAINS

- **Majestic Grande** (Bangkok, Thailand): The Majestic could rightly be called either a small-scale luxury hotel or a bloated boutique hotel. It's in a prime spot off bustling Sukhumvit, with rooms going for half the price of the large chains. See p. 59.

- **Baan Orapin** (Chiang Mai, Thailand): If you're going to travel on a budget, do it with style—Baan Orapin exudes an unhurried, colonial-era charm. Rooms are equipped with sturdy teakwood furnishings and four-poster beds, and the city's best bars and restaurants are on the riverfront a few steps away. See p. 156.

- **Day Inn Hotel** (Vientiane, Laos): There's a comfortable, laid-back feel here, and this many long-stay visitors can't be wrong. You'll find rooms for $32. See p. 200.

- **Madam Cuc** (Ho Chi Minh City, Vietnam): Not especially luxurious, but super friendly and helpful. They'll help you plan your sightseeing and you'll leave feeling like one of the family. See p. 344.

- **Goldiana** (Phnom Penh, Cambodia): It's no-frills, but friendly and cheap, set in a quiet neighborhood south of the town center. The hotel is popular with long-staying visitors and NGO workers. See p. 378.

- **Hangout@Mt Emily** (Singapore): Cheap doesn't have to be drab. Hangout has vibrantly colored rooms, clean facilities, a hip location not far from public transportation, and lots of facilities for travelers on a budget, including a very helpful staff.

- **Piccolo Hotel Kuala Lumpur** (Malaysia): Don't pay through the nose for a pool you'll never swim in or a fitness center you'll ignore. This moderately priced hotel has forgone fancy facilities to provide high-quality rooms in a fantastic location, in the heart of the city's fashionable Jalan Bukit Bintang. See p. 529.

- **Heeren House** (Melaka, Malaysia): Bargain or no bargain, this boutique hotel in the heart of the old city is the place to stay in Melaka if you want to really get a feel for the local atmosphere. See p. 540.

- **Telang Usan Hotel** (Kuching, Malaysia): An informal place, Telang Usan is homey and quaint, and within walking distance of many major attractions in Kuching. See p. 566.

- **Alila Manggis & Alila Ubud** (Bali): These twin resorts have nearly all the amenities of luxury properties but at rates ranging from $150 to $200 per night. You'll have to put up with slightly cramped rooms, but in return you'll get beautiful common areas, stellar service, excellent food, and expert spa treatments. And just in case you don't want to sit by the beautiful infinity pool at the Ubud property, the Alila offers a daily activity schedule with cooking classes, treks, and cultural lessons. See p. 619 and p. 608.

THE best LOCAL DINING EXPERIENCES

- **Street Food** (Bangkok, Thailand): On every street, down every alley, you'll find someone setting up a cart with an umbrella. Noodles, salads, and satay are favorites, and some hawkers set up tables and stools on the sidewalk for you to take a load off. See chapter 3.

- **Kua Lao** (Vientiane, Laos): Kua Lao serves traditional Lao cuisine in a restored colonial—it's the premier Lao restaurant in the country. The extensive menu goes on for pages. See p. 202.

- **Pho** (Vietnam): Don't leave the country without sampling one, if not many, bowls of this delicate noodle soup, made with thin rice noodles, chicken (*ga*) or beef (*bo*), a nutritious broth and several fresh accompaniments, according to the chef's whim or local flavor. See chapter 5.

- **Ngon Restaurant** (Ho Chi Minh City & Hanoi, Vietnam): It's loud and busy, but diners have their choice of food from the many authentic street stalls that line the central courtyard. Locals eat here; and though there is an English menu, go with a Vietnamese friend or ask for a recommendation from the friendly (but always busy) staff. See p. 349.

- **Hawker Centers** (Singapore): Think of them as shopping malls for food—great food. Walk around and select anything you want as it's prepared right before your eyes. See chapter 7.

- **Gurney Drive Food Stalls** (Penang, Malaysia): Penang is king for offering a variety of Asian cuisines, from Chinese to Malay, Indian, and everything else in between. See p. 552.

o **Warungs** (Bali): The Balinese equivalent of the greasy-spoon diner in America, *warungs* can be found on every street corner. The food can be authentic, delicious, and cheap. See chapter 9.

THE best MARKETS

o **Chatuchak Weekend Market** (Bangkok, Thailand): You can easily get lost and certainly spend hours wandering this labyrinth. Don't buy anything until you spend at least a half-day wandering down the endless aisles eyeballing the multitude of merchandise available. See chapter 3.

o **Night Bazaar** (Chiang Mai, Thailand): Most of those gorgeous handicrafts you find all over Thailand are made in the north, and at Chiang Mai's sprawling Night Bazaar, you'll find the widest selection and best quality. See chapter 3.

o **Morning Market** (Vientiane, Laos): Laos's famous market is three huge buildings with traditional tiered roofs. Silver handicrafts, fabrics, jewelry, electronics, books, and more occupy each building's several floors. The proprietors are friendly, gentle bargainers. See chapter 4.

o **Central Market** (Hoi An, Vietnam): On the banks of the busy Perfume River lies this entire city block of narrow, roofed aisles. Products of every description are for sale inside: handicrafts, household items, and services such as facials and massages. On the outskirts, an entire warehouse is devoted to silk and silk tailoring. See chapter 5.

o **Central Market** (Phnom Penh, Cambodia): This is where it all happens in Phnom Penh. The main building is a massive Art Deco rotunda with wings extending in all directions. It's an anthill of activity on any given day, and you can get some interesting bargains and unique finds. See chapter 6.

o **Arab Street** (Singapore): Sure, Singapore is a shopper's paradise, but it needs more places like Arab Street, where small shops lining the street sell everything from textiles to handicrafts. Bargaining is welcome. See chapter 7.

o **Central Market** (Kuala Lumpur, Malaysia): This is one-stop shopping for all the rich arts and handicrafts Malaysia produces—and it's air-conditioned, too. See chapter 8.

THE best SHOPPING BARGAINS

o **Antiques** (Thailand): Before you head out on vacation, visit some Asian galleries in your home country and take a look at the prices of the items you like. Once you're here, you'll be amazed at how little these things really cost. Most places will be glad to pack and ship purchases for you, and you'll still come out ahead. See chapter 3.

o **Tailored Silk Suits** (Thailand; also Hanoi, Hoi An, and Ho Chi Minh City, Vietnam): For a fraction of what you'd pay at home, you can have a lined silk (or wool) suit tailored in a day or less, including a fitting or two. Bring pictures of your favorite designer outfits for a clever copy, and pick up an empty suitcase or two for the trip home. See chapters 3 and 5.

everything has a price: HAGGLING

Prices are never marked in the small shops and at street vendors in Southeast Asia. You must bargain. The most important thing to remember when bargaining is to keep a friendly, good-natured banter between you and the seller. Before you start out, it's good to have some idea of how much your purchase is worth, to give you a base point for negotiation. A simple "How much?" is the place to start, to which the vendor will reply with the top price. Check at a few vendors before negotiating, and never accept the first price. Try a smile and ask, "Is that your best price?" Vendors will laughingly ask for your counteroffer. Knock the price down about 50%—they'll look shocked, but it's a starting point for bidding. Just remember to smile and be friendly, and remain willing to walk away (or fake it). *Caveat:* If it's a larger, more expensive item, don't get into major bargaining unless you're serious about buying. If the shopkeeper agrees on what you say you're willing to pay, it's considered rude not to make the purchase.

- **Hand-Woven Textiles** (Laos): The Laos hand-weave textured fabrics piece by piece on primitive wooden looms. Such painstaking work costs more than a few dollars, but, ranging from sophisticated silk to gaily colored ethnic prints, the designs are pure art and uniquely Laotian. See chapter 4.
- **Silver or Lacquer Handicrafts** (Vietnam): The workmanship is tops and the prices are low throughout Vietnam, particularly for lacquerware. Bargain hard and make sure that the silver is genuine. See chapter 5.
- **Silver Filigree Jewelry** (Malaysia): Silver is worked into detailed filigree jewelry designs to make brooches, necklaces, bracelets, and other fine jewelry. See chapter 8.
- **Pewter** (Malaysia). Malaysia is the home of Selangor Pewter, one of the largest pewter manufacturers in the world. Its many showrooms have all sorts of items to choose from. See chapter 8.
- **Fabric & Woodcarvings** (Bali): Even with the "rich man's tax" for tourists in Bali, just about anything you buy on the island is a bargain compared with the same stuff back home. Commissioned fabric and woodcarvings are a particularly good deal. See chapter 9.

THE hottest NIGHTLIFE

- **Patpong** (Bangkok, Thailand): Yes, *that* Patpong. If go-go bars and sex shows aren't your style, you'll still find plenty to do. After you're finished shopping in the crowded Night Market, you'll see plenty of restaurants, pubs, and discos that cater to folks who prefer more traditional nightlife. See chapter 3.
- **Ho Chi Minh City** (Vietnam): From the tawdry to the socialite scene, you'll find it in Ho Chi Minh City (Saigon). Most evenings begin with an elegant (but reasonably priced) French or Vietnamese dinner; then it's barhopping time in the compact downtown, mingling with trendy locals and fun-loving expats. See chapter 5.
- **Singapore:** Nightlife is becoming increasingly sophisticated in Singapore, where locals have more money for recreation and fun. Take the time to choose the place that suits your personality. See chapter 7.

WITHDRAWN

- **Bangsar** (near Kuala Lumpur, Malaysia): Folks in Kuala Lumpur know to go to Bangsar for nighttime excitement. A couple of blocks of concentrated restaurants, cafes, discos, pubs, and wine bars will tickle any fancy. See chapter 8.
- **Seminyak** (Bali): Certain nightclubs such as Hu'u Bar and Cocoon don't even get going until 2am, but there are plenty of options including Living Room and Sea Circus to keep you busy until then. See chapter 9.

INTRODUCING SOUTHEAST ASIA

While the rest of the world's continents fit into nice, tidy compartments, the nations that make up Southeast Asia—Cambodia, Indonesia, Laos, Malaysia, Singapore, Thailand, and Vietnam—often have more differences than similarities. Diverse geographical features, histories, religious and cultural heritages, economies, and politics across the region mean that the shortest journey offers cross-cultural comparison and new perspective.

Safety is a primary concern for travelers these days, and while it is important to stay updated on internal issues in any given country and to steer clear of any hot spots, the adventurous tourist paths through this vibrant region are ripe for exploration and replete with mystery, beauty, and ancient culture and wisdom.

THE REGION TODAY

Geographically, Southeast Asia is diverse and stunning. The lush tropical rainforests of peninsular Malaysia and Borneo are some of the oldest in the world. Beautiful islands and beaches are many, including large resort areas such as Thailand's Phuket or Indonesia's Bali, plus countless other gorgeous isles, atolls, and sandy strips that are relatively unexploited. Divers and snorkelers flock from around the world for stunning coral reefs bursting with colorful life in Thailand, Malaysia, and Indonesia. You can find adventures in the wild while jungle trekking, sea and river kayaking, or visiting ethnic villages and sacred peaks.

Southeast Asia is also a cultural melting pot, a crossroads of influences from China, south Asia, and Tibet. Consider the Sri Lankans, who transplanted Theravada Buddhism, with its serene and orthodox ways, from Myanmar to Thailand and Laos. Or the Indian traders, who brought ancient Hinduism to Cambodia, influencing the architecture of the magical city of Angkor. Or the Hindus who settled on Bali, mixing their dogma with local animism to create a completely unique sect. Meanwhile, seafaring Arab merchants imported Islam to coastal areas of Malaysia and Indonesia, adding another interesting facet to the region. In Vietnam, the only Southeast Asian nation to fall directly under the control of past Chinese empires, China's cultural influences are still strong. And, on top of that, Europeans from the late 1400s onward imported Western culture to cities such as Hong Kong, Singapore, Penang, and Melaka; the European colonial imprint is still visible in the architecture and cuisine of most countries in the region. Crossing an international border in Southeast Asia is stepping into another world.

Economic and political developments have changed the face of tourism in the region. While cosmopolitan stops such as Singapore, Kuala Lumpur, and Bangkok guarantee the best luxury hotels, finest dining, and most refined cultural attractions, up-and-coming cities such as Hanoi, Ho Chi Minh City (Saigon), and Chiang Mai promise cultural curiosities around every street corner as they struggle to balance traditional customs with modern development. Thailand's 3 decades of tourism development have created very familiar facilities for travelers, for example, but those looking for a more down-and-dirty experience can head off to nearby Cambodia or Laos, countries still off the beaten path of most tourist agendas. For every luxurious Bali, there's a laid-back Tioman Island (Malaysia). For every busy Bangkok, there's a charming Luang Prabang (Laos).

It is important, of course, to talk about those Southeast Asian nations that have political or safety concerns, and the sections that follow discuss political turmoil in more detail. Steer clear of any sectarian or political tension, and know that the relative stability of many countries in Southeast Asia is rather short-lived; flash political upheavals are not uncommon. Refer to your country's overseas travel bureau or to the U.S. State Department (for a current comprehensive list of warnings by country click "more" under Travel Warnings at www.travel.state.gov) to learn about current travel warnings in the area.

Thailand

Each year, Thailand sees more international travelers than any of its neighbors, though recently political instability and unfavorable exchange rates have made some visitors think twice before booking their trip. The country attracts all types—young professionals on hiatus, naive tourists prowling for that "One Night in Bangkok," and soul-searchers hanging around for the Buddhist dharma and Asian hospitality. Many trips to Southeast Asia either start here or end up here, and it is a good orientation.

Travelers usually arrive in **Bangkok,** staying for a few days to take in the city's bizarre mix of royal palaces and skyscrapers, pious monks amid rush-hour commuters, and sidewalk noodle vendors serving bankers in suits. That's not to mention the city's nightlife, with that seedy element that made the city infamous. Heading south, find the legendary beaches and resorts of **Phuket** island; **Ko Samui,** in the Gulf of Thailand, is a comparable alternative. Another attraction, the northern hills around **Chiang Mai,** presents a world of adventure trekking and tribal culture along well worn—but well worth-it—travel paths. Throughout the country, you'll have opportunities for **outdoor adventure** and **extreme sports,** organized by very professional firms that you can count on for safety and reliability.

And at the end of the day, there's that unbeatable taste of **Thai cuisine**—tangy soups, hearty coconut curries, and the freshest seafood.

Laos

In the past decade Laos has also put itself very firmly on the tourist map. Having said that, here is a country where foreigners are still greeted as gracious guests. It is also a country of immense natural beauty. The towns outside the capital are laid-back places where life goes on in much the same way it always has. Buddhism sets the pace and people are genuinely welcoming.

Some people feared that Laos would follow Thailand's accelerated development model, that the ethnic villages in the north would be turned into safari parks and the country's beautiful temples transformed into theme attractions. While development has been a mixed bag, there has been real awareness concerning the preservation of both culture and environment and that has paid off. The most obvious example of the results of this awareness is the city of **Luang Prabang**—a place of enduring grace.

For a capital city, **Vientiane** is still comparatively parochial. Development here is rampant compared to the rest of Laos, but nothing in comparison to that of equivalent capital cities in surrounding countries, including Phnom Penh and Hanoi. The jewel in the crown remains **Luang Prabang,** UNESCO World Heritage Site, a paradise of gorgeous Buddhist temples set amid shady streets lining the Mekong and Nam Khan rivers. If you have time, **Xieng Khouang,** east of Vientiane, is the home of Southeast Asia's Stonehenge, the **Plain of Jars,** huge mysterious stone monoliths that have somehow survived carpet bombing and the ravages of war. **Ecotourism** is growing rapidly, and some new and interesting avenues into the Lao jungle and rivers connect remote ethnic villages (especially in the north).

Vietnam

If the thought of Vietnam stirs flashbacks of televised war coverage or scenes from dark movies, think again. One of the fastest-growing destinations in the region also happens to be one of the most beautiful, friendliest, and safest places to travel.

Vietnam's major destinations fall in a line, and most visitors choose to travel from north to south, starting in Hanoi and ending in Ho Chi Minh City (Saigon), or vice versa. Convenient tourist buses connect the main coastal stops, and there are increasing options for individual travelers as well.

In the south, **Ho Chi Minh City,** or **Saigon,** is the gateway to the beautiful **Mekong Delta** region. Heading north, you'll pass through **Dalat,** a hill station in the cool mountains, and then on to **Mui Ne** or **Nha Trang,** the country's premier beach resorts. Farther north, **Hoi An** is one of the region's most charming towns and a picturesque labyrinth of cobblestone streets, historic buildings, and lots of shopping. Still farther, the former capital city at **Hue** is filled with many architectural gems of Chinese and European influence. The cultural amalgam is best defined in **Hanoi,** where Vietnamese, French, and Chinese cultures collide. From here, head east to see gorgeous **Halong Bay,** with hundreds of craggy rock formations jutting straight up from the sea; or travel to the far north to **Sapa,** where you visit Vietnam's hill-tribe people in the mountains that divide northern Vietnam from China.

Cambodia

In the last 30 years of the 20th century, Cambodia was one long story of tragedy, war, unrest, and strife. Those who did go faced a country in turmoil and it was not for the fainthearted. In recent times it has transformed, and, although still desperately poor and potentially unstable, the country is now firmly on the map in terms of tourism and investment of all sorts. Angkor Wat is Asia's premier cultural attraction bar none. The magnificent temple ruins of the mighty Angkor civilization of A.D. 800 to 1200 now draw immense crowds, and the nearby town of Siem Reap has become an incongruous oasis of five-star luxury in an often broken and barren land.

There is a dreadful legacy, but Cambodia is now looking to the future. The country is now enjoying a protracted period of peace not seen in many years. **Phnom Penh,** the capital, and **Siem Reap** are modern and even bustling while the country as a whole is safe. The countryside is opening up as the roads are surfaced and infrastructure improves. Provincial Cambodia is no longer just an adventure destination as it was only a few years ago. Many still limit their trip in Cambodia to the temples of Angkor, however. Convenient direct flights from the larger cities throughout the region simplify the process.

It's important to remember that parts of the country are still littered with UXO, unexploded ordnance, including dormant bombs and land mines. In the rural areas near the Thai border particularly, it's important to stay on well worn trails and use a guide. After peaceful elections in 2003 and 2008, the situation in Phnom Penh is stable, but visitors should stay informed before going, as the country has a history of flash political upheaval.

Singapore

All of Southeast Asia's cultures seem to converge on Singapore, making it perhaps one of the best places to begin your exploration of the region. Excellent **museums** explore Asian civilizations, Southeast Asian art, and even World War II history. The city's hundreds of restaurants provide a wealth of choices in terms of **cuisine,** offering a glimpse of many regional specialties in one stop. And some of the best regional **fine arts, crafts,** and **antiques** end up in Singapore showrooms.

Singapore gets trashed regularly by complaints that it is too Western, too modern, too sanitary—too Disneyland. Walk the streets of **Chinatown, Little India,** and the Malay Muslim area at **Kampong Glam,** and you can see where the buildings have been renovated and many former inhabitants have retired from traditional crafts. But some of these places have a few secrets left that are very rewarding if you are observant. Over the past 200 years, Singapore has reinvented itself from many contributing cultures. If you consider the country today, you'll realize it is still keeping up that tradition.

Malaysia

Possibly one of the most overlooked countries in Southeast Asia, Malaysia is one of our favorites for one very special reason: It's not Thailand. After so much time spent traveling around Thailand listening to every hawker yell, "Hello! Special for you!" and every backpacker bragging about $5 roach-infested guesthouses, we look forward to Malaysia just to escape the tourism industry. Beaches on the islands of **Langkawi** and **Sabah** are just as beautiful as Thailand's, and resorts here are equally fine. The quaint British colonial influences at **Penang, Malacca,** and **Kuching** (Sarawak) add to the beauty, as do the mysterious Arab-Islamic influences all over the country. That's not to mention an endless number of **outdoor adventures,** from mountain climbing to jungle trekking to scuba diving—in fact, the rainforest here is far superior.

Why is Malaysia so underestimated? To be honest, after experiencing the relative "freedom" and tolerance of Thai culture, many travelers find Malaysian culture too strict and prohibitive. We think it's a fair trade—in Thailand, when we talk to Thai people, we're often treated like tourists with fat wallets. In Malaysia, when we meet locals, we end up having interesting conversations and cherished personal experiences. And we don't have to suffer through blatant prostitution and drug abuse—the sad, sleazy side of the Thai tourism industry.

MYANMAR (BURMA): to go or not to go?

In preparing this guide, we were confronted with problematic political realities in Myanmar—realities that made us question the advisability of sending readers there. The brutality and unfairness of the military government of Myanmar have been met with sanctions and embargoes from the international community. Political leaders such as the resilient Aung San Suu Kyi are being punished, and any dissent is met with house arrest and prison.

Since the early 1990s, the junta has encouraged tourism, and a visit to Myanmar is in fact a unique glimpse into rich Buddhist tradition, ancient culture, and stunning natural beauty. But while some encourage tourism and believe that Western visitors give voice to the troubles of Burma, others shout for a moratorium on tourism to this troubled land, saying that visitors' dollars subsidize and support tyranny.

Because of the precarious political climate in Myanmar, we've decided to exclude the country from this edition. Those not so easily dissuaded, however, can find more information on the subject at the **Burma Project at the Open Society Institute** (www.soros.org/burma) or at www.burmadebate.org. If you do decide to go to Myanmar, we suggest sticking with a reputable international tour operator. Good regional providers include **Diethelm Travel** (1 Inya Rd., Kamayut Township; ✆ **951/527-110** or 951/527-117; fax 951/527-135; www.diethelmtravel.com) and **Exotissimo Travel** (#0303 Sakura Tower, 339 Bogyoke Aung San St., Kyauktada Township, Yangon; ✆ **951/255-427** or 951/255-388; fax 951/255-428; myanmar@exotissimo.com).

A word of caution: On April 23, 2000, a group of tourists was kidnapped from the diving resort at Sipadan Island, off the east coast of Sabah (Malaysian Borneo). Abu Sayyaf, the Filipino Muslim separatists who were responsible for the incident, still remain at large in the southern islands of the Philippines close to Borneo. Exercise caution when traveling to this area.

Bali (Indonesia)

Bali is undoubtedly one of the hottest spots in the world for honeymooners and jet-setters, with a plethora of luxury hotels at bargain rates, a cosmopolitan nightlife scene, and a growing number of gourmet restaurants. The island is also well known for beaches, lush rice paddies, and welcoming people.

Memories of the 2002 and 2005 terrorist attacks are fading fast though security still remains vigilant around the island. The **beaches** remain the stuff of legend, supporting dreamy resorts that cater to anyone from families to escapist honeymooners and well heeled paradise seekers. **Watersports** enthusiasts flock to Bali for surfing, snorkeling, scuba diving, and swimming, as well as kite surfing and windsurfing. Those who can pull themselves away from the seaside can venture into villages lively with local smiles and markets packed with eye-boggling handicrafts and treasures, or take off into the jungle or up among high volcanic peaks for rigorous trekking. The town of **Ubud** is set among delightful Hindu temples and gorgeous mountain scenery—famed for its terraced rice fields—and supports a community of local and expat artists. Bali still has much to offer, and the friendly Balinese islanders are eager to see a return of the Western visitors who've brought so much to this magical isle.

A SOUTHEAST ASIAN CULTURAL PRIMER

The diverse ethnic groups in the region, from socialite city dwellers to remote enclaves of subsistence farmers, have unique histories, cultural practices, and religions. The region is a cornucopia of cultures that have intertwined and adopted various elements, beliefs, and practices from one another.

Thailand

Over centuries, migrating cultures have blended to create what is known as "Thai" today. Early waves of southern Chinese migrants combined with Mon peoples from Burma, Khmers from Cambodia, Malays, and Lao people—it is said that Thailand's King Rama I could trace ancestry to all these—plus European, Indian, Han Chinese, and Arab families. Of the 75% of the population that calls itself Thai, a great number of people in northeastern Isaan are of Lao ancestry. In the past century, Thailand has also become home to many migrating hill tribes in the north—tribes who've come from Vietnam, Laos, Myanmar, and southern China, many as refugees. As you travel south toward the Malaysian border, you find Thai people who share cultural and religious affinity with their southern Malay neighbors. Also in the past 50 years, Thailand has seen a boom in Chinese immigrants.

The Thais are a warm and peaceful people, with a culture that springs from Indian and Sri Lankan origins. Early Thais adopted many Brahman practices, evident in royal ceremony and social hierarchy—Thailand is a very class-oriented culture. Even their cherished national story, the *Ramakien,* the subject of almost all Thai classical dances and temple murals, finds its origin in the Indian Hindu epic the *Ramayana.* Thai Buddhism follows the Theravada sect, imported from Sri Lanka along with the classic bell-shape stupa seen in many temple grounds.

Perhaps the two main influences in Thai life today are spirituality and the royal family. In nearly every household throughout the country, you'll find a spirit house to appease the spirit of the earth, a portrait of the king in a prominent spot and perhaps pictures of a few previous kings, a dais for Buddha images and religious objects, and portraits of each son as he enters the monkhood, as almost all sons do.

Laos, Vietnam & Cambodia

Together, the countries of Laos, Vietnam, and Cambodia make up one of the most ethnically diverse regions of Southeast Asia. Much of the architecture and art in Cambodia and Laos is influenced by Buddhism and includes some of the world's most renowned temples, along with exquisitely sculpted Buddha images. The temple complexes of Angkor Wat in Cambodia are among the architectural wonders of the ancient world, while the finest temples in Laos are found in the ancient capital of Luang Prabang.

Note: The ethnic minorities, or hill tribes, of northern Vietnam, Laos, and Thailand all share a common heritage with one another, originating from either Himalayan tribes or southern Chinese clans. You'll find startling similarities in the customs and languages of all these people.

LAOS In Laos, approximately half the population is ethnic Lao descended from centuries of migration, mostly from southern China. A landlocked country with few natural resources, Laos has had little luck entering the global trade scene and remains dependent on the international donor community. If you think the Thais are laid-back, you'll have to check the Laos for a pulse. In fact, Lao culture is most often compared with that of the Thais because the two share common roots of language and culture. Large communities of ethnic minorities live in agrarian and subsistence communities, particularly in the north, and carry on rich traditional crafts and practices.

VIETNAM   In Vietnam, the ethnic Vietnamese are a fusion of Viet, Tai (a southern Chinese group), Indonesian, and Chinese who first settled here between 200 B.C. and A.D. 200. Although Vietnam has no official religion, several religions have significantly impacted Vietnamese culture, including Buddhism, Confucianism, Taoism, and animism. Animism, which is the oldest religious practice in Vietnam and many other Southeast Asian countries, is centered on belief in a spirit world.

Ancient cultural traditions lean toward borrowings from the mandarins of old Chinese dynasties that claimed sovereignty over Vietnam. In the 1900s, the French added a new flavor to the mix. Modern Vietnam is defined by its pell-mell rush to capitalism.

CAMBODIA   The population of Cambodia is made up primarily of ethnic Khmers who have lived here since around the 2nd century A.D. and whose religion and culture have been influenced by interaction with Indians, Javanese, Thais, Vietnamese, and Chinese. The achievements of the ancient Angkor empire were a long time ago, and modern Khmer culture still struggles in the aftermath of many years of war and terror. Relative political stability is new here, and Cambodia has far to go to catch up economically and with the infrastructure of the other countries in the region. Basic medical necessities are still lacking. Time and effort by civil authorities and NGOs (nongovernmental organizations) will only tell. Life in Cambodia is marked by devout Buddhist ritual, much like its neighbors.

Singapore

Seventy-eight percent of Singaporeans trace their heritage to migrating waves from China's southern provinces, particularly from the Hokkien, Teowchew, Hakka, Cantonese, and Hainanese dialect groups. Back then, the Chinese community was driven by rags-to-riches stories— the poor worker hawking vegetables who opened a grocery store and then started a chain of stores and now drives a Mercedes. This story still motivates them today.

But it's not just Chinese who have dominated the scene. The island started off with a handful of Malay inhabitants; then came the British colonials with Indian administrators, followed by Muslim Indian moneylenders, Chinese merchants, Chinese coolie laborers, and Indian convict labor, plus European settlers and immigrants from all over Southeast Asia. Over 2 centuries of modern history, each group made its contribution to "Singaporean culture."

Today, as your average Singaporean struggles to balance traditional values with modern demands of globalization, his country gets raked over the coals for being sterile and overly westernized. Older folks are becoming frustrated by younger generations who discard their traditions in their pursuit of "The Five Cs"—career, condo, car, credit card, and cash. Temples and ethnic neighborhoods are finding more revenue from tourists than from the communities they once served. Although many lament the loss of the good old days, most are willing to sacrifice a little tradition to be Southeast Asia's most stable and wealthiest country.

BUDDHA & BUDDHISM in southeast asia

Born **Siddhartha Gautama Buddha** in the year 563 B.C., the historical Buddha was an Indian prince. A passing sage predicted the child's future as a great holy man, and his father, who wanted him to be a great king, kept him sheltered from suffering behind palace walls. As a child, he knew nothing of sickness and death. He married, had children, and lived a carefree life, though one plagued by a certain soul sickness and discontent. His journey began when he first spied a sick man and a corpse. Renouncing his princely cloaks, he concluded that life is suffering. Resolving to search for relief from earthly pain, he went into the forest and lived there for many years as a solitary ascetic, ultimately following his moderate "middle way" and achieving enlightenment and **nirvana** (escape from the cycle of reincarnation) while in meditation under the Bodhi tree.

Buddha's peripatetic teaching is the basis of all Buddhism. Upon his death,

two schools arose and spread throughout Asia. The oldest and probably closest to the original practice is **Theravada** (Doctrine of the Elders), sometimes referred to as **Hinayana** (the Small Vehicle), which prevails in Sri Lanka, Laos, Thailand, and Cambodia and posits the enlightenment of individuals in this life, one at a time. The other school is **Mahayana** (the Large Vehicle), practiced in eastern Asia and Vietnam, which speaks of group enlightenment (we all go at once).

Buddhism has one aim only: to abolish suffering. To do so, according to Buddhism, one must transcend the ego, the "self," and attachment to the fleeting pleasures in an ever-changing material world, in order to see things clearly—with wisdom—and find peace.

There is no god in Buddhism; the Buddha is but an example. Buddhist practices, particularly Theravada, center on meditation and require that individuals, according to Buddha himself, look

Malaysia

Malaysia's population consists primarily of ethnic Malays, labeled Bumiputeras, a political classification that also encompasses tribal people who live in peninsular Malaysia and Borneo. Almost all Malays are Muslim, and conservative values are the norm. The ruling government party supports an Islam that is open and tolerant to other cultures, but a growing minority favors strict Islamic law and government, further marginalizing the country's large Chinese and Indian population. These foreign cultures migrated to Malaysia during the British colonial period as trading merchants, laborers, and administrators. Today, Malaysia recognizes ethnic Chinese and Indian citizens as equals under national law. However, government development and education policies always seem to favor Bumiputeras.

Among the favorite Malaysian recreational pastimes are kite flying, using ornately decorated paper kites, and top spinning. Some still practice silat, a Malaysian form of martial arts.

Bali (Indonesia)

No country in Southeast Asia has a more ethnically diverse population than Indonesia, with more than 350 ethnic groups with their own languages and cultures scattered among the 6,000 inhabited islands of this vast archipelago of more than 14,000 islands.

within and come to understand the **Four Noble Truths:** the existence of suffering; its arising; the path to eliminating suffering; and its ultimate passing by practice of the Eightfold Path, a road map to right living and good conduct.

Buddhist philosophy pervades every aspect of life, morality, and thought in the countries of Thailand, Laos, and Cambodia. The monastic community, called the *sangha,* is supported by local people and serves as the cultural touchstone and often an important avenue of education. Monks live in the "supramundane," free from the usual human concerns of finding food, clothing, and shelter. Instead, they focus on the rigorous practice of meditation, study, and austerities prescribed by the Theravada tradition. Mahayana traditions from China hold important sway over life in parts of the Malay Peninsula, Thailand, and Vietnam.

Lay practitioners adopt the law of **karma,** in which every action has effects and the energy of past action, good or evil, continues forever and is "reborn." Merit is gained by entering the monkhood (which most males do for a few days or months), helping in the construction of a monastery or a stupa, contributing to education, giving alms, or performing any act of kindness, no matter how small. When monks go with their alms bowls from house to house, they are not begging, but offering laypersons an opportunity to **"make merit"** by supporting them.

Buddha images are honored and revered in the Eastern tradition and are said to radiate the essence of Buddha, ideals that we should revere and struggle to achieve; but the images themselves are not holy or spiritually charged, per se. Buddhism does not seek converts, and, as long as they follow some simple rules of conduct, tourists are welcome guests at most Buddhist fetes and festivals.

Of all the islands, Bali stands out for its especially rich cultural life, which is inextricably linked with its Hindu beliefs. Life here is marked by a unique flow of ritual; whether painting, carving, dancing, or playing music, it seems that all Balinese are involved in the arts or practice devout daily rituals of beauty. Flower offerings to the gods are a common sight, and the Balinese are forever paying homage to Hindu deities at more than 20,000 temples and during the 60 annual festivals on the island.

The majority of the island's population is native Balinese; there are quite a few people from other parts of Indonesia who are here for work opportunities. English is widely spoken in the tourist parts of Bali, which means that just about everywhere you go someone will speak enough to help you out.

Etiquette

"Different countries, different customs," as Sean Connery said to Michael Caine in *The Man Who Would Be King*. And although each destination covered in this book proves that rule by having its own twists on etiquette, some general pointers will allow you to go though your days of traveling without inadvertently offending your hosts. (For etiquette tips in individual countries, see the relevant chapters.)

GREETINGS, GESTURES & SOCIAL INTERACTION   In these modern times, the common **Western handshake** has become extremely prevalent throughout Southeast Asia, but it is by no means universal. There is a plethora of traditional greetings, so when greeting someone—an older man and, especially, a woman of any age—it's safest to wait for a gesture or observe those around you and then follow suit. In Muslim culture, for instance, it is not acceptable for men and women not related by blood or marriage to touch.

In interpersonal relations in strongly Buddhist areas (Laos, Vietnam, and Thailand), it helps to **take a gentle approach** to human relationships. A person showing anger or ill temper would be regarded with surprise and disapproval. A gentle approach will take you much further.

In countries with significant Muslim and Hindu cultures (Malaysia, Singapore, and Bali), **use only your right hand in social interaction.** Traditionally, the left hand is used only for personal hygiene. Not only should you eat with your right hand and give and receive all gifts with your right hand, but you should also make sure that you make all gestures, especially **pointing** (and, even more especially, pointing in temples and mosques), with your right hand. In all the countries discussed in this book, it's also considered more polite to point with your knuckle (with your hand facing palm down) than with your finger.

In all destinations covered in this guide, women seated on the floor should never sit with their legs crossed in front of them—instead, tuck your legs to the side. Men may sit with legs crossed. Both men and women should also **avoid showing the bottoms of the feet,** which are considered the most unclean part of the body. If you cross your legs while on the floor or in a chair, don't point your soles toward other people. Also be careful not to use your foot to point or gesture. **Remove your shoes** when entering a temple or private home. And don't ever step over someone's body or legs.

On a similar note, in Buddhist and Hindu cultures, the head is considered the most sacred part of the body; therefore, **do not casually touch another person's head**—and this includes patting children on the head.

DRESSING FOR CULTURAL SUCCESS The basic rule is simple: **Dress modestly.** Except perhaps on the grounds of resorts and in heavily touristed areas such as Bali's Kuta and Thailand's beaches, foreigners displaying navels, chests, or shoulders, or wearing short shorts or short skirts, will attract stares. Although shorts and bathing suits are accepted on the beach, avoid parading around in them elsewhere, no matter how hot it is.

In Singapore, wear your smartest clothes (looking poor does not make a good impression).

TEMPLE & MOSQUE ETIQUETTE When visiting the **mosques,** be sure to dress appropriately. Neither men nor women will be admitted wearing shorts. Women should not wear short skirts or sleeveless, backless, or low-cut tops. Both men and women are required to leave their shoes outside. Also, never enter the mosque's main prayer hall; this area is reserved for Muslims only. No cameras or video cameras are allowed, and remember to turn off cellphones. You should not plan to go to the mosques between 11am and 2pm on Friday, the Sabbath day.

Visitors are welcome to walk around and explore most **temples** and *wats.* As in the mosques, remember to dress appropriately—some temples might refuse to admit you if you're showing too much skin—and to leave your shoes outside. Photography is permitted in most temples, although some, such as Wat Phra Kaeo in Thailand, prohibit it. Never climb on a Buddha image, and if you sit down, never point your feet in the direction of the Buddha. Do not cross in front of a person who is in prayer. Also, women should never touch a monk, try to shake his hand, or even give something to one directly (the monk will provide a cloth for you to lay the item upon, and then he will collect it). Monks are not permitted to touch women or to speak directly to them anywhere but inside a temple or a *wat*.

SOUTHEAST ASIA IN POP CULTURE
Recommended Books & Films

BALI (INDONESIA)   *Bali Sekala and Nishkala: Essays on Religion, Ritual and Art,* by Fred B. Eiseman, Jr., is the seminal text on the labyrinth of beliefs and practices on the island. The last third of Elizabeth Gilbert's bestseller, *Eat, Pray, Love,* recently turned into a movie starring Julia Roberts, takes place in Bali's Ubud and gives a great sense of the place's people and culture.

CAMBODIA   Roland Joffe's 1984 classic movie *The Killing Fields* chronicles the lives of foreign journalists covering the fall of Phnom Penh and the subsequent experiences of a Cambodian journalist, Dith Pran, at the hands of the Khmer Rouge during the darkest of periods. *Lara Croft: Tomb Raider,* with Angelina Jolie, used Angkor as a set. In 2002, Matt Dillon made the indescribably complicated *City of Ghosts* using locations from all around the country. Cambodian director Rithy Pran made the most extraordinary documentary about Tuol Sleng. In *S21: The Khmer Rouge Killing Machine,* one of the only survivors of Toul Sleng, the artist Vann Nath, actually confronts the prison guards who did the torture and killing.

There are many, many books about Cambodia, plenty of them touching on the years of turmoil. Jon Swain's *River of Time* is a very affecting story of his lifelong love affair with Indochina. Nic Dunlop, a British photographer who quite by chance discovered the Khmer Rouge torturer-in-chief, Duch, writes a compelling story about that incident but touches on many of the wider implications in *The Lost Executioner.* One of the best biographies of Pol Pot is by Philip Short and is called *Pol Pot. The Pol Pot Regime,* by Ben Kiernan, is a very academic but very inclusive historical analysis of the whole era. Francois Bizot was a French ethnographer who was actually captured and imprisoned by the Khmer Rouge in 1973 (Duch again). His account, *The Gate,* gives some insight into their maniacal thinking. *When the War Was Over* is an immensely thoughtful account of the Khmer Rouge Years by *Washington Post* journalist Elizabeth Becker. There has also been a series of autobiographies by Khmer Rouge survivors. *Stay Alive My Son* by Pin Yathey, *First They Killed My Father* by Loung Ung, and *When Broken Glass Floats* by Chanrithy Him are among them but there are many others. *Angkor,* by George Coedes, is the premier read on the temples of Angkor. *Khmer: The Lost Empire of Cambodia,* by Thierry Zephir, makes a good guide and intro for a visit to Angkor.

LAOS   *Stalking the Elephant Kings,* by C. Kremmer, is a personal account of travel in Laos and one man's obsession to find the truth about the last dynasty—it's a good primer to Lao history and culture. *Another Quiet American,* by Brett Dakin, a witty account of recent travels in the country, paints the state of the nation through the eyes of a young American working as a consultant for the National Tourism Authority in Vientiane.

The Ravens: Pilots of the Secret War of Laos and *Air America: The Story of the CIA's Secret Airline,* both by C. Robbins, tell the heretofore untold tale of the undeclared war in Laos. And *Tragedy in Paradise: A Country Doctor at War in Laos* is a memoir by

Dr. Charles Weldon, recalling his experiences from 1963 to 1974 working hand in hand with Air America as chief of public health for USAID Laos.

MALAYSIA A witty and gripping travelogue, *Into the Heart of Borneo*, by Redmond O'Hanlon, follows two inexperienced travelers as they attempt a rugged trek into the deepest forests of Sarawak.

For a deeper look at Malaysian history, try *A History of Malaysia*, by Barbara Watson Andaya, or *The Long Day Wanes: A Malaysian Trilogy*, by Anthony Burgess, each of which mirrors the author's experiences and observations as a British civil servant during Malaysia's transition to independence.

SINGAPORE If you're having trouble finding books about Singapore in bookstores where you live, wait until you arrive and then browse local shelves, where you'll find tons of books about the country and its history, culture, arts, food, and local fiction. For interesting and informative reads that you can find (or order) through your neighborhood bookstore, here's a good place to start:

From Third World to First: The Singapore Story: 1965–2000, by Lee Kuan Yew, details the history and policies behind Singapore's remarkable economic success written by the man who was at the helm.

The Singapore Story: Memoirs of Lee Kuan Yew, by Lee Kuan Yew, offers an intimate account of Minister Mentor Lee's personal journey and will unravel some of the mysteries behind one of the world's most talked-about leaders.

King Rat, by James Clavell, is a novel set in Singapore during the Japanese Occupation that follows the story of an American POW as he struggles to outwit the system in a harsh prison camp.

Lord Jim, by Joseph Conrad, is a classic narrative of a man's struggle to find redemption in a Southeast Asian post.

THAILAND *Anna and the King*, the original late-19th-century work of Anna Leowens, governess for the children of the progressive King Rama IV, tells of the kingdom's opening to the West. Don't miss the film of the same name starring Jodie Foster (though due to gross historical inaccuracies, the film was banned from public release in Thailand).

Also banned in Thailand is *The Revolutionary King*, by William Stevenson, a biography of the revered King Bhumibol Adulyadej. Given unprecedented access to the king and royal family, Stevenson shows a side of the monarchy that few have seen. The book treats His Majesty as a real person (referring to him by his nickname, "Lek," meaning small) and delves into taboo subjects, such as the murder of the king's older brother Ananda, making it quite controversial.

The Beach, by Alex Garland, as well as the popular film of the same name featuring Leonardo DiCaprio, tells the tale of the impossibility of modern Utopia, the very thing that so many Asia adventurers seek. Though not about Thailand exclusively, Tiziano Terzani's *A Fortune-Teller Told Me* is a well crafted portrait of the interlocking cultures of Asia and of the Westerner's search for personal destiny.

Carol Hollinger's *Mai Pen Rai Means Never Mind* is a personal history of time spent in the kingdom some 30 years ago, but the cultural insights are quite current. *Patpong Sisters*, by Cleo Odzer, and *Sex Slaves*, by Louise Brown, are both interesting exposés of the Thai sex industry.

Books on Thai Buddhism are many. Try Phra Peter Parrapadipo's *Phra Farang*, literally "The Foreign Monk," which tells the story of an Englishman turned Thai Buddhist monk. The writings of Jack Kornfield, particularly *A Path with Heart*, are a good introduction.

VIETNAM *The Quiet American,* by Graham Greene, which was made into a Hollywood film starring Michael Caine in 2002, is a classic tale of espionage in the old colony. In fact, much of what is written—or popular—about Vietnam chronicles the country's recent strife, particularly the American War years. The list is long; below are but a few.

In Retrospect: The Tragedy and Lessons of Vietnam, by former American secretary of defense Robert S. McNamara and Brian DeMark, is quite popular in Vietnam (a copy stands in a glass case at the War Museum in Ho Chi Minh City), as it tells the tale of American deceit and misinformation from the perspective of one of its more remorseful arbiters. *A Bright Shining Lie,* by Neil Sheehan, is a similar explication. Pulitzer Prize–winning *Fire in the Lake,* by Francis Fitzgerald, is a sociological exploration of the war years and aftermath.

Personal accounts such as *Dear America: Letters Home from Vietnam,* by Bernhard Edelman, or the Vietnamese classic *The Sorrow of War,* by Bao Ninh, tell of the experiences of soldiers and civilians caught in the fray. *The Girl in the Picture: The Story of Kim Phuc and the Photograph That Changed the Course of the Vietnam War,* by Denise Chong, is self-explanatory.

Robert Olen Butler won a Pulitzer Prize for *A Good Scent from a Strange Mountain,* a collection of short stories recounting the legacy of war through disparate voices. This book is one of the best you can read while traveling in the country. *Catfish and Mandala,* by Andrew X. Pham, is a Vietnamese American's travel odyssey and coming to terms with the past.

The Vietnam War was fertile terrain for Hollywood in the 1980s, with award-winning classics such as Francis Ford Coppola's *Apocalypse Now, The Deer Hunter* with Robert DeNiro, and Oliver Stone's *Platoon* and *Born on the Fourth of July,* a true story about returnee Ron Kovic. *The Fog of War* is a uniquely candid hindsight look by Robert McNamara, the secretary of defense during the war. Films by Vietnamese directors such as Tran Anh Hung's *The Scent of Green Papaya* and *Cyclo* are more tranquil, studied views of Vietnamese culture. And *Indochine,* starring Catherine Deneuve, is a historic portrait of the tumultuous end of colonialism in Vietnam.

EATING & DRINKING

Southeast Asia is a real playground for adventurous eaters; from high-class hotel restaurants and power-lunch points to streetside stalls with local specialties, you'll find it all. The cuisine of each country is unique, and crossing borders often means a new course in manners, food, and culture. In this guide, we list the safest of options by and large, making sure to designate any dining that could be deemed "adventurous"—but the adventurous in fact have lots of opportunities to try new foods, from oddities such as freshly killed snake to fried crickets and grubs. It's not all that funky, though, and much of the best local cuisine is not found in restaurants but in markets and streetside stalls, something that puts some people off. Our advice: Be adventurous. When eating in open-air joints, just be careful that things are cooked fresh and aren't sitting out, and be careful of raw ingredients such as vegetables or some fish pastes. If you find yourself playing charades to get your food, laughing, smiling, and squatting on a tiny plastic stool, talking to locals and eating a meal that costs pennies to the approving nods of your new friends, then you're in the right place. Wherever possible, ask locals what's good, and you'll be in store for a fun cultural adventure.

Try *pho* and the many regional specials throughout Vietnam; enjoy cover-the-table spreads in Thailand and Malaysia, where spices are fiery and a meal is always an event; and don't miss crispy duck or *babi guling*—suckling pig—in Bali. The choices are endless. The usual varieties of international fare can be found throughout the region—in fact, every big city has its Chinese, Italian, sushi, and French. In parts of Indochina, Laos and Vietnam in particular, chefs carry on long traditions from colonial times, and the French cuisine is as good as you'll get anywhere. Chinese communities abound and, of course, so does good Chinese in its myriad forms—from dim sum to Peking duck.

All but the fanciest restaurants are open early until late. Tipping is not expected but always appreciated, and just rounding up the bill to the next dollar amount is often more than enough.

For drinkers, there are few restrictive laws or cultural taboos—in fact, drinking is a big part of most cultures in Southeast Asia. In Malaysia and much of Indonesia, however, Islamic rules do not permit the consumption of alcohol, but non-Muslim visitors are welcome to drink as long as they are respectful of their Muslim hosts. Local rice wines and whiskeys abound, and foreign guests are always invited. Sometimes the stuff is pretty potent—toxic, even—so be warned. European visitors left their mark on the region with brewing and distilling technologies, and each country produces its own local beers to go along with the many imports. Fresh fruit is falling off the trees in the tropical climes of Southeast Asia, so good fresh juices are available everywhere. Coffee is grown throughout the region, and though local roasting processes are a bit different, local brews are delicious. Tap water is not potable in most regions, but bottled water is available everywhere; and perhaps the best advice for travel in the region is to stay hydrated. If you're thirsty, then it's too late. Drink lots.

THAILAND

by Ron Emmons

Traffic and tranquillity, beaches and bargains, ancient palaces and stunning temples: Thailand has much to offer the millions who visit every year. The world caught on to Thailand's magic years ago, and foreign investors, with the encouragement of the Thai government, have seized on this fascination. Luxury resorts are popping up in virtually every town and island, turning once remote and unspoiled beaches and towns into bustling package-tour destinations, some virtually unrecognizable to those just a couple years removed from their last visit.

Bangkok's space-age airport, Suvarnabhumi, with the capacity to handle 45 million travelers a year (and eventually 100 million with planned expansion), has made Thailand an even more convenient destination for the growing number of visitors.

This increase in tourist numbers does not mean that Thailand has lost its charm, far from it. The authentic Thai way of life with its vibrant Buddhist culture is just outside the comfortable bubble of five-star resorts and luxury tour buses: All you have to do is wander the streets and soak it in.

In bustling Bangkok, find canal and riverside communities, a sprawling Chinatown, an ultramodern cityscape, and giant outdoor markets that are a heady mix of sights, sounds, and smells.

Beyond urban Thailand are flat plains carpeted with rice paddies and dotted with tiny villages; mountains of luxuriant teak forests where elephants once roamed wild; long stretches of white-sand beach; acres of coconut palms and rubber plantations; and clear-blue waters against towering rock cliffs. Rural life is languid and hospitable, and behind every warm Thai smile there is true kindness.

Outdoor-adventure opportunities abound: Sail, paddle, dive, and snorkel in the sea; trek to villages; ride the rivers; or go on four-wheel-drive adventures in the rugged upcountry. Rural Thailand is ripe for exploration by bus, train, car, motorbike, and boat, and visitors are limited only by their tolerance for adventure.

Gorgeous tropical island beaches play host to laid-back bungalow guesthouses and posh, Thai-style five-star resorts. The cuisine is captivating, a unique blend of sweet, sour, and salty tastes tempered with fiery spice. And whether shopping the sprawling bazaars or visiting Thailand's notorious nightlife, you're sure to have some *sanuk,* or fun, Thai-style.

GETTING TO KNOW THAILAND

The Lay of the Land

Thailand is in the center of Southeast Asia, roughly equidistant from China and India, and shares cultural affinities with both. It borders Myanmar (Burma) to the north and west, Laos to the northeast, Cambodia (Kampuchea) to the east, and Malaysia to the south. Thailand's southwestern coast stretches along the Andaman Sea, and its southern and southeastern coastlines border the Gulf of Thailand (still often called the Gulf of Siam).

Thailand covers approximately 514,000 sq. km (198,000 sq. miles)—about the size of France—and its shape is often compared to an elephant's head. The country is divided into six major geographic zones, within which there are 75 provinces.

NORTHERN THAILAND Northern Thailand (the forehead of the elephant) is a relatively cool, mountainous region at the foothills of the Himalayas. Like most of Thailand, the cool hills in the north are well suited for farming, particularly for strawberries, asparagus, peaches, litchis, and other fruits. At higher elevations, a few hill-tribe farmers still cultivate opium poppies (a crop that is ruinous to farmers who become addicted), though the Royal Projects agricultural program advanced by the king is introducing more productive crops such as cabbage and coffee. The cities in the north that are covered in this chapter are Chiang Mai and Chiang Rai.

THE CENTRAL PLAIN The Central Plain is an extremely fertile region, providing the country and the world with much of its abundant rice crop. The main city of the area is Phitsanulok, northwest of which are the impressive remains of Sukhothai, Thailand's first capital. To the south is Lopburi, an ancient Mon-Khmer settlement.

THE SOUTHEAST COAST The southeast coast features several seaside resorts, such as Pattaya and the islands Ko Samet and Ko Chang. They are nearer to Bangkok than the best beaches on the Southern Peninsula, so are quicker to reach.

WESTERN THAILAND On the opposite side of the country, west of Bangkok, are mountains and valleys carved by the Kwai River, made infamous during World War II by the "Death Railway," built by Allied prisoners of war who worked and lived under horrifying conditions, and a bridge (featured in the film *Bridge on the River Kwai*) over the river at Kanchanaburi. Just 80km (50 miles) north of Bangkok (which is in every way the center of the country, on the banks of the Chao Phraya River) is Ayutthaya, which was Siam's second capital after Sukhothai.

THE SOUTHERN PENINSULA The long, narrow Southern Peninsula (the elephant's trunk) extends south to the Malaysian border. It was on the west coast of the peninsula, in the Andaman Sea, that the "Christmas Tsunami" struck on December 26, 2004. The result of a 9.0 earthquake in Aceh Indonesia, the waves claimed 5,000 victims in Thailand alone. Coastal Phuket was buffeted by the waves, while areas in Phang Nga Province, particularly Khao Lak, as well as the popular resort island of Ko Phi Phi near Krabi, were flattened. However, reconstruction was fast and recovery of tourist centers is now complete.

The eastern coastline along the Gulf of Thailand extends more than 1,802km (1,120 miles), while the western shoreline runs 716km (445 miles) along the Andaman Sea. This region is the most tropical in the country, with heavy rainfall during monsoon seasons. The northeast monsoon, roughly from November to April, brings clear weather and calm seas to the west coast; the southwest monsoon, March to

Chiang Saen
Chiang Khong
Chiang Rai
Fang
GOLDEN
TRIANGLE
Mae Hong
Son
Pai
NORTHERN
HILLS
Chiang Mai
Lamphun
Lampang
Nan
Mae
Sariang
Phrae
Si Satchanalai
Uttaradit
Loei
Sukhothai
Phitsanulok
Tak
Mae Sot
Kamphaeng
Phet
Phetchabun
Khon Kaen
MYANMAR
(BURMA)
Nakhon Sawan
Phimai
Loppuri
Nakhon Ratchasima
(Khorat)
Ubon
Ratchathani
CENTRAL
PLAINS
Surin
Ayutthaya
Sam Rong
Nam Tok
Kanchanaburi
Nakhon
Pathom
Bangkok
Chon Buri
CAMBODIA
Cha-Am
Phetchaburi
Bangsaen
Hua Hin
Pattaya
Prachuap
Khiri Khan
Rayong
Chanthaburi
Koh Samet
EASTERN
SEABOARD
Chumphon
Ko Tao
Ko Chang
Trat
Ranong
Ko Phangngan
Ko Mak
Ko
Surin
Ko Kut
SURIN NATIONAL
MARINE PARK
Ko Samui
Khanom
**Phnom
Penh**
Surat
Thani
Gulf of Thailand
(Gulf of Siam)
Phangnga
Nakhon
Si Thammarat
SOUTHERN
PENINSULA
Phuket
Krabi
Ko
Phi Phi
Songkhla
*Andaman
Sea*
Had Yai
Pattani
Ko Tarutao
Narathiwat
TARUTAO
NATIONAL PARK
MALAYSIA
Sungai Kolok

LAOS

VIETNAM

Vientiane
Nong Khai
Udon
Thani
Ban Chiang
Nakhon
Phanom
Chi
ISAN
Mun

Ping
Chao Phraya
Wang
Yom
Noi Noi
Khwae Noi

*Andaman
Sea*

Mae

VIETNAM

0   100 mi
0   100 km

October, brings similar conditions to the east coast. There are glamorous beach resorts here (people visit them even during the rainy season, as it rarely rains all day), such as the western islands of Phuket and nearby Ko Phi Phi. The east-coast islands of Ko Samui and Ko Pha Ngan are similarly appealing.

ISAN Finally, Isan, the broad and relatively infertile northeast plateau (the ear of the elephant), is the least developed region in Thailand, bordered by the Mekong River (Mae Nam Khong in Thai). Isan is dusty in the cool winter and muddy during the summer monsoon. Fewer tourists make their way to Isan than any other part of the country, so we've opted not to cover it in this chapter.

A Look at the Past

Archaeologists believe that Thailand was a major thoroughfare for *Homo erectus* en route from Africa to China and other parts of Asia. Modern civilization did not arrive in Thailand until about 1,000 years ago, when waves of people migrated from central and southern China, settling primarily in what is now Vietnam, Laos, Thailand, and Myanmar (Burma). These people, who are called Tai, became dispersed over a vast area of space, sharing a cultural and linguistic commonality. The **early Tais** lived in nuclear families with household collectives, called *muang*, or villages, establishing loosely structured feudal states.

From the 6th century, Southeast Asia underwent a gradual period of **Indianization.** Merchants and missionaries from India introduced Brahmanism and Buddhism to the region, as well as Indian political and social values and art and architectural preferences. At the same time the **Mon,** migrants from Burma, were responsible for establishing Sri Lankan Buddhism in central Thailand.

By the early 9th century, the expansionist **Khmer** empire had risen to power in Cambodia, engulfing the region. Magnificent Khmer temples, originally built for the worship of Hindu deities before conversion to Buddhism and distinguished by their corncob-shaped *prang*, or towers, were constructed in outposts increasingly farther afield until the Khmer's eventual collapse in the 13th century. You can still find many Khmer ruins in Thailand, especially in Isan.

In 1259, several powerful centers of Tai power in northern Thailand, southern China, and Laos were united by **King Mengrai,** who established the first capital of the **Lanna Kingdom** at Chiang Rai in 1263, and later at Chiang Mai in 1296. The Lanna Kingdom saw the rise of a scholarly Buddhism, with strict adherence to orthodox ways. Citizens enjoyed the benefits of infrastructure projects for transportation and irrigation, developed medicine and law, and created artistic expression through religious sculpture, sacred texts, and poetry. But the Mongols, under the fierce expansionist leadership of **Kublai Khan,** forced their way into the region. Mengrai, forming strategic alliances with neighboring kingdoms, succeeded in keeping the Mongols at bay.

In the vacuum left by the departing Khmers, a tiny kingdom based in **Sukhothai** rose to fame after its crown prince, Rama, single-handedly defeated an invasion from neighboring Mae Sot at the Burmese border. Upon his coronation in 1279, **Ramkhamhaeng,** or "Rama the Bold," set the scene for what is recognized as the first truly Siamese civilization, mixing all the people of the central plains—Tai, Mon, Khmer, and indigenous populations, with threads of India and China interwoven in their cultural tapestry. In response to the Khmer's hierarchical rule, Ramkhamhaeng established himself as an accessible king. He was a devout Buddhist, adopting orthodox and scholarly Theravada Buddhism. A patron of the arts, the king commissioned many great Buddha images, initiated splendid architectural projects, and developed the modern Thai written language. After his death in 1298, his successors failed to rule wisely, and Sukhothai's brilliant spark faded almost as quickly at it had ignited.

Next came the kingdom of **Ayutthaya,** which swallowed what was left of Khmer outposts and the Sukhothai Kingdom. Incorporating the strengths of its population— Tai military manpower and labor, Khmer bureaucratic sensibilities, and Chinese commercial talents—the empire grew wealthy and strong. Following Khmer models, the king rose above his subjects atop a huge pyramid-shape administration. A fortified city was built, with temples that glittered as much as any in Sukhothai. This was the Kingdom of Siam that the first Europeans, the Portuguese, encountered in 1511.

Burmese invasion forces took Chiang Mai's Lanna Kingdom in 1558 and finally Ayutthaya in 1569. However, during the occupation, **Prince Naresuan,** descended from Sukhothai kings, in a historic battle scene atop an elephant, challenged the Burmese crown prince and defeated him with a single blow. Ayutthaya continued through the following 2 centuries in grand style, and while its Southeast Asian neighbors were falling under colonial rule, the court of Siam retained its own sovereignty. Thailand has the distinction of being the only Southeast Asian nation never to have been colonized, a point of great pride for Thais today. Unfortunately, the final demise of Ayutthaya was two more Burmese invasions in the 1760s.

The Siamese did not hesitate to build another kingdom. **Taksin,** a provincial governor, rose to power on the merits of his military excellence, his charisma, and a firm belief that he was divinely appointed to rule. Rebuilding the capital at Thonburi, on the western bank of the Chao Phraya River (opposite present-day Bangkok), within 3 years he reunited the lands under the previous kingdom. But Taksin suffered from paranoia—he had monks killed, along with eventually his own wife and children. Regional powers were quick to get rid of him—he was swiftly kidnapped, covered in a velvet sack, and beaten to death with a sandalwood club.

These same regional powers turned to **Chaophraya Chakri** in 1782 to lead the country. Crowned **King Ramathibodi,** he was the first king of Thailand's present dynasty, the **Chakri Dynasty.** He moved the capital across the river to Bangkok, where he built the **Grand Palace** and great temples. The city grew around a network of canals, with the river as the central channel for trade and commerce. Rama I reinstated Theravada Buddhist doctrine, reestablished the state ceremonies of Ayutthaya, and revised all laws. He also wrote the *Ramakien,* based upon the Indian *Ramayana,* a legend that has become the subject for many Thai classical arts.

King Mongkut (1851–68) with his son, **King Chulalongkorn** (1868–1910), led Siam into the 20th century as an independent nation, establishing an effective civil service, formalizing global relations, and introducing industrialization-based economics. It was King Mongkut who hired Anna Leonowens (of *The King and I*) as an English tutor for his children. Thai people want everyone to know that Mongkut was not the overbearing, pushover fop described in her account. Historians side with the Thais, for she is barely mentioned in court accounts—the story had its origins more in her imagination than in realty.

During the reign of **King Prajadhipok,** Rama VII (1925–35), the growing urban middle class became increasingly discontent. Economic failings and bureaucratic bickering weakened the position of the monarchy, which was delivered its final blow by the Great Depression. In 1932, a group of midlevel officials staged a coup d'état, and Prajadhipok abdicated in 1935.

Democracy had a shaky hold on Siam. Over the following decades, government leadership changed hands fast and frequently, many times the result of hostile takeover with the military at the helm. In 1939, the nation adopted the name Thailand—"Land of the Free."

During **World War II,** democracy was stalled in the face of the Japanese invasion in 1941. Thailand chose to side with the Japanese, but at the war's end, no punitive measures were taken against Thailand; the Thai ambassador in Washington had failed to deliver his country's declaration of war against the Allies.

Thailand managed to stay out of direct involvement in the **Vietnam War;** however, it continues to suffer repercussions from the burden of refugees. The U.S. pumped billions into the Thai economy, bringing riches to some and relative affluence to many, but further impoverishing the poor. Communism became an increasingly attractive political philosophy, and a full-scale insurrection seemed imminent. In June 1973, thousands of Thai students demonstrated in the streets, demanding a new constitution and the return to democratic principles. Tensions grew until October, when armed forces attacked a demonstration at Thammasat University in Bangkok, killing 69 students and wounding 800, paralyzing the capital with terror and revulsion.

The constitution was restored, a new government was elected, and democracy once again wobbled on. Many students, however, were not yet satisfied and continued to complain that the financial elite were still in control and still resisting change. In 1976, student protests again broke out, and there was a replay of the grisly scene of 3 years before at Thammasat University. The army seized control to impose and maintain order, conveniently spiriting away some bodies and prisoners, and another brief experiment with democracy was at an end. **Thanin Kraivichien** was installed as prime minister of a new right-wing government, which suspended freedom of speech and the press, further polarizing Thai society.

In 1980, **Prem Tinsulanonda** was named prime minister, and during the following 8 years, he managed to bring remarkable political and economic stability to Thailand. The Thai economy continued to grow steadily through the 1980s, fueled by Japanese investment and Chinese capital in flight from Hong Kong. Leadership since then has seen quite a few changes, including a military coup in 1991 and another crackdown in 1992. It was under **General Chavalit Yongjaiyudh**'s administration that the economic crisis hit Thailand in July 1997. While his government sat on its hands in indecision over how to proceed, connections between public officials and bad financial institutions became more apparent, and international investors lost confidence in Thailand. While in August 1997 Thailand accepted $17 billion in bailouts from the International Monetary Fund, political in-fighting stalled the government's action until November of the same year, when **Chuan Leekpai,** a previous prime minister, was elected into office again to try to straighten things out.

Economic stability was restored under the leadership of "the CEO Prime Minister" **Thaksin Shinawatra,** elected in 2000. From the outside, Thaksin's government appeared to be stable. Internally, however, discontent in the south and among the middle class in Bangkok was steadily growing over what was seen as the Thaksin regime's inherent corruption, subversion of democratic institutions, and inability to curb the increasing violence by Muslim separatists in the far south. This growing wave of discontent overtook the government in the form of an army-led coup on September 19, 2006, leaving the country under a military junta calling itself the **Council for National Security (CNS).** The CNS, headed by **General Sonthi Boonyaratglin** (with Prime Minister Surayad Chulanont as the junta's public face), dissolved Parliament, suspended the constitution, and placed restrictions on political gatherings. In December 2007, the **People's Power Party (PPP),** formed largely of Thaksin supporters and led by **Samak Sundaravej,** won a narrow victory in the general election. Samak was removed from office by the Constitutional Court in September 2008 and replaced by **Somchai Wongsawat,** a brother-in-law of Thaksin Shinawatra.

Thailand Today

Today, under a pyramid of king, nation, and religion, Thais enjoy far more freedom than any of their neighbors. King Bhumibol Adulyadej holds a position outside of government, but is recognized as the defender of all Thai people. On a few occasions, he has put his foot down when government monkey business has not been beneficial to his people.

Recently the monkeys have been working overtime, however, and Thailand's political situation has been in flux since the September 2006 coup, with the **People's Alliance for Democracy (PAD)** determined to bring down the PPP, which it sees as a proxy for Thaksin. For some months in late 2008, PAD supporters occupied Government House, and it seemed that the dissolution of parliament and new elections were likely. However, with hostilities between the PPP and PAD escalating, the future of Thailand's fragile democracy was insecure.

Thailand's People & Culture

Thailand is a true melting pot of people and cultures. Thais descended from people of southern China, who for centuries absorbed Mon, Khmer, Lao, Persian, Indian, and Malay people and influences. The hill-tribe peoples of the north descended from Tibeto-Burman people who migrated from the Himalayas.

RELIGION Thai culture cannot be fully appreciated without some understanding of Buddhism, which is followed by over 90% of the population. Although Buddhism first came to Thailand in the 3rd century B.C., when missionaries were sent from India, it was not until the 14th century that the *sangha* (monastic order) was established. Even Thai kings humbly don the monk's robes at age 13.

Other faiths in Thailand include Islam, Christianity, Hinduism, and Sikhism. Sunni Islam is followed by more than two million Thais, mostly in the south.

CUISINE Thai cuisine is the best of Chinese food ingredients and preparation combined with the sophistication of Indian spicing and topped off with red and green chilis. Basic ingredients include a cornucopia of shellfish, fresh fruits, and vegetables—asparagus, tamarind, bean sprouts, carrots, mushrooms of all kinds, various kinds of spinach, and bamboo shoots, combined with pungent spices such as basil, lemon grass, mint, chili, garlic, and coriander. Thai cooking employs coconut milk, curry paste, peanuts, and a variety of noodles and rice.

Among the dishes you'll find throughout the country are *tom yum goong,* a Thai hot-and-sour shrimp soup; satay, charcoal-broiled chicken, beef, or pork strips skewered on a bamboo stick and dipped in a peanut-coconut-curry sauce; spring rolls; *larb,* a spicy chicken or ground-beef concoction with mint and lime flavoring; salads, most with a dressing of onion, chili pepper, lime juice, and fish sauce; *pad thai* (fried noodles, usually served with shrimp, eggs, peanuts, fresh bean sprouts, and lime); *khao soi,* a northern curried soup served at small food stalls; a wide range of curries; spicy *tod man pla,* tasty fish cakes; sticky rice, served in the north and made from glutinous rice, prepared with vegetables and wrapped in a banana leaf; and Thai fried rice, a simple rice dish made with whatever the kitchen has on hand. "American fried rice" usually means fried rice topped with one egg, over easy, and meat. For dessert, the local fruit, from pineapple to papaya, is delicious. Also try local favorites such as rambutan (similar to litchi), jackfruit, and pungent durian.

A word of caution: Thais enjoy incredibly spicy food, normally much more fiery than is tolerated in even the most piquant Western cuisines. Protect your own palate by saying "Mai phet—farang," meaning "Not spicy—foreigner."

Etiquette

Disrespect for the royal family and religious figures, sites, and objects will cause great offense. While photography is generally permitted in temples, never stand above a Buddha image or point your feet in the direction of the Buddha. Women should never touch a monk; when you are handing a monk an offering, he will provide a cloth for you to lay the item upon, and he will collect it.

The traditional Thai greeting is called the *wai:* Place your palms together as in prayer, raise the tips of your fingers to your chin, and make a subtle bow from the waist while bending your knees slightly. It's also used to say thank you and goodbye. The person of lower social status initiates a *wai.* In general, you should not *wai* to children or to someone providing a service to you. Also, don't expect a monk to return a *wai;* they're exempt from the custom. In a business setting, a handshake is more appropriate. Note, too, that "Thai Time" dictates that appointments are loosely kept, and offense at someone's tardiness is met with confusion.

Address a Thai person by his or her first name preceded by "Khun." Don't be surprised if you are solely addressed by your first name—such as Mr. John or Ms. Mary. Close friends will use nicknames, which are much easier to remember.

Language

Thai is derived from Mon, Khmer, Chinese, Pali, Sanskrit, and, increasingly, English. It is a tonal language, with distinctions based on inflection—low, mid-, high, rising, or falling tone—rather than stress, which makes it very elusive to most speakers of Western languages. Central Thai is the official language, but there are regional dialects.

One interesting aspect of the language that can be confusing to first-time visitors is that the polite words roughly corresponding to our *sir* and *ma'am* are determined not by the gender of the person addressed, but by the gender of the speaker; females say *ka* and males say *khap* (the formal pronunciation is *khrap,* but the *r* is rarely heard in everyday usage). Unfortunately, there is no universal transliteration system, so you will see the usual **Thai greeting** written in Roman letters as *sawatdee, sawaddi, sawasdee, sawusdi,* and so forth.

USEFUL THAI PHRASES
Note: **All phrases end in *khap* for men and *ka* for women.**

Hello	**Sa-wa-dee-khap (male); sa-wa-dee-ka (female)**
Thank you	**Kop-koon-khap/ka**
How are you?	**Sa-bai-dee-mai-khap/ka**
I am fine	**Sa-bai-dee-khap/ka**
Excuse me	**Kor-toht-khap/ka**

I understand	Kao-jai-khap/ka
I don't understand	Mai-kao-jai-khap/ka
Do you speak English?	Khun-poot-pa-sa-angrit-dai-mai-khap/ka?
Where is the toilet?	Hawng-nam-yoo-tee-nai-khap/ka?
Do you have . . . ?	Mee . . . mai-khap/ka?
drinking water	nam-deum
coffee/tea with milk/sugar	cafe/cha sai nohm/nam-than
How much?	Tao-rai?
That's expensive/very expensive	Paeng/paeng maak
Can I get a discount?	Loht-dai-mai-khap/ka?
Bus station	Satani-rot-meh
Train station	Satani-rot-fai
Stop here	Yoot-tee-nee-khap/ka
Not spicy, please	Mai-pet-khap/ka

THE BEST OF THAILAND IN 2 WEEKS

Thailand is known worldwide for its Buddhist temples and beautiful beaches. Fortunately for visitors, the recent growth of no-frills airlines providing service throughout the country means that all the top spots are no more than an inexpensive hour-long flight from Bangkok. The following 2-week plan starts you off in Bangkok (temples) and then takes you south to Phuket, Ko Phi Phi, and Krabi (beaches). The last stop is Chiang Mai in the north (more temples), before you return to Bangkok or head to your next destination.

Days 1–3: Bangkok ★★★

Not to be missed, the capital is Thailand's most happening and vibrant city. It is also extremely congested, so you'll want to stay at a hotel with easy access to the BTS skytrain. On your first day, take the skytrain to Saphan Taksin pier on the Chao Phraya River and hop a tourist boat heading north. Stop off at **Wat Po** to see the giant **Reclining Buddha,** followed by the **Grand Palace** and **Wat Phra Kaeo,** which houses the **Emerald Buddha.** On your second day, start shopping. If it's the weekend, head to **Chatuchak Market,** a full day in itself. If it's a weekday, then **Sukhumvit Road** beckons—hit the malls during the day before strolling through infamous **Patpong** and its **Night Market.** On your third day, take a cruise upriver to the old capital of **Ayutthaya,** home to an array of temples in varying states of decay.

Days 4–5: Phuket ★★★

Fly directly to Phuket, one of Thailand's most beautiful islands. Relax by getting a massage or enjoying the beach (or both) during the day; then head to **Patong** for some adventurous nightlife. If you're up for it after a night on the town, a little daylight adventure can be had by kayaking in **Phang Nga Bay.**

Days 6–7: Ko Phi Phi ★★★

Hop a morning ferry to Phi Phi, and you'll be settled in at your resort by lunch. **Snorkeling** and **scuba diving** are the activities du jour. Leonardo DiCaprio fans should choose a day tour that stops at the locale where *The Beach* was filmed.

Days 8–9: Railay Beach ★★

A longtail boat from your resort drops you off at a ferry for the short hop back to the mainland and Railay Beach in Krabi Province. Spend the afternoon at one of the beach's **climbing schools,** battling gravity on sheer karst peaks. The next day, give your body a rest on the white sands of **Phra Nang Beach.** Wade out to **Happy Island** at low tide.

Day 10: Transit to Chiang Mai

There are no direct flights from Krabi to Chiang Mai, which means you'll have a stopover in Bangkok, a full day of travel, and a necessary break from the sun.

Days 11–13: Chiang Mai ★★★

Rent a bicycle or hire a tuk-tuk, and visit some of Chiang Mai's 300 temples. Don't miss **Wat Chedi Luang** and **Wat Phra Singh.** In the evening, browse the locally made handicrafts at the famous **Night Bazaar.** The next morning, hire a *songtao* for the drive to the top of **Doi Suthep** mountain and get blessed by a monk at **Wat Phra That.** If you've fallen in love with Thai food, take a half-day **cooking class;** if you're not shopped out, hop on a white *songtao* to **San Kamphaeng Road,** a retail paradise. To cap off your northern adventure (especially if you have an extra day or two), take a **jungle trek** and visit the local hill tribes.

Day 14: Bangkok or Beyond

Fly back to Bangkok to tie up any loose ends—for instance, sometimes it's easier to mail your souvenirs home than to lug them on the plane—or head to the next port of call on your Southeast Asian adventure.

PLANNING YOUR TRIP TO THAILAND

Visitor Information

The **Tourism Authority of Thailand (TAT)** publishes pamphlets and maps, as well as current schedules for festivals and holidays. Visit its useful website at **www.tourismthailand.org**. Once in the country, you'll also find many free tourist maps and resources.

Entry Requirements

All visitors to Thailand must carry a passport valid for at least 6 months with proof of onward passage (either a return or through ticket). Visa applications are not required if you are staying up to 30 days and are a national of one of 41 designated countries, including Australia, Canada, Ireland, New Zealand, the U.K., and the U.S. New Zealanders may stay up to 3 months. The **Immigration Division of the Royal Thai Police Department** has moved to the Government Center on Chaengwattana Rd. Soi 7 (*©* **021412-9889**), which is way out to the north of town and far from any public transport. A taxi from downtown costs around 300B, or from Mo Chit BTS about 100B. A visa extension costs a whopping 1,900B. It is best to always have a proper visa and exit the country by the date stamped in your passport (or make the proverbial "visa run" over border points with Myanmar, Laos, Cambodia, or Malaysia). Visitors who overstay their visa will be fined 500B for each extra day, payable in cash upon exiting the country. For exhaustive visa particulars, try the unofficial but informative site www.thaivisa.com.

Customs Regulations

Tourists are allowed to enter the country with 1 liter of alcohol and 200 cigarettes (or 250g of cigars or smoking tobacco) per adult, duty free. There are no restrictions on the import of foreign currencies or traveler's checks, but travelers need an export license for any antiques or art objects that they intend to take out of the country.

Money

The Thai unit of currency, the **baht,** is written on price tags and elsewhere as the letter B, sometimes crossed with a vertical slash (written "B" in this chapter, as in "100B"). One baht is divided into 100 satang, though you'll rarely see a satang coin. Yellow coins represent 25 and 50 satang; silver coins come in 1, 2, 5, and 10B (though the 2B coin is quite rare). Bank notes come in denominations of 20 (green), 50 (blue), 100 (red), 500 (purple), and 1,000 (khaki). This edition uses the rate of **35 baht = $1.**

ATMS All major banks throughout the country now have ATMs, which are also common in major tourist spots.

CURRENCY EXCHANGE The largest banks in Thailand—try **Bangkok Bank, Thai Farmers Bank, Siam Commercial Bank,** or **Bank of Ayudhya**—all perform debit and cash advance services through the MasterCard/Cirrus or Visa/PLUS networks. **Note:** Time changes between here and home can affect your ability to withdraw cash on 2 consecutive business days.

TRAVELER'S CHECKS Traveler's checks can be cashed in most banks or big hotels.

CREDIT CARDS Nearly all international hotels and larger businesses accept credit cards, though it's cash only in rural parts. Despite protests from credit card companies, many establishments add a 3% to 5% surcharge for payment. Use discretion in using your card—all major credit card companies list Thailand as a high-risk area for fraud. Don't let your card out of your sight, even for a moment, and be sure to keep all receipts. To report a lost or stolen credit card, call the emergency service numbers listed under "Lost & Found" in "Fast Facts: Thailand" (p. 42).

When to Go

CLIMATE Thailand has two distinct climate zones: tropical in the south and tropical savanna in the north. The northern and central areas of the country (including Bangkok) experience three distinct seasons. The hot season lasts from March to May, with temperatures averaging in the upper 90s Fahrenheit (mid-30s Celsius); April is the hottest month. This period sees very little rain, if any at all. The rainy season begins in June and lasts until October; the average temperature is 84°F (29°C), with 90% humidity. While the rainy season brings frequent showers, it's rare for them to last for a whole day or for days on end. Daily showers come in torrents, usually in the late afternoon or evening. The cool season, from November through February, has temperatures from the high 70s to low 80s Fahrenheit (mid- to upper 20s Celsius), with moderate and infrequent rain showers. In the north during the cool season (which is also the peak season for tourism), day temperatures can be as low as 60°F (16°C) in Chiang Mai and 41°F (5°C) in the hills.

The southern Malay Peninsula has intermittent showers year-round and daily ones during the rainy season (temperatures average in the low 80sF/high 20sC). If you're traveling to Phuket or Ko Samui, it will be helpful to note that the two islands alternate peak seasons. Optimal weather on Phuket occurs between November and April, when the island welcomes the highest numbers of travelers. Alternately, Ko Samui's good weather lasts from about February to October.

PUBLIC HOLIDAYS & EVENTS   Many holidays are based on the Thai lunar calendar, with numerous regional Buddhist fetes. The national holidays are **New Year's Day,** on January 1; **Makha Puja,** which falls in February; **Chakri Day,** on April 6; **Songkran,** the **Thai New Year,** celebrated from April 13 to April 15; **Coronation Day,** on May 5; **Visakha Puja,** which falls in May; **Asalha Puja,** which falls in July; **Her Majesty the Queen's Birthday,** on August 12; **Chulalongkorn Day,** on October 23; **His Majesty the King's Birthday,** on December 5; **Constitution Day,** on December 10; and **New Year's Eve,** on December 31.

Health & Safety

HEALTH CONCERNS   See the "Health & Safety" section in chapter 10 (p. 632) for information on the major health issues that affect travelers to Southeast Asia.

Don't drink the tap water in Thailand, even in the major hotels. Most hotels provide bottled water in or near the minibar or in the bathroom; use it for brushing your teeth as well as for drinking. Most restaurants serve bottled or boiled water and ice made from boiled water, but always ask to be sure. You may also want to exercise caution when eating from roadside and market stalls or in smaller local restaurants.

Air quality is not good in Bangkok, which has no emissions standards. Buses, trucks, and cars belch some toxic stuff, so visitors with respiratory concerns or sensitivity should take caution and consider donning a face mask. In recent years, Chiang Mai has also suffered badly from air pollution at the end of the dry season (Mar/Apr).

Thailand suffered fallout from the regionwide **SARS** scare in the winter and spring of 2003, but there have been no reported cases in the region since 2004. A number of cases of **avian influenza,** also called the **bird flu,** have been reported in Thailand, but the disease has been mostly isolated to people working in the poultry industry. Note that you cannot contract bird flu from consuming cooked chicken.

SAFETY CONCERNS   Visitors to Thailand should refer to their home country's overseas travel bureau or with the **U.S. State Department** (click the "more" button under "Travel Warnings" at **www.travel.state.gov** for a complete, up-to-date list by country) to learn more about the present situation in the area. The far south of Thailand has seen repeated attacks by Muslim extremists on the Buddhist population, police, and military. Attacks blamed on Muslim groups have moved north from the immediate border areas of Pattani, Narathiwat, and Yala provinces to Hat Yai in Songkhla Province, a major transit point in the south. Although these attacks were isolated incidents, they did target tourist areas; at least two foreign nationals were killed. Travel to the far south is generally discouraged.

The general political situation in Thailand, in both Bangkok and provincial capitals, is still very volatile, with members of the United Front for Democracy against Dictatorship (UDD, or "red shirts") and People's Alliance for Democracy (PAD, or "yellow shirts") looking to escalate conflict. Thus, tourists should always be aware of their surroundings (especially in crowded areas), avoid political gatherings of any size, and keep abreast of the current political situation before and during their trip. In addition to the U.S. State Department website (see above), local newspaper websites include **www.bangkokpost.com** and **www.nationmultimedia.com**.

Random violent crime in Thailand is rare; however, petty crimes such as purse snatching and pickpocketing are common. Overland travelers should take care on overnight buses and trains, popular targets for small-time thieves.

Road conditions vary throughout the country, but Bangkok is busy and chaotic. Crossing the streets can be the greatest risk on your trip; move slowly and exercise caution. In the beach towns, motorbike accidents are all too common—always wear a helmet if you decide to rent a vehicle.

Getting There

BY PLANE   In September 2006, the ultramodern **Suvarnabhumi International Airport** (say Su-va-na-*poom*) opened, and it now handles all international flights and many domestic flights into and out of Bangkok. However, due to "teething problems" at Suvarnabhumi, the old airport of **Don Muang** remains in service for nonconnecting domestic flights. **Thai Airways** (✆ **800/426-5204** in the U.S.; head office at 89 Vibhavadi Rangsit Rd., Bangkok, ✆ **02545-3691;** www.thaiair.com) covers virtually all Southeast Asian nations on its routes.

Note that while most international flights arrive in Bangkok, you can also fly direct to Phuket, Ko Samui, Hat Yai, and Chiang Mai from regional destinations such as Hong Kong, Singapore, Kuala Lumpur in Malaysia, Vientiane and Luang Prabang in Laos, and Phnom Penh and Siem Reap in Cambodia.

BY TRAIN   Thailand is accessible via train from Singapore and peninsular Malaysia. Malaysia's **Keretapi Tanah Melayu Berhad (KTM)** rail service begins in Singapore (✆ **652/6222-5165**), stopping in Kuala Lumpur (✆ **603/2267-1200**) and Butterworth (Penang; ✆ **604/323-7962**), before heading for Thailand, where it joins service with the State Railway of Thailand. Bangkok's **Hua Lamphong Railway Station** is centrally located on Krung Kassem Road (✆ **02223-3762**).

The ***Eastern & Oriental Express*** (✆ **800/524-2420** in the U.S., or 65/395-0678 in Singapore; www.orient-express.com) operates a 2-night/3-day journey between Singapore and Bangkok that makes getting there almost better than being there. The romance of 1930s colonial travel is joined with modern luxury on this luxurious train. Departures are limited; current fares start at $2,210 per person one-way during high season. There are also onward connections to Chiang Mai with a stop in Ayutthaya.

BY BUS   From every major city in peninsular Malaysia (and even Singapore), you can pick up a bus to Thailand. VIP buses cost more but have reclining seats and more legroom; traveling overland along the length of the southern peninsula is best by train, however. Buses connect with Laos over the Lao-Thai Friendship Bridge to Vientiane and at other southern border crossings, and with Cambodia via Poipet.

Getting Around

Transportation within Thailand is accessible, efficient, and inexpensive. If your time is short, fly. But if you have the time to take in the countryside and you care to see a bit of provincial living, travel by bus, train, or private car.

BY PLANE   Most convenient are domestic flights on **Thai Airways** (6 Larn Luang Rd., Bangkok; ✆ **02356-1111**), which connects Bangkok and 27 domestic cities, including Chiang Mai, Chiang Rai, Mae Hong Son, Phitsanulok, Loei, Surat Thani, and Phuket. **Bangkok Airways** (99 Moo 14, Vibhavadirangsit Rd., Chatuchak; ✆ **02270-6699**; www.bangkokair.com) connects Bangkok with Ko Samui, Phuket, Krabi, U Tapao (near Pattaya), Trat (for Ko Chang), Sukhothai, and Chiang Mai, and has international flights from seven Asian destinations. Budget airline **Air Asia** (✆ **02515-9999** in Bangkok; www.airasia.com) flies between Bangkok and Chiang Mai, Chiang Rai, Phuket, Krabi, Hat Yai, and several other destinations, both domestic and international, for supercheap (book ahead).

BY TRAIN   Bangkok's **Hua Lamphong Railway Station** (✆ **02223-3762,** or 1690 for information hot line; www.railway.co.th), easily reached by subway, is a convenient, user-friendly facility. Clear signs point the way to public toilets, pay phones, and a food court. A post office, an information counter, a police box, ATMs and money-changing facilities, convenience shops, a baggage check, and restaurants surround a large open area.

From this hub, the State Railway of Thailand provides regular service to destinations north as far as Chiang Mai, northeast to Nong Khai and Ubon Ratchathani, southeast to Pattaya, and south to Thailand's southern border with continuing service to Malaysia. Complete schedules and fare information can be obtained at their website or by calling Hua Lamphong Railway Station directly at the numbers listed above.

The various fare classes of trains are based on speed and comfort. The fastest is the Special Express, which is the best choice for long-haul, overnight travel. These trains cut travel time by as much as 60% and have sleeper cars, which are a must for the really long trips. Rapid trains are the next-best option. Prices vary by class, from air-conditioned sleeper cars in first class down to the straight-backed, hard seats in third class.

BY BUS   Thailand has a very efficient and inexpensive bus system, highly recommended for budget travelers and short-haul trips. Options abound, but the major choices are government or private, air-conditioned or non-air-conditioned. Most travelers use the private, air-conditioned buses. Buses are best for short excursions; long-haul buses are an excellent value, but they can be slow and uncomfortable.

Bangkok has three major bus stations, each serving a different part of the country. All air-conditioned public buses to the west and the southern peninsula arrive and depart from the **Southern Bus Terminal** (✆ **02894-6122**) at Putthamonthon Soi 1 in North Thonburi, about 10km (6¼ miles) west of the river over the Phra Pinklao Bridge from the Democracy Monument. Service to the east coast (including Pattaya) arrives and departs from the **Eastern Bus Terminal,** also known as **Ekamai** (✆ **02391-2504**), on Sukhumvit Road opposite Soi 63 (Ekamai BTS skytrain station). Buses to the north arrive and leave from the **Northern Bus Terminal,** aka **Mo Chit** (✆ **02936-2852**), Kampaengphet 2 Road, Mo Chit, near the Chatuchak Weekend Market, and a short taxi or bus ride from the Mo Chit skytrain station. VIP buses leave from locations in town.

BY CAR   Renting a car is a snap in Thailand, although self-driving in Bangkok traffic needs nerves of steel. Outside the city, it's a good option, though Thai drivers are quite reckless and American drivers must reorient themselves to driving on the left. Among the many car-rental agencies, both **Avis** (✆ **02251-1131**; www.avis thailand.com) and **Budget** (✆ **02203-9222**; www.budget.co.th) have convenient offices around the country.

telephone dialing AT A GLANCE

- **To place a call from your home country to Thailand:** Dial the international access code (011 in the U.S. and Canada, 0011 in Australia, 0170 in New Zealand, 00 in the U.K.), plus Thailand's country code **(66)**, and then the phone number (for example, a Bangkok number would be 011 66 2000-0000). *Important note:* When making international calls to Thailand, be sure to omit the 0 that appears before all phone numbers in this guide (thus you will only dial eight digits after the 66 country code).

- **To call a cellphone number in Thailand:** All Thai cellphone numbers are now 10 digits, beginning with 08, but don't forget to drop the 0 when calling from abroad (for example, 011 66 80000-0000).

- **To place a direct international call from Thailand:** Dial the international access code **(00),** plus the country code, the area or city code, and the number (for example, to call the U.S., you'd dial 00 1 000/000-0000).

- **International country codes are as follows:** Australia, 61; Cambodia, 855; Canada, 1; Hong Kong, 852; Indonesia, 62; Laos, 856; Malaysia, 60; Myanmar, 95; New Zealand, 64; the Philippines, 63; Singapore, 65; U.K., 44; U.S., 1; Vietnam, 84.

You can rent a car with or without a driver. All drivers are required to have an international driver's license. Self-drive rates start at around 1,000B per day for a small Honda sedan.

Local tour operators in larger destinations such as Chiang Mai, Phuket, and Ko Samui will rent cars for considerably cheaper than the larger, more well known agencies. Sometimes the savings are up to 50%. These companies rarely require international driver's licenses. Always ask if you will still be covered by their insurance policy.

Tips on Accommodations

Thailand accommodations run the gamut, but you can expect a high standard of comfort and service at affordable rates. In places such as Phuket and Ko Samui, rainy season brings discounts of 30% and 50%. You can negotiate with hotel reservations agents—there are always special discounts, packages, or free add-ons for extra value, and it never hurts to ask.

Tips on Dining

Larger Thai cities and towns play host to many Western restaurants, but go for authentic Thai wherever possible. One-dish meals such as noodle soup, fried rice, or noodles are popular for solo travelers, but Thai meals are best when shared family-style. There are many regional variations, but the most notable are the barbecue, sticky rice, and spicy papaya salads in Isan (the northeast) and the fiery coconut curries of the south; always ask about regional specials. Most family meals consist of a meat or fish dish (often a whole fish), fried or steamed vegetables, a curry, stir-fried dishes of meat and vegetables, and a soup, such as fiery *tom yum.* Meals are lengthy and boisterous affairs, and food is picked at slowly (often accompanied by local beer, rice wine, or strong whiskey). Table manners are casual and practical.

Be cautious with street eats: Check out the stall to see that it's clean and the ingredients are fresh. Most places temper spices for foreigners, but always ask.

You're not expected to tip at a Thai restaurant, but rounding up the bill or leaving 20B to 50B on top of most checks is acceptable.

Tips on Shopping

Shopping is a full-contact sport in Thailand. In markets and smaller shops, bargaining is the name of the game. If your suggested price is accepted, it is rude to walk away without finishing the sale. Keep in mind that in high-traffic tourist areas, prices are always inflated. In shopping malls and boutiques, prices are fixed. Some shops impose a 3% charge on credit card purchases.

[Fast FACTS] THAILAND

American Express
There is no specific agent that handles American Express services in Thailand anymore, but there is an **American Express** office at 388 Pahonyothin Rd., in Bangkok. You can reach the office at © **02273-5500** during business hours (Mon–Fri 8:30am–5pm) or call the customer service hot line (© **02273-5544**) with any problems or questions.

Business Hours Government offices (including branch post offices) are open Monday through Friday from 8:30am to 4:30pm, with a lunch break between noon and 1pm. Businesses are generally open from 8am to 5pm. Shops often stay open from 8am to 7pm or later, 7 days a week. Department stores are generally open from 10am to 9pm.

Drugstores Pharmacies carry brand-name medications; pharmacists often speak some English and are very helpful.

Electricity All outlets are 220 volts AC (50 cycles), with two flat- or round-pronged holes. If you use a 110-volt hair dryer, electric shaver, or battery charger, bring a transformer and an adapter. If you're bringing a laptop, don't forget a surge protector.

Embassies & Consulates Most countries have embassies in Bangkok; the U.S., Australia, Canada, and the U.K. also have consulates in Chiang Mai. Most embassies have 24-hour emergency services for their citizens. See "Fast Facts" in the Bangkok and Chiang Mai sections for contact information.

Emergencies Call © **1699** or 1155 for the tourist police. Don't expect many English speakers at normal police posts outside the major tourist areas. It is a good idea to contact your embassy in case of emergencies, both medical and legal.

Internet Access You'll find Internet cafes everywhere in Thailand. See the

"Fast Facts" sections in specific destination sections for details.

Language Central (often called Bangkok) Thai is the official language. English is spoken in the major cities at most hotels, restaurants, and shops, and is the second language of the professional class. See "Language," p. 34, for more information.

Liquor Laws The official drinking age in Thailand is 18, but laws are loosely followed—you can buy alcohol in most areas any time of day or night, with exceptions for certain Buddhist holidays and election days. All restaurants, bars, and nightclubs sell booze, and stores are licensed to sell alcohol from 11am to 2pm and 5pm to midnight. Nightspots close between midnight and 2am.

Lost & Found Your home embassy in Thailand is the place to contact if you've lost your travel documents and need them replaced. For more information, see "Embassies & Consulates," above.

If you have lost anything or had your valuables stolen, call the national police hot line at ☏ **1155**. Believe it or not, there have been several reports of lost items being returned to the appropriate consulate by taxi drivers and bus attendants.

To report a lost or stolen credit card in Thailand, call **American Express** (☏ **02273-5544**), **Diners Club** (☏ **02238-3660**), **MasterCard** (☏ **001-800-11-887-0663**), or **Visa** (☏ **001-800-441-4358**).

If you need emergency cash over the weekend, when all banks and American Express offices are closed, you can have money wired to you via **Western Union** (☏ **02/254-7000** in Bangkok), which has branches in Bangkok and in many provincial capitals. *A special warning:* Western Union's exchange rate is not favorable, so use this service only in an emergency.

Mail Airmail postcards to the U.S. cost 12B to 15B, depending on the size of the card; first-class letters cost 19B per 10 grams. Rates to Europe are about the same. Airmail delivery usually takes 7 days.

Air parcel post to the U.S. costs 950B per kilogram. Surface or sea parcel post costs 550B for 1 kilogram (and takes 3–4 months for delivery). International Express Mail (EMS) costs 600B for up to 250 grams and 700B for up to 500 grams, with delivery

guaranteed in 3 to 6 days. See individual destination sections for local post offices and their hours.

Shipping by air freight is expensive. Major international delivery services have their main dispatching offices in Bangkok, though they deliver throughout the country; these include **DHL Thailand,** Sathorn Road (☏ **02345-5000**); **FedEx,** Rama IV Road (☏ **1782** hot line); and **UPS Parcel Delivery Service,** 16/1 Sukhumvit Soi 44/1 (☏ **02728-9000**). Many businesses will also pack and mail merchandise for you at a reasonable price.

Newspapers & Magazines The major domestic English-language dailies are the *Bangkok Post* and the *Nation,* distributed in the morning in the capital and later in the day around the country. They cover the domestic political scene, as well as international news from AP, UPI, and Reuters wire services.

Police In an emergency, call the tourist police at ☏ **1699** or 1155 to connect with English speakers 24 hours a day.

Safety Petty crimes, such as purse snatching or pickpocketing, are common in Thailand. Overland travelers should take care on overnight buses and trains, popular targets for small-time thieves. Beware of inviting strangers to your hotel room—there are many incidents of drugging and robbery (especially by prostitutes).

Watch out for credit card scams: Carry a minimum of cards, don't allow them out of your sight, and keep all receipts. Don't carry unnecessary valuables, and keep those you do have in your hotel safe.

A special warning: Be wary of strangers who offer to guide you (particularly in Bangkok), take you to any shop (especially jewelry shops), or buy you food or drink. This most frequently occurs near tourist attractions. Without exception, this is a scam of some kind. These folks invariably want to sell you fake gems or waste your time and earn a commission. Just walk away.

See "Health & Safety," p. 632, for more tips on keeping yourself safe.

Taxes Hotels charge a 7% government value-added tax (VAT) and typically add a 10% service charge; hotel restaurants add 8.25% government tax. Smaller hotels quote the price inclusive of these charges.

Telephones The international country code for Thailand is **66**. Major hotels in Thailand offer international direct dialing (IDD), long-distance service, and in-house fax transmission. However, hotels levy a surcharge on local and long-distance calls, which can add up to 50% in some cases. Credit card or collect calls are a much better value, but most hotels add a hefty service charge for these too.

Major post offices have special offices or booths for overseas calls, as well as fax and telex service, usually open from 7am to 11pm. Guesthouses and travel agents in tourist areas offer long-distance calling or call-back service on their private line or use very affordable Net-to-phone connections of varying quality. Local calls can be made from any red or blue public pay phone. Card phones are your best bet; buy a Telephone Organization of Thailand (TOT) card, for use in yellow phones, anywhere.

For directory assistance, dial ✆ **1133**. See "Telephone Dialing at a Glance," p. 41, for details on how to make calls to and from Thailand.

Time Zone Thailand is 7 hours ahead of Greenwich Mean Time. During winter months, Bangkok is 7 hours ahead of London, 12 hours ahead of New York, and 15 hours ahead of Los Angeles.

Tipping If no service charge is added to your check in a fine-dining establishment, a 10% tip is appropriate. Airport or hotel porters expect tips, but 20B to 50B is acceptable. Feel free to reward good service wherever you find it. Tipping taxi drivers is not expected, but accepted. Carry small bills, as many drivers either don't have change or won't admit having any.

Toilets Virtually all restaurants and hotels have Western toilets. Some food shops and a few budget hotels have an Asian-style squat toilet—a hole in the floor with foot pads on either side. Near the toilet is a water bucket or sink with a small ladle. The water is for cleaning yourself and flushing the toilet. Don't count on these places having toilet paper. Shopping malls and department stores invariably have Western-style restrooms.

Water It is safer not to drink tap water, even in the major hotels. Most hotels provide bottled water in or near the minibar or in the bathroom; use it for brushing your teeth as well as for drinking. Most restaurants serve bottled or boiled water and ice made from boiled water, but always ask to be sure.

BANGKOK ★★★

With an estimated population of 8 million in a country of only 67 million, Thailand's capital is the urban and cultural heart of the land. Choked with traffic, polluted, and corrupt, it is more than 30 times bigger than any other city in the country. Central Bangkok is all columns of glass and steel, hulking shopping complexes, and hotels linked at the city center by an elevated monorail, the BTS skytrain, and a slick new subway.

Bangkok (known to Thais as *krung thep*) was founded when King Rama I moved the city across the river from Thonburi in 1782. Today, the capital's stunning temples share space with skyscrapers and Starbucks; luxury condominiums stand stridently just a stone's throw from labyrinthine slums along dirty canals; and glittering shopping malls cast their shadows over dusty open-air street bazaars. The city is less "Asian" than what many visitors often expect, but there are still gems to find in and among the new construction and suburban sprawl, and exploring Bangkok is certainly a highlight.

Getting There

Bangkok has a massive airport, three bus terminals, and a centrally located train station. Affordable taxis and tuk-tuks (three-wheeled, motorized trishaws) cruise the broad avenues. The BTS skytrain—the city's elevated rail line—and the new Bangkok subway have led to improved connections throughout the city, for example, between the domestic train station and the northern bus terminal.

BY PLANE Bangkok is a major hub for air travel in Southeast Asia, with around 100 airlines providing service. The ultramodern **Suvarnabhumi International Airport** (say Su-va-na-*poom;* www.bangkokairportonline.com; airport code BKK), with one of the largest terminal buildings in the world, is a city unto itself, and is located about 30km (19 miles) east of Bangkok.

Passengers will find the following services available upon arrival: luggage storage for 100B per day; currency-exchange banks with the same rates as those in town; ATMs; phone-rental booths; **Airport Information** (✆ 02132-1888) and **Tourism Authority of Thailand (TAT)** booths; Association of Thai Travel Agents desks; Thai Hotel Association desks; Thai and international restaurants; massage services; convenience stores; and the **Novotel Suvarnabhumi Airport Hotel** (✆ 02131-1111).

In August 2010, the much-delayed **express rail link** finally opened, providing the fastest way from the airport into town between 6am and midnight. The direct express train (150B) leaves every half-hour and takes just 15 minutes to the City Air Terminal in Makkasan, which is connected to the subway at Phetchaburi. The City Line service (15B–45B) leaves every 15 minutes and stops at eight stations, taking 30 minutes to the city center, linking with the skytrain at Phayathai.

Metered taxi stands are on Level 2 of the terminal building, and there is a 50B surcharge for airport service. The fare to most downtown destinations is around 250B to 300B, and the journey takes anywhere between 45 and 90 minutes.

Private limousine services have air-conditioned sedans for hire from booths in the arrivals hall. Trips to town start at 950B, but it is really worth taking this costly option only if there is an enormous queue for metered taxis.

The **Airport Express** bus is a convenient and inexpensive alternative, with regular departures from 5am to midnight. The four routes available are from Suvarnabhumi to Silom Road; to Khao San Road; to Sukhumvit Road; and to Hua Lamphong Railway Station (via Siam Center). Stops include many major hotels. Tickets cost just 150B.

The **transport center,** a 3km (1¾-mile) shuttle ride from the airport terminal, handles all city bus service to and from Bangkok, buses to outlying provinces, and all car-rental companies. Take a free airport shuttle from outside of the arrivals hall (Level 2).

City buses leave regularly and have clearly marked routes (the no. 552 bus is the most convenient for downtown Bangkok, stopping at the On Nut BTS station). **Interprovincial buses** with service to Pattaya (124B), Trat/Ko Chang (308B), and Nong Khai/Vientiane, Laos (454B) leave less frequently throughout the day.

Car-rental companies at Suvarnabhumi include **Avis** (✆ 02/251-2038), **Budget** (✆ 02/203-9251), and **Hertz** (✆ 02/266-5070). Daily rentals start at around 1,000B for a Toyota Soluna. Pickup and drop-off is at the transport center.

The old airport at **Don Muang** (www.donmuangairportonline.com; airport code DMK), located 24km (15 miles) north of the city center, is still used for nonconnecting domestic flights, so check your travel documents carefully to be sure which airport you are arriving at or leaving from. Being less crowded than before, it is relatively easy to get into the city center by **metered taxi** (stand in front of terminal; 50B surcharge; fare downtown around 200B–250B).

BY TRAIN The Thai rail network is extremely well organized, connecting Bangkok with major cities throughout the country. (You can also travel by train to Bangkok from Singapore, via Kuala Lumpur and Butterworth, Malaysia.)

All trains to and from the capital stop at **Hua Lamphong Railway Station** (☎ **1690** or 02223-3762), east of Chinatown at the intersection of Rama IV and Krung Kasem roads. The station has many services, including baggage check and a small food court. The information counter is helpful. From the station, connect to your destination by subway, metered taxi, or tuk-tuk. Be on the alert for scammers around the station.

BY BUS Bangkok has three major bus stations, each serving a different part of the country. Buses to the west and the southern peninsula arrive and depart from the **Southern Bus Terminal** (☎ **02894-6122**), on Putthamonthon Soi 1, west of the river over the Phra Pinklao Bridge from the Democracy Monument. Service to the east coast arrives and departs from the **Eastern Bus Terminal,** also known as **Ekamai** (☎ **02391-2504**), on Sukhumvit Road opposite Soi 63 (Ekamai BTS skytrain station). Buses to the north arrive at and leave from the **Northern Bus Terminal,** aka **Mo Chit** (☎ **02936-2852**), Kampaengphet 2 Road, Mo Chit, near the Chatuchak Weekend Market (easily reached by the BTS skytrain or the MRT subway).

City Layout

Vintage 19th-century photographs of Bangkok show the Chao Phraya River bustling with humble longtail boats and elaborate royal barges. Built along the banks of the broad, winding river, the city spread inland through a network of *klongs* (canals) that rivaled the intricacy—though never the elegance—of Venice.

The **Historic District,** along the Chao Phraya River, contains most of the city's historical sights, such as the Grand Palace, and most of the city's original *wats* (temples with resident monks). Following the river south, you'll run into the narrow lanes of Bangkok's **Chinatown** and, farther down, a row of the city's finest riverside hotels, including the Oriental and the Peninsula. Inland from the river, Bangkok's central **business district** is situated on Sathorn, Silom, and Surawongse roads, beginning at Charoen Krung (or "New") Road. Bangkok's main shopping thoroughfare, on **Rama I Road,** between Phayathai and Ratchadamri roads, sports huge modern shopping complexes such as CentralWorld and Siam Paragon. East of Rama I, **Sukhumvit Road** has acres of expat condos, restaurants, shopping, and nightlife.

Get to know the Thai word *soi,* meaning "lane." Larger thoroughfares in the city have names, and *sois* are the many numbered side streets along their length, odd and even numbers on alternate sides. For example, Sukhumvit Soi 5 is the home of the Amari Boulevard Hotel, while Sukhumvit Soi 8, a few minutes' walk east and across the street, is where you'll find Le Banyan restaurant. Note that closely numbered *sois* are not necessarily near each other.

STREET MAPS Nancy Chandler's *Map of Bangkok* (275B from www.nancychandler.net) is a detailed, colorful source for finding specific hotels, restaurants, and shopping. The free *Thaiways Map of Bangkok* is chock-full of adverts and detailed city maps with specific insets. Bus maps are plentiful and helpful if you go that route.

Getting Around

It can take more than 2 hours by taxi to get from one side of town to the other during rush hour, so it's best to avail yourself of the many new options below. Taxis are affordable, but at the wrong time of day (difficult to predict) can be a real nightmare.

BY SKYTRAIN The **Bangkok Mass Transit System (BTS skytrain)** is an elevated railway system high above the maddening traffic. Trains access Bangkok's

Bangkok Metro Lines

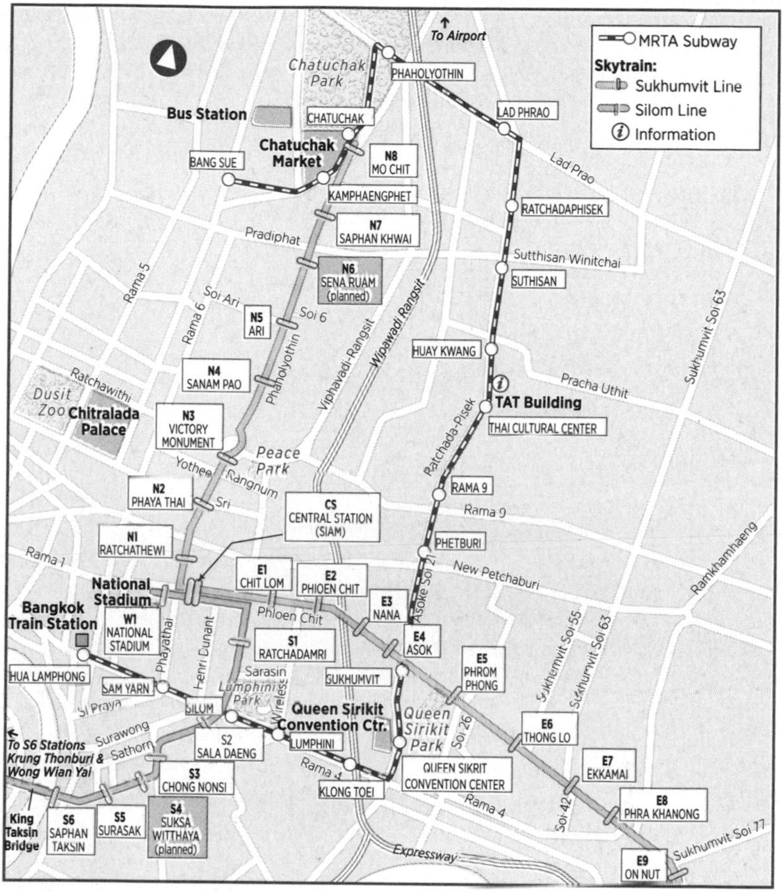

To Airport
MRTA Subway
Skytrain:
Sukhumvit Line
Silom Line
Information
Chatuchak Park
PHAHOLYOTHIN
Bus Station
CHATUCHAK
LAD PHRAO
Chatuchak Market
BANG SUE
N8 MO CHIT
Lad Prao
KAMPHAENGPHET
RATCHADAPHISEK
N7 SAPHAN KHWAI
Pradiphat
Sutthisan Winitchai
N6 SENA RUAM (planned)
SUTHISAN
Rama 5
Soi Ari
N5 ARI
Soi 6
Rama 6
Phaholyothin
Viphavadi-Rangsit
Wipawadi Rangsit
HUAY KWANG
Sukhumvit Soi 63
N4 SANAM PAO
Pracha Uthit
Ratchawithi
Dusit Zoo
Chitralada Palace
TAT Building
N3 VICTORY MONUMENT
Ratchada-Pisek
THAI CULTURAL CENTER
Peace Park
Yothee Rangnum
RAMA 9
N2 PHAYA THAI
Sri
Rama 9
CS CENTRAL STATION (SIAM)
N1 RATCHATHEWI
PHETBURI
Rama 1
New Petchaburi
Ramkhamhaeng
E1 CHIT LOM
E2 PHIOEN CHIT
National Stadium
Bangkok Train Station
E3 NANA
Asoke Soi 21
Phloen Chit
W1 NATIONAL STADIUM
Henri Dunant
E4 ASOK
S1 RATCHADAMRI
Sukhumvit Soi 55
Sukhumvit Soi 63
Phayathai
E5 PHROM PHONG
HUA LAMPHONG
Sarasin
SUKHUMVIT
SAM YARN
Lumphini Park
Wireless
Si Praya
SILOM
Queen Sirikit Convention Ctr.
Queen Sirikit Park
Soi 26
E6 THONG LO
To S6 Stations Krung Thonburi & Wong Wian Yai
Surawong
Sathorn
S2 SALA DAENG
LUMPHINI
Rama 4
E7 EKKAMAI
S3 CHONG NONSI
KLONG TOEI
QUEEN SIKRIT CONVENTION CENTER
Soi 42
King Taksin Bridge
S6 SAPHAN TAKSIN
S5 SURASAK
S4 SUKSA WITTHAYA (planned)
Rama 4
E8 PHRA KHANONG
Expressway
Sukhumvit Soi 77
E9 ON NUT

central areas and now connect with the **MRTA subway.** Single-journey tickets cost from 15B to 40B. Buy ticket cards at platform vending machines: Choose your numbered destination from a map, press the corresponding button on the map, and pay in a slot (get small change at the info counter as needed). Ticket cards let you through the turnstile and are required for exit, so be sure to hang onto them during the ride. Also available is a 1-day pass for 120B. The skytrain operates daily between 6am and midnight.

BY SUBWAY Bangkok's new subway line makes a reverse "C" though town, conveniently linking Hua Lamphong Railway Station with the Chatuchak Weekend Market and bus-terminal area, with connections to the BTS skytrain at Silom Road and on Sukhumvit at Asok. Hours of operation are 6am to midnight. Subway tokens cost between 15B and 39B, depending on distance traveled. Tap the token on the turnstile screen to enter, and put the token in the turnstile slot when exiting at your destination.

BY RIVERBOAT   Efficient and scenic, the public riverboats on the Chao Phraya are a great way to get around the sights in the city center and are a remarkable window on local life. Boats operated by the **Chao Phraya Express Company** (© **02623-6001-3;** www.chaophrayaexpressboat.com/en/home) trace the river's length, with stops at many piers (*tha* in Thai) both on the Thonburi side (west) and in central Bangkok (east). Good maps are posted at each stop. Most sightseers will board near Saphan Taksin BTS station, the last stop on the Silom Line as it meets the river. The major stops going into town from Saphan Taksin are Tha Ratchawong (in Chinatown off Ratchawong Rd.), Tha Thien (near Wat Po), Tha Chang (near the Temple of the Emerald Buddha), and Tha Maharaj (near Wat Mahathat). There is a range of boats available.

Tourist express boats, which run from Sathorn Pier (Central) to Phra Ahthit Pier every 30 minutes between 9:30am and 3pm, are the fastest and most convenient, with guides talking over a microphone about the sights you'll pass at riverside. Tickets are 150B, and are good for unlimited travel that day.

Express boats are long, white boats with pointed bow, bench seats, and open sides. They operate from 6am to 7pm. Mention your destination when you board, and the attendant will tell you if it's the right boat. Trips start at 12B to 31B.

Cross-river ferries are another category; these are useful for getting to places such as Wat Arun or other sights in Thonburi.

Private boats are also for hire for tours. See "Bangkok's Waterways," under "What to See & Do" (p. 66), for details.

BY BUS   Bangkok buses are cheap and frequent, if a bit confusing. Air-conditioned buses cost from 11B to 24B and save you from inhaling lots of exhaust fumes. Buy a map, bring small change, and be careful of pickpockets.

BY TAXI   Taxis are everywhere, or you can call © **1681** for a pickup. The meter starts at 35B for the first 3km (1¾ miles); thereafter, it's about 5B per kilometer. It is a good idea to have your hotel concierge or a Thai friend write out any destination in Thai. Avoid drivers who want to barter a flat fare. Tipping is appreciated.

BY CAR   You'd have to be a bit mad to drive yourself around Bangkok, what with the crazy traffic, left-side driving (if you're not used to it), and aggressive tactics of cabs and trucks. It is best to hire a car with a driver. Contact **Diethelm Travel** (© **02660-7000;** www.diethelmtravel.com), a leader in the region, for assistance.

BY TUK-TUK   As much a national symbol as the elephant, the tuk-tuk, a small, three-wheeled, open-sided vehicle powered by a motorcycle engine, is noisy (named for the putt-putt sound it makes), smoky, and offers lousy views, but can be good fun. Drivers whip around city traffic like kamikazes. They are not good for long hauls or during rush hour, but for short trips or off-peak hours, they're convenient and a real kick, especially for first-time visitors to Thailand.

All tuk-tuk fares are negotiated, usually beginning at 40B for short trips. Bargain hard, but remember you'll always end up paying more than locals. *Warning:* Tuk-tuk drivers are notorious for talking travelers into shopping trips (and collecting commissions). Drivers will offer a very low fare, but will waste your time by stranding you at small, out-of-the-way gem and silk emporiums, all places that scam you and where the driver gets a cut. Insist on being taken directly to where you want to go.

BY MOTORCYCLE TAXI   On every street corner, packs of drivers in colored vests play checkers, motorcycles standing by, waiting to shuttle passengers around the city. They are fast and can weave through traffic, but they are dangerous. Motorbike taxis are popular for short hops to the end of longer *sois,* or side streets, and cost from 20B for short trips. Put on the helmet, keep your knees tucked in, and hang on tight.

ON FOOT It is safe to walk around any part of town, but Bangkok is so spread out and the pollution so heavy that it's best to target a local area for pedestrian exploration.

Visitor Information & Tours

The **Bangkok Tourist Division** has offices at major tourist destinations throughout the city. Call ⟨℗ **02225-7612** with any questions, or check out www.bangkoktourist.com.

The **Tourism Authority of Thailand** (**TAT;** www.tourismthailand.org) offers general information about the provinces and operates a useful hot line at ℗ **1672.** It has two counters in Suvarnabhumi International Airport, open from 8am to midnight, and the head office (℗ **02250-5500**) is at 1600 New Phetchaburi Rd.

Numerous travel agencies offer local tours. **Diethelm Travel** (℗ **02660-7000;** www.diethelmtravel.com), a leader in the region, can arrange excursions of any length.

[FastFACTS] BANGKOK

American Express
There is an office with limited services at 388 Pahonyothin Rd.
(℗ **02273-5500**).

Bookstores **Asia Books** carries a wide selection of regional works at its main branch, 221 Sukhumvit Rd., between Soi 15 and 17 (℗ **02252-7277**), and its many outlets in town and throughout the country.

Bookazine has a good selection at its various locations, on the second floor of the Silom Complex, 191 Silom Rd. (℗ **02231-3153**); in Ploenchit on the second floor of Gaysorn Plaza, 999 Ploenchit Rd. (℗ **02656-1039**); and at 62 Khao San Rd. (℗ **02280-3785**).

Books Kinokuniya has shops in Pathumwan at the Isetan department store, on the sixth floor, CentralWorld, Ratchadamri Road (℗ **02255-9834**); at the Emporium shopping complex, third floor, 622

Sukhumvit Rd., Soi 24 (℗ **02664-8554**); and a huge outlet in the Siam Paragon mall (℗ **02610-9500**).

Numerous used bookstores willing to buy and trade can be found along Khao San Road and Soi Rambuttri in Banglamphu, Bangkok's main backpacker haunt.

Currency Exchange
Most banks will exchange foreign currency Monday through Friday from 8:30am to 3:30pm. Exchange booths affiliated with the major banks are found in all tourist areas, open daily from as early as 7am to as late as 9pm.

The largest banks in Thailand—such as **Bangkok Bank, Thai Farmers Bank, Siam Commercial Bank,** and **Bank of Ayudhya**—all perform debit and cash advance services through the MasterCard/Cirrus or Visa/PLUS networks.

Many international banks also maintain offices in Bangkok, including **Bank of America,** CRC Tower, 87/2 Wireless Rd. (℗ **02305-2800**); **JP Morgan Chase,** 20 Sathorn Nua Rd. (℗ **02684-2000**); **Citibank,** 399 Sukhumvit Rd. (℗ **02788-2000**); and **Standard Chartered Bank,** 90 Sathorn Nua Rd., Silom (℗ **02724-4000**). However, even if your bank has a branch in Thailand, you should make any special arrangements before leaving home.

Drugstores Bangkok has a great many pharmacies, though the drugs dispensed differ widely in quality, and generic knockoffs are common. Pack any prescription medications you require, and go to a hospital for refills.

Embassies **U.S.:** 95 Wireless Rd. (℗ **02205-4000;** http://thailand. usembassy.gov). **Canada:**

15th Floor, Abdulrahim Place, 990 Rama IV Rd. (($ℂ$) **02636-0540;** www. bangkok.gc.ca). **Australia:** 37 S. Sathorn Rd. (($ℂ$) **02344-6300;** www. thailand.embassy.gov.au). **New Zealand:** 14th Floor, M Thai Tower, All Seasons Place, 87 Wireless Rd. (($ℂ$) **02254-2530;** www. nzembassy.com/thailand). **U.K.:** 14 Wireless Rd. (($ℂ$) **02305-8333;** www. ukinthailand.fco.gov.uk).

Emergencies   In any emergency, first call Bangkok's **tourist police** at its direct-dial number (($ℂ$) **1155**) or at ($ℂ$) **02652-1721.** Someone at both numbers will speak English. Ambulance service is handled by private hospitals; see "Hospitals," below, or contact your hotel's front desk. For operator-assisted overseas calls, dial ($ℂ$) **100.**

Hospitals   The best facility going is luxurious **Bumrungrad Hospital,** 33 Soi 3, Sukhumvit Rd. (($ℂ$) **02667-1000;** www.bumrungrad. com). The **BNH Hospital** (Bangkok Nursing Home) is at 9 Convent Rd., between Silom and Sathorn roads, south of Rama IV Road (($ℂ$) **02686-2700;** www. bnhhospital.com). Bring your passport and be ready to put up a deposit as high as 20,000B. Bills must be settled before checking out.

Internet Access   Most shopping malls and even the smallest hotels these days have at least a few Internet terminals, and you can't take a step without hitting one in places such as Khao San Road, the backpacker area, or along busy Silom Road near Patpong. Prices usually range from 30B to 50B per hour. Big hotels charge exorbitant rates and are not worth it.

Luggage Storage
Suvarnabhumi International Airport offers luggage storage for 100B per day per bag, 24 hours a day. Most hotels will allow you to store luggage while away on trips in the countryside.

Mail   If you're shipping a parcel from Bangkok, take advantage of the packing service offered by the **General Post Office (GPO) Post & Telegraph Office,** Charoen Krung Road, open Monday to Friday 8am to 8pm, Saturday and Sunday 8am to 1pm. Small cardboard packing cartons start at just 10B; packing service is available during normal office hours. Telegraph and telephone service are available in the north end of the building. Ask at your hotel for branch offices located closer to you.

Newspapers & Magazines   *Bangkok Post* and the *Nation,* English-language dailies, both cover local, national, and international news, plus happenings around town, TV listings, and other useful information (30B). *Bangkok 101* (100B), found at most bookstores, is a good source of current information on what's happening in Bangkok, especially the entertainment and social scene. *BK Magazine* and *Look East* are slick monthly English-language magazines distributed free, listing events in the city and including features on Bangkok, with lesser coverage of other Thai cities and provinces.

Police   Call the **tourist police** at ($ℂ$) **1155** or 02652-1721, 24 hours a day, for assistance. English is spoken.

Safety   Bangkok is generally a safe city, but be careful of pickpockets as you would anywhere. Don't seek trouble—avoid public disagreements or hostility (especially with locals), and steer clear of large groups wearing red or yellow shirts.

Telephones   Beware of hotel surcharges on international calls, which can be up to 50% (check with the hotel operator). Your best bet is the yellow, blue, or gray phones found in front of most convenience stores and in public places; these accept prepaid cards or coins. For directory inquiries, dial ($ℂ$) **1133.** See "Fast Facts: Thailand," earlier in this chapter, for additional information.

Where to Stay

Bangkok supports a rich variety of hotels in all price categories—and luxury at a fraction of what you would pay elsewhere. Many hotels quote rates in U.S. dollars. Remember that prices listed here are the "rack rates" and should be considered only a guideline—be sure to search for discounts. Rates do not include the additional 7% value-added tax (VAT) and frequent service charge of 10%.

ALONG THE RIVER

Bangkok's most prestigious hotels are located beside the Chao Phraya River, which offers a quick getaway by river taxi to the main sights in the historic area, or linking with the skytrain at Saphan Taksin for other regions of the city for shopping and entertainment.

Very Expensive

The Mandarin Oriental, Bangkok ★★★ A high-ranking member in the pantheon of the world's finest hotels, the Oriental makes for perhaps the most memorable stay in Bangkok. Its history dates from the 1860s, when the original hotel, no longer standing, was established by two Danish sea captains soon after King Mongkut (Rama IV) opened Siam to world trade. The hotel has withstood occupation by Japanese and American troops and played host to a long roster of Thai and international dignitaries and celebrities. Rooms in the older wing, built in 1876, pack the most colonial richness and charm. Those in the newer buildings (ca. 1958 and 1976) are certainly more spacious, some with better views of the river, but they sacrifice some of that Oriental hotel romance. It's the level and range of service, however, that distinguishes the Oriental from other riverfront hotels, and everyone from honeymooners to corporate execs is treated like a diplomat. Even if you don't stay, stop by for high tea in the oldest building, now called the Authors' Wing and housing luxury suites. The area was recently renovated and is one of the best-preserved pieces of old Bangkok.

48 Oriental Ave., Bangkok 10500 (on the riverfront off Charoen Krung Rd./New Rd.). ℂ**02659-9000.** Fax 02659-9284. www.mandarin-oriental.com. 393 units. $389 standard; $459 deluxe; from $689 suite. AE, DC, MC, V. 5-min. walk or shuttle boat to Saphan Taksin BTS station. **Amenities:** 6 restaurants; lounge w/live jazz performances; babysitting; children's day-care center; concierge; executive-level rooms; state-of-the-art fitness center; 2 outdoor pools; room service; smoke-free rooms; luxurious spa w/sauna, steam, massage, and traditional Thai beauty treatments; 2 lighted outdoor tennis courts; cooking classes. *In room:* A/C, satellite TV, fridge, hair dryer, minibar, IDD phone.

The Peninsula Bangkok ★★★ Whether you land on the helicopter pad and promenade into the exclusive top-floor lounge, roll in from the airport in one of the hotel's Rolls-Royce limousines, or step lightly off the wood-decked custom barges that ply the Chao Phraya, you'll feel like you've "arrived" however you get to the Peninsula, one of Bangkok's most deluxe accommodations. Every possible amenity is available here, from elegant dining to great activities and top-of-the-line business services. The rooms, some of the largest in town, all have river views and are done in a refined Thai and Western theme—a good marriage of Thai tradition and high-tech luxury, with wooden paneling, silk wallpaper, and attractive carpets. The technical features may make you feel like you've walked into a James Bond movie: Bedside control panels operate everything from the three phones and voice mail to the TV and even the mechanized curtains. The large marble bathrooms have separate vanity counters and a large tub with a hands-free phone and built-in TV monitor. "Ask and it will be done"

Where to Stay & Dine in Bangkok

RESTAURANTS ◆
Baan Khanitha **29**
Bed Supperclub **18**
Biscotti **10**
Blue Elephant **35**
Cabbages & Condoms **15**
Crepes & Co **14**
Harmonique **38**
Hemlock **1**
Koi **25**
Le Banyan **15**
Le Normandie **37**
L'Opera **24**
Maha Naga **22**
Mango Tree **31**
May Kaidee **6**
Mrs Balbir **17**
Salathip **36**
Somboon Seafood **33**
Suda **21**
Vientiane Kitchen **23**

HOTELS ■
Amari Boulevard **13**
Arun Residence **7**
Bangkok Marriott Resort & Spa **42**
D&D Inn **4**
Dream **19**
Dusit Thani **30**
The Eugenia **20**
Federal **16**
Four Seasons Bangkok **10**
Grand Hyatt Erewan Bangkok **9**
Lamphu Tree House **3**
Luxx **34**
JW Marriott Bangkok **12**
Majestic Grande **11**
Mandarin Oriental **37**
Metropolitan Bangkok **27**
Millennium Hilton Bangkok **40**
Montien Hotel **32**
New Siam II Guesthouse **2**
Novotel Siam Square **8**
The Peninsula Bangkok **41**
Rikka Inn **5**
Royal Orchid Sheraton **39**
Shangri-La Bangkok **36**
The Sukhothai **28**
Tivoli **26**

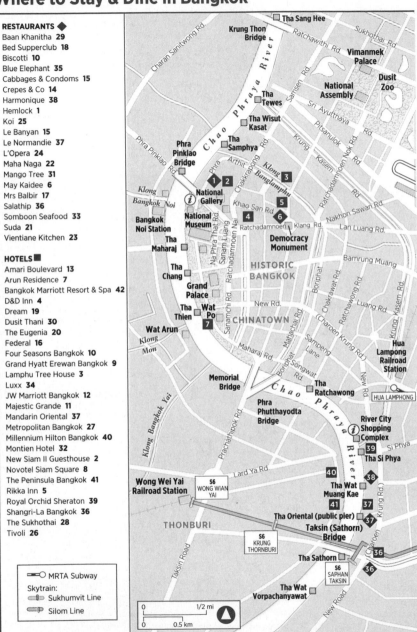

3

THAILAND | Bangkok

52

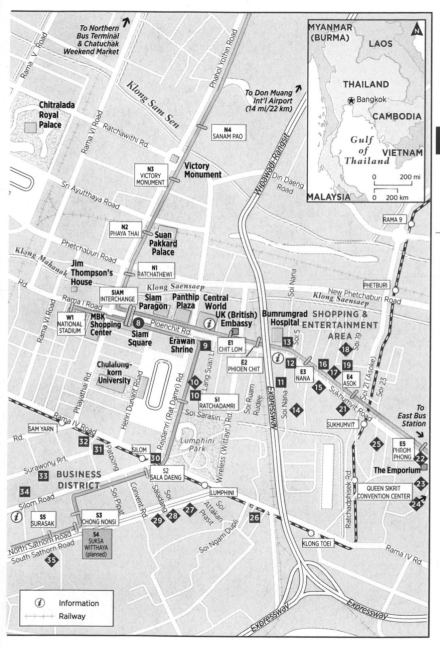

seems to be the rule about service, and the multilingual staff is friendly and very accommodating.

333 Charoennakorn Rd., Klongsan, Bangkok 10600 (just across the Chao Praya River from Saphan Taksin station). ✆ **866/382-8388** in the U.S., or 02861-2888 in Bangkok. www.peninsula.com. 370 units. 13,000B–15,000B grand deluxe; from 20,000B suite. AE, DC, MC, V. **Amenities:** 3 restaurants; 3 bars; babysitting; concierge; executive-level rooms; state-of-the-art fitness center; 60m (197-ft.) 3-tiered pool; room service; smoke-free rooms; full spa w/sauna, steam, massage, and aromatherapy; tennis court. In room: A/C, satellite TV, CD player, hair dryer, minibar, IDD phone, free Wi-Fi.

Expensive

Bangkok Marriott Resort & Spa ★★ ☺   On the banks of the Chao Phraya, across the river and a few miles downstream from the heart of Bangkok, this resort is somewhat removed from the action and best reached via longtail boat. It's a short trip downriver, but you feel the crazy city release you from its grip. Once you're at the property, the big city seems a distant memory. The three wings of the hotel surround a large landscaped pool area with lily ponds and fountains, and there is a wonderful spa. Boats go to and from the River City shopping mall every half-hour until evening.

257 Charoen Nakhorn Rd., at the Krungthep Bridge, Bangkok 10600 (on the Thonburi/west side of the Chao Phraya River, 15 min. by boat from River City). ✆ **888/236-2427** in the U.S., or 02476-0022. Fax 02476-1120. www.marriotthotels.com. 413 units. $245–$275 double; from $345 suite. AE, DC, MC, V. **Amenities:** 5 restaurants; 3 bars; bakery; babysitting; children's programs; concierge; fitness center w/ sauna; landscaped pool w/Jacuzzi; room service; smoke-free rooms; spa w/massage and beauty treatments; 2 outdoor lighted tennis courts; limited Wi-Fi (public areas only). In room: A/C, satellite TV, fridge, minibar, IDD phone.

Millennium Hilton Bangkok ★   Jutting into the Chao Phraya on the Thonburi side, the Hilton boasts some of the best views in the city, highlighted by the appropriately named rooftop jazz club ThreeSixty and the vertigo-inducing glass elevator that accesses it. All rooms and facilities are sleek, modern, and oriented toward the river. Like other Thai Hiltons, the guest rooms lack almost any Thai touches, but are comfortable nonetheless: soft carpeting, large bay windows, and mirror-laden marble bathrooms. The Beach, by the fourth-floor pool, has a unique 1-foot-deep shelf with loungers and tables placed in the water, so you can sun, soak your feet, enjoy a cocktail, and watch the boats cruise the river. There's regular ferry service to the main pier in the event that you tire of being a spectator and decide to join the game.

123 Charoennakorn Rd., Klongsan, Bangkok 10600 (on the Thonburi side of the Chao Phraya River, a 10-min. boat ride from Saphan Taksin pier). ✆ **02442-2000.** Fax 02442-2020. www.bangkok.hilton. com. 543 units. 5,000B deluxe; from 7,600B suite. AE, DC, MC, V. **Amenities:** 3 restaurants; 2 bars and cafe; babysitting; concierge; pool overlooking river; room service; spa w/sauna, steam, and massage. In room: A/C, satellite TV, hair dryer, Internet access, minibar.

Royal Orchid Sheraton Hotel & Towers ★   The Royal Orchid has magnificent views of the Chao Phraya and makes an excellent base for shopping or sightseeing. The recently refurbished rooms are spacious, pastel hued, and trimmed with warm teakwood, lending a refined and distinctly Thai ambience. The Sheraton Towers, a hotel within a hotel on the 26th through 28th floors (with its own check-in desk and express elevator), offers more ornate decor and a higher level of service for a premium; Sheraton Tower suites, for example, come with 24-hour butlers and personal fax machines. Facilities include the luxurious Mandara spa and a state-of-the-art fitness center. The large pool area makes it easy to forget the big, crowded city. Try the hotel's many fine-dining options. A walkway leads to the popular River City shopping complex next door.

2 Captain Bush Lane, Siphya Rd., Bangkok 10500 (next to River City mall). ℂ **800/325-3535** in the U.S., or 02266-0123. Fax 02236-8320. www.starwoodhotels.com. 734 units. 3,600B–6,000B double; from 6,600B suite. AE, DC, MC, V. Complimentary boat service to Saphan Taksin BTS station. **Amenities:** 4 restaurants; lounge; babysitting; concierge; executive-level rooms; 24-hr. fitness center w/sauna; 2 outdoor pools open 24 hr.; room service; luxurious spa w/private plunge pools, steam, massage, and beauty treatments; outdoor floodlit tennis court. *In room:* A/C, satellite TV, Internet access (495B/day), fridge, hair dryer, minibar.

Shangri-La Hotel, Bangkok ★★ The modern, opulent Shangri-La, on the banks of the Chao Phraya, boasts acres of polished marble and two towers with breathtaking views of the river. All units are outfitted with lush carpeting, teak furniture, and marble bathrooms. The views are terrific from the higher-floor deluxe rooms, and most have either a balcony or a small sitting room, making them closer to junior suites and a particularly good value for on-the-river upscale accommodations. For such an enormous place, the level of service and facilities is surprisingly good. The moody Chi Spa, whose design was inspired by Tibetan temple architecture, is one of the top hotel spas in town—highly recommended. The luxurious Krung Thep Wing adds another 17-story tower to the grounds, as well as a riverside swimming pool, restaurant, and breakfast lounge. Guests here register in their spacious rooms, surrounded by colorful Thai paintings and glistening Thai silk.

89 Soi Wat Suan Plu, Charoen Krung Rd. (New Rd.), Bangkok 10500 (adjacent to Sathorn Bridge, with access off Chaoren Krung Rd. at south end of Silom Rd.). ℂ **866/565-5050** in the U.S., or 02236-7777. Fax 02236-8579. www.shangri-la.com. 799 units. 6,000B–9,000B double; from 10,000B suite. AE, DC, MC, V. Next to Saphan Taksin BTS station. **Amenities:** 4 restaurants; lounge and bar; airport/city shuttle service; concierge; executive-level rooms; fitness center w/Jacuzzi, sauna, steam, massage, and aerobics classes; 2 outdoor pools w/outdoor Jacuzzi; room service; smoke-free rooms; spa; 2 outdoor floodlit tennis courts. *In room:* A/C, satellite TV, fridge, hair dryer, free Internet access, minibar.

Moderate

Arun Residence ★★ 🔑 This cool little arty hideaway comes with split-level suites, decorated in a colorful, unfussy, Thai-retro style, all with great views across to Wat Arun (Temple of Dawn), one of the city's most powerful icons. It's suited to those who want to feel at home in the thick of old Bangkok, as it's close to the major sights. Though public transport isn't on your doorstep, the twinkling river is right there in front of you, and the property's lush plants and sun-filled lounge offer a uniquely Thai experience.

36-38 Soi Phratu Nokyung, Maharaj Rd., Rattanakosin Island, Bangkok 10200. ℂ **02221-9158-9.** Fax 02221-4493. www.arunresidence.com. 6 units. 3,500B standard; 5,500B suite with roof garden. AE, MC, V. Taxi from Hua Lamphong MRT. **Amenities:** Restaurant. *In room:* A/C, satellite TV, DVD player, fridge, minibar, Wi-Fi.

BANGLAMPHU & KHAO SAN ROAD

Several of the major tourist sights are near here, making sightseeing on foot feasible,. It's quite a long ride from commercial Bangkok, though river taxis from Phra Ahthit Pier help to avoid the traffic jams. For budget travelers, the widest range of low-price accommodations is found in this area around Khao San Road. There are a number of good values, but the best of the lot is the **New Siam II Guesthouse** (50 Trok Rong Mai, Phra Ahtit Rd.; ℂ **02282-2795;** www.newsiam.net), with a pool and spotless fan and air-conditioned rooms going for 690B and 790B, respectively. Another good value is the new **Rikka Inn** (259 Khao San Rd.; ℂ **02282-7511-2;**

www.rikkainn.com), with compact but tastefully furnished rooms from 1,150B. The **D & D Inn** (68–70 Khao San Rd.; ✆ **02629-0526;** www.khaosanby.com) has clean but basic doubles starting at only 850B.

Inexpensive

Lamphu Tree House ★   Situated on the Banglamphu Canal, this attractive boutique hotel offers elegance and comfort at budget prices, though it lacks the range of facilities you'd find in a more expensive place. Rooms have teak-paneled walls and balconies, and there's a swimming pool and rooftop sun deck to help you unwind after a day of slogging the city's streets.

155 Wan Chat Bridge, Prachatipathai Rd., Phranakorn, Bangkok 10200 (5-min. taxi ride from Phra Ahthit Pier). ✆ **02282-0991-2.** Fax 02282-0993. 25 units. From 1,500B double. MC, V. **Amenities:** Restaurant; Internet access; outdoor pool; room service. *In room:* A/C, TV, minibar.

THE BUSINESS DISTRICT

Don't be put off by the "business district" name, which is merely to distinguish this area from the others. This part of town is connected by skytrain and subway and is home of Silom Road, the center of Bangkok nightlife.

Expensive

The Dusit Thani, Bangkok ★   Once upon a time, this was Bangkok's grandest address (and tallest building). Now this old girl just across from Lumpini Park has undergone an extensive renovation to put her in line with her flashy new neighbors. The location is ideal for shoppers, with several malls nearby, as well as for party people, as there are plenty of bars and nightclubs in the vicinity. Inside, the lobby has splashing fountains, and the large outdoor pool is surrounded by thick foliage—a great escape after a day of sightseeing. Refurbished rooms eschew the traditional Thai motif of years past for a more up-to-date business look, with club rooms adding high-speed Internet access and flatscreen TVs. The Devarana spa is world-class, and there are numerous quality in-house dining choices as well.

946 Rama IV Rd., Bangkok 10500 (at corner of Silom and Rama IV roads, opposite Lumpini Park). ✆ **02200-9000.** Fax 02236-6400. www.dusit.com/dusit-thani. 517 units. 7,900B–12,500B double; from 15,000B suite. AE, DC, MC, V. Near Sala Daeng BTS station. **Amenities:** 8 restaurants; bar; lounge; babysitting; concierge; executive-level rooms; driving range and putting green; fitness center; small landscaped pool; room service; spa w/massage, sauna, steam, and cafe; library w/high tea. *In room:* A/C, satellite TV w/VCR, fridge, hair dryer, Internet access, minibar.

Metropolitan, Bangkok ★   The Metropolitan is fashioned after the famed property in London and is one of Bangkok's hippest houses of style. The chic, modular lobby and crisply dressed staff could easily be mistaken for the velvet-rope crowd at an upscale urban club. Rooms are elegantly angular and quite stark at first glance, but there are lots of warm touches, such as earth-toned fabrics and overstuffed pillows, to offset the crisp, contemporary lines. Bathrooms are large, with big sunken tubs. This is a stylish getaway with some cool dining choices and the slick Met Bar, which is exclusively for the use of hotel guests.

27 S. Sathorn Rd., Tungmahamek, Sathorn, Bangkok 10120. ✆ **02625-3333.** Fax 02625-3300. www.metropolitan.bangkok.como.bz. 171 units. 8,580B–11,880B double; from 13,860B suite. AE, MC, V. Short cab ride from Sala Daeng BTS station, and just a short walk to the Lumpini subway stop. **Amenities:** 2 restaurants; bar; airport transfer; great fitness center; outdoor pool; room service; spa w/massage, Jacuzzi, sauna, and steam. *In room:* A/C, satellite TV w/DVD and CD players, fridge, minibar, Wi-Fi.

The Sukhothai ★★★   Find a welcome, if studied, serenity in this hotel's maze of low pavilions, contemporary lines, and earthy textures and tones. Broad, colonnaded public spaces surround peaceful lotus pools. Symmetry and simplicity form the backdrop for brick *chedis* (stupas or mounds), terra-cotta friezes, and celadon ceramics evoking the ancient kingdom of Sukhothai. Large guest rooms are done in fine Thai silk, mellow teak, and celadon tile. Gigantic luxurious bathrooms feature oversize tubs and two full-size wardrobes. The Sukhothai is second to none in service and privacy, and offers an indulgent spa experience as well.

13/3 S. Sathorn Rd., Bangkok 10120 (south of Lumpini Park, near intersection of Rama IV and Wireless roads, next to the YWCA). ℂ **02344-8888.** Fax 02344-8899. www.sukhothai.com. 210 units. 8,000B–10,000B double; from 11,000B suite. AE, DC, MC, V. **Amenities:** 4 restaurants; bar and lobby lounge; babysitting; concierge; executive-level rooms; state-of-the-art fitness center w/Jacuzzi, sauna, steam, massage, and aerobics classes; 25m (82-ft.) outdoor pool; room service; outdoor lit tennis court. *In room:* A/C, satellite TV w/in-house movies, fax, hair dryer, Internet access.

Moderate

Luxx ★★   This contemporary hideaway is the new face of Bangkok; its fashionably minimalist size and prime location appeal to the young and style conscious. Within walking distance of Silom's shops and night market, but away from the noisy main road, Luxx provides large airy rooms, flatscreen TVs, wooden barrel tubs, rain showers and pebble gardens in an eclectic mix of Thai-Zen minimalism. Such perks as Wi-Fi, iPod docks, and breakfast in bed confidently affirm its claims to evoke a "home away from home" feel.

6/11 Decho Rd., Bangrak, Bangkok 10500. ℂ **02635-8800.** Fax 02635-8088. www.staywithluxx.com. 13 units. 2,500B double; 4,100B suite. AE, DC, MC, V. Chong Nonsi BTS. **Amenities:** Room service; Wi-Fi. *In room:* A/C, satellite TV, DVD player, fridge, minibar.

Montien Hotel Bangkok ★   The Montien is a slick and comfortable business hotel in the very heart of Silom, right at the terminus of the two busy Patpong *sois.* Set up in two large wings, each with dark teak hallways and bright, pleasant rooms, the Montien has seen some good upgrades in recent years and offers lots of services and upmarket amenities at a price that would put you in a dull cell in other parts of the world. Unique here, too, are the resident psychics at the mezzanine level's Astrologers' Terrace, open daily from 10:30am to 7pm.

54 Surawong Rd., Bangkok 10500 (near Patpong). ℂ **02233-7060.** Fax 02236-5218. www.montien. com. 475 units. 3,000B–5,000B double; from 5,500B suite. AE, DC, MC, V. 10-min. walk to Sala Daeng BTS station. **Amenities:** 3 restaurants; bar; lounge and karaoke; babysitting; executive-level rooms; fitness center w/sauna; outdoor pool; room service. *In room:* A/C, satellite TV, fridge, hair dryer, Internet access, minibar.

Inexpensive

The Tivoli ★★ 🎒   The tiny Tivoli outdoes the competition. This wonderfully friendly, midsize hotel is set some way back from the fumes and traffic of Sathorn Road (and also accessible via Rama IV). Rooms are superbly decorated in a contemporary Thai style and offer exceptional value. The hotel helpfully provides a free tuk-tuk to those guests heading to the shops, extending a visa at immigration HQ, or seeing a doctor at nearby BNH hospital. It's a 5-minute ride to the Lumpini MRT station and an 8-minute ride to Silom in good traffic. Few Bangkok hotels of this range offer this luxury and service standard, plus the bonus of a rooftop swimming pool and spa.

71/2–3 Soi Sri Bumphen, Yen-Arkart Rd., Tungmahamek, Sathorn, Bangkok 10120. ℂ **02249-5858.** Fax 02249-5818. www.thetivolihotelbangkok.com. 133 units. 1,700B–2,700B double; 6,000B suite. AE, DC, MC, V. Sala Daeng BTS. **Amenities:** Restaurant; bar; pool; spa. *In room:* A/C, satellite TV, DVD player, fridge, hair dryer, Wi-Fi.

SUKHUMVIT ROAD: THE SHOPPING/EMBASSY AREA

Accessed along its entire length by the convenient skytrain, Sukhumvit Road is the heart of upscale, commercial Bangkok. Here you'll find many of the town's finest large shopping complexes, good restaurants, and thronging street life.

Expensive

The Eugenia   Set in a quiet *soi* off Sukhumvit, this delightful 19th-century, colonial-style house offers just a dozen rooms to discerning travelers who are looking for something a bit special for their stay in Bangkok. Rooms are equipped with period furnishings, part of the former owner's eclectic collection from travels around the world (it's now managed by lebua, who have several luxury properties in town). Communal areas include the garden pool, a teak pavilion, and the atmospheric DB Bradley Restaurant, named after a Presbyterian missionary who spent most of his life in Siam.

267 Sukhumvit Soi 31, Bangkok 10110 (btw. Sukhumvit and New Phetchaburi roads). ⓒ **02259-9017.** www.theeugenia.com. 12 units. 5,500B–7,200B suite. AE, DC, MC, V. 15-min walk to Asok BTS station. **Amenities:** Restaurant; lounge; pool; library. *In room:* A/C, satellite TV, hair dryer.

Four Seasons Hotel Bangkok ★★★   The Four Seasons is a modern palace. The impeccable service begins at the threshold, and an air of luxury pervades any stay in this modern city resort. Rooms are some of the most spacious in town, with Thai murals, plush carpeted dressing areas, and large bathrooms. Cabanas face the pool and terrace area, which is filled with palms, lotus pools, and all sorts of tropical greenery. If you can ignore the new condominium blocks overlooking the area, this is a real hideaway. The Four Seasons Spa is one of the best in Bangkok, and the inhouse dining is excellent. The executive upgrade for a nominal fee is well worth it.

155 Ratchadamri Rd., Bangkok 10330 (just south of Rama I Rd.). ⓒ **800/819-5053** in the U.S., or 02126-8866. Fax 02253-9195. www.fourseasons.com/bangkok. 354 units. 6,830B–16,800B double; 21,000B cabana; from 22,580B suite. AE, DC, MC, V. Adjacent to Ratchadamri BTS station. **Amenities:** 4 restaurants; lobby lounge w/high tea and live jazz; babysitting; concierge; executive-level rooms; state-of-the-art fitness center; landscaped outdoor pool; room service; smoke-free rooms; spa w/massage, sauna, and steam. *In room:* A/C, satellite TV, hair dryer, minibar, MP3 docking station.

Grand Hyatt Erawan Bangkok ★★★   Bangkok's old grande dame, the Grand Hyatt is tops in comfort, convenience, and style. Don't miss the Erawan shrine, a monument to prosperity and good luck dating from the 1956 construction of the previous hotel (the Erawan) on this site. The works of dozens of contemporary Thai artists grace hallways and spacious guest rooms, where earth-toned silks, celadon accessories, antique-finish furnishings, parquet floors, Oriental rugs, large bathrooms, and city views abound. Accommodations feature individual reading lights, Internet access, and compact control panels. In addition to the facilities one expects from a five-star hotel, there is a delightful fifth-floor pool terrace here, where a waterfall tumbles down a rocky wall into a full-size hot tub. The in-house dining is some of the best in the city, especially at Spasso, the Italian restaurant.

494 Ratchadamri Rd., Bangkok 10330 (corner of Rama I Rd.). ⓒ **02254-1234.** Fax 02254-6308. www. bangkok.grand.hyatt.com. 380 units. 6,600B–9,300B double; 13,100B suite; spa cottage 21,100B. AE, DC, MC, V. 5-min. walk to Chit Lom BTS station. **Amenities:** 6 restaurants; wine bar; lounge; babysitting; concierge; executive-level rooms; fitness center w/Jacuzzi, sauna, steam, and massage; rooftop pool and garden; room service; smoke-free rooms; outdoor spa; grass tennis court; helicopter service; 2 squash courts. *In room:* A/C, satellite TV, hair dryer, minibar.

JW Marriott Bangkok ★★ If you're looking for luxury but also need to stay wired for business back home (or you just have a bunch of high-tech gadgets), look no further than the JW Marriott. All rooms and common areas have wireless Internet access, and executive-level guests enjoy a lounge of their own. Rooms are decorated in a pleasing contemporary style with the plush bedding common to all Marriott properties and large marble-laden bathrooms. What makes them unique are the power strips that allow you to hook up your electronic devices to the room's flatscreen TV. For those looking for less sedentary perks, the hotel has a well equipped health club and spa. In-house dining is some of the best in the city, and the skytrain is a short walk away.

4 Sukhumvit Rd., Soi 2, Bangkok 10110. ✆ **02656-7700.** Fax 02656-7711. www.marriott.com. 441 units. 6,000B deluxe; from 8,000B executive; 60,000B royal suite. AE, DC, MC, V. Ploenchit BTS station. **Amenities:** 6 restaurants; 2 bars; babysitting; concierge; fitness center; outdoor pool; room service; spa w/sauna, steam, and attached juice bar. *In room:* A/C, satellite TV, hair dryer, minibar.

Moderate

Amari Boulevard Hotel ★ In the heart of the busy Nana shopping area of Sukhumvit Road (near the BTS Nana station), the Amari Boulevard is a good value. The newer, pyramid-shaped Krung Thep Wing has spacious rooms with terrific city views, while the original wing has less expensive rooms, some with a balcony. The hotel is in the heart of Sukhumvit's nightclub action, which can be a blessing or a curse depending on what you're here for. Also see its popular business address, the nearby **Amari Watergate** (✆ **02653-9000**).

2 Soi 5, Sukhumvit Rd., Bangkok 10110 (north of Sukhumvit Rd., on Soi 5). ✆ **02255-2930.** Fax 02255-2950. www.amari.com. 309 units. 3,199B–5,799B double; 7,900B suite. AE, DC, MC, V. 5-min. walk to Nana BTS station. **Amenities:** Restaurant; babysitting; concierge; fitness center; rooftop pool; room service. *In room:* A/C, satellite TV, fridge, minibar.

Dream Bangkok ★ This addition to the burgeoning hotel scene along Sukhumvit Road is at the cutting edge of modern style—indigo lights in the corridor and under-bed lighting create a true dreamlike aura. Just in case you're not ready to sleep, rooms are also equipped with large plasma TVs and high-speed Internet connections. Dining and drinking choices follow the stylish theme, with innovative dishes on the menu at Flava Restaurant and unusual cocktails in the Flava Lounge. There are also a gym and spa on the premises to help guests keep trim.

10 Sukhumvit Soi 15, Bangkok 10110. ✆ **02254-8500.** Fax 02254-8534. www.dreambkk.com. 195 units. $95–$115 double; $145–$245 suite. AE, DC, MC, V. Asok BTS or Sukhumvit MRT. **Amenities:** Restaurant; bar; concierge; gym; rooftop pool; spa. *In room:* A/C, satellite TV, minibar, Wi-Fi.

Majestic Grande ★★ 🦐 For location and price, you can't beat the Majestic Grande. Just off busy Sukhumvit Road and a short walk or shorter complimentary tuk-tuk ride to the skytrain, the Majestic is perfect for shoppers, sightseers, and partyers alike. Superior rooms are smaller than those in the more expensive hotels in the area, but the suites are very spacious, and all rooms are modern and superclean. Wood flooring around the beds is flanked by smooth marble leading to tidy bathrooms, some with separate tubs and showers. Facilities are also on the small side, but are all present and accounted for: pool, fitness center, business center, and two restaurants. A highly professional staff rounds out the plaudits, making the Majestic the top midrange choice on Sukhumvit.

12 Sukhumvit Soi 2, Bangkok 10110 (just south of Sukhumvit Rd.). ✆ **02262-2999.** Fax 02262-2900. www.majesticgrande.com. 251 units. 3,300B–4,100B double; from 8,500B suite. AE, DC, MC, V. 5-min.

walk from Ploenchit BTS station. **Amenities:** 2 restaurants; lobby lounge; babysitting; concierge; fitness center w/sauna, steam, Jacuzzi, and massage; small outdoor pool; room service. *In room:* A/C, satellite TV, hair dryer, minibar, Wi-Fi.

Novotel Bangkok on Siam Square ★★ This elegant and opulent high-rise hotel in the Siam Square shopping area is one of this French chain's best. Guest rooms are sharp: business chic dominated by earth tones, minus superfluous Thai touches. Bathrooms have the TV's sound wired in. Novotel is perfect for business or shopping trips and close to the skytrain. Don't miss CM2, one of the city's most popular nightclubs (located in the basement), which has live music 6 nights a week.

Siam Sq. Soi 6, Bangkok 10330 (in Siam Sq. off Rama I Rd.). ℭ **02209-8888.** Fax 02255-1824. www. novotelbkk.com. 423 units. $113–$163 double; from $170 suite. AE, DC, MC, V. Siam BTS station. **Amenities:** 3 restaurants; 4 bars; huge popular nightclub; babysitting; concierge; executive-level rooms; fitness center w/massage; Internet access; outdoor pool; room service; smoke-free rooms. *In room:* A/C, satellite TV, fridge, minibar.

Inexpensive

Federal Hotel ★ The Federal has been providing affordable lodgings with reasonable levels of comfort for about 50 years now, so the place runs very efficiently and staff are eager to help solve any problems. The lobby and restaurant on the first floor are classic 1960s design but thankfully rooms upstairs have been regularly renovated. Rooms are compact but well equipped with comfy beds and cable TV, and are set well back from street noise. There's a small but inviting pool, and free breakfast is included in the price.

27 Sukhumvit Soi 11, Bangkok 10110 (a 5-min. walk from Nana BTS). ℭ **02253-0175.** Fax 02253-5332. www.federalbangkok.com. 24 units. 1,300B–1,500B double. MC, V. **Amenities:** Restaurant; Internet access; small outdoor pool. *In room:* A/C, cable TV, minibar.

THE AIRPORT AREA

If you'd rather give Bangkok a miss, but need somewhere to rest up near the airport while waiting for a connecting flight, this is the only reasonable option.

Novotel Suvarnabhumi Airport Hotel ★ Located just a short walk or shuttle-bus ride from the airport terminal, the Novotel echoes Suvarnabhumi's massive proportions with its huge, bright, and delightfully tranquil lobby. The Novotel is as much a business hotel as a layover spot, sporting extensive convention and business facilities, as well as the airport's best dining options. Rooms are comfortable affairs, with soothing carpeting and large marble bathrooms. The spa has treatments catering to the weary traveler, and there's an attractive swimming pool. Day rates are also available, allowing visitors access to all hotel facilities.

999 Suvarnabhumi Airport Hotel, Moo 1, Nongprue Bang Phli, Bangkok 10540. ℭ **02131-1111.** Fax 02131-1188. www.novotel.com. 612 units. $168–$200 double; from $267 suite. AE, DC, MC, V. **Amenities:** 4 restaurants; lobby lounge; coffee shop; babysitting; children's programs; concierge; fitness center; outdoor pool; room service; spa w/massage and beauty treatments. *In room:* A/C, satellite TV, hair dryer, minibar, Wi-Fi.

Where to Dine

ALONG THE RIVER

Very Expensive

Le Normandie ★★★ FRENCH The ultraelegant Normandie, set atop the Oriental Hotel and enjoying fabulous views over the river, is the apex in formal dining in Thailand. The room glistens in gold and silver, from place settings to chandeliers.

dinner & lunch cruises ON THE CHAO PHRAYA

While there are a number of tour operators that offer dinner cruises along the Chao Phraya, if you want to eat the finest food, there are a couple of cruises that stand out. **Manohra Cruises** ★★ (257 Charoennakorn Rd., Bangkok 10600; 𝄴 **02477-0770;** www.manohra-cruises.com) operate three converted antique rice barges that cruise the river nightly, serving six Thai dishes that are delicious (and not overly spicy) in a relaxed and romantic setting. The set menu runs 1,990B per person, and the boats sets sail at 7:30pm. Book through their website or call to arrange a pick-up.

The **Horizon II** also makes evening cruises starting at 7:30pm (2,300B), though these are livelier and feature music and dancing. Contact the **Shangri-La Hotel** (𝄴 **02236-7777**) for more information.

Some of the highest-rated master chefs from France have made guest appearances here, adding their own touches to the menu. Choose from a limited selection of tempting daily specials, such as roast half Brittany lobster with caviar and frothy bisque. The set menu (both lunch and dinner) includes a cheese course, coffee, and a sinful dessert. Order any wine you can imagine from the extensive list.

At the Oriental, 48 Oriental Ave. (off Charoen Krung/New Rd., overlooking the river). 𝄴 **02659-9000.** Reservations required at least 1 day in advance. Jacket/tie required for men. Main courses 1,600B–2,500B; set lunch menu 1,150B; degustation menu 4,400B. AE, DC, MC, V. Daily noon–2:30pm and 7–10:30pm (closed Sun lunch). 10-min. walk from Saphan Taksin BTS station.

Expensive

Salathip ★★ THAI   Salathip, on the river terrace of the Shangri-La Hotel, is arguably Bangkok's most romantic Thai restaurant. Classical music and traditional cuisine are superbly presented in aging, carved-teak pavilions perched over a lotus pond and overlooking the river (there are also air-conditioned dining rooms). Set menus introduce you to a range of courses, from pomelo salad with chicken to your choice of Thai curries. There is live music nightly as well as Thai dancing and a culture show.

At the Shangri-La Hotel, 89 Soi Wat Suan Plu (overlooking Chao Phraya River, near Taksin Bridge). 𝄴 **02236-7777.** Reservations recommended. Main courses 420B–1,400B. AE, DC, MC, V. Daily 6:30–10:30pm. Saphan Taksin BTS station.

Moderate

Harmonique ★★ THAI   Hard to find, Harmonique is set in the courtyard of a century-old mansion and oozes character—a great stop if you're touring the riverfront or visiting the antiques stores of nearby River City. Enter through the crook of a dangling banyan tree to find courtyard seating and an open-air dining area with Thai antiques. The cuisine is Thai tailored to Western tastes, but it's still very good—the *tom yum* with fish is delicious, served only as spicy as you like and with enormous chunks of fish. The sizzling grilled seafood platter is nice and garlicky (chilis on the side). Harmonique also has good Western desserts such as brownies, great with a cool tea on a hot day. It's an atmospheric spot to relax.

22 Chaoren Krung Rd. (New Rd.), Soi 34. 𝄴 **02237-8175.** Main courses 80B–270B. AE, MC, V. Mon–Sat 11am–10pm. 15-min. walk from Saphan Taksin BTS station.

3

BANGLAMPHU & KHAO SAN ROAD

Khao San Road is Bangkok's busy backpacker ghetto and where you'll find every manner of food, from Israeli and halal cuisine to Italian fare and tasty Thai served streetside. Have a seat somewhere along the busy road, order a fruit shake, and watch the nightly parade of young travelers. **Cafe Primavera** (56 Phra Sumen Rd.; ℂ 02281-4718), around the corner from Phra Sumen Fort, serves excellent pizzas and pastas. Another renowned spot in this district is **May Kaidee** (111 Tanao Rd.; ℂ 02281-7699; www.maykaidee.com), which serves a great range of vegetarian dishes in no-frills surroundings at dirt-cheap prices. They have another branch, as well as a cookery school, at 33 Samsen Rd.

Inexpensive

Hemlock ★ THAI   The extensive and wide-ranging menu, which includes several vegetarian options, combined with a relaxing atmosphere and very reasonable prices, makes this a hot favorite for young Thais. It's also a good place to escape the hustle and bustle of nearby Khao San Road, though it's best to reserve at the weekend. If you're feeling adventurous, try the *yam hua plii* (banana flower salad)—a marvelous blend of tastes and texture.

56 Phra Ahthit Rd., Banglamphu. ℂ **02282-7507.** Reservations recommended. Main courses from 80B. MC, V. Mon–Sat 5pm–midnight. Ferry to Banglampoo Pier.

THE BUSINESS DISTRICT

Silom Road is where you'll find Patpong, the busy red-light district, a tourist night market, and a host of good dining choices.

Moderate

Baan Khanitha ★★ THAI   With one location on busy Sathorn Road and another (the original) on Sukhumvit Soi 23, Baan Khanitha offers authentic Thai in a comfortable, classy atmosphere. For starters, choose the *yam som o*, a tangy salad with pomelo, shrimp, and chicken. Then you can graduate to a curry, from spicy red to mellow yellow and green; light salads; and good seafood as you like it. Follow up with good Thai desserts. Thais actually come here, a rarity for upscale Thai eateries, and both places are always packed: a couple of good signs. Be sure to call ahead.

69 S. Sathorn Rd. ℂ **02675-4200.** There's another location at 36/1 Sukhumvit Soi 23. ℂ **02258-4128.** www.baan-khanitha.com. Reservations highly recommended. Main courses 240B–580B. AE, MC, V. Daily 11am–2pm and 6–11pm. 5-min. walk from Chong Nonsi BTS/Asok BTS, respectively.

Biscotti ★★ ITALIAN   This must be Bangkok's most stylish and consistently praised Italian restaurant. Its open kitchen and slick, minimalist decor give it a modern sophistication that few Italian restaurants in Bangkok can match. The long tables and polished wood floors give it a welcome, homely air. Equally unmatched are its

---

Bangkok Street Eats

Ask any Bangkokian to take you to his favorite restaurant, and you'll most likely be eating street side or in a small, open-air eatery. In fact, the many night bazaars and hawker stalls are where you'll find the best eats throughout Thailand. For the best open-air dining, try **Thong Lo,** a collection of busy stalls just adjacent to the Thong Lo BTS stop. **Suan Lum Night Bazaar,** next to Lumpini Park, is another good choice.

cuisine and top-class service, which don't come with too big a price tag, like so many others. Choose from the plate of miniature Italian appetizers (this can consist of anything from scallops, tuna, or beef); there's a great choice of fresh fish, a range of wood-fired pizzas, and an unending list of antipasti—not to mention homemade pastas and risottos. Save space for one of the irresistible desserts, or finish off with one of the excellent wines. It's smart, it's elegant, and it's utterly timeless.

The Four Seasons, 155 Ratchadamri Rd. © **02126-8866.** Reservations recommended. Main courses 280B–590B. AE, DC, MC, V. Daily noon–2:30pm and 6-10:30pm. Ratchadamri BTS.

Blue Elephant ★ THAI   The Blue Elephant franchises have been serving their brand of royal Thai cuisine throughout Europe and the Middle East since 1980. It was only in 2002 that the company opened a branch in Bangkok. Set in a 100-year-old colonial building that served as the Imperial Japanese Command Center during World War II, the restaurant is an oasis of refinement on busy South Sathorn Road. The dining rooms are decorated with traditional Thai-style statues and carvings, but they retain their colonial charm. The menu is a mix of classic Thai recipes and the chefs' original creations. If you have any questions about a particular dish, a member of the very professional waitstaff is always eager to assist.

The Blue Elephant has an excellent cooking school on the third floor of the building (see "Cultural Pursuits," p. 73).

233 S. Sathorn Rd. © **02673-9353.** www.blueelephant.com/bangkok. Reservations recommended. Main courses 340B–980B; set menus 1,150B–1,650B. AE, DC, MC, V. Daily 11:30am–2:30pm and 6:30–10:30pm. Surasak BTS station.

Mango Tree ★ THAI   In a lovely 80-year-old Siamese restaurant house with its own tropical garden, the Mango Tree offers a quiet retreat from the hectic Patpong area. Live traditional music and classical Thai decorative touches fill the house with charm, and the attentive staff serves well prepared dishes from all regions of the country. The mild green chicken curry and the crispy spring rolls are both excellent—but the menu is extensive, so feel free to experiment. Only trouble is, the food isn't exactly authentic—though it's still quite good.

37 Soi Tantawan, Bangrak (off west end of Surawong Rd.). © **02236-2820.** Reservations recommended. Main courses 220B–530B. AE, DC, MC, V. Daily 11:30am–midnight. 10-min. walk from Sala Daeng BTS station.

Somboon Seafood ★★ SEAFOOD   This one's for those who would sacrifice atmosphere for excellent food. Though it's packed nightly, you'll still be able to find a table, as the place is huge. The staff is extremely friendly—between them and the picture menu, you'll be able to order the best dishes and get the finest recommendations. Peruse the large aquariums outside to see all the live seafood options, such as prawn, fish, lobsters, and crabs (guaranteed freshness). The house specialty, chili crab curry, is especially good, as is the *tom yang goong* soup (spiced to individual taste).

169/7-11 Surawongse Rd. (just across from the Peugeot building). © **02233-3104.** Reservations not necessary. Seafood at market prices (about 900B for 2 people). No credit cards. Daily 4–11pm.

SUKHUMVIT ROAD: THE SHOPPING/EMBASSY AREA
Expensive

Bed Supperclub ★★ INTERNATIONAL   This is the coolest place in Bangkok, hands down. Come for a drink in the bar, at least, and stick around for when the place busts into a full-on club. It serves meals at one seating only (8:30pm); the best part is that, as the name suggests, you eat in long shared beds. You walk up a concrete gangplank to enter the giant cylinder-shaped building via large airplane airlocks. One side of the room is the bar, while the other is the dining area, where you'll be assigned your slot on one of the two big beds that line the walls. The two-story, glowing white-and-neon interior alone is unique. The "surprise" set menu changes every month (with three courses served Sun–Thurs and four courses on Fri and Sat) and rarely disappoints. Dessert is pure decadence of rich chocolate specials and cakes. The waitstaff wears tight spacesuits and angel wings, the music is funky trance spun by a DJ, and the food is fantastic.

26 Sukhumvit Soi 11, Klongtoey-Nua (at the end of Soi 11). ℮ **02651-3537.** www.bedsupperclub.com. Reservations required. Men should wear trousers, not shorts. Set menu 1,450B Sun–Thurs, 1,850B Fri–Sat. AE, MC, V. Tues–Thurs 7:30pm–midnight; Fri–Sat 7:30pm–2am. Dinner served promptly at 8:30pm (best to be early). Nana BTS station.

Koi ★★ JAPANESE   Modern modular Japanese pavilions set in a quiet, fountain-laden garden; slick black and blood-red interior; moody candle lighting; and beautiful people doing beautiful-people things at the bar. A case of style over substance? Not at all. One of the hippest restaurants in the city, Koi serves outstanding Japanese food with subtle California twists and some of the best sushi in town. One of the house specialty rolls is braised shrimp over a California roll, a circular sushi fort guarding helpless teriyaki shrimp, mushrooms, and asparagus. It's delicious, as is anything on the menu containing the words "sushi" or "chocolate cake." The service is decidedly unpretentious for a restaurant of such style.

26 Sukhumvit Soi 20, Klongtoey (a 5-min. walk down Soi 20). ℮ **02258-1590.** www.koirestaurantbkk. com. Reservations recommended. Main courses 320B–2,300B. AE, MC, V. Tues–Sat 6pm–midnight. Asok BTS station.

Le Banyan ★★ FRENCH   A spreading banyan tree on the edge of the gardenlike grounds inspires the name. The upscale dining area is warm in tone, with sisal matting and white-clapboard walls adorned with Thai carvings, old photos, and prints of early Bangkok. The house special is a dish for two: pressed duck with gooseliver, shallots, wine, and Armagnac to make the sauce. Other fine choices include a rack of lamb with herb-and-walnut crust and Swedish salmon with butter and lemon. There are daily specials and a list of fine wines as well. If you come on foot, you'll run the gauntlet of all the girly bars at the entrance of the *soi,* but find this little upscale gem and enjoy an evening of fine dining and effusive service.

59 Sukhumvit Soi 8 (1 block south of Sukhumvit Rd.). ℮ **02253-5556.** www.le-banyan.com. Reservations recommended. Main courses 360B–1,990B. AE, DC, MC, V. Mon–Sat 6:30–9:30pm. 10-min. walk from Nana BTS station.

Maha Naga ★★ THAI/WESTERN FUSION   Classy Maha Naga is an oasis of luxury Thai dining in the heart of the Sukhumvit area. The restaurant design features a fountain courtyard surrounded by high-peaked, lavishly decorated, and air-conditioned

Thai pavilions—it makes for a quiet, romantic evening or a fun night for private groups. The food is delicious, a bold marriage of Thai and Western traditions in dishes such as pork chop with a green papaya salad or baked duck breast and lychee in peanut curry sauce. Elsewhere, fusion dishes often come out rather bland, but the intriguing combinations at Maha Naga spark the imagination.

2 Sukhumvit Soi 29, Klongtoey. ℂ **02662-3060.** www.mahanaga.com. Reservations recommended. Main courses 380B–960B. AE, DC, MC, V. Daily 5:30pm–midnight. 5-min. walk from Phrom Pong BTS station.

Moderate

Cabbages & Condoms ★★ THAI   Locally known as C&C, this is a theme restaurant with a purpose. Opened by local hero Mechai Viravaidya, founder of the Population & Community Development Association, the restaurant helps fund population control, AIDS awareness, and a host of rural development programs. Set in a large compound, the two-story restaurant has air-conditioned indoor dining, but if you sit on the garden terrace, you'll be in a fairyland of twinkling lights—quite romantic. Share a whole fish done as you like or, for something on the sweet side, try the *gaang kua goong sapparot* (a sweet curry with shrimp and pineapple). There's also a large selection of vegetable and bean-curd entrees. As you arrive, be sure to check out the gift shop's whimsical condom-related merchandise. The restaurant hands out condoms instead of dinner mints.

10 Sukhumvit Soi 12. ℂ **02229-4610.** www.cabbagesandcondoms.com. Reservations recommended. Main courses 200B–350B. AE, DC, MC, V. Daily 11am–10pm. 15-min. walk from Asok BTS station.

Crepes & Co. ★★ ☺ EUROPEAN   Popular among Bangkok foreign residents (and their kids), this is the place to satisfy that sweet tooth, though the savory crepes are yummy, too. Crepes & Co. serves them light and fluffy and filled with any of dozens of combinations—all of them delicious. It also has good Mediterranean main courses, great coffee, and a nice selection of tea. Everything is excellent, and there's a choice of eating in the garden, lounge, or dining room.

18/1 Sukhumvit Soi 12. ℂ **02653-3990.** www.crepes.co.th. Reservations recommended. Main courses 250B–640B. AE, DC, MC, V. Daily 9am–midnight (Sun from 8am). 15-min. walk from Asok BTS station.

L'Opera ★ ITALIAN   With its sister restaurant in Vientiane, Laos, L'Opera Bangkok has been hosting visitors and expats since it first opened in the 1970s—back when Soi 39 was but a dusty little alley with cows grazing out front. Now it's a sophisticated enclave and it's got the formula just right: dim lights in a glassed-in pavilion; cool jazz; and good, affordable Italian food. Come with friends and fill the table. Start with a decadent seafood salad. For a main course, go for the fresh fish done as you like or any of the grilled items or fine pastas.

53/1 Sukhumvit Soi 39, Klongtoey. ℂ **02258-5606.** Main courses 220B–900B. AE, MC, V. Daily 11:30am–2pm and 6–10:30pm. 15-min. walk or 30B tuk-tuk ride from Phrom Pong BTS station.

Mrs. Balbir's ★ INDIAN   There's a cheerful atmosphere at this restaurant, thanks to the affable and effervescent owner, Mrs. (Vinder) Balbir, whose jolly banter accompanies any lunch or supper. The menu covers all sorts of Punjabi goodies such as biryani, dahl, chicken tikka masala, and deliciously smooth cheese and spinach dishes. All of Mrs. Balbir's food comes with homemade pickled onions and chutneys. She now also offers several Indo-Chinese dishes. As famous for being a TV chef as much as a restaurateur, Mrs. Balbir also runs highly enjoyable cooking classes from her home.

155/1-2 Sukhumvit Soi 11/1. ℂ **02651-0498.** www.mrsbalbir.com. Reservations recommended for dinner. Main courses around 300B. MC, V. Daily 11:30am–11pm. 5-min. walk from Nana BTS.

📎 **Anyone for Crickets?**

Grasshoppers, beetles that look like cockroaches, scorpions, ants, and grubs are favorite snacks for folks from Isan, in the northeast, where bugs are cultivated for the dining table and are an important source of protein. Don't miss the snack stands selling these on Sukhumvit or Khao San. How do they taste? Crickets are like popcorn, and the beetles are something like—hate to say it—crispy chicken.

Inexpensive

Suda ★ 🍴 THAI   In a time when restaurants are often judged for the appearance of their food rather than its taste, it's reassuring to find somewhere as reliable as Suda for a delicious and inexpensive meal. Order up a prawn tempura, fish cakes, and a spicy stir-fry, wash it down with a beer, and still get change from 500B. The decor wouldn't win any prizes but it's clean, comfortable, and congenial—the ideal solution when you're standing in front of Asok Station feeling hot, thirsty, and hungry.

Sukhumvit Soi 14. ✆ **02229-4518.** Main courses 70B–220B. No credit cards. Daily 10am–10pm. 3-min. walk from Asok BTS.

Vientiane Kitchen ★ LAOTIAN   The cuisine of Laos is the same as that of Isan, or northeastern Thailand, with sticky rice, grilled chicken, *som tam* (spicy green papaya salad), and *larb* (spicy ground pork salad) being a few of the most popular dishes. Isan food is generally very spicy, and there is plenty of scope for adventurous eaters to sample something out of the ordinary here, such as snails or red ants' eggs in a spicy salad. The place is large and barnlike, the decor is very simple (thatched roofs and bamboo chairs), and the clientele is an eclectic mix of Thais and foreigners. Most evenings there is entertainment in the form of *mor lam* music (a very rhythmic style from Isan and Laos) with accompanying dancers, and they will arrange a special blessing ceremony for anyone celebrating their birthday.

8 Napasap Yak 1, Sukhumvit Soi 36. ✆ **02258-6171.** www.vientianekitchen.com. Main courses 180B–350B. AE, MC, V. Daily noon–midnight. A 3-min. walk west from Thong Lo skytrain then 50m/164 ft. south down Soi 36.

What to See & Do

When Rama I established Bangkok as the new capital city in the 1780s, he built a new palace and royal temple on the banks of the Chao Phraya River. The city sprang up around the palace and spread outward from this point as population and wealth grew. Today, the area around Rattanakosin Island contains most of Bangkok's major historic sights, including a great number of **wats**, or Buddhist temples, that were built during the past 200 years. If you're short on time, the most interesting and easily accessible *wats* to catch are Wat Phra Kaeo, the royal *wat* that houses the Emerald Buddha at the Grand Palace, and Wat Po, home of the reclining Buddha.

BANGKOK'S WATERWAYS

The history of Bangkok was written on its waterways, and Bangkok was once known as the "Venice of the East." Most of these *klongs* (canals) have been paved over, but the magnificent Chao Phraya River (River of Kings) cuts through the heart of the city. On the Thonburi side (opposite Bangkok), the labyrinthine canals offer an intimate glimpse of traditional Thai life. You'll see people using the river to bathe and wash their clothes; floating kitchens in sampans serve rice and noodles to customers in other boats. Hire a private boat to see the busy riverside area and to tour the narrow canals of neighboring Thonburi. Boat charter is available at most of the riverside piers, but it is easiest to arrange hourly trips at the riverfront kiosk near the **River City** shopping mall, at the **Grand Palace** (② 02225-6179), or at the skytrain exit at the **Saphan Taksin BTS station.** Trips cost about 1,000B per hour, per boat (one to six persons). Be specific about destinations and times.

HISTORIC TREASURES

Jim Thompson's House ★ Jim Thompson was a New York architect who served in the OSS (Office of Strategic Services, now the CIA) in Thailand during World War II and afterward settled in Bangkok. He almost single-handedly revived Thailand's silk industry, employing Thai Muslims as skilled silk weavers and building up a thriving industry. After expanding his sales to international markets, Thompson mysteriously disappeared in 1967 while vacationing in the Cameron Highlands in Malaysia. Despite extensive investigation, his disappearance has never been resolved.

His Thai house is composed of six teakwood houses from central Thailand that were rebuilt according to Thai architectural principles, but with Western additions (such as window screens). In some rooms, the floor is made of Italian marble, but the wall panels are pegged teak. Visitors must join a guided tour through rooms filled with Thompson's splendid collection of Khmer sculpture, Chinese porcelain, Burmese carving (especially a 17th-c. teak Buddha), and antique Thai scroll paintings.

Soi Kasemsan 2 (on a small *soi* off Rama I Rd., opposite the National Stadium). ② **02216-7368.** www.jimthompsonhouse.com. Admission 100B. Daily 9am–5:30pm. National Stadium BTS.

National Museum ★★ The National Museum, a short (15-min.) walk north of the Grand Palace and the Temple of the Emerald Buddha, is the country's central treasury of art and archaeology. It was originally the palace that the brother of Rama I built as part of the Grand Palace complex in 1782. Rama V converted the palace into a museum in 1884. Today, it is the largest museum in Southeast Asia and takes quite a lot of time to see.

One important stop is the Red House, a traditional 18th-century Thai building that was originally the living quarters of Princess Sri Sudarak. Another essential stop is the Phuttaisawan (Buddhaisawan) Chapel, built in 1787 to house the Phra Phut Sihing, one of Thailand's most revered Buddha images, brought here from its original home in Chiang Mai. The main building of the royal palace contains gold jewelry, some from the royal collections, and Thai ceramics, including many pieces in the five-color *bencharong* style. The Old Transportation Room has ivory carvings, elephant chairs, and royal palanquins. There are also rooms of royal emblems and insignia, stone carvings, woodcarvings, costumes, textiles, musical instruments, and Buddhist religious artifacts. Fine art and sculpture are found in the newer galleries at the rear of the museum compound.

Na Phra That Rd. (about 1km/⅔ mile north of the Grand Palace). ② **02224-1333.** Admission 50B. Wed–Sun 9am–4pm. Free English-language tours: Buddhism/culture Wed 9:30am, art/culture/religion Thurs 9:30am; call the museum or check a newspaper for more details and current schedule.

Vimanmek Mansion ★ Built in 1901 by King Chulalongkorn the Great (Rama V) as the Celestial Residence, this beautiful golden-teakwood mansion was restored in 1982 for Bangkok's bicentennial and was reopened by Queen Sirikit as a private museum with a collection of the royal family's memorabilia. An intriguing and informative 1-hour guided tour takes you through a series of apartments and rooms (of

Exploring Bangkok

Grand Palace **8**
Jim Thompson's House **14**
Lumphini Stadium **17**
National Museum **5**
Patpong Night Market **16**
Ratchadamnoen Stadium **3**
Siam Paragon **15**
TAT Office (Tourist Authority of Thailand) **4**
Vimanmek Mansion **1**
Wat Arun (Temple of Dawn) **9**
Wat Banchamabophit (Marble Temple) **2**
Wat Mahathat **6**
Wat Pho (Temple of the Reclining Buddha) **10**
Wat Phra Kaeo **7**
Wat Saket **12**
Wat Suthat **11**
Wat Traimit (Golden Buddha) **13**

Tha Sang Hee
Krung Thon Bridge
Ratchawithi Rd.
Sukhothai Rd.
Charan Sanitwong Rd.
Chao Phraya River
Vimanmek Palace
1
Dusit Zoo
Samsen Rd.
Sri Ayutthaya Rd.
National Assembly
Tha Tewes
Pitsanulok Rd.
Ratchadamnoen Nok Rd.
Krung Kasem Rd.
Phra Pinklao Rd.
Tha Wisut Kasat
Tha Samphya
Phra Pinklao Bridge
Arthit Rd.
Klong Banglamphu
2
3
4
Chakrabongse Rd.
Nakhon Sawan Rd.
Klong
National Gallery
Khao San Rd.
Lan Luang Rd.
Klong
Bangkok Noi
Bangkok Noi Station
National Museum
5
Ratchadamnoen Klang Rd.
Na Phra That Rd.
Sanam Luang
Ratchadamnoen Nai
Democracy Monument
Bamrung Muang
Tha Maharaj
6
Tha Chang
7
HISTORIC BANGKOK
Boriphat Rd.
12
Chakrawat Rd.
Ratchawong Rd.
Luang Rd.
Krung Kasem Rd.
Grand Palace
8
11
New Rd.
Sanamchai Rd.
Mahachai Rd.
Sampeng Lane
(Charoen Krung Rd.)
Hua Lampong Railroad Station
Tha Thien
10
Wat Po
CHINATOWN
Wat Arun
9
Klong Mon
Maharaj Rd.
Boriphat Songwat Rd.
13
HUA LAMPHONG
Memorial Bridge
Chao Phraya River
Tha Ratchawong
River City Shopping Complex
Phra Phutthayodta Bridge
Si Phya
Tha Si Phya
Klong Bangkok Yai
Prachathipok Rd.
Lard Ya Rd.
Tha Wat Muang Kae
Wong Wei Yai Railroad Station
S6 WONG WIAN YAI
Tha Oriental (public pier)
Taksin (Sathorn) Bridge
(Charoen Krung Rd.)
THONBURI
Taksin Road
S6 KRUNG THONBURI
Tha Sathorn
S6 SAPHAN TAKSIN
Tha Wat Vorpachanyawat
New Road

MRTA Subway
Skytrain:
Sukhumvit Line
Silom Line

0   1/2 mi
0   0.5 km

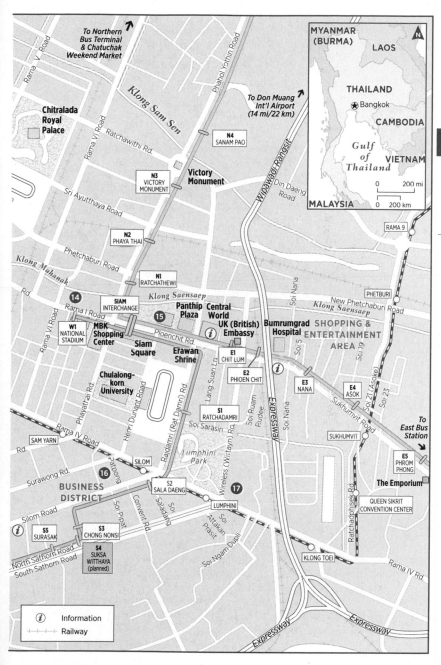

which there are 81 in all) in what is said to be the largest teak building in the world—the thought of all that gorgeous teakwood is staggering. The mansion is located in Dusit Palace Park, where the leafy grounds make for a peaceful stroll. While you're there, it's worth visiting other attractions such as the original and beautifully ornate **Abhisek Dusit Throne Hall,** which houses a display of Thai handicrafts, and the **Royal Elephant Museum,** where there's a small but fascinating array of pachyderm accessories; other museums scattered round the park feature photographs, clocks, fabrics, royal carriages, and other regalia.

193/2 Ratchavitee Rd., Dusit Palace grounds (opposite the Dusit Zoo, north of the National Assembly Building). *©* **02628-6300-9.** www.vimanmek.com. Dress code enforced. Admission 100B; included in Grand Palace fee. Daily 9am–4pm (ticket office closes 3:15pm).

Wat Phra Kaeo (Emerald Buddha Temple) and the Grand Palace ★★★

Built by Rama I when he established Bangkok as the new capital of Siam in 1782, this temple is a supreme example of Thai religious architecture and the most important place of worship for Thai Buddhists, while the palace is an inspired blend of European and Thai architecture. Today visitors walk through the temple compound, which is like a small city in itself, before going on into the grounds of the Grand Palace. Following a clockwise route, they pass the Phra Si Ratana Chedi (a golden bell-shaped Sri Lankan–style stupa), the Phra Mondop (a library with stunning Ayutthaya-style mother-of-pearl inlay doors), and the Royal Pantheon before arriving at the *bot* (ordination hall), which contains the **Emerald Buddha.**

This famed image, a .6m-tall (2-ft.) northern Thai–style image made from green jadeite, sits atop a towering gold altar. The statue dons a different costume for each of the three seasons in Thailand, changed by the king himself, who climbs up to the image because it can be lowered for no one.

Historians believe that artists created the statue in the 14th century, and its colorful history took it from Chiang Rai to Lampang, Chiang Mai, and Vientiane before Rama I finally captured the statue in a successful invasion of Laos and placed it in Wat Phra Kaeo. These days there is a constant fog of incense around the entrance to the *bot* as Buddhist devotees arrive to pay their respects to the nation's talisman.

Other significant features of the temple include 6m (20-ft.) *yaksas* (giant guardians) painted in gaudy colors, a *wihaan* (assembly hall) bejeweled with chipped porcelain mosaics, and a miniature model of Angkor Wat (the sprawling temple complex at the ancient Khmer capital), with its corncob-shaped *prangs*. Murals on the surrounding walls tell the story of the *Ramayana* (one of the two great epics of India).

From the temple complex, visitors pass through a small gate into the grounds of the **Grand Palace,** which was the official residence of all kings of Siam until 1946, when the royal family moved to Chitralada Palace. These days, the palace is used only for royal ceremonies. The focal point of the compound is the **Chakri Maha Prasad,** an intriguing mixture of Victorian architecture topped with Thai temple-style roofs that today house the ashes of royal family members. The **Amarinda Vinichai Hall,** in the Phra Maha Montien building to the left of the Chakri Maha Prasad, is the venue for the highest royal ceremonies, including coronations. The **Dusit Hall,** the last sight on this dizzying tour, is a perfect example of Thai architecture of the highest order, with an ornate roof that shimmers in the tropical sun.

Near the river on Na Phra Lan Rd. *©* **02224-1833.** Dress code applies. Admission 350B. Price includes admission to the Vimanmek Palace (near the National Assembly). Daily 8:30am–3:30pm. Take the Chao Phraya Express Boat to the Tha Chang Pier, then walk east and south.

BANGKOK'S TEMPLES

Wat Arun (Temple of Dawn) ★★★　The 86m-high (282-ft.) Khmer-inspired tower rises majestically from the banks of the Chao Phraya, across from Wat Po. This religious complex served as the royal chapel during King Taksin's reign (1868–82), when Thonburi was the capital of Thailand. The original tower was only 16m (52 ft.) high, but it was expanded during the rule of Rama III (1824–51) to its current height. The exterior is decorated with floral and decorative motifs made of colorful ceramic shards, which were donated to the monastery by local people at the request of Rama III. Wat Arun is a sight to behold shimmering in the sunrise, but the best time to view it is in late afternoon for sunset, when the main tower makes a striking silhouette.

West bank of the Chao Phraya, opposite Tha Thien Pier. www.watarun.org. Admission 50B. Daily 8am–5:30pm. Take a river taxi from Tha Thien (near Wat Po) or cross the Phra Pinklao Bridge and follow the river south on Arun Amarin Rd.

Wat Benchamabophit (Marble Temple)　Wat Benchamabophit, simplified for tourists as the Marble Temple because of the white Carrara marble from which it's constructed, is an early-20th-century temple designed by Prince Narai, the half brother of Rama V. It's the most modern and one of the most beautiful of Bangkok's royal *wats*. Unlike the older complexes, there's no truly monumental *wihaan* or *chedi* dominating the grounds. Many smaller buildings reflect a melding of European materials and designs with traditional Thai religious architecture. Even the courtyards are paved with polished white marble. Walk inside the compound, beyond the main *bot*, to view the many Buddha images that represent various aspects of regional styles. In the early mornings, monks chant in the main chapel, sometimes so intensely that it seems as if the temple is going to lift off.

Si Ayutthaya Rd. (south of the Assembly Bldg. near Chitralada Palace). Admission 20B. Daily 8am–5:30pm.

Wat Mahathat　Built to house a relic of the Buddha, Wat Mahathat is one of Bangkok's oldest shrines and the headquarters for Thailand's largest monastic order. Also the home of the Mahachulalongkorn Buddhist University, the most important center for the study of Buddhism and meditation, Wat Mahathat offers some programs in English (call for details).

Adjacent to it, between Maharat Road and the river, is the city's biggest **amulet market,** where a fantastic array of religious amulets, charms, talismans, and traditional medicine is sold. Every day, believers in their powers squat on the ground studying tiny images of the Buddha with magnifying glasses, hoping to find one that will bring good fortune or ward off evil.

Na Phra That Rd. (near Sanam Luang Park, btw. the Grand Palace and the National Museum). ℂ **02222-6011.** Donations welcome. Daily 9am–5pm.

Wat Pho (Temple of the Reclining Buddha) ★★★　Wat Pho (Wat Phra Chetuphon) was built by Rama I in the 16th century and is the oldest and largest Buddhist temple in Bangkok. Considered Thailand's first public university, the temple's many monuments and artworks explain principles of religion, science, and literature.

Most people go straight to the enormous Reclining Buddha in the northeast corner of the compound. It's more than 46m (151 ft.) long and 16m (52 ft.) high, and was built during the mid-19th-century reign of Rama III. The statue is brick, covered with layers of plaster and gold leaf; the feet are inlaid with mother-of-pearl illustrations of 108 auspicious *laksanas* (characteristics) of the Buddha. Behind the Buddha, a line of 108 bronze bowls, each also representing one of the *laksanas,* waits for visitors to drop coins.

Outside, the grounds contain 91 *chedis* (stupas or sacred mounds), four *wihaans,* and a *bot* (ordination hall). The Traditional Medical Practitioners Association Center teaches traditional Thai massage and medicine. Stop in for a massage (250B per hour) or ask about the massage courses.

Maharat Rd., near the river (2-min. walk west from Tha Tien Pier). ℂ **02225-9595,** or 02221-2974 (massage school). www.watpho.com. Dress code applies. Admission 50B. Daily 8am–5pm; massages offered until 5pm.

Wat Saket (Golden Mount) ★

Wat Saket is easily recognized by its golden *chedi* atop a fortresslike hill near the pier for Bangkok's east-west *klong* ferry. The *wat* was restored by King Rama I, and 30,000 bodies were brought here during a plague in the reign of Rama II. The hill, which is almost 80m (262 ft.) high, is an artificial construction begun during the reign of Rama III. Rama IV brought in 1,000 teak logs to shore it up because it was sinking into the swampy ground. Rama V built the golden *chedi* to house a relic of Buddha, said to be from India or Nepal, given to him by the British. The concrete walls were added during World War II to keep the structure from collapsing.

The Golden Mount, a short but breathtaking climb that's best made in the morning, is most interesting for its vista of old Rattanakosin Island and the rooftops of Bangkok. Every late October to mid-November (for 9 days around the full moon), Wat Saket hosts Bangkok's most important temple fair, when the Golden Mount is wrapped with red cloth and a carnival erupts around it, with food and trinket stalls, theatrical performances, freak shows, animal circuses, and other monkey business.

Ratchadamnoen Klang and Boripihat roads. Admission to Golden Mount 10B. Daily 9am–5pm.

Wat Suthat and the Giant Swing

This temple is among the oldest and largest in Bangkok, and Somerset Maugham declared its roofline the most beautiful. It was begun by Rama I and finished by Rama III; Rama II carved the panels for the *wihaan's* doors. It houses a beautiful 14th-century Phra Buddha Shakyamuni that was brought from Sukhothai, and the ashes of King Rama VIII, Ananda Mahidol, brother of the current king, are contained in its base. The detailed murals for which it is known were done during Rama III's reign.

The huge arch in front—also carved by Rama II—is all that remains of an original giant swing, which was used until 1932 to celebrate and thank Shiva for a bountiful rice harvest and to ask for the god's blessing on the next. The minister of rice, accompanied by hundreds of Brahman court astrologers, would lead a parade around the city walls to the temple precinct. Teams of men would ride the swing on arcs as high as 25m (82 ft.) in the air, trying to grab a bag of silver coins with their teeth. Due to injuries and deaths, the dangerous swing ceremony has been discontinued.

Sao Chingcha Sq. (near the intersection of Bamrung Muang and Ti Thong roads). Admission 20B. Daily 9am–8pm.

Wat Traimit (Golden Buddha)

Thirteenth-century Wat Traimit is notable only for its central statue, a nearly 3m-high (10-ft.), 5-ton Buddha in solid gold. The statue was discovered by accident in 1957 when an old stucco image was being moved from a storeroom by a crane, which dropped it and shattered the plaster shell, revealing the shining gold beneath. The graceful seated statue, which seems to glow with an inner light, was cast during the Sukhothai period and later covered with plaster to hide it from the Burmese.

Traimit Rd. (west of Hua Lamphong Railway Station, just west of the intersection of Krung Kasem and Rama IV roads). Admission 20B. Daily 9am–5pm. Walk southwest on Traimit Rd. and look for a school on the right with a playground; the *wat* is up a flight of stairs overlooking the school.

CULTURAL PURSUITS

Thai culture is not something to simply observe but also to participate in, and festivals, classes, and cultural activities abound. Check with the **TAT** (✆ **02250-5500**) or the **Bangkok Tourist Division** (✆ **02225-7612**) and keep an eye on magazines such as *BK Magazine* or local newspapers including the *Nation* and the *Bangkok Post* for major events during your stay.

THAI COOKING   Fancy a chance to learn cooking techniques from the pros? Thai cooking is fun and easy, and there are a few good hands-on courses in Bangkok. Learn about Thai herbs, spices, and unusual local veggies (you'll never look at a produce market the same way again). Lectures on Thai regional cuisine, cooking techniques, and menu planning complement classroom exercises to prepare all your favorite dishes. The best part is afterward, when you get to eat them. The **Blue Elephant** (✆ **02673-9353;** www.blueelephant.com) is one of the best in town, with classes starting at 2,800B.

THAI MASSAGE ★★★   A traditional Thai massage is a must-do for visitors. You don't just lie back and passively receive a Thai massage; instead, you are an active participant as masseuses manipulate your limbs to stretch each muscle, then apply acupressure techniques to loosen up tense muscles and get energy flowing. It's been described as having yoga "done" to you—your body will be twisted, pulled, and sometimes pounded in the process.

The home of Thai massage, **Wat Pho,** is school to almost every masseuse in Bangkok and offers massages in an open-air pavilion within the temple complex—a very interesting, though not always relaxing, experience (see "Bangkok's Temples," above; ✆ **02221-2974;** 250B per hour).

Bangkok supports some fine spas; most are in the larger hotels, though there are several day spas too. **Le Banyan Tree Spa** (✆ **02679-1052-4;** www.banyantree spa.com) and the **Shangri-La Hotel's Chi Spa** (✆ **02236-7777;** www.shangri-la. com) are among the best places, but they're just two of the many excellent spas in town.

There are countless massage places around Bangkok, many offering proficient services at very reasonable rates (around 200B per hour). Places that offer "ancient" or "traditional" Thai massage generally have well trained masseurs and masseuses who offer no extras, but if you are asked to pick a number from a group of dolled-up masseuses sitting behind a glass barrier, you can be sure the term "massage" is a euphemism for paid sex. Your chosen masseuse will then inform you of the "extras" available and the going rates.

THAI BOXING ★★   *Muaythai,* or Thai boxing, is Thailand's national sport. A visit to the two venues in Bangkok, or to the many fight-nights in towns all over Thailand (as much festival as sport), is a fun window into Thai culture. The pageant of the fighters' elegant pre-bout rituals, wailing musicians, and frenetic gambling activity are a real spectacle. In Bangkok, catch up to 15 bouts nightly at either of two stadiums. The air-conditioned **Ratchadamnoen Stadium** (Ratchadamnoen Nok Ave.;

© 02281-4205) hosts fights on Monday, Wednesday, Thursday, and Sunday, while the muggier **Lumpini Stadium** (Rama IV Rd.; © 02251-4303) has bouts on Tuesday, Friday, and Saturday. Tickets are 2,000B for ringside seats, 1,500B for second-class seats, and 1,000B for nosebleed seats. Go for second-class seats. Not for the squeamish.

MEDITATION   **Wat Mahathat** (see "Bangkok's Temples," above) serves as one of Thailand's largest Buddhist universities and has become a popular center for meditation lessons and practice, with English-speaking monks overseeing students of Vipassana, or Insight Meditation. Three-hour sessions begin daily at 7am, 1pm, and 6pm (© 02222-6011). Donations are requested.

Outdoor Activities

Most hotels, certainly the finest five-star properties, support quality fitness centers complete with personal trainers and top equipment. **California Wow,** on the fourth floor of Siam Paragon mall (© 02627-5999), is a large, convenient facility open to day visitors.

GOLF   Golf enthusiasts will be happy to know that you don't have to go far to enjoy some of Thailand's best courses; there are a number of courses, some of championship quality, in or near the city center.

- **Bangkok Golf Club** (© 02501-2828; www.golf.th.com), a short 35-minute drive from the city center, is an 18-hole course that's always popular and regularly plays host to local and regional tournaments. There's also a nine-hole, par-3 course that replicates some of the world's best-known short holes. Greens fees on weekdays are 1,700B and on weekends 2,500B.
- **Pinehurst Golf & Country Club,** 73 Moo 17, Phaholyothin Rd., Klong Luang, Pathum Thani (© 02516-8679; www.pinehurst.co.th), sports three 9-hole courses plus night golf. This prestigious club served as the venue for the 1992 Johnnie Walker Classic (greens fees: 1,600B weekdays, 2,100B weekends).
- **Green Valley Country Club,** 92 Moo 3, Bangna-Trad Rd., Samut Prakan (© 02312-5883-9), is one of the most convenient courses for Bangkok and Suvarnabhumi Airport and has some testing fairways and greens (greens fees: 2,500B weekdays, 4,000B weekends).

Shopping

With its abundance of Thai silk, good tailors, artwork, hill-tribe crafts, silver, gems, and porcelain, Bangkok pulls in shoppers from all over the world. Prices are comparatively low and the whole process is good fun—bargain hard. At the city's many **street bazaars,** you can find cheap batik clothing, knockoff watches, jeans, designer wear, and all sorts of souvenirs. Buy a bag to tote it all back home.

The best hotel shopping arcades are those at the **Oriental,** the **Four Seasons,** and the **Peninsula** hotels; prices in these places are high. For Thai silk, try the **Jim Thompson Thai Silk Company,** the town's most famous (main store: 9 Surawong Rd., near Silom; © 02632-8100; www.jimthompson.com).

Pick up a copy of Nancy Chandler's *The Market Map* (275B), with detailed insets of specific shopping areas. If you encounter problems with merchants, call the tourist police (© 1155).

SHOPPING AREAS

ALONG THE RIVER   One of the finest collections of art and antiques dealers anywhere in the kingdom is at **River City,** a low-rise mall of quirky shops at the riverside near Bangkok's finest hotels. Sticker shock is the rule, but you get what you pay for—and quality is what you get here. Nearby **Charoen Krung Road** hosts lots of high-end shopping venues for everything from jewelry and antiques to carpets and fine tailoring. All shops can arrange shipping.

SUKHUMVIT ROAD   This area is lined with shops from one end to the other, as well as some of Bangkok's biggest shopping malls (see "Department Stores & Shopping Malls," below). For antiques, stop in **L'Arcadia** (12/2 Sukhumvit Soi 23; ☎ 02259-9595), where you'll find fine Burmese and Thai furniture and carvings. For gems, try **Uthai's Gems** (28/7 Soi Ruam Rudee; ☎ 02253-8582), down Ruam Rudee, a busy shortcut *soi* parallel to Wireless just south of Ploen Chit.

SILOM ROAD   This area is packed with outdoor shopping (see the **Patpong Night Market,** discussed below). There are numerous fine jewelry shops, silk retailers, and tailors here.

MARKETS

Visiting Bangkok's many markets is as much a cultural as a consumer experience: The markets are where the Thai economy happens. Bargaining is fast and furious. The **Weekend Market (Chatuchak),** near the Mo Chit BTS stop, is the city's most famous, covering a vast area and overcrowded on any given Saturday or Sunday. The riverside **Chinatown** area is a labyrinth of shopping. **Khao San Road,** the popular backpacker area, is a great place to pick up anything from travel trinkets to cool T-shirts. **Patpong Night Market** (Patpong Soi 1, off Silom) is more an entertainment than a shopping experience, and sadly **Suan Lum Night Market,** which was once a great downtown alternative for any shoppers unable to visit the Weekend Market, has now been closed down.

DEPARTMENT STORES & SHOPPING MALLS

The size and opulence of Bangkok's many malls and shopping plazas are a shock to first-time visitors in search of the exotic. Highlights include the cavernous **Siam Paragon** (991/1 Rama I Rd., next to the Siam BTS stop; ☎ 02610-9000; www. siamparagon.co.th), one of the largest malls in Asia, with designer outlets, a gourmet market and food court offering everything from fast food to fine dining, an IMAX theater, a bowling alley, and even an opera theater.

 Jewelry Scams

For every reputable gem dealer in Bangkok, there are at least 100 crooks waiting to catch you in the latest scam. To avoid being ripped off, follow this simple rule: Refuse offers from touts for free city shopping junkets.

Next door are the sister shopping malls of **Siam Center** and **Siam Discovery Center** (Rama I Rd.; ☎ 02658-1000), both offering additional acres of high-end shopping.

Also near Siam, the **MBK Center** (at Rama I and Phayathai roads; National Stadium BTS station; ☎ 02620-9000; www.mbk-center. co.th) and its **Tokyu Department Store** are a real trip to teeny-bopper Thailand. This mall houses thousands of affordable local shops, making it a cross between a street market and a shopping mall.

The newest and biggest of Bangkok's monster malls is **Central World** (at Ratcha-damri and Rama I roads; ☎ **02635-1111;** www.centralworld.co.th), currently the biggest shopping complex in Southeast Asia with more than half a million square meters of retail space and parking for more than 7,000 cars. The complex, which includes 50 restaurants, 21 cinemas, a bowling alley, and a kids' zone, was badly dam-aged (as was Siam Paragon) by the riots of May 2010, but its rapid restoration is a sign of the city's resilience.

Bangkok After Dark

Despite legislation restricting bar hours, the action is still fierce and furious in Thai-land's hedonistic capital, and a rollicking good time can always be found. If the Bangkok debauch isn't your scene, know that the town is not all red-light district by any means: There are all kinds of events, clubs, and bars. Check *BK Magazine,* the *Bangkok Post,* or the *Nation* for current happenings.

THE PERFORMING ARTS

There are a number of Thai dance and dinner theaters for tourists (see "Dinner & Dance," p. 64, for specific recommendations).

There are two major theaters for Thai and international performances: the **National Theater** (1 Na Phra That Rd.; ☎ 02224-1342) and the **Thailand Cul-tural Center** (Thiem Ruammit Rd. off Ratchadaphisek Rd., Huai Khwang; ☎ 02247-0028), both with a regular schedule of performances. Contact them directly or check local papers. For a more Disneyfied take on the kingdom, sign up for the nightly extravaganza at **Siam Niramit** (Ratchada Theater, 19 Tiam Ruammit Rd.; ☎ 02649-9222; www.siamniramit.com); the 80-minute, eye-popping show costs 1,500B.

If you'd like a taste of Bangkok's bawdy nightlife without facing it full-on, consider a night out at a **ladyboy cabaret,** in which glamorous transvestites lip-sync to show tunes and prance across the stage in outrageous costumes. Check out **Calypso Cabaret** (☎ 02992-6999; www.calypsocabaret.com), who perform in the Asia Hotel at 269 Phayathai Rd.

THE BAR & CLUB SCENE

There are nighttime adventures to be found down any *soi* in town. If you'd like to unwind with an evening cocktail, check out what's happening at your hotel's lobby bar; many set up jazzy live music to entertain folks. Stop by the **Bamboo Bar,** at the Oriental (Oriental Lane off Charoen Krung Rd.; ☎ 02659-9000), or the **Living Room,** at the Sheraton Grande Sukhumvit (250 Sukhumvit Rd.; ☎ 02649-8888). Both present some of the best jazz in the city; the Living Room also hosts a weekly Sunday Jazzy Brunch Buffet from 11:30am to 3pm.

SILOM ROAD & PATPONG   There can be few better ways to get in the mood for a night out in Bangkok than by sipping on a sundowner at the **Sky Bar** (63rd Floor, State Tower, 1055 Silom Rd.; ☎ 02624-9555; dress code applies) while tak-ing in the sweeping cityscape and gazing down on the ant-sized people below. Ver-tiginous views are all the rage these days, and many of the city's high-rise buildings now feature rooftop bars or restaurants, with sky-high prices to match.

Few visitors leave Bangkok without a stroll around Patpong, the famous strip of go-go bars and night market with myriad vendors and blocks of bars and clubs. The Patpong scene centers on Soi Patpong 1 and Soi Patpong 2 between Surawong and Silom roads. It's the home of Bangkok's raunchier sex shows (mostly in the upstairs bars, which are infamous for scams so are best avoided), but most visitors come to wander the market area (lots of pirated goods) or peek in the downstairs go-go bars.

Despite its rep as a go-go center, there are lots of good bars in Patpong. **O'Reilly's Irish Pub** (62/1–4 Silom Rd., at corner of Soi Thaniya just east of Patpong; ℂ 02632-7515) is a lively bar full of locals and travelers, and features nightly drink specials. The **Barbican** (9/4–5 Soi Thaniya off Silom Rd.; ℂ 02234-3590) is a stylish hangout with great food and live music. **Molly Malone's,** across from Patpong on Convent Road (next to Silom Complex at 1/5–6 Soi Convent Silom; ℂ 02266-7160), caters to expats with live music after office working hours. If you crave margaritas, **Coyote on Convent** (1/2 Convent Rd.; ℂ 02631-2325) has 75 varieties to choose from.

Head to Silom Soi 4 (btw. Patpong 2 and Soi Thaniya off Silom Rd.), where you'll find small homegrown clubs spinning great music as well as the city's prominent gay clubs: **Telephone Pub** (114/11–13 Silom Soi 4; ℂ 02234-3279) and the **Balcony** (86–8 Silom Soi 4; ℂ 02235-5891).

SIAM SQUARE Siam Square, on Rama I Road between Henri Dunant and Phayathai roads, is where you'll find Bangkok's **Hard Rock Cafe** (424/3–6 Siam Sq. Soi 11; ℂ 02658-4090), featuring good live bands.

A great disco, **CM^2,** has nightly live or DJ music—a very popular place in the basement of the Novotel Bangkok on Siam Square (Siam Sq. Soi 6; ℂ 02209-8888). If you're more into jazz than disco, head for **Brown Sugar** (231/20 Sarasin Rd.; ℂ 02250-1825), a funky, compact bar where local and visiting jazzers perform nightly.

A little bit north of Siam Square, near the Victory Monument BTS station (a short cab ride up Phayathai Rd.), check out live jazz and blues at **Saxophone Pub and Restaurant** (ℂ 02246-5472).

KHAO SAN ROAD The backpackers on Khao San Road still party on despite restrictions on opening hours. Start at **Gulliver's,** on the corner of Khao San and Chakrabongse roads, and then explore the back lanes off Khao San for small dance clubs (some the size of broom closets) and hangouts. You'll find lots of travelers in their 20s and a perpetually laid-back atmosphere—anything goes. In the middle of Khao San, don't miss **Lava** (249 Khao San Rd.; ℂ 02281-6565), a popular basement dance club. For a mellower evening, head west of Khao San to riverside **Phra Athit Road,** where there are a number of small cafes with live music.

SUKHUMVIT ROAD One of the most happening areas of Bangkok, the small *sois* along busy Sukhumvit host Bangkok's top clubs and good bars. **Q Bar ★★** (34 Sukhumvit Soi 11; ℂ 02252-3274) is *the* place for the slick urban hip of Bangkok; its only rival is the similarly ab-fab **Bed Supperclub ★★★** (p. 63; 26 Sukhumvit Soi 11; ℂ 02651-3537). Both are ultramodern, have great expat DJs, and boom-boom-boom late into the night 7 days a week.

The **Conrad Hotel** (87 Wireless Rd., across from the U.S. Embassy; ℂ 02690-9999) is home to two of Bangkok's newest and best spots: **Club 87 Plus** is an ultrachic, ultraexclusive club, while the **Diplomat Bar ★** fills with, well, diplomats from the U.S. Embassy as well as Bangkok's hobnobbers.

For bars along Sukhumvit, try the **Bull's Head** (Sukhumvit Soi 33/1; ℂ 02261-0665), a fun local pub that draws crowds with frequent theme parties and a clubhouse attitude. The **Londoner Brew Pub** (Sukhumvit Soi 33; ℂ 02261-0238) is a popular brewpub, while the **Witch's Tavern** (Sukhumvit Soi 55; ℂ 02391-9791) packs 'em in—especially on weekends—with a range of beers and cocktails, as well as pub grub and live rock music.

If you're in the mood for dancing, **Royal City Avenue (RCA)** is a 2km (1¼-mile) stretch of bars, restaurants, and clubs between Rama IX and New Phetchaburi roads. Mostly frequented by young, well heeled Thais, RCA has clubs spinning everything from trance to American pop. It's always happening on the weekends and is decidedly un-sex-touristy.

On the other hand, if you're looking for something similar to the Patpong go-go scene, Sukhumvit has a couple of popular areas: **Soi Cowboy** (btw. Soi Asoke and Sukhumvit Soi 21), the oldest go-go scene dating from Vietnam War days; and **Nana Plaza,** just on Sukhumvit Soi 4.

Side Trips from Bangkok
EASY DAY TRIPS
See "Visitor Information & Tours" (p. 49) for recommended agencies that can make all the arrangements for the following excursions.

Muang Boran (© 02709-1644-8; www.ancientcity.com) ★★, or **Ancient City,** is roughly 45 minutes east of Bangkok in Samut Prakan. Best reached by group tour, Muang Boran is a collection of scaled-down replicas of more than 100 of Thailand's most famous and architecturally significant structures. The lush grounds housing the models cover 128 hectares (316 acres) in the shape of Thailand, with each structure generally set in its correct location. It makes a great antidote to Bangkok's hustle and bustle, and can easily occupy a whole day. Open daily 8am to 5pm. Admission is 350B for adults, 150B for children.

The **Floating Market at Damnoen Saduak** ★, Ratchaburi, is about 40 minutes south of Nakhon Pathom. Some tours combine the Floating Market with a visit to the Rose Garden or with the River Kwai sights (see below for more on each). At a real floating market, food vendors sell their goods from small boats to local folks in other boats or in *klong*-side homes. Damnoen Saduak is as precise a duplicate as you could imagine and great for photographers, though some find it a bit of a tourist trap.

One of Thailand's oldest towns, Nakhon Pathom is thought to be where Buddhism first established a following in the region, over 2,000 years ago. Thus, it is fitting that it should be home to the **Phra Pathom Chedi** (daily 6am–6pm; admission 40B), the tallest (120m/394 ft.) and most revered stupa in the kingdom. The site has been abandoned and rebuilt several times through the centuries, and the current structure was the work of Rama IV in 1853. Apart from its sheer enormity, the *chedi* impresses with its range of Buddha images in niches, all displaying different *mudras* (hand gestures). Located 56km/35 miles west of Bangkok, the *chedi* can be visited either on a tour or by train from Hua Lamphong Railway Station in Bangkok.

Kanchanaburi
120km (75 miles) NW of Bangkok

Really more than a day trip (best as an overnight), Kanchanaburi is home of the famed **Bridge over the River Kwai** and the notorious internment camps for Allied troops forced into servitude (and death) by the Japanese during World War II in an effort to link Burma and Thailand by rail. Made legendary by the film of the same name, the bridge that stands here today is just a rattletrap trestle that crosses the River Kwai (but that doesn't stop souvenir hawkers and the tourist infrastructure that has grown up around the bridge). A train ride across the bridge from Kanchanaburi and on to **Nam Tok** crosses sections of the line built by POWs and passes some lush tropical scenery. In Kanchanaburi itself is the Allied War Cemetery, where the dates on the gravestones set among manicured grounds tell a tragic tale of young lives cut

THE BANGKOK sex scene

Since the 1960s—namely since the Vietnam War—Bangkok has been the sin capital of Asia, with sex clubs, bars, massage parlors, and prostitutes concentrated in the **Patpong, Nana Plaza,** and **Soi Cowboy** districts. Sex is for sale in many quarters of Bangkok, and many first-time visitors are surprised at seeing the many older Western gentlemen strutting about town with lovely young Thai ladies.

Despite efforts by the government to tone down this image by restricting opening hours (most bars now close at midnight or 1am), Bangkok's skin trades are thriving. Go-go bars and clubs are really little more than fronts for prostitution, and very thinly veiled fronts at that. The men and women in the clubs are all available to take out of the bar for a "bar fine." "Modern" or "physical"

massage parlors are where patrons choose ladies by number from behind glass for an oil massage and more, with negotiations. If this is your scene, take great care: Apart from the condom thing (use one), prostitutes are known to slip you drugs (which happens), rob your hotel room while you're sleeping (which happens), or get you mixed up with illegal activities (which also happens). Child prostitution, slavery, and violence against sex workers are still common. If you encounter any problem, report it to the tourist police (✆ **1155**).

Note: A startling increase in HIV-positive cases in the past 20 years brought on mandated, as well as grass-roots efforts, to educate about the use of condoms, which has slowed the rate of increase, though AIDS is still a major concern among sex workers.

short. There are lots of good excursions in the area, many caves and waterfalls in the surrounding hills, and a few good hotels and riverside guesthouses; it's a popular escape from the heat, traffic, and pollution of Bangkok.

You can connect by train from Bangkok's **Hua Lamphong Railway Station** (✆ **1690** or 02223-3762) on regular weekend junkets starting in the early morning, or go by daily ordinary trains from **Thonburi Station** (formerly called Bangkok Noi; ✆ **02411-3102**), with slow, twice-daily connections to **Kanchanaburi Station** (✆ **03456-1052**) for 200B round-trip. There are also frequent regular buses from the **Southern Bus Terminal** (✆ **02894-1622**), but if you're going by road, it's perhaps best to opt for a rented car (see "Getting Around," p. 39).

For overnight lodging, consider the **Felix River Kwai Resort** (9/1 Moo 3, Tambon, Kanchanaburi; ✆ **03455-1000;** www.felixriverkwai.co.th). The Felix has rooms starting at 3,000B and is the best for comfort, but places such as the **VN Guesthouse** (44 Rongheeb Oil Rd., Soi 2; ✆ **034-514082;** www.vnguesthouse.net) offer basic rooms from 250B on a raft at the riverside, which are certainly far more atmospheric and adventurous. Budget guesthouses on dry land line the banks of the river south of the bridge.

Ayutthaya ★★
76km (47 miles) N of Bangkok

From 1350 until its fall to the Burmese in 1767, Ayutthaya was Thailand's capital and home to 33 kings and numerous dynasties. At its zenith and until the mid–18th century, Ayutthaya was a majestic city with three palaces and 400 splendid temples on an island threaded by canals—an awesome sight for early European visitors.

The architecture of Ayutthaya is a fascinating mix of Khmer (ancient Cambodian) and early Sukhothai style, with large corncob-shaped obelisks, called *prangs,* the hallmark. The town is encircled by water, and the central island area of Ayutthaya is itself the site; modern buildings and busy canalside streets are in and among the ruins of this once-great city. It is flat, so getting around by rented bicycle is a good choice. Highlights are **Wat Mahathat,** a crumbling but stunning example of the Ayutthaya style (don't miss the Buddha head embedded in the tree trunk), and **Wihaan Phra Mongkol Bopit,** which houses a massive Buddha. The **Ayutthaya Historical Study Center** and nearby **Chao Sam Phraya National Museum** offer useful background information. The TAT office at the museum offers a detailed map.

Train and bus connections are frequent from Bangkok's **Hua Lamphong Railway Station (℃ 1690** or 02223-3762) and **Northern Bus Terminal (℃ 02936-2852),** respectively.

All-day river cruises are a popular option to and from Ayutthaya. Contact **River Sun Cruises (℃ 02266-9125;** www.riversuncruise.co.th) directly or book through any riverside hotel; departure points are the **Oriental (℃ 02659-9000),** the **Shangri-La Hotel (℃ 02236-7777),** and the River City pier daily at approximately 7:30am (and include a stop at Bang Pa-In). The *Horizon II* from the Shangri-La makes four trips a week (Mon, Wed, Fri–Sat) from Ayutthaya to Bangkok (the outward journey is by minibus). The tour begins at 8am and costs 1,950B. For something more exclusive, the *Manohra* ★★ (℃ 02477-0770; www.manohracruises.com), a teak rice barge converted to a luxury floating hotel with staterooms, leaves every Monday and Thursday for a 3-day/2-night cruise to Ayutthaya; the cost is 69,000B for a double stateroom.

If you want to spend the night, the **Krungsri River Hotel** (27/2 Rojana Rd.; ℃ 03524-4333; www.krungsririver.com), near the train station, is a good choice. Convenient but basic is the **Ayothaya Hotel** (12 Naresuan Rd. Soi 2; ℃ 03523-2855), with rooms from 650B.

THE EASTERN SEABOARD

Tracing the coastline directly east of Bangkok, there are a few resort spots that are attractive as much for their proximity to Bangkok as anything. Closest is **Pattaya,** one of Thailand's earliest holiday developments and famous (or infamous) for its wild nightlife. The town is always hopping late into the night—guys come from all over the world to live it up. Continuing east from Pattaya, **Ko Samet,** in Rayong Province, but still within easy reach of Bangkok, is a small island with loads of basic bungalow resorts and a few high-end choices. It is a laid-back little retreat reached by a short ferry ride from the mainland at the town of Ban Phe (via Rayong). **Ko Chang,** Thailand's second-largest island and the last stop before Cambodia to the east, has earned a glowing reputation among travelers for its fabulous west-coast beaches that are now peppered with high-end resorts. Ko Chang is reached via the nondescript town of Trat.

Pattaya

147km (91 miles) E of Bangkok

The current incarnation of **Pattaya** claims its founders' day as June 29, 1959, when a few truckloads of American troops stationed in Isan arrived in overflowing trucks, rented houses along the beach, and had such a hoot that they told their friends. Word spread, and the town became the R & R capital for war-weary American troops over

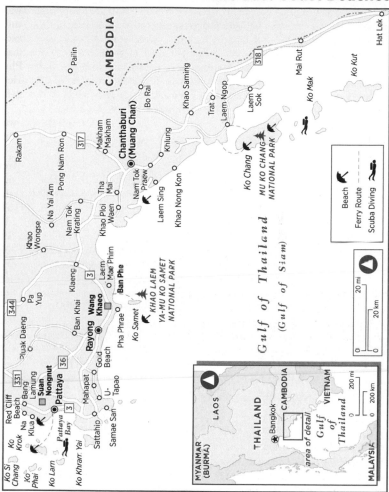

the next many years. The legacy of those early visitors is today's adult playground: hundreds of go-go clubs, beer bars, and massage parlors at beachside.

Tourism boomed in the 1980s, and because unchecked resort development was not accompanied by infrastructure upgrades, beaches became veritable toilets of raw sewage. Despite cleanup projects, the beach is still not at all pleasant.

In 2005, more than 5 million of Thailand's 11 million foreign tourists visited Pattaya. This number has only increased since the opening of Suvarnabhumi International Airport. Just an hour's drive away, Pattaya is as convenient a first stop when you step off the plane at Bangkok.

Pattaya supports a host of international resorts, retreats set in sprawling, manicured seaside gardens. It tries hard to be a family destination, and along with fine accommodations, there are some family activities here, but the mammoth sex-tourism industry kind of puts the kibosh on any wholesome family fun. Neighboring **Jomtien** and **Dongtan** beaches are popular alternatives with less seedy activities and cleaner beaches, but mostly just condominiums—good for day visits.

Pattaya Beach Road is the heart of the town, a long strip of hotels, bars, restaurants, and shops overlooking Pattaya Bay. Pattaya 2nd and Pattaya 3rd roads run parallel to Beach Road and form a busy central grid of small, crowded *sois* bound by North Pattaya Road and South Pattaya Road and bisected by Central Pattaya Road. At both the far northern and southern ends of the strip are two bluffs. Due south is condo-lined Jomtien Beach, a 15-minute ride from Pattaya.

GETTING THERE

BY PLANE   There are no flights to or from Bangkok, but if you are going to or from Phuket or Ko Samui, it's worth considering Bangkok Airways flights from **U-Tapao** airport, located about 30km (19 miles) south of Pattaya. From there, a minibus into town costs around 200B.

BY TRAIN   Weekday train service leaves from Bangkok's **Hua Lamphong Railway Station** at 6:55am and returns from Pattaya at 2:20pm (third class only). The 5-hour trip through the countryside is pleasant and costs only 31B. There's no service on the weekends. Call Hua Lamphong in Bangkok (✆ **1690** or 02223-3762) or in Pattaya (✆ **03842-9285**) for information. A shared *songtao* (covered pickup truck) to town from the Pattaya train station is just 30B.

BY BUS   Buses depart from Bangkok's **Eastern Bus Terminal** (Sukhumvit Rd., opposite Soi 63, at Ekamai BTS station; ✆ **02712-3928**) every half-hour from 5am to 11pm daily. For air-conditioned coach service, the fare is 113B. There's also regular bus service from Bangkok's **Northern Bus Terminal** (**Mo Chit;** ✆ **02936-3509**), as well as from the **Transport Center** at Suvarnabhumi Airport.

Air-conditioned buses to and from Bangkok use the bus station in Pattaya on North Pattaya Road (✆ **03842-9877**). A *songtao* to town is 40B.

BY TAXI   Cabs from Suvarnabhumi International Airport's taxi counter go for 1,050B. Any hotel concierge in Bangkok can negotiate a fare of about 1,500B with a metered taxi driver to take you to or from Pattaya resort, door to door.

GETTING AROUND

BY MINIBUS/SONGTAO   *Songtao* (called **baht buses** here) follow regular routes up and down the main streets. Fares in Pattaya start at 10B. It's about 40B to get to Jomtien (bargain hard). Some hotels operate minibuses as well.

BY CAR   **Avis** has an office at the Dusit Resort (✆ **03836-1628**), with self-drive rates from about 1,350B per day for a Toyota Vios. **Budget** has an office at 219/1–3 Moo 10, Liabchayhard Rd. (✆ **03871-0717**) and offers comparable rates. **Chalee Car Rent** (340–20 Moo 9, Pattaya 3rd Rd.; ✆ **03872-0413;** www.pattayacarrental. com) has a good reputation and, like many smaller firms in town, offers better rates (from 700B). Read contracts closely.

BY MOTORCYCLE   Let's be honest, Pattaya's busy roads are full of drunk and reckless foreign drivers on motorbikes, but the brave (or foolish) can rent 100cc motorcycles for 150B to 200B a day (no insurance). Big choppers and Japanese speed bikes (500cc) will go for 500B to 900B per day. Demand a helmet and, as always, "Renter beware."

Pattaya

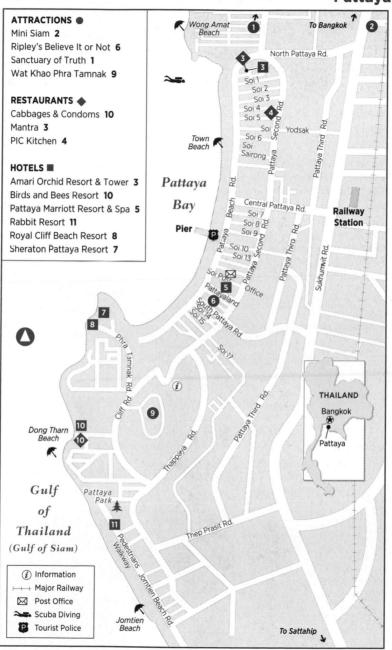

ATTRACTIONS ●
Mini Siam **2**
Ripley's Believe It or Not **6**
Sanctuary of Truth **1**
Wat Khao Phra Tamnak **9**

RESTAURANTS ◆
Cabbages & Condoms **10**
Mantra **3**
PIC Kitchen **4**

HOTELS ■
Amari Orchid Resort & Tower **3**
Birds and Bees Resort **10**
Pattaya Marriott Resort & Spa **5**
Rabbit Resort **11**
Royal Cliff Beach Resort **8**
Sheraton Pattaya Resort **7**

Wong Amat Beach
To Bangkok
North Pattaya Rd.
Soi 1
Soi 2
Soi 3
Soi 4
Soi 5
Soi
Yodsak
Soi 6
Soi Sairong
Town Beach
Pattaya Bay
Beach Rd.
Central Pattaya Rd.
Soi 7
Soi 8 Rd.
Soi 9
Soi 10
Soi 13
Pier
Pattaya Second
Pattaya Second Rd.
Pattaya Third Rd.
Pattaya Third Rd.
Sukhumvit Rd.
Railway Station
Soi Post
Pattayaland
Post Office
South Pattaya Rd.
Soi 14
Soi 15
Soi 17

Phra Tamnak Rd.
Cliff Rd.

Dong Tharn Beach

Gulf of Thailand
(Gulf of Siam)

Thappraya Rd.
Pattaya Third Rd.

Pattaya Park

Thep Prasit Rd.

Pedestrians Walkway
Jomtien Beach Rd.

Jomtien Beach

To Sattahip

THAILAND
Bangkok
Pattaya

(i) Information
┼─┼ Major Railway
⊠ Post Office
≋ Scuba Diving
🅿 Tourist Police

[Fast FACTS] PATTAYA

There are many independent **money-changing booths,** 24-hour **bank** exchange desks (with better rates), and **ATMs** at every turn in town. **Bangkok Pattaya Hospital** (✆ **03825-9999**) has full services and English-speaking staff. In Pattaya, the number for the **tourist police** is ✆ **1155** or 03842-9371. **Internet access** costs 30B to 60B per hour at a number of cafes along the water (try Soi Yamato). The **post office** is on Soi Post Office near the Royal Garden Plaza (✆ **03842-9340-1**).

WHERE TO STAY

Pattaya accommodations range from seedy to stylish. The town supports a few isolated, peaceful getaways as well. Reserve ahead in high season.

Very Expensive

Sheraton Pattaya Resort ★★   Perched in the hills south of Pattaya's main beach, the Sheraton is the top choice for a quiet and luxurious getaway. The guest rooms and pavilions descend the hillside, flanking a maze of gardens, waterfalls, and free-form swimming pools. Decorated in pleasing pastel peaches and sea greens, the guest quarters are spacious and contain oversize king-size or queen-size beds. There's an attractive man-made white-sand beach by the water. While the rocky waterfront isn't the most inviting place for a dip, the adventurous will find the water much cleaner than that of Pattaya's main beach.

437 Phra Tamnak Rd., Pattaya 20150 (on cliff, south end of Pattaya Bay). ✆ **03825-9888.** Fax 03825-9899. www.sheraton.com/pattaya. 156 units. 7,650B–12,000B double; from 37,664B villa. AE, DC, MC, V. **Amenities:** 3 restaurants; bar; babysitting; fitness center; 3 outdoor pools; room service; spa. *In room:* A/C, satellite TV w/DVD player, hair dryer, minibar, Wi-Fi and broadband Internet access (495B per day).

Expensive

Amari Orchid Resort & Tower ★   On the northern end of busy Pattaya, just out of the fray but close enough to walk there, the Amari has good amenities and a helpful staff, with rooms in both the Garden Wing and the new Ocean Tower. The open-air lobby of the Garden Wing is inviting and guest rooms are large, trimmed in dark wood with parquet floors and pleasing, contemporary lines. Rooms in the Ocean Tower are even more luxurious, with open-plan bathrooms, ultramodern fixtures and fittings, and superb views of the bay. Amari also has good in-house dining (see Mantra, under "Where to Dine," below).

Pattaya Beach, Pattaya 20150 (on the very northernmost end of the beachfront road). ✆ **03841-8418.** Fax 03841-8410. www.amari.com. 525 units. 2,898B–4,799B double; from 7,153B suite. AE, DC, MC, V. **Amenities:** 4 restaurants; 4 bars; babysitting; playground and kids' club; fitness center; Internet access; Jacuzzi; 2 outdoor pools; room service; smoke-free rooms; spa. *In room:* A/C, satellite TV, fridge, minibar.

Pattaya Marriott Resort & Spa ★★ ☺   Right in the center of Pattaya Beach, the Marriott has a quiet courtyard garden and landscaped pool area (with the largest pool in Pattaya)—so you can almost forget Pattaya city just beyond the walls. Spacious balconied rooms have views of the gardens or the sea and are done in a tidy, upscale style common to all Thai Marriotts, with lots of nice Thai touches and plush bedding. This resort makes for a great retreat full of all the requisite creature comforts. The adjoining Royal Garden Plaza means access to fine dining and entertainment.

218 Moo 10, Beach Rd., Pattaya 20260. ✆ **03841-2120.** Fax 03842-9926. www.marriott.com. 298 units. 4,520B–6,950B double; from 8,950B suite. AE, DC, MC, V. **Amenities:** 2 restaurants; 2 bars; babysitting; children's programs; executive-level rooms; large fitness center; pool w/swim-up bar; room service;

smoke-free rooms; spa w/Jacuzzi, sauna, and steam; 2 floodlit grass tennis courts; watersports equipment. *In room:* A/C, satellite TV w/in-house movies, fridge, minibar.

Rabbit Resort ★★ 🎁 The Rabbit Resort may be hard to find, but it's worth the search. This four-star boutique hotel on Dongtan Beach, in Jomtien, lies just south of Pattaya and is an ideal place for those needing a quiet retreat and escape from name-brand luxury resorts. Set on 1.6 hectares (4 acres) of oceanfront land, it has superb gardens graced by two pools. The rooms are mostly two-story Thai-style villas, decorated with antiques personally selected by the owners. The friendly Thai staff members are always willing to please and the proprietors are on hand to attend to special needs. The hotel serves complementary buffet breakfasts and has a grill house overlooking the sea.

318/84 Moo 12, Soi Dongtan Police Station, Jomtien 20260. ℰ **03825-1730-2.** Fax 03825-1628. www. rabbitresort.com. 49 units. 3,900B–8,900B off peak; 5,900B–12,900B high season. AE, DC, MC, V. **Amenities:** Restaurant; babysitting services; free Internet; 2 pools. *In room:* A/C, satellite TV, fridge, hair dryer, minibar.

Royal Cliff Beach Resort ★★★ Comprising the Royal Cliff Grand & Spa, the Royal Wing & Spa, the Royal Cliff Beach Hotel, and the Royal Cliff Terrace, this luxurious compound provides a range of accommodations and is tops in Pattaya. Each property has its own charm. High-end **Royal Cliff Grand** and all-suite **Royal Wing** are the best choices, catering to the well heeled business traveler. Everything is luxe, from the columned public spaces, chandeliers, and fountains to the large and opulent guest rooms. The Grand's spacious rooms are set in a contemporary, scallop-shaped tower and have marble bathrooms with separate shower stalls and twin sinks. The **Royal Cliff Beach Hotel,** the most affordable choice, is Pattaya's top family resort. Rooms here are also spacious, with bleached wood and pastel decor and large terraces, most with bay views. Two-bedroom suites are perfect for families. The beachfront **Royal Cliff Beach Terrace** was the resort's first property and is the most secluded. Rooms boast contemporary decor as well as nice ocean views. The property is far from town and very quiet.

353 Phra Tamnak Rd., Pattaya 20150 (on cliff, south end of Pattaya Bay). ℰ **03825-0421.** Fax 03825-0511. www.royalcliff.com. 1,072 units. 3,600B–7,200B double; from 14,400B suite. AE, DC, MC, V. **Amenities:** All Royal Cliff Beach Resort properties share all facilities, including 10 restaurants; 4 bars (2 w/live music); babysitting; children's playroom; concierge; golf course; 4-hole putting green; fully equipped fitness center; Jacuzzi; 5 outdoor landscaped pools; room service; smoke-free rooms; 2 spas; 7 outdoor lit tennis courts; watersports equipment; cooking school. *In room:* A/C, satellite TV, fridge, hair dryer, minibar.

Moderate

Birds and Bees Resort ★★ This fun, inviting resort was originally known as Cabbages & Condoms. It was built by Senator Meechai Viravaidya, a Thai activist in the field of sex education and rural development projects throughout Thailand. Rooms have a rustic feel, but all the required amenities are there. Its attraction mainly lies in its two pools, a semiprivate beach, and its tucked-away location in a quiet part of Pattaya. The property is very family-friendly and contains wishing wells, as well as an herb garden (with special exercise bikes designed to irrigate them). It is also home to the acclaimed Cabbages & Condoms restaurant (see below), which has a branch in Bangkok.

366/11 Moo 12, Phra Tamnak 4 Rd., Nongprue, Banglamung, Chonburi 20150 (south of town on Hu Gwang Bay). ℰ **03825-0556.** Fax 03825-0034. www.cabbagesandcondoms.co.th. 54 units. 2,500B–6,000B double; 6,000B–11,000B 1- and 2-bedroom suites. AE, MC, V. **Amenities:** Restaurant; 2 pools; room service. *In room:* A/C, satellite TV, fridge, minibar.

WHERE TO DINE

Busy Pattaya is chockablock with small storefront bars and eateries. You'll find the big fast-food chains well represented (including two Starbucks along the beachfront road). The **Royal Garden** shopping complex (south of town) and the large **Big C Festival Center** (on Pattaya 2nd Rd., north end of town) support a number of very familiar restaurants.

Expensive

Mantra ★★★ INTERNATIONAL   Part of Amari's expanding empire on the far north of the main beach, Mantra would be right at home 90 miles west in Bangkok or even 8,000 miles east in New York City. By far the most stylish restaurant in Pattaya, Mantra also serves the best food in town. The menu is eclectic: Australian beef, Indian curries, Peking duck, pizza, sushi, and dim sum are among the many choices prepared in open-air stations on the restaurant's main floor. The Sunday brunch is something special and worth the trip from Bangkok even if you're not staying in Pattaya. It's partially a buffet, as the salads, sandwiches, sushi, and desserts are all laid out, but you can also have main dishes cooked to order. Mantra's stylish bar is a happening place on the weekends, too.

At the Amari, 240 Moo 5, Pattaya Beach Rd. (north end of Pattaya). *(C)* **03842-9591.** www.mantra-pattaya.com. Dress code applies. Main courses 600B–4,600B; Sun brunch 1,490B. AE, DC, MC, V. Mon–Sat 5pm–1am; Sun 11am–3pm and 5pm–1am.

Moderate

Cabbages & Condoms Restaurant THAI   South of town on Hu Gwang Bay in the Birds and Bees Resort (see above), this is Pattaya's version of the much-lauded restaurant in Bangkok. Both are known not only for their food, but also for their efforts to educate Thais about HIV/AIDS. The mainly Thai cuisine is good, though, with wide choices ranging from seafood to regional specialties, though tastes are toned down for the foreign palate. The open-concept restaurant is set in the resort's tropical gardens and offers delightful views of the sea.

Birds and Bees Resort, 366/11 Moo 12, Phra Tamnak 4 Rd., Nongprue, Banglamung, Chonburi. *(C)* **03825-0556.** www.cabbagesandcondoms.co.th. Main courses 180B–350B. MC, V. Daily 11am–10pm.

PIC Kitchen ★ THAI   Named for the Pattaya International Clinic (PIC) Hospital next door (don't worry, they're unrelated), PIC has a nice atmosphere of small teak pavilions, both air-conditioned and open-air, and Thai-style floor seating or romantic tables. Delicious and affordable Thai cuisine is served a la carte or as lunch and dinner set menus. The spring rolls and deep-fried crab claws are mouthwatering. Other dishes come pan-fried, steamed, or charcoal-grilled, with spice added to taste. After dinner, head upstairs to the Jazz Pit and enjoy some live jazz (7pm–1am).

Soi 5 Pattaya 2nd Rd. *(C)* **03842-8374.** www.pic-kitchen.com. Main courses 180B–560B. AE, DC, MC, V. Daily 10am–2pm and 6pm–midnight.

WHAT TO SEE & DO

Wat Khao Phra Tamnak is a small temple complex on a hill (often referred to as Buddha Hill) high above Pattaya to the south, with an 18m (59-ft.) Buddha and fantastic views across the town and bay.

Though it in no way compares to the Ancient City (see "Side Trips from Bangkok," p. 78), **Mini Siam** (397 Moo 6, Sukhumvit Rd.; *(C)* **03872-7333;** www.minisiam. com) also features reproductions of some of the kingdom's most iconic buildings, though on a much smaller scale, and now there's a Mini Europe too, with models of places like the Eiffel Tower and the Leaning Tower of Pisa. It's great fun for kids. Admission is 300B (150B for kids).

For something completely unusual, **Ripley's Believe It or Not!** (Royal Garden Plaza, 218 Beach Rd., Third Floor; ☎ 03871-0294) is hilarious, with unusual exhibits and oddities, as well as a Haunted Adventure and an Infinity Maze. Kids will love this place too. It's open from 11am to 11pm daily; admission is 480B for adults, 380B for kids.

One of Pattaya's most striking sights is the **Sanctuary of Truth** ★ (206/5 Moo 5, Naklua; ☎ 03836-7229; www.sanctuaryoftruth.com), a 100m-tall (328-ft.) wood structure of intricately carved Thai, Khmer, Chinese, and Lao gods and goddesses. It's open daily from 8am to 5pm, and admission, including a horse-carriage ride around the building, costs 600B for adults, 350B for kids. Construction is ongoing; carpenters have worked on the structure since 1981 and expect to finish around 2025.

Out-of-town attractions include the **Pattaya Elephant Village** (☎ 03824-9818; www.elephant-village-pattaya.com), which stages elephant shows daily at 2:30pm (650B) and offers jungle treks as well. **Nong Nooch** (☎ 03870-9358-62; www.nongnoochtropicalgarden.com) is a picturesque botanical garden with well designed plant displays, plus a cultural show (traditional music and dance) and its own elephant show as well. Entrance tickets, including shows and hotel pickup at 8:30am or 2:30pm, cost 600B.

OUTDOOR ACTIVITIES

GOLF The hills around Pattaya are known as the "Golf Paradise of the East," with many international-class courses within a short 40km (25-mile) radius of the city.

○ **Bangpra International Golf Club,** 45 Moo 6, Tambon Bang Pra, Chonburi 20110 (☎ 03834-1149; www.bangpragolf.co.th), is the finest course in Pattaya, although it's a long drive from town (greens fees: 1,400B weekdays, 2,400B weekends).

○ **Laem Chabang International Country Club,** 106/8 Moo 4, Tambon Bung, Sri Racha (☎ 03837-2273; www.laemchabanggolf.com), is a 27-hole course designed by Jack Nicklaus with very dramatic scenery (greens fees: 2,500B weekdays, 3,000B weekends).

○ **Siam Country Club,** 50 Moo 9, Tambol Pong, Banglamung (☎ 03890-9700; fax 03890-9779; www.siamcountryclub.com), is a short hop from Pattaya and believed to be one of the country's most challenging courses (greens fees 2,750B weekdays, 3,300B weekends).

WATERSPORTS Efforts at cleanup are ongoing, but the bay in Pattaya is still quite polluted. It's sad that development ruined the one thing that attracts most visitors. Beach sand is coarse; swimming, if you dare, is best either at the very north of Pattaya Beach or a 15-minute drive south, over the mountain, to Jomtien Beach.

The bay is full of boats ready to take you to outlying islands such as **Ko Khrok, Ko Lan,** and **Ko Sok** for a day of private beach lounging or snorkeling starting at 500B per head on a full boat (more for a private charter). It'll cost you a bit more to access far-flung **Bamboo Island** or **Ko Man Wichai**—some 2,000B. Contact **Adventure Divers,** 391/77–78 Moo 10, Tappraya Rd., Nongprue Banglamung Chonburi 20260 (☎ 03836-4453), for scuba trips.

Paragliding around the bay behind a motorboat is a popular beachfront activity; a 5-minute flight costs from 500B. Jomtien Beach hosts **windsurfing** and **sea kayaking;** boards and boats are rented along the beach for rates starting at 400B per hour.

PATTAYA AFTER DARK

Pattaya is all flashing neon and blaring music down even the smallest *soi,* an assault on the senses. Places such as the south Pattaya pedestrian area, "Walking Street," are lined with open-air watering holes with bar girls luring passersby: The nightlife finds you in this town with an imploring, "You, mister, where you go?" Go-go bars are everywhere, and red-light "Bar Beer" joints are springing up as fast as local officials can close them down. The city is a larger version of Bangkok's Patpong, complete with "Boyz Town," a row of gay clubs in south Pattaya. The same debauchery that brings so many to Pattaya is pretty sad in the light of day, though, when bleary-eyed revelers stumble around streets once glowing with neon, now bleak and strewn with garbage.

There are a few spots without the sleaze. **Hopf Brewhouse** (219 Beach Rd.; © 03871-0650) makes its own fine brand of suds, and the in-house Hopf Band plays everything from old Herb Alpert tunes to newer jazzy sounds. **Shenanigan's** (© 03871-0641) is a fun Irish bar at the Royal Garden complex (near the Marriott), with the front entrance on Pattaya 2nd Road. **Henry J. Bean's** (on the beach at the Amari Orchid Hotel; © 03842-8161) has a live band and a light, friendly atmosphere.

The town's campy cabaret shows are touristy good fun. Pattaya's most beautiful *katoeys* (transsexuals) don sequined gowns and feather boas to strut their stuff for packed houses nightly. Both **Tiffany's** (464 Moo 9, 2nd Rd.; © 03842-1700-5) and **Alcazar** (78/14 Pattaya 2nd Rd., opposite Soi 4; © 03803841-0224) have hilarious shows much like those in other tourist towns in Thailand. Tickets start at 500B. If you're in the mood for a good set of blues music, make your way to the **Blues Factory** (Soi Lucky Star, off Walking St.; © 03830-0180; www.thebluesfactorypattaya. com), where two house bands will get you up off your seat.

Ko Samet ★

220km (137 miles) E of Bangkok on Hwy. 3 via Pattaya (or 185km/115 miles via Pattaya bypass)

Tiny **Ko Samet** first became popular with Thais from the poetry of Sunthon Phu, a venerated 19th-century author and Rayong native who set his best-known epic on this "tropical island paradise." Just 1km (⅔ mile) wide, Ko Samet is split by a rocky ridge, and the east coast is lined with bungalows and fancy resorts. Ko Samet is a national park (you'll pay 200B to enter Diamond Beach), but it's unclear what's being protected here since just about every square foot of beach has been developed. It's best to arrive on a weekday for ease in finding a room, as big groups from Bangkok pack the place on weekends and public holidays. This is quite simply because the island has far and away the best beaches within reach of the capital for a weekend getaway. The island is accessed by ferry from the town of **Ban Phe,** 35km (22 miles) east of Rayong city.

GETTING THERE

BY BUS   Buses leave Bangkok every hour between 5am and 7pm for the 3½-hour journey, departing from the city's **Eastern Bus Terminal (Ekamai),** on Sukhumvit Road opposite Soi 63 (© 02391-2504). The one-way trip to the ferry landing at Ban Phe costs 163B. If you're coming from Pattaya, you'll have to wait on the highway and flag down anything heading east.

BY MINIBUS **Samet Island Tour** (19/42–44 Soi Yamato [13/1] 2nd Rd., Pattaya; ℂ 03871-0676) runs regular routes from Pattaya to Ban Phe (trip time: 1 hr.; 460B round-trip, 1,200B day trip to Samet).

BY CAR Take Hwy. 3 east from Bangkok along the longer, more scenic coastal route (trip time: 3½–4 hr.), or the quicker route via Hwy. 3 east to Pattaya, then Hwy. 36 to Rayong, then the coastal Hwy. 3 to Ban Phe (trip time: about 3 hr.).

GETTING TO & GETTING AROUND THE ISLAND

From the **pier at Ban Phe** (ℂ 03889-6155), ferries leave for Ko Samet's northern ferry terminal at Na Dan every half-hour (trip time: 40 min.; 50B) or when full. The first boat departs at 8am and the last at 5pm. Several agents at the pier in Ban Phe sell passage directly to Vong Deuan beach, in the middle of the east coast for as little as 70B.

After arriving at the ferry terminal on the northern tip of Ko Samet, you can catch a *songtao* (covered pickup truck) to other beaches for between 20B and 50B. Or you can rent **motorbikes** for about 300B per day, though you'll need to be a confident rider, as Ko Samet's only road (down the east coast) is potholed and bumpy.

[FastFACTS] KO SAMET

There are ATMs at Na Dan pier and at the national parks office, and any resort can change money (at a worse rate). The **post office** is at the Naga Bar, along the main road south of Diamond Beach.

WHERE TO STAY & DINE

Ko Samet once featured only budget accommodations with basic facilities, but now the sky is the limit, with luxury resorts pampering to every whim. In general, rates are higher than at other beach resorts because food and water must be imported from the mainland. Hotel and transport touts pounce at the pier, so it's best to prebook accommodation to avoid this hassle.

All of the bungalows offer some sort of dining experience, mostly local food and beer, with some Western breakfast offerings. In the evenings on most beaches, tables are set up under twinkling lights alongside big seafood barbecues brimming with the day's catch. It's very pretty. Try **Jep's** on Ao Hin Khok.

Ao Kiew

Paradee ★ These are the most luxurious accommodations on Ko Samet. Reached by private speedboat (6,000B per person), the Paradee occupies a sliver of land at the southern tip of Samet that offers ocean access on both the east and west coasts (something for both sunrise and sunset enthusiasts). Most of the resort's thatch-roofed villas come with a private pool and Jacuzzi (some even with private butler), and all are spacious with imposing four-poster beds, sizable bathrooms, and furnished wood patios. Numerous high-tech amenities include flatscreen TVs, DVD players, and free broadband Internet access. The place is designed as a "couples" resort, so it's not the best place to take kids.

76 Moo 4, Tumbol Phe, Rayong, Ko Samet 21160 (on southern tip of island, best reached by direct boat). ℂ **03864-4283-8.** Fax 03864-4290. www.paradeeresort.com. 40 units. 15,500B garden villa; 18,100B garden villa with pool; 23,000B–27,000B beachfront villa with pool; 75,000B suite villa. AE, MC, V. **Amenities:** Restaurant; 2 bars; fitness center; Internet cafe; room service; spa; watersports equipment. *In room:* A/C, satellite TV w/DVD player, free Internet access, minibar.

Ao Prao

This is the only beach on the west coast, reached by either pickup or motorbike from the ferry or else directly by ferry. **Le Vimarn** (© 03864-4104; www.samedresorts.com), a hillside collection of cottages and villas, offers the highest standard on Ao Prao. Cottages start at 9,300B. Next door is the slightly more affordable **Ao Prao Resort** (© 03864-4100; www.samedresorts.com), Le Vimarn's sister property, with rooms from 6,400B. Contact either of these resorts for direct ferry service.

Vong Deuan

This area is the most happening beach in Samet. Busy, with lots of bungalows and open-air eateries, Vong Deuan has a good vibe in the evening and is a fun party spot on the weekend. The beach is about halfway down the island and can be reached by ferry directly from Ban Phe for just 60B one-way.

Vongduern Villa (© 03864-4260; www.vongduernvilla.com), at the southern end of the beach, has a variety of comfortable and clean rooms starting at just 1,200B. **Vongdeuan Resort** (© 03864-4171; www.vongdeuan.com) has rooms of a similar adequate standard.

Ko Chang ★

340km (211 miles) E of Bangkok

Trat's dramatic, wooded landscape crests at the Khao Bantat Range, which separates Thailand's easternmost province from neighboring Cambodia. The local economy relies on rubber and chili plantations, fish farming, and fishing. Memories of territorial conflicts with nearby Cambodia are fresh, but the situation is calm. Trat Province is the gateway to the tranquil, unspoiled acres of **Mu Ko Chang National Park,** 52 heavily wooded islands, most accessible by ferry from the cape at Laem Ngop. **Ko Chang,** Thailand's second-largest island with its highest point at 740m (2,428 ft.), is scenically beautiful and usually more peaceful than places such as Phuket and Ko Samui.

GETTING THERE

BY PLANE Bangkok Airways (© 02270-6699; www.bangkokair.com) flies three times a day from Bangkok to Trat (trip time: 1 hr., 5 min.) and reservations are necessary in the high season. Trat airport (© 03952-5776) is 20km (12 miles) from the pier at **Ao Thammachat** (for Ko Chang); a combined shuttle bus/ferry ticket costs 300B, which will take you directly to your resort on the island.

BY BUS There are hourly departures from Bangkok's **Eastern Bus Terminal (Ekamai)** to the pier at **Ao Thammachat** (© 02391-2504; trip time: 4–5 hr.). Less frequent buses leave from Bangkok's **Northern Bus Terminal** (© 02936-2852). Fares are between 200B and 250B. From Pattaya, you'll have to flag down eastbound buses along Sukhumvit Road; it's a 3½-hour trip. Pattaya tour companies can also arrange direct minivans.

BY CAR Take Hwy. 3 east from Bangkok to Chonburi, then Hwy. 344 southeast to Klaeng (bypassing Pattaya and Rayong), then the coastal Hwy. 3 east through Chanthaburi and south to Trat (trip time: about 5–6 hr.).

GETTING TO & GETTING AROUND THE ISLAND

There are now many ways to bypass Trat and go directly to or from Ko Chang from Bangkok. From Trat airport, **minivans** link passengers to one of two piers at Laem Ngop (a third is currently out of use), where during dry season (Oct–May),

Malaria?

Malaria is endemic to the heavily forested islands of Mu Ko Chang National Park and the jungle-covered foothills of Trat Province, but no cases have been reported in a number of years. It's all the buzz on the boat ride over, but don't believe the hype. Still, it is a good idea, as anywhere in Thailand, to avoid getting bitten. Bring insect repellent (with DEET if possible), and keep skin covered up at dusk and dawn.

weather-beaten ferries cross to the nearby islands of Ko Chang, and much farther afield, Ko Wai, Ko Kood, Ko Maak, and Ko Kham. From Trat, *songtaews* (shared pickups) journey between all piers for around 50B. On the island, white *songtaews* charge from 40B to 150B to take visitors to their hotels. In low season, if you are alone you may be obliged to charter the whole *songtaew* for 500B.

The ferry service departs Laem Ngop at regular intervals between 7am and 7pm (weather permitting), and the trip takes 30 to 40 minutes, costing 30B to 80B per person. If you are prone to seasickness, be warned that during the monsoon season (July–Sept) the crossing can be rough.

VISITOR INFORMATION

The **TAT** has an office in Trat (100 Moo 1, Trat-Laem Ngop Rd.; *©* **03959-7259**) and provides information about the nearby islands.

WHERE TO STAY & DINE

If you're arriving in the late evening and get stranded in Trat, the **Muang Trad Hotel,** 4 Sukhumvit Rd. (*©* **03951-1091**), 1 block south of the bus terminal, has rooms from 250B to 5,000B with fan or air-conditioning.

Amari Emerald Cove Resort & Spa ★★★   The Amari has an easy and effective formula for success in Thailand: well maintained, professionally staffed resorts with comfortable rooms and excellent dining. Well, maybe it's not that easy, but they sure make it look easy—and the Emerald Cove is a case in point. Some of the most attractive rooms in the Amari chain, with beautiful rosewood floors and comfortable modern furnishings, line an immaculately kept courtyard, the crown jewel being the beachfront 50m (164-ft.) lap pool. During the day, the ever-vigilant staff will assist you with your every need. At night, you have the choice of excellent Thai or Italian cuisine.

88/8 Moo 4, Ko Chang 23170. *©* **03955-2000.** Fax 03955-2001. www.amari.com/emeraldcove. 165 units. 5,376B superior; 6,575B deluxe; 14,575B suite. AE, MC, V. **Amenities:** 3 restaurants; 2 bars; babysitting; fitness center; Jacuzzi; large outdoor pool; children's pool; room service; sauna; spa. *In room:* A/C, satellite TV, hair dryer, minibar, Wi-Fi.

Panviman ★   The Panviman's spacious grounds are meticulously manicured, and the pool is a beautiful little meander flanked on one side by a casual bar, on the other by the resort's fine dining—everything oriented to great views of the sea (with the accompanying great sunsets). Check out the garden gnomes all about. Rooms are set in high-peaked, Thai-style buildings with arching *naga* roofs. They're done in tile and teak, each with a canopy bed, large sitting area, balcony, and huge stylish bathroom. It's not a private beach, but the resort is far south of central White Sand Beach, so even in high season you might have a vast stretch of sand to yourself.

8/15 Klong Prao Beach, Ko Chang 23170 (a short ride south of White Sand Beach on the west coast of the island). ✆ **03955-1290,** or 02910-8660 in Bangkok. Fax 03955-1283. www.panviman.com. 50 units. 10,500B deluxe; 12,500B deluxe pool access. MC, V. **Amenities:** Restaurant; bar; transfer services; fitness center; Internet access; Jacuzzi; outdoor pool; room service; watersports equipment. *In room:* A/C, satellite TV, fridge, minibar.

WHAT TO SEE & DO

Ko Chang, Thailand's second-largest island after Phuket, is the anchor of the 52-island **Mu Ko Chang National Park.** Thickly forested hills rise from its many rocky bays, forming a swaying hump reminiscent of a sleeping elephant (*chang* means elephant). Although they are not indigenous to the island, there are opportunities for elephant treks. The best choice by far is the **Ban Kwan Chang Elephant Camp.** The camp offers half-day tours that include feeding, bathing, and riding the elephants for 900B. Contact Jungle Way Bungalows at ✆ **08922-34795** (www.jungleway. com) for more information.

Cambodia is visible from the eastern shore of Ko Chang. **Hat Sai Khao (White Sand Beach),** on the island's west coast, is the most popular beach. Twenty minutes by boat farther south is **Hat Khlong Phrao,** with clusters of bungalows, an inland canal, and a fishing settlement. There is good snorkeling off Ko Chang's south coast; contact tour operators for details and to arrange passage by boat.

THE SOUTHERN PENINSULA: EAST COAST

Thailand's slim Malay Peninsula extends 1,250km (777 miles) south from Bangkok to the Malaysia border. The towns of **Cha-Am** and royal **Hua Hin** are just a short hop south of Bangkok, and the ancient temples of **Phetchaburi,** the last outpost of the Khmer empire, are a good day trip from there.

Passing through coastal towns such as Prachuap Kiri Khan and Chumphon, heading farther south you come to **Surat Thani,** a popular jumping-off point for islands in the east: Ko Samui, Ko Pha Ngan, and Ko Tao. As the beach resorts of Phuket dominate the tourist landscape on the west coast, **Ko Samui,** a developed but laid-back resort island in the Gulf of Thailand, dominates the east. Nearby **Ko Pha Ngan,** famed for its wild full-moon parties, is gaining prominence as a rustic resort destination, as is **Ko Tao** for its access to some of Thailand's best dive sites.

Hua Hin & Cha-Am

Hua Hin: 265km (165 miles) S of Bangkok, 223km (139 miles) N of Chumphon; Cha-Am: 240km (149 miles) S of Bangkok, 248km (154 miles) N of Chumphon

Hua Hin and **Cha-Am,** neighboring towns on the Gulf of Thailand, are together the country's oldest resort area. Developed in the 1920s as a relaxing getaway for Bangkok's elite, the beautiful seaside of "Thailand's Riviera" was a mere 3- to 4-hour journey from the capital by train, thanks to the southern railway's completion in 1916. The royal family was the first to embrace these two small fishing villages as the perfect location for both summer vacations and health retreats. In 1924, King Vajiravudh (Rama VI) built the royal Mareukatayawan Palace amid the tall evergreens that lined these stretches of golden sand. At the same time, the Royal Hua Hin Golf Course opened as the first course in Thailand. As Bangkok's upper classes began building summer bungalows along the shore, the State Railway opened the Hua Hin Railway Hotel for tourists, which stands today as the Sofitel Central Hua Hin Resort, and the

current king of Thailand spends much of his time at his regal residence just north of town. Today, the area's clean sea and beaches support some unique resorts, and nearby **Phetchaburi** (see "Side Trips from Hua Hin & Cha-Am," later in this section) is a fascinating and easy day trip to experience a bit of Thai history and culture.

Plan your trip for the months between November and May to get the most sunshine and least rain, but note that from about mid-December to mid-January, Hua Hin and Cha-Am reach peak levels and bookings should be made well in advance (at higher rates). This is also increasingly true for weekends year-round, as more and more weekenders from Bangkok are making Hua Hin their destination of choice.

GETTING THERE

BY PLANE Though there is an airport at Hua Hin, at the time of writing no flights were operating.

BY TRAIN Both Hua Hin and Cha-Am are reached via the train station in Hua Hin. Ten trains make the daily trek from Bangkok's **Hua Lamphong Railway Station** (🕿 **1690** or 02223-3762). The trip is just more than 4 hours.

The **Hua Hin Railway Station** (🕿 **03251-1073**), which is one of the town's most interesting sights, especially for its Royal Waiting Room, is at the tip of Damnoenkasem Road, which slices through the center of town straight to the beach. Pickup-truck taxis (*songtao*) or tuk-tuks to town start at 50B.

BY BUS The bus is the most efficient choice for travel from Bangkok. Buses depart from Bangkok's **Southern Bus Terminal** (🕿 **02894-6122**) regularly between 5am and 10pm (180B). There are also five daily buses to Cha-Am between 5am and 2pm (150B).

Buses from Bangkok pull up at the new bus station on the Petchkasem Road to the south of the town center (🕿 **03251-1654**). From here it's easy to find a *songtao* or tuk-tuk to take you to your destination. The Cha-Am bus station is on the main beach road (🕿 **03242-5307**).

Minibuses can be arranged at any hotel or travel agent in either Bangkok or Hua Hin. Minivan departures (🕿 **08163-30609**) leave every 30 minutes from the west side of the traffic circle at Bangkok's busy Victory Monument (a stop on the BTS skytrain) between 5:30am and 6pm and cost 200B.

BY CAR From Bangkok, take Route 35, the Thonburi-Paktho Highway, southwest and allow 2 to 4 hours, depending on traffic.

GETTING AROUND

Despite all the tourist traffic, **Hua Hin** is easy to navigate. The main artery, Petchkasem Road, runs parallel to the waterfront about 4 blocks inland. Wide Damnoenkasem Road cuts through Petchkasem and runs straight to the beach. On the north side of Damnoenkasem toward the waterfront, you'll find a cluster of guesthouses, restaurants, shopping, and nightspots lining the narrow lanes.

Smaller **Cha-Am** is a 25-minute drive north of Hua Hin along Petchkasem Road. Ruamchit Road, also known as Beach Road, hugs the shore and is lined with shops, restaurants, hotels, and motels. Cha-Am's resorts line the 8km (5-mile) stretch of beach that runs south from the village toward Hua Hin.

BY SONGTAO Pickup-truck taxis follow regular routes in Hua Hin, passing the railway station and bus terminals at regular intervals. Flag one down that's going in your direction. Fares range from 10B to 20B within town, while stops at outlying resorts will cost up to 50B. Trips between Hua Hin and Cha-Am are between 100B and 200B.

BY TUK-TUK Tuk-tuk rides are negotiable, as always, but expect to pay as little as 40B for a ride within town.

BY MOTORCYCLE TAXI Within each town, motorcycle-taxi fares begin at 20B. The taxi drivers, identifiable by colorful numbered vests, are a good way to get to your resort if you're in Cha-Am after hours (about 100B).

BY TRISHAW Trishaws, or *samlor,* can be hired for short distances in town (from 20B). You can also negotiate an hourly rate.

BY CAR/MOTORCYCLE **Budget** has a desk at the Hua Hin Grand Hotel, 222/2 Petchkasem Rd. (© 03251-4220). Self-drive rates start at around 1,300B. Cheaper alternatives can be rented from stands near the beach on Damnoenkasem Road. A 100cc motorcycle goes for around 150B to 200B per day.

VISITOR INFORMATION

The **Hua Hin Tourist Information Center** (© 03251-1047) is in the center of town, tucked behind the city shrine at the corner of Damnoenkasem and Petchkasem roads. Open daily from 8:30am to 8pm.

[Fast FACTS] HUA HIN & CHA-AM

In Hua Hin All major banks are along Petchkasem Road to the north of Damnoen-kasem Road, and there are many money-changers throughout the town. The main post office (© 03251-1350) is on Damnoenkasem Road near the Petchkasem intersection. Both Hua Hin and Cha-Am have Internet cafes along the more-traveled shopping streets. The **Hua Hin Hospital** (© 03252-0401) is located in the north of town along Petchkasem Road. Call the **Tourist Police** for either town at © 03251-5995.

In Cha-Am Banks are centered along Petchkasem Road, and the post office is on Beach Road. The **Thonburi Cha-Am Hospital** (© 03243-3903) is off Narathip Road. Internet access is available in a few places along Beach Road.

SPECIAL EVENTS

A free **jazz festival** is held annually in June over 2 or 3 days, featuring local and international bands. The event attracts thousands of visitors to a unique beach setting, with a stage usually set up in front of the Sofitel hotel. Spectators sit on the sand or can hire chairs. Extra jazz events take place around town at the same time. The event date varies annually. See www.huahinafterdark.com/events or contact the Hua Hin Tourist Information Center at © 03251-1047.

WHERE TO STAY

In Hua Hin

Chiva-Som International Health Resort ★★★ One of the finest high-end health resorts in the kingdom, Chiva-Som excels with its spa programs: From chi gong to chin-ups, muscle straining to massage, a stay at Chiva-Som is a chance to escape the workaday world and focus on development of body and mind. Upon check-in, you'll meet with a counselor who can tailor a program to fit your needs, goals, and budget or package you have booked (there is a wide range). Guests might focus on early morning yoga, stretching, and tough workouts, or go for gentle massages, aromatherapy, even isolation chambers and past-life regression workshops. The resort's spa cuisine is not all granola and oats, but delicious and healthy fare, and there is a nice bond that develops between guests and staff in weekly barbecues and frequent "mocktail" parties. Don't pass up the signature Chiva-Som massage.

73/4 Petchkasem Rd., Hua Hin 77110 (5-min. drive south of Hua Hin). © 03253-6536. Fax 03251-1154. www.chivasom.com. 57 units. All rates are quoted per person for a 3-night stay: 49,995B oceanview double; 62,865B pavilion; from 99,000B suite. Rates include 3 spa-cuisine meals per day, health and beauty consultations, daily massage, and participation in fitness and leisure activities. AE, DC, MC, V. **Amenities:** 2 restaurants; bike rental; concierge; golf course nearby; amazing fitness center w/personal trainers and exercise classes; ozonated indoor pool and outdoor pool; room service; smoke-free rooms; his-and-hers spas w/steam and hydrotherapy treatments, massage, beauty treatments, floatation, and medical advisement; watersports equipment; library. *In room:* A/C, satellite TV, fridge, minibar.

Anantara Resort Hua Hin ★★ The Anantara is a collection of teak pavilions surrounded by lily ponds, and from the hotel's most luxurious rooms and their wide balconies, you can hear chirping frogs and watch buzzing dragonflies. More affordable rooms cluster around a manicured courtyard. All accommodations are furnished in Thai style with teak-and-rattan furniture. Deluxe units have a garden view, while premium rooms feature large patios that are perfect for private barbecues. Suites have enormous aggregate bathtubs that open to guest rooms via a sliding door. Both suites and lagoon rooms offer exclusive use of the lagoon pool (adults only), as well as other fine perks. Fine-dining options are many, and the resort's spa is large and luxurious.

43/1 Petchkasem Beach Rd., Hua Hin 77110. ✆ **03252-0250.** Fax 03252-0259. www.anantara.com. 137 units. 6,300B–8,800B double; 10,800B superior lagoon; 14,800B suite. AE, DC, MC, V. **Amenities:** 4 restaurants; 3 bars; lounge; babysitting; children's playground; concierge; fitness center; Jacuzzi; 2 outdoor pools; children's pool; room service; smoke-free rooms; spa w/sauna, steam, and massage; outdoor floodlit tennis courts; watersports equipment and instruction. *In room:* A/C, satellite TV, fridge, hair dryer, minibar.

Hilton Hua Hin Resort & Spa ★★ Right in the heart of downtown Hua Hin, this massive tower overlooks the main beach. It's a Hilton, which means a fine room standard and courteous staff. Accommodations are spacious and well appointed, with balconies overlooking the sea. Spa suites are particularly classy, with sleek contemporary Thai decor. The marble lobby with quiet reflection pools is welcoming, the beachside pool is luxurious, and there are extensive indoor facilities and activities for rainy days. The Hua Hin Resort is a top international standard and the best location for strolling the main beach area, in-town shopping, and nightlife.

33 Naretdamri Rd., Hua Hin 77110 (on the main beach and in the heart of downtown shopping). ✆ **03253-8999.** Fax 02253-8990. www.huahin.hilton.com. 296 units. 8,400B–10,700B double; from 12,000B suite. AE, DC, MC, V. **Amenities:** 3 restaurants; 3 bars; babysitting; concierge; large fitness center; outdoor pool; room service; spa w/massage, Jacuzzi, sauna, and steam; 2 tennis courts. *In room:* A/C, satellite TV w/in-house movies, fridge, hair dryer, minibar, Wi-Fi and broadband Internet access.

Hua Hin Marriott Resort & Spa ★★ ☺ From the giant swinging couches in the main lobby to the large central pavilions, the Marriott is done in a grand, if exaggerated, Thai style. It attracts large groups, but is a good choice for families. Ponds, pools, boats, golf, tennis, and other sports venues dot the junglelike grounds leading to the open beach area. There is a good children's club, and the staff throughout the hotel seems to really enjoy kids, not just tolerate them. The hotel is relatively far from the busy town center, but provides shuttle service. Deluxe rooms are the best choice—large, amenity-filled, and facing the sea. Terrace rooms at beachside are worth the bump up. The spa is luxurious, too.

107/1 Petchkasem Beach Rd., Hua Hin 77110. ✆ **888/236-2427** in the U.S., or 03251-1881. Fax 03251-2422. www.marriott.com. 216 units. 6,800B–7,500B double; 8,000B–8,500B beachfront; from 18,000B suite. AE, DC, MC, V. **Amenities:** 4 restaurants; lounge; babysitting; children's playground and zoo; concierge; golf course nearby; fitness center; outdoor pool; room service; smoke-free rooms; spa; outdoor floodlit tennis courts; watersports equipment. *In room:* A/C, satellite TV, minibar.

Sofitel Centara Hua Hin Resort ★★★ The original Hua Hin Railway Hotel opened in the 1920s and is the classiest, most luxurious hotel going. There's a cool, calm colonial effect to the whitewashed buildings, shaded verandas and walkways, fine wooden details, red-tile roofs, and immaculate gardens with topiaries. A small museum contains photography and memorabilia, and the original 14 bedrooms are preserved for posterity. Subsequent additions and renovations over the years have expanded the place into a large and modern full-facility property without sacrificing a bit of its former charm. The original rooms have their unique appeal, but the newer rooms are larger, brighter, and more comfortable. With furnishings that reflect the hotel's old beach-resort feel, they are still modern and cozy. Sofitel's three magnificent outdoor pools are finely landscaped and have sun decks under shady trees. The spa, in its own beachside bungalow, provides full-service health and beauty treatments, and the fitness center is extensive.

1 Damnoenkasem Rd., Hua Hin 77110 (in the center of town by the beach). © **800/221-4542** in the U.S., or 03251-2021. Fax 03251-1014. www.sofitel.com. 249 units. $294–$334 double; from $375 suite. DC, MC, V. **Amenities:** 5 restaurants; lounge and bar; babysitting; kids' club; concierge; executive-level rooms; putting green and miniature golf; golf course nearby; fitness center; outdoor pool; room service; smoke-free rooms; spa w/massage; outdoor floodlit tennis courts; watersports equipment. *In room:* A/C, satellite TV, fridge, hair dryer, minibar.

In Cha-Am

Along the quiet stretch between Hua Hin and Cha-Am there are a number of fine resorts (and a growing number of condos). Cha-Am village itself is a bit raucous (the Ocean City, New Jersey, to Hua Hin's The Hamptons) and most stay outside of town.

Dusit Thani ★   Located about halfway between Cha-Am and Hua Hin, the Dusit has all the amenities of a fine resort. The elegant marble lobby features bronze horses and hunting tableaux; hall doors have polo mallet handles and other equine-themed decor. Guest rooms, renovated in 2007, carry the same theme and are spacious, with big marble bathrooms. Room rates vary with the view, although every room's balcony faces the lushly landscaped pool. Ground-floor rooms are landscaped for privacy, with private verandas leading to the pool and the beach. Suites are enormous, with elegant living rooms, and a full pantry and dressing area. For all its air of formality, the resort is great for those who prefer swimsuits and T-shirts to riding jodhpurs, and a relaxed holiday air pervades. All sorts of watersports are available on the quiet beach. It is a bit far from both Hua Hin and Cha-Am, but the resort is completely self-contained.

1349 Petchkasem Rd., Cha-Am 76120. © **03252-0009.** Fax 03252-0296. www.dusit.com. 296 units. 9,500B–11,500B double; from 19,000B suite. AE, DC, MC, V. **Amenities:** 4 restaurants; lounge; airport transfer; babysitting; executive floor; minigolf; golf course nearby; fitness center; huge outdoor pool; children's pool; room service; outdoor lit tennis courts; watersports equipment. *In room:* A/C, satellite TV, fridge, hair dryer, minibar.

WHERE TO DINE

The resorts have more restaurants than there is room to list; no matter where you stay, you'll have great in-house dining options. The main piers in both Hua Hin and Cha-Am are busy every morning, when fishing boats return with their loads. Nearby open-air restaurants on Naretdamri Road serve fresh seafood at a fraction of what you'd pay in Bangkok. In town, there are lots of small storefront eateries, tourist cafes, and seafood places along the beach. The **Night Market,** on Dechanuchit Road west of Petchkasem Road in the north end of Hua Hin, is a great spot for authentic local eats for very little.

Sawasdee ★ THAI/SEAFOOD   Located just across from the Hilton in the middle of Hua Hin, this place features a good range of Thai dishes with a particular emphasis on seafood. Prices are very reasonable and the taste is great—try the prawn cakes and the stir-fried crab. It's a family-run place and the staff is very attentive and helpful.

122/1-2 Naretdamri Rd. © **03251-1935.** Main courses 80B–320B. MC, V. Daily 11am–10pm.

WHAT TO SEE & DO

The stunning Khmer-style temples of **Phetchaburi** ★★ (described at the end of this section) are the most significant cultural sights near Hua Hin and Cha-Am, but most folks are here simply to escape Bangkok and enjoy the beaches.

The **Mareukatayawan Palace** ★, or the Teakwood Mansion (no phone; daily 8:30am–4:30pm; B30), located on the coast halfway between Hua Hin and Cha-Am, is one of the country's most attractive colonial buildings and a must-see for anyone interested in architecture. Built and designed in 1924 by King Rama VI, it served for many years as the royal summer residence and is now open to the public. A stroll through the beautifully preserved rooms with their polished teak floors, period furnishings, and shuttered windows is enough to be transported back to another era. Wander along the raised, covered walkway to the pavilions over the beach (formerly the royal changing rooms) and feel the fresh sea breeze on your face.

Pony riding is popular along the busy beaches at Hua Hin and Cha-Am. Frisky young fillies can be rented by the hour from 600B, but you'll need to bargain hard. At 100B for 10-minute kids' rides, you can ride with a Thai escort leading the pony (safest idea), or on your own if you're confident. If you're interested, take a walk down to the beach and you'll be besieged by young men eager to rent out their ponies.

The **Sofitel Centara Hua Hin Resort** (see "Where to Stay in Hua Hin," above), originally built in the 1920s for Thai royals and their guests, is itself an attraction. Visitors are welcome to tour the grounds or enjoy **high tea** in a quaint garden area (daily 3:30–6pm; 690B).

Shoppers will enjoy Hua Hin's 2-block-long **Night Market** ★ (on Dechanuchit Rd. west of Petchkasem Rd., in the north end of town), which is busy from dusk to late with small food stalls and vendors selling tasty treats and fun trinkets. On Damnoenkasem Road near the beach, you can also browse local handicrafts and batik clothing.

For nightlife, your best bet is Hua Hin. A 15-minute stroll through the labyrinth of *sois* between Damnoenkasem, Poolsuk, and Dechanuchit roads near the beach reveals all sorts of small places to stop for a cocktail, as well as lots of hostess bars that bring to mind Pattaya and Patpong in Bangkok.

OUTDOOR ACTIVITIES

GOLF   Hua Hin is a golf getaway for Bangkokians. It's best to make reservations. The larger hotels run shuttles to all courses.

- **Royal Hua Hin Golf Course,** Damnoenkasem Road near the Hua Hin Railway Station (✆ 03251-2475), was Thailand's first championship golf course, opened in 1924. Don't miss the many topiary figures along its fairways (greens fees: 2,200B).

- **Springfield Royal Country Club,** 193 Moo 6, Huay-Sai Nua, Petchkasem Rd., Cha-Am (✆ 03270-9222), designed by Jack Nicklaus in 1993, is in a beautiful valley setting—the best by far (greens fees: 3,500B).

WATERSPORTS   Most resorts forbid noisy jet skis, but the beaches are lined with young entrepreneurs renting them out for around 1,000B per half-hour. **Kiteboarding** is also becoming popular on the beach to the south of town; the season runs from November to April and a 3-day beginner's course costs 11,000B. Contact **Kiteboarding Asia** (✆ 08159-14593; www.kiteboardingasia.com) for more details.

Western Tours (☏ 03253-3303; www.westerntourshuahin.com) can arrange **snorkeling trips** to nearby islands for about 2,700B per person. Their office is at 11 Damnoenkasem Rd. in the city center.

SIDE TRIPS FROM HUA HIN & CHA-AM PHETCHABURI ★★

Phetchaburi dates from the same period as Ayutthaya and Kanchanaburi, and later served as an important military city. Phetchaburi's palace and historically significant temples are the highlights of an excellent day trip—it's just an hour from Hua Hin. The main attraction is **Phra Nakhorn Khiri,** a 19th-century summer palace of King Mongkut (Rama IV) in the hills overlooking the city, reachable by cable car. You'll also find a collection of important royal temples and the summer palaces of other kings. **Western Tours** (11 Damnoenkasem Rd.; ☏ 03253-3303) has a day excursion every Thursday that costs 1,500B.

KHAO SAM ROI YOT NATIONAL PARK

Just 40 minutes' drive south of Hua Hin, Khao Sam Roi Yot National Park, or the "Mountain of Three Hundred Peaks," offers great short hikes to panoramic views of the coast. Of the park's three caves, **Phraya Nakhon Cave** is the most interesting, housing a *sala* (pavilion) that was built in 1890 for King Chulalongkorn. **Western Tours** (11 Damnoenkasem Rd.; ☏ 03253-3303) runs trips on Tuesday and Saturday for 1,700B per person.

Surat Thani

644km (400 miles) S of Bangkok

Surat Thani was an important center of the Sumatra-based Srivijaya Empire in the 9th and 10th centuries. Today, it's known to foreigners as the main jumping-off point for the eastern islands **Ko Samui, Ko Pha Ngan,** and **Ko Tao** (each described in the following sections of this chapter), as well as the navigable jungles of **Khao Sok National Park.**

GETTING THERE & GETTING AROUND

BY PLANE Thai Airways (☏ 02545-3691 in Bangkok) and **Air Asia** (☏ 02515-9999 in Bangkok) both have daily flights from Bangkok to Surat Thani (trip time: 70 min.). You can get on a minibus to town for 70B. The local Thai Airways office is at 3/27 28 Karoonrat Rd. (☏ 07727-2610), just south of town.

BY TRAIN Ten trains to Surat Thani leave daily from Bangkok's **Hua Lamphong Railway Station** (☏ 1690 or 02223-3762; trip time: 13 hr.). A second-class sleeper (upper berth) is 758B; a second-class seat in a fan compartment is 438B. The Surat Thani train station is very inconvenient, but buses meet trains to transport folks to town for 20B; or if you roll in on the morning train, you can just hop on one of the travel-agent buses to the ferry.

BY BUS Two VIP 24-seater buses leave daily from Bangkok's **Southern Bus Terminal** (☏ 02894-6122; trip time: 10 hr.; 660B). Air-conditioned buses leave daily from Phuket's bus terminal off Phang-nga Road opposite the Royal Phuket City Hotel (☏ 07621-1977; trip time 4 hr.; 170B). Also from Phuket, minivans travel to Surat Thani daily (trip time: 4 hr.; 180B)—you can find them across from the Montri Hotel on Suthat Road. The bus terminal for most destinations is on Kaset II Road, a block east of the main road, but buses from Bangkok pull into the new bus station 2km (1¼ miles) southwest of town.

BY MINIVAN   The best way to travel between southern cities is by privately oper-ated air-conditioned minivans. They are affordable and run on regular schedules between Surat Thani and Chumphon, Ranong, Nakhon Si Thammarat, Hat Yai, and beyond. The best way to arrange these trips is by consulting your hotel's front desk. You can go door-to-door to the hotel of your choice, usually for around 200B.

BY CAR   Take Hwy. 4 south from Bangkok to Chumphon, then Hwy. 41 south direct to Surat Thani.

Surat Thani is built up along the south shore of the Tapi River. **Talad Mai Road,** 2 blocks south of the river, is the city's main street, with the TAT office at its west end and the bus station and central market at its east end. Frequent *songtao* run along Talad Mai; prices are based on distance, but rarely exceed 20B.

VISITOR INFORMATION

For information about Surat Thani, Ko Samui, and Ko Pha Ngan, contact the **TAT** office at 5 Talad Mai Rd., Surat Thani (℃ 07728-8818), near the Wang Tai Hotel.

[FastFACTS] SURAT THANI

Major **banks** along Talad Mai Road have ATMs and will perform currency exchanges. The **Post Office** and **Overseas Call Office** are together at the corner of Talad Mai and Chonkasem roads near the center of town. The **Taksin Hospital** (℃ 07727-3239) is at the north end of Talad Mai Road. The **tourist police** (℃ 07742-1281) are at 52/6–7 Taweera-jpakdee Rd.

WHERE TO STAY & DINE

For most, Surat Thani is just a stopping-off point for trips to the islands. If you have a layover, the best choice is the **100 Islands Resort & Spa** (19/6 Moo 3, Bypass Rd.; ℃ 07720-1150; www.roikoh.com), a fancy boutique hotel a couple of kilome-ters south of the town center, with attractive doubles beginning at 770B. Nearby, with similar rates and a swimming pool too, is the **Wang Tai Hotel** (1 Talad Mai Rd.; ℃ 07728-3020; www.wangtaisurat.com). More convenient to the market and town transport is the **Tapee Hotel** (100 Chonkasem Rd.; ℃ 07727-2575; www.tapee hotel.com) with basic but clean rooms from 440B.

WHAT TO SEE & DO

Surat is a typical small Thai city and, for most foreign visitors, little more than a transportation hub to the islands of Ko Samui and Ko Pha Ngan. However, if it is your only stop in Thailand (on the way to Ko Samui, for example), give the town a wander and see what Thai life is all about (take to the small streets and find a *wat*). Outside of town, popular day trips include the **Monkey Training College** (24 Moo 4, Tam-bon Thungkong; ℃ 07722-7351; www.firstmonkeyschool.com), where monkeys are trained to get coconuts.

Many foreigners make their way from Surat Thani to **Wat Suan Mokkha-balarama** (℃ 07753-1552; www.suanmokkh.org) near Chaiya, a meditation tem-ple where courses for foreigners are held during the first 10 days of each month. Day visitors are welcome at this forest monastery, but if you plan to sign up for the course, you'll need to do so well in advance. It's about 60km (37 miles) from Surat Thani.

SIDE TRIPS FROM SURAT THANI
Khao Sok National Park ★

Khao Sok, known for its stunning scenery and exotic wildlife, is convenient to both Surat Thani and Phuket. The park is some 646 sq. km (249 sq. miles) in area, traced by jungle waterways and steep trails among craggy limestone cliffs—imagine the jutting formations of Phang Nga Bay or Krabi, only inland. Rising some 1,000m (3,280 ft.), and laced with shaggy patches of forest, the dense jungle habitat of the park is literally crawling with life. Among the underbrush and thick vines hanging from the high canopy, tigers, leopards, golden cats, and even elephants still wander freely, and visitors commonly spot Malaysian sun bear, gibbons, langurs, macaques, civets, flying lemur, and squirrels. Keep your eyes peeled for the more than 200 species of birds, including hornbills, woodpeckers, and kingfishers. As for the flora, there is every variety—the rafflesia, the largest flower in the world and a parasite, finds vines from which to draw its nourishment (the largest are up to 1m/3¼ ft. wide).

One of the best ways to get up close with the varied fauna of the park is by kayak along the nether reaches of the large reservoir. Jungle animals are skittish, so your chances of seeing something rare by noisily tromping through the bush are slim at best. Contact the folks at **Paddle Asia** (18/58 Rasdanusorn Rd., in Phuket; (✆)/fax **07624-1519**; www.paddleasia.com) for details.

Ko Samui ★★★

84km (52 miles) E of Surat Thani

Ko Samui lies 84km (52 miles) off the east coast in the Gulf of Thailand, near the mainland commercial town of Surat Thani. The island is hilly, densely forested, and rimmed with coconut-palm plantations. Since the 1850s, Chinese merchants sailed from as far as Hainan Island in the South China Sea to trade coconuts and cotton, the island's two most profitable products.

Once a popular hippie haven of pristine beaches, idyllic bungalows, and thatched eateries along dirt roads, Samui is now an international resort area with all of the attendant comforts and crowding. If you came here as a backpacker in the past, you may not want to come back to see McDonald's and a Wal-Mart–style shopping outlet where hammocks once hung. An international airport was opened in 1988 and now greets up to 20 packed daily flights. Fine hotels and large resorts are popping up all over the island, making any comparisons with Phuket apt.

The high season on Ko Samui is from mid-December to mid-January. January through April months have the best weather, before it gets hot. October through mid-December is the wettest period, with November bringing extreme rain and winds that make the east side of the island rough for swimming. August sees a brief increase in visitors, a mini high season, but the island's west side is often buffeted by summer monsoons from the mainland.

GETTING THERE

BY PLANE **Bangkok Airways** (✆ **02270-6699** in Bangkok; www.bangkokair. com) connects Ko Samui with Bangkok and Phuket. **THAI Airways** (✆ **02356-1111** in Bangkok) now also has flights from Bangkok. There are more than a dozen flights a day.

Ko Samui Airport (✆ **07742-5011**) is a little slice of heaven—open-air pavilions with thatch roofs surrounded by gardens and palms. If you're staying at a larger resort, airport shuttles can be arranged when you book your room. There's also a convenient minivan service: Book your ticket at the transportation counter upon arrival, and you'll get door-to-door service for around 300B, depending on which beach you are going to. If you depart Ko Samui via the airport, a hefty 700B airport tax is added to your ticket charge.

BY FERRY   If you're traveling overland, there are several companies that run passenger and car ferries to Ko Samui from Surat Thani, a journey of around 2½ hours that costs around 200B to 250B. Most people buy a combination train and boat or bus and boat ticket from Bangkok. **Songserm** (*©* **02280-8073** in Bangkok) operates ferries connecting Surat Thani, Ko Samui, Ko Pha Ngan, Ko Tao and Chumphon.

Picking up the ferry in Chumphon makes the overland journey shorter and allows passengers to get a glimpse of Ko Samui's neighboring islands of Ko Pgha Ngan and Ko Tao. One company that operates this route is **Lomprayah** (*©* **07742-7765** in Ko Samui; www.lomprayah.com). The bus goes from Bangkok to Chumphon, from where a catamaran goes to Ko Tao and Ko Pha Ngan before arriving at Ko Samui. The complete journey takes around 12 hours and costs 1,200B.

GETTING AROUND

With a total area of 233 sq. km (90 sq. miles), you can trace Samui's entire coastline by car in about 2½ hours. The Ko Samui Airport is in the northeast corner of the island. The hydrofoils, car ferry, and express boats arrive on the west coast, in or near (depending on the boat) **Nathon,** just a tiny town with a few banks, the TAT office, and the main post office (few visitors spend much time here). The main road (Hwy. 4169, also called the "ring road") circles the island. The long east-coast stretch between **Chaweng** and **Lamai** beaches is the most popular destination for visitors and, consequently, where you'll find the greatest concentration of hotels and bungalows. The south coast has a few little hideaways, too.

BY SONGTAEW   *Songtaews* are the most efficient way to get around the island, though drivers regularly overcharge, so you need to be on your guard. A short ride shouldn't cost more than 20B, while from one side of the island to the other costs around 80B. They advertise their destinations—to such beaches as Lamai, Chaweng, and Mai Nam—with colorfully painted signs, and all follow Route 4169, the ring road, around the island, either clockwise or counterclockwise. You can hail one anywhere along the highway or along beach roads. Most stop running regular routes after sundown, after which some will hang around outside the discos in Chaweng to take night owls home to other beaches, but negotiate the fare first, or you'll get taken for a ride in more than one sense.

BY TAXI   Metered taxis loiter outside most resorts and on virtually every street corner in Chaweng, but most drivers refuse to switch the meter on. If you're used to Bangkok's metered taxis, the prices here will come as a shock. A ride between beaches will set you back 200B with some bargaining; rides to and from the airport usually run 400B to 500B. Thus taxis are a good option only if you need to get somewhere quickly; otherwise, stick to *songtaews*.

BY CAR   Ko Samui's roads are narrow, winding, and poorly maintained, with few lights at night to guide you. Road accidents are many, but renting a car is a far better idea than going by motorcycle. Your defensive-driving skills will be required to navigate around slow-moving trucks and motorcycles at the side of the road, not to mention the occasional wandering dog.

Ko Samui

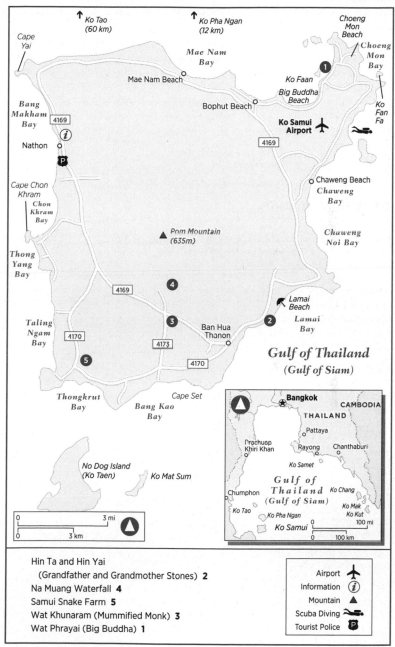

Ko Tao
(60 km)

Ko Pha Ngan
(12 km)

Choeng
Mon
Beach

Cape
Yai

*Choeng
Mon
Bay*

*Mae Nam
Bay*

Mae Nam Beach

Ko Faan

*Bang
Makham
Bay*

4169

Bophut Beach

Big Buddha
Beach

Ko
Fan
Fa

(i)

Nathon

Ko Samui
Airport

4169

*Cape Chon
Khram*

Chaweng Beach

*Chon
Khram
Bay*

*Chaweng
Bay*

▲ *Pom Mountain*
(635m)

*Chuweng
Noi Bay*

*Thong
Yang
Bay*

4169

④

*Lamai
Beach*

③

*Taling
Ngam
Bay*

4170

Ban Hua
Thanon

②

*Lamai
Bay*

4173

⑤

4170

Gulf of Thailand
(Gulf of Siam)

*Thongkrut
Bay*

Cape Set

*Bang Kao
Bay*

▲ **Bangkok**
★

CAMBODIA

THAILAND

Pattaya

Prachuap
Khiri Khan

Rayong

Chanthaburi

Ko Samet

No Dog Island
(Ko Taen)

Ko Mat Sum

*Gulf of
Thailand*
(Gulf of Siam)

Ko Chang

Chumphon

Ko Mak
Ko Kut

Ko Tao

Ko Pha Ngan

100 mi

Ko Samui

100 km

0   3 mi

▲

0   3 km

Hin Ta and Hin Yai
(Grandfather and Grandmother Stones) **2**
Na Muang Waterfall **4**
Samui Snake Farm **5**
Wat Khunaram (Mummified Monk) **3**
Wat Phrayai (Big Buddha) **1**

Airport	✈
Information	*(i)*
Mountain	▲
Scuba Diving	🤿
Tourist Police	Ⓟ

Budget Car Rental has an office at the Samui Airport (*©* **07796-1502**). It rents a host of vehicles, starting with a Honda Jazz at 1,400B a day. **Avis** also has an office here (*©* **08470-0816-1**) and charges similar rates. Beachside rental companies and travel agents rent for as low as 800B per day, but don't expect solid insurance coverage.

BY MOTORCYCLE Road accidents injure or kill an inordinate number of tourists and locals each year on Ko Samui, mostly motorcycle riders. Still, two wheels and a motor is still the most popular way to get around the island. The roads on Ko Samui are busy, so stay left and close to the shoulder of the road to make way for passing cars and trucks. And go easy: Racing around the island lands many in the hospital, or worse. The fine for not wearing a helmet is 500B, but it's enforced irregularly. Travel agencies and small operators rent motorcycles in popular beach areas for as little as 150B per day.

VISITOR INFORMATION

The **TAT** information center is on Thawirat Road, just north of the main ferry terminal in Nathon (*©* **07742-0504**). You'll also find a host of free small-press magazines and maps at retailers throughout Ko Samui.

[FastFACTS] KO SAMUI

All the major **banks** are in Nathon along Thawirat Road. In Chaweng, you'll find numerous money-changers and ATMs; try Krung Thai Bank, opposite Starbucks. Hotels and guesthouses also accept traveler's checks. If you need medical attention, **Samui International Hospital** (*©* **07723-0781-2**; www.sih.co.th) is a fine facility in North Chaweng with English-speaking physicians who also make house calls.

For **Internet access,** most resorts and hotels provide a service, sometimes free for guests. Otherwise, there are countless coffee shops offering free Wi-Fi or terminals with rates of around 60B per hour. The main **post office** is on Chonwithee Road in Nathon, but you probably won't hike all the way back to the main pier for posting. Any hotel or guesthouse will handle it for you, and stamps can be purchased in small provision shops in beach areas.

WHERE TO STAY

Twenty years ago, there were but a few makeshift beachside bungalow compounds along the nearly deserted coast of Samui. Today, luxury resorts stand shoulder to shoulder with homey guesthouses, chic modern facilities next to motel cellblocks, all vying for supremacy over the choicest beachside real estate. Even if your budget is tight, you can still enjoy the same sand as those in the more exclusive joints.

Cape Yai

Four Seasons Samui ★★★ Located on a steep hillside in the extreme northwest corner of the island, this resort is not the place to go if you want to be in the thick of the nightlife, but for anyone looking for a relaxing break, it is an ideal choice. All villas and suites enjoy expansive views out to sea, and guests have a choice of swimming at the beach (for resort guests only) in the lovely communal pool, or in their private infinity pool attached to each villa. Rooms are furnished in typically sumptuous Four Seasons style, and are equipped with large, flatscreen TVs, Wi-Fi, and wine coolers. Buggies are on hand to run guests up and down the steep hill, and service is both personal and extremely efficient.

219 Moo 5, Angthong, Ko Samui 84140. ℂ **07724-3000.** Fax 07724-3002. www.fourseasons.com/kohsamui. 74 units. From 18,700B 1-bedroom villa; 44,200B beach villa. AE, MC, V. **Amenities:** 2 restaurants; bar; health club; outdoor pool; room service; spa; 2 tennis courts; water sports; library. *In room:* A/C, satellite TV/DVD player, minibar, Wi-Fi.

Mae Nam Bay

Mae Nam Bay is 12km (7½ miles) from the ferry pier, at the midpoint of Samui's north shore, facing nearby Ko Pha Ngan. The beach is narrow and long, with coarse sand and shaded by trees. The water is deep enough for swimming.

Coco Palm Resort   A good midrange choice, Coco Palm's bungalows are basic and comfortable. The place attracts lots of families on a budget, but is still quite peaceful. Deluxe bungalows are worth a bump-up; though still with just shower-in-room bathrooms, they are airy and have vaulted cathay ceilings. Seaside bungalows are worth the additional jump in price for their location.

26/4 Moo 4, Mae Nam Beach, Ko Samui 84330. ℂ **07724-7288.** Fax 07742-5321. www.cocopalmsamui.com. 94 units. 2,300B–4,200B bungalow; 5,500B–9,000B villa. MC, V. **Amenities:** Restaurant; transfer service; small outdoor pool. *In room:* A/C, TV, minibar, no phone.

Mae Nam Resort ★ 🔥   These 36 bungalows form a secluded little village in overgrown jungle gardens with tall, lush greenery. Each has teak paneling and floors, rattan furnishings, a small bathroom with polished stone walls, and a small deck. Beachfront bungalows will have you stepping off your balcony right into the silky, palm-shaded sand for very little, considering that the neighboring Santiburi Dusit Resort's beachfront villas run about 50,000B. Okay, so Mae Nam Resort can't compare to five-star luxury, but it's still the same sand and view.

1/3 Moo 4, Mae Nam Beach, Ko Samui 84330 (next to the Santiburi Dusit Resort). ℂ **07724-7287.** Fax 07742-5116. www.maenamresort.com. 36 units. 1,600B–2,000B double; 3,000B family bungalow. AE, MC, V. **Amenities:** Restaurant; transfer service; room service. *In room:* No phone.

Santiburi Golf Resort and Spa ★★★   The design of the sprawling Santiburi is influenced by late Thai architecture, with spacious and airy interiors—a simplicity accented with luxurious Jim Thompson Thai silks and tidy floral arrangements. The top villas front the beach, while the others are set among lush greenery around a central pool and spa. Each bungalow is a luxe suite, with living and sleeping areas divided by glass and flowers. The bathroom is masterfully outfitted in wood and black tiles, the centerpiece a large, round sunken tub. Guests can take advantage of windsurfing and sailing on the house, while golfers can enjoy the best 18 holes on the island at the nearby Santiburi Samui Country Club. The resort also has its own gorgeous Chinese junk, anchored in the bay for dinner cruises or for hiring out to tour surrounding islands. For a more affordable but equally indulgent stay, try Santiburi's sister property, **Bophut Resort & Spa,** just a short hop down the beach.

12/12 Moo 1, Tambol Mae Nam, Ko Samui 84330. ℂ **07742-5031.** Fax 07742-5040. www.santiburi.com. 71 units. 8,880B–16,080B suite; 12,780B–50,400B villa. AE, DC, MC, V. **Amenities:** 3 restaurants; 2 bars; lounge; babysitting; concierge; fitness center; Internet access; Jacuzzi; outdoor pool; room service; sauna; spa; outdoor floodlit tennis courts; watersports equipment. *In room:* A/C, satellite TV w/DVD player and DVD library, fridge, hair dryer, minibar, Wi-Fi.

Bophut Beach

Bophut Beach is on the north coast just east of Mae Nam. The beach is thin and the sand is coarse, but the little commercial strip is fun and convenient.

Peace Resort ★★ ☺   Owned and managed by a caring family, the Peace Resort has an ambience that justifies its name. The free-standing bungalows are really more like small luxury suites, and are particularly favored by families. All have vaulted ceilings with design schemes that are either finely crafted wood or cooler, almost Mediterranean numbers in pastel tiles with designer flat-stone masonry and smooth stucco. Spring for a larger seaside room. The central pool is not particularly large, but it's cozy and near the beach, and there's a kids' play area. There's a small, open-air restaurant where you can enjoy a cool drink, the company of good friends, and the calm of this tranquil bay with the big Buddha winking from the next beach.

Bophut Beach, Ko Samui 84320 (central Bophut). ℂ **07742-5357.** Fax 07742-5343. www.peaceresort. com. 122 units. 3,600B–6,200B bungalow; 12,200B beachview villa. MC, V. **Amenities:** Restaurant; bar; babysitting; kids' club and playground; Internet access; outdoor pool; room service; spa (across the road). *In room:* A/C, satellite TV, fridge, minibar, no phone.

Cape Samrong

Situated in the extreme northeast of the island, Cape Samrong is about as far away from it all as you can get on Samui.

Six Senses Samui ★★★   Set on a gently sloping headland among 8 hectares (20 acres) of lush vegetation, this resort was proclaimed "Best in the World" by Condé Nast's Readers' Travel Awards in 2008. Those who voted for it were impressed not only by its lovely location and environmental friendliness, but also by its sophisticated ambience and extensive leisure facilities. These facilities include private pools beside most villas and suites, a spa with a comprehensive range of treatments and activities such as aquarobics, island tours, diving trips, and cooking classes. All the villas are equipped with every imaginable comfort and are attended by personal butlers, while the views are simply fabulous.

9/10 Moo 5, Baan Plai Laem, Boput, Ko Samui 84320 (northeast tip of island). ℂ **07724-5678.** Fax 07724-5671. www.sixsenses.com. 66 units. 12,216B–20,114B villa; from 27,906B suite. AE, DC, MC, V. **Amenities:** 2 restaurants; 2 bars; gym; pool; spa; watersports; cooking classes; library. *In room:* A/C, satellite TV w/DVD player, Wi-Fi.

Tongsai Bay

Tongsai Bay is a scenic cove dominated by the hillside Tongsai Bay resort. The beach itself is uninspiring with very rough sand, but it's quite private.

The Tongsai Bay ★★   The luxe Tongsai Bay resort dominates this stunning, rocky section of coast. Built theatrically down a hillside, the white-stucco, red-tile-roofed bungalows and buildings are reminiscent of the Mediterranean, though the palm trees are pure Thai. Between the half-moon cove's rocky bookends, the coarse-sand beach invites you to idle away the days. The all-suite resort has some touches that set it apart—each unit has plenty of outdoor terrace space, with sea views or a private walled courtyard. Terrace suites have outdoor tubs, while the Tongsai Grand Villas have not only tubs but also gazebos; the Tongsai Pool Villas manage to add on a private pool to boot. The villas are designed in harmony with nature, some even with small stands of trees growing through the middle of them. Service is tiptop: From the landscapers to management, there is no friendlier staff on the island.

84 Moo 5, Ban Plailaem, Bophut, Ko Samui 84320 (northeast tip of island). ℂ **07724-5480.** Fax 07742-5462. Bangkok reservations office: ℂ 02381-8774; fax 0281-8772. www.tongsaibay.co.th. 85 units. 11,000B beachfront suite; 14,000B cottage suite; 22,000B Tongsai Grand Villa; 25,000B Tongsai Pool Villa. AE, DC, MC, V. **Amenities:** 3 restaurants; 2 bars; fitness center; Internet cafe; outdoor pool; room service; spa w/massage and beauty treatments; outdoor floodlit tennis court; watersports. *In room:* A/C, satellite TV w/DVD player, fridge, hair dryer, minibar.

Choeng Mon

Choeng Mon is a gracefully shaped crescent about 1km (⅔ mile) long. Palm trees shading sunbathers reach right to the water's edge; swimming is excellent, with few rocks near the central shore. Choeng Mon is isolated, but there are many good local services and transport.

Imperial Boat House Hotel ★   You've got a pretty interesting concept here—34 authentic teak rice barges have been dry-docked and converted into charming free-standing suites. The less expensive rooms in the three-story buildings are fine but not nearly as atmospheric. Hotel facilities are extensive, the beach is one of the nicest on the island, and if you can't get a boat suite, at least you can swim in the boat-shaped swimming pool.

83 Moo 5, Tambon Bophut, Ko Samui 84320 (southern part of beach). ℂ **07742-5041.** Fax 07742-5460. www.imperialhotels.com. 210 units. 3,659B double; 4,458B honeymoon suite; 5,720B boat suite. AE, DC, MC, V. **Amenities:** 2 restaurants; bar; babysitting; concierge; fitness center; Jacuzzi; 2 outdoor pools; room service; sauna; spa; watersports equipment. *In room:* A/C, satellite TV, fridge, hair dryer, minibar.

Sala Samui ★★   If you are on your honeymoon, are celebrating your anniversary, or are just in love and want to get away from it all, look no further than the Sala Samui. Pool villas offer the most privacy, with daybeds, outdoor bathrooms (use the mosquito nets in the evenings), and small pools set in a secluded courtyard. Bedrooms are minimally decorated, with whitewashed walls offset by wood trimming and furnishings. If you do decide to leave your luxury lair, the resort offers two common swimming pools and access to a lovely part of the beach. Honeymooners are a large part of the clientele here, and the staff goes out of its way to make each couple feel welcome.

10/9 Moo 5, Bophut, Ko Samui 84320. ℂ **07724-5888.** Fax 07724-5889. www.salaresorts.com. 69 units. 13,400B deluxe; 8,100B–9,700B pool villa; from 13,700B suite. AE, MC, V. **Amenities:** Restaurant; bar; fitness center; 2 outdoor pools; room service; spa w/massage; watersports equipment. *In room:* A/C, TV, hair dryer, minibar.

Chaweng & Chaweng Noi Bays

The beaches at Chaweng are the most popular and most overdeveloped on Samui. If you came to get away from it all, go elsewhere. Still, most of the resorts here are private, cozy, affordable, and convenient to the busy strip. North Chaweng beaches are rocky; the south, where Chaweng Noi is located, is better for swimming.

Amari Palm Reef Resort & Spa ★★   This resort is located in North Chaweng and features luxury suites at beachside as well as an oceanside pool and dining. Accommodations in the main block and new blocks across the road are not particularly luxurious, though they're very clean with parquet floors. Suites face the sea and are designed in a seamless marriage of contemporary and traditional Thai, with large decks giving way to huge glass sliders, lovely sunken seating areas, massive plush beds, and designer bathrooms with separate shower, tub, and his-and-hers sinks. The rocks and coral along the beach mean you'll have to take a bit of a walk for swimming, but the scenery is lovely, and you can expect the same high standard of service as at all Amari hotels. The resort is far enough from the Chaweng strip to be quiet and comfortable (but close enough to party). Great for families.

Chaweng Beach, Ko Samui 84320 (north end of the main strip). ℂ **07742-2015.** Fax 07742-2394. www.amari.com. 187 units. 4,398B superior; 5,573B deluxe; 16,428B suite. AE, MC, V. **Amenities:** 2 restaurants; 2 bars; babysitting; bike rental; kids' club; fitness center; 2 outdoor pools; smoke-free rooms; spa w/massage, Jacuzzi, sauna, and steam; dive center. *In room:* A/C, satellite TV, fridge, hair dryer, minibar, IDD phone.

Baan Chaweng ★ This newish place is a very good midrange choice. You're right in the heart of Chaweng here, but far enough removed from the thumping bass to get a peaceful night's sleep. Quiet paths lead past rooms and bungalows, through the lovely gardens and palms of the main courtyard, to a cozy beachfront pool and restaurant. Guest rooms are comfortable and sparsely decorated, though not displeasingly so. Superior units are in modern two-story blocks farthest removed from the beach, while free-standing deluxe bungalows and villas take the prime spots and are not a bad upgrade. The hotel's restaurant, Leelawadee, has terrace seating right on the beach and serves very good seafood.

90/1 Moo 2, Chaweng Beach, Ko Samui 84320 (middle of Chaweng Beach). ✆ **07742-2403.** Fax 07742-2404. www.baanchaweng.com. 94 units. 3,500B superior; 4,050B–6,000B villa; 13,000B beachfront suite. Rates include breakfast. AE, MC, V. **Amenities:** Restaurant; babysitting; Internet access; pool; spa. *In room:* A/C, satellite TV, hair dryer, minibar.

Coral Bay Resort ★ Far from the boom-boom bass of Chaweng but close enough to commute, the Coral Bay—a collection of large, upscale thatch bungalows—crests a picturesque hill on the northern end of Chaweng. Rooms are in rows along the hillside (a bit of trudging to get to some); each has a large balcony, some shared with adjoining rooms. The decor is lavish, with bamboo and coconut-inlaid cabinets, intricate thatch, and fine hangings; some rooms feature graphic mosaics as well: There's nothing like it on Samui. Spring for a deluxe unit with canopy bed. Bathrooms are small garden landscapes with waterfall showers and designer flat-stone masonry. The central pool area is high above the rock-and-coral beach below (not good for swimming), and large thatch pavilions house the open lobby and fine dining.

9 Moo 2, Bophut, Chaweng Beach, Ko Samui 84320 (north end of Chaweng as the road crests the first big hill). ✆ **07723-4555.** Fax 07723-4558. www.coralbay.net. 56 units. 6,850B–8,500B deluxe bungalow; from 8,750B family bungalow; all rooms add beachfront surcharge. AE, MC, V. **Amenities:** 2 restaurants; bar; babysitting; kids' club; Internet access; Jacuzzi; pool; sauna; smoke-free rooms; spa; library. *In room:* A/C, fridge, minibar.

Jungle Club ★ Set high on a hill behind Chaweng Noi Beach, this attractive resort offers accommodations to suit all budgets, from a very basic jungle hut with just a fan, mattress, and mosquito net, to a sturdier jungle bungalow, a spacious jungle house, and luxurious lodges and villas. The setting is truly idyllic, but it is so isolated (only 4WD vehicles and motorbikes can get up the hill) that you'll need to take a shuttle down to the beach or town (free at 10:30am and 6pm; other times 50B/100B). The resort is under French/Thai management and its popular restaurant attracts many visitors to enjoy the view, the romantic, candle-lit setting and the range of Thai and French dishes.

Chaweng Noi Beach, Soi Panyadee School, Ko Samui 84320 (call for pickup). ✆ **08189-4232-7.** www.jungleclubsamui.com. 11 units. 600B jungle hut; 1,200B–1,600B bungalow/house; 2,900B–3,500B lodge/villa. AE, DC, MC, V. **Amenities:** Restaurant; Internet access; pool. *In room:* A/C, satellite TV w/ DVD player (lodge and villa), fridge, minibar.

The Library ★★★ This ravishingly minimalist resort offers a startlingly different contemporary slant. Designed by a Bangkok architect, its rooms are divided into studios and suites, and in keeping with the hotel's name, the resort's main feature is a library featuring an array of books and DVDs. State-of-the-art rooms (with Jacuzzis and rain showers) provide an extraordinary range of luxuries, from huge plasma TVs and iMacs, to light boxes and self-controlled colored lighting. It's cool, it's original, and it appeals to those with a leaning toward techno-Zen. The red-tiled pool, while innovative, somehow brings to mind Agatha Christie.

14/1 Moo 2, Bophut, Ko Samui, 84320. ☎ **07742-2767-8.** Fax 07742-2344. www.thelibrary.co.th. 13 units. 14,000B studio; 16,000B suites. AE, MC, V. **Amenities:** Restaurant; bar; fitness room; pool; library. *In room:* A/C, satellite TV w/DVD player.

Poppies Samui ★★   The famed Balinese resort runs this popular annex in Samui. On the south end of busy Chaweng, Poppies is indeed an oasis. Luxury cottages, all the same, have thatch roofs and Thai-Balinese appointments. Renovations have brought new floors, remodeled bathrooms, and flatscreen TVs. Although rooms are set close together, they're well situated for optimum privacy. This is a popular honeymoon choice, and the service and standards throughout are tops. The central pool is small but cozy, and the hotel dining is some of the best going (see "Where to Dine," below).

P.O. Box 1, Chaweng, Ko Samui 84320 (on the south end of the Chaweng strip). ☎ **07742-2419.** Fax 07742-2420. www.poppiessamui.com. 24 units. 9,750B double; rates vary depending on season. AE, MC, V. **Amenities:** Restaurant; babysitting; pool; room service. *In room:* A/C, satellite TV, fridge, hair dryer, minibar.

Sandalwood Luxury Villas ★★   Set back from the coast on a hill with sweeping views over the gentle curve of Chaweng Beach, this complex of just 10 individually decorated villas offers the ultimate in personalized service to its guests. Some villas have a private pool, others share one, and some feature Jacuzzis on the terrace. Bathrooms are all marble and granite, and furnishings are a pleasing fusion of traditional and contemporary styles. There are two infinity pools on-site, as well as an inviting restaurant and boutique spa. They also offer cookery classes and can help plan your island sightseeing.

211 Moo 4, Tambon Maret, Ko Samui 84320 (behind Chaweng Beach). ☎ **07741-4016.** Fax 07741-4017. www.sandalwoodsamui.com. 10 units. 7,078B–10,673B villa. AE, DC, MC, V. **Amenities:** Restaurant; bar; babysitting; 2 infinity pools; room service; spa; cooking classes. *In room:* A/C, satellite TV, DVD player w/free in-house movies, fridge, hair dryer, minibar, Wi-Fi.

Lamai Bay

The long sand beach on Lamai Bay is comparable to Chaweng's, but caters more to the young backpacker set. There are a few comfy new resorts among the budget bungalows, however, and the wide range of services, cafes, and nightlife makes Lamai a good base for a comfortable stay.

Banyan Tree ★★★   With so many luxury resorts scattered around the coast of Ko Samui, the word "breathtaking" may seem clichéd, but it's totally apt to describe this fabulous property. The stylish villas and suites, each with its own private pool, are perched on a series of terraces, and all enjoy superb views across the palm-fringed beach to the limpid waters of the gulf. Villas range from a large 130 sq. m (1,400 sq. ft.) to a massive 316 sq. m (3,400 sq. ft.) in the Sanctuary Pool Villa. Interiors are decorated in a blend of modern lines and Thai accents such as silk cushions and bamboo furnishings that is very easy on the eye. Every detail is considered here, right down to your choice of pillow and bath menu, making every guest feel like royalty. Sands, The Edge, and Saffron restaurants promise exciting culinary adventures, and the resort also features The Rainforest, Samui's only hydrotherapy spa.

99/9 Moo 4, T. Maret, Ko Samui 84310. ☎ **07791-5333.** Fax 07791-5388. www.banyantree.com. 78 units. 30,270B–39,180B pool villas; 113,130B sanctuary pool villa. **Amenities:** 3 restaurants; bar; babysitting; kids' club; gym; outdoor pool; kids' pool; spa; library. *In room:* A/C, satellite TV, DVD player, minibar, Wi-Fi.

Rocky's Boutique Resort ★★   Rocky's offers affordable luxury with two beautiful pools and individually designed one- to four-bedroom villas, which cascade down a rocky hillside to a private sandy beach. Just 5 minutes north of Lamai, it's easily accessible—but a hard slog up steep hills for villa residents. The resort boasts a one-to-one staff/guest ratio and great views from the private villa terraces. The hotel longtail boat can whisk you to the Marine Park or secluded beaches (for a price).

438/1 Moo 1, Lamai, Tambon Maret, Ko Samui 84310. ℂ **07741-8367.** Fax 07741-8366. www.rockyresort.com. 50 units. 5,476B gardenview; 7,582B oceanview suite; 9,520B beachfront suite; 14,996B deluxe villa. AE, MC, V. **Amenities:** Restaurant; bar; babysitting; bike and jeep rental desk; 2 pools. *In room:* A/C in some, satellite TV, CD player, Wi-Fi.

Spa Samui Resorts ★ 🍴   For long-term stays or just a daytime spa visit, the Spa Samui Resorts offers a "healthy good time." This laid-back spa resort just north of Lamai has been around for years and is still in full swing, a rustic grouping of old bungalows and open-air dining and massage pavilions, but it now has a more comfortable property in the south of Lamai, high in the hills above town, as well as new two-bedroom villas with private pools. Rooms at the new resort range from simple, affordable bungalows to large private suites with balconies. All rooms are fitted with a colonic board for daily enemas. The spa has a cozy pool, herbal steam bath in a stone grotto, massage, body wraps, and facial treatments. All of the spa services are available for day visitors as well. The onsite vegetarian Spa Restaurant serves excellent dishes with particular care to cleansing the body.

Lamai Beach, Ko Samui 84320 (just south, in the hills over Lamai Beach). ℂ **07723-0855.** Fax 07742-4126. www.thesparesorts.net. 73 units. 800B–2,000B double; 2,800B suite; from 5,000B villa. MC, V. **Amenities:** Restaurant; juice bar; pool; sauna; spa. *In room:* A/C, fridge, minibar.

West Coast
Baan Taling Ngam Resort ★★★   Built on the side of a west-facing hill (great for sunsets!), this remote resort's accommodations include deluxe rooms and suites, along with one- to three-bedroom beach and cliff villas. The hilltop lobby and restaurant, as well as the guest rooms, have fantastic views of the sea and resort gardens, and the main pool appears to spill over its edges into the coconut-palm grove below. Guest rooms combine Thai furniture, fine textiles, and louvered wood paneling, including the sliding doors to the huge tanning terrace. The resort's only drawback is that the beach is small, and you're a bit cut off from the "action" on the east coast of the island—at least a 30-minute drive away. The resort has a fine spa, plus kayaks, windsurf boards, and mountain bikes for guests' use. International and Thai cuisine is served at the Lom Talay and at the Promenade, which both provide a setting for a memorable meal.

295 Moo 3, Taling Ngam Beach, Ko Samui 84140. ℂ **07742-9100.** Fax 07742-3220. www.baan-taling-ngam.com. 70 units. 8,407B double; 12,265B–21,540B villa. AE, DC, MC, V. **Amenities:** 2 restaurants; lounge; babysitting; bike rental; concierge; fitness center; Jacuzzi; 7 pools; room service; sauna; spa w/ massage; outdoor floodlit tennis courts; watersports equipment; library. *In room:* A/C, satellite TV, fridge, minibar.

Lipa Lodge Resort   Situated on the quiet west coast, this small resort is hard to beat if you're looking for an affordable and tranquil escape. In business for over 35 years, the owners have learned the art of giving personal attention, and with just 11 bungalows, there's no chance of its getting crowded. As the resort was founded by an award-winning chef, you can look forward to great tastes in the restaurant, and the infinity pool is just the spot to watch a spectacular sunset. Bungalows are comfortable and well equipped, and each has a private balcony.

75/4 Moo 3, Tambon Lipa Noi, Ko Samui 81410. ✆ **07748-6167.** www.lipalodgeresort.com. 11 units. 3,200B–5,300B double; 6,200B family bungalow. V, MC. **Amenities:** Restaurant; airport transfer; Internet; infinity pool; library. *In room:* A/C, satellite TV, DVD player, minibar.

WHERE TO DINE
Fisherman's Village

Take time out any evening to wander through "Fisherman's Village," as the village of Bophut on the north coast is now known, where you'll find several atmospheric pubs and small upmarket restaurants along the water's edge. You can savor excellent Italian dishes at **Villa Bianca** (✆ **07724-5041**), or, if it's Thai cuisine served in a stylish setting you're after, pop into **Starfish and Coffee** (✆ **07742-7201**) in the center of the street. Americans dreaming of a down-home diner and a burger they can get their teeth into should check out **The Shack** (✆ **07724-6041**), which also grills fresh seafood, ribs, and imported steaks.

Tongsai Bay

Chef Chom's ★ THAI   Even if you're not fortunate enough to stay at the Tongsai Bay resort, Chef Chom's makes a trip to this corner of the island worthwhile. Chom descends from a long line of cooks, some of whom worked in the palace kitchen of Princess Vibhavadee Rangsit in Bangkok. The menu is a mix of southern Thai (spicy) and royal Thai (sweet) cuisines and utilizes only the freshest ingredients. For a nice selection of tastes, try the Tongsai Platter, which offers six distinct dishes, including the excellent *gai hor bai toey* (chicken in pandanus leaves). The cool ocean breezes, candlelight, and soft Thai classical music in the background all make for a romantic evening.

At the Tongsai Bay resort, Moo 5, Ban Plailaem, Bophut (northeast tip of island). ✆ **07724-5480.** Reservations recommended in peak season. Main courses 250B–490B. AE, MC, V. Daily 7–10pm.

Chaweng Beach

Chaweng is where you'll find the most variety, from McDonald's to fine dining.

Betelnut ★ INTERNATIONAL   At this innovative restaurant, you might be greeted by Jeffrey Lord, owner, proprietor, and rollicking raconteur who delivers fine wit and witticisms along with excellent victuals. The delicious sesame-encrusted salmon katsu is indicative of the international fare here. The blackened tuna with salsa and the soft-shell crabs with green papaya and mango salad are also good choices. Come with friends, order a spread of dishes, and pick from among the fine wine selections for a great evening. If you're having difficulty choosing between all the appetizing alternatives, go for the five-course tasting menu, which will set you back around 2,000B.

Buri Rasa Village Resort, Chaweng Beach. ✆ **07741-3370.** Main courses 475B–1,200B. AE, DC, MC, V. Daily 6–11pm.

Poppies ★ THAI/INTERNATIONAL   Known for its Balinese flair, Poppies is equally famous for fresh seafood by the beach. The romantic atmosphere under the large thatch pavilion is enhanced by soft lighting and live international jazz music. Though it specializes in fresh seafood, the kitchen also offers international and Thai classics, as well as a sizable vegetarian menu. Thai dishes are tempered to the Western palate, but say, *"Ow pet"* ("I want it spicy"), and chef Wantanee will crank up the heat for you.

South Chaweng Beach. ✆ **07742-2419.** Reservations recommended. Main courses 220B–1,350B. AE, MC, V. Daily 11:30am–10:30pm.

Zico's ★★ BRAZILIAN   For a wild night out, this unique Brazilian-themed restaurant is a riot of music, drink, and dance, with Brazilian performers shaking their tail feathers from table to table. Roving waiters, called *passadors,* come around with massive skewers of meat and trays of delicacies (you can also choose from the extensive salad bar). For a set price, you pick what you like, and as much as you like, by laying a small disc on the table with the green side up for "More please," and the red side up for "Enough for now, thanks." Quite an experience.

38/2 Moo 3, Chaweng Beach (on the south end of Chaweng across from the Centara Resort). ℂ **07723-1560.** Unlimited buffet 790B. MC, V. Daily 6:30pm–midnight. Dance shows at 8, 9, 10, and 11pm.

Lamai Beach

Cliff Bar & Grill ★ INTERNATIONAL/MEDITERRANEAN   In a fantastic setting on a hill between Chaweng and Lamai Beaches, this is the perfect spot to while away a breezy afternoon or evening, nibbling your way through a seafood platter or gorging yourself on an imported T-bone steak and sipping on an ice-cold glass of wine or fruit juice. Prices are a bit steep, but the combination of glorious views and well prepared food makes it worth it.

124/2 T. Maret, Lamai Beach, Koh Samui 84330. (On the coast road btw. Chaweng and Lamai beaches). ℂ **07741-4266.** www.thecliffsamui.com. Main courses 350B–1,290B. MC, V. Daily 9am–midnight.

WHAT TO SEE & DO

Busy Samui supports all kinds of activities, from scuba diving to bungee jumping, jungle trekking to cooking schools. Most folks come here for beach fun and frolic, and you'll find all kinds of such activities—sailing, jet skis, and parasailing—right at beachside.

The gold-tiled **Wat Phrayai (Big Buddha),** 15m (49 ft.) tall, sits atop Ko Faan (Barking Deer Island), a small islet connected to the shore by a dirt causeway almost 305m (1,000 ft.) long. Though of little historic value, it's an imposing presence on the northeast coast and is one of Samui's primary landmarks. It's easy to reach: Just hop on any *songtaew* going to Big Buddha Beach. You can't miss it.

Ko Samui's famed **Hin Ta** and **Hin Yai,** or Grandfather and Grandmother Rocks, shaped like the male and female sexual organs—are at the far southern end of Lamai Beach. To get there, flag down any *songtaew* to Lamai Beach.

The **Mummified Monk** at Wat Khunaram is certainly worth a visit if you're bent on seeing roadside oddities. He died in the meditation mudra, legs folded lotus-style, and was embalmed that way; you can see him behind glass in a small pavilion at the right as you enter **Wat Khunaram,** itself a worthy example of a typical Thai town temple. At the entrance to the monks' pavilion, a few coins are the cost of the resident monk's blessing with water. Take off your shoes, smile, and kneel, and he will put water on your head and give you a blessing. The *wat* is along the main road, Route 4169, as it shoots inland far south of Lamai.

A few kilometers northwest of Wat Khunaram along Route 4169 are two roads leading up to **Na Muang Waterfalls I and 2;** number one features a large bathing pool (be careful of sharp rocks) at its base, while number two has impressive cascades. You can walk the steamy 5km (3-mile) trek from the coast road to the falls or take the easier route on the back of an elephant (any travel agency in town can arrange this).

Samui's **snake farm** is at the far southwest corner of the island on 4170 Road (ℂ **07742-3247**), with daily shows at 11am and 2pm; tickets cost 250B.

For daily Thai cooking and fruit-carving lessons, the **Samui Institute of Thai Culinary Arts** (**SITCA**; ⓒ 07741-3172; www.sitca.net) is a professional operation and a great way to have fun—especially if your beach plans get rained out. Lunch and dinner courses cost 1,950B each.

OUTDOOR ACTIVITIES

KAYAKING **Blue Stars Sea Kayaking,** 169/1 Moo 2, Chaweng Beach Rd. (ⓒ **07723-0497;** www.bluestars.info), is easy to contact through most booking agents and takes people to the Mu Ko Ang Thong National Marine Park for kayaking and snorkeling. The rubber canoes are perfect for exploring the caverns beneath limestone cliffs. The full-day trip costs 2,200B for adults, 1,400B for children.

SCUBA DIVING & SNORKELING Local aquanauts agree that the best scuba diving is off **Ko Tao,** a small island north of Ko Pha Ngan and Ko Samui, and many of the operations on Samui coordinate with larger on-site dive centers there while also offering good day trips from Samui. Conditions vary with the seasons (Oct–Mar are the best months). The cluster of tiny islands northwest of Samui, **Mu Ko Ang Thong National Marine Park,** is often a more reliable destination. Follow the advice of a local dive shop on where to go, as many have schools on Samui and offer trips farther afield. You can try **Samui International Diving School** (ⓒ **07741-3050;** www.planetscuba.net); **Easy Divers** (ⓒ 07741-3373; www.easydivers-thailand.com); or **Discovery Dive Center** (ⓒ 07741-3196; www.discoverydivers.com) at the Amari Palm Reef Resort.

THE SPA SCENE

Traditional massage is available in any number of storefronts in Chaweng and everywhere along the beach. Expect to pay between 200B and 400B per hour for services.

Ban Sabai, at Big Buddha Beach (ⓒ **07724-5175;** www.ban-sabai.com), is a great choice for a relaxing seaside massage. It offers all treatments, from aromatherapy to body waxing, in its lush, Thai-style compound. Personal attention is this spa's hallmark, and the well informed staff can tailor a program to your every need. Treatments start at 1,100B for a 1-hour neck and shoulder massage. There is another branch at Baan Taling Ngam Beach on the west coast.

The **Spa Resort,** in Lamai (ⓒ **07723-0855;** www.thesparesorts.net), has been a leader on the island for years and continues to provide good, affordable day programs, as well as its signature fasting retreat and all-inclusive packages. **Tamarind Retreat** (ⓒ **07742-4221;** www.tamarindretreat.com) is a more exclusive (and expensive) choice set apart in a jungle area just off the beach at Lamai.

KO SAMUI AFTER DARK

Any given evening along the Chaweng strip is certain to be disrupted at least a few times by roaming pickup trucks with crackling PA systems blaring out advertisements in Thai and English for local **Thai boxing** bouts. Grab one of their flyers for times and locations, which vary.

For bars and discos, Chaweng is the place to be. A mainstream kind of fun seems to always be happening at the **Reggae Pub** (indicated on just about every island map—back from the main road around the central beach area). In this huge thatch mansion, the stage thumps with funky international acts, the dance floor jumps (even during low season, it does a booming business), and the upstairs pool tables are good for sporting around. Just outside is a collection of open-air bars, also found along

Chaweng's beach road. The **Green Mango** has its own street, just off the beachfront road in the northern end of Chaweng, and boom-boom-booms late every night as the town's number-one dance location. A good place to meet that special someone or two.

Most beachside bars consist of a younger backpacker crowd lounging on cushions in the sand. Of these, the **Ark Bar** (© **07742-2047**), across from the Center Point shopping center, is the most happening. The Irish-owned **Tropical Murphy's** (© **07741-3614**), across from McDonald's in south Chaweng, is indeed a slice of Ireland along the Chaweng strip. It's always full and open late; it's the best place to have a friendly pint and be assured you won't have to scream over the thumping bass of house music. Good Irish bands visit from time to time.

Many of Samui's hotels and resorts have cultural shows featuring Thai dance that can be magical. If you like sequins and glamour, Samui puts on some entertaining *katoey* (drag queen) shows as well. **Christy's Cabaret** (© **08167-6218-1**), at the north end of Chaweng, puts on a gala extravaganza of high camp that's free of charge. Come well before the show starts at 10pm to get a good seat, and be prepared to make up for the free admission with cocktail prices.

Over at Lamai Beach, there's everything from beer bars of the sleazier variety to mud wrestling, Thai lady boxing, and a few decent music venues. **Fusion** breaks the mold with acid jazz, funk, soul, and drum 'n' bass nights, and just behind it at the **Super Sub Club,** decent DJs, a good drink selection, and professional dancers (not go-go girls) whip the crowd up into a frenzy till the small hours. Sports fans may be impressed by the gigantic screen that looms over the beer garden here. **Bauhaus** has cheap drinks and holds foam parties and attracts football fans to its screens in high season.

Sunday afternoons, be sure to truck on over to the **Secret Garden Party ★★**, on Big Buddha Beach (© **07724-5255**), for live music and a barbecue on the beach. Many a famous performer (Gerry played here, man!) has jumped up on stage, and there have been times when the pub has hosted thousands. It's not exactly "secret," but still highly recommended. Festivities usually kick off around 4pm.

SIDE TRIPS FROM KO SAMUI
Mu Ko Ang Thong National Marine Park ★

Forty islands northwest of Ko Samui have been designated a national park. Mu Ko Ang Thong National Marine Park is known for its scenic beauty and rare coral reefs. Many of these islands are limestone rock towers (similar to Phang Nga Bay off Phuket), once used by pirates marauding in the South China Sea.

You can book a private boat from Nathon Pier, or you can take a day trip via sea kayak, paddling through the scenery for better views. The latter runs about 2,200B with **Blue Stars Sea Kayaking** (see "Outdoor Activities," above).

Ko Pha Ngan ★

75km (47 miles) E of Surat Thani

Visible from Ko Samui and about two-thirds its size, with similar terrain and flora, Ko Pha Ngan has some beautiful beaches and, along the farther reaches of the island—the rugged north and west coasts, accessible only by bumpy road or special boat—a few cozy resorts and a measure of rustic tranquillity.

The southeastern peninsula of **Haad Rin** is the locus of the monthly **Full Moon Party,** a multiday beachside rave with all the Day-Glo, strobe lights, and debauchery you can handle; attendance at the raves, especially in high season, numbers in the thousands. Partyers move to the mix of a European DJ, gobbling tabs of Ecstasy and magic mushrooms, and letting loose, very loose: something like Ibiza meets a Phish show at the beach. The aftermath of the party is a beautiful white-sand beach strewn with party garbage and buzzing with flies.

If you're interested in attending, boats from Ko Samui leave at regular intervals all day and night (stopping at around 1am), and many revelers just make a night of it, crash on the beach, and come back to Samui in the morning. *A word of warning:* Beware of theft at Full Moon Parties—do yourself a favor, and lock all your valuables in a hotel safe.

Just Say "Mai!"

"Mai" means "no." Thai authorities hope to put a stop to Haad Rin's monthly Full Moon Parties (and other "Half-Moon" and "No-Moon" excuses to rave). This means undercover drug busts by the very guy who just sold you that bag of oregano and bribing your way out of police custody.

GETTING THERE

BY BOAT Frequent boats link Surat Thani, Ko Samui, Ko Pha Ngan, Ko Tao, and Chumphon. From Samui's Nathon Pier, the trip to Ko Pha Ngan takes 45 minutes and costs 200B. Contact **Songserm,** in Ko Samui (℡ 07742-0157). Special boats from Samui's Big Buddha Beach and Bophut Beach also make regular trips for 100B, more during Full Moon Parties at inflated rates. *Note:* Unfortunately, the muster point in Pha Ngan is not well organized, just a bare pier and one gruff attendant. Come armed with the patience of Buddha, especially anytime near the full moon.

GETTING AROUND

Jeep and **motorbike** rentals on Ko Pha Ngan are available anywhere in Haad Rin or near the ferry pier at Thong Sala, on the southwest coast. Jeeps start at 1,000B; regular motorbikes go for 150B to 200B. Be warned, however, that the island roads are steep and treacherous, especially the popular southern reaches east of Thong Sala near Haad Rin. Many interior roads, including the trek to the secluded Thong Nai Pan area in the north, are hilly, muddy tracks. *Songtaews* follow regular routes between Thong Sala ferry pier and Haad Rin, as well as up the west coast; rides start at 50B, more at night or during party time.

[FastFACTS] KO PHA NGAN

There are several banks with exchange and ATM services along both the main street of Thong Sala and in Haad Rin. **Internet access** is chockablock around the island; prices are 1B to 2B per minute. The **tourist police** operate a small information kiosk on the north end of the ferry offices at Thong Sala pier; call ℡ 07742-1281 for info or ℡ 1155 in an emergency.

WHERE TO STAY & DINE

Cheap eats abound in busy Haad Rin, but your best bet for a good meal outside of your resort is limited to mostly budget storefronts blaring DVD movies at high decibels. One bright spot is **Om Ganesh** (℡ 07737-5123), near the main ferry pier. It has great curries and set menus (all-you-can-eat Indian *thali* meals) for little: authentic, delicious, and very popular. For something a little classier, try **Me'n'u**

(☎ 08928-9133), located at Ban Hin Kong, about 5km (3 miles) from the ferry, where the menu features items like seared scallops and Japanese tuna loin tartare.

Ban Tai Beach

Just east of the ferry landing at Thong Sala, Ban Tai Beach is a quiet stretch of sand on the island's southwest coast. The water is shallow and not great for swimming, but the beaches are lovely, and there are a few convenient little resorts far from the hub-bub of Haad Rin but close enough to visit. A couple of attractive options are **First Villa** (145/1 Moo 1, Ban Tai Beach; ☎ 07737-7225; www.firstvilla.com), with basic bungalows from 1,200B, or nearby **Milky Bay Resort** (103/4 Moo 1, Ban Tai Beach; ☎ 07737-7726; www.milkybaythailand.com), which is a bit more upmarket and has rooms starting at 2,700B.

Haad Rin

Haad Rin is a narrow peninsula on the island's southeast tip, with a large number of bungalows on both the west and east sides and busy shopping streets and footpaths leading between them. There are lots of small bungalow resorts, all quite basic, as well as some pockets of luxury. Without a doubt the most beautifully designed resort in this area is the **Sarikantang Resort** (129/3 Moo 6, Seekantang Beach; ☎ 07737-5055-57; www.sarikantang.com), with superb oceanview suites and seaview villas at 4,600B to 5,400B. For something a bit simpler and cheaper, try the **Phanganburi Resort & Spa** (120/10 Haad Rin Nai Beach, Haad Rin; ☎ 07737-5481), with superior rooms from 3,150B. Or check out hilltop **Sea Breeze Bungalow** (94/11 Moo 6, Haad Rin; ☎ 07737-5419; www.seabreezekohphangan.com), a quiet, lofty perch high enough above town for a bit of quiet but close enough to walk down and join the festivities. Rooms with air-conditioning start at 2,000B (rates double at full moon times).

The **Sanctuary** (P.O. Box 3, Ko Pha Ngan 84280; ☎ 08127-1361-4; www.the sanctuarythailand.com) bills itself as an alternative boutique resort. It offers all kinds of healthy activities such as yoga, massage, and fasting programs. Accommodations range from 200B for dorms to family houses starting at 1,500B. You'll need to arrange a taxi boat from Haad Rin to Haad Tien (50B).

Northeast Coast

Secluded on its own stretch of beach 17km (11 miles) from the ferry pier and north of busy Haad Rin, this area features great beaches with a few budget stops as well as the island's best resorts. Thong Nai Pan is a scenic choice, easily reached by boat (contact Panviman) or, less easily, by bumpy dirt road. **Panviman ★** (22/1 Moo 5, Thong Nai Pan Noi Bay; ☎/fax 07744-5101; www.panviman.com) is one of the best hotels on Pha Ngan and has picturesque rooms overlooking the bay, lots of services, and a tiered pool area. Another comfortable option is the **Santhiya Resort & Spa ★★** (22/7 Moo 5, Banthai; ☎ 07742-8999; www.santhiya.com), where the teak villas are scattered among 7.3 hectares (18 acres) of grounds and deluxe rooms start at 12,000B.

Northwest Coast

The northwest coast has good beaches and is far from the monthly "do" at Haad Rin, a relief for many. Resorts here are quiet, affordable, and growing in number and quality of amenities. **Green Papaya** (Haad Salad, on the far northwest of the island; ☎/fax 07737-4230; www.greenpapayaresort.com) is a mellow little courtyard hotel with rooms from 4,600B. The next-door **Salad Beach Resort** (☎ 07734-9274; www.phangan-saladbeachresort.com) also has smart rooms at slightly cheaper rates.

WHAT TO SEE & DO

The rugged roads of Pha Ngan beg to be explored, and interior roads connect small towns worth seeing as a window into a way of laid-back island living that is slowly disappearing.

Wat Kow Tahm ★ is a well known international meditation center and temple compound just north of the road near Thong Sala pier. Since 1988, Steve and Rosemary Weissmann (from the U.S. and Australia, respectively) have been offering courses in Insight Meditation, or Vipassana. The emphasis is on the development of compassionate understanding through the practice of formal walking and sitting meditation. There are frequent Dharma talks and 10- and 20-day retreats for meditators of all experience levels; prices start at 5,000B for 10 days. The temple is also open to day visitors and has an overlook with one of the best views on the island. Check the informative website at www.watkowtahm.org, or address inquiries to Retreats, Wat Kow Tahm, P.O. Box 18, Ko Pha Ngan, Surat Thani 84280.

Ko Tao ★

Tiny Ko Tao developed differently from its neighbors—it skipped the slow-growth years of thatch shacks and candlelit meals and went straight to corrugated tin roofs and video-playing bars. There are still lots of rustic choices on the island, but the current trend is small, all-inclusive resorts owned and operated by dive companies with head offices in Samui and elsewhere. Visitors spend their days out on the water on **scuba tours** to the fine coral sites around the island, then return to the comfort of private bungalows where they can relax and debrief after the day's exploration (many of these places even have air-conditioned classrooms for studying diving specifics). Avoid Ko Tao in the stormy November-to-December season, when the monsoon whips up and winds cloud the normally transparent seas.

Songserm (✆ **07742-0157** on Ko Samui, 07750-6205 in Chumphon, or 07745-6274 on Ko Tao) connects from nearby islands. From Chumphon, the fare is 450B; from Ko Samui, 400B; and from Ko Pha Ngan, 250B. Once you get to the main town, you'll find scuba operators and accommodations booking offices.

For advance booking with a dive service, contact a dive office such as **Big Blue Diving Ko Tao** (in Mae Haad; ✆ **07745-6415;** www.bigbluediving.com) or **Easy Divers** (in Mae Haad at the catamaran jetty; ✆ **07745-6010;** www.thaidive.com).

The Far South & On to Malaysia

From Surat Thani going south, Thailand slowly gives way to Malay culture; Buddhism, predominant elsewhere in the kingdom, is replaced by rich Islamic influence, a gradual process without any precise border. **Nakhon Si Thammarat** is an ancient Buddhist city of note with many temples worth visiting. The far southern **Hat Yai** is a major transport hub and a destination more popular with Malay and Singaporean tourists, mostly a stopover for onward travel to (or connecting from) Malaysia.

Warning: Bomb attacks have targeted tourist areas in Hat Yai. In April 2005, a bomb was set off in Hat Yai International Airport, killing two, and in September 2006, six separate bombs killing four people, including a Canadian, were detonated in downtown Hat Yai. While these were isolated events, and most of the violence occurs farther south in the border areas with Malaysia, caution is advised if you plan on using Hat Yai as a transit point.

NAKHON SI THAMMARAT

Nakhon Si Thammarat, one of the oldest cities in southern Thailand, has long been a religious capital. **Wat Mahathat** houses a hair of the Buddha and is the town's central attraction and important pilgrimage point for Thai Buddhists. This region is the locus for traditional Thai puppet play, and **Ban Nang Thalung Suchart Subsin** (Mr. Subsin's House of Shadow Plays), 110/18 Si Thammasok Soi 3 (✆ 07534-6394), makes for an interesting visit.

Nok Air connects Nakhon Si Thammarat with Don Muang airport in Bangkok. All north-south **trains** make a stop here, and affordable **minivans** can be arranged from any hotel (the best way to get around the south).

Thai Hotel (1375 Ratchadamnoen Rd.; ✆ 07534-1509; www.thaihotel-nakorn. com) is a basic and convenient standard lodging, with fan rooms starting at 260B.

HAT YAI

It's a town full of tourists behaving badly, mostly men from nearby Malaysia and Singapore attracted by this rowdy, slightly sleazy, inexpensive, consumer playground. For Westerners, Hat Yai is mostly a gateway to Malaysia by train or bus, or a stepping-off point for rugged Tarutao National Park. Hat Yai's busy **Night Market** is certainly worth a wander, and the beaches at nearby **Songkhla** are not a bad day trip.

Hat Yai International Airport welcomes frequent flights from Malaysia and Singapore via Silk Air, Malaysia Airlines, and Thai Airways, and there are connections available to Bangkok and Phuket.

Five trains depart daily from Bangkok's **Hua Lamphong Railway Station** (✆ 1690 or 0223-3762) to Hat Yai, which is a major rail hub, and there are daily connections with Malaysia. Minibuses connect from other parts of the region, and long-distance buses connect from Bangkok's **Southern Bus Terminal** (✆ 02894-6122).

A number of fine hotels cater to Malay tourists. Try the **Novotel Centara** (3 Sanehanusom Rd.; ✆ 07435-2222), with rooms from $75 a night, or the popular backpacker haunt, **Cathay Guest House** (93/1 Niphat Uthit 2 Rd.; ✆ 07424-3815), with singles from 160B.

Hat Yai is also the gateway to **Tarutao National Park,** a chain of 51 islands originally settled by sea gypsies and later used as prison colonies. The jumping-off point for Tarutao is Ban Pak Bara, a port city reached by bus from Hat Yai.

THE SOUTHERN PENINSULA: WEST COAST

This stunning length of coast, overlooking the Andaman Sea and dotted by some of the finest resorts in the country, is now well known for the tragic events of December 2004, when a massive tsunami struck the shores here, leaving a path of destruction. Many lives were lost and this long, heavily populated coast was left in ruins. Today, there are few signs left of the destruction, as resorts were quick to rebuild and remodel post-tsunami. In the unlikely event of another tsunami, the government has installed an early warning system, and evacuation routes to high ground are well marked.

The island of **Phuket** was one of the earliest tourist developments in the kingdom, and from humble origins has grown into a top international resort area: the best choice for comfort and services on the west coast. Phuket may be Thailand's largest

The Southern Peninsula: West Coast

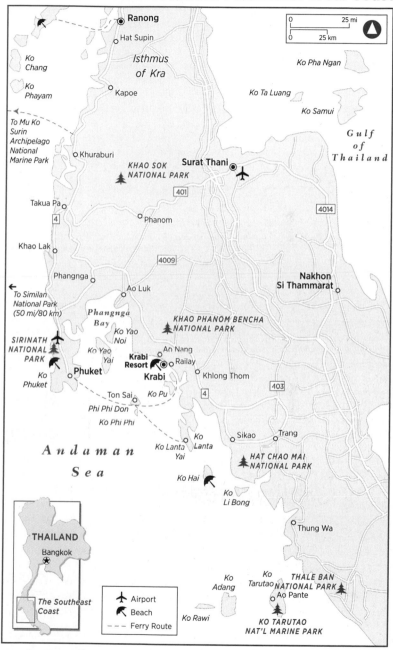

Ranong
Hat Supin
Ko Chang
Ko Phayam
Isthmus of Kra
Kapoe
Ko Pha Ngan
Ko Ta Luang
Ko Samui
To Mu Ko Surin Archipelago National Marine Park
Khuraburi
KHAO SOK NATIONAL PARK
Surat Thani
Gulf of Thailand
Takua Pa
401
4014
Phanom
Khao Lak
4009
Phangnga
To Similan National Park (50 mi/80 km)
Ao Luk
Nakhon Si Thammarat
Phangnga Bay
Ko Yao Noi
KHAO PHANOM BENCHA NATIONAL PARK
Ko Yao Yai
SIRINATH NATIONAL PARK
An Nang
Krabi Resort
Railay
Phuket
Krabi
Khlong Thom
Ko Phuket
403
Ton Sai
Ko Pu
4
Phi Phi Don
Ko Phi Phi
Andaman Sea
Ko Lanta Yai
Ko Lanta
Sikao
Trang
HAT CHAO MAI NATIONAL PARK
Ko Hai
Ko Li Bong
Thung Wa

THAILAND
Bangkok
The Southeast Coast

Ko Adang
Ko Tarutao
THALE BAN NATIONAL PARK
Ao Pante
Ko Rawi
KO TARUTAO NAT'L MARINE PARK

Airport
Beach
Ferry Route

and best-known island, though it is but one of many in the brilliant blue Andaman Sea; rocky islets, atolls, and leafy jungle coastline play host to a roster of island resorts and getaways. It is a great area to island-hop via bus and ferry connections, and there are opportunities for snorkeling, trekking, and laid-back luxury in every quarter.

The province of **Krabi** encompasses all the land east of Phuket, including Ko Phi Phi and Ko Lanta, but "Krabi" typically refers to the small port town and nearby beaches of the Krabi Resort area and Ao Nang Beach. In places such as Railay Beach, you'll find dynamic stone-tower landscapes (popular among rock climbers), great beaches, and a range of resorts. It's a popular alternative to busy Phuket.

About equidistant from Krabi and Phuket, the island of **Ko Phi Phi** followed Phuket's development model, though on a smaller scale. Phi Phi was hit hard by the tsunami, but has quickly been rebuilt.

Ko Lanta is a large island southeast of Krabi Town. Once lined only with budget resorts and bungalows, it now hosts a number of luxury resorts with more under construction.

The high season on the west coast is from November to April—bookings must be made in advance, especially on Phuket, and discounted rates are hard to come by. Still, western winter months are the time for water activities, when the Andaman is calm and the skies are clear (and when the snow falls thick in many parts of the world). In superpeak season, from the Christmas holiday to about January 10, most places tack on steep surcharges.

Phuket ★★

At its best, this island in the Andaman Sea is idyllic: It has long sandy beaches (some with dunes), warm water, excellent snorkeling and scuba diving off Ko Similan, good windsurfing conditions, mountains, fine resorts, and some of the best seafood in all of Thailand. At its worst, it is overdeveloped and overrun with tour groups; its raucous nightlife and areas such as busy Patong's pulsing commercial strip can be a bit too much for those in search of beachside tranquillity.

Over the years, the Thai government has granted economic incentives to encourage developers to shape the island into an international first-class resort. The 2004 tsunami was merely a speed bump, development-wise, as today construction continues to spread to previously remote beaches, and tourism numbers are back to pre-tsunami days. As groups pour in from Singapore, Hong Kong, and Europe, the backpackers head off to nearby Ko Phi Phi and Krabi, or to islands on the eastern gulf such as Samui and Pha Ngan.

But many of the resorts are attractive and elegant and designed to give you the illusion of tropical solitude in busier areas. It's nearly impossible to find a totally secluded beach, but there are a number of very attractive and comfortable facilities with a high level of service—not a bad trade-off for those in search of all the luxuries. If you're on a family holiday, Phuket is a good choice.

GETTING THERE

BY PLANE **Thai Airways** (© **02545-3691** in Bangkok for domestic reservations) flies at least 10 times daily from Bangkok, from 7am to 9:30pm (trip time: 1 hr., 20 min.), and has a daily flight from Chiang Mai (trip time: 2 hr.). It also connects Phuket with international flights to and from Frankfurt, Hong Kong, Perth, Singapore, and Tokyo. The local Thai Airways office in Phuket is at 78 Ranong Rd. (© **07636-0400**).

Phuket

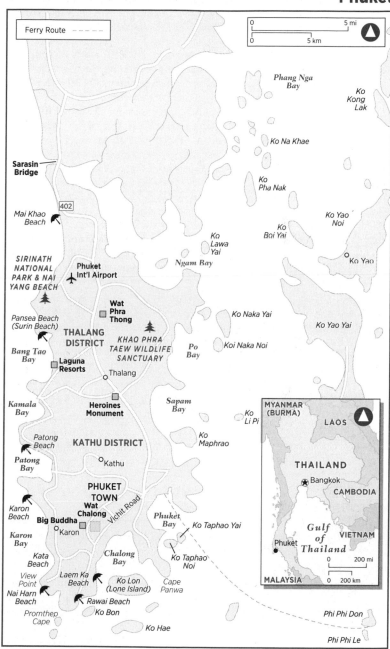

Ferry Route --- -- ---

0   5 mi
0   5 km

Phang Nga
Bay

Ko
Kong
Lak

Ko Na Khae

Ko
Pha Nak

Sarasin
Bridge

Ko Yao
Noi

Mai Khao
Beach

Ko
Boi Yai

Ko
Lawa
Yai

402

Ko Yao

SIRINATH
NATIONAL
PARK & NAI
YANG BEACH

Ngam Bay

Phuket
Int'l Airport

Wat
Phra
Thong

Ko Naka Yai

Ko Yao Yai

Pansea Beach
(Surin Beach)

THALANG
DISTRICT

KHAO PHRA
TAEW WILDLIFE
SANCTUARY

Po
Bay

Koi Naka Noi

Bang Tao
Bay

Laguna
Resorts

Thalang

Kamala
Bay

Heroines
Monument

Sapam
Bay

Ko
Li Pi

MYANMAR
(BURMA)

LAOS

Patong
Beach

KATHU DISTRICT

Ko
Maphrao

Patong
Bay

Kathu

THAILAND

Bangkok

PHUKET
TOWN

Wat
Chalong

Vichit Road

CAMBODIA

Karon
Beach

Big Buddha

Karon

Phuket
Bay

Ko Taphao Yai

Karon
Bay

Gulf
of
Thailand

VIETNAM

Kata
Beach

Chalong
Bay

Ko Taphao
Noi

Phuket

View
Point

Laem Ka
Beach

Ko Lon
(Lone Island)

Cape
Panwa

0   200 mi

Nai Harn
Beach

Rawai Beach

MALAYSIA

0   200 km

Promthep
Cape

Ko Bon

Ko Hae

Phi Phi Don

Phi Phi Le

Silk Air (© 07630-4018-20) has daily connections with Singapore.

Bangkok Airways (© 02270-6699 in Bangkok, or 07742-2235 on Ko Samui) connects Phuket with both Ko Samui and Bangkok at least twice daily. The Bangkok Airways office in Phuket is at 158/2–3 Yaowarat Rd., Phuket Town (© **07622-5033,** or 07620-5401 at Phuket Airport).

Air Asia (© 02515-9999; www.airasia.com) and **Nok Air** (© **02900-9955;** www.nokair.com) also connect Phuket with Bangkok daily.

The attractive, modern **Phuket International Airport** (© 07732-7230-7; www.phuketairportonline.com) is in the north of the island, about a 40-minute drive from Phuket Town or from Patong Beach. It has banks, money-changing facilities, car-rental agents (see "Getting Around," below), and a post office. The Phuket Tourist Business Association booth can help you make hotel arrangements if you haven't booked a room in advance.

Many resorts will pick you up at the airport upon request for a fee, usually steep, though some include this with your rate. However, there are other options for getting to your hotel from the airport. The cheapest way is the **minibus,** which operates every hour on the hour from 9am to 11pm daily. Stopping between Patong, Kata, Karon, and Phuket Town, prices run from 120B to 180B, depending on how far you're going (180B gets you as far south as Kata Beach). **Taxi** service from the airport will cost between 400B to Phuket Town and 650B to Kata Beach. The **airport bus** connects with Phuket Town and costs 85B. Buses depart roughly every hour from 6:30am to 9:30pm.

BY BUS   Three air-conditioned 24-seat VIP buses leave daily from Bangkok's **Southern Bus Terminal** (© 02894-6122), best as an overnight, and cost from 1,000B. Regular air-conditioned buses cost 630B. Standard buses make frequent connections to Surat Thani and nearby towns on the mainland (trip time from Surat: 6 hr.; 170B).

The intercity bus terminal (Phangnga Rd.; © 07621-1480) is east of Phuket Town just opposite the Royal Phuket City Hotel. For information on how to get from here to the beaches, see "Getting Around," below.

BY MINIVAN   Minivans to and from Surat Thani, Krabi, Nakhon Si Thammarat, Ranong, and other southern cities leave on regular schedules throughout the day. In each city, minivan operators work with the hotels and arrange free pickup, so it's best to book through your hotel front desk or a travel agent (especially since the operators who man the phones at minivan companies rarely speak English). Tickets from destinations in the south, such as Surat Thani and Hat Yai, go for between 150B and 350B.

GETTING AROUND

Public transportation is a problem on Phuket that never seems to get solved. If you've spent any time in other parts of the country, you'll know that the covered pickup trucks that cruise the streets picking up and dropping off passengers are called *song-taews,* while the noisy motorized three-wheel demons are known as tuk-tuks—not so on Phuket. Here, the people call the pickup trucks **tuk-tuks,** while *songtaews* are the giant colorful buses that ply the main roads (a few people also call them **baht buses**). Tuk-tuk drivers, in an attempt to generate more business, have lobbied successfully for exclusive rights to transport people *between* beaches, the lone exception being between Kata and Karon. This means the *songtaews* are permitted to travel only from each beach to Phuket Town—you can't hop from beach to beach on them. For these trips, you have to negotiate with the tuk-tuk drivers (see below for tips).

BY SONGTAEW The local bus terminal is in front of the Central Market on Ranong Road in Phuket Town. Fares to the most popular beaches range from 25B to 40B. *Songtaews* leave when full, usually about every 30 minutes, from 7am to 6pm between Phuket Town and the main beaches on the west coast. Other than the route through Karon and Kata beaches, they do not operate routes between beaches.

BY TUK-TUK & DAIHATSU MINI Within Phuket Town, tuk-tuk trucks cost about 30B to 60B for in-town trips: a good way to get to the bus station or to Phuket Town's restaurants. In the west-coast beaches, tuk-tuks and small Daihatsu mini-trucks roll around town honking at any tourist on foot, especially in Patong, and charge more, about 300B from Patong Beach to Karon Beach, with higher prices late at night.

BY MOTORCYCLE TAXI Drivers, identifiable by colored vests, make short trips in Phuket Town or along Patong Beach for 20B to 40B.

BY CAR Because of the poor and expensive transportation system on Phuket, self-driving is popular, but extreme caution applies. Roads between the main beaches in the west and connecting with Phuket Town across the center of the island are danger-ously steep and winding, with more than a few hairpin turns, lots of traffic, and motorbikes zipping around unpredictably. As in other parts of the kingdom, drivers pass aggressively, even on blind curves, so you need to be very defensive and alert at all times.

Avis has a counter at Phuket Airport (© **07635-1244;** www.avisthailand.com). Plan on spending around 1,600B per day for a Toyota Vios. **Budget** (© **07620-5396**) is considerably cheaper (around 1,000B for a basic midsize); it has an airport location, an office in Phuket Town, and a counter at the Patong Merlin Hotel (44 Thaweewong Rd., Patong). Both companies offer sedans, and both also have sound insurance coverage available, which is highly recommended.

BY MOTORCYCLE Also along the Patong strip, the same car-rental guys will provide you with a motorbike for cheap. A 100cc Honda scooter goes for 200B per day, while a 400cc Honda CBR or a 600cc Honda Shadow chopper will set you back at least 600B per day. Significant discounts can be negotiated if you plan to rent for a longer time. Wear your helmet (there are sometimes-enforced fines of 500B for going without), keep to the left, and let cars pass. Exercise caution: You're sure to meet up with a few road-rashed travelers in any beach area, and there is no quicker way to end a vacation than on slippery, treacherous roads, especially for inexperienced riders.

 Special Event

If you are on Phuket in October, don't miss the **Vegetarian Festival,** a colorful tradition passed down from early Thai-Chinese settlers. For 9 days, not only do devotees refrain from meat con-sumption, but many also submit to physical self-mutilation through walk-ing over coals and practicing extreme body-piercing with long skewers or swords, all acts of merit making and penance to the spirits who helped early inhabitants ward off malaria. Early morning processions follow through the streets of Phuket Town, with onlookers clad in white for the occasion.

ISLAND LAYOUT

Phuket Town, the island's commercial center, is in the southeast. Picturesque stretches of sand dot the western coast from Nai Harn, on the southern tip, to Mai Khao, about 30km (19 miles) north. From south to north on the west coast, you'll find Kata Noi, Kata, Karon, Patong, Kamala, Surin, and a number of other beaches all along this coastline. A busy coastal road links the popular resorts in the south, but destinations north of Patong require short detours from the coast. Inland, the island also has plenty of interest, including regimented rows of rubber trees at the roadside, as well as wilder areas like the **Khao Phra Taew Wildlife Reserve,** where animal lovers might like to visit the **Gibbon Rehabilitation Project** (see "What to See & Do," later in this chapter).

THE BEACHES There's a beach for everyone in Phuket, from exclusive hideaways with luxury hotels to backpacker lodgings and even campgrounds. Each beach is distinct—selecting the appropriate area makes all the difference.

Nai Harn Beach, in the far south of the busy west coast of Phuket, is an isolated area with a few fine resorts. Going north from here, you'll find **Kata Noi Beach, Kata Yai Beach,** and **Karon Beach.** Developed but not overwhelmingly so (far from over-the-top Patong), these beaches are home to resorts large and small. Sandy beaches are long and picturesque; the water is deep, with some nice wave breaks. This beach area has more restaurants than the remote bays, and some shopping, nightlife, and travel-agent options as well. But you won't find rowdy crowds here—and even with all the development, the area manages to maintain a laid-back character.

North of Kata and Karon bays, you'll pass through **Relax Bay,** a small cove with a few resorts, before rolling down the mountain to **Patong Beach,** the most famous (perhaps infamous) strip on the island. Patong's draw is its raucous nightlife, busy shops and restaurants, and brash neon-radiating pulse: Can you hear the bass? Accommodations run the gamut here.

Farther north from Patong, **Kamala Bay, Surin Beach,** and **Pansea Beach** have more secluded resorts on lovely beaches for those who still want the convenience of nearby Patong but cherish the serenity of a quiet resort. Just north is **Bang Tao Beach,** home to the Laguna Resort Complex of luxury hideaways. Beautiful **Nai Thon** and **Nai Yang** beaches are often deserted, and, finally, in the far north is **Mai Khao Beach,** the island's longest and quietest strip of sand.

VISITOR INFORMATION

The **TAT** office in Phuket Town is at 191 Thalang Rd. (© **07621-1036**), but it's also easy to find information through any hotel concierge or tour desk. You'll find lots of free maps on offer (all filled with advertisements). For driving around the island, pick up the very detailed *Periplus Editions Map of Phuket* at any bookstore. Restaurants and hotel lobbies are good places to pick up a number of free local publications: *Phuket Food-Shopping-Entertainment* is packed with dining suggestions and ads for many of the island's activities; *What's on South* has some useful information on Phuket, Ko Phi Phi, and Krabi; *Art & Culture South* has some great tips for shoppers; and there are a few fun ultraglossy local magazines for sale.

[FastFACTS] PHUKET

Currency Exchange
Banks are in Phuket Town, with many larger branches on Ranong and Rasada roads. There are bank offices at the airport, as well as branches of major Thai banks at Kata, Karon, and Patong beaches. See each destination section for more information. Money-changers are in major shopping areas on each beach and at most resorts, but banks offer the best rates.

Hospitals The **Bangkok Hospital** (2/1 Hongyok-Uthit Rd., off Yaowarat Rd. in Phuket Town; ✆ **07625-4425;** www.phukethospital. com) has English-speaking staff and high-quality facilities, and accepts international medical insurance.

Internet Access Most hotels and guesthouses now offer Wi-Fi services, either free or for a fee.

Otherwise, there are plenty of Internet cafes in tourist areas with rates varying from 50B to 200B per hour.

Mail The general post office in Phuket Town is at the corner of Thalang and Montri roads.

Police The emergency number for the **tourist police** is the fast-dial four-digit ✆ **1155.**

WHERE TO STAY

The island's accommodations and restaurants below are divided by beach area, to help you simplify your choices. Hotel listings provide high-season rack rates, an almost fictitious fee but a good point of departure for gauging price. Expect to pay from 30% to as much as 50% below the listed rates, especially in low season.

Phuket Town

Most just pass through the island's commercial hub, but it's worth considering as a base, since you can get to all the beaches easily, and it has some of the island's best dining options (see "Where to Dine," later in this section).

If you're looking for a budget spot, the **Talang Guesthouse** (37 Talang Rd.; ✆ **07621-4225;** www.thalangguesthouse.com) is an old standby at the town center with fan rooms starting at 350B. Rooms are basic, but this Sino-Portuguese shophouse has lots of character and makes a convenient base to explore the town. The **Old Town Guesthouse** (42 Krabi Rd.; ✆ **07625-8272;** www.phuketoldtown hostel.com) is under the same management and has slightly higher rates.

Royal Phuket City Hotel ★ For a small town such as Phuket, this hotel is surprisingly cosmopolitan. A true city hotel, Royal Phuket's facilities include one of the finest fitness centers going, a full-service spa with massage, a large outdoor swimming pool, and a very professional business center. Above the cavernous marble lobby, guest rooms are smart—in contemporary hues and style, though views of the busy little town below can't compare with the beachfront just a short ride away. The Red Onion coffee shop on the 19th floor offers great panoramas, while the White Palm Restaurant serves authentic Chinese cuisine. Few indeed stay in Phuket Town, but if you're stuck here, go for style.

154 Phang-Nga Rd., Amphur Muang, Phuket 83000 (to the east of Phuket Town, across from the inter-city bus terminal). ✆ **07623-3333.** Fax 07623-3335. www.royalphuketcity.com. 251 units. 2,200B–2,800B double; from 5,000B suite. AE, DC, MC, V. **Amenities:** 2 restaurants; lobby lounge; babysitting; executive-level rooms; golf course nearby; fitness center w/sauna, steam, massage, and spa; outdoor pool; room service; smoke-free rooms. *In room:* A/C, satellite TV, fridge, hair dryer, minibar.

Nai Harn Beach

Far to the south, Nai Harn Beach is a good escape, with a range of accommodations on offer. Adjacent beaches on the eastern side of the island, **Rawai** and **Chalong,** are also home to a few good, high-end resorts: **Evason Phuket & Bon Island** (100 Vised Rd.; © **07638-1010;** fax 07638-1018; www.sixsenses.com/evason-phuket) is a luxury, family-friendly enclave and popular day-spa destination, with room rates starting at around 5,000B; and **Mangosteen** (99/4 Moo 7, Soi Mangosteen; © **07628-9399;** fax 07628-9389; www.mangosteen-phuket.com) is another gorgeous spa resort, where rooms start at around the same price.

Just up the coast road from the Royal Yacht Club are quaint seaside, forest bungalows at **Baan Krating Phuket Resort** (11/3 Moo 1, Viset Rd.; ©/fax **07628-8264;** www.baankrating.com). Offering good facilities such as a free-form pool, this is a good value getaway. Rooms start at 2,699B.

The Royal Phuket Yacht Club ★★★   Perched above the northern edge of Nai Harn Beach, the Royal Yacht Club is one of the earliest luxury accommodations in Phuket, yet it still rivals nearly anything on the island for setting and comfort. The pagoda-style foyer overlooks terraced gardens overflowing with pink and white bougainvillea. Common areas have terra-cotta tiles and open views. Interiors are spacious and decorated with cheerful fabrics and tasteful furniture; bathrooms are huge, many with sunken tubs. All rooms have large balconies for viewing the beach and Promthep Cape.

23/3 Viset Rd., Nai Harn Beach, Phuket 83130 (above Nai Harn Beach, 18km/11 miles south of Phuket). © **07638-0200.** www.puravarna.com. 110 units. 7,360B–10,000B double (varies with view); 10,800B–29,200B suite. AE, DC, MC, V. **Amenities:** 3 restaurants; lounge; airport transfer; babysitting; fitness center; Internet; outdoor pool; room service; spa; 2 outdoor lighted tennis courts; extensive watersports equipment. In room: A/C, satellite TV, fridge, hair dryer, minibar.

Kata Beach

One of Phuket's best tourist beaches, Kata is a wide strip of soft sand and rolling surf. Rent an umbrella, get a massage, or grab a kayak or surfboard and hit the waves (there's good surf May–Oct). Unfortunately, the best beachfront real estate is taken up by the sprawling **Phuket Club Med** (© **07633-0455**), an all-inclusive, club-style resort (www.clubmed.com), but the beach is open to all. After dark, Kata comes alive in the bars and music cafes along the beach roads.

Kata Country House   Set in an attractive garden, this smart place offers decent-sized rooms with rustic furnishings at budget prices. The wood or concrete bungalows are the best bet, though standard and superior rooms in two-story blocks are also excellent value. The only downside is that it's tucked away behind Club Med and about a 10-minute walk from the beach, but there's a spa and swimming pool on-site.

82 Kata Rd., Kata Beach, Phuket 83100. © **07633-3210.** Fax 07628-4221. www.katacountryhouse.com. 88 units. 1,600B standard room; 2,600B bungalow. MC, V. **Amenities:** Restaurant; Internet; outdoor pool; spa. In room: A/C, satellite TV, fridge.

Katanoi Bay Inn   The Katanoi offers basic, motel-style rooms adjacent to the Katathani Hotel. Most rooms have balconies and firm beds. There is little in the way of facilities, but quiet Kata Noi Beach is just across the road for great snorkeling and watersports.

69/1 Kata Noi Rd., Kata Noi Beach, Phuket 83100 (Kata Noi is south of Kata Yai Beach). © **07633-3308-9.** Fax 07633-3545 www.katanoibayinn.com. 28 units. From 1,200B double. MC, V. **Amenities:** Restaurant; Internet cafe. In room: A/C (some), satellite TV, fridge, no phone.

Katathani Hotel ★★★ The Katathani is the best option on the cul-de-sac of lovely Kata Noi Beach, a haven of quiet luxury. Rooms are contemporary, but cozy—all with large balconies and cozy indoor sitting areas. Wide, well groomed lawns surround sizable pools and lead to the graceful curve of the pristine cove. There is a nightly poolside buffet. The Katathani's best feature is that it is right on the beach and all rooms have good sea views. However, it is usually quite crowded and very popular with families, so this is not the resort for a quiet, romantic getaway.

14 Kata Noi Rd., Kata Noi Beach, Phuket 83100 (north end of Kata Noi Beach). ℰ **07633-0124-6.** Fax 07633-0426. www.katathani.com. 479 units. From 9,750B double; 12,000B–28,050B suite. AE, DC, MC, V. **Amenities:** 6 restaurants; 5 bars; airport transfer; babysitting; golf course nearby; fitness center; Internet; 6 outdoor pools; room service; aromatherapy spa; 2 outdoor lighted tennis courts; watersports equipment; library. *In room:* A/C, satellite TV, hair dryer, minibar.

The Boathouse: 182 Koktanod Rd., Kata Beach, Phuket 83100 (south end of Kata Yai Beach). ℰ **07633-0015.** Fax 07633-561. www.boathousephuket.com. 38 units. 9,000B double; 17,500B suite; 25,000B dolphin pool villa. **Villa Royale:** 12 Kata Noi Rd., Kata Noi Beach, Phuket 83100. ℰ **07633-3568.** www.villaroyalephuket.com. 27 units. 14,000B–25,000B suite. AE, DC, MC, V for both. **Amenities:** 3 restaurants; lounge; airport transfer; babysitting; golf course nearby; fitness center; outdoor pool; room service; spa; library. *In room:* A/C, satellite TV, fridge, hair dryer, minibar, Wi-Fi.

Mom Tri's Boathouse (aka "The Boathouse") and Villa Royale ★★★ At the quieter south end of Kata Beach, this small inn has been a longtime favorite with many returning visitors. More inn than resort, there's a real home-style feeling here. Comfortable, attractive rooms all face the sea, each with a terrace overlooking a courtyard pool and beach beyond; they're not particularly luxurious, but they are clean and adequate. For a very special stay, there's **Villa Royale,** a collection of extravagant suites. These huge rooms are perched over a steep cliff with stunning views of the sea and are sumptuously decorated in a unique mix of local materials: dark teak, mosaics of bamboo and coconut, black tile with stone inlay, and elegant textiles. The Boathouse, the first-floor restaurant, is an old favorite for visiting connoisseurs (see "Where to Dine," later in this chapter). They offer fun cooking classes, too.

Sawasdee Village ★★ 🏨 Just a short walk from Kata Beach, you'll pass a small portico of stone with some Khmer statuary; walk in and you'll find a little Eden. Before reaching the rooms at the lush central courtyard, you'll walk past the hotel's restaurant, spa, and pretty garden. The garden surrounds a small pool with ornate fountains bordered with fine masonry and overflowing with greenery. Garden rooms are midsize and stylish, with canopy beds. Bathrooms are shower-only and not too small. The stunning new triple-pool-access **Baray Villas** are enormous, featuring a delightful blend of Arabic and Thai design and private butlers. There are elegant Thai touches throughout the compound, such as *salas* for relaxing and sliding doors that connect each room to the courtyard.

38 Katekwan Rd., Kata Beach, Phuket 83100 (down a small road north of the sprawling Club Med). ℰ **07633-0979.** Fax 07633-0905. www.phuketsawasdee.com. 54 units. 5,200B garden room; 17,000B Baray Villas. **Amenities:** 2 restaurants; bar; small outdoor pool; spa; free Wi-Fi. *In room:* A/C, fridge, minibar, no phone.

Karon Beach

Karon Beach is a long, straight stretch of beach lined with upper- and midrange hotels and resorts. You'll find heaps of tailors, gift shops, small restaurants, Internet service, and minimarts on the north end of the beach.

Andaman Seaview Hotel ★★ Here's one that is highly recommended if you can book it (it's often full in high season). Bright and airy public spaces—done in Mediterranean hues of light blue and white, a Sino-Portuguese theme—are flanked by ponds and give way to a large central courtyard, garden, and meandering pool. Some rooms overlook the pool area and are large and nicely appointed, better than most in this category. Deluxe units are massive, featuring marble bar areas and his-and-hers sinks. Bright primary colors dominate and everything sparkles. There is a charm throughout that is less about luxury than about the warm welcome, tidy appearance of the place, and friendly crowd. The restaurant is a de rigueur hotel coffee shop, but you'll want to dine at poolside—in fact, do everything at poolside. You're just across the street from Karon Beach here.

Karon Rd., Phuket 83100 (along the main strip at Karon Beach). ℂ **07639-8111.** Fax 07639-8177. www.andamanphuket.com. 161 units. 8,300B superior double; 11,500B deluxe double. AE, MC, V. **Amenities:** Restaurant; poolside bar; small fitness center; Internet access; Jacuzzi; 2 outdoor pools; room service; small spa. *In room:* A/C, satellite TV, fridge, minibar.

Golden Sand Inn One of only a few acceptable budget accommodations on this part of the island (they're either getting converted into swanky digs or falling into disrepair as in Patong), the Golden Sand is clean, reasonably quiet, and well maintained. The location isn't bad, on the northernmost end of Karon and not far from all the town services and the beach. Rooms are large and like those in a beat-up roadside motel. It does have a nice coffee shop, though, and a small pool. Off-season rates are cheap-cheap.

Karon Beach, Phuket 83100 (across highway from north end of beach above traffic circle). ℂ **07639-6493.** Fax 07639-6117. www.phuket-goldensand.com. 125 units. 1,600B–2,300B double; 3,500B family room. AE, DC, MC, V. **Amenities:** Restaurant; pool. *In room:* A/C, TV, minibar.

Karona Resort and Spa ★ Tucked in a little side street where Karon and Kata beaches meet, the Karona Resort is a low-luxe find, with simple rooms surrounding a tiered central pool, all just a short walk from Karon Beach and the busy Kata strip. Deluxe rooms, in a block overlooking the pool, are worth the upgrade—you'll get a few more amenities, such as a safe. They also have good, affordable spa treatments, and the place is quite stylish and the service good for the price. Long-stay discounts apply.

6 Karon Soi 2, Karon Beach, Phuket 83100. ℂ **07628-6406.** Fax 07628-6411. www.karonaresort.com. 96 units. 3,000B–4,000B double; 6,500B–10,500B suite. MC, V. **Amenities:** Restaurant; bar; Internet; outdoor pool; room service; spa. *In room:* A/C, satellite TV, fridge, minibar.

Marina Phuket ★★ These simple cottages tucked in the jungle above a scenic promontory between Kata and Karon beaches are quite comfortable, and offer four room types. They are the best choice of the many choices nearby. Rates vary according to the view, but all have a jungle bungalow charm, connected by hilly walkways and boardwalks past the lush hillside greenery (keep your eyes peeled for wildlife). It is a hike down to the rocky shore and the swimming isn't great, but they have a good seaside restaurant, On the Rock (see "Where to Dine," later in this chapter), and their in-house **Marina Divers** (ℂ **07633-0272;** www.marinadivers.com) is a PADI International Diving School, which conducts classes, rents equipment, and leads good multiday expeditions. Heavy discounts apply during low season.

47 Karon Rd., Karon Beach, Phuket 83100 (on bluff at south end of Karon Beach Rd.). ℂ **07633-0625.** Fax 07633-0516. www.marinaphuket.com. 92 units. $160–$300 double; $650 grand villa. MC, V. **Amenities:** 2 restaurants; free Internet; pool; room service. *In room:* A/C, satellite TV, minibar.

Mövenpick Resort & Spa ★★ Occupying a huge area right opposite the center of Karon Beach, this Swiss-run, luxury hotel is ideal for those who want everything on-site. Rooms range from gardenview doubles in the main building to plunge-pool villas done out with Balinese-style, thatched roofs, and massive, two-bedroom family suites. Guests have a choice of two attractive pools to swim in or lounge around, as well as several restaurants and bars scattered around the site. There's a play zone for kids and a spa, a fitness room, and PADI diving courses for adults run by the reliable Euro Divers.

509 Patak Rd., Karon Beach, Phuket 83100. ✆ **07639-6139.** Fax 07639-6122. www.moevenpick-phuket.com. 362 units. From 7,900B double; from 10,800B plunge pool villa; 21,000B family suite. AE, MC, V. **Amenities:** 4 restaurants; 3 bars; airport transfer; play zone; fitness room; 2 outdoor pools; spa; 2 tennis courts. *In room:* A/C, satellite TV, Internet; minibar.

Relax Bay (aka Karon Noi)

Le Meridien Phuket Beach Resort ★ ☺ Le Meridien Phuket is tucked away on secluded Relax Bay, just to the north of Karon Beach, with a lovely 549m (1,800-ft.) beach and 16 hectares (40 acres) of tropical greenery. The advantages of a larger resort are its numerous facilities—two big pools, watersports, four tennis courts, a putting green and practice range, and a fine fitness center. The disadvantage is the crowds. The staff is helpful but harried, and can often be found "dug in" behind the front desk like soldiers in a trench readying for the onslaught of the many big groups here. The resort caters to families, though, and there are lots of activities and a good day-care center that kids love. The large complex combines Western and traditional Thai architecture, and 80% of the rooms face the ocean. Each cheerful room has modern furnishings of rattan and teak, as well as a balcony with wooden deck chairs. No fewer than 10 restaurants give you all kinds of dining options.

29 Soi Karon Nui, P.O. Box 277, Relax Bay, Phuket 83000. ✆ **0800/656-469** or 07637-0100. Fax 07634-0479. www.lemeridien.com. 470 units. 6,863B–10,593B double; from 10,656B suite. AE, DC, MC, V. **Amenities:** 10 restaurants; 4 pubs; babysitting; bike rental; excellent children's center; concierge; golf driving range and on-site pro; miniature golf; fitness center; 2 large outdoor pools; room service; smoke-free rooms; spa; outdoor floodlit tennis courts; watersports equipment. *In room:* A/C, satellite TV, fridge, hair dryer, minibar.

Patong Beach

Patong's got it all, but it's all stacked in a heap and glowing with neon. The area pulses with shopping, dining, and nightlife activity late into the evening. In the downtown area, it's all touts catcalling and the beeping horns of passing tuk-tuks wanting to take you for a ride (quite literally); but Patong does have tons of services and some good accommodations (the best find creative ways to make you feel like you're not in Patong).

The downside of Patong's cleanup after the 2004 tsunami for budget travelers is that most places that needed to rebuild have also upgraded their facilities, so there are now virtually no inexpensive hotels left on this beach. If you need to find cheap lodgings, you'll fare better in Phuket Town or on the beaches farther south at Kata and Karon. Of what budget accommodation remains, the following offer reasonable value.

Andatel Patong (41/9 Rat-U-Thit 200 Pee Rd.; ✆ **07629-0480;** www.andatel hotel.com) is one good central option with rooms around 2,000B; reservations are necessary in high season. **Kelly's Hotel** (47/1 Nanai Rd.; ✆ **08703-12154** mobile; www.kellyshotelphuket.com) is a bit of a trek from the beach but has helpful management, a small pool, and free Wi-Fi; room rates are 1,260B to 3,500B.

Amari Coral Beach Resort & Spa ★★ The Coral Beach gets the nod for its wonderful location atop the rocks high above Patong, at the southern tip well away from the din of Patong's congested strip, but close enough for access to the mayhem. The beachfront below is rocky, but it's a good place to search for sea creatures at low tide. The whole resort, from the very grand terraced lobby to the guest rooms and fine pool, is situated toward incredible views of the huge bay below. The rooms have sea-foam tones, cozy balconies, and all the comforts of home. The hotel's Italian restaurant, **La Gritta** (see "Where to Dine," below), is consistently good, and there are Thai and international options too.

2 Meun-ngern Rd., Phuket 83150 (south of and uphill from Patong Beach). ℂ **07634-0106.** Fax 07634-0115. www.amari.com/coralbeach. 197 units. 6,400B–8,100B double; from 10,900B suite. AE, DC, MC, V. **Amenities:** 4 restaurants; lounge; babysitting; fitness center; 2 outdoor pools; room service; spa; 2 outdoor floodlit tennis courts. *In room:* A/C, satellite TV, minibar.

Burasari Resort ★★ Welcoming staff make the Burasari a great choice if you prefer it chic and petite; just don't expect a sea view. This teeny-weeny resort-styled hotel has been squeezed into the middle of a *soi* just off the main drag, and styled as a contemporary hanging-garden resort. The stylish rooms set amid a narrow courtyard of waterfalls, pools, and greenery are delightful, fusing a blend of contemporary and rustic Thai design—however, the basic rooms are rather small. If size matters to you, opt for one of the Mood Collection rooms, which are more spacious. For this convenient location, just a stroll to the beach and madness of the main street, it represents good value.

18/110 Ruamjai Rd., Patong, Phuket 83150. ℂ **07629-2929.** Fax 07629-2930. www.burasari.com. 186 units. 3,910B–5,950B double; 5,950B–8,670B elite; 9,095B mood collection. AE, DC, MC, V. **Amenities:** 2 restaurants; 2 bars; lobby lounge; airport transfer; babysitting; fitness room; 2 outdoor pools; room service; spa. *In room:* A/C, satellite TV, DVD player, fridge, hair dryer, minibar, Wi-Fi.

Impiana Resort ★★ The Impiana is the only high-end property in Patong with direct beachfront access. It was heavily damaged by the 2004 tsunami, shutting its doors for almost a year, but it's now better than ever. Cabanas have been refitted with polished stone floors, vaulted ceilings, and recessed lighting. Each is fashioned in a pleasingly minimal contemporary boutique style. The beach is only steps away, a major selling point, but there is also a beachfront infinity-edge pool if the strip gets too crowded. The location means that you are right in the thick of things, but the rooms are far enough removed from the main drag for privacy.

41 Thaweewongse Rd., Patong Beach, Phuket 83150 (middle of Beach Rd.). ℂ **07634-0138.** Fax 07634-0178. www.impiana.com. 70 units. 10,500B–14,800B double; from 16,600B suite. AE, DC, MC, V. **Amenities:** 2 restaurants; 2 bars; babysitting; concierge; Internet access; pool; room service; spa; water-sports equipment. *In room:* A/C, satellite TV, fridge, hair dryer, minibar.

Novotel Coralia Phuket ★ Set high in the hills on the north end of Patong, the Novotel is a lovely hideaway. It's typical of Accor hotels anywhere: good service and comfortable rooms done in a local style. What sets this apart is the three-tiered pool at the center of the property and its dynamic view of the beach and sea from this towering point. The lobby is under an enormous steep Thai roof, and from its luxury massage pavilions to the many fine-dining choices, guests are constantly wrapped in comfort and reminded of Thai culture.

Kalim Beach Rd., Patong Beach, Phuket 83150 (on the hill north of town, just as the road heads uphill). ℂ **07634-2777.** Fax 07634-2168. www.novotelphuket.com. 215 units. 4,735B–6,735B double; from 8,435B suite. AE, MC, V. **Amenities:** 3 restaurants; 3 bars; babysitting; kids' club; fitness center; Internet access; pool w/multiple tiers; room service; sauna; 2 tennis courts. *In room:* A/C, satellite TV, fridge, minibar.

Kamala Beach

Kamala Beach was hit hard by the 2004 tsunami, but reconstruction was swift and now this attractive beach just a short hop from Patong hosts some of Phuket's most modern and inviting resorts.

Paresa Resort ★★★ Just when you think you've seen the ultimate in luxury resorts, a smart-thinking developer comes up with a dream resort to trump all others. This beautiful complex offers a range of exclusive suites, villas, and residences that are designed with privacy and comfort in mind. The buildings seem to grow out of the hillside on which they are built, and the structures are composed of earth-tone brick-work, solid wood floors, and soaring, pavilion-style ceilings. Rooms are huge and well lit, with modern furnishings, and each has its own private infinity plunge pool. There's also an "energy pool," which apparently recharges and revitalizes the body through use of a rose quartz crystal positioned in the pool's center. Guests have a choice of Italian or Thai restaurants for dining, and the spa features a range of innovative treatments that leave guests in perfect shape to enjoy their recluse. They also offer 5- to 7-night cookery school "retreats" with prices starting at 72,000B for two people.

49 Moo 6, LayiNakalay Rd., Kamala, Phuket 83150. ☎ **07630-2000.** Fax 07630-2001. www.paresa resorts.com. 49 units. 15,569B–30,880B suite; 25,274B villa; 37,780B residence. AE, DC, MC, V. **Amenities:** 2 restaurants; bar; shuttle service; fitness center; pool; room service; spa; library. *In room:* A/C, satellite TV, hair dryer, MP3 docking station.

Surin Beach

Surin Beach is a pretty beach just north of Kamala and about 25km (16 miles) from Phuket Town. The northernmost bay, often called Pansea Beach, has coconut planta-tions, steep slopes leading down to the beach, and small, private coves dominated by two of the most secluded and divine hotels on the island.

Amanpuri ★★★ Amanpuri has long been billed as the address of note for inter-national celebrities; however, by today's standards of luxury and style, some may find it falling short considering the high prices it demands. The teak-filled rooms are certainly masterfully designed in a traditional Thai style, with teak and tile floors, sliding doors, and well chosen antiques. But they are a tad small in the light of the oversized villas now on offer and can be musty in the rainy season; some may also find the ubiquitous concrete decor too stark. These things apart, the Aman style is still omnipresent: The spacious villas are sumptuously decorated and their private pools are all extremely elegant; private *salas* are perfect for romantic dining or secluded sunbathing. The Aman Spa offers six large spa suites, a grand herbal steam bath, and sauna.

Pansea Beach, Phuket 83000 (north end of cove). ☎ **07632-4333.** Fax 07632-4100. www.aman resorts.com. 70 units. $850 garden pavilion; from $1,250 seaview pavilion; from $2,550 2-bedroom villa. AE, DC, MC, V. **Amenities:** 3 restaurants; airport transfer; babysitting; golf course nearby; fitness center; pool; room service; spa; outdoor lighted tennis courts; watersports equipment; Wi-Fi (in public spaces); library. *In room:* A/C, CD/DVD player, fridge, minibar.

The Chedi Phuket ★★★ Like its august sister resort and immediate neighbor (Amanpuri), the Chedi commands an excellent view of the bay and has its own pri-vate stretch of sand. It's perhaps a more kid-friendly option than Amanpuri, plus the site enjoys shady wooden walkways under the trees. From the exotic lobby, with col-umns and a lily pond, to sleek private bungalows, it is one of the most handsome properties on the island. True, the quality comes with a big price tag, but this roman-tic getaway has all the details down pat. Each room is a thatched minisuite with a lovely private sun deck and top amenities. The black-tile swimming pool is large and luxurious. The fine service here caters to the likes of honeymooners and celebrities, and everyone is treated like a VIP. While it may not be as outwardly impressive as its ritzy neighbor, The Chedi is quiet, comfortably informal, and unpretentious, with fine-dining options.

118 Moo 3, Surin Beach Rd., Cherng Talay, Thalang, Phuket 83110 (next to the Amanpuri). © **07632-4017.** Fax 07632-4252. www.chediphukethotel.com. 108 units. From 7,980B hillside cottage; from10,560B superior cottage; from 12,960B deluxe cottage; from 15,600B beach suite; from 14,760B 2-bedroom cottage. AE, DC, MC, V. **Amenities:** 3 restaurants; bar; airport transfer; babysitting; kids' club; outdoor pool; room service; spa; 2 outdoor lighted tennis courts; watersports equipment; library. *In room:* A/C, satellite TV, Internet, minibar.

Bang Tao Bay (Laguna Resort Complex)

Twenty minutes south of the airport and just as far north of Patong Beach on the western shore of Phuket, this isolated area is Phuket's "integrated resort" of five high-end properties that share some of the island's most top-rated facilities. Among them you'll find world-class spas, countless restaurants, and the island's best golf course. The grounds are impressively landscaped, and the hotel properties are scattered among the winding lagoons, all navigable by boat. The best thing about staying here is that you can dine at any of the fine hotel restaurants, connecting by boat or free shuttle, and be charged on one simple bill at whatever resort you're staying at.

Banyan Tree Phuket ★★★ Banyan Tree is possibly Phuket's most famous hide-away for honeymooners, sports stars, and high society. Private villas with walled courtyards, many with private pools or Jacuzzis, are spacious and grand, and lavishly styled in teakwood with outdoor bathtubs. The main pool is truly impressive—a free-form lagoon, landscaped with greenery and rock formations—with a flowing water canal. A small village in itself, the spa provides a wide range of beauty and health treatments in luxurious rooms—you can request a private massage in your room or in outdoor pavilions. The resort can arrange barbecues at your villa, or you can dine at the Tamarind Restaurant, which serves delicious, light, and authentic health food. The Banyan Tree garners many international awards, especially for its Green Initiative and eco-friendly stance.

33/27 Moo 4, Srisoonthorn Rd., Cherngtalay District, Amphur Talang, Phuket 83110 (north end of beach). © **800/591-0439** or 07632-4374. Fax 07632-4375. www.banyantree.com. 150 units. 20,653B–84,633B villas. AE, DC, MC, V. **Amenities:** 6 restaurants; lounge; airport transfer; babysitting; golf course; fitness center; outdoor pool; room service; spa; 3 outdoor lit tennis courts; watersports equipment. *In room:* A/C, satellite TV, fridge; minibar, Wi-Fi.

Dusit Thani Laguna Resort ★★★ ☺ The Dusit hotel group has some fine properties in Thailand, and the Dusit Thani Laguna is no exception. Opt for a deluxe room with a balcony and ocean view and you'll find rates are reasonable. Suites are large and luxurious, while the new oceanfront pool villas are veritable palaces, occupying almost 300 sq. m (3,229 sq. ft.). The hotel offers four excellent restaurants; of note is their quaint Italian restaurant, La Trattoria, serving authentic Italian cuisine in a chic, but laid-back pavilion decorated in cool whites and blues. The well land-scaped gardens have an especially delightful waterfall and an excellent pool. The grounds open onto a wide, white-sand beach flanked by two lagoons. Facilities for families are excellent, with a whole gamut of entertainment including computer games.

390 Srisoonthorn Rd., Cherngtalay District, Phuket 83110 (south end of beach). © **07636-2999.** Fax 07636-2900. www.dusit.com. 254 units. 9,700B–13,700B double; 19,700B suite; 46,000B villa. AE, DC,

MC, V. **Amenities:** 4 restaurants; lounge; airport transfer; babysitting; bike rental; kids' club; pitch and putt on premises and golf course nearby; fitness center; Internet; outdoor pool; room service; spa; outdoor lighted tennis courts; watersports equipment. *In room:* A/C, satellite TV, fridge, minibar.

Sheraton Grande Laguna Phuket ★★ This is a sprawling, luxury campus of two- and three-story pavilions. Rooms are quite large with tiled floors, cozy sitting areas, and large balconies; some bathrooms have sunken tubs. The hotel design carefully traces the natural lines, coves, and jetties of its surrounding lagoon, and the area is quiet and private. A fair-size pool meanders through the resort and there are good amenities for kids of all ages, from a kids' club (called VIK, or Very Important Kids) to beach games and sailboat rental at the lagoon. With its professionalism and an enormous range of outlets, plus casual eateries and cafes (including a good bakery), the Sheraton is a fine, familiar choice.

10 Moo 4, Srisoonthorn Rd., Cherng Talay, Talang, Phuket 83110. ✆ **07632-4101.** Fax 07632-4108. www. starwoodhotels.com. 419 units. $267–$373 double; from $528 villa. AE, DC, MC, V. **Amenities:** 6 restaurants; bar and lounge; airport transfer; babysitting; bike rental; kids' club; golf course nearby; fitness center; free-form outdoor pool; room service; spa; 2 outdoor lighted tennis courts; watersports equipment/rentals. *In room:* A/C, satellite TV, fridge, hair dryer, minibar, Wi-Fi.

Layan Beach

Phuket Pavilions ★★ "No tan lines" is the catchphrase at this intimate escape, by which guests should understand that they can enjoy total privacy within the grounds of their spacious pool villa. The resort is situated on a hill just north of the Laguna complex, and while it's a bit of a trek from the beach, most guests will settle for lounging around the luxurious pavilions. Furnishings are supermodern and comfortable, and each pavilion has its private pool within stepping distance of the bedroom, as well as fantastic views out to sea. Buggies are on hand to run guests to the Plantation Club restaurant or 360° Lookout bar, and spa treatments are offered in specially constructed rooms beside each private pool.

31/1 Moo 6, Cherng Talay, Phuket 83110. ✆ **07631-7600.** Fax 07631-7601. www.thepavilionsresorts.com. 49 units. 15,000B–18,000B pool villa; 52,250B 3-bedroom pool villa. AE, MC, V. **Amenities:** Restaurant; bar; spa service; library. *In room:* A/C, satellite TV/DVD player, kitchenette, Wi-Fi.

Nai Yang Beach

Hat Nai Yang National Park is a long stretch of shoreline peeking out from underneath a dense forest of palms, casuarina, and other indigenous flora. It's become an area known for the yearly release of baby turtles into the wild. This area is good if you want to leave the crowds behind, but be warned that it is isolated and quite rustic. For accommodations, there are two top-line options. The secluded **Adamas Resort & Spa** (✆ **07631-6000;** www.adamasresortspa.com) has luxury rooms from 5,800B. The **Indigo Pearl** (✆ **07632-7006;** www.indigo-pearl.com) also has a range of luxurious suites, villas, and pool pavilions, with rates starting at 10,800B.

Mai Khao Beach

Mai Khao is a marvelous, endless beach on the northwestern shore near the airport. It's where sea turtles lay their eggs during March; efforts are ongoing to protect the breeding grounds, since turtle eggs are a local delicacy.

JW Marriott Resort & Spa ★★★ Relaxation. If ever a resort fully embodied this ethos, it is the Marriott. The resort is set on a desolate and wind-swept stretch of Mai Khao Beach, and the sounds of birds and flowing water follow you wherever you step. Comfortable spots to curl up and read are around every corner, from daybeds on stairwell landings to reading nooks in each beautifully appointed room. There are no services outside of the hotel, and it is a 30-minute drive to Phuket Town or the southern beaches—there are regular shuttles—but the resort facilities are so complete that guests needn't leave. Rooms are private getaways with open-plan bathrooms and the aforementioned reading corner, with Thai cushions and lovely balconies that give way to sumptuous gardens: a hidden Eden. Enjoy the very professional service, fine spa treatments, sports, activities, and dining.

Mai Khao, Talang, Phuket 83110. © **07633-8000.** Fax 07634-8348. www.marriott.com. 265 units. 9,800B–11,900B deluxe double; from 17,800B suite. AE, DC, MC, V. **Amenities:** 6 restaurants; 3 bars; babysitting; complimentary bikes; children's center and kids' club; teen activity center w/computers; concierge; executive-level rooms; top-notch fitness center w/lots of activities; Jacuzzi; 3 outdoor pools; room service; sauna; smoke-free rooms; extensive spa; 2 tennis courts; watersports equipment (Hobie Cat and runabouts). *In room:* A/C, satellite TV w/in-house movies, fridge, hair dryer, minibar.

WHERE TO DINE

From tip to tip, north to south, it's more than a 1-hour drive on Phuket, but hired tuk-tuks, hotel transport, or even self-drive vehicles mean that for dining and nightlife, you can choose from any establishments on the island. The beach areas in the west are chockablock with small storefront eateries, while Patong features everything from the obligatory McDonald's and Starbucks to designer sushi chains.

Phuket Town

Though it's a long ride from the west-coast beach areas, a night out in Phuket Town is worth it for some fine meals and a taste of local culture.

Blue Elephant ★★★ 📷 THAI   Most people like to splurge on a meal sometime during their vacation, and the new branch of the Blue Elephant in Phuket Town offers the perfect opportunity. The restaurant is housed in a splendid Sino-Portuguese mansion, a former governor's residence that provides the perfect setting for a culinary treat. Whether you opt for the fresh lime sea bass, the *tom yam koong* or mussaman lamb, you'll find yourself smiling as the tastes explode in your mouth. Besides classic Thai dishes, you'll find some fusion and many Indian-influenced choices on the menu. The Royal Thai Banquet Set Menu, at 1,650B, is an excellent way to get a taste of several dishes. As at their Bangkok branch, there's a highly regarded cookery school based here.

96 Krabi Rd., Tambon Talad Neua, Phuket 83000. © **07635-4355-7.** Reservations recommended. Main courses 560B–680B. AE, DC, MC, V. Daily 11:30am–2:30pm and 6:30–10:30pm.

Ka Jok See ★★ 🍴 THAI   A truly special find, Ka Jok See is a smart and intimate European-styled venue set in an old Sino-Portuguese house. This classy Thai restaurant run by Khun Lek has been here for years and hides mysteriously behind a facade dripping with ivy. Patronized by well heeled local professionals, it's so well known there is no sign. Though its name means stained glass, the decor opts for ceilings of huge wooden beams, giant plants, and candlelight instead of painted glass. A great selection of music sets the stage for a romantic evening, one that's well worth a venture from the beach.

26 Takua Pa Rd., Phuket Town (a short walk from central Rasada Rd.). © **07621-7903.** Reservations recommended. Main courses 350B. MC, V. Tues–Sat 6:30–10:30pm.

Kata & Karon Beaches

The busy road between Kata and Karon (as well as the many side streets) is packed with small cafes and restaurants serving affordable Thai and Western food. Stop by **Euro Deli** (58/60 Karon Rd.; © **07628-6265**) for a good sandwich; it's open from 10am to 11pm.

The Boathouse ★★★ THAI/INTERNATIONAL   So legendary is the Thai and Western cuisine at the Boathouse that the inn where it resides (see **Mom Tri's Boathouse and Villa Royale** in "Where to Stay," earlier in this section) offers popular vacation packages for visitors who wish to come and take lessons from its chef. A large bar and separate dining area sport nautical touches, and through huge picture windows or from the terrace diners can watch the sun set over the watery horizon. The cuisine combines the best of East and West and utilizes only the finest ingredients. If you're in the mood for the works, the Phuket lobster is one of the most expensive dishes on the menu, but is worth every baht. The Boathouse also has an excellent selection of international wines—more than 800 labels. And if that doesn't tickle your taste buds, **Mom Tri's Kitchen,** another upscale venture from the folks at the Boathouse, is just up the hill and serves similar fine cuisine from its luxury perch. *Bon appétit.*

At the Boathouse Inn, Kata Beach. ✆ **07633-0015.** www.momtriphuket.com. Reservations recommended during peak season. Main courses 550B–1,600B; seafood at market prices. AE, DC, MC, V. Daily 6:30am–11pm. No children after 8pm.

On the Rock   Part of the Marina Phuket Resort (see "Where to Stay," earlier in this section), this unassuming little restaurant serves excellent Thai meals from a scenic deck high above the south end of Karon Beach. Laid-back and charmingly rustic, it offers some of the best views of the beach below. Try the seafood basket, a medley of grilled and fried ocean critters. There are steaks and French entrees such as chicken *cordon bleu,* but stick with the better Thai dishes for a great meal in a great atmosphere.

47 Karon Rd., Karon Beach (on bluff at south end of Karon Beach Rd.). ✆ **07633-0625.** Fax 07633-0516. www.marinaphuket.com. Reservations necessary. Main courses 250B–800B. AE, MC, V. Daily 8am–11pm.

Ratri Jazztaurant ★★ THAI   Perched high at the top of a precipitous hill slope, Ratri is worth the (hideously steep) 1km (2/3-mile) climb for their classic Thai dishes, most of which pack an explosively spicy punch. There's an enthusiastic live jazz band that plays late into the night. The music is great, but if you are looking forward to some dinnertime conversation, it makes that hard (you should go before sunset, in that case). There's a full wine cellar and cigar bar (so nonsmokers beware). The somewhat surly service is the only drawback.

Patak Rd., Kata Hill (behind Big One convenience store). ✆ **07633-3538.** www.ratrijazztaurant.com. Main courses 230B–580B. MC, V. Daily 3pm–late; live band 8:30pm–late.

Patong Beach

Some of the best seafood dining in busy Patong doesn't come from any upscale restaurant, but from the small **food stalls** at the north end of Patong along busy Rat-U-Thit Road. It's really just a collection of outdoor restaurants sharing a large open-air dining area. Visitors who approach or show any interest will be attacked with menus and implored to choose from among the restaurants. It can be a bit off-putting, but just pick a menu or a kind face (the others will disperse) and order from a wide selection of fresh seafood, prepared as you like it. It's good food at a fraction of restaurant prices.

Baan Rim Pa ★★★ THAI   In a beautiful Thai-style teak house, Baan Rim Pa offers dining in a romantic indoor setting or from outdoor terraces with gorgeous views of the bay. Among high-end travelers, the restaurant has long been one of the most popular stops on the island, so be sure to reserve your table early. The Thai cuisine features seafood, plus a variety of other meat and vegetable dishes, including a rich duck curry and a sweet honey chicken dish. The seafood basket is a fantastic assortment of prawns, mussels, squid, and crab. The owner also runs two other restaurants on the cliffside next to Baan Rim Pa: **Da Maurizio** (✆ 07634-4079) and **Joe's Downstairs** (✆ 07661-8245).

223 Prabaramee Rd., on the cliffs just north of Patong Beach. ✆ **07634-0789**. www.baanrimpa.com. Reservations necessary. Main courses 370B–1,750B. AE, DC, MC, V. Daily noon–midnight.

La Gritta ★ ITALIAN   Similar to the Amari chain's other fine Italian restaurants of the same name, this one is notable for its views of Patong Beach below—the best in town, really. It's classic northern Italian cuisine: antipasti, salads, soups, grilled entrees, and pastas accompanied by an extensive wine list. The cooks use all fresh ingredients and serve a colorful antipasti plate that makes a great shared appetizer. **Note:** For a romantic evening, La Gritta is best visited after 8pm, unless your idea of romantic is listening to the lobby band rip through Ricky Martin's *oeuvre*.

At the Amari Coral Beach Resort, 2 Meun-ngern Rd., south of and uphill from Patong Beach. ✆ **07634-0106**. Main courses 330B–850B. AE, MC, V. Daily 11am–midnight.

Pan Yaah THAI   Here is a good escape from busy Patong and some real Thai home cooking. The restaurant is a wooden deck overlooking the bay some 2km (1¼ miles) north of central Patong, with perhaps the best view in town. The menu is classic Thai, with some one-dish meals like fried rice or noodles, but best enjoyed with friends sharing a number of courses, such as spicy *tom yam* soup with prawns, stir-fried dishes, and whole fish cooked to order. Prices are reasonable and service is friendly and laid-back.

249 Prabaramee Rd., Patong (2km/1¼ miles north of Patong along the coast). ✆ **07634-4473**. Main courses 200B–380B. MC, V. Daily 11am–11pm.

Sala Bua ★ THAI   The lunch menu here features light Thai dishes, plus Western sandwiches and burgers. More pricey evening fare includes southern Thai-style seafood favorites—local Phuket lobster, huge juicy tiger prawns, and fresh fish steaks in a variety of local preparations—expensive, but a good value. The imported New Zealand tenderloin is award-winning. For dessert, try the sticky-rice sushi rolls with sweet coconut milk and mango. Sala Bua is a far more intimate option than the crowded seafood joints across the street.

At the Impiana Phuket Resort, 94 Thaweewong Rd., Patong Beach (at the north end of the beach). ✆ **07634-0138**. Reservations recommended on weekends. Main courses 485B–2,250B. AE, DC, MC, V. Daily 6am–midnight.

Bang Tao Bay (Laguna Resort Complex)

The many hotel restaurants of the five-star properties in the Laguna Resort Complex could fill a small guidebook on their own. You can't go too wrong in any of the hotels, really, and here, more than anywhere, it's a question of getting what you pay for; from superluxurious fine dining to laid-back grills or snack corners, everything's covered. One restaurant just outside the complex is worth mentioning, however—it's where all the hotel managers eat when they get out of work.

Tatonka ★★ INTERNATIONAL   The food at Tatonka is billed as "globe-trotter cuisine," and dining here is indeed a foray into the realm of a culinary nomad, Harold Schwarz. "Fusion" is a battered term in restaurant parlance, but Harold's dishes are a creative melding of Mediterranean, Pan-American, and Asian influence. The emphasis is on variety: Selections from the tapas menu include vegetable quesadillas, California crab cakes, stuffed calamari cups, wonton wafers, and rolls. The menu is updated frequently and depends on what is fresh that day, but may feature anything from Peking duck to pizza, gazpacho to Thai *tom yum koong* (hot-and-sour soup with shrimp). Ask what's good and enjoy.

382/19 Moo 1, Srisoonthorn Rd., Cherngtalay (at the entrance of the Laguna Resort Complex in Bangtao Bay). ℭ **07632-4349.** www.phuket.com/tatonka. Main courses 275B–560B. MC, V. Thurs–Tues 6–10:30pm.

WHAT TO SEE & DO

There's lots to do on Phuket. Beach and outdoor activities top the list, and you'll find the beachfront areas full of tour operators, each vying for your business and offering similar trips (or copycat tours). Opportunities abound to visit the island's rustic bays, explore the many beaches, and take day trips to the jungle interior or to scenic Phang Nga Bay to the north.

If Phuket is your only destination in Thailand, you'll certainly want to get to some of the small rural temples and to **Phuket Town,** though the island's sights pale in comparison to culturally rich places such as Bangkok or Chiang Mai. It's certainly worth taking a stroll around the tastefully restored **Old Town** in the center of Phuket Town, where the Sino-Portuguese architecture is particularly attractive since the ugly electric cables that once spoiled the view have gone underground. Thalang and Dibuk Roads have the best examples.

There are a few Buddhist temples around the island that are quite notable. The most famous one among Thai visitors is **Wat Chalong,** on the Bypass Road, about 8km (5 miles) south of Phuket Town. Chalong was the first resort on Phuket, back when the Thais first started coming to the island for vacations, and the temple still remains a center of Buddhist worship, bursting into life during Buddhist holy days. Just up the road from here is the newly completed **Big Buddha,** a 45m (148-ft.) statue of a sitting Buddha, perched on top of a hill with some of the island's best views. Also worth visiting is **Wat Phra Thong,** along Hwy. 402 in Thalang, just south of the airport—it's the most unique temple on the island, famed for its half-buried Buddha (only head and shoulders are aboveground). On the main road south of Thalang stands the **Heroines Monument,** which commemorates two local women who defended the island against a Burmese invasion in 1785.

Sea gypsies, the indigenous people of the southern islands, are fast disappearing from Phuket as commercial-fishing interests and shoreline development continue to push them out of their traditional environment. Gypsy villages are simple: floating shacks and longtail boats. Visits to some of the larger settlements in Phang Nga Bay are included in many island day trips, though it's more like a trip to the zoo than a meaningful cultural encounter.

For a view of gorgeous **Phang Nga Bay,** book a trip aboard the *June Bahtra,* a restored Chinese sailing junk, to cruise the islands. Full-day trips include lunch and hotel transfers. Adults pay 3,700B, not including alcoholic beverages. Contact **Asian Oasis,** 128/3 Chalermprakiat Rd., Patong (ℭ **07637-6192;** www.asian-oasis.com), to book. For a different perspective of Phang Nga Bay, see "Sea Kayaking" under "Outdoor Activities," below.

Sirinath National Park, 90 sq. km (35 sq. miles) of protected land in the northwest corner of the island, offers a peaceful retreat from the rest of Phuket's tourism madness that includes the beaches of Mai Khao, Nai Thon, and Nai Yang. There are two fantastic reasons to make the journey out to the park. The first is for Phuket's largest coral reef in shallow water, only 460m (1,500 ft.) from the shore. The second is for the slim chance of spotting a green, hawksbill, or critically endangered giant leatherback turtle, which occasionally nest here in December and January. Park headquarters is a very short hop from Phuket Airport off Hwy. 402.

The **Gibbon Rehabilitation Project** ★★ (© **07626-0492**; www.gibbon project.org), off Hwy. 4027 at the Bang Pae waterfall in the northeastern corner of the island, cares for mistreated gibbons, placing them in more caring and natural surroundings (among other gibbons). Volunteer guides offer tours. Open daily from 9am to 4:30pm; it's located within the **Khao Phra Taew Wildlife Sanctuary,** and donations for the project are appreciated.

At **Butterfly Garden & Insect World** (71/6 Moo 5, Yaowarat Rd.; © **07621-0861;** www.phuketbutterfly.com), you get a crash course in the history and life cycles of insects followed by a walk through an enclosed garden housing thousands of butterflies bred on the premises. Don't forget your camera. Open daily from 9am to 5pm. Admission is 300B for adults and 150B for children 4 to 10.

OUTDOOR ACTIVITIES

Most of the noisier watersports activities are concentrated along Patong Beach—so swimmers can enjoy most of the other beaches without the buzz of a jet ski or powerboat. **Jet skis** are technically illegal, but can still be rented for 15 minutes at about 800B. A 10-minute **parasailing** ride is around 1,000B, and you can rent outboard runabouts by the hour or the day. **Hobie Cats** go for 700B per hour, **windsurfing** boards for 250B per hour. There are no specific offices to organize these activities, just small operators with hand-painted signs at the beaches, and prices are negotiable.

BUNGEE JUMPING The **Jungle Bungy Jump** awaits! If you have the nerve to jump out 50m (164 ft.) over the water, call the "bungee hot line" at © **07632-1351** (phuketbungy.com). It's in Kathu, near Patong. The charge is 2,100B per jump. It has a 100% safety record—knock wood.

GOLF There are some fine courses on Phuket; golf junkets bring vacationing expats and international tourists alike.

o **Laguna Phuket,** 34 Moo 4, Srisoonthorn Rd., at the Laguna Resort Complex on Bang Tao Bay (© **07627-0991;** fax 07627-0992; www.lagunaphuketgolf.com), is the best option, a par-71 resort course (greens fees: 3,900B, plus caddie fee; guests of the Laguna Resort Complex receive a discount).

o **Blue Canyon Country Club,** 165 Moo 1, Thepkasattri Rd., near the airport (© **07632-8088;** fax 07632-8068; www.bluecanyonclub.com), has two world-class tracks, the Lakes and Canyon courses—the latter host to the Johnnie Walker Classic in 1994 and 1998, won by Tiger Woods (greens fees: 4,000B Lakes course, 5,600B Canyon course).

o **Phuket Country Club,** 80/1 Moo 7, Vichitsongkram Rd., west of Phuket Town (© **07631-9200;** fax 07631-9206; www.phuketcountryclub.com), an older course that dates from 1989, has beautiful greens and fairways, plus a giant lake (greens fees: 3,500B).

HORSEBACK RIDING A romantic and charming way to see Phuket's jungles and beaches is on horseback. **Phuket Riding Club,** 95 Viset Rd., Chaweng Bay (© **07628-8213;** www.phuketridingclub.com), and **Phuket Laguna Riding Club,** 394 Moo 1, Bangthao Beach (© **07632-4199**), welcome riders of all ages and experience levels and can provide instruction for beginners and children. Prices start at 800B per hour.

SCUBA DIVING   With access to the nearby **Similan Islands,** Phuket is a popular scuba destination and one of the most affordable (and safe) places to get certified. There are three decompression chambers on the island and a strong dive community. The problem is, there are around 40 companies, and all can arrange day trips to the nearby coral wall and wrecks, as well as overnight or long-term excursions to the Similan Islands (as well as PADI courses, Divemaster courses, 1-day introductory lessons, and open-water certification). Open-water courses can cost as little as 8,500B.

Many storefront operations are just consolidators for other companies, so ask if they have their own boats and whether they're PADI certified. Also check on the ratio of divers to instructor or Divemaster; anything more than five to one is not acceptable, and it should be more like two to one for beginner courses. Below are a few choices:

○ **Scuba Cat** (94 Thaweewong Rd., Patong Beach; ℰ **07629-3121;** www.scuba cat.com) has got the best thing going on Phuket. With more than 10 years of experience, a large expat staff, and its own fleet of boats, it's a very professional outfit offering the full range of day trips and luxury live-aboards for anyone from beginner to expert (and at competitive prices). You can't miss the small practice pool in front of its beachside Patong office (in fact, you have to cross a small bridge to get in the place). The staff is very helpful and welcoming.

○ **Dive Asia** (main office: 24 Karon Rd., Kata Beach; ℰ **07633-0598;** fax 07628-4033; www.diveasia.com) is another reputable firm on Phuket. The dive packages include live-aboard trips to the Similan Islands and 4-day PADI certification courses, in addition to full-day dives around Phuket.

○ **Sea Bees Diving** (Chalong pier; ℰ **07638-1765;** fax 07628-0467; www.sea-bees. com) is also a good outfit offering day trips from 3,750B for divers, 2,400B for nondivers.

SEA KAYAKING   **Phang Nga Bay** ★★, a 1½-hour drive north of Phuket (3 hr. by boat), is a great location for day trips by sea kayak. The scenery is stunning, with limestone karst towers jutting precariously from the water's surface, creating more than 120 small islands. These craggy rock formations (one of them was the backdrop for the James Bond classic *The Man with the Golden Gun*) look straight out of a Chinese scroll painting. Sea kayaks are perfect for inching your way into the many breathtaking caves and chambers that hide beneath the jagged cliffs. All tours include the hour-plus rides to and from Phang Nga, the cruise to the island area, paddle guide, kayak, and lunch. The company that pioneered the cave trips is **Sea Canoe** (125/461 Baan Tung Ka–Baan Sapam Rd.; ℰ **07652-8839;** fax 07652-8841; www. seacanoe.net). It's much imitated, but still the best choice for day trips through island caves to central lagoons (called *hongs*). The standard day trip runs 3,200B per person. It's touristy, you'll be sitting two to a kayak, and you'll be paddled by a guide going in and out of the caves, unless you'd rather paddle alone, in which case it's 2,950B. The scenery is great and the caves are stunning. It also offers multiday and sunset dinner trips.

The folks at **Paddle Asia** (18/58 Thanon Rasdanusorn; ℰ/fax **07624-1519;** www.paddleasia.com) make Phuket their home and do trips throughout the region, with a focus more on custom adventure travel, not day junkets. It has great options for anyone from beginner to expert. On any trip, you'll get to paddle real decked kayaks, not inflatables. A highlight is its trip to Khao Sok National Park (p. 101), a

3-day adventure in which you'll see lots of monkeys and birds. In Phuket, it can arrange either offshore paddling to outlying islands or custom adventures.

ELEPHANT TREKKING   Fun trips into Phuket's interior include **elephant trekking,** a perennial favorite for children, and a great time for adults too. Elephants are not indigenous to Phuket, so what you get here is more or less a pony ride, but arguments over captive elephant-tour programs aside, the kids dig it (and the elephants do better here than when paraded around city streets for owners to collect coins). **Siam Safari Nature Tours** (45 Chaofa Rd., Chalong; ℂ **07628-0116;** www.siamsafari.com) coordinates daily treks on elephants, Land Rovers, river rafts, and traditional wooden junks. The four-in-one half-day safari is a 6-hour trip that includes elephant trekking through jungles to rubber estates, jeep touring to see local wildlife, watching trained monkeys pick coconuts, and a relaxing cruise on a wooden junk to Chalong Bay. A full-day tour includes canoeing and elephant trekking in Khao Sok National Park, with a Thai lunch.

YACHTING   The crystal-blue waters of the Andaman Sea near Phuket are an old salt's dream. Every December, Phuket hosts the increasingly popular **King's Cup Regatta,** in which around 100 international racing yachts compete. For more information, check out www.kingscup.com.

There are lots of options for chartering yachts in Phuket. For details, contact **Asia Marine** (c/o Phuket Boat Lagoon, 20/8 Thepkasattri Rd., Tambon Ko Kaew, Phuket 830; ℂ **07623-9111;** www.asia-marine.net).

THE SPA SCENE ★★★

If you've come to Phuket to escape and relax, there's no better way to accomplish your goal than to visit one of the island's spas. Even the smallest resort now offers full spa services (of varying quality), and you can find good, affordable massage along any beach and in storefronts in the main tourist areas.

For luxury treatments, one of the most famous and exclusive facilities here is the **Banyan Tree Spa** (p. 73; ℂ **07632-4374** for reservations; www.banyantreespa. com). In secluded garden pavilions, you'll be treated regally and can choose from many types of massage, body and facial treatments, or health and beauty programs. Expect to pay for the luxury—figure at least 6,000B per individual treatment.

In Phuket Town, the **Cher Aim Spa Village** (16 Wichitsongkram Rd.; ℂ **07624-9670;** www.cheraimspavillage.com) offers a wide variety of treatments ranging from massage to seaweed and mud wraps, all in a relaxing garden setting. Highly recommended.

Another affordable place is the **Body & Mind Day Spa** (558/7–12 Patak Rd., Karon Beach; ℂ **07639-8274;** www.body-mindspa.com), where a soothing 1-hour foot massage costs 600B.

SHOPPING

Patong Beach is the center of handicrafts and souvenir shopping on Phuket; the main streets and small *sois* are chockablock with storefront tailors, leather shops, jewelers, and ready-to-wear clothing boutiques. Vendors line the sidewalks, selling everything from batik clothing, T-shirts, and pirated CDs to local arts, northern-hill-tribe handicrafts, silver, and souvenir trinkets. *Be warned:* Everywhere in Patong, they have the nasty habit of hassling passersby. Prices are a bit inflated, but a bit of haggling gets you the same cool goods that you'd otherwise find only in the far north or in Bangkok.

PHUKET AFTER DARK

From the huge billboards and glossy brochures, **Phuket FantaSea ★★** (© 07638-5111 for reservations; www.phuket-fantasea.com), the island's premier theme attraction, could be touristy and ridiculous—it is. But it's fun in the same way Atlantic City can be fun. This big theme park has a festival village lined with glitzy shops, games, entertainment, and snacks. A wander here will keep you busy until the show starts. There's a huge buffet in the palatial Golden Kinaree Restaurant; afterward, visitors proceed to the Palace of the Elephants for the show. The in-your-face advertising for the place alone is enough to put you off (witness the trucks driving around town with loudspeakers and posters plastered on anything flat), but it's worth a trip. Many places include transport in the price of the ticket. The show is at Kamala Beach, north of Patong, on the coastal road. The stage is dark on Thursdays. The park opens at 5:30pm, the buffet begins at 6:30pm, and the show is at 9pm. Tickets for the show are 1,500B, while dinner and transfer fees usually add 400B for adults and 200B for children. Ask about the rates at any hotel concierge, as they often have deals.

Dino Park Mini Golf (© 07633-0625; www.dinopark.com) is for kids young and old. There's golf for the kids, and a restaurant and bar for mom and dad. It's located on the south of Karon Beach, next to the Marina Phuket Resort.

Phuket's resident cabaret troupe can be found at **Simon Cabaret,** 8 Sirirach Rd., Patong Beach (© 07634-2011; www.phuket-simoncabaret.com). There are shows at 7:30 and 9:30pm nightly for 800B adults, 600B kids; it's on the south end of Patong. It's a featured spot on every planned tour agenda, so it draws busloads. The glitzy transsexual show caters mostly to Asian tourists—the lip-sync numbers of popular Asian pop songs keep the audience roaring. It can be a lot of fun. In between the comedy are dance numbers with pretty impressive sets and costumes; performers are available for photos after the show.

You can catch Thai boxing at **Patong Boxing Stadium** (2/59 Sai Nam Yen Rd., Patong; © 07634-5578; www.boxingstadiumpatong.com). Bouts start every Monday and Thursday night at 9pm and go on until late. Fight-night info is all over town, and admission is 1,300B to 1,500B.

Patong nightlife is wild. Lit up like a little Las Vegas, the beach town hops every night of the week. Shops and restaurants stay open late, and tourists choose from an array of bars, nightclubs, karaoke lounges, snooker halls, massage parlors, go-go bars, and dance shows a la Bangkok's Patpong or the streets of Pattaya. Bangla Road, perpendicular to the beach road on the north end of Patong, is the little red-light district in town, where the hostess girls line up and reel in passersby (it goes something like: "Hey, handsome man, where you go?"). It's pretty seedy, but it's a funny scene. A few bars about halfway down the road are always packed for views of the informal tabletop dancing. The curvaceous, costumed dancers are mostly transsexuals. (*Important:* No photos.)

Molly Malone's (© 07629-2771) and **Scruffy Murphy's** (© 07629-2590), both along the main strip in Patong, are the obligatory beachside Irish pubs. Good

The Best Sunset

On a good day, from the cliffs atop Promthep Cape on the southern tip of the Island, the view of the sky as it changes colors at sunset—from gold to scarlet and purple—can compete with the best fireworks. The place isn't exactly a secret, so get here half an hour before sundown for a good viewing spot.

atmosphere, good service, good pints. Both are fine places to start the night, end the night, or spend the whole night (they'll wake you up at closing time). There are also a few discos in town; just ask around to find out what's going on.

Krabi

814km (506 miles) S of Bangkok, 211km (131 miles) SW of Surat Thani, 165km (103 miles) E of Phuket, 42km (26 miles) E of Ko Phi Phi

Krabi is a popular alternative to busy Phuket. Ferries and minivans connect the town of Krabi (few stay here) to the nearby beach and tourist strip at **Ao Nang** and to the farther-flung beaches: **Railay Beach ★★**, the famed "climbers' beach" with its stunning karst towers, is accessed by boat, while **Khlong Muang Beach,** only recently developed, is north of Ao Nang. Many travelers heading for **Ko Phi Phi** and **Ko Lanta** also set out from Krabi port.

GETTING THERE

There are boat and bus connections between Krabi and Phuket, as well as connections via Surat Thani with the east-coast islands of Ko Samui and Ko Pha Ngan.

BY PLANE   **Thai Airways** (✆ **02545-3691**) flies at least twice daily from Bangkok, as does **Bangkok Airways** (✆ **02270-6699**), which also has flights to Ko Samui and Pattaya. Budget carrier **Air Asia** (✆ **02515-9999**) has daily connections to both Bangkok and Kuala Lumpur. From the airport, you can catch a shuttle bus to town for 100B. Taxis start at 350B.

BY BUS   Two air-conditioned VIP (top-line buses with plenty of legroom and reclining seats) 24-seater buses leave daily from Bangkok's **Southern Bus Terminal** (✆ **02894-6122;** trip time: 12 hr.; 1,100B to Krabi Town). Frequently scheduled air-conditioned minibuses leave daily from Surat Thani to Krabi (trip time: 2¾ hr.; 180B). Three air-conditioned minibuses leave daily from Phuket Town to Krabi (trip time: 3½ hr.; 250B).

BY BOAT   Daily ferries leave from Ko Phi Phi to Krabi (trip time: 1½ hr.; 150B), as well as from Ko Lanta (trip time: 2½ hr.; 170B).

GETTING AROUND

Krabi Town is the commercial hub in the area, but few stay here. There is frequent *songtaew* service between Krabi Town and Ao Nang Beach; just flag down a white pickup (trip time: 45 min.; 50B). **Railay Beach** is not on an island, but is cut off by its high cliffs from the mainland and is reachable only by boat from the pier in Krabi Town (45 min.) or from the beach at Ao Nang, at the small pavilion across from the Prah Nang Inn (20 min.). **Khlong Muang Beach** is some 25km (16 miles) from Krabi Town.

[FastFACTS] KRABI

Most services in Krabi Town are on Utarakit Road, paralleling the waterfront (to the right as you board the ferry). Here you'll find the **TAT Office** (✆ **07562-2163**) and a number of **banks** with ATM service. The **post office** and **police station** (✆ **07563-7208**) are south on Utarakit Road, to the left as you leave the pier. There are also a few banks in Ao Nang, near the Phra Nang Inn.

WHERE TO STAY & DINE

Outside of the resorts, your dining options are just small storefront eateries and tourist cafes. In Ao Nang, try **Sala Bua and Lo Spuntino** for a great choice of Thai or Italian fare, or stop in any of the small beachside eateries. In Railay, there are lots of little beachside bars and restaurants as well.

Railay Beach

Sand Sea Resort (℡ 07581-9463; www.krabisandsea.com), just next to Rayavadee, is typical of the good midrange bungalows here, with clean air-conditioned rooms from 3,550B. **Diamond Cave Resort** (℡ 07562-2589; www.diamondcave-railay.com), at the north end of Railay Beach, has small private bungalows with a fan from 2,400B. If you're looking for hotel-style accommodations, the **Railay Princess Resort & Spa** (℡ 07562-2570) has tidy rooms overlooking the pool for 3,199B.

Rayavadee ★★★   Rayavadee is one of the finest resorts in Thailand. Handsome two-story rounded pavilions are large and luxurious, offering every modern convenience and utmost privacy; the first-floor sitting areas have a central hanging lounger with cushions, while second-story bedrooms are all silk and teak. Private bathrooms come complete with Jacuzzi tubs and luxury products. The resort grounds lie at the base of towering cliffs on the island's most choice piece of property, a triangle of land in which each point accesses the beach. It all comes with an over-the-top price tag, though—and the sun sets the same for the bungalow dwellers next door. Still, everything at Rayavadee *is* excellent, and from your airport pickup and private boat transfer to great dining and professional service, you'll get the regal treatment.

214 Moo 2, Tambol Ao Nang, Amphur Muang, Krabi 81000 (30 min. northwest of Krabi Town by longtail boat or 70 min. from Phuket via the resort's own launch). ℡ **07562-0740.** Fax 07562-0630. www.rayavadee.com. 102 units. 22,300B deluxe pavilion; 28,300B hydropool pavilion; 35,000B family pavilion; from 72,000B specialty villa. AE, DC, MC, V. **Amenities:** 4 restaurants; lounge; concierge; fitness center; Jacuzzi; outdoor pool w/children's pool, room service; sauna; spa; outdoor floodlit tennis courts; watersports equipment and scuba center; cooking school; library. *In room:* A/C, satellite TV, fridge, minibar.

Ao Nang Beach

Centara Grand Beach Resort & Villas Krabi   Accessible only by boat, this resort sits on its own private beach (Pai Plong Bay), which is over 500m (1,640 ft.) long, and has views of limestone outcrops and gorgeous white sands. There are many types of rooms, but all are big and airy and feature ample terraces for lounging. It's certainly away from it all, but provides all the facilities guests might need, including daily newspapers and Wi-Fi access. There's a complimentary boat to shuttle guests to the mainland if they want to go exploring.

396-396/1 Moo 2, Ao Nang. ℡ **07563-7789.** Fax 07563-7800. www.centarahotelsresorts.com. 192 units. 13,000B–16,000B double; 32,000B–55,000B villa. AE, DC, MC, V. **Amenities:** 4 restaurants; bar; fitness center; pools; room service; spa; watersports and dive center; Wi-Fi. *In room:* A/C, flatscreen TV, minibar.

Khlong Muang Beach

Sofitel Krabi Phokeethra   Occupying a prime spot on Khlong Muang Beach, this Sofitel property is a perfect blend of Western luxury and authentic Thai atmosphere. The elegant colonial design and spacious rooms give the place an aura of sophistication and relaxation. It boasts a 7,000-sq.-m (75,350-sq.-ft.) pool, a wide range of dining and drinking choices, a fitness center, and great spa. Rooms range between 45 sq. m and 150 sq. m (484 sq. ft. and 1,615 sq. ft.) and feature teakwood floors and comfortable furnishings.

Klong Muang Beach, Nong Talay, Krabi 81000 (15km/9⅓ miles north of Ao Nang, 26km/16 miles from Krabi Town). © **07562-7800.** Fax 07562-7899. www.sofitel.com. 276 units. $150–$215 double; $273–$606 suites. AE, DC, MC, V. **Amenities:** 3 restaurants; 5 bars; children's playground; fitness center; outdoor pool; spa; tennis courts. *In room:* A/C, satellite TV, fridge.

WHAT TO SEE & DO

Most head straight for the beaches to relax and play. Popular activities are day boat trips, snorkeling, and rock climbing at Railay.

Just a short tuk-tuk ride northeast of Krabi Town, however, you'll find **Wat Tham Sua (Tiger Temple),** a hilltop pilgrimage point and meditation center. The beaches and stunning cliffs of **Railay Beach ★★** are certainly worth a day trip even if you don't stay there (see "Where to Stay & Dine," above). In the daytime, longtail boats pick up passengers at Ao Nang Beach for the 20-minute, 80B ride. From the docks in Krabi Town, it's a 40-minute, 200B ride (high season only).

The craggy karst cliffs of Railay make it one of the best-known **rock-climbing** spots in the region (if not the world). It's "sport climbing" done on mapped routes, with safety bolts already drilled into the rock; a number of companies offer full- and half-day courses. There are many routes suitable for beginners too. Start with a lesson at **King Climbers** (© **07566-2096;** www.railay.com) or **Hot Rock** (© **07566-2245;** www.railayadventure.com). Half-day courses begin at about 1,000B, while full-day courses are from 1,800B.

If you visit Railay, don't miss secluded **Phra Nang Beach ★,** one of the most scenic beaches in Thailand. Access from Railay is by a footpath that wraps around the Rayavadee resort. Monkeys hop around the beachfront trees here; at low tide, you can walk across a sandbar to nearby **Happy Island,** which also has a number of sport-climbing routes.

Full-day **boat trips** and **snorkeling** can be arranged at any beachfront tour agent or hotel near Krabi. You'll be taken to a few small coral sites and any number of secluded coves, starting at 1,000B for a half-day. Day kayak tours to outlying islands like **Ko Hong,** costing around 1,800B per person, are also becoming popular. Contact **Koh Phi Phi Tour** (© **07562-0507**) or **Sea Kayak Krabi** (© **07563-0270**) for details.

Ko Phi Phi ★★

42km (26 miles) W of Krabi, 160km (99 miles) SW of Phuket

Phi Phi was devastated by the 2004 tsunami; most of the central isthmus of this tiny island was wiped out and the loss of life was considerable. Soon after the tsunami, there was talk that development would be curbed and the island would only be open to day trips. The talk was short-lived, however, and nowadays Phi Phi is back and better (or worse) than ever.

Phi Phi is two islands: **Phi Phi Don** is the main barbell-shaped island whose central isthmus (the barbell handle) is packed with amenities; all visitors arrive at the busy ferry port in Phi Phi Don's Loh Dalam Bay. The sandy beaches at Ton Sai Bay, just opposite, are good for swimming. Smaller **Phi Phi Lei** is south of the main island and famed for its coveted swallow nests and the courageous pole-climbing daredevils who go get them (the nests fetch a hefty price for the making of a gourmet soup). The smaller island is protected as a natural park, but is visited as part of most day trips.

Phi Phi is where the filmmakers of *The Beach* staged their Hollywood version of tropical Utopia, and some tours will take you to Makan, the site of the filming. Small beachfront outfits rent snorkel gear and conduct longtail boat tours to quiet coves for as little as 500B.

GETTING THERE

Ferries make regular connections from Phuket, Krabi, and Ko Lanta. Boats from the pier in central Krabi Town run at least three times daily (usually at 9am, 10:30am, and 2:30pm) for 450B. Boats from Ao Nang/Railay (high season only) depart at 9am and charge the same price. From Phuket, ferries leave from the pier near Phuket Town at 8:30am, 1:30pm, and 2:30pm, with rates at around 400B. And from Ko Lanta, two boats a day leave at 8am and 1pm, costing 450B.

[Fast FACTS] KO PHI PHI

Services on Ko Phi Phi are in Ton Sai Village, on the central isthmus of Phi Phi Don. **Siam Commercial Bank** has an ATM; there are a number of currency-exchange booths as well. **Internet cafes** are ubiquitous and average 120B per hour. A small **post office** can be found toward the middle of the village. The **tourist police** booth is next to the main pier.

WHERE TO STAY & DINE

Ton Sai Village is the commercial center of Phi Phi and has been overrun with budget accommodations, turning it into a virtual backpacker ghetto. The best of the budget set is the **Phi Phi Hotel** (© 07561-1233), with comfortable rooms starting at 1,800B. The island's best resorts are on the isolated beaches in the northeast corner of the island and can be reached by longtail boat from Ton Sai pier. Some ferries from Krabi or Phuket will drop you off directly at your resort.

While the nicer resorts usually have the best food on the island, it's always fun to mix things up. Ton Sai Village is developing a wide variety of dining choices. Most are simple beachside cafes, but **Le Grand Bleu,** by the main pier, stands out as the best of the bunch, serving fine French fare with a good selection of wines. For all of your bread needs, **Pee Pee Bakery** is an old standby.

Very Expensive

Zeavola ★★ The only true luxury resort on the island, located in its far northeast corner, Zeavola is trying to create a return to traditional 1950s Thai living. Sand walkways cut through palm trees, and scaevola plants lead to free-standing thatch-roofed teak suites. Each is luxuriously appointed with polished teakwood floors, oversize daybeds, and both indoor and outdoor rain showers. What makes the suites truly unique, however, are the rustic flourishes: old-fashioned copper piping, wooden taps, pottery sink basins, and *mon ing* cushions (the traditional triangular Thai pillows) for the patios. This rustic theme extends to the fine hillside spa but not, for obvious reasons, to the resort's first-class PADI dive center and private dive boat. *Hint:* The beachfront suite trades privacy for the sea view; some garden suites have partial ocean views without the loss of privacy.

11 Moo 8, Laem Tong, Ko Phi Phi, Krabi 81000. © **07562-7024.** Fax 07562-7025. www.zeavola.com. 52 units. 9,900B village suite; 10,900B garden suite; 16,400B beachfront suite; 20,900B pool villa suite. AE, MC, V. **Amenities:** 2 restaurants; saltwater pool; spa; watersports equipment; Wi-Fi and broadband Internet access. *In room:* A/C, TV w/DVD/CD player, hair dryer, minibar.

Expensive

Holiday Inn Resort Phi Phi Island The Holiday Inn has a lot of things going for it—a great location on beautiful Laem Tong beach, lovely manicured lawns, and hammocks gently swaying under beachfront palm trees. Unfortunately, the bungalows are rather basic and uninspired, with guesthouse-quality bathrooms. The restaurants offer decent fare, though. Bottom line: unparalleled location, but lodgings are a little lacking. Try Phi Phi Island Village (see below) first.

Laem Tong Beach, Ko Phi Phi, Krabi 81000. ℂ **07562-7300.** Fax 07562-7397. www.phiphi.holidayinn. com. 77 bungalows. 7,500B–9,400B bungalow; 10,200B suite. AE, MC, V. **Amenities:** 2 restaurants; 2 bars; fitness center; outdoor pool; room service. *In room:* A/C, minibar.

Phi Phi Island Village Beach Resort & Spa ★ Set on quiet Loh Ba Kao Bay just south of Laem Tong Beach, Phi Phi Island Village offers a variety of elevated wood-and-cement huts spread among the palms. The bungalows are large and comfortable with all of the creature comforts (it's the only resort on this part of the island with satellite TV), but they're starting to show their age—just normal wear and tear—which is understandable since this was the first resort on the island. Of all of the island's resorts, this one offers the most facilities, making it thoroughly self-sufficient and the best option for an extended stay on Phi Phi.

Loh Ba Kao Bay (20 min. by longtail boat from main pier), Ko Phi Phi, Krabi 81000. Phuket office: 89 Satoon Rd., Phuket 83000. ℂ **07621-5014.** Fax 07621-4918. www.ppisland.com. 100 units. 6,900B–10,000B bungalow; 17,500B beachfront suite; 21,500B pool villa. AE, MC, V. **Amenities:** 3 restaurants; 3 bars; babysitting; Internet cafe; Jacuzzi; outdoor pool; sauna; spa. *In room:* A/C, satellite TV, minibar.

OUTDOOR ACTIVITIES

Next to lounging on the beach, **snorkeling** and **scuba diving** are the most popular activities in and around Phi Phi, though some folks get their kicks **rock climbing** or **cliff jumping,** both of which can be arranged through local tour companies. *Warning:* Unsurprisingly, cliff jumping results in many accidents, but the tour company that takes you to the cliff won't pay your hospital bills. Most resorts offer free snorkeling equipment, or you can rent from one of the storefronts on Ton Sai Bay. **Moskito Diving** (ℂ 07560-1154; www.moskitodiving.com) caters to all experience levels and offers a variety of day trips as well as live-aboards on its state-of-the-art 26m (85-ft.) dive boat. Other PADI-certified outfits include **Phi Phi Scuba** (ℂ 07560-1148; www.ppscuba.com) and **Blue View Divers** (ℂ 07581-9395; www.blueviewdivers.com).

Ko Lanta

70km (43 miles) SE of Krabi

Small Muslim fishing villages dot the east coast of Lanta Yai (Big Lanta), a fast-developing region of the south. You'll have to cross Lanta Noi (Small Lanta) to get to the main beach areas of Lanta Yai. Business is booming, and where there were once only backpacker haunts, luxury and midrange bungalows are slowly taking over. Much of the development is taking place in the protected Moo Ko Lanta National Marine Park, meaning that the new construction must meet environmental impact standards. Local laws also govern the height and size of new resorts, an attempt to keep the island looking as natural as possible.

GETTING THERE

Minivans from Krabi Town and Trang make connections to Lanta; the cost is from 350B for bus/boat/bus door-to-door service. After two short ferry crossings, most transport stops in **Saladan,** near the ferry pier on the northern tip of Lanta Yai. In the high season, daily ferries connect Ko Lanta with Ko Phi Phi (450B). You can also connect with Phuket via Phi Phi. In the low season, minivan or an expensive chartered boat is your only option.

WHERE TO STAY
Very Expensive

On developing Phra Ae Beach, **Layana Resort & Spa** (272 Moo 3, Saladan; ⓒ **07560-7100;** www.layanaresort.com) offers first-class accommodations and is the best on the beach. Luxury pavilions and suites start at 11,300B.

Pimalai Resort & Spa ★★   From Krabi Town or the airport, you can ride in style: first by luxury van, then by picturesque private boat ride directly to the resort in high season (a short four-wheel-drive ride to another pier in low season). Getting here is an adventure in itself that pays dividends when you check in to your own room. A fine marriage of comfort and proximity to nature, the large, free-standing villas are partly walled compounds with rooms done in hardwoods and luxurious bathrooms with outdoor showers. Each unit has a large veranda, some overlooking the sea or at least within earshot of the crashing surf of the picturesque beach below (a good swimming beach). The high-end suites are spectacular. The resort is thoroughly self-contained, with a library, a beautiful spa, and good day trips.

99 Moo 5, Ba Kan Tiang Beach, Lanta Yai Island, Krabi 81150 (on the far southeast coast of Lanta Yai). ⓒ **07560-7999.** Fax 07560-7998. www.pimalai.com. 121 units. 14,000B deluxe; 27,000B–37,000B pavilion suite; from 36,000B villa. AE, DC, MC, V. **Amenities:** 4 restaurants; 5 bars; mountain-bike rental; fitness center; Internet access; Jacuzzi; pool; room service; spa w/massage; watersports equipment; library. *In room:* A/C, satellite TV (some w/DVD players), fridge, minibar.

Moderate/Inexpensive

Budget accommodations along the west coast of Lanta are basic bungalows starting as low as 300B, with new places opening all the time. **Moonlight Bay Resort** (69 Moo 8, Klongtob; ⓒ **07566-2590**) is one of the better bungalow resorts and offers cozy accommodations and basic services starting at 2,000B.

CENTRAL THAILAND

Going north from Bangkok, travelers tracing the route of the Chao Phraya River travel back in time as they push upstream and beyond. Starting with the ruins of **Ayutthaya** (see "Side Trips from Bangkok," p. 78), you travel through the vast Central Plains to the nation's greatest architectural wonder, **Sukhothai,** which was the very founding point of the Thai kingdom in 1238. Even farther north, you climb into a range of hills that constitute the foothills of the Himalayas and enter the former kingdom of Lanna (meaning "a million rice fields"), with its distinctive culture and dialect, centered around Chiang Mai (covered below).

　　Phitsanulok, 377km (234 miles) north of Bangkok, is the commercial hub of the region, but apart from a visit to the town's noted **Wat Yai,** an important destination for Buddhist pilgrims because of its revered **Phra Phuttha Chinnarat** Buddha image, there's little to detain visitors on their way to Sukhothai. The **Phitsanulok Station** (ⓒ 05525-8005) is served by regular rail connection from Bangkok's **Hua**

Lamphong Railway Station (☎ 1690 or 02223-3762). If you're stuck for the night, try **Topland Hotel** (68/33 Akathodsarod St.; ☎ **05524-7800;** www.topland hotel.com), with rooms going for 2,000B.

Sukhothai ★★★ & Si Satchanalai ★

Sukhothai: 427km (265 miles) N of Bangkok, 58km (36 miles) E of Phitsanulok; Si Satchanalai: 56km (35 miles) N of Sukhothai

The emergence of Sukhothai (which means "Dawn of Happiness" in Pali) in 1238 as an independent political state signified the birth of the first unified kingdom now known as Thailand. Today, Sukhothai is the country's best-known historical site; it is to Thailand what Angkor Wat is to Cambodia.

New Sukhothai, built along the banks of the Yom River, is the access point for the main attraction, **Sukhothai Historical Park** (or Muang Kao, which means Old City), situated some 12km (7½ miles) west of the town center.

Si Satchanalai Historical Park, also along the Yom River, is 56km (35 miles) north of New Sukhothai. Another legacy of the Sukhothai Kingdom, the ancient city is crumbling—but that's part of its charm, and it's certainly worth the 1-day detour. If you're traveling from Phitsanulok, the drive takes you across wide plains of rice paddies, cotton fields, and mango and lemon groves—a glimpse into another era.

GETTING THERE

BY PLANE   **Bangkok Airways** has a private airport near Sukhothai, with at least one daily flight connecting Sukhothai with Bangkok. For information, call ☎ **02270-6699** in Bangkok or ☎ **05564-7224** at the Sukhothai airport.

BY TRAIN   The nearest railway station is at Phitsanulok (see above). From Phitsanulok's intercity bus terminal on Hwy. 12, buses leave hourly for the 1-hour trip to New Sukhothai (58B).

BY BUS   Three daily air-conditioned buses leave from Bangkok's **Northern Bus Terminal** (☎ **02936-2852**) for the 7-hour trip (295B). Four daily air-conditioned buses leave from Chiang Mai's **Arcade Bus Terminal** (☎ **05324-2664**) for the 5½-hour trip (274B).

The Sukhothai bus station is about 1km (2/3 miles) north of New Sukhothai. Public *songtao* charge 20B for the ride to Old Sukhothai.

BY CAR   Take Singhawat Road west from Phitsanulok, then Hwy. 12.

WHERE TO STAY & DINE

Sukhothai Heritage Resort (999 Moo 2, Tambon Klongkrajong, Sukhothai 64110; ☎ **05564-7567;** www.sukhothaiheritage.com) is located next to the airport, in an idyllic rural setting about 20km (12 miles) from the town. Well equipped rooms, all with a view of the pool, start at 2,900B. In New Sukhothai, **Lotus Village** (170 Ratchathanee St.; ☎ **05562-1484;** www.lotus-village.com) has basic fan-cooled and air-conditioned rooms from 900B and 1,200B, respectively. They can also arrange drivers and certified park guides.

In the superinexpensive category, **Ban Thai Guesthouse** (38 Pravet Nakhon Rd.; west side of Yom River; ☎ **05561-0163**) is a collection of A-frame teak bungalows starting from just 250B. It's quite basic, but a good place to get useful local info.

As in most small cities and towns in Thailand, you can find good eats at the central market from early 'til late. **Dream Cafe** (86/1 Singhawat Rd.; ☎ **05561-2081**) is a great choice, with a refined atmosphere and great eats.

Special Event

Loi Krathong is a visually delightful 3-day festival held nationwide on the full moon of the 12th lunar month— in late October or November—in honor of the water goddess. Crowds gather at ponds, canals, rivers, and temple fountains to float small banana-leaf boats bearing candles, incense, a flower, and a coin in offering to wash away the past year's sins. This festival dates from the Sukhothai era, and is celebrated here with a spectacular light and sound show in the historical park.

EXPLORING SUKHOTHAI ★★★

Named a UNESCO World Heritage Site in 1991, the Sukhothai Historical Park has been restored and maintained by the government's Fine Arts Department to make the monuments accessible to the public.

You can reach the historic park of Sukhothai by public bus, three-wheeled motorcycle taxi *(samlor),* private car, or bicycle. The *samlor* that cruise around New Sukhothai can be hired to trek you out to the monuments and take you for a 4-hour tour around the park for about 500B.

The historical park is open daily from 6am to 6pm. Purchase a combination ticket with admission to the National Museum, Historical Park (all areas), and Si Satchanalai Historical Park for 350B—a good value and valid for 30 days. A basic map is available at the museum, but better maps are to be found at the bike-rental shops near the entrance. Since the site is too spread out for walking, it's best to go by guided tour in a car, *samlor,* or rented bicycle (about 30B per day, available at the entrance). There are also irregular tram tours (20B per person).

A network of walls and moats defines the perfect rectangle that is the central city. The **Ramkhamhaeng National Museum,** with its detailed models and artifacts from the site, is a good place to start. **Wat Mahathat,** composed of several small towers and *chedis,* is an imposing monument and the site's most important. The 15m (49 ft.) seated Buddha at **Wat Sri Chum,** located to the northwest of the old city, is one of the nation's most evocative and photogenic sights. Don't miss the temples, pottery kilns, and small pilgrimage mounds outside the city walls. A visit to **Sri Satchanalai,** some 56km (35 miles) north, makes for a good day trip.

NORTHERN THAILAND

If lazy beach days aren't your thing, the historic cities of **Chiang Mai, Chiang Rai,** and the small but interesting **Golden Triangle** (Sop Ruak), a former center of the opium trade, are a welcome change for visitors who want to experience Thailand's rugged rural beauty.

The majority of northern Thais trace their heritage to the Tai people who migrated from southern China in waves between the 1st and 8th centuries. King Mengrai, a brilliant leader who united the Tai tribes, established the first capital of the Lanna Kingdom at Chiang Rai in 1262. It was about this time that Kublai Khan invaded Burma. For added protection, King Mengrai forged ties with the Sukhothai Kingdom to the south, and in 1296 he moved his capital to Chiang Mai. For the next century, the Lanna Kingdom absorbed most of the northern provinces and, in alliance with Sukhothai, held off invasion from the Mons and Khmers. After taking control of Sukhothai, Ayutthaya tried to conquer Chiang Mai and failed each time. The Lanna Kingdom enjoyed wealth and power until 1556, when the Burmese captured the capital. It remained in their hands until 1775, when King Taksin, assisted by King Kawila from Lampang, took it for Siam.

North of Chiang Mai and its satellite cities, travelers enter a mountainous region that promises lots of adventure. Rugged hills, proximity to Myanmar (Burma) and Laos, and the diverse ethnic hill-tribe groups living here distinguish northern Thailand from the rest of the country. The mighty Mekong River flows southeast from the Golden Triangle, the former opium-producing region straddling Myanmar and Laos, and the river traces a path through dense jungles and teak forests. This is the land of elephants, ancient Lanna culture, backwater border towns, and adventure around every turn.

Northern Thailand is home to the majority of Thailand's more than half a million members of **ethnic hill tribes,** which are classified in six primary groups: the Karen, Akha, Lahu, Lisu, Hmong (Meo), and Mien (Yao), each with subgroups that are linked by history, lineage, language, costume, social organization, and religion. With close ethnic, cultural, and linguistic ties to the cultures of their Lao, Chinese, Burmese, and Tibetan ancestors and neighbors, each group retains, to this day, traditional costume, religion, art, and daily practices.

Keep in mind that November through February are the best months for trekking, with March and April being the least crowded, but also the hottest, months. ***Trekkers beware:*** During the rainy season, June through October, paths become mudslides due to frequent showers, and leeches abound.

Chiang Mai ★★★

Chiang Mai (New City) was founded in 1296 by King Mengrai as the capital of the first independent Thai state, Lanna (Kingdom of One Million Rice Fields). It became the cultural and religious center of the northern Tai, those who had migrated from southern China to dwell in Thailand, and remained through the turbulent period of recurring Burmese attacks. The Burmese were occupiers; in fact, Burmese influence on culture is still strong. Ongoing Thai-Burmese conflicts led to alliances with Siam and, in 1932, the province became an integral part of the Kingdom of Siam.

These days, Chiang Mai is a booming town of some 250,000 people (in a province of some 1.7 million). Most residents are native born, but an increasing number of transplants from Bangkok are drawn to the slower pace and friendly locals. Chiang Mai's heart is the Old City, an area surrounded by vestiges of walls and moats originally constructed for defense; yet Chiang Mai is also a modern city with a growing infrastructure of modern shopping malls and condominiums. The contrast is part of the town's charm.

GETTING THERE

BY PLANE   Lao Airlines (✆ **05322-3401**) connects Chiang Mai to Luang Prabang five times each week, while **Air Asia** (✆ **05392-2170**) has daily flights to Kuala Lumpur (Malaysia). **Silk Air** (✆ **05390-4985**), the regional arm of Singapore Airlines, connects with Singapore.

Within Thailand, **Thai Airways** (240 Prapokklao Rd.; ✆ **05392-0937**), **Bangkok Airways** (✆ **05327-6176,** or 02270-6699 in Bangkok), and budget carriers **Air**

Asia (✆ **02515-9999** in Bangkok) and **Nok Air** (✆ **02627-2000**) fly from Bangkok to Chiang Mai daily (trip time: 1 hr., 10 min.) and make regional connections.

The **Chiang Mai International Airport** has several banks for changing money, a post and overseas call office, and an information booth. Taxis from the airport charge a flat 150B to town. Buy a ticket from the taxi booth in the arrivals hall, and then proceed to the taxi queue.

BY TRAIN   Of the seven daily trains from Bangkok to Chiang Mai, the 8:30am Sprinter (trip time: 12 hr.) is the quickest, but you sacrifice a whole day to travel and spend the entire trip in a seat. A second-class air-conditioned seat will run 611B.

Other trains take between 13 and 15 hours. For overnight trips, second-class sleeper berths are a good choice, costing 881B for a lower berth with air-conditioning, 791B for an upper berth with air-conditioning. In Bangkok, contact **Hua Lamphong Railway Station** (℃ **1690** or 02223-3762) up to 90 days in advance. For local train information in Chiang Mai, call ℃ **05324-4795.** Reservations cannot be made over the phone, but you can check availability.

BY BUS Buses from Bangkok to Chiang Mai are many and varied—from rattle-trap, open-air numbers to fully reclining VIP vehicles. The trip takes about 10 hours. From Bangkok's **Northern Bus Terminal** (℃ **02936-2852**), there are numerous departures (about 700B for VIP bus). There's also frequent service between Chiang Mai and Mae Hong Son, Phitsanulok, and Chiang Rai.

Chiang Mai's **Arcade Bus Terminal** (℃ **05324-2664**) is on Kaeo Nawarat Road, 3km (1¾ miles) northeast of Tha Pae Gate; some buses arrive at **Chang Puak Station** (℃ **05321-1586**), north of Chang Puak Gate on Chotana Road.

GETTING AROUND
The heart of Chiang Mai is the **Old City,** completely surrounded by a moat and a few remains of the massive wall, laid out in a square aligned with the cardinal directions. Several of the original gates have been restored and serve as handy reference points, particularly **Tha Pae Gate** to the east. All major streets radiate from the Old City.

The main business and shopping area is the 1km (⅔-mile) stretch between the east side of the Old City and the **Ping River.** Here you will find the Night Bazaar, many shops, trekking agents, hotels, and restaurants. To the west of town and visible from anywhere in the city is the imposing wall of **Doi Suthep** mountain, where, at its crest, you'll find the most regal of all Chiang Mai Buddhist compounds, **Wat Phra That Doi Suthep.**

BY TAXI Chiang Mai's metered taxis are an odd breed in that they don't use their meters and don't stop for people flagging them in the street. Still, it's the most comfortable way to get around and not too expensive—a ride from one side of town to the other shouldn't cost more than 150B. Phone **05327-9291** to book one.

BY SONGTAEW *Songtaews* (covered pickups) cover all routes. These red pickup trucks fitted with two long bench seats are also known locally as *seelor* (four wheels). Hail one going in your general direction and tell the driver your destination. (*Tip:* Have your hotel or guesthouse concierge write your destination in Thai before you head out.) Ask the price and bargain hard.

BY TUK-TUK The ubiquitous tuk-tuk (motorized three-wheeler) is the next best option to the *songtaew.* Fares are negotiable—you will have to bargain hard to get a good rate—but expect to pay at least 40B for any ride.

BY CAR Avis (℃ **05320-1798**) has an office conveniently located at the airport, while **Budget** (℃ **05320-2871**) will deliver; prices start at around 1,400B. **North Wheels** (70/4–8 Moonmuang Rd.; ℃ **05387-4478**) is a good choice and typical of the more budget services in town.

BY MOTORCYCLE Many guesthouses along the Ping River and shops along Chaiyaphum Road (north of Tha Pae Gate in the Old City) rent 100cc to 150cc motorcycles for about 150B per day (with discounts for longer periods); 250cc Hondas (and larger) are also available. Wear a helmet.

BY BICYCLE   Cycling in the city is fun and practical, especially for getting around to the temples within the Old City. Bikes are available at any of the many guesthouses in or around the Old City; they go for about 50B per day.

VISITOR INFORMATION

The **TAT** office is at 105/1 Chiang Mai-Lamphun Rd. (✆ **05324-8604**), 400m (1,300 ft.) south of the Nawarat Bridge on the east side of the Ping River. Around town, you can find lots of free local magazines with maps and lists of events.

[Fast FACTS] CHIANG MAI

Bookstores   Backstreet Books (✆ **05387-4143**) and **Gecko Books** (✆ **05387-4066**) are neighbors on Chang Moi Kao, a side street north of Tha Pae Road just before it meets Tha Pae Gate. Both have a good selection of new and used books and do exchanges at the usual rate: two for one, depending on the condition. **Bookzone** (318 Tha Pae Rd.; ✆ **05325-2418**) is strong on guidebooks and Thai culture. The **Suriwong Book Centre** (54 Sridonchai Rd.; ✆ **05328-1052**) also has a comprehensive selection of English-language books.

Consulates   U.S.: 387 Wichayanond Rd. (✆ **05325-2629**). **Canada:** 151 Chiang Mai–Lampang Superhighway, T. Tahsala (✆ **05385-0147**). **Australia:** 165 Sirimangklachan Rd. (✆ **05322-1083**). **U.K.:** 198 Bumrungraj Rd. (✆ **05326-3015**).

Currency Exchange For convenient bank ATMs and money-changers, go to Chang Klan Road (the Night Bazaar street).

Emergencies   In case of emergency, dial ✆ **1699** to reach the tourist police.

Hospitals   Chiang Mai hospitals offer excellent emergency and general care, with English-speaking nurses and physicians. The best private hospital is **McCormick,** on Kaeo Nawarat Road (✆ **05392-1777**), out toward the Arcade Bus Terminal.

Internet Access   In the Old City, there are numerous small, inexpensive cafes with service sometimes costing only 30B per hour. Many hotels and restaurants also provide Wi-Fi or free Internet service for guests and customers.

Mail   The most convenient branch is at 186/1 Chang Klan Rd. (✆ **05327-3657**). The general post office is on Charoen Muang (✆ **05324-8719**), near the train station.

WHERE TO STAY

Near the Ping River

The Chedi, Chiang Mai ★★   When you first see it, the Chedi resembles a fortress with windowless, wood-clad walls providing protection from the onslaught of tuk-tuks and noise beyond. However, the interior reveals a sleek modern hideaway with little to remind you that you are in fact still in Chiang Mai. Reflecting pools and manicured gardens line an inner courtyard dominated by an 80-year-old whitewashed colonial building. Formerly the British consulate, it now houses the hotel's bar and restaurant and provides a welcome charm to the otherwise stark exterior architecture. Airy rooms are decorated in a chic contemporary Asian style that is more focused on "contemporary" than "Asian." Stunning black-marble bathrooms open up to the bedroom by way of folding teak doors, and balconies overlook a riverfront swimming pool surrounded by lotus ponds (try for a fourth-floor room for the best view). Added perks such as butler service, complimentary minibar, and free laundry service make the very spacious suites worth the steep price tag.

123 Charoen Prathet Rd., Chiang Mai 50100 (on the river 5 blocks south of Tha Pae Rd.). ✆ **05325-3333.** Fax 05325-3352. www.ghmhotels.com. 84 units. 16,235B deluxe; 24,411B suite. AE, DC, MC, V. **Amenities:** Restaurant; 2 bars; lounge; babysitting; fitness center; outdoor pool; room service; spa. *In room:* A/C, satellite TV, hair dryer, minibar, Wi-Fi and broadband Internet access.

Butterfly ★   The east bank of the River Ping is the most sought-after location in town for hotels and restaurants, and no place has a better spot than Butterfly with its 125m (410 ft.) river frontage, even if the resort is about 6km (3¾ miles) north of the city center (a free shuttle is on hand to run guests into town). Rooms are tastefully equipped with solid wooden floors, canopy beds, traditional textiles, and private balconies, offering a great combination of privacy and luxury. There's a pool, restaurant, and bar, plus an extensive riverside lawn, and the area is shaded by an enormous tree; all in all it's the perfect spot to chill out.

181 Moo 6, San Pisua, Chiang Mai 50300. ✆ **05311-5270.** Fax 05311-5271. www.stayatbutterfly.com. 19 units. 4,800B deluxe; 6,900B villa. AE, MC, V. **Amenities:** Restaurant; bar; free bike use; concierge; lap pool; plunge pool. *In room:* A/C, fridge, hair dryer, Wi-Fi.

dusit D2 ★★   The Dusit hotel chain is trying to appeal to a younger, hipper crowd by updating its image, and inclusion in Condé Nast's annual hot list is testimony to its success. From the lobby to the restaurants to the guest rooms, every corner of the hotel is bathed in a postmodern minimalist cool. Oranges and browns are the dominant colors, and the furniture and decor seamlessly blend sharp lines with rounded edges—everything flows. More important, the style of the furnishings does not translate into a lack of comfort. Rooms are very livable and have all the finer creature comforts: daybeds, flatscreen TVs with DVD players, and well stocked bathrooms. An upgrade to the club deluxe level allows access to the chic club lounge, with free cocktails and Internet service. Dusit's famous Devarana Spa is the one part of the hotel that retains the traditional Thai elegance. The hotel's staff exudes a laid-back cool, but is very attentive and helpful.

100 Chang Klan Rd., Chiang Mai 50100 (2 blocks south of Tha Pae Rd., 2 blocks west of river, just north of Night Bazaar). ✆ **05399-9999.** Fax 05399-9900. www.dusit.com. 131 units. 4,000B deluxe; 5,300B club deluxe; from 6,500B suite. AE, DC, MC, V. **Amenities:** Restaurant; bar; babysitting; concierge; fitness center; outdoor pool; room service; spa. *In room:* A/C, satellite TV w/DVD player, hair dryer, Internet access, minibar.

Le Meridien ★   With an ideal location on Chang Klan Road, right next to the Night Bazaar, this place is an imposing new presence in central Chiang Mai. With typical Le Meridien flair, the design both outside and inside is very pleasing on the eye, and the spacious and well lit rooms are packed with state-of-the-art furnishings and fittings, including high-definition TVs and high-speed Internet access. The muted earth tones of the decor are very restful, and some upper-floor rooms have wonderful views of the nearby mountain, Doi Suthep. The hotel's restaurants and bars offer an appetizing array of culinary delights, exotic cocktails, and fruit infusions.

108 Chang Klan Rd., Chiang Mai 50100. ✆ **05325-3666.** www.starwoodhotels.com. 384 units. 3,555B–6,399B double; 9,243B–11,613B suite. AE, DC, MC, V. **Amenities:** 2 restaurants; 2 bars; babysitting; fitness facility; pool; sauna; spa. *In room:* A/C, satellite TV, hair dryer, minibar.

Ping Nakara ★   Taking its inspiration from the teak boom in Chiang Mai in the late 19th century, this award-winning new boutique property has an elegant colonial design, with delicately carved woodwork around the eaves and balconies. The theme

Where to Stay & Dine in Chiang Mai

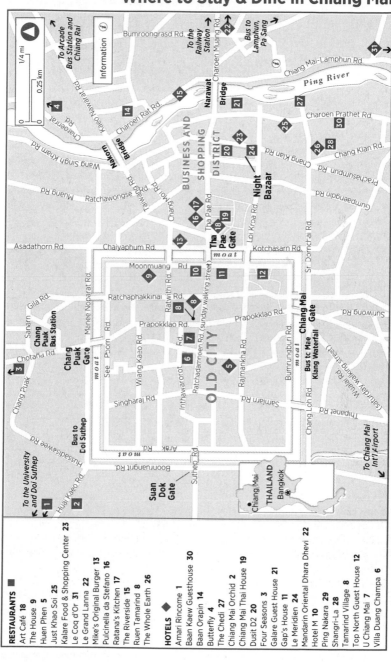

RESTAURANTS ■
Art Café **18**
The House **9**
Huen Phen **5**
Just Khao Soi **25**
Kalare Food & Shopping Center **23**
Le Coq d'Or **31**
Le Grand Lanna **22**
Mike's Original Burger **13**
Pulcinella da Stefano **16**
Ratana's Kitchen **17**
The Riverside **15**
Ruen Tamarind **8**
The Whole Earth **26**

HOTELS ◆
Amari Rincome **1**
Baan Kaew Guesthouse **30**
Baan Orapin **14**
Butterfly **4**
The Chedi **27**
Chiang Mai Orchid **2**
Chiang Mai Thai House **19**
Dusit D2 **20**
Four Seasons **3**
Galare Guest House **21**
Gap's House **11**
Le Meridien **24**
Mandarin Oriental Dhara Dhevi **22**
Hotel M **10**
Ping Nakara **29**
Shangri-La **28**
Tamarind Village **8**
Top North Guest House **12**
U Chiang Mai **7**
Villa Duang Champa **6**

continues in the rooms, where old-style telephones, fans, and carpets hark back to another era. Other fixtures and fittings are thoroughly modern, however, from the flatscreen TV and minibar to hushed but efficient air-conditioning units and Jacuzzis in top-end rooms. All of the 19 rooms are named after different Thai flowers and are individually decorated, giving each a separate identity. Hotel facilities include an infinity pool, an Ayurvedic spa, a small but smart restaurant, and a cozy library, while the high staff-to-guest ratio guarantees prompt and attentive service.

135/9 Charoen Prathet Rd., Chiang Mai 50100. © **05325-2999.** Fax 05325 2111. www.pingnakara.com. 19 units. 4,900B–6,900B double. AE, MC, V. **Amenities:** Restaurant; bar; infinity pool; spa; library. *In room:* A/C, satellite TV, DVD player (and in-house movies on request), minibar, Wi-Fi.

Shangri-La ★ Located in a lush garden setting in the heart of the city's business district, the Shangri-La is a city resort designed to facilitate both business and leisure for visitors. It is just a 10-minute ride from the city's airport and within easy reach of all major sights, and combines a broad range of facilities such as the CHI Spa with Shangri-La's inimitable service. They offer special packages for honeymooners and golfers, as well as excellent dining and drinking options. Horizon club rooms are worth the upgrade for perks such as a personal concierge and access to the club lounge. These rooms occupy the top three floors—ask for a mountain view.

89/8 Chang Klan Rd., Chiang Mai 50100. © **05325-3888.** Fax 05325-3800. www.shangri-la.com. 281 units. 4,100B–4,900B double; 5,600B–6,100B horizon club rooms; 8,850B suite. AE, DC, MC, V. **Amenities:** Restaurant; 3 bars; babysitting; kids' corner; pool; spa; tennis court. *In room:* A/C, high-speed Internet access, minibar.

Baan Orapin Bed & Breakfast ★★ 🛍 If you're looking for a more intimate and personal stay in Chiang Mai, the Baan Orapin is a real gem. Owned and operated by Khun Opas Chao, who spent more than a decade studying and working in the U.S. and U.K., the hotel is set on land that has been in his family for more than 100 years. Two-story Lanna-style buildings surround the 90-year-old mansion and attached gardens. While the rooms and suites are rustic in comparison with the larger resorts and hotels, they are stylish and extremely clean, with sturdy teakwood furniture, mosquito netting for the beds, and handicrafts to add some local flavor. Large bathrooms are outfitted in beautifully polished, locally made green-and-blue tiling. Khun Opas is a wealth of information about the town and its history; he and his staff will bend over backward to attend to your every need.

150 Charoenraj Rd., Chiang Mai 50100 (east side of river, north of Nawarat Bridge). © **05324-3677.** Fax 05324-7142. www.baanorapin.com. 15 units. 2,400B superior; from 2,800B suite. AE, MC, V. **Amenities:** Restaurant; Internet access; small pool. *In room:* A/C, satellite TV, fridge.

Baan Kaew Guesthouse ★ This motel-style guesthouse, an enclosed compound in a quiet neighborhood just a short walk south of the Night Bazaar, has a well tended garden and a manicured lawn. Rooms are very simple but spotless, with new floor coverings (guests are asked to remove shoes before entering) and tiled bathrooms with hot-water showers. Breakfast is served in a shaded pavilion. You're close to the market, but the place is quiet.

142 Charoen Prathet Rd., Chiang Mai 50100 (south of Loy Kroh Rd. opposite Wat Chaimongkol; enter gate, turn left, and find guesthouse well back from street). © **05327-1606.** Fax 05327-3436. www. baankaew-guesthouse.com. 20 units. 800B double. No credit cards. **Amenities:** Restaurant (breakfast only). *In room:* A/C.

Chiang Mai Thai House ★ 🍴 Set on a quiet *soi* 2 blocks from Tha Pae Gate and a 10-minute walk to the Night Bazaar, the Thai House is somewhere between a guesthouse and a hotel. Opened in 2005, the rooms and bathrooms (the all-in-one shower variety) are spotless, and a quick perusal of the house rules shows management is dead set on keeping them that way. Spacious air-conditioned rooms have wood floors and small fridges, with first-floor air-conditioning units sporting an attached small garden sitting area. Fan rooms are just as spacious and a good choice during the cooler months. Hallway balconies overlook the relaxing pool area. The tour desk can help book excursions ranging from rafting and cycling to all-day cooking classes. The restaurant serves decent Thai fare. Overall, this is a great value.

5/1 Tha Pae Rd., Soi 5, Chiang Mai 50100 (2 blocks east of Tha Pae Gate). © **05390-4110.** Fax 05390-4110, ext. 200. www.chiangmaithaihouse.com. 38 units. 400B double with fan; from 700B double with A/C. AE, MC, V. **Amenities:** Restaurant; small outdoor pool. *In room:* TV, Internet access.

Galare Guest House   This Thai-style, three-story, brick-and-wood motel has broad covered verandas overlooking a pleasant garden and courtyard. Rooms are small but have air-conditioning and king-size beds. Even with linoleum floors, it is very comfortable. The restaurant serves breakfast, lunch, and dinner on a covered deck overlooking the river. An in-house trekking agency organizes trips to hill-tribe villages, as well as local tours of Chiang Mai; ask about discounts in the off season.

7 Charoen Prathet Rd., Soi 2, Chiang Mai 50100 (on river south of Thapae Rd.). © **05381-8887.** Fax 05327-9088. www.galare.com. 35 units. 950B–1,150B double. MC, V. **Amenities:** Restaurant; computer w/Internet access. *In room:* AC, TV, fridge, no phone.

In the Old City

Tamarind Village ★★   Passing down a long, shaded lane lined with new-growth bamboo, follow meandering walkways among the whitewashed buildings of this stylish little hideaway in the heart of the Old City. It's hard to believe that you're in Chiang Mai. Rooms at the Tamarind are marvels of concrete flatwork burnished to an almost shining glow. Complemented by straw mats and chic contemporary Thai furnishings, they make for a pleasing, minimalist feel (if you're a minimalist, that is). Bathrooms are spacious, with double doors connecting to the vaulted-ceilinged guest rooms. There's an almost Mediterranean feel to the whole complex, what with all of the arched, covered terra-cotta walks joining buildings in a village-style layout. The village also has a full-service spa with Jacuzzi and sauna facilities. Add that to the already excellent poolside restaurant, **Ruen Tamarind** (see "Where to Dine," below), and you have the makings of a unique city resort.

50/1 Ratchadamnoen Rd., Sri Phoom, Chiang Mai 50200 (a short walk toward the center of the Old City from Tha Pae Gate). © **05341-8896.** Fax 05341-8900. www.tamarindvillage.com. 45 units. 6,000B–8,000B double; from 14,000B suite. MC, V. **Amenities:** Restaurant; bar; outdoor pool; spa. *In room:* A/C, satellite TV, fridge, hair dryer, minibar, Wi-Fi.

Hotel M ★   Formerly the Montri Hotel, this was the earliest address of note for foreigners in Chiang Mai because of its central location beside Tha Pae Gate. Now after a long overdue makeover, it once again offers comfortable rooms at affordable rates. Thick mattresses promise a good rest, though you should ask for a back-facing room to get away from street noise and, on higher floors, enjoy a mountain view. Dark parquet floors are standard throughout, and bathrooms are of the shower-in-room style.

2-6 Ratchadamnoen Rd., Chiang Mai 50100 (just northwest across from Tha Pae Gate). © **05321-1070.** Fax 05321-6417. www.hotelmchiangmai.com. 75 units. 3,000B–3,600B double. MC, V. **Amenities:** Restaurant. *In room:* A/C, satellite TV, fridge, minibar, Wi-Fi.

U Chiang Mai ★   With an ideal location right in the center of the Old City, this new place makes it easy to walk to the city's main temples, and the Sunday Walking Street sets up right in front. Rooms are tastefully equipped in Lanna style and guests have use of the gym, infinity pool, and spa facilities. Added touches like breakfast whenever and wherever you like it and free Wi-Fi make this an attractive option.

70 Ratchadamnoen Rd., Sri Phum, Chiang Mai 50200. ℭ **05332-7000.** Fax 05332-7096. www.uhotels resorts.com. 41 units. From 4,199B double. MC, V. **Amenities:** Restaurant; bar; gym; outdoor pool; spa. *In room:* A/C, satellite TV, minibar.

Villa Duang Champa ★   This cute, refurbished colonial house is full of character and superbly located for sightseeing in the heart of the Old City. There are just 10 rooms in the main building, each with different furnishings and decor, and two cozy wooden villas out back. Some of the well equipped rooms have small balconies and others have views of the nearby mountain, Doi Suthep. The place lacks amenities like a restaurant and bar, but there are plenty of places just a few steps away, and the friendly staff are happy to give advice.

82 Ratchadamnoen Rd., Sri Phum, Chiang Mai 50200. ℭ **05332-7198-9.** Fax 05332-7197. www.villa duangchampa.com. 12 units. 2,400B–3,200B double. MC, V. *In room:* A/C, satellite TV, fridge.

Gap's House   Gap's House is tucked down a quiet lane just inside the city wall near Tha Pae Gate. Long popular among budget travelers, the hotel boasts a calm atmosphere, with a leafy central garden area surrounding a large, teak Lanna pavilion. Rooms are in free-standing teak houses and feature woven rattan beds and small tiled bathrooms. Some rooms are getting a bit tatty and management is rather indifferent, but it's still a cheap, atmospheric choice in the town center, and its cooking classes are particularly popular. No advance bookings are accepted, so call on arrival.

3 Rajadamnern Rd. Soi 4, Chiang Mai 50000 (1 block west of Thapae Gate on left). ℭ/fax **05327-8140.** www.gaps-house.com. 20 units. 470B–700B double. MC, V. **Amenities:** Vegetarian restaurant; cooking classes. *In room:* A/C, no phone.

Top North Guest House   South of Tha Pae Gate and down one of the Old City's narrow lanes, laid-back Top North is comfortable and affordable. The small central pool is a find in this category and is a popular hangout for backpackers. Rooms are large and clean, with tile floors and bathrooms with tubs. Time is not kind to budget hotels, however, and some of the furnishings look like they've gone a few rounds with an angry, caged ape. Cheaper rooms don't have air-conditioning or TV, but all at least have hot-water showers. Top North's extras include a good tour operation, an Internet cafe, and a bar that shows DVDs in the evenings. Its sister property, **Top North Hotel** (ℭ **05327-9623-5**), is an old standby just south of the Tha Pae Gate within the Old City; it offers a slightly higher class of rooms at slightly higher rates.

15 Moon Muang Rd., Soi 2, Chiang Mai 50100. ℭ **05327-8684.** Fax 05327-8485. www.topnorthgroup. com. 90 units. 400B–500B double. MC, V. **Amenities:** Restaurant; bike and motorcycle rental; Internet cafe; outdoor pool. *In room:* A/C, TV.

West Side/University Area
Amari Rincome Hotel ★   This tranquil hotel complex is a favorite because of its elegant, yet traditional, Thai atmosphere. The public spaces are decorated with local handicrafts, and the professional staff wears intricately embroidered costumes. Superior rooms are elaborately adorned with Burmese tapestries and carved-wood

accents in local style, but are looking a little worn. Renovated deluxe rooms are more in keeping with Amari's high standards: business beiges with plush carpeting and modern Lanna decorations. There is a gorgeous garden and pool area, the dining at La Gritta is great, and the hotel is near some of the better upscale shops and galleries in town. The staff is as professional as they come, will know your name from the moment you cross the threshold, and can help with any eventuality (tours, transport, and so on).

1 Nimmanhaemin Rd., off Huay Kaeo Rd., Chiang Mai 50200 (near superhighway northwest of Old City). © **05322-1130.** Fax 05322-1915. www.amari.com. 158 units. 3,800B–4,800B standard/superior; 6,400B deluxe; 14,200B suite. AE, DC, MC, V. **Amenities:** 2 restaurants; lounge; babysitting; concierge; executive-level rooms; 2 outdoor pools; room service; smoke-free rooms; outdoor floodlit tennis court. *In room:* A/C, satellite TV, fridge, hair dryer, minibar.

Chiang Mai Orchid ★

The Orchid has attractive facilities and friendly service and is just next to one of the town's most popular hangouts, the Kad Suan Kaew (Central) shopping complex. Spacious, quiet rooms are pleasantly decorated with local woodcarvings. The lobby and other public spaces are furnished with clusters of chic, low-slung rattan couches and decorated with flowers. The Orchid covers all the bases in terms of amenities, including dining, car rental, and a knowledgeable tour desk.

23 Huay Kaeo Rd., Chiang Mai 50200 (northwest of Old City, next door to Kad San Kaew/Central shopping complex). © **05322-2099.** Fax 05322-1625. www.chiangmaiorchid.com. 266 units. $70–$88 double; from $225 suite. AE, DC, MC, V. **Amenities:** 3 restaurants; lounge and pub; babysitting; children's playground; fitness center; outdoor pool; room service; sauna. *In room:* A/C, satellite TV, fridge, minibar.

Outside Chiang Mai

Four Seasons Resort Chiang Mai ★★★

Northern Thailand's first five-star resort is isolated from the bustle of the city on 8 hectares (20 acres) of landscaped grounds in the Mae Rim Valley. The beautiful central area features terraced rice paddies and even a resident family of water buffalo used to work the fields. Two-story Lanna-style pavilions overlook the tranquil scenery. Spacious suites are understatedly elegant with polished teak floors and vaulted ceilings, decorated with traditional Thai fabrics and art, each with an adjoining private *sala*. Bathrooms are particularly large and luxurious. The location gives full access to the picturesque Mae Rim Valley, which guests can explore by borrowing a complimentary mountain bike. If you're worried about being far from Chiang Mai, there are regular shuttles to and from the main business and shopping district. There's even a fine cooking school. The *pièce de résistance* is the luxurious Lanna Spa, which offers a standard of luxury and service without rival in the region.

Mae Rim–Samoeng Old Rd., Mae Rim, Chiang Mai 50180 (20 min. north of city off Chiang Mai–Mae Rim Rd.). © **800/819-5053** in the U.S., or 05329-8181. Fax 05329-8190. www.fourseasons.com/chiangmai. 80 units. 20,000B–26,500B pavilion suite; 33,000B pool villa; from 70,000B 2-bedroom residence. AE, DC, MC, V. **Amenities:** Restaurant; bar; babysitting; mountain bikes; children's activities; concierge; fitness center w/sauna and steam; 2 pools; complimentary shuttle; room service; spa w/steam, massage, and salon; 2 outdoor floodlit grass tennis courts; library. *In room:* A/C, satellite TV w/in-house movies, fridge, hair dryer, minibar.

Mandarin Oriental Dhara Dhevi, Chiang Mai ★★★

Lying east of town off the busy San Kamphaeng Road, this spectacular resort is a re-creation of an idealized Lanna palace and its attendant village. Upon arrival, a horse-drawn cart whisks you across a moat into the miniature city, dropping you off at the lavishly decorated lobby.

A reproduction of a Burmese palace, it is quite impressive and—like the nearby spa, a teakwood extravagance modeled after the Mandalay Palace—wholly unique in a resort setting. Accommodations are of the suite-only variety, roughly divided between the villas and pavilions and the colonial suites. Villa suites are grand, two-story teakwood rice barns, while pavilion suites are impressive takes on traditional Thai houses, each incorporating different ethnic influences on Lanna architecture. All have attached Thai-style *salas* and are appointed as if for royalty, in rich teak, silk, and all the finest fittings. Pastel tones, chandeliers dangling from towering ceilings, and stunning open-plan marble bathrooms give these rooms a sense of refinement unmatched in Chiang Mai.

51/4 San Kamphaeng Rd., Moo 1, T Tasala, Chiang Mai 50000. © **05388-8888.** Fax 05388-8999. www. mandarinoriental.com. 123 units. 22,000B–97,500B colonial suite; 22,000B–95,500B villa; from 63,000B residence; 309,000B royal residence. AE, MC, V. **Amenities:** 4 restaurants; 2 bars; babysitting; children's center; concierge; health club; outdoor pool; room service; extensive spa; tennis court; cooking school; library. *In room:* A/C, satellite TV, fridge, hair dryer, minibar.

WHERE TO DINE

Northern-style cuisine is strongly influenced by the Burmese and ethnic minorities who live in the area. Northern Thais often prefer sticky rice to steamed rice, and eat it with their fingers. Among the most distinctive northern Thai dishes are *gaeng haeng lay* (pork curry with ginger); *sai ua* (Chiang Mai sausage); and *khao soi* (a spicy, curried broth with crispy and egg noodles), which is usually eaten at lunchtime; as well as many distinctive meat and fish curries. The formal northern meal is called *khan toke,* referring to the custom of sharing a variety of main courses with guests seated around a *khan toke* (a low, lacquered table).

Near the Ping River

Just Khao Soi NORTHERN THAI   If you'd like to try Chiang Mai's signature dish, *khao soi,* but don't trust those hole-in-the-wall places where they sell it, then head for this place, which elevates the dish to fine-dining status. You might be paying several times the going rate, but it's still reasonably cheap, and you get to choose from different strengths of broth and a wide range of accompanying side dishes and condiments, all served on a giant artist's palette. Add the spotless, smart surroundings and attentive staff, and you have the perfect setting in which to enjoy this memorable dish.

108/2 Charoen Prathet Rd. (1 block east of the Night Bazaar). © **05381-8641.** Main courses 99B–249B. MC, V. Daily 11am–11pm.

Le Coq d'Or ★★ FRENCH   In a romantic English-country-house setting, Le Coq d'Or is second to none in Chiang Mai for excellent atmosphere, food, presentation, and service. Jazz musicians perform each evening 7 to 10pm except Sundays, and professional waiters serve from a list of imported beef, lamb, and fish prepared in French and Continental styles. Presentation is done on fine white linen and real china. Try the chateaubriand, rare, with a delicate gravy and béarnaise on the side. The poached Norwegian salmon is a fine light choice. For starters, try the foie gras or a salmon tartar wrapped in smoked filet and served with toast, a sour-cream-and-horseradish sauce, and capers. A nice wine list complements the menu.

11 Soi 2 Ko Klang Rd. (2-min. drive south of the Mengrai Bridge, on the east side of the river). © **05314-1555.** www.lecoqdorchiangmai.com. Reservations recommended for weekend dinners. Main courses 600B–5,200B. AE, DC, MC, V. Daily noon–2pm and 6–10pm.

Le Grand Lanna ★★★ 🛏 THAI Located a short ride east of town in the luxury Mandarin Oriental Dhara Dhevi, this classy place is a good stop before, or after, a trip to the craft workshops at San Kamphaeng. The restaurant provides icy-cool air-conditioned rooms inside, or terrace seating outside, with cooling mist-spraying fans and umbrellas. Evening meals are candlelit, with flaming torches and the dulcet tones of traditional music accompanying your choice of food. For starters, try pomelo salad (if needed, ask to reduce the spiciness); then try the *gaeng hang lan mop*, a dry, fiery red curry that will knock your socks off and which is best mollified by a sweet mango chutney. Also don't pass up their signature *sai ua*, or Chiang Mai spicy sausage. Follow up with great homemade ice-cream made of local litchi (lychee) or taro (yam). If you're short of time or money, come for a drink, at least.

Mandarin Oriental Dhara Dhevi Hotel, 51/4 Chiang Mai-San Kamphaeng Rd. (4km/2½ miles east on Charoen Muang). ℭ **05388-8888.** www.mandarinoriental.com/chiangmai/dining. Main courses 500B–1,200B. AE, MC, V. Daily 11:30am–2:30pm and 6:30–10:30pm.

The Riverside ★★ THAI/INTERNATIONAL Casual and cool is what the Riverside is all about. Something of a Chiang Mai institution, it has recently lost most of its river frontage, but has opened an attractive alternative across the road to accommodate its many fans. There's live music, from blues to soft rock, plus great Thai and Western food (including burgers) and a full bar. Even if you just stop by for a beer, it's a convivial place that always draws an eclectic mix of Thais, travelers, and expats. Riverside also operates a dining cruise at 8pm (board at 7:15pm) for 110B per person (55B for kids); drinks and dining are a la carte.

9-11 Charoenrat Rd. (east side of river, north of Nawarat Bridge). ℭ **05324-3239.** www.theriversidechiangmai.com. Reservations recommended. Main courses 95B–280B. AE, MC, V. Daily 10am–1am.

The Whole Earth ★ 🛏 VEGETARIAN/INDIAN Featuring Asian foods, mostly Indian and Thai, prepared with light, fresh ingredients in healthy and creative ways, this 30-year-old Chiang Mai institution is a real find. The restaurant is set in a traditional Lanna Thai pavilion and has an indoor air-conditioned nonsmoking section, and a long open-air veranda with views of the gardens. The menu is extensive, and everything on it is good. Try the spicy house vegetarian curry with tofu wrapped in seaweed and finish with a fresh mango lassi.

88 Sri Donchai Rd., A. Muang. ℭ **05328-2463.** Main courses 220B–360B. MC, V. Daily 11am–10pm.

Around the Old City

The House ★★ PACIFIC RIM/FUSION This wonderful supper-only bistro was established by a resident Dane who immediately upped the culinary standards in Chiang Mai. Set in an old 1960s edifice that's been lovingly restored, the main dining room has large windows with gorgeous drapes, silk cushions, and candlelit tables; upstairs there are two rooms which are even cozier. An internationally trained Thai chef works his magic on a constantly evolving menu of regionally influenced classical dishes, a medley of grilled items and imported steaks, and lamb and seafood when available—there are fabulous desserts to boot. Outside is a Moorish souk-styled lounge bar with lights in the trees, and a separate tapas bar for snacks. This refined dining spot, with its romantic nooks and funky furnishings, caters to the discerning traveler.

199 Moon Muang Rd. (north of Thapae gate on the inside edge of the city moat). ℭ **05341-9011.** www.thehousethailand.com. Main courses 450B–850B. MC, V. Daily 6pm–midnight.

Huen Phen ★ THAI   Huen Phen, near Wat Phra Sing, is an authentic local choice. At lunchtime the basic eatery out front serves good *khao soi,* Chiang Mai's famed noodle stew, as well as *khanom jeen namneua,* a spicy beef broth with noodles. In the evenings, typical northern Thai dishes such as *gaeng hang lay* (pork curry with ginger) are served in the atmospheric house, which is set back from the road and is full of local crafts and furnishings.

112 Rachamankha Rd. ℂ **05381-4548.** Main courses 30B–80B. No credit cards. Daily 8:30am–4pm and 5-10:30pm.

Mike's Original Burger AMERICAN   This is the only cheeseburger (outside the U.S.) that can compare to a real American burger (McDonald's does not count, by the way). Just a simple streetside counter, Mike's serves hot dogs as well as the afore-mentioned burgers; however, if you're a vegetarian, your only option is the condiments. It's a convenient stop before exploring the *wats* or after exploring a couple of bottles of Beer Singh, though the open setting on a busy street corner is not ideal.

Chaiyaphum Rd. (at corner of Changmoi Rd., just north of Tha Pae Gate). No phone. Main courses 120B–185B. No credit cards. Daily noon–3am.

Pulcinella Da Stefano ★ ITALIAN   Da Stefano's is in a narrow lane off Tha Pae Road; it's a lively and popular place with an extensive catalog of northern Italian cuisine, including steaks, excellent pizzas, and pastas. Portions are big, the wine list is deep, and there are good daily set menus and specials. Meet lots of young back-packers splurging after long, rugged journeys in the north.

2/102 Chang Mai Kao Rd. (just to the east of Tha Pae Gate). ℂ **05387-4189.** Main courses 120B–530B. AE, MC, V. Daily 11:30am–10:30pm.

Ruen Tamarind ★ THAI/INTERNATIONAL   Part of Tamarind Village (see "Where to Stay," earlier in this chapter), Ruen Tamarind offers a fine selection of northern Thai cuisine with a couple of international favorites thrown in for the less adventurous. A must-try is the *tort mun pla,* or fried fish cakes, a common dish with a delicious twist: The cakes are marinated with small chunks of banana and are served with peanut sauce. In the evenings, the restaurant's candlelit tables spread onto the hotel's lovely pool deck. Live jazz is performed every night.

At the Tamarind Village, 50/1 Ratchadamnoen Rd., Sriphoom (a short walk toward the center of the Old City from Tha Pae Gate). ℂ **05341-8896.** Main courses 240B–580B. MC, V. Daily 7am–11pm.

Snacks & Cafes

Kalare Food & Shopping Center (Chang Klan Rd., opposite the Night Bazaar; ℂ **05327-2067**) is where you'll find a small food court next to the nightly Thai culture show, which starts around 8:30pm. **Ratana's Kitchen** (320–322 Tha Pae Rd.; ℂ **05387-4173**) is a popular place on the town's main street where the huge menu includes filling sandwiches, tasty curries, and refreshing fruit shakes. Right across from Tha Pae Gate, the **Art Cafe** (291 Tha Pae Rd.; ℂ **05320-6365**) serves everything from pizza to enchiladas and is a good spot for people-watching.

WHAT TO SEE & DO
The Wats

Chiang Mai has more than 300 *wats* in and around the city, one of the largest con-centrations of religious buildings in the country; to make things even more intriguing, many of them are very, very old. In one full day, you can get around all the main

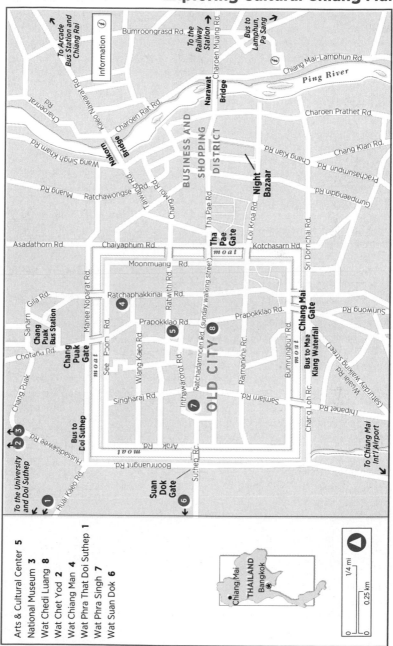

Arts & Cultural Center **5**
National Museum **3**
Wat Chedi Luang **8**
Wat Chet Yod **2**
Wat Chiang Man **4**
Wat Phra That Doi Suthep **1**
Wat Phra Singh **7**
Wat Suan Dok **6**

attractions in the Old City by tuk-tuk or even on foot, if you keep up a good pace. However, there's a saying that "if you haven't visited **Wat Phrathat Doi Suthep,** you haven't visited Chiang Mai," so allow at least half a day to take a look at the north's most-visited temple perched 1000m (3,280 ft.) above the city (see "Side Trips from Chiang Mai," later in this chapter).

Wat Chedi Luang ★★   Because this temple is in the heart of the Old City, most visitors begin their sightseeing here, where there are two *wats* of interest. This complex, which briefly housed the Emerald Buddha now at Bangkok's Wat Phra Kaeo, dates from 1411 when the original *chedi* (mound) was built by King Saen Muang Ma. The already-massive edifice was expanded to 84m (276 ft.) in height in the mid-1400s, only to be ruined by a severe earthquake in 1545, just 11 years before Chiang Mai fell to the Burmese. A recent restoration gives an idea of its former grandeur, with elephant statues around its base and Buddha images in niches, though it still lacks a spire. To the left just inside the entrance to the temple compound, a towering tree stands over a small building that houses Chiang Mai's City Pillar.

Wat Pan Tao, right next door, has a lovely teak *wihaan* (assembly hall), with beautiful glass mosaics in the form of a peacock over the main door. After leaving the temple, walk around to the monks' quarters on the side, taking in the traditional teak northern architecture and delightful landscaping.

Prapokklao Rd., south of Ratchadamnoen Rd.

Wat Chet Yot (Seven Spires) ★★   Wat Chet Yot is one of the city's most elegant sites, though it's quite a way from the city center. The seven-spired *chedi* for which the temple is named was built during the reign of King Tilokkarat in the late 15th century (his remains are in one of the smaller *chedis*), and in 1477, the World Sangkayana convened here to revise the doctrines of the Buddha. The unusual design of the main rectangular *chedi* with seven peaks was copied from the Maha Bodhi Temple in Bodh Gaya, India, where the Buddha achieved enlightenment. The temple also has architectural elements of Burmese, Chinese Yuan, and Ming influence. The extraordinary proportions, the stucco bas reliefs of cross-legged deities appearing to float on the wall of the *chedi,* and the juxtaposition of the other buildings make Wat Chet Yot a masterpiece.

On the superhighway near the Chiang Mai National Museum (north of the intersection of Nimmanhaemin and Huai Kaeo roads, about 1km/⅔ mile on the left).

Wat Chiang Man ★   Chiang Mai's oldest *wat* was built during the 13th century by King Mengrai, the founder of Chiang Mai, on the spot where he first camped. Like many of the *wats* in Chiang Mai, this complex reflects varied architectural styles. Some of the structures are pure Lanna, while others show influences from as far away as Sri Lanka; notice the typical row of elephant supports around the base of the gold-capped *chedi.* Wat Chiang Man is most famous for its two tiny Buddha images: **Phra Saetang Khamani,** a miniature crystal image, and the marble **Phra Sila,** which are just 10cm and 30cm high (4 ft. and 12 ft.), respectively. They are both housed in the small *wihaan* that stands to the right as you enter the compound, but unfortunately it is often closed.

Ratchaphakkinai Rd., in the Old City, near the north moat.

Wat Phra Singh ★★★   This compound was built during the zenith of Chiang Mai's power and is one of the more venerated temples in the city. It's still the focus of many important religious ceremonies, particularly during the Songkran Festival. More than 700 monks study here, and you will probably find them both friendly and curious. King Pha Yu, of Mengrai lineage, built the *chedi* in 1345, principally to house the cremated remains of King Kam Fu, his father. As you enter the grounds, look to the right at the 14th-century **scripture library,** frequently given as the best example of Lanna religious architecture. The delicately sculptured figures around the base are thought to have been made during King Muang Kaeo's reign in the early 16th century. The library is raised up on this base to keep the fragile *sa* (mulberry bark) manuscripts elevated from flooding and vermin.

To the left of the main *wihaan* as you enter, and tucked back from view, is the 200-year-old **Wihaan Lai Kham** (Gilded Hall), housing the venerated image of the **Phra Singh,** brought to the site by King Muang Ma in 1400 and after which the temple is named. The original Buddha's head was stolen in 1922, but the reproduction in its place doesn't diminish the homage paid to this figure during Songkran. The small building is perfectly proportioned, and its golden bargeboards shimmer in the morning sun. Inside are murals illustrating the stories of Sang Thong (the Golden Prince of the Conch Shell) and Suwannahong. These images convey a great deal about the religious, civil, and military life of 19th-century Chiang Mai during King Mahotraprathet's reign.

Samlarn and Ratchadamnoen roads.

Wat Suan Dok   This complex is special less for its architecture (the buildings, though monumental, are undistinguished) than for its contemplative spirit and pleasant surroundings. The temple was built amid the pleasure gardens of the 14th-century Lanna Thai monarch, King Ku Na. Wat Suan Dok houses quite a few monks who study at the northern campus of the Mahachulalongkorn Buddhist University and are keen to practice their English with visitors. Among the main attractions in the complex are the *bot,* toward the back of the compound, with a very impressive **Chiang Saen Buddha** (one of the largest bronzes in the north), dating from 1504, and some garish murals. Behind the enormous, hangarlike *wihaan* are numerous *chedis* containing the ashes of Chiang Mai's royal family, which look particularly impressive when seen in silhouette against the setting sun. There is also an informal "monk chat," (www.monkchat.net) where monks and lay visitors can share views, every Monday, Wednesday, and Friday from 5 to 7pm.

Suthep Rd. (from the Old City, take the Suan Dok Gate and continue 1.6km/1 mile west).

Museums

Chiang Mai City Arts and Cultural Center   In a shuttered colonial building adjacent to the Three Kings Monument in the heart of the Old City, this museum houses a permanent exhibit that walks visitors through a tour of prehistory to the present. Another section houses short-term local exhibits of all types.

Prapokklao Rd.*C* **05321-7793.** Admission 90B. Tues–Sun 8:30am–5pm.

Chiang Mai National Museum   While its collection of historic treasures is not nearly as extensive as that of Bangkok's National Museum, this quick stop does provide something of an overview of the region, the city, and its history. The Lanna Kingdom, Tai people, and hill tribes are highlighted in simple displays with English explanations.

Just off the superhighway northwest of the Old City near Wat Chet Yot. *C* **05322-1308.** Admission 100B. Wed–Sun 9am–4pm.

Cultural Pursuits

THAI COOKING If you love Thai food and want to learn how to make it, look into a class at the **Chiang Mai Cookery School ★**, the oldest establishment of its kind in Chiang Mai. It has five 1-day courses, each designed to teach Thai cooking basics but with a different menu—of up to seven dishes—so you can attend as many days as you want and still gain quite a bit of skill. You'll have hands-on training and a lot of fun. Classes start at 10am and last until 4pm; they cost 990B for the day. Contact the main office at 47/2 Moonmuang Rd., opposite the Tha Pae Gate (✆ **05320-6388;** fax 05320-6387; www.thaicookeryschool.com).

THAI MASSAGE Northern-style Thai massage is something closer to yoga, in which your muscles are stretched and elongated to enhance flexibility and relaxation. There are a number of schools in Chiang Mai. Try the **International Training Massage (ITM),** where a 5-day course is 3,500B. Contact the school at 17/7 Morakot Rd., Hah Yaek Santitham (✆ **05321-8632;** fax 05322-4197; www.itmthaimassage.com).

MEDITATION The **Northern Insight Meditation Center** at Wat Rampoeng is a well respected center for learning Vipassana meditation, but you'll need enough resolve to see through the 26-day course. Participants are assigned very sparse private rooms; they are asked to wear white, loose-fitting clothes (available at the temple store); and basic meals are served at 6 and 10:30am only (there isn't an evening meal). Though the dhamma is given for free, you will be asked to make a contribution for board and lodging of whatever amount you see fit. Located to the west of town, the temple is best reached by tuk-tuk, *songtaew,* or rented motorbike (Wat Rampoeng, Tambol Suthep, Chiang Mai; ✆ **05327-8620).**

OUTDOOR ACTIVITIES

ELEPHANT RIDING One of Thailand's greatest treasures, the domesticated Asian elephant has worked alongside men since the early history of Siam, and these gentle giants are an important symbol of the kingdom. There are a total of 14 elephant camps near Chiang Mai, some with animals in rather dire condition. One of the best is the **Thai Elephant Conservation Center,** on the road to Lampang (see "Side Trips from Chiang Mai," below), where visitors can watch shows and also work with the animals. **Patara Elephant Camp** (✆ **08199-22551;** www.pataraelephant-farm.com), located on the Samoeng Road to the southwest of town, runs a pricey (5,800B) but enjoyable program called "Elephant owner for a day," in which you spend a day feeding, caring for, and riding your own elephant bareback.

GOLF Golf is a hugely popular activity in Chiang Mai, especially among the many Western retirees and vacationing Thais. All courses below are open to the public and offer equipment rental. Call ahead to reserve a tee time.

- **Summit Green Valley Country Club,** 186 Moo 1, Chotana Rd., in Mae Rim, 20 minutes north of town on Route 107 (✆ **05329-8220;** fax 05329-7426; www.summitgreenvalley.com), is in excellent condition with flat greens and fairways that slope toward the Ping River (greens fees: 1,800B weekdays, 2,400B weekends).

- **Chiang Mai Highlands Golf & Spa Resort,** 167 Moo 2, Tambol On-Nuar (✆ **05326-1354;** fax 05326-1363; www.chiangmaihighlands.com), is a hillside course about 20 minutes east of town off Hwy. 1317 (greens fees: 2,800B).

- **Royal Chiang Mai,** 165 Moo 5, Chiang Mai-Phrao Rd., 26km (16 miles) north of Chiang Mai (✆ **05384-9301;** fax 05384-9308; www.royalchiangmai.com), is a fine 18-hole course (greens fees: 1,400B weekdays, 1,800B weekends).

TREKKING For jungle trekking, a number of outfitters arrange trips from Chiang Mai. **Contact Travel** (54/5 Moo 2, Tambol Tasala, Chiang Mai; ✆ 05385-0160; fax 05385-0166; www.activethailand.com) is in a category all its own—it can combine treks and village stays with multisport adventures by jeep, bicycle, and kayak.

Small operators that cater to the backpacker market offer tours and treks for as little as 1,000B per day. This can mean you'll be in a large group, with care and feeding at a lower standard, but that's budget trekking for you. **Eagle House** (16 Chiang Mai Kao Rd., Chiang Mai; ✆ 05387-4126) and **Queen Bee Travel Service** (5 Moonmuang Rd., Chiang Mai; ✆ 05327-5525) are both good.

THE SPA SCENE

Most hotels offer massage and beauty treatments, and there are lots of streetside massage places of varying quality and reputation. The **Four Seasons Resort** (Mae Rim–Samoeng Old Rd.; ✆ 05329-8181) has some of the finest spa facilities in Thailand, and though it comes with a high price tag, the quality and service are unbeatable. **Oasis Spa** (✆ 05392-0111; www.chiangmaioasis.com), with two convenient locations, is more affordable, has a variety of treatments, and comes highly recommended. **Let's Relax,** in Chiang Mai Pavilion (145/27 Chang Klan Rd., on the second floor above McDonald's; ✆ 05381-8498), has good rates and makes for a nice break from shopping.

SHOPPING

If you plan to shop in Thailand, save your money for Chiang Mai. Quality craft pieces and handmade traditional items still sell for very little, and large outlets for high-end goods abound in and around the city. Many shoppers pick up an affordable new piece of luggage to tote their finds home. If you find that huge standing Buddha or oversize Thai divan you've been searching for, don't worry: All stores can arrange shipping.

The **Night Bazaar ★★**, on Chang Klan Road between the Old Town and the river, is the city's premier attraction. Shopping starts around 6pm each night and slows down at about 11pm. The actual Night Bazaar is a modern, antiseptic, three-story building, but the street is lined with stalls for several blocks north and south. There are thousands of pirated audiotapes and videodiscs, acres of burnished brown "bone" objects, masks, woodcarvings, opium pipes, opium weights—you name it.

If you're in town on a weekend, head for one of the popular **Walking Streets ★**, where thousands of stalls are set up to sell locally made crafts, while food vendors and musicians add to the atmosphere. On Saturday it's at **Wualai Road,** running southwest from Chiang Mai Gate on the south side of the Old City, and on Sunday, there's an even bigger market along **Ratchadamnoen Road** in the heart of the Old City. These streets are closed to traffic from around 4 to 11pm.

AROUND THE OLD CITY Small shops and boutiques line the areas around the Night Bazaar and Old City. If you're looking for quality tribal arts in the form of textiles and ritual artifacts, check out **Lost Heavens** (228–234 Tha Pae Rd.; ✆ 05325-1557). **Nova Collection** (201 Tha Pae Rd.; ✆ 05327-3058) carries a line of decorative jewelry in contemporary styles with Asian influences and also has 1- to 5-day courses in jewelry making. **Princess Jewelry** (147/8 Chang Klan Rd.; ✆ 05327-3648) offers customized and ready-made jewelry and personalized service. For silk, try **City Silk** (336 Tha Pae Rd., 1 block east of the gate; ✆ 05323-4388).

WEST SIDE Across from the Amari Rincome Hotel, **Nantawan Arcade** (95 Nimmanhaemin Rd.) has many notable antiques, crafts, and curio shops that make for fun browsing. Note the gorgeous giant bamboo furniture in the window of **Gerard Collection** (6/23–24 Nimmanhaemin Rd; ℰ **05322-0604;** www.thaibamboo. com). **Gong Dee Gallery** (Nimmanhaemin Rd. Soi 1; ℰ **05322-5032**) has a fine collection of gifts and original artwork. Try **Ginger** (6/21 Nimmanhaemin Rd.; ℰ **05321-5635**) for fine designer clothing and jewelry.

SAN KAMPHAENG ROAD Shopaholics will be thrilled by the many outlets along the Chiang Mai–San Kamphaeng Road (Rte. 1006). Rent your own wheels or hop on the white *songtaews* that follow this busy road due east of town. After several miles, you'll reach the many shops, showrooms, and factories extending along a 9km (5⅔-mile) strip. These feature anything from lacquerware to ready-made clothes, silver to celadon pottery.

For pottery, try **Baan Celadon** (7 Moo 3, Chiang Mai–San Kamphaeng Rd.; ℰ **05333-8288**) and **Siam Celadon** (38 Moo 10, Chiang Mai–San Kamphaeng Rd.; ℰ **05333-1526**). For silver pieces, **Louis Silverware** (99/1 Chiang Mai–San Kamphaeng Rd.; ℰ **05333-8494**) has traditional silversmiths on the premises so you can see the various stages of the jewelry-making process. The **Thai Silk Village** (120/11Moo 3, Chiang Mai–San Kamphaeng Rd.; ℰ **05333-8357**) takes you from silkworm to loom to scarf.

CHIANG MAI AFTER DARK

The east bank of the River Ping is the center of nighttime activity. The following are just a few bars and clubs among the many to choose from. **Good View** (13 Charoenrat Rd.; ℰ **05324-1866**) and the **Riverside** (9/11 Charoenrat Rd.; ℰ **05324-3239**) are both popular riverfront restaurants that feature live music. Blues and reggae fans should head straight for **Le Brasserie** (37 Charoenrat Rd.; ℰ **05324-1665**), where resident guitarist Took gets everyone in the groove.

There are lots of small bars, clubs, and go-go joints, as well as McDonald's and some fancy hotel restaurants, in the vicinity of the Night Bazaar (Chang Klan Rd.). If you get tired and hungry while you're shopping, drop by the **Kalare Food & Shopping Center** (Chang Klan Rd., opposite the Night Bazaar; ℰ **05327-2067**), which has free cultural dance shows nightly at around 8:30pm.

For a more studied cultural performance, the **Old Chiang Mai Cultural Center,** 185/3 Wulai Rd. (ℰ **05320-2993;** www.oldchiangmai.com), stages a good show at 8pm every night for 420B, which includes dinner (starting at 7pm). Enjoy a *khan toke* meal accompanied by live music and dance. Yup, it's touristy, but a rollicking good time.

During the cool season (Nov–Feb), the **Imperial Mae Ping Beer Garden** (153 Sridonchai Rd.; ℰ **5328-3900**) is a pleasant spot to enjoy a pitcher of beer. If you're in the mood for dancing, head for **Warm Up** (40 Nimmanhaemin Rd.; ℰ **05340-0676**), where live bands and DJs keep the young crowd (mostly students from the nearby university) on their toes. Back in town, **Spicy** (Chaiyaphum Rd., just north of Tha Pae Gate; no phone) is the place to go when everywhere else is closed (around 2am).

Outside of town in Doi Suthep–Pui National Park, the controversial **Chiang Mai Night Safari** (ℰ **05399-9000;** www.chiangmainightsafari.com) offers a chance to ride around in open-air trams and perhaps glimpse any of the 60 species of animals on show in the poorly lit pens, including giraffes, Asian elephants, impalas, and

THE mae hong son LOOP

Seasoned travelers, given the option, never backtrack, and the "loop" through the rugged hills north and west of Chiang Mai is ideal for that very reason. Connecting the towns of Pai and Mae Hong Son, the circuit continues to out-of-the-way Mae Sariang before returning to Chiang Mai. For all but the adventurous, going by tour or by hired car with a driver is recommended, though a self-drive means freedom to take side trips and explore at one's own pace. The road is serpentine and precipitous, and calls for good driving skills (watch for anything from smoke-belching buses to buffalo to landslides). Give yourself 4 days to do it, staying at least a night in each town.

Your first stop is **Pai,** 135km (84 miles) northwest of Chiang Mai. It's very popular with backpackers and is characterized by scenic views and a laid-back vibe. Overnight rafting trips on the Pai River with **Thai Adventure Rafting** (16 Moo 4, Rangsiyanon Rd.; ✆ **05369-9111;** www.thairafting.com) are popular July through January.

Guesthouses abound in Pai. Try **Rim Pai Cottages,** in the town center (✆ **05369-9133;** www.rimpaicottage. com). One of the best high-end choices is **Belle Villa Resort** ★★ (113 Moo 6, Tumbol Viengtai; ✆ **05369-8226-7;** www.bellevillaresort.com), just outside of town, with cozy stilted cottages starting from 2,850B.

Between Pai and Mae Hong Son, you'll find the **Lod,** or **Spirit Cave,** some 8km (5 miles) north of the highway near Soppong. This large, awe-inspiring cave is filled with colorful stalagmites and stalactites; the small caverns will keep you exploring for hours. Hire a guide with a lantern at the entrance; you'll pay 150B, plus 300B for ferry crossings.

Mae Hong Son, the next stop on the loop, sits close to the border with Myanmar and is the largest town amid the scenic woodlands, waterways, and unique hill-tribe villages of the area. The town is famed for cool weather and an eerie morning mist (the town's nickname is "city of three mists"). It's a good base for trekking. Contact **Rose Garden Tours** (86/4 Khunlumprapas Rd.; ✆/fax **05361-1681;** www.rosegarden tours.com), which arranges treks and visits to nearby **Padaung Villages,** peopled by the famed **"long-necked Karen."**

The best place to stay in town is the luxury **Imperial Tara Mae Hong Son Hotel** ★★ (149 Moo 8, Tambol Pang Moo; ✆ **05368-4444;** www.imperial hotels.com/taramaehongson), with rooms from 2,550B. A good in-town budget choice is **Bai Yoke Chalet** (90 Khunlumprapas, Chong Kham; ✆ **05361-3132**), where you'll pay 1,000B and up.

Mae Sariang is just a cozy river town and the best halfway stopover on the long southern link between Mae Hong Son and Chiang Mai. Driving in the area, along Route 108, takes you past pastoral villages, scenic rolling hills, and a few enticing side trips to small local temples and waterfalls. Mae Sariang offers only basic accommodations, of which the **Riverhouse Hotel** (77 Langpanich Rd.; ✆ **05362-1201;** www.riverhousehotels. com) is your best choice. Rooms start at 1,800B, and the resort's restaurant, Coriander in Redwood, is the best place to eat in town.

maybe even a cheetah. Reports of animal deaths due to mishandling and the ill-conceived plan to serve rare species at the park's restaurant have caused public outcries and protests. The park is open daily from 11am to 11pm. Admission is 500B for adults and 300B for children.

SIDE TRIPS FROM CHIANG MAI

If you have time for only one day trip, Wat Phra That Doi Suthep, Chiang Mai's famed mountain and temple, is the best choice.

Wat Phra That Doi Suthep ★★★

The jewel of Chiang Mai, Wat Phra That Doi Suthep sparkles in the sun on the slopes of Doi Suthep mountain. At just over 1,000m (3,280 ft.), the temple occupies an extraordinary site with a cool refreshing climate, expansive views over the city (weather permitting), and the mountain's idyllic forests, waterfalls, and flowers.

In the 14th century, during the installation of a relic of the Buddha in Wat Suan Dok (in the Old City), the holy object split in two, with one part equaling the original size. A new *wat* was needed to honor the miracle. King Ku Na placed the new relic on a sacred white elephant and let it wander freely through the hills. The elephant climbed to a promontory on Doi Suthep, trumpeted three times, made three counter-clockwise circles, and knelt down, thus choosing the site for Wat Phra That Doi Suthep.

The site is highly revered, and Thai visitors come in droves to make their offerings—usually flowers, candles, incense, and small squares of gold leaf that are applied to a favored Buddha or to the exterior of a *chedi*—and to be blessed.

The site is open from 6am to 8pm, and the entrance fee is 30B, or 50B including tram fare (which avoids the climb up 306 steps). To get here, take a *songtaew* (50B) from Huay Kaeo Road in front of Chiang Mai University. Dress respectfully, meaning no shorts or sleeveless tops. In the cool season, take a sweater or jacket, as it gets cold up there. Go early or late to avoid the crowds.

Lampang ★

The sprawling town of Lampang (originally called Khelang Nakhon) was once famous for its exclusive reliance on the horse and carriage for transportation long after the car was introduced. In fact, old-style horse buggies can still be rented near the center of town next to the City Hall. Sprawling Lampang has some of the finest Burmese temples in Thailand, and short tours by horse and carriage are popular.

About 37km (23 miles) east of town, don't miss the **Thai Elephant Conservation Center** (© **05424-7875**). The center is less touristy than other camps, though there are daily shows at 10am, 11am, and 1:30pm (adults 80B; children 40B), and you can watch them bathing at 9:45am and 1:15pm. Visitors can take a ride on an elephant, and there are also homestay programs for anyone who wants to learn how to be an elephant mahout, though these must be booked well in advance. Call for more information.

Doi Inthanon National Park ★★

Thailand's tallest mountain, **Doi Inthanon**—at 2,565m (8,415 ft.)—is 106km (66 miles) south of Chiang Mai, but can be visited on a day trip, as there's a road that runs to the top. The 482-sq.-km (186-sq.-mile) national park provides a habitat for hundreds of unusual birds and plants, and beside the road to the summit are some impressive waterfalls and inviting nature trails. For Thais, the novelty of a visit here is the chance to shiver in the lower temperatures at the top. At the base of the mountain, the 30m-high (98-ft.) **Mae Klang Falls** is a popular picnic spot with food stands. Admission to the national park is 200B.

Chiang Rai ★

180km (112 miles) NE of Chiang Mai, 780km (485 miles) NE of Bangkok

Chiang Rai is Thailand's northernmost province. The Mekong River makes its borders with Laos to the east and Myanmar (Burma) to the west. The smaller yet scenic Mae Kok River, which supports many hill-tribe villages along its banks, flows right through the provincial capital of the same name.

Chiang Rai lies some 565m (1,854 ft.) above sea level in a wide fertile valley, and its cool, refreshing climate, tree-lined riverbanks, and popular Night Market lure travelers weary of traffic congestion and pollution in Chiang Mai. Although Chiang Rai has some passable hotels and restaurants and a few small attractions, most just use this as a base for trips to Chiang Saen and the Golden Triangle.

GETTING THERE

BY PLANE   Thai Airways (© 05371-1179) has three daily flights from Bangkok to Chiang Rai (trip time: 80 min.). **Air Asia** (© 02515-9999) has at least one daily flight. The **Chiang Rai International Airport** (© 05379-8000) is 8km (5 miles) north of town. Taxis to town are around 200B.

BY BUS   Three air-conditioned, VIP 24-seat buses leave daily from Bangkok's **Northern Bus Terminal** (© 02936-2852) to Chiang Rai (trip time: 11 hr.; 900B). Buses leave from Chiang Mai's **Arcade Bus Terminal** (© 05324-2664) roughly every hour between 6am and 5:30pm (trip time: 3½ hr.; 106B non-A/C, 191B A/C, 295B VIP). Chiang Rai's **Khon Song Bus Terminal** (© 05371-1224) is near the Night Market in the center of town, though most buses, including those from Bangkok, now stop at a new bus station (© 05377-3989) 6km (3¾ miles) south of town. A shuttle service (10B) operates between the two stations, and tuk-tuks and *samlor* (motorized pedicabs) connect to hotels for 30B to 100B, depending which station you arrive at.

BY CAR   The fast, not particularly scenic, route from Bangkok is Hwy. 1 north, direct to Chiang Rai. A slower, but more scenic, approach on blacktop mountain roads is Route 107 north from Chiang Mai to Fang, then Route 109 east to Hwy. 1.

GETTING AROUND

Chiang Rai is a small city, with most services grouped around the main north-south street, Phaholyothin Road. The Mae Kok River forms the north edge of town, and several luxury resorts line its banks. The town is compact enough to explore on foot; however, there are *samlor* and **tuk-tuks,** which charge 40B to 80B in town.

BY MOTORCYCLE   A good choice to get out of town. **Soon Motorcycle,** 197/2 Trairat Rd. (© 05371-4068) charges 150B per day for a 100cc motorbike.

BY CAR   **Budget** has a branch at the Golden Triangle Inn (see "Where to Stay & Dine," below; 590 Phaholyothin Rd.; © 05374-0442), with standard rates beginning at 1,500B for a Honda Jazz.

VISITOR INFORMATION

The **TAT** (© 05374-4674) is at 448/16 Singhakai Rd., near Wat Phra Singh on the north side of town. Good free maps and info are available anywhere.

[FastFACTS] CHIANG RAI

To exchange currency, look for the several **banks** on Phaholyothin Road in the center of town, open daily from 8:30am to 10pm. The **Overbrook Hospital** (✆ **05371-1366**) is on the north side of town at Singhakai and Trairat roads, west of the TAT. There are a few **Internet cafes** along the main drag, Phaholyothin Road, with average service going for 30B per hour. The **tourist police** (✆ **05371-7779**) is on Uttarakit Road, near the town center. The **post office** is also on Uttarakit Road.

WHERE TO STAY & DINE

With the exception of the expensive resorts along the river, most Chiang Rai hotels are within walking distance of the sights and shopping. As for dining options, after 7pm the **Night Market** is the best for budget eats, but beyond that there are a few good restaurants to choose from.

Look for a branch of Bangkok's **Cabbages & Condoms** (620/25 Thanalai Rd.; ✆ **05371-9167**), a good Thai restaurant that promotes its humanitarian work. The **Golden Triangle Cafe** ★, at the Golden Triangle Inn (see below), serves great regional treats from a menu that is a short course in Thai cuisine. **BaanChivitMai Bakery** (✆ **05371-2357**), conveniently located across from the old bus station, offers an all-day breakfast menu, breads and pastries, and Internet service.

Tip: Be sure to sample the town's delicacies, such as *kaeng hang lay* or Burmese-style pork curry; litchis, which ripen in June and July; and the sweet *nanglai* pineapple wine.

Dusit Island Resort, Chiang Rai ★   Chiang Rai's longest-standing resort hotel occupies a large delta island in the Mae Kok River and offers a comfortable and tranquil base for exploration. The lobby is grand, with panoramic views of the water. Rooms are luxuriously appointed with pastel cottons and teak trim. The resort has manicured grounds, a pool, and numerous facilities that make the place quite self-contained. Tenth-floor dining at the Peak offers sweeping views, while the Chinatown restaurant serves good Cantonese. Stop by the Cellar Pub & Games Room in the evening.

1129 Kraisorasit Rd., Amphur Muang, Chiang Rai 57000 (over bridge at northwest corner of town). ✆ **05360-7999.** Fax 05371-5801. www.dusit.com. 268 units. 4,700B–5,100B superior/deluxe double; from 7,700B suite. AE, DC, MC, V. **Amenities:** 4 restaurants; 2 lounges and pub; babysitting; concierge; executive-level rooms; fitness center w/Jacuzzi, sauna, steam, and massage; outdoor pool; room service; smoke-free rooms; floodlit tennis courts. *In room:* A/C, satellite TV, fridge, Internet, minibar.

Golden Triangle Inn ★★   The Golden Triangle Inn is set in its own quiet little garden patch. Large rooms have terra-cotta floors and traditional-style furniture and decor; they are cozy but rather Spartan (no TV, for example) and not luxurious. The staff is helpful, the Thai restaurant is excellent, and the in-house travel agency, Golden Triangle Tours, is a good choice in town for arranging travel in the area.

590 Phaholyothin Rd., Amphur Muang, Chiang Rai 57000 (2 blocks north of bus station). ✆ **05371-1339.** Fax 05371-3963. www.goldenchiangrai.com. 39 units. 900B double. MC, V. **Amenities:** Restaurant. *In room:* A/C, no phone.

The Legend ★★ 🏨   The Legend is a unique and attractive rural boutique resort. Rooms are private sanctuaries with smooth-finish concrete and stucco walls; the end result is a crisp, modern look, with many natural touches. Some rooms overlook the river, others line a narrow garden pond, and all have great indoor and outdoor sitting areas, which allow for a constant connection with your surroundings. There are a few different configurations, including huge private pool villas and family suites, but all include large outdoor shower areas, some with a Jacuzzi tub, and large, luxuriant canopy beds. One highlight is the small infinity edge pool at the center of the resort. They have a great spa with outdoor *salas* and indoor treatment rooms, and the resort runs a number of day trips and activities. It may not have the reputation, or all the facilities, of the nearby Dusit, but it has endless charm.

124/15 Moo 21, Kohloy Rd., Chiang Rai 57000. © **05391-0400.** Fax 05371-9650. www.thelegend-chiangrai.com. 76 units. 3,900B–5,900B studio; 8,100B pool villa. MC, V. **Amenities:** Restaurant; bar; babysitting; outdoor pool; room service; spa. *In room:* A/C, satellite TV, fridge, minibar, Wi-Fi.

Le Meridien ★★ ☺ In an idyllic setting by the Kok River just a kilometer from the town center, Le Meridien is a clever blend of contemporary chic and traditional design. Spread out over five wings, the resort's rooms enjoy views of a private lake, lush lawns, and the lazy river from the balconies. The rooms themselves are spacious with stylish furnishings, including walk-in closets, desks, and high-speed Internet access. There are plenty of activities on-site, such as spa treatments, yoga classes, and a well equipped gym, as well as trekking, boat tours, and biking tours in the hills around. There's also a shuttle service into town to see the sights or go shopping.

221/2 Moo 20, Kwaewai Rd., Tambon Robwieng, Chiang Rai 57000. © **05360-3333.** www.lemeridien.com. 159 units. 7,450B–9,750B double; 14,750B suite. AE, MC, V. **Amenities:** 2 restaurants; 2 bars; shuttle service; kids' club; fitness center; outdoor pool; spa; library. *In room:* A/C, satellite TV/DVD player, Internet, minibar.

WHAT TO SEE & DO

There are a number of fine *wats* in town: **Wat Phra Kaeo,** on Trairat Road in the northwest quadrant, is the best known of the northern *wats* because it once housed the Emerald Buddha now at Bangkok's royal Wat Phra Kaeo. **Wat Phra Singh,** a restored 15th-century temple, is 2 blocks east of Wat Phra Kaeo. The Burmese-style **Wat Doi Tong** (Phra That Chomtong) sits atop a hill above the northwest side of town, up a steep staircase off Kaisornrasit Road, and offers an overview of Chiang Rai and a panorama of the Mae Kok Valley. It's said that King Mengrai himself chose the site for his new Lanna capital from this very hill. This is also the site of Chiang Rai's City Pillar.

The **Mae Kok River** is one of the most scenic attractions in the area. You can hire a longtail boat for day trips to outlying villages. Most of the **hill-tribe villages** within close range of Chiang Rai have long ago been set up for routine visits by group tours (not recommended), but there are a few good outfitters. The best operation is **Golden Triangle Tours,** at the Golden Triangle Inn, 590 Phaholyothin Rd. (© 05371-3918; www.goldenchiangrai.com). It offers everything from 1-day hill-tribe treks to weeklong adventures.

Chiang Saen ★★ & the Golden Triangle

239km (149 miles) NE of Chiang Mai, 935km (581 miles) NE of Bangkok

The small village of **Chiang Saen** has a sleepy, rural charm, as if the waters of the Mekong carried a palpable calm from nearby Myanmar (Burma) and Laos. Chiang Saen was abandoned for the new Lanna Thai capitals of Chiang Rai and then Chiang Mai, in the 13th century, and today the decaying regal *wats*, crumbling fort walls, and overgrown moat contribute greatly to its appeal. After visiting the museum and local sights, most travelers head north along the Mekong to the **Golden Triangle,** the north's prime attraction. It is actually less mysterious than its reputation and more like a row of souvenir stalls leading to a giant riverside golden Buddha statue, but if you stand at the crook of the river, you can see Laos on the right and Myanmar (Burma) on the left.

GETTING THERE

BY BUS Buses from Chiang Rai's **Kohn Song Bus Terminal** (℡ **05371-1224**) leave every 15 minutes from 6am to 6pm (trip time: 1½ hr.; 38B). The bus drops you on Chiang Saen's main street; the museum and temples are within walking distance.

BY CAR Take Route 110 north from Chiang Rai to Mae Chan, then Route 1016 northeast to Chiang Saen.

GETTING AROUND

Route 1016 is the village's main street, also called Phaholyothin Road, which terminates at the Mekong River. Along the river road there are a few guesthouses, eateries, and souvenir, clothing, and food stalls.

BY BICYCLE/MOTORCYCLE It's a great 45-minute bike ride from Chiang Saen to the prime nearby attraction, the Golden Triangle. The roads are well paved and pretty flat. You'll see a few rental outlets along the river that charge 50B to B80 per day.

BY SAMLOR Motorized pedicabs hover by the bus stop in town to take you to the Golden Triangle for around 80B one-way.

BY SONGTAEW These pickup-truck taxis can be found on the main street across from the market; rides to the Golden Triangle cost only 20B.

BY LONGTAIL BOAT Longtail-boat captains wait down by the river and offer Golden Triangle tours to visitors. One popular option is a trip to the Golden Triangle with a short stop at a Lao village on the way, costing 800B for 2 hours. The village is just a couple of market stalls, but you can find interesting cheap Chinese goods, Lao silks, or the "I bought this in Laos" souvenir. Without the stop in Laos, the half-hour boat trip to the Triangle costs 500B (600B return).

VISITOR INFORMATION

The nearest **TAT** office is in Chiang Rai. You can pick up a useful map at the Chiang Saen National Museum (see below).

[Fast FACTS] CHIANG SAEN

There's a **Siam Commercial Bank** in the center of the main street, Phaholyothin Road (Rte. 1016), close to the bus stop and **post office.** You'll also see currency-exchange booths at the Golden Triangle.

WHERE TO STAY

For a different experience, consider a stay at the **Four Seasons Tented Camp Golden Triangle ★★★** (℡ **05391-0200;** www.fourseasons.com/goldentriangle), a superluxe, all-inclusive resort. Getting to the camp requires a Kurtzian ride up the

Some visitors make Chiang Rai or Chiang Saen their last port of call in Thailand before heading overland to rugged but inviting Laos. It is possible to travel downriver 70km (43 miles) to Chiang Khong, a small border town from which you can catch a boat into the "Land of a Thousand Elephants," Laos. Buses and local *songtaew* make the connection to Chiang Khong from either Chiang Rai or Chiang Saen. For more information, see chapter 4, "Laos."

Mekong; once there, you will be pampered and wined and dined between mahout (elephant handling) classes.

The next step down from the luxurious Anantara Resort is the **Imperial Golden Triangle Resort** ★ (222 Golden Triangle, Sop Ruak; ✆ **05378-4001;** www.imperialhotels.com), about 11km (7 miles) northwest of Chiang Saen. It's a clean but uninspired hotel, with rooms starting at 2,500B. There are great views of the river from the top floor. In tiny Chiang Saen, the **Chiang Saen River Hill Hotel** (714 Moo 3, Tambol Viang; ✆ **05365-0826**) has clean, attractive air conditioned rooms from 1,200B. It's a 5-minute *samlor* ride from the bus stop.

Anantara Resort Golden Triangle ★★★ The Anantara is a triumph of upscale local design. The resort features fine local weavings, carved teak panels, and expansive views of the juncture of the Ruak and Mekong rivers. The balconied guest rooms have splendid views and are so spacious and private, you'll feel like you're in your own bungalow. Tiled foyers lead to large bathrooms; the bedrooms are furnished in teak and traditional fabrics. It shares an elephant camp with the Four Seasons Camp and also offers mahout classes.

229 Moo 1, Chiang Saen, Chiang Rai 57150 (above river, 11km/7 miles north of Chiang Saen). ✆ **05378-4084.** Fax 05378-4090. www.goldentriangle.anantara.com. 77 units. From 11,400B double; 17,900B suite. AE, DC, MC, V. **Amenities:** 2 restaurants; lounge and bar; airport transfer; babysitting; bike rental; fitness center; Internet; outdoor pool; room service; spa; outdoor lit tennis courts. *In room:* A/C, satellite TV w/in-house movies, fridge, hair dryer, minibar.

WHAT TO SEE & DO

Allow a half-day to see all of Chiang Saen's historic sights before exploring the Golden Triangle. The **Chiang Saen National Museum** (702 Phaholyothin Rd.; ✆ **05377-7102;** closed Mon–Tues) is a good first stop, with an overview of artifacts from 15th- to 17th-century Lanna Thai. Admission is 100B.

The main temples of Chiang Saen are all within walking distance, though lesser-known sites are scattered around a wide area. **Wat Pa Sak** is the best preserved; the oldest is **Wat Phra Chedi Luang.** All are fine examples of Lanna temples.

The infamous **Golden Triangle,** 12km (7½ miles) northwest of Chiang Saen, is the point where Thailand, Myanmar (Burma), and Laos meet at the confluence of the broad, slow, and silted Mekong and Mae Ruak rivers. Once a no man's land of the international drug trade, the area is a unique vantage point for life in the north.

The **Hall of Opium** ★★ (✆ **05378-4444;** www.maefahluang.org), located 11km (7 miles) northwest of Chiang Saen, is a sprawling, state-of-the-art museum located almost opposite the Anantara Resort that offers an intriguing experience. After passing through a long, dark tunnel that illustrates the positive and negative effects of the drug, visitors continue through interactive exhibits, as well as halls detailing the cultivation of poppies and the history of the opium trade. Through its hard-hitting displays, the museum encourages visitors to reflect on the substance that made this region infamous. Open Tuesday to Sunday 8:30am to 5:30pm (last entry 4pm); admission 200B.

LAOS

by Daniel White

Wherever it is you have traveled from, arriving in Laos seems to naturally involve slowing down. For many years recent history conspired to pass Laos by. For the French occupiers, it was simply a buffer between British-influenced Siam and the lucrative territories of Tonkin and Cochin Indochina. During the regional conflicts of the '50s and '60s, Laos was ravaged by war and by massive American bombing.

After the communist takeover in 1975, the paralysis of a socialist planned economy hindered development and ensured a minimum of outside investment. In the past 10 years the level of development and interaction with the outside world has been incredibly rapid. These days, it is fast becoming the crossroads of the region. Infrastructure connecting China, Vietnam, and Thailand is moving on apace; there are now two bridge crossings over the Mekong, and the Golden Triangle is becoming a pivotal junction for all the countries it encompasses.

The days of Cold War isolation are now a very distant memory as tourists flood into Laos to enjoy the cultural riches of **Luang Prabang,** the laid-back charm of **Vientiane,** and the enigmatic mysteries of the **Plain of Jars.** At present the population stands at an approximate 5.7 million. It remains very much a land of misty mountains, beautiful French colonial–built towns, glittering Buddhist temples, and some fairly surreal Stalinist government management. Luang Prabang was made a UNESCO World Heritage Site in 1995, ensuring that any development did not deface or deform its nature as a breathtaking blend of cultures, architecture, and history. Vientiane is certainly far busier than it was, but it's still not actually very busy at all. Vang Vieng has become a hideaway for the backpacker-hippy crowd who gather in the shadow of spectacular limestone outcrops that line the Nam Song River. It has become very busy indeed.

Buddhism and Theravada Buddhist ritual are central to life in Laos. The Communist Pathet Lao wisely never made any attempt to suppress it on taking power in 1975, and from the 1950s actually attempted to co-opt the Buddhist clergy to their cause. Almost every Lao male will spend some time as a monk at some point in his life. Monks remain revered, and in anywhere that is near a *wat* or temple you will see people making their early morning food donations as the monks go on their alms round.

Laos is very much a one-party state ruled by an all powerful and largely aging elite with absolute power to crush any dissent. The Lao People's Revolutionary Party (LPRP) is led by President Chummaly Sayasone as the head of state, while Bouasone Bouphavanh is the Prime Minister and head of government presiding over the National Assembly elected (in Soviet style, there being no legal opposition) in 2006. The real power is the 10-member Politburo and to some extent the 52-member Central Committee, all of whom are appointed and operate behind firmly closed doors.

Laos today is a curious mixture of the ancient and the modern. A historically tolerant and relaxed people are ruled in understated but very authoritarian style by a leadership that tolerates no dissent. Although the cities are modernizing fast and infrastructure all over the country is improving, education levels remain low to nonexistent while rural poverty remains high. Laos is certainly moving into the 21st century in the cities lining the Mekong. In many remote areas, they have yet to experience electricity.

GETTING TO KNOW LAOS
The Lay of the Land

Comprising 147,201 sq. km (56,835 sq. miles), roughly the size of Great Britain or the state of Utah, Laos shares borders with China and Myanmar in the north and the northwest, Cambodia in the south, Thailand in the west, and Vietnam in the east. The country is divided into 16 provinces. Seventy percent of its land is mountain ranges and plateaus, and with an estimated population of nearly 5.7 million, Laos is one of the most sparsely populated countries in Asia. Natural landmarks include the Annamite Mountains along the border with Vietnam, as well as the Mekong River, which flows from China and along Laos's border with Thailand. About 55% of the landscape is pristine tropical forest, sheltering such rare and wild animals as elephants, leopards, the Java mongoose, panthers, gibbons, and black bears.

A Look at the Past

Laos can trace its history as a unified state to the Kingdom of Lane Xang Hon Khao ("one million elephants under a white parasol"). Formed in 1353 by an exiled prince named Fa Ngum, its capital was Muang Xiang Thong, later renamed Luang Prabang, or "Great Prabang," in honor of a gold Buddha image *(prabang)* given to the kingdom by the court at Angkor. For 300 years, Lane Xang was an important and powerful trading center, occupying present-day Laos as well as parts of northern Thailand, Vietnam, and Cambodia.

In 1707, a secession crisis caused the kingdom to split into three smaller principalities: Vientiane, Luang Prabang, and Champasak. Over the next 100 years, Siam gradually established domination over these minikingdoms, sacking Vientiane in 1828 after a rebellion by their handpicked king.

Toward the end of the 19th century, Siamese hegemony was replaced by French rule. By 1907, through treaty as well as force, Siam was obliged to cede all lands east of the Mekong to the French, who in turn united this territory and named it Laos.

World War II saw the occupation of French Indochina by the Japanese, who forced King Sisavangvong to declare Laos's independence in 1945. Japan's surrender later that year created a power vacuum, which the French and the recently organized Lao Issara ("Free Laos") movement, headed by former prime minister Prince Phetsarath, hoped to fill. Early the next year, the French defeated the combined forces of the

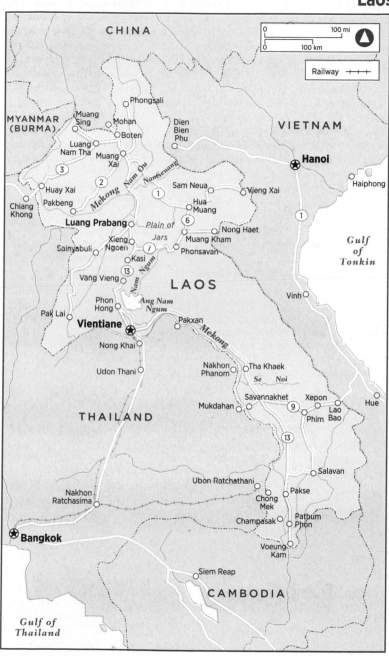

Laos Issara and Vietminh, and Prince Phetsarath, along with his half brothers Prince Souvannaphouma and Prince Souphannavong, set up a government-in-exile in Thailand.

Over the next 7 years, the French gradually granted sovereignty to Laos, culminating in full independence in 1953. During this period, Souvannaphouma returned to Laos to negotiate with the French, while Souphannavong (the "Red Prince") set up the Lao Patriotic Front (widely known as the Pathet Lao) in northwestern Vietnam. Accompanying invading Vietminh forces, the Pathet Lao soon established a stronghold in the northeastern town of Sam Neua.

The late 1950s and early 1960s saw numerous attempts at coalition building between the neutralists, rightists, and communists mediated by Prince Phetsarath, but these governments all collapsed. The Second Geneva Convention held in 1961 and 1962 reestablished Laos's neutrality and formed another coalition government under Souvannaphouma. This one failed as well, and the country descended into civil war. The Pathet Lao, with help from North Vietnamese troops still in Laos in violation of the Geneva Conventions, took control over most of eastern and northeastern Laos.

As the civil war and the wider Indochina conflict intensified, the U.S. began its secret bombing campaign over eastern Laos, targeting communist bases and the Ho Chi Minh trail. From 1964 to 1973, the U.S. dropped more tonnage of bombs on Xieng Khouang, Huaphan, and Phongsali provinces than were dropped on the whole of Europe during World War II. It is estimated that an average of one bombing run was flown every 8 minutes for 9 years.

With the U.S. trying to end its involvement in the region, a cease-fire was reached in 1973, and by 1975, with the U.S. fully withdrawn, the whole of Laos fell to the Pathet Lao. The Lao People's Democratic Republic (LPDR) was formed with Kaysone Phomvihane, a longtime behind-the-scenes communist organizer, installed as prime minister and Prince Souphannavong as president. Draconian political and economic policies followed, including the relocation of many members of the previous government, including the royal family, into "reeducation camps" (the king died within 4 years). An additional 10% of the population fled the country, with an estimated 250,000 eventually settling in the U.S.

During the 1980s and 1990s, progressively more liberalized economic policies were introduced to stir the stagnant economy, producing a more capitalist system. Tourism was also embraced, as the government could not ignore the tourist boom occurring throughout Southeast Asia, especially in neighboring Thailand. Concerted governmental efforts, as well as improved relations with Thailand and the resultant Thai-Lao Friendship Bridge connecting Nong Khai and Vientiane, have helped Laos court the tourist dollar. While only an estimated 33,000 travelers visited Laos in 1991, more than one million arrived in 2008, bringing in more than $150 million and making tourism one of the leading sources of foreign exchange. Unfortunately, the relaxation of economic policies has not gone hand-in-hand with the easing of political controls. Although they have been inept at implementing strict socialist doctrine, the communist People's Revolutionary Party retains a stranglehold on power to this day.

The Lao People & Culture

A study conducted by a group of Russian ethnologists estimated that there are more than 100 distinct ethnic groups in Laos, but it is commonly believed that Laotians fall into 68 different groups. Only 47 groups have been fully researched and identified; sadly, many are disappearing by attrition or intermarriage. All Lao ethnicities fit into one of three categories. The lowlanders are **Lao Loum,** the majority group, who live along the lower Mekong and in Vientiane. The **Lao Theung,** low mountain dwellers, live on mountain slopes, and the **Lao Soung** are the hill tribes, or *montagnards.* Eighty percent of the population lives in villages or small hamlets, practicing subsistence farming.

The earliest Lao religions were animist, and most hill tribes still practice this belief, often in combination with Buddhism. In minority villages, you'll see elaborate spirit gates, small structures of bamboo and wood often depicting weapons to protect the village (tread lightly if you come across one of these markers, as they are of great significance; touching or even photographing them is a major faux pas). Buddhism predominates, though, and 60% to 80% of all Laotians are practicing Theravada Buddhists. In the morning, monks walk the streets collecting food or alms, eagerly given by the Laotians, who believe it will aid them in the next life. Laotians worship regularly and can often be seen making temple visits. Most young males spend at least 3 months in a *wat,* or monastery, usually around the time of puberty or before they marry. Impressive religious art and architecture are created in a singular Lao style, particularly the "standing" or "praying for rain" Buddha, upright with hands pointing straight down at the earth.

Music and dance are integral to the Lao character, and you'll get a taste of it during your stay. Folk or *khaen* music is played with a reed mouth organ, often accompanied by a boxed string instrument. The *lamvong* is the national folk dance, in which participants dance in concentric circles. Don't miss a **Baci ceremony,** in which a circle of celebrants chant and sing to honor or bless an event.

Laotians are friendly and easygoing, but you might find it hard to make a close friend. Language will usually be a barrier. Solo travelers probably have the best chance of making entry into society, and any effort with the Lao language goes a long way. While Laos suffered brutally throughout its colonial history and most horrifically during the Vietnam War, the Lao people want to move on to peace and prosperity rather than dwell on the past. It's very unlikely that an American will be approached with recrimination, but memories are still fresh. Lao people still deal with war fallout literally and figuratively, a result of the unexploded bombs (UXO) that litter 50% of the country.

Etiquette

Laos is a very conservative place on a tight social leash. Education is low and generally people are not very worldly and are easily shocked. Dress modestly. You will see that people of both sexes dress conservatively, showing little skin above the elbow or mid calf. You as a foreigner can get away with shorts and T-shirts, but if they are excessively short or dirty you will garner a fairly negative reaction. It's all about respect in the end. Avoid open displays of affection. The usual rules of respect for religion apply. Take your shoes off when entering a temple (and indeed a private home). Women should never make any physical contact with a monk. It is also important not to point the soles of your feet at another person and certainly not at a Buddha image. Never step over food or people. The feet are seen as being dirty while the head is sacred. Don't pat people on the head even if it is meant as a gesture of affection. The traditional greeting is called the "nop" or "wai," and if you can master it you will be considered very polite. You don't do it to waitresses or children. It is a sign of respect for your equals and social superiors. To perform a nop, place your hands together at chest level as if you are praying, bow your head to your hands, and bend your upper body slightly. In a business setting, a handshake is also appropriate. When you beckon someone, do not do it the Western way. Flap your whole hand downward with your palm flat. If you do it with your hand or finger pointing up, it is interpreted as either very impolite or as a sexual gesture.

As in neighboring countries the concept of face is pivotal, and even if it means things take longer, try to engineer things so that no one loses face. Also, anger is very counterproductive. With the basic levels of education and the generally laid-back attitude in Laos, you will find that things don't always get done, in terms of service, as one might expect in the West. Build some tolerance and wiggle room into your schedule so as to avoid high blood pressure or disappointment.

Language

The Lao language resembles Thai, with familiar tones and sounds found in each. While some vocabulary words might cross over, the two tongues—spoken and written—are quite distinct. However, many Lao understand Thai (learned from school texts and TV), so if you've picked up some words and phrases in Thailand, they'll still be useful here; people will understand and correct you with the appropriate Lao phrase.

Thankfully, many people in Vientiane and Luang Prabang speak English, and some older citizens might be able to speak French.

Like Thai, Lao has no officially recognized method of Roman alphabet transliteration. As a result, even town and street names have copious spelling irregularities, so for the vocabulary below, only phonetic pronunciations are listed. Most Lao will understand you, even without proper tones, and will appreciate your efforts to speak their language.

When trying to figure out the correct pronunciation of certain names, it's helpful to remember that the original transliteration of Lao was done by Francophones, so consider the French pronunciation when faced with a new word. For example, in Vientiane (pronounced Wee-en-*chan*), the wide central avenue spelled Lane Xang is pronounced *Lahn Sahng*. Also in Vientiane, Mixay sounds like *Mee*-sigh. Phonexay is *Pawn*-sigh. It takes a while, but it's easy to pick up.

ENGLISH	LAO
Hello	**Sa bai dee**
Goodbye	**Laa gawn**
Thank you	**Khawp jai**
Thank you very much	**Khawp jai lai lai/khawp jai deuh**
You're welcome/it's nothing	**Baw pen nyahng**
No problem	**Baw mi banhaa**
How are you?	**Sa bai dee baw?**
I'm fine/I'm not fine	**Sabai dee/baw sabai**
Yes	**Chow**
No	**Baw/baw men**
Excuse me	**Khaw toht**
I don't understand	**Baw kao jai**
Do you speak English/French?	**Passah Angit/Falang dai baw?**
How do you say that in Lao?	**Ani passah Lao ee-yahng?**
Where is the toilet?	**Hawng nam yoo sai?**
May I wear shoes here?	**Sai gup pen nyanhg baw?**

ENGLISH	LAO
Where are you going?	**Pai sai?**
I'm going traveling/to the market/to eat	**Pai tiao/pai talat/pai gin kao**
I want to go to . . .	**Koi yak pai . . .**
Do you have . . . ?	**Mii . . . baw?**
drinking water	**nam-deum**
a room	**hawng**
I would like . . .	**Kaaw . . .**
coffee (black)/with cream	**café dahm/café sai nom**
tea	**nam saa**
How much kip/baht/dollar?	**Tao dai keep/baht/dollah?**
Expensive/too expensive	**Paeng/paeng poht**
Can you make it cheaper?	**Loht dai baw?**
Help!	**Soi neh!**
Call the police!	**Toh-ha tam louat!**

THE BEST OF LAOS IN 1 WEEK

Tourism in Laos is still a relatively new phenomenon, and as such, the number of tourist "spots" is still very limited. The only stop that must be included on any Laos itinerary is the ancient capital of Luang Prabang. While some visitors get stuck for weeks or even months in Luang Prabang, the suggested plan below calls for only a couple of days there out of 1 week in the country. This gives you enough time to hit the two most important and interesting cities, Vientiane and Luang Prabang, as well as mix in some outdoor adventure along the caves and rivers in and around Vang Vieng.

Day 1: Vientiane ★★

After arriving in **Vientiane,** start the day by visiting the city's oldest temple, **Wat Si Saket.** Check out the thousands of miniature Buddha statues. After that head for the former royal temple **of Wat Pra Keo,** which previously housed the famous Emerald Buddha Image that is now in Bangkok. On the way to the famous and sacred structure of **That Luang Stupa,** you can stop to take a look at the imposing **Patuxai Monument,** a huge structure very closely echoing the Arc de Triomphe in Paris. As the sun goes down, make your way to the Mekong for a relaxing aperitif before enjoying a meal at one of the many superb restaurants the city has to offer.

Days 2 & 3: Vang Vieng ★

Travel by road to **Vang Vieng,** maybe with a stop over at the 11th-century archeological site of **Vang Xang.** On arrival at Vang Vieng, you can cross the **Nam Song River,** and then enjoy a short walk or trek through the breathtaking and eerie karst scenery to **Tam None cave** and nearby hill villages. Today ends with a spectacular view of the **sunset** over the **Nam Song River.** Enjoy a quiet dinner in one of the quiet restaurants in town, although in all honesty Vang Vieng is a little disappointing on the food front. Pick one by the river, near the hospital, unless you like noise. Spend your third day drifting down the Nam

Song River on inflated tractor-tire inner tubes. For some reason this has become a "must do" in Vang Vieng over the years. It is best interspersed with drink stops to enjoy the stunning scenery.

Day 4: Route 13 ★★★

Travel by road on the truly spectacular **Route 13** to **Luang Prabang.** It is one of Asia's most beautiful drives. You will need to start early. The scenery is rarely equaled, with a mixture of steep terraced fields and hill-tribe villages making for some stunning views and some interesting stops along the way.

Days 5 & 6: Luang Prabang ★★★

Spend the day wandering the spellbinding city of **Luang Prabang,** enjoying the faded colonial charm of the place, including the city's oldest temple, the magnificent **Wat Xieng Thong.** In the afternoon take **a cruise** on the **Mekong River,** enjoying the special tranquillity of the area as well visiting the mysterious **Pak Ou caves,** crammed with thousands of gold Buddha statues. Along the way, make a stop at the village of **Ban Xang Hai,** where they make the local rice wine. Once back in Luang Prabang, take a short drive to **Ban Phanom,** well known for its hand weaving. In the evening wander through the **Night Market** where handicrafts, jewelry, and souvenirs of all sorts amount to a shopaholics' nirvana. The following morning, visit the **National Museum** at the former **Royal Palace,** which houses a superb collection of Lao cultural artifacts dating from the days of the early kings right through to the last one. In the afternoon, take a look at the impressive stupa of **Wat Visoun** and the shrine of **Wat Aham,** and then climb up to the top of **Phousi Hill** for an exploration of the sacred, gilded stupa, and a beautiful sunset view of the city and the Mekong River.

Day 7: Buddha Park

Take a morning flight back to Vientiane. Drive the 24km (15 miles) out of town to **Xieng Khuan** or **"Buddha Park".** Enjoy the strange creation of a philanthropic eccentric whose vision is realized in this bizarre collection of Buddhist and Hindu sculptures. To finish off your trip, take a leisurely afternoon **stroll along the Mekong** watching life on the river go by, stopping for refreshment at one of the many cafes along the banks.

PLANNING YOUR TRIP TO LAOS

Visitor Information

The Lao Tourism Authority serves as more of an administrative arm of the government than an information service for visitors. It provides some basic brochures if contacted at the **National Tourism Authority of Lao P.D.R.,** 08/02 Lane Xang Ave., P.O. Box 2511, Vientiane, Lao P.D.R. (☎ **021/212-248** or 212-251; fax 021/ 212-769; www.tourismlaos.org). The information office in Vientiane has a few good English speakers and is not a bad place to start.

The official Visit Laos website, **www.visit-laos.com,** is sponsored by both the Lao government and private organizations. This site is detailed and accurate, and provides links to other sources of information in the region. For current domestic and international news and government affairs, log on to **www.laoembassy.com,** sponsored and

Booking Air Travel in Laos

Making your own air arrangements from Vientiane or Luang Prabang is simple, and most travel offices can help for a small fee.

Lao Airlines has offices in Vientiane at 2 Pangkham Rd. (✆ 021/212-051, or 212-052 for reservations; www.lao airlines.com), the best place to book domestic flights. Smaller booking offices, such as **Lao Air Booking Co.** (43/3 Setthathirath Rd., just south of Namphu in Vientiane; ✆ **021/216-761**), are good for purchasing regional connections on international carriers.

maintained by the Lao Embassy in Washington, D.C. Below are Lao embassy and consulate locations overseas.

- **In the U.S.:** 2222 S St. NW, Washington, DC 20008 (✆ **202/332-6416;** fax 202/332-4923; www.laoembassy.com); or 317 E. 51st St., New York, NY 10022 (✆ **212/832-2734;** fax 212/750-0039; www.laoembassy.com).

- **In Australia:** 1 Dalmain Crescent, O'Malley, Canberra, ACT 2606 (✆ **02/6286-4595;** fax 02/6290-1910).

- **In Thailand:** 520/502/1–3 Soi Sahakarnpramoon, Wangthonglang, Bangkok 10310, Pracha Uthit Road (end of Soi Ramkhamhaeng 39; ✆ **539-6667-8** or 539-7341; fax 539-3827 or 539-6678; www.bkklaoembassy.com).

Organized Tours & Travel Agents

In chapter 10, we outline major tour operators that organize trips throughout the region (p. 640). Getting around underdeveloped Laos can be difficult, making organized travel the simplest option here.

Independent travel is quite feasible, though, and the same companies that organize group tours can help with hotel and travel arrangements and even create independent tour itineraries.

The most established and widely represented agencies provide basic, mainstream tours to most provinces for either short trips or extended visits. Destinations include in and around Vientiane, Luang Prabang, Xieng Khouang (Plain of Jars), and Champasak, plus visits to Laos's hill tribes, adventure trips, and ecotourism excursions. When arranging travel with even the larger tour operators, be absolutely clear about the specifics (meals included, driver's expenses, taxes, and so forth). Many tour companies offer the world and come up short. Below are recommended tour operators that offer Laos itineraries.

- **Diethelm Travel,** Namphu Square, Setthathirath Road, P.O. Box 2657, Vientiane (✆ **021/213-833** or 020/248-9197; fax 021/217-151; www.diethelmtravel.com), is open Monday through Friday from 8am to noon and 1:30 to 5pm, Saturday from 8am to noon, and operates almost like a de facto tourist information and help center. The folks here are the most professional in the country and can arrange deluxe, personalized trips that cover all the necessities. Offices are in all major towns (locations are listed in the sections on each town in this chapter).

- **Exotissimo Travel,** Pangkham Street, Vientiane (✆ **021/241-861;** fax 021/262-001; www.exotissimo.com), is a slick and helpful French-owned company. It offers fine upscale group, individual, classic, and ecotourism itineraries.

- **Green Discovery,** 54 Setthathirath Rd., Nam Phu Fountain Circle, Vientiane (*©* **021/223-022;** www.greendiscoverylaos.com), offers exciting rafting, kayaking, climbing, cycling, and trekking excursions ranging from 1-day trips to 1-month expeditions. The helpful international staff caters to both budget travelers and well heeled adventurers.

Entry Requirements

Visitors need a passport with at least 6 months' future validity and a visa to visit Laos. A tourist visa for Laos with 30 days' validity can be issued at certain entry points or via a travel agent, or you can apply at a Lao embassy or consulate. If you use a travel agent, the visa will cost between $30 and $40 depending on your nationality and in which city you apply. Getting a visa on arrival is perfectly possible at most overland crossings between Thailand and Laos, including the entry points at Huay Xai, Vientiane, Savannakhet, Tha Khek, and Vieng Tao. It is also available at Vientiane, Luang Prabang, and Pakse airports, costing $37, in cash only. You also need one passport photo. It is also available at the Boten crossing with China and at the main international crossings from Vietnam. Visa on arrival is not available at the Paksan crossing at present, nor the southern road or river crossings from Cambodia. That may change shortly, but at the time of writing, if you are planning a trip overland from Cambodia to Laos, make sure you get a visa in Phnom Penh before making your way up the Mekong. Check the Lao Embassy site at **www.laoembassy.com** for details.

You can extend a tourist visa either through the immigration office in Vientiane or through a travel agent. The cost is $2 a day if you do it yourself (Vientiane only). It's a fairly relaxed process. It will be nearer $3 per day if you use a travel agent, which is a necessity if you are outside Vientiane. All tourist visas are single entry only. If you want to stay in Laos longer than a month, it's no problem to cross to Thailand and come back into Laos on a new tourist visa for another 30 days. If you do overstay your visa, you will be fined a fairly hefty $10 a day and it mounts up pretty quickly. If you're calculating an overstay of anything other than a day or two, then you are better off leaving within the expiration date of your visa and crossing over to Thailand to enter on a fresh one.

There is no departure tax if leaving by land on either a bridge or a boat, although one is sometimes touched for an illicit but small "fee" of some sort, particularly after dark or on a weekend. If you're flying out of either Vientiane or Luang Prabang international airport, there is a departure tax of $10, but since early 2009 this fee has been incorporated into the price of the air ticket at the point of sale.

CUSTOMS

You may bring 500 cigarettes, 100 cigars, or 500 grams of tobacco; 1 liter of alcohol; two bottles of wine; and unlimited amounts of money, all for personal use, into Laos without taxation or penalty—not that the Customs officials do much, if any, searching. However, if you purchase silver or copper items during your stay, you might be required to pay duty upon exiting Laos, according to their weight. Antiques, especially Buddha images or parts thereof, are not permitted to leave the country.

Money

The **kip** (pronounced *keep*), the official Lao unit of currency, comes in denominations of 500, 1,000; 2,000, 5,000, and, only recently issued by the Lao government, 10,000, 20,000, and 50,000 notes. The new notes are an improvement, but with the current exchange rate at approximately **8,000 kip = $1,** that still means that the largest unit of currency is just $6.25. For your larger purchases, you'll want to use **U.S. dollars,** accepted widely, or **Thai baht,** commonly accepted but more popular near the border. Be prepared to handle bricks of Lao cash when you exchange foreign currency.

Laos is still very much a cash country, especially outside Vientiane. A new government decree requires service providers to list prices in Lao kip, but virtually all hotel and guesthouse rates, upmarket restaurant prices, transportation charges, and expensive items' price tags can quote prices in U.S. dollars as well. Use kip for smaller purchases, local transportation, and pocket money. Remember to exchange your kip into dollars or baht before leaving Laos. Kip cannot be exchanged outside of the country.

CURRENCY EXCHANGE The main bank in Laos is the **Bank Pour Le Commerce Extérieur.** They exchange cash and traveler's checks and issue U.S. dollars in all the major towns. They also advance money on MasterCard and Visa and charge 3% commission. The **Joint Development Bank** also changes cash and traveler's checks. Both banks also now have **ATMs** in Vientiane, Luang Prabang, Pakse, Savannakhet, and Tha Khek. In fact, ATMs are springing up at a very rapid rate. Many accept both Visa and MasterCard. They are not particularly useful if you are drawing money from a foreign account since they only issue Lao kip with a daily limit in the region of 700,000 kip, and the transaction charges are very high. Bank **exchange booths** are far better. They are rapid and can issue U.S. dollars as well as Lao kip. In Luang Prabang many travel agents also change money and traveler's checks, as well as advancing cash on a credit card.

CREDIT CARDS Credit cards are gaining wider acceptance at hotels and restaurants, but many places are still cash-only.

When to Go

High season for tourism is November through March and the month of August, when weather conditions are favorable, plus the Lao New Year in the middle of April. Accommodations run at full capacity and transportation can be overbooked at these times.

CLIMATE Laos's tropical climate ushers in a wet monsoon season lasting from early May to October, followed by a dry season from November to April. In Vientiane, average temperatures range from 71°F (22°C) in January to 84°F (29°C) in April. The northern regions, which include Xieng Khouang, get chilly from November to February and can approach freezing temperatures at night in mountainous areas. Beginning in mid-February, temperatures gradually climb, and April can see temperatures over 100°F (38°C). In order to avoid the rain and heat, the best time to visit the south is probably November through February. In the mountains of the north, May through July means still-comfortable temperatures.

PUBLIC HOLIDAYS & EVENTS Businesses and government offices close for these holidays, but restaurants remain open. Ask about local festivals; on the full moon of each month, called a *boun,* there's always a festival somewhere—not to be missed.

o **International New Year's Day:** January 1, nationwide. Your standard countdown and party, sans Dick Clark.

- **Lao New Year (Pimai Lao):** Full moon in mid-April, nationwide. The Luang Prabang festivities include a procession, a fair, a sand-castle competition on the Mekong, a Miss New Year pageant, folk performances, and cultural shows. Make sure you're booked and confirmed in hotels before you go.
- **Buddhist Lent (Boun Khao Phansa):** At local temples, worshipers in brightly colored silks greet the dawn on Buddhist Lent by offering gifts to the monks and pouring water into the ground as a gesture of offering to their ancestors. Lent begins in July and lasts 3 months. Monks are meant to stay at their temple throughout this time, for more rigorous practice. Lent ends in the joyous **Boun Ok Phansa** holiday in September, usually commemorated with boat races (see below), carnivals, and the release of hundreds of candle-bearing paper and bamboo floats on the country's rivers.
- **Dragon Boat Races (Bun Song Hua):** Held at different times in late summer and early fall in every riverside town, these races celebrate the end of Buddhist Lent. Teams of 50 paddle longboats in a long sprint, and winners parade through town. The **Vientiane Boat Race Festival** (Vientiane and Savannakhet) is held the second weekend in October. The **Luang Prabang Boat Races** are held in early September along the Nam Kan, with a major market day preceding the races and festivities throughout the night on race day.
- **That Luang Festival:** Full moon in early November, Vientiane. This major Buddhist fete draws the faithful countrywide and from nearby Thailand. Before dawn, thousands join in a ceremonial offering and group prayer, followed by a procession. For days afterward, a combined trade fair and carnival offers handicrafts, flowers, games, concerts, and dance shows.
- **Hmong New Year:** End of November/beginning of December, in the north. Although this is not a national holiday, it's celebrated among this northern hill tribe.
- **National Day:** December 2, nationwide. The entire country celebrates a public holiday, while in Vientiane you'll find parades and dancing at That Luang temple.

Health & Safety

HEALTH CONCERNS See chapter 10's "Health & Safety" section (p. 632) for information on the major health issues that affect travelers to Southeast Asia and recommended precautions for avoiding the most common diseases. It's also a good idea to check the most recent information at the **Centers for Disease Control** (click "Travelers' Health" at **www.cdc.gov**).

No water in Laos is considered potable, so stick with bottled water. Also, Lao cuisine uses many fresh ingredients and garnishes, and condiments made from dried fish that might have been stored under unsanitary conditions. Exercise caution when eating from roadside and market stalls and smaller local restaurants.

In Laos, medical facilities are scarce and rudimentary. Emergency medical facilities exist in Vientiane, but outside the capital you'll require medical evacuation. Contact information is provided under "Fast Facts: Laos," below.

SAFETY CONCERNS Visitors to Laos should refer to their home country's overseas travel bureau or check with the **U.S. State Department** (click the "more" option under "Travel Warnings" at **www.travel.state.gov** for a complete, up-to-date list) to learn more about the present situation in the area. Laos is not a dangerous destination, but it's important to remember that the current climate of calm and openness to visitors is historically quite new. Visitors should keep an ear to the ground when in the country.

Travelers in the countryside should also remember that bus and boat breakdowns are frequent. Additionally, road conditions and poor infrastructure make rural travel unpredictable. Hospital facilities, even in the capital, are rudimentary at best, and any serious medical conditions require evacuation. UXO, unexploded ordnance left from years of conflict, is still a major concern, especially in Xieng Khouang near the Plain of Jars. It should also be mentioned that Lao Airlines has yet to pass any international standards for safety.

Getting There

Official land borders are with China, Vietnam, Cambodia, and Thailand. Not all of the smaller border points are open to Western nationals, although this is changing fast.

BY PLANE In most cases, to get to Laos you will need to get to Bangkok in Thailand first since it is the major regional hub for onward travel all over the region. There are three international airports in Laos:

- Wattay International Airport (VTE; ✆ 021/512-165)
- Luang Prabang International Airport (LPQ; ✆ 071/212-856)
- Pakse International Airport (PKZ; ✆ 031/212-844).

Lao Airlines is the national carrier and has domestic flights to all airports in the country, as well as to Thailand, Cambodia, China, and Vietnam. In addition, **Thai Airways International, Vietnam Airlines,** and **China Eastern Airlines** serve Vientiane, while **Bangkok Airways** and Vietnam Airlines serve Luang Prabang. **Air Asia** (www.airasia.com) run flights from Kuala Lumpur to Vientiane.

- Vietnam Airlines (1st Floor, Lao Plaza Hotel, Samsenthai Rd.; ✆ **021/217-562;** www.vietnamairlines.com), 8am to noon and 1:30 to 4:30pm Monday to Friday and 8am to noon on Saturday.
- Lao Airlines (Pangkham Rd.; ✆ **021/512-028;** www.laoairlines.com), 8am to noon and 1 to 4:30pm Monday to Saturday.
- Thai Airways International (Luang Prabang Rd.; ✆ **021/222-527**), 8am to 5pm Monday to Friday and 8am to noon on Saturday.
- China Eastern Airlines (Luang Prabang Rd.; ✆ **021/212-300;** www.flychina eastern.com).
- Bangkok Airways (57/6 Sisavangvong; ✆ **071/253-334** or 253-253; www.bangkok air.com).

BY TRAIN In 2009, the extension of the railway line from Bangkok to Nong Khai and across the border to Laos was completed. No one ever used it though, since there is a great deal more trouble involved in crossing the border by train than simply getting off in Nong Khai and crossing the border by foot, bus, or taxi. It is now being retired, and both the line and the **Thanalaeng station** will become sidings for a proposed new high-speed rail link, connecting China and Thailand through Laos.

Take any train between Bangkok and Nong Khai, and then use road transport into Laos. From Nong Khai, take a local tuk-tuk from the railway station to Nong Khai bus station, costing 50B. A shuttle bus runs from the bus station across the Friendship Bridge to Laos every 20 minutes throughout the day. It costs about 30B, and it stops at Thai immigration 5 minutes after leaving the bus station and then crosses the Friendship Bridge, arriving at Lao customs and immigration. You then remove your luggage from the bus and go through Lao customs. Once through, take another tuk-tuk to your chosen hotel.

When traveling southbound, leave central Vientiane at least 3 hours before your train leaves Nong Khai for Bangkok, in order to allow time for border formalities and the various bus/taxi journeys.

BY BUS   Getting from any major Thai town or city to any border crossing with Laos is a very simple task since buses are frequent, cheap, efficient, and ubiquitous. Buses from Bangkok's Morchit Northern Bus Terminal take about 9 hours and usually leave Bangkok in the evening and travel overnight. Tickets are 500B to 1,000B depending on the quality of facilities on the bus. There are also buses to all major cities in Vietnam from Vientiane, Luang Prabang, Savannakhet, and Pakse.

Getting Around

What was said about getting around in Laos only 5 years ago is now largely history. Until recently, going anywhere was hard work. The national airline was considered to be dangerous and the roads were bone-jarringly bad and occasionally beset by armed bandits, particularly on the way to Luang Prabang. Those perceptions should now be consigned to the dustbin of history, although a simple Internet search will show that cyber-consciousness takes some years to update itself. Most of the roads to major destinations are adequate and surfaced. Lao Airlines may not be a world leader, but it has been overhauled dramatically from the days when the words "Lao Aviation" struck terror into the heart of any nervous flyer. Indeed, their slogan is now a reassuring "You're Safe with Us." The river, where one is allowed to navigate it, was always the winner in terms of getting around Laos, and that hasn't changed. As roads improve, river travel declines. Roads are quicker and cheaper.

BY PLANE   The national carrier, Lao Airlines (Pangkham Rd., Vientiane; $\textcircled{C}$ **021/512-028;** www.laoairlines.com) is the only domestic airline in Laos.

BY BUS   The bus system has vastly improved over the past few years in coverage, speed, and comfort. Having said that, taking a long-distance bus in Laos can still seem like a pretty arduous option, and they are very slow and often quite crowded. Quality really varies. In addition to people, you can sometimes find yourself on a bus also packed with great piles of goods being transported from one place to another. Also, the buses are very slow. Unless you are very tough or in a big hurry, it pays in terms of blood pressure to plan your trips in short stages.

On major routes minibuses will parallel the public buses for a few more dollars. They are certainly faster, although not much more comfortable since you will still be crammed in and they swing around the bends in a way that can make your head spin.

Air-conditioned, Thai-style VIP buses (often from the magnificently named "King of Bus" company) ply the routes between major towns. On the long journey from Champasak to Vientiane, there are many companies offering sleeper buses with your own curtained-off bunk. The VIP buses are best booked through a travel agent or your hotel. VIP buses vary considerably between genuinely well appointed air-conditioned luxury to vehicles piled high with luggage and added chaos. When you are in the mountainous north, whichever of these options you take, the driver will most likely be issuing all passengers a plastic bag or two. That is because these mountain roads bring whole new vistas of meaning to the words *travel sick.*

Finally, there is that mainstay of Lao transport, the *songthaew*. This is a van with a covered rear with two benches (the word means "two rows" in Lao and Thai) on either side facing each other. They tend to cover smaller local journeys, although you certainly can take them all the way on longer routes if you are feeling particularly sociable.

BY CAR One alternative is to hire a private car with a driver (self-drive vehicles are virtually impossible to find). Contacts for car hires are listed in each corresponding section that follows.

BY BOAT The river used to be the main means of transport in Laos. This was largely because the roads were truly dreadful or nonexistent. That has changed rapidly as the whole country progresses to being sealed and paved, and road transport undercuts river transport in terms of both money and time. The journey down from Huay Xai in the north to Pakbeng remains very popular, and a number of companies run vessels of varying luxury. You can book a ticket from a travel agent on the Thai side of the border in Chiang Khong before you cross. This is not recommended because you won't see what you are getting. For the normal tourist boat you can simply walk through immigration in Huay Xai and then wander down to where the boats are moored and buy a ticket for $20. Boat traffic south of Luang Prabang is virtually nonexistent. Elsewhere in the country you can charter your own boat, but that is expensive and logistically complicated. If you are in a hurry, the quickest way to move is by **Lao "speedboat"**—a narrow flat-bottomed skiff with an outsize car engine bolted to the back that skims the surface of the water at 80kmph (50 mph), shooting rapids and narrowly missing boulders. These craft are very dangerous, with a track record of accidents, and are not recommended. At the time of writing, the speedboat service on the route from Huay Xai to Luang Prabang had been suspended due to noise disruption and accidents. It is still running on the Nam Ou River from Phonsaly to Muong Khua.

---

 telephone dialing AT A GLANCE

○ **To place a call from your home country to Laos:** Dial the international access code (011 in the U.S. and Canada, 0011 in Australia, 0170 in New Zealand, 00 in the U.K.), plus Laos's country code **(856),** the city or local area code (**21** for Vientiane, **71** for Luang Prabang), and the phone number (for example, 011 856 21/000-000). *Important note:* Omit the initial "0" in all Laos phone numbers when calling from abroad.

○ **To place a call within Laos:** Dial the city or area code preceded by a **0** (the way numbers are listed in this book), and then the local number (for example, 021/000-000).

○ **To place a direct international call from Laos:** Dial the international access code **(00),** plus the country code, the area or city code, and the number (for example, to call the U.S., you'd dial 00 1 000/000-0000).

○ **International country codes are as follows:** Australia, 61; Cambodia, 855; Canada, 1; Hong Kong, 852; Indonesia, 62; Malaysia, 60; Myanmar, 95; New Zealand, 64; the Philippines, 63; Singapore, 65; Thailand, 66; U.K., 44; U.S., 1; Vietnam, 84.

Tips on Accommodations

Book your hotel early during peak season (Aug and Nov–Mar), using travel agents and tour operators as necessary. Also be aware that most hotels in Luang Prabang are full during the Lao New Year, when thousands of tourists, both foreign and Lao, pour into the city for the festivities. Both standards and prices are generally good.

Tips on Dining

Lao cuisine is varied and interesting, with sticky rice (or glutinous rice) a staple. Lao fare mixes Thai and Chinese traditions, with a bit of French thrown in for good measure (and a few unique regional favorites). Try it at real restaurants whenever possible—the street stands aren't up to the standards of those in either Vietnam or Thailand. French colonial influence is clear in the many excellent Continental options in Vientiane and Luang Prabang.

Tips on Shopping

You'll undoubtedly leave with a few pieces of hand-woven Lao textiles, handcrafted silver, and other lovely objects. Many things are one of a kind, so if you see something you like, get it. Remember that the Lao do, of course, haggle. For foreigners, the starting price might be high, but bargaining here is not as relentless as it is in Laos's neighboring countries.

[FastFACTS] LAOS

American Express The country's one Amex representative is **Diethelm Travel,** Namphu Square, Setthathirath Road, Vientiane (☎ **021/213-833** or 021/215-920; www.diethelm travel.com).

Business Hours With a few exceptions, hours are 8:30am to noon and 1:30 to 5pm Monday through Friday, 8am to noon on Saturday. Restaurants are open from about 11am to 2pm and 6 to 10pm daily; many are closed for lunch on Sunday.

Drug Laws Opium is openly grown in northeast Laos and is easily available, as is marijuana. Neither is legal, and although you might see many travelers indulging, it is highly recommended that you don't.

You could face high fines or jail if you're caught.

Electricity Laos runs on 220-volt electrical currents. Plugs are two-pronged, with either round or flat prongs. If you're coming from the U.S. and you must bring electrical appliances, bring your own converter and adapter. Outside of Vientiane and Luang Prabang, electricity is sketchy, and sometimes available for only a few hours a day. A surge protector is a must for laptops.

Embassies U.S.: Thatdam Bartholonie Road, Vientiane (☎ **021/267-000;** fax 021/212-584; http://vientiane.usembassy. gov). **Australia:** Nehru Road, Bane Phonsaly, Vientiane (☎ **021/413-600;** www.laos.embassy.gov.au).

The Australian embassy also assists nationals of Canada, New Zealand, and the U.K.

Emergencies In Vientiane, dial ☎ **191** for police, ☎ **190** for fire, and ☎ **195** for an ambulance. For medical evacuation, call **Lao Westcoast Helicopter Company** (☎ **021/512-023;** www.laowestcoast.com) in Vientiane.

Hospitals Medical facilities in Laos are very basic indeed. Most foreigners living in Laos go to Thailand for treatment of all but the most trivial of ailments. The Friendship Bridge connecting Vientiane to Nong Khai in Thailand is open from 6am to 10pm. If there is a real medical emergency, crossing out of hours is allowed. Many travelers go to AEK International Hospital ($\mathcal{C}$ **+66-42/342-555**) or the North Eastern Wattana General Hospital ($\mathcal{C}$ **+66-1/833-4262,** both of which are in Udon Thani about 55km (34 miles) from the border. Both hospitals have English-speaking staff. For less complex medical procedures, Nong Khai Wattana Hospital in Nong Khai, Thailand ($\mathcal{C}$ **+66-1/833-4262**) is also an option.

Within Laos, the International Medical Clinic operated by Mahosot Hospital is situated on the banks of the Mekong on Fa Ngum Road ($\mathcal{C}$ **021/214-022;** open 24 hr.). The Australian Embassy also operates a modern medical clinic. It is situated at Km 4 on Thadeua Road in Watnak Village ($\mathcal{C}$ **021/353-840;** Mon–Fri 8:30am–12:30pm and 1:30–5pm). Most doctors and hospitals in Laos require payment in cash, regardless of whether you have health insurance The Australian Embassy Clinic accepts both MasterCard and Visa.

Internet Access   You can find Internet cafes in the main tourist towns. The cheapest service is found in Vientiane and Luang Prabang, where connections are generally fast. Wireless access is now available in both cities, but connections are slow.

Language   The national language of Laos is *Lao,* which is similar to Thai. Many people understand Thai, and in Vientiane and Luang Prabang, many speak English. Some older people speak French. See "Language," p. 182, for more information.

Liquor Laws   There are no real liquor laws in Laos, but most bars refuse to admit patrons age 17 and under. Bars usually close around midnight.

Mail   A letter or postcard should take about 10 days to reach the U.S. Overseas postage runs about 33,000 kip ($3.80) for 100 grams, and up to 138,000 kip ($16) for 500 grams. Postcards are 8,500 kip ($1). The mail system is not very reliable In Laos. If you can, you are better off mailing from Thailand. Outgoing mail takes 10 to 15 days to reach Europe or America. When posting a parcel, you must leave it open for a customs inspection. There is an Express Mail service to most Western countries which is faster than standard mail and also automatically registers your letter. **FedEx** ($\mathcal{C}$ **021/223-278**) and **DHL** ($\mathcal{C}$ **021/216-830**) have offices in the major cities. Post offices tend to be open 5 days a week between 8am and noon and 1 and 4pm. You can recognize them by their mustard-colored signs.

Safety   Laos is an extremely safe country by any standard. Violent or even petty crime is not a big risk for tourists. There have been rare instances of robbery or rape in remote areas, however. Thus, solo travelers should take care when off the beaten path, even on a day hike. Petty crime does exist. Watch your belongings, and don't leave valuables in your hotel rooms. When trekking in the north near the Plain of Jars or in the south around the Ho Chi Minh trail, beware of unexploded bombs. Don't stray into remote areas, and don't touch anything on the ground. See "Health & Safety," p. 188, for more information.

Telephones   The international country code for Laos is **856.** Most newer hotels have international direct dialing at surcharges of about 10%. Collect calls are impossible, and the long-distance companies haven't made it to Laos yet. Internet cafes often have Internet phone service at 2,000 kip per minute and charge 2,000 kip for callback service. See "Telephone Dialing at a Glance," p. 191, for details.

Phone booths in Laos accept only prepaid phone cards, even for local calls. You can buy phone cards at the post office, telephone office, and minimarts. Laos has no coins.

Laos has bypassed the need to upgrade the landline system by investing heavily in the **mobile phone network.** There are a number of operators and you can buy a local SIM card for $5. Recharge cards are also cheap and widely available. There are a number of providers. **Laotel** and **ETL** Mobile have the best coverage. **Tigo** has agreements with more than 100 International phone networks. They also have a low-cost international rate of 2000 kip per minute to many countries, if you buy their SIM card and dial "177" instead of "+". Their coverage is still said to be poor away from larger towns. **ETL Mobile** (www.etllao.com) is known to have better coverage in rural and remote parts of Laos.

Time Zone Laos is 7 hours ahead of Greenwich Mean Time, in the same zone as Bangkok. That makes it 12 hours ahead of the U.S. Eastern Standard Time during the winter months, and 3 hours behind Sydney.

Tipping Tipping has arrived in Laos, particularly in Vientiane. Feel free to tip bellhops, chauffeurs, and tour guides, and to leave 5% to 10% or round up your bill in upscale restaurants. Foreign currency, especially U.S. dollars, is appreciated.

Toilets You'll find Western toilets (sit-down style) in most hotels for foreigners. Out in the boonies, it's mostly the Asian-style squat toilets. Bring your own toilet paper. Sanitary hand wipes or lotions are a good idea, too. You'll notice a bowl and a pail of water nearby for flushing (put two or three buckets in). On rural roads, buses just pull to the side for bathroom breaks. In villages, find a convenient tree.

Water Drink only boiled or bottled water. Be wary of ice in any but the finest restaurants. Some people even use boiled or bottled water for tooth brushing.

VIENTIANE ★★

Vientiane (Wee-en-*chan*) is often described as one of the world's most laid-back capitals. It is small, pleasant, and compact. Although it lacks the splendors of Luang Prabang, it does have its own unique charm. Even though it is a long way from the sea, by this stage in its course the Mekong River is very wide, meandering, and rather mesmerizing. Upon arrival, whether by land or by air, make your way to **Chanthabuli,** the central district by the river. Here you will find guesthouses, hotels, restaurants, and Internet cafes. Once you're there, most things you want to reach will be within easy walking distance.

Having said that, for better or worse, the slow march to modernity is in progress, as the massive influx of foreign aid and manpower from both foreign governments and NGOs reshapes the city and dramatically affects those who inhabit it. Although change comes slowly to Vientiane, traffic is now increasing in the center of town. The city is largely closed down by 11pm. The essential nature of Vientiane is relaxed, but for how many more years that will remain the case is uncertain. Compared to either Hanoi or Phnom Penh, it remains a village, and that encapsulates its essential charm.

Getting There

For more information on arriving by plane or by train, see p. 189.

BY PLANE Vientiane is Laos's major international hub for air travel. If you're arriving via **Wattay International Airport** in Vientiane, a taxi to town will cost $5.

BY BUS The **Northern Bus Station** (✆ 021/260-555) connects Vientiane with all destinations in Laos. The bus station at the **Morning Market** (✆ 021/216-507), which is called **Talat Sao** in Lao, is the hub for local buses as well as those linking Vientiane with Nong Khai and Udonthani in Thailand via the Friendship Bridge.

Getting Around

The city lies on the east side of the Mekong River (the western bank is Thailand). The main streets, running parallel to each other, are Samsenthai and Setthathirath, with Lane Xang, the north-south artery, intersecting them. The heart of the city is Nam Phu Fountain, and many of the directions in this chapter are given in relation to it.

Central Vientiane is easily covered on foot. You can also hire a **tuk-tuk,** a covered cart behind a motorbike, or a **jumbo,** a bigger version of the same. Drivers charge about 10,000 kip to 20,000 kip around town; settle the price before you ride. Bikes are a great way to get around town. Both bicycle and motorcycle rentals are available at many storefronts along Fa Ngum Road near the river or along Samsenthai.

Visitor Information & Tours

There is a tourist information office on Lane Xang Avenue, just north of the Morning Market. Also see "Organized Tours & Travel Agents" (p. 185) for tour providers in Laos, all of which have helpful offices in Vientiane. The *Vientiane Times* (www.vientiane times.org.la) is the local English-language paper with listings of local events.

[Fast FACTS] VIENTIANE

American Express Vientiane's Amex representative is **Diethelm Travel,** Namphu Square, Setthathirath Road (℡ **021/213-833;** www.diethelmtravel.com).

ATMs There's a **Banque Pour Le Commerce Extérieur Lao (BCEL)** ATM on Setthathirath Road (across the street from Joma Café); the maximum withdrawal is 700,000 kip. The newly opened **Australia New Zealand Bank Vientiane (ANZV)** has two ATMs at their Lang Xang Avenue branch near the Victory Monument (at Blvd. Khounboulan intersection).

Currency Exchange **Banque Pour Le Commerce Extérieur Lao (BCEL)** is on Pangkham Street down by the river, just west of the Lane Xang Hotel (℡ **021/213-200**). At BCEL and most other banks, you can exchange money in all major currencies, change traveler's checks to U.S.

dollars, and get cash advances on Visa and MasterCard; commission rates start at 3%. You can also exchange money at **Banque Setthathirath,** near Wat Mixay. All banks are open Monday through Friday from 8:30am to 3:30pm. Other banks line Lane Xang Avenue; exchange counters dot the city.

Emergencies For police, dial ℡ **991;** for fire, dial ℡ **190;** and for an ambulance, dial ℡ **195.** For medical evacuation, call **Lao Westcoast Helicopter Company** (℡ **021/512-023**).

Internet Access There are numerous Internet cafes on riverside Fa Ngum or on parallel Setthathirath or Samsenthai (each 1 block farther from the river). Connections are generally good. Expect to pay around 100 kip to 300 kip per minute at most Internet cafes. Hotel business centers

charge at least three times this rate. Free Wi-Fi access is increasingly available in restaurants and hotels. **Sticky Fingers** and **Full Moon Café** on François Nginn Street are the best of the bunch at present.

Mall The general post office is at the corner of Khou Vieng Road and Lane Xang Avenue, opposite the Morning Market. Hours are Monday through Friday from 8am to noon and 1 to 5pm, Saturday and Sunday from 8am to noon. EMS and FedEx services are just next door.

Telephones The city code for Vientiane is **21.** The central telephone office, where you can place local and international direct dial (IDD) calls, is located on Setthathirath Road just east of Nam Phu Circle (Nam Phu Fountain). It's open from 8am to 10pm daily. You can also send faxes.

Where to Stay

Vientiane has some good options that range from luxury rooms to backpacker dives. Book ahead, especially in late November and early December, and ask for a discount if you come during the rainy season (some places post their low-season rates). Hotels accept U.S. dollars, Lao kip, or Thai baht. Be warned that the prices listed below do not always include a government tax of 10% or any additional service charges (sometimes applicable in high season).

EXPENSIVE

Don Chan Palace ★ Vientiane has a law prohibiting building higher than seven floors, but somehow the Malaysian company behind the Don Chan Palace managed to circumvent the rule—maybe because the hotel is technically on an island in the river. From the outside this 14-floor hotel is a tragedy, and really blights the skyline. Constructed in 2004 for the ASEAN conference, it really is a mystery as to why it was allowed to come into being in the first place—the best explanation is a misplaced desire for international prestige. When you are actually in the Don Chan Palace, the view is better because you can no longer see the hotel itself. Rooms are business-hotel standard, with muted colors and few traditional Lao touches, but they're comfortable nonetheless. Ask for a room on the Mekong/sunset side, where you can enjoy the scenery from your own small balcony.

Unit 6 Piawat Village, Sistanak District, Vientiane. ✆**021/244-288.** Fax 021/244-111. www.donchanpalace laopdr.com. 239 units. $120–$190 double; $250–$550 suite; $1,800–$2,000 Presidential suite. AE, MC, V. **Amenities:** 3 restaurants; bar and disco; bakery; coffee shop; concierge; outdoor gym; indoor pool; sauna; spa; shuttle-bus service (to city center and airport). *In room:* A/C, satellite TV, hair dryer, Internet access, minibar.

Green Park Boutique Hotel ★★ Combining the traditional and the contemporary into a seamless whole can be difficult, but the Green Park has succeeded in doing just that. Raised tile pathways set among jar fountains lead from the elegant reception area to the central courtyard, where contemporary Lao-style pavilions surround a lovely swimming pool and adjacent reflecting pool. Stylish guest rooms boast rich wood floors, beautiful Lao silks draped over chic teakwood furniture, and all the modern conveniences, including free wireless Internet access. Cozy balconies have views of the pools and the newly planted frangipani trees that dot the surrounding garden areas.

248 Khouvieng Rd., P.O. Box 9698, Vientiane. ✆ **021/264-097.** Fax 021/263-064. www.greenpark vientiane.com. 34 units. $140 classic; $150–$160 deluxe; $290 suite. Internet rates available. AE, MC, V. **Amenities:** Restaurant; lounge; free airport transfers and shuttle service to town; Jacuzzi; outdoor pool; spa. *In room:* A/C, satellite TV, hair dryer, minibar, Wi-Fi.

Lao Plaza Hotel ★ Popular with business travelers, the Lao Plaza is the most familiar international hotel in Laos. It's in a convenient central location, and the accommodations are bland but comfortable. Sizable rooms are either beige or blue, with solid wood furniture, thick rugs, firm beds, and small marble-tile bathrooms with terry-cloth robes. The pool is big and inviting. The May Yuan restaurant has admirable Chinese food, while a cheery cafe has buffet meals and a deli/bakery. The Plaza is sufficiently self-contained and convenient to any destination in town, and one of only a few accommodations in Laos where you might forget that you're in Laos.

63 Samsenthai Rd., P.O. Box 6708, Vientiane. ✆ **021/218-800.** Fax 021/218-808. www.laoplazahotel. com. 142 units. $180–$206 superior single/twin; $225–$256 plaza single/twin; $344–$569 suite; $725 presidential suite. AE, MC, V. **Amenities:** 3 restaurants; bar; popular nightclub; beer garden; bakery;

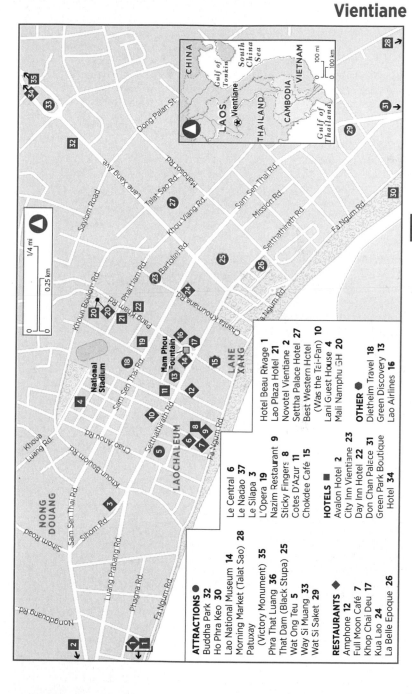

Vientiane

ATTRACTIONS ●
Buddha Park **32**
Ho Phra Keo **30**
Lao National Museum **14**
Morning Market (Talat Sao) **28**
Patuxay
   (Victory Monument) **35**
Phra That Luang **36**
That Dam (Black Stupa) **25**
Wat Ong Teu **5**
Way Si Muang **33**
Wat Si Saket **29**

RESTAURANTS ◆
Amphone **12**
Full Moon Café **7**
Khop Chai Deu **17**
Kua Lao **24**
La Belle Epoque **26**

Le Central **6**
Le Nadao **37**
L'Opera **19**
Nazim Restaurant **9**
Sticky Fingers **8**
Cotes D'Azur **11**
Chokdee Café **15**

HOTELS ■
Avalon Hotel **2**
City Inn Vientiane **23**
Day Inn Hotel **22**
Don Chan Palace **31**
Green Park Boutique
   Hotel **34**

Hotel Beau Rivage **1**
Lao Plaza Hotel **21**
Novotel Vientiane **2**
Settha Palace Hotel **27**
Best Western Hotel
   (Was the Tai-Pan) **10**
Lani Guest House **4**
Mali Namphu GH **20**

OTHER ●
Diethelm Travel **18**
Green Discovery **13**
Lao Airlines **16**

gym; Internet access (in business center); Jacuzzi; nice pool; sauna; smoke-free rooms. *In room:* A/C, satellite TV, hair dryer, Internet access (Plaza rooms free), minibar.

Novotel Vientiane ★   The building itself is from the French era and very stylish. The foyer is cavernous with a sweeping staircase with a very 1940s retro feel. Somehow one expects Humphrey Bogart to emerge from the dining room and say something cynical—it's that kind of a place. The fantastic pool area is leafy and atmospheric. The lobby is decorated in a classic Art Deco theme, with stylish woodwork. Renovated rooms have fine wood furniture and marble bathrooms. They also come with perks such as free laundry, a minibar, and Internet access. The mildly wriggling fly in the ointment is that some of them are a little dark and there are reports that the beds are rather rocklike to sleep on. Adjoining the lobby is a well appointed Continental restaurant with indoor and outdoor by-the-pool seating. It's a bit far from town but has very convenient amenities and good transportation.

Unit 9, Samsenthai Rd., P.O. Box 585, Vientiane. © **800/221-4542** or 021/213-570. Fax 021/213-572. www.novotel.com. 172 units. $112 standard; $133 superior; $181 executive; $242 executive suite. AE, MC, V. **Amenities:** Restaurant; 3 bars; free transport to the town center; babysitting; health club; Internet access (in business center); nice outdoor pool; room service; sauna; tennis;. *In room:* A/C, satellite TV, hair dryer, Internet access, minibar.

Settha Palace Hotel ★★★   This is the best hotel in Vientiane. It was first built in the early 20th century under the French. As you walk up the leafy driveway, you will be greeted by the sight of a genuine London minicab, used to ferry guests to the airport. Restoration to an "Indochine" ideal (one which very likely never existed in reality) is a rabidly popular exercise in the hospitality industry across Laos and Cambodia, but in the Settha Place they really get it right. The pool area is leafy and calm and the service is superb yet casual. Rooms are cozy, with antique details, dark-wood reproduction furnishings, and stalwart four-poster beds. They have all the facilities that an international hotel should offer but somehow seem to proffer them in a personal style. Bathrooms are small but still have separate showers. The hotel's elegant restaurant, La Belle Epoque (p. 200), serves excellent Continental cuisine.

6 Pangkham (P.O. Box 161), Vientiane. © **021/217-581.** Fax 021/217-583. www.setthapalace.com. 29 units. $220 deluxe; $320 junior suite; $420 suite. AE, MC, V. **Amenities:** Restaurant; bar; Internet access (in business center); Jacuzzi; outdoor pool (nonguests welcome for $7.50); room service. *In room:* A/C, satellite TV, minibar, Wi-Fi.

MODERATE

Best Western ★ 🗡   Until a recent takeover in mid-2010, this was called the Tai-Pan Hotel. It combines businesslike practicality with a certain amount of style. It is tastefully and efficiently designed, well equipped, with friendly staff. If you are on business and want to be near the center of town, the Best Western will give you everything you need. Neither fancy nor glamorous, it is about getting things done. That does not mean that it is soulless—the designers obviously put a lot of thought into combining functionality and style, and that combination is very successful. The rooms are large and come with all the conveniences you would need. The pool and the business center are good and the foyer has just enough painted-on retro charm to do justice to its old town location.

2-12 François Nginn Rd., Ban Mixay, Muong Chanthabury, Vientiane. © **021/216-906.** Fax 021/216-223. www.bestwestern.com. 44 units. $74 double; $78 deluxe; $85 junior suite. AE, MC, V. **Amenities:** Restaurant; bar; airport transfers; health club; Internet access; Jacuzzi; small pool; sauna; conference rooms; computer rental. *In room:* A/C, satellite TV, minibar.

4

LAOS | Vientiane

City Inn Vientiane ★★ 🎁 This brand-new hotel is a stylish option for downtown Vientiane. The decor is minimalist with a touch of traditional Laos. Double rooms are spacious, with unfinished stone floors, cream-colored walls, and contemporary wood furniture. Cool rattan furniture and traditional Lao silk bed throws round out the look, alongside modern comforts such as flatscreen TVs and American standard tubs and sinks. The large lobby has sparkling white floors and Scandinavian-style furniture mixed with dark-wood accents. This is a great place to check into for a few days. Longer-stay/serviced apartments are also available.

Pangkham Rd. (across from Days Inn), Lane Xang Ave., P.O. Box 3925, Vientiane. ☎ **021/218-333.** Fax 021/218-444. 40 units. $65 deluxe; $100–$112 suite. MC, V. Free parking. **Amenities:** Restaurant; bar; sauna; smoke-free rooms. *In room:* A/C, TV, minibar.

Hotel Beau Rivage Mekong ★★ The Beau Rivage is beautifully situated by the river. It is also very eccentric in a way that works. Floor-to-ceiling windows grace both the lobby area and many of the rooms, letting light from across the Mekong flood the building. This is probably the only riverside hotel where they have really thought about maximizing the enjoyment of the river views. There are also art exhibits scattered around. With Wi-Fi throughout, it works if you are engaged in either business or leisure, and being a bit up the river it is very quiet. The rooms feature pastel shades, which has the potential to plunge the whole enterprise into the realm of the nauseatingly twee. The Beau Rivage somehow succeeds in not being too kitschy, however. The bar/restaurant is delightfully appointed in a rustic and very comfortable fashion. In true boutique style the Beau Rivage has an attached spa.

Fa Ngum Rd., P.O. Box 9015, Vientiane. ☎ **021/243-350.** Fax 021/243-345. www.hbrm.com. 16 units. High season $50–$61 double; low season $45–$52 double. MC, V. **Amenities:** Restaurant; bar; spa. *In room:* A/C, TV, minibar, Wi-Fi.

Lani Guest House This hotel stands out from the crowd simply because they are doing something quite different from everyone else. It is down a shaded lane in a slightly rambling old villa. The place is airy with atmosphere with statues and handicrafts scattered artfully around both the rooms and the communal areas. The rooms in the house are large, airy, and pleasant. Those in an adjoining annex are a bit dark. It is a lovely place but somewhat overpriced. They have, however, done very well to create something special for a niche market. The Lani inspires real enthusiasm among those who stay there often and does get a lot of repeat customers. In keeping with its pleasant but slightly snooty outlook, the Lani Guest House does not have TVs, but it does have wireless Internet throughout.

281 Setthathirath Rd., Ban Haysok, Vientiane. ☎ **021/214-919.** www.laniguesthouse.com. 12 units. $35–$40 double; $25–$30 single. MC, V. **Amenities:** Internet. *In room:* A/C.

INEXPENSIVE

Avalon Hotel ★ 🍴 This brand-new minihotel is the best option in this price range. It's about 2 blocks away from the main tourist drag, which is either a good thing or a bad thing depending on your love/tolerance of loud music and chatty travelers. Double rooms are nice, but the corner twins are worth the upgrade—they're bigger and have better views. Each room is named for a flower, and quotations offering pearls of wisdom are pasted to the walls or fridges. The staff is eager to please; some have excellent English, and others get an A for effort.

Phnom Penh Rd., Ban Anou, Vientiane. ☎ **021/263-597.** Fax 021/263-596. www.avalonbooking.com. 30 units. $15 standard; $30–$35 double/twin; $65 suite. Internet rates available. MC, V. **Amenities:** Restaurant. *In room:* A/C, satellite TV, fridge (not available in single rooms), Wi-Fi.

Day Inn Hotel ★ 🛏 This charming little inn in the shadow of the Lao Plaza was once the Indian embassy, and it retains some of that urban, colonial dignity in its large, airy rooms, with their high ceilings and tall French doors. Though it's all a bit simple, and the bright sea-green color scheme is a little overpowering, you're in an ideal downtown location. Rooms (with orange, blue, or pink walls) are furnished in basic but tidy wicker, with hard beds and clean bathrooms (some with a tub). The Day Inn is like an upscale guesthouse, really, but it has the standard in-room amenities of a proper hotel. Ask for a room in the front, where doors and windows open to small private balconies. The staff is extremely cheerful and very helpful, making this an all-around pleasant stay.

059/3 Pangkham Rd., P.O. Box 4083, Vientiane. © **021/223-848.** Fax 021/222-984. dayinn@laopdr. com. 32 units. $40–$45 double/twin; $60 suite. MC, V. **Amenities:** Restaurant; Internet access in lobby. *In room:* A/C, satellite TV, minibar.

Mali Namphu Guest House ★★★ 🖋 Mali Namphu is a beautiful French villa right in the center of town. They have the renovation to Indochine style exactly right, and at $30, this place is a steal. The atmospheric ocher building is constructed around a shaded courtyard with a very Parisian-looking terrace on which you can sit and enjoy your very Parisian-looking coffee. The staff is very friendly. They also have an unusually efficient website operation if you wish to book in advance.

114 Pangkham Rd. © **021/215-093.** Fax 021/263-297. www.malinamphu.com. 40 units. $30 double. MC, V. **Amenities:** Restaurant; bar; executive-level rooms; Internet; room service. *In room:* A/C, satellite TV, fridge, minibar.

Where to Dine

When it comes to food, you might consider Vientiane to be the equivalent of the Holy Grail. Dining is one of the great pleasures of this town. The quality of cuisines of all types is unsurpassed in Southeast Asia, with both Luang Prabang and Phnom Penh coming a close second. What is particularly distinctive is that in addition to Laotian cuisine, there is a plethora of French restaurants serving what is genuinely gourmet fare at prices that will leave you gasping in astonishment. The standards are incredibly high.

EXPENSIVE

La Belle Epoque ★★ FRENCH/CONTINENTAL In the atmospheric Settha Palace Hotel (p. 198), you can't beat the atmosphere of La Belle Epoque—colonial elegance mixed with Vientiane's laid-back charm. The service is efficient, and the menu covers a wide range of Continental specialties, with meat, game, and seafood prepared to order. Imported Australian steaks and salmon top a fine list of specialties, such as grilled lamb with ratatouille or terrine of duck liver marinated in wine. Try one of the creative appetizers, such as the goat-cheese pastry. Don't pass up the crème brûlée. You would pay an arm and a leg for such a meal anywhere but here. The Sunday poolside buffet brunch (11am–2pm) is a steal at $18; price includes pool admission.

Settha Palace Hotel, 6 Pangkham St. © **021/217-581.** Reservations recommended. Main courses $7.50–$25. AE, MC, V. Daily 7am–10:30pm.

Le Nadao ★★ FRENCH Le Nadao means "Stars in the Ricefield," and indeed this little star now plays host to Vientiane's best and brightest businesspeople and dignitaries. The dining room is a converted teak house, very rustic and soothing, with a corrugated metal ceiling showing through rough slats, warm indirect lighting, and live local music. The menu is classic French. You might start with calamari pan-fried in cream Catalonian style, followed by roast partridge in a rich gravy with potatoes and a lightly fried Mekong filet with lemon, capers, and local organic brown rice. Dessert is chocolate mousse—so rich you'll melt—or a unique "tulip" of pastry with local fruit and ice cream. Bring someone special and make a long evening of it.

Patouxay (on the west side of the Victory Monument roundabout). ℂ **021/213-174.** Main courses $4-$30. MC, V. Daily noon–1:30pm and 7-10:30pm.

L'Opera ★★ ITALIAN   For more than 10 years, L'Opera has been serving "real Italian" cuisine and garnering nothing but praise. It features homemade egg-noodle pasta, fine grilled and broiled entrees, daily specials, and fantastic desserts and espresso. There is also a large selection of pizza Lao, which is a surprisingly good combination of tomatoes, cheese, chiles, Lao sausage, and pineapple. The ambience is a rather formal Italy-meets-Lao, with linen tablecloths, brick walls, and wood-beam ceilings in a large, open setting. Lao staff in fine restaurants often act as if their foreign patrons are armed and dangerous, but here the service is confident and professional. Groups of four or more can try the Opera Menu of nine different special appetizers, pastas, and main courses for $25 per person.

On the Fountain Circle. ℂ **021/215-099.** Main courses $6–$18. AE, MC, V. Daily 11:30am–2pm and 6-10pm.

MODERATE

Amphone ★ LAO   The Amphone serves authentic Lao cuisine to a gourmet standard (in the Luang Prabang style) in beautiful surroundings. If you are a serious foodie with serious intent to sample Lao food at its most artistic, this is where your quest might end. The building is modern but artfully harks back to the French colonial era. Outside is a wooden deck with soft lighting adjoining the main restaurant itself. Try the steamed fish citronella in banana leaves or the spicy Lao salad. The staff is as charming as the food is good.

37 Ban Xieng Gneun (located on the small alley beside Jazzy Brick). ℂ **020/771-1138.** Main courses 35,000 kip–65,000 kip. No credit cards. Daily noon–2pm and 6-10pm.

Chokdee Café ★★ 📷 BELGIAN   From the Tin Tin and Asterix cartoons on the wall, to the fridge full of excellent beers brewed by Catholic monks, the Chokdee Café rarely lets you forget the glories of Belgian culture. The food is superb with a real feeling of home cooking. Best of all, on Fridays and Saturdays they do a spectacular *moules marinieres* (mussels in white wine sauce with Belgian fries, cooked the way only Belgians know how). This is a Belgian culinary flagship. Weekend "Moules" nights at the Chokdee have become something of a weekly ritual for expats, and the place is usually packed. You have to book your meal a day in advance because the energetic young Belgian owner goes all the way to Thailand to purchase the fresh ingredients to-order, list in hand.

19/3 Fa Ngum. ℂ**020/501-7575.** Main dish 35,000 kip–60,000 kip. MC, V. Mon–Sat 9am-10pm.

The Cote d'Azur Pizzeria ★★★ 🍴 FRENCH   This is an extremely traditional provincial French restaurant serving real top-range provincial French cuisine at unbelievably modest prices. There is a very regular Gallic crowd who obviously recognize this. If you were to encounter French culinary artistry of this sort in New York or London (or even Paris), your wallet would be considerably lighter and you would still not feel cheated. Even by the astonishingly high standards of French restaurants in

Vientiane, the Cote d'Azur stands out. Neither the decor nor the atmosphere is particularly inspired (in fact, it's a bit gloomy), and the owners are suitably indifferent and shoulder-shrugging in a very French style. This is a place devoted to food and food alone. Every dish we tried here, be it the goat-cheese salad, the Mediterranean-style oysters cooked with a delicious and light tomato-and-herb garnish, or the steak, was simply breathtaking.

62/63 Fa Ngum. © **021/217-252.** Main courses 50,000 kip–70,000 kip. MC, V. Mon–Sat 11am–2pm and 5:30–11pm.

Full Moon Café ★ INTERNATIONAL   This cafe is relaxed, with plenty of cushions and very, very comfortable bench seating. It is a great place to unwind in the air-conditioning during the day in hot season or, indeed, get things done on the laptop. You will see quite a number of people working on their computers here, taking advantage of the wireless Internet. The menu is not particularly inspired, describing itself as Asian fusion, but it is perfectly acceptable. The salads are good and the Thai food is well prepared and straightforward. It is a well conceived place offering casual comfort in an understated but thoughtful style.

020 François Nginn Rd. © **021/243-373.** Main courses 32,000 kip–50,000 kip. MC, V. Mon–Sat 9am–midnight (kitchen closes at 10:30pm).

Khop Chai Deu ★ LAO/INTERNATIONAL   This restaurant/bar housed in an old French villa forms something of a focus point in Vientiane—it's very large, very popular, and very central. In reality, it is more of a restaurant complex than one single place. There is an outside bar and terrace, an inside room with a live band, and upstairs a large balcony and two more inside restaurant areas. The food is an eclectic mix of Lao, Western, Indian, and Chinese but is hugely average across the board. The building itself lends a certain elegance to the whole operation and the service is very good. They have sub menus within the main menu such as "the expatriates relief" and the "backpacker's experience." They also have an extensive range of fried insect dishes on offer, including crickets and larvae, a delicacy in Laos and northeastern Thailand.

54 Setthathirath Rd., southwest of Nam Phu Fountain. © **021/251-564.** Main courses 25,000 kip–50,000 kip. MC, V. Daily 7am–10:30pm. Bar open later.

Kua Lao ★★ LAO   Kua Lao serves excellent Lao fare in a traditional atmosphere. This restaurant, set in a restored colonial mansion, offers music and Lao dancing each evening. It's a bit of tourist kitsch, but the staff is very kind, and their desire to infuse your dining experience with Lao culture is quite genuine. Nowhere else will you find such an extensive menu of Lao food with English descriptions (and pictures), and many will appreciate the numerous options for vegetarians, not to mention a whole page of tempting Lao desserts. Try the *laap* (or *larp*), a mince of fish, chicken, or beef mixed with spices and mint; it's excellent when accompanied by a basket of sticky rice and eaten by hand. If you're going upcountry or heading out to the boondocks, this is a good place for a primer on Lao cuisine.

111 Samsenthai Rd. (at the intersection with Chanta Khoumane). © **021/214-813.** www.kualao.laopdr. com. Main courses $6–$12; set menu $15. MC, V. Daily 11am–2pm and 5–11:30pm.

Le Central ★★ FRENCH/CONTINENTAL   Le Central scored a coup by stealing one of the chefs from La Belle Epoque. His new twists on Asian favorites (deep-fried spring roll filled with goat cheese and cashew nuts) and a nice selection of French and Chilean wines complement the Continental main menu. The aforementioned spring rolls are excellent; the braised lamb shank is melt-in-your-mouth tender.

However, the highlight of the meal will undoubtedly be the Chef's Specialty: chocolate volcano cake with custard and gingerbread ice cream. Outstanding. Even if you eat dinner somewhere else, the freshly baked cakes and pies are worth a look for dessert.

077/8 Setthathirath Rd. © **021/243-703.** Main courses $8-$22. MC, V. Daily 11:30am-2pm and 6:30-10pm.

Le Silapa ★★ 🏠 FRENCH/CONTINENTAL   For cozy atmosphere and authentic French cuisine, this is a find in Vientiane (if you can find it). The effusive French proprietor will make you feel welcome. There's a great wine list to go with tasty meals such as whitefish subtly garnished with capers, lemon, and parsley. The food is a lot more sophisticated than you might expect from such an unassuming storefront.

17/1 Sihom Rd., Ban Haysok. © **021/219-689.** Main courses $8.50-$19. MC, V. Mon-Sat 11:30am-2pm and 6-10pm.

Sticky Fingers ★★ INTERNATIONAL   This incredibly chic but relaxed restaurant and cafe is very popular for a very good reason. The food is unique and delicious, the staff is cool and friendly, and the Australian management is very welcoming in an understated and very Australian way. Real thought and genuine taste have gone into this place and it shows. The menu includes plenty of light, healthy, salad-oriented dishes but also has a section of "comfort foods" for those missing their fish and chips, ribs, or burgers. There is a full range of cocktails, including the signature "tom yam martini," an inspired concoction with chili and lemon grass. This works very well indeed and is as good a way to start a night on the town. They also have wireless Internet at a reasonable speed.

10/3 François Nginn Rd. © **021/215-972.** Main courses 40,000 kip-62,000 kip. No credit cards. Tues-Sun 10am-11pm.

INEXPENSIVE

Nazim Restaurant ★ INDIAN   For Indian cuisine at affordable prices, Nazim has largely cornered the market in Laos and now has branch locations in Vang Vieng, Nong Kiaow, Pakse, and Luang Prabang. The food can be very good and authentic if they have the right ingredients. If they don't, then they tend to improvise and the results can be bizarre. The staff can sometimes act as if taking your order is an unspeakable bother, but the prices are reasonable, making this a popular backpacker spot. On a good day the *masala dosa* is very good. If you like sweet Indian *masala chai* (tea with milk and sugar all boiled up together), then the Nazim won't disappoint.

Fa Ngum Rd. © **021/223-480.** www.nazim.laopdr.com. Main courses 18,000 kip-55,000 kip. No credit cards. Daily 10:30am-10:30pm.

SNACKS & CAFES

Joma Bakery Café, across from the fountain on Setthathirath Road (© **021/215-265**), is renovated and spruced up, with fine breads and good coffee, as well as wireless Internet access. Next door is the newly opened **Dao-Fa** (© **021/215-651**), offering the same fine crepes and pastas as its sister branch in Luang Prabang. Nice toasted baguette sandwiches can be had at **Le Banneton** (Nokeokuman Rd.; © **021/217-321**). The **Scandinavian Bakery** (© **021/215-199**), off Nam Phu Fountain Circle, has good fresh bread and is always packed with travelers. It's a good place to pick up a foreign newspaper and people-watch on the terrace. The **Swedish Bakehouse** (74/1 Pangkham Rd.; © **021/215-231**) is another tasty European option that also serves decent pizza. **Xayoh Café,** just across from the Lao National

Culture Hall (✆ 020/612-051), serves pub grub of all sorts and is a good place to relax and have a beer or a coffee anytime. For excellent desserts, including a chocolate and wine sampler, try **Le Central** (see above).

What to See & Do

Most sights are within the city limits, which means you'll be able to cover them by bicycle or even on foot, getting to know the city intimately—and getting to know the city intimately might be the real attraction in this little burg.

Buddha Park ★★ 📱☺ Buddha Park is a fanciful sculpture garden full of Hindu and Buddhist statues, and it is a concrete testament to the obsession of Luang Pu, a shamanist priest who conceived and started building the park in the 1950s. The statues are captivating, whether they are snarling, reposing, or saving maidens in distress (or carrying them to their doom—it's hard to tell). The huge reclining Buddha is outstanding; you can climb on his arm for a photo. There is also a large pumpkin-esque dome to climb, itself filled with sculptures. The dusty and bumpy bus ride here provides clear views of Thailand across the Mekong.

About 24km (15 miles) southeast of town (take bus no. 14 from the Morning Market). Admission 5,000 kip plus an additional 2,000 kip to use a camera. Daily 7:30am–5:30pm.

Ho Phra Keo ★★ Built by King Setthathirath in 1565, Phra Keo was constructed to house an emerald Buddha that the king took from Thailand (which the Thais took back in 1779). Today there are no monks in residence, and the *wat* is actually a museum of religious art, including a Khmer stone Buddha and a wooden copy of the famous Luang Prabang Buddha. In the garden, there's a transplanted jar from the Plain of Jars (p. 227).

On Setthathirath Rd., opposite Wat Si Saket. Admission 5,000 kip. Daily 8am–noon and 1–4pm.

Lao National Museum This slightly haphazard museum is housed in an interesting old colonial structure built by the French as the office of the police commissioner. The Museum of the Revolution has photos, artifacts, and re-creations of the Lao struggle for independence against the French and Americans. The exhibits (firearms, chairs used by national heroes, and the like) are rather scanty, barely scratching the surface of such a complicated subject, but most are captioned in English. The museum features everything from dinosaur bones and sandstone sculptures of the Hindu god Shiva to machine guns and black-and-white photos of the Pathet Lao soldiers in action against the U.S.-backed regime. Archaeological finds and maps presented on the first floor help make a visit here worthwhile. There are also numerous artifacts such as pots, drums, and tools, as well as an ethnographic section. Additionally, there are some exhibits on cultural and historical sites like the Plain of Jars and Wat Phou, which provide visitors with insights into the rich cultural heritage of Laos. The second floor is divided into a series of galleries, each displaying artifacts and pictures of periods dating back as far as 1353, including the history of the Lao kingdom of Lan Xang up to 1707, the division of Lan Xang into three principalities, the rule of the Thais, the French colonial period, the first Indochina War, U.S. intervention, the successful liberation of the country in 1975, and finally the period of national development since 1975. There are a lot of interesting historical photos with captions making it absolutely clear who were the "colonialist" and "imperialist" aggressors.

Samsenthai Rd., near the Lao Plaza Hotel. Admission 10,000 kip. Daily 8am–noon and 1–4pm.

Morning Market (Talat Sao) ★★ Newly renovated and full of surprises around every corner, the Morning Market is the hub of local commerce and really where the action is. Here you can find anything from the Thai version of a Britney Spears CD to a Buddhist keepsake from one of the tourist shops or trinket salesmen. Great deals can be found on Lao silks if you bargain hard. This is the Laos version of mall culture, and sometimes the everyday tool department or stationery area gives a special glimpse into daily life. Enjoy a good wander and hassle-free shopping. There are few touts, but, as always in crowded places, mind your valuables.

On Talat Sao Rd., off Lane Xang Ave. Daily 8am–5pm.

Patuxay (Victory Monument) ★ This monument was completed in 1968 and rather cheekily the government of the day constructed it with cement actually donated by the Americans to build the airport. This is why it is sometimes laconically referred to as the "vertical runway." It is dedicated to those who fought in the war of independence against the French. Ironically, the monument is an arch modeled on the Parisian Arc de Triomphe. Its detailing is typically Lao, however, with many *kinnari* figures—half woman, half bird. It's an imposing sight, and you can climb to the top for panoramic views of the city (though it's closed by sunset, when the views would be best). Once you're on top, numerous signs forbid the use of cameras (government paranoia, perhaps), but no one seems to take heed.

At the end of Lane Xang Ave. Admission 5,000 kip. Daily 8am–4pm.

Phra That Luang ★★ This is the preeminent stupa in Laos, a national symbol that's an imposing 44m (144 ft.) high. It is not the original; the first, built in 1566 by King Setthathirath over the ruins of a 12th-century Khmer temple, was destroyed when the Siamese sacked Vientiane in 1828. It was rebuilt by the French in 1900, but the Lao people criticized it as not being true to the original. It was torn down in 1930 and remodeled to become what you see today. As you approach, the statue in front depicts Setthathirath. After you enter the first courtyard, look to the left to see a sacred Bodhi tree, the same variety Buddha was sitting under when he achieved enlightenment. It has a tall, slim trunk, and the shape of its foliage is almost perfectly round. According to the Laotians, Bodhi trees appear only in sacred places; legend has it that the site originally housed a stupa containing a piece of the Buddha's breastbone. The stupa is built in stages. On the second level, there are 30 small stupas, representing the 30 Buddhist perfections, or stages to enlightenment. That Luang is the site of one of Laos's most important temple festivals, which takes place in early November.

At the end of That Luang Rd. Admission 5,000 kip. Daily 8am–noon and 1–4pm.

That Dam (Black Stupa) That Dam is a large stupa at the center of a quiet roundabout at the end of Thanon Chanta Khumman. It is believed to be inhabited by a seven-headed dragon who tried to protect the Lao from the raging armies of Siam who invaded in 1827 (if so, it certainly failed the test). That Dam means "Black Stupa," a name that is self-explanatory.

In the center of the traffic circle at the intersection of Chanta Khumman and Bartholomie Rd.

Wat Ong Teu ★ Wat Ong Teu is in a particularly propitious place. It is surrounded by four temples: Wat Inpeng to the north, Wat Mixay to the south, Wat Haysok to the east, and Wat Chan to the west. It is named after a huge bronze Buddha (*ongteu*) in the *sim* (ordination hall). It's a mighty 5.8m (19 ft.) high. This is why it is called "Temple of the Heavy Buddha." It is also known for its beautifully carved wooden facade. The temple was first constructed in the early 16th century during the reign of King Setthathirath. Like almost every other temple in Vientiane, it was destroyed in later wars with the Thais. The temple was then rebuilt in the 19th and 20th centuries. Wat Ong Teu Mahawihan is also the home base of the Patriarch of Lao Buddhism and serves as a center for Buddhist studies.

Intersection of Setthathirath and Chau Anou roads. Daily 8am–5pm.

Wat Si Muang   Another 1566 Setthathirath creation, this wat houses the foundation pillar of the city. According to legend, a pregnant woman Nang Si, but called "Si," inspired by the gods to sacrifice herself, jumped into the pit right before the pillar was lowered. To this day, Si Muang is still worshiped as a kind of patron saint, and the *wat* that is constructed on the place where she supposedly died is named after her. There is no sign here to recount the story of Si Muang. There is only a pile of old bricks next to a small statue of her at the back of the temple. Wat Si Muang is the site of a colorful procession 2 days before the That Luang festival every November.

East on Samsenthai, near where it joins Setthathirath. Daily 8am–5pm.

Wat Si Saket ★★   This is generally considered to be the oldest temple in Vientiane, built between 1818 and 1824. It is constructed in a Bangkok rather than a Lao style. Its creator, King Anouvong, was really just a vassal of the Thai court until he came to the throne in 1824 and fomented rebellion in 1826. It may have been the Thai nature of this *wat* that dissuaded the Siamese from destroying it when they sacked the city in 1828. Wat Si Saket is surrounded on all four sides by a thick-walled cloister with more than 2,000 ceramic and silver Buddha images housed in a seemingly endless series of small niches. More than 300 seated and standing Buddhas of varying sizes and materials rest on long shelves below the niches, most of them sculpted or cast in the characteristic Lao style. Most of the images are from 15th- to 16th-century Luang Prabang. At the rear of the *sim* is an altar with several more Buddha images, bringing the total number of Buddhas at Wat Si Saket to 6,840. The interior walls are dotted with hundreds of Buddha niches similar to those in the cloister, as well as "jataka" murals (paintings depicting stories of the Buddha's past lives). Si Saket is also home to a museum.

At the corner of Setthathirath Rd. and Lane Xang Ave. Admission 5,000 kip. Daily 8am–noon and 1–4pm.

4

LAOS | **Vientiane**

The **Lao Plaza Hotel** (✆ 021/218-800) has a basic gym and good outdoor pool open to day visitors. Settha Palace's outdoor pool also offers day rates. There are a number of small massage storefronts along Fa Ngum Road, but for good spa treatments, try **Papaya Spa** (✆ 021/216-550; www.papayaspa.com), a Vientiane trendsetter.

Shopping

Laos is famous for its hand-woven silk textiles. You can buy them as fabric or in ready-made wall hangings, accessories, and clothing. Finely crafted silver and ornamental objects are also popular souvenirs. The main shopping streets are **Samsenthai** and **Setthathirath,** around the Nam Phu Fountain area and the **Morning Market** (p. 205), where you can find the best deals on Lao silks.

Perhaps best known (not just in town but worldwide) is **Carol Cassidy: Lao Textiles,** off Setthathirath on Nokeo Koummane Road (✆ 021/212-123; www. laotextiles.com). Since 1990, Carol has employed local weavers who create fine contemporary pieces, using traditional Lao motifs as a base. The colonial house alone is worth a visit, and be sure to stroll through the busy workshop area where up to 10 weavers work the looms and are happy to chat.

Satri Lao Silk, at 79/4 Setthathirath Rd., has fabrics, clothing, and housewares. **Couleur d'Asie,** Namphu Square (✆ 021/223-008), has a fine ready-to-wear line. The unusual furniture and artworks displayed at **T'shop Lai Gallery,** Vat Inpeng Road (✆ 021/223-178), are also worth a visit. And the **Mixay Boutic,** Ban Mixay (✆ 021/216-592), sells a host of silks, clothing, and souvenirs from its two shops in the town center. You can also watch the looms at work in the weaving studio.

For a unique shopping experience in Vientiane, contact Sandra Yuck at her private studio, **Caruso,** housed in a charming colonial property west of the hospital on Fa Ngum Road (✆ 021/223-644; www.carusolao.com). Sandra carries a line of ebony wood boxes, trays, and accessories, as well as unique Lao bedspreads.

Monument Books, 124/1 Nokeokuman Rd. (✆ 021/243-708), next door to the Vayakorn Guesthouse, has the best selection of guidebooks, novels, and newspapers. For foreign goods, check out **Phimphone Minimart,** 110/1 Samsenthai Rd. (✆ 021/219-045), or the **AM Minimart,** on Lane Xang Avenue, just past the Morning Market.

Vientiane After Dark

Vientiane was long known as a city that was firmly shut by midnight. Although it is still definitely a place that tends to close very early, there are now quite a number of venues where you can drink, dance, or talk until 1am, or even quite a lot later if the police are not in the throes of one of their periodic crackdowns. A lot of the restaurants and bars are indivisible. Be aware that there is a fair aspect of sleaze among one or two of the later-night venues.

At dusk, wander down to the riverside quay on Fa Ngum Road. The **Lane Xang Sunset Cruise** (✆ 020/771-1003) boards at 4:30pm and the fee is $8, including a snack and one drink. They also run a **Dinner Cruise** boarding at 7:30pm costing $12, including your meal but excluding drinks.

4

LAOS

Vientiane

Back on land, there are a few places to meet and greet. The **Khop Chai Deu** (p. 202), on the southwest corner of the Nam Phu Fountain, is a hot spot for expats and travelers, and a good place to find out what's going on in town. For a more laid-back atmosphere, try **Jazzy Brick** (43/1 Ban Xieng; ℂ 020/771-1138), across from Khop Chai Deu. Locals and expats mingle at **Bor Pen Yang** (ℂ 021/216-373) on Fam Ngu Road, a slightly sleazy rooftop bar with pool tables and cheap beer. For a proper cocktail and a view of the Mekong, head to the **Spirit House** (Fam Ngu Rd.; ℂ 021/243-795) next to Hotel Beau Rivage. For live music, try **Chess Café,** on Sakkaline Road, just off Fa Ngum Road east of town, or **On the Rock,** an intimate affair on Luang Prabang Road. In addition to having a name that sounds curiously like a typing error, **The Wind West** (Luang Prabang Rd.; ℂ 020/2000-77) also has very dim lighting, and a superb live band. This is the late-night venue of choice for expats and you don't see many tourists here. It closes, officially, at midnight. In reality it goes on until about 2am. **Lunar 36** (6 Ban Piawat, Fa Ngum Rd.; ℂ 021/244-288), on the roof of the monstrous Don Chan Palace Hotel, does tasteless tackiness with wild abandon. It is a booming, packed, modern nightclub and it is the most popular disco in town, open until the small, wee hours. There is, however, no dance floor. People jiggle around the tables where they drink in a style borrowed from Thailand. **Future Nightclub** (Luang Prabang Road) is another deafening, thumping nightclub with frenetic lighting situated just past the Novotel. It gets very busy even on weekdays. Be aware that the Future has an aspect of very marked sleaze about it. You will not be harassed, however, if you wish to jiggle in peace. It ostensibly closes at 1:30am. In practice they are often open longer.

VANG VIENG ★

Set on the Nam Song River, Vang Vieng is stunningly beautiful. Across the fast-moving water rises a complex of karst, Limestone Mountains rippling into the distance to a great height, their summits often wreathed in trails of cloud. As the river makes its way north, you can see the Limestone Mountains disappearing into the mist. The area is famous for caving, kayaking, rock climbing, and trekking. It also lies at the start of one of Asia's great mountain journeys: the spectacular drive to Luang Prabang. Beautiful as it is, the development of Vang Vieng is a serious cause for concern and it is held up across Southeast Asia as the way not to allow things to happen. While you have the amazing scenery on one side of the river in Vang Vieng itself, you also have a fairly tawdry situation, with hordes of backpackers taking drugs and drinking. The best place to stay is on the road near the river, unless noise, drugs, and television are of more interest to you than all things Lao.

Getting There

Vang Vieng is a 3-hour bus ride north on Hwy. 13 from Vientiane. There are numerous daily departures from the **Morning Market** (ℂ 021/216-507), and tickets are about 60,000 kip on a VIP bus and 100,000 kip on a minibus. The new Vang Vieng **Bus station** (ℂ 023/511-341) is just outside of town on Route 13 heading north about 2km (1¾ miles) from the main junction, and there are plenty of tuk-tuk drivers there who can take you to the town center or the guesthouse of your choosing.

Visitor Information & Tours

Diethelm Travel (see "Planning Your Trip to Laos," p. 184) includes Vang Vieng in many of its tours and can make any custom arrangements. The town itself is brimming with small operators. For good ecotours, contact the local branch of **Green Discovery** (see "Outdoor Activities," below).

Where to Stay

Ban Sabai Bungalow   This is in a great location, but the resort itself, though quite "boutique" and upscale, is a little cramped. The bungalows are also arranged around a central pond that just screams mosquitoes after 6pm, so doors are best kept firmly shut. They are, however, very pleasant and well furnished in a suitably rustic fashion. There is no TV. The resort features a riverside restaurant with great views. The menu is both European and Asian.

Ban Sisavang (along the river just south and west of the town center). ℂ **023/511-088.** www.xayoh group.com. 13 units. $28–$34 standard; $33–$41 superior; $36–$44 deluxe; $42–$52 super deluxe. MC, V. **Amenities:** Restaurant; bar. *In room:* A/C.

Bungalow Thavansouk ★   Really more of a small village than a resort, this pleasant, rambling complex is right on the river. There is a real range of rooms, some of which are superb and some of which are disappointing, so it's important to take a look at a few before making your decision. Some of the doubles are spacious and light with great views, but the singles in the second tier from the water are dark and a little hokey. The riverfront suites are superb, with a wooden deck outside with loungers from which you can gaze at the astonishingly beautiful view across the river. The attached Sunset restaurant and bar serves good local fare and is a happening spot at dusk. The whole place has a relaxed and pleasant atmosphere.

Ban Sisavang (along the Nam Song just south and west of the town center). ℂ **023/511-096.** Fax 023/511-215. www.thavonsouk.com. 44 units. 410,000 kip–450,000 kip double riverfront; 300,000 kip–330,00 kip gardenview double; 700,000 kip–750,000 kip suite. MC, V. **Amenities:** Restaurant; concierge (can arrange tours and all rentals); Internet access (in business center). *In room:* A/C, TV, minibar (not available in gardenview rooms).

The Elephant Crossing Hotel ★★★   The best hotel in Vang Vieng, the Elephant Crossing is relaxed and thoughtfully conceived. The rooms are simple but elegant with floor-to-ceiling windows that let in a fantastic amount of light. The ocher tiled floors create a vaguely Mediterranean feel. Each room has a pleasant attached balcony. Standard rooms are the popular option for their views from the top two floors of the hotel. The decision to place deluxe rooms on the lower floors was based on weight. The garden fronting the hotel is very quiet and a great place if you have children and want to keep an eye on them. The staff and management are relaxed and helpful. Above all, the Elephant Crossing just seems to have an intangibly welcoming atmosphere. A leisurely repast at the riverside restaurant is a fantastic way to start and/or end the day.

Ban Viengkeo (along the Nam Song, next door to Ban Sabai Bungalows). ℂ **023/511-232.** Fax 023/511-232. www.theeelephantcrossinghotel.com. 31 units. $45–$50 double; $80 suite. MC, V. **Amenities:** Restaurant; bar; concierge (can arrange tours). *In room:* A/C, TV, minibar.

The Villa Nam Song Resort   The Villa Nam Song is a beautiful resort in a beautiful location. The rooms, set in a lush tropical garden, are light and airy, with picture windows leading on to views both mesmerizing and splendid, while the Terrace Bar is the ideal place for either tea or cocktails.

Riverside Rd. ℂ **023/511-637.** Fax 023/511-016. www.villanamsong.com. 16 units. $100 double; $90 single; $120 triple. MC, V. **Amenities:** Restaurant; Internet. *In room:* A/C, fridge.

Where to Dine

Whereas Vientiane is world-beating when it comes to dining and Luang Prabang can certainly hold its own, Vang Vieng is notable for the fairly mundane quality of its restaurants. You don't eat badly in Vang Vieng, it's just that you don't eat very well either. There are lots of small eateries of the storefront variety all over town, and you can get decent, basic travelers' fare (fried noodles, rice, and faux-Western food) for next to nothing. **Sanaxay,** on the main drag (✆ 023/511-440), draws crowds with its cozy lounge seats and Lao, Thai, and Western menu. Nearby **Nazim Restaurant,** 15 Ban Sansavang (✆ 023/511-214), serves the same good, affordable Indian cuisine as its other locations in Laos. **Xayoh Café,** at the main intersection in town (✆ 023/511-403), serves reliable but dreary burgers and basics. For Lao fare, try **Nokeo,** across from the old market (✆ 020/241-1203), or **Phay Kam,** on the west side of the old airstrip (✆ 023/511-095), a locals' favorite.

Outdoor Activities

Ecotour operators offering kayak tours now line the main road, but the folks at **Green Discovery,** at the main intersection in town (Setthathirath Rd.; ✆ 023/511-440; www.greendiscoverylaos.com), are your best bet for a fun day in inflatable two-person kayaks on the small rapids of the Nam Song. The trip will take you to some of the local caves, including one where you'll actually swim, wearing a headlamp. A more relaxing option is to spend a half-day tubing down the river. This is by far the most popular activity in Vang Vieng. Transportation is provided upriver—all you have to do is let the current bring you back to town. Another good half-day excursion is a visit to **Phu Kham Cave,** located about 7km (4⅓ miles) from town. Best reached by bicycle, the cave contains a bronze reclining Buddha as well as a swimming hole out front where you can cool down after the journey. The scenery along the way is spectacular.

LUANG PRABANG ★★★

When talking of Luang Prabang, it is hard not to employ superlatives, and pretty much everyone who has spent time in the town does. It is a place where history, atmosphere, and terrain combine to create something of astonishing beauty. Set in the northern mountains where the Nam Khan tributary joins the Mekong, the surrounding hills are rugged, jungle clad, and spectacular. The town itself is a magical mixture of some of the most ancient and exquisite Buddhist temples in the region, combined with the sort of intimate French colonial architecture that creates an atmosphere of timeless beauty. Luang Prabang was designated a UNESCO World Heritage Site in 1995 so mercifully development has been monitored and the ingredients that define this uniquely beautiful place have not been negatively tampered with. Add into this mix of perfect architectural yin and yang the fact that the streets are not crowded with traffic, since buses and lorries are not allowed. Noise levels are low and stress levels even lower. Even with all the development of facilities purely designed for tourism, the soul of Luang Prabang is intact, and the feel of the city has remained unaltered over the past 15 years. The massive increase in restaurants and the introduction of a Thailand-style night market are part of inevitable changes as the city becomes ever more established on the Indochina tourist circuit, but, in all, Luang Prabang remains an unmatched success story in terms of tourism and the preservation of history and culture.

Luang Prabang

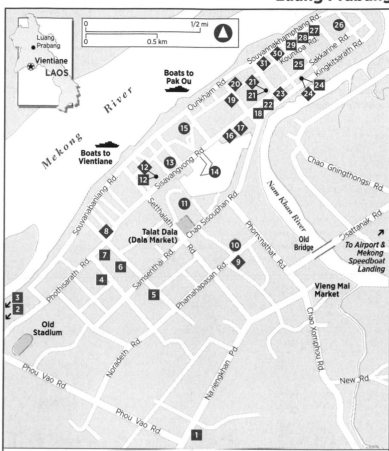

ATTRACTIONS ●

Mount Phousi (Phu Si) **12**
Royal Palace Museum **13**
Traditional Arts &
 Ethnology Centre **9**
Wat Mai **11**
Wat Wisunalat/Visounarath **14**
Wat Xieng Thong **28**
Night Market **15**

RESTAURANTS ◆

Couleur Café
 and Restaurant **17**
Indochina Spirit **5**

L'Elephant **22**
Les 3 Nagas **24**
Tamarind Café **19**
Tamnak Lao Restaurant **20**
Villa Santi **18**
The Blue Lagoon Café **21**
Vieng Kheam Khong

HOTELS ■

Ancient Luang Prabang **10**
Apsara **25**
Grand Luang Prabang
 (Xieng Keo) **1**
La Résidence Phou Vao **8**

Le Calao **27**
Les 3 Nagas **24**
Maison Souvannaphoum **4**
Mouang Luang Hotel **7**
Sayo Guesthouse **26**
Satri House **6**
Villa Maly **3**
Villa Santi Hotel **18**
Villa Santi Resort **2**
Lotus Villa Hotel **23**
Villa Sokxai **29**
3-Nagas **24**

Getting There

BY PLANE Luang Prabang International Airport (📞 071/212-173) is about 4km (2½ miles) from town. You can hire a **tuk-tuk** for $5. Going the other way, get your guesthouse or hotel to organize a tuk-tuk. It should cost about $3.

Luang Prabang has fairly good international connections with a number of cities and towns within the wider region, as well as a few domestic routes to elsewhere in Laos; the principal one of course being Vientiane.

Lao Airlines (Phamahapatsaman Rd.; 📞 071/212-172 or 212-173; www.lao airlines.com) runs routes to Thailand including **Bangkok** (one flight a day there and back), **Chiang Mai** (one flight a day there and back), and **Udon Thani** (two flights a week). To Cambodia they fly only to **Siem Reap** (two flights a day there and back). To Vietnam they fly to **Hanoi** (one flight a day there and back). Domestic connections from Luang Prabang are to **Vientiane** (at least three flights a day) and **Pakse** (two flights a week). There are also infrequent flights to **Phongsali** and **Xieng Khuang.**

Bangkok Airways (57/6 Sisavangvong Rd.; 📞 071/253-334 or 253-253; www. bangkokair.com) also flies twice daily between **Bangkok** and Luang Prabang. You can book online at their website. **Vietnam Airlines** (Luang Prabang International Airport; 📞 071/213-048; www.vietnamairlines.com) flies to and from Luang Prabang from both **Hanoi** and **Siem Reap** five times a week.

BY BUS/MINIVAN In the past there were problems of murder and banditry on the road from Vientiane to Luang Prabang. This is now ancient history and it is perfectly safe. To get to Luang Prabang from **Vientiane,** take a bus from the **Northern Bus Terminal.** The journey takes about 10 hours through some of the most breathtaking scenery in Asia on Route 13. If you suffer from travel sickness, then be sure to bring the right pills or you are in line for 10 hours of pure, unremitting, queasy hell. This road may be beautiful, but it also winds interminably. There are **two main bus stations** in Luang Prabang: one for traffic to and from the south called **Naluang,** the other for traffic to and from the north called **Kiew Lot Sai Nuan.** To get from one station to another, take a tuk-tuk for around 10,000 kip per person. Double that fare at night. A faster alternative to a public bus is to take a **minibus.** You can buy a ticket from most travel agents and some guesthouses. The journey on a minibus is faster, but it can also be pretty cramped. A minibus to **Vang Vieng** takes 5 hours and costs 60,000 kip. To **Vientiane** takes about 7 hours and costs $18. In terms of travel sickness, the minibuses may well be worse than the regular buses since the drivers swing them around the bends at speed.

BY BOAT One of the nicest and most popular ways to get to Luang Prabang is to cross the border from far north of Thailand to Laos (Chiang Khong to Huay Xai) and take a boat up or down the Mekong through spectacular and scenic countryside. If you take the **slow boat** (recommended), then it will take 2 days and you overnight in the small town of Pakbeng. In **Huay Xai** the slow boats leave from a pier just next to immigration and the 2-day journey costs $20. Slow boats to Huay Xai going the other way leave from the pier at the end of Thanon Khitsarat in the center of town. If you want to spend considerably more money, but enjoy considerably more comfort, you can take a trip with **Luangsay Cruises** (50/4 Sakkarine Rd.; 📞 071/252-553; www.luangsay.com), which offers a 2-day or 3-day luxury Mekong jaunt going in both directions. The Lao/German company **Mekong Sun Cruise** (2/2 Sakkarine Rd.; 📞 071/254-768; www.cruisemekong.com) also runs high-end river trips on all

Where the Streets Have No Names

In **Luang Prabang,** though you'll see street signs, the same road can change names as it progresses through the city, making things confusing. For example, the main street starts as Chao Fa Ngum, then transforms into Sisavangvong, and then on to Sakkarine Road, as it progresses up the main isthmus. Locals use village names, not streets, to navigate, and villages are commonly named for the local temple or *wat.*

Once you get your head around this village structure, life becomes considerably simpler. When checking into your hotel, get a business card or ask the name of the local *wat* to tell taxi and tuk-tuk drivers. Also note that the Western spelling of many street and *wat* names is very inconsistent. Once you find the wat specified, you are nearly there.

navigable stretches of the Mekong and indeed the Nam Ou. Alternatively, you can take a **Lao speedboat.** These are flat-bottom skiffs with an outsize outboard motor attached. They are best avoided because they are, quite simply, very dangerous indeed. Tickets can be bought at all travel agents and cost 400,000 kip to Huay Xai and 250,000 kip to Pakbeng only. Going from Luang Prabang, speedboats leave from the pier at Ban Don, a 15-minute tuk-tuk ride from the center of town. Going to Luang Prabang from Huay Xai, they leave from a pier about 2km (1¼ miles) south of immigration.

Note: At the time of writing, speedboat services from Huay Xai to Luang Prabang have been suspended indefinitely.

Getting Around

To get to the airport costs $5 in a **tuk-tuk;** however, they stack many people in the vehicle. Going the other way costs considerably less and is best done through reception at your hotel. Apart from that, Luang Prabang is pleasantly walkable wherever it is you may want to go. It is possible to hire **bicycles** if you wish for about $2. You can hire **motorbikes** but they are very expensive, costing $20 a day for a small stepthrough 110cc scooter. **Tuk-tuks** cost between 50¢ and $1 for short trips around town depending on your bargaining skills. Tuk-tuk drivers in Luang Prabang are rapacious.

Visitor Information & Tours

In addition to the following recommendations, small tour offices with good budget ticket services are chockablock in the center of town. Try **All Lao Services** (5/7 Sisavangvong Rd.; ✆ **071/252-785;** fax 071/253-523) for ticketing, rentals, and Internet access.

o **Diethelm Travel,** Sakkarine Road, near the Villa Santi (✆ **071/212-277;** fax 071/212-032; www.diethelmtravel.com). The top agent in town, Diethelm arranges city tours and excursions to out-of-town sights.

o **Exotissimo Travel,** 44/3 Ban Vat Nong, Khemkong Rd. (✆ **071/252-879;** fax 071/252-879; www.exotissimo.com).

4

LAOS

Luang Prabang

Currency Exchange

The **Bank Pour Le Commerce Extérieur** (BCEL; Sisavangvong Rd.; Mon–Fri 8:30am–3:30pm) exchanges cash and traveler's checks and issues U.S. dollars. They advance money on **MasterCard** and Visa and charge 3% commission. The nearby **Lao Development Bank** (Sisavangvong Rd.; Mon–Fri 8:30am–3:30pm) also exchanges cash and traveler's checks but does not advance money on credit cards. All along the main restaurant drag of Sisavangvong Road, there are small exchange booths open until 9pm that will change cash and traveler's checks, and make advances on MasterCard and Visa. The one attached to the Luang Prabang Bakery seems to offer the best rates. There are ATMs all over the center of the city, but they are not your best bet for getting cash from home. They issue only kip (with a limit of 700,000). They also levy quite a hefty charge on top of any charges your own bank might levy.

Emergencies

For police, dial © **071/212-453**; for a medical emergency, call © **071/252-049**. The levels of healthcare in Luang Prabang are low. If you are afflicted by anything serious, you will need to get to Thailand. There are two hospitals in town offering rudimentary healthcare. The **Provincial Hospital** (Setthathirath Rd.; © **071/252-049**) and the **Chinese Hospital** (Ban Phu Mok; © **071/254-026**) can deal with relatively simple and nonserious ailments.

Internet Access

There are Internet cafes all over central Luang Prabang charging 100 kip a minute before 10pm and 300 kip per minute afterward. A few places have free Wi-Fi, notably **L'étranger: Books and Tea** (see "Where to Dine," later in this chapter), but even there, connections are often patchy.

Mail

The post office is on the corner of Photisarath and Kitsalat roads, across from Luang Prabang Travel and Tourism. Hours are Monday through Friday from 8am to noon and 1 to 5pm, Saturday from 8am to noon.

Telephones

The city code for Luang Prabang is 71. The telephone center in town consists of two booths around the corner from the post office on Kitsalat Road. You can buy local and international phone cards in an office across the street.

Where to Stay

Luang Prabang is absolutely packed with hotels and guesthouses. In high season, however, it is also absolutely stuffed with visitors, so finding a place in any budget range can be a bit of a trial if you haven't prebooked. The main concentration of accommodation is along the peninsula dissected by Sisavangvong Road on the banks of both the Mekong and the Nam Khan rivers and all the crossroads in between. Most operations slash their rates by more than half in low season (Apr–Oct) when it is actually quite nice to visit as long as you manage to dodge the rain. Those hotels that take credit cards will generally charge you an extra 4% on top of your bill. Quite a number of the more "boutique"-style hotels deliberately do not have TVs in the rooms so as to maintain a traditional and tranquil atmosphere.

EXPENSIVE

Grand Luang Prabang (Xieng Keo) ★ The princely accommodations of the Grand Luang Prabang offer a garden landscape that provides a wonderful cocoonlike ambience. It is big enough to wander around and even get lost in. The courtyard pool is also a tad more spacious than those of other resorts in town, but the Grand does fall short on the amenities. All rooms have private balconies with fabulous views overlooking the mountains and the Mekong River. Go for the Mexong Deluxe suites, which are the same price as the Deluxe units but have the added bonus of better views, being situated in the guesthouse closest to the river.

Baan Xiengkeo, Khet Sangkalok (about 6km/3¾ miles south of the town center), Luang Prabang. ⓒ **071/253-851.** Fax 071/253-027. www.grandluangprabang.com. 78 units. $80–$120 deluxe; $230 suite. AE, MC, V. **Amenities:** Restaurant; outdoor pool. *In room:* TV, hair dryer, minibar.

La Résidence Phou Vao ★★ This sumptuous five-star hotel is built slightly up a hill with great views of the mountains beyond Luang Prabang. Exquisitely designed and furnished in a muted "Indochine" style, La Residence Phou Vao offers top-of-the-range luxury in a very relaxed environment. Shallow ponds trace the courtyards that connect the buildings, and bushes of bougainvillea, palm, and frangipani frame views of Phoussi hill in the distance. The views are especially lovely from the pool area and the balconies of the more choice rooms. The accommodations are like small suites, decorated with a bamboo-and-wood inlaid headboard, fine rosewood furniture, and retro fixtures such as fans and mosquito netting. The large marble bathrooms feature oversize stone tubs and dark-teak sink stands. Private balconies come with low, Lao-style divans.

Phou Vao St., P.O. Box 50, Luang Prabang. ⓒ **071/212-194.** Fax 071/212-534. www.residencephouvao. com. 34 units. $260–$370 garden view; $290–$450 mountain view; $340–$500 mountain pool view; $390–$630 suite. AE, MC, V. **Amenities:** Restaurant; bar; babysitting; Internet access (in business center); outdoor pool; limited room service; spa w/sauna and steam room; library. *In room:* A/C, satellite TV, fridge, minibar, Wi-Fi.

Les 3 Nagas ★ This is a class act aiming for a subdued boutique, homey style. It is a pleasing marriage of contemporary design and Lao heritage, featuring dark-wood floors, traditional "torchis" walls, and clay tile roofs. Simplicity reigns, with elegant touches and attention to the smallest of details. The rooms are large and airy with dark wooden floors offset by whitewashed walls and predominantly light-colored furnishings with the odd splash of colorful silk. The wooden balconies are huge, with comfortable chairs and loungers. Eight rooms are located in The Khamboua House, a jewel of traditional Lao architecture. Built in 1903, it opens onto a beautiful 500-square-meter (5,380-sq.-ft.) garden edging the Nam Khan River. The other seven rooms are located in The Lamache House, built originally in 1898 to host the then–royal family, and converted into an ice-cream factory in the 1930s.

Just farther along the peninsula from "restaurant row," P.O. Box 772, Luang Prabang. ⓒ **071/253-888.** www.alilahotels.com/3nagas. 15 units. $195–$315 double; $265–$430 junior suite; $360–$575 executive suite. MC, V. **Amenities:** Restaurant; cafe/bar; bike rental; Internet access; outdoor pool. *In room:* A/C, fridge, hair dryer, Internet access, minibar.

Maison Souvannaphoum ★ Set among the trees and manicured gardens just off Nam Phou fountain, the Maison is steeped in history and colonial charm. Until 1975 the private residence of Prince Souvannaphouma, former prime minister in the Royal Lao Government, the old L'Hotel Souvannaphoum was given a face-lift and is now under the Colours of Angsana banner. The beautifully restored La Residence wing offers one twin and three suites, the largest of which, the Maison Suite, was the prince's bedroom. Rooms in the newer Garden Wing are small but elegant. Spacious marble balconies, furnished with comfortable wicker chairs, overlook the gardens and a small, but inviting, swimming pool. Unfortunately, the spa is not up to Angsana's

4

normally high standards. Due to UNESCO restrictions, it is housed in tents set close to the main road, rendering the treatment areas noisy and lacking in privacy.

Rue Chao Fa Ngum (on Namphu Sq.), P.O. Box 741, Luang Prabang. © 071/254-609. Fax 071/212-577. www.angsana.com. 24 units. $216 garden room and verandah room; $260 Champa room; $310 La Residence twin; $360 suite. AE, MC, V. **Amenities:** Restaurant; bike rental; small pool; spa; Wi-Fi; boutique. *In room:* A/C, satellite TV, hair dryer, minibar.

Satri House ★   This royal residence–turned–boutique hotel has an authentic edge over the competitors. As a UNESCO-protected Heritage House, it is both limited and liberated in terms of amenities and decor. There's no minibar because fridges would be against the rules, but the walls are adorned with authentic royal memorabilia such as Buddha carvings from the royal temple and original furniture decorates rooms and public spaces. The family suite is large and luxe, with an intriguing black wooden corner bathtub. Satri House is owned by the same woman behind the Satri Lao boutiques scattered around town.

57 Photisarath Rd., Luang Prabang. © 071/253-491. Fax 071/253-418. www.satrihouse.com. 25 units. $240 deluxe; $300 junior suite; $480 satri house suite. 15 units. AE, MC, V. **Amenities:** Outdoor pool. *In room:* A/C.

Villa Maly ★   The newest resort in Luang Prabang offers colonial Indochine style injected with a burst of color and whimsy. The former royal residence is composed of six single- and two-story houses placed around an outdoor courtyard pool. Rooms are done in shades of pastel pinks or greens, and offset with creamy gray floors and beams. Those on the second floor have sloped ceilings, lending a cozy, cabin feel. The lamps and mahogany furnishings are retro European style (circa 1950s). Granite-floor bathrooms are ultrachic, with brightly painted walls partially dividing rain-shower cubicles from the toilet and a hammered gold basin perched on a giant porcelain jar serving as the sink. Book a corner room overlooking the central courtyard swimming pool; otherwise, you'll be stuck with a dismal view of neighboring vacant lots.

B.P. 158, Luang Prabang. © 071/253-904. Fax 071/254-912. www.villa-maly.com. 33 units. $250–$278 superior; $280–$381 deluxe. AE, MC, V. **Amenities:** Restaurant; electric bike rental; nice outdoor pool; spa; boutique. *In room:* A/C, satellite TV, hair dryer, minibar, Wi-Fi.

Villa Santi Hotel ★   For charm and convenience, the Villa Santi is the top in-town residence. Formerly the home of Lao princess Manilay, this low-key villa reopened in 1992. Whether in the original building, in the nearby annex, or at the latest venture some 6km (3¾ miles) from town (see Villa Santi Resort, below), you'll find peaceful elegance and a connection with culture and nature. The decor is deluxe colonial, with overstuffed pillows, fine linens, mosquito netting, local weaving, parquet floors, and rosewood furniture. The tile bathrooms are small but neat. Nice touches include old-fashioned sun umbrellas available for borrowing, plus fresh flowers in every room. The newer annex just across the street has common balcony sitting areas and a charm all its own. Only four rooms have king-size beds, so be sure to specify when you book if that's what you want. The downtown location is terrific, right in the thick of things.

Sakkarine St., P.O. Box 681, Luang Prabang. © 071/212-267. Fax 071/252-158. www.villasantihotel.com. 20 units. $170 double; $280 suite. Special Internet rates available. AE, MC, V. **Amenities:** Restaurant; bar; limited room service. *In room:* A/C, fridge, minibar.

Villa Santi Resort ★★   This resort is a roomier rural companion to the popular downtown Villa Santi and similarly sophisticated, without being stuffy. Tucked among lush rice paddies and picturesque hills, this little Eden has a tranquil stream that tiptoes through the grounds, a placid pond, and an open garden area. The buildings seem at ease with the surroundings, and from the open-air, high-ceilinged lobby to the two-story villas scattered about, there's a certain harmony to the place. Rooms are larger versions of those at the downtown Villa Santi, with similar tile floors, dark rosewood trim, and local decoration. The hotel has laid claim to the largest swimming pool in town and plans to add tennis courts and a fitness center in the near future. The staff is kind and courteous, and will ensure efficient transport to and from town (as with the other resorts, distance is the biggest drawback here).

Santi Resort Rd., Ban Nadeuay, P.O. Box 681 (6km/3¾ miles from town, a 10-min. drive), Luang Prabang. © **071/253-470.** Fax 071/253-471. www.villasantihotel.com. 67 units. $170 deluxe double; $180 suite. AE, MC, V. **Amenities:** Restaurant; bar; limited room service. *In room:* A/C, satellite TV w/in-house movies, fridge, hair dryer, minibar.

MODERATE

Ancient Luang Prabang ★★
Right at the heart of town near the night market, this is a good option in the midrange. Each room is named after an animal of the Chinese zodiac and they are airy and light. As is so often the case, the decor here is dark wood and creamy textiles broken up by the odd splash of pastel colors. Although the toilet is enclosed, the bathroom is open to the room, which we thought was curious. Not a place for the shy or modest if sharing. The breakfast terrace has a good view of the night market below and Wat Phousi. It's a great place to observe the daily life of the city.

Sisavangvong Rd., Ban Pakarm, Luang Prabang. © **071/212-264.** Fax 071/212-804. www.ancientluang prabang.com. 12 units. High season $75-$85 double; low season $65 double. MC, V. **Amenities:** Restaurant; bar. *In room:* A/C, satellite TV w/DVD player, fridge, hair dryer, minibar, Wi-Fi.

Apsara ★★
Set on the Nam Khan River side of the Luang Prabang isthmus, rooms are split between two beautiful colonial buildings. Superior units are like loft spaces with high ceilings, old wood floors, and fashionable room dividers separating the bathroom area from the living space. Modern dark-wood furniture is highlighted by four poster beds covered with hand-woven silks and plush pillows. Smaller standard rooms are just as airy. French doors leading to either a patio by the road or a second-floor balcony let in an abundance of light, especially in the morning. The bar and restaurant are top-notch, but early-to-bedders beware: Two second-story rooms are immediately above the restaurant and can be noisy until closing time. Large families or groups should inquire about the nearby Villa Savanh, a three-bedroom traditional house that the hotel rents on a nightly basis.

Kingkitsarath Rd. (on the Nam Khan River), Ban Wat Sene, Luang Prabang. © **071/254-670.** Fax 071/254-252. www.theapsara.com. 13 units. $70–$85 standard; $80 superior downstairs; $130 superior upstairs. MC, V. **Amenities:** Restaurant; bar. *In room:* A/C.

Le Calao ★★
With this restored 1904 villa, Indochine atmosphere comes naturally. Nothing is contrived. Built a little bit up a hill, it has charm, light, and class. This slightly faded grandeur and old-world atmosphere are helped by the rather dotty old-world management. The Calao does not need to engage in being boutique, because it naturally and effortlessly ticks all the boxes that boutique aspires to. It could be a film set. Imagine it is all in black and white and then keep an eye out for Lauren Bacall. The rooms are light, whitewashed, and airy, with large balconies from which you can contemplate the panorama of the Mekong River. In keeping with the time warp you have just entered, don't expect TV or Internet. At the Calao neither has yet been invented. The restaurant at the front, La Cave des Chateaux, used to

serve excellent provincial French food with a gourmet touch, but now it is simply the Le Calao Restaurant, and Le Cave des Chateaux exists only in Vientiane.

Khaem Khong Rd. (on the Mekong River, close to Wat Xieng Thoung), Luang Prabang. © **071/212-100.** Fax 071/212-085. www.le-calao.com. 6 units. $70–$80 double; $75 family suite. V. **Amenities:** Cafe/bar. *In room:* A/C.

Lotus Villa Hotel ★★   This is a new hotel that was constructed in exact imitation of the decaying French house it replaced. The approach is boutique but very understated, with a creative approach to every detail. The tiled rooms are light, spacious, and airy. The windows are large, with lovely Mekong sunset views. There are rooms in the main house and also in a block set in the rear among a satisfyingly jungly garden with seating in the central area where breakfast is served. What makes this project special is not just the pleasant atmosphere and thoughtful design put in place by its friendly Australian owners, but also the commitment to minimizing environmental impact. Every detail of the running of the hotel has been considered and ways have been sought to keep the footprint low.

Ban Phone Heuang. © **071/255-050.** www.lotusvillalaos.com. 17 units. $53–$89 double; $140–$220 suite. MC, V. **Amenities:** Breakfast restaurant; Internet. *In room:* A/C.

Mouang Luang Hotel ★   A 10-minute walk from town on a quiet street north of the Souvannaphoum, the Mouang Luang is adorned with traditional Lao temple–style roofs. The rooms are clean, with parquet floors and marble-tiled bathrooms (all with smallish tubs). Streetside rooms have balconies. There's an open-air Lao restaurant in the back, and just above it is an enormous balcony reserved for Baci ceremonies. Mouang Luang has the distinction of being one of the only hotels in town with a pool (there's a charge of $5 for nonguests). The staff is very friendly, and the place is popular with groups. If it's full, try **Le Parasol Blanc,** its sister property (© **071/252-124**).

Bounkhong Rd., P.O. Box 779, Luang Prabang. © **071/212-791.** Fax 071/212-790. mgluang@laotel.com. 35 units. $72–$95 deluxe. AE, DC, MC, V. **Amenities:** Restaurant; outdoor pool. *In room:* A/C, TV, minibar.

INEXPENSIVE

Sayo Xieng Mouane Guesthouse ★   This is a very popular guest house. It is set in an old French villa and the rooms are spacious, with very high ceilings and plenty of light. They also feature four-poster beds if you are suddenly feeling a little bit like Henry VIII and wish to relax. The upstairs family rooms have a mezzanine area, which is great for children who wish to create their own den, or couples in the throes of divorce. There are actually a number of related guesthouses run by the same people, and they all have "Sayo" in the name, and they are all good.

In front of Vat Xieng Mouane (btw. Sisavangvong Rd. and the Mekong), P.O. Box 1060, Luang Prabang. © **071/252-614.** www.sayoguesthouse.com. 27 units. $30–$70 double. No credit cards.

Villa Sokxai   This is a basic guesthouse in an attractive colonial building. Clean rooms have wood floors, soft beds, and both air-conditioning and a fan. Try for an upstairs room overlooking the balcony and Wat Phon Heuang—this is one of the first spots where monks receive their morning alms, and the hotel staff can help you buy sticky rice if you'd like to make merit. At dusk, you can sit on the balcony and listen to the hypnotic chanting drone of the evening prayers. One drawback is the Sokxai's poorly run reservations system; you should confirm your reservation more than once before arriving. If it's full, look for its sister hotel, **Villa Sokxai 2,** on the other side of Mount Phousi.

Sakhalin Rd. (across from Wat Pho Heuang), Ban Kilee, Luang Prabang. ©/fax **071/254-309.**
sokxaigh@yahoo.com. 7 units. $35–$50 double; $45–$60 family suite. No credit cards. In room: A/C.

Where to Dine

Luang Prabang has its own very distinctive style of cuisine, and there are many places in the city that can demonstrate just how rich that tradition is. Some are very expensive by Lao standards but they are also very good indeed, often combining northern Lao tradition with that of France. It is an explosively delicious combination. There are also very modestly priced places (our favorites are along the Mekong itself). Here you can sample the famous Luang Prabang sausage, the delicious fermented fish stew, and many other Lao culinary concoctions. You will eat better across the board in Vientiane than in Luang Prabang, but that is no denigration of the ancient northern capital. Vientiane just happens to be a fantastic culinary aberration whereas Luang Prabang is very much about local tradition.

EXPENSIVE

L'Elephant ★★ FRENCH   This stylish bistro is where it's at for fine dining in Luang Prabang. Run by French expats, it has a laid-back, retro-chic atmosphere inside a high-ceilinged colonial shell. There are daily and weekly specials, and just about everything is good, especially the imported steaks. Good cheeses and wines are also imported, though local stock is used whenever possible. A range of tasty dishes, from coq au vin to grilled buffalo to a vegetarian savory baked eggplant, covers all the bases. The menu is mainly French but with some Lao touches as with the lamb shank braised with Indochina cardamom or the duck breast roasted with "Mak Toum" and Grand Marnier. L'Elephant is very expensive for Laos, but more than worth it. Be sure to make a reservation—it's often fully booked.

Ban Vat Nong. © **071/252-482.** www.elephant-restau.com. Reservations recommended. Main courses $15–$25. MC, V. Daily 11am–2:30pm and 6–10pm.

Les 3 Nagas ★★ LAO   The 3 Nagas hotel is in two buildings on opposite sides of Sisavangvong Road. It has two attached restaurants, one in each building. While one is concentrated wholly on Luang Prabang cuisine (although with some nods to French haute cuisine delivery) the other (Mango 3 Nagas) performs as bistro serving a more modern mixture with the emphasis on fusion cuisine. Start your meal with betel-leaf soup before moving on to sautéed local mushrooms (when in season), laap, and grilled delicacies, from chicken satay to whole chunks of hearty river fish, lightly marinated in lemon grass and chiles. For dessert, go for the Lao-style crème brûlée, a custard of pumpkin and coconut that's divine. Great coffee, too.

In Les 3 Nagas hotel, just farther along the peninsula from "restaurant row." © **071/252-079** or 071/253-888. www.alilahotels.com/3nagas. Main courses $8–$25. AE, MC, V. Daily 7am–10pm.

MODERATE

Apsara ★ LAO/INTERNATIONAL   This, like L'Elephant, is often cited as the best restaurant in town, and there is a fair amount of legitimacy behind that claim. The menu is not large but it is very well thought out and beautifully conceived at every level. For a starter the cauliflower soup spiced with roast cumin is simply delicious in an understated way. For something really Lao go for the Luang Prabang buffalo sausages. For main course try the braised river fish, or if you wish to try something completely left-field, abandon Asia altogether and try the Moroccan tagine of young goat served with couscous. The wine cellar is suitably impressive. The decor is muted but stylish, with Lao silk offset by sparkling white tablecloths and with dark-wood folding doors open to the Mekong.

Kingkitsarath Rd. ℂ **071/254-670.** Main courses $6.50–$15. MC, V. Daily 6:30am–10pm.

The Blue Lagoon Café WESTERN/ASIAN   Here, nouvelle cuisine characterized by small but artfully presented portions is the order of the day. The restaurant itself is situated in a tropical garden with rattan chairs and candlelit dark-wood furniture. A surprisingly eclectic menu of Asian and European dishes comes to you as a feast for the eyes before you start to chow down on the artwork. Both the simmering Indian curry and the steak cordon bleu are reported to be exceptional, as is the choice of wine.

Ban Choumkhong. ℂ **071/253-698.** www.blue-lagoon-cafe.com. Main courses 100,000 kip. MC, V. Daily 10am–10pm.

Couleur Café and Restaurant ★ LAO/FRENCH   This unassuming but atmospheric down-alley bistro features affordable fine dining. The decor is elegantly sparse, with colonial-size high ceilings and walls adorned with the work of local artists. Though run by a young French expat, the bistro has Lao specialties such as steamed fish with coconut in banana leaf, or perhaps fried prawns in oyster sauce. Both are served with sticky rice, of course. Eggplant, mushrooms, and crispy green beans are combined in a tasty Casserole Luang Prabang. Order up some Mekong seaweed for an interesting appetizer, and ask about the fine Lao whiskey and imported wines. It's a quiet little getaway for next to nothing.

48/5 Ban Vat Nong. ℂ**071/254-694.** Main courses 35,000 kip–100,000 kip. MC, V. Daily 11am–2:30pm and 4:30–10:30pm.

Indochina Spirit ★ LAO/THAI/WESTERN   Housed in a restored 70-year-old wooden home, Indochina Spirit, as its name suggests, dishes up as much atmosphere as it does good grub. This gorgeous Lao home has been put to lovely use and now features traditional Lao music most evenings from 7:30 to 8pm (check the chalkboard in front to make sure). Indochina Spirit has done a great job with the simple local decor inside and charming garden dining outside. The menu is an ambitious list of Lao, Thai, and Western dishes. It's a good place to have a drink, enjoy an affordable appetizer plate, and hear some good sounds before strolling the city at night.

Ban Vat That 52, opposite the fountain across from Maison Souvannaphoum. ℂ **071/252-372.** Main courses $5–$12. MC, V. Daily 8am–10pm.

Tamnak Lao Restaurant ★★ LAO   This is generally considered to be one of the best places in Luang Prabang to sample expertly prepared authentic Lao cuisine. This is a little odd since it is Australian owned and run. There is also a Western menu, but it is the Lao food that stands out here. The steamed fish in lemon grass gets rave reviews, but pretty much anything on the menu will further your knowledge of what authentically prepared Lao food tastes like. If you want to extend your knowledge even further than that, they also run cooking classes where you can learn about ingredients and cooking methods, starting with the Lao staple of staples—sticky rice. Go to their website for up-to-date information.

Sakhalin Rd., Ban Wat Sene. ℂ **071/252-525.** www.tamnaklao.yolasite.com. Main courses 30,000 kip–80,000 kip. MC, V. Daily 8am–10pm.

INEXPENSIVE

Vieng Kheam Khong ★★★ ◙ LAOS   There are a host of restaurants lining the Mekong and many are good. The Vieng Kheam Khong is very popular and this is borne out by the fact that you will see many local people here, as well as foreigners. Always a good sign. There is a seating area by the roadside, but far nicer is a softly lit wooden deck overlooking the river. The food is authentically Lao and authentically delicious. The Luang Prabang sausage is interesting if you have also tasted Chiang Mai sausage in Thailand. It has an almost woody taste, gently seasoned as compared to its fierier Thai cousin. The Lao stew (whether fish, chicken, or pork) is also a good option. **Beware:** Although it is not that spicy, they do add whole unseeded chilies, and if you accidentally bite into one, you might find yourself in discomfort.

549 Ban Xieng Moune. © **071/212-726.** Main courses 25,000 kip. No credit cards. Daily 9am-10:30pm.

Tamarind Café LAO   Open only for breakfast and lunch, this excellent little place offers a range of Lao-style tapas or little sample plates of many different Lao tastes. They also serve refreshing and original fruit drinks. Staff is brisk and not unfriendly. The kitchen is small, so sit back and enjoy the fine views of Wat Nong while you wait for your food.

Ban Wat Nong. © **020/777-0484.** www.tamarindlaos.com. Main courses 27,000 kip-40,000 kip. No credit cards. Mon-Sat 11am-6pm. Dinner available only for groups that have prebooked.

SNACKS & CAFES

For atmosphere, there is nowhere better than **L'étranger: Books and Tea** in Ban Vat Aphay on the backside of Phousy Hill (the opposite side from the main street and royal palace) near the Nam Khan River. Have a pot of tea or a cocktail (don't miss the *lao-lao* margarita) in their atmospheric upstairs teahouse and gallery; it's also a good place on a steamy afternoon to relax on the floor against a cozy Lao cushion while perusing one of the old *National Geographic* magazines. Young travelers descend for the films, played each day at 7pm. They also have the best free wireless Internet in town.

The **Luang Prabang Bakery,** 11/7 Sisavangvong Rd. (© **071/212-617**), serves some good pizza as well as a host of baked goods. Farther east, the **Scandinavian Bakery,** 52/6 Sisavangvong (© **071/252-223**), and chic, air-conditioned **Joma** (© **071/252-292**) both serve similar fine coffee and baked goods.

The same team of expats who run L'Elephant (see above) own **Le Café Ban Wat Sene** (© **071/252-482**), an atmospheric, open-air space. Their desserts and coffee are excellent, as are their light lunch specials of sandwiches and salads. They also offer wireless Internet access. Find them just across from the elementary school.

The best place in town for authentic French crepes, savory or sweet, is **Dao Fa,** on Sisavangvong Road (© **071/252-656**), also a good spot for people-watching. It has excellent Mediterranean entrees and homemade pastas cooked to order, too.

At the midtown end of Sisavangvong Road just in front of Wat Phousi near the Hmong Market are a series of **street stalls** selling delicious **baguette sandwiches** (baguette being "khao ji" in Lao) with a variety of fillings and plenty of healthy salad and mayo for between 10,000 kip and 15,000 kip. Next to them are others serving **fresh fruit shakes.** You pick your own fruit combination from the choice laid out, and they then put it in the blender.

What to See & Do

Mount Phousi ★★   Rising from the center of town, Phousi has temples scattered on all sides of its slopes and a panoramic view of the entire town from its top. **That Chomsi Stupa,** built in 1804, is its crowning glory. Taking the path to the northeast, you will pass **Wat Tham Phousi,** which has a large-bellied Buddha, Kaccayana. **Wat**

📎 Make Merit

Watching the monks on their daily morning alms round has become very popular in Luang Prabang. Although this ritual is observed all over Laos, Cambodia, and Thailand the sheer numbers of monks and the incredibly atmsopheric situation make this a great place to observe the scene. The problem has been that with all the tourists attending and trying to get photos, the whole event has on occasion turned into a bit of a circus. This is offensive because it is a working religious ceremony with important meaning in the lives of local people. If you do wish to take part, try and observe some simple rules.

o Observe the ritual in silence and with respect. Even better, learn about what the ceremony actually means in the daily life of a Therevada Buddhist Monastery in Southeast Asia, and only then consider the reasons for your actions.

o Buy the rice at the local market earlier in the morning rather than from street vendors along the monks' route. The reason for this is that some of the more rapacious local vendors are selling old and unsafe food to the tourists to make a bigger profit. This may be bad karma for the vendors, but it does also mean that you might be putting the monks in hospital.

o Don't get in the way of the monks' procession or people giving alms.

o Do not photograph the monks too intrusively; camera flashes might be disturbing for both the monks and those giving alms.

o Dress appropriately; your shoulders, chest, and legs should be covered.

o Do not make physical contact with the monks.

Phra Bat Nua, farther down, has a yard-long footprint of the Buddha. Be prepared for the 355 steps to get there. Try to make the hike, which will take about an hour with sightseeing, in the early morning or late afternoon to escape the sun's burning rays. A great spot for sunset, if you don't mind sharing the experience with hordes of other tourists.

Photisarath Rd., across from the Palace Museum. Admission 20,000 kip. Daily dawn–dusk.

Royal Palace Museum ★★   The palace, built for King Sisavang Vong from 1904 to 1909, was the royal residence until the Pathet Lao seized control of the country in 1975. The last Lao king, Sisavang Vattana, and his family were exiled to a remote region in the northern part of the country where they perished in a gulag. The palace remains as a repository of disparate treasures—rather scanty but still interesting. You can begin your tour by walking the length of the long porch; the gated open room to your right has one of the museum's top attractions, a replica of a golden standing Buddha that was a gift to King Fa Ngum from the Khmers of whom he was a vassal. Known as "The Prabang" (thus the town's name), which translates to "holy image," the original was cast in Sri Lanka in the 1st century A.D.

Don't miss the busts of the last dynasty of kings. The central throne room is done in colorful glass mosaics dating from a renovation in the 1930s. Past the throne rooms is a compound of large, spartan bedrooms with what little finery was left after the departure of the last king. The temple at the compound entrance is a gilded wedding cake, and the large Soviet-made statue of Sisavang Vong, the first king under the Lao constitution, has a stiff raised fist like a caricature of Lenin.

The palace hosts a growing troupe of dancers who sometimes perform at the Royal Theater next door. Also, on occasion, tourists can take part in a Baci ceremony and view the historical reenactment of the *Ramayana*. Inquire at the Museum reception.

Photisarath Rd. ☏ **071/212-470.** Admission 30,000 kip. Mon–Sat 8–11am and 1:30–4pm. **Warning:** At 11am the museum will kick you out, and you'll have to pay *again* to come back after lunch.

The Traditional Arts and Ethnology Centre (TAEC) ★★ This museum is a fantastic place to learn about the various ethnic minorities of Laos. The modest-size center is housed in the 1920s former residence of a French colonial judge. Staff is extremely friendly and can answer any questions you have. The handful of exhibits are well curated, displaying traditional clothing, weaving looms, and household wares. Accompanying explanations are in Lao and English. Entry fees and donations go directly toward running TAEC and promoting cultural diversity and preservation. There's a small shop in the back selling textiles and housewares purchased directly from artisan communities.

Photisarath Rd. ☏ **071/253-364.** www.taeclaos.org. Admission 30,000 kip. Tues–Sun 9am–6pm.

Wat Mai ★★ Wat Mai is one of the jewels of Luang Prabang. Its golden bas-relief facade tells the story of Phravet, one of the last avatars, or reincarnations, of the Buddha. This *wat* held the Pra Bang Buddha from 1894 until 1947. Stop by at 5:30pm for the evening prayers, when the monks chant in harmony.

Photisarath Rd., near the Lane Xang Bank. Admission 30,000 kip. Daily dawn–dusk.

Wat Wisunalat/Visounarath ★ Wisunalat is known for its absolutely huge golden Buddha in the *sim*, the largest in town at easily 6m (20 ft.) tall. The *wat* was constructed in 1512 and held the famous Pra Bang Buddha from 1513 to 1894. On the grounds facing the *sim* is the famous **That Makmo,** or watermelon stupa, a survivor since 1504. Wat Aham is a few steps away from the Wisunalat *sim*.

At the end of Wisunalat Rd. Admission 10,000 kip. Daily 8am–5pm.

Wat Xieng Thong ★★ Xieng Thong is the premier *wat* of Luang Prabang. Built in 1560 by King Say Setthathirath, it is situated at the tip of Luang Prabang's peninsula where it juts out into the Mekong. Xieng Thong survived numerous invading armies, making its facade one of the oldest originals in the city. To the left of the main temple, find the "red chapel" and its rare statue of a reclining Buddha that dates back

taking refuge: MAKING FRIENDS AT THE TEMPLE

The particular beauty of the sleepy peninsula of Luang Prabang is in its peace. Time spent here is about soaking up the atmosphere and taking leisurely walks along dusty lanes lined with French colonial buildings. Another great local activity is to stop in at a temple—any temple, really—and meet with the monks or young novices. The monks are great sources of information and insight into Laos culture, and Buddhism. Language is a big part of their training, and they study Pali and Sanskrit as well as English and French (and even Chinese and Japanese). Novices are keen to practice their English or even get help with their homework. Women should be careful not to touch or sit too close to monks and novices, but all are welcome in the temple.

to the temple's construction. The statue is one of the premier Buddha images in the country, with an attitude sublime; the piece actually traveled to the World's Fair in Paris in 1931. The glass mosaics adorning all external buildings date from only the 1950s, but are fun depictions of popular folk tales and Buddhist history; note the "tree of life" on the side of the main temple. Facing the courtyard from the temple steps, the building on the right contains the funeral chariot of King Sisavang Vong with its seven-headed *naga* (snake) decor. The chariot was carved by venerated Lao sculptor Thid Tun. There are also some artifacts inside, including ancient marionettes.

At the end of Xieng Thong Rd. Admission 20,000 kip. Daily 8am–6pm.

SIGHTS OUTSIDE THE CITY

Other sights outside of town include **Wat Phon Phao (Peacefulness Temple),** a golden stupa on a hilltop about 5km (3 miles) away, best viewed from afar—though the view back to town from its height is worth the trek. From here, visit nearby **Ban Phanom Weaving Village,** a now-commercialized weaving collective where you can find deals on Lao Ikat patterns and hand-woven bags. Just past Ban Phanom and hidden in a jungle riverside area (signs point the way down the embankment), find the **Tomb of Henri Mouhot,** the 19th-century French explorer credited with the rediscovery of Cambodia's Angkor Wat. He died in Luang Prabang of malaria while hunting the source of the Mekong. **Day trips across the Mekong** to small temples and villages are also popular and can be arranged with boat drivers at quayside.

Kuangsi Waterfall ★★   As famous now for its recent collapse as anything, Kuangsi was a tower of champagne-glass limestone formations until the whole structure fell in on itself in 2003. Locals say that tour operators became too greedy and neglected local spirits, called Pi. The falls are still beautiful, but less so. The ride here, however, is quite spectacular. You'll have to travel by *songthaew* for $5 per person if shared, or by boat and tuk-tuk for the same fee.

Another option, **Tad Se Waterfall,** is 21km (13 miles) from town and good for swimming, even if it's less spectacular in height than Kuangsi. During the rainy season, the falls are stunning. Hire a driver for about $5, or pay a bit extra for a ferryboat.

36km (22 miles) south of town. Admission 10,000 kip. Daily dawn–dusk.

Pak Ou Caves ★★   This longtail boat ride 25km (16 miles) up the Mekong is a great day trip. This stretch of river is stunningly beautiful, and from the base of the cave entrance, you get a view of the high cliffs and swirling water of the Nam Ou River as it joins the Mekong. Inside the caves are enshrined a pantheon of Buddha statues, many of them in the standing pose. Basically, this is where Buddhas that have been damaged or are simply worn out are laid to rest. Guesthouses and travel agents can book you on a tour, or you can go down to the waterfront yourself and try to get a better deal with a boatman directly. You are unlikely to succeed. They have been doing it far longer than you have. The half-day trip often includes a visit to a weaving village or the former stoneware-jar-making village of Ban Xang Hai. They don't make jars anymore but they do make a potent form of the local firewater, *lao-lao*. If you overdo this, you might end up floating in the river rather than floating down it. The average inclusive tour price from a travel agent is 100,000 kip per person.

25km (16 miles) from town on the Mekong. Admission 20,000 kip.

The newly opened spa at **La Résidence Phou Vao** (p. 215) is by far the most luxurious in town. Like the hotel itself, treatments are pricey but well worth the money. The **Red Cross of Luang Prabang,** near Wat Visoun to the southeast of the city, offers traditional massage and herbal sauna to raise money for its education programs. The Red Cross is the cheapest place in town, in addition to funding a good cause. The herbal sauna is open daily from 4:30 to 8:30pm; a 1 hour massage (9am–8:30pm) costs just $3.

Outdoor Activities

Luang Prabang is a good base for exploring the mountainous north. The folks at **Green Discovery,** in the center of town (✆ 071/212-093; www.greendiscovery laos.com), are the experts. They offer tours and connections to the far north in Luang Namtha, in addition to multisport adventures along the Mekong and the picturesque Nam Ou out of Nong Kiaw (east of Luang Prabang).

Shopping

Luang Prabang is a good place to find unique hand-woven textiles. The **Night Market** opens at dusk each evening, near Wat Mai along Photisarath Road at the town center. Everything from good silk to jewelry to T-shirts sells for a song.

Ban Lao Natural Products, on the Mekong riverfront (✆ 030/514-555), offers locally produced handmade silks, handicrafts, clothing, and naturally made soaps and beauty products, while promising fair trade with its local producers to help increase sustainable development. **Kopnoi,** in Ban Aphay on the backside of Mount Phousi by the Nam Kham River, also offers a diverse product line, including jewelry and clothing, and promotes the exportation of products made in Laos (it also has an art gallery upstairs).

Natural papermaking has taken the town by storm, and **Baan Khily Gallery,** on the eastern end of Sisavangvong Road (✆ 071/212-611), is where longtime German expat Oliver Bandmann produces and exhibits. Ask about papermaking classes.

Caruso, Sandra Yuck's inspired collection of housewares, furnishings, and silk, has an outlet in a renovated colonial along Sisavangvong, as well as a display area above Ban Vat Sene (see "Snacks & Cafes," above). And **Ban Mixay** (✆ 071/253-535) is a branch of the popular Vientiane boutique that sells the same quality silks, clothes, and handicrafts. **Ock Pop Tok** (73/5 Ban Wat Nong; ✆ 071/253-219) carries pretty contemporary clothing and silks.

Lisa Regale (✆ 071/253-224) has a collection of ready-to-wear silk, including some very unique antique pieces, at her gallery behind Wat Xieng Thong.

Satri Lao Silk, on "restaurant row," has good, affordable cloth, while **Naga Creations** (✆ 071/212-775) presents an eclectic mix of jewelry. **Walkman Village** (✆ 020/567-3909) is the place to find jackets, packs, and other travel gear before heading up north.

Luang Prabang After Dark

Talking about "nightlife" in Luang Prabang amounts, virtually, to an oxymoron. The town starts to wind up business by 9:30pm, is looking very sleepy by 10pm, and by

11pm streets are looking utterly dark and deserted. There are, however, a few places to drink and party. Backpackers fill the quiet lanes of **Ban Wat That,** the old silver-smith quarter near the Mekong on the east end of town, and you'll sometimes find people up late. Take a walk down any alley for budget guesthouses and adjoining bamboo bars. **Lemongrass,** near the Sala Prabang, is an attractive wine bar with a small sitting area overlooking the Mekong, but the best selection of vino is at **Pack Luck Wine Bar** (Sakkaline Rd., opposite Bangkok Airways; ℂ 071/254-839). Restaurant Luang Prabang always seems to attract a large after-dinner crowd enjoying a Beer Lao or four. The Hive, just next door to L'étranger and run by the same team, plays drum-and-bass and hip-hop for a young crowd until late into the evening. It also hosts live music if they can dig up some musicians. Nearby, the **House** (Ban Vat Aphay; ℂ 071/255-021) is a newcomer to the scene and has a good selection of Belgian beer. Luang Prabang boasts a couple of "nightclubs," but they are closed by midnight. At the back of the **Muangsua Hotel** (Phu Vao Rd.) is a darkened disco where a band plays loud Thai and Lao pop and people emerge from the murky fringes to engage in the *ramvong* (traditional Lao and Khmer circle dancing) as well as more free-form boogie. When the locals get their en-masse synchronized moves together, it is really quite impressive. The **Dao Fah** (Rte. 13 near Southern Bus Station) is a modern Thai-style disco where music is played at deafening volume, whether by a live band or by a spiky-haired DJ, and Luang Prabang's young and hip congregate moodily.

NORTH OF LUANG PRABANG

These days, the main roads all over northern Laos are very good. The whole area is a place of remote mountains, karst-lined rivers, and a diversity of ethnic groups.

Heading north from Luang Prabang is the **Nam Ou River.** Taking a slow boat up, down, or both ways takes you through areas of breathtaking scenery. Limestone karsts tower over steep river valleys. There are also plenty of villages along the way peopled by a diverse variety of ethnicities. In the upper reaches during hot season when the water is low, white sandy beaches are revealed—the perfect place for a dip. During rainy season when the river is high and road transport becomes difficult, the Nam Ou still retains its role as a major trade and transport route, and, as with the Mekong, the water also flows through terrain too mountainous for road construction.

Nong Kiaow boasts one of the most beautiful settings in Asia. It is surrounded by towering limestone mountains fronting fantastic river views. There is not much to do in the town itself and facilities are still very basic. At nighttime the town remains almost entirely unlit. The journey from Luang Prabang is stunning. If you go by road, it takes about 3 hours. Taking the boat takes twice as long, but it is the journey, not the destination, that is the reason to be heading this way in any case. There are a number of caves near Nong Kiaow worth a visit. One was the scene of tragedy during the last Indochina war when a bomb struck, incinerating all those sheltering inside. The village temple is also worth looking at since it is 250 years old, making it one of the oldest surviving *wats* in the region. One of the best things to do here is take the boat tour up the Nam Ou past Moung Ngoi to the canyons. Boat tours can be easily set up riverside. All the accommodations and restaurants in Nong Keaow are clustered around the bridge over the Nam Ou where the boats arrive and depart. The **Nong Kiau River Side** (ℂ 020/570-5000; www.nongkiau.com; 320,000 kip double) is the best place in town. It has comfortable rooms, great views, and wireless Internet. The **Sunset Guest House** (Riverside; ℂ 071/600-033; 200,000 kip double; 100,000 kip single) is also an excellent option. It is spruce and tastefully decorated. A large balcony restaurant overlooking the river serves traditionally prepared Lao food.

Muang Ngoi Neua is a pleasant, sleepy town with no road access. The lack of motorbikes and pickups gives it a very ethereal feel. Limited electricity means that the day starts at sunrise and the town shuts down by 9 or 10 at night. No phones and no Internet add to the feeling of being constructively lost. In fact, there is no infrastructure at all, so make sure you bring everything you need. Historically, Muang Ngoi was part of the Ho Chi Minh Trail, so it was quite heavily bombed during the war, and locals often lived in caves to avoid the falling fire from the sky. Some of these caves can now be visited. **Accommodation** here is basic. There are a series of guesthouses offering simple bamboo huts for between $2 and $5 a night. They are all very much the same and they all serve food. The **Ning Ning Guesthouse** has hot showers, which makes it luxe in this neck of the boonies.

Three days' travel up the Nam Ou River is the far northern town of **Phongsali.** This remote mountainous place is home to the greatest variety of hill-tribe ethnicities in all of Laos. You will see that in the variety of tribal dress you see around you. There is also a strong Chinese influence. The picturesque Chinese Quarter of cramped, cobblestone streets lined with small, low-roofed houses is really quite atmospheric and decorative in a pleasingly simple style. It gets pretty cold up here at 1,400 feet in the winter months so a pullover or a fleece, or both, is a must. Chinese is a far more widely spoken language here than Lao and Phongsali are—to all intents and purposes, a Yunnanese town in both feel and culture. Phongsali is a good base for trekking trips to explore this wild and remote region. It is a tough place to get to, but the rewards are worth the hardship. A visit to the **Museum of Tribes** (Mon–Fri 8–11:30am and 1:30–4:30pm; 20,000 kip) is well worth the effort if you want some background to the patchwork of ethnicities in Phongsali Province. If you are feeling fit, take a stab at hiking up **Phou Fa** itself. It is a mere 400 steps up. The views from the top are spectacular. The **Phongsali Hotel** (𝄇 088/412-042; 50,000 kip double, 30,000 kip single) is Chinese built and austere. The restaurant serves adequate Lao and Thai food. The **Viphaphone Hotel** (𝄇 088/210-111; 80,000 kip double) is the best in town, although that does not mean it is actually particularly good in the larger scheme of things. The rooms are big, with Western-style toilets and hot showers. The **Phou Fa Hotel** (𝄇 020/569-5315; 50,000 kip double) is built on a hill and used to be the Chinese consulate and is suitably fortified given the fractious history of the area. The views are fantastic from the garden, and the restaurant is acceptable.

PHONSAVAN & THE PLAIN OF JARS

Xieng Khouang has the dubious distinction of being one of the most heavily bombed provinces in the most heavily bombed country on earth. For centuries, it has been at the crossroads of war, culminating in the U.S.'s "secret war" against the Pathet Lao and North Vietnamese Army. The former capital city of Muang Khouang was so thoroughly destroyed by American bombing raids that the capital was moved in 1975 to Phonsavan, itself heavily damaged. However, the people do not seem to harbor any ill will and have taken the tragedy of the war years in stride, incorporating the remnants of war into their daily lives. Halved bombshells serve as pig troughs, ammunition cases function as lunchboxes, metal tracks airlifted for makeshift runways are converted to convenient driveways, and there is even a village dedicated to and decorated by found shrapnel and bomb material. Today, Xieng Khouang is gaining recognition as home to the **Plain of Jars,** a little-understood group of archaeological sites of enormous stone jars, or drums, buried in the earth. **Phonsavan,** which has virtually no buildings remaining from the prewar years, is merely a base from which to explore the area and not much else. The jars themselves are a fun and interesting mystery. A visit to this region is certainly educational: You'll learn about the Hmong rebels, the mysterious recent history, and the many demining projects. Spring for a good guide to take you around to the many sites. *Note:* Higher altitude and weather patterns mean that it can get chilly here, especially in the rainy season, so bring a few layers.

Getting There

BY PLANE   Lao Airlines (✆ 021/212-051; www.laoairlines.com) flies to Xieng Khouang from Vientiane ($85) five times weekly, and Luang Prabang (same price as Vientiane) twice weekly, with return flights now offered to both cities. Schedules change with the seasons. Make sure you reconfirm your flight out *every day until you leave* to guarantee a seat back (flights overbook in the high season and get canceled in the low season).

BY BUS   Daily buses connect Phonsavan with Vientiane (6–8 hr.) and Luang Prabang (6–8 hr.). Route 7, a spur of the main north-south artery, Route 13, begins 150km (93 miles) north of Vientiane; the road, once a contender for the world's worst, is now in great condition. The ridge-top scenery is spectacular, but buses are overcrowded and slow. The road is also prone to landslides, so ask travel agents and fellow travelers about current conditions before setting out.

Visitor Information & Tours

At **Sousath Travel,** adjoining Maly Guesthouse, a short ride south from the town center (✆ 061/312-031; fax 061/312-395), the effusive Mr. Sousath is the definitive source on local history and a true steward of the jar sites; he has been featured in a number of local history and archaeology books and was in a documentary, *Ravens,* about the covert CIA pilots who flew from the area during the Vietnam War. A tour with Mr. Sousath himself, if you are so fortunate, is one of the town's most interesting activities. A car and driver can be arranged.

   Diethelm Travel, on the main road in Phonsavan (✆ 061/211-118; www.diethelmtravel.com), meets its usual high standards and can cater guided tours to any sights, local or remote.

   Local guides will come and find you upon arrival or if you're wandering central Phonsavan. Make sure they have been certified by the government, be specific about the itinerary, and barter for price. Freelance guides usually charge about $30 for tour and transport.

   For information on the ongoing unexploded ordinance (UXO) cleanup effort in Xieng Khouang, talk to the knowledgeable staff at the **Mines Advisory Group (MAG),** on the main road. MAG has been working in Laos since 1994 to clear the country of the deadly remnants of the U.S.'s "secret war" that continue to kill to this day.

[Fast FACTS] PHONSAVAN

Currency Exchange   There are a few foreign exchange counters on the main road (Rte. 7) near the central market, and **Lane Xang Bank** has a branch near the post office.

Internet Access   Internet access is hard to come by, but there are a few spots where you can log on. Connections are of the dial-up variety, slow and prone to disconnecting in the middle of an e-mail. Patience is essential. Try **Hot Net,** near the main intersection, the cheapest in town at 18,000 kip per minute ($2.10 per hour).

Where to Stay & Dine

Budget accommodations line the main street (Rte. 7), and if you don't care to dine at your hotel, take a short stroll and you'll find a few good noodle and snack shops near the town center, **Sangha Restaurant** being the best. For Western dishes, stop by **Craters,** next door to the Mines Advisory Group and owned by an Australian expat who used to work for MAG.

Maly Hotel   Owned and operated by local historian and raconteur Mr. Sousath, this is a good, low-luxe, but comfortable base for exploring the jars. Built pell mell in a series of additions, the rooms vary and the decor runs the gamut from comfortable wooden lodge to musty cell. Ask to see your room before checking in. A few luxe setups have floor-to-ceiling windows and fine views. Bathrooms are guesthouse basic with fickle solar showers. Good Lao and Western food can be found in the popular lobby restaurant, whose walls are covered with land mines and various other objects of destruction. The staff is friendly and helpful, and the convenient offices of **Sousath Travel** are the best place in town to arrange for a guide. Don't miss any chance to chat with Mr. Sousath.

A short ride south from the town center, P.O. Box 649, Phonsavan. ✆ **061/312-031.** www.malyht.laotel. com. 24 units. 150,000 kip–500,000 kip double. MC, V. **Amenities:** Restaurant. *In room:* TV.

Vansana Plain of Jars Hotel ★   Perched on a hill just off the main road, the Vansana is luxurious by local standards. The rooms are no-frills but clean. Standard units sport tile floors and balconies facing the town below. Suites are a good upgrade, with the extra $10 getting you a fireplace in the living area, a valuable addition during the winter months. The main drawback is the lack of an in-house travel agency for trips to the jars, but the town center is just a short stroll down the hill. A good choice.

Atop a hill northwest of the town center, Phonsavan. ✆ **061/213-170.** Fax 061/213-174. www.vansana hotel-group.com. 38 units. 400,000 kip double; 500,000 kip suite. MC, V. **Amenities:** Restaurant; bar; shuttle service. *In room:* A/C, satellite TV, minibar.

What to See & Do

Thought to date back some 2,000 years, the archaeological finds at the **Plain of Jars** are stunning and mysterious. Hundreds of stone jars of varying sizes, the largest a bit more than 2.7m (9 ft.) high, cover a plateau stretching across 24km (15 miles). Jars have been found in 15 different sites in the area so far. A guide is required to visit these sites, and it's nice to have one around if only to allay any fears over land mines (all areas within the sites are safe, though) and to get some perspective on local history. You can cover the main sites in a day, but you might want to take a few days and explore the surrounding Hmong villages. **Na Sala,** a busy Hmong village, is a good destination. Be sure to go with a guide who can translate and make introductions.

Plain of Jars: Site 1 ★★ If you're short on time, this is the one to see. Set on a high hill is one of the largest of the jars, called the Doloman jar, amid a cockeyed collection of 300 jars. It's all quite surreal and a unique photo op; a visit here gives you a great perspective on the surrounding countryside. Burn scars still dot the area, and legend has it that a few enterprising members of the American military once tried to lift one of the jars with a helicopter and failed. This is the easiest site to access and the most picturesque.

11km (6¾ miles) from town, near Ban Hang Village. Admission 10,000 kip.

Plain of Jars: Sites 2 and 3 ★ These sites are both off the beaten track and require some fancy driving and a bit of picturesque rice-paddy and pasture walking to reach, but they are certainly worth it. Site 2 is situated near a small waterfall and has some 60 jars in a grove atop a small hill. Site 3 will have you crossing a bamboo bridge and picking your way through fields to get to open pasture on a high hill with some 100 jars.

Site 2 is 22km (14 miles) from town, and Site 3 is just a short drive from there. Both have admission fees of 10,000 kip.

PAKSE & CHAMPASAK

South of Vientiane, Route 13 traces the Mekong River as it forms the border with Thailand. The river passes through **Savannakhet,** a French colonial administrative center and now an increasingly bustling transit point on the land route to Vietnam. From there Route 13 heads on south to Pakse, a midsize town, before reaching the wide Mekong flood plain, where the river spreads into hundreds of rivulets before cascading over the dynamic **Phapheng Falls** to Cambodia. What brings many to this little-visited region is **Wat Phou,** a pre-Angkorian ruin on a hilltop overlooking the river near the town of **Champasak.** The city of **Pakse** is the best base for exploring the region. **Si Phan Don,** in the far south, literally means "the 4,000 Islands." Here, the Mekong spreads out like the branches of a tree, and you'll find stunning waterfalls and quaint island towns such as **Don Khong.**

Getting There

BY PLANE **Pakse Airport** is situated 2km (1¼ miles) from town heading north up Road 13. **Lao Airlines** (Road 1; ✆ 031/212-252; Mon–Fri 8–11:30am and 1:30–4:30pm) has daily flights to **Vientiane** and twice weekly to **Luang Prabang.** A one-way flight to Vientiane costs $129. There are also international flights to **Siem Reap, Ho Ch Minh City,** and **Bangkok.** A jumbo from the center of town costs about a dollar. **Departure tax** on international flights is $10.

BY BUS Hotels, restaurants, and travel agents lining Road 13 sell bus tickets with an inclusive shuttle to the terminal or pickup point. The **VIP bus** to Vientiane (you can't miss it—it's huge, luridly decorated, and costs 150,000 kip) picks up in town. The **Northern Bus Terminal** is located 8km (5 miles) to the north of the airport. Regular buses to Vientiane cost 100,000 kip. We recommend you take the VIP sleeper bus. It's a long way. For excursions to the Bolaven Plateau, all destinations south and to the remote east of the country head to the **Southern Bus terminal** 13km (8 miles) out of town heading south. Tickets to **Champasak** cost 10,000 kip and the bus to **Don Kong** (the drop-off point for "the 4,000 Islands") costs 40,000 kip. The **VIP Bus Terminal** is along Route 11 heading near the BCEL Bank, although

Luxury on the Mekong

The **Vat Phou Cruise** (www.vatphou. com) operated by the folks at **Luang Say Cruises** (℃ 021/215-958 in Vientiane; www.asian-oasis.com) is a 3-day, 2-night excursion between Pakse and the 4,000 Islands (Si Phan Don) in the far south. The boat is large and luxurious, with a top deck replete with quiet corners in which to relax and enjoy the passing scenery. Private staterooms are small but air-conditioned and comfortable. All trips begin in Pakse. Trips include stops at small villages, the unique pre-Angkorian ruins of Oum Muong, and, of course, the south's premier attraction, Wat Phou. The food is ample, guides are informative and professional, and service is very friendly.

the buses pick up and drop off in town as well. Pakse is also just a short ride from the **Thai border** and a few hours by bus from **Ubon Ratchathani.**

Where to Stay

The wonderfully eccentric **Champasak Palace Hotel,** 1km (⅔ mile) east of town on Route 13 (℃ 031/212-263), on the banks of the Se Don River, has rooms ranging from $40 to $200. In the heart of town, the elegant and efficient **Hotel Pakse** (Street 5, Ban Watlouang; ℃ 031/212-131; www.paksehotel.com) is Pakse's most practical and comfortable, with rooms ranging from $28 to $53. The **Sala Champa** (Road 14; ℃ 031/212-273) is a slightly rambling affair in one of Pakse's few old French colonial villas. Prices for double rooms range from $15 to $28.

What to See & Do

Wat Phou ★★   Predating the temples of Angkor (sometime before the 9th c.), this stunning hilltop site is a highlight in Laos. Wat Phou was built in homage to the Hindu god Shiva, on grounds once used for animist worship. Some archaeologists posit that the temple is also homage to the Mekong and a copy of a similar site along the Ganges in India. The compound is symmetrical, with a broad causeway as the central axis and expansive reflecting *barays,* or ponds, now gone dry, as flanks. The approach to the main temple site passes between two pavilions, crumbling but still grand, before ascending the steep central stair.

The upper level is the main sanctuary, which was converted to Buddhism in the 13th century and now houses nonhistoric Buddhist statues and an altar. The temple exterior is decorated in fine reliefs of Apsara, alluring mythical female dancers. The sanctuary was reportedly a site of human sacrifices from the pre–Wat Phou temple era. Today, in a ceremony conducted on the fourth day of the waxing moon in the sixth lunar month, a bull is ritually slaughtered by members of a nearby Mon-Khmer (an ethnic group closely related to the Khmer) tribe in honor of the founding father of the temple. The view of the surrounding Mekong basin is spectacular. Don't miss the spring at the base of the cliff behind the main temple. The water is thought sacred and visitors anoint themselves to receive a blessing. There is a small museum at the entrance featuring artifacts from the original site.

14km (8⅔ miles) southwest of Champasak; 45km (28 miles) from Pakse. Admission 30,000 kip. Daily 8am–4pm.

VIETNAM

by Ron Emmons

For many Westerners, Vietnam was a war. Now, though, it has come into itself as a destination, with beauty, idiosyncrasies, and a people longing to put Vietnam's many conflicts and occupations behind them. Its mountains, jungles, and coastlines range from virtually untouched to well groomed and welcoming, and the country now offers anything a traveler might hope for. Villages remain quaint and hospitable. Major cities are cosmopolitan but retain much of their old charm; a duck off a main street can lead a visitor down old stone corridors, into bustling markets, or through neighborhood enclaves with individual personalities. Ethnic hill tribes live much the way they always have, albeit with some finding themselves now melding into something not old, not new, but simply different. Where it might have once been said that Vietnam was struggling to put its past behind it, there is now plenty of evidence to say that it has finally succeeded. Even a short trip to this multifaceted country will confirm this.

Vietnam's more than 2,000 years of history was shaped by occupation: The Chinese, French, and Americans left a brutal imprint on the Vietnamese story, but also left a rich cultural footprint. Chinese and French food, language, and architecture have been assimilated smoothly into the already fascinating Vietnamese culture. An ancient Confucian university, a Zen monastery, a Buddhist temple built in the Hindu style, a Vietnamese puppet show, French country chalets, and gourmet restaurants—you'll find them all in Vietnam.

Vietnam has 54 ethnic minority groups, mostly living in rural, mountainous areas. The distinct clothing, language, and customs of each indigenous group present another side of the country entirely. The Cham Kingdom, an Indian- and Khmer-influenced nation, also made what is present-day Vietnam its home from the 2nd to the 18th century, leaving a stunning legacy of art and architecture.

Besides its rich cultural legacy, this is a land of abundant natural beauty. From plunging mountains and craggy limestone formations to dense jungles, vast river deltas, and pristine beaches, Vietnam's ecological treasures alone are worth a trip. Adventure- and outdoor-travel outfitters abound, and many visitors come to trek, bicycle, and paddle their way to scenic serenity.

If you want to see the country's past in terms of its wars, you can easily do so. Many sights, such as the tunnel city of **Vinh Moc,** near **Hue;**

crumbling pillboxes of the **DMZ** (demilitarized zone); or old Viet Cong hide-outs in the **Mekong Delta** or in the areas outside Ho Chi Minh City (Saigon) serve as somber reminders of the past. American veterans and history buffs of all nationalities visit former bases and battle sites. The Vietnamese, though, have moved on; the sentiment is almost a public policy, and you'll hear it like a mantra. You might have a chance to talk about the wars on a casual basis with people, and some might even share their stories, but expect no recrimination.

Instead, the Vietnamese are going forward to establish their country as a strong nation at peace. Since the inception of *doi moi,* the Communist Party's policy of loosening stringent economic restrictions and opening trade, Vietnam has enjoyed exponential growth. From the smallest northern village to the colorful capital of **Hanoi** and frantic **Ho Chi Minh City (Saigon)** in the south, all are rushing for a slice of the pie. National infrastructure is improving, foreign investment flowing, and tourism booming. The central business districts rank with any in the world for quantity of glass and steel, and they're peopled by an increasing number of Western businesspeople. Expat residents bring along their pocketbooks and appetites, and local hotels and restaurants rise to the challenge.

Travel here is a breeze; English speakers are many, and, although the touts are plenty, you'll have your pick of tour guides, ticket agents, and drivers. Vietnam's relatively good roadways and efficient, inexpensive air system—indeed, its very shape—put much of this small country within easy reach of the casual traveler. Vietnam also hosts an ever-expanding collection of impressive, luxury resorts.

So, whether you want to close a chapter on the past, experience a lively ancient culture, see beautiful countryside, get your adventure fix, or just enjoy a bit of beachside or cosmopolitan comfort, Vietnam has it all. Now is the time to go: The word is out, and the number of visitors is steadily swelling. Be sure to bring your camera—the whole country is a photo op on the go.

GETTING TO KNOW VIETNAM
The Lay of the Land

Vietnam is an S-shaped strip of land that borders China in the north, Laos in the west, and Cambodia in the southwest. Covering about 331,520 sq. km (128,000 sq. miles), it is roughly the size of Italy. It has a varied and lush topography, with two deltas, tropical forests, craggy mountains, rock formations, and a coastline that stretches for 3,260km (2,026 miles), much of it white-sand beaches. Vietnam also claims thousands of islands off its coast.

THE REGIONS IN BRIEF

THE NORTH   The scenic northern highlands have craggy mountains hovering over sweeping green valleys. The inhabitants of the region are predominantly ethnic minorities, scratching out a living from subsistence farming and still somewhat isolated from civilization. Popular tourism destinations are **Sapa** and **Dien Bien Phu,** the former French military garrison. Vietnam's tallest mountain, Fansipan (3,143m/10,312 ft.), hovers over Sapa near the border with China in the northwest, part of the mountain range the French dubbed the "Tonkinese Alps." The **Red River Delta** lies to the east of the highlands. It is a triangular shape off the **Gulf of Tonkin,** an extension of the South China Sea. In the gulf is spectacular **Halong Bay,** 3,000 limestone formations jutting from still blue waters. South of the highlands but still in the northern region is **Hanoi,** Vietnam's capital city.

THE CENTRAL COAST South of Hanoi is the central coastline, location of major cities **Hue, Hoi An,** and **Danang.** Hue is Vietnam's former capital and Imperial City (1802–1945). Hoi An, a major trading port in the mid–16th century, still shows the architectural influences of the Chinese and Japanese traders who passed through and settled here, leaving buildings that are perfectly preserved. Danang, Vietnam's fourth-largest city, is a port town whose major attractions include the museum of Cham antiquities and nearby China Beach.

THE SOUTH-CENTRAL COAST & HIGHLANDS The central highlands area is a temperate, hilly region occupied by many of Vietnam's ethnic minorities. Travelers are most likely to visit historic **Dalat,** a resort town nestled in the Lang Bien Plateau, established by the French at the turn of the 20th century as a recreation and convalescence center. On the coast is **Nha Trang,** Vietnam's preeminent sea resort.

THE MEKONG DELTA Farthest south, the Mekong Delta is a flat land formed by soil deposits from the Mekong River. Its climate is tropical, characterized by heat, high rainfall, and humidity. The delta's sinuous waterways drift past fertile land used for cultivating rice, fruit trees, and sugar cane. The lower delta is untamed swampland. The region shows the influences of ancient Funan and Khmer cultures, as well as the scars from war misery, particularly in battles with neighboring Cambodia. **Ho Chi Minh City (Saigon),** Vietnam's largest cosmopolitan area, lies just past its northern peripheries.

A Look at the Past

Vietnam began in the Red River Valley, around the time of the 3rd century B.C., with a small kingdom of Viet tribes called Au Lac. The tiny kingdom was quickly absorbed into the Chinese Qin Dynasty in 221 B.C., but as that dynasty crumbled, it became part of a new land called Nam Viet, ruled by a Chinese commander. In 111 B.C., it was back to China again, this time as part of the Han empire. It remained part of greater China for the next thousand years or so. The Chinese form of writing was adopted (to be replaced by a Roman alphabet in the 17th c.), Confucianism was installed as the leading ideology, and Chinese statesmen became the local rulers. Few effectively challenged Chinese rule, with the exception of a nobleman's two daughters, the Trung sisters, who led a successful but short-lived revolt in A.D. 39.

In A.D. 939, the Chinese were finally thrown out and the Vietnamese were left to determine their own destiny under a succession of dynasties. The kingdom flourished and strengthened, enough for the Vietnamese to repel the intrusion of Mongol invaders under Kublai Khan from the north, and armies from the kingdom of Champa from Danang and the east, in the mid–13th century. Gathering strength, Vietnam gradually absorbed the Cham empire and continued to move south, encroaching upon Khmer land, taking the Mekong Delta, and almost extinguishing the Khmer as well. There followed a brief period of Chinese dominance in the early 1400s, but the biggest risk to the country's stability was to come from the inside.

Torn between rival factions in court, the country split along north-south lines in 1545; the north followed the Le Dynasty, while the south followed the Nguyen. The country was reunited under Emperor Gia Long in 1802, but by the 1850s, the French, already settled and on the prowl in Indochina, launched an offensive that resulted in the Vietnamese accepting protectorate status 3 decades later.

Although the French contributed greatly to Vietnamese infrastructure, the proud people of Vietnam bridled under colonial rule. In 1930, revolutionary Ho Chi Minh

Vietnam

responsible TOURISM

Tourists in Vietnam are a relatively new species, and it's important to respect local culture and try to minimize our impact on the country. Try to keep personal ideologies and political debate quiet. Vietnamese are proud of their triumph over outside threats, autonomy that came at a great cost in lives and suffering, and the doors are just opening after a long period of isolation (because of both external sanctions and internal policies). The common sentiment among Vietnamese, most of whom were born after the end of conflict with the United States, is to forget the past and push on into an ever brighter future, economically and socially. There are, however, many monuments to Vietnam's years of struggle. When visiting monuments to war—or one of the many sights that depict or revisit the years of struggle against the Chinese, French, or Americans—it's important to practice restraint. Refrain from jokes, try to go in smaller groups, and engage in debates or personal feelings in discreet tones or at a later time. In places such as **Ho Chi Minh's Mausoleum** in Hanoi, the monument to the **My Lai Massacre** in central Vietnam, at the tunnels of **Cu Chi** and **Vinh Moch,** in the **Hoa Lo Prison Museum** (formerly known as the **Hanoi Hilton**), or in the **War Remnants Museum** in Ho Chi Minh City, discretion is not only requested, but often enforced (visitors have been known to receive actual hand slaps and barked orders at Ho Chi Minh's Mausoleum).

Our strongest impact as visitors is through our money and how we spend it. Giving gifts in Vietnam, particularly to young people or the many who approach foreign visitors with calls of help, is a double-edged sword. Where it might gratify in the short term to help someone and fill a few outstretched hands with sweets or school supplies, it sets up a harmful precedent and props up the image of foreign visitors as walking ATMs. You will be followed and harried in Vietnam quite a bit, and in some areas, particularly Hanoi, the young

found fertile ground to establish a nationalist movement. As in China, World War II and occupation by the Japanese in 1940 helped fuel the movement by creating chaos and nationalist fervor. Upon the retreat of the Japanese, Ho Chi Minh declared Vietnam an independent nation in August 1945.

The French did not agree, however, and the two sides fought bitterly until 1954. The French, having lost a decisive battle at Dien Bien Phu, agreed to a cease-fire at the Geneva Convention that year. The two sides determined that the country would be split north and south at the 17th Parallel, with the Viet Minh (League for the Independence of Vietnam) having control of the north and the French supporters having control of the south. Elections were to be held in 2 years to determine who would lead a new, unified Vietnam.

Because of resistance to the American-supported regime in the south, led by Ngo Dinh Diem, the elections were never held. The communists continued to gain power, and Diem was assassinated, putting the southern regime in peril. Finally, in 1965, American president Lyndon Johnson dispatched the first American combat troops to Danang to prop up the south. The Soviet Union and China weighed in with assistance to the north. The rest is history. After a decade of heavy fighting that took 58,000 American lives and as many as four million Vietnamese lives, the communists took Saigon on April 30, 1975. In 1976, north and south were officially reunited.

book-and-postcard salesmen and touts are part of organized gangs and very persistent (although the hard sell has lessened with the increased number of tourists). Saying a polite but firm "no" to persistent hawkers goes a long way toward alleviating the problem.

Among **Vietnam's ethnic minorities** in the Central Highlands and the far north, be most careful about your impact. These communities are on the fringes of Vietnamese culture, distinct enclaves where ancient practices of animistic faiths still hold sway. Photographers should be sure to ask before snapping portraits or images of ceremonial sights; increasingly, asking for permission to photograph is met with pleas for money, but say "no" and move on. It's important not to assault locals with a camera, however uniquely attired and exotic they may be. Gifts of clothes or medicines might seem helpful but only diminish already-eroding ancient cultures and customs. Learn about these people and their traditions as much as you can before traveling among them. Keep an open mind and be ready to learn, not teach. Below are a few good guidelines for environmental and cultural stewardship:

Don't litter: sounds simple, but in a country where you will rarely find a public trash receptacle (most things are discarded on the street and swept up en masse), it is difficult. On rural hiking trails or in national parks, tie a garbage bag to the outside of your pack and pick up wrappers along the way. Don't preach, but if locals ask what you are doing—and they certainly will—explain that you are keeping the park clean and that it is something that anyone can do.

Wherever possible, try to **support the local economy**—eat at local joints, buy essentials such as bottled water and soap at small mom-and-pop shops, and even try public transport (if you are a hearty soul). Don't buy any animal products, such as snake wines or lizard-skin bags, and try to find out if souvenirs are produced locally.

Rather than enjoying the newfound peace, Vietnam invaded Cambodia after border skirmishes in 1978. China, friend of Cambodia, then invaded Vietnam in 1979.

In the mid-1980s, Vietnam began moving toward *doi moi*, a free-market policy, to save itself from bankruptcy. To further ingratiate itself with the international community, it withdrew its army from Cambodia in 1989, and as the 1990s began, the country began opening to the world. It reorganized its economy toward a market-oriented model, sought diplomatic relations, and in 1991 signed a peace agreement with Cambodia. In 1994, America capitulated and lifted its long-standing trade embargo against Vietnam, and the two countries established diplomatic relations in 1995. Vietnam also joined ASEAN (Association of Southeast Asian Nations).

Vietnam Today

The modern portrait of this once-troubled land is rosy. Today, Vietnam is the world's third-largest rice exporter, and the country is tentatively finding its way in the global economy. Normalization of ties between the U.S. and Vietnam in 1995 was followed by a series of ongoing resolutions and agreements contingent upon Vietnamese complicity with international human rights and trade standards. President Clinton visited the reunified country in 2000, the first U.S. president since Richard Nixon in 1969, and Vietnam is now a member of the World Trade Organization (WTO).

American Secretary of Defense Donald Rumsfeld met with Vietnam's defense minister in Washington in 2003, and the USS *Vandergrift* pulled into port in Ho Chi Minh City at about the same time, the first U.S. navy ship to dock in a Vietnamese port since hasty withdrawal in 1975. Since then, diplomatic visits have been frequent, including Secretary of State Hilary Clinton's visit in October 2010 to sign trade agreements.

The road has not always been smooth, however: Pell-mell growth in certain industries—catfish and shrimp hatcheries, for example—circumvents international standards, disrupting markets and raising U.S. ire; and continued reports of humanitarian violations are under close international scrutiny.

Per capita income in Vietnam is estimated at around $1,300 per person, but that figure increases steadily each year, especially in urban centers. However, rural poverty and lack of good medical services are still major problems. Recent international airline agreements and direct flights to the U.S. and Europe signify further international cooperation. As a stable, safe, rapidly developing nation, Vietnam appeals to travelers of all tastes and budgets.

Vietnam's People & Culture

Vietnam has a cultural landscape as varied and colorful as its topography. The Viet ethnic group is well in the majority, comprising about 88% of the population, but there are 54 other ethnic minority groups, many of whom are hill tribes living in villages largely untouched by modern civilization.

Though Vietnam has rushed into modernization over the past several years, the economy has remained largely agrarian, with farmers, fishermen, and forestry workers accounting for 70% of the workforce and most of the population still residing in small villages. The Vietnamese have a strong sense of family and of community, and are accustomed to close human contact and far-reaching interrelationships. This might be one of the reasons why, despite centuries of occupation by foreigners, Vietnamese cultural traditions have survived. Moreover, outsiders are still welcomed. Americans, in fact, will get a wide smile and a thumbs up, although the reception is better in the south than in the north.

RELIGION Approximately 70% of all Vietnamese are Buddhists, mainly Mahayana practitioners of Chinese influence (see "Buddha & Buddhism in Southeast Asia," p. 20). About 10% are Catholics, and the rest are Confucianists, animists (believing in gods of nature), or followers of the unique Vietnamese religion Cao Dai (see the listing on the Cao Dai Holy See Temple, p. 355), an interesting combination of the major world faiths. Islam and Protestantism also have small pockets of believers. While we're on the topic of -isms, it's hard for the casual observer to see any observance of communism at all, other than the prevalence of state-owned entities and the bureaucratic hoops you might have to jump through.

CUISINE Each region has its specialties, but the hallmarks of Vietnamese food are light, fresh ingredients, heavy on the rice, pork, and fish, with garnishes such as mint, coriander, fish sauce, and chile pepper. Two of the local dishes you're most likely to encounter are *pho,* a noodle soup in a clear broth, and *bun cha,* fresh rice noodles with barbecued pork in sauce. Chinese-influenced dishes can be found, including hot pot, a cook-your-own group activity in which fresh vegetables and chunks of meat and fowl are dipped into boiling broth and then consumed. The French have left their mark as well: Along with excellent restaurants, you'll find espresso coffee and crusty French bread on every street corner.

THE ARTS Ancient, distinctive Vietnamese art forms remain today, like **water puppetry,** with wooden hand puppets actually dancing across water, and *cheo,* traditional **folk opera.** There is an emerging interest in fine arts, with countless galleries in almost every major Vietnamese city, and an emphasis on traditional techniques such as lacquer and silk painting and wood blocking. Vietnamese **music,** using string and woodwind instruments, bamboo xylophones, and metal gongs, is delicate, distinctive, and appealing. **Literature** has existed since the forming of the nation in folklore, proverbs, and idioms singular to each village and ethnic group, and passed down from century to century. Many of the old tales have been translated and printed in books that you can easily find in foreign-language bookstores.

ETIQUETTE Although the Vietnamese are generally tolerant of foreign ways, they dress very modestly. Foreigners wearing hot pants or displaying navels, chests, or shoulders will attract stares. Swimsuit thongs and nude beach bathing are out of the question. Some temples flatly refuse to admit persons in shorts, and some smaller towns such as Hoi An post signs asking tourists to dress "appropriately," which means you might have a run-in with the police if you don't.

LANGUAGE The ancient Vietnamese language, though not complex structurally, is tonal and therefore difficult for many Westerners to master. In its earliest written form, it was based on the Chinese pictographic writing forms—you'll see remnants of that tradition on temple walls—but in the 17th century, a French scholar developed the Roman alphabet that is used today. It may look like you can read this stuff, but the system of accent marks is quite involved. Today, most city dwellers seem to speak at least a little English, the older generation speaks some French, and, with growing influence from China (the Chinese compose more than 50% of all visitors here), younger people are increasingly studying Mandarin. Students especially will be eager to practice English with you. Solo travelers, being less intimidating, are at an advantage; they'll get many opportunities (and invitations) to have a squat on a street corner, drink a "Bia Hoi" (beer Hoi), and meet people.

USEFUL VIETNAMESE PHRASES

ENGLISH	VIETNAMESE	PRONUNCIATION
Hello	**Xin chao**	Seen chow
Goodbye	**Tam biet**	Tam bee-et
Thank you	**Cam on**	Cahm un
You're welcome	**Khong co gi**	Kawng koe gee
Yes	**Vang**	Bahng
No	**Khong**	Kawng
Excuse me	**Xin loi**	Seen loy
I don't understand	**Toi khong hieu**	Toy kawng hew
When?	**Luc nao?**	Look now?
Where is . . . ?	**O dau . . . ?**	Er dow . . . ?
drinking water	**nuoc khoang**	nook kwang
hotel	**khach san**	kak san
restaurant	**nha hang**	nya hahng
toilet	**nha ve sinh**	nya vay shin

ENGLISH	VIETNAMESE	PRONUNCIATION
Turn right	**Re phai**	Ray fie
Turn left	**Re trai**	Ray chrai
How much?	**Bao nhieu?**	Baugh nyew?
I need a doctor	**Toi can bac si**	Toy cahn back see

THE BEST OF VIETNAM IN 2 WEEKS

Vietnam's serpentine curve along the South China Sea is the perfect shape for a linear trip that starts in Hanoi and ends in Ho Chi Minh City, often called by its former name, Saigon. Vietnam encompasses the cultures of more than 50 ethnic groups, was ruled by both the Chinese and the French, and is the prototypical Indochinese country. That's a lot to take in.

Days 1-2: Hanoi ★

Stay in a guest room in the old wing of the **Sofitel Metropole.** The hotel is a short ride or walk from the **Old Quarter,** which you can explore by foot or by cyclo pedicab. Reserve your sleeper berth on a night train to Lao Cai and Sapa for the next night. Then stretch your legs with a walk around **Hoan Kiem Lake** and end your first evening with dinner at **Green Tangerine,** just to the north of the lake. Spend the next day exploring Hanoi's attractions—the **Ho Chi Minh Museum and Mausoleum,** the **Vietnam National Museum of Fine Arts,** the **Hoa Lo Prison**—and grabbing lunch at **Quan An Ngon,** where many local dishes are on offer. Take an early dinner at **Club de L'Oriental,** a smart upscale Vietnamese restaurant. Thus fortified, board your night train to Lao Cai for **Sapa.**

Days 3-4: Sapa ★★★

You'll arrive before dawn at the border town of Lao Cai; from there, take a minivan to Sapa, a hub of hill-tribe (and tourist) activity in the Tonkinese Alps. Stay at the **Topas Eco-Lodge,** 18km (11 miles) out of town. Rest in the morning, trek in the afternoon, and spend the evening relaxing at the simple, green resort, which overlooks a quiet, plunging valley of jungle and terraced rice fields. The next morning, go trekking with a guide and learn about different minority tribes along the way. Catch the return night train to Hanoi.

Day 5: Transit to Halong Bay

If you plan it right, you can arrive in Hanoi in the early morning and be on your way to Halong Bay not long after.

Days 6-7: Halong Bay ★★

The spires and coves of Halong Bay can best be experienced aboard the replica French junk *Halong Jasime.* Swim (but watch out for the jellyfish!), watch the sun set from the top deck, and fall asleep to the lull of the sea.

Days 8-9: Hue ★★

Return to Hanoi to catch an evening flight to Hue, the old imperial capital. Stay at **La Résidence,** an Art Deco gem with an excellent restaurant, **Le Parfum.**

Dine here, on the edge of the Perfume River, and relax with a spa treatment or nighttime dip in the pool. The city has a dish named after it, *bun bo Hue,* so be sure to sample this during your stay. Spend your second day exploring the walled **Citadel** and **Imperial City** by foot and the **tombs of the Nguyen Dynasty emperors** by boat. Or make a trip to the **DMZ** of the American war (the Vietnam War).

Days 10–11: Hoi An ★★

Take an early morning bus to Hoi An, which features the southern stretches of **China Beach** and the UNESCO World Heritage Site **old town.** The **Hoi An Riverside Resort** is a good bet, located at equal distances from both the beach and the town, making getting to either a pleasant bike ride. Schedule your trip to coincide with a full moon in order to see the city's **lantern festivals.** Take a quick evening flight from nearby Danang to Saigon.

Days 12–13: Ho Chi Minh City (Saigon) ★★

Saigon is Vietnam's most chaotic city; come here for cosmopolitan buzz mixed with nostalgia for the city's past, typified in design by the new **Park Hyatt,** where you can grab dinner or drinks at any of the hotel's venues. Spend your first day on the must-sees: the **Vietnam History Museum;** the **War Remnants Museum;** and **Cholon,** the Chinese district. Have a drink or snack on the rooftop bar of the **Majestic** or the **Rex**—either will give you a feel for long-gone Saigon. On your second day, take a tour of the **Mekong Delta,** try Vietnamese *pho* from any street vendor, and cap off your travels at the **Q Bar,** in the old opera house.

Day 14: Return to Hanoi

A daytime flight back to Hanoi will put you on track for a flight home in the evening. Sleep on the plane—you'll have earned the rest.

PLANNING YOUR TRIP TO VIETNAM

Visitor Information

Vietnam's national tourism administration has a fairly good website at **www.vietnam tourism.com**, but it's more bureaucracy than information. It operates mainly through state-run tourism agencies, **Saigontourist** (www.saigon-tourist.com) and **Hanoi Tourism** (www.hanoitravel.com.vn), which have offices all over Vietnam and provide comprehensive tours and booking services. For more online info, click on "Vietnam" at the Mekong subregion's cross-referenced site, **www.visit-mekong. com**.

The website of the Vietnam Embassy in the U.S., **www.vietnamembassy-usa. org**, is very helpful. Below are the Vietnam embassy and consulate locations overseas.

- **In the U.S.:** 1233 20th St. NW, Ste. 400, Washington, DC 20036 (© **202/861-0737;** fax 202/861-0917; www.vietnamembassy-usa.org); 866 United Nations Plaza, Ste. 435, New York, NY 10017 (© **212/644-0594;** fax 212/644-5732); or 1700 California St., Ste. 430, San Francisco, CA 94109 (© **415/922-1577;** fax 415/922-1848; www.vietnamconsulate-sf.org).

- **In Canada:** 470 Wilbrod St., Ottawa, Ontario K1N 6M8 (© **613/236-0772;** fax 613/236-2704).
- **In the U.K.:** 12–14 Victoria Rd., London W8-5RD (© **0207/937-1912;** fax 0207/937-6108).
- **In Australia:** 6 Timbarra Crescent, O'Malley, Canberra, ACT 2606 (© **2/6286-6059;** fax 2/6286-4534); or Ste. 205, level 2, Edgecliff Centre, 203–233 New South Head Rd., Edgecliff, NSW 2027 (© **02/9327-2539;** fax 02/9328-1653).
- **In Thailand:** 83/1 Wireless Rd., Bangkok 10330 (© **02/251-7202** or 251-5836; fax 02/251-7201 or 02/650-7525).

Entry Requirements

Residents of the U.S., Canada, Australia, New Zealand, and the U.K. need both a passport and a prearranged visa to enter Vietnam. A single-entry tourist visa lasts for 30 days and costs $65; $110 will get you a multiple-entry visa for 90 days. You'll pay a bit more through an agent, but will save yourself some paper shuffling (it can be done for a nominal fee at any travel agency in Bangkok). Getting a visa takes 5 to 7 days for processing. Applicants must submit an application, a passport, and two passport photos. Tourist visas can be extended twice, each time for 30 days (best done through a travel agent). Multiple-entry business visas are valid for up to 3 months, but require a sponsor in Vietnam. Visas are good for any legal port of entry. *Note:* The visa begins on the date that you specify on your application.

Customs Regulations

If you're entering the country as a tourist, you do not need to declare any items for personal use. You must declare cash in excess of $7,000 or the equivalent. You can also import 400 cigarettes, 1.5 liters of alcohol, and perfume and jewelry for personal use. Antiques are forbidden from export.

Money

The official currency of Vietnam is the **dong (VND),** which comes in notes of 500,000, 200,000, 100,000, 50,000, 10,000, 5,000, 1,000, 500, and 200VND. At press time, the exchange rate was **19,495 Vietnamese dong = $1.** The U.S. dollar is used as an informal second currency, and most items that cost more than a few dollars are priced in the greenback. Prices in this guide are listed as they are quoted, in either U.S. dollars or Vietnam dong.

ATMS Tourist areas have ATMs that dispense cash in Vietnam dong.

CURRENCY EXCHANGE You can exchange currency at banks in any city. Every hotel, no matter how small, will also change money at a slightly lower rate (or charge a small commission). Don't accept torn or very grubby bills. A service charge of anywhere between $1 and $4 will be levied.

TRAVELER'S CHECKS Banks everywhere can cash traveler's checks in U.S., Canadian, and Australian dollars or pounds sterling. Vendors and retailers usually don't accept traveler's checks, however.

CREDIT CARDS Credit cards are accepted at major hotels, in upmarket restaurants, by tour operators, in most big Hanoi and Ho Chi Minh City outlets, and increasingly outside these two major cities as well. Any Vietcombank branch, as well as big foreign banks, will handle credit card cash advances.

tours for VIETNAM VETERANS

U.S. veterans are returning to Vietnam—some to see how the story ended, others to stage memorial services, find closure by crossing the 17th Parallel, or just experience Vietnamese culture this time around.

Tours of Peace (TOP; ☎ 520/326-0901), a nonprofit organization started by Jess DeVaney, a retired U.S. Marine, runs tours where veterans not only come to terms with their past by visiting important sights in the Mekong Delta and the DMZ (among others), but also participate in the future. The folks at TOP believe that through helping others, we heal ourselves, so humanitarian aid projects are part of every tour. Financial assistance is available. Check www.topvietnamveterans.org, or write to TOP Vietnam Veterans, 8000 S. Kolb Rd., Ste. 43, Tucson, AZ 85756-9275.

Another popular veterans' tour operator is **Vietnam Battlefield Tours** (5150 Broadway St. #473, San Antonio, TX 78209-5710; ☎ **210/568-9500;** www.vietnambattlefieldtours.com).

To report lost or stolen credit cards, call the nearest branch of **Vietcombank.** Otherwise, you can go to a post office to place a collect call to the card's international toll-free collect number for cash and a card replacement. The following international numbers are operational 24 hours: **Visa** Global Customer Assistance Service (☎ **443/641-2004**) and **MasterCard** Global Services (☎ **636/722-8372**). Note that foreigners aren't permitted to make collect calls, so you'll have to get a local to assist you. Or you can use AT&T, whose access number in Vietnam is ☎ **1/201-0288.** For **American Express,** visit or call the nearest representative, listed later in this chapter in "Fast Facts: Vietnam."

When to Go

September through April are the peak months, but with a range of climatic variation in the different regions of the country, there are always areas of Vietnam where you can find favorable weather.

CLIMATE   Vietnam's climate varies greatly from north to south. The north has four distinct seasons, with a chilly but not freezing winter from November to April. Summers are warm and wet. The south (which means from Nha Trang on down) has hot, humid weather throughout the year, with temperatures peaking March through May into the 90s (30s Celsius). The south has a monsoon season from April to mid-November. Vietnam is also affected by weather to the east, bearing the brunt of Pacific typhoons, especially August through September.

If you follow a south-north or north-south sweep, you might want to avoid both the monsoons and heat in the south by going sometime between November and February. If you're planning a beach vacation, however, keep in mind that the surf on the south-central coast (China Beach, Nha Trang) is too rough for watersports from October to March (but brings out the windsurfers in droves). Dalat, a hill station in central Vietnam, stays cool all year; and Sapa, in the far north, is at some altitude and gets quite chilly. Otherwise, prepare for heat.

PUBLIC HOLIDAYS & EVENTS   Public holidays are **New Year's Day** (Jan 1); **Tet/Lunar New Year,** the 4-day state holiday that falls between late January and mid-February; **Saigon Liberation Day** (Apr 30); **International Labour Day** (May 1); and **National Day of the Socialist Republic of Vietnam** (Sept 2). Government offices and tourist attractions are closed at these times.

While **Tet,** the Lunar New Year, is Vietnam's biggest holiday, it's very much a family-oriented time, something like American Thanksgiving. Folks travel far to get home for some of mom's cooking. Beginning on the evening exactly 3 days from the Lunar New Year and lasting for 4 days, much of the country closes down, including stores, restaurants, and museums, and tickets for transport as well as accommodations may be difficult to find.

Health & Safety

HEALTH CONCERNS   Your biggest safety precaution is to take care with food. Drink only bottled or boiled water, without ice. Wash your hands often. And follow this adage: Boil it, cook it, peel it, or forget it.

You will need to get special vaccinations if rural areas are on your itinerary. The following vaccinations are important for Vietnam: **hepatitis A** or **immune globulin (IG)** and **typhoid.** Injections for **Japanese encephalitis** are recommended if you plan to visit rural areas during the rainy season, as well as **rabies** in rural areas where you might be exposed to wild animals. You should also consider booster doses for **tetanus-diphtheria, measles,** and **polio.**

According to the Centers for Disease Control, travelers in Vietnam should take an oral prophylaxis for **malaria** if traveling extensively in rural parts; malaria is not a problem anywhere in the Red River Delta, in coastal areas north of Nha Trang, nor in any of the major cities: Ho Chi Minh City (Saigon), Hanoi, Haiphong, Nha Trang, or Danang. Consult a physician, but the common recommendations for malarial preventive are as follows: **atovaquone/proguanil (Malarone), doxycycline, mefloquine (Larium),** or **primaquine** in special circumstances. Side effects abound, so be sure to discuss with a medical professional and follow any treatment regimen to the letter. The best prevention is to cover exposed skin and use an insect repellent that contains DEET (diethylmethyltoluamide).

See the Health & Safety" section in chapter 10 (p. 632) for more information on the major health issues that affect travelers to Southeast Asia.

SAFETY CONCERNS   Vietnam is a safe destination, but take heed of the following: First, the traffic is deadly, so be cautious when crossing the street anywhere; in big cities, pedestrians cross in groups and, if alone, wade out into the street and maintain a steady pace. Second, women should play it safe and avoid going out alone late at night. Third, and most important, beware of unexploded mines when hiking or exploring, especially through old war zones such as the DMZ or My Son. Don't stray off an established path, and don't touch anything you might find lying on the ground. Before you depart, you may want to check with your home country's overseas travel bureau or with the **U.S. State Department** (click "more" under "Travel Warnings" at **www.travel.state.gov** for a complete, up-to-date list) to keep abreast of travel advisories and current affairs that could affect your trip.

Violent crime isn't common in Vietnam, but petty thievery, especially against tourists, is a risk. Pickpocketing is rampant, and Ho Chi Minh City (Saigon), in particular, has a special brand of drive-by purse snatching via motorbike. Don't wear flashy jewelry or leave valuables in your hotel room, especially in smaller hotels. There are small-time rackets perpetrated against tourists by taxi and cyclo drivers, usually in the form of a dispute on the agreed-upon price after you arrive at your destination. Or else the driver doesn't seem to have change. Simply agree on a price by writing it down first, and always smile and demand change.

Getting There

BY PLANE   A cooperative treaty between the U.S. and Vietnam means that there are now direct flights between the two ex-enemies. **United Airlines** flies from the U.S. West Coast.

Most travelers connect to Vietnam via Bangkok, Hong Kong, Taipei, or Tokyo. See the "Getting There" section (p. 624) in chapter 10 for more international flight tips. **Malaysia Airlines, Singapore Airlines, Thai Airways,** and **EVA Air** fly regular routes from the big hubs. **Vietnam Airlines** connects Vietnam (Ho Chi Minh City) with Vientiane, Phnom Penh, Siem Reap, Bangkok, Kuala Lumpur, Singapore, and Manila.

Reconfirmation for flights should be made 72 hours before departure from Vietnam, though some airlines do not require it. The $14 departure tax for international flights is included in ticket prices.

BY BUS   From Laos, it is possible to enter Vietnam overland via a bus ride from Savannakhet in the south. It's 520km (323 miles) to Danang ($27) or 405km (252 miles) to Hue ($22). Buses leave at midnight. In Laos, contact **Savanbanhao Tourist Co. (𝒞 041/212-202).** The overnight is long and bumpy, and the road often washes out in rainy season, so be sure to ask around first.

BY BOAT   A convenient boat service now connects Vietnam with neighboring Cambodia by way of one of the larger tributaries of the Mekong between Phnom Penh, Cambodia's capital, and the Mekong Delta border town Chau Doc. The trip takes all day and costs $15. Contact the **Capitol Guesthouse (𝒞 023/217-627),** Cambodia's budget-travel cafe, or make more luxury arrangements on a private outboard speedboat with the **Victoria Chau Doc Hotel (𝒞 076/3865-010;** www. victoriahotels-asia.com). Be sure to have a prearranged Vietnam visa. The boat leaves Phnom Penh daily at 1:30pm, and offers an interesting adventure with great perspective on Indochine river life.

Getting Around

The large number of tour operators—from big, inefficient government operations to slick, high-end tour companies and on down to the many budget tourist cafes—means that getting around Vietnam is quite easy. Stay with well established agencies or the recommendations listed under "Visitor Information" in each section of this chapter. Before booking any kind of transport, be sure to confirm details: meal inclusions, air-conditioning, and so on.

BY PLANE   **Vietnam Airlines** is the country's principal domestic air carrier; its prices are reasonable and the service is good. **Jetstar Pacific** is a low-cost carrier that also operates some of the busier routes such as Hanoi to Ho Chi Minh City. Seats are usually easy to come by if you book a few days in advance. Purchasing tickets is also very easy; all travel agents book for a nominal fee, and many major hotels have Vietnam Airlines agents in the lobby.

BY TRAIN   Vietnam's major rail network runs from Hanoi to Ho Chi Minh City (Saigon), with stops in Hue, Danang, and Nha Trang. To give you an idea of timing, from Hanoi all the way to Saigon takes 34 hours on the express train; from Hanoi to Hue is about 14 hours on an overnight express. For more details, visit **www.vr.com.vn.**

"Motorbike? Motorbike? Where you go?" You'll hear it on every street corner in most cities, the relentless pleas of the motorbike-taxi drivers. These guys drive like maniacs, but, especially for the individual traveler, there is no better way to get around any town in Vietnam. They're called Xe Om or Honda Om in Vietnamese, with Om meaning "hug"—thus, it's really a "hugging taxi." These huggers will, after bargaining, take you on a short ride at rates starting from 10,000VND, or around 40,000VND per hour. Thanks to a recent law, helmets are now widely used. But don't be afraid to tap the guy's shoulder and give a "slow-down" hand signal.

The train is an interesting way to get around, although not much cheaper than flying. Soft-sleeper berths and special tourist cars are available on most routes and are worth the upgrade. Hard-sleeper berths are a good value, but you're stacked three high and cannot sit when the bunks are down. Air-conditioning will cost more per ticket, but is definitely worth it.

It's not difficult to buy tickets at any station, but most hotels and tour agencies will gladly simplify the process and arrange tickets for you for only a nominal fee (check each section of this chapter for contacts). If you're going from Hanoi to Lao Cai (Sapa) near the China border, be sure to check out the luxury cars on the *Victoria Express*, run by the **Victoria Sapa Resort** (© 020/387-1522; www.victoriahotels-asia.com), though you'll need to book a room at their resort to get a place. See "Getting There" in specific destination sections for more info.

BY BUS/MINIVAN   Public buses are recommended to only the most intrepid travelers. Local transport is slow, crowded, and prone to breaking down.

Begun as small storefronts making arrangements for early backpackers in the 1990s, Vietnamese **tourist cafes** are the best option for seat-in-coach tours. Now franchised, with offices dotting the country, these convenient outfits run **open-tour bus tickets** that connect all the major points: Ho Chi Minh City (Saigon), Dalat, Phan Thiet, Nha Trang, Hoi An, Danang (optional), Hue, and Hanoi. You can travel in either direction, north to south or vice versa, for under $30. The buses leave at set times (most in the morning, though a few overnights are possible); you just decide the day before if you want to be on one. This gives you tremendous freedom to plan your own itinerary. In recent years, **Sinh Café,** which now has computerized reservations services, has really beat out the pack, but all of the cafes match prices and often consolidate services. **Queen Café, Kim Café,** and **TM Brothers** (in the south) all have comparable service. Check "Visitor Information & Tours" in the destination sections that follow.

BY CAR   For maximum freedom and adaptability on your travels, rent a car with a hired driver (self-drive is not yet possible in Vietnam). Rates are reasonable, making this a good way to see things outside urban centers or to take a 1-day city tour of major sights. All major hotels and travel agents can arrange rental.

Tips on Accommodations

Vietnam is gaining in popularity among travelers and tourists (tourist arrivals for 2010 were up over 30% on 2009), so book early, especially during the high season of

November and December; accommodations ranging from the glitziest five-stars to the grungiest guesthouses are often booked up and are able to demand high rates. Always ask about seasonal reductions or promotional rates; low-season discounts can be as high as 50%. **Note:** A 20% VAT was instituted for hotels and restaurants in 1999, but expect variation in how it's followed. Some establishments might add the full 20%, while others might charge as little as 10%, and still others will ignore it entirely. Be sure to inquire. Our accommodation listings apply a pricing system as follows:

- Very expensive = over $200
- Expensive = $100 to $200
- Moderate = $50 to $100
- Inexpensive = under $50

Tips on Dining

Many of the world's finest culinary traditions are represented in Vietnam, including French, Chinese, Japanese, and, of course, Vietnamese. Local French cuisine is affordable and authentic. There are some interesting new upscale Vietnamese food venues, but ask locals where to eat, and you'll get a blanket recommendation for the local market or street stalls. Regardless of whether you are with locals or at high-end eateries, try local delicacies such as *bun bo* (cold rice noodles with fried beef), *banh khoi* (crispy thin rice-based crepes filled with chopped meat and shrimp), and *chao* (rice porridge with garnishes of meat, egg, or chiles). Note that many upscale places levy a 10% government tax plus a 5% service charge; some places might absorb the tax in their prices, while others add the full 20% VAT, which was instituted in 1999. Our restaurant listings apply a pricing system as follows:

- Very expensive = over $20
- Expensive = $10 to $20
- Moderate = $3 to $10
- Inexpensive – under $3

Tips on Shopping

Bring an empty suitcase—or buy one in-country for peanuts. Vietnam offers fabulous bargains on silk, as both fabric and made-to-order clothing, as well as lacquerware, silver, and fine art. Hanoi is probably best for most buys, particularly paintings; save the lacquerware and home furnishings for Ho Chi Minh City (Saigon). Furthermore, all prices are negotiable except for those in the most upscale shops; the more relentless bargainers can walk away with incredible deals on some unique finds.

In 2004, Vietnam committed to the Berne Convention for the Protection of Literary and Artistic Works, a consortium of more than 150 nations working together to protect international copyright. Any stroll through a local market will tell you that this

---

 Smoker's Paradise

There is no such thing as "nonsmoking" in Vietnam. Only top-end restaurants serving Western cuisine are likely to have a nonsmoking section, and even then it's unlikely that there will be any partition or distance to contain the fumes. Some hotels offer nonsmoking guest rooms or floors. Inquire when booking, especially at hotels popular with business travelers, as the rooms can get pretty musty.

telephone dialing AT A GLANCE

- **To place a call from your home country to Vietnam:** Dial the international access code (011 in the U.S. and Canada, 0011 in Australia, 0170 in New Zealand, 00 in the U.K.), plus Vietnam's country code **(84)**, the city or local area code (**4** for Hanoi, **8** for Ho Chi Minh City, **54** for Hue, **511** for Danang, **510** for Hoi An, **63** for Dalat, **58** for Nha Trang), and the phone number (for example, 011 84 4/000-0000).

- **To place a call within Vietnam:** Dial the city or area code preceded by a **0** (the way numbers are listed in this book), and then the local number (for example, 04/000-0000). Note that not all phone numbers have seven digits after the city code.

- **To place a direct international call from Vietnam:** Dial the international access code **(00)**, plus the country code, the area or city code, and the number (for example, to call the U.S., you'd dial 00 1 000/000-0000).

- **International country codes are as follows:** Australia, 61; Cambodia, 855; Canada, 1; Hong Kong, 852; Indonesia, 62; Laos, 856; Malaysia, 60; Myanmar, 95; New Zealand, 64; the Philippines, 63; Singapore, 65; Thailand, 66; U.K., 44; U.S., 1.

- **Phone numbers in Vietnam:** In late 2008 all phones in Vietnam added an extra digit between the area code and the actual number; however, many websites have been slow to update this information. Most numbers (from the government's service provider) have added a 3, though a few numbers using other companies have added, a 2, 4, 6, or 9.

pledge is a tall order. Vietnamese have long followed the socialist ideal that all intellectual property—literary, artistic, or scientific—benefits the collective and should be shared; in fact, copying, under the communist regime, was encouraged. Today, this means rampant pirating of CDs and DVDs for resale. The tide is slowly turning, however, and Customs checks (upon return to Western countries) are increasingly sensitive to pirated material.

[FastFACTS] VIETNAM

American Express Amex is represented by **Exotissimo Travel** (in Hanoi at 26 Tran Nhat Duat St.; ℂ **04/3828-2150;** in Ho Chi Minh City at **Exotissimo,** 64 Dong Du, District 1; ℂ **08/3827-2911**). *Be warned:* It does not provide complete travel services, but can direct you if you lose your card. Hours are Monday through Friday from 8:30am to 5:30pm.

Business Hours Vendors and restaurants tend to be all-day operations, opening at about 8am and closing at 9 or 10pm. Government offices, banks, travel agencies, and museums are usually open from 8 to 11:30am and 2 to 4pm.

Drug Laws Possessing drugs can mean a jail sentence, and selling them or possessing quantities in excess of 300 grams means a death sentence. Don't take any chances.

Electricity Vietnam's electricity carries 220 volts, so if you're coming from the U.S., bring a converter and an adapter. Plugs have either two round prongs or two flat prongs. If you're toting a laptop, bring a surge protector as well. Big hotels will have all these implements.

Embassies **U.S.:** 1st Floor, Rose Garden Tower, 170 Ngoc Khanh St., Hanoi (© **04/3850-5000;** http://vietnam.usembassy.gov). **Canada:** 31 Hung Vuong St., Ba Dinh District, Hanoi (© **04/3734-5000;** www.vietnamembassy-canada.ca). **Australia:** 8 Dao Tan, Ba Dinh District, Hanoi (© **04/3831-7755;** www.vietnam.embassy.gov.au). **New Zealand:** 63 Ly Thai To (© **04/3824-1481**). **U.K.:** 31 Hai Ba Trung St., 4th Floor, Hoan Kiem District, Hanoi (© **04/3936-0500;** http://ukinvietnam.fco.gov.uk/en).

Emergencies Nationwide emergency numbers are as follows: For police, dial © **113;** for fire, dial © **114;** and for ambulance, dial © **115.** Operators speak only Vietnamese.

Hospitals Vietnamese healthcare is not yet up to Western standards. However, there are competent clinics in Hanoi and Ho Chi Minh City (Saigon), with international, English-speaking doctors and dentists. If your problem is serious, it is best to get to either one of these cities as quickly as possible. The clinics can arrange emergency evacuation. If the problem is minor, ask your hotel to help you contact a Vietnamese doctor. He or she will probably speak some English, and pharmacies

throughout the country are surprisingly well stocked and require no prescriptions (check expiration, though).

International SOS has a 24-hour service center and both Vietnamese and foreign doctors. In Hanoi, go to 1 Dang Thai Mai, West Lake (24-hr. hot line © **04/3934-0666**). In Ho Chi Minh City (Saigon), go to 167A Nam Ky Khoi Nghia St., District 3 (24-hr. hot line © **08/3829-8424**). Also in Hanoi, the **French Hospital,** 1 Phuong Mai St. (© **04/3577-1100,** or emergency line 04/3574-1111), provides fine medical attention at a fraction of the cost of SOS.

Internet Access There are heaps of Internet cafes in cities throughout Vietnam, the best in popular guesthouse and hotel areas. Cafe rates are dirt-cheap—usually around 4,000VND per hour. In rural areas, it can be as much as 30,000VND per hour, and hotel business centers usually charge at least triple that. Take a short walk in most towns, and you can find affordable service.

Language Vietnamese is the official language of Vietnam. Older residents speak and understand French, while young people are busily learning Chinese these days. Although English is widely spoken among folks in the service industry in Hanoi and Saigon, it is harder to find in other tourist destinations. Off the beaten track, arm yourself with a phrase book and as

many Vietnamese words as you can muster. See "Language," p. 239, for more information.

Liquor Laws There are virtually no age-restriction laws limiting when or where you can buy or consume drink. It's not uncommon to find that your motorbike or taxi driver has had a few, so be cautious, especially at night.

Mail A regular airmail letter will take about 10 days to reach North America, 7 days to reach Europe, and 4 days to reach Australia or New Zealand. Mailing things from Vietnam is expensive. A letter up to 10 grams costs 13,000VND to North America, 11,000VND to Europe, and 9,000VND to Australia or New Zealand; postcards, respectively, cost 8,000VND, 7,000VND, and 6,000VND. Express services such as **FedEx** and **DHL** are easily available and are usually located in or around every city's main post office.

Police You won't find a helpful cop on every street corner—just the opposite. Count on them only in cases of dire emergency. Police can even be part of the problem. Especially in the south, you and your car/motorbike driver might, for instance, be stopped for a minor traffic infraction and "fined." If the amount isn't too large, cooperate. Corruption is the rule, and palm greasing and graft pose as police process. Be aware.

Safety Vietnam is a generally safe destination, but watch out for crazy traffic, especially in big cities, and for unexploded mines in rural areas. Women should avoid going out alone at night. Beware of pickpockets, especially in Ho Chi Minh City (Saigon), where drive-by purse snatching is rampant. Don't wear flashy jewelry or leave valuables in your hotel room, especially in smaller lodgings. See "Health & Safety," p. 244, for more tips on keeping yourself safe.

Telephones The international country code for Vietnam is **84.** Most hotels offer international direct dialing, but with exorbitant surcharges of 10% to 25%. It is far cheaper to place a call from a post office. There are plenty of phone booths that accept phone cards (local and international), which can be purchased at any post office or phone-company branch. A local

call costs 1,000VND per minute. See "Telephone Dialing at a Glance," p. 248, for details.

Time Zone Vietnam is 7 hours ahead of Greenwich Mean Time, in the same zone as Bangkok. It is 12 hours ahead of the U.S. Eastern Standard Time during the winter months, and 3 hours behind Sydney.

Tipping Tipping is common in Hanoi and in Saigon. In a top-end hotel, feel free to tip bellhops anywhere from 10,000VND to 15,000VND. Most upscale restaurants throughout the country now add a service surcharge of 5% to 10%. If they don't, or if the service is good, you might want to leave another 5%. Taxi drivers will be pleased if you round up the bill (again, mainly in the big cities). Use your discretion for tour guides and others who have been particularly helpful.

Toilets Public toilets (*cau tieu*) are nonexistent in Vietnam outside of tourist attractions, but you'll be welcome in hotels and restaurants. In rural areas, squat-style toilets prevail. You'll often see a tub of water with a bowl next to the toilet. Throw two or three scoops of water in the bowl to flush. Finally, bring your own paper and antiseptic hand wipes—just in case.

Water Water is not potable in Vietnam. Outside of top-end hotels and restaurants, drink only beverages without ice, unless the establishment promises that it manufactures its own ice from clean water. Bottled mineral water is everywhere. Counterfeits are a problem, so make sure you're buying the real thing, with an unbroken seal. A sure sign is typos. "La Vile" water speaks for itself.

HANOI ★★★

Vietnam's capital, Hanoi, ranks among the world's most attractive and interesting cities. Originally named Thang Long, it was first the capital of Vietnam in 1010, and even when the nation's capital moved to Hue under the Nguyen Dynasty in 1802, the city continued to flourish, especially after the French took control in 1888. In 1954, after the French departed, Hanoi was declared Vietnam's capital once again. The city boasts 1,000 years of history, and that of the past few hundred years is marvelously preserved.

Hanoi has a reputation, doubtless accrued from the American war years, as a dour northern political outpost. While the city is certainly less developed than chaotic Ho Chi Minh City (Saigon), and there are some vestiges of Soviet-influenced concrete monolith architecture, there are also beautiful streets and neighborhoods in Hanoi with a gracious, almost regal flavor. The city is dotted with dozens of lakes small and large, around which you can usually find a cafe, a pagoda or two, and absorbing vignettes of street life. Hanoi's 6.5 million residents all seem to be in constant motion, as part of the endless stream of motorbike and bicycle traffic, but there are plenty of quiet corners and tranquil neighborhoods to explore.

Among Hanoi's sightseeing highlights are the **Ho Chi Minh Museum and Mausoleum,** the **Temple of Literature,** the **Vietnam National Museum of Fine Arts,** the grisly **Hoa Lo Prison** (also known as the infamous Hanoi Hilton), and the **Old Quarter,** whose ancient winding streets are named after the individual trades once practiced there. Hanoi is also Vietnam's cultural center: The galleries, puppetry, music, and dance performances are worth a stay of at least a few days. You might also want to use the city as a base for excursions to Halong Bay, to Cuc Phuong nature reserve, or north to Sapa.

Getting There

BY PLANE Hanoi, along with Ho Chi Minh City (Saigon), is a major international gateway. For details, see Vietnam's "Getting There" section (p. 245). The **Noi Bai International Airport** is located about a 45-minute drive outside Hanoi. If you haven't booked a transfer through your hotel, you can take an airport taxi for about $15. To save a few dollars, hop on the Vietnam Airlines minivan into town. It costs $2 for a drop-off at the Vietnam Airlines office, but sometimes for an extra buck you can get the driver to take you to your hotel.

BY TRAIN Located on the western edge of Hoan Kiem District, **Hanoi Railway Station** (120 Le Duan; ℂ **04/3942-3697**) is a terminal stop on the Reunification Railroad. For 534,000VND, you'll get a comfortable, air-conditioned soft-berth to Hue, or pay 1,160,000VND for the same to Ho Chi Minh City (Saigon). Buying tickets at the stations is easy (but takes time); any travel agent can handle it for a small fee.

BY BUS Numerous open-tour options are available in tourist cafes in the Old Quarter on Hang Bac or Hang Be streets. Services and prices are similar: About $27 gets you an open-tour ticket from Hanoi to Ho Chi Minh City (Saigon), with all stops in between. See "Visitor Information & Tours," below.

Getting Around

Hanoi is divided into districts. Most sights and accommodations are in **Hoan Kiem District** (downtown), centered around picturesque Hoan Kiem Lake, or in **Ba Dinh District** (west of town) or **Hai Ba Trung District** (south of town). Most addresses include a district name. You'll want to plan your travels accordingly, as getting from district to district can be time-consuming and expensive.

BY BUS Hanoi has only buses in the way of public transport. They are extremely crowded, and using them is difficult if you don't speak Vietnamese.

BY TAXI Taxis can be hailed off the street, at hotels, and at major attractions. The meter should read around 15,000VND to start, then jump around 9,500VND to 11,000VND for every kilometer thereafter. The three most reputable companies are **Hanoi Taxi** (ℂ **04/3853-5353**), **Hanoi Tourist Taxi** (ℂ **04/3856-5656**), and **Mai Linh** (ℂ **04/3822-2666**). You (or the concierge) can call ahead for pickup. Make sure the cabby turns on the meter. Be sure to get your change; drivers often seek a surreptitious tip by claiming they don't have the change. Tell the driver that you'll wait until it's obtained, and it will materialize. *Warning:* Stick with accredited taxi companies; some independents rig meters. If you have any problems, take your case to the concierge of your hotel.

BY CAR Renting a car with driver is convenient. Rates start at around $35 per day (or $5 per hour, minimum 3 hr.). If an upscale hotel quotes you more, call a tourist cafe (combination eatery and travel agent) or any travel agent.

Hanoi

Church ✝
Post Office ✉

West Lake

Tran Quoc Pagoda

6 7

Lake Truc Bach

■ **Quan Thanh Pagoda**

Thuy Khue

Quan Thanh

8

Phan Dinh Phung

Duong Hung Vuong

Hoang Dieu

Nguyen Tri Phuong

4

5

BA DINH DISTRICT

1

Ong Ich Khiem

3

Doi Can

2

Le Hong Phong

Kim Ma ✉

Duong Tran Phu

Dien Bien Phu

44

Trinh Hoai Duc

Nguyen Thai Hoc

45

46

Nguyen Khuyen

Quoc Tu Giam

N Thinh Hao

Ton Duc Thang

Lake Van Chuong

Duong Le Duan

CHINA

▲ **Hanoi** ★

Gulf of Tonkin

LAOS

South China Sea

THAILAND

Kham Thien

CAMBODIA

DONG DA DISTRICT

VIETNAM

Gulf of Thailand

Ngo Cho Kham Thien

0   100 mi
0   100 km

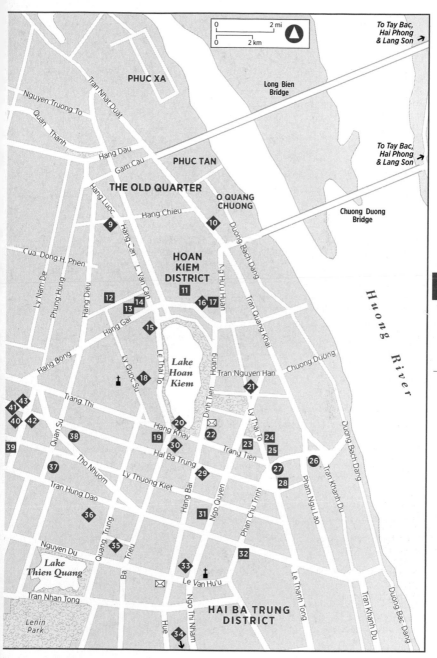

PHUC XA

Long Bien
Bridge

To Tay Bac,
Hai Phong
& Lang Son

Nguyen Truong To

Quan Thanh

Tran Nhat Duat

Hang Dau

Gam Cau

PHUC TAN

THE OLD QUARTER

O QUANG
CHUONG

To Tay Bac,
Hai Phong
& Lang Son

Hang Luoc

Hang Chieu

9

10

Chuong Duong
Bridge

Cua Dong

H. Phen

Hang San

Ly Van Can

Hang Bo

HOAN
KIEM
DISTRICT

Ng Hu'u Huan

Duong Bach Dang

Huong River

Ly Nam De

Phung Hung

Hang Dieu

12

14

13

11

16 **17**

Tran Quang Khai

Hang Gai

15

Hang Bong

Ly Quoc Su

Le Thai To

Lake Hoan Kiem

Huong

Tran Nguyen Han

Chuong Duong

18

†

21

Dinh Tien

Ly Thai To

Duong Bach Dang

Trang Thi

43

41

40 **42**

Ts Quang

38

39

20

Hang Khay

19

30

Hai Ba Trung

22

Trang Tien

23

24

25

26

Tran Khanh Du

Pham Ngu Lao

27

28

Tho Nhuom

Ly Thuong Kiet

37

Tran Hung Dao

Hang Bai

29

Ngo Quyen

Phan Chu Trinh

36

Quang Trung

Ba Trieu

31

Nguyen Du

35

*Lake
Thien Quang*

32

Le Thanh Tong

Tran Khanh Du

Duong Bach Dang

Tran Nhan Tong

33

†

Le Van Hu'u

Hue

Ngo Thi Nham

HAI BA TRUNG
DISTRICT

*Lenin
Park*

34

BY MOTORBIKE Motorcycle taxis are a cheap and easy way to get around the city, but they go like madmen, so this is only for the brave. With haggling, expect to pay about 10,000VND for short trips, or $1 to $2 by the hour. Self-rental at the tourist cafes starts at $6 for the day and is only for the fearless.

BY CYCLO Cyclos are two-seated carts powered by a man on a foot-pedal bike riding behind you. Flag them down anywhere (these guys find you). Being trundled along among whizzing motorcycles isn't always very comfortable, but it's a fun option for touring the Old Quarter. Pay as low as 15,000VND for a short ride, 30,000VND for a longer haul, or by the hour for about 60,000VND. If you're inclined, they'll let you try to ride just for fun.

BY BICYCLE Rental costs about $1 from a hotel or tourist cafe. The traffic is daunting, but the brave learn quickly how to join the flow.

Visitor Information & Tours

Most tour companies are based in Ho Chi Minh City (Saigon); however, many have branches in Hanoi as well. Operators can usually assist with local tours as well as countrywide services.

o **Ann Tours** (79 Pham Hong Thai St., Ba Dinh District; ☎ 04/3715-0950; fax 08/3832-3866; www.anntours.com). This company offers private tours to Halong Bay and everywhere else in the country. Their personal and efficient service has earned them rave reviews.

o **Buffalo Tours** (94 Ma May, Hoan Kiem District; ☎ 04/3828-0702; www.buffalo tours.com). This reputable outfit offers a range of standard tours and some good eco-adventures, like cycling, trekking, and kayaking. Its boat, *Jewel of the Bay*, is a great choice for trips in Halong. Friendly and professional staff.

o **Exotissimo Travel** (26 Tran Nhat Duat St., Hoan Kiem District; ☎ 04/3828-2150; fax 04/828-2146; www.exotissimo.com). Comprehensive, upscale services.

o **Handspan** (80 Ma May St., Hoan Kiem District; ☎ 04/3926-2828; fax 04/926-2383; www.handspan.com). A good option for organized trips around Hanoi or adventures to the northern hills and Halong Bay.

o **Queen Travel** (65 Hang Bac, Hoan Kiem District; ☎ 04/3826-0860; fax 04/826-0300; www.azqueentravel.com). One of Hanoi's longest-established tour operators, Queen can arrange anything from a half-day city tour to a 2-week 4WD exploration of remote northern villages.

o **Topas Outdoor Adventures** (52 To Ngoc Van St.; ☎ 04/3715-1005; fax 04/715-1007; www.topas-adventure-vietnam.com). This Danish company is very professional and extremely friendly. It's best known for upscale trekking tours around Sapa but also offers Halong Bay cruises.

BUDGET TOURS

Another good option for tours and transport or for 1- or 2-day excursions is to book with one of the tourist cafes, which are small eateries, Internet cafes, and travel agents all rolled into one. For a good, affordable seat-in-tour coach, try these:

o **Sinh Café** (40 Luong Ngoc Quyen, Hoan Kiem District; ☎ 04/3926-1568; fax 04/3926-1621; www.thesinhtourist.vn).

o **Kim Tours** (137 Hang Bac, Hoan Kiem District; ☎ 04/3926-0804; www.kim tours.net).

[FastFACTS] HANOI

American Express

The local Amex representative, **Exotissimo Travel,** 26 Tran Nhat Duat St. (✆ **04/3828-2150**), does not provide complete travel services, but can direct you if you lose your card. Hours are Monday through Friday from 8:30am to 5:30pm.

Currency Exchange

Major banks in Hanoi include **Australia New Zealand Bank (ANZ),** 14 Le Thai To St. (✆ **04/3825-8190**); **Citibank,** 17 Ngo Quyen St. (✆ **04/3825-1950**); and **Vietcombank,** 198 Tran Quan Khai (✆ **04/3934-3137**). ATMs are located at ANZ Bank, at Citibank, and in various locations throughout the city. Money-changing offices abound in places such as Hang Bac, in the heart of the backpacker area of

the Old Quarter—**Hanoi Sacombank,** 87 Hang Bac (✆ **04/3926-1392**), is typical of many. Black-market money-changers may approach you outside the major banks. Best to just avoid the temptation, as you'll often be left with a few counterfeit or out-of-circulation notes in the mix.

Emergencies

For police, dial ✆ **113;** for fire, dial ✆ **114;** and for ambulance, dial ✆ **115.**

Internet Access

Most budget and midrange hotels offer free Internet or Wi-Fi use to their guests, though top-end hotels tend to charge for the service. Small Internet storefronts are numerous throughout the city, especially in the Old Quarter on Hang Bac or Hang Be, with rates starting at about 4,000VND per hour.

Mail

The general post office is at 75 Dinh Tien Hoang St., Hoan Kiem District (✆ **04/3825-7036**). It's open daily from 6:30am to 10pm. You can also send faxes or telexes and make international phone calls. **FedEx** (✆ **04/3557-8899**) is located at 5B Le Van Thiem St., Thanh Xuan District.

Telephones

The city code for Hanoi is **4.** Most hotels provide international direct dialing, although none allows you to access an international operator or AT&T (whose Vietnam access code is 12010288). To do that, you will have to go to the general post office (see above). There are public phone booths throughout the city for local calls; these accept phone cards purchased from the post office.

Where to Stay

Hanoi has everything from historical charm to slick efficiency to budget hole in the wall. Amenities and cleanliness levels are high and prices low, making Hanoi a good place for an upgrade. Most hotels charging more than $15 per night will have a phone, air-conditioning, an in-room safe, and a hair dryer. Children 11 and under usually stay free. Prices shown here are rack rates, and discounts abound—just ask. Note that hotels charge a VAT of up to 20%.

VERY EXPENSIVE

In addition to the top-rated hotels listed below, options on the pricier end include the mammoth **Melia Hanoi** (✆ 04/3934-3343; www.meliahanoi.com), the plush **Hotel Nikko** (✆ 04/3822-3535; www.hotelnikkohanoi.com.vn), and the **Hanoi Horison Hotel** (✆ 04/3733-0808; www.accorhotels.com).

Hilton Hanoi Opera ★★ The Hilton is a reproduction colonial that makes an elegant arc around the perimeter of the splendid Hanoi Opera building. The inside matches the fine facade, with a lobby done on a grand scale. Rooms are outfitted with richly colored carpet, unique cushioned wallpaper, subdued lighting, and faux Chinese lacquer cabinets. Those on the fifth floor have balconies. Suites are much larger and nicely appointed. Daily newspaper delivery, voice mail, and in-room broadband Internet access keep business travelers up to speed. Leisure travelers can enjoy the inviting courtyard pool, get tips from the helpful concierge, and take advantage of in-house tour services with Exotissimo (open 8am–8pm, daily).

1 Le Thanh Tong St., Hoan Kiem District, Hanoi. *©* **800/774-1500** in the U.S., or 04/3933-0500. Fax 04/3933-0530. www.hilton.com. 269 units. $185 double; $225 executive room; $310 suite. AE, MC, V. **Amenities:** 2 restaurants; bar; cafe; babysitting; concierge; executive-level rooms; fitness center; outdoor pool; room service. *In room:* A/C, satellite TV, hair dryer, high-speed Internet, Wi-Fi.

Sofitel Metropole Hanoi ★★★   Hanoi's top choice. Built in 1901, the Metropole is a historic treasure. It's where invading, liberating, or civil armies have found billet and raised their flags, where the first film was shown in Indochina, where Charlie Chaplin spent his honeymoon, where Jane Fonda and Joan Baez took cover in a bomb shelter, and where heads of state and embassy officials resided for many years. In fact, the history of the Metropole is the history of the past 100 years in Hanoi.

The hotel has been through numerous renovations, and a new building was added in 1994. Rooms in the new wing are more spacious, but go for the old wing and walk into a bit of history: Your medium-size room will have wood floors, cane furniture, classic fixtures, and high ceilings. The staff couldn't be nicer or more efficient. The pool is small, but the adjoining Bamboo Lounge is an oasis of calm in the city center. Le Beaulieu is popular for classic French fare, while the Spices Garden is a great place to sample local delights (the lunch buffet is a safe and tasty place to try Hanoi street fare including *pho* and *bun cha*). The downtown location can't be beat, and there's a nice mix of tourists and businesspeople here.

15 Ngo Quyen St., Hoan Kem District, Hanoi. *©* **800/221-4542** in the U.S., or 04/3826-6919. Fax 04/3826-6920. www.sofitel.com. 364 units. $230–$390 double; from $580 suite. AE, DC, MC, V. **Amenities:** 3 restaurants; 3 bars; babysitting; concierge; top-notch health club and spa; nice courtyard pool; room service; smoke-free rooms; Wi-Fi. *In room:* A/C, satellite TV, fridge, hair dryer, high-speed Internet, minibar.

EXPENSIVE

De Syloia Hotel ★   The De Syloia is a cozy little treasure just south of the city center. Rooms are large and clean—not especially luxurious, but comfortable with tidy carpet, dark-wood appointments, and large bathrooms with tubs (deluxe rooms have Jacuzzis). The lobby is compact and clean but not particularly atmospheric, and the whole setup is a Hanoi minihotel gone upscale, with a good standard throughout. The staff is friendly on a good day, and the amenities are limited, but this is a popular choice away from the downtown traffic.

17a Tran Hung Dao St., Hoan Kem District, Hanoi. *©* **04/3824-5346.** Fax 04/3824-1083. www.desyloia. com. 33 units. $105–$130 double; $140 suite. Internet rates available. AE, MC, V. **Amenities:** Restaurant; bar; exercise room; room service. *In room:* A/C, satellite TV, fridge, hair dryer, minibar, free Wi-Fi.

InterContinental Hanoi West Lake ★★   InterContinental offers a sweet resortlike atmosphere in busy little Hanoi. The hotel is one of Hanoi's newest five-star hotels and was tapped by Condé Nast for its 2008 Hot List. For a romantic treat, splurge on a suite on one of the island pavilions connected to the main building via Venetian-style bridges. All rooms come with private balconies and most have fabulous views of West Lake. Rooms on the top floor ("Atelier rooms") have high, sloping ceilings, giving the space a cozy cabin feel. Located about a 20-minute cab ride away from Hanoi's Old Quarter, this hotel is a perfect getaway from the hustle and bustle of city life. The outdoor Sunset Bar is quickly becoming a weekend destination for local expats.

1A Nghi Tam, Tay Ho District, Hanoi. © **04/6270-8888.** Fax 04/6270-9999. www.intercontinental.com. 359 units. $105–$147 double; from $189 suite. AE, MC, V. **Amenities:** 3 restaurants; outdoor bar; cafe; lounge; babysitting; concierge; executive-level rooms; health club; Jacuzzi; outdoor pool; room service; sauna; smoke-free rooms; spa. *In room:* A/C, satellite TV, fridge, hair dryer, minibar, Wi-Fi.

Maison D'Hanoi ★★   One of the city's newer offerings, this place is a clever blend of French colonial with Asian Art Deco styles. The spacious lobby sets the tone, and the rooms are both elegant and luxurious, with nice touches like firm but comfortable beds, padded headboards, and silk table lamps. While geared principally toward businessmen, it has an excellent location for sightseeing too, being just a short walk from Hoan Kiem Lake and the Old Quarter. There's free Internet service throughout the hotel and a restaurant that serves up attractive and tasty dishes. For a real indulgent stay, ask for the boutique penthouse apartment on the top floor.

35–37 Hang Trong St., Hoan Kiem District, Hanoi. © **04/3938-0999.** Fax 04/3938-0989. www.hanova hotel.com. 55 units. $140–$160 double; $180–$220 suite. AE, MC, V. **Amenities:** Restaurant; babysitting; Internet; room service; smoke-free rooms; spa. *In room:* A/C, satellite TV, hair dryer, Internet, minibar.

Mövenpick Hotel Hanoi ★★   This hotel chain has had considerable success in Southeast Asia with its well chosen locations and sumptuously furnished rooms, and this newish place in Hanoi is no exception. Conveniently located near the railway station and 5 minutes from downtown, the colonial-style building features elegant rooms with wooden floors, classy drapes, and flatscreen TVs. One of the hotel's quirkiest features is a women-only floor that has direct access to the fitness center, and another plus is the delightful Mangosteen Restaurant with its mouthwatering buffet lunches and dinners.

83A Ly Thuong Kiet St., Hoan Kem District, Hanoi © **04/3822-2800.** Fax 04/3822 2022. www. moevenpick-hotels.com. 154 units. $130 superior; $150 premium deluxe; $240 suite. AE, MC, V. **Amenities:** 2 restaurants; 2 bars; babysitting; concierge; gym; room service; dry sauna; smoke-free floors. *In room:* A/C, satellite TV, fridge, hair dryer, minibar, Wi-Fi.

Sheraton Hanoi ★   Just a 10-minute ride north of town, this smart, upscale hotel sits on a peninsula jutting into Hanoi's picturesque West Lake in a neighborhood popular with the local expat community (which means good restaurants and services in the area). The hotel makes up for any inconvenience of being far from town by being completely self-contained, with fine-dining options, a top fitness center, and services that cover all bases, from local touring to business support. Rooms are done in an ultratidy, contemporary style typical of Sheraton hotels—certainly nothing spectacular, but cozy and familiar nonetheless. All units have fine views of the lake. Bathrooms are large, with big tubs, separate showers, and wood and granite detail. In-house dining is tops; a shuttle bus to town runs three times daily and taxis are available 24 hours.

K5 Nghi Tam, 11 Xuan Dieu Rd., Tay Ho District, Hanoi. © **04/3719-9000.** Fax 04/3719-9001. www. sheraton.com. 299 units. $119–$190 double; from $325 suite. AE, DC, MC, V. **Amenities:** 2 restaurants; bar; babysitting; concierge; executive-level rooms; health club; Jacuzzi; outdoor pool; room service; sauna; smoke-free rooms; tennis court. *In room:* A/C, satellite TV, fridge, hair dryer, minibar, Wi-Fi ($15 a day).

Zephyr Hotel ★★ 🛎   This downtown boutique property is a real find. Nine floors overlook the southern end of central Hoan Kiem Lake. It's perfect for luxury travelers who want to be in the middle of things but can't bear the thought of an Old Quarter minihotel (though many of these hotels are being upgraded, they can still be pretty beat-up and rooms very noisy from the busy streets below). Thin office-style carpets in rooms are a drawback, but beds have big fluffy duvets, and the built-in wooden cabinetry is sleek and contemporary. Deluxe rooms are quite luxurious, and two of them have balconies. Upper floors are best—some have great views. The first-floor restaurant serves international fare and a very good buffet breakfast. The place is like a large international hotel stuffed into the space of a Hanoi minihotel. The staff is very efficient, and you couldn't ask for a better downtown location.

4 Ba Trieu St., Hoan Kiem District, Hanoi. © **04/3934-1256.** Fax 04/3934-1262. www.zephyrhotel.com. vn. 43 units. $123 superior double; $143 deluxe; $178 Zephyr suite. AE, MC, V. **Amenities:** Restaurant; bar (top-floor lounge); exercise room. In room: A/C, satellite TV, fridge, high-speed Internet, minibar.

MODERATE

Green Mango ★★ 🏠 Tucked away in the labyrinthine streets of the Old Quarter, this little gem is a one-stop sleep, eat, and party location. With just a handful of stylish rooms upstairs and one of the city's most celebrated restaurants and bars downstairs, this place is ideal for short-stay visitors who prefer to avoid getting caught up in the city's traffic. Most rooms are compact but well equipped, with wooden floors, flatscreen TVs, and Wi-Fi. If you prefer a bit more space, go for the Deluxe Sweet room. Rates include a delicious breakfast, and airport pickups can be arranged for $20.

18 Hang Quat St., Haon Kiem District, Hanoi. © **04/3928-9916.** Fax 04/3928-9915. www.greenmango. vn. 7 units. $50–$100 double. MC, V. **Amenities:** Restaurant, bar, room service. In room: A/C, cable TV, minibar, Wi-Fi.

Hoa Binh Hotel ★ Built in 1926, the Hoa Binh is an atmospheric choice. Comfort and history meet at a good level, and whether you're walking up the creaky grand staircase or opening French doors onto a balcony overlooking the busy street, you know that you're in Hanoi here. Sizable rooms have original light fixtures, molded ceilings, and glossy wood furniture. Everything is done a bit low-luxe, however: The shiny polyester bedspreads, velveteen drapes, and spongy mattresses detract from the overall effect. Bathrooms are plain and small but spotless. The hotel is in a prime downtown location, and the bar has a view of the city. Ask to see a room before checking in, as they vary in size, shape, and degree of smoke or mustiness; in general, though, this is a good bet. It's popular with tour groups.

27 Ly Thuong Kiet St., Hoan Kiem District, Hanoi. © **04/3825-3315** or 3825-3692. Fax 04/3826-9818. www.hoabinhhotel.com. 103 units. $60–$75 double; $90–$100 suite. Rates include breakfast. AE, MC, V. **Amenities:** 2 restaurants; 2 bars; concierge; room service; sauna; smoke-free rooms. In room: A/C, TV, fridge, hair dryer, minibar, Wi-Fi.

Queen Hotel ★ Typical of many lodgings in the Old Quarter, this former backpacker's haunt has been made over and reborn as a classy boutique hotel with a distinctive lobby where vintage bicycles and scooters are on display. The central location is ideal, and the breezy roof garden and cosy communal lounge make it feel like a home away from home. Rooms are equipped with wooden floors and traditional furnishings, and each has a small balcony. Rooms out back are a bit quieter, away from the traffic noise. The owner is both an architect and one of the city's most knowledgeable tour operators, so it's well worth signing up here for a customized tour of the north.

65 Hang Bac St., Hoan Kiem District, Hanoi. *C* **04/3826-0860.** Fax 04/0826-0300. www.azqueen travel.com. 15 units. $65–$100 double. Rates include breakfast. AE, MC, V. *In room:* A/C, satellite TV, DVD player, hair dryer, minibar, Wi-Fi.

INEXPENSIVE

Classic Street Hotel 🏷️
Furnished like a traditional Vietnamese house, this place makes guests feel at home right away and offers some quiet sitting areas apart from the cozy, carpeted rooms. Lodgings are not luxurious but very adequate for the price and include all major comforts such as bathtubs, hot-water bathrooms, and cable TV. There's a small restaurant where guests can enjoy a free breakfast before heading out to explore—and one of this hotel's best points is that it is right in the heart of the action, on the edge of the Old Quarter and a few steps from Hoan Kiem Lake.

41 Hang Be St., Hoan Kiem District, Hanoi. *C* **04/3825-2421.** Fax 04/3934-5920. www.classicstreet-phocohotel.com. 22 units. $33–$38 double. MC, V. **Amenities:** Restaurant, room service. *In room:* A/C, cable TV, fridge, hair dryer, Wi-Fi.

Hong Ngoc Hotel ★★
With four locations all in the heart of the Old Quarter, this is a good no-frills option close to Hoan Kiem Lake. The incredibly friendly staff has a can-do attitude and will help you with any detail, such as renting a car, motorcycle, or bicycle. Rooms are compact, but all have dark-wood trim and the quality amenities of a proper hotel. Larger suites are a good choice. Bathrooms are small and clean. This is top notch downtown affordability, a minihotel with attitude—like a terrier who thinks himself a Great Dane.

14 Luong Van Can St., Hoan Kiem District, Hanoi. *C* **04/3826-7566.** Fax 04/38245362. 40 units. 30–34 Hang Manh St., Hoan Kiem District. *C* **04/3828-5053.** Fax 04/3828-5054. 53 units. 39 Hang Bac St., Hoan Kiem. *C* **04/3926-0322.** Fax 04/3926-1600. 25 units. 95-7 Nguyen Trong To St. *C* **04/3716-4143.** Fax 04/3716-4187. 28 units. www.hongngochotel.com. $30–$60 double; $60–$100 suite. MC, V. **Amenities:** Restaurant; Internet (free in lobby), room service. *In room:* A/C, satellite TV, fridge, minibar, Wi-Fi.

Where to Dine

It's hard to have a bad meal in Hanoi. The French influence is everywhere, with both classical French and Vietnamese fusion fare, all priced for any budget. Almost every ethnic food variation is well represented in the city as well.

Hanoi has savory specialties that must be sampled. For that, hit the streets and dine in small local eateries. *Pho,* by far the most popular local dish, is noodles with slices of beef *(bo)* or chicken *(ga),* fresh bean sprouts, and condiments. *Bun cha,* a snack of rice noodles and spring rolls, has made the **Dac Kim** restaurant (at 1 Hang Manh, in the Old Quarter) city-renowned. And don't miss **Cha Ca,** Hanoi's famed spicy fish fry-up (p. 262).

EXPENSIVE

Bobby Chinn ★★ CALIFORNIA/VIETNAMESE/FRENCH
After several years enjoying a prime location beside Hoan Kiem Lake, Bobby Chinn's has now moved north to Tay Ho district near West Lake. Chinn the chef has become something of a celebrity in recent years with lots of TV appearances, and his restaurant is definitely a hangout for hi-so socialites, though the boss is not there in person so often these days. Some may find the decor of rich drapes on the walls and ceilings a bit over the top, but there's no denying the appeal of the delightfully eclectic menu of fine French and Vietnamese-inspired dishes, all with a playful, cross-cultural flair. To start, try the

rib sampler or "symphony of flavors" from the tapas menu. Main courses such as pan-roasted salmon with wasabi mashed potatoes, or perhaps green tea–smoked duck, have a certain Franco-Japanese appeal and promise a new taste sensation.

77 Xuan Dieu, Tay Ho District. ℭ **04/3719-2460.** www.bobbychinn.com. Reservations recommended. AE, MC, V. Main courses $15-$30. Daily 11am-midnight.

Club de L'Oriental ★★★ VIETNAMESE   This is upscale Vietnamese food at its best—beautiful colonial decor, properly trained staff, and amazing food. The fresh spring rolls are the best in town. For mains I highly recommend the grilled chicken in lemon leaves served with a dipping plate of salt and pepper in a sprinkle of lime juice, a light but savory dish. On the richer side, try the sautéed prawns in tamarind sauce. The main floor has a handful of tables set up around an open kitchen, seats around which are perfect for couples or single diners. For an intimate but chilly experience, reserve a table in the wine cellar.

22 Tong Dan, Hoan Kiem District. ℭ **04/3826-8801.** Fax 04/3826-8802. Reservations recommended. Main courses $8.25-$50. AE, MC, V. Daily 11am-2pm and 6-11pm.

Green Tangerine ★★ FRENCH   The Green Tangerine is set in a lovingly restored 1928 colonial right in the center of the Old Quarter. Its small courtyard, just a few steps off busy Hang Be, is great for an afternoon drink, while the air-conditioned dining room is a real sanctuary for a luxurious meal. It's very popular with expats, and that makes for a constantly evolving menu to keep up with repeat customers. Dishes might include a lovely bass enhanced with ginger served with slices of zucchini and potatoes piled like a layer cake. The creamy Cointreau-flavored frozen yogurt served in a green tangerine shell is delicious and refreshing. The set menus are popular and good value. Everything here is rich and delicious.

48 Hang Be, Hoan Kiem District. ℭ **04/3825-1286.** Main courses $7.90-$20. AE, MC, V. Daily 11am-10:30pm.

La Badiane ★★ FRENCH   Local chef Benjamin Rascalou's excellent restaurant is housed in an old colonial villa divided into a small garden courtyard on the ground floor and a pair of intimate dining rooms upstairs. The three set-price dinner menus include flavorful options like coffee-marinated lamb. Service is also top-notch here, which is quite an accomplishment for such an intimate place. Rascalou is well known in Hanoi for his innovative menus at Green Tangerine, where he worked as head chef for 6 years before starting his own restaurant.

10 Nam Ngu St. ℭ **04/3942-4509.** Reservations recommended. Main courses $14-$18; set menus $11 lunch, $23-$29 dinner. AE, MC, V. Daily 11:30am-2pm and 6-10pm.

La Verticale ★★ FUSION   Every time I come here it's buzzing with French-speaking patrons happily tucking into their meal and sipping their wine. Chef Didier Corlou (formerly of Le Beaulieu in the Sofitel Metropole) has done well. His food is at once an homage to the lightness of local cuisine and the rich gastronomic traditions of his native France. The presentation of dishes is decidedly flamboyant, but adds to the special dining experience. This place is excellent value given the quality of food, but if you're looking to save on the bill (or your waistline), skip the appetizers; main portions are generous and come with a *mis en bouche* anyway.

19 Ngo Van So St. ℭ **04/3944-6317.** www.verticale-hanoi.com. Main courses $16-$33. AE, MC, V. Daily 10am-2pm and 6:30-10pm.

Le Café des Arts de Hanoi ★ BISTRO/CONTINENTAL After strolling around Hoan Kiem Lake, stop off its northwest end for a drink or a bite at this friendly bistro-style eatery, run by French expats and open all day. Spacious, with tiled floors and shuttered windows looking into the narrow Old Quarter street below, the cafe has casual rattan furniture and a long, inviting bar. It doubles as an art gallery, which explains the interesting paintings hanging throughout. The Vietnamese art crowd also adds some attractive local color. Most inviting, however, is the excellent food. A three-course set lunch costs $10. There are also daily specials, and bistro standbys such as omelets or a *croque madame*—toasted bread and cheese sautéed in egg—and house specialty *salade bressare* (very fresh chicken and vegetables in a light mayonnaise sauce). You'll also find good house wine by the glass.

11B Ngo Bao Khanh, Old Quarter, Hoan Kiem District. ℂ **04/3828-7207.** Main courses $10–$25. MC, V. Daily 8am–11pm. Bar open until midnight.

Press Club ★★ CONTINENTAL Subdued and elegant, this place says "power lunch"—and offers cuisine and prices to match. The indoor restaurant is sizable yet private, done in dark tones of maroon and forest green with solid wood furniture and detailing. There is outdoor seating on the terrace, facing a stage that features regular live acts. The menu is full of sumptuous Continental standards: antipasto starters, goat-cheese salad, tuna steak, smoked trout and baked grouper, and various wood-grilled imported steaks and meat dishes. Unique is the "deconstructed" Vietnamese *pho* noodle soup with lobster, foie gras, and truffle. For dessert, try the white-chocolate sticky rice or rich rice pudding. The service here is impeccable.

The **Deli,** on the third floor, is a good place to enjoy a relaxed lunch of sandwiches or gourmet pizzas, not to mention the Aussie pie with chips or "Mom's Meatloaf." Breakfast is served all day. A good choice for a casual dose of home.

59A Ly Thai To St., Hoan Kiem District. ℂ **04/3934-0888.** www.hanoi-pressclub.com. Reservations recommended. Main courses $16–$32. AE, MC, V. Restaurant: ground floor daily 11am–2pm and 6–11pm; terrace Mon–Fri 9am–11pm, Sat–Sun 3–11pm. Deli: daily 6:30am–10pm.

Wild Rice (Lá Luá) ★ ASIAN FUSION Nothing about Lá Luá portends to be authentic Vietnamese, and everything from the decor to the dining is in fact an amalgam of traditions and customs. The place looks like an upmarket L.A. bistro borrowing Japanese themes, with tall stands of bamboo encased in glass, slate floors, and white walls that shine with the mellow glow of indirect lighting. The food is good, Vietnamese-influenced fare. Try the barbecued squid or beef with coconut or the deliciously spicy and savory grilled chicken in chile with lemon grass. Presentation is Zen simple: white linen with black chopsticks, a plate, a bowl, and a candle. It's all a bit studied, really, but the food is very good.

6 Ngo Thi Nham St., Hai Ba Trung District. ℂ **04/3943-8896.** Fax 04/3943-6299. Main courses $16–$35. AE, MC, V. Daily 11am–3pm and 6–11pm.

MODERATE

Al Fresco's ☺ TEX-MEX Run by Australian expats, Al Fresco's is two floors of friendly, casual dining. With checkered tablecloths, oldies music, and a great view from the second floor to the street below, this is the place to bring the kids (or yourself) when they're in need of a taste of home. The place serves good Tex-Mex fare, excellent imported Aussie steaks, and pizza, chicken wings, and the like. Ribs are the house specialty. The burgers are the real deal, with all the fixings. Desserts are good

THE best AUTHENTIC LOCAL FARE

Hanoi's local cuisine is some of the best in Vietnam, and the finest local dishes are served at small one-dish restaurants, usually just open-air joints at streetside, where you might wonder why there's a line out the door. To Vietnamese, it's about the food, not the atmosphere. Standards of hygiene might appear poor, but do as locals do and wipe down bowls and chopsticks with a napkin before digging in. Eating on the street means you might have some tummy trouble, but if you stick to the few places recommended below, you should be okay.

The ubiquitous *pho*—noodle soup served with slices of beef *(bo)* or chicken *(ga)*, fresh bean sprouts, and condiments—can be found anywhere. And don't miss *cha ca*, Hanoi's famed spicy fish fry (see Cha Ca La Vong below).

Banh Cuon ★, 14 Hang Ga St. (✆ **04/3828-0108**), consists of minced pork and mushrooms rolled into soft rice crepes topped with crispy fried garlic and coriander. Cut-up pieces are dipped in a tasty fish sauce. The stuffing-to-crepe ratio at this streetside eatery is a bit on the low side, but it is still great value for the money at 25,000VND a plate.

Bun Bo Nam Bo ★★, 67 Hang Dieu St. (✆ **04/3923-0701**), serves only one main course: *bun bo*, a dish of fresh rice noodles with herbs and spices, topped with beef and crispy fried garlic that costs only 28,000VND. Sound simple? It is. It's the subtlety of the flavors of this dish and the stock that brings 'em here in droves. Just order by holding up as many fingers as you want bowls of *bun bo*, take a seat at the low tables in the brightly lit interior, and wait. A spartan atmosphere, but a rich and delicious dish worth hunting down. No credit cards. Daily 7am to 10:30pm.

Cha Ca La Vong ★★, 14 Cha Ca St. (✆ **04/3825-3929**), is on a street called Cha Ca, and it serves one dish—you guessed it—*cha ca*. Cha ca is a delicate white fish, fried at high heat in peanut oil with dill, turmeric, rice noodles, and peanuts—and it's delicious. The place is pretty grungy, and to call the service "indifferent" would be to sing its praises, but that's the beauty here: It's all about the food. You order by saying how many of you there are (expect to pay 80,000VND per person) and how many bottles of beer or soda you'd like. Then it's do-it-yourself, with some gruff guidance, as you stir in the ingredients on a

old standbys such as brownies a la mode. The wine list is heavy on Australian and inexpensive South American reds.

23 Hai Ba Trung St., Hoan Kiem District. ✆ **04/3826-7782.** Main courses 92,000VND–220,000VND. MC, V. Daily 8:30am–11pm.

Highway 4 ★ VIETNAMESE Named after the highway that snakes through North Vietnam, this place is more than a restaurant—it's a complete dining experience. Explore a range of traditional Vietnamese dishes, such as steamboat and oven-baked claypot, while relaxing in a typically Vietnamese interior. If you are suitably impressed by the quality of the food, you can also sign up for cookery classes here. To complete the cultural immersion program, choose one of the Son Tinh rice wines in herbal and fruit flavors—a range of liquors produced exclusively by Highway 4. They claim that the high quality of distillation and absence of artificial additives guarantee a clear head the next day, though if you want to be sure, stick to the herbal frying pan over a charcoal hibachi right at the table. It's a rich dish and great with some hot sauce (go easy on it at first). Just say "Cha Ca," and any cab-driver can take you there. Avoid copy-cats: The original Cha Ca La Vong is the only game in town. No credit cards. Daily 10am to 2pm and 4 to 10pm.

Pho Gia Truyen ★★, 49 Bat Dan St. (on the west side of the Old Quarter near the old citadel wall), is a very pop-ular storefront *pho* stand in Hanoi's Old Quarter. If you've seen the Japanese film *Tampopo* about the making of the per-fect noodle soup, or the *Seinfeld* epi-sode about New York City's "Soup Nazi" who, because of his quality broth, chose his customers instead of vice versa, you'll have an idea what it's like. The line is around the block day and night. The formula is simple: delicious cured beef, fresh noodles, and spices. Just order "one please" (it is *pho* with beef or nothing) and carry your own bowl to an open slot at a crowded table. The place is as shabby as any little noodle stand, but when you pull those first noodles off the chopsticks and follow with a spoon-ful of broth, you'll know why you came. No phone. One bowl of beef *pho* is 25,000VND. Daily 6am to 11pm.

Restaurant Lau Tu Xuyen, 163 Yen Phu, with another location at 199 Duong Nghi Tam (⊘ **04/3714-0289**), is a fun adventure. Way out on the eastern shore of West Lake (about 40,000VND by taxi from the city center), this big warehouse of a restaurant is the best place in town to enjoy the real *lau,* or Vietnamese hot pot. Go with a Vietnamese friend or be open to some creative charades with your waitress; there's no English menu and foreign visitors are rare. The official directions for cooking hot pot? As my friend says, "You just put." Add what-ever you like—fresh seafood, beef, poul-try, and vegetables—to a shared pot of boiling broth on a hot plate in the center of the table. They also can bring out a barbecue setup for small kabobs. You order like you would order dim sum, choosing plates of raw ingredients off a tray. The place is packed in the evenings, especially in the winter (this is Vietnam's version of stew) and on weekends. The entry is just adjacent to the Thang Loi Lakeside hotel. The local draft beer flows freely and costs little. Make a night of it and end with a walk in this busy expat neighborhood. Expect to pay about $5 per person in a group. No credit cards. Daily 11am to 10pm.

teas or fruit juices. There are now four branches (see website for details of others); this one is conveniently located on the eastern side of the Old Quarter.

3 Hang Tre St. ⊘ **04/3926-4200.** www.highway4.com. Main courses 35,000VND–365,000VND. AE, MC, V. 10am–midnight.

Hoa Sua ★ VIETNAMESE/FRENCH   Do a good deed, enjoy a great feed. You'll find lots of good French and Vietnamese dishes at this popular cafe in the south end of town. Started in 1995, Hoa Sua is also an NGO and training school for disadvan-taged youth, with more than 700 students a year on its various programs. Because working at the restaurant is like a final exam for these students, the young staff is as friendly as they come and every detail is well attended to. The food is great, the atmosphere in the courtyard or on one of the patios in this sprawling faux colonial is very laid back, and the price is right. Lunch and dinner specials are written on a chalk-board, and everything—from good steak and chips, to sandwiches, to Vietnamese curry specials or fried seafood—is delicious. Best of all, the profits go to good use, providing scholarships for students and upgrading the school's service standard.

28A Ha Hoi St. ℰ **04/3942-4448.** www.hoasuaschool.com. Main courses 45,000VND–180,000VND. MC, V. Daily 7am–10pm.

Indochine ★ VIETNAMESE   Set in a beautifully restored colonial, this place is a longtime tourist favorite. The food, like that at many restaurants in Hanoi, is Vietnamese cuisine toned down for foreign palates, but Indochine does it well. The spring rolls are great, as are both the banana-flower salad and the crispy fried prawn-cakes with ginger. Ask about daily specials. With indoor and patio seating and traditional Vietnamese performances in the evening (call ahead for times), Indochine is well worth a visit for the beautiful colonial setting alone. Take a cab; it's hard to find. **Warning:** The restaurant fills with tour groups at lunchtime, which brings a rise in noise level and a drop in service quality.

16 Nam Ngu St., Hoan Kiem District. ℰ **04/3942-4097.** Main courses $3–$6.50. MC, V. Daily 11:30am–2pm and 5:30–10pm.

Khazanna ★★ INDIAN   The current incarnation of this restaurant serves a fine menu of northern and southern Indian dishes, complemented by the tidy Indian-themed decor and the excellent service and presentation: The curries are served in small metal crocks with brass ladles. The affordable lunch menu brings in crowds of businesspeople. In the evening, choose from an extensive selection of curries, grilled dishes, and naan (bread). Everything's good here.

1C Tong Dan St., Hoan Kiem District. ℰ **04/3934-5657.** Main courses 100,000VND–200,000VND. MC, V. Daily 11am–2:30pm and 6–10:30pm.

Mediterraneo ★ ITALIAN   You'll find a tasty but typical range of northern Italian fare at this mellow streetside cafe on Nha Tho, Hanoi's stylish cafe area (called Church St.). Prosciutto with melon, tomato, and homemade mozzarella is a good starter. Follow with good homemade pasta, a choice of grilled dishes, or pizza. It's affordable, cozy, and casual. There are daily specials and a good wine list too.

23 Nha Tho St. (near the Cathedral), Hoan Kiem District. ℰ **04/3826-6288.** Main courses $6–$15. AE, MC, V. Daily 10am–11pm.

Seasons of Hanoi ★ VIETNAMESE   The atmosphere is picture-perfect at Seasons: intimate, candlelit, earth-toned surroundings in a casual yet beautifully restored colonial with authentic native furniture. The spring rolls are heaven, as are the tempura soft-shell crabs. The kitchen serves great fish the way you like it—fried, boiled, on kebabs, or in hot pots. Try the sautéed eel with chile and lemon grass or the fried chicken in pandanus leaves. Presentation is elegant and the wine list long. **Tip:** Sit on the first floor to avoid the group tours that take over the second floor.

95B Quan Thanh St., Ba Dinh District. ℰ **04/3843-5444.** Reservations recommended, especially for groups. Main courses 60,000VND–120,000VND. AE, MC, V. Daily 11am–2pm and 6–10pm.

INEXPENSIVE

Chim Sao (L'Oiseau Siffleur) ★ 🎁 VIETNAMESE   This charming restaurant serves authentic Vietnamese dishes in a home-style ambience. Rotating art hangs on unfinished walls, and guests have to remove footwear before heading upstairs to sit on floor pillows and dine over squat tables. The English translations of dishes rarely do them justice—the "tofu with egg salted" is actually a delightful dish of cubed, battered tofu that is lightly fried for a crisp exterior. Other must-try dishes are the caramelized pork served in a piping-hot clay pot and the "mountainous flower rice"—sticky rice served with a sprinkle of crispy fried garlic.

65 Ngo Hue, Hoan Kiem District. © **04/3976-0633.** Main courses 40,000VND–70,000VND. No credit cards. Daily 10am–10pm.

Pho 24 ★ VIETNAMESE   If you are desperate to try a bowl of *pho* but can't bring yourself to step into one of those grungy dives, then here's the answer. Starting in 2003, this franchise serving Vietnam's national dish has gradually spread across the country (and also has branches in Hong Kong, Seoul, and Jakarta) and now operates more than 70 branches throughout the country; this is the most convenient in Hanoi. All locations are air-conditioned and spotlessly clean, and even if the various options on the menu are all standardized, most customers find these noodles lip-smacking good. In fact, you'll notice that customers are often Vietnamese rather than foreigners, so they must be doing something right. You can customize your *pho* by ticking selected ingredients on the menu, and then sit back and slurp away. A basic bowl will set you back around 30,000VND.

1 Hang Khay St., 2 blocks west of Hoan Kiem Lake. © **04/3747-4840.** Main dishes 30,000VND–50,000VND. MC, V. Daily 7am–10pm.

Quan An Ngon ★★ VIETNAMESE   *Ngon* means delicious in Vietnamese, and this lively restaurant with its extensive menu lives up to its name. The concept is simple and spot-on for visitors—to provide a range of classic Vietnamese dishes that are usually served at street stalls in a comfortable and hygienic environment. Sit at the elbow-to-elbow tables in the open air or else inside, where it's cooler and quieter. The bustling courtyard, filled with Vietnamese professionals and students, is surrounded by well stocked, clean food stalls, reminiscent of what you might find, at random, on the street, but without some of the, uh, hygiene concerns. Try the pancakes; try the noodles; try as much as you can. Everything on the menu is good, the staff is on the ball, and the prices are reasonable, so visitors can get a wide-ranging sample of Vietnamese fare. The place is often crowded with locals so it pays to arrive outside peak eating hours.

Note: Seafood fanatics, head to sister restaurant **Hai San Ngon** (199a Nghi Tam St., Tay Ho District; © **04/3719-3169;** daily 10:30am–10:30pm), which serves good fish and prawn dishes (*Hai San* is Vietnamese for seafood) in an atmospheric outdoor setting.

18 Phan Boi Chau St., Hoan Kiem District. © **04/3942-8162.** Main courses 26,000VND–115,000VND. MC, V. Daily 7am–10pm.

Tamarind Café ★ VEGETARIAN   Even if you're not a vegetarian, this welcoming cafe's inventive menu will tickle your fancy. Vegetarian wonton soup and two-color soup (spinach and sweet potato) take the chill off Hanoi winter nights and go great with the selection of sandwiches. Other inventive options include "ratatofu" (ratatouille over tofu) and an all-day breakfast served with delicious homemade fruit condiments. Fruit shakes and excellent teas round out the meal. This is a great place to take a break while exploring the hectic Old Quarter. There are streetside tables out front and funky seating in back. A good place to meet other travelers and pick up advice.

80 Ma May St., Hoan Kiem District. © **04/3926-0580.** Main courses $3–$5. MC, V. Daily 6am–11pm.

have you tried the SNAKE?

Six kilometers (3¾ miles) to the east of Hanoi, across the Red River, lies the town of **Le Mat,** also known as the "snake village." Among shanty houses and winding alleys, you'll find Chinese-style roofs sheltering the elegant dining areas of flashy little restaurants, all strangely tucked away. What's the big secret? The town is the hub of the very taboo snake industry. The Vietnamese taboo is not much different from that in the West (something like "Eat snake? Ooooh, yuck!"). Snake is also considered a male aphrodisiac, a kind of fried Viagra, so at night it's not uncommon to see groups of businessmen drunk as skunks piling into these places for a bit of medicine.

So, here's the drill. Finding it is half the battle (or adventure). Any taxi driver will be happy to take you to his friend's place in anticipation of a commission. Feel free to ask to see another restaurant (some of them are pretty disgusting), but expect to pay about $5 to get here. There are lots of restaurants in Le Mat, but try **O Sin** (© **04/3827-2984**).

You'll be greeted by a friendly owner who'll usher you back to the cages and put on quite a show of stirring up the snakes before selecting one he thinks will feed your party. He'll then quote you a ridiculous price, but expect to pay somewhere between $10 and $15 per person, after bargaining.

Then the show begins. Before your eyes, the owner kills the snake, drains the blood into a jar of rice whiskey, and systematically disembowels the animal, extracting the liver and showing you the still-beating heart before adding it to the whiskey/blood concoction. The guest of honor eats the heart and takes the first sip of whiskey. Thus begins a lengthy seven-course meal, starting with fried snake skin, grilled snake filet, snake spring rolls, snake soup with rice cake, minced snake dumpling, and copious amounts of rice whiskey. It's a decent meal, really, and certainly something to brag about.

Be warned that many of these places are part of the underground market in endangered species, but the snakes are common cobras found everywhere in Vietnam. Be clear with the driver about where you want to go (in other words, not to a brothel afterward), and don't pay until you arrive at your destination.

SNACKS & CAFES

For great coffee and desserts, try **Moca Café,** 14–16 Nha Tho St., Hoan Kiem District (© **04/3825-6334**). This area has become the popular spot for a growing little bohemian community in Hanoi, and businesses are sprouting up all along Nha Tho, the street that extends from St. Joseph's Cathedral. **Paris Deli,** 13 Nha Tho St., Hoan Kiem District (© **04/3928-6697**), is a popular spot with great breads and deli sandwiches.

One of the main attractions around Hoan Kiem Lake is **Fanny's Ice Cream,** 48 Ly Thai To St., Hoan Kiem District (© **04/3828-5656**), on the west side of the lake. Fanny's serves exquisite gelato-style ice cream. You can also find local ice-cream shops along Trang Tien between the lake and the Press Club. For 5,000VND, enjoy a cone and be part of the local scene.

Pepperonis, 29 Ly Quoc Su St., Hoan Kiem District (© **04/3928-5246**), serves the pizza that backpackers have been longing for along the tough travel trails throughout Asia. The pizza is cheap and best on the popular bar street, across from Café des Arts.

Little Hanoi, 21–23 Hang Gai St., Hoan Kiem District (✆ **04/3828-8333**), just north of the lake, is a little local-style fast-food joint, with basic but tidy bamboo-and-wood decor. It's not on the menu, but insiders know to order the *pho ga* (chicken noodle soup), which is outstanding here. This is a good place for a light meal (and a good central meeting point). Little Hanoi delivers too.

Highland's Coffee is the local version of Starbucks and a popular place to beat the heat. Find it at lakeside (38–40 Ly Thai To St., Hoan Kiem District; ✆ **04/3828-7043**) or in a hip outdoor courtyard between the Hilton and the Hanoi Opera House (✆ **04/3933-4947**).

What to See & Do

Remember that state-owned attractions usually close for lunch from 11:30am to 1:30pm. Be sure not to accept any extraneous pamphlets or unwanted guides at sights; all come with a nominal but frustrating fee.

BA DINH DISTRICT

Army Museum ★★   This museum, opened in 1959, presents the Vietnamese side of the country's struggle against colonial powers. There are three buildings of odds and ends from both the French and the American wars here, including evocative photos. Most interesting, though, is the actual war equipment on display, including aircraft, tanks, bombs, and big guns, some with signs indicating just how many of which enemy the piece took out. Outside, you'll see a spectacular display of downed French and U.S. aircraft wreckage. Also on the grounds is Hanoi's ancient flag tower (Cot Co), constructed from 1805 to 1812. The exhibits have English translations, which makes this an easy and worthwhile visit.

28A Dien Bien Phu St., Ba Dinh District. ✆ **04/3823-4264.** Admission 20,000VND. Tues–Thurs and Sat–Sun 8–11:30am and 1:30–4:30pm.

Ho Chi Minh Mausoleum ★★   In an imposing, somber, granite-and-concrete structure modeled on Lenin's tomb, Ho lies in state, embalmed and dressed in his favored khaki suit. He asked to be cremated, but his wish was not heeded. A respectful demeanor is required, and the dress code mandates no shorts or sleeveless shirts. For foreign visitors, the point of a visit here is to see how deeply Vietnam's greatest national hero is adored by the local people, who often become emotional on leaving the chamber where Ho rests. ***Note:*** The mausoleum is usually closed in October and November, when Ho goes to Russia for body maintenance of an undisclosed nature. The museum might be closed during this period as well. Also note the very limited opening hours.

On Ba Dinh Sq., Ba Dinh District. Tues–Thurs and Sat 8–11am. Last visitors admitted at 10:15am.

Ho Chi Minh Museum ★★   English-language explanations help to piece together the fragments of Ho's life and cause at this museum tribute; you'll see personal items, photos, and documents detailing the rise of the nation's communist revolution. The rhetoric is laid on a bit thick, but all in all it's an interesting and informative display. Completely unique to Vietnam are the conceptual displays symbolizing freedom, reunification, and social progress through flowers, fruit, and mirrors. Have a look.

3 Ngo Ha (left of 1 Pillar Pagoda, near Ba Dinh Sq.), Ba Dinh District. ✆ **04/3846-3757.** Admission 15,000VND. Tues–Thurs and Sat–Sun 8–11:30am and 2–4pm.

Ho Chi Minh's Residence ★★   Ho's residence, the well known house on stilts, stands in stark contrast to the adjacent Presidential Palace, a gorgeous French colonial building built in 1901 for the resident French governor. Shunning the glorious structure nearby, Ho instead chose to live here from 1958 to 1969. Facing an exquisite landscaped lake, the structure does have its charm, and the spartan room is an interesting glimpse into the life of this enigmatic national hero. The basement was a meeting place for the Politburo; upstairs are the bedroom and a study. Little details including his phone and walking cane are kept behind glass. Behind the house is a garden of fruit trees, many of them exotics imported from other lands, including miniature rosebushes and areca trees from the Caribbean.

Behind the Presidential Palace at Ba Dinh Sq., Ba Dinh District. Admission 5,000VND. Tues–Sun 8–11am and 2–4pm.

Hun Tiep Lake and the Downed B-52   This place won't blow you away for its size or beauty; in fact, what brings many here is that it's an ordinary neighborhood, a maze of quiet lanes broken only by a small pond and, in the brackish water, the wreckage of an American B-52 shot down during the Christmas air raids of 1972. Many folks, veterans among them, find that a visit here puts a perspective on the war and that the rusting wreckage brings our abstract historical impressions back to the concrete present; others see landing gear, struts, and metal sheathing in a grungy pond. There's a partly submerged memorial plaque, and the area is cordoned off, though there are no entrance fees as yet. Most taxi drivers know it, or else some creative charades will get the point across. Drivers will drop you off at the head of the alley (Lane 55) leading to the site (a handwritten sign reads B-52 with an arrow).

Located just south of West Lake along Hoang Hoa Tham Rd., and a short walk down Lane 55 heading south, Ba Dinh District.

One-Pillar Pagoda ★   To the right of the Ho Chi Minh Museum is the unique One-Pillar Pagoda, a 1049 wooden structure that sits on stilts over a lake. A king of the Ly Dynasty, Ly Thai Thong King, had it built after having a dream in which Bodhisattva Avalokitesvara, the goddess of mercy, presented him with a lotus flower. The existing pagoda is a miniature reproduction of the original, which was said to represent a lotus emerging from the water. It is certainly interesting, and a prayer here is said to bring fertility and good health. It's best to wear something full length (skirt or trousers), not shorts.

Right of Ho Chi Minh Museum, near Ba Dinh Sq., Ba Dinh District.

Vietnam National Museum of Fine Arts ★★   This very worthwhile museum features Vietnamese art of the 20th century, up to the 1970s or so. While the presentations are a bit crowded and rustic, there are explanations in English. Much of the art is outstanding, although you won't really see any works of an innovative or controversial nature. Entire rooms are devoted to the Vietnamese style of lacquer and silk painting, wood block, and folk art. Techniques are explained—a nice touch. Interesting also are the modern works of wood statuary interspersed among the exhibits. Some are patriotic in nature, depicting daily life or events during the war or done in Soviet-influenced caricature, with heavy-limbed peasants striking triumphant poses. The top floors are devoted to prehistoric artifacts and Buddhist sculptures, some of which are huge and impressive. Don't miss the famous 11th-century goddess of mercy (Kouan Yin), with her thousand arms and eyes, in the far-left room on the second floor. Best of all, the museum itself is in an old colonial, and, unless there's a

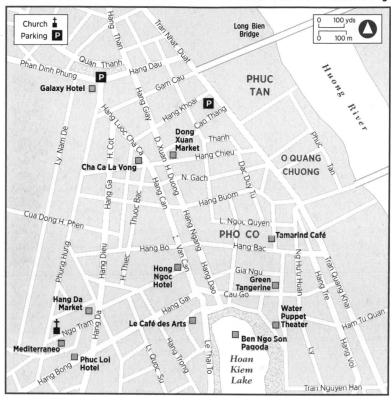

Church ☩
Parking ℙ

0 100 yds
0 100 m

Long Bien Bridge

Hang Than
Tran Nhat Duat
Phan Dinh Phung
Quan Thanh
Hang Dau
Gam Cau

Galaxy Hotel

PHUC TAN

Huong River

Hang Giay
Hang Khoai
Cao Thang

Ly Nam De
Hang Luoc
Cha Ca
H. Cot
D. Xuan H.Duong
Dong Xuan Market
Thanh

Cha Ca La Vong
Hang Chieu

O QUANG CHUONG

PHUC TAN

N. Gach

Hang Ga
Hang Can
Hang Buom

Cua Dong
H. Phen
Thuoc Bac
Hang Ngang
L. Ngoc Quyen

PHO CO
Tamarind Café

Phung Hung
Hang Dieu
H. Thiec
Hang Bo
Van Can
Hang Dao
Hang Bac

Hong Ngoc Hotel

Gia Ngu
Green Tangerine
Cau Go

Hang Da Market

Hang Gai

Ngo Tram
Hang Da
Le Café des Arts

Water Puppet Theater

Ng Huu Huan
Hang Tre
Tran Quang Khai
Ham Tu Quan

Mediterraneo

Hang Bong
Phuc Loi Hotel
L. Quoc Su
Hang Trong
Le Thai To

Ben Ngo Son Pagoda

Hoan Kiem Lake

Ly
Hang Voi

Tran Nguyen Han

5

VIETNAM | Hanoi

tour group milling around, you can stroll around in relative serenity and rest on one of the many benches provided (no napping). The gift shop has some modern works by well known artists for sale.

66 Nguyen Thai Hoc St., Ba Dinh District. ✆ **04/3733-2131.** www.vnfineartsmuseum.org.vn. Admission 20,000VND. Daily 8:30am–5pm.

West Lake ★★   In Hanoi, West Lake is second only to Hoan Kiem as a nerve center for the city, steeped in legend and sporting several significant pagodas. Vietnam's oldest pagoda, **Tran Quoc,** was built in the 6th century and is located on Cayang Island in the middle of the lake, a beautiful setting. An actual fragment of the Bodhi tree under which Buddha achieved enlightenment was given as a gift from the prime minister of India in 1959 and now grows proudly in the main courtyard. Constructed by an early Zen sect and a famous center for dharma study, and later an imperial feasting grounds, the temple has a visitors' hall, two corridors, and a bell tower; it still houses a group of diligent monks. (Avoid wearing shorts here as this might offend sensibilities.) Farther along the lake, **Quan Thanh Temple,** by the northern gate, was built during the reign of Le Thai To King (1010–28). It is dedicated to Huyen Thien Tran Vo, the god who reigned over Vietnam's northern regions.

Renovated in the 19th century, the impressive temple has a triple gate, courtyard, and 3.6m (12-ft.) bronze statue of the god. West Lake is also a hub of local activity, particularly on weekends, when families go paddle boating here.

Bordered by Thuy Khue and Thanh Nien sts., Ba Dinh District. Free admission. Park is always open.

DONG DA DISTRICT

Temple of Literature and National University (Van Mieu–Quoc Tu Giam) ★★ If Vietnam has a seat of learning, this is it. There are two entities here: Van Mieu, a temple built to worship Chinese philosopher Confucius in 1070; and Quoc tu Giam, literally "Temple of the King Who Distinguished Literature," an elite institute established in 1076 to teach the doctrines of Confucius and his disciples. It existed for more than 700 years as a center for Confucian learning. Moreover, it is a powerful symbol for the Vietnamese, having been established after the country emerged from a period of Chinese colonialism that lasted from 179 B.C. to A.D. 938. It's a testament to the strong cultural heritage of the Mandarins; as such, it stands for independence and a solidifying of national culture and values.

What exists today is a series of four courtyards that served as an entrance to the university. Architecturally, it is a fine example of classic Chinese with Vietnamese influences. Still present are 82 stone stelae—stone diplomas, really—erected between 1484 and 1780, bearing the names and birthplaces of 1,306 doctoral laureates who managed to pass the university's rigorous examinations. Beyond the final building, known as the sanctuary, the real university began. Damaged in the French war, it is currently being restored.

Quoc Tu Giam St., Dong Da District. ℂ **04/3845-2917.** Admission 5,000VND. Daily 7:30am–5:30pm.

HOAN KIEM DISTRICT

Hanoi Opera House This gorgeous Art Nouveau building was built near the turn of the 20th century. Unfortunately, to get inside, you'll have to attend a performance, but that should be enjoyable as well (see "Hanoi After Dark," p. 274).

1 Trang Tien St. (at Le Thanh Tong St.), Hoan Kiem District. ℂ **04/3933-0113.**

Hoa Lo Prison (Hanoi Hilton) ★★ For sheer gruesome atmosphere alone, this ranks near the top of the must-see list. It was constructed by the French in 1896 mainly to house political prisoners; the Vietnamese took it over in 1954. It was subsequently used to house prisoners of war. From 1964 to 1973, it was a major POW detention facility for American soldiers, who gave it the ironic nickname Hanoi Hilton. U.S. Sen. John McCain was a particularly famous inmate, as was Pete Peterson, the ambassador to Vietnam, and Lt. Everett Alvarez, officially the first American pilot to be shot down over Vietnam. Their stories are told from the Vietnamese perspective in photographs and writings grouped in one small room. To the west is the guillotine room, still with its original equipment, and the female and Vietnamese political prisoners' quarters. The courtyard linking the two has parts of original tunnels once used by a hundred intrepid Vietnamese revolutionaries to escape in 1945. Only part of the original complex is left (look for the gateway marked MAISON CENTRALE); the rest of the original site was razed and is ironically occupied by a tall, gleaming office complex (Hanoi Towers) popular with foreign investors. There are basic English explanations, but this is a good spot to have a guide, who is certain to be armed with a tale or two.

1 Hoa Lo St., off Quan Su St., Hoan Kiem District. ℂ **04/3824-6358.** Admission 5,000VND. Tues–Sun 8–11:30am and 1:30–4:30pm.

FLYING DRAGONS & THIEVING TURTLES:
hanoi's founding

Originally, Hanoi was called Thang Long, or **"the Ascending Dragon."** The dragon that ascended, so the story goes, created civilization as we know it along the Red River Valley, and then plunged to his sleep in Halong Bay, thereby creating the grand karst slopes—today a UNESCO World Heritage Site. The dragon is the symbol of the city, and you'll find references to it wherever you go.

Hanoi's other important creation myth is one oddly echoed by the legendary tale of King Arthur and his rise to the throne after receiving the sword Excalibur from the Lady of the Lake. "Strange women lying in ponds distributing swords is no basis for a system of government," says Eric Idle's character in Monty Python's spoof of the Arthur legend, and Hanoi's mandate granted by a giant turtle in Hoan Kiem is equally ridiculous, but a great one for putting the kids to bed to at night.

Le Loi, the first king of a united Viet people, asked the powers in heaven to help him vanquish the Chinese in the 2nd century A.D. His answer came from a giant turtle that rose from the depths of Hoan Kiem Lake and offered him the sword that he would use to drive the Chinese out. (Vietnamese history is full of valiant tales about driving the Chinese out.) When Le Loi returned to the lake to give thanks, the turtle rose again out of the water and took a firm jaw hold of the sword and dragged it to the watery depths, a sign that the citizens could lay down their arms and the city would prosper in peace. The turtle fooled old Le Loi, because the Vietnamese would suffer under Chinese oppression for centuries to come. The myth is best depicted at the **Thang Long Water Puppet Theater** (p. 274). Don't miss the preserved turtle that weighs around 250kg at Ngoc Son Temple on a small island in Hoan Kiem Lake. See the section on **Hoan Kiem** (p. 270) for details on the lake's temples and sights, and note that most addresses in this chapter are given in relation to the lake, so you should get to know it during your stay in the Vietnamese capital.

National Museum of Vietnamese History   This is an exhaustive repository of Vietnamese historic relics nicely displayed with some bare-bones explanations in English. Housed in a building that was the French consulate until 1910 and a museum in various incarnations since, the collection walks you from prehistoric artifacts and carvings to funerary jars and some very fine examples of Dong Son drums from the north, excavations of Han tombs, Buddhist statuary, and everyday items of early history. It's the kind of place where schoolchildren are forced to go (be careful if you see buses out front), and for anyone but history buffs, you might feel just as bored as the kids. For those on any kind of historical mission in Vietnam, it's best to contact a tour agency and book a knowledgeable guide for an excellent overview and a good beginning to any trip.

1 Trang Tien St. (just east of the opera house), Hoan Kiem District. ⓒ **04/3825-3518.** Admission 20,000VND. Tues–Sun 8–11:30am and 1:30–4:30pm.

Old Quarter and Hoan Kiem Lake ★★★   The Old Quarter evolved from workshop villages clustered by trades, or guilds, in the early 13th century. It's now an area of narrow, ancient, winding streets, each named for the trade it formerly featured. Even today, streets tend to be for silk, silver, or antiques. It's a fascinating slice of centuries-old life in Hanoi, including markets that are so pleasantly crowded that the street itself narrows to just a few feet. The entire quarter is like a living museum and is the city's most popular attraction, as well as home to many hotels and restaurants.

Hoan Kiem Lake (Lake of the Restored Sword), immediately south of the Old Quarter, is considered the center of the city. In the mid–15th century, it's said, the gods gave emperor Le Thai To a magical sword to defeat Chinese invaders. While the emperor was boating on the lake one day, a giant tortoise reared up and snatched the sword, returning it to its rightful owners and ushering peace into the kingdom. Stroll around the lake in the early morning or evening to savor local life among the willow trees and see elders playing chess or practicing tai chi. In the center of the lake is the Tortoise Pagoda; on the northern part is Ngoc Son Pagoda, reachable only by the bright-red Huc Bridge (Bridge of the Rising Sun). One of the most striking sights at the temple is the preserved carcass of an enormous turtle that supposedly once lived in the lake.

Bordered by Tran Nhat Duat and Phung Hung sts., Hoan Kiem District.

Quan Su Pagoda ★   Chua Quan Su (aka the Ambassadors' Pagoda) is one of the most important temples in the country. Constructed in the 15th century along with a small house for visiting Buddhist ambassadors, in 1934 it became the headquarters of the Tonkin Buddhist Association, and today it is headquarters for the Vietnam Central Buddhist Congregation. The active pagoda is usually thronged with worshipers; the interior is dim and smoky with incense. To the rear is a school of Buddhist doctrine. To show respect, visitors of any stripe are welcome to buy sticks of incense and make offerings at the various altars and sand urns. It's easy to just follow suit, and folks will be glad to show you what to do.

73 Quan Su St. (at intersection with Tran Hung Da), Hoan Kiem District.

OUTSIDE THE CITY CENTER
Vietnam Museum of Ethnology ★★★   To learn more about the 54 ethnic minorities populating Vietnam's hinterlands, make the jaunt out to this sprawling compound (go by cab). It's the city's newest museum and so engaging that it's well worth the journey. The different ethnic groups' history and customs are explained in photos, videos, and displays of clothing and daily implements. Out back are a number of re-creations of the village homes, from a low Cham house to the towering peak of a thatched Bahnar communal home. You'll come away with a good historical perspective on the many groups in the far north and central highlands, as well as in parts of neighboring Laos and Thailand, and the experience will help you to identify different groups when you go trekking in the hills.

Nguyen Van Huyen, 6km (3¾ miles) west of town. ℂ **04/3756-2193.** www.vme.org.vn. Admission 25,000VND; guide 50,000VND; camera or video player 50,000VND. Tues–Sun 8:30am–5:30pm.

Outdoor Activities
Wake up early and join the hordes of people doing tai chi, stretching, walking, and running in the parks of Hanoi. This town is a great place for people-watching and a little morning wake-up; the best spots are near the Botanical Gardens, Reunification Park (formerly Lenin Park), and Hoan Kiem Lake. Get your run in before about 6:30am, though, before traffic starts to snarl. Or rent a bicycle from almost any hotel for about $1 a day.

Shopping

Hanoi is a fine place to shop for silk, silver, lacquerware, embroidered goods, and ethnic minority crafts. Silk is of good quality and an easy buy. Shops will tailor a suit in as little as 24 hours, but allow yourself extra time for alterations. Many of the shops are clustered along **Hang Gai Street** (Silk Street), on the northeast side of the Old Quarter. A silk suit will run from about $35 to $75, depending on the silk, and a blouse or shirt will cost $15 to $20. Virtually every shop accepts MasterCard and Visa. Bargain hard for all but the silk; offer 50% of the asking price and end up paying 70% or so.

Khai Silk, with branches in various hotel lobbies and at 96 Hang Gai St. (✆ 04/3825-4237) and 121 Nguyen Thai Hoc St. (✆ 04/3823-3508), is justly famous for its selection, silk quality, and relatively pleasant store layout. Also try **Thanh Ha Silk** (114 Hang Gai St.; ✆ 04/3928-5348) and **Oriental House** (28 Nha Chung; ✆ 04/3828-5542). **Tan My** (16 Hang Trong St.; ✆ 04/3828-8848; www.tanmyembroidery.com) has exquisite embroidery work, especially for children's clothing and bedding. **Craft Link** (43 Van Mieu St.; ✆ 04/3843-7710; www.craftlink.com.vn) features handmade products by ethnic minorities as well as traditional Vietnamese handicrafts. Near the Sheraton, check out the high-end boutiques along Xuan Dieu Street, such as **Pearl Ha** at #65, which displays some neat clothing and accessories.

For decorative items and souvenirs, shopping is chockablock on the streets surrounding Hoan Kiem Lake. One good place to start is **Nha Tho Street,** also called "Church Street" since it terminates at the town's largest cathedral. Here you'll discover silk and housewares designers among the cozy cafes. Unique lacquerware and furnishings can be found at **La Casa** (12 Nha Tho St.; ✆ 04/3828-9616; www.lacasavietnam.com). In the Old Quarter, **Vietnamese House** (92 Hang Bac St.; ✆ 04/3826-2455; www.vietnamesehouse.com) has a good selection of jewelry, ceramics, and antiques. These are just a few of the many options here.

Some standout local labels include **Ipa-Nima** (34 Han Thuyen St.; ✆ 04/3933-4000; www.ipa-nima.com), a whimsical bag boutique whose wares have been featured in *Vogue* and stocked by Bergdorf's and Bendel's. **Tina Sparkle** (17 Nha Tho St.; ✆ 04/3928-7616) is their sister store on Church Street. Nearby **Song** (27 Nha Tho St.; ✆ 04/3928-8733) offers an array of resortlike cotton and hemp separates. Song has international clout: It's carried by Saks in the U.S.

For fine ceramics and lacquerware, look to **Hanoi Moment** (101 Han Gai St.; ✆ 04/3928-7170). Wood, stone, and brass lacquer reproduction sculptures of religious icons are sold at **KAF Traditional Sculptures and Art Accessories** (31B Ba Trieu St.; ✆ 04/3822-0022).

ART GALLERIES Vietnam has a flourishing art scene, and Hanoi has many galleries featuring oil, silk, watercolor, and lacquer paintings. Don't forget to bargain here. Keep in mind that most paintings are not originals, but copies of works by well known Vietnamese artists.

Galleries are chockablock in the Old Quarter and on the perimeters of Hoan Kiem. Try **Van Linh Gallery** (13 Hang Gai St.; ✆ 04/3928-7013) or **Van Gallery,** its sister shop on Trang Tien near the Dan Chu Hotel. Nearby **Green Palm Gallery** ★ (39 Hang Gai St.; ✆ 091/321-8496; www.greenpalmgallery.com) is an excellent gallery with reliable selections and knowledgeable staff.

54 Traditions Gallery ★ (30 Hang Bun St.; ✆ **04/3715-0194**) is the best, arguably the only, place to buy minority art pieces. It is an ethnographic museum, library, and gallery all rolled into one.

Others include **Thanh Mai** (64 Hang Gai St.; ✆ **04/3825-1618**), **Apricot Gallery** (40B Hang Bong St.; ✆ **04/3828-8965**), and **Thang Long** (41 Hang Gai St.; ✆ **04/3825-0740**) in the Old Quarter.

BOOKSTORES   Due to copyright infringement, there's a scant choice of English-language books in Hanoi, but check out the **Bookworm** (44 Chau Long St.; ✆ **04/3715-3711**; www.bookwormhanoi.com), a longtime expat favorite, or one of the many shops lining Trang Tien or Ma May streets, where you'll find backpacker book repositories and some good deals on photocopied bootlegs. Also try the few similar shops on Bao Khan Street, a popular nightlife area.

CONVENIENCE STORES   To pick up good snacks for a long train or bus ride, check out **Intimex** (22–23 Le Thai To St.; ✆ **04/3825-6148**), a spiffy grocery down a small alley on the west side of Hoan Kiem Lake. Another place worth exploring for tasty treats is **Citimart** (Hanoi Towers, 49 Hai Ba Trung).

Hanoi After Dark

When it comes to nightlife, Hanoi is no Saigon, but there are a variety of pleasant watering holes about town as well as a few rowdy dance spots.

Hanoi is also the best city in which to see **traditional Vietnamese arts** such as opera, theater, and water-puppet shows. Invented during the Ly Dynasty (1009–1225), the art of water puppetry is unique to Vietnam. The puppets are made of wood and really do dance on water. The shows feature traditional Vietnamese music and depict folklore and myth. Book tickets for the popular puppets at least 5 hours ahead.

Real cinema can be found at **Hanoi Cinematheque** (22A Hai Ba Trung St.; ✆ **04/3936-2648**), south of Hoan Kiem Lake.

THE PERFORMING ARTS

The **Hanoi Opera House,** or Hanoi Municipal Theatre (1 Trang Tien St., Hoan Kiem District; ✆ **04/3933-0113;** www.hanoioperahouse.org.vn), hosts performances by local and international artists. The **Hanoi Traditional Opera** (15 Nguyen Dinh Chieu, Ba Dinh District; ✆ **04/3943-4205**) has shows on Monday, Wednesday, and Friday at 8pm.

Central Circus (in Reunification Park, Hai Ba Trung District; ✆ **04/3822-0277**) has shows at 8pm every day except Monday. It's a real circus done on a small scale, so see it only if you're desperate to entertain the kids.

Thang Long Water Puppet Theater ★★★ 🎫   This might sound like one for the kids, but there is something enchanting about the lighthearted comedy and intricately skilled puppetry of this troupe. They perform numerous vignettes of daily life in the countryside as well as ancient tales, including the legend of Hoan Kiem Lake and the peaceful founding of the city of Hanoi. Puppeteers use bamboo poles, pulleys, and string to extend their puppets from behind the proscenium and up through the surface of a small pond that forms the stage. You will be amazed at their ingenuity, and it doesn't take much to suspend disbelief and get caught up in a magical hour of escape. The kids will like it, too. In high season, buy tickets early. The theater is poorly slanted, which means that although seats in the front cost a bit more, you'll have a better view—and not look at the back of someone's head—from the middle or the back (pick from a seating chart at the ticket office). You'll also get a better effect of verisimilitude from the back, where it looks more real.

57B Dinh Tien Hoang St., Hoan Kiem District. ☏ **04/3824-9494.** Fax 04/3824-5117. www.thanglong waterpuppet.org. Admission 40,000VND–60,000VND; extra for camera or video. Shows daily at 3:30, 5, 6:30, 8, and 9:15pm.

BARS, PUBS & DISCOS

Bao Khanh Street, just down a short lane in the northwest corner of Hoan Kiem Lake (near Café des Arts), is home to lots of popular bars. Some are a bit seedy, but there are a few comfortable places. Most popular is the **Funky Monkey** (31 Hang Thung; ☏ **04/3928-6113**), which has music, pool tables, and pizzas. Also check out **Polite Pub** (5 Bao Khanh; ☏ **04/3825-0959**), open from 5pm until late, and **Amazon Bar** (across from Café des Arts; ☏ **04/3928-7338**).

For a night out with the boys, the **Spotted Cow** (23C Hai Ba Trung, next to Al Fresco's; ☏ **04/3824-1028**) is a good choice—there's just drinking and darts here.

For a more upscale experience, sip a cocktail at the famous **Press Club** (59A Ly Thai To; ☏ **04/3934-0888**), or drop by the **Green Mango** (18 Hang Quat St.; ☏ **04/3928-9916**), a relaxing lounge bar where they mix up some mean cocktails. An atmospheric spot for a sundowner is **Sunset Bar** (at the Inter-Continental West Lake, 1A Nghi Tam; ☏ **04/3829-3939**), an outdoor venue with a gorgeous lakeside setting; don't forget your mosquito repellent.

In the heart of the Old Quarter, **Minh's Jazz Club** (31 Luong Van Can St.; ☏ **04/3825-7655;** www.minhjazzvietnam.com) has no cover charge and features saxophonist Quyen Van Minh and his son Dac playing jazz standards in a convivial setting, with a good food-and-drinks menu as well.

The **ILU Bar & Lounge** (18 Yen Phu St., 37 Pho Duc Chinh; ☏ **04/3715-0656**) is a hidden treasure just north of the city center. Walk through the parking garage, take the elevator to the seventh floor, and then climb a flight of stairs to get to ILU's spacious balcony overlooking West Lake.

Finally, **Le Pub** (25 Hang Be; ☏ **04/3926-2104**), in the southeast corner of the Old Quarter, is one of those rare travelers' oases where the beer is refreshingly chilled, the music fits the mood, and the tale-telling rolls on into the night.

Side Trips from Hanoi

HALONG BAY ★★

A Vietnamese fable tells that the towering limestone rock formations, called karst, at Halong were formed with the crash landing of a dragon sent by the gods of early Vietnamese animism to protect the country from an invading navy. The picturesque area did in fact play host to some important Vietnamese naval victories against Chinese forces, but the bay is most famous today for its UNESCO World Heritage status, its emerald-green water, and 3,000 islands of towering limestone in the Gulf of Tonkin. Needless to say, the weather in the bay affects the experience, but unfortunately it is frustratingly unpredictable, and the region is often prone to days of cloud and rain.

The bay itself is a 4-hour drive from Hanoi; a visit usually includes an overnight stay of at least 1 night (though it can be done in a long day trip). Given the logistics, the trip is best done through an agent or with a group. If you book a tour with an overnight stay, you'll probably cruise on a junk for 4 to 6 hours along the bay, stopping to explore two grottoes. You might pause for swimming or kayaking as well. Overnight trips can cost anywhere from $40 to upwards of $300; it depends on whether you travel to the bay by bus or with a private driver, and what standard of comfort you enjoy while afloat in the bay. The cheapest way to go is to make your own way to Halong City, then join a day tour from there; it's not difficult to do and is a good idea for adventurous types.

Sinh Café (✆ **04/3926-1568;** www.thesinhtourist.vn) does a fine job on the low end, but don't expect much. Our recommendation is to contact the helpful folks at **Buffalo Tours** (✆ **04/3828-0702;** www.buffalotours.com/jewel). Its high-end boat, *Jewel of the Bay*, runs overnight trips that include kayaking, touring, and fine dining, costing around $160 per person. Buffalo is just one of a handful of operators; **Handspan** (✆ **04/3962-2828;** www.handspan.com) runs similar tours from Hanoi, and **HuongHai** (www.halongtravels.com) manages a fleet of junks.

For a luxury experience on the water, look no further than the *Halong Ginger.* Unlike the *Emeraude* (see below), *Halong Ginger* is a small, intimate affair. The boat is equipped with only 10 cabins, pushed to either side of a central deck to ensure that each room has a private, unobstructed view of the ocean. You can book through their website at www.cruisehalong.com or offices (✆ **04/3933-5561;** fax 04/3984-4538). You should save around 25% if you book through a travel agent. *Halong Jasmine* was added in late 2007—rooms on this larger junk are bigger and some have private balconies. The company's latest venture, *Halong Violet,* was launched in 2009, boasting a library, spa, gym, Jacuzzi and balcony.

The other high-end experience is aboard the *Emeraude,* a copy of a French steamer that once plied these waters in the early 20th century. *Emeraude*'s 55m (180-ft.) boat offers real luxury in each of its 38 cabins, and it comes with prices to match. The 2-day, 1-night cruise is well worth it, though. Go to www.emeraude-cruises.com, or contact the office at ✆ **04/3935-1888;** fax 04/3935-5342.

Ecotourism is taking off here, and the steep karst outcrops of the bay are not only beautiful, but also ideal for exploration. You might want to consider one of the 3-day **sea-kayaking** and **rock-climbing** adventures that are becoming popular here. Contact Buffalo Tours or Handspan for memorable packages starting from around $200 for multiday trips.

CAT BA ISLAND

Cat Ba Island, to the south of Halong Bay, is an increasingly popular destination for foreign tourists who want to combine a tour of the bay with spending some time on a beach, trekking in a national park, or rock climbing. During the past decade, the small fishing village of Cat Ba with its picturesque harbor has seen the opening of several budget hotels, restaurants, and bars. Several tour companies in Hanoi use these hotels to accommodate guests on their tours instead of overnighting on a boat, though there are plenty of independent travelers who make their way here as well. Ask at any tour operator in Hanoi for information about bus and high-speed ferry services. About half the island is occupied by Cat Ba National Park, and it's easy to join a group to spend a day trekking through the lush terrain. The island's few beaches would not win any prizes for beauty but are fine for a day's relaxation.

CUC PHUONG NATIONAL PARK

Cuc Phuong, established in 1962 as Vietnam's first national park, is a lush mountain rainforest with more than 250 bird and 60 mammal species, including tigers, leopards, and the unique red-bellied squirrel. The park's many visitors—and poachers—might keep you from the kind of wildlife experience you might hope for in the brush, however. It's still the perfect setting for a good hike, and the park features goodies such as a 1,000-year-old tree, a waterfall, and Con Moong Cave, where prehistoric human remains have been discovered. Cuc Phuong is a good day trip from Hanoi, and some tourist cafes offer programs for $40 to $50 per person depending on the size of the group. It is also possible to overnight here in the park headquarters.

HOA LU

From A.D. 968 to 1010, Hoa Lu was the capital of Vietnam under the Dinh Dynasty and the first part of the Le Dynasty. Located in a valley surrounded by awesome limestone formations, it's known as the inland Halong Bay—it's a similarly picturesque sight, but much easier to reach. Most of what remains of the kingdom are ruins, but there are still temples in the valley that were renovated in the 17th century. The first honors Dinh Tien Hoang and has statues of the king. The second is dedicated to Le Dai Hanh, one of Dinh's generals and the first king of the Le Dynasty, who grabbed power in 980 after Dinh was mysteriously assassinated. Hoa Lu can easily be seen on a day trip from Hanoi. Seat-in-coach tours from a tourist cafe run about $20 per person.

SAPA ★★★ & THE FAR NORTH

The north and northwest highland regions are popular destinations for hardy travelers. In addition to the breathtaking **Tonkinese Alps** and off-the-map destinations such as **Dien Bien Phu,** some of the main attractions are the **villages of the ethnic minority hill tribes.**

Sapa is a small market town that has been a gathering spot for many local hill tribes for nearly 200 years. Hmong and Yao people, among others, still come here to conduct trade, socialize, and attend an ephemeral **"love market"** where young men and women choose one another for marriage (these days, it's not likely you'll see anything but a staged re-creation of it). Seeing this, French missionaries as early as 1860 said, "Mon Dieu!" and set up camp to save souls; their stone church still stands sentinel and is well attended at the center of town. Sapa, with its refreshingly cool climate, later became a holiday escape for French colonists, complete with rail connection, upscale hotels, and a tourist bureau as early as 1917. The outpost was retaken by the Vietnamese in 1950 and attacked and destroyed later by the French, followed by a brief occupation by Chinese troops. The town reopened for tourism in the 1990s.

Now connected by luxury train with Hanoi, Sapa boasts good accommodations and is a great jumping-off point for trekking and ecotours. Even a 1- or 2-day trip, bracketed by overnight train journeys from Hanoi, will give you a unique glimpse of local hill-tribe culture. Trek out to nearby villages with or without a guide, or meet with the many hill-tribe people who come to town to sell their wares. Hill-tribe costumes are colorful embroidered tunics embellished with heavy silver ornaments that signify marital status or place in the group's hierarchy.

Finally, the Tonkinese Alps are a feast for the eyes: The hills striated by terraced rice farms in vast, green valleys are like a stairway up to **Mount Fansipan,** Vietnam's tallest mountain, which, at 3,143m (10,312 ft.), smiles down on all the proceedings. *Note:* Bring a few layers here, as it can get quite chilly, especially in the winter months.

Getting There

BY TRAIN   The *Victoria Express* train from Hanoi to Sapa—with wood-paneled luxury sleeping cars and a restaurant billed as the finest dining between the two towns—is an exciting option, though it is available only to guests staying at the resort. Trains depart daily except Saturday at around 9pm with a similar return schedule, making possible convenient 2- or 3-day trips with overnight transport. Prices range from $145 for a midweek round-trip in superior class to $230 in a deluxe compartment on the weekend. Contact the Victoria Sapa Resort (© **20/3871-522;** www.victoriahotels-asia.com) for details and reservations.

A number of standard and tourist trains also make the overnight run from Hanoi. You can make arrangements with any travel agent for a small fee, or do it yourself at the **Hanoi Railway Station** (120 Le Duan; © **04/3942-3949**), located where the western edge of Hoan Kiem District meets Dong Da District. Prices range from $11 for a hard-sleeper to $18 for a soft-berth with air-conditioning. Trains passing through Lao Cai also continue north and make connections in China. (**Note:** This requires a Chinese visa.)

To get to Sapa from the train station in Lao Cai, you'll need to transfer by tourist bus for the 2-hour ride (40,000VND). The road is cut into the hillside and is bumpy and windy, but the views of the terraced rice farms of the valley are beautiful as you ascend (get a seat on the left going up and right going down for the best views).

Note: All trains to Sapa leave from the **Hanoi Railway Station** at 120 Le Duan St., often confused with Hanoi's other station. Be sure to show your taxi driver the correct address.

BY BUS   Hanoi's tourist cafes all run frequent buses to Sapa for $12 one-way. Some include Sapa in larger tours of the north. You get what you pay for, though—the train is still the best option.

BY CAR   Any tourist cafe or travel agent in Hanoi can arrange trips by private jeep or a combo jeep-and-train tour. Apart from Sapa, the vast tracts of the north are untouristed and best visited with a tour company. Look under "Visitor Information & Tours" in the Hanoi section (p. 254). **Ann Tours, Buffalo Tours, Queen Travel,** and **Handspan** all offer comprehensive itineraries. Avoid the temptation to book budget tours with the tourist cafes, especially for areas off the beaten track.

Visitor Information & Tours

There are a few storefront Internet cafes on Cau May Street in Sapa. All hotels provide exchange service for traveler's checks and even credit card cash advances.

For tours and trekking in the region, the Danish outfit **Topas Travel** (24 Muong Hoa, Cau May, Sapa; © **020/3871-331;** fax 020/3871-596; www.topastravel.vn), with offices worldwide and experienced guides, is a great option. Whether it's a day trek to nearby villages, an extended tour with homestays in villages, or the 5-day push to the top of Fansipan, these guys can cover it.

Where to Stay

EXPENSIVE

Topas Eco-Lodge ★★   Set atop a hill overlooking terraced rice fields 18km (11 miles) from now-bustling Sapa, the Eco-Lodge's biggest assets are peace and quiet—in nearly no other place in all of Vietnam can you experience silence like this. Each

5

Sapa & the Far North

VIETNAM

villa is made of locally quarried stone and blond wood. Decks overlook the deep valleys and plunging mountains of Sapa, and the few other residences you'll see are those of the hill tribes, far in the distance. When night falls, darkness is complete, and the only light comes from the stars overhead and a few wood fires down in the valley. At the Eco-Lodge, simplicity is the rule: Each villa is powered by solar panels. All guests eat the same dish at mealtime, with vegetables that come from the lodge's own garden. Make reservations by e-mail or fax only.

24 Muong Hoa, Sapa, Lao Cai Province. © **020/3871-331.** Fax 020/3872-405. www.topasecolodge. com. 25 units. $90–$140 double. AE, MC, V. **Amenities:** Restaurant; bar. *In room:* No phone.

Victoria Sapa Resort ★★★   This is Sapa's crème de la crème and one of the nicest rural resorts in Indochina, set on a small hill with panoramic views of the town. The standards here, from the comfortable rooms and fine dining to the incredible hilltop health club and pool, are without rival. Situated around a cozy courtyard, all bedrooms have balconies and wood floors offset by saturated wall colors, cane and fine wooden finishes, and local weavings and artwork that remind guests of the local hill-tribe culture. The bathrooms are large, with granite counters, wood fixtures, and even a small heater to warm up the tiles. If you're here with the kids, you'll appreciate the huge family rooms, with up to six beds and bunks (which can be rearranged). Suites feature elegant canopy beds and sitting areas. With amenities including a billiards table, comfortable reading nooks, and scenic viewing points here and there, this hotel is so inviting that many prolong their stay. Don't miss having at least one meal in the Ta Van restaurant.

At the top of the hill overlooking town, Sapa District, Lao Cai Province. © **020/3871-522.** Fax 020/3871-539. www.victoriahotels-asia.com. 77 units. $195–$205 double; from $260 suite. Promotional rates available. AE, MC, V. **Amenities:** Restaurant; bar; babysitting; kids' playroom; health club; Internet access; indoor/outdoor heated pool; sauna; smoke-free rooms; tennis court. *In room:* Satellite TV w/ in-house movies, fridge, hair dryer, minibar.

MODERATE

Bamboo Sapa Hotel   This good midrange standby is a large concrete block near the town center. Built in 2002, its rooms are clean and spacious, done in shiny tile. Most have balconies, and all are oriented to the valley view. Shower-in-room–style bathrooms are large and clean; mattresses are sturdy, firm foam; and the staff is quite friendly. A good in-house tour operator, **Sapa Travel,** can plan any trip. An open-air restaurant under the lobby holds fun cultural dance shows.

18 Muong Hoa St., Sapa, Lao Cai Province. © **020/3871-075.** Fax 020/3871-945. www.sapatravel.com. 60 units. $55–$95 double; $225 executive suite. MC, V. **Amenities:** Restaurant; bar; bike rental. *In room:* A/C, central heating, satellite TV, hair dryer, minibar.

Cha Pa Garden ★ 🛏   As there are only four rooms in this renovated colonial villa, staying here is an intimate experience—more like lodging with sophisticated friends than in a hotel. It was Sapa's first boutique hotel to open and still sets a high standard for others to follow. Rooms are equipped with solid and stylish furnishings, and the leafy garden is a definite plus. There are no sweeping views over the valley, but its central location makes it easy to get around. They offer market trips as well as half- and 1-day tours, and the cozy restaurant features an open fireplace.

23b Cau May St., Sapa, Lao Cai Province. © **020/387-2907.** Fax 020/387-2906. www.chapagarden. com. 4 units. $65–$80 double. MC, V. **Amenities:** Restaurant. *In room:* Central heating, satellite TV, minibar.

INEXPENSIVE

Cat Cat View The view: That's what it's all about here. At this guesthouse with rooms of varying standards, buildings are stacked like an unlikely pile of children's blocks against a steeply sloping hill. There's something for everyone here—from $25 basic boxes to a two-bedroom apartment for $180. Most rooms have fantastic views, as well as big windows, balconies, and fireplaces. Stop for a coffee even if you don't stay the night; the bar here has the best view in town.

Cat Cat Rd. (at the base of the town on the way down to the Cat Cat Village), Lao Cai Province. © **020/3871-946.** Fax 020/3871-133. www.catcathotel.com. 40 units. $25–$60 double; $180 apartment. No credit cards. **Amenities:** Restaurant; bar. *In room:* Satellite TV.

Royal Sapa Hotel ★ It's backpacker central at this little five-story tower in the heart of town, the very terminus of central Cau May Street. The sparse tile-and-concrete decor, busy hallways, and hit-or-miss service are a bit of a turnoff, but the price is right and deluxe rooms have great mountain views. The hotel's Muong Hoa Restaurant also has good views and the food is good, basic traveler fare (fried rice, fried noodles, international dishes, and beer). Every room has a balcony; some even come with a fireplace. Ask about Royal trains and travel services.

54 Cau May St., Sapa, Lao Cai Province. © **020/3871-313.** Fax 020/3871-788. www.royalsapahotel. com. 32 units. $25–$35 double. No credit cards. **Amenities:** Restaurant. *In room:* TV.

Where to Dine

Baguettes et Chocolat ★ FRENCH The folks from **Hoa Sua** (p. 263), a popular restaurant designed as a training center for disadvantaged youth, have done an excellent job with this cozy cafe. Open sandwiches, pizzas, salads, and omelets top a fine menu heavy on good French cuisine. Seating is in a cool "no shoe" area with rattan couches and white pillows (don't turn up here spattered in mud from a trek!), or you can sit outside. For lovers of strong coffee and fluffy pastries, this place is a must—take your pick from the tempting selection on display. If you're heading off on a trek, why not treat yourself and order a picnic hamper from here to take with you? There are also a few smart rooms for rent upstairs.

Thac Bac St., near the hilltop terminus of central Cau May St., Sapa. © **020/3871-766.** www.hoasua school.com. Main courses 50,000VND–160,000VND. No credit cards. Daily 7am–9pm.

What to See & Do

The town itself is the attraction here. Sapa's small alleys are eminently strollable, if a bit steep, and a short walk in any direction offers great views. On any given day, **Cau May Street** (the main drag) and the **central market area** are teeming with hilltribe folks in their spangled finery, putting on the hard sell for some great weaving, fine silver work, and interesting trinkets such as mouth harps and flutes. Especially on the weekend, it can be quite a scene. On the high end of Cau May is the **Mission Church ★**, an aging stone edifice. This was the church of the early French missionaries and is still a popular meeting point for locals. Masses are held on Saturday night and throughout the day on Sunday.

At the base of the hill below the town of Sapa is **Cat Cat Village ★**, with a small waterfall that makes a good spot to kick back. This Hmong village is accessible by road most of the way, and cement path for the rest. The whole trip can be made in just a few hours and offers a unique glimpse of rural life. Admission (paid at the top of the hill) is 5,000VND. You can either walk all the way down or hire a motorbike or car taxi for pickup and drop-off.

The premier day trip in this area is from **Lao Chai to Ta Van ★**, a good opportunity to traipse around the rice terraces and experience a bit of rural village life. Hire a car or motorbike for the 6km (3¾-mile) ride down the valley from Sapa to the Hmong village of Lao Chai (some folks even walk it); it's a nice ride in itself, with great views of the lush terraces. From there, follow the valley for another 3km (1¾ miles) to the next town of Ta Van. The short trek leads through the picturesque hilltribe villages of Hmong, Zay, and Dao people. It's good to have a guide along to explain any customs and perhaps translate for you. You're sure to see other tourists on the trail (which puts many people off), but this is a good example of the many great treks in the area. Ask at your hotel or contact **Topas Travel** (℃ **020/3871-331;** www.topastravel.vn) for longer, less touristy options. A ride to or from Lao Chai or a ride back from Ta Van will cost about $5 by motorbike taxi or $25 by jeep; contact any hotel for a guide.

A worthwhile side trip from Sapa, some 100km (62 miles) from town, is the very popular **Bac Ha Market,** a more authentic version of Sapa's market, held early on Sunday mornings and attended by the appropriately named Flower Hmong, whose flamboyant dress takes some beating. **Mai Chau,** a gorgeous valley, is home to ethnic Tai people; it's about 4 hours from Hanoi, from where frequent tours take visitors to overnight in stilt houses. **Dien Bien Phu,** to the far northwest, is a former French commercial and military outpost, as well as the site of Vietnam's decisive military victory over the French. You can fly directly to Dien Bien Phu from Hanoi, though it's visited more by domestic tourists than overseas visitors.

HUE ★★

Hue (pronounced *hway*) was once Vietnam's Imperial City, the capital of the country from 1802 to 1945 under the Nguyen Dynasty, and is culturally and historically significant. While much of Hue—tragically including most of the walled Citadel and Imperial City—was decimated during the French and American wars, there is still much to see. Perhaps most captivating is simply observing daily life on the **Perfume River,** its many dragon boats, houseboats, and longtail vessels dredging for sand. You can visit some of the attractions, including the **tombs of Nguyen Dynasty emperors,** by boat. The town has a reputation throughout Vietnam for its sophisticated culture, and many visitors are attracted by the locals' laid-back attitude, as well as the low-slung, colorful, colonial-style buildings and local cuisine, which is also distinctive.

While in Hue, you might want to plan a full-day **American war memorial excursion** to the nearby demilitarized zone **(DMZ),** the beginning of the **Ho Chi Minh trail,** and underground tunnels at **Vinh Moc.**

Getting There

BY PLANE **Vietnam Airlines** connects to Hue from both Hanoi and Ho Chi Minh City (Saigon). A taxi from the airport costs around 200,000VND. There's also an airport bus that will drop you off and pick you up from your hotel; it covers the half-hour trip for 45,000VND. Book through your hotel or any tour operator.

BY TRAIN Trains to Hue depart daily from both Hanoi and Ho Chi Minh City (Saigon). The trip from Hanoi to Hue takes 14 hours on the express trains, which depart nightly at 7 and 11pm; these trains have soft-berth compartments with air-conditioning for about $35. From Saigon, in a soft-berth, it's about $50, which is a good way to go.

BY CAR If you're coming from the south, Vietnamtourism Danang can arrange a car for the 2-hour ride from Danang to Hue for $40. Contact travel agents in any section to rent a car with driver.

BY BUS Many travelers choose to take a nerve-rattling overnight bus or minivan from Hanoi to Hue. Tickets are $14 through one of Hanoi's tourist cafes; the trip takes an excruciating 10 hours. Hue is a major stop on any open-tour ticket, and open-tour cafe buses connect with Danang and Hoi An for $9, or Nha Trang for $15; these are long, bumpy trails but are cheap and convenient.

Getting Around

Taxis are much cheaper here than in Hanoi: 10,000VND starting out and 10,000VND for each kilometer thereafter. Flag 'em down or call **Gili** (✆ **054/382-8282**) or **ThanhDo** (✆ **054/385-8585**). Because Hue is relatively small, renting a cyclo by the hour for around 20,000VND also works well. Even the tiniest hotel provides motorbike rentals at about $5 per day and bicycles for $1 to $2.

Visitor Information & Tours

A number of tour companies in Hue can book boat trips and visits to the DMZ for you. Every hotel will also be able to assist you, although the tour companies will be cheaper, especially for car services. Hue's most efficient group, as well as the most expensive, is the **Huong Giang Tourist Company** (17 Le Loi St.; ✆ **054/383-8485;** www.charmingvietnam.com), which organizes good, personalized tours to the tombs and the DMZ at a premium (or you can join one of its group tours). A half-day tour by car and boat, with guide, to the Citadel and Thien Mu Pagoda is $25 for one, $30 for two. A private boat up the Perfume River will cost $29. On the budget end, **Sinh Café** (12 Hung Vuong St.; ✆ **054/384-5022;** www.thesinhtourist.vn) takes big groups upriver for as little as $2 each and has very reasonable junkets to the DMZ.

[FastFACTS] HUE

Currency Exchange Most hotels in Hue will change currency, but at a poor exchange rate. **Vietcombank** is at 78 Hung Vuong St. (✆ **054/381-1900**). There's a branch of **Vietinbank** at 2 Le Quy Don (✆ **054/221-0620**) that has several ATMs and foreign exchange facilities, and is also a Western Union representative.

Internet Access Sinh Café (60 Nguyen Tri Phuong; ✆ **054/384-8626;** www.thesinh tourist.vn) has good service for 10,000VND per hour. There are also many good spots on Hung Vuong (the main tourist street south of the river), Pham Ngu Lao Street (just across from the Century Riverside), and Doi Cung Street.

Mail There are mini–post offices in both the Century and Huong Giang hotels. The main post office, at 8 Hoang Hoa Tham St., is open from 7am to 9pm.

Telephones The city code for Hue is **054.** You can place IDD calls at the post office (see above) and from most hotels.

Where to Stay

Considering the volume of travelers coming through this town, there isn't much in the way of quality accommodations, apart from a few notable exceptions. Budget choices abound, but there are some real duds. Always ask to see the room first, before

Hue

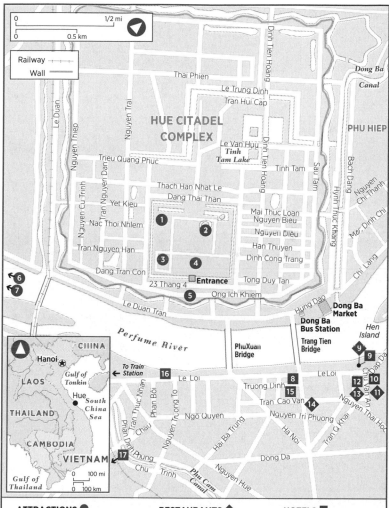

ATTRACTIONS ●
Citadel & Imperial City **1**
Flag Tower **5**
Forbidden Purple City **2**
Imperial Tombs **7**
Mieu Temple **3**
Thai Hoa Palace **4**
Thien Mu Pagoda **6**

RESTAURANTS ◆
Hoa Mai **9**
La Carambole **13**
Mandarin Café **14**
Tropical Garden **11**

HOTELS ■
Hotel Saigon Morin **8**
Huong Giang Hotel **9**
Imperial Hotel **15**
La Residence **16**
Orchid Hotel **10**
Pilgrimage Village **17**
Sports 1 Hotel **12**

checking in. Hotel amenities are limited, but most have basic tour services and include breakfast. Prices are flexible, so press for a discount.

EXPENSIVE

Hotel Saigon Morin ★ The Saigon Morin is a government-run, refurbished colonial block near the main bridge in town. The hotel forms a large courtyard around a central garden and pool area, and the good-sized rooms are equipped with fine linens, wood floors, and stylish bathrooms that connect to the room via a fun "peekaboo" shuttered opening. More than 100 years old, the Morin was originally the colonist's address of note; photos of that bygone era line the halls. The street in front of the Morin was where a young Ho Chi Minh carried his first placard in protest of foreign occupation (if he could only see the place now). The exterior maintains some of that old charm, but common areas are brash and busy, neon lit, and cluttered with souvenir stalls—all kinds of fun, though. Service is a bit hit-or-miss, but usually friendly.

30 Le Loi St., Hue. ⓒ **054/382-3526.** Fax 054/382-5155. www.morinhotel.com.vn. 184 units. $120–$160 double; from $250 suite. Internet rates available. AE, MC, V. **Amenities:** Lobby restaurant; outdoor buffet area; 2 bars/cafes (1 on roof w/good views); concierge; small gym; Internet access; small outdoor pool; room service; sauna. *In room:* A/C, satellite TV, fridge, hair dryer, Internet access, minibar.

Huong Giang Hotel ★ This hotel is a veritable Asian wonderland, so enamored is it of heavy carved wood and bamboo furnishings in its faux "imperial" theme. Tacky? Yes, but also kind of fun. Standard rooms are clean and comfortable, but the bathrooms are a disappointing dormitory style, with plastic shower curtains and no counter space. Try to get a good deal on one of the Royal Suites, with carved-wood walls, grandiose furniture with inlaid mother-of-pearl, and a massive wood room divider—sort of a minipagoda right in your room. (The words *emperor* and *bordello* both leap to mind.) The Royal Restaurant, worth a photo just for its gaudy gold-and-red-everything design alone, is for prearranged group dinners; its costumed staff serves a fancy traditional dinner at a hefty price (popular in town). The Terrace Bar is the best place in Hue to have a drink and watch life on the river. Be sure to splurge for a riverview room and enjoy a fine meal at the Hoa Mai Restaurant (reviewed below). To lay some money on a horse race, seek out the e-casino.

51 Le Loi St., Hue. ⓒ **054/382-2122** or 382-3958. Fax 054/382-3102. www.huonggiangtourist.com. 165 units. $80 gardenview double; $90 riverview double; $150–$200 suite. AE, MC, V. **Amenities:** 3 restaurants; 2 bars; concierge; basic health club; Internet access (in business center); pool; sauna. *In room:* A/C, cable TV, fridge, hair dryer, minibar.

Imperial Hotel ★★ This newish five-star hotel is a gem for Hue city. Rooms are spacious and the marble entrances that segue into classic wooden floors are a nice touch. The overall decor is antique Oriental: carved wooden chairs, imperial yellow silk bed throws and accent pillows, ornate dragons carved into pillars in the lobby. Modern amenities such as flatscreen TVs and angular glass shower cubicles round out the room. Spring for a Deluxe Riverview room and request a corner unit on a higher floor—the view is fantastic. For an unrivaled lookout over the Perfume River, grab a drink at the top-floor panorama bar.

8 Hung Vuong St., Hue. ⓒ **054/388-2222.** Fax 054/388-2244. www.imperial-hotel.com.vn. 194 units. $100–$120 cityview/riverview deluxe; from $180 suite. AE, MC, V. **Amenities:** 2 restaurants; 2 bars; concierge; exercise room; small outdoor pool; room service; spa and sauna. *In room:* A/C, satellite TV, fridge, hair dryer, minibar, Wi-Fi.

La Résidence Hôtel & Spa ★★★   Once home to France's envoy to central Vietnam, or Annam, La Résidence has been rethought and added onto and is now one of the best-designed boutique hotels in the country. Warm colors and dark wood combine with unobtrusive, elegant Art Deco patterns befitting a colonial villa, while black-and-white pictures on the wall are reminiscent of Indochina. Nooks and crannies of private space abound, so a guest can easily find a quiet corner to himself. Rooms are spacious, with clean lines, parquet floors, and views of the Perfume River and the Citadel. The cuisine at Le Parfum is carefully prepared and excellent; the staff is exceptional.

5 Le Loi St., Hue. ✆ **054/383-7475.** Fax 054/383-7476. www.la-residence-hue.com. 122 units. From $125 double; $215–$285 suite. AE, MC, V. **Amenities:** Restaurant; bar; bike and motorbike rental; concierge; nice gym; outdoor saltwater pool; room service; spa; Wi-Fi. *In room:* A/C, satellite TV, fridge, hair dryer, minibar.

The Pilgrimage Village ★★   This is the place to come if you're looking for a luxurious, secluded getaway. The resort offers cozy villas and bungalows spread out over manicured grounds. The villa deluxe rooms—with spacious interiors, decadently large bathrooms, and private balconies—are excellent value. Get one on the second floor for the cabin-esque sloping roofs. Higher-end huts and bungalows come with outdoor rain showers and stone bathtubs. For a special getaway, splurge on one of the three traditional Vietnamese pool houses. The houses are more than 150 years old and were transported here from nearby villages. They come with a bevy of perks, such as a free hour of spa services and tai chi classes on request. Pilgrimage Village is one of the only independently owned and operated hotels in the area. It's a 10-minute ride to the town center, but there are shuttle buses to run guests around, and it's close to two of the best tombs in Hue. For the best Hue has to offer, it's a battle between here and La Résidence Hôtel & Spa (see above): luxurious local charm in a natural setting versus chic colonial digs with a breathless view over Perfume River. You decide.

130 Minh Mang St., Hue. ✆ **054/388-5461.** Fax 054/388-7057. www.pilgrimagevillage.com. 99 units. $179 villa deluxe; $260 bungalow; $312 villa family deluxe; $663 pool house. AE, MC, V. **Amenities:** 2 restaurants; 2 bars; free airport transfer for house, hut, and bungalow rooms; concierge; fitness center; spacious 40m (131-ft.) outdoor pool; room service; luxurious spa w/Jacuzzi and sauna. *In room:* A/C, satellite TV, fridge, hair dryer, minibar, Wi-Fi.

INEXPENSIVE

Orchid Hotel ★   This popular minihotel is good value for the money. Rooms are comfortable and beds are done up nicely, with charming textiles and accent pillows. There are a few things that veer toward the tacky side, such as faux-wood-finish floors and leopard-print bathrobes, but these are more than made up for by the provision of computers and Wi-Fi in rooms and a superattentive staff. Family rooms or triple rooms are excellent value, as they are double the size of standard rooms and also have small balconies. Another nice touch is free afternoon cake and fruit for all guests.

30A Chu Van An St., Hue. ✆ **054/383-1177.** Fax 054/383-1213. www.orchidhotel.com.vn. 18 units. From $35 double; $52 family room. Rates include breakfast. MC, V. **Amenities:** Cafe. *In room:* A/C, TV/DVD, fridge, minibar, Wi-Fi.

Sports 1 Hotel   This place is good value and is one of the town's better budget hotels. The rooms are tidy, beds are decent, and the blond faux-wood interior is pretty inviting. Bathrooms are spotless, which is a major bonus in this price range. The location puts you in the midst of backpackers, which means a good selection of local eateries and popular watering holes. Try to get one of the few rooms that have river views and a decent-size balcony.

15 Pham Ngu Lao St., Hue. ℂ **054/382-8096.** Fax 054/383-0199. www.huesportshotel.com. 30 units. $32 double; $39 family room. MC, V. **Amenities:** Restaurant; bar. *In room:* A/C, satellite TV, hair dryer, Wi-Fi.

Where to Dine

Hue cuisine is unique, with a focus on light ingredients in choices such as the popular fresh spring rolls; *bun bo Hue,* a noodle soup with pork, beef, and shredded green onions; and *banh khoai,* a thin, crispy pancake filled with ground meat and crispy vegetables. Local dishes are best at streetside—there are a few good spots with English menus along the river and in the backpacker area, along Hung Vuong.

MODERATE

Hoa Mai Restaurant ★★ VIETNAMESE   Hoa Mai is decked out in kitschy bamboo furnishings and set in an open area on the top floor of the Huong Giang Hotel. Great views of the Perfume River accompany the good Vietnamese fare. Try *banh rom hue,* triangular fried rolls stuffed with ground meat, shrimp, and vegetables. Daily special set menus are a good idea and can feature such dishes as fried cuttlefish with grapefruit, crab soup, and shrimp with fig and rice cake. Be sure to choose a table near the riverside window and away from any banquet-size setups that say RESERVED.

At the Huong Giang Hotel, 51 Le Loi St., 3rd floor. ℂ **054/382-2122.** Main courses $3–$10; set menus $10–$15. AE, MC, V. Daily 7am–11pm.

Tropical Garden ★★ VIETNAMESE   Though a popular tour-bus stop, Tropical Garden has a nice laid-back feel. The restaurant serves fine Vietnamese fare from an English-language menu, plus stages a live music show nightly. Even when it's packed, there are enough intimate corners that you'll feel comfortable. The place specializes in "embarrassing entrees," the kind of flaming dishes that would impress that eccentric uncle of yours (spring rolls served on toothpick skewers around the rind of a hollowed pineapple with a candle in the middle, a la a Halloween jack-o'-lantern). It's all good fun, so just go with it. The food is good, but a bit overpriced for a la carte items. Set menus are quite reasonable and walk you through some house specialties, such as the banana-flower soup, the grilled chicken with lemon leaf, and the steamed crab with beer. As an appetizer, don't miss the grilled minced shrimp with sugar cane wrapped in rice paper and served with peanut sauce—unique and delicious. Service is a bit hit-or-miss, either fawning or forgetful.

27 Chu Van An St. ℂ **054/384-7143.** Fax 054/382-8074. Main courses $3–$6; set menus $8–$20. AE, MC, V. Daily 8:30am–11pm.

INEXPENSIVE

La Carambole ★★ VIETNAMESE/CONTINENTAL   Good music is the first thing you might notice at La Carambole; I heard an unlikely mix from CCR to Beck on one relaxing evening. The decor is cheerful: cool indirect lighting, red tablecloths, and playful mobiles hanging from the ceiling, all as welcoming as the kind waitstaff. The French proprietor, Christian, and his wife, Ha, will certainly make you feel at home, and the comfort items on the menu—spaghetti, burgers, pizzas, and various French-style meat-and-potatoes specials—will stick to your ribs. The set menus are a good deal (salad and pizza at $6, for example), and portions are ample. There's a game table, and you're sure to meet lots of other travelers here.

19 Pham Ngu Lao St. ☏ **054/381-0491.** Fax 054/382-6234. Main courses 30,000VND-140,000VND; set menus $6-$10. No credit cards. Daily 7am-11pm.

Mandarin Café ★ VIETNAMESE/CONTINENTAL   In a busy storefront just a short walk from the riverside (near the Hotel Saigon Morin), Mandarin is always full of young backpackers, and for a reason: Good, affordable Vietnamese fare, predominantly one-dish items such as fried rice or noodles, top a roster of comfort foods. Have a banana pancake and be one with the universe. Owner Mr. Cu (pronounced *Coo*) is a practiced photographer; his works, classic images of rural Vietnam, line the walls and are for sale as postcards or prints. For the amateur shutterbug, the images are inspiring, and the best part is that Mr. Cu is more than happy to share secrets and talk shop. Come here for both a casual meal and conversation with fellow travelers.

24 Tran Cao Van St. ☏ **054/382-1281.** mandarin@dng.vnn.vn. Main courses 20,000VND-50,000VND. AE, MC, V. Daily 6:30am-10pm.

What to See & Do in the Citadel & Imperial City ★★★

The Citadel is often used as a catchall term for Hue's Imperial City, built by Emperor Gia Long beginning in 1804 for the exclusive use of the emperor and his household, much like Beijing's Forbidden City. The city actually encompasses three walled enclosures: the Exterior Enclosure, or **Citadel;** the Yellow Enclosure, or **Imperial City,** within that; and, in the very center, the **Forbidden Purple City,** where the emperor actually lived. The Citadel itself is a square 2km (1¼-mile) wall, 7m (23 ft.) high and 20m (66 ft.) thick, with 10 gates. Ironically, it was constructed by a French military architect, though it failed to prevent the French from destroying the complex many years later. The main entrance to the Imperial City is the Noon Gate (Cua Ngo Mon, the southwest gate); this is where you can get a ticket and enter the site. Admission is 55,000VND. Hours are daily from 7am to 5:30pm.

Flag Tower ★★   The focal point of the Imperial City, a large rampart to the south of the Noon Gate, this tower was built in 1807 during Gia Long's reign. The yellow flag of royalty was the first to fly here and was exchanged for and replaced by many others in Vietnam's turbulent history. It's a national symbol.

Forbidden Purple City ★   Once the actual home of the emperor and his concubines, this second sanctum within the Citadel is a large open area dotted with what's left of the king's court. Almost completely razed in a fire in 1947, the sanctum is now a few buildings among the rubble. The new **Royal Theater** behind the square, a reconstruction of the razed original, hosts performances of *nha nhac* (courtly dance) at 9am, 10am, 2:30pm, and 3:30pm (admission 50,000VND). To the left as you head north is the partially restored **Thai Binh Reading Pavilion,** notable mostly for its beautifully landscaped surroundings, including a small lake with a Zen-like stone sculpture, and the ceramic-and-glass mosaic detailing on the roof and pillars favored by flamboyant emperor Khai Dinh.

Mieu Temple ★★   Constructed in 1921 to 1922 by Emperor Minh Mang, this temple has funeral altars paying tribute to 10 of the last Nguyen Dynasty emperors, omitting two who reigned for only days, with photos of each emperor and his empress(es) and various small offerings. The two empty glass containers to the side of each photo should contain bars of gold, probably an impractical idea today.

Across from the Mieu is Hien Lam, or the Glorious Pavilion, to the far right, with the **Nine Dynastic Urns** in front. Cast from 1835 to 1837, each urn represents a

Nguyen emperor and is richly embellished with all the flora, fauna, and material goods that Vietnam has to offer, mythical or otherwise.

Noon Gate (Cua Ngo Mon) ★★ One of 10 entrances to the city, this southern entrance is the most dynamic. It was the royal entrance, in fact, and was built by Emperor Gia Long in 1823. It was used for important proclamations, such as announcements of the names of successful doctoral candidates (a list still hangs on the wall on the upper floor) and, most memorably, the announcement of the abdication of the last emperor, Bao Dai, on August 13, 1945, to Ho Chi Minh. The structure, like most here, was damaged by war but is now nicely restored, with classic Chinese roofs covering the ritual space, complete with large drums and an altar. Be sure to climb to the top and have a look at the view.

Thai Hoa Palace Otherwise known as the Palace of Supreme Harmony, this structure was built in 1833 and is the first one you'll approach at the entrance. It was used as the throne room, a ceremonial hall where the emperor celebrated festivals and received courtiers; the original throne still stands. The Mandarins sat outside. In front are two mythical *ky lin* animals, which walk without their claws ever touching the ground and have piercing eyesight for watching the emperor, tracking all good and evil he does. Note the statues of the heron and turtle inside the palace's ornate lacquered interior: The heron represents nobility and the turtle represents the working person. Folklore has it that the two took turns saving each other's lives during a fire, symbolizing that the power of the emperor rests with his people, and vice versa.

Thien Mu Pagoda ★★ Often called the symbol of Hue, Thien Mu is one of the oldest and loveliest religious structures in Vietnam. Set on the bank of the Perfume River 4km (2½ miles) southwest of the Citadel, it was constructed beginning in 1601. The Phuoc Dien Tower in front was added in 1864 by Emperor Thieu Tri. Each of its seven tiers is dedicated to either one of the human forms taken by Buddha or the seven steps to enlightenment, depending upon whom you ask. There are also two buildings housing a bell that reportedly weighs 2 tons, plus a stele inscribed with a biography of Lord Nguyen Hoang, founder of the temple.

Once past the front gate, observe the 12 huge wooden sculptures of fearsome temple "guardians"—note the real facial hair. A complex of monastic buildings lies in the center, offering glimpses of the monks' daily routines. Stroll all the way to the rear of the complex to look at the graveyard at the base of the Truong Son mountains and to wander through the well kept garden of pine trees. Hours are daily from 8am to 5pm, but try not to go between 11:30am and 2pm, when the monks are at lunch, because the rear half of the complex will be closed.

What to See & Do at the Imperial Tombs ★

As befits its history as an Imperial City, Hue's environs are studded with tombs of past emperors. They are spread out over a distance, so the best way to see them is to hire a car for a half-day or take one of the many organized boat tours up the Perfume River. Altogether, there were 13 kings of the Nguyen Dynasty, although only 7 reigned until their death. As befits an emperor, all had tombs of stature, some as large as a small town. Most tomb complexes usually consist of a courtyard, a stele (a large stone tablet with a biography of the emperor), a temple for worship, and a pond.

Tomb of Khai Dinh ★★ Emperor Khai Dinh himself wasn't particularly revered, being overly extravagant and flamboyant (reportedly he wore a belt studded with lights that he flicked on at opportune public moments). His tomb, completed in 1931, is a gaudy mix of Gothic, baroque, Hindu, and Chinese Qing Dynasty architecture at the top of 127 steep steps—a reflection of the man himself. Inside, the two main rooms are completely covered with fabulous, intricate glass and ceramic mosaics in designs reminiscent of Tiffany and Art Deco. The workmanship is astounding. The outer room's ceiling was done by a fellow who used both his feet and his hands to paint, in what some say was a sly mark of disrespect for the emperor. While in most tombs the location of the emperor's actual remains are a secret, Khai Dinh boldly placed his under his de facto tomb itself.

Admission 55,000VND. Summer daily 6:30am–5:30pm; winter daily 7am–5pm.

Tomb of Minh Mang ★★   Minh Mang reigned from 1820 to 1841 and his tomb is perhaps the biggest and most elaborate of all, set in 15 hectares (37 acres) of parkland and lakes. A processional way leads across three mounds topped with buildings. First is the stele house, where the emperor's achievements are recorded in stone (these achievements included fathering more than 140 children by his various wives and concubines). After that comes the principal temple, and finally the elegant Minh Lau, or "Pavilion of Pure Light," which is surrounded by frangipani trees—a symbol of longevity. From here a pathway crosses a crescent-shaped lake to the tomb mound itself.

Admission 55,000VND. Summer daily 6:30am–5:30pm; winter daily 7am–5pm.

Tomb of Tu Duc ★★   With the longest reign of any Nguyen Dynasty emperor, from 1848 to 1883, Tu Duc was a philosopher and scholar of history and literature. His reign was unfortunate: His kingdom unsuccessfully struggled against French colonialism, he fought a coup d'état by members of his own family, and although he had 104 wives, he left no heir. The "tomb" was constructed from 1864 to 1867 and also served as recreation grounds for the king, having been completed 16 years before his death. In fact, he actually engraved his own stele. The largest in Vietnam, at 20 tons, it has its own pavilion in the tomb. The highlight of the grounds is the lotus-filled lake ringed by frangipani trees, with a large pavilion in the center. The main cluster of buildings includes Hoa Khiem (Harmony Modesty) Pavilion, where the king worked; it still contains items of furniture and ornaments. Minh Khiem Duong, constructed in 1866, is said to be the country's oldest surviving theater. It's great fun to poke around in the wings.

Taking a Boat to the Tombs

Expect to pay between $2 and $4 for a shared boat ride to the temples (depending on which agent you use), *plus* 55,000VND for *each* tomb. Be prepared for when the boat pulls to shore at the first two tombs; you'll have to hire one of the motorcycle taxis at the bank to shuttle you to and from the site. You will not have enough time to walk there and back, so you're basically at their mercy. Haggle as best you can—about 10,000VND is a good starting point.

There are also pieces of original furniture lying here and there, as well as a cabinet with household objects: the queen's slippers, ornate chests, and bronze and silver books. The raised box on the wall is for the actors who played emperors; the real emperor was at the platform to the left.

Admission 55,000VND. Summer daily 6:30am–5:30pm; winter daily 7am–5pm.

Shopping

All along Le Loi Street, you'll see souvenir stalls that vary from the cute to the kitschy. Look out in particular for conical "poem" hats, for which Hue is famed. You can find good deals on commemorative spoons and velvet Ho Chi Minhs here, but nothing too traditional or authentic. There are a few good silversmiths, however. A few tailors are based in and among the souvenir shops, or you can stop by **Seductive** (40 Le Loi St.; ✆ 054/382-9794), a small, ready-to-wear silk boutique. **Bambou Company** (21 Pham Ngu Lao St., next to La Carambole) produces unique T-shirts of local theme and design.

Hue After Dark

The best view in town is at the **Imperial Hotel**'s (8 Hung Vuong St.; ✆ **054/388-2222**) panorama bar. Across from the major riverside hotels is the **DMZ Café** (44 Le Loi; ✆ **054/382-3414**), which stays up late like a beer-swilling frat party. Along Hung Vuong, you'll find a few backpacker bars open 'til midnight, but overall this is a pretty sleepy town. **Bar Why Not?** (21 Vo Thi Sau St.; ✆ **054/824-793**) is a cool open-air joint at the intersection of Pham Ngu Lao and Vo Thi Sau (near La Carambole); it has a good pool table and hot dogs cooked to order. **Café on Thu Wheels** (3/34 Nguyen Tri Phuong; **054/383-2241**) is a small and welcoming bar run by enthusiastic Thu, a good spot to meet other travelers and sup a local beer. **Brown Eyes** (56 Chu Van An St.; ✆ **054/827-494**) is a late-night bar and cafe that attracts a young clientele.

Side Trips from Hue

Except for the remains of its fabulous Imperial City, Hue in itself has sadly seen the worst of the French and American wars. Most of the star attractions other than the Citadel, therefore, involve half- or full-day trips outside the city.

THE DMZ & VINH MOC TUNNELS ★★

If you're old enough to remember the Vietnam War, you'll know Hue from the large-scale battles waged there. A day trip to the nearby DMZ and Vinh Moc Tunnels is a sobering revisit to that tumultuous time.

Under the Geneva Accords of 1954, an agreement struck to bring peace to Indochina after its struggle with French colonists, Vietnam was divided into North and South along the **17th Parallel.** What was meant to be a short-term political fix became a battle line, and the 17th Parallel, aka the **DMZ** or demilitarized zone, became a tangle of barbed wire and land mines bombed and defoliated into a wasteland. Today, the area is slowly recovering and completely unremarkable except for its history. Nearby are strategic sites with names you may recognize: the Rockpile, Hamburger Hill, Camp Carroll, and Khe Sanh, a former U.S. Marine base that was the site of some of the war's most vicious and deadly fighting. If you take a tour of the area, you will also visit Dakrong Bridge, an official entryway into the Ho Chi Minh trail. *Warning:* The route over Hwy. 9 to the sites is narrow and bumpy. Rethink this trip if it's a rainy day or if you are faint of either heart or stomach.

Most tours to the DMZ area include a visit to the **Vinh Moc Tunnels,** a site that is a testament to human tenacity. Like the tunnels in the south at Cu Chi (p. 356), soldiers and civilians took to the underground, literally, digging over 1.6km (1 mile) of tunnels from 1965 to 1966 to support Viet Cong troops and confound U.S. battalions at this strategic position near the line of north-south demarcation. Up to 20m (about 66 ft.) below the surface, multilevel tunnels formed a real community haven, with "living rooms" for families, a conference and performance room, a field hospital, and exit points inland and along the coast. Visitors walk through about 300m (984 ft.) of the tunnels in a main artery that is 1.6m high by 1.2m wide (5¼×4 ft.), going down three levels. It's dirty, clammy, and a bit claustrophobic—dress accordingly. A museum at the entrance has photos and testimony of survivors. Admission is 25,000VND.

These sites are some 60km (37 miles) north of Hue. Contact Hue tourist cafes such as **Sinh Café** for group excursions, or for a good private tour try **Huong Giang Tourist Company** (see "Visitor Information & Tours," earlier in this section).

LANG CO BEACH

A good day stop along Route 1A between Hue and Danang/Hoi An, Lang Co Beach is a sweeping expanse of sand where you can dip your toes and take a rest en route. The absence of group tours and touts is the main draw. For a cozy overnight getaway, try the **Lang Co Beach Resort** (© **054/387-3555;** www.langcobeachresort.com.vn), where oceanview rooms go for $110.

DANANG & CHINA BEACH

Danang, the fourth-largest city in Vietnam, is one of the most important seaports in the central region. It played a prominent role in the American war, serving as the landing site for the first American troops officially sent to Vietnam. Danang has nothing in the way of charm and has no major attractions except for the **Cham Museum,** which has become just a quick stop on the tourist-cafe buses between Hoi An and Hue. **Furama Resort,** a short ride from the city center, is one of the finest high-end resorts in Indochina, though it now faces stiff competition from places like the beautiful **Nam Hai Resort** in nearby Hoi An.

China Beach, or **My Khe** as it's known locally, is worth a stop. This former U.S. recreation base has a light-sand coast with excellent views of the nearby Marble Mountains and is just beginning to draw international visitors.

Getting There

BY PLANE   You can fly to Danang from both Hanoi and HCMC. A taxi from the airport costs about $3.

BY BUS   If you're traveling on an open-tour ticket, Danang is not a specified stop, but you can be dropped off at the Cham Museum. You'll have to call the office in either Hue or Hoi An for pickup when you're ready to leave. Travelers to Laos should contact **Vietnamtourism** for buses to Savannakhet (about $25).

BY CAR   Danang is about 2 hours by car from Hue. You'll pay around $30 for the trip. From Hoi An, it's about an hour and costs $15. This ride makes a good day trip along with the Marble Mountains (see "What to See & Do," below). Contact **Vietnamtourism** for good rentals.

Visitor Information & Tours

There are few tour offices in Danang because most major tour operations are based at nearby Hoi An or Hue. Any hotel can help out with onward travel, either by private car, by minivan, or through budget cafes. Tours can also be booked with any concierge.

Vietnamtourism Danang (83 Nguyen Thi Minh Khai; ℂ **0511/382-3660;** fax 0511/382-1560) can arrange trips to the Marble Mountains and My Son. **An Phu Tourist** (20 Dong Da; ℂ **0511/381-8366;** anphu_cndn@yahoo.com) is the local tourist-cafe contact and can arrange any low-budget connections.

[FastFACTS] DANANG

Currency Exchange   The **Vietcombank** branch is at 140 Le Loi St. (ℂ **0511/382-2110**).

Internet Access   Most hotels provide Internet service, either free or for a fee; otherwise, look along Dong Da Street adjacent to the An Phu Tourist office (20 Dong Da St.).

Telephones   The city code for Danang is **0511.**

Where to Stay

EXPENSIVE

Furama Resort Danang ★★★   Just a short ride southwest of Danang and situated in elegant relation to a beautiful sandy beach, the Furama greets you in style with a grand lobby that is more or less the gilded frame to the beautiful scenery: sand, sun, and sky. Whether you're a sailor, a beach bum, or a comfort junkie, you'll find what you want. There are two gorgeous swimming pools: one a multitiered minimalist still life overlooking the open beach, and the other a faux lagoon, complete with small waterfall and bridge. It's a good place to just relax, but there is always something to do, too: The hotel offers local tours, yoga, tai chi, a spa, and a full salon. Rooms are large and comfortable with wood floors, Vietnamese-style furniture, and sliding doors to balconies that overlook the ocean or pool. Large marble bathrooms have all the amenities. Prices are determined by view; oceanfront units are only steps from the beach and well worth it. Note that watersports are available only February through September—the surf is far too rough the rest of the year. Resort amenities are extensive, but they have to be, as the site is quite isolated. There are shuttles to the city, but there isn't much to entice in bustling Danang.

68 Ho Xuan Huong St. (ocean side 11km/6¾ miles southwest of town), Danang. ℂ **0511/384-7333.** Fax 0511/384-7220. www.furamavietnam.com. 198 units. $185–$210 garden view; $265 ocean view; $300–$560 suite. AE, MC, V. **Amenities:** 3 restaurants; 3 bars; concierge; luxe health club; Internet access; 2 outdoor pools; room service; sauna; 4 tennis courts; watersports rental. *In room:* A/C, satellite TV, fridge, hair dryer, minibar.

MODERATE

Bamboo Green Harbourside ★★   A convenient choice in Danang proper, Bamboo Green is operated by Vietnamtourism. Rooms are large, with beige carpets and light-wood furnishings (try to overlook the hideous poly bedspreads). The nice-size marble bathrooms are spotless. Ask for a room on the top floor for a city view. Hotel features include a big restaurant with decent Asian/Vietnamese fare, good tour services, and a friendly staff. Overall, this is as cozy as any midrange U.S. chain.

177 Tran Phu St., Danang. ℂ **0511/382-2996** or 382-2722. Fax 0511/382-4165. www.bamboogreenhotel. com. 70 units. $60 superior; $70 deluxe; $100 suite. AE, MC, V. **Amenities:** 2 restaurants; bar; room service; sauna. *In room:* A/C, satellite TV, fridge, hair dryer, minibar.

Saigon Tourane Hotel ★   Popular with European tour groups, this nondescript, friendly, three-star standard hotel offers comfort at low cost. The rooms are carpeted and clean, and they come with tidy, good-size bathrooms; some upper-floor units have city views. Nonetheless, it's all a bit low-luxe, with a general atmosphere marked by failing neon signs and worn carpets that speak of the volumes that pass through. The hotel is owned by Saigontourist; thus, guests are well connected and can make any necessary arrangements with little hassle. The staff couldn't be more kind. Be sure to ask for a room away from the karaoke—far away.

5 Dong Da St. (on the north end of town), Danang. ✆ **0511/382-1021.** Fax 0511/389-5285. www.saigon tourane.com.vn. 82 units. $50–$80 double; $110 suite. No credit cards. **Amenities:** 2 restaurants; bar; basic gym; sauna; smoke-free rooms. *In room:* A/C, satellite TV, fridge, hair dryer, minibar.

Where to Dine

If you're at the **Furama Resort,** that's where you'll find the best fine dining, but beachside seafood shacks adjacent to the property also serve good barbecue for a fraction of resort prices. In Danang proper, choices are few, but they do exist. **Apsara** (222 Tran Phu; ✆ **0511/356-1409**) is the fanciest restaurant in the city, serving mostly seafood in smart surroundings, with live traditional music each evening. **Kim Do** (180 Tran Phu St.; ✆ **0511/382-1846**), a long-standing popular Chinese restaurant, serves good stir-fries and steamed Cantonese specials. A notable find are the small storefronts adjacent to the Cham Museum that serve good duck and rice dishes. If you're craving comfort food, make your way to **Bread of Life** (12 Le Hong Phong; ✆ **0511/356-5185;** www.breadoflifedanang.com), where the menu features Western breakfasts, pizzas, burgers, pancakes, and sandwiches made with freshly baked bread; it's operated by deaf staff and proceeds go to fund projects for the deaf.

What to See & Do

Cham Museum ★★   The Cham Museum was established in 1916 (originally the Ecole Française d'Extreme Orient) to house the relics of the powerful Champa kingdom that once ruled vast tracts of central Vietnam. The museum has the largest collection of Cham sculpture in the world, in works ranging from the 4th to the 14th century, which spills over into a rough outdoor setting that suits the evocative, sensual sculptures well. The more than 300 pieces of sandstone artwork and temple decorations were largely influenced by Hinduism and, later, Mahayana Buddhism. Among the cast of characters, you'll see symbols of Uroja, or "goddess mother," usually breasts or nipples; the linga, the phallic structure representing the god Shiva; the holy bird Garuda; and Ganesha, child of the god Shiva, with the head of an elephant. Note the masterpiece Tra Kieu altar of the late 7th century, with carved scenes telling the story of the epic *Ramayana*. There is also a permanent photo exhibit of the many Cham relics at various locations throughout Vietnam.

At Tran Phu and Trung Nu Vuong sts. Admission 30,000VND. Daily 7am–5pm.

Marble Mountains ★   The "mountains" are actually a series of five marble and limestone formations, which the locals liken to the shape of a dragon at rest. The hills are interlaced with caves, some of which are important Buddhist sanctuaries. These caves, like so many in the country, served as shelter for the Viet Cong during the American war. The highest mountain, Thuy Son (admission 15,000VND), is climbable via a series of metal ladders beginning inside the cave and extending to the surface at the top. Ling Ong Pagoda, a shrine within a cave, is a highlight. The quarries in Non Nuoc village, at the bottom of the mountains, are as interesting as the caves. Fantastic animals and fanciful statues of folk tales and Buddhist figures are carved from the rock. Try to get a good look before you're set upon by flocks of hawkers. What's more, even if you're interested in the items they hawk—incredibly cheap mortar-and-pestle sets, some very nice chess sets, turtles, and small animals—any amount of marble adds considerable weight to luggage. You can easily see the mountains as part of your trip en route to or from Hoi An; most cafe-tour buses stop here.

11km (6¾ miles) south of Danang and 9.5km (6 miles) north of Hoi An along Hwy. 1. All tours stop here.

HOI AN ★★

A visit to this old-world gem, which was designated a UNESCO World Heritage Site in 1999, is a sure cultural highlight of any Vietnam tour. From the 16th to the 18th century, Hoi An was Vietnam's most important port and trading post, particularly of ceramics with nearby China. Today, it is a quaint, picturesque town of some 844 structures protected as historic landmarks, and the unique influence of Chinese and Japanese traders who passed through (or settled) can still be felt.

Hoi An is small enough to cover easily on foot, with many nooks and crannies, shops, and gastronomic delights to discover. Wander among historic homes and temples, lounge in an open-air cafe, gaze at the exotic foods in the market, or take a sampan ride down the lazy river. You can still see local craftspeople at work in some parts of the city. In the afternoons when school is out, the streets are thronged with skipping children, the girls in their *ao dai* (silk costumes).

On the full moon of every month, local shop owners turn off the electricity and hang lanterns bearing their shop's name; a candlelight lantern procession, complete with a few small floats, makes its way through the old town and along the riverfront. It's worth timing a visit to enjoy the spectacle and the postprocessional festivities.

Getting There

BY PLANE/TRAIN Major transport connections go through Danang. From there, you can take a car to Hoi An for about $15.

BY BUS Hoi An is a major stop on all open-tour cafe buses. Connection with Danang is just $3.

Getting Around

Hoi An is so small that you'll be able to memorize the map in an hour or two. Most hotels and guesthouses rent **bicycles** for 20,000VND a day, a great way to explore the outer regions of the city or Cua Dai Beach. **Motorbikes** are $5 to $7 per day and are not difficult to drive in this tiny, calm city, though some streets are off-limits to motorized vehicles. Car hire (with driver) is also available through most hotels; expect to pay around $50 a day.

Visitor Information & Tours

- **Hoi An Ancient Town** (1 Nguyen Truong To, ℂ **0510/386-1327;** or 12 Phan Chu Trinh St., ℂ **0510/386-2715**) sells the Hoi An World Cultural Heritage tickets. A one-ticket purchase offers limited admission to the town's museums, old houses, and Chinese assembly halls. Ticket booths are at 78 Le Loi, 30 Tran Phu, 12 Phan Chu Trinh, 10 Nguyen Hue, and 5 Hoang Dieu. For more information about the tickets, see "What to See & Do," later in this chapter.
- **Hoi An Tourist Service Company,** inside the Hoi An Hotel (10 Tran Hung Dao St.; ℂ **0510/386-1445;** fax 0510/386-1636), is a reliable operation that books

Hoi An

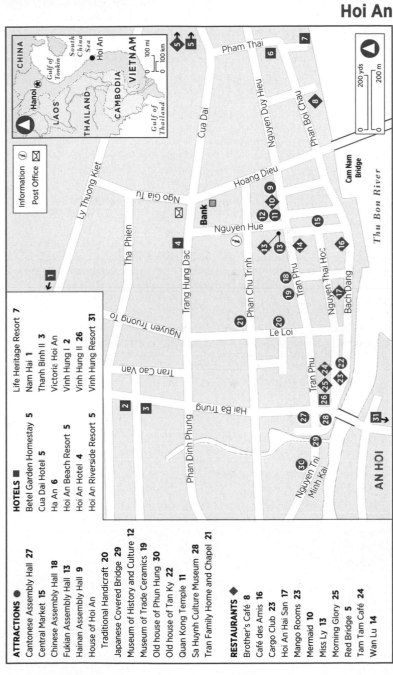

ATTRACTIONS ●

Cantonese Assembly Hall **27**
Central Market **15**
Chinese Assembly Hall **18**
Fukian Assembly Hall **13**
Hainan Assembly Hall **9**
House of Hoi An
 Traditional Handicraft **20**
Japanese Covered Bridge **29**
Museum of History and Culture **12**
Museum of Trade Ceramics **19**
Old house of Phun Hung **30**
Old house of Tan Ky **22**
Quan Kong Temple **11**
Sa Huynh Culture Museum **28**
Tran Family Home and Chapel **21**

HOTELS ■

Betel Garden Homestay **5**
Cua Dai Hotel **5**
Ha An **6**
Hoi An Beach Resort **5**
Hoi An Hotel **4**
Hoi An Riverside Resort **5**
Life Heritage Resort **7**
Nam Hai **1**
Thanh Binh II **3**
Victoric Hoi An
Vinh Hung I **2**
Vinh Hung II **26**
Vinh Hung Resort **31**

RESTAURANTS ◆

Brother's Café **8**
Café des Amis **16**
Cargo Club **23**
Hoi An Hai San **17**
Mango Rooms **23**
Mermaid **10**
Miss Ly **13**
Morning Glory **25**
Red Bridge **5**
Tam Tam Café **24**
Wan Lu **14**

5

VIETNAM | Hoi An

every type of tour of the city and surrounding areas, including China Beach and the Marble Mountains.

- **Sinh Café** (587 Hai Ba Trung St.; *C* **0510/386-3948**) provides bus tours and tickets onward.

[Fast FACTS] HOI AN

Currency Exchange   The **Vietcombank** (642 Hai Ba Trung St.) has an ATM, changes most major currencies, and does credit card cash advances. Hours are Monday through Saturday from 7:30am to 7pm. **Incombank** exchanges money at 9 Le Loi St. and **Vietincombank** does likewise at 4 Hoang Diet St. **Exchange Bureau #1,** across from the Hoi An Hotel at 37 Tran Hung Dao, has exchange services and an ATM. There is also an ATM at the post office.

Internet Access   Along Le Loi, you'll find service at around 6,000VND per hour. On the northern end of town, **Min's Computer** (125 Nguyen Duy Hieu; *C* **0510/391-4323**) is a reliable spot.

Mail   The post office is at the corner of Trang Hung Dao and Huong Dieu streets; open Monday through Saturday from 6am to 9:30pm.

Telephones   The city code for Hoi An is **0510.** You can place international calls from the post office listed above and from most hotels.

Where to Stay

Hoi An has seen a recent boom in upscale resorts, with more on the way along Cua Dai Beach. Large-scale new construction in Hoi An proper is prohibited by UNESCO, but smaller hotels are going upmarket, and there are a few new options closer to town.

VERY EXPENSIVE

The Nam Hai ★★★   This is the best luxury resort in Hoi An, and a contender for best in the land. Individual villas are discreetly laid out over an immaculately tended 35 hectares (86 acres). Staff is incredibly friendly and quick to be of service at the first sign of a furrowed brow. The one-bedroom villa is a chic affair of granite stone floors, local dark wood, and brown, cream, and green colors. The centerpiece is a raised six-column platform topped with lattice woodwork and draped in silk curtains. Behind it are the bed and a bathtub done in traditional crushed eggshell lacquer. The outdoor tropical rain shower is an excellent place to rinse off sand and sea salt. Facilities are comprehensive, from the swivel flatscreen TV to the loaded iPod and Bose speakers. Activities include tennis tournaments and cooking classes—a nice touch, as sometimes you want to do more than lounge poolside.

Multibedroom pool villas are excellent value if you are traveling as a family or group, as they come with superluxurious "club benefits" like return airport limousine transfer, a personal butler, complimentary minibar, and evening cocktails and canapés with free-flowing champagne and wine.

Hamlet 1, Dien Duong village, Dien Ban District, Quang Nam Province. *C* **0510/3940-000.** Fax 0510/3940-999. www.thenamhai.com. 100 units. $750-$850 1-bedroom villas; $1,350-$3,900 1- to 5-bedroom pool villas. AE, DC, MC, V. **Amenities:** 2 restaurants; bar; bikes; health club; high-speed Internet; 3 outdoor pools; room service; spa; 4 tennis courts; library. *In room:* A/C, on-demand movies and satellite TV, fridge, hair dryer, minibar, MP3 docking station, Wi-Fi.

EXPENSIVE

Hoi An Beach Resort ★   Opened in 2000, this is the flagship of Hoi An Tourist, a government-owned company, and it's their answer to recent upscale development in town. The resort is across the road from Cua Dai Beach and close to the small "restaurant row" and popular tourist sunbathing area. Everything here—from the casual open-air restaurant to the more expensive rooms and suites—faces the De Vong River as it approaches the sea, offering a unique glimpse of everyday riverside life. At the bar and upscale access point to the beach, you can sit in private chairs without harassment from beachside sellers. All rooms here are nice, but the villas are certainly worth the few extra dollars: They're quite large, with high ceilings and private balconies. Villas and suites have vaulted ceilings, and some have separate entrances with a shower area for cleanup after the beach. Service and general standards are comparable to the high-end competition in town. It's a popular choice for large European tours and can get a bit wild in the busy season, but it's all good fun. There are frequent shuttles to town.

1 Cua Dai, Cua Dai Beach, Hoi An. © **0510/392-7011.** Fax 0510/392-7019. www.hoianbeachresort.com. vn. 121 units. $110 garden deluxe double; $195 river- or oceanview villa; $255 riverview suite. AE, MC, V. **Amenities:** Restaurant; 2 bars; babysitting; bike rental; concierge; small health club; Internet; Jacuzzi; 2 large outdoor pools; room service; sauna; spa. In room: A/C, satellite TV, fridge, hair dryer, minibar.

Hoi An Hotel ★★   Still the best and most convenient in-town address, the Hoi An Hotel was the first high-end hotel and works hard to keep that reputation. As a result, it's pretty busy here, with lots of tour groups. The friendly staff does a great job, though, and handles large numbers with a modicum of grace. Don't expect anything fancy, but rooms are unusually large and impeccably clean, with tile floors and comfortable beds. The newest building has upscale rooms with dark-wood floors and a fun, contemporary Chinese theme (but the older rooms are just as good). The central pool is large, though often overcrowded. The folks at the tour desk are very helpful.

10 Tran Hung Dao St., Hoi An. © **0510/386-1445.** Fax 0510/386-1636. www.hoiantourist.com. 160 units. $96 $138 double; $198 suite. AE, MC, V. **Amenities:** Restaurant; garden bar; babysitting; concierge; Jacuzzi; nice courtyard pool; room service; tennis court; Wi-Fi. In room: A/C, satellite TV, fridge, hair dryer, minibar.

Hoi An Riverside Resort & Spa ★★   For tranquil and intimate surroundings, you'll find no better place than this lush little resort between road and river outside of Hoi An. The place has a cozy feel, as if guest rooms kind of grew around the winding path of the garden and courtyard pool. Rooms are neat and clean, not especially big, but with nice views of the meandering bend in the river or the quiet garden. Vietnamese- or Japanese-themed accommodations have small, spotless bathrooms and nice wood appointments throughout. The staff is invisible, meaning that this place carries on like an immaculately trimmed golf course that gets a once-over each night. The Song Do restaurant serves fine Vietnamese and Continental fare; a visit to the Faifo bar harks back to another era. The central pool is a relaxing spot—great after wandering the town labyrinths. The staff is very professional and informative. The resort offers Vietnamese cooking lessons and lazy canoe trips on the picturesque river.

175 Cua Dai Rd. (3km/1¾ miles from town), Hoi An. © **0510/386-4800.** Fax 0510/386-4900. www. hoianriverresort.com. 63 units. $159 Vietnamese standard; $169 Japanese standard; $189 superior (river view); $259 deluxe (river view). Internet rates available. AE, DC, MC, V. **Amenities:** Restaurant; bar; babysitting; health club; Internet access; outdoor pool; room service; small library. In room: A/C, satellite TV, fridge, minibar.

Life Heritage Resort Hoi An ★ Life Resort is the only resort within walking distance of Hoi An—a good start. It shut down in 2008 for renovations, and the resulting look is fabulous (enough to be included in Condé Nast's 2010 Gold List). The dark-wood furniture and warm accent colors such as orange and dark champagne are a welcome addition to the formerly spartan decorations. Rooms are split-level, with the slightly raised sleeping area done in cool slate tiles. Bathrooms are large, open-plan affairs. Views of the river are good, and deluxe units have quiet sitting areas out front that are perfect for meditation or a respite from the noonday sun. The dining outlets, housed in a faux-colonial block at riverside, are atmospheric; the quiet, air-conditioned cafe has good coffee and desserts. For location alone, this is a great choice.

1 Pham Hong Thai St., Hoi An. ℂ **0510/391-4555.** Fax 0510/391-4515. www.life-resorts.com. 94 units. $159 garden view; $178–$213 junior suite, depending on view; $303–$333 grand suite, depending on view. Internet rates available. AE, MC, V. **Amenities:** 2 restaurants; bar; babysitting; Internet access; outdoor pool; room service. *In room:* A/C, satellite TV, fridge, minibar.

Victoria Hoi An Beach Resort & Spa ★★ It's peace and palm trees just a short ride from ancient Hoi An. The comfortable Victoria, with top-notch amenities and lots of activities, begs at least a few nights' stay. Guest rooms have it right in every detail, from fine rustic decor to in-room sandals and beach robes. Rooms are either the bungalow variety in low-slung buildings at beachside or set in parallel two-story rows to mimic Hoi An's ancient streets—not displeasing, but a bit like a theme park. Prices reflect beachside proximity, but even the least expensive units are laid-back and classy. Some bungalows are decorated in French country style, with canopy beds and wicker; others are unique Japanese rooms, with open-timber construction, bamboo floors, and large tubs. There is a certain flow to this property, from beach to garden, rooms to common spaces, which invites guests to wander; everything's connected by catwalk. Convenient shuttles connect to town frequently, or you can sign up for an excursion by motorcycle with sidecar. Other perks include a private boat for transfer to town, kite-surfing equipment, and cooking courses.

Cua Dai Beach (5km/3 miles from town), Hoi An. ℂ **0510/392-7040.** Fax 0510/392-7041. www.victoria hotels-asia.com. 109 units. $170–$235 double depending on view; $280–$300 suite. **Amenities:** Restaurant; 3 bars; babysitting; children's play area; nice health club; Jacuzzi; large outdoor beachside pool; room service; spa; 2 tennis courts; watersports rental; Wi-Fi; small library. *In room:* A/C, satellite TV, fridge, minibar.

MODERATE

Betel Garden Homestay ★ Homestays are becoming increasingly popular in Vietnam among visitors tired of impersonal hotels, and Betel Garden certainly offers a more personal and friendly environment than your average high-rise hotel. Located a 10-minute walk from the town center, it features services like free Wi-Fi, free use of bicycles, and free laundry, small things that are very pleasing. Rooms are well equipped and comfortable, with shady porches surrounded by a leafy garden. Staff are superfriendly and helpful.

161 Tran Nan Tong St., Hoi An. ℂ **0510/392-4165.** www.betelgardenhomestay.com. 7 units. $45–$80 double. MC, V. **Amenities:** Restaurant; free use of bicycles; outdoor pool; room service. *In room:* A/C, cable TV, hair dryer, minibar, Wi-Fi.

Cua Dai Hotel ★★ Located on the beach road just out of town, the Cua Dai is a good marriage of affordability and comfort. It's easy to settle in here, with the open sitting areas furnished in wicker and the basic but comfy rooms. The very kind staff will make you feel right at home, too, and can help with any travel need. The only drawback is the busy road out front, but all units have double-paned windows and are relatively quiet. Rooms in the new wing in back have fine wooden appointments and creative, local decor; older rooms in the main building are quite large, basic, and comfortable. Cua Dai makes a good base to explore or meet the many expats and long-stay travelers here on cultural or humanitarian missions.

18A Cua Dai St., Hoi An. ℂ **0511/393-6741.** www.cuadai-hotel.com. 24 units. $38–$66 double. MC, V. **Amenities:** Restaurant; bike/motorbike available; outdoor pool. *In room:* A/C, TV, fridge, minibar.

Ha An ★ This colonial-style place with a courtyard entry is just a short walk from town. Rooms in the faux colonial-style building are compact but tidy and comfortable. The Ha An is basically like minihotels everywhere, but slightly more spacious and with nice touches such as rattan furniture and attractive wall hangings. Unique are the DVD players and movies available to borrow. The hotel restaurant is cozy and the staff aims to please. This is one of the best midrange options in town, and a convenient alternative if you can't afford to splash out at neighboring Life Resort.

06–08 Phan Boi Chau St. (just outside the entrance to Life Resort). ℂ **0510/386-3126.** Fax 0510/391-4280. www.haanhotel.com. 24 units. $50–$80 double. MC, V. **Amenities:** Small courtyard restaurant and bar; bikes; Internet; outdoor pool table. *In room:* A/C, TV, DVD player, fridge, minibar.

Vinh Hung I and II ★ Standard rooms in both Vinh Hung I and Vinh Hung II are large, with wooden appointments and cool retro features such as mosquito nets and Chinese latticework balconies. Vinh Hung I, a downtown property set in an old wooden Chinese house, is a Hoi An institution; its two signature rooms are almost museum pieces and are alone worth a visit, but they're not especially luxe or comfortable. Vinh Hung II is a tour-group favorite and often full—and for good reason (the central pool is unique in this category). Popularity means heavy use, though, and the place is getting a bit rough around the edges. The Vinh Hung Resort (see below) is an improvement on an old theme.

Vinh Hung 1: 143 Tran Phu St., Hoi An. ℂ **0510/386-1621.** Fax 0510/387-4094. 6 units. $90–$100 double. Vinh Hung II: Hai Ba Trung St., Hoi An. ℂ **0510/386-3717.** Fax 0510/386-4094. www.vinhhung resort.com. 31 units. $40–$50 double. AE, MC, V. **Amenities:** Restaurant; small outdoor pool. *In room:* A/C, TV.

Vinh Hung Resort ★ Chinese-style entrepreneurs follow the "start small; go big" model, and that's what the folks at Vinh Hung have done. Their small in-town properties (Vinh Hung I and II, above) are popular, so they've turned that income back into this latest project: a self-contained, midlevel resort on Hoi An Island. The area is just a 10- to 15-minute walk from the canal bridge at Hoi An's center. Deluxe rooms are the best bet—large and tidy, with wood floors, Chinese tapestries, and carpeted sitting areas. High-end rooms are enormous, some with Jacuzzis. Ask for one overlooking the wide river. Although services are limited, and everything is a bit compact, Vinh Hung Resort is an affordable and convenient getaway. Rental kayaks make for a unique commute to the town center, or you can catch a ferry to town if you prefer.

111 Ngo Quyen, on Hoi An Island (across the small bridge connecting to town near Bach Dang St. and a short ride to the opposite end of the island), Hoi An. ℂ **0510/391-0577.** Fax 0510/386-4094. www. vinhhungresort.com. 82 units. $75–$105 double (depending on view); $130 suite. AE, MC, V. **Amenities:** Restaurant; 2 bars; babysitting; small fitness center; Internet access; Jacuzzi; 2 outdoor pools; room service; sauna; tennis court; kayak rental (guests can paddle to town). *In room:* A/C, satellite TV, fridge, Internet, minibar.

INEXPENSIVE

Thanh Binh II Hotel ★ The Thanh Binh II is a better deal than its sister property, the **Thanh Binh I** (✆ **0510/391-6364**), which has a good location on Le Loi Street but just basic rooms. This three-story building has a Chinese-inspired lobby, with carved dark-wood furnishings and cafe tables. Upstairs are the very clean, spacious guest rooms. The decor is a color-coordinated mishmash, but there's not a musty smell to be found, the bathrooms are tidy, and the staff is really friendly. For fun, ask about a suite: a huge room that sports wood paneling, carved Chinese-style furnishings, a mosquito net over the bed, a nice balcony with beaded curtains, and, in the center of everything, a large wooden carving of a fat, happy Buddha. Another location, **Thanh Binh III**, is at 98 Ba Trieu St. (✆ **0510/391-6777**).

712 Hai Ba Trung St., Hoi An. ✆ **0510/391-6364.** www.thanhbinhhotel.com.vn. 35 units. $15–$25 double. AE, MC, V. **Amenities:** Restaurant, pool. In room: A/C, TV, fridge, minibar.

Where to Dine

Hoi An is a feast for the stomach as well as for the eyes. Local specialties include *cao lau* (rice noodles with fresh greens, rice crackers, and croutons), *banh bao,* which means "white rose" (dumplings of shrimp in clear rice dough), and savory fried wontons. Good, fresh seafood is available everywhere (don't miss the morning market). There are some new high-end options in town alongside the popular standbys, and each of the resorts has its own fine dining (see "Where to Stay," above).

The riverfront road, **Bach Dang,** has become the de facto "restaurant row," where you're sure to be besieged by friendly but persistent touts who will literally try to drag you into their restaurants. Since many places here are comparable in price and cuisine (fried rice and noodles), it's sometimes fun to let the restaurant choose you. **Note:** If you do eat on Bach Dang but you'd like a quieter meal, choose a table a bit off the street and say a calm "no, thank you" to the many young Tiger Balm and chewing gum salesmen.

EXPENSIVE

Brother's Café ★★★ VIETNAMESE Serving fine Vietnamese fare, Brother's Café is the town's top choice for both cuisine and atmosphere. A bland streetside facade gives way to the lush garden sanctuary formed by this grand U-shaped colonial by the river. Indoor seating is upscale Indochina of a bygone era, while the courtyard is dotted with canvas umbrellas to shade you on a balmy afternoon. The food is gourmet Vietnamese at its finest, with changing daily set menus and great specials; be sure to ask for a recommendation. It's a good place to try local items such as White Rose (a light Vietnamese ravioli) or *cao lao* noodles. Groups can order family-style. Ask the friendly staff about the cooking school here.

27-29 Pham Boi Chau St. ✆ **0510/391-4150.** Main courses $8–$20. AE, MC, V. Daily 7am–11pm.

Mango Rooms ★★ INTERNATIONAL This is the hippest little restaurant between Ho Chi Minh and Hanoi. Owner and chef Duc spent his formative years in Texas before earning his stripes in hotels and fine-dining establishments. He brings to Hoi An his own blend of cuisines, putting words like *salsa* and Vietnamese *nuoc mam* (fish sauce) in jarring juxtaposition, and serving up cool combinations of California cuisine, down-home barbecue, and Pacific Rim—all stylishly presented in a fashion that would make the grade among the finest bistros of New York or San Francisco. Try the likes of La Tropicana, a chicken breast with lemon grass and garlic; the "Asian sins" of rice noodles pan-fried with vegetables, garlic, onion, and sweet basil;

or seared tuna in rice paper. There are fresh-fish specials daily. The drinks list is long and the cocktails are divine. Try the delicious sticky rice with mango for dessert.

111 Nguyen Thai Hoc (with an entrance on riverside Bach Dang just across from Tam Tam Café). © **0510/391-0839.** Main courses 200,000VND–300,000VND. No credit cards. Daily 8am–midnight.

MODERATE

Café des Amis ★★ VIETNAMESE What's on the menu? There isn't one. It's your choice of set menu—seafood, meat, or vegetarian—and the details are, well, a surprise. And the surprise is always good—one of the best meals in Vietnam (just read the straight dope from the many people who sign the lengthy guest book). You might enjoy a leisurely dinner of savory clear soup, fried wontons with shrimp, broiled fish, stuffed calamari, and scallops on the half shell. Sit back and surrender yourself to the surprises of the effusive Mr. Kim and his attentive staff. Mr. Kim is a practiced raconteur with rich material from his years as a taster for the army and a chef for heads of state. He is careful to explain the intricacies of each dish and even demonstrates how to eat some of the more unique entrees. A meal here makes for a memorable evening.

52 Bach Dang St. © **0510/386-1616.** Set menu 120,000VND–150,000VND. No credit cards. Daily 6am–10pm.

Cargo Club ★ INTERNATIONAL This atmospheric place—a unique, open-air patisserie and French cafe—is part of Ms. Vy's Hoi An empire, which includes the Mermaid and Morning Glory restaurants (p. 302) and the Cua Dai Hotel (p. 298). The stylish storefront serves light meals in a casual lounge, while upstairs is a refined restaurant specializing in contemporary Vietnamese cuisine. Sandwiches are made from fresh bread baked on-site. Seafood dishes abound, such as the crab in five spices or jumbo shrimp with tamarind sauce. Curries and good veggie dishes round out a good, affordable menu. If you dine upstairs, you can sit on the cool balcony overlooking the river.

107-109 Nguyen Thai Hoc St. © **0510/391-1227.** www.restaurant-hoian.com. Main courses 42,000VND–195,000VND. MC, V. Daily 7:30am–11pm.

Hoi An Hai San ★★ VIETNAMESE/CONTINENTAL *Hai-san* means "seafood" in Vietnamese and "hello" in Swedish. The owners, Swedish expat Calle and his Vietnamese wife, Hoa, offer just that: "Hello, seafood!" This is one of the few spots on Bach Dang that won't try to drag you in—instead, it's the food that brings folks here. Everything's good: grilled tuna with ginger, garlic, and lemon grass, served in a light coconut milk; sea scallops in cream sauce, a favorite; and Swedish lingonberry ice cream. It's a good place to linger and watch the goings-on on busy Bach Dang.

64 Bach Dang St. © **0510/386-1652.** Main courses 40,000VND–250,000VND. No credit cards. Daily 10am–10pm.

Miss Ly (aka Cafeteria 22) ★ VIETNAMESE You're greeted here by the kind proprietor herself, always dressed to the nines and welcoming. The menu is limited, but that means everything is always fresh in this hole-in-the-wall cafe in the heart of the old town. It's the best place in Hoi An to try the town's famous fried wontons, a rice pastry stuffed with meat, shrimp, and onion and topped with Miss Ly's special sauce, onion, and tomato—messy and delicious. Since Ly has been at it for many years now, she has just the right formula. There's nothing fancy here, and that's just the appeal for folks who tire easily of trumped-up atmosphere and overpriced versions of local fare. Come meet Ly and try the real deal.

22 Nguyen Hue St. © **0510/386-1603.** Main courses 45,000VND–100,000VND. No credit cards. Daily 8am–11pm.

Morning Glory ★★★ VIETNAMESE   Set in a French-style colonial building in the heart of Hoi An's old district, this low-key eatery serves Vietnamese street food with a twist: It's as healthy and fresh as it is authentic. The menu includes tips from Ms. Vy on the health properties of ingredients, and recommendations (for example, for cooling the body in hot weather, try the traditional dessert Che, made with soft tofu and ginger syrup). We highly recommend the grilled pork with fresh rice paper, the *banh xeo* (crepe-style pancakes stuffed with shrimp, bean sprouts, and other veggies), the "caramel" mackerel in a clay pot, and the whole grilled trout—grilled and smothered in lemon grass, chile peppers, lime, and peanuts, it is perfection. It's not the cheapest meal in town, but not a megasplurge either. If you like what you eat, stick around and take a **cooking class**—a chance to bring some of Vietnam home to your kitchen.

106 Nguyen Thai Hoc St. © **0510/3241-555.** www.restaurant-hoian.com. Main courses 45,000VND–195,000VND. MC, V. Daily 9am–10pm.

Red Bridge ★★ 🎁 VIETNAMESE   In an idyllic riverside location a couple of kilometers from the town center, this place is definitely worth tracking down, both for its tempting menu and for the opportunity to join an afternoon cookery class. Call for a pickup in town at midday and enjoy the 20-minute boat cruise to the restaurant, then settle into one of three open-air pavilions to scan the options. These include *banh xeo* (crispy Hoi An pancakes) or countryside soups for starters, lemon grass beef or seafood hot pot for mains. Take your swimsuit, as there's a decent pool for guests' use. Note that although the restaurant is open for lunch daily, dinner is by appointment only.

Thon 4, Cam Thanh, Hoi An. © **0510/393-3222.** www.visithoian.com/redbridge. Main courses 80,000VND–140,000VND. MC, V. Daily 11:30am–2:30pm.

Tam-Tam Café ★★ ITALIAN/CONTINENTAL/VIETNAMESE   Tam-Tam is both a cozy restaurant and a laid-back bar. The brainchild of three French expats, it is set in a historic building and serves tasty, familiar food. The decor is authentic local style, with hanging bamboo lamps, a high ceiling, and fantastic wooden figurines. The dinner menu, served in a separate room with checkered tablecloths, is simple—generous portions of homemade pastas, steaks, and salads—but the food is delicious. Desserts include flambéed crepes, sorbet, and hot chocolate. There are two barrooms; the bigger one to the left of the entry has a pool table, a book-swap shelf, and comfortable lounge chairs and sofas—it's the place to hang out in Hoi An. The extensive drinks menu features all kinds of bang-for-the-buck rum specials. There's even a small counter on the balcony where you can sip a cocktail and watch life go by on the street below. Even if it's just for a coffee, don't miss this place.

110 Nguyen Thai Hoc St., 2nd Floor. © **0510/386-2212.** Main courses 35,000VND–170,000VND. AE, MC, V. Daily 24 hr.

INEXPENSIVE

Mermaid (Nhu Y) Restaurant ★★ VIETNAMESE   This quiet spot in the heart of downtown is an unassuming, ivy-draped storefront that serves some of the best authentic Vietnamese food in town (for next to nothing). The tuna filet, cooked in a banana leaf with turmeric, is scrumptious; the spring rolls are light and fresh, with a whole jumbo shrimp in each; and the Mermaid serves a most unique dish called white eggplant: It's eggplant covered in spring onion, garlic, and chile, and then pressed, sliced, and served in a light oil.

02 Tran Phu St. © **0510/3861-527.** www.restaurant-hoian.com. Main courses 20,000VND–70,000VND. No credit cards. Daily 10am–10pm.

Wan Lu ★ VIETNAMESE   It's an open-air place, and the atmosphere is a little rough, but it serves a nice selection of local favorites, all for next to nothing. Try the special, *cao lao*, a thick but tender white noodle in light soy with fresh vegetables, garnishes, and croutons. This is where the locals eat it—but if it's not your cup of tea, then you're out less than a dollar. The portions are big and everything's authentic, right down to the kindness in this little mom-and-pop joint. There are no touts here; it's the food that brings 'em in.

27 Tran Phu St. © **0510/386-1212.** Main courses 8,000VND–25,000VND. No credit cards. Daily 7am–9pm.

What to See & Do

Hoi An is like a living museum; in fact, the atmosphere in the old town smacks of a theme park, which puts many visitors off. Nevertheless, the whole town is an attraction, its narrow streets buzzing with open-air crafts shops, woodworkers, and carvers based in lovely historic buildings. Most Hoi An buildings have been lovingly restored and transformed into cafes, art galleries, and silk and souvenir shops, while retaining their dignity. If you're an artist, bring your sketch pad and watercolors; photographers, bring plenty of memory cards. Tran Phu and Nguyen Thai Hoc streets are crowded with the shops of the original Chinese merchants and clan associations.

WORLD CULTURAL HERITAGE SIGHTS

The **Hoi An World Cultural Heritage Organization** (www.hoianworldheritage. org.vn/en) has the dilemma of financing restorations and maintaining the old portions of the town. It sells a 75,000VND ticket that allows limited admission to the sights within the old town, each of which is listed below. "Limited" means a "one from column A, one from column B" formula. That is, one ticket gets you one of the three museums, one of the two assembly halls, one of the four old houses, plus a choice of the tiny temple on the Japanese Covered Bridge or the Quan Cong Temple, plus the local handicrafts workshop. In order to see everything, you'd have to purchase four tickets, though for most people, one is enough (look for those locations with the most stars to see the most interesting in each category). See "Visitor Information & Tours," earlier in this chapter, for where to buy tickets.

Museums

Museum of History and Culture ★   This tottering building, erected in 1653, houses works that cover 2,000 years of Hoi An history, from Cham relics to ancient ceramics and photos of local architecture. The English-language explanations are scanty. If you're seeing only one museum, make it the Museum of Trade Ceramics (see below). One interesting tidbit: The name Hoi An literally means "water convergence" and "peace."

7 Nguyen Hue St. Daily 7am–6pm.

Museum of Trade Ceramics ★★★   Located in a traditional house, this museum describes the origins of Hoi An as a trade port and displays its most prominent trade items. Objects are from the 13th to the 17th century and include Chinese and Thai works as well. While many of the exhibits are in fragments, the museum does have very thorough descriptions in English, giving you a real sense of the town's origins and history. Furthermore, the architecture and renovations of the house are thoroughly explained, and you're free to wander through its two floors, courtyard, and anteroom. After all the scattered explanations at the other historic houses, you'll finally get a sense of what Hoi An architecture is all about.

80 Tran Phu St. Daily 7am–6pm.

Sa Huynh Culture Museum ★ After local farmers around Hoi An dug up some strange-looking pottery, archaeologists identified 53 sites where a pre-Cham people, called the Sa Huynh, buried their dead in ceramic jars. The two-room display here includes some of the burial jars, beaded ornaments, pottery vessels, and iron tools and weapons that have been uncovered. English descriptions are sketchy. Upstairs, the little-visited Museum of the Revolution includes such intriguing items as the umbrella "which Mr. Truong Munh Luong used for acting a fortune-teller to act revolution from 1965 to 1967." Huh? This is for connoisseurs only.

149 Tran Phu St. Daily 8am–6pm.

Old Houses

Old House of Phun Hung ★ This private house, constructed in 1780, comprises two floors of various architectural influences. The first floor's central roof is four-sided, showing Japanese influence, while the upstairs balcony has a Chinese rounded "turtle shell" roof with carved beam supports. The house has weathered many floods; in 1964, during a particularly bad bout, its third floor served as a refuge for other town families. The upstairs is outfitted with a trapdoor for moving furniture rapidly to safety. Although tour guides at every house make such claims, the family really does seem to live here.

4 Nguyen Thi Minh Khai St. Daily 7am–6pm.

Old House of Tan Ky ★ There have been either five or seven generations of Tans living here, depending on whom you speak with. Built more than 200 years ago, the four small rooms are crammed with dark-wood antiques. The room closest to the street was for greeting visiting merchants. Farther in are the living room, then the courtyard, and, to the back, the bedroom. The first three are open to the public. A guide, who will greet you at the door, will hasten to explain how the house is a perfect melding of three architectural styles: ornate Chinese detailing on some curved roof beams, a Japanese peaked roof, and a simple Vietnamese cross-hatch roof support. The mosaic decorations on the wall and furniture are aged, intricate, and amazing. This is the most popular of the old houses, so visit early or late in the day to avoid the crowds.

101 Nguyen Thai Hoc St. Daily 7am–6pm.

Tran Family Home and Chapel ★★★ In 1802, a civil service mandarin named Tran Tu Nhuc built a family home and chapel to worship his ancestors. A favorite of Viet Emperor Gia Long, he was sent to China as an ambassador, and his home reflects his high status. Elegantly designed with original Chinese antiques and royal gifts such as swords, two parts of the home are open to the public: a drawing room and the ancestral chapel. The house does a splendid job of conveying all that is interesting about these people and their period; it has even been featured in a fashion magazine. The drawing room has three sections of sliding doors: the left for men, the right for women, and the center, open only at Tet and other festivals, for dead ancestors to return home. The ancestral altar in the inner room has small boxes behind it containing relics and a biography of the deceased; their pictures hang, a little spookily, to the right of the altar. A 250-year-old book with the family history resides on a table to the right of the altar. In back of the house are a row of plants, each buried with the placenta and umbilical cord of a family child, so that the child will never forget its home. As if it could.

21 Le Loi St. (at corner of Phan Chu Trinh St.). Daily 7am–6pm.

Assembly Halls
Cantonese Assembly Hall (Quang Trieu/Guangzhou Assembly Hall) Built in 1885, this hall is quite ornate and colorful. All of the building materials were brought here from China and then reassembled. The center garden sports a fountain with a dragon made of chipped pottery. Inside, look for the statues depicting scenes from famous Cantonese operas and, in the rooms to each side, the ancestral tablets of generations past.

176 Tran Phu St. Daily 7am–6pm.

Fukian Assembly Hall (Phuc Kien) ★ This is the grandest of the assembly halls, built in 1697 by Chinese merchants from Fukian Province. It is a showpiece of classical Chinese architecture, at least after you pass the first gate, which was added in 1975. It's loaded with animal themes: The fish in the mosaic fountain symbolizes scholarly achievement, the unicorn flanking the ascending stairs symbolizes wisdom, the dragon symbolizes power, the turtle symbolizes longevity, and the phoenix symbolizes nobility. The main temple is dedicated to Thien Hau, goddess of the sea, on the main altar. To the left of her is Thuan Phong Nhi, a goddess who can hear ships within a range of thousands of miles; on the right is Thien Ly Nhan, who can see them. Go around the altar for a view of a fantastic detailed miniature boat. There are two altars to the rear of the temple, the one on the left honoring a god of prosperity and the one on the right honoring a goddess of fertility. The goddess of fertility is often visited by local couples hoping for children. She is flanked by 12 fairies or midwives, each responsible for one of a baby's functions: smiling, sleeping, eating, and so forth.

46 Tran Phu St. Daily 7am–6pm.

More World Cultural Heritage Sights
Japanese Covered Bridge ★★★ The name of this bridge in Vietnamese, Lai Vien Kieu, means "Pagoda in Japan." No one is quite sure who first built it in the early 1600s (it has since been renovated several times), but it is usually attributed to Hoi An's Japanese community. The dog flanking one end and the monkey at the other were considered sacred animals by the ancient Japanese. A guide claimed this was because most Japanese emperors were born in the Asian zodiac year of either the monkey or the dog, though we later read that perhaps the animals' presence means construction began in the year of the dog and was completed in the year of the monkey. The small temple inside is dedicated to Tran Vo Bac De, god of the north, beloved (or cursed) by sailors because he controls the weather. There's a tiny temple here that requires an admission ticket, but the Quan Cong Temple (below) throws up more of interest.

At the west end of Tran Phu St.

Quan Cong Temple ★ This temple was built in the early 1600s to honor a famous Chin Dynasty general. Highlights inside are two gargantuan 3m (10-ft.) wooden statues flanking the main altar, one of Quan Cong's protector and one of his adopted son. They are both fearsome and impressive. The temple was reportedly a stop for merchants who came in from the nearby river to pay their respects and pray for the general's attributes of loyalty, bravery, and virtue.

24 Tran Phu St. (at corner of Nguyen Hue). Daily 7am–6pm.

Handicraft Workshop ★   Included in the Hoi An Old Town ticket price is a visit to this workshop, where locals are busy making silk lanterns and embroidering panels to show visitors the traditional process of such crafts. It's located in a 200-year-old Chinese trading house, and there are a couple of cultural performances each day at 10:15am and 3:15pm, featuring traditional musicians and dancers.

9 Nguyen Thai Hoc. *C* **0510/391-0216.** Daily 7am–6pm.

OTHER ATTRACTIONS

Central Market ★★   If the old town feels a bit like a tourist trap, this is the place to escape to, as it's one of the most colorful and authentic fresh markets in the entire country. There are endless stalls of exotic foodstuffs and services, plus a special shed for silk tailoring at the east end (these tailors charge much less than the ones along Le Loi). Check out the ladies selling spices—curries, chile powders, cinnamon, peppercorns, and especially saffron. But don't buy from the first woman you see; the stuff gets cheaper the deeper you go into the market. Walk out to the docks to see activity there (best early in the morning), but be careful of fish flying through the air, and stand back from the furious bargaining (best before 7am).

At Nguyen Hue and Tran Phu sts. along the Thu Bon River, on the southeast side of town.

Chinese Assembly Hall ★   This hall was built in 1740 as a meeting place for all of the resident Chinese, regardless of their native province.

64 Tran Phu St. Daily 8am–5pm.

Hainan Assembly Hall   The Chinese merchants from Hainan Island, in the South China Sea east of Danang, built this hall. Although it is newer than most and is mainly made of concrete, it is still worth a visit.

178 Nguyen Duy Hieu St. Daily 8am–5pm.

House of Hoi An Traditional Handicraft ★★   This is basically a silk shop with an interesting gimmick: On the first floor, you can see a 17th-century silk loom and a working, machine-powered cotton one. On the second floor, you can see where silk comes from: There are trays of silkworms feeding, then a rack of worms incubating, and then a tub of hot water where the pupae's downy covering is rinsed off and then pulled, strand by strand, onto a large skein. It's cool. The shop has a good selection of silks, both fine and raw, in many colors and weights good for clothing and for home interiors.

41 Le Loi St. Daily 8am–5pm.

Shopping

Southeast Asia is packed with would-be Buddhists, travelers on a real spiritual mission espousing lives of detachment from material desires. However, even these folks can't resist the "one suit, two shirts, trousers, and a tie package" when they leave Hoi An. Shopaholics just wander the streets in a daze, mesmerized by all the goodies on display.

Hoi An is a silk mecca. The quality and selection are the best in the country, and you'll have more peace and quiet at fittings here than in Hanoi. **Silk suits** are made to order within 24 hours for about $50 to $100, though if you give them longer you will find the quality is better; **cashmere wool suits** are around $85. There are countless shops, and the tailoring is all about the same quality and speed. A good way to choose a shop is by what you see out front—if you spot a style you like, it will help with the ordering. Make sure you take the time to specify your style, down to the stitch (it can come back looking pretty cheap without specifics). Try any of the shops along Le Loi; to recommend one in particular would be like choosing one snowflake over another. The tailoring is very fast, but not always great, so plan to have two or three fittings. Be choosy about your cloth, or go to the market and haggle over it yourself (try **Hoi An Cloth Market** at 1 Tran Phu St.). It's not a bad idea to bring an actual suit or piece of clothing that you'd like to have copied. *Tip:* Get measurements from friends and relatives for good gifts.

If you have a hard time choosing from among the many budget tailors, consider **Yaly Couture** (47 Nguyen Thai Hoc St.; ✆ **0510/391-0474**). It has higher prices, but its quality comes with more of a guarantee.

After shopping for your new suit, seek out one of the town's skilled cobblers, who make **custom shoes** at affordable rates. You'll find them near the market on Tran Phu Street.

Tran Phu Street is also lined with **art galleries** and vendors of good **pottery** and **carved wood.** Along the river, lots of places sell blue-and-white **ceramics** and other handicrafts. Try **Reaching Out** (103 Nguyen Thai Hoc St.; ✆ **0510/386-2460**), a fair-trade gift shop that employs artisans with disabilities. The nearby **Bambou Company** (96 Nguyen Thai Hoc St.) produces unique (Western-size) T-shirts of local theme and design. Regardless of how cumbersome your finds are—like those lovely **Chinese lanterns**—shopkeepers are masters at packing goods for travel and to fit in your luggage, and will do so before you've even agreed on a price or decided to buy. Haggle hard.

Hoi An After Dark

For the most part, Hoi An is a town that sleeps early, but there are a few good nightspots. **Tam-Tam Café** (p. 302) is a popular spot for travelers, expats, and locals. Another late-night tourist hangout, **Hai's Scout Café** (98 Nguyen Thai Hoc St.; ✆ **0510/386-3210**), features your standard bar drinks, cappuccino, and great baked treats. **Treat's Café** (158 Tran Phu St.; ✆ **0510/386-1125**) is usually hopping; it even has a pool table and a guillotine (for show, of course). The owners of Treat's also run **Same Same Not Different Bar** (93 Tran Hung Dao; ✆ **0510/386-2278**).

The **Yellow Star Café** (73 Nguyen Thai Hoc St.; ✆ **0510/391-0430**) serves drinks, yummy Western food, and desserts like lemon tart, while the next-door **ChamPa** (75 Nguyen Thai Hoc St.; ✆ **0510/386-2974**) has a cozy atmosphere, good wine, and a pool table. **Lounge Bar** (102 Nguyen Thai Hoc St.; ✆ **0510/3910-480**) is a chic, laid-back stop, while nearby **Mango Rooms** (111 Nguyen Thai Hoc St.; ✆ **0510/391-0839**) is similarly hip and mellow.

Side Trips from Hoi An

CUA DAI BEACH ★★

Cua Dai Beach is a 25-minute bike ride from Hoi An on a busy road with views of lagoons, rice paddies, and stilt houses. Take Tran Hung Dao Street to Cua Dai Street to the east of town and follow it for 3km (1¾ miles). The beach is thin and crowded with hawkers, but there are cozy deck chairs (for a small fee). The sand, surf, and setting, with views of the nearby Cham Islands, are worth the trip. In season (Mar–Sept), tour companies will tout boat excursions to the **Cham Islands,** a group of seven islands about 13km (8 miles) east of Hoi An; most people join a snorkeling trip for about $20 to $30 a head. Contact the tourist cafes in town for details. Boat trips on the Thu Bon River are another option.

MY SON ★★

My Son, some 40km (25 miles) from Hoi An and 71km (44 miles) from Danang, is an important temple complex of the Cham people, a once-powerful Hindu empire. The temples were constructed as a religious center for citizens of the Cham capital, Danang, from the 7th to the 12th century during the height of Cham supremacy. My Son (pronounced *Mee Sun*) might also have been used as a burial site for Cham kings after cremation. Originally, there were more than 70 towers and monuments at the site, but bombing during the war with the U.S. (the Viet Cong used My Son as a munitions warehouse) has sadly reduced many to rubble. Additionally, much of the statuary has been removed to the Cham Museum in Danang. The complex is a very serene and spiritual setting, however, and what does remain is powerful and evocative. It's not hard to imagine what a wonder My Son must once have been.

Much of what remains today are structures built or renovated during the 10th century, when the cult of Shiva, founder and protector of the kingdom, was predominant in the Cham court. Each group had at least the following structures: a *kalan,* or main tower; a **gate tower** in front of that, with two entrances; a *mandapa,* or meditation hall; and a **repository building** for offerings. Some have towers sheltering stelae with kingly epitaphs. A brick wall encircles the compound.

Architecturally, the temple complex shows Indian influences. Each temple grouping is a microcosm of the world. The foundations are earth, the square bases are the temple itself, and the pointed roofs symbolize the heavens. The entrance of the main tower faces east, and surrounding smaller towers represent each continent. A trench, representing the oceans, surrounds each group. Vietnamese architecture is represented in decorative patterns and boat-shaped roofs.

Group A originally had 13 towers. A-1, the main tower, was a 21m-high (69-ft.) masterpiece before it was destroyed in 1969. Group B bears the marks of Indian and Indonesian influence. Note that B-6 holds a water repository for statue-washing ceremonies. Its roof is carved with an image of the god Vishnu sitting beneath a 13-headed snake god, or naga. Group C generally followed an earlier architectural style called Hoa Lai, which predominated from the 8th to the beginning of the 9th century. Groups G and H were the last to be built, around the end of the 13th century.

Arrange a half-day trip to My Son with any tourist agent in Hoi An (see "Visitor Information & Tours," earlier in this section). Entrance to the site is 75,000VND; a private half-day tour with a guide is around $40 per person for two people. The half-day seat-in-coach tour by **Sinh Café** costs about $5 per person and is nothing more than a ride here, with no explanations. Less frequent tours also depart from Danang.

NHA TRANG ★

Welcome to Vietnam's Ocean City. The capital of Khanh Hoa Province, Nha Trang has a full-time population of about 300,000, but it far exceeds that with the heavy local and international tourist influx, especially in summer. While it's not a particularly charming town, the surf isn't bad and the beach is breathtaking, with views of more than 20 surrounding islands. There is a growing collection of high-end hotels

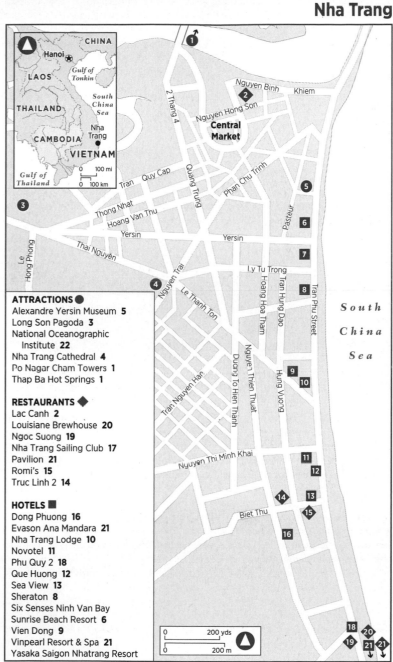

ATTRACTIONS ●
Alexandre Yersin Museum **5**
Long Son Pagoda **3**
National Oceanographic
   Institute **22**
Nha Trang Cathedral **4**
Po Nagar Cham Towers **1**
Thap Ba Hot Springs **1**

RESTAURANTS ◆
Lac Canh **2**
Louisiane Brewhouse **20**
Ngoc Suong **19**
Nha Trang Sailing Club **17**
Pavilion **21**
Romi's **15**
Truc Linh 2 **14**

HOTELS ■
Dong Phuong **16**
Evason Ana Mandara **21**
Nha Trang Lodge **10**
Novotel **11**
Phu Quy 2 **18**
Que Huong **12**
Sea View **13**
Sheraton **8**
Six Senses Ninh Van Bay
Sunrise Beach Resort **6**
Vien Dong **9**
Vinpearl Resort & Spa **21**
Yasaka Saigon Nhatrang Resort

5

VIETNAM | Nha Trang

and resorts here, as well as good budget options. Dining is all about fresh seafood, and the choice of restaurants is huge.

Nha Trang is also a very popular vacation spot for Vietnamese; especially in the summer months, the town is chockablock with tourists and young kids out cruising the strip on motorbikes—a bit much for folks looking to relax. It's a fine place to spend 2 or 3 days frolicking in the surf, snorkeling and diving, or taking a cruise around the nearby islands.

Culturally, there are a few things to keep you occupied. The **Pasteur Institute** offers a glimpse into the life and work of one of Vietnam's most famous expats; also interesting are the **Long Son Pagoda, Nha Trang Cathedral,** and the well preserved **Po Nagar Cham Temple.**

If you're traveling in the off season, from October to March, note that the surf is far too rough for swimming and sports—you might want to rethink stopping at Nha Trang at all.

Getting There

BY PLANE Nha Trang is 1,350km (839 miles) from Hanoi and 450km (280 miles) from Ho Chi Minh City (Saigon). There are daily connections on **Vietnam Airlines** (in Nha Trang at 91 Nguyen Thien Thuat St.; © **058/382-6768**). The Nha Trang airport, once in the center of town, has traded places with a larger military facility and is now called **Cam Ranh Airport,** some 35km (22 miles) south of town. The 30-minute taxi ride costs around 250,000VND, while irregular shuttle buses cover the trip for 40,000VND. The larger resorts offer more affordable group connections or limousine service.

BY TRAIN Nha Trang, a stop on the *Reunification Express,* is 12 hours from Ho Chi Minh City (Saigon) on a soft-sleeper for 340,000VND, and 20 hours from Hanoi for 954,000VND. Buy your ticket at least a day in advance at the Nha Trang train station, at 17 Thai Nguyen St. (© **058/382-2113**), or from any travel agent. There is a convenient overnight connection with Ho Chi Minh.

BY CAR/BUS If you drive from Hoi An to Nha Trang, the 10-hour trip will cost about $120. An arduous 12-hour bus or minibus ride with an open tour bus will cost only $10. There are overnight schedules to Ho Chi Minh City and Hoi An; the trip is long and tiring, but it's a good option if you're short on time and don't want to waste your precious daylight hours looking out the window of a tour bus.

Getting Around

The main street in Nha Trang, **Tran Phu,** runs along a 4km (2½-mile) beach lined with the myriad hotels and beach attractions that make the town center. **Biet Thu Street,** perpendicular to Tran Phu, is where you'll find lots of budget hotels, cheap restaurants, and tour operators.

Taxis tend to congregate around the major hotels. Renting a **bicycle** from your hotel for around 30,000VND a day is a good option, as are cyclos, which you can rent for about $3 per hour from your hotel. A **cyclo** ride across town will cost about 15,000VND. In addition, **motorcycle taxis** can be had for $2 to $3 per hour and on short trips starting at 10,000VND. *Warning:* Nha Trang cyclo and motorbike taxi riders are notorious for their extracurricular activities as pimps and drug dealers, especially after dark.

Visitor Information & Tours

All hotels in Nha Trang can book city tours, day boat trips, or onward travel to your next destination.

One-day city tours visit Long Son Pagoda, the Oceanographic Institute, and the Po Nagar Cham Towers. Country tours take you to Ba Ho Waterfall and secluded Doc Let Beach, as well as Monkey Island. *Important:* No matter what anyone tells you, Monkey Island is not worth the trip, especially if you like animals and don't like wasting your time (you can just buy a "monkeys on bikes" postcard and be done with it).

For bus tickets and connection to Dalat, contact **TM Brothers Café** (22B Tran Hung Dao St.; ✆ **058/381-4556**), **Sinh Café** (2A Biet Thu St.; ✆ **058/352-2982**), or **Khanh Hoa Tourism** (1 Tran Hung Dao St.; ✆ **058/352-6753**).

[Fast FACTS] NHA TRANG

Currency Exchange The local **Vietcombank** branch is at 17 Quang Trung St. (✆ **058/382-1483**). Hours are 7:30 to 11am and 1:30 to 4pm. It offers the usual currency and traveler's-check exchange, as well as credit card cash advances. Along Biet Thu, some of the tour operators will cash traveler's checks and change money—rates are the same as at the bank (except for a small service fee), and they're open longer hours.

Internet Access Biet Thu has a cluster of Internet cafes that charge around 6,000VND per hour, and most budget hotels offer free Wi-Fi.

Mail The main post office is at 4 Le Loi St. (✆ **058/382-3866**). Hours are Monday through Saturday from 6:30am to 10pm. **DHL** express services and Internet access are available. There is another branch at 50 Le Thanh Ton St.

Telephones The city code for Nha Trang is **058**.

Where to Stay

There are hundreds of hotels in Nha Trang, most quite basic and geared to the summer influx of Vietnamese vacationers. At the top end, the Evason Ana Mandara Resort (see below) and its sister property, the Six Senses Ninh Van Bay, stand in a class of their own. New places are opening constantly, and the keen competition ensures that rates are very competitive and there are some great deals to be found at all levels.

VERY EXPENSIVE

Evason Ana Mandara ★★★ ☺ One of the finest resorts in the region, the Ana Mandara is a real seaside dreamscape. The name means "beautiful home" in the Cham language, and, though it comes with a high price tag, the hospitality extended here is quite sincere. The staff is very kind, and such personalized service in a beautiful beachside setting, with fine dining and a host of activities, means you won't want to leave. There's a large, luxurious pool and a spa with outdoor massage areas, but it's the little things that make this resort special: in-room touches such as slippers and umbrellas, the basin of rainwater on your private veranda for rinsing sandy feet, and the burning incense in the open-air lobby. Each room is double-height and airy with wood beams, rattan ceiling, and stylish furniture. Bathrooms have a large window facing a private outdoor enclosure, like your own Zen garden. Thirty-six units face the beach, while others look onto a courtyard with exotic plants. The Pavilion (p. 315) has the best food and atmosphere in town; the beachside eatery is tops, too. The resort offers lots of great excursions, including informative market tours where guests can learn about Vietnam cuisine and find out where it all comes from. Tai chi and yoga classes are also available.

Beachside, off Tran Phu Blvd., Nha Trang. ✆ **058/352-2222.** Fax 058/352-5828. www.sixsenses.com. 74 units. $248–$447 double; $477 Ana Mandara suite. AE, DC, MC, V. **Amenities:** 2 restaurants; 2 bars; concierge; health club; Jacuzzi; 2 large outdoor pools w/hot tub; room service; sauna; smoke-free rooms; fine spa; tennis court; watersports rentals; library w/games. *In room:* A/C, satellite TV/DVD, fridge, hair dryer, free Internet, minibar.

Six Senses Ninh Van Bay ★★★ This cluster of private villas, hidden in a secluded cove in Ninh Van Bay to the northeast of the city, can be reached only by boat and is as good as it gets in Nha Trang. Each three-room villa has its own private pool, outdoor shower, and butler, and the Hideaway premise to keep natural surroundings intact means you almost feel marooned. All units at this resort, a sister to Evason Ana Mandara (see above), share a pristine beach, but it's the surrounding forest and mountains that make the place special. Choose a villa on the beach, on the hillside, or perched on huge boulders on the water. The spa menu is extensive, and the service is top-notch. It's a great place for a honeymoon—or to get hitched, as there's a wedding chapel on-site. *A word of warning:* Once you're here, it's hard to leave. No boats run after dark, and there's only one restaurant and bar. Not the place for partygoers, but a nice place to disappear for a day or two.

Ninh Van Bay, Ninh Hoa, north of Nha Trang. ✆ **058/372-8222.** Fax 058/372-8223. www.sixsenses. com. 58 units. $688–$1,104 villa; $2,240 presidential suite. AE, DC, MC, V. **Amenities:** 3 restaurants; 2 bars; health club; Internet access; Jacuzzi; outdoor pool; room service; sauna; smoke-free rooms; fine spa; tennis court; watersports rentals; library. *In villa:* A/C, satellite TV/DVD, fridge, hair dryer, free Internet, minibar.

VinPearl Resort & Spa ★ ☺ This flashy new resort is geared mostly to Asian tourists, but might also appeal to Western families with active kids, as there's a huge amusement park here too (with free access to guests). It is on Hong Tre (Bamboo Island), just off the coast of Nha Trang, and everything on the island, from construction materials to the very water that comes out of the taps, is transported by large tankers—an incredible undertaking. Guests connect via a fleet of sturdy, high-speed crafts or by a new, 3,320m-long (10,900-ft.) cable car that offers dramatic views. Rooms are large and comfortable, though plain. The resort is designed in an arc around the vast central pool, which at 5,700 sq. m (61,350 sq. ft.) is reputedly the largest in Southeast Asia, with fun slides, meandering river areas, and bridges, all overlooking a secluded bay. The VinPearl offers lots of activities, group trips, a top-notch watersports facility, a scuba school, and a variety of classes, from yoga to "crazy cricket" (you have to ask what it is). Dining is familiar but uninspired. The resort is so far a favorite with wealthy Vietnamese weekenders and Korean group tours, but time will tell if Westerners go for it too.

Hon Tre Island, Nha Trang. Connect by boat or cable car from the pier on beachside Tran Phu, just south of Evason Ana Mandara. ✆ **058/359-8188.** Fax 058/359-8199. www.vinpearlland.com. 485 units. $235–$280 double (depending on view); $425 junior suite; $2,265 presidential suite. AE, MC, V. **Amenities:** 2 restaurants; 3 bars; babysitting; children's center; concierge; health club; Internet access; Jacuzzi; enormous outdoor pool; room service; sauna; smoke-free rooms; luxe Shiseido Spa; tennis courts; extensive watersports rental. *In room:* A/C, satellite TV, fridge, hair dryer, minibar, Wi-Fi.

EXPENSIVE

Sheraton ★★ ☺ With a choice location overlooking the gorgeous swath of beach, this new Sheraton has muscled in among other top-end hotels and will offer stiff competition with its modern design, comprehensive facilities, and efficient service. Though deluxe rooms are impressive enough, with eye-pleasing decor of yellow and beige and deep mattresses on the bed, it's worth considering an upgrade to a club room or suite, where you'll enjoy advantages such as superior views, better bathroom amenities, access to the Club Lounge for complimentary breakfast, and free use of the fitness center. Executive suites include a Jacuzzi surrounded by floor-to-ceiling windows for a fabulous view. There's a spectacular rooftop pool and several dining options covering a wide range of cuisines.

26-28 Tran Phu St., Nha Trang. ✆ **058/388-0000.** Fax 058/388-2222. www.starwoodhotels.com. 284 units. 3,400,000VND deluxe; 4,600,000VND club room; from 5,400,000VND suite. AE, MC, V. **Amenities:** 3 restaurants; 3 bars; babysitting; children's club; concierge; fitness center; large rooftop pool; children's pool; room service; spa; cooking school. *In room:* A/C, satellite TV, minibar, Wi-Fi.

Sunrise Beach Resort Nha Trang ★★ The grand edifice of the Sunrise Beach Resort is all polished marble and white columns. The massive hotel is 10 floors of pomp, a bit like an oversize mafia don's palace, but everything about the place is shiny and new. Large rooms are simple and tastefully decorated in a soothing off-white, all with great views of oceanside Tran Phu Street and the beach. The second-floor circular pool is surrounded by ostentatious columns, but makes for a luxurious getaway. Dining options are many, and the rooftop rotunda houses a classy lounge with views of the big blue beyond.

12 Tran Phu St., Nha Trang. ✆ **058/820-999.** Fax 058/822-866. www.sunrisenhatrang.com.vn. 120 units. $125–$140 double; from $180 suite. AE, MC, V. **Amenities:** 3 restaurants; 2 bars; babysitting; small health club and spa; Internet access; outdoor pool; room service. *In room:* A/C, satellite TV, fridge, minibar.

Yasaka Saigon Nhatrang Resort Hotel & Spa ★ On the main strip overlooking Tran Phu and the ocean blue, this Japan/Vietnam joint venture bridges the gap between the ultraluxe resorts and the low-end minihotels—a good compromise. Rooms have all the basic amenities and are about as cozy as your favorite highway hotel chain back home. Upper-level units have good views of the sea, some with balconies; the vista from corner suites is quite spectacular and worth the upgrade. The standard superior rooms are comfortable, if bland; the deluxe rooms, on higher floors, are the best bet for atmosphere. Service is friendly, there are lots of good on-site dining options (the Red Onion on the rooftop is a local favorite), the pool is small but inviting, and it's just a short hop across busy Tran Phu Street to the beach.

18 Tran Phu St., Nha Trang. ✆ **058/382-0090.** Fax 058/382-0000. www.yasanhatrang.com. 201 units. $118–$198 double; from $250 suite. Rates include breakfast. AE, MC, V. **Amenities:** 4 restaurants; bar; nightclub; small health club; Jacuzzi; outdoor pool w/ocean view; room service; sauna; tennis court. *In room:* A/C, satellite TV w/in-house movies, fridge, minibar, Wi-Fi.

MODERATE

Nha Trang Lodge Hotel ★ This well run, 12-story high-rise has average-size rooms in chain-hotel style, with clean carpets, floral bedspreads, and marble finishes in the bathroom. Spring for an oceanview room with balcony (on an upper floor away from street noise, if possible). It's a nice, uninspired, affordable standard here—a bit like the younger, less-accomplished brother of the Yasaka (see above).

42 Tran Phu St., Nha Trang. ⓒ **058/352-1500** or 352-1900. Fax 058/352-1800. www.nhatranglodge. com. 121 units. $65–$85 double; $140 suite. AE, MC, V. **Amenities:** Restaurant; bar; small fitness center; Internet; outdoor pool; room service; sauna. *In room:* A/C, satellite TV, fridge, minibar.

Novotel ★ Along with the Sheraton, Novotel is the new kid on the block in Nha Trang, but its design makes all its neighbors appear so 20th century. With its clean lines, predictably reliable service, and affordable rates, it provides a solid midrange choice. Like most of the town's top hotels, it enjoys a prominent position on Tran Phu, overlooking the palm-lined beach, and all rooms have their own balcony from which to admire the view. It caters to both vacationers and businesspeople, with facilities such as an outdoor pool, a spa, Wi-Fi, and a conference center. The hotel is also equipped with ramps, allowing access to those with disabilities; overall this is a good choice for a stress-free base on the beach.

50 Tran Phu St., Nha Trang. ⓒ **058/625-6900.** Fax 058/625-6901. www.novotel.com. 158 units. $77–$145 double. AE, MC, V. **Amenities:** Restaurant; 2 bars; fitness center; outdoor pool; room service; sauna; spa. *In room:* A/C, satellite TV, minibar, Wi-Fi.

Phu Quy 2 ★ If you'd like to enjoy panoramic views of NhaTrang's beautiful beach without the high price tag, consider this midrange alternative, where most rooms are small but equipped with all the comforts you'd expect of a top-end resort such as bathtubs, solid furnishings, and free Internet. With two other budget properties in town, the Phu Quy team is well experienced in providing attentive service for guests, and can help plan your stay to get the most out of the town. There's a tiny rooftop pool, and needless to say, the best views are from rooms near the top of the 15-story building.

1 Tue Tinh St., Nha Trang. ⓒ **058/352-5050.** Fax 058/352-5722. www.phuquyhotel.vn. 60 units. $38–$100 double (depending on view and size). MC, V. **Amenities:** Restaurant; bar; small rooftop pool; room service; smoke-free rooms. *In room:* A/C, satellite TV, hair dryer, free Internet, minibar.

Que Huong Hotel A Khanh Hoa Tourism property, like the Vien Dong Hotel (see below), this is a bright, bland, four-story block just across the street from the beach—quiet and convenient. Rooms surround a large central courtyard and pool. All are average size, with clean but worn carpets, pastel tones, nice padded wooden furniture, and balconies. There are signs of wear here and there, like crumbly tile bathrooms, but the suites are huge and a nice option for families (some even have two bathrooms). This is the land of the tour group, though, and the staff is not versed in individual graces; in high season, the front desk is run like a busy deli: "Next!" That said, it's affordable, clean, and close to the beach, and the pool is quite lovely. Nice amenities include an Asian/Continental restaurant, a small pool hall, a fun little disco, and capable travel agents in the lobby.

60 Tran Phu St., Nha Trang. ⓒ **058/382-5047.** Fax 058/382-5344. www.nhatrangtourist.com.vn. 56 units. $40 double; $75 suite. MC, V. **Amenities:** Restaurant; bar/club/karaoke lounge; Internet access; nice outdoor pool; sauna; tennis. *In room:* A/C, satellite TV, fridge, hair dryer, minibar.

INEXPENSIVE

Dong Phuong Hotel ★ It's function, not form, in this motel-style block that's typical of the budget accommodations in town (this is one of three properties of the same name and standard in Nha Trang). Rooms are bright but spartan, with not much more than a bed and a shower-in-room style of bathroom. Some units have a good city view. If you're lucky, you'll be blessed with a classy nude done in painted tile mosaic in the bathroom (the only decoration we could find throughout). Family rooms are a good value, and the penthouse room adjoins a huge rooftop area with 360-degree views of town. It's your standard minihotel service, though: just rooms.

103 Nguyen Thien Thuat St., Nha Trang. ✆ **058/352-6986** or 352-6247. Fax 058/352-6986. dong phuongnt@dng.vnn.vn. 47 units. $6–$18 double; $25 deluxe (family). MC, V. **Amenities:** Restaurant. *In room:* A/C, satellite TV, fridge, hair dryer.

Sea View Hotel   Here's another good and clean option in a convenient location. The Sea View is right in the heart of the busy backpacker area, and you'll have to be on a higher floor to get any actual sea view, but rooms are large, simple, and clean, with tile floors and shower-in-room-style bathrooms. Some units have balconies. Amenities are few, but the hotel is handy for shops and restaurants.

4 Biet Thu St., Nha Trang. ✆ **058/352-4333.** Fax 058/352-2335. seaviewhotel@dng.vnn.vn. 60 units. $12–$20 double. MC, V. *In room:* A/C, satellite TV, fridge.

Vien Dong Hotel   The Vien Dong is showing its age after years of heavy tour-group use, but it's still a relatively comfortable three-star with all the amenities. The large pool is a highlight. Smallish rooms have simple wood furnishings and sturdy foam mattresses. Bathrooms are clean but bare. A college dorm room comes to mind. Suites are not worth the extra cost. An inviting outdoor restaurant features cultural music and dance shows. You're sure to meet other travelers here, and the general atmosphere is friendly, which helps. The staff, though taxed by the many groups coming and going, is kind and helpful, and a buffet breakfast is included in the price.

1 Tran Hung Dao St., Nha Trang. ✆ **058/352-3606** or 352-1608. Fax 058/352-1912. www.nhatrang tourist.com.vn. 100 units. $28–$38 double. AE, MC, V. **Amenities:** Large restaurant; open-air poolside bar; bike rental; Internet access (1,000VND/10 min.); big outdoor pool; room service; tennis courts. *In room:* A/C, satellite TV, fridge, hair dryer, minibar.

Where to Dine

EXPENSIVE

Pavilion ★★★ ASIAN/CONTINENTAL   Without question the finest dining on this beautiful stretch of coast, the Pavilion is the jewel in the crown of the Evason Ana Mandara Resort, serving exquisite cuisine in elegant, natural surroundings. Whether you're perched on the oceanfront veranda, shaded by a canvas umbrella in the courtyard, or dining by candlelight over the open ocean on the seaside jetty, the location alone is breathtaking. The food is creatively prepared and beautifully presented. The ever-evolving roster of local and seasonal specials means anything from homemade minestrone soup and green mango salad to a South Indian clay-pot curry for two. A highlight is the roast lobster wrapped in Parma ham, served with bok choy and a light sauce made of fennel and ginger. This is the best choice for romantic ambience and fine dining.

At the Evason Ana Mandara Resort, Tran Phu Blvd. ✆ **058/352-2222.** Main courses $14–$35. AE, MC, V. Daily 6am–11pm.

MODERATE

Louisiane Brewhouse ★ ECLECTIC/PUB   This beachfront place is an excellent spot to laze away a sunny afternoon sampling the many goodies on offer from well turned-out Vietnamese dishes to Japanese sushi or Western dishes like chicken escalope or pizza and filling sandwiches or yummy cakes. As the "brewhouse" tag suggests, there are also locally brewed beers on offer, and there's also a swimming pool and pool table for guests' use. If you hang around till evening, you'll likely catch a live band drawing in the after-dark partygoers.

29 Tran Phu, Nha Trang. ℂ **058/352-1948.** www.louisianebrewhouse.com.vn. Main courses 50,000VND–200,000VND. MC, V. Daily 7am–1am.

Ngoc Suong ★★ SEAFOOD   Nha Trang has dozens of good seafood restaurants, but this one, part of a supersuccessful national chain, leads the pack. Whether in the very pleasant thatched outdoor pavilion or the vaguely nautical, softly lit interior, it's "seafood as you like it" served by a helpful, friendly staff, and there are often musicians serenading diners with gentle jazz or classical music. Whole fish and crustaceans can be chosen by pointing at the large tank and smiling greedily; the day's catch, including shrimp and crab, is ordered by the pound, grilled, fried, or boiled with basic spices such as tamarind or pepper and lemon. The oysters, if available, are small but succulent. There are tempting set menus as well—a good idea if you go in a group. The name of the restaurant refers to a delicate marinated whitefish salad, one of the specialties and a great appetizer. This is a popular local and expat favorite.

96A Tran Phu (south of the town center at beachside). ℂ **058/352-5677.** Main courses 50,000VND–250,000VND. MC, V. Daily 10am–midnight.

Nha Trang Sailing Club ★ VIETNAMESE/CONTINENTAL   Stop by this open-air bar/restaurant for a real Western breakfast, if nothing else. A good bet is the pancakes, not greasy (as usual) and served with real butter. Other menu items include tasty (though not authentic) burgers and macaroni and cheese, plus the usual Nha Trang seafood selections. There are now different "stations" for dining here, including good Japanese eats, an Italian menu, and even an Indian menu. The setting, in a large hut just off the beach, can't be beat. You can lounge on the beach, buy or swap a book from the well stocked rack, and book a boat tour or a day of scuba with Rainbow Divers. The bar swings at night.

72-74 Tran Phu St. ℂ **058/382-6528.** Main courses 50,000VND–220,000VND. MC, V. Daily 7am–11pm. Bar until 2am.

Truc Linh 2 Restaurant ★ VIETNAMESE   The eclectic menu here has everything from the backpacker standbys of fried rice and noodles to sirloin steak and T-bone. There's a seafood smorgasbord out front from which you can choose your own jumbo shrimp, crab, squid, and fresh fish of the day and then have it weighed and cooked to your taste. It's got fondue and clay-pot specials, barbecued beef on clay tile, and delicious rice-paper spring rolls with shrimp. Truc Linh now has four outlets, of which this is the most atmospheric, and it has made such a name for itself that even folks from the top-end resorts stop by to check what the fuss is all about.

18A Biet Thu St. ℂ **058/352-1089.** Main courses 50,000VND–180,000VND. No credit cards. Daily 6am–11pm.

INEXPENSIVE

Lac Canh ★★ CHINESE/VIETNAMESE   Two words: grilled shrimp. The Chinese-influenced Vietnamese cuisine here is all about the ingredients, so go for the basics: fresh seafood in a light marinade that you grill yourself on a rustic, cast-iron brazier. The new location is a little more airy, but try to sit outdoors because the atmosphere is smoky. This is definitely the town's "greasy spoon," packed with both locals and tourists, and it makes for a fun evening.

44 Nguyen Binh Khiem. ℂ **058/821-391.** Main courses 30,000VND–130,000VND. No credit cards. Daily 9am–9:30pm.

Romy's Ice Cream and Coffee Bar ★ ☺ VIETNAMESE/WESTERN This ice-cream parlor, in the middle of the backpacker area, is a good place to meet fellow wanderers over a snack or breakfast. The owners and staff are friendly, the list of fruit shakes is as long as a sunny beachside day, and the ice cream is tops. Opt for the strawberry shake for a quick pick-me-up.

1C Biet Thu. ℂ **058/352-7677.** Ice-cream dishes 25,000VND–90,000VND. No credit cards. Daily 10am–11pm.

What to See & Do

Alexandre Yersin Museum ★★ Here you can get an inkling of the work of one of Vietnam's greatest heroes, surprisingly a non-native. Swiss doctor Alexandre Yersin founded Dalat, isolated a plague-causing bacteria, and researched agricultural methods and meteorological forecasting, all to the great benefit of the Vietnamese. He founded the institute in 1895. On display are his desk, overflowing library, and scientific instruments.

In the Pasteur Institute, 10 Tran Phu St. ℂ **058/382-2355.** Admission 26,000VND. Mon–Fri 8–11am and 2–4:30pm; Sat 8–11am.

Lang Son Pagoda ★ The main attraction at this 1930s pagoda is the huge white Buddha on the hillside behind it, the symbol of Nha Trang. Around the base of the Buddha are portraits of monks who immolated themselves to protest the corrupt Diem regime. After climbing the numerous flights of stairs, you'll be rewarded with a bird's-eye view of Nha Trang.

Thai Nguyen St. Free admission. Daily 8am–5pm.

National Oceanographic Institute This museum of all things aquatic is housed in an attractive colonial building to the south of town, right beside the Cau Da wharf where boats head out to the islands. You can feast your eyes on such oddities as the skeleton of a humpback whale, as well as watch horseshoe crabs and zebra sharks patrolling the tanks outside. Many of the colorful species on display are found in the nearby bay, so you may be able to identify those you have seen while diving or snorkeling.

1 Cau Da, Nha Trang (6km/3¾ miles south of the city center). ℂ **058/359-0037.** Admission 15,000VND adults, 7,000VND kids. Daily 6am–6pm.

Nha Trang Cathedral Set on a small hill overlooking the train station in the west of town, this imposing edifice was built in the late 1920s in a French Gothic style. A path spirals up to the entrance, passing numerous tiny gravestones strewn with flowers, and inside the cavernous exterior, the stained-glass panels cast a rainbow light across the pews. Its sheer size is an indicator of the strong hold that Catholicism has in Vietnam, and it's worth a look as it's on the way to the Lang Son Pagoda.

Corner of Nguyen Trai and Thai Nguyen sts. Daily 6am–6pm.

Po Nagar Cham Towers ★★ Starting in the 8th century, the Cham people, an early Hindu empire in central Vietnam built the Po Nagar Cham temple complex to honor Yang Ino Po Nagar, mother of the kingdom. Set on the site of an earlier wooden temple burned by the Javanese in A.D. 774, there were originally 10 structures here; today, just 4 remain. The main tower, or Po Nagar Kalan, is one of the tallest Cham structures ever built. Its square tower and three-story cone roof are exemplary of Cham style. It has more remaining structural integrity than many sites, giving you a

who are the CHAM?

With little written history, what we do know of the Cham is from Chinese written texts and from the splendid religious art attributed to the Champa Kingdom (note the many Khmer-style towers scattered along Vietnam's central coastline). The Cham people settled in central Vietnam in the 2nd century A.D. and fought Chinese incursions from their stronghold in and around Danang.

The Cham belong to the Malayo-Polynesian language family and have their own Sanskrit-based script. Cham communities lived by rice farming, fishing, and trading pepper, cinnamon bark, ivory, and wood with neighboring nations via Hoi An. Hinduism was their dominant religion, with Buddhist influences and an infusion of Islam starting in the 14th century. In the middle of the 10th century, internal warfare, as well as battles against both Khmer to the south and Dai Viet to the north, began to erode the Champa kingdom. By the mid–15th century, it had been almost entirely absorbed into Vietnam.

The Cham today are an ethnic minority; many are still Hindu, but many have converted to Islam. Cham enclaves subsist by fishing, farming, and sales of handicrafts. The premier Cham site is at **My Son** (see "Side Trips from Hoi An," p. 308) and the biggest collection of Cham artifacts can be seen at the **Cham Museum in Danang** (p. 293), but the best-preserved Cham towers are located around Nha Trang and Phan Thiet,.

good idea of how it might have looked in all its glory. In the vestibule, you can see two pillars of carved epitaphs of Cham kings; in the sanctuary, there are two original carved doors. The statue inside is of the goddess Bharagati (also called Po Nagar) on her lotus throne. It was carved in 1050. The Po Nagar temples are still in use by local Buddhists, and the altars and smoking incense add to the intrigue of the architecture. Detracting from the whole experience are the souvenir stands and crowds of hawkers.

2 Thang 4, at the end of Xom Bong Bridge (2km/1¼ miles north of the city center). Admission 10,000VND. Daily 7:30am–5pm.

Thap Ba Hot Springs   Just north of the Po Nagar Cham Towers, a small side road leads a couple of kilometers to this area of hot springs that have been organized into a variety of healthy experiences. The place is hugely popular among Vietnamese and Japanese visitors. If you've never had a mud bath, then here's your chance to roll around in a tub of the stuff for half an hour, which staff claim will do wonders for your skin due to the minerals contained in the messy ooze. After letting the stuff dry, wash it off with a powerful shower, then head for the mineral water swimming pool or stand under a mineral waterfall. The key mineral here is sodium silicate chloride, which is supposed to ease rheumatism, arthritis, and stress. Prices depend on the treatment chosen (usually around $5–$15).

25 Ngoc Son St., Nha Trang (call for hotel pickup). ✆ **058/383-4939.** Daily 7am–8pm.

Outdoor Activities

Diving is big in Nha Trang, in season (Mar–Sept). There are a number of professionally run operations here; whether you're a beginner or an expert, make your choice based on safety more than anything. **Rainbow Divers** (90A Hung Vuong St.; ☎ 058/352-4351; www.divevietnam.com) has taken advertising to the level of pollution in Nha Trang, with seemingly every storefront claiming a connection, but these guys really are among the best in town. **Sailing Club Divers,** based at the **Nha Trang Sailing Club** (☎ 058/382-6528; see "Where to Dine," above) is another reliable company, as is the Evason Ana Mandara Resort, where the expert, mostly expat staff can devise dives for any and all.

Perhaps the most popular activity in Nha Trang is a **day boat cruise** to some of Nha Trang's 20 surrounding islands, which can cost as little as $7 a person, including hotel pickup and drop-off, a seafood lunch, and snorkeling-equipment rental. Some of these trips are famed for being little more than daytime raves, particularly those organized by **Mama Linh** (23C Biet Thu; ☎ 058/352-2844), which includes a live band, dancing, and a "floating bar"—a crew member perched on an inflated inner tube topping up swimming guests' plastic cups with cheap wine. Several other tour operators offer slightly more low-key tours at similar rates, while **Con Se Tre Tourist** (100/16 Tran Phu; ☎ 058/352-7522) runs more upmarket tours at $25 a person. The day of motoring through lovely bays to three or four different islands generally includes some snorkeling off **Hon Mun,** a big seafood lunch off **Hon Mot,** and a swim on a small beach at **Hon Tam.** Beer and drinks are available all day. Last stop on the tour is usually **Hon Mieu,** where you can visit the **Tri Nguyen Aquarium** (admission 25,000VND), a wonderfully kitschy building where you can marvel over the sharks, groupers, turtles, and colorful sea anemones. Just about everyone in town will want to book you on one of these tours, so ask at any hotel front desk and be sure to nail down all specifics (meals, transport included, and so forth).

For sailing, contact the **Nha Trang Sailing Club** (☎ 058/382-6528) or the **Evason Ana Mandara Resort** (☎ 058/352-2222). Go for a Hobie Cat if it's available and hire a captain if you are not experienced; the strong ocean breezes and choppy waters will make for a memorable sail. Runabouts and jet skis are also available.

For all other watersports, just take a walk along the municipal beach and check out the guys renting out jet skis, parasailing rides, kayaks, and windsurf equipment. There's a convenient spot right in front of the **Louisiane Brewhouse** (see "Where to Dine," above).

Nha Trang After Dark

Nha Trang is Vietnam's party town, and for some reason bars here stay open long after those in Saigon and Hanoi have locked up for the night; it's not unusual to watch the sun rise over the South China Sea before owners bring down the shutters. The **Nha Trang Sailing Club** (72–74 Tran Phu St.) has open-air bamboo huts and a dance scene on some nights until late. Another beachfront location that gets hopping at night is the **Louisiane Brewhouse** (see "Where to Dine," above), where there's home-brewed beer every night and live music some nights. **Crazy Kim Bar** (19 Biet Thu St.; ☎ 058/381-6072), in the backpacker area, is also open late and asks customers to "Be hot. Be cool. Be crazy. Just be." There are many versions of that mantra around town, and it's popular with the diving crowd and the few expats here. **Guava,** next door to Kim's at 17 Biet Thu, has a similar scene, and the nearby **Why Not Bar?** at 24 Tran Quang Khai is often the last place in town to close.

DALAT ★

Known as "Le Petit Paris" by the early builders and residents of this hillside resort town, Dalat is still considered a kind of luxury retreat for city dwellers and travelers tired from trudging along sultry coastal Vietnam. In Dalat, you can play golf on one of the finest courses in Indochina, visit beautiful temples, and enjoy the town's honeymoon atmosphere and delightfully hokey tourist sights.

At 1,500m (4,920 ft.) elevation, Dalat is mercifully cool year-round—there's no need for air-conditioning here—and is a unique blend of pastoral hillside Vietnam and European alpine resort. Alexander Yersin, the Swiss physicist and bacteriologist who first traipsed across this pass, recommended establishing a town here in 1893 as a resort for French colonials weary of the Vietnamese tropics. His advice was taken by the Governor General of Indochina, Paul Doumer, and from the early 20th century it became a hugely popular escape for the French colonials oppressed by the heat and humidity of Saigon. In and around town are still scattered the relics of colonial mansions (some of them lovingly renovated), as well as some serene pagodas in a lovely natural setting—you've escaped from big-city Vietnam for real here. You can also visit the small villages of a few ethnic minorities, including the Lat and the Koho, who live in and around the picturesque hills surrounding Dalat.

Dalat is a top resort destination for Vietnamese couples getting married or honeymooning. If the lunar astrological signs are particularly good, it's not unusual to see 10 or so wedding parties in a single day. Many of the local scenic spots, such as the Valley of Love and Lake of Sighs, pander to the giddy couples. The waterfalls swarm with vendors, costumed bears, and "cowboys" complete with sad-looking horses and fake pistols. A carnival air prevails. It's tacky, but it's one of those "so bad that it's good" feelings that's kind of fun. For most foreign visitors, the attraction of Dalat is the opportunity to participate in some adventure sports (see "Visitor Information & Tours," below) and as a base for deeper exploration of the Central Highlands.

Getting There

BY PLANE   The only direct flights to Dalat are from Ho Chi Minh City (flight time: 50 min.). You can reach **Vietnam Airlines** at © **063/383-3499.** The airline operates a minibus to and from the airport, which is about 30km (19 miles) south of town, for 35,000VND, while a taxi is around $12; the journey takes about 30 to 45 minutes.

BY BUS/CAR   Dalat is connected by open-tour bus from Ho Chi Minh City and Nha Trang. Buses stop at Po Klong Garai, an old Cham temple site near Phan Rang, where the road turns inland for the hills of Dalat. The trip from Nha Trang (to the north) or Ho Chi Minh City (to the south) takes 7 hours and costs $8 to $9 at any tourist cafe. Alternatively, you can hire a private car for the trip and save about an hour. It's a picturesque ride, but a bit of a bone-shaker; if your time is limited, opt for a flight.

Getting Around

There are no cyclos in Dalat (the streets are too steep), but walking is very pleasant in the cool air. You can reach most of the city sights, such as the market and the lake, on foot. Try **Mai Linh Taxi** (© **063/351-1111**) if you need a cab in town.

Dalat is a good place to rent a **motorbike,** which will cost about $6 to $8 per day, with discounts available if you rent for several days; ask at your hotel. This is a good, adventurous way to get to all the funky sights outside the city. The winding roads will have you feeling like you're born to be wild, if you can forget that you're riding the motorcycle equivalent of a hair dryer. Be sure to check the brakes and the horn: You should beep-beep all the way to warn people of your presence.

Another option is to get a **motorbike with driver** (look for blue jackets with an Easy Rider logo). You'll pay about $1 to $2 per hour, or you can fix a rate for the day and the destinations. A **car with driver** runs about $30 per day. Because most sights are outside city limits, it makes sense to take a half- or full-day tour through your hotel or a tourist cafe.

Visitor Information & Tours

ECOTOURS

Young U.S. expats Brian and Kim, of **Phat Tire Ventures** (109 Nguyen Van Troi St.; ℂ **063/382-9422;** fax 063/382-0331; www.phattireventures.com), can arrange anything from day treks to jungle expeditions, mountain biking (they have a stable of top-quality bikes and hold daily clinics), rock climbing, white-water rafting, rappelling, or canyoning. Daily rates for most activities start at around $40 and include lunch, transport, and a knowledgeable guide. Safety and environmental stewardship are their trademark.

BUDGET TOURS

- **Sinh Café** (4A Bui Thi Xuan St.; ℂ **063/382-2663**) has an information and tour office adjacent to Trung Cang Hotel, the company's budget accommodations.
- **TM Brothers** (58 Truong Cong Dinh St.; ℂ **063/382-8383**) can book standard budget tours for you from its office on "cafe street."
- **Da Lat Travel Service** (34 Hoa Binh Sq.; ℂ **063/351-0993**) is located near the central market.

[FastFACTS] DALAT

Currency Exchange   **Vietcombank** is at 6 Nguyen Thi Minh Khai St. (ℂ **063/351-0586;** daily 7:30–11am and 1:30–4:30pm). You can exchange traveler's checks here and you'll also find an ATM that accepts most cards. There are plenty of other ATM machines scattered around town, including in the main post office.

Internet Access   Most hotels and guest houses provide Internet access, in many cases for free. If you're stuck, try **Viet Hung Café,** 7 Nguyen Chi Thanh, where Internet use is free with the purchase of coffee or tea.

Mail   The main post office is at 14 Tran Phu St., across from the Novotel. Open Monday through Saturday from 7:30am to 5:30pm.

Telephones   The area code for Dalat is **063.**

Where to Stay

With its long history as a resort area for both foreigners and Vietnamese, Dalat offers some choice lodgings, and there are some great deals to be found. There are plenty of minihotels, and several upmarket places in the hills outside the city center. Efforts are underway to restore and preserve the many 1950s-era French colonial homes, and some are converting to guesthouses. *Note:* No Dalat hotels have air-conditioning; with the year-round temperate weather, none is needed.

VERY EXPENSIVE

Sofitel Dalat Palace ★★★   Opened in 1922 as the address of choice for French colonists on holiday and once headquarters of the occupying Japanese, this recently renovated beauty, with its understated old-world opulence, is one of the finest five-star choices in all of Indochina. From the huge fireplace and mosaic floor in the lobby to the hanging tapestries and 500 oil reproductions of classic European art, it's a French country château with a Southeast Asian colonial flair. The large rooms, with glossy original wood floors, are finished with fine fabrics and throw rugs, and all beds are crowned with an ornate wooden housing for an ornamental mosquito net. Lakeview units open to a huge shared veranda with deck chairs. Service is superb. All in all, this is an exquisite place that should not be missed. The in-house dining at Le Rabelais (p. 324) is unrivaled, and Larry's Bar, a great little grotto with a pool table, darts, and good pub grub, is a neat place to while away an evening.

12 Tran Phu St., Dalat. 🕐 **063/382-5444.** Fax 063/382-5666. www.accorhotels.com. 43 units. $340–$390 double; $510–$600 suite. Ask about discounts and specials. AE, DC, MC, V. **Amenities:** Restaurant; 2 bars; babysitting; kids' playroom and outdoor playground; concierge; golf arrangements; heated outdoor pool; room service; tennis. *In room:* Satellite TV, Wi-Fi, fridge, hair dryer, minibar.

EXPENSIVE

Ana Mandara Villas ★★   For a real taste of colonial living, the Villas provide an experience unrivaled in Dalat. It's as though the designers made a trip back to the 1930s, bought up an entire neighborhood, and brought the whole place into the present. Seventeen renovated villas are spread over 14 hectares (35 acres) a short ride from central Dalat, and all are as distinct as their first owners. Each is a thematic homage to French colonialist professions, from winemakers to archaeologists to the Citroën family, which used to sponsor a race from Paris to Vietnam. All the original structures have been retained, so floors are polished with age and creak in a nostalgic way that can't be replicated by new construction. Most villas are designed with guest rooms sharing a common area, but a private butler in each building means that even the most reclusive visitor will be satisfied.

Le Lai St., Ward 5, Dalat. 🕐 **063/355-5888.** Fax 063/355-5666. www.anamandara-resort.com. 65 units. $98–$179 double; $258–$394 suite. AE, DC, MC, V. **Amenities:** Restaurant; bar; airport transfers; babysitting; children's center; gym; heated outdoor pool; room service; spa. *In room:* Satellite TV/DVD, hair dryer, minibar.

Mercure Dalat Du Parc ★★   Formerly the Novotel Dalat, this is a scaled-down version of the Sofitel Palace (with which it shares amenities), located just across the road. Lovely renovations in 1997 converted the 1932 building, which was originally the Hotel Du Parc. The lobby has a unique wrought-iron elevator. The smallish rooms have attractive historical touches: glossy wood floors, tastefully understated wood furniture, and high molded ceilings. A superior room (the lowest standard) is a bit cramped and not the greatest value, but deluxe rooms are clean, classy, and worth the upgrade. The bathrooms are efficient and spotless, with sleek granite and dark-wood trim. Everything is tidy and convenient, with local artwork throughout and a warm, homey atmosphere. The staff is businesslike and friendly, and the hotel shares fine amenities with neighboring Sofitel Dalat Palace (see above).

7 Tran Phu St., Dalat. 🕐 **063/382-5777.** Fax 063/382-5888. www.mercure.com. 140 units. $112–$138 double; $168 suite. Ask about discounts and specials. AE, MC, V. **Amenities:** 2 restaurants; 2 bars; concierge; golf arrangements; heated outdoor pool; room service; sauna; smoke-free rooms; tennis. *In room:* Satellite TV, fridge, hair dryer, minibar, Wi-Fi.

MODERATE

Empress Hotel ★   This Hong Kong/Vietnamese joint venture is an upscale but affordable oasis just a stone's throw from the lake and close to all the action. Tucked into the side of a hill, the hotel has rooms that form a courtyard, with the steep gable of a European lodge–style reception and restaurant on one side and two floors of rooms (all facing the courtyard) on the other. The comfortable accommodations have dark-wood walls, terra-cotta tile floors, rattan furniture, nice local artwork, and elegant bedspreads. Bathrooms are large, with granite counters and nice fixtures, some with tubs and others an open arrangement with a combined shower/toilet area (like a guesthouse, but spotless). The suites are large and luxe, with a sunken tub and sitting area, but the deluxe rooms are a better deal, with views of the stone courtyard and lake below. Go for a room on the second floor, as those on the first are getting a bit musty.

5 Nguyen Thai Hoc St., Dalat. ✆ **063/833-888.** Fax 063/829-399. empresdl@hcm.vnn.vn. $45–$55 double; $61–$112 suite. 20 units. AE, MC, V. **Amenities:** Restaurant. *In room:* Satellite TV w/in-house movies, fridge, hair dryer, minibar.

Ngoc Lan Hotel ★   Enjoying superb views over the lake, this once-crumbling property has been cleverly restored to four-star status and is now one of the top spots to stay in town. It's just a few steps from the central market and well positioned for an exploration of Dalat's winding streets. The bright and breezy rooms have wooden floors, shuttered windows, flatscreen TVs, Wi-Fi, and well chosen artwork on the walls; some also have balconies. Facilities such as the fitness center are equipped with the latest gear, making them a pleasure to use. The smart restaurant prepares tasty Vietnamese and international cuisine, and staff are eager to help you plan your stay.

42 Nguyen Chi Thanh St., Dalat. ✆ **063/383-8838.** Fax 063/382-4032. www.ngoclanhotel.vn. 91 units. $65–$95 double; $125–$385 suite. AE, MC, V. **Amenities:** Restaurant; bar; concierge; conference rooms; fitness center; room service. *In room:* Satellite TV, minibar, Wi-Fi.

INEXPENSIVE

Chau-Au Europa ★   This cozy little hideaway is just around the corner from the imposing Ngoc Lan Hotel (see above), and many rooms enjoy the same views over the lake, though furnishings are not comparable. The real pull, here, however, is the friendly family who works tirelessly to ensure guests' comfort. There's a range of rooms here, from windowless closets to spacious, breezy units with good views. Facilities are limited, but all the basics, like hot-water showers and free Wi-Fi in the rooms, are here.

76 Nguyen Chi Thanh St., Dalat. ✆ **063/382-2870.** 16 units. $10–$25 double. No credit cards. *In room:* Satellite TV, Wi-Fi.

Dreams I & II ★   If you want value for money, look no further, but you'd better book ahead, as these superfriendly minihotels have developed quite a reputation among travelers in Vietnam. So what's the draw here? Quite simply it's the owner's drive to make everyone's stay as enjoyable as possible, which means providing free use of Internet terminals, free Wi-Fi, huge free breakfast, plus use of Jacuzzi and sauna for all guests, as well as sound advice on local attractions. The well maintained rooms feature double-glazing for a quiet sleep, and some have massage showers in the bathroom.

151 and 164b Phan Dinh Phung St., Dalat. ✆ **063/383-3748.** www.dreamshoteldalat.com. 20 units. $25 double. Rates include breakfast. No credit cards. **Amenities:** Free Internet; Jacuzzi; sauna. *In room:* A/C, satellite TV, minibar, Wi-Fi.

Where to Dine

The huge variety of local ingredients, particularly fruit and vegetables, makes for fresh-tasting food and some culinary delights in Dalat. Many excellent, small restaurants are located on **Phan Dinh Phung Street,** and some of the best dining is at the stalls in the **central market.** Do try the artichoke tea and strawberry jam, two local specialties (and good souvenirs to take home from the market).

Café de la Poste ★★ CONTINENTAL/VIETNAMESE   This cozy, colonial gem, part of the **Sofitel Dalat Palace hotel** (p. 322), is located in an open, airy corner building across from the post office (go figure). It's more restaurant than cafe, really, and has a great selection of light choices, sandwiches, and desserts (don't miss the cheesecake), along with hearty entrees such as T-bone steak and fresh pasta. The salads are big and fresh, and the French onion soup is great. Rather stick with Vietnamese? Head upstairs to the elegant **Y Nho Y,** where several gourmet options await. It's pricey for Dalat, but worth it.

12 Tran Phu St. ✆ **063/382-5444.** Main courses $8–$42. AE, MC, V. Daily 6am–10pm.

Da Quy ★ ASIAN/WESTERN   Just a few steps down Truong Cong Dinh Street from the market brings you to this little gem of a place, where the food and service are top-notch but the check is embarrassingly low. The decor is low-key elegant, with crisp tablecloths topped with glowing candles, and the service is refreshingly unpushy. Try the venison with lemon grass, or one of the baked clay-pot dishes, or even one of the many Western dishes, but save room for one of their tasty desserts. Add a warming bottle of local wine, and you've got the recipe for a cheap and cheerful evening in Dalat.

49 Truong Cong Dinh St., Dalat. ✆ **063/351-0883.** Main courses $2–$10. Daily 7am–10pm.

Le Rabelais ★★ FRENCH   A meal at Le Rabelais is a genuine French colonial fine-dining experience. Prices are high, but so is the standard of preparation and service. The Sofitel people work closely with local organic farms; thus, all dishes are prepared with the finest fresh produce. In the tradition of the original 1922 Langbian Palace Hotel, Le Rabelais serves from a limited menu, which ensures that everything is done just right. Beginning with a tantalizing *amuse bouche,* dinner is a slow progression of delicious courses. The lobster bisque is rich, and the beef sirloin succulent and satisfying in a savory pepper sauce. The wine list is long and, unusual in this region, the staff knows the right suggestions for any given meal; in fact, the service here is efficient and professional, attentive without fawning or hovering, and meticulous with every detail. It's a great place to take that special someone for an evening of candlelit opulence. Follow up with coffee or after-dinner drinks and cigars down in the very atmospheric Larry's Bar.

At the Sofitel Dalat Palace, 12 Tran Phu St. ✆ **063/382-5444.** Main courses $25–$47; set menus $65–$85 dinner, $22 lunch. AE, MC, V. Daily 6am–10pm.

Long Hoa ★★ VIETNAMESE/CONTINENTAL   On a busy street just opposite the hilltop cinema, this small bistro has checkered tablecloths and a cozy atmosphere. The owner, a vivacious, self-taught linguist, is very welcoming and will talk you through the menu, travel recommendations, or local lore in the language of your choice. You'll feel like a regular, or you will become one, even if you're in town for only a few days. The menu is grouped by ingredients (chicken, beef, fish) and lists any kind of sauté or steamed dish you can imagine, as well as a variety of hot pots and soups for those cold Dalat nights. It's inexpensive, excellent local fare with a French flair. Don't miss the homemade yogurt, a real treat.

6 Duong 3 Thang 2 (Duy Tan). ☏ **063/382-2934.** Main courses 40,000VND–110,000VND. No credit cards. Daily 11am–2:30pm and 5–9pm.

Lyla Hotel and Restaurant de Famille ★ ☺ VIETNAMESE/CONTINEN-TAL   This is real family dining, heavy on good French, in a closed, quiet dining room along Dalat's busy cafe street and a longtime expat favorite. Try a "real" Continental meal of French onion soup (absolutely delicious), fries with mayonnaise, and a niçoise salad. The menu features great steaks, pasta, and seafood, too. Very family friendly.

18A Nguyen Chi Thanh. ☏ **063/383-4540.** Main courses 45,000VND–95,000VND. MC, V. Daily 7am–10pm.

Ngoc Hai Restaurant ★ VIETNAMESE/CHINESE   Just down the street from the market, this local spot is two floors of bright, clean indoor/outdoor dining. It's nothing spectacular, but the staff is friendly and the menu is ambitious; ask for anything, and you'll hear hearty replies of "Have, have." Selections from the Western end of the spectrum include roasted chicken with potatoes and a mock-up of British fish and chips, but go for the Chinese-influenced Vietnamese stir-fries, one-dish meals, and soups. Reasonable set menus are a safe bet. Good veggie selections, too.

6 Nguyen Thi Minh Khai St. ☏ **063/382-5252.** Main courses $5–$15; set menus 160,000VND. No credit cards. Daily 9am–10pm.

V Café ★★ 🏫 CONTINENTAL   It's good for the budget and good for the tummy here at homey V Café. Where else can you sit at a table with linen and candles and enjoy a great burger for a couple of bucks? You'll also find the only burritos in town here. The owner, V, and her husband, Michael, a longtime expat, serve up hospitality smothered in gravy and will welcome you as their own. The place is full of travelers and expats.

1/1 Bui Thi Xuan St. (across from Sinh Cafe). ☏ **063/352-0215.** www.vcafedalatvietnam.com. Main courses 40,000VND–100,000VND. No credit cards. Daily 6:30am–10pm.

SNACKS & CAFES

Nguyen Chi Thanh Street is lined with cafes, one indistinguishable from the next in many ways. Each building hangs over the main market street and all serve ice cream, tea, and beer to ogling couples. Try **Artista Cafe** (9 Nguyen Chi Thanh St.; ☏ **063/382-1749**) for good ice cream, classic rock, and friendly folks. Just next door, the **Viet Hung Internet Café** (☏ **063/383-5737**) has laid-back porch seating.

What to See & Do

Much of what there is to see in Dalat is natural: Lakes, waterfalls, and dams dominate the tourist trail. Sights are spread over quite some distance, so consider booking a tour or renting your own car or motorbike with driver. *Note:* Avoid visiting pagodas between 11:30am and 2pm, when nuns and monks have their lunch. You might disturb them and also miss a valuable opportunity for a chat. You should also leave 1,000 or 2,000 dong in the donation box near the altar.

Bao Dai's Palace ★   Completed in 1938, this monument to bad taste provided Bao Dai, Vietnam's last emperor, with a place of rest and respite with his family. It has never been restored and, indeed, looks veritably untouched since the emperor's ousting and hasty exile; on a busy weekend in high season, you might get a rush by pretending you're here to liberate the place and are part of the looting masses—it's not hard to imagine, with the crowds ignoring any velvet ropes and posing for pictures in the aging velvet furniture. You'll be asked to go in stocking feet or wear loose shoe covers, which make it fun for sliding around the home's 26 rooms, including Bao Dai's office and the bedrooms of the royal family. You can still see the grease stains on Bao Dai's hammock pillow and the ancient steam bath in which he soaked. The explanations are in English; most concern Bao Dai's family members. There is pathos in reading them and piecing together the mundane fate of the former royals: One prince has a "technical" job, while another is a manager for an insurance company. There are three other Bao Dai palaces in town, the Sofitel Dalat Palace hotel among them, but this is the best choice.

South of Xuan Huong Lake and up the hill behind "Crazy House." No phone. Admission 8,000VND. Daily 7–11am and 1:30–4pm.

Dalat Market (Cho Da Lat) ★★★ Huge, crowded, and stuffed with produce of all varieties, this is the top stroll-through destination in Dalat. Come see all the local specialties—and even have a try. Some of the vendors will be happy to give you a sample of local wine or a few candied strawberries. Dalat in general is low on the annoying touts who plague the big towns and tourist sights in Vietnam, and entreaties from the merchants here are friendly; you can walk around without too much hassle since the locals are doing all the shopping.

Central Dalat. Daily early morning to night.

Dalat Railway Station (Cremaillaire Railway) Built in 1943, the Dalat station offers an atmospheric slice of the area's colonial history. You can see an authentic old wood-burning steamer train on the tracks to the rear, and stroll around inside looking at the iron-grilled ticket windows, empty now. Although the steamer train no longer makes tourist runs, a newer Japanese train makes a trip to Trai Mat and the Linh Phuoc Pagoda (see below). The round-trip costs 80,000VND and it leaves five times a day (7:45am, 9:50am, 11:55am, 2pm, and 4:05pm).

Near Xuan Huong Lake, off Nguyen Trai St. Daily 8am–5pm.

French Quarter ★★ The whole town has the look and feel of a French replica, but on the ridge-running road, Tran Hung Dao, don't miss the derelict shells of the many French colonial summer homes; it's where the connected and successful came to escape the Saigon summer heat. Some of them have now been painstakingly renovated, while others are gradually being overrun by creepers, but they are a beautiful and eerie reminder of the recent colonial past. The road itself, one you'll take to many of the sights outside of town, offers panoramic views.

Follow Tran Hung Dao Rd. a few miles southeast from town. Some of the houses are on private roads at the ends of promontories. Best visited by motorbike or car with driver.

Lake of Sighs (Ho Than Tho) ★ This lake has such romantic connotations for the Vietnamese that you would think it was created by a fairy godmother rather than French dam work. Legend has it that a 15-year-old girl named Thuy drowned herself after her boyfriend of the same age, Tam, fell in love with another. Her gravestone supposedly still stands on the side of the lake, marked with the incense and flowers left by other similarly heartbroken souls (even though the name on the headstone reads THAO, not THUY). The place is crammed with honeymooners in pedal boats and motorboats.

Northeast of town, along Ho Xuan Huong Rd. Admission 5,000VND. Daily 7am–5pm.

Lam Ty Ni Pagoda (Home of Thay Vien Thuc, "The Crazy Monk")   A visit with the man is a highlight for some and just plain creepy for others. The temple itself is nothing special, though the immaculate garden in the back is nice, but the real attraction is the studio of Mr. Thuc, a Vietnamese Zen practitioner who seems to be painting, drawing, and scribbling his way to nirvana. It's a rare glimpse into the inner sanctum of a true eccentric, and though locals say that he's not a real monk, just a painter and salesman, it's an interesting visit. A polyglot afflicted with graphophilia perhaps (a language genius who can't stop drawing), Mr. Thuc has a message of peace and connectedness characteristic of the Zen sect, and he conveys that message in Vietnamese, Chinese, French, English, Japanese, German, and Swedish as he continually cranks out poems with small stylized drawings while you talk with him. For $1 (bargain if you will), he'll scribble an original before your eyes and pose for a photo. You're free to ask questions, browse his stacks of finished works in the studio, and sign the guest book.

2 Thien My. ☎ **063/382-1775.** Free admission, but most feel obliged (or compelled) to buy one of his paintings.

Linh Phuoc Pagoda ★   Here is another example of one of Vietnam's fantasyland glass-and-ceramic mosaic structures. Refurbished in 1996, this modern temple features a huge golden Buddha in the main hall, plus three floors of walls and ceilings painted with fanciful murals. Go to the top floor for the eye-boggling Bodhisattva room and views of the surrounding countryside. In the garden to the right, there is a 3m-high (10-ft.) dragon, made entirely out of broken beer bottles, climbing in and out of a small lake. You'll find very cool little nooks and crannies to explore.

At the end of Trai Mat St. (20 min. by car or bike). Daily 8am–5pm.

Prenn Falls ★   The falls are quite impressive, especially after a good rain. You can ride a rattletrap cable car over them if you're brave, or else follow a stone path behind the falling water (prepare to get your feet wet). That's a minor thrill, of course, but the true Prenn experience is all about staged photos for Vietnamese tourists: couples preening, boys acting macho, and girls looking wan and forlorn. Professional photographers run the show and pose their willing actors on a small wooden bridge, on the back of a costumed horse, with an arm around a guy in a bear suit, on a small inflatable raft in front of the falls, or perched in one of the cool treehouses high above (be careful of the loose rungs when climbing up). Come here to have a laugh and observe until you find out that, as a foreign tourist, it's you that's being observed; in that case, say "Xin Chao" or return a few hellos and go from there (you'll be getting your photo snapped for sure). You might walk away with some new chums, not to mention some tourist tchotchkes, if that's your wont (plastic samurai sword, anyone?).

At the foot of Prenn Mountain pass, 10km (6¼ miles) from Dalat. Admission 6,000VND. Daily 7am–5pm.

Thien Vuong Pagoda ★   Otherwise known as the Chinese Pagoda, built as it was by the local Chinese population, this 1958 structure is unremarkable except for its serene setting among the hills of Dalat and the very friendly nuns who inhabit it. It does have three awe-inspiring sandalwood Buddhist statues that have been dated to the 16th century: Dai The Chi Bo Tat, god of power; Amitabha or Sakyamuni, Buddha; and Am Bo Tat, god of mercy. Each is 4m (13 ft.) high and weighs 1½ tons.

3km (1¾ miles) southeast of town at the end of Khe Sanh St. Daily 9am–5pm.

Truc Lam (Bamboo Forest) Zen Monastery ★★ What's refreshing here is that you can walk around Truc Lam with no harassment, unlike many other temples and most pagodas in Vietnam. This is a working temple, and though it's packed with tourists at certain times of the day, you'll be wandering amid meditation halls and classrooms that are utilitarian, not museum pieces. You'll get to see monks at work and have an informative glimpse into the daily rhythms of temple life. The complex was completed in 1994 with the aim of giving new life to the Truc Lam Yen Tu Zen sect, a uniquely Vietnamese form of Zen founded during the Tran Dynasty (1225–1400). Adherents practice self-reliance and realization through meditation. The shrine, the main building, is notable mainly for its simple structure and peaceful air. There is a large relief sculpture of Boddhidarma, Zen's wild-eyed Indian heir, at the rear of the main temple. The scenery around the monastery, with views of the nearby man-made lake, Tuyen Lam Lake, and surrounding mountains is breathtaking. Truc Lam can be reached by a scenic **cable car ride** from the top of Robin Hill overlooking Dalat; the 12-minute glide down over the pine forest is a great experience too, and costs 75,000VND for the round-trip.

Near Tuyen Lam Lake, 6km (3¾ miles) from Dalat. A popular spot on any countryside tour. Daily 7am–5pm.

Valley of Love ★★ The Valley of Love is scenic headquarters in Dalat and a popular stopover for honeymooners. It's a good place to find some real bizarre kitsch, the kind whose precedent can only be roadside America. We're talking guys in bear suits and huge-headed cowboys with guns that spout "bang" flags. There are a few nice paths among the rolling hills and quaint little lakes, and everyone enjoys the antics of Vietnamese honeymooners zipping around on motorboats and posing for pictures with guys in fuzzy jumpsuits. Don't miss it.

Phu Dong Thien Vuong St., about 3.2km (2 miles) north of town center. Admission 10,000VND. Daily 6am–5pm.

Xuan Huong Lake ★★ Once a trickle originating in the Lat village, Dalat's centerpiece, Xuan Huong, was created from a dam project that was finished in 1923, demolished by a storm in 1932, and reconstructed and rebuilt (with heavier stone) in 1935. You can rent swan-shaped pedal boats to glide over the lake, and in high season even canter around the lake in a pony and trap. A walk around its 7km (4⅓-mile) perimeter is a pleasant way to spend an hour or two, and the route passes the **Dalat Flower Garden** (admission 10,000VND; daily 7:30am–4pm), where there's yet another opportunity for a few more cheesy photos.

Central Dalat.

Outdoor Activities

Dalat is the perfect setting for hiking and mountain biking. Check with the folks at **Phat Tire Ventures** (109 Nguyen Van Troi St.; ℂ **063/382-9442;** see "Visitor Information & Tours," earlier in this section) for remote jungle treks to hill-tribe towns, good mountain biking, white-water rafting, or any kind of day trip. This company is extremely amenable and can customize to your needs.

Golfers can try the impressive 18-hole course at the **Dalat Palace Golf Club** (© **063/382-1201**). One round costs Sofitel Palace or Mercure Dalat guests $65 to $75; all others pay $95 to $105; prices include caddie fees. Call for reservations. Rental clubs and shoes are available, as are private lessons (by appointment), which begin at $30 for a half-hour. There is a nice driving range too.

PHAN THIET TOWN & MUI NE BEACH ★

This is one of the best laid-back getaways in Vietnam. The town of Phan Thiet itself is a bustling little fishing port—quite picturesque and good for a day's visit—but you'll want to get out to the long, sprawling, sandy stretch of beach to the east: Mui Ne. This is a popular weekend getaway from nearby Saigon, and development in recent years has been rapid. You'll find some very nice upscale resorts and comfy little boutique bungalow properties.

A couple of top-class golf courses are a big draw, and the consistent winds of Mui Ne bay bring kite- and windsurfers from all over the world. Farther east and north along the coast are vast sand dunes, like a beachside Sahara, and inland is the famous and strangely verdant **Lotus Lake** amid the towering, shifting sands—a good day trip. These spots, as well as other small fishing villages and some local Cham ruins, make for great day trips.

Getting There

Mui Ne is just 3 to 4 hours by bus or car from Ho Chi Minh City (Saigon), though heavy traffic and road work can sometimes make the journey much longer. The tourist-cafe buses connect here from Nha Trang and Dalat as well as Saigon, and **Sinh Café** covers all the bases from its **Mui Ne Resort** (144 Nguyen Dinh Chieu St., Ham Tien, Mui Ne; © **062/384-7542;** www.thesinhtourist.vn). Any hotel front desk can make the necessary arrangements for car rental or bus tickets.

Where to Stay

The Novotel is the only international standard hotel in Phan Thiet proper; most people head straight for Mui Ne, about 9km (5¾ miles) to the east, where you'll find a growing clutch of luxury resorts in every price range scattered along the 10km (6¼-mile) beach. For a splurge, the Princess D'Annam is about as away-from-it-all as you can get. **Warning:** The wind conditions that are so good for wind- and kitesurfing occasionally play havoc with the beach at Mui Ne, and high tides can sometimes smother the golden sands and encroach on resort gardens; look for previous guests' comments on the resort that appeals to you. **Note:** Some resorts do not have official addresses, in which case they are listed by their distance from Phan Thiet.

VERY EXPENSIVE

Princess D'Annam ★★★   This newish resort, located in a supremely remote coastal region about 30km (19 miles) south of Mui Ne, sets the luxury standard for coastal retreats in Vietnam. Standard suites are spacious, with raised wraparound wooden foundations for the king-size bed and daybed. The bathroom is equally large, with separate rain showers and a deep tub shaped like an inverted trapezoid. Everything is white or cream, with silk textiles in shades of gold and pale blue throughout. Life-size sepia photographs of Vietnam life adorn the walls. Sumptuous villas are connected via a narrow stone path, surrounded by a lush tropical garden that is home to a rainbow of butterflies. There's a spectacular spa right on the beach, and pleasing views of a 19th-century lighthouse on an offshore island.

Hon Lan, Tan Thanh Commune, Ham Thuan Nam district, Binh Thuan Province. ☎ **062/368-2222.** Fax 062/368-2333. www.princessannam.com. 57 units. $465 suite; $675–$1,370 villa. AE, MC, V. **Amenities:** Restaurant; 2 bars; babysitting; spacious children's playroom; concierge; health club; 3 outdoor pools; spa; 2 tennis courts. *In room:* A/C, TV, fridge, hair dryer, minibar, Wi-Fi.

EXPENSIVE

Coco Beach Resort ★★ ☺
On the main strip in Mui Ne, Coco Beach doesn't look like much from the road—just a wall to keep out the noise—but it is a real seaside oasis. It was the first to build along the strip here, and it's still the best. Rooms are wooden bungalows on stilts, each with a comfy balcony, vaulted ceiling, thatch roof, and mosquito net. They're intimate and tidy, offering an authentic rustic luxury (plus maintenance here is tops—no musty smells). Bathrooms are small but clean, with glass shower stalls. Prices vary depending on proximity to the beautiful beach, where you'll find private lounge chairs and umbrellas. Service is attentive and genuine, the best along the main strip of Mui Ne. The resort's two restaurants, the seaside Paradise Beach Club and the more upscale Champa, are the best in town (see "Where to Dine," below). The quiet garden is a good place to just relax after a day of swimming or boating. There's even an open-air massage facility at the center.

58 Nguyen Dinh Chieu St. ☎ **062/384-7111.** Fax 062/384-7115. 34 units. $125 bungalow; $250 2-room villa (long-stay rates available). AE, MC, V. **Amenities:** 2 restaurants; pool/beach bar; babysitting; children's programs; Internet access; Jacuzzi; outdoor pool; room service; library. *In room:* A/C, fridge, minibar.

Pandanus Resort
The best of a new clutch of resorts at the foot of the famous Red Sand Dunes north of Phan Thiet, this large property is as self-contained as any in Mui Ne proper, but a bit more remote. The resort is spread out, with ponds and manicured greens; the central pool area is cozy; and the beach is expansive, though dirty and unused. Rooms vary greatly, but all are comfortable, with cool terra-cotta tile offset by dark-wood trim.

Quarter 5, Mui Ne, Phan Thiet. ☎ **062/384-9849.** Fax 062/384-9850. www.pandanusresort.com. 134 units. $99–$119 double; $149–$229 suite; $179 bungalow. AE, MC, V. **Amenities:** Restaurant; 2 bars; free shuttle service; free use of bike; small fitness center; Jacuzzi; outdoor pool; room service; sauna; spa; tennis court. *In room:* A/C, satellite TV, fridge, hair dryer, minibar, Wi-Fi.

Victoria Phan Thiet Beach Resort & Spa ★★
Just as the road descends from Phan Thiet to meet the sandy beaches of Mui Ne, the Victoria stands on a quiet knoll overlooking the sea. The grass-and-garden property is traced by small brick paths leading to upscale bungalows. The layout is unique, with catwalks connecting the main buildings, most made of rough stone. The overall atmosphere is laid-back, private, and very family-friendly. Two different pool areas are great places to while away the day, or you can pamper yourself at the massage facility in a seaside grove. Guest rooms are large, private bungalows, some with two tiers and all done in terra cotta and dark wood; the decor is refined comfort with nice touches, such as stylish indirect lighting disguised as pottery, private outdoor showers, and local artwork. Family bungalows have multiple sleeping areas and pullout couches. The newer rooms, farther from the beach, are double-height and quite spacious. The beach is rocky, but the resort overlooks its own quiet cove and has beachside thatch awnings. Come for the weekend and you'll want to stay for the week.

Km 9, Phu Hai, Phan Thiet. ☎ **062/381-3000.** Fax 062/381-3007. www.victoriahotels-asia.com. 59 units. $190–$240 bungalow; $500–$750 villa. AE, MC, V. **Amenities:** Restaurant (indoor/outdoor dining); large thatched-roof poolside bar areas; babysitting; children's club; small health club; two outdoor pools, one w/Jacuzzi; spa; tennis court; watersports equipment; Wi-Fi. *In room:* A/C, satellite TV, fridge, minibar.

MODERATE

Mui Ne Sailing Club Resort ★   This seaside spot is owned by the same Aussie folks who run the popular Sailing Club in Nha Trang. Accommodations range from air-conditioned units in an attractive thatched house to top-notch seaside bungalows. Ask to see your room before checking in, as some are a bit musty. All units have terra-cotta tile with bamboo matting, cloth hangings, and bamboo floor lamps. There is an American Southwest feel in the artful beveled edges of the plaster walls and in the similarly rounded built-in nightstands. Large bathrooms are nicely appointed in tile and stripped-wood trim; they're separated from the bedroom by hanging cloths, a nice touch. The high-end bungalows are the best choice and worth the upgrade. The pool is small but set in a picturesque courtyard adjoining the open-air colonial-style restaurant. The owners have also added a spa, though no sauna. This is a popular stop for windsurfers and kite surfers—both rentals and lessons are available.

24 Nguyen Dinh Chieu St., Phan Thiet. ☎ **062/384-7440.** Fax 062/384-7441. www.sailingclubvietnam.com. 29 units. $85 double room; $120–$170 bungalow, depending on view. AE, MC, V. **Amenities:** Restaurant; bar; babysitting; Internet access; outdoor pool; room service; spa; watersports and kiteboarding rentals; Wi-Fi. *In room:* A/C, satellite TV, minibar.

Novotel Ocean Dunes & Golf Resort ★   "Fore!" Sandwiched between Nick Faldo's golf course and an open lawn and sandy beach, the Novotel is a popular choice for both golfers and Saigon expats on holiday. It's got all the amenities of a resort, but rooms and facilities are in a "traditional" hotel style, with clean carpets and floral prints. The original hotel is an old Soviet-era resort, thus the concrete-block rooms—comfy, but small and not particularly luxe. Every unit has a balcony, though, and prices vary according to the view of the beach or the golf course. The property is on the fringe of Phan Thiet, but it's insulated by the surrounding golf course and far from any road (so no honking). Unfortunately, it's about 9km (5⅔ miles) to the popular beaches of Mui Ne. The beach here is narrow and rocky, but the pool area is expansive and great for kids (there's even a jungle gym). The hotel has lots of activities and rents jet skis and sailboats as well.

1 Ton Duc Than St., Phan Thiet. ☎ **062/382-2393.** Fax 062/382-5682. www.accorhotels.com. 123 units. From $63 golf/seaview double; from $135 villa. AE, MC, V. **Amenities:** Restaurant (indoor/outdoor seating); 2 bars; babysitting; children's club and playground; concierge; golf course; health club; outdoor pool; room service; smoke-free rooms; 2 tennis courts; watersports equipment rental; Wi-Fi. *In room:* A/C, TV, fridge, hair dryer, minibar.

Saigon Mui Ne Resort ★   The Saigon Mui Ne is the most popular spot in town for larger group tours. Run by Saigontourist, the resort has all the amenities, but not a lot of charm. Rooms are comparable to any in this category in town, but there's that hazy indifference of a government-run, tour-group hotel. The good news: the affordable rates and the many amenities. The sprawling property has manicured lawns and tidy bungalows with terra-cotta tile floors, wrought-iron furniture, and bathrooms with granite counters and bamboo latticework. The hotel-block rooms are spacious, but go for a bungalow with balcony, ideally facing the sea or the pool area.

56–97 Nguyen Dinh Chieu St., Ham Tien, Phan Thiet. ☎ **062/384-7303.** Fax 062/384-7307. www.saigonmuineresort.com. 87 units. $80–$175 double (bungalow or hotel block); $185–$270 family room.

AE, MC, V. **Amenities:** Restaurant; beachside bar; Internet access; Jacuzzi; nice courtyard pool; room service; sauna; tennis court. *In room:* A/C, TV, fridge, minibar.

INEXPENSIVE

Budget options are tough to find in Mui Ne, as most resorts aim at the well heeled market. The scene is constantly changing, but gone are the days of a $10 basic room in a guesthouse—expect to pay more like $20 minimum. If you come by open-tour bus, you'll be dumped at the hotel run by the tour company. It gets cheaper and more rustic the farther east you go on the main road.

Sinh Café operates the **Mui Ne Resort** (144 Nguyen Dinh Chieu St., Ham Tien; ✆ **062/384-7542;** www.thesinhtourist.vn), a 48-room hotel on the farthest end of Mui Ne. If you come by one of its buses, they'll presume you want to stay here. Rooms start at $40 and aren't a bad bet. There's a pool and all the basics. A festive atmosphere prevails (lots of young partyers).

Another good budget choice is **Thai Hoa Resort** (56 Huynh Thuc Khang St., toward the east end of the bay; ✆ 062/384-7008; www.thaihoamuineresort.com). Facilities are limited, but it's a quiet spot and has a small pool, with rates beginning at $30.

Where to Dine

In addition to the recommendations below, **Sandals Restaurant** at the **Mui Ne Sailing Club** (24 Nguyen Dinh Chieu St.; ✆ 062/384-7440) serves an intriguing range of fusion dishes in a nice open-air building at poolside overlooking the ocean. Farther east, **Full Moon Beach** (84 Nguyen Dinh Chieu St.; ✆ 062/384-7008) is a good stop for coffee or breakfast on your way to Lotus Lake or the big dunes north of town. New places are opening all the time; a couple of smart new places worth checking out are **Sankara** (78 Nguyen Dinh Chieu St.; ✆ 062/374-1122; www. sankaravietnam.com) and **Snow** (109 Nguyen Dinh Chieu St.; ✆ 062/374/3123).

Thatched-roof eateries line the main beachside road in Mui Ne. **Luna d' Autunno** (51A Nguyen Dinh Chieu St.; ✆ 062/384-7591), a popular Saigon pizzeria, has a cool restaurant under a high thatched roof. **Good Morning Vietnam Restaurant** (Km 11.8, Ham Tien; ✆ 062/384-7585), a branch of Vietnam's pizza and pasta franchise, serves affordable, familiar meals. The **Hot Rock** (Km 12.5, across from Bien Xanh Resort; ✆ 062/384-7608) is a good late-night hangout where you can get basic Western fare such as fresh, grilled seafood.

Paradise Beach Club ★ SEAFOOD   Set in a soothing seaside pavilion at the popular Coco Beach Resort (see "Where to Stay," above), the Paradise Beach Club is the place for fine fresh seafood and barbecue. Choose from a raw bar and have it cooked to order. The menu covers everything from light snacks and sandwiches to hearty Western meals. For dessert, check out the unique sundaes. The resort's more upscale restaurant, **Champa,** is also a great choice, but only for dinner.

At the Coco Beach Resort, 58 NguyenDinh Chieu St. ✆ **062/384-7111.** Main courses 50,000VND–125,000VND. MC, V. Daily 11am–3pm and 6:30–10pm.

Rung (Forest) ★ ☺ SEAFOOD/EXOTIC   This must be Mui Ne's most atmospheric restaurant, with such a jungle feel to it that kids will want to explore. Minority crafts are on display among the vines and creepers, and the menu is no less exotic. Of course, there's the obligatory seafood section, but there's also the chance to taste unusual dishes like crocodile, snake, and turtle. If you're having trouble deciding, opt for a combination platter such as a farmer's meal or pottery master's meal (both

130,000VND). Unique to this restaurant is Vietnamese water music, an ingenious system of levers, pulleys, and bamboo pipes that creates a pleasant background melody for customers. They also often stage performances of traditional music.

67 Nguyen Dinh Chieu St. © **062/384-7589.** www.forestrestaurant.com. Main dishes 60,000VND–160,000VND. Daily 10am–3pm and 6–11pm.

What to See & Do

At **Cape Mui Ne ★★**, some 20km (12 miles) northeast of Phan Thiet, you'll find Mui Ne's sprawling sand dunes. A trip out this way brings you through lots of quaint seaside villages that are worth a look. Coming from Mui Ne Beach, you'll first reach the small fishing village with a fine little rural market—great in the early morning. Heading inland away from the beach, you'll come to the towering **Red Dunes ★★**. A walk to the top offers views of the town and surrounding countryside; you're sure to be followed by a gaggle of friendly (or pestering) kids trying to sell you a postcard or interest you in the idea of renting one of their plastic sleds for the ride down the steep dune slopes—kind of fun. From the Red Dunes, if you have time, take a long and bumpy ride to unique **Lotus Lake ★★**. The views of the coast are dynamic, and this unique verdant lake in the parched silver dune makes the trip worth it. It's a long day, though. Ask at any hotel for tour arrangements. Expect to pay $25 to $30 per person for two or more to go to visit the dunes and lake.

At the highest point on the road between Phan Thiet Town and Mui Ne Beach, you won't miss the **Po Shanu Cham Towers,** impressive spires of crumbling brick set back from the road. The towers date from the end of the 13th century and are worth a stop if you weren't able to catch any of the Cham sites near Hoi An or Nha Trang. Any taxi will be happy to make a brief diversion on the way. The country's most famous Cham tower—**Po Klong Garai**—stands some 2 hours' drive up the coast near Phan Rang; all hotels can arrange tours.

Phan Thiet Market is a large but pretty standard central market in town. This is where you can pick up a bottle of locally made *nuoc mam* (fish sauce). Go early for the bringing in of the day's catch, and don't forget your camera.

Outdoor Activities

The wind conditions in Mui Ne are steady and strong in the dry season (Oct–May), and the beach has become a real kite-surfing and windsurfing mecca (it's over 12-knot winds for two-thirds of the year). **Jibe's** (90 Nguyen Dinh Chieu St.; © **062/384-7405;** www.windsurf-vietnam.com), a popular rental shop, windsurfer club, and bar, is a good place to check in or rent a board. It's also a great opportunity for first-time kite surfers, though the experience doesn't come cheap: A 10-hour package including a week's lodging costs around $700, or you can take 5 hours over 3 days with room for $350. The focus is on safety, of course, and the savings are significant here (similar lessons elsewhere cost a mint).

Sailors will want to contact the folks at the **Mui Ne Sailing Club** (24 Nguyen Dinh Chieu St.; © **062/384-7440**), or at any hotel or resort, about renting Hobie Cat and Laser sailboats, windsurfers, jet skis, and runabouts.

Finally, there are two outstanding golf courses in the vicinity: the Nick Faldo–designed **Ocean Dunes Golf Course** (1 Ton Duc Than St., Phan Thiet; © **062/382-2393**) at the Novotel Dunes Hotel is a big draw in town, while the superb new **Sealinks Golf Course** (© **062/374-1666;** www.sealinkscity.com) at the beginning of Mui Ne's beach strip is inspired by links courses in Scotland, though the gorgeous views are unmistakably tropical.

HO CHI MINH CITY (SAIGON) ★★

Ho Chi Minh City—or Saigon, as it is once again commonly known—is a relatively young Asian city, founded in the 18th century. Settled mainly by civil war refugees from northern Vietnam as well as Chinese merchants, it quickly became a major commercial center. When the French took over the country they called Cochin China, Saigon became the capital. After the French left in 1954, Saigon remained the capital of South Vietnam until national reunification in 1975.

Saigon is still Vietnam's commercial headquarters, brash and busy, with a keen sense of its own importance. Located on the Saigon River, it's Vietnam's major port and largest city, with a population of around seven million people. True to its reputation, the city is noisy, crowded, and dirty, but the central business district is rapidly developing in steel-and-glass precision to rival any metropolis on the globe. Still, the old Saigon survives in wide downtown avenues flanked by pristine colonials. Hectic and eclectic, this place has an attitude all its own.

Some of Saigon's tourism highlights include the **Vietnam History Museum;** the grisly **War Remnants Museum; and Cholon,** the Chinese district, with its pagodas and exotic stores. **Dong Khoi Street**—formerly fashionable Rue Catinat during the French era and Tu Do, or Freedom Street, during the American war—is still lined with grand colonial hotels, chic shops, and cafes. The food in Saigon is some of the best Vietnam has to offer, the nightlife sparkles, and the shopping is good. The city is also a logical jumping-off point for excursions to other southern destinations: the Mekong Delta (p. 356), the Cu Chi Tunnels (p. 356), and Phan Thiet Town and Mui Ne Beach (see previous section).

Getting There

BY PLANE Most regional airlines connect with Ho Chi Minh, including Malaysian Airlines, Thai Airways, Singapore Airlines, Lao Airlines, Garuda Indonesia, Philippine Airlines, and Cathay Pacific. **Vietnam Airlines** usually has the best fares, thanks to government controls; to confirm or book flights, you can call its local office at the 16th Floor, Sun Wah Building, 115 Nguyen Hue, District 1 (© **08/3832-0320;** fax 08/3848-6945). If you're flying to Vietnam directly from North America, check with **United Airlines** and **Cathay Pacific** for good fares and itineraries. Domestically, Ho Chi Minh City (Saigon) is linked by Vietnam Airlines flights from Hanoi, Hue, Danang, Hoi An, Nha Trang, and Dalat. The budget airline **Jetstar Pacific** (177 Vo Thi Sau St., District 3; © **08/6290-7349**) also flies to the major cities.

At the **Tan Son Nhat International Airport,** you can change foreign currency for VND, or get cash from an ATM machine with your credit card. Arranging a hotel limousine to greet you will certainly make life a bit easier, but taxis are plentiful outside the arrivals hall. The trip to town is around $5. To get to the airport, if you can't find a cab on the street, call **Mai Linh Taxi** (© **08/3822-6666**).

BY BUS/MINIVAN By bus, Saigon is about 5½ hours from Dalat, the nearest major city. All of the open-tour buses connect here, of course, and line the streets around the Pham Ngu Lao area. See "Visitor Information & Tours," below.

BY CAR Self-drive car hire is not yet possible in Vietnam, but hiring a car with English-speaking driver can be the best way to explore the country. Contact **Budget** (www.budget.com.vn) for rates. For city tours and 1-day tours out of town, any hotel can fix you up with a tour group.

Getting Around

Saigon is divided into districts, as is Hanoi, and is relatively easy to navigate. Be sure to know the district along with the address of your destination, and try to group your sightseeing accordingly (avoid crisscrossing districts in a day). Most of the hotels, bars, shops, and restaurants are in District 1, easily covered on foot, while sightseeing attractions are spread among Districts 1, 3, and 5 (Cholon).

BY TAXI   Taxis are clustered around the bigger hotels and restaurants. They cost 15,000VND to start and 11,000VND or so for every kilometer thereafter. If you need to call ahead, try **Mai Linh Taxi** (✆ 08/3822-6666) or **Vina Taxi** (✆ 08/3811-1111).

BY CAR   You can simplify your sightseeing efforts if you hire a car and driver for the day from **Ann Tours** or **Saigontourist** (see "Visitor Information & Tours," below).

BY MOTORBIKE/BICYCLE   Saigon is cursed with the country's most chaotic traffic, so you might want to think twice before renting a motorbike or bicycle. You can, however, hop a **motorcycle taxi**—a quick trip is 10,000VND, while hourly booking can be in the ballpark of 60,000VND with some haggling. It's a bit hair-raising sometimes, but a good way to get around.

BY CYCLO   Cyclos are available for an hourly rental of about 80,000VND, but they simply are not a good option in Saigon, especially outside District 1. First, drivers have an odd habit of not speaking English (or indeed, any other language) halfway through your trip and taking you to places you never asked to see, or driving around in circles pretending to be confused. Second, riding in a slow, open convey-ance amid thousands of motorbikes and cars is unpleasant and dangerous—plus cyclo passengers are low to the ground and in the front, functioning something like a bumper. Third, drive-by thefts from riders are common even during daylight hours.

Visitor Information & Tours

Every major tourist agency has its headquarters or a branch in Saigon. All will be able to book tours and travel throughout the city and the southern region, and usually the countryside as well.

- **Ann Tours** (58 Ton That Tung St., District 1; ✆ 08/3925-3636; fax 08/3832-3866; www.anntours.com) has a great reputation that is well deserved. It special-izes in custom tours for individuals and small groups. It can be relatively expensive, but that's compared to the seat-in-coach cattle-drive tours. These guys will help you with virtually anything you want to do in Vietnam. Ask for director Tony Nong, and tell him Frommer's sent you.

- **Exotissimo Travel** (80–82 Phan Xich Long St., Phu Nhuan District; ✆ 08/3995-9898; fax 08/3995-9184; www.exotissimo.com) can arrange just about any tour or international itinerary. It's popular with expats and has convenient offices through-out the region.

- **Sinhbalo Adventure Travel** (283/20 Pham Ngu Lao St., District 1 [down a small alley off the main street]; ✆ 08/3837-6766; fax 08/3836-7682; www.sinhbalo.com) is a superefficient setup specializing in cycling and motorbike tours, but their in-depth knowledge can help to customize any itinerary.

Ho Chi Minh City (Saigon)

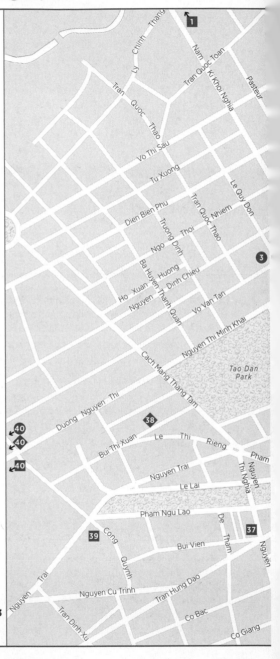

BUDGET TOURS

○ **Sinh Café** (246–248 De Tham St., District 1; ℂ **08/3838-9597** or 08/3836-9322; www.thesinhtourist.vn) is a backpacker's choice for inexpensive travel and tours. On paper, the tours seem exactly the same as others offered through private tour agents, but the price tags are cheaper.

○ **TNK** (216 De Tham St., District 1; ℂ **08/3920-4766;** www.tnktravelvietnam.com) is just another of the many options.

[FastFACTS] HO CHI MINH CITY (SAIGON)

American Express
Amex is represented in Saigon by **Exotissimo Travel** (80–82 Phan Xich Long St., Phu Nhuan District; ℂ **08/3995-9898**). *Be warned:* It does not provide complete travel services, but can direct you if you lose your card. Hours are Monday through Friday from 8am to 5pm.

Currency Exchange
You can change money in banks, hotels, and jewelry stores. The exchange rate in Saigon is better than in many smaller cities. There's a convenient currency-exchange storefront at 4C Le Loi St., right in the town center—a good spot for the right rates on traveler's checks.

Major banks include **ANZ Bank,** 11 Me Linh Sq., District 1 (ℂ **08/3829-9319**); **Citibank,** 115 Nguyen Hue St., District 1 (ℂ **08/3824-2118**); **HSBC,** 235 Dong Khoi St., District 1 (ℂ **08/3829-2288**); and **Vietcombank,** 29 Ben Chuong Duong, District 1 (ℂ **08/3829-7245**). ANZ Bank, Citibank, and HSBC all have **ATMs** dispensing dollars and VND around the

clock, though **ANZ** is the only one that doesn't have extra service charges on top of your withdrawal.

Embassies & Consulates For embassies, see "Fast Facts: Vietnam," p. 249. Consulates are all in District 1, as follows: **U.S.,** 4 Le Duan St. (ℂ **08/3822-9433**); **Canada,** 10th Floor, 235 Dong Khoi St. (ℂ **08/3827-9899**); **Australia,** 5B Ton Duc Thang St. (ℂ **08/3829-6035**); **New Zealand,** 9th Floor, 235 Dong Khoi St. (ℂ **08/3822-6907**); and **U.K.,** 25 Le Duan St. (ℂ **08/3823-2604**).

Emergencies For police, dial ℂ **113;** for fire, dial ℂ **114;** and for an ambulance, dial ℂ **115.** Have a translator on hand, if necessary; operators don't speak English.

Internet Access
Almost every upscale hotel provides Internet services, but you can bet they charge a pretty penny. Ironically, most budget hotels and some midrange hotels offer free Internet use or Wi-Fi. You won't find any service on Dong Khoi, but a

short walk in any direction brings you to storefronts that charge an average of 10,000VND per hour. Service in the Pham Ngu Lao backpacker area is fast and cheap; Internet cafes line De Tham and charge around 5,000VND per hour.

Mail The main post office is at 2 Coq Xu Paris, District 1 (ℂ **08/3827-1149**), just across from Notre Dame Cathedral. It's open daily from 7:30am to 8pm. All services are available here, including long-distance calling and callback. The building itself is a historic landmark (see "What to See & Do," later in this chapter). Postal service is also available in most hotels and at various locations throughout the city.

Safety The biggest threat to your health in Saigon is likely to be the traffic. Cross the wildly busy streets at a slow, steady pace. If you're having a really hard time getting across, find a local who is crossing and stick to his heels.

Pickpocketing is a big problem, especially the motorbike drive-bys in which someone slashes the shoulder strap of your bag and drives off. Keep your bag close and away from traffic. Hang on to your wallet, don't wear flashy jewelry, and be especially wary in crowded places like markets. Women should avoid wandering around alone past 11pm or so. Contact your consulate or hotel if you have a serious problem. If you insist on going to the local police, bring a translator. Know that the Saigon police tend to throw up their hands at "minor" infractions such as purse snatching or thievery.

Telephones The city code for Saigon is **08.**

Where to Stay

Saigon has the best variety of accommodations in Vietnam, from deluxe business and family hotels to spotless smaller options. Most upmarket hotels are clustered around Dong Khoi Street in District 1, as are many restaurants, shops, and bars. Budget lodgings can be found in the area around De Tham Street, still in District 1 but about a kilometer (⅔ mile) west of the center. Restaurant and bar prices around here are also much cheaper than downtown.

Remember that prices listed here are the "rack rates" and should be considered only a guideline. Internet, group, and standard promotional rates are the rule. Especially in the off season (Mar–Sept), expect discounts of up to 50%. Note that many hotels levy a VAT of up to 20%.

VERY EXPENSIVE

Caravelle Hotel ★★ Named for a type of light, fast ship, this sleek downtown hotel gives you that very impression. A French company built the original in 1956 and, after honeymoon years as the town's address of note, the place became a shabby hangout for wartime journalists and then fell into obscurity as the Doc Lap (Independence) Hotel in postwar years. In 1998, the Caravelle was renovated beyond recognition and is now an extremely attractive, efficient, and well appointed hotel. Business travelers and well heeled tourists enjoy the plush rooms, with neutral furnishings and marble bathrooms; higher floors have great views. In 2008, the hotel underwent a complete overhaul again, well timed to stand up to new competition from the nearby Park Hyatt and Sheraton. The best addition: incredibly comfortable Posturepedic mattresses and 400-thread-count linen. This is one of the best places to catch a proper night's sleep. The classic character of the old hotel lives on in the rooftop Saigon Saigon bar, an open-air colonial throwback with rattan shades, low-slung chairs, and twirling ceiling fans. If you let your imagination go, you might just see Graham Greene sidling up to the bar.

19 Lam Son Sq., District 1, Ho Chi Minh City. ⓒ **08/3823-4999.** Fax 08/3824-3999. www.caravellehotel. com. 335 units. $188–$245 double; suites from $305. AE, DC, MC, V. **Amenities:** 2 restaurants; 3 bars; executive-level rooms; health club; Jacuzzi; lovely rooftop pool; room service; sauna; spa. In room: A/C, satellite TV, fridge, hair dryer, minibar.

Equatorial ★ This huge building is a long way from downtown Saigon, in the far reaches of District 5, but the Equatorial has long been a popular business address for regional and international conventioneers. It covers all the bases, with good amenities and services, and now offers one of the city's most exciting dining options at its Orientica Seafood Restaurant (see "Where to Dine," later in this chapter) and an international buffet at the Chit Chat Café. Deluxe rooms are not so much luxurious and opulent as tidy, utilitarian, and cozy, though the suites are very classy. The lobby bar is always busy with foreigners, and there's a spa and decent pool to help guests to unwind after a busy day.

242 Tran Binh Trong St., District 5, Ho Chi Minh City. © **08/3839-7777.** Fax 08/3839-0011. www. equatorial.com. 333 units. $220–$390 double; from $520 suite. MC, V. **Amenities:** 2 restaurants; 2 bars; airport transfer; concierge; health club; Jacuzzi; outdoor pool w/swim-up bar; room service; smoke-free floors; spa; Wi-Fi in lobby and restaurants. *In room:* A/C, satellite TV, hair dryer.

Park Hyatt Saigon ★★★ This is, hands down, the best business hotel in the city. From the modern black *ao dai* uniforms of reception staff to the nonbranded, black-top water bottles in the bathroom, everything at the Park Hyatt is sleek, modern, and sophisticated. Lines are clean and elegant, and teak floors and antique glass combine with traditional lacquer to create instant nostalgia. The rooms, which feel like a Vietnamese residence, are spacious and well appointed; some have verandas that open directly onto the pool. Modern features include soundproof windows and flatscreen TVs. That outdoor pool—with midstream jets to massage you while you swim—and the accompanying landscaped green space give the place a resort feel. On-site restaurants include Square One, which serves seafood and Vietnamese along with grilled steaks, and Opera, which is strictly Italian down to its exclusively Italian wine list. The Park Hyatt lacks a wartime or French colonial history, so any nostalgia you may feel here is carefully designed. That said, the hotel is becoming the hot spot for international jet-setters (the private driveway and back entrance help). Still, you don't have to be the biggest superstar in the world to find the Park Hyatt a good choice for a luxury stay in the center of Saigon.

2 Lam Son Sq., District 1, Ho Chi Minh City. © **08/3824-1234.** Fax 08/3823-7569. www.saigon.park. hyatt.com. 252 units. $320–$450 double; $620–$2,600 suite. AE, MC, V. **Amenities:** 2 restaurants; bar/lounge; babysitting; concierge; executive-level rooms; best health club in town; Internet access; Jacuzzi; outdoor pool; room service; spa; cooking classes. *In room:* A/C, flatscreen satellite TV, hair dryer, high-speed Internet access, minibar.

Sheraton Saigon Hotel & Towers ★★ The tallest, and one of the newest, hotels in Ho Chi Minh City, the Sheraton is the talk of the town. Everything is done on a grand scale, from colossal meeting rooms and top business facilities to plush guest rooms. It's high-end comfort from a brand that you can bank on. Rooms have it all: flatscreen TVs, broadband Internet, large desks, and great views of town. Bathrooms are huge, with separate shower and tub. Rooms in the new towers feature ultracontemporary style and comfort. The Sheraton seemingly covers every amenity, from a host of fine-dining options to the spa area (with squash courts and an outdoor pool) to the popular nightspot, which plays host to live bands every night. From the moment your car pulls up out front, you'll know you've arrived: Every guest here is given the red-carpet treatment.

88 Dong Khoi St., District 1, Ho Chi Minh City. © **08/3827-2828.** Fax 08/3827-2929. www.starwood hotels.com. 470 units. $215–$280 deluxe; from $430 suite. AE, MC, V. **Amenities:** 5 restaurants; 4 bars; babysitting; concierge; executive-level rooms (w/separate check-in); health club; Jacuzzi; outdoor pool; room service; smoke-free rooms; spa; steam room. *In room:* A/C, satellite TV, fridge, hair dryer, Internet access ($15 a day), minibar.

Sofitel Plaza Saigon ★★ The Sofitel chain is famous in Southeast Asia for finding grand old colonial dames and converting them into the most charming hotels. This is not one of them. Opened in 1999, the Sofitel Plaza is one of the shiny towers on the Saigon skyline; what it lacks in colonial charm, however, it more than makes up for in luxury, convenience, and comfort. Accommodations are handsome, with fine Art Deco touches such as the curving, clean-lined desks in most rooms. You'll never lack any amenity here, and the staff is helpful and professional. In a convenient spot just across from the former U.S. and French embassies, this is a popular choice for the international business crowd and long-stay executives, who enjoy the sleek executive floor with private lounge, buffet, drinks, and business services.

17 Le Duan Blvd., District 1, Ho Chi Minh City. ⓒ **800/221-4542** in the U.S., or 08/3824-1555. Fax 08/3824-1666. www.sofitel.com. 286 units. $196 superior; $260 club room; from $420 suite. AE, MC, V. **Amenities:** 2 restaurants; bar; babysitting; concierge; executive-level rooms; health club; Internet access (in business center); luxury rooftop pool; room service; sauna; smoke-free rooms; spa. *In room:* A/C, satellite TV, fridge, minibar.

EXPENSIVE

Grand Hotel ★★ This 1930s colonial, another owned by Saigontourist, is done just right (well, close, at least). The renovated Grand has a serene atmosphere, with some choice features such as the lovingly restored iron elevator at the center. The Grand is at its best when taking advantage of its long history, thus rooms in the older block are much more charming than the bland, chain-hotel units in the new wing. Deluxe rooms clustered in the old building near the elevator have classic high ceilings, wood floors, and a comfortable colonial charm. All units are big, with simple dark-wood furniture—and without the musty smell that plagues many Saigon hotels. The bathrooms are small, but have plenty of counter space. The lobby is bright, the staff is friendly, and the location on Dong Khoi couldn't be better. The quiet atmosphere suggests leisure rather than business travelers, though, and the hotel boasts all the right amenities, including the central courtyard's small but peaceful pool area, a unique escape from busy Ho Chi Minh City.

8 Dong Khoi St., District 1, Ho Chi Minh City. ⓒ **08/3823-0163.** Fax 063/3827-3047. www.grandhotel. vn. 107 units. $100 $115 deluxe; from $130 suite. AE, MC, V. **Amenities:** 2 restaurants; bar; small health club; Jacuzzi; nice outdoor courtyard pool; room service; sauna. *In room:* A/C, satellite TV, fridge, hair dryer, minibar, Wi-Fi.

Hotel Majestic ★ This 1925 landmark, on the riverside corner of Dong Khoi Street (formerly Rue Catinat), still has some historical charm despite many renovations—and it's a real picture-postcard colonial from the outside. Owned by Saigontourist, the Majestic is always full, as it's a good, affordable, atmospheric choice. Botched details abound on the inside, however, like tacky decor, but the rooms and facilities are still classy and comfortable for the price. High ceilings, original wood floors, and retro fixtures are a nice touch. Bathrooms are large, with tubs and old-style taps. The small courtyard pool area is lined with picturesque shuttered windows and walkways; in fact, the best choices are the deluxe rooms facing this quiet spot. Suites are just larger versions of deluxe rooms, while standards are small and quite basic. Buffet meals at the fine restaurant, Cyclo, are accompanied by either piano or traditional music and sometimes dance. The staff has a genuine desire to make your stay memorable, whether that means explaining the eccentricities of Vietnamese cuisine or hailing you a taxi. Don't miss the great views from the rooftop bar, a good spot to have a chat and popular for weddings and parties.

1 Dong Khoi St., District 1, Ho Chi Minh City. ⓒ **08/3829-5517.** Fax 08/3829-5510. www.majesticsaigon. com.vn. 175 units. $168–$228 double; $268–$438 suite. AE, DC, MC, V. **Amenities:** 2 restaurants; 3 bars; free airport pickup; babysitting; basic health club; Internet access; small courtyard pool; sauna; spa. *In room:* A/C, satellite TV, fridge, hair dryer, minibar, Wi-Fi.

May Hotel ★   This is one of the best of a clutch of new hotels in downtown Saigon, with a good location just a couple of blocks east from fashionable Dong Khoi Street. Rooms have pleasant, light-wood furniture and spacious bathrooms, and deluxe rooms also have a small balcony. As the place is new, all facilities such as the large pool on the 15th floor and the gym on the 14th floor are in tiptop condition. There's a business center offering high-speed Internet connections, and the staff can help with transport arrangements around town.

28–30 Thi Sach St., District 1, Ho Chi Minh City. ☎ **08/3823-4501.** Fax 08/3823-4502. www.mayhotel. com.vn. 117 units. $100–$120 double; $160 suite. AE, MC, V. **Amenities:** Restaurant/bar; gym; pool; room service; sauna; Wi-Fi. *In room:* A/C, satellite TV, fridge, minibar.

Mövenpick Saigon Hotel ★   Swiss hotelier Mövenpick recently took over management of this former CIA and U.S. Army quarters and has given it a much-needed face-lift (some taxi drivers still know the hotel by its former name: Omni). The carpeted rooms are extremely comfortable and boast sleek new furniture, flatscreen TVs, bathrooms fitted with marble countertops, rain-shower heads, and glass partitions to lend the room a spacious feel. The lobby retains its colonial flavor and Art Deco details, while a small casino features state-of-the-art gaming machines. Dining options include Japanese, Cantonese, Vietnamese, and international cuisine, and there's a well equipped gym and wellness studio next to the large pool. The only drawback is the location; it's just 10 minutes from the airport, but you're in District 3 and some 15 minutes from the city center. There are often special offers such as 3 nights for 2—check out the website for details.

253 Nguyen Van Troi St., Phu Nhuan District (District 3), Ho Chi Minh City. ☎ **08/3844-9222.** Fax 08/3844-9198. www.moevenpick-hotels.com. 278 units. $120 deluxe; $150 executive deluxe rooms. AE, DC, MC, V. **Amenities:** 4 restaurants; bar; babysitting; executive-level rooms; health club; Internet access; Jacuzzi; outdoor pool; room service; sauna. *In room:* A/C, TV, fridge, hair dryer, minibar.

New World Hotel Saigon ★★   President Clinton called this first-rate hotel home during his brief stay in Saigon; it's a fine choice, indeed, whether you're a business traveler, tourist, or world leader. The location is in the very center of town, a short walk from **Ben Thanh Market** (p. 350). A popular park is right out front, and there's a nice bustle and feeling of connectedness to the place that's rarely found at the self-contained luxury hotels. The impeccable rooms are done in a soothing array of neutrals, while the bathrooms are a sharp contrast in black-and-gray marble. The fat pillows are a little mushy and the beds are a bit too firm, but you can't have everything. The executive floors have a lounge and an impressive list of perks: all-day refreshments, free pressing, computer hookups, and free access to financial newswire information. Service is ultraefficient. It's also one of the few hotels that asks straightaway if you'd like a nonsmoking room.

76 Le Lai St., District 1, Ho Chi Minh City. ☎ **08/3822-8888.** Fax 08/3823-0710. www.newworldsaigon. com. 538 units. $149–$189 double; from $229 suite. AE, DC, MC, V. **Amenities:** 2 restaurants; bar; babysitting; concierge; executive-level rooms; health club; outdoor pool; room service; sauna; spa; lighted tennis court. *In room:* A/C, satellite TV, fridge, Internet access, minibar.

Norfolk Hotel ★★   This snappy little business hotel has one of the highest occupancy rates in town, and for good reason: It's affordable, it's convenient, and it covers all the bases. Rooms are large and bright, furnished in slightly mismatched chain-hotel style, but everything is like new. The beds are soft and deluxe, the TVs are large, and the bathrooms are small but finished in marble. The staff is efficient and helpful.

The Corso Restaurant on the ground floor offers a good range of Asian and international dishes, as well as monthly themes and special menus. It's perfect for the business traveler or tourist seeking lots of amenities—all at reasonable prices. Book early.

117 Le Thanh Ton St., District 1, Ho Chi Minh City. ☏ **08/3829-5368.** Fax 08/3829-3415. www.norfolk hotel.com.vn. 104 units. $100–$120 double; $180 suite. Promotional and Internet rates available. AE, MC, V. **Amenities:** Restaurant; bar/club; concierge; room service; smoke-free rooms; spa. *In room:* A/C, satellite TV, fridge, free Internet access, minibar.

Renaissance Riverside Hotel Saigon ★

Managed by Marriott, the Renaissance Riverside is a convenient downtown address. The lobby is done in a colonial theme with a grand spiral staircase connecting to the mezzanine. Rooms have black-and-white tile entries, tidy carpeting, and light furnishings done in cool pastels. Electronic control panels near the headboard might remind you of a 1970s bachelor pad. Bathrooms have black-marble counters. You could be anywhere, really—everything's nice in the same way an upscale hotel might look in Bangkok, Paris, or Pittsburgh; nevertheless, the amenities, such as the small rooftop pool and health club, are good. The Riverside is a popular business hotel, which means smoking everywhere: All public spaces are a bit musty, even on designated nonsmoking floors. If you want a nonsmoking room, ask to see it before checking in. Don't miss the dim sum lunch at the fine Cantonese restaurant, Kabin.

8-15 Ton Duc Thang St., District 1, Ho Chi Minh City. **08/3822-0033.** Fax 08/3823-5666. www. renaissancehotels.com/sgnbr. 319 units. $160–$215 double; from $375 suite. AE, MC, V. **Amenities:** 2 restaurants; cafe; bar; babysitting; concierge; executive-level rooms; health club; rooftop pool w/great city view; room service; smoke-free rooms; nice spa/massage facility. *In room:* A/C, satellite TV, fridge, minibar.

Rex Hotel ★

The Rex has an unorthodox history: It used to be a French garage, was expanded by the Vietnamese, and then was used by the United States Information Agency (and some say the CIA) from 1962 to 1970. The hotel was transformed in a massive renovation and opened in 1990 as the hugely atmospheric government-run place it is today. In 2008 it was subject to yet another makeover to bring it in line with other five-star hotels in town, and a new wing was added. There are a variety of rooms, some with wooden floors and others carpeted, but all are large and clean, and feature local art on the walls. Wi-Fi and satellite TV come as standard. The Rex has a fabulous location downtown, across from a square that has a lively carnival atmosphere at night. It is also known for its rooftop bar, with its panoramic Saigon view. The shopping arcade on the first floor (stand-alone shops from Marc Jacobs, Chloe, and Balenciaga) is a dangerous distraction for shopaholics. The Cochinchine Spa provides a range of treatments that are a great relief after a busy day of sightseeing.

141 Nguyen Hue Blvd., District 1, Ho Chi Minh City. ☏ **08/3829-2185.** Fax 08/3829-6536. www.rex hotelvietnam.com. 286 units. $115–$155 double; $220–$2,000 suite. AE, MC, V. **Amenities:** 3 restaurants; 2 bars; babysitting; small health club; Jacuzzi; outdoor pool; room service; sauna; smoke-free rooms; tennis court. *In room:* A/C, satellite TV, fax machine, hair dryer, Wi-Fi.

MODERATE

Bong Sen Hotel Annex

This small annex to the large Saigontourist-owned Bong Sen provides many of the same amenities as the top-end hotels at a lower price. Rooms are very basic but tidy, with light-wood furniture, thin carpet, and blue-tile bathrooms. Everything is on the small side, though, and the economy rooms have only one small window (even a junior suite isn't much bigger). Make sure you're getting the Annex and not the main Bong Sen, which, though recently renovated, isn't much of a value. Service is indifferent, but this is a good place to just lay your head for cheap. You can arrange any travel necessities elsewhere.

61-63 Hai Ba Trung St., District 1, Ho Chi Minh City. ☏ **08/3823-5818.** Fax 08/3823-5816. www.bongsen hotel2.com. 57 units. $55-$65 double; $90 junior suite. AE, MC, V. **Amenities:** Restaurant. *In room:* A/C, TV, fridge, hair dryer, minibar.

Palace Hotel ★★   This hotel is a standout for its location and price. The Palace has been around since 1968; in fact, it was popular with U.S. soldiers on R & R during the war years. Fortunately, it has been refurbished frequently, most recently in 2006 when all rooms were treated to a swanky, Art Deco–style renovation to "Signature" status. The upgrade from superior to deluxe is well worth it—the cheaper room has only one tiny window that makes it feel somewhat cavelike, while the deluxe comes with a great street view and a small balcony. Staff here is ultrafriendly.

56-66 Nguyen Hue St., District 1, Ho Chi Minh City. ☏ **08/3829-2860.** Fax 08/3824-4229. www.palace saigon.com. 144 units. $85-$95 double; $105-$140 suite. AE, MC, V. **Amenities:** 2 restaurants; 2 bars; rooftop pool; room service. *In room:* A/C, TV, fridge, minibar, free Wi-Fi.

INEXPENSIVE

If you're on a tight budget, head for **De Tham,** a backpacker haven loaded with guesthouses and minihotels; a fan-cooled room with a cold-water shower goes for as little as $5 per night, or an air-conditioned room with hot water for around $15. Most of these places are very basic (and a bit noisy from street traffic) but tidy, well run, and friendly.

An An Hotel ★   This long-running minihotel is a cut above the rest in the budget district, and recently they opened a second branch around the corner at 216 De Tham St. with slightly smaller (and cheaper) rooms. Facilities include solid furnishings, free Wi-Fi, and satellite TV, and rooms on the upper floors have city views. The staff are eager to help guests in any way they can, and there's a travel desk of TNK Travel in the lobby of the second branch.

40 Bui Vien St., District 1, Ho Chi Minh City. ☏ **08/3837-8087.** Fax 08/3837-8088. www.ananhotel.vn. 58 units. $25-$50 double. *In room:* A/C, satellite TV, hair dryer, minibar, free Wi-Fi.

Hong Hoa Hotel ★★   This minihotel is a decent choice in the De Tham budget district. Rooms are small but tidy, with real wood furniture and tile floors. It's backpacker basics here—low foam beds and little charm—but the satellite TV and IDD phones are a real luxury in this price range. It's a funny spot: If it looks like two addresses, it is, with one entrance through a small grocery storefront on busy De Tham and the other off Pham Ngu Lao. The hotel is cozy, safe, and friendly, and if you stay long enough, you'll be adopted (and certainly learn some Vietnamese). If the place is full, which is more often than not the case, try the neighboring **Lan Anh** (252 De Tham St.)—another friendly, family-run place.

185/28 Pham Ngu Lao St., 250 De Tham St., District 1, Ho Chi Minh City. ☏ **08/3836-1915.** www.hong hoavn.com. 7 units. $17-$25 double. Rates include tax and service charge. MC, V. **Amenities:** Popular Internet center (free access for guests). *In room:* A/C, satellite TV, free Wi-Fi.

Madam Cuc ★★ 💼   The congenial Madam Cuc has a simple policy that works so well that her rooms are almost always full. It's this: Treat all guests like family, remembering their names, helping out with transport arrangements, and providing a nourishing, free breakfast (as well as a basic lunch and dinner if you happen to be around!) and Internet use. This personal treatment brings a steady stream of repeat customers, and there are now three branches of Madam Cuc's within a short walk of each other in the budget district. Rooms are basic but well maintained, with air-conditioning, satellite TV, and hot-water showers. Reserve through their website to avoid disappointment, and ask for a room out back to escape from the constantly honking car horns on the street.

127 Cong Quynh, District 1, Ho Chi Minh City (main branch). © **08/3836-8761.** Fax 083836-0658. www.madamcuchotels.com. 90 units. $25–$30 double. No credit cards. **Amenities:** Free Internet use. *In room:* A/C, satellite TV, minibar.

Spring Hotel (Mua Xuan) ★★   If you don't care about fancy amenities and want to be downtown, look no further than the Spring, with nicer rooms than those at many hotels twice the price. Accommodations are neat and clean, with comfy beds, big TVs, and solid dark-wood or rattan furniture. The floral motif isn't bad, and the carpeted floors are impeccably clean. The lowest-priced "economy" rooms have no windows. Suites are large, with couches in separate sitting rooms. Go as high up as you can to escape street noise, which is the hotel's one failing (the elevator's kind of slow, too). The Spring has an unsettling Greco-Roman motif, with statues and filigree here and there; if the lobby's hanging ivy, colonnades, and grand staircase are a bit over the top, the rooms are a bit more toned down and utilitarian. A short walk from Dong Khoi and the central business district, this is a popular choice for long-term business travelers. The staff couldn't be nicer or more helpful.

44–46 Le Thanh Ton St., District 1, Ho Chi Minh City. © **08/3829-7362.** Fax 08/3822-1583. 45 units. $35–$60 double; $74 suite. Rates include breakfast. AE, MC, V. **Amenities:** Restaurant; bar; room service; Wi-Fi. *In room:* A/C, TV, fridge, minibar.

Where to Dine

Saigon has the largest array of restaurants in Vietnam, with virtually every world cuisine represented, and for many visitors their most exciting discoveries in the city are of a culinary variety. The area around **Dong Khoi** has lots of fine-dining choices, including **Vietnam House,** 93–95 Dong Khoi (© **08/3829-1623**), an excellent introduction to Vietnamese cuisine, and the oh so posh **On the 6,** 6 Dong Khoi St. (© **08/3823-8866**), run by Chef Didier Corlou of La Verticale (p. 260) fame and formerly of Le Beaulieu.

Ask locals where to eat, though, and they'll point you to the **Ben Thanh Market** or a local vendor on wheels; for them, eating is about taste, not ambience. Ho Chi Minh's famous street stalls serve local specials such as *mien ga,* vermicelli, chicken, and mushrooms in a delicate soup; *lau hai san,* a tangy seafood soup with mustard greens; and, of course, *pho,* Vietnam's staple noodle soup.

EXPENSIVE

Amigo ★★ ARGENTINE/STEAKHOUSE   This is one of those expat gems you'll want to seek out. It serves some of the best steaks you'll ever have—anywhere. The roomy two-floor downtown setting has an Argentine steakhouse theme, laid-back but classy. The friendly staff and chummy atmosphere around the imposing bar will make you feel at home. But it's the food that sells this place: imported steak done just how you like it, chargrilled to perfection (not pan-fried, as is common in this part of the world). The filet mignon with red shallots would hold its own in the heart of Chicago. There's also a full raw bar and a roster of seafood specials and salads. Entrees come with baked potatoes and corn; for a real slice of home, follow up with apple strudel or ice-cream roulade. The great wine list features Argentine and Chilean reds, among others; there's also a full-service bar.

55 Nguyen Hue St., District 1. ✆ **08/3829-0437.** Main courses 320,000VND–510,000VND. AE, MC, V. Daily 11am–2pm and 5–11pm.

Hoi An ★★ VIETNAMESE   Run by the same folks who bring you Mandarin just around the corner (see below), Hoi An serves a similar complement of fine, authentic Vietnamese; here the focus is on central Vietnam's lighter fare and cuisine from Hoi An, Hue, and Saigon. On busy Le Thanh Ton just north of the town center, the building is a nice re-creation of a traditional Vietnamese home, and the upstairs dining room is an interesting faux-rustic blend of wood and bamboo. Presentation here is original; witness the hollowed coconut used to serve fine crab and asparagus. Try the drunken shrimp, large prawns soaked in rice whiskey and pan-fried tableside. Order a cover-the-table meal for a group, and you're sure to go away smiling. Call ahead to ask about the authentic Vietnamese classical music (most nights).

11 Le Thanh Ton St., District 1. ✆ **08/3823-7694.** Main courses $9.50–$48. AE, MC, V. Daily 11:30am–2pm and 5:30–11pm.

Mandarin ★★ VIETNAMESE/CHINESE   On a quiet side street between busy Le Than Thon and the river, cross the threshold at Mandarin and enter a quaint, elegant oasis that will have you forgetting the city outside. The decor is an upscale Chinese motif with timber beams, fine screen paintings, and artwork. It's plush but not stuffy; you'll feel comfortable in casual clothes or a suit. The staff is attentive but doesn't hover and is helpful with suggestions and explanations. Ask about daily specials and set menus. Don't miss the excellent spicy sautéed beef, served in bamboo with rice, or the famed duck done in sweet "Mandarin style." The steamed lobster in garlic is as good as it sounds; the seafood steamboat for four is a real coup. The restaurant features a live classical trio (call ahead for the schedule).

11A Ngo Van Nam, District 1. ✆ **08/3822-9783.** Fax 08/3825-6185. Main courses $8.80–$55; set menus from $35 per person (minimum 2 people). AE, MC, V. Daily 5:30–10pm.

Orientica ★★ VIETNAMESE/SEAFOOD   The first thing that strikes you about this restaurant, located on the second floor of the Equatorial Hotel, is the vibrant decor of red, silver, and black, portraying the restaurant's theme of "fire, water, and ice." The specialty is seafood, and guests choose their meal either from a bed of ice or directly from a water tank. They can then watch the chefs prepare their food at the city's only teppanyaki "fire bar." Since opening in 2007, the restaurant has been showered with awards, including "Best Culinary Establishment of the Year 2009" at the Vietnam Culinary Challenge. It's a bit of a ride from the city center, but for those who make it, it's a rewarding journey.

Equatorial Hotel, 242 Tran Binh Trong St., District 5, Ho Chi Minh City. ✆ **08/3839-7777.** Main courses $18–$42. AE, DC, MC, V. Daily 11:30am–2:30pm and 6:30–10:30pm.

Square One ★★ VIETNAMESE/WESTERN   You don't come to Square One to eat, you come to spend an evening paying homage to good food. The cooks behind the glass partitions look confident and are constantly in motion, grilling seafood, changing charcoal, or wrapping fish in giant pandanus leaves. The menu is divided into traditional Vietnamese starters and mains and Western dishes. The spring rolls— pork, bean sprouts, and mint wrapped in fresh rice paper, then wrapped in a cabbage leaf and tied together with a strip of pandanus leaf—are light, crunchy, and incredibly fresh. Vietnamese dishes are meant to be shared, so expect large portions for main courses (the red grouper, grilled to perfection and served with a zesty chile sauce, is more than enough for two people). Early evening, chill lounge music segues into a funkier upbeat tempo after 9pm. Get a table facing one of the open kitchens—it's better than people-watching.

Park Hyatt Hotel. ✆ **08/3824-1234.** Main courses $10-$36; hefty steaks on the Western menu $34-$85. AE, MC, V. Daily noon-2:30pm and 6-10:30pm.

Xu ★★ VIETNAMESE/FUSION   Co-owner Bien Nguyen left school at 15 to work in the food-and-beverage industry. An old French couple took him under their wing and taught him, as he puts it, "the A to Z of F and B." Saigon is grateful to that couple and to Bien, who has created one of the finest restaurants Saigon has on offer. The food is innovative and yet retains the traditional taste and feel of Vietnamese eats. Highly recommended is the tamarind braised beef cheeks, accompanied by pumpkin mash, bok choy mushrooms, and pumpkin flower—a delicate combination of tastes and textures. The decor is modern, with retro wooden chairs fixed with deep-purple velvet cushions. The lounge is a great place for pre- and after-dinner drinks. The first-floor coffee bar is good for a casual grilled sandwich at lunch.

71-75 Hai Ba Trung, District 1. ✆ **08/3824-8468.** www.xusaigon.com. Main courses 225,000VND-435,000VND. Set dinner 800,000VND (8 courses); 500,000VND (4 courses) AE, MC, V. Daily 11am-midnight.

MODERATE

Al Fresco's ★ ☺ WESTERN   Just like the popular Al Fresco's in Hanoi, this new location in the heart of Saigon (just a stone's throw from the Sheraton) is Vietnam's answer to TGI Friday's. Burgers, steaks, popular ribs, good pizzas, pastas, and hearty salads all stick to your ribs. Worthwhile starters include chicken wings, satay, and fried calamari. Al Fresco's is the best choice for Western comfort foods or for something familiar—kids love it. Expat management and ultrafriendly waitstaff make a visit here a welcome slice of home.

27 Dong Du, District 1. ✆ **08/3822-7318.** www.alfrescosgroup.com. Main courses 175,000VND-385,000VND. MC, V. Daily 8:30am-11pm.

Augustin ★ FRENCH   On the quaint "restaurant row" of Ngueyen Thiep (just off Don Khoi), this bright, lively restaurant is a favorite with French expats and tourists, as it's just a few steps from all the top hotels. The food is simple yet innovative French fare, including beef *pot-au-feu* and sea bass tartare with olives. Try the seafood stew, lightly seasoned with saffron and packed with fish, clams, and shrimp. The seating is quite cozy, especially since the place is always full, and the Vietnamese staff is exceptionally friendly, speaking both French and English. The menu is bilingual, too. A large French wine list and classic dessert menu finish off a delightful meal.

10 Nguyen Thiep, District 1. ✆ **08/3829-2941.** Main courses 135,000VND-260,000VND. No credit cards. Daily 11:30am-2pm and 6-10:30pm.

Lemongrass VIETNAMESE   Also located on "restaurant row" in the downtown area, this place has three floors of subdued fine dining—a great place to duck out of the midday sun. The atmosphere is candlelit and intimate, very Vietnamese, with cane furniture and tile floors, yet it's not overly formal. Set lunches are an affordable and light option: soup, spring rolls, and a light curry for around $5. The extensive menu emphasizes seafood and seasonal specials. Particularly outstanding are the deep-fried prawns in coconut batter and the crab sautéed in salt-and-pepper sauce. Go with a group, if possible, and sample as many delicacies as possible.

4 Nguyen Thiep St., District 1. ✆ **08/3822-0496.** Main courses 150,000VND-390,000VND; lunch set menus from 100,000VND. AE, MC, V. Daily 11am-2pm and 5-10pm.

The Refinery ★ FRENCH   This French bistro is built in the former headquarters of the leading opium refinery (hence the name) of old Indochina. They've got a great selection of light and filling food that's made just right. The eggplant with tomato-mint sauce, goat's cheese, and brown and wild rice is a perfect blend of healthy starches and cheesy indulgence. Being a bistro, they're always ready to serve a coq au vin at the drop of a hat. The understated decor makes for casual, intimate dining.

74/7 Hai Ba Trung St. (walk through the traditional yellow gate; it's on your left after about 100m/328 ft.), District 1. 𝄐 **08/3823-0509.** Main courses 100,000VND–250,000VND. MC, V. Daily 10am–midnight.

Skewers ★ MEDITERRANEAN   The best food at this chic bistro does in fact come on skewers; barbecue entrees, particularly the lamb kabobs, are delicious. Also try the moussaka, baked Moroccan sea bass, good pastas, vodka-flamed beef, or ribs dipped in honey. All the flame-bursting barbecuing is done in an open-air kitchen at the front of the restaurant—fun to watch. The salads are delicious, and the light meals and starters include great dips such as hummus and baba ghanouj. The atmosphere is candlelit and cozy, a great spot for a romantic evening.

9A Thai Van Lung St., District 1. 𝄐 **08/3829-2216.** www.skewers-restaurant.com. Main courses 85,000VND–160,000VND. MC, V. Mon–Fri 11:30am–2pm; daily 6–10:30pm.

Song Ngu ★ VIETNAMESE/SEAFOOD   Ask any Saigonese, and they'll help you find Song Ngu. Offset from a relatively quiet street, the restaurant is a popular place for locals and tour groups (who sit in a separate room). It's an old standby for good reason: Though the interior is nothing special, the food is anything but bland. The chefs are imaginative, the ingredients are fresh, and the portions are plentiful. And if it comes out of the water, Song Ngu does it right. Crab spring rolls, scallops, and steamed clams with lemon grass are a good start, but for the indecisive, there's an extensive list of the chef's recommendations.

70 Suong Nguyen Anh St., District 1. 𝄐 **08/3832-5017.** www.songngu.com. A la carte dishes 90,000VND–420,000VND. MC, V. Daily 11am–2pm and 5–10pm.

Temple Club ★★ VIETNAMESE   For atmosphere alone, the Temple Club is a must-see in Ho Chi Minh. As the name suggests, this is a turn-of-the-20th-century Chinese temple with original wood and masonry. The ceiling is high, the walls are exposed brick, the floor is terra cotta draped in antique throw rugs, and there are some great Buddhist tapestries and statuary on display. Patrons gather at a classic wooden bar and in a formal but comfortable dining room, as well as in the lounge area in the back for coffee and dessert. The cuisine is standard Vietnamese from all parts of the country. Abandon your diet and order the Hue-style spring rolls, pork filling in lattice wrappers fried to crispy perfection. The *tom me,* prawns in tamarind sauce, is a smart choice as well. The banana-coconut-cream pudding with sesame seeds is a decadent dessert, and the coffee is the real thing.

29 Ton That Thiep St., District 1. 𝄐 **08/3829-9244.** Main courses 130,000VND–220,000VND. AE, MC, V. Daily 10am–2pm and 5–11pm.

Warda ★ LEBANESE   Don't be surprised if as you walk into this place you get the urge to break into a belly dance. Beaded turquoise curtains mark the entrance to a semicircle cave of mirrors (the bathrooms, naturally), and there's an outdoor terrace protected by a patterned awning that looks like something out of Arabian Nights. The food is as sumptuous as the decor. The fish and pear tajine, a braised sea bass marinated in olive oil, parsley, and chile, with thin pear slices, is divine. The fish falls apart at the mere touch of your fork. Drinks have a hint of Arabic style, such as bitter saffron or rose martinis. If you've got a sweet tooth, you'll love the crispy phyllo pastry filled with almond paste for dessert, and for those watching the waistline, an order of apple-flavored shisha should round out the evening quite nicely.

71/7 Mac Thi Buoi St., District 1. ✆ **08/3823-3822.** Main courses 125,000VND–250,000VND. MC, V. Daily 9am–midnight.

INEXPENSIVE

Ngon Restaurant ★★★ 🏢 VIETNAMESE *Ngon* means "delicious," and, for authentic Vietnamese, this restaurant lives up to its name and is the best in Vietnam. This Ho Chi Minh institution is always packed with both locals and tourists; it has even built a new location nearby to handle the overflow. The atmosphere is chaotic: a cacophony of chattering guests, shouting waiters, and clanging pots and pans. Fans blow mist to quell the smoky cooking fires of the open-air kitchen. Seating is a mix of regular tables in the colonial and those on the balcony or in the courtyard out back. The main building is surrounded by cooking stations, each serving a regional specialty; it's like someone went around the country head-hunting all of the best street-side chefs. Waitstaff simply act as liaisons among the many cooks. The menu is a survey course in Vietnamese cooking, and the tuition is low. Go with a Vietnamese friend, if you can, or someone who can explain the regional specialties. If you're alone, just point and shoot; everything is good. There's Hue-style *bun bo*, cold noodles with beef; a catalog of *pho*, noodle soup; and all kinds of seafood prepared the way you like. Meals here are best done as leisurely, multicourse affairs, but stop by for a snack if you're visiting the Reunification Palace or any sights downtown. Don't miss it, but be prepared to wait for a seat.

138 Nam Ky Khoi Nghia, District 1. ✆ **08/3829-9449.** Main courses 26,000VND–235,000VND. AE, MC, V. Daily 7am–10:30pm.

Restaurant 13 ★ VIETNAMESE With all the upscale eateries popping up downtown, you might miss out on an old-school standby like this little storefront. Tucked between high-rises and just off Dong Khoi, it's one of many restaurants whose name is its street number (if this one is busy, try no. 19). The atmosphere is plain, but the kitchen serves excellent traditional Vietnamese food without any bells, whistles, or sticker shock. The place is jolly and filled with locals, tourists, and expats. Ask what's good, or try the seafood, anything done in coconut broth, or the sautéed squid with citronella and red pepper. The food is carefully prepared and the waitstaff is very professional for this price range.

13 Ngo Duc Ke, District 1. ✆ **08/3823-9314.** Main courses 25,000VND–88,000VND. No credit cards. Daily 7am–10:30pm.

SNACKS & CAFES

When touring the city, stop to savor a moment at **Au Parc** (23 Han Thuyen St., District 1; ✆ **08/3829-2772**), a lovely spot nestled in a two-story colonial house between the Reunification Palace and the Notre Dame Cathedral. It serves great fruit smoothies and buzzes with expats at lunchtime.

Bun Bo Xu ★ (28 Cao Ba Quat, District 1; ✆ **08/3822-1539**) is a new eatery from the folks behind Xu (see above). Head here to try *Bon bo Hue*, a savory beef and noodle dish from the former Imperial city, in an upscale environment.

Café Central, on the ground floor of the Sun Wah Tower (115 Nguyen Hue St., District 1; ✆ **08/3821-9303**), is a great little international deli. Stop in for breakfast or a sandwich any time; the kind staff makes you feel like you've stepped into an old greasy spoon (with all the same standbys on the menu).

Fanny, just below the Temple Club (48 Ton That Thiep St., District 1; ✆ 08/3821-1633), serves the real-deal French glacé.

Centro (11–13 Lam Son Sq., District 1; ✆ 08/3827-5946) is a cozy, upmarket coffee corner right next to the Caravelle Hotel.

La Fenetre Soleil (2nd Floor, 135 Le Thanh Ton, District 1, Ho Chi Minh City [entrance at 125 Nam Ky Khoi Nghia]; ✆ 08/3822-5209) is tricky to find but worth the hunt; a real offbeat place that functions as a chill-out cafe by day and a trendy bar at night.

Mojo (88 Dong Khoi St., District 1; ✆ 08/3827-2828) is a funky little place that serves hearty crust-free sandwiches and excellent frosted coffee. It's a great place to do some people-watching.

What to See & Do

IN DISTRICT 1

Ben Thanh Market ★★   The clock tower over the main entrance to what was formerly known as Les Halles Centrale is the symbol of Saigon, and the market might as well be, too. Opened first in 1914, it's a crowded place, a boon for pickpockets with its narrow, one-way aisles, and loaded with vendors clamoring to sell you postcards and cheap goods (T-shirts, aluminum wares, silk, bamboo, and lacquer). There will be so many people calling out to you that you'll feel like the belle of the ball—or a wallet with legs. The wet market, with its selection of meat, fish, produce, and flowers, is interesting and hassle free; no one will foist a fish on you. In open-air stalls surrounding the market are some nice little eateries. The adventurous can try all kinds of local specialties for next to nothing.

At the intersection of Le Loi, Ham Nghi, Tran Hung Dao, and Le Lai sts., District 1. Daily early morning to night.

General Post Office (Buu Dien) ★   In this grand old colonial building, you can check out the huge maps of Vietnam on either side of the main entrance and the huge portrait of Uncle Ho in the rear. The specialty-stamps counter has some great collector sets for sale. It's directly opposite the Notre Dame Cathedral, so you can tick off two places with one visit.

2 Coq Xu Paris, District 1. Daily 7:30am–8pm.

Ho Chi Minh Municipal Theater (Saigon Opera House)

This magnificent building, which dominates Lam Son Square with its sweeping arched entrance and classical statues, was built at the turn of the 20th century and renovated in the 1940s. Its three stories hold 1,800 seats. Today, it hosts very little in terms of performances, but it is a stalwart atmospheric holdout amid steel-and-glass downtown.

At the intersection of Le Loi and Dong Khoi sts.

Ho Chi Minh City Museum ★

Originally built in 1890 by the French as a commercial museum, then turned into a governor's palace, a committee building, and later the Revolutionary Museum, the institution today covers a broad range, from archaeology to ethnic survey and documents from the city's founding in the 1600s. The second floor is heavy on Vietnam's battle against the Americans, with displays of weaponry and memorabilia from the period that show Vietnamese ingenuity, such as bicycle parts transformed into mortars and documents concealed in the inner tubes of motorbikes. The grounds around the museum are picturesque, which explains the many young couples posing for wedding photos, and there is an interesting collection of captured U.S. fighter planes, tanks, and artillery in the main courtyard. Underneath the building is a series of tunnels (closed to the public) leading to the Reunification Palace, once used by former president Ngo Dinh Diem as a hide-out before his execution in 1962.

65 Ly Tu Trong St., District 1. ✆ 08/3829-9741. Admission 15,000VND. Daily 8am–5pm.

Notre Dame Cathedral ★

The neo-Romanesque cathedral was constructed between 1877 and 1883 using bricks from Marseilles and stained-glass windows from Chartres. It is possibly the most-photographed building in Ho Chi Minh City, though its towering spires are now dwarfed by modern, glass and steel buildings. A statue of the Virgin Mary stands in the small park fronting the Cathedral; take a close look at her eyes, as locals have sworn that on more than one occasion they have seen her shed tears. Sunday services are in Vietnamese and English.

Near the intersection of Dong Khoi and Nguyen Du sts., District 1. Sun services 5:30, 6:30, 7:30, and 9:30am, and 4, 5:15, and 6:30pm.

People's Committee Building

The Hotel de Ville was constructed by the French between 1902 and 1908, and this fantastic and ornate example of colonial architecture is one of Saigon's most iconic sights, standing proudly at the head of Nguyen Hue Boulevard. It's not open to the public as it's now occupied by government offices, but all the attraction is on the outside anyway.

Le Thanh Ton St., at the junction with Nguyen Hue Blvd., District 1.

Reunification Palace ★

Designed as the home of former president Ngo Dinh Diem, the U.S.-backed leader of South Vietnam in the 1960s, this building is most notable for its symbolic role in the fall of Saigon in April 1975, when its gates were breached by North Vietnamese tanks and the victor's flag hung on the balcony. This was the moment when the war ended with victory for the north. Built on the site of the French governor general's home, called the Norodom Palace, the current modern building, designed when "modern" meant "sterile," was completed in 1966. Like the

Bao Dai Palace in Dalat, the Reunification Palace is a series of rather empty rooms that are nevertheless interesting because they specialize in period kitsch and haven't been gussied up a bit. The private quarters, dining rooms, entertainment lounges, and president's office look like everybody just up and left. Most interesting is the war command room, with its huge maps and old communications equipment, as well as the basement labyrinth. All visitors need to join a guided tour, which kicks off with a patriotic video about Viet Cong triumphs leading up to the capture of the palace.

106 Nguyen Du St., District 1. No phone. Admission 15,000VND. Daily 7:30–11am and 1–4pm.

Vietnam History Museum ★★ Housed in a rambling pagoda-like structure, the museum presents a clear picture of Vietnamese history, with a focus on the south. Highlights include an excellent selection of Cham sculpture and the best collection of ancient ceramics in Vietnam, as well as some priceless Buddha images from all over Asia. Weaponry from the 14th century on is displayed; one yard is nothing but cannons. One wing is dedicated to ethnic minorities of the south, including photos, costumes, and household implements. Nguyen Dynasty (1700–1945) clothing and housewares are also on exhibit, as are archaeological artifacts from prehistoric Saigon. Its 19th- and early-20th-century histories are shown using photos and, curiously, a female corpse unearthed as construction teams broke ground for a recent housing project. There are even some general background explanations in English, something missing from most Vietnamese museums. There's also a small **water puppet theater** on the premises, so when you arrive, check to see if there'll be a performance (costing around $1) while you're there.

2 Nguyen Binh Khiem, District 1. (© **08/3829-8146.** Admission 15,000VND. Daily 8–11am and 1–4:30pm.

IN OTHER DISTRICTS

Cholon (District 5) ★★ Cholon is probably the largest Chinatown in the world. It exists in many ways quite apart from Saigon. The Chinese began to settle the area in the early 1900s and never quite assimilated with the rest of Saigon, which causes a bit of resentment among the greater Vietnamese community. You'll sense the different environment immediately, and not only because of the Chinese-language signs.

A bustling commercial center, Cholon is a fascinating maze of temples, restaurants, jade ornaments, and medicine shops. Gone, however, are the brothels and opium dens of bygone days. You can lose yourself walking the narrow streets, but it makes sense to take a cyclo by the hour to see the sights.

Start at the **Binh Tay Market** ★★, on Phan Van Khoe Street, which is even more crowded than Ben Thanh and has many of the same goods, but with a Chinese flavor. You'll see a lot more produce, along with medicines, spices, cooking utensils, and plenty of hapless ducks and chickens tied in heaps, but not so much in the way of souvenirs. From Binh Tay, head up to Nguyen Trai, the district's main artery, to see some of the major temples on or around it. Be sure to see Quan Am, on Lao Tu Street off Luong Nhu Hoc, for its ornate exterior. Back on Nguyen Trai, Thien Hau Pagoda is dedicated to the goddess of the sea and was popular with seafarers making thanks for their safe trip from China to Vietnam. Finally, as you follow Nguyen Trai Street past Ly Thuong Kiet, you'll see the Cholon Mosque, the one indication of the district's small Muslim community.

Bordered by Hung Vuong to the north, Nguyen Van Cu to the east, the Tau Hu Channel to the south, and Nguyen Thi Nho to the west, District 5.

Giac Lam Pagoda ★ Giac Lam, built in 1744, is the oldest pagoda in Saigon. The garden in front features the ornate tombs of venerated monks, as well as a Bodhi tree. Next to the tree is a regular feature of Vietnamese Buddhist temples, a gleaming white statue of Quan The Am Bo Tat (Avalokitesvara, the goddess of mercy) standing on a lotus blossom, a symbol of purity. Inside the temple is an eerie funerary chamber, with photos of monks gone by, and a central chamber chock-full of statues. Take a look at the outside courtyard as well.

118 Lac Long Quan St., District 5. Daily 8am–5pm.

Jade Emperor Pagoda (Phuoc Hai) ★★ One of the most interesting pagodas in Vietnam, the Jade Emperor is filled with smoky incense and fantastic carved figurines. It was built by the Cantonese community around the turn of the 20th century and is still buzzing with worshipers, many lounging in the front gardens. Take a moment to look at the elaborate statuary on the pagoda's roof. The dominant figure in the main hall is the Jade Emperor himself; referred to as the "god of the heavens," the emperor decides who will enter and who will be refused. He looks an awful lot like Confucius, only meaner. In an anteroom to the left, you'll see Kim Hua, a goddess of fertility, and the King of Hell in another corner with his minions—he undoubtedly gets those the Jade Emperor rejects. It's spooky.

73 Mai Thi Luu St., District 3. Daily 8am–5pm.

War Remnants Museum ★★ This museum has a comprehensive collection of the machinery, weapons, photos, and documentation of Vietnam's wars with both the French and the Americans, though the emphasis is heavily on the latter. It was once called the War Crimes Museum, which should give you an idea of whose side of the story is being told here. Short of being outright recrimination, this museum is a call for peace and a hope that history is not repeated—visitors are even asked to sign a petition against the kind of aerial carpet-bombing that so devastated the people of Vietnam. The exhibit begins to the right of the entrance with a room listing war facts: troop numbers, bomb tonnage, and statistics on international involvement in the conflict and numbers of casualties on both sides. Next is a room dedicated to the journalists who were lost in wartime. The exhibits are constantly evolving; one room is devoted to biological warfare, another to weaponry, and another to worldwide demonstrations for peace. The explanations, which include English translations, are very thorough. There is a large collection of bombs, planes, tanks, and war machinery in the main courtyard. Kids will love it, but you might want to think twice before taking them inside to see things like wall-size photos of the My Lai massacre and the bottled deformed fetus supposedly damaged by Agent Orange. There is also a model of the French colonial prisons, called the Tiger Cages, on the grounds.

28 Vo Van Tan St., District 3. ℂ **08/3930-5587.** Admission 15,000VND. Daily 7:30am–noon and 1:30–5pm.

Outdoor Activities

There are two excellent 18-hole golf courses at the **Vietnam Golf & Country Club.** The clubhouse is at Long Thanh My Ward, District 9 (ℂ **08/6280-0124;** fax 08/6280-0127). Fees are $110 during the week for nonmembers, and $145 on Saturday and Sunday. Save a few bucks and play on Golf Day (Wed) for $70; women play for $68 Thursdays.

Tennis enthusiasts can find courts at **Lan Anh International Tennis Court** (291 Cach Mang Than Tam, District 10; ✆ **08/3862-7144**).

The best gym in town is at the **Park Hyatt** (p. 340); this as well as the pool and well equipped gym and spa at the **Caravelle Hotel** (p. 339) are available for non-guests at a day rate of $20 to $30.

Shopping

Saigon has a good selection of silk, fashion, lacquer, embroidery, and housewares. Prices are higher than elsewhere in Vietnam, but the offerings are more sophisticated. Stores are open daily from around 8am to 7pm. Credit cards are widely accepted, except in the markets.

Dong Khoi is the city's premier shopping street. Formerly Rue Catinat, it was a veritable Rue de la Paix in colonial times. Notable shops include **Mystere** (141 Dong Khoi St.; ✆ **08/3823-9615**) for its beautiful silverware and scarves. Down the way is **Tombo** (145 Dong Khoi St.), which has a huge selection of affordable bags. **Authentique Interiors** (38 Dong Khoi St.; ✆ **08/3823-8811**) specializes in fine pottery and table settings. **Tuyet Lan** (99 Dong Khoi St.; ✆ **08/3827-4253**) has a quality selection of ready-made clothing and can, of course, whip something up for you in a day. **Khai Silk** (107 Dong Khoi St.; ✆ **08/3829-1146**) has a fine outlet right in the heart of the city and offers ready-to-wear and fitted silk clothing. For top-notch lacquerware and lacquer furniture, visit **Dragon Smile** on a parallel street to Dong Khoi (74/5 Hai Ba Trung St.; ✆ **08/3823-1788**). Nearby Le Thanh Ton Street is another shopping avenue. Look for **Kenly Silk** (132 Le Thanh Ton St.; ✆ **08/3829-3847**), a brand-name supplier with the best ready-to-wear silk garments in the business. **Liti** (76E Le Thanh Ton St.; ✆ **08/3824-7114**) has a handsome assortment of antique lace, jewelry, and knickknacks such as blenders and 1950s sunglasses. Next door, Hanoi-based **Song** (76D Le Thanh Ton St.; ✆ **08/3824-6986**) carries gorgeous, original cotton and hemp designs.

Another local label worth checking out is **Ipa-Nima** (85 Pasteur St.; ✆ **08/3824-2701**), which stocks colorful bags and totes.

ART GALLERIES The **Ho Chi Minh Fine Arts Museum** (97A Pho Duc Chinh St., District 1; ✆ **08/3829-4441;** Tues–Sun 9am–4:45pm; admission 10,000VND) is the place to start if you're truly keen; the evolving collection features area artists' works in sculpture, oil, and lacquer—a good glimpse into the local scene. **Lac Hong Art Gallery,** on the ground floor of the museum (✆ **08/3821-3771;** www.lachonggallery.com), features the works of many famous Vietnamese artists.

There are galleries throughout the city, many clustered around Dong Khoi and near the major hotels. Reproduction artists are everywhere. Here are a few popular galleries in town: **Apricot Gallery** (50–52 Mac Thi Buoi St., District 1; ✆ **08/3822-7962;** www.apricotgallery.com.vn), **Gallery Quynh** (1 Ly Tu Trong St., District 1; ✆ **08/3824-8306;** www.galeriequynh.com), **Lotus Gallery** (67 Pasteur St., District 1; ✆ **08/3829-2695**). If these pique your curiosity, pick up a copy of *Vietnam Discovery* or *The Guide* for further listings.

BOOKSTORES Ho Chi Minh City's official foreign-language bookstore, **Xuan Thu** (185 Dong Khoi St., across from the Continental Hotel; ✆ **08/3822-4670**), has a few classics, as well as some foreign-language newspapers. There are also several small bookshops on De Tham Street in the backpacker area, but in general good reading material in English is hard to find. Bring it from home or exchange with other travelers.

Ho Chi Minh City After Dark

When Vietnam made a fresh entry onto the world scene in the mid-1990s, Ho Chi Minh City quickly became one of the hippest party towns in the East. The mood has sobered somewhat recently, with police trying to make sure every place closes by midnight, but it's still fun. Everything is clustered in District 1; ask expats in places such as **Saigon Saigon** (see below) or check out publications like *The Word* or *Asia Life* to find out about any club happenings. As for cultural events, Saigon is sadly devoid of anything really terrific, except for a few cultural dinner and dance shows.

BARS & CLUBS   Head to the basement of the central opera house for **Q Bar** (7 Cong Truong Lam Son; ✆ 08/3823-3479; www.qbarsaigon.com), the town's hippest club. It's a funky catacomb with good music, cocktail nooks, and an eclectic mix of people.

Atop the Caravelle Hotel (old building), **Saigon Saigon** (19 Lam Son Sq.; ✆ **08/3823-4999**) is a very popular spot featuring live music and a terrific view. Next door at the Sheraton, **Level 23** (88 Dong Khoi St.; ✆ **08/3827-2828**) is a double-height rotunda overlooking town. Good live bands play here—it's Indochina meets the Hard Rock Cafe on any given evening.

Pacharan (97 Hai Ba Trung St.; ✆ **08/3825-6024**), a swanky Spanish tapas bar downtown, is a great place to start your evening. **Vasco's Bar,** next to the Refinery restaurant (74/7D Hai Ba Trung St.; ✆ **08/3824-2888**), is an atmospheric choice. On Dong Du Street, a side street off Dong Khoi, you'll find the **Amber Room** (59 Dong Du St.; ✆ **08/6291-3686**) and **Zan Z Bar** (41 Dong Du St.; ✆ **08/3822-7375**), both classy cocktail lounges.

Don't miss the brick-walled Irish pub **O'Briens** (74/A2 Hai Ba Trung St.; ✆ **08/3829-3198**) for pints and pizza. **Sheridan's** (19 Le Thanh Ton St.; ✆ **08/3823-0793**) is another friendly watering hole with character.

The Pham Ngu Lao area stays up late, and **Allez Boo** (195 Pham Ngu Lao; ✆ **08/3837-2505**) is always up till the wee hours, as is their sister bar **Go2** at 187 De Tham, just a short stagger down the street.

THE PERFORMING ARTS   A few hotels and restaurants stage traditional music and dance shows for the benefit of their guests, but there's no convenient show in town that gives you the full works. For that you'll need to contact the **Binh Quoi Tourist Village** (✆ **08/3556-6020**; www.binhquoiresort.com.vn), run by Saigon-tourist, and book an evening cruise to the village about 8km (5 miles) north of the city center, where you'll be entertained while dining by dancers and musicians.

Side Trips from Ho Chi Minh City

See "Visitor Information & Tours," earlier in this section, for tour providers to the following sights.

Cao Dai Holy See Temple ★★   The Cao Dai religion is less than 100 years old and is a broad, inclusive faith that sprang from Buddhist origins to embrace Jesus, Mohammed, and other, nontraditional, latter-day saints such as Louis Pasteur, Martin Luther King, Jr., and Victor Hugo. Practitioners of Cao Daism are pacifists, pray four times daily, and follow a vegetarian diet for 10 days out of every month. Cao Daism is practiced by only a small percentage of Vietnamese people, mostly in the south, but you'll see temples scattered far and wide—easily recognizable by the all-seeing eye, which, oddly enough, looks something like the eye on the U.S. dollar. Often included with trips to the Cu Chi Tunnels (see below), the temple at Tay Ninh is the spiritual center—the Cao Dai Vatican, if you will—and the country's largest. Visitors are welcome at any of the four daily ceremonies (the noon ceremony is the most convenient), but all are asked to wear trousers covering the knee, remove their shoes before entering, and act politely, quietly observing the ceremony from the balcony area. The temple interior is a colorful wedding cake, with bright murals and sculpted dragons leaping off of pillars. Cao Dai supplicants wear either white suits or colorful robes, each color denoting what root of Cao Daism they practice: Buddhist, Muslim, Christian, or Taoist.

About 90km (56 miles) northwest of Ho Chi Minh City. Daily dawn–dusk.

Cu Chi Tunnels ★★ Vietnamese are proud of their resolve in their long history of struggle against invading armies, and the story of the people of Cu Chi is indicative of that spirit. The Cu Chi area lies near the end of the Ho Chi Minh trail and was the base from which Ho Chi Minh guerillas used to attack Saigon. As a result, the whole area became a "free fire zone" and was carpet-bombed in one of many American "scorched-earth" policies. But the residents of Cu Chi took their war underground, literally, developing a network of tunnels that, at its height, stretched as far as Cambodia and included meeting rooms, kitchens, and triage areas, an effective network for waging guerilla warfare on nearby U.S. troops. The U.S. Army's 25th Infantry Division was just next door, and there are detailed maps denoting land that was U.S.-held, Vietminh-held, or in dispute.

Visitors first watch a war-era propaganda film that is so over the top, it's fun. The site supports a small museum of photos and artifacts, as well as an extensive outdoor area of guerrilla snares and reconstructions of the original tunnels and bunkers. Dress appropriately if you choose to get down in the tunnels; the experience is dirty and claustrophobic. There is also a shooting range where, for $1 per bullet, you can try your hand at firing anything from a shotgun to an AK-47. A half- or full-day trip can be arranged with any tour company in Saigon, often including a visit to the Cao Dai Temple (see above).

About 65km (40 miles) northwest of Ho Chi Minh City. Daily dawn–dusk. Admission 65,000VND.

THE MEKONG DELTA

Don't leave without seeing the Mekong Delta, even if it's for just a day. The delta is a region of waterways formed by the Mekong River, covering an area of about 60,000 sq. km (23,200 sq. miles) and with a population of 17 million, most engaged in farming and fishing. Often called the breadbasket of Vietnam, the Mekong Delta accounts for more than an estimated 50% of rice production. The land is characterized by bright-green rice paddies, fruit orchards, sugar cane fields, and vegetable gardens, and its waters are busy with boats and fish farms.

The region's urban centers, Can Tho and Chau Doc, are good bases for tours and exploration of the countryside by road and canal. As you cruise slowly along the meandering canals, you'll see locals living right beside the water on stilt houses or houseboats—a fascinating glimpse into a way of life that has survived intact for hundreds of years. In the many floating markets, trade is conducted from boat to boat in areas teeming with activity and sellers touting their wares. Delta people are friendly and unaffected, and their cuisine is delicious—lots of good seafood, of course.

Coming south from Ho Chi Minh City (Saigon) on a day tour, the town you'll probably head for is **My Tho,** where there are several islands in the river, though several tour buses push on a bit farther to **Cai Be Floating Market.** If you have time to overnight, you should try to make it down at least as far as **Can Tho,** the delta's largest city. It has a bustling riverfront and waterway, and around Can Tho are several other floating markets. **Chau Doc** is another picturesque town and a popular gateway to Cambodia. Look for unique floating markets, weaving villages, and expansive fish farms, all visited on tours.

Visitor Information & Tours

To cope with the necessary logistics, going with a travel agent is your best bet in the Mekong Delta. They offer everything from day trips to 3-day tours. Our pick is **Ann Tours** (58 Ton That Tung St., District 1; ✆ **08/3833-2564;** fax 08/3832-3866; www.anntours.com) for custom excursions that take you off the beaten path; prices start at $50 per day with a group.

    Sinhbalo Adventure Tours (283/20 Pham Ngu Lao St., District 1 [down a small alley off the main street]; ✆ **08/3837-6766;** fax 08/3836-7682; www.sinhbalo.com) runs Delta trips to homestays in quiet areas that include kayaking and cycling, or they can arrange a customized itinerary.

    The tourist cafes all run standard, affordable trips to the Mekong Delta. Contact **Delta Adventure Travel** (267 De Tham St., District 1; ✆ **08/3920-2112;** www.deltaadventuretours.com) for 2- and 3-day tours starting at $23 per day (with optional connection to Cambodia).

Where to Stay

Victoria Hotels (www.victoriahotels-asia.com) has two properties on the Mekong Delta, in Can Tho (✆ **0710/381-0111**) and Chau Doc (✆ **076/386-5010**). New but colonial-style rooms and services at riverside come priced from just $165. Nothing compares.

CAMBODIA

by Daniel White

I f ever a country could be in possession of charisma, then this troubled but fascinating Southeast Asian kingdom has it in droves. Where for 3 decades misfortune and war obscured a rich history and vibrant culture, for the past decade that perception of the country has been in a state of constant revision. It is a nation at peace, no longer a proxy battleground for world superpowers.

GETTING TO KNOW CAMBODIA

The Lay of the Land

About the size of Missouri, some 181,035 sq. km (69,900 sq. miles), Cambodia has 20 provinces that are bordered by Laos in the north, Vietnam in the east, Thailand to the west, and the Gulf of Thailand to the south.

The mighty Mekong River enters from Laos to the north and nearly bisects the country. It divides into two main tributaries at Phnom Penh before it traces a route to the delta in Vietnam, and most areas of population density lie along the valleys and fertile plains of this great river and its tributaries. Near Siem Reap, the Tonle Sap Lake is the largest lake in Southeast Asia. In the monsoon summer months, when the Mekong is swollen from the snows of Tibet, the river becomes choked with silt and backs up on the Mekong Delta. The result is an anomaly: The Tonle Sap River relieves the pressure by changing the direction of its flow and draining the Mekong Delta hundreds of miles in the opposite direction and into the Tonle Sap Lake.

The northeast of the country, Ratanakiri Province, and areas bordering Vietnam are quite mountainous and rugged, as are the Thai border areas defined by the Dangrek Mountains in the northwest and the Cardamom Mountains in the southwest.

A Look at the Past

Cambodia is populated by people of the **Mon-Khmer** ethnic group, who probably migrated from the north as far back as 1000 B.C. The area they settled was part of the kingdom of Funan, an empire that extended into Laos and Vietnam, until the 6th century, when it was briefly absorbed into

a nation called Chenla. It then evolved into its glorious Angkor period in the 8th century, from which sprung many of Cambodia's treasures, most notably the lost city of Angkor, once the seat of a vast empire.

The story of Khmer civilization is one of a slow decline from the zenith of the powerful Angkor civilization of the 11th century. At its height it covered all of the lands of what are now Cambodia and Laos, 80% of what is now Thailand, huge tracts of what is now Burma, and most of what is now southern Vietnam. It stretched from the South China Sea to the Andamans. The late 12th century was marked by internal rebellions, decay, and infighting. Angkor was lost to the Kingdom of Siam in 1431. Vietnam also had a hand in controlling the kingdom, to some degree, beginning in the 17th century. The French took over completely in 1863, followed by the Japanese during World War II, and then the French again in 1945. Cambodia finally regained independence in 1953 under the leadership of **Prince Norodom Sihanouk.**

When the French were ejected from Indochina, Vietnam was split between the communist north and the American-backed south. The south became a cold war battleground as pro-Hanoi guerrillas and North Vietnamese regulars attempted to wrest control of the area from the Saigon-based regime. North Vietnamese forces increasingly used outposts in Cambodia as bases from which to attack the Saigon regime. From March 1969 onward, Cambodia was bombed heavily and indiscriminately by American forces, in an effort to dislodge them. The North Vietnamese simply withdrew farther into neutral Cambodia to escape the rolling thunder of the American B52s, and Sihanouk had no way of stopping them. A U.S.-backed military coup followed in 1970, installing the disastrous Lon Nol as leader. At the time, the American press joked, "The only thing we know about Lon Nol is that Lon Nol spelled backward is Lon Nol." In 1975, after 5 years of savage fighting, the now infamous **Khmer Rouge,** led by the tyrannical and paranoid **Pol Pot regime,** took over Cambodia, and renamed it **Democratic Kampuchea.** This was the dawn of 4½ years of untrammeled horror for the Cambodian people. Opposition—even imaginary opposition—was brutally crushed, resulting in the death of more than two million Cambodians. The inhumanity of the Khmer Rouge beggared belief then, and it still does. Khmer Rouge rule and the wars that came both before and after decimated Cambodia on every level. Cambodia became, and still is, one of the world's poorest nations, with a mainly agrarian economy and a literacy rate of about 35%.

In response to Khmer Rouge infractions into its country, communist Vietnam invaded Cambodia in 1978, chased the Khmer Rouge out of power, and occupied the country until 1989, installing a client regime led first by **Heng Samrin** and then by **Hun Sen** as prime minister. The Khmer Rouge went back to the jungles and in a cobbled-together alliance with both former Lon Nol factions and Sihanouk factions, continued to wage war and prolong the torture of Cambodia for another decade. This unholy, but anti-Soviet, alliance (in which the Khmer Rouge provided the muscle) was backed by the U.S., China, and the Western powers. When Vietnam departed Cambodia at the end of the Cold War, the **United Nations** stepped in and engineered a fragile coalition government between the Sihanouk and Hun Sen factions after elections were held in 1993. The United Nations Transitional Authority in Cambodia, or **UNTAC,** left Cambodia in a worse mess than they found it, with **two prime ministers** in place: Hun Sen of the CPP and Prince Ranariddh of FUNCIN-PEC. They vied with each other for ultimate power as the Khmer Rouge calculated its chances of a return to rule from the jungles of the Thai border. In 1997, Hun Sen broke the deadlock and seized total power for himself in what is often misnamed a "coup." The Khmer Rouge was already waning and they were soon finished. Pol Pot died a deservedly ignominious, fly-blown, jungle death in 1998.

There were **elections** in **1998, 2003,** and **2008.** Hun Sen and the CPP won all three times and his grip on power remains almost total. Whether that's a good thing or not is often a point of debate, but the fact is that since 1998 the hard-won stability that now exists benefits many ordinary Cambodian people. The other side of the coin is that there is almost no respect for human rights in Cambodia, and corruption is rampant from the very top to the very bottom. In many ways Cambodia is run on similar lines to the mafia and, these days, there is only one Godfather—Hun Sen. In 2004 the mercurial King Sihanouk abdicated in favor of his son, **Norodom Sihamoni,** who has gained respect for the quiet dignity with which he fulfills his duties, although Sihanouk, or "Papa" as many Cambodians refer to him, remains a seminal figure. Maybe Sihanouk was the last God King of the Khmer.

Cambodia Today

From 2001 to 2004, Cambodia's economy grew at a rate of 6.4%. Although the growth rate slowed dramatically by 2009, in 2010 the country is still booming. This boom, driven mostly by garment exports, construction, and tourism, seems to be entirely unregulated in nature, and it is only a tiny and increasingly wealthy elite who benefit to any great extent. The situation in rural Cambodia remains bleak. Basic medical services are nonexistent, and education and job training are out of reach for rural peasantry. The major challenge for Cambodia over the next decade will be creating an economic environment in which enough jobs can be created to handle Cambodia's demographic imbalance. More than 50% of the population is under 21 years old. As so often has been the case in Cambodia's recent history, one step taken forward can often result in two steps being taken back. Having said that, there is a whole new generation who are the first in nearly a century not to experience war, and as things change and develop, that is something that remains of indescribable value.

The Khmer People & Culture

The name *Cambodia* is an Anglicized version of the French *Cambodge,* which is an adaption of the Khmer *Kampuchea.* Both the people and the language they speak are known as *Khmer.* Cambodia is one of the most ethnically homogenous nations in Asia, with 96% of its population being ethnically Khmer. Apart from that, there are communities of Vietnamese, Chinese, and Cham (both Muslim and Buddhist), plus animist hill-tribe groups in Ratanakiri and Mondulkiri. The Khmers have been in this area since the start of recorded history, long before the Thais or Vietnamese migrated here. This fairly straightforward story of Khmer ethnicity gives the Khmers a strong sense of collective self, despite all the upheavals they have undergone. Even a thousand years later a pride in the cultural achievements of Angkor is central to Khmer identity. There are also many Khmers living in the northeastern Thai provinces of Buriram, Surin, and Si Saket, as well as Vietnam's Mekong Delta. Ethnically, these provinces are Khmer but were dislocated as a result of the ebb and flow of empire.

Etiquette

Traditions and practices in Cambodia, like those in neighboring Thailand and Laos, are closely tied with Theravada Buddhism. It is a very conservative country where modesty is the order of the day. You can dress skimpily or with undue attention to hygiene, but it won't do you any favors in terms of other's perception of you. Likewise, openly public displays of affection will embarrass people.

As with other countries in the region, the concept of "face" governs social interaction on every level. You will get things done faster if you go out of your way to make sure that you don't cause someone to lose face. Don't get angry and show it. It's utterly counterproductive. Things in Cambodia often don't run efficiently and there are cultural and historical reasons for that. Build in plenty of wiggle room in terms of how

---

 "Heritage Friendly" Establishments

Much of Cambodia's ancient history has been lost, thanks to its violent past and the continued looting and trafficking of Khmer artifacts. To help prevent this, look for the "Heritage Friendly" logo. This logo was created by the Heritage Foundation (www.heritagewatch.org), an organization working to preserve Khmer antiquities and culture. The presence of the logo indicates that a business or organization has met certain standards that help protect Cambodian heritage.

you plan your timing and schedule. Another thing to remember is that a Cambodian reaction to uncertainty or embarrassment is to giggle or laugh. They are not laughing at you; it's just their way of dealing with it. Smile and joke as much as you can. It's the Cambodian way, and people will be more willing to help you.

When you beckon someone, don't do it the Western way. Flap your whole hand downward with your palm flat. If you do it with your hand or finger pointing up it is interpreted as either very impolite or as a sexual gesture.

As in all Buddhist countries, the head is considered holy while the feet are considered dirty. Don't go around touching people's heads even if it's just patting a child on the head. Likewise, don't point the soles of your feet at anyone and certainly not at a Buddha image. Cambodians tend to sit on the floor with their feet tucked to the side. Don't step over someone and don't step over food. It's considered very rude.

If you are in a temple, dress modestly. Have respect for monks in general. Women should not touch them.

Language

Khmer is part of the Mon-Khmer language group, a subdivision of the South East Asian Austro Asiatic classification. Unlike Thai, Vietnamese, or Lao, it is not tonal, although it does have a bewildering number of consonants—33 to be exact. Once you get your head around the often-guttural pronunciation and bizarre vowel sounds, it's not a difficult language to pick up. The grammar is very simple, no tenses, no different endings or singular or plural. Khmer is a satisfyingly substantial language with plenty of rolling of the r's. If you do master a bit of Khmer, the rewards are big. You will be very popular indeed, especially if you can crack a joke or two. Written Khmer script is based on Pallava script from South India. It is very complex and very ancient. Although many Cambodians used to speak French, that is no longer the case. The second language of choice is English these days, and it is amazing how many people have learned to speak it—especially the young.

USEFUL KHMER PHRASES

ENGLISH	KHMER	PRONUNCIATION
Hello	**Soa s'day**	Sew sadday
Goodbye	**Lia haoy**	Lee howie
Thank you	**Awk koun**	Awk coon
Thank you very much	**Awk koun chelan**	Awk coon chalan
How are you?	**Sohk sabai?**	Sook sabai?
I am fine	**Sohk sabai**	Sook sabai
Yes (man)	**Baat**	Baht
Yes (woman)	**Jaa**	Jya
No	**Ah te**	Ah tay
I'm sorry	**Sohm to**	Sum tow
Toilet?	**Bawngku uhn?**	Bangku oon?
Do you have . . . ?	**Men awt men?** (lit. do you have or don't you?)	Mien ought mien?
Water?	**Tuhk sot?**	Took sawt?

| How much? | **Th'lai pohnmaan?** | Tlai bawn mahn? | **6** |
| Can you make it cheaper? | **Som joh th'lai?** | Sum joe tlai? | |

CAMBODIA | The Best of Cambodia in 1 Week

THE BEST OF CAMBODIA IN 1 WEEK

If time is of the essence, you are best off doing fewer things well than tearing around doing everything badly. On a first visit, Cambodia can be a bit overwhelming, so the best way to ease into that is to fly to Siem Reap and start your trip with the Angkor Wat complex.

Day 1: Siem Reap ★★★

Get up before dawn and start with the sunrise over **Angkor Wat** itself. As the sky glows red, this spectacular structure will reveal itself first in silhouette and then in all its immense glory. Then head to one of the world's most seriously enigmatic buildings while the light is still soft—**the Bayon.** Clambering over this astonishing structure as the enormous serene faces of a God King watch your every move is another part of the high-impact start to your journey. A short trip northwest of the Bayon is **the Baphuon.** This was the central structure of Angkor before the rest of Angkor Thom was built. After that, take in the **Terrace of the Leper King.** Early afternoon is a good time to see **Ta Phrom**, built by **Jayavarman VII** in tribute to his mother. In the evening you could take in some **classical dancing** or simply enjoy the lively restaurants, cafes, and nightlife of Siem Reap town.

Day 2: Angkor Wat ★★★

In the morning take in some more temples. **Preah Khan** is a large and important complex full of intriguing passages lined with carvings. The temple mountain of **Pre Rup** rears out of the flatlands, and if you climb it you not only get to see detailed and richly preserved carvings, but also get good views of the surrounding countryside. After that, decide which temple you like most and go back there, whether that's Angkor Wat itself, the Bayon, or Ta Phrom. In this short amount of time, you can only get a taste of the place, but there are always highlights and favorites. After lunch go wander around the **markets** and **boutiques** of **Siem Reap.**

Day 3: Phnom Penh

In the morning, fly to Phnom Penh. If you arrive in time for lunch, head to the riverfront around Sisowath Quay, where you can eat while becoming accustomed to the frantic bustle of the city. After you have finished your food, walk the few yards to 178 Street, have a peek at the art galleries and boutiques, and take a look around the stunning collection of Angkorian and pre-Angkorian sculpture in the National Museum. The Royal Palace just next door is your next port of call. Then take a moto up to Wat Phnom, the namesake heart of Phnom Penh. Since you are already near the river, head back to Sisowath Quay for some well deserved refreshment. Look out for Phnom Penh's only elephant, the much-loved lady named Sambo. Phnom Penh is replete with restaurants, bars, and nightlife of all sorts. Plan your evening according to your tastes.

Day 4: Phnom Penh

Cambodia is a country of incredible history but some of it is simply horrific. If you are to have any understanding of this place, you will need to visit **Tuol Sleng,** also called **S21.** You may leave the building weeping at the thought of the fate of all those faces staring out of the fading black-and-white photographs, but you will understand more about Cambodia. You can follow that with a trip to "Choeng Ek," or the **Killing Fields,** where the terrified victims of S21 were bludgeoned into an undeserved oblivion. If you are with younger children, then of course these places should be skipped. With older children it's a tough call and should be handled carefully because it is all very real. After lunch, take a cruise down the **Mekong.** In the evening cross the Japanese Bridge to **Prek Leap** and have dinner at one of the popular traditional Khmer restaurants.

Day 5: Phnom Penh/Sihanoukville

If you aren't all shopped out from Siem Reap, take a swing around **Psar Toul Tom Pong,** often referred to as the **Russian Market.** After lunch, take the bus to **Sihanoukville,** arriving in the late afternoon in time to have an aperitif while watching the sun sink over the Gulf of Thailand.

Day 6: Sihanoukville

Relax on the beach, and try some crab or lobster cooked right in front of you by passing vendors.

Day 7: Sihanoukville/Kampot

Either continue to relax on the beaches of Sihanoukville, or make the short drive over to **Kampot** to enjoy the riverine atmosphere of this small elegant town before taking the bus back to Phnom Penh for your flight out.

PLANNING YOUR TRIP TO CAMBODIA

Visitor Information

You'll find a wealth of information at **www.gocambodia.com,** or click on "Cambodia" at **www.visit-mekong.com.** The Cambodian Embassy to the U.S. sponsors **www.embassyofcambodia.org.** Below are Cambodian embassy and consulate locations overseas.

- **In the U.S.:** 4530 16th St. NW, Washington, DC 20011 (© **202/726-7742;** fax 202/726-8381; www.embassy.org); or 866 United Nations Plaza, Ste. 420, New York, NY 10017 (© **212/223-0676;** fax 212/223-0425).
- **In Australia/New Zealand:** 5 Canterbury Crescent, Deakin, ACT 2600, Canberra (© **02/6273-1259;** fax 02/6273-1053; www.embassyofcambodia.org.nz/au.htm).
- **In Thailand:** #185, Rajdammri Rd., Lumpini Patumwan, Bangkok 10330, Thailand (© **02/254-6630;** fax 02/253-9859).

Organized Tours & Travel Agents

Many visitors choose to see Cambodia with the convenience of a guided tour, which is a good idea: It's not only safer and easier, but also means that you won't miss the finer details of what you're seeing and can visit rural Cambodia in as much comfort as possible. Being part of a larger group tour is a good, affordable option. Even if you travel independently, you might want to sign up with a local tour operator (like Diethelm or Exotissimo, below) once you're in Cambodia. Below are recommended tour operators that offer Cambodia excursions.

INTERNATIONAL

o **Abercrombie & Kent,** 1520 Kensington Rd., Ste. 212, Oakbrook, IL 60523-2141 (*C* **800/554-7016** or 630/954-2944; fax 630/954-3324; www.aandktours. com).

o **Asia Transpacific Journeys,** 2995 Center Green Court, Boulder, CO 80301 (*C* **800/642-2742** or 303/443-6789; fax 303/443-7078; www.asiatranspacific. com).

REGIONAL

o **Diethelm Travel,** House #65, St. 240, P.O. Box 99, Phnom Penh (*C* **023/219-151;** fax 023/219-150; www.diethelmtravel.com), or House #4, Rd. #6, Krum #1, Sangkat #2, Phum Taphul, Siem Reap (*C* **063/963-524;** fax 063/963-694).

o **Exotissimo Travel,** SSN Center, 66 Norodom Blvd., 6th Floor, Phnom Penh (*C* **023/218-948;** fax 023/426-586; www.exotissimo.com), or 300 Airport Rd. N.6, Siem Reap (*C* **063/964-323;** fax 063/963-621).

Entry Requirements

All visitors are required to carry a passport and visa. A 1-month tourist visa can be issued on arrival at the Phnom Penh or Siem Reap airports for about $20. A visa on arrival is also available at overland border crossings from both Thailand and Vietnam. Bring two passport photos for your application, or be prepared to pay a few extra dollars. There is also an overland crossing between Laos and Cambodia via Stung Treng, a trip that is becoming increasingly popular since the roads are now good on both sides of the border. Visa on arrival is now available when heading into Cambodia from Southern Laos.

Tourist visas can be extended three times for a total of 3 months. Any travel agent can perform the service for a small fee. Business visas, for just $25 upon entry, can be extended indefinitely.

You can also apply for an e-visa online. Instead of applying through a Cambodian Embassy, you simply complete the online application form and pay with your credit card. After receiving your visa through e-mail, print it out and bring it with you on arrival. To apply for an e-Visa, applicants need to have a passport valid for at least 6 months, a recent passport-size photo (JPEG/PNG format), and a valid credit card (Visa/MasterCard). The visa costs $20 and there is a $5 processing fee. It is important to note this visa is good only for arrival to Siem Reap and Phnom Penh international airports and by land from Thailand at Poipet/Aranyaprathet, Koh Kong/Had Lek, and Vietnam at Bavet/Svay Rieng. It is not valid for any other border crossings. To apply for an e-visa, go to www.mfaic.gov.kh.

Customs Regulations

For visitors 18 and older, allowable amounts of goods when entering are as follows: 200 cigarettes or the equivalent quantity of tobacco; one opened bottle of liquor; and a reasonable amount of perfume for personal use. Currency in possession must be declared on arrival. Cambodian Customs on the whole is not stringent. Due to a long, sad history of theft from the Angkor temples, it is forbidden to carry antiques or Buddhist reliquaries out of the country, but Buddhist statues and trinkets bought from souvenir stalls are fine.

Money

Cambodia's official currency is the **riel,** but the Cambodian economy is tied to the fate of its de facto currency, the **U.S. dollar.** Greenbacks can be used anywhere. The normal exchange rate used is **4,000 riel = $1.** Prices for all but the smallest purchases are in U.S. dollars and are listed as thus in this chapter. The **Thai baht** is also widely accepted in the western region of the country.

It's important to have riel for smaller purchases, but there is no point in exchanging large amounts of foreign currency into the local scrap. You'll commonly receive small change in riel as well. The riel comes in denominations of 100, 200, 500, 1,000, 2,000, 5,000, 10,000, 50,000, and 100,000. You cannot change Cambodia's riel outside the country, so anything you carry home is a souvenir.

ATMS ATMs are now available at major banks all over the country. They are also appearing in shops, hotels, and even restaurants in Phnom Penh, Siem Reap, and Sihanoukville.

CURRENCY EXCHANGE You can change traveler's checks in banks in all major towns. Because the U.S. dollar is the de facto currency, it's not a bad idea to change traveler's checks to dollars for a 1% or 2% fee and make all purchases in U.S. cash.

TRAVELER'S CHECKS Traveler's checks are accepted in most major banks for exchange, but not commonly at individual vendors. American Express is a good bet and is represented by **Diethelm** (see "Organized Tours & Travel Agents," above).

CREDIT CARDS Cambodia has a cash economy, but credit cards are becoming more widely accepted. Most large hotels and high-end restaurants accept the majors, but you'll want to carry cash for the majority of transactions—and certainly in the countryside.

When to Go

CLIMATE Cambodia's climate falls under the pattern of the southern monsoons that also hit neighboring Thailand and Vietnam from May to November. Between November and February the weather is pleasantly warm and dry. After February it starts to heat up, and by April it is oppressively hot. The best time to go is from December to February.

CLOTHING CONSIDERATIONS Keep it light and loose; it's always hot. "Less is more" applies here; bulky luggage is an albatross in Cambodia. Light cotton is best and it is important to keep in mind that Cambodians value modesty and cleanliness. Carry a hat and sun protection, particularly if you're spending long hours sightseeing around temples.

PUBLIC HOLIDAYS & EVENTS **Khmer New Year** is in the middle of April. The **Angkor Festival** is held at the end of July. **King Sihanouk's Birthday** is October 31. **Independence Day** is November 9 (1953) and is celebrated throughout the country like the American Fourth of July. There are water festivals and boat races at the end of November, including a huge festival in Phnom Penh.

Health & Safety

DRUGS   Marijuana has long been available in Cambodia and has only recently been made illegal. Stronger drugs, such as heroin, methamphetamine, and cocaine are now available in the major cities, and it is likely you will be approached, especially if you look young. Be aware that if you are caught with any illegal substance, you will be facing either jail or a hefty sum of money to get yourself off the hook.

HEALTH CONCERNS   See chapter 10's "Health & Safety" section (p. 632) for information on health concerns and general issues that affect the region. Remember that no tap water in Cambodia is considered potable, so stick with bottled water. It's also a good idea to check the most recent information at the **Centers for Disease Control** (click "Travelers' Health" at **www.cdc.gov**).

Health considerations should comprise a good part of your trip planning for Cambodia, even if you're going for only a few weeks. If rural areas are on your itinerary, you'll need to get special vaccinations far enough in advance to give them time to take effect. If you follow the guidelines here and those of your doctor, there's no reason you can't have a safe and healthy trip.

Malaria is not a concern in Phnom Penh and any of the larger towns, but upcountry, especially around the Thai border, it's quite common. Many travelers take preventive medication. An **antimalarial prophylaxis** is recommended in affected areas. Take **atovaquone proguanil** (brand name **Malarone**), **doxycycline**, or **mefloquine** (brand name **Lariam**). If you plan to travel extensively in the rural areas on the western border with Thailand, primaquine is the only effective preventive.

Other mosquito-borne ailments, such as **Japanese encephalitis** and **dengue fever,** are also prevalent. Your best protection is to wear light, loose-fitting clothes from wrist to neck and ankles; use a bug repellent with DEET; and be particularly careful at sunset or when out and about early in the morning.

Hepatitis is a concern, as it is anywhere. Reliable statistics on **AIDS** are not out, but with rampant prostitution and drug abuse, Cambodia is certainly fertile ground for the disease. Recent efforts to educate needle users about the dangers of substance abuse and the importance of clean needles, as well as increased condom use, are positive signs, but statistics show that the tide of new AIDS cases is still rising.

SAFETY CONCERNS   It is recommended that you check with your home country's overseas travel bureau or with the **U.S. State Department** (for a complete, updated list click "more" under "Travel Warnings" at **www.travel.state.gov**) to keep abreast of travel advisories and current affairs that could affect your trip.

If you encounter problems during your visit, go to your country's embassy. Addresses for embassies in Phnom Penh are listed under "Fast Facts: Cambodia" (p. 371).

   Medical Safety & Evacuation Insurance

The Cambodian medical system is rudimentary at best and nonexistent at worst. Make sure that you have medical coverage for overseas travel and that it includes emergency evacuation. For more information on insurance, see p. 631. There are a few clinics in Phnom Penh and Siem Reap, but for anything major, evacuation to Bangkok is the best option.

SOME IMPORTANT safety tips

○ Remember that the police and military of Cambodia are not there to protect and serve. Any interaction with the constabulary usually results in frustration and/or your coming away shorter by a few dollars. Contact your embassy for major problems, and call for police assistance only in cases of theft or extreme danger. Demand a ticket if threatened with a fine of any sort (although often, especially for small traffic infractions, it's best to just cough up a buck or two).

○ Women should take extra caution in Cambodia, as recent years have seen an increase in sexual assaults on foreign women, in both Phnom Penh and Siem Reap, and even in the Angkor temple complex. Don't travel alone, and try not to isolate yourself in areas around the temples.

○ Rural travel is really opening up, and you'll find a warm welcome in even the most remote hamlet. It is worth remembering that you're really on your own out in the sticks, with no hospitals and limited support services available should you be involved in any kind of an accident.

○ Especially at night, travelers should stay aware, just as they would in any big city. Purse snatching is not uncommon in Phnom Penh. If you are riding pillion on a motorcycle, make sure nothing is dangling that can be grabbed (such as a camera or a shoulder bag) because you could get pulled off the bike altogether if you are targeted. Pickpockets are as proficient here as anywhere in the region, so take care.

○ Land mines and unexploded ordnance (UXO) can be found in rural areas in Cambodia, but especially in Battambang, Banteay Meanchey, Pursat, Siem Reap, and Kampong Thom provinces. Don't walk in heavily forested spots or in dry rice paddies without a local guide. Areas around small bridges on secondary roads are particularly dangerous.

The days of the Khmer Rouge taking backpackers hostage are long gone, and the general lawlessness and banditry that marked Cambodia as inaccessible and dangerous have abated. Having said that, in general travelers should still take same caution.

Getting There

BY PLANE International flights to Cambodia from neighboring countries are numerous and affordable. Cambodia's two main hubs, **Siem Reap International Airport** and **Phnom Penh International Airport,** are served by the following: **Siem Reap Airways** (a subsidiary of **Bangkok Airways**), **Bangkok Airways, Thai Airways,** and **Air Asia** from Thailand; **Malaysia Airlines** and **Air Asia** from Kuala Lumpur; **Lao Airways** and **Vietnam Airlines** from Vientiane; **Vietnam Airways** from Ho Chi Minh and Hanoi; **Silk Air** from Singapore; and **EVA Air** from Taipei. **Shanghai Air** and **China Southern** provide connections between Phnom Penh and points in mainland China. **Dragon Air** flies from Hong Kong. **Asiana Airlines** and **Jetstar** connect with South Korea. There is a $25 international departure tax.

BY BUS Getting from **Bangkok** to either **Siem Reap** or **Phnom Penh** is very easy and straightforward. Take a standard bus from Morchit Northern Bus Terminal in Bangkok (near either Morchit BTS Skytrain or Chatuchak MRT subway stations). Buy a ticket to **Aranyaprathet** taking about 5 hours. Once in Aranyaprathet, take a tuk-tuk for between 50 and 100 baht to the border. You can also take a minibus direct from the Khao San Road area, which is faster but very uncomfortable. Once you have completed immigration formalities and are in **Poipet** on the Cambodian side of the border, you have the option of taking a regular **bus,** a shared or **private taxi,** or a seat in a crowded **pickup truck** to your onward destination. There is a free shuttle bus from the border to the place where the buses and taxis are parked. It takes between 2 and 3 hours to get to **Siem Reap,** 4 hours to **Battambang,** and 9 hours to **Phnom Penh.** Buses also run from the **Koh Kong/Had Lek** border to both **Sihanoukville** and **Phnom Penh** via the new **National Highway 48** to **Srey Ambal.** To get to the **Had Lek** border from **Bangkok,** take a regular bus from **Ekamai Bus Terminal** to **Trat** and from Trat take a **minibus** (1 hr.) to the border.

Buses connect with neighboring **Vietnam** at the Moc Bai border area—at the town of Svay Rieng on the Cambodian side. From Saigon in Vietnam, contact **Saigontourist** (✆ **08/829-8914**) or **Sinh Café** (✆ **08/369-420**) for direct connection to Cambodia—Sinh Café and Capitol Tour (also called Capitol Guesthouse) are in cahoots and one carrier takes up your transport at the border. Going in either direction (to or from Cambodia), you'll cross the border around noontime and the $6 bus drops you at your destination sometime after 3pm. The overland border procedure is quick and easy going into Cambodia. You just have to fill out some forms and pay the 2,000 VND tax (payable in any currency). Going from Cambodia to Vietnam, ask at any travel agent or hotel and be sure that you have a prearranged visa for Vietnam. Visa is available on arrival at all land crossings into Cambodia.

BY BOAT Daily boat connections run between **Chau Doc** in **Vietnam** and the town of **Neak Loeung,** some 2 hours east of Phnom Penh in Cambodia. You can arrange the trip through any budget travel agent in Vietnam. Budget tour operators **Sinh Café** (✆ **08/369-420** in Ho Chi Minh City) and **Capitol Tour** (#14, Rd. 182, Phnom Penh; ✆ **023/217-627**) are now working together, so when you cross borders, the other company adopts you. It's an all-day journey in a diesel-belching tour boat, but views of life on the wide, lazy Mekong are worth it. *Also note:* A visa is available on arrival when you enter Cambodia, but you have to have a prearranged visa for entry to Vietnam.

On the luxury end coming from Chau Doc to Phnom Penh, contact the **Victoria Chau Doc Hotel** (✆ **076/865-010**) for expensive, private transfer on a speedy runabout boat.

Getting Around

BY PLANE These days the Thai carrier, **Bangkok Airways,** and its subsidiary, **Siem Reap Airways,** are the only domestic operators. The company has a monopoly on all flights to **Siem Reap** from **Bangkok** and internally, and charges accordingly. The only domestic route now running is between Phnom Penh and Siem Reap. There is a $6 domestic departure tax in both Phnom Penh and Siem Reap.

BY BUS Long-distance buses now go to all major towns in Cambodia. They tend to operate from the central market area in most towns. In **Phnom Penh** different

○ **To place a call from your home country to Cambodia:** Dial the international access code (011 in the U.S. and Canada, 0011 in Australia, 0170 in New Zealand, 00 in the U.K.), plus Cambodia's country code **(855),** the city code (**23** for Phnom Pehn, **63** for Siem Reap), and the six-digit phone number (for example, 011 855 23 000-000). *Important note:* Omit the initial "0" in all Cambodian phone numbers when calling from abroad.

○ **To place a call within Cambodia:** Dial the city or area code preceded by a **0** (the way numbers are listed in this book), and then the local number (for example,

023 000-000). Note that all phone numbers are six digits after the city code.

○ **To place a direct international call from Cambodia:** To place a call, dial the international access code **(00),** plus the country code, the area or city code, and the number (for example, to call the U.S., you'd dial 00 1 000/000-0000).

○ **International country codes are as follows:** Australia, 61; Canada, 1; Hong Kong, 852; Indonesia, 62; Laos, 856; Malaysia, 60; Myanmar, 95; New Zealand, 64; the Philippines, 63; Singapore, 65; Thailand, 66; U.K., 44; U.S., 1; Vietnam, 84.

companies leave from different parts of town, although **Psar Thmei** (Central Market) is where you will find the departure points for both **Sorya** and **GST Express.** The seats are made for midgets and on a long journey they can get very uncomfortable. **Mekong Express** (leaving from Sisowath Quay on the corner of St. 102) are a bit more expensive but offer bigger seats, and it's worth the extra dollar or two to use them. The easiest way to buy tickets is through your hotel or guesthouse or a travel agent.

BY CAR/MOTORBIKE It is possible to hire a car with a driver. The best way to do this is through your hotel or a travel agent. It will cost between $20 and $30 a day. Another practical way to get around is by motorcycle, although you should be an experienced motorcyclist if you choose to do this and it's important to drive slowly. Bikes generally range from step-throughs to 250cc dirt bikes. The most established place in town to rent is **Lucky! Lucky!** (413 Monivong Blvd.). Road travel in Cambodia used to be a real test of physical endurance. This is no longer the case and most of the main roads are sealed and in very good condition. Once off the main roads, you can still expect a bumpy ride choked by huge amounts of dust in dry season and sliding around in glutinous mud when it rains.

BY BOAT The boat from Phnom Penh to Siem Reap leaves the pier on Sisowath Quay (near St. 104 opposite the River View Guest House) at 7am. It costs $30 to $35 and takes between 4 and 6 hours. The boat from Siem Reap to Battambang is very much the slow, expensive, and awkward option, particularly at the height of the dry season from April to May when the waters are low and one often has to transfer to lighter and smaller vessels in the middle of the journey. The ferry leaves Siem Reap at 7:30am, costs $16, and takes 8 to 10 hours.

Tips on Accommodations

Cambodia offers excellent value on midrange accommodation in **Phnom Penh, Siem Reap, Battambang,** and **Sihanoukville.** Competition is fierce and for $15 to $75, you can find some really good deals with all the modern conveniences, satellite TV, and these days even Wi-Fi Internet (although don't expect it to be fast). The standards are particularly high in **Battambang,** where a rash of recent hotel construction and renovation means that there are a great many excellent choices. At the high end **Siem Reap** offers the best concentration of five-star accommodation in Asia, while **Phnom Penh** is home to some classic colonial-style hotels such as the **Raffles Le Royale.** The rates quoted in this book are the standard rates given, but one can almost always get a better deal if one contacts them in advance. The **budget travelers** are also well catered to since the whole of Cambodia has become solidly lodged on the backpacker circuit over the past 12 years.

Tips on Dining

In this old French colony the foreign cuisine is often French, affordable, and often quite good. In Phnom Penh and Siem Reap one can now find restaurants serving food from pretty much all corners of the globe, although the authenticity of many remains approximate. There's also good Thai, Chinese, and Vietnamese, and tourist centers are chockablock with storefronts that serve up reasonable facsimiles of Western favorites such as omelets and pancakes.

Tips on Shopping

There are lots of antiques stores and boutiques in the major tourist centers, but shopping for trinkets and memorabilia is best at the big markets: the Russian Market and Central Market in Phnom Penh, and the Old Market in Siem Reap.

[FastFACTS] CAMBODIA

American Express For basic American Express services (such as reporting lost checks) contact **Diethelm Travel,** House #65, St. 240, P.O. Box 99, Phnom Penh (© **023/219-151;** www.diethelmtravel.com).

Business Hours Vendors and restaurants tend to be all-day operations, opening at about 8am and closing at 9 or 10pm. Government offices, banks, travel agencies, and museums are usually open from 8am to 4 or 5pm, with an hour break for lunch.

Drug & Liquor Laws There is no minimum legal drinking age in Cambodia. When it comes to drugs, however, availability can look like permission, but it's often not the case. It's said that you can bribe your way out of (or into) anything in corrupt Cambodia, but it's best not to test that theory. Police are crooked and may be the ones who sell (out of uniform) in order to collect the bribe. Like anywhere, dabbling in this arena makes you friends in all the wrong places, and

Cambodia is not a good place to have the wrong friends.

Electricity Cambodia runs on 220-volt European standard electricity, with rounded, two-prong plugs. If you're coming from the U.S., bring an adapter, as well as a surge protector for delicate gadgets.

Embassies **U.S.:** #1, St. 96, Sangkat Wat Phnom, Phnom Penh (© **023/728-000;** http://cambodia. usembassy.gov). **U.K.:** #27–29, St. 75, Sangkat Srah Chak, Phnom Penh

(☏ **023/427-124;** http://ukincambodia.fco.gov.uk/en). **Australia:** #11, St. 254, R V Senei Vannavaut Oum, Phnom Penh (☏ **023/213-470;** http://cambodia.embassy.gov.au). The Australian embassy also assists nationals of Canada and New Zealand.

Emergencies   In Phnom Penh, dial ☏ **117** for police, ☏ **119** for an ambulance.

Hospitals   You'll want to take care of any medical or dental issues before arriving in Cambodia. The **SOS Clinic** in Phnom Penh, #161, St. 51 (☏ **023/216-911**), is your best bet in a pinch.

Internet Access   Reliable service can be found in the major centers, with prepaid wireless connections a recent innovation. More and more restaurants and hotels now also have Wi-Fi access. Don't expect connections to be fast.

Language   The Cambodian language is "Khmer." English is spoken widely and French is often spoken by the older generation. See "Language," p. 362, for more information.

Mail   Hotels usually sell stamps and send postcards for guests. See specific cities for locations of post offices.

Police   Khmer police exist to harass and collect, not to protect and serve. Contact them only in the event of a major emergency, by calling ☏ **117.** Otherwise, call your embassy.

Safety   Once a place where violence and banditry were an everyday occurrence, Cambodia has become much safer in recent years, but stay on your toes. It's best not to be out on the roads too late at night. Beware of unexploded bombs and mines in rural areas. Also remember to lock valuables in hotel safes since opportunistic theft is widespread. In the event of trouble, comply and report any incidents to local officials. See "Health & Safety," p. 367, for more information.

Telephones   The international country code for Cambodia is **855.** Phones in the major centers are reliable, and international direct dial is common—for a very hefty price. Many Internet cafes can organize Web-based calls. Most hotels levy exorbitant surcharges of 10% to 25%. See "Telephone Dialing at a Glance," p. 370, for details.

Time Zone   Cambodia is 7 hours ahead of Greenwich Mean Time, in the same zone as Bangkok. It is 12 hours ahead of U.S. Eastern Standard Time during the winter months, and 3 hours behind Sydney.

Tipping   Tipping is not obligatory, but it is appreciated. A blanket 10% to 20% is exorbitant. It's best to just round up the check, or leave a buck or so.

Toilets   In rustic areas toilets tend to be rustic too and are generally of the squat variety. As in most of Asia, toilet paper is not the norm since people perform their ablutions with water and their left hand. It's not a bad idea to bring your own toilet paper and antibacterial lotion if this is a practice you do not wish to follow. Western style toilets are the norm in hotels and restaurants across the country.

Water   No tap water is potable. Don't even brush your teeth with it. Buy bottled water, which is widely available.

PHNOM PENH

The trading city of Chaktomuk, Phnom Penh replaced Angkor Thom as the Khmer capital in the 15th century, when the empire was in decline and Angkor itself was under attack from the armies of Ayutthaya. The city has long been a vital hub at the confluence of three rivers: the Mekong, Tonle Sap, and Bassac.

In the '50s and '60s Phnom Penh was considered the most beautiful city in Asia. Wide, lazy boulevards shaded by trees and French-built villas set among pre-war Art

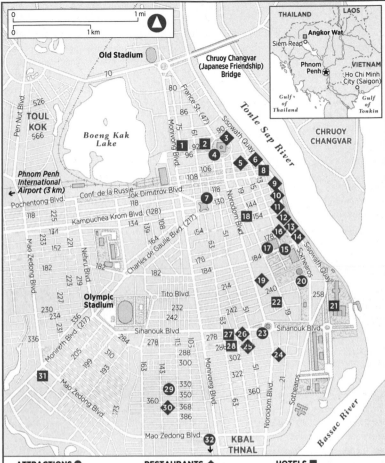

ATTRACTIONS ●
Central Market **7**
Independence Monument **23**
"The Killing Fields,"
    Choeung Ek Memorial **32**
National Museum **17**
Royal Palace **15**
Silver Pagoda **20**
Tuol Sleng, Museum of
    Genocide **29**
Wat Phnom **4**

RESTAURANTS ◆
Boddhi Tree **30**
Cantina **11**
Comme á la Maison **25**
FCC (Foreign
    Correspondents Club) **13**
Le Deauville **3**
Mith Samlanh (Good Friends)
    Restaurant **16**
Pacharan **14**
Tamarind Café **19**
Van's Restaurant **5**
Malis **24**
Khmer Surin **26**
Kandal House **9**
Happy Herb's **10**

HOTELS ■
Amanjaya Pancam Hotel **12**
Golden Gate Hotel **27**
Goldiana **28**
Hotel Cambodiana **21**
Hotel Inter-Continental
    Phnom Penh **31**
The Pavilion **22**
Raffles Hotel Le Royal **1**
Sunway Hotel **2**
Royal Guesthouse **18**
Indochine 1 **8**
Juliana **6**

Deco monoliths gave the city a unique feel. Above all, it was "slow" in the nicest possible way. In the 1960s when war raged in Vietnam, but had yet to engulf its neighbor, Phnom Penh was the R & R destination of choice for those involved in the continuing horror.

Until recently, Phnom Penh was still often described as "sleepy." Now it is anything but. In fact, it would be better described as absolutely frenetic and intense. There has been a massive increase in vehicles and population over the past 5 years, and Phnom Penh is now very much a boomtown. In many ways the city is overtaking Bangkok and Manila for the prize of having the most congested and claustrophobic city streets in Asia. It often feels like it has actually reached a point of permanent gridlock. All this is quite a shock to the system, and in many ways Phnom Penh feels like a city that is reeling from the relentless pressure. Having said that, it is of a very manageable size and once you get your bearings it is actually pretty easy, although sometimes slightly hair-raising, to get around.

Getting There

BY AIR   All major airlines in the region connect here. **Phnom Penh International Airport** is about a 20-minute drive from the city center (if the traffic is thin). A **taxi** costs $9, while a **tuk-tuk** costs $7. Vehicles entering the airport are monitored. You pay at a counter in arrivals and hand the voucher to the driver waiting in the queue at the front.

BY BOAT   **Hydrofoil river boats** connect **Phnom Penh** with **Siem Reap** and leave early every morning from the main dock on the north end of town. This used to be the major way to get from Phnom Penh to Siem Reap when the roads were bad. Tickets are available from both travel agents and hotels or you can purchase directly at the quay. The price is in the region of $35.

BY BUS   Different companies leave from different parts of town, although **Psar Thmei (Central Market)** is where you will find the departure points for both **Sorya** (© 023/210-359) and **GST Express** (© 023/355-379). **Mekong Express** (© 023/427-518), leaving from Sisowath Quay on the corner of Street 102, is generally reputed to be the most comfortable and swift, but you will pay slightly more. **Sorya** (or **Ho Wah Genting** as they used to be called) and **GST** offer a slightly cheaper but less salubrious option.

Getting Around

With the increase in crowds and traffic in the past few years, getting around Phnom Penh can be a fairly wild experience. **Motorcycle taxis** are everywhere and are often the quickest mode of transport. Just hail one from the sidewalk. Most trips around town will cost less than a dollar during the day. At night you normally double the fee. A gentler but slower way to see the sites is by **cyclo.** They operate under the same rules and pretty much the same rates as the motorcycle taxis. The **tuk-tuk** (correctly called a **"remorque"**) is a fairly new development in Phnom Penh and they are available everywhere. The name is taken from the Thais, but these tuk-tuks have little in common with the noisy, Bangkok two-stroke three-wheeler. Cambodia's tuk-tuks are a two-wheeled surrey pulled by a standard motorbike attached through a fairly ingenious coupling device. Pay between $2 and $5 for trips around town; a ride farther out, say the Killing Fields, will set you back $15. Metered **taxis** have now made an appearance on the streets of Phnom Penh, although they are few and far between.

There are many unofficial cabs. All guesthouses and hotels will be able to get you a car within half an hour. A ride to the airport costs between $5 and $7.

Visitor Information & Tours

DELUXE

- **Diethelm Travel,** House #65, St. 240, P.O. Box 99, Phnom Penh (☎ **023/219-151;** fax 023/219-150; www.diethelmtravel.com), or House #4, Rd. #6, Krum #1, Sangkat #2, Phum Taphul, Siem Reap (☎ **063/963-524;** fax 063/963-694).
- **Exotissimo Travel,** #46, Norodom Blvd., Phnom Penh (☎ **023/218-948;** fax 023/426-586; www.exotissimo.com).

BUDGET

- **Capitol Guesthouse Tours,** #14, AEO, Rd. 182, Sangkat Beng Prolitt (☎ **023/217-627**). This is the town's budget travel cafe and a good place to arrange inexpensive rural and local tours and onward connections by bus and boat. Remember that you get what you pay for, but the services are convenient.
- Small tour operators and ticket shops abound along Sisowath. For flights and other services, try **K.U. Travel & Tours** (#77, St. 240; ☎ **023/723-456;** fax 023/427-425; www.kucambodia.com) in the cafe and gallery area.

[FastFACTS] PHNOM PENH

American Express For basic American Express services (such as reporting lost checks), contact **Diethelm Travel,** House #65, St. 240, P.O. Box 99, Phnom Penh (☎ **023/219-151;** www.diethelmtravel.com).

Currency Exchange ATMs are everywhere now in Phnom Penh and they accept all internationally recognized cards. Those of the **Canadia Bank** levy the lowest transaction charges. All ATMs dispense U.S. dollars. **ANZ Bank** has many reliable international ATMs in town, the most convenient being at their riverside branch, 265 Sisowath Quay (☎ **023/726-900**). Canadia Bank, at #265–269 St. 114 (☎ **023/215-286**), and **Mekong Bank,** at 1 St.

114 (☎ **023/217-112**), are also in the downtown area and can cash traveler's checks and give cash advances. A **Western Union** office is at 327 Sisowath Quay (☎ **023/990-688**).

Emergencies For police, dial ☎ **117;** for fire, dial ☎ **118.** For the expat hot line, dial ☎ **023/724-793.**

Hospitals The **International SOS Medical and Dental Clinic,** #161, St. 51 (☎ **023/216-911**), is the best place for minor emergencies. **Naga Clinic,** #11, St. 254 (☎ **011/811-175**), is another. For any major emergency or injury, however, you'll want to arrange medical evacuation.

Internet Access Internet outlets line the riverside Sisowath Street. Hourly

access starts at $1. **Friendly Web,** near Capitol Guesthouse, has good access from its office at #199 EO, St. 107 (☎ **012/843-246**), at the corner of Road 182. **Sunny Internet Cafe,** 351 Sisowath Quay (☎ **023/986-629**), has several flat screen computers with fast ADSL connections in a bright location.

Mail The post office is located in the north end of town on Street 13, east of Wat Phnom. It's open daily from 6:30am to 5pm, and has standard delivery service and an international phone. **DHL** has an office at House 353, St. 110 (☎ **023/427-726**). **FedEx** is at #701D Monivong Rd. (☎ **023/216-712**).

Pharmacies There are pharmacies all over town,

but many are unreliable. The best pharmacy by far is **Pharmacie De La Gare** (81Eo Monivong Boulevard; ℂ **023/430-205**). This is a very professional outfit run to French standards.

Where to Stay

There are some choice hotels in town, from old, upscale gems to budget minihotels. Many are centered between the riverfront area of **Sisowath Quay** and **Norodom Boulevard.** This is the heart of town, but it is busy and can be noisy. To enjoy a less frenetic pace, head down to the area of **Boeung Keng Kang,** south of Lucky Market and Sihanouk Boulevard (heading directly south down 51 St. from Psar Thmei takes you straight there). Although still central, the streets are leafy and quiet and there is little traffic. In upmarket hotels the rates vary considerably by season, by offer, and by method of booking. Some charge 10% VAT.

VERY EXPENSIVE

Raffles Hotel Le Royal ★★ Built in 1929, this is Phnom Penh's most atmospheric hotel, an authentic Art Deco and colonial classic. It reopened and expanded with a new wing in 1997, and everything from the vaulted ceilings in the lobby to the classic original central stairs breathes history and charm. Rooms are done with fine tiled entries, high ceilings, indirect lighting, a sitting area with inlaid furniture, and ornate touches such as antique wall sconces and fine drapery. Landmark rooms, just one step above the standard, are a good choice in the older building and are larger, with nice appointments including claw-foot tubs. There are also some interesting theme suites named for famous visitors, including Stamford Raffles. Even Jacqueline Kennedy has a room dedicated to photos and memorabilia of her 1967 visit. The central pool area is a tranquil oasis divided by a pavilion, and the amenities throughout are excellent.

92 Rukhak Vithei Daun Penh (off Monivong Blvd.), Sangkat Wat Phnom, Phnom Penh. ℂ **023/981-888.** Fax 023/981-168. www.phnompenh.raffles.com. 170 units. $290 double; $330 landmark; $380–$1,700 suite. AE, MC, V. **Amenities:** 2 restaurants; bar; babysitting; concierge; health club; Internet access (in business center); Jacuzzi; 2 outdoor pools; room service; sauna. *In room:* A/C, satellite TV, fridge, hair dryer, minibar.

EXPENSIVE

Hotel Cambodiana ★★ The Cambodiana nearly has it all. With a convenient location, atmosphere, and all the amenities, this is a good jumping-off point for the sights downtown. The building looks like a giant gilded wedding cake, and its vaulted Khmer-style roofs dominate the sky in the southern end of downtown. The large riverside pool is great, and there are some fine choices in international dining. All rooms have picture windows and good views of town or the river. They're priced according to their view of the river, and executive floors are maintained to high standards. Everything is tidy, but the decor is a chain-hotel style in plain wood and office carpeting. Deluxe riverview rooms are your best bet. Wireless Internet access (with prepaid cards) is available in all public spaces.

313 Sisowath Quay, Phnom Penh. ☎ **023/426-288.** Fax 023/426-392. 236 units. $175 deluxe; $420 suite; $500 executive suite. AE, MC, V. **Amenities:** 4 restaurants; bar; concierge; executive-level rooms; small health club; Internet access (in business center); Jacuzzi; outdoor pool; limited room service; sauna; tennis court. *In room:* A/C, satellite TV, fridge, minibar.

Sunway Hotel ★★ The Sunway is a very comfortable high-end choice. Just west of Wat Phnom in the north end of town, the facade and entry are grand, and the small wrought-iron chandelier suspended in the cool marble of the lobby completes the fine effect. The Sunway covers all the bases for amenities, with a good health club and large downstairs salon and massage area. The dining room and laid-back lobby lounge are stylish and inviting. Rooms are chain-hotel bland, but large, clean, and very comfortable, with white walls, carpeting with a tight geometric design, and wooden valances. Bathrooms are large, with combination tub/showers and granite counters.

#1, St. 92, Sangkat Wat Phnom, P.O. Box 633, Phnom Penh. ☎ **023/430-333.** Fax 023/430-339. www.phnompenh.sunwayhotels.com. 138 units. $140–$170 deluxe; $280–$850 suite. AE, MC, V. **Amenities:** Restaurant; cafe; bar/lounge (w/live entertainment on Sat); babysitting; concierge; health club; Jacuzzi; room service; sauna; spa. *In room:* A/C, satellite TV, fridge, minibar.

MODERATE

Amanjaya Pancam Hotel ★★ Riverside at Sisowath Quay, this three-story corner building is a true house of style. The porous laterite walls of the lobby, the same stone used in Angkor, and Buddhist statues throughout contribute to a cool boutique vibe. Though sparse in services and amenities, the rooms are spacious, done in rich red silk hangings and bedspreads that contrast boldly with the dark-wood trim and floors. All units have king-size beds. The suites are enormous and worth the extra outlay. Bathrooms are immaculate affairs done in wood and tile, with neat tub/shower units in standard rooms and a separate shower and tub in suites, delineated by unique stone paths in concrete. Accommodations vary in size and shape, with the corner suites the best, offering panoramic views of the river and busy street below. Noisy traffic is the only drawback.

#1, St. 154, Sisowath Quay, Phnom Penh. ☎ **023/219-579.** Fax 023/219-545. www.amanjaya-pancam-hotel.com. 21 units. High season $155–$250 double; low season $120–$220 double. MC, V. **Amenities:** Restaurant; limited room service. *In room:* A/C, satellite TV, fridge, minibar.

Juliana Hotel ★ The Thai-owned Juliana is a good distance from the center of town and popular with both group tours and regional businessmen. Rooms are situated around a luxuriant central pool shaded by palms and with a terrace and lounge chairs. Standard rooms aren't especially attractive, with their aging red carpeting and the nicks and scrapes of heavy use. That said, superior and deluxe rooms are large and well appointed, with tidy carpet and light-wood trim. Be sure to request a non-smoking room—and check it out before checking in. Calling itself a "city resort" isn't quite accurate, but the Continental restaurant is inviting and the pool is a standout, even if the rooms don't quite pass muster.

16 Juliana 152 Rd., Sangkat Vealvong, Phnom Penh. ☎ **023/880-530-31.** Fax 023/366-070-72. www.julianacambodia.com. 118 units. $79–$89 superior; $99–$109 deluxe; $109–$119 executive; $250 suite. AE, MC, V. **Amenities:** 2 restaurants; small lobby bar; babysitting; small health club; Internet access (in business center); outdoor pool; room service; sauna; smoke-free rooms. *In room:* A/C, satellite TV, fridge, minibar.

The Pavilion ★★ 🏄 This hotel is your best choice in town in this price range. The Pavilion is a renovated former royal residence tucked away on a quiet street overlooking a nearby pagoda and the Royal Palace. Walk through large wooden doors and white stone walls into the central oasis of gardens, four-poster daybeds with mosquito nets, and an inviting outdoor pool. Rooms are ultrachic, especially given their price tags. Furniture is made from sugar-palm wood and hot water is provided by rooftop solar panels. Rooms on the second floor have lovely views of traditional rooftops and neighboring colonial houses. A few rooms in the new building have private pools.

227 St. 19. 🕐 **023/222-280.** www.thepavilion.asia. 20 units. High season $75–$90 double; $100 suite/private pool room; low season $60–$70 double; $85 suite. MC, V. **Amenities:** Restaurant; bar; free Wi-Fi. *In room:* A/C, satellite TV, fridge, minibar, free Wi-Fi.

INEXPENSIVE

Golden Gate Hotel The standard rooms here are basic but clean and quite livable. The Golden Gate also has deluxe rooms that are larger but just as plain. This is a popular spot for long-staying expat business visitors and NGO workers, as the suites, with kitchenette and small living room, are like one-room apartments. Accommodations are outfitted in either tile or office-style carpeting and have mismatched but tidy upholstered and rattan furniture. Bathrooms are the small shower-in-room type typical of guesthouses. The best choice is a deluxe room on a higher floor (with view). Be sure to ask to see the room first, as they really vary.

#9, St. 278, Sangkat (just south of the Independence Monument), Phnom Penh. 🕐 **023/7211-161.** Fax 023/721-005. www.goldengatehotels.com. $28 standard; $35 deluxe; $45 suite. MC, V. **Amenities:** Restaurant; Internet access (in business center); limited room service. *In room:* A/C, satellite TV, fridge, minibar.

Goldiana ★★ The Goldiana is one of the best budget choices in the Cambodian capital. The hotel is just south of the Victory Monument and a short ride from the main sights. It is not luxurious, but it is squeaky-clean. Rooms are very large, with either carpeting or wood flooring. The hotel's standard of maintenance, unlike that of similar properties in town, is meticulous. Bathrooms are small but comfortable, with a tub/shower combo and granite tile. The third-floor pool is a real bonus in this category. The lobby is a designer muddle of heavy curtains, large pottery with fake flowers, mirrors, and bright-colored carved wood, but it acquires a certain appeal once it becomes familiar. The staff is kind and helpful and is used to the questions and concerns of long-staying patrons, tourists, and business clients.

#10–12, St. 282, Sangkat Boeng Keng Kang I, Phnom Penh. 🕐 **023/219-558.** Fax 023/219-558. www.goldiana.com. 148 units. $53 double; $76–$109 suite. MC, V. **Amenities:** Restaurant; basic gym; Internet access (in business center); outdoor rooftop pool; room service. *In room:* A/C, TV, fridge, minibar.

Indochine 1 🏄 This newly renovated hotel is in an excellent location right on the riverfront. While prices are low, the rooms are very clean and come with a flatscreen TV, hot water, and A/C. The staff is friendly and security is good. The cheaper rooms lack windows, but at the prices they are charging it remains very good value indeed, given its location.

#251, Sisowath Quay. 🕐 **023/427-292.** Fax 023/427-292. 16 units. $12–$25 double. *In room:* A/C, satellite TV.

Royal Guesthouse ★ 🏠 This is a rambling palace for those on a budget. It has been around since the days when UN soldiers wandered the streets of a city that was intermittently lit by the power of generators and punctured by the sound of occasional gunfire. These days it is one of the premier accommodation choices for the financially challenged. The rooms range from the poky but cheap to whole-family suites. One thing they all have in common is that they are spotlessly clean. At the Royal Guesthouse you won't find luxury but you will find comfort at a very reasonable price. The rooms also have satellite TV with the full package of channels, which is a good deal in this lowly price range. The downstairs restaurant serves basic Asian and western fare and the breakfasts are really quite good.

#91, St. 154. ☎ **023/218-026.** 35 units. $6–$15 double. **Amenities:** Restaurant; bar. *In room:* A/C, satellite TV, fridge.

Where to Dine

Between remnants of French colonialism and the more recent influx of humanitarian-aid workers, international cuisine abounds in the Cambodian capital. There are simply hundreds of restaurants in Phnom Penh of all cuisine types. The mind-boggling choice reaches a crescendo along the riverfront from the Royal Place to the Siem Reap boat pier. Around the residential area of Boeng Keng Kang south of Sihanouk Boulevard and centered around 51 Street are a number of restaurants set alongside quiet, leafy streets. It makes a real change from the bustle of the riverside and the city center.

EXPENSIVE

FCC (Foreign Correspondents Club) ★ CONTINENTAL   Housed in one of the most beautiful French colonial buildings in town, the FCC is as much a tour stop as a restaurant. Opened first in 1993, it was once a bona fide press club, but that is no longer the case. It is a multi-floor affair of restaurant, bar, and shops done in dark wood and terra cotta. There are low reclining chairs in the cafe area, a fine-dining room, and a bar that serves as the centerpiece. It is open on three sides with fantastic views of the Tonle Sap and the Mekong beyond and is dramatically breezy in rainy season. The food is uninspired but adequate. The upstairs bar is very popular in the evening, and the whole place is abuzz with activity day and night. They also have an excellent permanent art collection, and regular photo and art exhibitions.

#363, Sisowath St. ☎ **023/724-014.** www.fcccambodia.com. Main courses $8–$17. MC, V. Daily 6am–midnight.

Malis ★★ KHMER   Malis is Phnom Penh's gourmet Cambodian dining experience at a price. Artfully prepared contemporary and traditional Khmer cuisine from the kitchen of the hugely renowned Cambodian chef, Luu Meng, is served in stylish, elegant surroundings. The presentation of the dishes is superb. The staff claim the Battambang Steak in Cambodian spices and the Roast Chicken as their signature dishes. Try the "Mak Mie," or crispy fried noodles topped with stir-fried mince pork and fresh herbs with Malis Chili sauce. In reality, Malis is fusion cuisine, using Khmer roots to create something new.

136 Norodom Blvd. (near Independence Monument to the south). ☎ **023/221-022.** Fax 023/221-121. www.malis-restaurant.com. Main courses $6.50–$68. AE, MC, V. Daily 7am–11pm.

Van's Restaurant FRENCH   This newcomer to the scene is set in the impressive French colonial grandeur of the former Banque de l'Indochine. Van's serves French haute cuisine in truly glorious surroundings. Traditional French fare such as Filet de Beouf au Poivre (beef steak with heavy pepper sauce) or Lapin en Gibelotte (rabbit

in a heavy stew with white wine) is unlikely to do wonders for your waistline but is undoubtedly part of the overall experience of this splendid place. They also specialize in Escargots de Bourgogne (snails in garlic butter) and Pate de Foie Gras either hot or cold. The main dining room is a series of beautifully laid-out tables, the tablecloths and napkins gleaming white, the wine glasses sparkling. There is a balcony surround on the corner, where you can dine closer to the buzz of the city below.

#5, St. 102. ✆ **023/722-067.** www.vans-restaurant.com. Main courses $9.50–$15. AE, MC, V. Daily 11am–2:30pm and 5:30–11:30pm.

MODERATE

Cantina ★★★ MEXICAN   There are many restaurants and cafes along the river-front, but Cantina stands out. In the early days of tourism development, many places copied the pizza parlor formula of Happy Herb's—Phnom Penh's first and most original pizza joint. Cantina (next door to Happy Herb's) completely shattered the mold, offering up tacos, tostadas, and burritos using plenty of fresh ingredients and genuine meso flower flown over specially from Mexico via the States. If you want excitement, try the gringas—two corn quesadillas served on a smoking-hot metal platter. In addition to the truly superb Mexican food, the cocktails are simply legendary. Cantina serves some of the best Margaritas in Asia. While enjoying one, check out the photos on the walls—there's stunningly good work by great photographers.

#347, Sisowath St. ✆ **023/222-502.** www.cantinacambodia.com. Main courses $3.25–$6.25. No credit cards. Sun–Fri 2:30–10pm.

Comme à la Maison ★ CONTINENTAL   Part restaurant, part patisserie, and part cafe, Comme à la Maison is set on a giant leafy veranda with simple ocher floor tiles and light rattan furniture. The atmosphere is very relaxing, with classical arias wafting across the garden. It is best for light lunches. The chevre chaud (hot goat's cheese) salad with croutons, walnut, apple, and pesto comes highly recommended, but there are many other tasty options. Although Comme à la Maison is certainly very Gallic, the food served is in contrast to many of the more traditional French restaurants with their heavy saturated sauces. Comme à la Maison also features mildly heartier French entrees, meats, and cheese platters, as well as good pizzas and pastas, but it all remains light. Follow up with fresh yogurt, fruit, and good desserts. The quiet courtyard area is at the top of the list for escaping the chaos of busy Phnom Penh.

#13, St. 57 (around the corner from Goldiana, southwest of town center). ✆ **023/360-801.** www.commealamaison-delicatessen.com. Main courses $5–$9.50. No credit cards. Daily 6am–10:30pm.

Happy Herb's Pizza ★★ WESTERN/INTERNATIONAL   The first of the famous "Happy" Phnom Penh pizza joints with a great location overlooking the river serves Khmer food, salads, pasta, and, of course, pizza. "Happy" Pizza is sprinkled with marijuana, just so you know. These days this is largely a historical gimmick, an eccentric remnant of the wild days of UNTAC. Happy Herb's has been much copied but never bettered. The feta salad is superb and the normal pizza, with absolutely no marijuana whatsoever, remains the best in Phnom Penh by a very long way indeed.

#345, Sisowath Quay. ✆ **012/921-915.** Main courses $3.50–$5.50. Daily 11am–midnight.

Kandal House ★★★ WESTERN/KHMER   This small hole in the wall eatery offers a fine range of solid fare, from British fish and chips to Italian pasta and American burgers. Where it really excels, however, is in the quality of their excellent traditional Khmer dishes. The *amok* (similar to an American hamburger) here comes highly recommended. They also have a good handle on Thai food and do a good job with both green curry and yellow curry.

#239BEo Sisowath Quay. ☏ **016/800-111.** Main courses $4.50. MC, V. Daily 9am–11pm.

Khmer Surin ★★★ KHMER/THAI   A long-running Khmer and Thai restaurant that simply gets better and better, Khmer Surin is set in a large Khmer traditional-style building on leafy 57 Street. It serves a fantastic range of regional dishes in beautifully crafted, but endearingly rustic, surroundings. At the Khmer Surin they keep the Thai and Khmer menus separate so that you know from which country the dish originates. Surin is actually a province of Thailand bordering Cambodia to the north that is largely ethnic Khmer in makeup. The dishes range from the simple Thai such as "Rad Na Gai" (large flat noodles with chicken in gravy) to Khmer favorites such as "Trey Dom Rai" (whole fish fried with tamarind sauce). Try the "Trey Chhlounh" or deep-fried peacock eel direct from the Tonle Sap.

#9, St. 57. ☏ **023/993-163.** Main courses $3.50–$8.50. Daily 10am–10pm.

Le Deauville ★ FRENCH   This open-air French bar and brasserie, on the north end of the Wat Phnom roundabout, is a good, mellow choice for affordable French and Khmer dishes. The atmosphere is unpretentious and cozy, with a large open bar at the center and tables scattered in the streetside courtyard (and shielded from the traffic by a wall of potted greenery). Daily lunch set menus give you a choice of salad and entree, including local specialties such as Mekong fish with lime or beef medallions. The restaurant serves good pizzas and spaghetti, and its wine list fits just about any taste or budget. Le Deauville is also a popular spot for a casual drink in the evening.

Kj St. 94 (just north of Wat Phnom). ☏ **012/843-204.** Main courses $4.50–$9. V. Daily 11am–2pm and 6–10pm.

Pacharan ★★ SPANISH   This is Phnom Penh's only Spanish restaurant serving tapas. Part of the FCC group, they've got all the favorites: *patatas bravas,* cured meats, Spanish tortillas—the list goes on. In keeping with tapas spirit, portions are small, and you're meant to order different plates to share among friends. The chicken *croquettas* are perfectly crispy. If you have room, try the chocolate tart, a healthy portion of rich chocolate served with a side of vanilla ice cream. They also have a fine selection of Spanish wines.

389 Sisowath Quay. ☏ **023/224-394.** Tapas $3.50–$11. MC, V. Daily 11am–midnight.

Tamarind Café ★ FRENCH/MEDITERRANEAN   Good tapas, *meze* (Middle Eastern appetizers), salads, and a host of French and Mediterranean entrees make Tamarind's cool perch, overlooking busy Street 240, an excellent choice. The pastas and pizzas are delicious, and fresh salads and light menu items are just right on a hot day. The bar is always busy and stays open late.

#31, St. 240. ☏ **012/830-139.** Main courses $5–$15. MC, V. Daily 10am–midnight.

INEXPENSIVE

Boddhi Tree ★ ASIAN/KHMER   You can easily combine lunch here with a trip to nearby Tuol Sleng prison (p. 384), a site that doesn't inspire an appetite, really, but the Boddhi Tree is a peaceful oasis and not a bad spot to collect your thoughts after visiting vestiges of Cambodia's late troubles. Named for the tree under which the

Buddha "saw the light," this verdant little garden courtyard and rough-hewn guest-house has comfy balcony and courtyard seating, where it seems to serve up as much calm as the coffee, tea, and light fare that make it so popular. There are daily specials and often visiting chefs. All the curries are good, as are the great baguette sandwiches.

#50, St. 113, Beong Keng Kong (across from Tuol Sleng Museum). ℂ **023/211-397.** Main courses $2.50–$5.50. No credit cards. Daily 7am–9pm.

Friends (Mith Samlanh) Restaurant ★★ KHMER/INTERNATIONAL This friendly little gem is not to be missed. It's an NGO project where Khmer street kids are given shelter and taught useful skills for their reintegration into society. The food is great, with an ever-changing menu of local and international favorites such as spring rolls, fried rice, good salads, and a host of desserts. Stop by to cool off and have a light bite while touring the city center (it's right across from the National Museum). The place is a cozy open-air colonial in a courtyard decorated with the kids' murals. You might even find yourself giving English lessons, laughing, and smiling with these young survivors. They also run a boutique next door called **Friends and Stuff,** which sells reconditioned electronics and new crafts from their training center.

#215, St. 13 (near entrance to National Museum). ℂ **012/802-072** or 023/426-748. www.streetfriends. org. Main courses $4–$5. No credit cards. Daily 11am–9pm.

SNACKS & CAFES

Java Café and Gallery (#56, E1 Preah Sihanouk Blvd.; ℂ **012/833-512** or 023/987-420) is a good spot in town to relax and escape the midday heat. Just south of the main sights (near the Independence Monument), this popular second-story oasis has casual seating on a large balcony and an open gallery interior. It serves real coffee and cappuccino, as well as good cakes and other baked goods. Evenings can feature live music. Open daily 7am to 10pm.

The **Deli,** at #13, St. 178 (ℂ **012/851-234**), is an expat favorite for a good sandwich and excellent pastries.

The **Shop** is a nice little stop on popular Street 240 (ℂ **023/986-964**), on the north end of Sisowath Quay. It serves fine baked goods and great teas and coffees in a friendly and comfortable storefront at each location. There are neat details, such as butcher-block tables and fresh flowers, and the Shop can arrange picnic lunches for day trips from Phnom Penh.

Fat Boy at #124, St. 130 (ℂ **012/704-500**) is a submarine sandwich shop that is making waves. It serves up the best American-style subs in town, generously

---

 Prek Leap

For an interesting evening of local fun and frolic, cross the Cambodian–Japanese Friendship bridge on the Tonle Sap River in the north end of town, and follow the main road a few short clicks to the town of **Prek Leap,** a grouping of large riverside eateries that's always crowded with locals on the weekend. Some of these places put on popular variety shows, combining the universal language of slapstick with a good chance to eat, talk, and laugh with locals. The restaurants serve good Khmer and Chinese fare. Go by taxi and pick the most crowded place—the more, the merrier.

made-to-order on fresh-baked just-like-home breads and rolls. Imported roast beef, turkey, ham, salami, Italian subs, tuna salad, cheeses, and a big selection of sauces and add-ons. The Fat Boy sub packing a full kilo of meat is for real aficionados of the sub at its finest and indeed its largest.

The **Sugar Palm** (#19, St. 240; ✆ **023/220-956**) serves good Khmer dishes streetside, or from its upstairs balcony. The interior also functions as a gallery, with local crafts on display. This is a great place to relax and enjoy real Khmer atmosphere.

What to See & Do

Phnom Penh is fairly compact and most sights are not far from the central riverfront area. You can walk but be prepared for a fairly nerve-wracking time dealing with the traffic. Alternatively, hire a tuk-tuk or motodup for the day. The Russian market is in the south of town away from the center. Nearby, **Tuol Sleng** and the **Killing Fields** can be visited together.

Central Market This Art Deco behemoth (called Psar Thmei in Khmer, meaning "New Market"), built in 1937, is a city landmark and, on any given day, a veritable anthill of activity. The building is a towering cruciform rotunda with four wings. The eastern entrance is the best spot to find T-shirts, hats, and all manner of trinkets and souvenirs, as well as photocopied bootlegs of popular novels and books on Cambodia. Goldsmiths and watch-repair and -sales counters predominate in the main rotunda, and you can find some good deals. Spend some time wandering the nooks and crannies, though, and you're sure to come across something that strikes your fancy, whether that's a chaotic hardware shop, a cobbler hard at work with an awl, or just the cacophony and carnival-barker shouts of salesmen and haggling shoppers. Be sure to bargain for any purchase.

Btw. sts. 126 and 136 in town center. Daily 5am–5pm.

Independence Monument Built in the late 1950s to commemorate Cambodia's independence from the French on November 9, 1953, this towering obelisk is crowned with Khmer Nagas and was designed to deliberately echo Angkorian architecture. The area is at its most majestic when all lit up at night (or from afar while squinting).

South of town center at intersection of Norodom and Sihanouk boulevards.

"The Killing Fields," Choeung Ek Memorial ★★ This was originally a Chinese cemetery before becoming an execution ground for the Khmer Rouge during their maniacal reign under Pol Pot from 1975 to 1979. Victims were bought here in trucks and forced to kneel by freshly dug pits. They then had their throats slashed or were bludgeoned to death one by one under the harsh light of fluorescent tubes. Choeung Ek is one of many mass graves all over the country dating from the days of Democratic Kampuchea. Most towns will have at least one. Many remain undiscovered or known only to local people. This particular site is a collection of innocuous-looking mounds, near a towering monument of catalogued human skulls. There is some debate as to the taste or relevance of this display. As a sign of respect, you take your shoes off before mounting the steps to view the monument up close. Human skulls, arranged by age and gender, are arranged at eye level, while other bones are placed on higher levels. The Killing Fields are often visited in conjunction with a tour of Tuol Sleng (see below).

15km (9⅓ miles) south of Phnom Penh. Arrange a private car or motorcycle. Admission $3; guides available (highly recommended) in exchange for donations. Daily 8am–5:30pm.

National Museum ★★★ The National Museum of Phnom Penh, opened in 1920 by King Sisowath, is an important storehouse for artifacts and statuary from all regions of Cambodia and housed in a beautiful French colonial building. This grand red sandstone edifice has a beautiful collection of Khmer pieces displayed around a pretty central courtyard. From the entrance, begin on your left with a room of small prehistoric artifacts and follow the galleries around clockwise. More than 5,000 exhibits are on display, including Angkorian-era statues, lingas, Buddhas, apsaras, and other artifacts, most notably the legendary statue of the "Leper King." There are good accompanying descriptions in English, but this is not a bad place to have a knowledgeable guide. Just ask at the ticket desk.

Just north of Royal Palace at St. 178, and a short walk from the river. Admission $3. Daily 8am–5pm.

Royal Palace and Silver Pagoda ★★★ This glittering downtown campus was the ostentatious jewel in the crown of Cambodia's monarchy. Built in the late 1860s under the reign of Norodom, the site comprises elaborate gilded halls, with steep tile roofs, stupa-shaped cupolas, and golden temple *nagas*. The grand **Throne Hall** at the center is the coronation site for Khmer kings. Featured here are the many royal busts and the gilded umbrella used to shade the king when in procession. The French built a small exhibition hall on the temple grounds, a building that now houses the many gifts given to the monarchy. Just inside the door, there is an original Cézanne canvas that has suffered terrible water damage and hangs in a tatty frame like an unwanted diploma. The balcony of the exhibition hall is the best bird's-eye view of the gilded temples. The facade of the neighboring **Royal Residence** is just as resplendent and is still the home of the now-abdicated King Sihanouk and his son and successor.

The **Silver Pagoda** is just south of the palace; entrance is included with the Royal Palace ticket. The floors of this grand temple are covered with 5,000 blocks of silver weighing more than 6 tons. The temple houses a 17th-century Buddha made of Baccarat crystal, and another made almost entirely of gold and decorated with nearly 10,000 diamonds. The temple courtyard is encircled by a covered walkway with a contiguous mural of Cambodia's history and mythology. On the southern end of the complex is a small hill covered in vegetation and said to be a model of the sacred Mount Meru.

Btw. sts. 240 and 184 on Sothearos (entrance on east side facing the river). Admission $3; $5 with still camera; $7 with video camera. Daily 7:30–11am and 2–5pm.

Russian Market This bustling market in the south end of town is comparable to the Central Market and equally worthy of a visit. The real deal on souvenirs can be had here, though it takes hard haggling to get the best prices on items such as opium paraphernalia, carvings, and ceramics. It's all authentic-looking, even if it's not genuine. In hot season the temperature reaches ovenlike levels.

South of town center btw. sts. 440 and 450. Daily dawn–dusk.

Tuol Sleng, Museum of Genocide ★★ It is important to visit this profoundly disturbing place if you wish to understand modern Cambodia. It is an experience that brings you close to the darkest depths of mankind's capacity for brutality. The grounds of this former high school are just as the Vietnamese found them in 1979 at the end of Cambodia's bloody genocide. Under the Khmer Rouge, this former school became one of the most notorious interrogation centers, where unbelievable cruelty was used to extract "confessions" before victims were slaughtered in the Killing Fields. It was called S21 by the Khmer Rouge and it was by no means the only facility of this sort in Democratic Kampuchea. S21 was one part of a larger organized killing apparatus. From 1975 to 1979, an estimated 17,000 prisoners were tortured and killed at Tuol Sleng, or were executed in the nearby Killing Fields. A great number were actually Khmer Rouge themselves accused of disloyalty by the increasingly paranoid leadership. Some very senior Khmer Rouge cadres (even those close to Pol Pot in his Parisian days) and veterans of the "freedom" struggle were bought here and tortured and then killed with a sledgehammer blow to the back of the head. So were their wives and so were their children. Many were just ordinary Khmer citizens required to confess to crimes about things they would never have known to exist. Often they would be tortured for being spies for the CIA or the KGB or both. Most would never have heard of either, being beaten, horrifically mutilated, drowned, or electrocuted until they confessed to whatever sinister, paranoid fantasies the savage agents of "Angkar," or the "Organization," dreamed up to please their increasingly demented masters. If you don't come with a guide, you might want to hire one at the entrance, although you're free to roam the grounds on your own. The prison population of Tuol Sleng was carefully catalogued; in fact, the metal neck brace employed for holding subjects' heads in place for their admittance photographs is on display. There are some written accounts in English and paintings made by a survivor called Vann Nath. He was saved only because the Khmer Rouge used his talents to make propaganda paintings of Pol Pot. In addition to his artwork, there are gory photos of the common torture practices in the prison. Perhaps what is most haunting is the look in the eyes of the newly arrived; one wing of the buildings is dedicated to these very arrival photos: thousands of people staring at you across history. Some look nervous. Some look terrified. Others look bewildered. Many are infants. Children did not escape the savagery of this dreadful place. This sight is overwhelming, so be prepared. There are a few Westerners among them—hapless yachtsmen or hippies, transporting who knows what, who took a disastrous wrong turn into the wrong waters. The upper galleries contain the roughly constructed cells, the manacles, and the small metal boxes used for defecation that were part and parcel of daily life for all inmates before they were taken away and murdered. To the left as you enter are a series of former classrooms used for torture. There are grisly pictures of what the Vietnamese found when they arrived. Victims still chained to the metal beds on which they had been tortured and then murdered before their persecutors made a hasty exit to save their own skins from the invading Vietnamese army. The trial of the camp commandant, Duch, took place in 2010. He pleaded guilty, although proffered the perennial excuse of torturers worldwide, that he was simply "following orders." The depth of suffering is truly unfathomable.

South of town at corner of sts. 350 and 113. Admission $2; guide fees vary, but are usually $2–$3 per person. Daily 8am–noon and 1–5pm.

Wat Phnom ★★ Legend has it that in the 14th century, a woman named Penh found sacred Buddhist objects in the nearby river and placed them here on the small hill that later became a temple. Well, the rest is history. *Phnom*, in fact, means "hill," so the name of the city translates to "Penh's Hill."

The temple is a standard Southeast Asian *wat,* with *nagas* (snakes) on the cornered peaks of the roof and didactic murals of the Buddha's life done in Day-Glo allegories along interior walls. Don't miss the central ceiling, which, unlike the bright walls, is yet to be restored and is gritty and authentic.

During the day the whole area is a hive of activity. At night it is badly lit and in the past has been notorious for robberies.

Outdoor Activities

If your hotel lacks an outdoor pool, head to the **Clark Hatch Fitness Center** (✆ **023/424-888**) at the Hotel InterContinental. This place has it all in the way of equipment. Daily visitors are invited for a fee ($10 weekdays, $15 weekends), with pool and sauna included. It's open daily from 6am to 10pm.

Shopping

Shops and galleries are growing in number in the developing capital. The best shopping in town, for everything from souvenirs and trinkets to the obligatory kitchen sink, is at any of the large local markets (see the Central Market and Russian Market under "What to See & Do," above).

All along Street 178, interesting little outlets are springing up, including a few affordable silk dealers such as **Lotus Pond** (#57Eo, St. 178; ✆ **023/426-782**). At **Asasax Art Gallery** (#192, St. 178; ✆ **023/217-795;** www.asasaxart.com.kh), you'll see unique local works.

Street 240 is also developing its own cafe culture. It has antiques shops and boutiques, such as **Bliss** (#29, St. 240; ✆ **023/215-754**), which sells some unique beaded and embroidered cushions and quilts.

Near the Independence Monument, **Bazar** (28 Sihanouk Blvd.; ✆ **012/776-492**) has a small but refined collection of Asian antiques and furniture.

For CDs, DVDs, and cool T-shirts and hip-hop fashions, stop by the **Boom Boom Room** just across from the Golden Gate Hotel (#1C, St. 278; ✆ **012/709-906**).

For essentials and Western groceries, stop by the **Lucky Market** (#160, Sihanouk Blvd.; ✆ **023/215-229**). For fresh organic produce and fine canned goods, try **Veggy's** (#23, St. 240; ✆ **023/211-534**).

Monument Books (#111, Norodom Blvd.; ✆ **023/217-617**) has a great selection of new titles; it's a good spot to find books on Khmer language and culture. Stop by the **London Book Centre** (#51, St. 240; ✆ **023/214-258**), among the new bistros and cafes, to exchange or buy new and used books; there's a good selection here.

Phnom Penh After Dark

Phnom Penh has a reputation for booming nightlife. Booming it is, but a large part of that is actually pretty seedy. There are, however, a number of very classy options.

Most restaurants also have bars, and those along the riverfront will be open as late as midnight. **Cantina** (p. 380) is a convivial spot and very popular. **Kandal House** (p. 380) is cozy and friendly.

There are a number of large discos you can visit if you feel a boogie impetus coming on. They are not your best bet, though, since they are expensive and not very pleasant. It is better to head to one of the bars with a dance floor. Upstairs at the **Riverhouse Lounge** (#6, St. 110 [corner of Sisowath]; ✆ **023/212-302;** daily 4pm–2am) is the coolest disco in town. The setting is marvelous, the river glittering before you as you sip one of their very respectable cocktails on the balcony.

Rubies Wine Bar (#13, St. 19; ☏ **092/319-769;** Tues–Sun 5:30pm–late) is a sophisticated little place on the corner of Street 240, among the upmarket boutiques. It has an impressive array of wines and spirits.

Side Trips from Phnom Penh
MEKONG RIVER CRUISE

In the evening you will see a number of boats lit up like Christmas trees chugging slowly up and down the Tonle Sap. Cruises taking in great views of the Royal Palace, National Museum, and floating villages along the banks are becoming ever more popular, as is dinner afloat. You can find these boats of many different sizes and levels of quality along the waterfront between Street 178 and Street 130. They are also at the ferry terminal opposite Street 104. They have small signs up and may also hail you as you walk by. Costs start at about $10 per hour. **Kanika** (☏ **012/848-802**) runs a unique catamaran for parties and dinner cruises. Proceeds go to Seametrey NGO projects. **Experience Mekong Boat** (☏ **012/432-456;** www.cambodiaby boat.com) offers tours of various sorts, including a look at how the boats are built and general life on the river.

OUDONG

Following defeat at Angkor by the Thais, the Khmer capital moved to Oudong, and kings ruled from here for more than 100 years until the power center shifted to nearby Phnom Penh in 1866. The area was a monastic center, and the 13th-century temples, like most others, pale in comparison to those of the Angkor complex. Still, the hills of Oudong offer breathtaking views. It's an hour west of Phnom Penh and is best reached by rented vehicle.

PHNOM CHISOR & TONLE BATI

If you have been or are going to Angkor Wat, these temples will pale in comparison, but the ride through the countryside and among rural villages makes for a good day trip. Tonle Bati (33km/21 miles south of Phnom Penh) is a small collection of Angkor-style temples. Admission is $3. Nearby Phnom Chisor is a group of 10th-century ruins atop a picturesque hill. Phnom Penh travel agents can make all the arrangements.

SIEM REAP & ANGKOR WAT ★★★

The ruins of the ancient city of Angkor, capital of the Khmer kingdom from 802 to 1295 A.D., are one of the world's acknowledged marvels. The "City of God-Kings," heart of the "Water Kingdom," Angkor boasts some of the largest religious monuments ever constructed. It was built as a microcosm of the universe. Angkor Wat itself, the largest religious building in the world, represents Mount Meru.

The temples are served by the nearby town of Siem Reap, some 6km (3¾ miles) to the south. Siem Reap means "Siam Defeated" and refers to the 16th-century victory that solidified the Khmer kingdom even though the Thais were to triumph once again as empires ebbed and flowed. Not long ago, Siem Reap was a quiet, dusty town of rutted roads and dark nights. It now supports a host of large five-star hotels and resorts, restaurants in great number, and the kind of goods, services, shops, galleries, and spas that make the little city an island of luxury in parched and desperately poor western Cambodia.

A 3- or 4-day visit will suffice (though many do it in less time) to come away with a newfound love for its mystery, religion, and some of the most spectacular sunrises known to man.

Getting There

BY PLANE **Bangkok Air** (in Phnom Penh, ℂ **023/722-545;** in Siem Reap, ℂ **063/965-422;** www.bangkokair.com) and its subsidiary **Siem Reap Air** (in Phnom Penh, ℂ **023/723-963;** in Siem Reap, ℂ **063/965-427;** www.siemreapair. com) is currently the only airline running the 1-hour connection to Siem Reap from Phnom Penh. One-way fares are $58 to $85. If you just want to see the great temples at Angkor, the process is simplified with international arrivals: **Vietnam Airlines** (www.vietnamairlines.com) flies directly from Ho Chi Minh City. **Bangkok Air** flies directly from Bangkok. **Lao Airlines** (www.laoairlines.com) flies in from Vientiane. **Air Asia** (www.airasia.com) and **Malaysia Airlines** (www.malaysiaairlines.com) fly from Kuala Lumpur. **Silk Air** (www.silkair.com) flies from Singapore. *Note:* The international departure tax (from both Phnom Penh and Siem Reap) is $25; the domestic tax is $6.

BY BOAT A ride on the 5-hour boat connection between Phnom Penh and Siem Reap costs $30 to $35. Contact any hotel or travel agent (they all sell the same tickets at the same price). The trip connects to Siem Reap via the great Tonle Sap Lake. Siem Reap also connects with Battambang, to the south and west, via the Tonle Sap and the Sangker River. In the rainy season when the water is high, the ride is relatively straightforward, but in the dry season (Feb–May) it can take 8 hours or more and isn't recommended. Book your ticket at any tour agent or the front desk of your hotel or guesthouse. The price is $14.

BY BUS **Mekong Express** (ℂ **023/427-518**) connects Phnom Penh and Siem Reap with daily luxury buses ($11 for the 5½-hr. ride). **Neak Krorhorm Travel and Tour** (in Phnom Penh, ℂ **023/219-496;** in Siem Reap near the Old Market, ℂ **063/964-924**) provides similar services. The road from Siem Reap to Poipet on the Thai border, which was appalling for years, has now finally been improved and is perfect. Once into Thailand, you can travel on to Bangkok by minibus from the crossing or you can travel on into Aranyaprathet by tuk-tuk and catch a regular bus from the bus station. Any all-in fares, either from Bangkok to Siem Reap or the reverse, are not recommended as they come rife with scams and rip-offs.

Getting Around

You'll need some kind of wheeled conveyance to make your way around Siem Reap and to and from the temples. Any hotel front desk or travel agent can make arrangements for you.

A **rented car with driver** is about $25. A **motorcycle taxi** is a good, cheap option for $10 per day, and there are also **tuk-tuks,** for about $15 per day.

Riding your own motorbike was once the most popular choice, but local officials put a stop to it, citing the many road accidents. **Bicycles** are still a possibility, however, and the temple roads are flat and well paved. Bikes rent for $2 to $3 per day from guesthouses and hotels. Take care in the scorching midday heat and drink plenty of fluids.

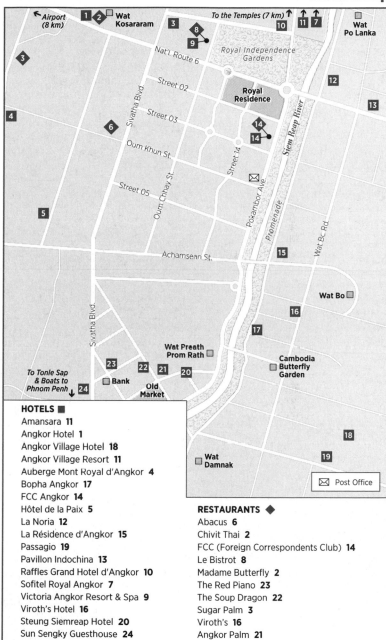

HOTELS ■

Amansara **11**
Angkor Hotel **1**
Angkor Village Hotel **18**
Angkor Village Resort **11**
Auberge Mont Royal d'Angkor **4**
Bopha Angkor **17**
FCC Angkor **14**
Hôtel de la Paix **5**
La Noria **12**
La Résidence d'Angkor **15**
Passagio **19**
Pavillon Indochina **13**
Raffles Grand Hotel d'Angkor **10**
Sofitel Royal Angkor **7**
Victoria Angkor Resort & Spa **9**
Viroth's Hotel **16**
Steung Siemreap Hotel **20**
Sun Sengky Guesthouse **24**

RESTAURANTS ◆

Abacus **6**
Chivit Thai **2**
FCC (Foreign Correspondents Club) **14**
Le Bistrot **8**
Madame Butterfly **2**
The Red Piano **23**
The Soup Dragon **22**
Sugar Palm **3**
Viroth's **16**
Angkor Palm **21**

Navigating central Siem Reap around Psar Chas is easy because it is compact. The town as a whole is very spread out, though. However, there is no shortage of willing available wheels.

Visitor Information & Tours

Contact either of the following agencies for information and tours.

- **Diethelm Travel,** House #4, Airport Rd. #6, Krum #1, Sangkat #2, Phum Taphul, Siem Reap (© **063/963-524;** fax 063/963-694; dtc@dtc.com.kh). All local and regional services.
- **Exotissimo Travel,** #300, Airport Rd. #6, Siem Reap (© **063/964-323;** fax 063/963-621; www.exotissimo.com). All local and regional services.

[Fast FACTS] SIEM REAP

Currency Exchange

You can change traveler's checks in some hotels and in any bank; **Canadia Bank** (on the western side of the Old Market; © **063/964-808**) is the kindest in terms of fees charged. **ANZ Royal Bank** (566–570 St. Tep Vong; © **023/999-000**) is the best option for service. **ANZ** has several ATMs around town, including one at the central branch and two 24-hour ATMs in the heart of the backpacker district just south of Red Piano Bar. **Cambodia Commercial Bank (CCB;** 130 Siwatha Blvd.; © **063/380-154**) and **Mekong Bank** (43 Siwatha Blvd.; © **063/964-420**) can do credit card cash advances as well.

Doctors & Hospitals
Royal Angkor International Hospital (#6, Airport Rd.; © **063/761-888;** www.royalangkorhospital.com) provides 24-hour emergency care, ambulance, translation, and evacuation. Check on their website before departure to make sure your insurance covers you under their terms and conditions.

Emergencies There is a tourist police station near the entrance to the temples. For local police, dial © **117.** In the event of a medical emergency, contact **International SOS Clinic,** in Phnom Penh (© **023/216-911**).

Internet Access Small storefront offices surround the central market area. Most are open early to late

(7am–midnight). More and more places offer free Wi-Fi to customers, including **Le Tigre de Papier, The Blue Pumpkin,** and **Molly Malone's.**

Mail The post office is located on Pokambor Avenue, at riverside near the town center (next to the FCC; see "Where to Dine," p. 379). It's open daily from 7am to 5pm and can handle foreign and domestic regular and parcel post.

Telephones The area code for Siem Reap is **63.** Most hotels have international direct dialing (IDD). Many of the Internet cafes around the Old Market have better rates and offer callback service or Internet phones.

Where to Stay

Not surprisingly, the accommodation scene in Siem Reap has exploded since peace broke out in Cambodia at the end of the last century, and now the choices of places to stay is astronomical in all categories. Having said that, in the high season high-end hotels often fill up, so be sure to book ahead. In low season be sure to ask for a discount. Most hotels levy a 10% VAT. Budget travelers are also amply catered to, but again in high season you may have to try a few different guesthouses before you find a room.

VERY EXPENSIVE

Amansara ★★★ If there's one place to splurge in Southeast Asia, Amansara is it. Transformed into an ultraluxury resort from former King Norodom Sihanouk's private guesthouses, the space at Amansara alone is worth it. Suites—there are no "rooms" here—are elegant and minimalist, with bas-reliefs on creamy walls, dark-wood trim, and polished stone floors. The separate shower looks out onto a courtyard or a private saltwater swimming pool. The dining is fabulous here, in a restaurant that was once King Sihanouk's private screening room (in his heyday, he was a prolific filmmaker). What really sets Amansara apart is the way it brings Khmer culture—both ancient and modern—inside the walls. Lectures and performances are frequent occurrences, the library is stocked with helpful books, and the staff members feel more like friendly neighbors than anything else. It's all done on a first-name basis, without being obtrusive.

Road to Angkor, Siem Reap. ✆ **063/760-333.** Fax 063/760-335. www.amanresorts.com. 24 units. High season $800 suite, $1,000 pool suite; low season $750 suite, $950 pool suite. AE, MC, V. **Amenities:** Restaurant; bar; Internet access (in library); central outdoor pool and 25m (82-ft.) lap pool; room service; spa. *In room:* A/C, fridge, hair dryer, minibar, Wi-Fi.

Hôtel de la Paix ★★ Hôtel de la Paix is a modern, cutting-edge hotel, in sharp contrast to most high-end accommodations in town. The lobby contains black and white tiles and stark white walls that are shockingly broken by neon pink lights behind the lobby lounge. Room interiors have a similar monochromatic scheme, but with accent pillows in deep purple and silver wall hangings and lamps. Suites come with white marble bathtubs that lie a couple of feet away from the foot of the bed. Around the corner is the funky stone shower console with tropical shower head.

Sivatha Blvd. ✆ **063/966-000.** Fax 063/966-001. www.hoteldelapaixangkor.com. 107 units. $373 deluxe; $460 deluxe/courtyard suite; $553 duplex spa suite. AE, MC, V. **Amenities:** Restaurant; lounge; cafe; babysitting; concierge; fitness center; Jacuzzi; outdoor pool; sauna; spa. *In room:* A/C, satellite TV, DVD player in suites, fridge, hair dryer, minibar, MP3 docking station.

La Résidence d'Angkor ★★ Formerly the Pansea, La Résidence d'Angkor is a stylish, self-contained sanctuary managed by the people at Orient-Express. You'll cross a small moat to enter the cool interior of the steeply gabled, dark-wooden lobby with its grand Angkor-inspired reliefs. The tranquil central courtyard is lined with palms and dominated by a small but stylish pool. The resort area is small, but everything from the gardens to the room decor is tidy and designed for quiet privacy. Rooms are large, well appointed, open, and elegant, with cloth divans, retro fixtures, and nice local touches. Spacious bathrooms connect with the bedrooms via a bamboo sliding door, and another glass slider opens to a small private balcony with views of the courtyard and lounges. The lobby restaurant offers fine dining. There are some great sitting areas for drinks, as well as a library with books, chess, and a conference table.

River Rd., Siem Reap. ✆ **063/963-390.** Fax 063/963-391. www.residencedangkor.com. 55 units. $185–$285 deluxe riverside; $205–$365 deluxe garden side; $250–$325 poolside. AE, MC, V. **Amenities:** Restaurant; bar; Internet access (in business center); outdoor pool; room service; library. *In room:* A/C, satellite TV, fridge, hair dryer, minibar.

Raffles Grand Hotel d'Angkor ★★★ For luxury, atmosphere, and convenience, there is no better choice in Siem Reap. Rebuilt in 1994 from the shell of a classic 1929 structure, this is authentic old Indochina that's neither museum piece nor overly stuffy. Right in the center of town, the imposing colonial facade gives way to a marble lobby with an open metal elevator—an original period piece that's still functional. Staterooms are large, with classic French doors and windows, tiled entries, fine furnishings, and an almost out-of-place high-tech entertainment module. Landmark rooms, a step up, are similar but have four-poster beds, a balcony with rattan furniture, and nice touches such as porcelain bathrooms and antique detail.

1 Vithei Charles de Gaulle, Khum Svay Dang Kum, Siem Reap. © **063/963-888.** Fax 063/963-168. www.raffles.com. 119 units. $265–$350 double; $465–$700 suite; $2,000 2-bedroom villa. AE, MC, V. **Amenities:** 4 restaurants; 2 bars; kids' club; concierge; health club; Jacuzzi; outdoor pool; sauna; spa; 2 tennis courts; Wi-Fi. *In room:* A/C, satellite TV, fridge, hair dryer, minibar.

Sofitel Angkor Phokeethra Golf and Spa Resort ★★ Sofitel is famed for bringing life back to the classic hotels of old Indochina, but in Siem Reap, it started totally afresh. The lobby is an old-world Indochine replica with an antique Khmer pagoda and a menagerie of overstuffed European furniture. The courtyard pool is large, open, and fun, including a short river meander crossed by a small bridge and a swim-up bar. Rooms are spacious, with dark-wood floors and rich touches such as designer throw rugs and elegant built-in cabinetry. All bathrooms are large, with tubs and granite counters. Be sure to find a moment, preferably near the magic hour of sunset (though any time will do), to take it all in from the island pagoda in the central pond.

Vithei Charles de Gaulle (on the way to temples, just north of town center), Khum Svay Dang Kum, Siem Reap. © **063/964-600.** Fax 063/964-610. www.sofitel.com. 238 units. High season $565 superior, $647 luxury, $682–$1,500 suite; low season $276 superior, $332 luxury, $431–$550 suite. AE, MC, V. **Amenities:** 5 restaurants; 2 bars; concierge; 18-hole golf course; health club; Jacuzzi; large outdoor pool; 24-hr. room service; sauna; smoke-free rooms; small library. *In room:* A/C, satellite TV w/in-house movies, fax, fridge, hair dryer, minibar.

Victoria Angkor Resort & Spa ★★ Victoria Angkor is a tasteful replica of a French colonial–era hotel, but with all of the amenities and functionality of a modern resort. Public spaces are done in earth tones, rattan and wood accents, and Art Deco floor tiles in mustard yellow tones. A large central atrium with period-piece elevator and towering courtyard staircase greets the visitor to this downtown campus. The central pool is a private oasis surrounded by a mini-jungle, with massage *salas* nestled in the flora. Rooms are large, luxurious, and decorated with retro oil paintings. Floors are wood with a border of fine tile that matches luxurious woven bedspreads. All rooms have balconies. Colonial suites have individual themes and the best ones are the corner suites with large, covered outdoor balconies. Fine dining at their Le Bistrot (see below) is tops.

Central Park, P.O. Box 93145, Siem Reap. © **063/760-428.** Fax 063/760-350. www.victoriahotels-asia. com. 130 units. $155–$165 double; $445 poolview or gardenview suite. AE, MC, V. **Amenities:** 2 restaurants; bar; babysitting; children's center; concierge; Jacuzzi; large outdoor saltwater pool; room service; spa. *In room:* A/C, satellite TV, fridge, hair dryer, minibar.

EXPENSIVE

Allson Angkor Hotel ★ Of the many newer hotels along the airport road, Route 6, the Angkor Hotel is the best—and only slightly more expensive than the rest. It's large and ostentatious, with high, Khmer-style roofs and large reproductions of temple statuary in the entry. Everything is clean and comfortable, if a bit sterile. Guest rooms are bland but spacious, but the bathrooms are a little small. Ask for a room facing the pool or in the new building in the back. The Angkor Hotel is a good, comfortable step down from the glitzier properties in town, and the best choice if they're full. The lobby is always busy with tour groups, but the staff remains friendly and expedient. The hotel is sufficiently self-contained, with all of the basic amenities and services, an outdoor pool, and a good restaurant.

Rte. 6, Phum Sala Kanseng, Siem Reap. © **063/964-301.** Fax 063/964-302. www.angkor-hotel-cambodia. com. 169 units. $70–$85 deluxe; $60–$75 superior; $130–$160 junior suite. V. **Amenities:** Restaurant; bar; basic gym; Internet access (in business center); outdoor pool; tours. *In room:* A/C, TV, fridge, hair dryer, minibar.

Angkor Village Hotel ★★ For comfortable, rustic atmosphere, Angkor Village is without rival. Located in a quiet neighborhood not far from the main market, this hideaway is a unique maze of wood bungalows connected by covered boardwalks surrounding a picturesque pond. Rooms have high bamboo ceilings, wood beams, built-in cabinetry, and decorative touches such as traditional Khmer shadow puppets and statuary. Top units have balconies overlooking the central pond. The pool is small but picturesque, set in a verdant courtyard at the rear. L'Auberge de Temples, on a small island in the central pond, serves fine French and Khmer cuisine. The hotel's **Apsara Theatre Restaurant,** just outside the gate, has Khmer-style banquet dining and performances of Khmer Apsara dancing nightly.

Wat Bo Rd., Siem Reap. © **063/963-5613.** Fax 063/963-363. www.angkorvillage.com. 52 units. $79–$189 double. AE, MC, V. **Amenities:** Restaurant; bar; Internet access (in business center); outdoor pool; limited room service; small library. *In room:* A/C, fridge, hair dryer, minibar.

Angkor Village Resort ★★ ☺ This place brings all of the taste and class of the Angkor Village Hotel (see above) into a resort atmosphere. A serpentine pool, hidden by lush gardens, is its premier attraction, but the Khmer architecture, attention to detail in local wood, and spacious breathing room all make it a good bet. Room rates are the same for bottom- or top-floor rooms, but the top floor is a better choice, with four-poster beds and higher ceilings reminiscent of a Khmer home. The resort is a bit off the beaten path, but not far from the town center, and is linked to its sister hotel and her offerings.

Phum Traeng, Siem Reap. © **063/963-561.** Fax 063/963-363. www.angkorvillage.com. 80 units. Double $159–$209. AE, MC, V. **Amenities:** Restaurant; bar; Internet access (in business center); outdoor pool; room service; spa; small library. *In room:* A/C, fridge, hair dryer, minibar.

MODERATE

FCC Angkor ★ This hotel is located beside the popular restaurant of the same name. Herb- and fruit-named rooms (Basil, Lychee, and so on) have low beds on wooden frames, and the decor is decidedly modern—flatscreen TVs, geometric Scandinavian-style furniture, vases stuffed with wooden sticks, and canvas block color paintings on the walls. The bathrooms are top-notch. There's a long and narrow outdoor pool, and all rooms come with either poolside or garden balconies.

Pokambor Ave. (next to the Royal Residence and just north of the post office). © **063/760-280.** Fax 063/760-281 www.fcccambodia.com. 31 units. $145–$175 pool view; $125–$165 garden view; $225–$280 suite. MC, V. **Amenities:** Restaurant; bar; outdoor saltwater pool. *In room:* A/C, satellite TV/DVD, fridge, minibar, Wi-Fi.

Steung Siemreap Hotel ★★ 🎁 This is a brand-new hotel, in two separate buildings along a pretty square, that does a great job of looking aged. Although this is not a new or even an uncommon concept, at the Steung Siemreap they manage it rather well. Downstairs, attractive checkered red and cream tiles are complemented by muted dark-wood furnishings. The rooms are large and very bright, lit by French windows. The furnishings are uncluttered and the feel is spare but not Spartan. The space, light, and location make this hotel a real contender in the higher echelons of the midrange category.

St. 9, Psar Chas. © **063/965-169.** Fax 063/965-151. www.steungsiemreaphotel.com. 76 units. $70 superior single; $80 superior double; $90 deluxe single; $100 deluxe double; $130 triple; $180 junior suite; $200 colonial suite; $250 Steung Siemreap suite. MC, V. **Amenities:** Restaurant; bar; concierge; small health club; Internet; outdoor pool; room service. *In room:* A/C, satellite TV, fridge, minibar.

Viroth's Hotel ★★ 🍴 A hotel that is this chic and this cheap is a rarity. The hotel is a small boutique affair, making for a private, intimate experience. Rooms are minimalist and modern: cool gray stone floors, white walls, sleek geometric furniture. But soft touches such as a floor vase of dried palm leaves, dark-brown leather desktops, and coffee-colored duvet covers keep it warm and inviting. One corner is painted a contrasting maroon color and marks the shower console. Most rooms have private balconies. The best room in the house is no. 3, on the ground floor. It comes with a large, poolside terrace and cozy lounge beds. The rooftop restaurant is lit with fairy lights at night and is an excellent place to spend the evening, looking out over the rooftops of Siem Reap.

0658 Wat Bo Village (behind City River Hotel). © **063/778-096.** Fax 063/760-774. www.viroth-hotel. com. 7 units. $80 double. MC, V. **Amenities:** Restaurant; bar; high-speed Internet; rooftop Jacuzzi; small outdoor pool; room service; small spa. *In room:* A/C, satellite TV, in-house phone only, Wi-Fi.

INEXPENSIVE

The downtown area of Siem Reap, on either side of the main road, is brimming with budget accommodations.

Auberge Mont Royal d'Angkor ★★ ☺ Down a quiet lane just to the west of the town center, this inn is a much better choice than the larger tourist hotels in this category. The cozy, Canadian-owned hotel features a genial staff, an inviting restaurant, and standard rooms that are quite chic for the low price tag. Terra-cotta tile covers the open areas, while atmospheric touches include canvas lamps, carved wood beds, and traditional hangings, curtains, and bedspreads. Deluxe rooms are worth the upgrade.

497 Taphul, P.O. Box 34, west of town center, Siem Reap. © **063/964-044.** www.auberge-mont-royal. com. 30 units. $29–$37 standard; $56–$66 pool villa; $47–$57 deluxe. AE, MC, V. **Amenities:** Restaurant; bar. *In room:* A/C, satellite TV, fridge, minibar, no phone.

Bopha Angkor ★ With its popular nightly dance show and Khmer restaurant, there is a certain cultural-theme-park vibe to this place, but nevertheless, Bopha Angkor is tidy, affordable, and quite genuine about providing a culturally infused visit to Siem Reap. Rooms are arranged in a U-shaped courtyard around a lush garden. Private spaces are large and feature fun local accents such as mosquito nets and souvenir-shop trinkets on the walls. Bathrooms are small. The hotel is close to the Old Market area.

#0512, Acharsvar St. (across canal from market), Siem Reap. © **063/964-928.** Fax 063/964-446. www.bopha-angkor.com. 38 units. $55–$91 double; $120 suite. MC, V. **Amenities:** Restaurant; bar; Internet access. *In room:* A/C, satellite TV, fridge, minibar.

La Noria ★★ With a similar sister property, Borann Auberge de Temples, La Noria is a mellow group of bungalows connected by a winding garden path. The guesthouse is near the town center, but you wouldn't know it in the hush of this little laid-back spot. Rooms are basic but tidy, with pleasing traditional decor and nice touches such as terra-cotta floors, wooden trim, small balconies, and fine hangings.

Bathrooms are small but clean, with a guesthouse-style shower-in-room setup. The place is light on amenities, though it does have a small pool and makes up for any deficiency with simple charm. The open-air restaurant is a highlight, serving good Khmer and French food. The hotel is affiliated with Krousar Thmey "New Family," a humanitarian group doing good work, and there is a helpful information board about rural travel and humanitarian projects.

Down small lane off Rte. 6 to the northeast of town, Siem Reap. ✆ **063/964-242.** Fax 063/964-243. 28 units. www.lanoriaangkor.com. $39 double. MC, V. **Amenities:** Restaurant; Internet access; outdoor pool. *In room:* A/C (optional).

Passagio ★　This unpretentious little workhorse of a hotel is convenient to downtown and adjoins its own helpful travel agent, Lolei Travel. Rooms are large and tidy and not much more, but that's the beauty here: three floors that are something like an American motel, complete with tacky hotel art. The one suite has a bathtub; all others have stand-up showers in bathrooms that are nondescript. The friendly staff can arrange any detail and is eager to please.

Watdamanak Village (across river to east of town), Siem Reap. ✆ **063/760-324.** Fax 063/760-163. 17 units. www.passaggio-hotel.com. $32–$47 double; $45 family room. AE, MC, V. **Amenities:** Restaurant (breakfast only); free airport pickup; Internet access (in business center). *In room:* A/C, satellite TV, fridge, minibar, no phone, Wi-Fi.

Pavillon Indochine ★★　This converted traditional Khmer house and garden is the closest you'll get to the temples. It's quite peaceful, even isolated, in a quiet neighborhood. Really it's an upscale guesthouse, charming and surprisingly self-contained, with a good restaurant and a friendly, knowledgeable French proprietor whose staff can help arrange any detail in the area. Just a few years old, the rooms are large, clean, and airy, with terra-cotta tile and wood trim. The courtyard has a picturesque garden dotted by quiet sitting areas with chairs or floor mats and comfy pillows. A good information corner lists the current happenings in town and at the temples.

Wat Thmei, on back road to temples, Siem Reap. ✆ **012/804-952.** www.pavillon-indochine.com. 24 units. $50–$65 double; $70–$85 suite. AE, MC, V. **Amenities:** Restaurant. *In room:* A/C, TV/DVD, no phone (mobile phone available upon request).

Sun Sengky Guesthouse　This is a no-nonsense, well run, and very cheap option, with secure parking right near Psar Chas on Sivatha Road. There are few frills—just TV, fridge, and air-conditioning—but the rooms are large and new with an outside veranda. The wide, white-tiled corridors are certainly not going to win any prizes for subtlety of decoration, but they might win some for light, bright functionality.

#15, Sivatha Rd. ✆ **063/964-034.** 27 units. $10 double with fan; $15 double with A/C. **Amenities:** Restaurant; bar. *In room:* A/C, satellite TV, fridge.

Where to Dine

Dining in Siem Reap is not a pricey affair. In addition to the choices listed below, all of the major hotels have fine upscale restaurants. The area around the Old Market is a cluster of storefront eateries, all affordable and laid-back.

EXPENSIVE

Le Bistrot de Siem Reap ★★ FRENCH　The atmosphere in this restaurant is wonderfully charming, with old French music playing lightly in the background, light gray walls with the ceiling trim and accent walls painted warm maroon, and black lacquer tables with mixed wooden and rattan chairs. The walls are adorned with old posters advertising voyages to the Far East, but the cuisine is a superb culinary trip to France. The wine list is a work in progress, so ask for a recommendation. They also have a good selection of Cuban cigars. It's a wonderful, tasty slice of old Indochine.

Victoria Angkor Resort and Spa, Central Park, P.O. Box 93145, Siem Reap. © **063/760-428.** Main courses $18–$26. AE, MC, V. Daily 6:30–10:30pm.

MODERATE

Abacus ★ ASIAN/FRENCH This restaurant is set in a traditional Cambodian stilt house. There is a central bar made of volcanic stone and a few tables with rattan chairs on the first floor, underneath the house. Terrace seating upstairs is divided among various small, cozy rooms. The menu is written on a chalkboard and you can choose from a good selection of either Asian rice bowls or Western mains with a couple of side dishes. The breaded fish is light and tender, served with a tangy tamarind sauce; the eggplant is grilled with rosemary and cracked pepper (ask them to go easy on the salt); and the sautéed spinach with chopped garlic is a good, healthy injection of greenery.

Oum Khun St. © **012/644-286.** Main courses $5–$17. No credit cards. Daily 11am–late.

Chivit Thai ★★ THAI This is authentic Thai in an atmospheric, traditional wood house. The food is great, the prices are low (try one of the set menus), and there's casual floor seating and a rustic but comfortable dining room, romantic in the candlelight. Name your favorite Thai dish, and they do it here—and do it well. The *tom yum* (sweet, spicy Thai soup) is excellent.

House #129, Rd. 6, next to Angkor Hotel. © **012/830-761.** Main courses $2.50–$5. No credit cards. Daily 7am–10:30pm.

FCC (Foreign Correspondents Club) CONTINENTAL The glowing white, modern cube would be at home in a nouveau riche California suburb, but it is a bit jarring canalside in the center of Siem Reap. The menu is the same as the original FCC in Phnom Penh, with generic soups, salads, and Western standards like pasta, steaks, and wood-fired pizzas. The first-floor compound continues to expand, and now supports some of the finest shopping in the city. Also, check out their cool billiards room, which is like a modernist installation behind glass, or their big-screen television surrounded by large lounge chairs at poolside.

Pokambor Ave. (next to the Royal Residence). © **063/760-280.** www.fcccambodia.com. Main courses $8–$24. MC, V. Daily 6am–midnight.

Madame Butterfly ★★ KHMER/THAI Serving the finest authentic Khmer- and Thai-influenced cuisine in town, Madame Butterfly is very pleasant—its setting alone is worth a visit. Located in a converted traditional wooden home, the seating is in low rattan chairs and the decor is characterized by a tasteful collection of Buddhist and Khmer artifacts. The whole effect is casually romantic. The menu reads like a short course in local cuisine, heavy on the curries and hot pot dishes. The helpful staff and French proprietor will gladly explain the daily specials. Look for the delicious poached fish in coconut sauce with sticky rice; the divine *masaman* curry; or the rich *mchou pous,* a chicken and shrimp bisque. For a leisurely evening, this is a great pick.

Short ride west on Airport Rd. #6. © **016/909-607.** Lunch is by reservation only. Main courses $3–$10. MC, V. Daily 11:30am–2pm and 5:30–10:30pm.

The Red Piano ★★ INTERNATIONAL Imported steaks, spaghetti, sandwiches, salads, and international specialties like good Indian samosas or chicken cordon bleu round out a great menu. Everything is good, and this place is always hoppin' late into the evening. Due to popular demand (it's sometimes hard to get a seat and they take no reservations), they've expanded onto a second floor, and renovations throughout give the place a tidy, upscale charm.

50m (164 ft.) northwest of the Old Market. © **063/963-240.** Main courses $3.75–$9.75. No credit cards. Daily 7am–midnight.

The Sugar Palm ★★ TRADITIONAL KHMER   Sugar Palm occupies the second floor of a spacious house and offers a warm and inviting ambience with subdued, covered lighting, a wall painted in sunny yellow, and vaulted ceilings. The furniture and bar are done in dark sugar-palm wood. Most of the seating is on the wraparound balcony, partially covered from the outside world with roll-down bamboo blinds. On the menu, the pomelo salad is excellent (fleshy pomelo tendrils are played off the sharp taste of dried shrimp and crunchy chopped peanuts; strips of spicy red pepper give it an extra kick). For an entree, try the chicken stir-fried with ginger.

Ta Phul Rd. (400m/1,300 ft. south of the Caltex gas station). © **063/964-838.** Main courses $4–$6. MC, V. Daily 11:30am–3pm and 5:30–11pm. Bar stays open late.

Viroth's Restaurant ★★ KHMER   Like its sister hotel two streets down (p. 394), Viroth's Restaurant boasts a sleek and stylish interior. The French and Khmer owners were the original purveyors of popular Angkor Café (see "Dining at the Temples" below). The food is traditional Khmer cuisine and mighty tasty. The *amok* fish is a perfect blend of coconut milk and lemon grass and, unlike at other restaurants, the fish is completely deboned. The spacious dining area is on a raised wooden platform and flanked on one side by a wall of bamboo rods. Ceiling and floor fans keep a cool breeze going and send ripples through the strips of sheer saffron sheets suspended from the ceiling and hanging between tables. The dessert menu is Western—if it's available, try the lime sorbet, which comes with thin strips of zesty lime rind.

246 Wat Bo St. (behind La Résidence Hotel). © **063/760-774.** Main courses $3–$5.50. MC, V. Daily 10am–2pm and 5–10pm.

INEXPENSIVE

Angkor Palm ★★★ KHMER   This gem serves Khmer food at its finest in elegant surroundings. Light, bright traditional Khmer furnishings and comfortable rattan chairs in a beautiful colonial villa in a central location set the scene. Kompong Chnang native, Monsieur Bun Try, the owner, spent much of his life in Paris and has combined traditional Khmer values with French panache and applied these qualities to presenting the best side of Khmer culinary tradition. The starters are the size of main courses. There are plenty of nice presentation touches such as artfully folded napkins and satisfyingly heavy cutlery. The staff is charming and attentive.

Pithnou St. opposite the northern end of the Alley. © **063/761-436.** www.angkorpalm.com. Main dish $3–$6. MC, V. Daily 10am–10pm.

The Soup Dragon ★ VIETNAMESE/KHMER   This is a longtime popular Pub Street cafe, now with three floors and excellent views of the Old Market area. Authentic Vietnamese staples such as pho (noodle soup), fresh spring rolls, and all manner of wok-fried dishes are the mainstays. There are two floors of open-air dining overlooking the center of town and they are always packed. There is also a large rooftop area. The place opens into a casual bar in the late evening and, whether to just escape the heat at noontime or to talk late into the night, Soup Dragon is a good place to enjoy cool drinks and good food.

#369, Group 6, Mondol 1 (north of the Central Market). ✆ **063/964-933.** Main courses $2.50–$8. No credit cards. Daily 6am–10pm.

DINING AT THE TEMPLES

Across the busy parking lot closest to Angkor Wat, you're sure to spot the snazzy **Angkor Café** (✆ **012/946-227**). This little gallery and souvenir shop serves—for a mint by Khmer standards—good coffee, tea, and sandwiches.

For a very affordable and hearty meal while touring the temples, try **Sunrise Angkor** (✆ **012/946-595**), one of many open-air eateries and the first one you'll see behind and to the left of Angkor Café. It has good breakfasts for very low prices.

In and among all the major temples, you'll see lots of small, bamboo-roofed eateries, and all will implore you to enter.

SNACKS & CAFES

For a good breakfast, real coffee, baked goods, and snacks, try **Blue Pumpkin** (#365, Mondol 1; ✆ **063/963-574**), a posh cafe north of the market that's also a great stop for sandwiches to go (perfect for a temple picnic).

Butterflies Garden Restaurant ★   Don't miss this netted enclosure with a butterfly farm and meticulous menagerie of local flora and fauna, including a pond filled with Japanese carp. There are detailed descriptions of all plants and some individual butterflies. The restaurant serves drinks and offers a small lunch menu.

Just across the Siem Reap River north of the Old Market. ✆ **063/761-211.** Entrance costs $2. No credit cards. Daily 8am–5pm.

What to See & Do

Angkor Wat is the Disneyland of Buddhist temples in Asia. The temple complex covers 97 sq. km (37 sq. miles) and requires at least a few busy days to thoroughly explore the major sites. Everyone has his or her favorite, but a few must-sees are highlighted below. Be sure to plan carefully and catch a sunrise or sunset from one of the more prime spots; it's a photographer's dream. *Note:* The temples are magnificent, and days spent clambering around are inherently interesting, but be careful not to come away from a visit to ancient Angkor with a memory of an oversize rock collection or jungle gym. There's much to learn about Buddhism, Hinduism, architecture, and Khmer history; it's useful to hire a well informed guide or join a tour group. There are also subtleties to temple touring, and a good guide is your best chance to beat the crowds and catch the intricacies, or be in the right place for the magic moments of the day. Contact your hotel front desk or one of the tour agencies listed at the beginning of this section.

THE TEMPLES

Entrance fees for Angkor Wat are as follows: A 1-day ticket is $20, a 3-day ticket is $40, and a 1-week ticket is $60. Tickets are good for all sites within the main temple compound, as well as Banteay Srei, to the north, and the outlying temples of the Roluos Group. The main temple area opens at 5am and closes at 6pm.

Angkor Wat ★★★   The symbol of Cambodia, the four spires of the main temple of Angkor are known the world over. In fact, this is the most resplendent of the Angkor sites, one certainly not to miss even on the most perfunctory of tours.

the magic hours AT ANGKOR WAT

The skies over Angkor always put on a show. With just a little planning, you can see the dawn or the day's afterglow framed in temple spires, glowing off the main *wat,* or reflected in one of the temple reservoirs. Photographers will swoon. Here are a few hints for catching the magic hours at the temples.

The sunrise and sunset views from the upper terraces of **Angkor Wat,** the main temple, are among the best, though it's a tough climb for some. At dusk, temple staff start clearing the main temple area just as the sun dips. Smile, avoid them, and try to stay for the afterglow.

For the classic photographers' view of the main temple, Angkor Wat, at sunset—with the image of the temple reflected in a pool—enter the first wall of the temple compound, walk halfway down the front gangway, and then take a right, down a set of stairs, and out into the field. The view from the water's edge, with warm light bouncing off the temple, is stunning.

It's a bit crowded, but the views from **Phnom Bakeng (Bakeng Hill),** just a short drive past the entrance to Angkor Wat, are amazing at both sunrise and sunset. It's a good little climb up the hill; those so inclined can go by elephant.

The open area on the eastern side of **Banteay Kdey** looks over one of Angkor's many reservoirs, this one full and a great reflective pool for the rising glow at sunrise.

For the best view of the temples, hands down, contact **Helicopters Cambodia Ltd.** ★ at ✆ **023/213-706.** For a hefty fee, you can see the sites from any angle you choose. Balloon rides are also available.

Built under the reign of Suryavarman II in the 12th century, this temple, along with Bayon and Baphuon, is the pinnacle of Khmer architecture. From base to tip of the highest tower, it's 213m (669 ft.) of awe-inspiring stone in the definitive, elaborate Khmer style.

The famous bas-reliefs encircling the temple on the first level depict the mythical "Churning of the Ocean of Milk," a legend in which Hindu deities stir vast oceans in order to extract the elixir of immortality. This churning produced the Apsaras, Hindu celestial dancers, which can be seen on many temples.

The most measured and studied of all the sites, Angkor Wat is the subject of much speculation: It's thought to represent Mount Meru, home of Hindu gods and a land of creation and destruction. Researchers measuring the site in *hat,* ancient Khmer units of measure, deduce that the symmetry of the building corresponds with the timeline of the Hindu ages—as a map or calendar of the universe, if you will. The approach from the main road crosses the *baray* (reservoir) and is an ascending progression of three levels to the inner sanctum. The T-shirt hawkers are relentless, and the tricky steps and temple height are a challenge to those with vertigo, but the short trip is inspiring and the views from the top are breathtaking. **Note:** There is a guide rope on the southern face (and often a long line up).

Angkor Thom ★★★   The temple name means "the great city" in Khmer and is famed for its fantastic 45m (148-ft.) central temple, Bayon. The vast area of Angkor Thom, over a mile on one side, is dotted with many temples and features; don't miss the elaborate reliefs of the **Terrace of the Leper King** and the **Terrace of Elephants.**

The **Bayon** is a Buddhist temple built under a later king, Jayavarman VII (1190), but the temple nevertheless adheres to Hindu cosmology and can be read as a metaphor for the natural world. It has four huge stone faces, with one facing out and keeping watch at each compass point. The curious smiling image, thought by many to be a depiction of Jayavarman himself, is often considered the enigmatic Mona Lisa of Southeast Asia. Bayon is also surrounded by two long walls with bas-relief scenes of legendary and historic events, probably painted and gilded originally. There are 51 smaller towers surrounding Bayon, each with four faces of its own.

Just north of the Bayon is the stalwart form of the **Baphuon,** a temple built in 1066 that is in the process of being put back together in a protractive effort that gives visitors an idea of what original temple construction might have been like.

Ta Prohm ★★★   The jungle foliage still has its hold on this dynamic temple. Ta Prohm was the only one that was left in such a ruinous state when early archaeologists freed the rest of the Angkor Wat temples from the jungle. Ta Prohm is a favorite for many; in fact, the ruinous roots appeal to most. As large around as some tree trunks, the roots of fig, banyan, and kapok trees cleave massive stones in two or give way and grow over the top of temple ramparts. It's quite dramatic, and there are a few popular photo spots where the collision of temple and vine are most impressive. Sadly, Ta Prohm was looted quite heavily in recent years, and many of its stone reliquaries have been lost.

ATTRACTIONS FARTHER AFIELD

Banteay Srei ★★   True temple buffs won't want to miss this distinct complex: The 10th-century buildings of Banteay Srei are done in a style unique to the high spires of Angkor. The site is a collection of low walls surrounding low-rise peaked structures of deep-red sandstone. Translated as the "Citadel of Women," it has well preserved relief carvings on the squat central buildings and intricate tellings of ancient Hindu tales. Go with a guide who can explain the finer details of temple inscriptions.

32km (20 miles) north of the main temples of Angkor Wat.

Kabal Spean 🎎   Known as the "River of a Thousand Linga" (a *linga* is a phallic symbol representing the Hindu god Shiva), Kabal Spean lay undiscovered by Westerners until a French researcher stumbled across it recently. Dating from the early 11th century, the relief carvings that line the streambeds are said to purify the water before it fills the reservoirs (called *barays*) of Angkor. It's the journey here that's really interesting, along rough roads through rural villages north of Banteay Srei, and there's also a fun 30-minute forest hike to the first waterfall. Khmer folks come to picnic, and it's a good spot to swim or follow the path that trips along the brook; from there, you can view the many carvings in relief on the banks and creek bed.

5km (3 miles) north of Banteay Srei. Admission $3.

Land Mines Museum   You won't find signs leading you to this seemingly impromptu museum; Cambodian officials prefer their own rhetoric to that of the owner and curator, Mr. Akira. The museum itself is just a corrugated-roof area stacked high with disarmed ordnance and detailed data on the country's UXO (unexploded ordnance). Most interesting is the small grove out back, an exhibit of how mines are placed in a real jungle setting. The museum is a call to action for demining in the country. Resist any temptation to volunteer (unless properly trained), but you can chat with Mr. Akira, peruse his recent book on the subject, and sign a petition (he's hoping to achieve NGO status). It's an interesting visit.

On the main road to the temples, just before the checkpoint and a few miles east. Free admission (voluntary contributions). Daily 7am–5pm. Go by motorbike or taxi.

Roluos Group These three temples are best viewed in the context of Angkor architecture's progression, as the forefathers of the more dynamic of Angkor's main temples. A visit to these temples is included in the main temple ticket, but will cost you a bit extra for transport.

13km (8 miles) east of the town center.

Shopping

The **Old Market,** in the center of Siem Reap, is the best place to find Buddhist trinkets, souvenirs such as T-shirts, and even good books on the temples. Just outside the market, you'll see a whole array of small storefront boutiques.

Large, mall-style souvenir venues line the road just north of town on the way to the temples. These are a good stop for the obligatory collector's spoon or plastic replica of the temples.

The **Lazy Mango Bookshop,** a block west of the Old Market (lazymangobooks@ yahoo.com), is where you can exchange that novel you've been dragging around for a new one.

Siem Reap After Dark

Siem Reap is a town where most visitors are up with the sun and out visiting the temple sites, but there are an increasing number of good evening options.

Having spent the day looking at the stone variety of Apsaras, why not spend an evening checking out the living ones? A number of places around town hold shows of **Apsara Dance.** At **Angkor Village** dancers in traditional gilded costume practice their slow, elegant art. This comes combined with a fine set Khmer menu in the traditional indoor banquet-house theater. To make reservations for the nightly show, call ✆ 063/963-561. Dinner begins at 7pm, and the show starts at 7:30pm (tickets cost $22). **The Raffles Grand Hotel D'Angkor** has a similar show in an open pavilion on the lawn at the front of the hotel ($32 including dinner). Times and performances vary so be sure to call ✆ 063/963-888 in advance. Most hotels have a performance space, and many small restaurants have shows of varying quality.

Dr. Beat (Beatocello) Richner plays the works of Bach and some of his own comic pieces between stories and vignettes about his work as director of the **Kantha Bopha Foundation,** a humanitarian hospital just north of the town center. Admission is free, but donations are accepted in support of their valiant efforts to serve a steady stream of destitute patients, mostly children, who suffer from treatable diseases such as tuberculosis. Dr. Richner is as passionate about his music as he is about his cause. You're in for an enjoyable, informative evening. Performances are every Saturday at 7:15pm just north of the town center on the road to the temples.

Pub Street is now beginning to resemble the party towns of Thailand, with throbbing music, boisterous backpackers, and touts. There are now quite a number of bars open into the small hours. **The Angkor What?** (Pub St., 1 block west of the Old Market; ✆ 012/490-755) was the first—and is still the most popular. **World Lounge** (✆ 012/865-332), in the same area, also rocks late and has a free pool table. **Dead Fish Tower** (✆ 063/963-060), on the main road heading toward the temples, is set up like the rigging of a tall ship, with precarious perches, funky nooks, and unique drinks. **Laundry** (✆ 016/962-026), on a side street to the north of the Old Market, is the funky side of Siem Reap and it's open nightly. **Linga** (North of Old Market; ✆ 012/246-912) is a gay bar that attracts a decent mixed crowd to their two-story corner location overlooking the small side street and the traffic on Mundul 1 Village St. The walls have psychedelic paintings of Buddhist monks. **Molly Malone's** (Bar St., across the street and west of Red Piano Bar; ✆ 063/965-576) often stages local expats playing live music, a mix of original songs and covers of crowd pleasers. **Temple Club** (Central Pub St.; ✆ 063/965-570) is many things to many people. During the day it is an open-air bar and restaurant. They have traditional Apsara dance performances between 7:30 and 9:30pm. Then, at around 10pm the sound system kicks in, blasting out techno-pop at maximum volume. If you want to boogie until 4am, you can do it here. They also have live sports on TV and three pool tables. At **Funky Munky** (Corner of Pub St. near the Old Market; ✆ 092/276-751) there are more than 50 cocktails to choose from, and during high season the place is packed. It is open from midday to the wee hours of the morning.

BATTAMBANG

Battambang is small and the center is easy to navigate by foot. If you want to venture further afield, motodups are plentiful until after 8pm, when you might consider hiring one for the duration of the evening to save the hassle of tracking one down on the dark and leafy outskirts.

Getting There

Daily ferries leave in each direction to and from **Siem Reap** at 7am. This is becoming a major tourist draw in Cambodia. The fare is $19 to $25 per person. The **bus** journey from **Siem Reap** takes about 3 hours. Bus companies running the route are **Neak Krorhorm, Mekong Express,** and **Rith Mony.** Tickets can be bought from the company offices for $4 to $5 just north of Psar Nath on Route #5. From **Phnom Penh,** several bus companies (including **Phnom Penh Sorya, GST, Neak Krorhorm, Mekong Express,** and **Capitol Tours**) run frequent daily services to Battambang. The first bus leaves at 6:30am and the last at 2:30 or 3pm. The journey takes 5 hours. In Battambang, buses depart from the various transportation company offices around town. From **Siem Reap** a **taxi** costs $40 to $50 and takes 3 to 4 hours. From **Phnom Penh** a **taxi** all to yourself costs $35 to $45. A seat in a shared taxi costs $7 per person and takes 4 hours.

Getting Around

As with most other towns in Cambodia, the main transport choice is the cheery motodup, renting a car with a driver, or a motorcycle. Your hotel can arrange either a car or a motorcycle. **Cars** cost around $20 per day and **motorcycles** rental from $5 to $8 per day. The **motodups** are everywhere during the day but seem to evaporate at night. If you are going any distance for the evening, it may be a good idea to hire a driver for the evening at about $5. A ride in town should range from $1 to $2. Many hotels rent out **bicycles** for $1.50 a day. There are now **tuk-tuks** in Battambang, and if there are a few of you, they are a sensible option.

ATMs There are a number of ATMs ringing Psar Nath. Each bank has one and this is where their offices are located. The best one to use is the **Canadia Bank** since they have the lowest charges.

Hospitals The **Polyclinique Visal Sokh** (Junction of St. 3 and NH#5 north of Psar Nath; ☎ **053/952-401**) is your first port of call if you need medical attention. They have a pharmacy and an ambulance, and some English is spoken. If it is anything serious, head to Thailand.

Internet Cyber cafes are plentiful on Street 1 and the adjoining roads. They cost about $1.50 an hour and speeds are variable. The **Bus Stop Guesthouse** on Street 2 has free Wi-Fi and it is very fast. The **Gecko Cafe** also has swift Wi-Fi.

Mail The main **Post Office** is situated near the river just where Street 1 forks after the museum just near the main junction between the Old Stone Bridge and the Old Iron Bridge. It is open Monday to Friday 6am to 5pm and Saturday 8am to noon.

Telephone Internet cafes are equipped for **long-distance calls.** There are also scores of shops selling mobile SIM cards and phones all over the center of town. A new SIM card costs as little as $2 and is your best option if you want to make local calls.

Tourist information The **Tourist Office** (St. 1; ☎ **053/730-217;** Mon–Fri 7–11am and 2–5pm) is situated in a French villa. The actual information they provide is a little thin, however.

Where to Stay & Dine

Development has been fast in Battambang and there are now a huge number of affordable and good quality hotels—maybe the best choice in all of Cambodia.

La Villa (185 Pom Romchek; ☎ **053/730-151**) is the best luxury option in Battambang—a beautiful colonial French villa on the east bank of the river. The **Teo Hotel** (St. 3; ☎ **053/952-288**) holds a special place in the hearts of those journalists, de-miners, and NGO workers who knew Battambang in more troubled times. This was largely because in those days it was the only place to stay. It still remains a good option. The **Seng Hout Hotel** (1008B St. 2; ☎ **092/530-293**) is a brand-new hotel and is one of the best options in town for both price and comfort. It is in an excellent situation just north of Psar Nath. The rooms are very big and very light. Best of all, they have factored in a number of very attractive outside sitting areas. The **Bus Stop** (149 St. 2; ☎ **053/730-544;** www.busstopcambodia.com) is an excellent guesthouse run by an Australian-Khmer couple with constructive contributions from their boisterous young son. The **Spring Park Hotel** (east bank of the river, Old NH#5; ☎ **012/849-999**) is a good option. It is immensely good value even by Battambang standards.

When it comes to dining, Battambang may not rival either Phnom Penh or Siem Reap for choice, but it certainly has a few quality restaurants that stand out. The **Bus Stop** (149 St. 2; ☎ **053/730-544;** www.busstopcambodia.com) is an Australian-style restaurant/pub that serves up huge portions of fantastic home cooking. The **Gecko Cafe** (St. 3; ☎ **092/719-985;** www.geckocafecambodia.com) is a wonderful old French colonial that makes the most of its location. Most of the Gecko Bar is located on a wraparound corner balcony. The food is light with a combination of pasta, burgers, and sandwiches. The **Riverside Balcony Bar** (St. 1; ☎ **053/730-313**) is an all-wooden Khmer house right on the river half a kilometer south of the

Teo Hotel. One of the best bars in Cambodia, its giant dark-wood veranda exudes relaxed grandeur. The food is not the main draw here, although the burgers are very good and there's a good selection of Tex-Mex offerings and pasta. It's the perfect place to enjoy a gin and tonic or glass of wine as the light fades, the crickets chirp, and the tropical night begins to fall. The **White Rose** (St. 2; ℂ **012/536-500**) is a no-nonsense Khmer restaurant with an encyclopedic menu embracing Chinese, Thai, and Vietnamese dishes as well as Cambodian. It is justifiably famous for its magnificent range of healthy fruit shakes—the best in Cambodia. Try the guava. It's superb, but then so are many of the others. **Pomme d'Amour** (63 St. 2, 5; ℂ **012/415-513**) is a relative newcomer to the Battambang scene and serves excellent French provincial food in quirky but tasteful surroundings.

What to See & Do

The atmospheric **colonnaded streets** and beautiful **French colonial villas** of Battambang are an attraction in themselves. It is a great city in which to stroll. The **bamboo train** is an improvised form of transportation that cuckoos the now-defunct railway tracks. It is made up of a small bamboo cart powered by a motorcycle engine that rides the railroad tracks picking up and dropping off passengers, cargo, animals, motorcycles, and pretty much anything else along the way. You can find these marvels of invention at various intersections around town. The motodups will know where they are. **Ek Phnom** (admission $2) is an atmospheric Angkorian pile that dates from the 11th century and was constructed as a **Hindu temple** under **Suryavarman I** and is really quite impressive. The temple consists of *prasats,* or towers, on a platform with some bas-relief carvings in very good condition. The river-road drive to Ek Phnom from Battambang passes through small villages and rice paddies, and it is an absolutely stunning little journey, a real slice of genuine rural Cambodia. **Phnom Banan** is a mountaintop temple dating from the 11th century that consists of five *prasats*. Its elevated location gives good views in all directions. The hilltop temple of **Phnom Sampeou Mountain** on the road to the old Khmer Rouge stronghold of Pailin affords fantastic views of the surrounding area. About halfway up the hill are the "killing caves." This was an execution ground during the years of Democratic Kampuchea. The Battambang **Provincial Museum** is on the riverfront in the center of town and houses a large collection of Angkorian and pre-Angkorian statues and carvings.

After Dark

Battambang is very quiet after 9pm. The **Bus Stop** stays open until midnight if there are customers, and it can get quite busy. The **Riverside Balcony Bar** is also a place that caters to a crowd if there is one. The main nightspot dancing venue is the **Sky Disco** (ℂ **012/862-777**; daily 8pm–1am) near the Khemara Hotel. This is a modern Thai-influenced affair with some pretty strange playlists. It can get busy on the weekend and is a good place (well, the only place) to expend energy and work up a dance-induced sweat.

SIHANOUKVILLE

Also called Kompong Som, Sihanoukville was first founded in the '50s as a deep-sea port. The main beach areas are where the action is, particularly around **Ochheuteal Beach.** This beach and the district behind it is now replete with any number of hotels, guesthouses, restaurants, and nightlife venues.

Getting There

The **bus station** is located in the northeast of the downtown area next to Psar Leu. It is essentially a large, dusty parking lot. You will be greeted by platoons of motos and tuk-tuks. A ride to Ochheuteal Beach costs between $1 and $2 by motorbike and $3 to $5 by tuk-tuk. Traveling from **Phnom Penh,** National Route #4 has long been one of Cambodia's best roads. It was constructed in the '60s and for a long time was virtually Cambodia's only decent road. **Sorya** and **GST** run services from Psar Thmei (Central Market) in Phnom Penh. The journey takes about 4 hours and costs $4.50. **Mekong Express** also runs two buses a day for $6, and if you are tall it might be worth considering since the seats on Sorya and GST buses are mostly suited to leprechauns and pygmies.

Getting Around

Sihanoukville is very spread out. There are plenty of **motos** and **tuk-tuks.** A moto from the beach to town or vice versa costs $1 in the daytime and $2 at night. A ride from Ochheuteal Beach to Victory Beach costs $3. A tuk-tuk costs double that. They do struggle up the hills, however. You can hire a small motorcycle from most guesthouses for $5 a day.

[FastFACTS] SIHANOUKVILLE

ATMs   There are ATMs all around Sihanoukville. They take all international cards. The best one to use is **Canadia Bank** since they have the lowest charges.

Hospitals   The **CT Clinic** (47 Boray Kamakor; ℰ **034/934-222;** open 24 hr.) should be your first port of call if in need.

Internet   There are **Internet cafes** scattered around all areas where there are tourists. The excellent **Beach Club Resort** has **Wi-Fi** in the restaurant by the pool.

Mail   The main **post office** (Ekareach St. at the intersection of Mittapheap and Kampuchea-Soviet St.) is open Monday to Friday 6am to 5pm and Saturday 8am to noon.

Where to Stay & Dine

Accommodation in Sihanoukville is of a very high standard at attractive rates. The best area to stay is around Ochheuteal Beach. The town itself is unpleasant. **The Independence Hotel** (St. 2 Thnou, Sagkat #3, Khan Mittapheap; ℰ **034/934-300**) is restored and has an excellent location on a private strip of sand on Independence Beach. The hotel used to be a showpiece of the Royal family and once played host to elite dignitaries. **Sokha Beach Resort** (St. 2 Thnou, Sangkat 4, Mittapheap District, Sihanoukville; ℰ **034/935-999;** www.sokhahotels.com) provides luxury and real seclusion, since the place has a beach all to itself. The **Reef Resort** (road from Golden Lion to Serendipity; ℰ **012/315-338;** www.reefresort.com.kh) is casual and laid-back. They also have a good selection of Mexican food. The **Beach Club Resort** (St. 23 Tola; ℰ **034/933-634;** www.beachclubcambodia.com) is light, bright, and thoughtfully conceived. The poolside, open-air restaurant is relaxed with excellent food and zipping Wi-Fi Internet.

Dining in Sihanoukville means good seafood, and there are lots of oceanside budget stops. They mainly serve the same seafood barbecue with barracuda, shrimp, and baked potato or rice for a standard $3. It is uniform but it is also delicious. **Sokha**

Beach Resort (see above) also has a fine seafood restaurant if you wish to go upmarket. Eateries of all sorts are spread around town and near all the beaches. **Mick and Craig's** (just adjacent to the Golden Lion Traffic circle at the head of the road leading to Serendipity Beach; ✆ 012/727-740) has a casual open-air setup with good tunes, a busy bar, and a billiards area. **Cantina Del Mar** (Otres Beach; ✆ 023/222-502; www.cantinacambodia.com) is sister to the riverfront Cantina in Phnom Penh and offers delicious fish tacos and tostadas in a rough-and-ready beachfront house on glorious Otres Beach. **Holy Cow** (Ekareach St. btw. Ochheuteal and town; ✆ 012/478-510) is situated in an old Khmer house on the busy road from Ochheuteal to town. It is a laid-back restaurant/cafe serving a mixture of European and Khmer dishes. **Les Feuilles** (23 Tola St. [south end]; ✆ 034/933-910) is set 2 blocks back from the southern end of Ochheuteal Beach and does excellent provincial French food. **Happa Restaurant and Wine Bar** (road to Serendipity; ✆ 034/934-380) serves teppanyaki-style cuisine—the Japanese art of cooking on the iron skillet.

What to See & Do

There are excellent **diving and snorkeling** opportunities around Sihanoukville and the surrounding islands. Reefs encrusted with coral are a feature of nearby islands, supporting an abundance of marine life including stingrays, moray eels, dolphins, and even the odd whale. First-rate dive sites can be found around the islands, such as **Koh Rung Samloem** and **Koh Kon,** all within a 2-hour boat journey. The very best sites are **at Koh Tang, Koh Prins,** and **Condor Reef** and are 4 to 6 hours away. **The Dive Shop** (road to Serendipity Beach near the Golden Lions; ✆ 012/161-5517; www.diveshopcambodia.com), **EcoSea Dive** (225 Ekareach near Ochheuteal Beach and the Golden Lions; ✆ 012/654-104; www.ecoseadive.com), and **Scuba Nation** (Mohachai Guesthouse on Serendipity Beach Rd.; ✆ 012/604-680; www.divecambodia.com) can provide equipment, tours, and training.

The **fishing** in the waters around Sihanoukville is excellent. It is best in the dry season when the weather is fair. If you want to take a day trip, you can get a tourist boat right off of the beach or arrange it through your guesthouse or a tour operator. Prices start at $6 to $10. The standard tour will take you to one to three islands for snorkeling, swimming, and lunch. **The Fisherman's Den Sports Bar** (downtown; ✆ 034/933-997) offers fishing and other kinds of boat trips on a 16m (54-ft.) Western-style fishing boat with shower, toilet, wet bar, and all necessary equipment.

Sihanouk National Park is more often called Ream National Park because that is the district in which it is located. It was established in 1993. It encompasses a large portion of the coastal area, including sandy beaches, mangrove forests, the **Prek Tuk Sap Estuary,** offshore coral reefs, and two islands (**Koh Thmei** and **Koh Seh**). It is also the habitat of elusive creatures such as **macaques, sun bears, dolphins, mouse deer, pangolin,** and more than a hundred species of birds, and some say that it is also home to a **tiger,** although there are no proven sightings. Guesthouses and tour operators in Sihanoukville offer a number of tours of the park, including **jungle trekking** and **riverboat trips** along the Prek Tuk River, through the jungle and mangroves, and on to the sea. The nearby **Kbal Chhay waterfalls** are spectacular and refreshing in wet season, although in dry season they virtually cease to exist. It is a good place for a picnic. Tours may be arranged through a tour operator directly through the Park at the **Park Office** (located 23km/14 miles north of Sihanouk Ville,

500m/1,640 ft. off Route 4 on Airport Road, opposite the entrance to the airport; ✆ 012/875-096 or 012/215-759). The Park office is open daily from 7am to 5pm.

After Dark

Sihanoukville is a late-night party town, although venues are spread out and the streets are dark. Be aware that in some places there is an underlying vibe of either serious drug abuse or prostitution or both, and Sihanoukville has long had a negative reputation in this regard. The sound systems along **Ochheuteal Beach** blast late into the night and often early into the morning, and there are often beachside parties. **Golden Lions Plaza,** a few blocks back from the beach, is home to a number of late-night drinking dens. **Utopia,** on the road to Serendipity, is a very late-night bar/ disco, with an unpleasant and druggy vibe. **Victory Hill** is now home to a slew of depressing and sleazy "hostess" bars and resembles the Thai sex-tourist capital of Pattaya. One of the most bizarre places to party in Sihanoukville is at **The Airport** on Victory Beach. This Russian-owned place is a disco hangar in which there is a real Antonov 24 prop plane.

KAMPOT

Kampot is a great place to spend a couple of days winding down. A neat grid of French colonial villas and houses lines the Kampong Bay River on the opposite bank, backed by low mountains and magnificent lingering sunsets. A strip of small cafes, restaurants, and guesthouses lines the **riverfront.**

Getting There

Sorya Transport leaves the station across from Central Market (Psar Thmei) in **Phnom Penh** and takes 4 to 5 hours. From Kampot, buses leave from the **central bus stand.** The first service is at 7:30am, the last one at noon. It is a long journey since the bus has to take the long way around via Kep, because of vehicle restrictions on bridges on the more direct routes. From or to Phnom Penh, a seat in a **shared taxi** costs $7 both ways.

Getting Around

Kampot is tiny and you can walk everywhere. If you wish to explore, you can rent a **motorcycle.** Many decide to stay in Kampot and do **Kep** as a **day trip** since Kampot is a friendlier place to overnight, unless you actually want the evening isolation that Kep offers. The countryside around Kampot is delightful and well worth a day's two-wheel pottering even though Bokor is off-limits. There are a couple of places near the main traffic circle that rent out bikes, including **Sean Ly Motor Rental Shop** (#27, D Soeng Ngoc Rd.; ✆ 012/944-687), just south of the central traffic circle, and **Cheang Try** (✆ 012/974-698) next door. Renting a small step-through, 100cc machine costs $5 a day. A 250cc dirt bike costs $11 to $12 a day.

Where to Stay & Dine

Blissful Guesthouse (a short walk east of the river, past the "2000" monument; ✆ 012/513-024; www.blissfulguesthouse.com) is an old colonial villa fashioned with heavy wooden beams. **Bokor Mountain Lodge** (Riverfront Dr. [riverside at the center of Kampot]; ✆ 033/932-314) is also an old colonial building overlooking the river. **Le Manguiers** (riverside on the eastern bank 1.6km/1 mile from town;

© 012/330-050; www.mangokampot.com) is legendary among expats in Cambodia. It is a superb rustic hideaway on the river's edge. Rustic villas set in gardens and rice fields are atmospheric and peaceful.

The Sri Lankan **Bamboo Light Café** (River Rd. near the bridge; *©* **012/681-530**) offers cheap and tiptop eats, curries being red or yellow, mild or fiery—prepared to your tastes. The **Bokor Mountain Lodge** (see above) offers high-end fine dining in Kampot. The **Rusty Keyhole** (River Rd.; *©* 012/679-607) is a popular Western-run cafe and restaurant, serving Western and Asian food at a very reasonable price. For good Khmer food, stop by the open-air **Restaurant Phnom Kam Chay Thmey** (*©* **012/602-505**), an affordable joint right next to the bridge. After dinner and a brief walk around town, you'll find that there are a number of little bars dotted around the place. They are easy to find since they are the only things with lights ablaze on the otherwise dark streets.

What to See & Do

Bokor Mountain is the main attraction in and around Kampot. Unfortunately, at the time of writing, it is largely closed to visitors as the road is being repaired. Bokor Hill Station was built by the French as a high-altitude compliment to the fashionable seaside resort of Kep across the bay. Both are now faded and crumbling in a very atmospheric fashion. The whole area around Kampot is dotted with limestone mountains rising steeply out of the deep green of the rice fields. Some of these contain caves with bizarre rock formations, and Buddhist shrines such as **Phnom Chhork, Phnom Sla Ta'aun,** and **Phnom Sasear.** If you cross the river and drive north for a couple of kilometers, you reach the scenic area of **Tek Chhou Falls.** They are not really spectacular since they don't fall very far, but it is a very pleasant area by the river to enjoy a sandwich and a cold beer. Twenty to 40 minutes by local boat from Kep is **Rabbit Island.** A place of white sandy beaches and coconut palms, it is a fairly idyllic day trip from either Kampot or Kep. Seafood here is great. Most likely, when you order crab on Rabbit Island, your restaurateur will wade out into the tepid ocean and haul your lunch directly from one of the crab pots. A boat for the return trip costs $20. Guesthouses also offer a package for $7.

KEP

Only a half-hour's scenic drive from Kampot is the place that was once considered the Cambodian Riviera. Now it is crumbling and pocked with bullet holes. Kep (and indeed much of Southern Cambodia) was a fierce battleground over the years of war, and the derelict feel still remains, although developers are moving in fast and things are changing. Kep is better done as a short relaxed day trip from Kampot. It is a pretty drive from one to the other in any case. Where Kep is a world-beater is when it comes to seafood. They fish some of the best crab in the world off Kep. And Kampot is world renowned as producing the best pepper on the globe. The killer recipe doesn't take much working out and **Kep crab in Kampot pepper** lives up to anyone's expectations.

Getting There & Getting Around

Kep is situated around a loop in the main road from Kampot to Vietnam. Approaching Kep from Kampot, you turn right off the main road (Rte. 33) at the roundabout with the "White Horse Monument" at its center. The diversion takes you first past the crab market, then on to the main beach. From Kampot take a **tuk-tuk,** a **moto,** or a **taxi.** Alternatively, hire your own motorcycle (p. 407) so that you have the freedom to stop where you like and explore.

There are no banks, ATMs, or medical services in Kep. They got mains electricity only in 2007 so the town is also a little behind when it comes to Internet. There is a Department of Tourism Office just near the central roundabout. It is in a fine building but is rarely open. Your hotel or guesthouse remains your main source of information if staying in Kep. In short, facilities in Kep are sparse.

Where to Stay & Dine

There has been something of an explosion in accommodation in Kep, no doubt in anticipation of development to come. While there are many places of a good or even excellent standard, unless it is real quiet and seclusion you seek, nearby Kampot remains a more practical option. **Knai Bang Chatt** (Phum Thmey Sangkat Prey, Thom Khan Kep; ✆ 012/879-486; www.knaibangchatt.com) is the best luxury option in Kep. The **Veranda Natural Resort** (opposite ASPECA orphanage and far up the hillside; ✆ 012/888-619; www.veranda-resort.com) is on a hilltop overlooking the bay. **Le Flamboyant** (Beach Rd. before the crab market turnoff; ✆ 012/230-357) offers unique bungalows, with outdoor showers and lounging beds on rooftop verandas. **Le Bout de Monde** (near the ASPECA orphanage and far up the hillside; ✆ 011/964-181; www.leboutdumondekep.com), meaning the "end of the world," lives up to its name in rustic Gallic style. Those on a budget might want to consider **The Botanica** (Beach Rd. before the Crab Market turnoff; ✆ 016/562-775; www.kep-botanica.com), which is made up of a pleasantly rustic series of bungalows.

All the hotels and guesthouses double up as restaurants, but the real Kep dining experience comes with the **fresh seafood served on the seafront.** Both the **crab market** and the **esplanade** in town in front of the beach are places to enjoy this wonderful aquatic bonanza.

SINGAPORE

by Jennifer Eveland

A fascinating mix of contrasts, Singapore lies at the crossroads of East and West, and as a result, it hums with a unique culture that is equal parts Oriental and Occidental. From the steel-and-glass skyscrapers that rise above Chinatown's historic narrow lanes to vibrant Little India's burst of sights, sounds, and smells, the old blends seamlessly with the new in Singapore. In 1 day, it is possible to trek through a rainforest, visit various places of worship from a multitude of religions that exist together in harmony, and stop in a sleek mall on Orchard Road to buy a new outfit in time for a sumptuous dinner prepared by a Michelin-starred chef. Singapore has always been, and will always be, a nation that blends the best of all worlds into one nation.

In its haste to modernize, Singapore often appears to have sold its Asian soul in exchange for a Western lifestyle. On the surface, the terrain is unremarkably globalized and consumer driven; its rows of shiny shopping malls flank wide, manicured avenues dotted with McDonald's and Starbucks. But for those who pause to take a closer look, Singapore's cultural heart is alive and well beneath the polished veneer. Singapore's Chinese are still driven by ancient values that respect the family, authority, and success merited by hard work. Its Malays share openly their warm ideals of generosity, hospitality, and joy among friends and family. And the city's Indians possess a culture steeped in thousands of years of traditional beauty and passion for life. Add to this the spirit of Arabs and Armenians, Bugis and British, various Europeans and Eurasians, and many more—a multitude of cultures that, combined, defines what it means to be Singaporean.

Singapore strives to honor its past while keeping one eye firmly focused on the future. Amid its efforts to grow the nation's economy and its people's standard of living are huge plans for tourism development. Already it hosts stellar world-class institutions, such as the Asian Civilisations Museum, the Singapore Arts Museum, and the award-winning Singapore Zoo and Night Safari. In 2010, two enormous casino complexes—the Marina Bay Sands, which dominates the downtown city skyline, and Resorts World Sentosa, on the city's family-fun island getaway—opened, changing the dynamic of the city.

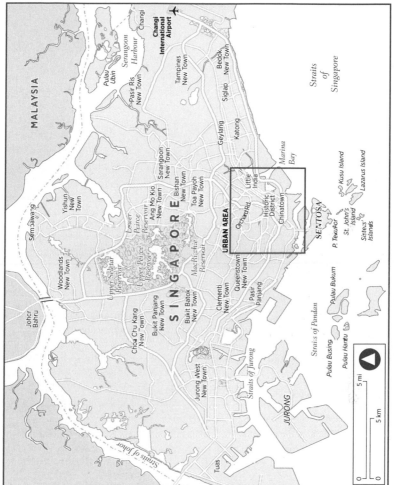

GETTING TO KNOW SINGAPORE

The Lay of the Land

On a world map, Singapore is nothing more than a speck nestled in the heart of Southeast Asia, at the tip of the Malaysian peninsula. In the north, it's linked to Malaysia by two causeways over the Straits of Johor, which are its only physical connection to any other body of land. The country is made up of 1 main island, Singapore, and around 60 smaller ones, some of which—like Sentosa, Pulau Ubin, Kusu, and St. John's Island—are popular retreats. The main island is shaped like a flat, horizontal diamond, measuring in at just over 42km (26 miles) from east to west and almost 23km (14 miles) north to south. With a total land area of only 693 sq. km (268 sq. miles), Singapore is shockingly tiny.

Singapore's geographical position, sitting approximately 137km (85 miles) north of the Equator, means that its climate features uniform temperatures, plentiful rainfall, and high humidity.

Singapore is a city-state, which basically means the city *is* the country. The urban center starts at the Singapore River at the southern point of the island. Within the urban center are neighborhoods that are handy for visitors to become familiar with: the Historic District, Chinatown, Orchard Road, Kampong Glam, and Little India.

THE CITY   The urban center of Singapore spans quite far from edge to edge, so walking from one end to the other—say, from Kampong Glam to Chinatown—will be too much for a relaxed walk. But within each neighborhood, the best way to explore is by foot, wandering along picturesque streets, in and out of shops and museums.

The main focal point of the city is the **Singapore River,** which is located at the southern point of the island. It was along the banks of this river that Sir Stamford Raffles landed and built his settlement for the East India Trading Company. In 1822, Raffles developed a Town Plan which allocated neighborhoods to each of the races who'd come to settle. The lines drawn then remain today, shaping the major ethnic enclaves held within the city limits.

On the south bank of the Singapore River, old go-downs, or warehouses, line the waterside. Behind these, offices and residences sprang up for the Chinese community of merchants and coolie laborers who worked the river- and sea-trade; this area is still known as **Chinatown** today.

Neighboring Chinatown is **Tanjong Pagar,** a small district where wealthy Chinese and Eurasians built plantations and manors. With the development of the steamship, Keppel Harbour was built here to receive the larger vessels, and the neighborhood developed into a commercial and residential area filled with workers who supported the industry.

In the early days, both Chinatown and Tanjong Pagar were a hive of activity. Row houses lined the streets with shops on the bottom floor and homes on the second and third floors. Chinese coolie laborers commonly lived 16 to a room, and the area flourished with gambling casinos, clubs, and opium dens where they could spend their spare time and money. Indians also thronged to the area to work on the docks, a small reminder that although races had their own areas, they were never exclusive communities.

As recently as the 1970s, the shops here housed Chinese craftsmen and artists. On the streets, hawkers peddled food and other merchandise. Calligraphers set up shop on sidewalks to write letters for a fee. Housewives would bustle, running their daily errands. Overhead, laundry hung from bamboo poles.

Today both of these districts are gentrified by comparison. New towns have siphoned residents off to the suburbs, and though the old shophouses have been preserved, they're now tenanted by law offices and architectural, public relations, and advertising firms.

The **north bank** of the river was originally reserved for colonial administrative buildings and is today commonly referred to as the **Historic District.** The center point was the Padang, the field on which the Europeans would play sports and hold outdoor ceremonies. Around the field, the Parliament Building, Supreme Court, City

Hall, and other municipal buildings sprang up in grand style. Government Hill, the present-day **Fort Canning Hill,** was home of the governors. The Esplanade along the waterfront was a center for European social activities and music gatherings. These days, the Historic District is still the center of most of the government's operations.

To the northwest of the Historic District, in the area along **Orchard** and **Tanglin** roads, a residential area was created for Europeans and Eurasians. Homes and plantations were eventually replaced by apartment buildings and shops, and in the early 1970s luxury hotels ushered tourism into the area in full force. In the 1980s, huge shopping malls were erected along the sides of Orchard Road, turning the Orchard-scape into the shopping hub it continues to be. The Tanglin area is where you'll find most of the foreign embassies in Singapore.

The natural landscape of **Little India** made it an ideal location for an Indian settlement. Indians were the original cattle hands and traders in Singapore, and this area's natural grasses and springs provided their cattle with food and water while bamboo groves supplied necessary lumber to build pens. Later, with the establishment of brick kilns, Indian construction laborers flocked to the area to find work. Today many elements of Indian culture persist, although Indians make up a small percentage of the current population. Shops, restaurants, and temples still serve the community, and on Sundays Little India is a wonderful mob scene, when all the workers have their day off and come to the streets here to socialize and relax.

Kampong Glam, neighboring Little India, was given to Sultan Hussein and his family as part of his agreement to turn Singapore over to Raffles. Here he built his *Istana* (palace) and the Sultan Mosque, and the area subsequently filled with Malay and Arab Muslims who imported a distinct Islamic flavor to the neighborhood. The area is still a focal point of Muslim society in Singapore, thanks to Sultan Mosque, and the Istana has become an exhibit celebrating Malay culture. **Arab Street** is a regular draw for both tourists and locals who come to find deals on fabrics and local and regional crafts.

SUBURBAN SINGAPORE   With rapid urbanization in the 20th century, plantations and farms turned into suburban residential areas, many with their own ethnic roots. In the immediate outskirts of the main urban area are older neighborhoods, such as **Katong, Geyland,** and **Holland Village,** which features prewar homes with charming architectural details. Beyond these are the newer suburbs, called **HDB New Towns.** The HDB, or Housing Development Board, is responsible for creating large towns, such as **Ang Mo Kio** and **Toa Payoh,** which are clusters of government-subsidized housing that have sprung up around the island, supported by their own shops, schools, and clinics, and many of them connect by the subway system.

Etiquette

While in Singapore, try to use only your right hand in social interaction. Why? Because in Indian and Muslim societies, the left hand is used only for bathroom chores. Not only should you eat with your right hand and give and receive all gifts with your right hand, but you should make all gestures, especially pointing (and especially in temples and mosques), with your right hand. By the way, you should also try to point with your knuckle rather than your finger, to be more polite.

In cosmopolitan Singapore, most people will shake hands in greeting, but it's good to remember that Muslim women are not allowed to touch men to whom they are not related by blood or marriage. Unless they initiate a handshake, a simple smile and nod is fine.

Also, it's common for Singaporeans to exchange business cards. Always receive cards with two hands, and always treat the card with respect. Don't stash it in your pocket without paying attention to it.

If you're touring during the day, shorts and a T-shirt are fine; however, if you plan to enter a temple or mosque, you will be required to cover your legs and upper arms. If you're dining in a restaurant or attending a business function, the dress code is "dress casual," meaning slacks and a pressed shirt for men, and a dress, slacks, or a skirt for women. For most business meetings for men, a suit and tie are still necessary, but you needn't wear your jacket anywhere. For women, business suits are also expected.

If you would like to offer a gift to a Singaporean, consult your hotel concierge for appropriate recommendations. For example, avoid giving sweets or foods to Muslim friends, unless you are certain the gift is *halal* (permitted within Islamic dietary practices). For the Chinese, it's trickier. Gifts should never be knives, clocks, handkerchiefs, or white flowers. (The sharp blades of knives symbolize the severing of a friendship; in Cantonese, the word for "clock" sounds the same as the word for "funeral"; handkerchiefs bring to mind tears and sadness; and white is the color of funeral mourning).

The main rules regarding table manners revolve around the use of chopsticks. Don't stick them upright in any dish, don't gesture with them, and don't suck on them. Dropped chopsticks are also considered bad luck. South Indian food can be eaten with your hands, but make sure you wash them first, and, again, always use your right hand.

Language

Singapore's four official languages are Malay, Chinese (Mandarin dialect), Tamil, and English. Malay is the national language, while English is the language for government operations, law, and major financial transactions. Most Singaporeans are at least bilingual, with many speaking one or more dialects of Chinese, plus English and some Malay.

THE BEST OF SINGAPORE IN 1 WEEK

If your time in Singapore is limited, I recommend that you bypass the museums and head straight for the streets, where you'll find a living museum of sorts, with local people, food, shops, and places of worship, plus a couple of interesting cultural displays. Stop first at a **Singapore Tourism Board (STB) Visitors' Centre** to pick up copies of their walking tour pamphlets, one for each of Singapore's ethnic neighborhoods.

Day 1–2: Settle into Singapore

After arriving in Singapore, take it easy while spending some time wandering through the city's streets. **Arab Street** is lined with shops that sell Malaysian and Indonesian batik cloth and home decor items, baskets, carved wood, objets d'art, and other gifts. Just off Arab Street, you can't miss the towering onion dome of **Sultan Mosque.** The most historic in Singapore, its grounds are open, so feel free to explore within its walls, including the ablutions area. The **Malay**

Heritage Centre is inside the restored palace of the original sultanate. The staff here is really nice and can also chat about the local Malay culture from their personal experiences.

Days 3–4: Chinatown ★

The streets surrounding the **Chinatown Heritage Center** are packed with souvenir shops with tons of curious finds, plus some beautiful art and antiques galleries. A Chinatown must is a stop at **Yue Hwa.** This Chinese emporium is practically a museum of Chinese handicrafts, filled with floor after floor of fabulous shopping. Excellent buys here include ready-made silk clothing, embroidered handbags, carved jade, and pottery.

Day 5: Little India ★★

Explore life at ground level with a stroll through Little India. The heart of Singapore's Indian community is **Serangoon Road.** This long strip is where the locals come to buy spices, flowers, Bollywood DVDs, saris, and all kinds of ceremonial items that make excellent gifts. This is one of the few authentic old neighborhoods in Singapore, un-"modernized" by the government. Midway down Serangoon Road you'll find **Sri Veerama Kaliamman,** the brightly colored temple humming with devotees all times of the day. Take off your shoes to explore the dioramas inside. Farther along Serangoon Road, **Mustafa Centre** is a frenzied Indian emporium. Explore the basement sari fabric department and groceries section with row after row of boxed curry mixes. Or check out Mustafa's three floors of elaborate gold jewelry.

Day 6: Natural Singapore ★★

Early risers beat the heat and get a nearly private tour of the **Singapore Botanic Gardens'** beautiful displays of tropical plants, shady trees, vivid blooms, and delicate bonsai. It opens at 5am! Visit the National Orchid Garden while you're there. Later in the day, take the rare opportunity to see the area's nocturnal wildlife. **Night Safari** is the one place where all Singaporeans bring their foreign visitors, and it's rare for someone to walk away unimpressed.

Day 7: Try to Leave

Say goodbye to Singapore, and prepare for your return flight home.

PLANNING YOUR TRIP TO SINGAPORE

Visitor Information

The long arm of the **Singapore Tourism Board (STB)** reaches many overseas audiences through its branch offices, which will gladly provide brochures and booklets to help you plan your trip, and through its detailed website, at **www.yoursingapore.com**.

After you arrive in Singapore, several visitor centers are staffed to assist, beginning with information desks at the Arrival Halls in Terminals 1, 2, and 3 at Changi Airport, open daily from 6am to 2am. Other visitor centers are located in the city as follows: at the junction of Orchard and Cairnhill roads (cater-cornered from the Meritus Mandarin Hotel), open daily from 9:30am to 10:30pm; in Little India at the

Urban Singapore Neighborhoods

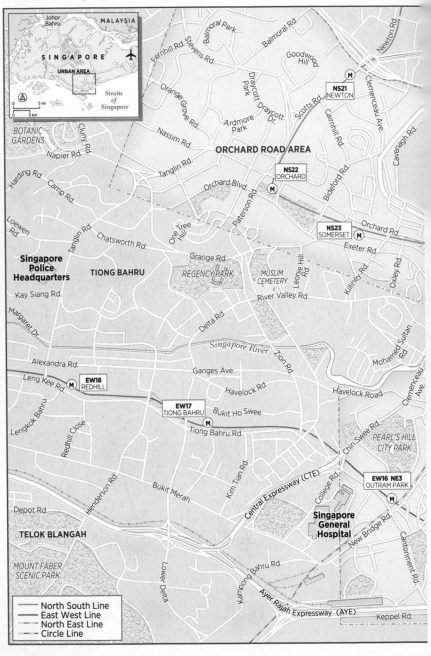

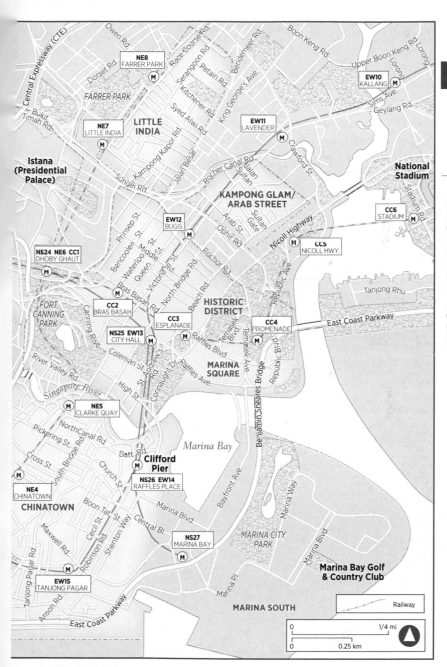

InnCrowd Backpackers' Hostel, at 73 Dunlop St., open daily from 10am to 10pm; and at Suntec Galleria, open from 10am to 6pm daily.

STB operates a 24/7 information hot line that is toll-free within Singapore at ✆ **1800/736-2000.** STB has up-to-date information, but if you need accurate information about travel timetables, I recommend you call airlines, ferry services, bus companies, or train stations directly.

Entry Requirements

To enter Singapore, you must have a passport valid for at least 6 months from your date of entry. To acquire a passport, contact one of the following Passport Offices:

- **Australia** Australian Passport Information Service (✆ **131-232,** or visit www.passports.gov.au).
- **Canada Passport Office,** Department of Foreign Affairs and International Trade, Ottawa, ON K1A 0G3 (✆ **800/567-6868;** www.ppt.gc.ca).
- **Ireland Passport Office,** Setanta Centre, Molesworth Street, Dublin 2 (✆ **01/671-1633;** www.foreignaffairs.gov.ie).
- **New Zealand Passports Office,** Department of Internal Affairs, 47 Boulcott St., Wellington, 6011 (✆ **0800/225-050** in New Zealand or 04/474-8100; www.passports.govt.nz).
- **United Kingdom** Visit your nearest passport office, major post office, or travel agency or contact the **Identity and Passport Service (IPS),** 89 Eccleston Sq., London, SW1V 1PN (✆ **0300/222-0000;** www.ips.gov.uk).
- **United States** To find your regional passport office, check the U.S. State Department website (http://travel.state.gov/passport) or call the **National Passport Information Center** (✆ **877/487-2778**) for automated information.

Customs Regulations

There's no restriction on the amount of currency you can bring into Singapore. For those over 18 years of age who have arrived from countries other than Malaysia and have spent more than 48 hours outside Singapore, allowable duty-free concessions are 1 liter of spirits; 1 liter of wine; and 1 liter of port, sherry, or beer, all of which must be intended for personal consumption only. There are no duty-free concessions on cigarettes or other tobacco items. If you exceed the duty-free limitations, you can bring your excess items in upon payment of goods and services tax (GST) and Customs duty.

PROHIBITED ITEMS It is important to note that Singapore has some very unique prohibitions on the import of certain items. While pretty much every country in the world, including Singapore, prohibits travelers from bringing items like plutonium, explosives, and firearms through Customs—the same goes with agricultural products such as live plants and animals, controlled substances, and poisons—Singapore adds to the list any type of printed or recorded pornography; pirated movies, music, or software; and toy or decorative guns, knives, or swords. A detailed rundown of prohibited items can be found on the Net at the Ministry of Home Affairs home page: **www.mha.gov.sg.**

Money

The local currency unit is the **Singapore dollar.** It's commonly referred to as the "Sing dollar," and retail prices are often marked as S$ (a designation we've used throughout this book). Notes are issued in denominations of S$2, S$5, S$10, S$50,

Singapore's Drug Policy

With all of the publicity surrounding the issue, Singapore's strict drug policy shouldn't need recapitulation, but here it is: Importing, selling, or using illegal narcotics is absolutely forbidden. Punishments are severe, up to and including the death penalty (automatic for morphine quantities exceeding 30 grams, heroin exceeding 15 grams, cocaine 30 grams, marijuana 500 grams, hashish 200 grams, opium 1.2 kilograms, or methamphetamines 250 grams). If you're carrying smaller sums (anything above: morphine 3 grams, heroin 2 grams, cocaine 3 grams, marijuana 15 grams, hashish 10 grams, opium 100 grams, or methamphetamines 25 grams), you'll still be considered to have intent to traffic and may face the death penalty if you can't prove otherwise. If you're crazy enough to try to bring these things into the country and you are caught, no measure of appeal to your home consulate will grant you any special attention.

S$100, S$500, and S$1,000. S$1 bills exist but are rare. Notes vary in size and color from denomination to denomination. Coins are issued in denominations of S1¢, S5¢, S10¢, S20¢, S50¢, and the fat, gold-colored S$1. Singapore has an interchangeability agreement with Brunei Darussalam, so don't be alarmed if you receive Brunei currency with your change, as it's legal tender. The exchange rate used throughout this chapter is **S$1.49 = $1**.

It's not an absolute necessity to buy Singapore dollars before your trip, because you can find ATMs that accept cards from the Cirrus and Plus networks at the Arrival Halls of all Changi Terminals as you exit the baggage claim area.

In town, it's best to exchange currency or traveler's checks at a local authorized money-changer, found in most shopping malls throughout the city. They'll give you the best rate. You'll lose money with the high rates at banks, hotels, and shops.

The easiest and best way to get cash away from home is from an ATM (automated teller machine). Check online for ATM locations in Singapore. It's a good idea to check your daily withdrawal limit before you depart. **Note:** Remember that banks impose a fee every time you use a card at another bank's ATM, and that fee can be higher for international transactions (up to US$5 or more) than for domestic ones (where they're rarely more than US$2). In addition, the bank from which you withdraw cash may charge its own fee. For international withdrawal fees, ask your bank.

Major credit cards are widely accepted at hotels, restaurants, and shops, and even at many attractions and in taxis. Beware of hidden credit card fees while traveling. Check with your credit or debit card issuer to see what fees, if any, will be charged for overseas transactions. Recent reform legislation in the U.S., for example, has curbed some exploitative lending practices. But many banks have responded by increasing fees in other areas, including fees for customers who use credit and debit cards while out of the country—even if those charges were made in U.S. dollars. Fees can amount to 3% or more of the purchase price. Check with your bank before departing to avoid any surprise charges on your statement.

When to Go

A steady supply of business travelers keep occupancy rates high year-round in Singapore. However, some hotels report that business travel gets sluggish during the months of July and August, when they target the leisure market more aggressively. This is probably your best time to negotiate a favorable rate. Peak season for travel falls between December and June, with "super-peak" beginning in mid-December and lasting through the Chinese Lunar New Year, which falls in January or February, depending on the moon's cycle. During this season, Asian travel routes are booked solid and hotels are maxed out. Favorable deals are rare because much of Asia takes annual leave at this time.

WEATHER   Because Singapore is 137km (85 miles) north of the Equator, you can pretty much guarantee that it's hot. In terms of seasonal variations, you've got some months that are not as warm as others, but for the most part, they're all still hot.

What does vary greatly is rainfall. Singapore lies between two monsoon winds. The Northeast Monsoon arrives at the beginning of November and stays until mid-March, when temperatures are slightly cooler (relatively speaking) than other times of the year. The heaviest rainfall occurs between November and January, with daily showers that sometimes last for long periods of time; at other times, it comes down in short, heavy gusts and goes quickly away. Wind speeds are rarely anything more than light. The Southwest Monsoon falls between June and September. Temperatures are much higher and, interestingly, it's during this time of year that Singapore gets the *least* rain (with the very least reported in July).

HOLIDAYS   There are 11 official public holidays: **New Year's Day** (Jan 1); **Chinese New Year** or **Lunar New Year** (2 days in Jan or Feb); **Good Friday** (Fri before Easter Sun); **Labor Day** (May 1), **Vesak Day** (May or June), **National Day** (Aug 9), **Hari Raya Puasa** (also called Eid al-Fitr, Aug), **Deepavali** (Oct or Nov), **Hari Raya Haji** (also called Eid al-Adha, Nov), and **Christmas Day** (Dec 25). On these days, expect government offices, banks, and some shops to be closed.

Health & Safety

Singapore's healthcare system is exemplary, with many tourists coming each year to seek medical treatment. All hospitals have international accreditation. By and large, Singapore no longer has problems with most of the tropical world's nastiest scourges. Food is clean virtually everywhere, tap water is potable, restaurants and food vendors are regulated by the government, and many other airborne, bug-borne, and bite-borne what-have-yous have been eradicated.

Singapore doesn't require that you have any vaccinations to enter the country but recommends immunization against diphtheria, tetanus, hepatitis A and B, and typhoid for anyone traveling to Southeast Asia in general. If you're particularly worried, follow their advice; if not, don't worry about it.

o **BUGS, BITES & OTHER WILDLIFE CONCERNS**   Although you have no risk of contracting malaria in Singapore (the country's been declared malaria-free for decades by the World Health Organization), there is a similar deadly virus, **dengue fever,** that's carried by mosquitoes and for which there is no immunization. A problem in the Tropics around the world, dengue fever is controlled in Singapore with an aggressive campaign to prevent the responsible mosquitoes from breeding. Still, cases of infection are reported each year, almost all of them occurring in suburban neighborhoods and rural areas. Symptoms of dengue fever include sudden fever and tiny red, spotty rashes on the body. If you suspect you've contracted dengue, seek medical attention immediately. If left untreated, this disease can cause internal hemorrhaging and even death. Your best protection is to wear insect repellent that contains DEET, especially if you're heading out to the zoo, the bird park, or any of the gardens or nature preserves, especially during the daytime. A newer threat, **chikunguniya,** also a mosquito-borne virus, has also posed a danger here in recent years, but incidents have been rare. Symptoms are similar to those of dengue fever.

o **DIETARY RED FLAGS**   The government rates restaurants, street vendors, and hawker centers on their standards of cleanliness and hygiene practices—look for decals on display in windows or at stalls. (A is for excellent.) Regardless, the use of chili and spices in local food can cause Delhi-belly. If you suffer a bout of **diarrhea,** it could be from many causes: weakness from jet lag, adjustments to the climate, new foods, spices, or an increase in physical activity. Always carry Imodium, or a comparable antidiarrheal, but most important, don't forget to drink plenty of water to avoid dehydration. If symptoms include painful cramps, fever, or rash, seek medical attention immediately; otherwise, it'll probably just clear up by itself. *Note:* People who are sensitive to MSG, be warned that it's used often in cooked food. If you need to ask about it, locally it's called Ajinomoto, after its Japanese manufacturer.

o **SUN EXPOSURE**   Singapore's climate guarantees heat and humidity year-round; you should remember to take precautions. Give yourself plenty of time to relax and regroup on arrival to adjust your body to the new climate (and to the new time, if there is a time difference for you). Also drink plenty of water. Avoid overexposure to the sun. The tropical sun will burn you like thin toast in no time at all. You may also feel more lethargic than usual. This is typical in the heat, so take things easy and you'll be fine. Be careful of the air-conditioning, though. It's nice and cooling, but if you're prone to catching a chill, or find yourself moving in and out of air-conditioned buildings a lot, you can wind up with a horrible summer cold.

o **VIRAL INFECTIONS**   Severe Acute Respiratory Syndrome, or **SARS,** hit Singapore hard in 2003, killing 33 people in Singapore and effectively closing the region to tourism. However, Singapore had mobilized the entire country to take daily precautions against the spread of the disease in an effort that was highly lauded by the World Health Organization (WHO), and today casual travelers face no threats of contracting this disease in Singapore. Cases of **Asian bird flu,** or Avian influenza, have been reported all over Asia Pacific, with countries culling more than 100 million poultry to contain outbreaks. Avian influenza is an acute viral infection affecting birds and poultry. Cross-infection to humans is rare; however, it does happen among people who have come in contact with sick or dead birds. To protect the country, Singapore keeps a close watch on its poultry farms and has developed safe channels for the import of all poultry products to make sure infected meats and eggs don't cross its borders.

GETTING THERE

BY PLANE   Singapore's award-winning **Changi International Airport** (© **65/6542-4422;** www.changiairport.com; airport code: SIN) is a major transportation hub for many of the world's largest passenger airlines, so flights from all corners of the globe are convenient.

Compared to other international airports, Changi is a dream come true, providing clean and very efficient facilities. Expect to find in-transit accommodations, restaurants, duty-free shops, money-changers, ATMs, car-rental desks, accommodations assistance, and tourist information all marked in English with clear signs. There is even a spa, pool, and butterfly garden. Three terminals are connected by a Skytrain system, so it is easy to get around the airport.

The best deals are offered through Asian carriers. Compare fares at Japan Airlines (www.jal.co.jp), Korean Air (www.koreanair.com), Cathay Pacific Airways (www.cathaypacific.com), Malaysia Airlines (www.malaysiaairlines.com), and Thai Airways International (www.thaiair.com). Otherwise, I've listed information for a few major airlines below.

Singapore's national carrier, **Singapore Airlines** (© **65/6223-8888** in Singapore; © **800/742-3333** in the U.S. and Canada, © **0844/800-2380** in the U.K., © **131011** in Australia, or © **0800/808-909** in New Zealand; www.singaporeair.com), is arguably one of the finest airlines in the world, with reliable service that is second to none. It's the most luxurious way to fly to Singapore, but sometimes the most expensive as well. It connects major cities in North America, Europe, Australia, and New Zealand to Singapore with daily flights.

GETTING INTO TOWN FROM THE AIRPORT Most visitors to Singapore will land at **Changi International Airport,** which is located toward the far eastern corner of the island. It takes around 30 minutes to reach the city by car from the airport. If you're driving, you'll traverse the wide Airport Boulevard to the Pan-Island Expressway (PIE) or the East Coast Parkway (ECP), past public housing estates and other residential neighborhoods in the eastern part of the island, over causeways, and into the city center.

A taxi trip to the city center will cost around S$22 to S$25, which is the metered fare plus an airport surcharge, usually S$3 to S$5, depending on the time of pickup. If you've got a lot of people and luggage, **CityCab** offers a six-seater maxicab to anywhere in the city for a flat rate of S$35. You can inquire at the taxi queue or call © **65/6535-3534.**

There's an **airport shuttle,** a coach that traverses between the airport and all major hotels. Booking counters at all three terminals are open 24 hours daily. When you book your trip into town, you can also make an advance reservation for your departure. Pay S$9 for adults or S$6 for children at Terminal 1, © **65/6543-1985;** Terminal 2, © **65/6546-1646;** or Terminal 3, © **65/6241-3818;** as well as the Budget Terminal, © **65/6546-7656.**

The city is easily accessible by public transportation. The **MRT,** Singapore's subway system (www.smrt.com.sg; see map, inside back cover), operates to the airport, linking you with the city and areas beyond. STB will tell you the trip takes 30 minutes, but really, give yourself at least an hour, because you'll need time to wait for the train to arrive, then you'll have to transfer trains at Tanah Merah station, and if you're arriving in Terminal 1, you'll need to hop on yet another train—a shuttle between terminals. After you get to your station in town, you'll still have to find your way, with your luggage, to your hotel. Personally, I think it's a pain in the neck, but hey, it costs only about S$2.70 to town. Trains operate roughly from 6am to midnight daily.

A couple of **buses** run from the airport into the city as well. SBS bus no. 36 is the best, with an express route to the Historic District and along Orchard Road. Pick up the bus in the basement of any terminal. The trip will take over an hour, and you'll need to get exact change before you board. A trip to town will be roughly S$2.

For arrival and departure information, you can call **Changi International Airport** at © **65/6542-4422.**

BY TRAIN While most visitors to Singapore will arrive by air, some will come via train from Malaysia. The **Keretapi Tanah Melayu** (KTM) operates a rail system that connects Singapore all the way up the Malay peninsula, with stops in Kuala Lumpur, Penang, and even connections to service in Thailand to Bangkok. Train passengers will stop for immigration at the checkpoint at Woodlands, just across the strait from Malaysia. In July 2011, the **Singapore Railway Station** on Keppel Road will be relocated to Woodlands, but at press time, no details were released. Woodlands is in the far north of the island, quite a way from the city center, so expect a taxi to be pricey.

For train information from Kuala Lumpur, call **KL Sentral** railway station at © 603/2267-1200. In Bangkok, call the **Hua Lamphong Railway Station** at © 622/223-7010.

BY BUS Buses from Malaysia will drop off passengers at any number of points around the city, depending on the bus operator—there is no proper inbound bus station. For bus service from major Malaysian cities, refer to bus listings in each section. Operators will be able to tell you where you will be dropped off.

GETTING AROUND

The many inexpensive mass transit options make getting around Singapore pretty easy. Of course, taxis always simplify the ground transportation dilemma. They're also very affordable and, by and large, drivers are helpful and honest, if not downright personable. The **Mass Rapid Transit (MRT) subway service** has lines that cover the main areas of the city and out to the farther parts of the island. Buses present more of a challenge because there are so many routes snaking all over the island, but they're a great way to see the country while getting where you want to go.

Of course, if you're just strolling around the urban limits, many of the sights within the various neighborhoods are within walking distance, but walking between the different neighborhoods can be a hike, especially in the heat. The STB Visitors' Centres carry a variety of free city maps and walking-tour maps of individual neighborhoods to help you find your way around.

Stored-value EZ-Link fare cards can be used on both the subway and buses, and can be purchased at TransitLink offices in MRT stations. These save you the bother of trying to dig up exact change for bus meters. The card does carry a S$5 initial cost and a S$3 deposit—for a S$15 initial investment, you'll get S$7 worth of travel credit.

A better deal is the **Singapore Tourist Pass,** a card that allows unlimited travel on MRT trains and public buses for 1, 2, or 3 days. The cost is S$8 per day, with a refundable S$10 deposit. Passes can be purchased at the following MRT stations: Changi Airport, Orchard, Chinatown, City Hall, Raffles Place, HarbourFront, and Bugis, and at the STB Visitors' Centres at Changi Airport and Orchard Road.

BY TAXI Taxis are by far the most convenient way to get around Singapore. Fares are cheap, cars are clean, and drivers speak English. Taxi stands can be found at every hotel, shopping mall, and public building; otherwise, you can flag one down from the side of the road. Most destinations in the main parts of the island can be reached fairly inexpensively, while trips to the outlying attractions can cost from S$10 to S$15 one-way. That said, I caution against becoming too dependent on them. During the morning and evening rush, you can wait a maddeningly long time in the line, and sometimes if you're at a destination outside the main city area, they're few and far between. If it's raining, you might as well stay put; you'll never get a cab.

If you do find yourself stranded, there are a few things you can do. If you're at an attraction or a restaurant, you can ask the cashier or help desk to call a taxi company and book a cab for you. If you're near a phone, you can make your own booking: Call **CityCab and Comfort** (© **65/6552-1111**), **TIBS** (© **65/6555-8888**), or **SMRT** (© **65/6555-8888**). During peak times, I have the best luck with SMRT. There's an extra charge for the booking, anywhere between S$2.50 and S$3.50.

Taxis charge the metered fare, which is from S$2.80 to S$3 for the first kilometer (⅔ mile) and S20¢ for each additional 300 to 400m (984–1,312 ft.) or 45 seconds of waiting. Extra fares are levied on top of the metered fare, depending on where you're going and when you go.

BY TROLLEY For sightseeing trips around town, your best bet is the **SIA Hop-on bus.** Plying between Suntec City, the Historic District, the Singapore River, Chinatown, Orchard Road and the Singapore Botanic Gardens, Little India, and Sentosa, the Hop-on comes every 30 minutes between the hours of 9am and 9pm daily. Unlimited rides for 1 day cost S$12 adults and S$6 children. If you flew Singapore Airlines to get here, you have to pay only S$6 adults and S$3 children if you flash your boarding pass. Buy your tickets from the bus driver when you board. For info, call **SH Tours,** © **65/6734-9923.**

BY MASS RAPID TRANSIT (MRT) The MRT is Singapore's subway system. It's cool, clean, safe, and reliable, providing service around the central parts of the city, extending into the suburbs around the island. There are stops along Orchard Road into the Historic District, to Chinatown and Little India—chances are, there will be a stop close to your hotel (see the map on the inside back cover for specifics).

Fares range from S70¢ to S$2, depending on which stations you travel between. System charts are prominently displayed in all MRT stations to help you find your appropriate fare, which you pay with an EZ-Link fare card. Single-fare cards can be purchased at vending machines inside MRT stations. See above for information on stored-fare cards for multiple trips. (*One caution:* A fare card cannot be used by two people for the same trip; each traveler must have his own.)

MRT operating hours vary between lines and stops, with the earliest train beginning service daily at 5:15am and the last train ending at 12:47am. For more information, call the **TransitLink Hot Line** at © **1800/225-5663** (daily 24 hr.).

BY BUS Singapore's bus system comprises an extensive web of routes that reach virtually everywhere on the island. Use an EZ-Link stored-value card to pay for your trips, and a TransitLink Guide to find your way around (see above for more details). All buses have a gray machine with a sensor pad located close to the driver. Tap your EZ-Link card when you board and alight, and the fare will be automatically deducted. It'll be anywhere between S80¢ and S$1.80. If you're paying cash, be sure to have exact change; place the coins in the red box by the driver and announce your fare to him. He'll issue a ticket, which will pop out of a slot on one of the TransitLink machines behind him. If you're not sure how much your fare should be, the driver can assist.

For more information, contact either of the two operating bus lines during standard business hours: **Singapore Bus Service** (**SBS;** © **800/287-2727**) or the **Trans-Island Bus Service** (**TIBS;** © **800/482-5433**).

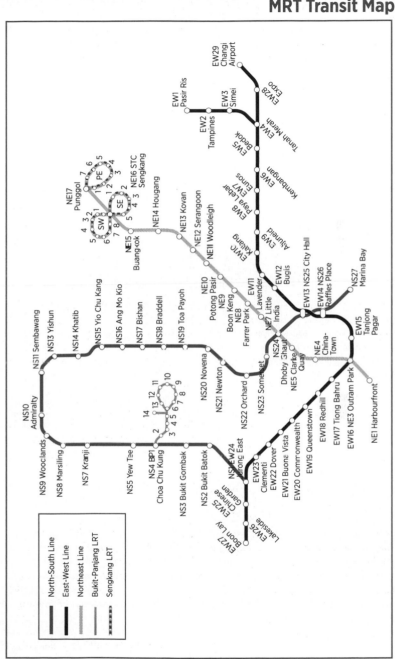

telephone dialing AT A GLANCE

- **To place a call from your home country to Singapore:** Dial 011 (the international access code), then 65 (Singapore's country code), and then the eight-digit number. The whole number you'd dial would be 011-65/XXXX-XXXX.

- **To place international calls** from Singapore: First dial 001 and then the country code (U.S. or Canada 1, U.K. 44, Ireland 353, Australia 61, New Zealand 64). Next, dial the area code and number. For example, if you wanted to call the British Embassy in Washington, D.C., you would dial ℂ 001-1-202/588-7800.

- **To place a call to Malaysia from Singapore:** It is not necessary to use IDD service, as there is a trunk cable between Singapore and peninsular Malaysia. To place a call, dial 02 to access the trunk cable, then the area code *with the* zero prefix, followed by the seven- or eight-digit local number. For example, to call the Malaysia Tourist Centre in Kuala Lumpur, dial ℂ 02-03-2164-3929. For calls to Malaysian Borneo, you must still use IDD.

- **For directory assistance** within Singapore, dial ℂ **100.** Dial ℂ **104** for assistance with numbers in other countries.

- **For operator assistance** in making a call, dial ℂ **104** if you're trying to make an international call and ℂ **100** if you want to call a number in Singapore.

- **For toll-free numbers,** be aware that numbers beginning with 1800 within Singapore are toll free, but calling a 1-800 number in the States from Singapore is not toll free. In fact, it costs the same as an overseas call.

BY RENTAL CAR Visitors to Singapore rarely rent cars for sightseeing, because it's just not convenient. Local transportation is excellent and affordable, you don't have to adjust to local driving rules and habits, and there's no need to worry about where to park. Still, if you must, contact **Avis** at ℂ **1800/737-1668**); they operate counters in all three Changi Airport terminals daily 7am to 11pm.

[FastFACTS] SINGAPORE

Area Codes Singapore's country code is 65. Tiny Singapore has no regional area codes.

Business Hours Shopping centers are open Monday through Saturday from 10am to 9pm and stay open until later on some public holidays. Banks are open from 9:30am to 4pm Monday through Friday and from 9am to 12:30pm on Saturday. Restaurants open at lunchtime from around 11am to 2:30pm, and for dinner they reopen at around 6pm and take the last order sometime around 10pm. Government offices are open from 9am to 5pm Monday through Friday and from 9am to 1pm on Saturday. Post offices conduct business from 8:30am to 5pm on weekdays and from 8:30am to 1pm on Saturday. Some keep extended hours until 8pm.

Drinking Laws The legal age for purchase and consumption of alcoholic beverages is 18; proof of age is rarely requested.

Electricity Standard electrical current is 220 volts AC (50 cycles). Local electrical outlets are made for plugs with three square prongs. Consult your concierge to see if your hotel has converters and plug adapters in-house for you to use. If you are using sensitive equipment, do not trust cheap voltage transformers. Nowadays, a lot of electrical equipment—including laptop computers—comes with built-in converters, so you can follow the manufacturer's directions for changing them over.

Embassies & Consulates Contacts for major embassies in Singapore are as follows: **Australian High Commission,** 25 Napier Rd. (☎ **65/6836-4100;** www.singapore. embassy.gov.au); **British High Commission,** 100 Tanglin Rd. (☎ **65/6424-4200;** http://ukinsingapore. fco.gov.uk); **Canadian High Commission,** One George St. #11–01 (☎ **65/6854-5900;** www.singapore. gc.ca); and **U.S. Embassy,** 27 Napier Rd. (☎ **65/6476-9100;** http://singapore. usembassy.gov).

Emergencies For **police,** dial ☎ **999.** For **medical** or **fire** emergencies, call ☎ **995.**

Hospitals If you require hospitalization, the centrally located **Mount Elizabeth Hospital** is near Orchard Road at 3 Mount Elizabeth (☎ **65/6737-2666**); for accidents and emergencies, call (☎ **65/6731-2218**). You can also try **Singapore General Hospital,** Outram Road (☎ **65/6222-3322**);

for accidents and emergencies, call (☎ **65/6321-4311**).

Insurance Before you travel, it's a good idea to check with your airline, credit card issuers, and any medical plan you have in your home country to find out what kind of coverage you have for things like flight delays, loss of luggage, theft, accident, or illness while traveling. Additional travel insurance can be purchased on an annual basis or per trip through your insurance company.

Internet & Wi-Fi Almost all major hotels in Singapore supply high-speed broadband Internet access in-room, usually at extra cost. Some newer and more expensive hotels will have Wi-Fi (wireless Internet connections) in room, while others will support Wi-Fi throughout certain public spaces.

Language Singapore's four official languages are Malay, Chinese (Mandarin dialect), Tamil, and English. Malay is the national language, while English is the language for government operations, law, and major financial transactions. Most Singaporeans are at least bilingual, with many speaking one or more dialects of Chinese, plus English and some Malay.

Mail Most hotels have mail services at the front counter. **Singapore Post** (www.singpost.com.sg) is very reliable and has centrally located offices that include #B2–62 ION

Orchard, 3 Orchard Turn (in Singapore, four-digit hotline ☎ **65/1605**); Chinatown Point, 133 New Bridge Rd. #02–41/42/43/44 (☎ **65/6538-7899**); Change Alley, 16 Collyer Quay #02–02 Hitachi Tower (☎ **65/6538-6899**); and Suntec City Mall #03–01/03, 3 Temasek Blvd. (☎ **65/6332-0289**). Plus, there are four branches at Changi International Airport.

The going rate for international airmail letters to North America, Europe, Australia, and New Zealand is S$1.10 for 20 grams, plus S35¢ for each additional 10 grams. Postcards and aerogrammes to all destinations are S50¢.

Newspapers & Magazines Local English newspapers available are the *International Herald Tribune, The Business Times, The Straits Times, Today,* and *USA Today International.* The *Asian Wall Street Journal* has limited distribution in Singapore. Most of the major hotels carry it, though, so ask around and you can find one. *I-S Magazine* is a good resource for nightlife happenings. The STB Visitors' Centres carry a few free publications for travelers, including *Where Singapore, This Week Singapore,* and *Singapore Business Visitor.* Major bookstores and magazine shops sell a wide variety of international magazines.

Packing In the tropics, it's best to wear loose-fitting clothes that are made of natural materials.

Expensive restaurants require "dress casual" wear, meaning collared shirts and long trousers for men and slacks and blouses, skirts, or dresses for women. I recommend packing a light jacket or sweater, as many shopping malls, theaters, and restaurants are air-conditioned and are sometimes cold. For shoes, slip-ons are the easiest when touring temples and mosques, which require you to take them off at the door. An umbrella is necessary year-round. For more helpful information on packing for your trip, download our convenient Travel Tools app for your mobile device. Go to www.frommers.com/go/mobile.

Police For emergencies, call ✆ **999.** If you need to call the police headquarters, dial ✆ **1800/255-0000.**

Smoking It's against the law to smoke in public buses, elevators, theaters, cinemas, shopping centers, government offices, and taxi queues. In addition, all restaurants, hawker centers, bars, and nightclubs are smoke free, with the exception of designated smoking areas. Establishments with outdoor seating can allocate 20% of this space for a smoking area. Nightclubs can have smoking rooms inside their premises, but this room cannot exceed 10% of the club's total floor space. It is not legal to bring any quantity of duty-free cigarettes into Singapore.

Taxes Many hotels and restaurants will advertise rates followed by "++." The first + is the goods and services tax (GST), which is levied at 7% of the purchase. The second + is a 10% gratuity charge. See information on the GST Tourist Refund Scheme later in this chapter, which lets you recover the GST for purchases over S$100 in value.

Telephones Hotels, with the exception of backpacker hostels, all have in-room telephones with International Direct Dialing (IDD) service. This is the most convenient way to make international calls, but is also the most expensive, as the hotel will always add its own surcharge to your telephone bill.

Public telephones can be found in booths on the street or back near the toilets in shopping malls, public buildings, or hotel lobbies. Local calls cost S10¢ for 3 minutes at coin- and card-operated phones. International calls can be made only from public phones designated specifically for this purpose. International public phones will accept either a stored-value phone card or a credit card. Phone cards for local and international calls can be purchased at Singapore Post branches, 7-Eleven convenience stores, or money-changers—make sure you specify local or international phone card

when you make your purchase.

Time Zone Singapore Standard Time is 8 hours ahead of Greenwich Mean Time (GMT). International time differences will change during daylight saving or summer time. Basic time differences are: New York –13, Los Angeles –16, Montreal –13, Vancouver –16, London –8, Brisbane +3, Darwin +1, Melbourne +2, Sydney +3, and Auckland +4. For the current time in Singapore, call ✆ **1711.**

Tipping While tipping is not exactly discouraged at hotels, at bars, and in taxis, it is not the norm here. A gratuity is automatically added into guest checks, but servers rarely see any of it. While tipping is not expected, I typically leave the small bills behind in restaurants and bars, I tell the cabby to "keep the change," and I always give bellhops at least S$2 per bag in all hotels. It is always appreciated.

Toilets Clean and safe public toilets can be found in all shopping malls, hotels, and public buildings. Smaller restaurants may not be up on their cleanliness, and beware of the "squatty potty," the Asian-style squat toilet, which you see in the more "local" places. Carry plenty of tissues with you, as they often run out. Very rarely will you still find a pay toilet around. If you do, it's usually S20¢ per entry, S30¢ if you'd like tissue.

WHERE TO STAY

Competition is fierce among hotels in the Garden City, driven by a steady stream of business and convention travelers, many of whom stay at international hotel chains. These companies invest millions in a never-ending cycle of renovations, constantly upgrading their super-royal-regal executive facilities, all in an attempt to lure suits and CEOs and—eventually, it is hoped—land lucrative corporate accounts.

Good-quality budget accommodations are not a high priority on the island. Between the business community's demand for luxury on the one hand and the inflated Singaporean real estate market, room prices tend to be high. What this means for leisure travelers is that you may end up paying for a business center you'll never use or a 24-hour stress-reliever masseuse you'll never call—and all this without the benefit of a corporate discount rate.

Making Hotel Reservations Online

The website www.asiarooms.com offers the best rates I've seen for Internet bookings, particularly for hotels in the very expensive and expensive categories; however, they don't have deals for every hotel property. It's worth it to browse and compare.

RATES, TAXES & SERVICE CHARGES All rates listed are in Singapore dollars. Most do not include what locals call "++" taxes and charges: the 10% service charge and 7% goods and services tax (GST). Some budget hotels will quote discount rates inclusive of all taxes, and Internet booking sites normally include taxes as well.

The Historic District

VERY EXPENSIVE

Raffles Hotel ★★ Walking into Raffles has a palpable sense of event. Liveried Sikh doormen usher you through the ornate wrought-iron portico into a lobby that seems faithfully unaltered from the hotel's 1930s heyday. If price is no object, then Raffles will deliver a blend of luxury, history, and colonial ambiance no other hotel can match. Only residents are allowed into the private inner lobby, or to stroll across the polished teak verandas overlooking tropical courtyards to suites decorated with a small elegant lounge, period furnishings, and a lovely four-poster bed. Although suites are on the small side, every detail is true to the hotel's heritage, making a stay here the ultimate in romance. Butlers provide customized service for each suite. There is a small landscaped rooftop pool and a spa that can arrange individualized treatments with the utmost discretion. Residents also have the benefit of eight exceptional dining choices in house. A stay at Raffles is an event in itself.

1 Beach Rd., Singapore 189673. © **800/232-1886** in the U.S. and Canada, or 65/6337-1886. Fax 65/6339-7650. www.raffleshotel.com. 103 suites. From S$740 suite. AE, DC, MC, V. Next to City Hall MRT. **Amenities:** 8 restaurants; 2 bars; free airport transfers; babysitting; concierge; health club w/ Jacuzzi, sauna, steam, and spa; outdoor pool; room service. *In room:* A/C, TV w/satellite programming and in-room VCR, hair dryer, high-speed Internet, minibar.

The Ritz-Carlton, Millenia Singapore ★★★ No one could accuse the Ritz-Carlton of looking like just another international hotel. A little less than 3 hectares (7 acres) of landscaped grounds give a sense of peace, despite its busy Marina Bay location. Inside the award-winning Kevin Roche's building, the lobby and public areas showcase extraordinary art: Hockney and Warhol brush shoulders with more than

Where to Stay in Urban Singapore

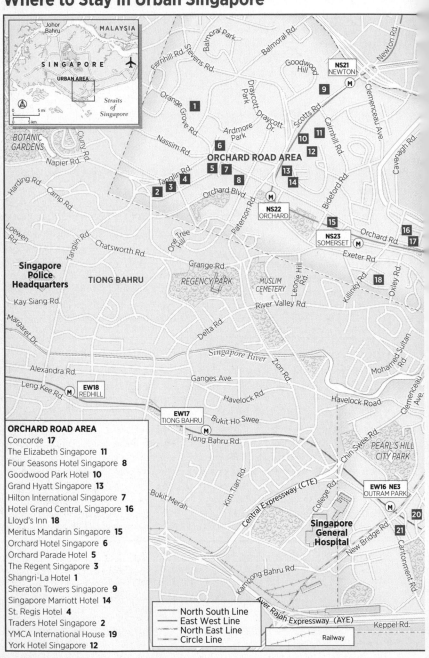

ORCHARD ROAD AREA

Concorde **17**
The Elizabeth Singapore **11**
Four Seasons Hotel Singapore **8**
Goodwood Park Hotel **10**
Grand Hyatt Singapore **13**
Hilton International Singapore **7**
Hotel Grand Central, Singapore **16**
Lloyd's Inn **18**
Meritus Mandarin Singapore **15**
Orchard Hotel Singapore **6**
Orchard Parade Hotel **5**
The Regent Singapore **3**
Shangri-La Hotel **1**
Sheraton Towers Singapore **9**
Singapore Marriott Hotel **14**
St. Regis Hotel **4**
Traders Hotel Singapore **2**
YMCA International House **19**
York Hotel Singapore **12**

North South Line
East West Line
North East Line
Circle Line

Railway

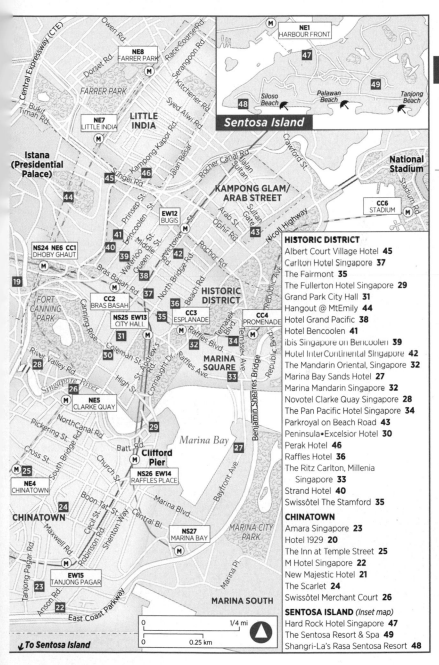

Sentosa Island

HISTORIC DISTRICT

Albert Court Village Hotel **45**
Carlton Hotel Singapore **37**
The Fairmont **35**
The Fullerton Hotel Singapore **29**
Grand Park City Hall **31**
Hangout @ MtEmily **44**
Hotel Grand Pacific **38**
Hotel Bencoolen **41**
ibis Singapore on Bencoolen **39**
Hotel InterContinental Singapore **42**
The Mandarin Oriental, Singapore **32**
Marina Bay Sands Hotel **27**
Marina Mandarin Singapore **32**
Novotel Clarke Quay Singapore **28**
The Pan Pacific Hotel Singapore **34**
Parkroyal on Beach Road **43**
Peninsula•Excelsior Hotel **30**
Perak Hotel **46**
Raffles Hotel **36**
The Ritz Carlton, Millenia
    Singapore **33**
Strand Hotel **40**
Swissôtel The Stamford **35**

CHINATOWN

Amara Singapore **23**
Hotel 1929 **20**
The Inn at Temple Street **25**
M Hotel Singapore **22**
New Majestic Hotel **21**
The Scarlet **24**
Swissôtel Merchant Court **26**

SENTOSA ISLAND *(Inset map)*
Hard Rock Hotel Singapore **47**
The Sentosa Resort & Spa **49**
Shangri-La's Rasa Sentosa Resort **48**

↓ **To Sentosa Island**

4,000 works by international artists. You can't miss Dale Chihuly's vivid glass tendrils, which exude from the walls of the lounge and restaurant areas on either side of the lobby. Guest rooms are quiet and larger than most in Singapore, and each has stunning views of either the Kallang or the Marina bays. Decor and furnishings are sumptuous and comfortable, from big wood-posted beds dressed in crisp white linens, to lounges, walk-in closets, and, for Club rooms, even Bulgari toiletries. Best of all are the huge octagonal picture windows placed next to the bathtub in every room, surely the most luxurious way possible to unwind after a long day's business or sightseeing.

7 Raffles Ave., Singapore 039799. ☏ **800/241-3333** in the U.S. and Canada, 800/241-33333 in Australia, 800/241-33333 in New Zealand, 800/234-000 in the U.K., or 65/6337-8888. Fax 65/6338-0001. www.ritzcarlton.com. 610 units. S$420 double; from S$470 suite. AE, DC, MC, V. 10-min. walk to City Hall MRT. **Amenities:** 3 restaurants; lobby lounge; airport transfers; babysitting; concierge; health club w/ sauna, steam, and massage; outdoor Jacuzzi; outdoor pool; room service; outdoor lighted tennis court. *In room:* A/C, TV w/satellite programming and in-house movies, hair dryer, high-speed Internet, minibar.

EXPENSIVE

The Fullerton Hotel Singapore ★★

The historic Fullerton, which rivals Raffles in luxury and architecture, is regularly voted one of Asia's top hotels. Superb views in almost every direction include the Singapore River and historic district, the city skyline, and the harbor. Built in 1928 as the General Post Office, its location, immense size, and classical Doric columns are testament to its vital role in the colonial government. The restoration and hotel conversion have been done beautifully, with lofty, elegant public spaces and guest rooms cleverly arranged to fit the original structure. Rooms are oases of comfort, stylish and contemporary with flatscreen TVs, PlayStations, large desks, and Philippe Starck fittings in the enormous bathrooms. Facilities are excellent, too, with a state-of-the-art gym and spa and an infinity pool that overlooks the river. Standards of service are second to none. A range of restaurants offer fine dining, sophisticated bars, and a great location for business and pleasure.

1 Fullerton Sq., Singapore 049178. ☏ **800/44-UTELL** (448-8355) in the U.S. and Canada, 800/221-176 in Australia, 800/933-123 in New Zealand, or 65/6733-8388. Fax 65/6735-8388. www.fullertonhotel. com. 400 units. S$388 double; S$1,180 suite. AE, DC, MC, V. 5-min. walk to Raffles Place MRT. **Amenities:** 3 restaurants; bar and lobby lounge; airport transfers; babysitting; concierge; health club w/ Jacuzzi, sauna, and steam; outdoor infinity pool w/view of the Singapore River; room service; spa w/ massage and beauty treatments. *In room:* A/C, TV w/satellite programming and in-house movies, hair dryer, high-speed Internet, minibar.

Hotel Grand Pacific ★

Formerly The Allson Hotel, this continues to be a strong tourist-class hotel in the city's historic district despite a big jump in price. Deluxe guest rooms have been completely redecorated with contemporary furnishings, including a few pieces from the old Allson, namely the attractive Ming-style end tables that remind guests that they're in Asia. Premium rooms are more European in flavor, with free Internet and soft drinks. Bathrooms are very small but clean, with combined tub/shower. The small pool area and even smaller gym have received some maintenance touch-ups. There are no views here, but all windows are built with double glass to block the sound from the busy street below.

101 Victoria St., Singapore 188018. ☏ **65/6336-0811.** Fax 65/6339-7019. www.hotelgrandpacific.com. sg. 450 units. S$320 double; from S$720 premium. AE, DC, MC, V. 5-min. walk from Bugis Junction MRT. **Amenities:** 3 restaurants; lounge; babysitting; concierge; health club w/Jacuzzi, sauna, steam, and massage; small outdoor pool; room service. *In room:* A/C, TV w/satellite programming and in-house movies, hair dryer, high-speed Internet, minibar.

The Mandarin Oriental Singapore ★★★   The Mandarin Oriental is the most elegant of the Marina Bay atrium-style hotels, with its subdued lobby of dark polished marble, rich fabrics, and stunning orchid arrangements. Even the central elevator lobby is surrounded by softly trickling pools. The king- and queen-size bedrooms have a sophisticated contemporary Asian look, with beautiful silk prints and upholstered wicker chairs. Oceanview rooms overlook the Singapore Flyer and the bay, though only suites have balconies. The newly refurbished city-facing rooms have attractive modern oak partitions and marble bathrooms. The Mandarin Oriental's restaurants and bars are excellent (though expensive), and its hushed, exotic spa is to die for. Service is superb.

5 Raffles Ave., Marina Sq., Singapore 039797. ⓒ **800/526-6566** in the U.S. and Canada, 800/123-693 in Australia, 800/2828-3838 in New Zealand or the U.K., or 65/6338-0066. Fax 65/6339-9537. www. mandarinoriental.com/singapore. 524 units. S$379 double; from S$879 suite. AE, DC, MC, V. 10-min. walk to City Hall MRT. **Amenities:** 4 restaurants; bar and lobby lounge; airport transfers; babysitting; concierge; health club; outdoor pool; room service; spa w/Jacuzzi, sauna, and steam. *In room:* A/C, TV w/satellite programming and in-house movies, hair dryer, high-speed Internet, minibar.

MODERATE

Carlton Hotel Singapore ★★   This Carlton property comprises three buildings, or wings. Leisure travelers will be most interested in the value-priced superior and deluxe rooms in the Main Wing. The Executive Wing is for exclusive club rooms, while the Premier Wing is for exclusive Carlton Premier guests. Rooms in all categories are about the same size. All public spaces have been upgraded, including the lobby entrance, alfresco coffee shop, and tiny wine and cigar room. The location, in the center of the historic district, is great. Ask for a room with a view of the city.

76 Bras Basah Rd., Singapore 189558. ⓒ **65/6338-8333.** Fax 65/6339-6866. www.carltonhotel.sg. 627 units. S$220 double; from S$320 suite. AE, DC, MC, V. 5-min. walk to City Hall MRT. **Amenities:** 2 restaurants; lobby lounge; airport transfers; babysitting; concierge; health club w/sauna, steam, and massage; outdoor pool; room service. *In room:* A/C, TV w/satellite programming and in-house movies, hair dryer, high-speed Internet access, minibar.

The Fairmont ★★★   Close to the sights of the historic district, Fairmont is directly above an MRT hub and next to the enormous Raffles City shopping center replete with restaurants, supermarkets, and swish stores. Rooms in the North Tower have an attractive and contemporary Asian flavor, while South Tower rooms have polished wooden floors, Bose sound systems, and Heavenly Beds with 10 layers of goose feathers. Ask for a harbor view in the South Tower to enjoy the best views of the financial district skyscrapers overlooking Marina Bay. The Willow Stream Spa has plunge pools, a huge range of Asian and European treatments, and a state-of-the-art fitness center that's open around the clock. Business facilities are outstanding, with a dedicated executive floor with its own lounge, complimentary use of meeting rooms, in-room espresso machines, and a private gym.

2 Stamford Rd., Singapore 178882. ⓒ **65/6339-7777.** Fax 65/6337-1554. www.fairmont.com/singapore. 769 units. S$290 double; from S$1,000 suite. AE, DC, MC, V. City Hall MRT. **Amenities:** 12 restaurants; martini bar, lobby lounge, and a live jazz venue; airport transfers; babysitting; concierge; outdoor pool; room service; spa w/gym, Jacuzzi, sauna, steam, and massage. *In room:* A/C, TV w/satellite programming and in-house movies, hair dryer, high-speed Internet access, minibar.

Grand Park City Hall ★   Formerly the Grand Plaza Parkroyal and the Parkroyal on Coleman Street, this property changed hands in 2007. Built on top of (and incorporating) 2 blocks of prewar shophouses, there are still hints of shophouse detail throughout the lobby. The hotel is located at the corner of Coleman and Hill streets, close to the Armenian Church, the Asian Civilisations Museum, and Fort Canning Park—plus there's a shuttle to Orchard Road. Guest rooms are of smaller size than average, have decent closet space, and sport sharp Italian contemporary furniture in natural tones, with homey touches like snuggly comforters on all the beds.

10 Coleman St., Singapore 179809. ℂ **65/6336-3456.** Fax 65/6339-9311. www.parkhotelgroup.com/gpch. 326 units. S$200 double; from S$550 suite. AE, DC, MC, V. 5-min. walk to City Hall MRT. **Amenities:** 3 restaurants; lobby lounge; airport transfers; babysitting; concierge; health club; outdoor pool w/view of Armenian Church across the street; room service; spa w/Jacuzzi, sauna, steam, and massage. *In room:* A/C, TV w/satellite programming, high-speed Internet, minibar.

Hotel InterContinental Singapore ★

InterContinental has brilliantly incorporated a block of prewar shophouses into its design. While the hotel remains unmistakably modern and efficient, it's been admirably successful in infusing signatures of the local Peranakan style, evident in the carved panels dotted around the hotel, and the use of ornate fabrics and porcelain in the vivid Peranakan palette. Deluxe rooms on the upper floors are large, pleasant, and well equipped, but in my view, it's worth paying extra to get one of the Shophouse rooms or suites in the original part of the building. Although they are slightly smaller, they have been beautifully and atmospherically renovated, with wooden floors, oriental rugs, and good reproduction antiques. The Club Lounge has recently been relocated to the second floor of the old building. For an additional charge, guests can enjoy complimentary breakfast, afternoon tea, and cocktails here.

80 Middle Rd., Singapore 188966 (near Bugis Junction). ℂ **800/327-0200** in the U.S. and Canada, 800/221-335 in Australia, 800/442-215 in New Zealand, 800/0289-387 in the U.K., or 65/6338-7600. Fax 65/6338-7366. www.intercontinental.com. 406 units. S$200 double; from S$480 suite. AE, DC, MC, V. Bugis MRT. **Amenities:** 3 restaurants; bar and lobby lounge; airport transfers; babysitting; concierge; health club w/Jacuzzi, sauna, and massage; outdoor pool; room service. *In room:* A/C, TV w/satellite programming and in-house movies, hair dryer, high-speed Internet, minibar.

Marina Mandarin Singapore ★★

The atrium of the Marina Mandarin is a colossal 21-story space, but it is peaceful and serene for its size and busy location due to the natural light that streams through skylights and bird song from caged Chinese nightingales. The rooms are spacious and attractive, with crisp white bed linen offset by dark-wood furniture, Asian fabrics, and frosted-glass walls around the well equipped bathrooms. Premier Suites are more Western in flavor, using light wood and gold and white fabrics. Venus rooms offer women travelers comforts and conveniences, including bath oils, custom pillows, and hair tongs. Each room has a balcony—ask for a harborview room. The Marina Mandarin has the Marina Square and Millennium Walk shopping malls on its doorstep. Though it's a fair walk from this area to the MRT (subway), it's possible to do most of the journey via air-conditioned malls, and taxis are plentiful here.

6 Raffles Blvd., Marina Sq., Singapore 039594. ℂ **65/6845-1000.** Fax 65/6845-1001. www.meritushotels.com.en 575 units. S$220 double; from S$510 suite. AE, DC, MC, V. 10-min. walk to City Hall MRT. **Amenities:** 3 restaurants; English pub and lobby lounge; airport transfers; babysitting; concierge; health club; outdoor pool; room service; spa w/Jacuzzi, sauna, steam, and massage; outdoor lighted tennis courts. *In room:* A/C, TV w/satellite programming and in-house movies, hair dryer; high-speed Internet, minibar.

The Pan Pacific Hotel Singapore ★★

Public spaces here are awash with color; the lobby has a checkerboard-inlay reception counter, vibrant carpeting, and a lobby lounge with walls of lights that change colors. Guest rooms are large, with wood paneling in geometric panels, Asian-inspired fabrics, and large oval desktops with

Herman Miller chairs. New entertainment centers allow you to hook up your laptop to the TV and iPod to the stereo. Hands down, Pan Pac has Singapore's best business center—a full floor designated for private offices, with full secretarial services, every piece of office equipment you'd need, plus meeting rooms and even snacks and cocktail lounges. The hotel's restaurants include top choices in Singapore, like the highly regarded Rang Mahal Indian restaurant and the Chinese restaurant Hai Tien Lo. The rooftop pool has a huge open sun deck and a spa and fitness center with pool view.

7 Raffles Blvd., Marina Sq., Singapore 039595 (near Suntec City). © **800/327-8585** in the U.S. and Canada, 800/525-900 in Australia, 800/969-496 in the U.K., or 65/6336-8111. Fax 65/6339-1861. www. singapore.panpacific.com. 784 units. S$240 double; from S$700 suite. AE, DC, MC, V. 10-min. walk to City Hall MRT. **Amenities:** 6 restaurants; lobby lounge; airport transfers; babysitting; concierge; health club w/Jacuzzi, sauna, steam, massage, and spa treatments; outdoor pool; room service; 2 outdoor lighted tennis courts. *In room:* A/C, TV w/satellite programming and in-house movies, hair dryer, high-speed Internet, minibar.

Parkroyal on Beach Road   Formerly known as The Plaza, the Parkroyal is just across from the color and great restaurants of Arab Street and Kampong Glam. It's 15 minutes' walk to the MRT (subway), so you'll need to take buses or taxis just about everywhere else—but the trade-off is that if you stick around, you can take advantage of the attractive recreation and relaxation facilities, which include a huge swimming pool and a lovely sun deck decorated in a lazy-days Balinese-style tropical motif, and a Bali-themed poolside cafe, cooled by ceiling fans. Two gyms to the side have plenty of space and new equipment, but the most exquisite facility of all is the exotic Bali-inspired spa. Other hotel facilities include outdoor and indoor Jacuzzis, a sauna, and a steam room.

7500A Beach Rd., Singapore 199591. © **65/6298-0011.** Fax 65/6296-3600. www.parkroyalhotels.com. 350 units. S$221 double; from S$500 suite. AE, DC, MC, V. 15-min. walk to Bugis MRT. **Amenities:** 2 restaurants; lounge; airport transfers; babysitting; concierge; health club; outdoor pool; room service; spa w/Jacuzzi, sauna, steam, and massage. *In room:* A/C, TV w/satellite programming and in-house movies, hair dryer, high-speed Internet, minibar.

Perak Hotel ★   This small hotel on the edge of Little India feels like a quaint bed-and-breakfast. Its location in a row of white and blue shophouses gives it charm, and there are nice decorative touches, with local fabrics and simple wooden furniture. As with most conversions, guests need to accept a few quirks as well: The atmospheric wooden floors can be noisy, and the guest rooms, though clean and tidy, are small, with tiny and basic bathrooms. Superior rooms are pleasant, with shuttered windows, but many standard rooms rely on skylights instead. It's popular with the friendly backpacking crowd who gather in the lobby and cafe to chat and make use of the free Internet.

12 Perak Rd., Singapore 208133. © **65/6299-7733.** Fax 65/6392-0919. www.peraklodge.com. 34 units. S$221 double; S$221 triple. Rates include breakfast. AE, DC, MC, V. 5-min. walk to Bugis or Little India MRT. **Amenities:** Cafe; high-speed Internet. *In room:* A/C, TV.

Swissôtel The Stamford ★   With more than a thousand rooms and 73 floors, this immense tower is the tallest hotel in Southeast Asia. The Stamford has completed a much-needed face-lift, and rooms now feel urban and vibrant with sleek designer furnishings. Each guest room has a small balcony with unbeatable views of the island, from the historic Padang beneath to the business district and the iconic Marina Bay Sands. If that's not enough, just head upstairs to the New Asia bar. At 226m (741 ft.), you can see almost the entire island and beyond. This hotel is in a great location, over the City Hall MRT and Raffles City Mall, and it also shares many of its facilities—including swimming pools and restaurants—with its sister hotel, the Fairmont.

2 Stamford Rd., Singapore 178882. ✆ **800/637-9477** in the U.S. and Canada, 800/121-043 in Australia, or 65/6338-8585. Fax 65/6338-2862. www.swissotel.com. 1,200 units. S$270 double; S$800 suite. AE, DC, MC, V. City Hall MRT. **Amenities:** 12 restaurants; martini bar, lobby lounge, and a live jazz venue; airport transfers; babysitting; concierge; outdoor pool; room service; spa w/gym, Jacuzzi, sauna, steam, and massage. *In room:* A/C, TV w/satellite programming and in-house movies, hair dryer, minibar.

INEXPENSIVE

Albert Court Village Hotel ★ 🌶

This eight-story boutique hotel has revitalized a block of charming prewar shophouses and given it Western-style comforts. Decorators placed local Peranakan touches everywhere, from the carved teak furnishings in traditional floral design to the antique china cups used for tea service in the rooms. As in most heritage hotels in Singapore, guest rooms aren't large, but details like the teak molding, bathroom tiles in bright Peranakan colors, and old-time brass electrical switches give this place real charm. Albert Court offers new courtyard rooms in the renovated houses that front the hotel's courtyard; these rooms contain all the local touches that make this hotel stand out from the rest. This hotel is just across the street from Little India.

180 Albert St., Singapore 189971. ✆ **65/6339-3939.** Fax 65/6339-3252. www.stayvillage.com. 210 units. S$190 double; from S$238 suite. AE, DC, MC, V. 5-min. walk to either Bugis or Little India MRT. **Amenities:** 3 restaurants; small lobby lounge; babysitting; room service. *In room:* A/C, TV w/satellite programming, hair dryer, high-speed Internet, minibar.

Hangout@Mt Emily

The coolest of the budget choices, this hotel is located in an artsy part of town. Room decor here is funky and functional, with bright colors and minimalist furnishings that brighten up tiny rooms and make them feel less cluttered. All private rooms have en suite bathrooms with small standing showers. There are no TVs in the rooms, but the hotel has a hangout room with TV, PCs, a pool table, vending machines, a kitchenette, and seating all around. The hotel restaurant, the elegant **Wild Rocket** (✆ **65/6339-9448**), serves excellent moderately priced Asian fusion cuisine.

10A Upper Wilkie Rd., Singapore 228119. ✆ **65/6438-5588.** Fax 65/6339-6008. www.hangouthotels. com. S$141 double; S$235 room with 5 single beds. Breakfast included. MC, V. 10-min walk to Dhoby Ghaut MRT. **Amenities:** Restaurant; Internet cafe. *In room:* Wi-Fi (free).

Hotel Bencoolen

Bencoolen is the signature backpacker hotel on a block that's best known for budget accommodations. A tiny lobby has a reception desk, a bellhop, and one computer for Internet access. Upstairs, the rooms are equally small, with barely room to move around a queen-size bed, only a narrow closet for clothes, and a tiny TV hanging from the ceiling. King-size rooms have space for a small desk, while family rooms have one queen and one slightly oversize single bed squeezed in. Decor is stark. Small bathrooms are newly tiled as well but are already beginning to show some age. Don't expect views or creature comforts—the Bencoolen is a good, clean place to sleep before hitting the city again. The hotel has a rooftop restaurant.

47 Bencoolen St., Singapore 189626. ✆ **65/6336-0822.** Fax 65/6336-2250. www.hotelbencoolen.com. 74 units. S$198; S$298 family. MC, V. 10-min. walk to City Hall or Dhoby Ghaut MRT. **Amenities:** Restaurant; bar; concierge; sauna; smoke-free rooms. *In room:* A/C, TV, hair dryer, Wi-Fi.

ibis Singapore on Bencoolen

This new hotel is okay value for leisure travelers. Affordable rooms are small and sparsely decorated, with minimalist built-in furnishings, wood floors, bay windows, flatscreen TVs, and complimentary Wi-Fi in every room. Spotless bathrooms have glass-enclosed standing showers and small vanities with not much room for your things. The location is good, however, along Bencoolen's popular stretch of budget hotels, all within walking distance of many major attractions and the Dhoby Ghaut MRT interchange. It gets the job done.

170 Bencoolen St., Singapore 189657. ✆ **65/6339-3584.** Fax 6884-9962. www.ibishotel.com. 538 rooms. S$188 double. AE, DC, MC, V. 10-min walk to Dhoby Ghaut or City Hall MRT. **Amenities:** Restaurant; bar. *In room:* A/C, TV w/satellite programming, hair dryer, Wi-Fi (free).

Novotel Clarke Quay Singapore ★

This hotel towers over the Singapore River just next to Clarke Quay (a popular spot for nightlife, dining, and shopping) and is a stroll away from the Historic District. Guest rooms are a good size, some with space for four single beds. All have small balconies with good views of the river, the financial district, Fort Canning Park, or Chinatown, and even standard rooms have large bathrooms like those you typically see in more deluxe accommodations. Decor is Western contemporary in shades of brown, green, and tan, with small desks next to floor-to-ceiling picture windows. The main lobby is an elevator ride up from the ground level. A recently renovated adjacent shopping mall has groceries in the basement and a few handy shops.

177A River Valley Rd., Singapore 179031 ✆ **800/515-5679** in the U.S. and Canada, or 65/6338-3333. Fax 65/6339-2854. www.novotel.com. 398 units. S$198 double; from S$398 suite. AE, DC, MC, V. 5-min. walk to Clarke Quay MRT. **Amenities:** Restaurant; lobby lounge; airport transfers; babysitting; concierge; health club; Jacuzzi; outdoor pool; room service. *In room:* A/C, TV w/satellite programming, hair dryer high-speed Internet, minibar.

Peninsula • Excelsior Hotel ★★ ✦

As its rather uninspiring name suggests, this huge hotel was created when two of the city's busiest tourist-class hotels merged, combining their lobby and pools and other facilities into one giant value-for-money property popular with tour groups. The location really is excellent, in the Historic District within walking distance to Chinatown and Boat Quay, with some fantastic views over the city, the Singapore River, and the marina. A long-overdue renovation has been completed, bringing rooms up-to-date, some with huge wood headboards and lounges built into cozy bay windows, but most with very plain, but tidy, standard furnishings. My one problem with this hotel is the pool, which is small and separated only by glass from the hotel lobby, which makes for a very self-conscious swim. This remains a very popular hotel for large tour groups.

5 Coleman St., Singapore 179805. ✆ **65/6337-2200.** Fax 65/6336-3847. www.ytchotels.com.sg. 600 units. S$200 double; from S$350 suites. AE, DC, MC, V. 5-min. walk to City Hall MRT. **Amenities:** Restaurant; bar and lobby lounge; babysitting; concierge; health club w/Jacuzzi; 2 outdoor pools; room service. *In room:* A/C, TV w/satellite programming, hair dryer, high-speed Internet, minibar.

Strand Hotel ★

The Strand is definitely one of the better backpacker places in Singapore. The lobby doesn't look or feel like a budget hotel, with marble floors, a smart bellhop, and a long reception desk. There's also an inviting cafe to one side, plus a small gift shop. Guest rooms are the largest I've seen in a budget hotel in Singapore—in fact, they are larger than a lot of more expensive rooms as well. Rooms are simply furnished, but decoration is exuberant (the rooms with purple walls and leopard-skin headboards may not be to everyone's taste). Unless you're a bona fide exhibitionist, don't go for the "special room," with the bathtub/shower separated from the main room by only a thin glass wall. Anybody for a free show?

25 Bencoolen St., Singapore 189619. ✆ **65/6338-1866.** Fax 65/6338-1330. 130 units. S$160 double; S$200 3-person sharing. AE, DC, MC, V. 10-min. walk to City Hall or Dhoby Ghaut MRT. **Amenities:** Restaurant; room service. *In room:* A/C, TV.

Chinatown

MODERATE

Amara Singapore   Amara, located in the Shenton Way financial district, attracts primarily business travelers, so if your vacation includes a little business too, this hotel puts you closer to the action. If you're simply in town for a vacation, Amara doesn't offer the best location or environment, but the focus on business travelers means there are some better value weekend rates available, as well as a two-room suite that's useful for families. The top eight floors of this hotel are reserved for the corporate set; they have not only better views, but also modern decor and services attractive to business visitors. Tropical 6 rooms aimed at the leisure traveler are spacious and closer to the pleasant pool area, but offer little in terms of views.

165 Tanjong Pagar Rd., Singapore 088539. © **65/6879-2555.** Fax 65/6224-3910. www.amarahotels. com. 338 units. S$230 double; from S$480 suite. AE, DC, MC, V. 5-min. walk to Tanjong Pagar MRT. **Amenities:** 2 restaurants; lounge; airport transfers; babysitting; concierge; health club w/Jacuzzi, jogging track, sauna, steam, and massage; outdoor pool; room service; outdoor lighted tennis courts. *In room:* A/C, TV w/satellite programming and in-house movies, hair dryer, high-speed Internet, minibar.

The Inn at Temple Street ★★   They've done a lovely job with this modest boutique hotel. In the heart of Chinatown's tourism hustle and bustle, step into the small lobby to be greeted by pretty antiques and Chinese porcelain. To the side of the lobby, a popular cafe serves Western and local meals three times a day. The friendly front desk handles everything from business center services to arranging laundry, tours, and postal services, but never seems frazzled. Naturally, there's no elevator and rooms can fairly be described as tiny, but they are quite modern for this type of hotel, with keycard locks, in-room safe, tea and coffee, minibar, TV, and room service. Decor is atmospheric, too, with carved wooden bedsteads and pretty fabrics. I like the black-and-white-tiled bathrooms, though you'll need to opt for a deluxe room if you want a bathtub rather than a shower. Attractive, affordable, and friendly.

36 Temple St., Singapore 058581. © **65/6221-5333.** Fax 65/6225-5391. www.theinn.com.sg. 42 units. S$208 double; S$248 family. AE, DC, MC, V. 5-min. walk to Chinatown MRT. **Amenities:** Restaurant; lounge; room service; smoke-free rooms. *In room:* A/C, TV, hair dryer, minibar, Wi-Fi.

M Hotel Singapore ★★   If work brings you to the Shenton Way downtown business district, then M Hotel is your best bet. Cornering the international business travel market, everything here is designed to make life easier for those with places to go and people to see. Rooms feature large, comfortable workspaces in clutter-free tones (blond wood furnishings, bone upholstery, tan carpeting), with some splashes of darker textiles for variety. Broadband Internet access and laptop safes make for extra convenience. The 11th floor is reserved for unwinding, with pool, spa, and fitness center all in sanitary contemporary white with glass-and-chrome accents everywhere. Good weekend deals are available, but leisure travelers won't find much to inspire in the financial district evenings or weekends. Operated by local firm Haatch, the spa has an excellent menu and reputation for quality. M Hotel's restaurants are packed for power lunches, so book in advance.

81 Anson Rd., Singapore 079908. © **866/866-8086** in the U.S. and Canada, 800/147-803 in Australia, 800/782-542 in New Zealand, 800/8686-8086 in the U.K., or 65/6224-1133. Fax 65/6222-0749. www. millenniumhotels.com. 413 units. S$270 double; S$600 suite. AE, DC, MC, V. 10-min. walk to Tanjong Pagar MRT. **Amenities:** 3 restaurants; bar; babysitting; health club w/rock-climbing wall; outdoor pool w/2 Jacuzzis; room service; spa. *In room:* A/C, TV w/satellite programming, hair dryer, high-speed Internet, minibar.

New Majestic Hotel ★★   The Art Deco New Majestic Hotel is achingly stylish, with a shining white lobby dotted with a collection of classic chairs that represent the best of 20th-century design. The guest rooms are large, each designed by a Singaporean artist with an unlimited budget. The popular Wayang room, named after traditional Chinese opera, is scarlet and black, with walls entirely covered in fine red silk. Fashion designer Daniel Boey's Pussy Parlour is a confection of fuchsia and electric blue, with silk crepe sheets and a Champagne bar in red lacquer. There are also more understated and practical rooms, though they're no less creative. High-quality amenities include Kiehl's toiletries, Bose systems, espresso machines, and iPod docking stations. The New Majestic proudly boasts "Singapore's smallest pool." The only pool permitted in a conservation building, this compact rectangle of mosaic tiling is placed above the restaurant and features glass portholes in its floor.

31-37 Bukit Pasoh Rd., Singapore 089845. ℭ **65/6511-4700.** Fax 65/6227-3301. www.newmajestic hotel.com. 30 units. S$250 double; from S$550 suite. AE, MC, V. 1-min. walk to Outram Park MRT. **Amenities:** Restaurant; concierge; health club; outdoor pool. *In room:* A/C, TV w/satellite programming, hair dryer, minibar.

Swissôtel Merchant Court ★   Merchant Court is beautifully located in the city center, within easy walking distance of Chinatown and the historic and financial districts. Colorful Clarke Quay opposite offers a superb range of restaurants, cafes, and nightlife, and Robertson and Boat Quays are a short, pleasant stroll along the river. A mall and the MRT are right on the doorstep. All that convenience means it's a busy, buzzing part of town, particularly at night, but the large attractive pool and terrace area gives some room to relax and the Willow Stream Spa is excellent. Standard (Classic) rooms are simple and pleasant—not large, but with good-sized bathrooms. Renovated business rooms are larger and more stylish, with striking geometric carpets and wall panels, and there's an Executive Lounge on the top floor. Although the hotel is largely geared toward business travelers, if you give advance notice, staff can create a special Kids Room, accessorized with bright rugs, age-appropriate toys, and DVDs.

20 Merchant Rd., Singapore 058281. ℭ **800/637-9477** in the U.S. and Canada, 800/121-043 in Australia, 800/637-94771 in the U.K., or 65/6337-2288. Fax 65/6334-0606. www.swissotel-merchantcourt. com. 476 units. S$260 double; from S$680 suite. AE, DC, MC, V. Clarke Quay MRT. **Amenities:** Restaurant; bar; babysitting; health club and spa w/Jacuzzi, sauna, steam, massage, and beauty treatments; outdoor pool; room service. *In room:* A/C, TV w/satellite programming and in-house movies, hair dryer, high-speed Internet.

INEXPENSIVE

Hotel 1929 ★ 👔   This trendy, inexpensive little place is a real gem in Chinatown, operated by the same people behind the swish New Majestic. Though its target market is very different, there are some clues to the shared parentage in its love of vintage chairs and retro design. The hotel's shophouse location means that rooms are small and quirkily shaped—many of the toilets are extremely close to the shower, but clever design and an eye for detail makes for pleasant, well organized spaces with real personality. Some of the cheapest rooms have no windows, and facilities are limited to a Jacuzzi and sun deck—though its busy and sometimes noisy location doesn't really lend itself to sunbathing. Staff is friendly and helpful, and the Ember restaurant is popular.

50 Keong Saik Rd., Singapore 089154. ℭ **65/6347-1929.** Fax 65/6327-1929. S$198 double; from S$250 suite. AE, DC, MC, V. 5-min. walk to Outram Park MRT. **Amenities:** Restaurant; Jacuzzi. *In room:* A/C, TV, hair dryer, minibar.

The Scarlet   Glamour drips from every chandelier onto the polished black marble floors of this groovy little boutique hotel. Swirling patterns of gold and blood red velvet compete for attention in the lobby and its equally stylish lounge. The location, in a row of original shophouses, means that guest rooms are very small and skylights are the only source of daylight in first-floor deluxe rooms. Unless you're in a premium deluxe or a suite, you'll have a shower rather than a bathtub, but rooms are well designed and comfortably decorated in sophisticated muted color schemes and equipped with flatscreen TVs, DVD, and broadband. Suites are opulent, with swaths of silk drapery, funky lounge areas, and ornate gilt frames. There's not much in the way of facilities (a Jacuzzi and a tiny gym, "Flaunt," and a pleasant rooftop bar and restaurant), but Chinatown and the fashionable haunts of Club Street are just around the corner.

33 Erskine Rd., Singapore 069333. ✆ **65/6511-3333.** Fax 65/6511-3303. www.thescarlethotel.com. 84 units. S$185 double; from S$550 suite. AE, DC, MC, V. 10-min. walk from Chinatown MRT. **Amenities:** 2 restaurants; lounge; concierge; executive-level rooms; health club; outdoor Jacuzzi. *In room:* A/C, TV w/ satellite programming, high-speed Internet, minibar.

Orchard Road Area
VERY EXPENSIVE

Four Seasons Hotel Singapore ★★★   The Four Seasons has a residential atmosphere, and there's a sense of intimacy and peace that's unusual among international hotels. The hotel is smaller than many of its competitors, and the personable staff delivers ultraefficient service. Located just off Orchard Road, extensive gardens block out much of the sights and sounds of the city center. As well as the elegant pools, there are indoor and outdoor tennis courts (with a resident professional), a spa, and a fully staffed fitness area. A 2008 refurbishment added state-of-the-art entertainment systems and plasma TVs. Premier rooms and suites are huge, with antiques and artworks selected from the Four Season's large collection. Superior rooms are also unusually large and comfortable, decorated in tasteful ivory and chestnut with high ceilings and the kind of comforts that come at a premium elsewhere. Consider a standard room here before a suite in a less expensive hotel.

190 Orchard Blvd., Singapore 248646. ✆ **800/332-3442** in the U.S., 800/268-6282 in Canada, or 65/6734-1110. Fax 65/6733-0682. www.fourseasons.com. 254 units. S$550 double; from S$720 suite. AE, DC, MC, V. 10-min. walk to Orchard MRT. **Amenities:** 2 restaurants; bar; airport transfers; babysitting; concierge; Singapore's best equipped fitness center; Jacuzzis; 2 outdoor pools; room service; spa w/sauna, steam, massage, and full menu of beauty and relaxation treatments; 2 outdoor lighted tennis courts and 2 indoor air-conditioned tennis courts. *In room:* A/C, TV w/satellite programming and in-room LaserDisc player w/complimentary disks available, hair dryer, minibar, Wi-Fi.

St. Regis Hotel ★★★   Singapore's top luxury city hotel opened in early 2008. Touted as a six-star property, it's distinctly palatial and ornate, with patterned fabrics and carpeting, dainty crockery, and huge chandeliers. Guests are chauffeured in Bentleys. Guest rooms feature walnut furniture, Jim Thomson silks, and plush couches, and are full of gadgets, with Bose sound systems, plasma TVs, and lighting panels. Enormous marble-clad bathrooms have flatscreen TVs in the mirror facing the bathtub. Each floor is serviced by discreet and expert butlers. Grand Deluxe rooms overlook the greenery of the exclusive Tanglin and Nassim areas. Toiletries are from the in-house Remède spa, with a wet lounge, which is complimentary for guests. While you're there, consider the Remède's version of a hot stone massage, which uses huge silken pebbles of pure jade. Facilities are of the high standard that you would expect, though the pool area is overlooked by nearby towers.

29 Tanglin Rd., Singapore 247911. © **877/STREGIS** (787-3447) in the U.S. and Canada; 800/221-637 in Australia; 800/450-561 in New Zealand; 800/325-78734 in the U.K.; or 65/6506-6888. Fax 65/6506-6708. www.starwoodhotels.com. 299 units. S$440 double; from S$650 suite. AE, DC, MC, V. 15-min. walk to Orchard MRT. **Amenities:** 3 restaurants; 2 bars; airport transfers; babysitting; concierge; health club; outdoor pools w/Jacuzzi; room service; spa w/wet room, sauna, steam, massage, and comprehensive menu of treatments; 2 indoor air-conditioned tennis courts. *In room:* A/C, plasma TVs w/satellite programming and in-room entertainment center, hair dryer, minibar, Wi-Fi.

Shangri-La Hotel ★★★ On 6 hectares (15 acres) of tropical gardens, the Shang's 750 rooms are spread across three wings, each tailored to meet the needs of different travelers. The vast lobby features columns that rise up from the marble floor, and a series of sparkling chandeliers overhead. The Tower Wing rooms are aimed at the business traveler, with modern blond wood, uncluttered appearance, and large work areas. Bay windows offer floor-to-ceiling views over the city. Leisure travelers prefer the tropical feel of the Garden Wing, where large rooms have balconies that overlook the gardens. Celebrities, government leaders, and high rollers favor the ultraexclusive Valley Wing, which has a separate private driveway and entrance, butler service, complimentary champagne bar, and personalized stationery. Its rooms and suites are some of the largest in Singapore, elegant and supremely comfortable with luxurious bathrooms and separate dressing rooms. The hotel's Limousine airport transfer is free to Tower Wing guests.

22 Orange Grove Rd., Singapore 258350. © **800/942-5050** in the U.S., 866/344-5050 in Canada, 800/222-448 in Australia, 800/442-179 in New Zealand, or 65/6737-3644. Fax 65/6737-3257. www. shangri-la.com. 750 units. S$385 Tower double; S$435 Garden double; S$645 Valley double; from S$1,000 suite. AE, DC, MC, V. 10-min. walk to Orchard MRT. **Amenities:** 5 restaurants; lobby lounge; free airport transfer; babysitting; concierge; health club; outdoor pool; room service; spa with Jacuzzi, sauna, steam, and massage; 4 outdoor lighted tennis courts. *In room:* A/C, TV w/satellite programming and in-house movies, hair dryer, high-speed Internet, minibar.

Singapore Marriott Hotel ★★ The towering green-and-scarlet–roofed pagoda of the Marriott is a landmark at the corner of Orchard and Scott roads. Geared strongly toward business travelers, its ultracentral location, next to Orchard MRT, makes sightseeing convenient, too. The cosmopolitan lobby is perfect for informal meetings or a comfortable coffee stop. Crossroads Café, which spills from the hotel onto the sidewalk, is one of Singapore's most popular spots to see and be seen. The pagoda tower means that rooms aren't large, though they are cozy and inviting and equipped with all the comforts and conveniences you'd expect for business travel. Leisure travelers may prefer the pool-terrace rooms and suites. These elegant little cabins are surprisingly resortlike, considering the Orchard Road location. Each has a poolside veranda, wooden floors with rugs, skylights over the open-plan bathroom, and walls of carved stone.

320 Orchard Rd., Singapore 238865. © **800/228-9290** in the U.S. and Canada, 800/251-259 in Australia, 800/22-12-22 in the U.K., or 65/6735-5800. Fax 65/6735-9800. www.singaporemarriott.com. 373 units. S$450 double; from S$640 suite. AE, DC, MC, V. Orchard MRT. **Amenities:** 4 restaurants; bar w/ live jazz, lobby lounge, and dance club w/live bands; airport transfers; babysitting; concierge; health club w/Jacuzzi, sauna, steam, and massage; outdoor pool w/Jacuzzi; room service. *In room:* A/C, TV w/ satellite programming and in-house movies, hair dryer, high-speed Internet, minibar.

EXPENSIVE

Grand Hyatt Singapore ★★ The unusual lobby, with glass windows set at right angles and a reception desk hidden around the corner, brings good feng shui to this excellent hotel. In public spaces, floors of polished cream or black marble are offset by deep wood and streams trickling slowly over hand-chiseled rocks. Guest rooms in the Terrace Wing are decked out in shades of cream and gray with good work desks and big marble bathrooms. Even better are the Grand Wing rooms, which are really suites with separate living areas, small walk-in closets, Bang & Olufsen TVs, and a separate work area. The free-form pool is beautifully landscaped, with wooden decks and loungers that sit in shallow water. The Japanese-designed Damai spa and state-of-the-art fitness center overlook the incredible five-story waterfall that sits in the center of the hotel. This is an oasis just steps away from the busiest intersection in the city.

10 Scotts Rd., Singapore 228211. ✆ **800/223-1234** in the U.S. and Canada, or 65/6738-1234. Fax 65/6732-1696. www.singapore.grand.hyatt.com. 663 units. S$390 double; from S$450 Grand Deluxe. AE, DC, MC, V. Near Orchard MRT. **Amenities:** 5 restaurants; 2 bars; live music bar; airport transfers; babysitting; concierge; health club w/Jacuzzi, sauna, and steam; landscaped outdoor pool; room service; spa; 2 outdoor lighted tennis courts. In room: A/C, TV w/satellite programming and in-house movies, hair dryer, high-speed Internet, minibar.

Meritus Mandarin Singapore ★ This tour group favorite is brilliantly located in the center of Orchard Road. A renovation project launched in 2008 has moved the main lobby around the corner to Orchard Link, and a fifth-floor linkway now connects the hotel's two wings. The first four floors have been converted into a high-end fashion mall, and guest rooms have received refurbishment as well. Try for a Premier room, on higher and much quieter floors, which are more spacious and luxurious. The tower and rooftop revolving restaurant was a landmark when it opened in 1973. Sadly, it no longer revolves, but the Chatterbox restaurant still offers Singaporean specialties such as chicken rice with remarkable 360-degree city views.

333 Orchard Rd., Singapore 238867. ✆ **65/6737-4411.** Fax 65/6732-2361. www.asiatravel.com/singapore/mandarin. 1,051 units. S$380 double; from S$1,410 suite. AE, DC, MC, V. Near Orchard MRT. **Amenities:** 4 restaurants; revolving observation lounge and lobby lounge; airport transfers; babysitting; concierge; health club w/Jacuzzi, sauna, steam, and massage; outdoor pool; room service. In room: A/C, TV w/satellite programming and in-house movies, minibar.

Orchard Hotel Singapore ★ There's a pleasant buzz about the Orchard Hotel. Perhaps it's the giant wrought-iron clock in the center of the lobby, ticking away the time in London, Tokyo, Singapore, and New York that gives the Orchard an air of a very plush railway station. The Orchard Wing houses standard (superior) rooms. These aren't huge, but make good use of space with comfortable contemporary furniture and an intriguing round window that lets daylight into the bathrooms. A few Superior rooms have a more Asian feel and local touches like painted wooden furniture. The larger and plusher Executive Deluxe and Club rooms are mostly housed in the Claymore Wing. The hotel's upper Orchard Road location means that views aren't spectacular, but there's a large pool, a fitness center, and a great attached shopping mall that has useful cafes, restaurants, and salons. The staff is friendly and helpful, though at times overworked, so allow plenty of time for checkout.

442 Orchard Rd., Singapore 238879. ✆ **800/637-7200** in the U.S. and Canada, 800/655-147 in Australia, 800/442-519 in New Zealand, or 65/6734-7766. Fax 65/6733-5482. www.orchardhotel.com.sg. 672 units. S$305 double; S$520 suite. AE, DC, MC, V. 5-min. walk to Orchard MRT. **Amenities:** 2 restaurants; lobby lounge; babysitting; concierge; health club w/sauna; outdoor pool; room service. In room: A/C, TV w/satellite programming, minibar.

The Regent Singapore ★ The Regent is tucked between Cuscaden and Tanglin roads, at the northern end of Orchard Road—you'll have to hike about 10 minutes to get to the center of things. But check out the lobby in this place! It's a huge three-level atrium affair with windows on three sides, a skylight, fountains, plenty of small private meeting nooks, and raised walkways straight out of *The Jetsons*. The guest rooms have high ceilings and are decorated with Chinese motifs in refurbished fabrics, but the bathrooms are smaller than at most other comparable hotels and the place is showing its age slightly. You have to request coffee-/tea-making facilities in your room; otherwise, the service is free in the tea lounge, which also serves a high tea the old-fashioned way, with silver-tray service.

1 Cuscaden Rd., Singapore 249715. © **800/545-4000** in the U.S. and Canada, 800/022-800 in Australia, 800/440-800 in New Zealand, 800/917-8795 in the U.K., or 65/6733-8888. Fax 65/6732-8838. www. regenthotels.com. 441 units. S$335 double; from S$470 suite. AE, DC, MC, V. 15-min. walk to Orchard MRT. **Amenities:** 2 restaurants; very cool bar; lobby tea lounge; airport transfers; babysitting; concierge; health club w/steam and massage; outdoor pool; room service. *In room:* A/C, TV w/satellite programming and in-house movies, hair dryer, high-speed Internet.

MODERATE

Concorde Formerly Le Meridien, this Orchard Road hotel has undergone several stages of renovation in recent years. Public areas, including the impressive atrium lobby, haven't changed much, and it's a shame there are no plans yet to overhaul the rather shabby shopping arcade outside. Business facilities have a way to go to make the Concorde a great choice for business travelers, but if you're here to shop, then you can't beat this location; the Concorde's large refurbished rooms makes an enviably convenient place to stash your shopping bags before heading to the Historic District nearby.

100 Orchard Rd., Singapore 238840. © **65/6733-8855.** Fax 65/6732-7886. www.concordehotel.com. sg. 407 units. S$260 double; from S$363 suite. AE, DC, MC, V. 5-min. walk to Dhoby Ghaut MRT. **Amenities:** 2 restaurants; lobby lounge; airport transfers; babysitting; concierge; health club w/sauna; outdoor pool; room service. *In room:* A/C, TV w/satellite programming and in-house movies, hair dryer, minibar.

The Elizabeth Singapore The Elizabeth is European in style, although the lobby has a huge and distinctly Asian waterfall that cascades down to a rock garden below and a gift shop that's good for Asian souvenirs. Executive-floor rooms were refurbished in 2008, as were the four large suites, which are large, if relatively unadventurous, spaces with dark-wood furniture. If you need the space, these can be a good deal. Unfortunately, the hotel has no plans yet to invest in the standard (Superior) rooms, which are becoming rather worn and dark since their last refit in 2005. The facilities are nothing to write home about; there are a few workout machines next to the pool area and no business center (although Internet is available and the friendly staff at reception will help with faxes). There is a restaurant, but most would prefer to head to Orchard Road, a short but slightly hilly stroll away.

24 Mount Elizabeth, Singapore 228518. © **65/6738-1188.** Fax 65/6732-3866. www.theelizabeth.com. sg. 256 units. S$228 double; from S$298 suite. AE, DC, MC, V. 10-min. walk to Orchard MRT. **Amenities:** Restaurant; lobby lounge; babysitting; concierge; health club; outdoor pool; room service. *In room:* A/C, TV w/satellite programming, hair dryer, high-speed Internet, minibar.

Goodwood Park Hotel ★ The Goodwood Park is a National Landmark, built in 1900 as the Teutonia Club, and may be Raffles's closest rival for historical significance. Guest rooms are large and lovely, overlooking the main pool or the Mayfair pool. Spacious Poolside Suites are decorated in a classic European style, and several open directly onto the gardens and main pool terrace. *One caveat:* The main pool is also overlooked by the glass walls of the main lobby, so if you prefer privacy, choose a room beside the Balinese-inspired Mayfair pool. If you're in Singapore for a week or more, the large one-bedroom Parklane Suites, housed in a separate wing, can be a bargain. While Goodwood doesn't come close to matching the business and fitness centers of other hotels in its price range, its four restaurants are highly rated by locals, particularly the dim sum served at the Min Jiang restaurant. The staff at Goodwood Park is particularly friendly and helpful.

22 Scotts Rd., Singapore 228221. ℂ **800/772-3890** in the U.S., 800/665-5919 in Canada, 800/89-95-20 in the U.K., or 65/6737-7411. Fax 65/6732-8558. www.goodwoodparkhotel.com. 235 units. S$260 double; from S$450 suite. AE, DC, MC, V. 5-min. walk to Orchard MRT. **Amenities:** 6 restaurants; bar and lobby lounge; airport transfers; babysitting; concierge; tiny health club; 2 outdoor pools; room service; spa. *In room:* A/C, TV w/satellite programming and in-house movies, hair dryer, minibar.

Hilton International Singapore   This Hilton doesn't measure up with some of their other properties worldwide and definitely can't compete with other hotels in this price category in Singapore. The most famous feature of the Hilton is its glamorous shopping arcade, where you can find your Donna Karan, Louis Vuitton, Gucci—all the greats. With all this, the guest rooms should be pretty sumptuous, no? Well, no. The rooms are simpler than you'd expect, with nothing flashy or overdone. Floor-to-ceiling windows are in each, and although views in the front of the hotel are of Orchard Road and the Thai Embassy property, views in the back are not so hot. In this day and age, when business-class hotels are wrestling to outdo each other, Hilton has a lot of catching up to do.

581 Orchard Rd., Singapore 238883. ℂ **800/445-8667** in the U.S., or 65/6737-2233. Fax 65/6732-2917. www.singapore.hilton.com. 423 units. S$295 double; from S$645 suite. AE, DC, MC, V. Near Orchard MRT. **Amenities:** 2 restaurants; lobby lounge; airport transfers; babysitting; concierge; health club w/ sauna and steam; outdoor pool; room service. *In room:* A/C, TV w/satellite programming and in-house movies, hair dryer, minibar.

Hotel Grand Central, Singapore   The Grand Central certainly ain't grand, but you can't get much more central than smack in the middle of Orchard Road (though, strictly speaking, the lobby is tucked into a lane just around the corner). Permanently busy, its predominantly regional guests throng the small lobby while the staff does its best to keep up. As well as a seafood restaurant, the lobby has a useful tour desk and travel agent, and there's a rooftop pool. Standard guest rooms are backpacker basic, with decent beds, central air-conditioning, and TVs. Not somewhere you'd be tempted to linger, but why would you, with the center of Singapore on the doorstep? Premium rooms have been refurbished with LCD TVs and other standard amenities.

22 Cavenagh Rd./Orchard Rd., Singapore 229617. ℂ **65/6737-9944.** Fax 65/6733-3175. www.grand central.com.sg. 390 units. S$230 double; S$450 family suite. AE, DC, MC, V. 5-min. walk to Somerset or Dhoby Ghaut MRT. **Amenities:** Restaurant; lounge; health club w/Jacuzzi and steam; outdoor pool. *In room:* A/C, TV w/in-house movies, minibar.

Orchard Parade Hotel ★★ 🥐 ☺   This Mediterranean-style gem is right at the top of Orchard Road. I recommend its family studios; they are large and comfortable, with a king-size bed and lounge seating area, dining area, and spacious bathroom, plus two extra single beds behind a partition. There's a balcony too, though the view over the busy junction of Tanglin and Orchard Road isn't exactly peaceful. Deluxe double rooms are also spacious, pleasant, and bright, though the bathrooms are fairly basic. Views are variable, so specify at booking if that's important to you. Standard double and twin rooms tend to face the building at the back of the hotel, so your view's likely to be of concrete. On the sixth-floor roof there's a colorful terra-cotta-tiled pool area, and the terrace outside is convenient for coffee shops and family restaurants—plus, of course, you have all of Orchard Road to choose from. It's a 10-minute walk to the Botanic Gardens and Orchard MRT.

1 Tanglin Rd., Singapore 247905. © **65/6737-1133.** Fax 65/6733-0242. www.orchardparade.com.sg. 387 units. S$238 double; S$378 family studio; from S$358 suite. AE, DC, MC, V. Orchard MRT. **Amenities:** 5 restaurants; lobby lounge; babysitting; concierge; health club; outdoor pool; room service. *In room:* A/C, TV w/satellite programming, hair dryer, minibar.

Sheraton Towers Singapore ★★

Sheraton's lobby is lined with service awards. With the deluxe (standard) room, they'll give you a suit pressing on arrival, daily newspaper delivery, shoeshine service, and complimentary movies. These refurbished rooms are handsome, with textured walls, plush carpeting, and a bed luxuriously fitted with down pillows and dreamy 100% Egyptian cotton bedding. Upgrade to a Tower room, and you get a personal butler, complimentary nightly cocktails and morning breakfast, free laundry, free local calls, your own pants press, and free use of the personal trainer in the fitness center. The cabana rooms, off the pool area, have all the services of the Tower Wing in a very private resort room. Each of the 23 one-of-a-kind suites features a different theme: Chinese regency, French, Italian, jungle, you name it. Although Sheraton is a luxe choice, you can find better deals, pricewise.

39 Scotts Rd., Singapore 228230. © **800/325-3535** in the U.S. and Canada, 800/073-535 in Australia, 800/325-35353 in New Zealand, 800/353535 in the U.K., or 65/6737-6888. Fax 65/6737 1072. www. sheraton.com. 413 units. S$290 double; from S$600 suite. AE, DC, MC, V. 5-min. walk to Newton MRT. **Amenities:** 3 restaurants; lobby lounge; airport transfers; babysitting; concierge; health club w/sauna and massage; outdoor pool; room service. *In room:* A/C, TV w/satellite programming and in-house movies, hair dryer, high-speed Internet, minibar.

Traders Hotel Singapore ★★

Traders doesn't look like a value-for-money hotel, with its smartly designed lobby and restaurants, but that's how it advertises itself— and it's certainly a bargain for leisure travelers in Singapore. Most of the rooms are moderately small, although there are five triple rooms with child-size sofa beds. Superior (standard) rooms are located on the lower floors, with their Deluxe counterparts benefiting from slightly better views. The only major problem with Traders (and its neighbors) is the distance from the main part of Orchard Road and the subway, but they do offer an hourly free shuttle bus to and from Orchard MRT and Ngee Ann/Takashimaya, and weekday shuttles to various business parks. Better still, this value hotel has a cross-signing arrangement with the nearby Shangri-La hotel and the Rasa Sentosa resort on Sentosa Island, giving you access to their awesome pools, spas, and fitness centers, plus the latter's beachfront location.

1A Cuscaden Rd., Singapore 249716. © **800/942-5050** in the U.S. and Canada, 800/222-448 in Australia, 0800/442-179 in New Zealand, or 65/6738-2222. Fax 65/6831-4314. www.shangri-la.com. 547 units. S$265 double; from S$400 suite. AE, DC, MC, V. 15-min. walk to Orchard MRT. **Amenities:** 2 restaurants; bar and lobby lounge; airport transfers; babysitting; concierge; health club w/Jacuzzi, sauna, steam, and massage; outdoor pool; room service; spa. *In room:* A/C, TV w/satellite programming, hair dryer, high-speed Internet access, minibar.

York Hotel Singapore ★

This charming little hotel has gotten even better in the past year, thanks to a modernization program that's smartened up the 407 rooms and extended the business and fitness facilities. Pale, contemporary furnishings in neutral colors lend a calming atmosphere to the guest rooms. Superior rooms aren't particularly large, so if you want more space, upgrade to one of the spacious deluxe or colorful cabana rooms that look out over the pool. The York's location, 10 minutes' walk from Orchard Road, offers a good compromise between accessibility and a moderately relaxing environment. Staff here is extremely professional and courteous. All these improvements mean that rates have risen to match and the York isn't the steal it used to be, but it remains a consistently good value option. The buffet breakfast seems to be disproportionately expensive—try to get an inclusive rate or head to Orchard Road instead.

21 Mount Elizabeth, Singapore 228516. © **800/223-5652** in the U.S. and Canada, 800/553-549 in Australia, 800/447-555 in New Zealand, 800/89-88-52 in the U.K., or 65/6737-0511. Fax 65/6732-1217. www.yorkhotel.com.sg. 407 units. S$285 double; from S$300 suite. AE, DC, MC, V. 10-min. walk to Orchard MRT. **Amenities:** Restaurant; lobby lounge; babysitting; health club; Jacuzzi; outdoor pool; room service. *In room:* A/C, TV w/satellite programming, minibar.

INEXPENSIVE

Lloyd's Inn   This two-story bungalow is in a quiet residential area just a few blocks from Orchard Road. Lloyd's is a budget motel in every sense, with few facilities. Open-air corridors form a pleasant little courtyard, and standard rooms are small, with a definite budget feeling, though all have en suite bathrooms, TV, air-conditioning, and phones. Deluxe rooms are a better size and have a small fridge. Published rates include the "++" taxes (see "Taxes & Service Charges," earlier in this chapter), although there's an extra 2% charge for credit cards and rooms are charged in advance. The welcome is friendly and low-key. No pool, no fitness center, no nothing—you got your room, that's what you got.

2 Lloyd Rd., Singapore 239091. © **65/6737-7309.** Fax 65/6737-7847. www.lloydinn.com. 34 units. S$90–S$110 double. MC, V. 10-min. walk to Somerset MRT. *In room:* A/C, TV.

YMCA International House ☺   With a superb location at the lower end of Orchard Road, this budget gem is very convenient for sightseeing and getting around by mass transit. The guest rooms have been renovated and have private bathrooms that are better than I've seen at some much pricier hotels. All rooms have air-conditioning, a telephone (with free local calls), color television, and a stock-it-yourself refrigerator, but be warned, all standard double-occupancy rooms are twin beds only. The dormitories are small, dark, and quiet, with two bunk beds per room. Across the hall are men's and women's locker rooms for showering. Most of the public areas have no air-conditioning, including the old fitness facility, billiards center, and squash courts—so be warned: They can become unbearably hot. The rooftop pool is nothing to write home about, but a full-time lifeguard is on duty. There's a coffee shop in the lobby. The staff is amazingly friendly.

1 Orchard Rd., Singapore 238824. © **65/6336-6000.** Fax 65/6337-3140. www.ymcaih.com.sg. 111 units. S$159 double; S$190 family room; S$190 superior room. AE, DC, MC, V. 5-min. walk to Dhoby Ghaut MRT. **Amenities:** 2 restaurants; babysitting; small gym; Internet center; outdoor pool. *In room:* A/C, TV, fridge.

Sentosa Island

Sentosa's Island getaway gets bigger every year, with new attractions, hotels, and facilities being added all the time. Thanks to a huge land reclamation and building project, the island itself is expanding geographically, too. Sentosa's hotels are geared toward couples on romantic breaks and young families, attracted by the beach resort feel and the accessibility of the city.

Hard Rock Hotel Singapore   Hard Rock is all about the drama, from the dark lobby pulsating with rock and pop music to guest rooms fit for a glamorous star, with tactile black, purple, blue, and gold wall decor and fabrics, crystal chandeliers, and specially designed mood lighting. Entertainment systems feature large-screen LCD TVs with the hotel's video channel, CD players, and iPod docking stations. The Simmons "Cool Max" mattresses are very comfortable. Hard Rock is one of six hotels inside Resorts World Sentosa, so guests have easy access to Universal Studios Singapore, the 24-hour casino, and tons of dining, shopping, and entertainment venues.

8 Sentosa Gateway, Singapore 098269. ✆ **65/6577-8899.** Fax 65/6577-8890. www.hardrockhotel singapore.com. 300 units. S$470 double; from S894 suite. AE, MC, V. **Amenities:** 2 restaurants; 2 bars; airport transfers; babysitting; kids club; concierge; fitness center; huge lagoon pool. *In room:* A/C, TV w/satellite programming and in-house movies, hair dryer, high-speed Internet, minibar.

The Sentosa Resort & Spa ★★   At this hotel, fashioned after the luxury resorts of Phuket, Thailand, designers have done a great job combining clean, modern lines with tropical touches and courtyard gardens to produce a sophisticated getaway with relaxing charm. Lazy terraces and cozy alcoves tucked all over the grounds invite guests to unwind in privacy—perfect for intimate candlelit dinners that can be requested anywhere you like. The centerpiece is Spa Botanica; its garden massages, treatments, and frangipani baths are repeatedly voted some of the world's best. The standard guest rooms in the five-story hotel building are small but stunning, featuring camphor burl-wood doors and accents, Thai silk screens in natural browns and greens, and granite-and-tile bathrooms with deep tubs and separate showers. Ask for views of the golf course, which are prettier than the views of the hotel courtyards and buildings. The four Garden Villas are supremely romantic and luxurious. Butlers wait 'round-the-clock to serve you—a standard feature for all rooms.

2 Bukit Manis Rd., Sentosa, Singapore 099891. ✆ **65/6275-0331.** Fax 65/6275-0228. www.thesentosa. com. 205 units. S$270 double; from S$550 suite; S$1,825 villa. AE, DC, MC, V. **Amenities:** 3 restaurants; bar; lounge; airport transfers; babysitting; concierge; golf at nearby facilities; health club w/20m (66-ft.) lap pool, Jacuzzi, and sauna; gorgeous midnight blue-tiled outdoor pool w/views of the harbor; room service; luxury spa w/private pool, mud baths, steam, Jacuzzis, exercise and relaxation classes, salon, beauty treatments, and massage; 2 outdoor lighted tennis courts w/coach. *In room:* A/C, TV w/satellite programming and in-house movies, hair dryer, high-speed Internet, minibar.

Shangri-La's Rasa Sentosa Resort ☺   Set on an immaculate white-sand beach fringed with coconut palms, this is Singapore's only true beachfront hotel. Great outdoor activities make the Rasa Sentosa particularly attractive, with a sea-sports center, offering windsurfing, sailing, and paddle skiing. There's a large free-form swimming pool in the gardens, a jogging track, aqua-bike rentals, an outdoor Jacuzzi, and a fully equipped spa with gym, sauna, body and facial treatments, hydromassage, and massage therapies. For children, there is a separate pool with water slides (no lifeguard, though), a playground, a nursery, and a games room.

This hotel has undergone a massive renovation with a completely new look from head to toe. It will still be under Shangri-La's apt management, so this will likely continue to be a good bet. The resort is connected to Singapore's downtown by frequent and free shuttles.

101 Siloso Rd., Sentosa, Singapore 098970. ✆ **800/942-5050** in the U.S. and Canada, 800/222-448 in Australia, 800/442-179 in New Zealand, or 65/6275-0900. Fax 65/6275-1055. www.shangri-la.com. 459 units. S$425 superior (hill view); from S$625 suite. AE, DC, MC, V. **Amenities:** 3 restaurants; poolside bar and lobby lounge; airport transfers; babysitting; children's center; golf at nearby facilities; health club; outdoor lagoon-style pool w/children's pool and Jacuzzi; room service; spa w/sauna, steam, and massage. *In room:* A/C, TV w/satellite programming and in-house movies, hair dryer, high-speed Internet, minibar.

THE best OF SINGAPORE'S SPAS

In the mid-1990s, spas began making a splash in the Singapore hotel scene. By the millennium, every luxury hotel was either planning a full-blown spa facility or at least offering spa services to its residents. At the same time, day spas sprouted up in shopping centers, and despite the economic downturn, these businesses have stayed afloat. Now the Singapore Tourism Board is positioning Singapore as an urban spa hub in Southeast Asia, luring visitors from the region and beyond with luxurious facilities that go above and beyond the call of relaxation and hedonistic pampering. Here are the best among the many:

Singapore's most celebrated spa is the **Willow Stream Spa** (The Fairmont, Level 6, 2 Stamford Rd., ✆ **65/6336-4477;** and Swissôtel Merchant Court, Level 2, 20 Merchant Rd., ✆ **65/6239-1780;**

www.willowstream.com). This spa at The Fairmont is the largest spa in Singapore, with Southeast Asian–inspired interiors and treatments—over 1,000 to choose from.

The Willow Stream Spa is convenient if you want to stay in the city center; however, if you want more of a retreat spa experience, **Spa Botanica** (2 Bukit Manis Rd., The Sentosa, ✆ **65/6371-1318;** www.spabotanica.com) is a gorgeous pick. It is located at the Sentosa, a scenic resort dripping with laid-back yet elegant tropical Southeast Asian decor. Spa Botanica has 6,000 sq. m (64,583 sq. ft.) of designated spa space, with pools, mud baths, and treatment pavilions nestled in lush gardens. Treatments center around natural recipes for beauty and relaxation, including spice and floral treatments.

WHERE TO DINE

Singapore claims an estimated 2,000-plus eating establishments, so you'll never go hungry. But to simply say, "If you like food, you'll love Singapore!" doesn't do justice to the modern concept of eating in this city. Here you'll find a huge selection of local, regional, and international cuisine, served in settings that range from bustling hawker centers to grand and glamorous palaces of gastronomy. The food is authentic, and many times the dining experience is entertainment in its own right. Various ethnic restaurants, with their traditional decor and serving styles, hold their own special sense of theater for foreigners; but Singaporeans don't stop there, dreaming up new concepts in cuisine and ambience to add fresh dimensions to the fine art of dining.

Tips on Dining

In many foreign destinations, the exotic cuisine isn't the only thing that keeps you guessing. Here, I give you the ground rules on Singapore dining.

HOURS Most restaurants are open for lunch as early as 11am but close around 2:30 or 3pm to give them a chance to set up for dinner, which begins around 6pm. Where closing times are listed, that is the time when the last order is taken. If you need to eat at odd hours, food centers serve all day and some hawker centers are open all night.

TIPPING It's not expected here. Restaurants always add a gratuity to the bill. Sometimes I just leave the small change, but it's not expected.

RESERVATIONS Some restaurants, especially the more fashionable or upscale ones, may require that reservations be made up to a couple of days in advance. Reservations are always recommended for Saturday and Sunday lunch and dinner, as eating is a favorite national pastime and a lot of families take meals out for weekend quality time.

ATTIRE Because Singapore is so hot, "smart casual" (a local term, meaning a shirt and slacks for men and a dress or skirt/slacks and blouse for women) is always a safe bet in moderate to expensive restaurants. For the very expensive restaurants, "smart elegant" is required, which in Singapore means jacket and tie for men and a dressier outfit for women. For the cheap places, come as you are, as long as you're decent.

ORDERING WINE WITH DINNER Singaporeans have become more wine savvy in recent years and have begun importing estate-bottled wines from California, Australia, New Zealand, Peru, South Africa, France, and Germany. However, these bottles are heavily taxed. A bottle of wine with dinner starts at around S$50, and a single glass runs between S$15 and S$25, depending on the wine and the restaurant. Chinese restaurants usually don't charge corkage fees for bringing your own.

Historic District
VERY EXPENSIVE

Inagiku ★★ JAPANESE   Inagiku serves Japanese food that rivals some of Tokyo's best restaurants. The dining room is subdued and artistic, with recessed spotlights designed to illuminate the dish in front of you to maximum effect. It's all very cultured, despite some unfortunately chosen elevator music. Inagiku's kitchen is separated into teams, one specializing in sushi and sashimi that's outstandingly fresh and expertly prepared. The *tokusen sashimi moriawase* is a stunning assortment of fresh seafood presented in an ice-filled shell. The tempura—firm, fresh seafood and vegetables fried in batter that is incredibly light—is excellent. Lunchtime set menus offer a more affordable way to dine here, and the quality remains just as high. If sashimi isn't your thing, try the tenderloin and lobster. Separate dishes of succulent beef, followed by meaty shelled lobster smothered in a rich cheese sauce, make it the ultimate surf and turf. In addition to sake, there is a good selection of wines.

Raffles The Plaza, Level 3, 80 Bras Basah Rd. ✆ **65/6431-6156.** Reservations recommended. Set lunch S$48-S$170; set dinner S$280-S$350. AE, MC, V. Daily noon-2:30pm and 6:30-10:30pm.

EXPENSIVE

KU DÉ TA ★★★ PAN ASIAN   A visit to this restaurant, sister to Bali's famous KU DÉ TA, will be one of your most memorable experiences in Singapore. The view from the top of Marina Bay Sands is a stunning 360-degree panorama of the tropical sunset against glittering skyscrapers. KU DÉ TA calls its food "avant-garde"—it's a very contemporary take on the best cuisines of Asia, with dishes like seared Black Angus beef tataki, jumbo soft-shell crab served with green chili mayonnaise, and bamboo-roasted black cod in red miso. Dishes are served Asian-style for all to share. After hours, this place becomes a very sexy nightclub. SkyPark fees are waived for guests.

SkyPark at Marina Bay Sands North Tower, 1 Bayfront Ave. ✆ **65/6688-7688.** www.kudeta.com.sg. Reservations required. Most dishes S$15-S$40. AE, MC, V. Mon-Fri noon-2:30pm and 6-11pm; Sat-Sun 6-11pm.

Lei Garden ★★ CHINESE/CANTONESE   Lei Garden lives up to a great reputation for the highest-quality Cantonese cuisine in one of the most elegant settings, nestled within **CHIJMES** (later in this chapter). Highly recommended dishes are

Where to Dine in Urban Singapore

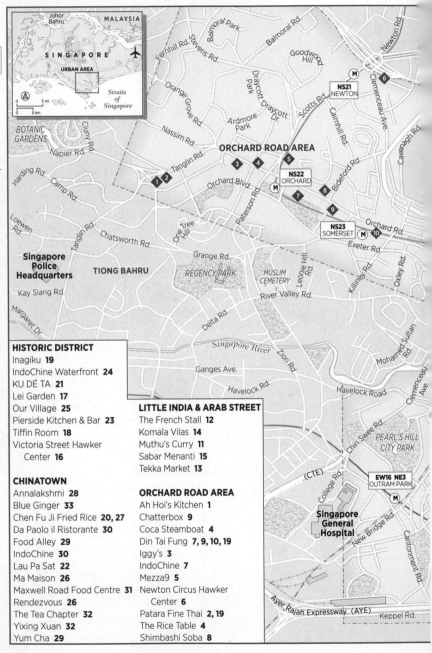

HISTORIC DISTRICT
Inagiku **19**
IndoChine Waterfront **24**
KU DÉ TA **21**
Lei Garden **17**
Our Village **25**
Pierside Kitchen & Bar **23**
Tiffin Room **18**
Victoria Street Hawker
　Center **16**

CHINATOWN
Annalakshmi **28**
Blue Ginger **33**
Chen Fu Ji Fried Rice **20, 27**
Da Paolo il Ristorante **30**
Food Alley **29**
IndoChine **30**
Lau Pa Sat **22**
Ma Maison **26**
Maxwell Road Food Centre **31**
Rendezvous **26**
The Tea Chapter **32**
Yixing Xuan **32**
Yum Cha **29**

LITTLE INDIA & ARAB STREET
The French Stall **12**
Komala Vilas **14**
Muthu's Curry **11**
Sabar Menanti **15**
Tekka Market **13**

ORCHARD ROAD AREA
Ah Hoi's Kitchen **1**
Chatterbox **9**
Coca Steamboat **4**
Din Tai Fung **7, 9, 10, 19**
Iggy's **3**
IndoChine **7**
Mezza9 **5**
Newton Circus Hawker
　Center **6**
Patara Fine Thai **2, 19**
The Rice Table **4**
Shimbashi Soba **8**

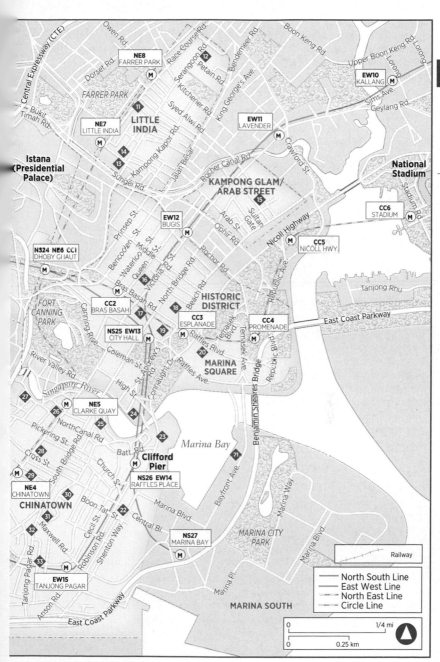

Istana (Presidential Palace)

FARRER PARK

LITTLE INDIA

KAMPONG GLAM/ARAB STREET

National Stadium

Tanjong Rhu

HISTORIC DISTRICT

FORT CANNING PARK

MARINA SQUARE

Singapore River

Marina Bay

Clifford Pier

MARINA CITY PARK

CHINATOWN

MARINA SOUTH

NE8 FARRER PARK	EW10 KALLANG
NE7 LITTLE INDIA	EW11 LAVENDER
EW12 BUGIS	CC6 STADIUM
N324 NE6 CC1 DHOBY GHAUT	CC5 NICOLL HWY.
CC2 BRAS BASAH	CC4 PROMENADE
NS25 EW13 CITY HALL	CC3 ESPLANADE
NE5 CLARKE QUAY	NS26 EW14 RAFFLES PLACE
NE4 CHINATOWN	NS27 MARINA BAY
EW15 TANJONG PAGAR	

East Coast Parkway

Benjamin Sheares Bridge

Railway	
——	North South Line
——	East West Line
----	North East Line
····	Circle Line

0 — 1/4 mi
0 — 0.25 km

the fried shrimp with tangerine peel and black-bean sauce, and crispy roasted kuro-buta pork. If you reserve 24 hours in advance, try the beggar's chicken, a whole stuffed chicken wrapped and baked in a lotus leaf covered in yam, which makes the chicken moist with a delicate flavor you won't forget. Also try the barbecued Beijing duck, which is exquisite. Dim sum here is excellent. A small selection of French and Chinese wines is available.

30 Victoria St., CHIJMES #01-24. ✆ **65/6339-3822.** Reservations required. Small dishes S$22–S$68. AE, DC, MC, V. Daily 11:30am–2:30pm and 6–10:30pm.

Tiffin Room ★ NORTHERN INDIAN   Tiffin curry came from India and is named after the three-tiered containers that Indian workers would use to carry their lunch. The tiffin-box idea was adopted by the British colonists, who changed around the recipes a bit so they weren't as spicy. The cuisine that evolved is pretty much what you'll find served at Raffles's Tiffin Room, where a buffet spread lets you select from a variety of curries, chutneys, rice, and Indian breads. Highlights include the red snapper with almond and cashew-nut sauce, and south Indian spring chicken cooked with coconut, but there's a vast array of vegetarian dishes to choose from, too. The restaurant is just inside the lobby entrance of Raffles Hotel and carries the trademark Raffles elegance throughout its decor. Very British Raj.

Raffles Hotel, 1 Beach Rd. ✆ **65/6412-1816.** www.raffles.com. Reservations recommended. All meals served buffet-style. Breakfast S$45; lunch S$60; high tea S$55; dinner S$75. AE, DC, MC, V. Daily 7–10:30am, noon–2pm, 3:30–5:30pm (high tea), and 7–10pm.

MODERATE

IndoChine Waterfront ★★★ VIETNAMESE/LAO/CAMBODIAN/FRENCH   IndoChine Waterfront shares the stately Empress Place Building with the Asian Civilisations Museum, enhancing the sophistication of its chic oriental decor. The views over the water make for true romance. The menu combines the best dishes from the Indochinese region, many with hints of the French cuisine that was added into regional palates during colonial days. Their two most popular dishes are the house specialty beef stew ragout and the pepper beef with sweet-and-sour sauce. More traditional Vietnamese favorites, like spring rolls and prawns grilled on sugar cane, are fresh starters. After dinner, don't miss the Vietnamese coffee; it's mind-blowingly delicious. The only weakness here is the slightly lackluster service, but the concept and food have proved so popular that IndoChine now has several bars and restaurants around the city. After Waterfront, the best are in a quaint Chinatown shophouse (49B Club St.; ✆ **65/6323-0503**) and Wisma Atria (Orchard Rd. #01–18/23; ✆ **65/6238-3470**).

1 Empress Place, Asian Civilisations Museum. ✆ **65/6339-1720.** www.indochine.com.sg. Reservations required. Main dishes S$18–S$39. AE, DC, MC, V. Sun–Fri noon–3pm; Sun–Thurs 6:30–11:30pm; Fri–Sat noon–2:30pm and 6:30pm–12:30am.

Pierside Kitchen & Bar ★ SEAFOOD   A light and healthy menu centers on seafood prepared with fresh flavors in a wide variety of international recipes, like the house specialty cumin-spiced crab cakes with marinated cucumber and chili or the lobster linguini. A new menu has added some new favorites, including Maine lobsters with sweet basil and chili and chargrilled octopus. Nothing can compete with the view, really—the panoramic view of the Esplanade Theatres and the marina is lovely. After sundown, the alfresco dining area cools off with breezes from the water, and the stars make for some romantic dining. Relax, enjoy the scenery, and linger over rasp-berry and lychee soufflé or the divine seven textures of dark chocolate.

Unit 01-01, One Fullerton, 1 Fullerton Rd. © **65/6438-0400.** www.piersidekitchen.com. Reservations recommended. Main courses S$24–S$38. AE, DC, MC, V. Mon-Thurs 11:30am–2:30pm and 7–10:30pm; Fri-Sat 7–11pm.

INEXPENSIVE

Our Village ★ NORTHERN INDIAN   With its antique white walls stuccoed in delicate and exotic patterns and glistening with tiny silver mirrors, you'll feel like you're in an Indian fairyland here. Even the ceiling twinkles with silver stars, and hanging lanterns provide a subtle glow for the heavenly atmosphere—it's a perfect setting for a delicate dinner. Every dish here is made fresh from hand-selected imported ingredients, some of them coming from secret sources. In fact, the staff is so protective of its recipes, you'd almost think their secret ingredient was opium— and you'll be floating so high after tasting the food that it might as well be. There are vegetarian selections as well as meats (no beef or pork) prepared in luscious gravies or in the tandoor oven. The dishes are light and healthy, with all-natural ingredients and not too much salt.

46 Boat Quay (take elevator to 5th floor). © **65/6538-3058.** Reservations recommended on weekends. Small dishes S$14–S$22. AE, MC, V. Mon-Fri noon–1:45pm and 6–11:30pm; Sat-Sun 6–11:30pm.

Chinatown

MODERATE

Da Paolo Il Ristorante ★★★ ITALIAN   This Italian-owned place in trendy Club Street is coolly elegant, with whitewashed walls and starched linens, but has a casual, comfortable feel. The pasta is made fresh every morning and often served with fresh seafood in classic and modern Italian style. The house specialty of fresh squid-ink spaghetti, lightly dressed with olive oil and garlic, is divine and the home-made tiramisu shouldn't be missed. The owners have other branches that are equally satisfying: **Da Paolo il Giardino** (501 Bukit Timah Rd., #01–05 Cluny Court, beside the Singapore Botanic Gardens; © **65/6463-9628**) and **Da Paolo la Terrazza** (44 Jalan Merah Saga, #01–56, at Chip Bee Gardens in Holland Village; © **65/6476-1332**).

80 Club St. © **65/6224-7081.** www.dapaolo.com.sg. Reservations recommended. Main courses S$20– S$40. AE, DC, MC, V. Mon-Sat 11:30am–2:30pm and 6:30–10:30pm.

INEXPENSIVE

Annalakshmi INDIAN VEGETARIAN   The motto at this communal eatery is "Eat as you wish. Pay as you feel." A group of volunteers cooks and serves southern Indian vegetarian cuisine, rich and spicy vegetable curries with dosai, oothappam, or vada breads, to diners who decide after the meal how much they would like to donate to the restaurant. It's a warm and friendly place, full of charm, and with an antimammon stance that is refreshing in worldly Singapore. Fridays, Saturdays, and Sundays lunch and dinner are served buffet-style; other days it's a la carte.

133 New Bridge Rd., #B1–02 Chinatown Point, Podium A. © **65/6339-9993.** Reservations not necessary. S$1–S$20. No credit cards. Daily 11am–3pm and 6–9:30pm.

Blue Ginger ★ PERANAKAN   The standard belief is that Peranakan cooking is reserved for home-cooked meals, and therefore restaurants are not as plentiful—and, where they do exist, are very informal. Not so at Blue Ginger, where traditional and modern mix beautifully. Located in a shophouse, the decor combines clean and neat lines of contemporary styling with paintings by local artists and touches of Peranakan flair like carved wooden screens. The cuisine is Peranakan from traditional recipes, making for some very authentic food—definitely something you can't get back home. A good appetizer is the *kueh pie tee*: bite-size "top hats" filled with turnip, egg, and prawn with sweet chili sauce. A wonderful entree is the *ayam panggang* "Blue Ginger," really tender grilled, boneless chicken thigh and drumstick with a mild coconut-milk sauce. One of the most popular dishes is the *ayam buah keluak* (my favorite), a traditional chicken dish made with a hard black Indonesian nut with sweetmeat inside. The favorite dessert here is *durian chendol,* red beans and *pandan* jelly in coconut milk with *durian* purée. Served with shaved ice on top, it smells strong—though they can make a durian-free version for guests who aren't fans of the pungent fruit.

97 Tanjong Pagar Rd. ℭ **65/6222-3928.** www.theblueginger.com. Reservations recommended. Small dishes S$3.20–S$38. AE, DC, MC, V. Daily noon–2:30pm and 6:30–9:45pm.

Chen Fu Ji Fried Rice SINGAPOREAN   With bright fluorescent lighting, the fast-food ambience is nothing to write home about, but the riverside views are pleasant, and after you try the fried rice here, you'll never be able to eat it anywhere else again, ever. These people take loving care of each fluffy grain, frying the egg evenly throughout. The other ingredients are added abundantly, and there's no hint of oil. On the top is a crown of shredded crabmeat. If you've never been an aficionado, you'll be one now. The spicy chicken with cashew nuts and spring onions is delicious, and their soups are also very good. There is an additional branch, the **Chen Fu Ji Noodle House,** at Suntec City Mall, 3 Temasek Blvd. #03–020 Sky Garden (ℭ **65/6334-2966**), and the true devotee can grab a bowl before boarding a plane at Changi's Terminal 2 transit lounge (ℭ **65/6542-8097**).

#02–31 Riverside Point, 30 Merchant Rd. ℭ **65/6533-0166.** Reservations not accepted. Small dishes S$10–S$20. AE, DC, MC, V. Daily noon–2:30pm and 6–9:45pm.

Ma Maison ASIAN/FUSION   This cozy little timber-paneled place is tucked away in a mall between the Historic District and Chinatown. Try to get a window seat for views over the river and Clarke Quay, while you browse an eclectic menu that ranges from hamburgers and pasta to *tonkatsu,* a pork cutlet in light Japanese breadcrumbs, fried and served with rice, pickles, and shredded cabbage. Most of the Western dishes have an Asian twist to them and are often served with rich Japanese-style tomato or brown sauce. The house special is a comforting, rich beef stew. The predominantly Japanese staff is friendly and attentive.

6 Eu Tong St., The Central #03–96. ℭ **65/6327-8122.** Reservations recommended on weekends. Main courses S$13–S$22. AE, DC, MC, V. Daily 11:30am–3pm and 6–10pm.

Rendezvous MALAY/INDONESIAN   Line up to select from a large number of Malay dishes, cafeteria-style, like sambal squid in a spicy sauce of chili and shrimp paste, and beef *rendang,* in a dark spicy curry gravy. The waitstaff will bring your order to your table. The old-style coffee shop setting instills a sense of nostalgia for locals. On the wall, black-and-white photos trace the restaurant's history back to its opening in the early 1950s. It's a great place to experiment with a new cuisine.

6 Eu Tong Sen St. #02–72, The Central (above Clarke Quay MRT). ℭ **65/6339-7508.** Reservations not necessary. Meat dishes sold per piece S$4–S$7. AE, DC, MC, V. Daily 11am–9pm. Closed on public holidays.

Yum Cha ★ CHINESE   Dim sum aficionados swear by Yum Cha's crystal chive dumplings, tiny translucent parcels of chunky fresh prawns and herbs, as well as the soft-shell crabs and delicious steamed dumplings filled with meat and clear broth called *xiao long bao.* The main attraction certainly isn't the service, which tends to be a little brusque at the best of times, even more so on weekends, when the place is packed with families and groups of friends. Get there early to compete for the attention of the trolley-wielding waitresses (especially if you want help with ordering) and try to leave room for the gorgeous miniature baked egg tarts.

20 Trengganu St. ℭ **65/6372-1717.** Reservations recommended. Small dishes S$2.50–S$8. AE, DC, MC, V. Daily 8am–10:30pm.

Little India & Arab Street
INEXPENSIVE

The French Stall ★★ 🔪 FRENCH   Well known among Singapore's expatriate residents, The French Stall is a surprising find in Little India. In a corner coffee shop, this alfresco bistro is homey and comfortable. The simple French fare includes favorites such as escargots, ratatouille, beef bourguignon, and chicken-liver pâté, which are prepared well and served in good portions for a very affordable price. A small selection of reasonably priced wines are served by the bottle or glass. Leave room for homemade desserts like tiramisu and profiteroles in chocolate sauce.

544 Serangoon Rd. (opposite the Shell petrol station). ℭ **65/6299-3544.** Reservations not necessary. Main courses S$16–S$22. MC, V. Tues–Sun 3–6pm (desserts only) and 6–10pm.

Komala Vilas ★ SOUTHERN INDIAN   Komala Vilas is famous with Singaporeans of every race. Don't expect the height of ambience—it's pure fast food, local-style—but to sit here during a packed and noisy lunch hour is to see all walks of life come through the doors. Komala serves vegetarian dishes in southern Indian style, so there's nothing fancy about the food; it's just plain good. Order the *dosai*, a huge, thin pancake used to scoop up luscious and hearty gravies and curries. Even for carnivores, it's very satisfying. What's more, it's cheap: Two samosas, *dosai*, and an assortment of stew-style gravies (*dhal*) for two are under S$10, with tea. For a quick fast-food meal, this place is second to none.

76–78 Serangoon Rd. ℭ **65/6392-6980.** www.komalavilas.com.sg. Reservations not accepted. Dosai S$2.05; lunch for 2 S$14. No credit cards. Daily 7am–10:30pm.

Muthu's Curry Restaurant SOUTHERN INDIAN   Muthu's is a local institution that is synonymous with one local delicacy: fish-head curry, a giant fish head floating in a huge portion of delicious curry soup, its eye staring and teeth grinning. The cheek meat is the best part of the fish, but to be truly polite, let your friend eat the eye. The list of accompanying dishes is long and includes crab *masala,* chicken *biryani,* and mutton curry, with fish cutlet and fried chicken sold by the piece. We're not talking the height of dining elegance here, but Muthu's really has come a long way since its simple coffee shop opening, with its recent shift to newer, larger digs, with matching tables and chairs, and waitstaff taking orders on PDAs! I miss the old grotty ambience, but still it's a good place to try this dish. Go either at the start or toward the end of mealtime so you don't get lost in the rush and can find staff with more time to help you. There's another branch in town at 3 Temasek Blvd., #B1–056, Suntec City Mall (ℭ **65/6835-7707**).

138 Race Course Rd. ℭ **65/6392-1722.** www.muthuscurry.com. Reservations recommended. Small dishes S$4–S$13; fish-head curry from S$20. AE, DC, MC, V. Daily 10am–10pm.

Sabar Menanti INDONESIAN/MALAY   Nasi padang originated in Padang, Sumatra, where rice was served with vegetables and meats stewed in delicious coconut-based gravies alongside tangy fried chicken, barbecued fish in chili, and the most famous dish of all, beef rending, chucks of beef in a "dry" coconut and chili sauce. This place serves the most authentic nasi padang in Singapore, but you must come early before they run out. Join the queue and choose your dishes, and servers will scoop out your choices on a plate of rice. You will be charged by your individual selections.

48 Kandahar St. ☎ **65/6396-6919.** www.sabarmenanti.com.sg. Reservations not accepted. Meal for one S$5.50–S$11. No credit cards. Daily 11am–2pm.

Orchard Road Area

VERY EXPENSIVE

Iggy's ★★★ CONTEMPORARY EUROPEAN   Deliciously exclusive, Iggy's invites gourmands to dine at one of only six tables. Behind glass doors, culinary works of art are prepared in a kitchen that is twice the size of the dining room. White truffles, *foie gras,* beef *tartare,* venison, hearts of palm, and other treasured ingredients are crafted into dishes as sumptuous as they are artful. (In 2010, Iggy's was rated the number-one restaurant in Asia by *The Miele Guide* and ranked number 28 in *S Pellegrino World's 50 Best Restaurants.*) Owner Ignatius Chan is Singapore's most beloved sommelier; the wine selection is exceptional. The tantalizing dessert bar also has an open kitchen concept. Guests can also dine in the cozy lounge.

581 Orchard Rd., The Hilton, Level 3. ☎ **65/6732-2234.** www.iggys.com.sg. Reservations required. Prices vary according to seasonal availability. 7-course dinner menu S$195. AE, MC, V. Mon–Fri noon–1:30pm and 7–9:30pm; Sat 7–9:30pm.

EXPENSIVE

Mezza9 ★★ FUSION   This is your best bet if your party can't agree on what to eat because Mezza9 offers an extensive menu that includes Chinese steamed treats, Japanese, Thai, deli selections, Italian, fresh seafood, and Continental grilled specialties. Start with big and juicy raw oysters on the half-shell. If you want to consider more raw seafood, the combination sashimi platter is also very fresh. Grilled meats include various cuts of beef, rack of lamb, and chicken dishes, with a host of delicious sides to choose from. The enormous 400-seat restaurant has a warm atmosphere, with glowing wood and contemporary Zen accents, but service can be harried. Before you head in for dinner, grab a martini in their *très* chic martini bar.

Grand Hyatt, 10 Scotts Rd. ☎ **65/6732-1234.** www.singapore.grand.hyatt.com. Reservations recommended. Main courses S$40–S$100. AE, DC, MC, V. Daily noon–3pm and 6–11:30pm.

MODERATE

Ah Hoi's Kitchen SINGAPOREAN   I like Ah Hoi's for its casual charm and its selection of authentic local cuisine. The menu is extensive, specializing in local favorites like fried black pepper *kuay teow* (noodles), *sambal kang kong* (a spinachlike vegetable fried with chili), and fabulous grilled seafood. The alfresco poolside pavilion location gives it a real "vacation in the Tropics" sort of relaxed feel—think of a hawker center without the dingy florescent bulbs, greasy tables, and sludgy floor. Also good here is the chili crab—if you can't make it out to the seafood places on the east coast of the island, it's the best alternative for tasting this local treat. Make sure you order the fresh lime juice. It's very cooling.

Traders Hotel, 1A Cuscaden Rd., Level 4. ☎ **65/6831-4373.** Reservations recommended. Small dishes S$12–S$35. AE, DC, MC, V. Daily noon–2:30pm and 6:30–10:30pm.

Chatterbox SINGAPOREAN   If you'd like to try the local favorites but don't want to deal with hawker food, then Chatterbox is the place for you. This restaurant is located in the Meritus Mandarin Hotel. Their Hainanese chicken rice is highly acclaimed, and the other dishes—like *nasi lemak, laksa,* and carrot cake—are as close to the street as you can get. For a quick and tasty snack, order *tahu goreng,* deep-fried tofu in peanut chili sauce. This is also a good place to experiment with some of those really weird local drinks. *Chin chow* is the dark brown grass jelly drink; *chendol* is green jelly, red beans, palm sugar, and coconut milk; and *bandung* is pink rose syrup milk with jelly. For dessert, order the ever-favorite sago pudding, made from the hearts of the sago palm.

Mandarin Hotel, 333 Orchard Rd. *C* **65/6831-6291.** Reservations recommended for lunch and dinner. Main courses S$21–S$48. AE, DC, MC, V. Sun–Thurs 5pm–1am; Fri–Sat 24 hr.

Coca Steamboat ★ CHINESE/SINGAPOREAN   Beloved by Singaporeans, a steamboat is a tureen of stock that's kept simmering at the table. Diners choose a flavor of stock and add side vegetables, fish, and meats, which are dipped into the broth to cook, then eaten. The best part of the meal is at the end, when the flavored stock is enjoyed as a soup on its own or with rice. Coco has a huge range of side dishes and consistently good, fresh ingredients, from simple cuts of meat to authentic Singaporean staples like fish balls. I particularly like the duck breast and the wontons, and there's a good selection of unusual mushrooms. Throw caution to the winds and pick some old favorites and new flavors, dipped in the signature chili sauce if you like it spicy. Not a place to choose if you're in a hurry, but great fun for families and groups.

International Bldg., 360 Orchard Rd., #02-05. *C* **65/6738-2588.** Reservations recommended. Lunch buffet S$20–S$25, dinner buffet S$33–S$45. AE, DC, MC, V. Daily 11am–3:45pm and 4–10pm.

Patara Fine Thai THAI   Patara may say "fine" dining in its name, but the food here is home cooking: not too haute, not too traditional. Seafood and vegetables are the stars here. Deep-fried *garoupa* (grouper) is served in a sweet sauce with chili that can be added sparingly upon request. Curries are popular, too. The roast duck curry in red curry paste with seasonal fruits is juicy and hot. For something really different, Patara's own invention, the Thai taco, isn't exactly traditional, but it is good, filled with chicken, shrimp, and sprouts. Their green curry, one of my favorites, is perhaps the best in town. Their Thai-style iced tea (which isn't on the menu, so you'll have to ask for it) is fragrant and flowery. A small selection of wines is also available. Patara has another outlet at Swissôtel The Stamford, Level 3, Stamford Road (*C* **65/6339-1488**).

#03-14 Tanglin Mall, 163 Tanglin Rd. *C* **65/6737-0818.** www.patara.com.sg. Reservations recommended for lunch, required for dinner. Small dishes S$12–S$39. AE, DC, MC, V. Daily noon–2:30pm and 6–10pm.

INEXPENSIVE

Din Tai Fung ◢ DIM SUM   Taiwan-based Din Tai Fung has outlets all over the Asia Pacific region, including nine in Singapore—the Paragon Shopping Centre location was its first here. Famous for excellent quality dim sum at an affordable price, this eatery has become a standard for Singaporean Chinese. The menu is not extensive, but covers all the bases: dumplings and buns, rice and noodle dishes, soup, cold dishes, and vegetables. Other convenient locations are **Wisma Atria** (435 Orchard Rd., #02–48/43; *C* **65/6732-1383**), **Raffles City Shopping Centre** (252 North Bridge Rd., #B1–08/09/10; *C* **65/6336-6369**), **313 @ Somerset** (313 Orchard Rd., #B2–01/02/03; *C* **65/6509-6696**), and **Resorts World Sentosa** (26 Sentosa Gateway, #01–217/222; *C* **65/6686-3565**).

Paragon Shopping Centre, #B1-03/06, 290 Orchard Rd. *C* **65/6836-8336.** Reservations recommended. S$5–S$14. MC, V. Mon–Fri 11am–9:30pm; Sat–Sun 10am–9:30pm.

The Rice Table ★ MALAY/INDONESIAN/DUTCH   Indonesian Dutch rijst-tafel, meaning "rice table," is a service of many small dishes (up to almost 20) with rice. Traditionally, each dish would be brought to diners by beautiful ladies in pomp-ous style. Here, busy waitstaff brings all the dishes out and places them in front of you—feast on favorite Indo-Malay wonders like beef *rendang,* chicken satay, *otak otak,* and *sotong assam* (squid) for a very reasonable price. It's an enormous amount of food and everything is terrific. You will pay extra for your drinks and desserts.

International Bldg., 360 Orchard Rd., #02-09/10. ✆ **65/6835-3783.** www.ricetable.com.sg. Reserva-tions not necessary. Set lunch S$18; set dinner S$29. AE, DC, MC, V. Daily noon–2:15pm and 6–9:15pm.

Shimbashi Soba 🍴 ☺ JAPANESE   It's easy to identify Shimbashi's specialty from the chef who works behind a glass wall, preparing fresh soba noodles at every stage from the grindstone that mills the wheat into flour to the table where he kneads and rolls the dough before slicing each noodle by hand. Glance at the walls, and you'll see photos of the fields in Hokkaido and Tasmania where the buckwheat grew. Whether you slurp them hot in a clear, tasty broth or munch them cold and dipped in sauce, these are the best in town. Reservations aren't accepted, and if you hit the lunchtime or evening rush, you might have to wait, but the line moves quickly. The busy waitstaff are really friendly and pleasant with kids.

#B1-41 Paragon, 290 Orchard Rd. ✆ **65/6735-9882.** Reservations not accepted. Set meals S$15–S$30. AE, DC, MC, V. Daily 11:30am–9:30pm.

A Little Farther Out

Many travelers will choose to eat in town for convenience, and although there's plenty of great dining in the more central areas, there are some other really fantastic dining finds if you're willing to hop in a cab for 10 or 15 minutes.

EXPENSIVE

Halia ★ CONTINENTAL/FUSION   You really need to come to Halia, most notable for its location within the aromatic ginger garden of the Singapore Botanic Gardens, for a daytime meal—a weekend breakfast buffet, relaxing lunch, or weekday high tea, if you want to enjoy the lush greenery of the surroundings. Cuisine is con-temporary fare, with ginger permeating quite a few of the recipes—*halia* being "gin-ger" in Malay. The specialty of the house is the chunks of seafood stewed in Asian flavors of chili and lemon grass served over a bed of *papardelle* pasta. To get there, ask the taxi driver to take you along Tyersall Avenue, and look for the HALIA signboard at the Tyersall Gate near the Ginger Garden.

1 Cluny Rd., in the Singapore Botanic Gardens, Tyersall Gate. ✆ **65/6476-6711.** www.halia.com.sg. Reservations recommended. Main courses S$34–S$120. AE, DC, MC, V. Mon–Fri noon–3pm; high tea 3–5pm; dinner 6:30–10:15pm; Sat–Sun breakfast/brunch 9am–3:30pm.

MODERATE

Long Beach Seafood Restaurant SEAFOOD   They really pack 'em in at this place. Tables are crammed together in what resembles a big indoor pavilion, complete with festive lights and the sounds of mighty feasting. This is one of the best places for fresh seafood of all kinds: fish like *garoupa* (grouper), sea bass, marble goby, and kingfish, and other creatures of the sea, from prawns to crayfish. The chili crab here is good, but the house specialty is really the pepper crab, chopped and deliciously smothered in a thick concoction of black pepper and soy. Huge chunks of crayfish are also tasty in the black pepper sauce and can be served in variations like barbecue, sambal, steamed with garlic, or in a bean sauce. Don't forget to order buns so you can sop up the sauce. You can also get vegetable, chicken, beef, or venison dishes to complement, or choose from their menu selection of local favorites. Long Beach now has several branches, including at Dempsey Hill (25 Dempsey Rd., opposite the Botanic Gardens; ℗ **65/6323-2222**).

1018 E. Coast Pkwy. ℗ **65/6338-9398.** www.longbeachseafood.com.sg. Reservations recommended. Seafood is sold by weight according to seasonal prices; most nonseafood dishes S$11–S$22. AE, DC, MC, V. Daily 11am–3pm; Sun–Fri 5pm–12:15am; Sat 5pm–1:15am.

Original Sin ★ MEDITERRANEAN/VEGETARIAN   This cozy place is a perennial favorite with Singapore's expatriate population. Located in Holland Village, Singapore's expat enclave, this particular restaurant is a favorite, with generous portions of baba ghanouj, *tzatziki,* and hummus served with olives, feta, and pita bread. And although the menu features standard Mediterranean fare like moussaka and risotto dishes, people always seem to go for the pizzas, which are loaded with interesting Middle Eastern toppings. The owners also run another restaurant in Chip Bee Gardens, the casual bistro-style Italian **Michelangelo's** (Block 44, Jalan Merah Saga #01–60; ℗ **65/6475-9069**).

Block 43 Jalan Merah Saga, #01-62, Chip Bee Gardens, Holland Village. ℗ **65/6475-5605.** www. originalsin.com.sg. Reservations recommended. Main courses S$22–S$28. AE, DC, MC, V. Tues–Sun 11:30am–2:30pm and 6-10:30pm; Mon 6–10:30pm.

UDMC Seafood Centre ★★ SEAFOOD   Eight seafood restaurants are lined side by side in 2 blocks, their fronts open to the view of the sea outside. UDMC is a fantastic way to eat seafood Singapore-style, in the open air, in restaurants that are more like grand stalls than anything else. Eat the famous local chili crab and pepper crab here, along with all sorts of squid, fish, and scallop dishes. Noodle dishes are also available, as are vegetable dishes and other meats. But the seafood is the thing to come for. Of the eight restaurants, there's no saying which is the best, as everyone seems to have his own opinions about this one or that one (I like Jumbo, at the far eastern end of the row; call ℗ **65/6442-3435** for reservations, which are recommended for weekends). Have a nice stroll along the walkway and gaze out to the water while you decide which one to go for.

Block 1202 E. Coast Pkwy. No phone. Seafood dishes are charged by weight, with dishes starting from around S$14. AE, DC, MC, V. Daily 5pm–midnight.

INEXPENSIVE

Samy's Curry Restaurant ★ SOUTHERN INDIAN   There are many places in Singapore to get good southern Indian banana leaf, but none quite so unique as Samy's out on Dempsey Road. Samy's is situated in a huge, high-ceilinged, open-air hall, with shutters thrown back and fans whirring above. Wash your hands at the back and have a seat, and soon someone will slap a banana-leaf place mat in front of you. A blob of white rice will be placed in the center, and then buckets of vegetables, chicken, mutton, fish, prawn, and you-name-it will be brought out, swimming in the richest and spiciest curries to ever pass your lips. Take a peek in each bucket, nod your head yes when you see one you like, and a scoop will be dumped on your banana leaf. Eat with your right hand or with a fork and spoon. When you're done, wipe the sweat from your brow, fold the banana leaf away from you, and place your tableware on top. Samy's serves no alcohol, but the fresh lime juice is nice and cooling, and lassi, the flavored yogurt drink, helps to counteract the spiciness.

Block 25 Dempsey Rd., Civil Service Club. ℗ **65/6472-2080.** www.samyscurry.com. Reservations not accepted. Sold by the scoop or piece, S80¢–S$4. V. Daily 11am–3pm and 6–10pm. No alcohol served.

HAWKER CENTERS These large groupings of informal open-air food stalls were Singapore's answer to fast and cheap food in the days before McDonald's and are still the best way to sample every kind of Singaporean cuisine. The traditional hawker center is an outdoor venue, usually under cover with fans whirring above, and individual stalls each specializing in different dishes. In between rows of cooking stalls, tables and stools offer open seating for diners.

CAFE SOCIETY In Singapore, traditions such as British high tea and the Chinese tea ceremony live side by side with a growing coffee culture. These popular hangouts are all over the city. Following are a few places to try.

BRITISH HIGH TEA Two fabulous places to take high tea in style are at **Raffles Bar & Billiard Room** at Raffles Hotel, 1 Beach Rd. (© **65/6412-1816**), and **Equinox** at Swissôtel The Stamford, 2 Stamford Rd. (© **65/6431-6156**). Both places are lovely, if pricey. The buffet will cost anywhere from S$33 to S$38, more at peak seasons. High tea is served in the afternoons from 3 to 5 or 5:30pm.

CHINESE TEA There are a few places in Chinatown where tea is still as important today as it has always been in Chinese culture. **The Tea Chapter,** 9–11A Neil Rd. (© **65/6226-1175**), and **Yixing Xuan,** 30–32 Tanjong Pagar Rd. (© **65/6224-6961**), offer tranquil respites from the day and cultural insight into Chinese tea appreciation.

CAFES Western-style coffee joints have been popping up left and right all over the island, so coffee-addicted travelers can rest assured that in the morning their favorite blends are brewing close by—as long as you don't mind spending up to S$7 for a cup of brew. **Starbucks,** the **Coffee Bean & Tea Leaf,** the **Coffee Club, Spinelli,** and many more international chain cafes have outlets in just about every shopping mall in the city.

WHAT TO SEE & DO

Of Singapore's many sights and attractions, the city's many old buildings and well presented museum displays bring history to life. Chinese and Hindu temples and Muslim mosques welcome curious observers to discover their culture as they play out their daily activities, and the country's natural parks make the great outdoors easily accessible from even the most urban neighborhood. That's the best benefit of traveling in Singapore: Most attractions are situated within the heart of the city, and those that lie outside the urban center still can be easily reached.

A *note:* Many of the sights to see in Singapore are not of the "pay your fee and see the show" variety, but rather historic buildings, monuments, and places of religious worship. The places of worship listed in this chapter are open to the public and free of entrance charge. Expect temples to be open from sunup to sundown. Visiting hours are not specific to the hour, but unless it's a holiday (when hours may be extended), you can expect these places to be open during daylight hours.

The Historic District

Armenian Church ★ Of all colonial buildings, the Armenian Church (more formally called the Church of St. Gregory the Illuminator) is one of the most beautiful examples of early architectural style here. Designed by George Coleman, one of Singapore's most prolific and talented architects, it is his finest work. Although there were many alterations in the last century, the main style of the structure still dominates. The round congregation hall is powerful in its simplicity, its long louvered windows letting in cooling breezes while keeping out the imposing sunlight. Roman Doric columns support symmetrical porticos that protect the structure from rain. All in all, it's a wonderful achievement of combined European eclectic tastes and tropical necessity.

The first permanent Christian church in Singapore, it was funded primarily by the Armenian community, which was at one time quite powerful. Today few Singaporeans can trace their heritage back to this influential group of immigrants. The church was consecrated in 1836, and the last appointed priest serving the parish retired in 1936. Although regular Armenian services are no longer held, other religious organizations make use of the church from time to time. The cemetery in the back of the church is the burial site of many prominent Armenians, including Ashgen Agnes Joaquim, who discovered the Vanda Miss Joaquim, Singapore's national flower.

60 Hill St., across from the Grand Plaza Park Hotel. No phone. Free admission. 15-min. walk from City Hall MRT.

Asian Civilisations Museum ★★★   If you have time for only one museum, this is the one I recommend. This fantastic and well executed exhibit of Southeast Asian culture highlights the history of the region and explores the Chinese, South Indian, and Islamic heritage that helped to shape regional cultures here. Well planned galleries showcase fine arts, furniture, porcelain, jade, and other relics with excellent descriptions.

The Empress Place Building that houses the museum stood as a symbol of British colonial authority as sea travelers entered the Singapore River. The stately building housed almost the entire government bureaucracy around the year 1905 and was a government office until the 1980s, specifically the Registry of Births and Deaths and the Citizenship Registry.

Don't forget to stop at the Museum Shop (© **65/6336-9050**) to browse exquisite ethnic crafts of the region. Also, check out the museum's website to find out more about their free lecture series.

1 Empress Place. © **65/6332-7798.** www.acm.org.sg. Admission S$8 adults, S$4 children and seniors; discounted admission Fri 7–9pm. Mon 1–7pm; Tues–Sun 9am–7pm (extended hours Fri 9am–9pm). Free guided tours in English Mon 2pm, Tues–Fri 11am and 2pm, with an extra tour on weekends at 3pm. 5-min walk from Raffles Place MRT.

Cathedral of the Good Shepherd   This cathedral was Singapore's first permanent Catholic church. Built in the 1840s, it unified many elements of a fractured parish. In the early days of the colony, the Portuguese Mission thought itself the fount of the Holy Roman Empire's presence on the island, and so the French bishop was reduced to holding services at the home of a Mr. McSwiney on Bras Basah Road, a dissenting Portuguese priest held services at a certain Dr. d'Ameida's residence, and the Spanish priest was so reduced that we don't even know where he held his services. These folks were none too pleased with their makeshift houses of worship and so banded together to establish their own cathedral—the Cathedral of the Good Shepherd. Designed in a Latin cross pattern, much of its architecture is reminiscent of St. Martin-in-the-Fields and St. Paul's in Covent Garden. The archbishop's residence, in contrast, is a simple two-story bungalow with enclosed verandas and a portico. Also on the grounds are the residents' quarters and the priests' residence, the latter more ornate in design, with elaborate plasterwork.

4 Queen St. (at the corner of Queen St. and Bras Basah Rd.). © **65/6337-2036.** Free admission. Open to the public during the day. 5-min. walk from City Hall MRT.

Urban Singapore Attractions

HISTORIC DISTRICT
Armenian Church **19**
Asian Civilisations Museum **31**
Boat Quay **29**
Cathedral of the Good Shepherd **14**
CHIJMES (Convent of the
  Holy Infant Jesus) **16**
City Hall (Municipal Building) **23**
Clarke Quay **28**
Esplanade Park **25**
Fort Canning Park **18**
Hill Street Building **21**
Kuan Yin Thong
  Hood Cho Temple **12**
Marina Bay Sands **42**
Merlion Park **32**
National Museum of Singapore **13**
Old Parliament House **27**
The Padang **24**
Peranakan Museum **17**
Raffles Hotel **15**
Raffles Landing Site **30**
Singapore Art Museum **13**
Singapore Flyer **26**
Singapore Philatelic Museum **20**
Sri Thandayuthapani Temple **3**
St. Andrew's Cathedral **22**
Statue of Raffles **31**
Supreme Court **23**
Victoria Theatre and Concert Hall **31**

CHINATOWN
Al-Abrar Mosque **39**
Chinatown Heritage Centre **34**
Jamae Mosque **35**
Lau Pa Sat Festival Pavilion **41**
Nagore Durgha Shrine **40**
Sacred Buddha Tooth Temple **37**
Singapore City Gallery **38**
Sri Mariamman Hindu Temple **36**
Thian Hock Keng Temple **40**
Wak Hai Cheng Bio Temple **33**

LITTLE INDIA
Abdul Gafoor Mosque **8**
Sakya Muni Buddha Gaya
  (Temple of a Thousand Lights) **4**
Sri Perumal Temple **5**
Sri Veerama Kaliamman Temple **6**

ARAB STREET & KAMPONG GLAM
Alsagoff Arab School **9**
Hajjah Fatimah Mosque **10**
Malay Heritage Centre
  (Istana Kampong Glam) **11**
Sultan Mosque **11**

ORCHARD ROAD AREA
ION Sky **1**
The Istana and Sri Temasek **7**
Peranakan Place **2**

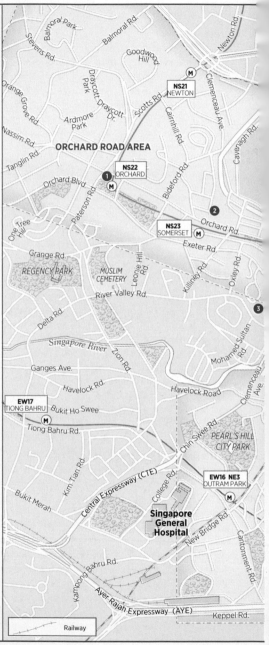

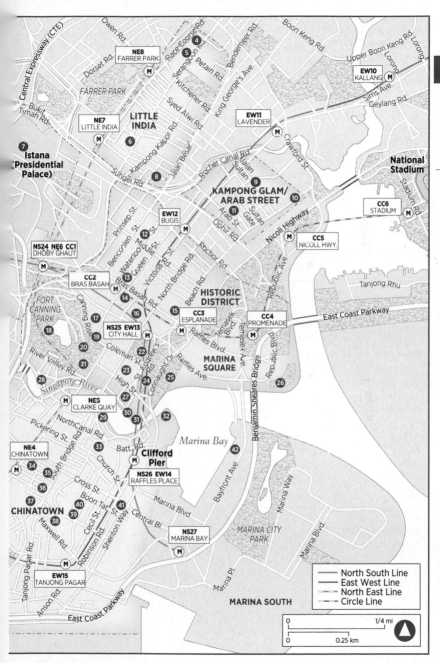

NE8
FARRER PARK

EW10
KALLANG

FARRER PARK

NE7
LITTLE INDIA

LITTLE INDIA

EW11
LAVENDER

National Stadium

Istana (Presidential Palace)

KAMPONG GLAM/ ARAB STREET

CC6
STADIUM

EW12
BUGIS

CC5
NICOLL HWY.

NS24 NE6 CC1
DHOBY GHAUT

CC2
BRAS BASAH

HISTORIC DISTRICT

CC3
ESPLANADE

CC4
PROMENADE

FORT CANNING PARK

NS25 EW13
CITY HALL

Tanjong Rhu

MARINA SQUARE

NE5
CLARKE QUAY

MARINA SQUARE

NE4
CHINATOWN

Clifford Pier

Marina Bay

NS26 EW14
RAFFLES PLACE

CHINATOWN

NS27
MARINA BAY

MARINA CITY PARK

EW15
TANJONG PAGAR

MARINA SOUTH

North South Line
East West Line
North East Line
Circle Line

0 .... 1/4 mi

0 .... 0.25 km

CHIJMES (Convent of the Holy Infant Jesus) As you enter this bustling enclave of retail shops, restaurants, and nightspots, it's difficult to imagine this was once a convent which, at its founding in 1854, consisted of a lone, simply constructed bungalow. After decades of buildings and add-ons, this collection of unique yet perfectly blended structures—a school, a private residence, an orphanage, a stunning Gothic chapel, and many others—was enclosed within walls, forming peaceful courtyards and open spaces encompassing an entire city block. Legend has it the small door on the corner of Bras Basah and Victoria streets welcomed hundreds of orphan babies, girl children who just appeared on the stoop each morning, born either during inauspicious years or to poor families. In late 1983, the convent relocated to the suburbs, and some of the block was leveled to make way for the MRT Headquarters. Thankfully, most of it survived and the Singapore government, in planning the renovation of this desirable piece of real estate, wisely kept the integrity of the architecture. For an evening out, the atmosphere at CHIJMES is exquisitely romantic.

A note on the name: CHIJMES is pronounced "Chimes"; the "Chij," as noted, stands for Convent of the Holy Infant Jesus, and the "mes" was just added on so they could pronounce it "Chimes."

30 Victoria St. ✆ **65/6337-7810.** Free admission. 5-min. walk from City Hall MRT.

City Hall (Municipal Building)   During the Japanese Occupation, City Hall was a major headquarters, and it was here in 1945 that Adm. Lord Louis Mountbatten accepted the Japanese surrender. In 1951, the Royal Proclamation from King George VI was read here declaring that Singapore would henceforth be known as a city. Fourteen years later, Prime Minister Lee Kuan Yew announced to its citizens that Singapore would henceforth be called an independent republic.

City Hall, along with the Supreme Court, was judiciously sited to take full advantage of its prime location. Magnificent Corinthian columns march across the front of the symmetrically designed building, while inside, two courtyards lend an ambience of informality to otherwise officious surroundings. For all its magnificence and historical fame, however, its architect, F. D. Meadows, relied too heavily on European influence. The many windows afford no protection from the sun, and the entrance leaves pedestrians unsheltered from the elements. In defining the very nobility of the Singapore government, it appears the Singaporean climate wasn't taken into consideration.

At press time, City Hall and the Supreme Court were undergoing a massive renovation that will transform them into a new National Art Gallery, which will house the nation's collection of Southeast Asian art and provide a platform for major international exhibitions. The project is slated for completion in 2013.

3 St. Andrew's Rd., across from the Padang. Entrance is not permitted. 5-min. walk from City Hall MRT.

Fort Canning Park   These days, Fort Canning Park is known for great views over Singapore, but in days past it served as the site of Raffles's home and the island's first botanic garden. Its history goes back even farther, though: Excavations have unearthed ancient brick foundations and artifacts that give credence to the island natives' belief that their royal ancestors lived and were buried on the site. Atop the hill, a mysterious *keramat,* or sacred grave, marks what is believed to be the burial site of Iskander Shah (also known as Parameswara), the Palembang ruler who came to Singapore in the late 1300s before settling in Melaka.

From the start, Raffles chose this hill to build his home (at the site of the present-day lookout point), which later became a residence for Singapore's diplomats and governors. In 1860, the house was torn down to make way for Fort Canning, which was built to quell British fears of invasion but instead quickly became the laughing-stock of the island. The location was ideal for spotting invaders from the sea, but defending Singapore? Not likely. The cannons' range was such that their shells couldn't possibly have made it all the way out to an attacking ship—instead, most of the town below would have been destroyed. In 1907, the fort was demolished for a reservoir. Today the only reminders of the old fort are some of the walls and the Fort Gate, a deep stone structure. Behind its huge wooden door you'll find a narrow stair-case that leads to the roof.

Raffles also chose this as the location for the first botanic garden on the island, with ambitious plans to develop commercial crops, particularly spices. The garden was short-lived due to lack of funding; however, the park still has a pretty interesting selection of plants and trees, like the cannonball tree with its large round seed pods, and the cotton tree, whose pods open to reveal fluffy white "cotton" that was com-monly used for stuffing pillows and mattresses. In many parts, these plants are well marked along the pathways. Also look for the ASEAN sculpture garden; five members of the Association of Southeast Asian Nations each donated a work for the park in 1982 to represent the region's unity.

Fort Canning was also the site of a **European cemetery.** To make improvements in the park, the graves were exhumed and the stones placed within the walls sur-rounding the outdoor performance field that slopes from the Music and Drama Society building. A large Gothic monument was erected in memory of James Napier Brooke, infant son of William Napier, Singapore's first law agent, and his wife, Maria Frances, the widow of prolific architect George Coleman. Although no records exist, Coleman probably designed the cupolas as well as two small monuments over unknown graves. The Music and Drama Society building itself was built in 1938. Close by, in the wall, are the tombstones of Coleman and of Jose D'Almeida, a wealthy Portuguese merchant.

Inside the park, the **Battle Box** is an old World War II bunker that displays in wax dioramas and a multimedia show the surrender of Singapore. It's open daily from 10am to 6pm; adults S$8, children S$4 (✆ **65/6333-0510**).

The National Parks Board gives free guided tours of the park, but not the Battle Box, every last Saturday of the month at 4pm; call ✆ **65/6332-1302** to register.

51 Canning Rise. ✆ **65/6332-1302.** www.nparks.gov.sg. Free admission. Major entrances are from behind the Hill Street Building, Percival Rd. (Drama Centre), National Library Carpark, and Canning Walk (behind Park Mall). Dhoby Ghaut or City Hall MRT.

Hill Street Building   Originally built to house the British Police Force, the build-ing was sited directly across from Chinatown for easy access to quell the frequent gang fights. Later it became home to the National Archives, and it is believed that inquisitions and torture were carried out in the basement during the Japanese Occu-pation. Former National Archives employees claimed to have seen ghosts of tortured souls sitting at their desks.

Today this colorful building houses the Ministry of Information, Communications and the Arts (MICA), and the National Arts Council. Inside the courtyard, check out ARTrium@MICA, with galleries displaying Singaporean, Southeast Asian, and Euro-pean fine arts. It's air-conditioned!

140 Hill St. at the corner of River Valley Rd., on Fort Canning Park. www.artriumatmica.com. Free admis-sion. 5-min. walk from Clarke Quay MRT.

Kuan Yin Thong Hood Cho Temple   It's said that whatever you wish for within the walls of Kuan Yin Temple comes true, so get in line and have your wish ready. It must work, as there's a steady stream of people on auspicious days of the Chinese calendar. The procedure is simple (watch others to catch on): Wear shoes easily slipped off before entering the temple and join the queue. When it is your turn, light several joss sticks, bow with them, and make a wish before placing them in the urn provided. Pick up the cylindrical container filled with wooden sticks and shake it until one stick falls out—each stick has a number. Give this number to the interpretation office and they will hand you a piece of paper with verses in Mandarin and English. This will tell you your general fortune, plus a clue as to whether your wish will come true. (For a small fee, interpreters outside can help with the translation.) Now for the payback: If your wish comes true, you're supposed to return to the temple and offer fruits and flowers to say thanks (oranges, pears, and apples are a thoughtful choice, and jasmine petals are especially nice). So be careful what you wish for. After you're back home and that job promotion comes through, your new manager might nix a trip back to Singapore to bring fruits to this little temple. To be on the safe side, bring the goods with you when you make your wish.

178 Waterloo St., about 1½ blocks from Bras Basah Rd. Free admission. Open to the public during the day. 15-min. walk from Bugis MRT.

Marina Bay Sands ★★★   The newest and most imposing structure on the Singapore skyline, this "integrated resort" comprises three hotel towers with more than 2,500 five-star guest rooms and suites; a 1.2-hectare (3-acre) SkyPark; an enormous four-level world-class convention and exhibition center; a high-fashion luxury shopping mall; two theaters; a museum; almost 60 venues for dining and nightlife; and one of Singapore's two new casinos.

The 24-hour **casino** is abuzz with lights and sounds from 1,600 slot machines; more than 500 tables offering baccarat, roulette, Sic-Bo, "Singapore stud poker" (**Note:** poker is not on offer here), noncommission baccarat, and Money Wheel; new electronic, or "Rapid Table Games," with touch screens and computerized wagers for playing baccarat, roulette, and Sic-Bo; and invitation-only salons for high-stakes games, all located on four floors, one of which is nonsmoking. You must be 21 years or older to enter. While foreigners can enter the casino for free, Singapore citizens and residents must pay S$100 levy for 24 hours of access, a policy designed to decrease the temptation for Singaporeans to gamble their savings away (you will be asked to present your passport). There's also a dress code prohibiting beachwear, flip-flops, casual shorts. and sleeveless T-shirts. There are three main entrances to the casino via the shopping mall, outside of which you'll find banks of conveniently located ATMs.

The **Sands SkyPark ★★**, a cantilevered garden on top of the hotel blocks, is large enough to park four-and-a-half Airbus 380s nose-to-tail. The open-air observation deck is open to the public, with views from the 56th floor over the city's skyline, the Marina Bay, and out to the sea. Some areas are limited to hotel guests only (such as the mind-blowing rooftop infinity pool that appears to be spilling over the edge), but there are a couple of dining establishments that are open to the public, including **KU DÉ TA** (p. 449) and **Sky on 57** (© **65/6688-8868**), an offering by Justin Quek, one of Singapore's most celebrated chefs. Tickets to the Sands SkyPark are S$20 for adults, S$14 for children, and S$17 for seniors, purchased at the Basement 1, beneath Hotel Tower 3. It's open daily from 10am to 10pm, but closes during extreme rain.

The integrated resort also includes **The ArtScience Museum**—the curious lotus-shaped building at the water's edge—which contains 4,600 sq. m (49,500 sq. ft.) of gallery space for permanent and touring exhibits that merge science and technology concepts with art and design.

The complex is home to some interesting permanent **art installations** that are incorporated into the architectural design. An art map is available that will point out pieces such as Ned Kahn's mesmerizing 260,000 aluminum flaps attached to the buildings' facades, waving in the breeze to create undulating visual effects.

2 Bayfront Ave. ✆ **65/6688-8868.** www.marinabaysands.com. 5-min. walk from Marina Bay MRT.

National Museum of Singapore ★★★   The premises of the National Museum are as interesting as the exhibits inside. Originally, the museum was housed in the 120-year-old main building, which makes up the facade fronting Stamford Road. Later the building was expanded to more than twice its original size with the addition of a striking modernist wing to the rear of the building. Cleverly, the new wing is invisible from the front. An ingenious glass-ceilinged walkway connects the old and new wings and provides a perfect point to view the magnificent Victorian dome with its stained-glass panels and zinc fishtail tiles. The large History Gallery, based in the new wing, tells the story of Singapore from two points of view: from a historian and from the "man on the street," accompanied by state-of-the-art multimedia exhibits designed to bring history to life and make it accessible for all visitors. You decide which story you'd like to hear, then choose the corresponding audio headset that will guide you through the exhibit. The four Living Galleries are on the second floor of the old wing and show objects and elements of everyday Singaporean life: food, fashion, film, and photography. The museum conducts free guided tours in English Monday through Friday at 11am and 2pm, and on Saturday and Sunday at 11:30am, 2pm, and 3:30pm; the tour takes 1 to 1½ hours. The building itself is a mix of colonial and contemporary architecture; a free tour that focuses just on the architecture is offered Friday through Sunday at 3:30pm.

93 Stamford Rd. ✆ **65/6332-3659.** www.nationalmuseum.sg. Admission S$10 adults, S$5 children and seniors; free admission to the Living Galleries daily 6–8pm. History Gallery daily 10am–6pm; Living Galleries daily 10am–8pm. 5-min. walk from Dhoby Ghaut or City Hall MRT.

Old Parliament House   The Old Parliament House is probably Singapore's oldest surviving structure, even though it has been renovated so many times it no longer looks the way it was originally constructed. It was designed as a home for John Argyle Maxwell, a Scottish merchant, but he never moved in. In 1822, Raffles returned to Singapore and was furious to find a residence being built on ground he'd allocated for government use. So the government took over Maxwell's house for its court and other offices. In 1939, when the new Supreme Court was completed, the judiciary moved into Maxwell's House (as it became officially known); then, in 1953, following a major renovation, the small structure was renamed Parliament House and was turned over to the legislature.

The original house was designed by architect George D. Coleman, who had helped Raffles with his Town Plan of 1822. Coleman's design was in the English neo-Palladian style. Simple and well suited to the Tropics, this style was popular at the time with Calcutta merchants. Major alterations have left very little behind of Coleman's design, replacing it with an eclectic French classical style, but some of his work survives.

Today the building has been transformed once again—The Arts House at the Old Parliament has been lovingly restored, with spaces for visual and performance arts, plus special cultural events. A small gallery retells the story of the building. A couple of highbrow eateries offer a variety of Thai, Vietnamese, and Western cuisine. Singapore's parliament now operates out of the new Parliament Building just next door.

The bronze elephant in front of the Old Parliament House was a gift to Singapore in 1872 from His Majesty Somdeth Phra Paraminda Maha Chulalongkorn (Rama V), supreme king of Siam, as a token of gratitude following his stay the previous year.

1 Old Parliament Lane, at the south end of the Padang, next to the Supreme Court. © **65/6332-6900.** www.theartshouse.com.sg. Free admission, guided tour S$8; extra charge for tickets to events. Mon–Fri 10am–8pm; Sat 11am–8pm. 15-min. walk from City Hall MRT.

The Padang   This large field has witnessed its share of historical events. Bordered on one end by the Singapore Recreation Club and on the other end by the Singapore Cricket Club, and flanked by City Hall, the area was once known as Raffles Plain. Upon Raffles's return to the island in 1822, he was angry that resident Farquhar had allowed merchants to move private residences into the prime area he had originally intended for government buildings. All building permits were rescinded, and the Padang became the official center point for the government quarters, around which the Esplanade and City Hall were built.

Today the Padang is mainly used for public and sporting events—pleasant activities—but in the 1940s, it felt more forlorn footsteps when the invading Japanese forced the entire European community onto the field. There they waited while the occupation officers dickered over a suitable location for the "conquered." They ordered all British, Australian, and Allied troops, as well as European prisoners, on the 22km (14-mile) march to Changi.

An interesting side note: Frank Ward, designer of the Supreme Court, had big plans for the Padang and surrounding buildings. He would have demolished the Cricket Club, Parliament House, and Victoria Hall & Theatre to erect an enormous government block if World War II hadn't arrived, ruining his chances.

St. Andrew's Rd. and Connaught Dr. Free admission. 5-min. walk from City Hall MRT.

Peranakan Museum   This small branch of the Asian Civilisations Museum (see earlier in this chapter) illuminates the fascinating culture of the Peranakans, people born of intermarriages between Chinese immigrants and locally born Malays. The result is a rich blend of traditions, cuisine, and decorative influences. Look for the incredibly beautiful carved teak wedding furniture and the distinctive porcelain decorated in typical Peranakan colors of pink, blue, green, and yellow. The clothing is vivid yet delicate, featuring intricate embroidery and beading. It's a great insight into a culture that appeared and flourished for a brief period of time in a tiny part of the world. The collection is nicely laid out in a lovely building that was the former Tao Nan School, which dates from 1910.

39 Armenian St. © **65/6332-7591.** www.peranakanmuseum.sg. Admission S$6 adults, S$3 children and seniors; discounted admission Fri 7–9pm. Mon 1–7pm; Tues–Sun 9am–7pm (extended hours Fri 9am–9pm). 15-min. walk from City Hall MRT.

Raffles Hotel ★★   Built in 1887 to accommodate the increasing upper-class trade, Raffles Hotel was originally only a couple of bungalows with 10 rooms but, oh, the view of the sea was perfection. The owners, Armenian brothers named Sarkies, already had a couple of prosperous hotels in Southeast Asia (the Eastern & Oriental in Penang and the Strand in Rangoon) and were well versed in the business. It wasn't long before they added a pair of wings and completed the main building—and reading rooms, verandas, dining rooms, a grand lobby, the Bar and Billiards Room, a ballroom, and a string of shops. By 1899, electricity was turning the cooling fans and providing the pleasing glow of comfort.

As it made its madcap dash through the 1920s, the hotel was the place to see and be seen. Vacancies were unheard of. Hungry Singaporeans and guests from other hotels, eager for a glimpse of the fabulous dining room, were turned away for lack of reservations. The crowded ballroom was jumping every night of the week. During this time Raffles's guest book included famous authors like Somerset Maugham, Rudyard Kipling, Joseph Conrad, and Noël Coward. These were indeed the glory years, but the lovely glimmer from the chandeliers soon faded with the stark arrival of the Great Depression. Raffles managed to limp through that dark time—and, darker still, through the Japanese Occupation—and later pull back from the brink of bankruptcy to undergo modernization in the '50s. But fresher, brighter, more opulent hotels were taking root on Orchard Road, pushing the "grand old lady" to the back seat.

In the 1990s, Raffles was brought back to its former glory, restored and sensitively expanded over the course of a 3-year, multimillion-dollar project. History-minded renovators selected 1915 as a benchmark and, with a few changes here and there, faithfully restored the hotel to that era's splendor. Today the hotel's restaurants and nightlife draw thousands of visitors daily to its open lobby, its theater playhouse, the Raffles Hotel Museum, and exclusive boutiques. Its 13 restaurants and bars—especially the Tiffin Room and Raffles Grill—are excellent, as is its famous Bar and Billiards Room and Long Bar. If you're arriving by taxi, ask the driver to take you to the front door of the hotel, where you'll be met by Raffles's fabulous Sikh doormen.

1 Beach Rd. © **65/6337-1886.** www.raffles.com/singapore. City Hall MRT.

Raffles Landing Site   The polymarble statue at this site was unveiled in 1972. It was made from plaster casts of the original 1887 figure located in front of the Victoria Theatre and Concert Hall (see below) and stands on what is believed to be the site where Sir Stamford Raffles landed on January 29, 1819.

North Boat Quay. Free admission. 15-min. walk from City Hall MRT.

St. Andrew's Cathedral   Designed by George Coleman; erected on a site selected by Sir Stamford Raffles himself; named for the patron saint of Scotland, St. Andrew; and primarily funded by Singapore's Scottish community, the first St. Andrew's was the colonials' Anglican Church. Completed toward the end of the 1830s, its tower and spire were added several years later to accord the edifice more stature. By 1852, because of massive damage sustained from lightning strikes, the cathedral was deemed unsafe and torn down. The cathedral that now stands on the site was completed in 1860. Of English Gothic Revival design, the cathedral is one of the few standing churches of this style in the region. The spire resembles the steeple of Salisbury Cathedral—another tribute from the colonials to Mother England.

The plasterwork of St. Andrew's inside walls used a material called Madras *chunam,* which, though peculiar, was a common building material here in the 1880s. A combination of shell lime (without the sand) was mixed with egg whites and coarse sugar or jaggery until it took on the consistency of a stiff paste. The mixture was thinned to a workable consistency with water in which coconut husks had steeped and was then applied to the surface, allowed to dry, and polished with rock crystal or smooth stones to a most lustrous patina.

The original church bell was presented to the cathedral by Maria Revere Balestier, the daughter of famed American patriot Paul Revere. The bell is now on display in the National Museum of Singapore.

11 St. Andrew's Rd., across from the Padang. ℂ **65/6337-6104.** Free admission. Open during daylight hours. City Hall MRT.

Singapore Art Museum ★   The Singapore Art Museum (SAM) opened in 1996 to house an impressive collection of more than 6,500 pieces of art and sculpture, most of it by Singaporean artists. Limited space requires the curators to display only a small number at a time, but these are incorporated in interesting exhibits to illustrate particular artistic styles, social themes, or historical concepts. A large collection of Southeast Asian pieces rotates regularly, as well as visiting international exhibits. Besides the main halls, the museum offers up a gift shop with fine souvenir ideas, a cafe, a conservation laboratory, an auditorium, and the E-mage Gallery, where multimedia presentations include not only the museum's own acquisitions, but other works from public and private collections in the region as well. A new wing, 8Q, in neighboring Queen Street, opened in 2008 to highlight the work of living Asian artists and experimental art forms. It also contains a Children's Gallery with a hands-on approach. Once a Catholic boys' school established in 1852, SAM has retained some visible reminders of its former occupants: Above the front door of the main building, you can still see inscribed "St. Joseph's Institution," and a bronze-toned, cast-iron statue of St. John Baptist de la Salle with two children stands in its original place.

71 Bras Basah Rd. ℂ **65/6332-3222.** www.singart.com. Admission S$10 adults, S$5 children and seniors; free admission Fri 6–9pm. Sat–Thurs 10am–7pm; Fri 10am–9pm. Free guided tours in English Mon 2pm, Tues–Thurs 11am and 2pm, with additional tours Fri 7pm and Sat–Sun 3:30pm. 10-min. walk from City Hall and Dhoby Ghaut MRT.

Singapore Flyer ★★★   The new must-have accessory for the world's most ambitious cities is a giant observation wheel, and Singapore has built itself the world's largest, standing proudly at Marina Bay. But in a typically Singaporean cultural twist, just 6 months after the multimillion-dollar wheel started to revolve in 2008, it was stopped and yet more millions were spent on reversing the turning direction. Why? Because feng shui masters observed that the Flyer was turning away from the financial center and taking Singapore's riches with it. The U-turn was a good move; the geomancers are happy and passengers now get to appreciate views that stretch up to 45km (28 miles) to Malaysia and Indonesia before enjoying impressive views of the city skyline and the harbor on the way back down—definitely the highlight of the trip. If you need a reminder of Singapore's enduring importance as a trading center, count the number of giant container ships waiting off the east coast to berth at the docks. It takes about 30 minutes to complete the circle, and the glass cabins are large enough to stroll around in while the world moves leisurely past.

30 Raffles Ave. ℂ **65/6734-8829.** www.singaporeflyer.com. Admission S$30 adults, S$21 children. Daily 8:30am–10pm. Bus 106, 111, or 133 from Raffles Hotel to Temasek Ave. Free shuttle buses every half-hour from St Andrew's Cathedral 10am–11pm. MRT.

Singapore Philatelic Museum   This building, constructed in 1895 to house the Methodist Book Room, underwent a $4.7-million restoration to become the Philatelic Museum in 1995. Exhibits include a fine collection of old stamps issued to commemorate historically important events, first-day covers, antique printing plates, postal service memorabilia, and private collections. Visitors can trace the development of a stamp from idea to the finished sheet, and can even add a picture to holiday postcards to mail from the last operational colonial postbox in Singapore. Special-edition folios featuring indigenous trees, flowers, and wildlife make pretty and compact souvenirs. Free guided tours are available upon request.

23B Coleman St. ℂ **65/6337-3888.** www.spm.org.sg. Admission S$5 adults, S$4 children and seniors. Mon 1–7pm; Tues–Sun 9am–7pm. 10-min. walk from Clarke Quay MRT.

Statue of Raffles This sculpture of Sir Stamford Raffles was erected on the Padang in 1887 and moved to its present position after getting in the way of one too many cricket matches. During the Japanese Occupation, the statue was placed in the Singapore History Museum (then the Raffles Museum) and was replaced here in 1945. The local joke is that Raffles's arm is outstretched to the Bank of China building, and his pockets are empty. (*Translation:* In terms of wealth in Singapore, it's Chinese 1, Brits 0.)

Behind the Victoria Theatre and Concert Hall, 9 Empress Place. Free admission. 10-min. walk from City Hall, Clarke Quay and Raffles Place MRT.

Supreme Court The Supreme Court stands on the site of the old Hotel de L'Europe, a rival of Raffles Hotel until it went bankrupt in the 1930s. The court's structure, a classical style favored for official buildings the world over, was completed in 1939. With its spare adornment and architectural simplicity, the edifice has a no-nonsense, utilitarian attitude, and the sculptures across the front, executed by the Italian sculptor Cavaliere Rodolpho Nolli, echo what transpires within. Justice is the grandest, standing 2.7m (8¾ ft.) high and weighing almost 4 tons. Kneeling on either side of her are representations of Supplication and Thankfulness. To the far left are Deceit and Violence. To the far right, a bull represents Prosperity, and two children hold wheat, to depict Abundance.

Two-and-a-half million bricks were used in building this structure, but the stone-work is fake—it's actually a type of plaster that is molded to look like granite. A dome, a copy of the one at St. Paul's Cathedral in London, covers an interior courtyard, which is surrounded by the four major portions of the Supreme Court building.

There is currently no public access to the Old Supreme Court building, but visitors are permitted to attend court hearings, which are held in the modern court building, provided appropriate dress and etiquette codes are observed.

1 St. Andrew's Rd., across from the Padang. ℂ **65/6336-0644.** 10-min. walk from City Hall MRT.

Victoria Theatre and Concert Hall Designed by colonial engineer John Bennett in a Victorian Revival style that was fashionable in Britain at the time, the theater portion was built in 1862 as the Town Hall. Victoria Memorial Hall was built in 1905 as a memorial to Queen Victoria, retaining the same style of the old building. The clock tower was added a year later. In 1909, with its name changed to Victoria Theatre, the hall opened with an amateur production of the *Pirates of Penzance*. Another notable performance occurred when Noël Coward passed through Singapore and stepped in at the last moment to help out a traveling English theatrical company that had lost a leading man. The building looks much the same as it did then, though of course the interiors have been modernized. It was completely renovated in 1979, conserving all the original details, and was renamed Victoria Concert Hall. It housed the Singapore Symphony Orchestra until the opening of the Esplanade–Theatres on the Bay, when they shifted to the larger digs. Browse the SISTIC website at www.sistic.com.sg for events information and ticketing.

11 Empress Place, at the southern end of the Padang. No phone. www.vch.org.sg. Free admission to lobby areas. Concert tickets priced depending on performance and seat location. 15-min. walk from City Hall MRT.

Along the River

The Singapore River had always been the heart of Singapore even before Raffles landed, but for many years during the 20th century, life here was dead—quite literally. Rapid urban development that began in the 1950s turned the river into a giant sewer, killing all plant and animal life in it. In the mid-1980s, though, the government began a large and very successful cleanup project; shortly thereafter, the buildings at Boat Quay and Clarke Quay, and later Robertson Quay, were restored.

Boat Quay ★ Known as "the belly of the carp" by the local Chinese because of its shape, this area was once notorious for its opium dens and coolie shops. Nowadays, thriving restaurants boast every cuisine imaginable and the rocking nightlife offers up a variety of sounds—jazz, rock, blues, Indian, and Caribe. **Note:** Pronounce *quay* like *key.*

Located on the south bank of the Singapore River btw. Cavenagh Bridge and Elgin Bridge. Free admission. 5-min. walk from Clarke Quay MRT.

Clarke Quay The largest of the waterfront developments, Clarke Quay was named for the second governor of Singapore, Sir Andrew Clarke. In the 1880s, a pineapple cannery, an iron foundry, and numerous warehouses made this area bustle. Today, with 60 restored warehouses hosting restaurants, bars, and nightclubs, the Quay still hops. **River House,** formerly the home of a *towkay* (company boss), occupies the oldest structure, a beautiful building that's become a popular bar and restaurant run by the Indochine group. During the day, children can play in the water jets that shoot up from the floor in Clarke Quay's central hub, but when the fountains are switched off, the area is used for special events and occasional markets.

Also here, **G-Max Reverse Bungy** (3E River Valley Rd.; ✆ **65/6338-1146;** www.gmax.co.nz) will strap you and two buddies into a cage and fling you around at the end of giant bungee cords for only S$45 each. You'll go up 60m (197 ft.) high at 200kmph (124 mph). Whoo! Despite its name, the next-door **Xtreme Swing** is slightly less extreme, propelling five people above the river and back for S$45 a time, though it's still not for the fainthearted. Open Monday to Thursday 2pm to 1am, Friday 2pm to 3am, Saturday 1pm to 3am, and Sunday 1pm to 1am.

River Valley Rd. west of Coleman Bridge. ✆ **65/6337-3292.** www.clarkequay.com.sg. Free admission. Clarke Quay MRT.

Esplanade Park Esplanade Park and Queen Elizabeth Walk were established in 1943 on land reclaimed from the sea. Several memorials are located here. The first is a fountain built in 1857 to honor **Tan Kim Seng,** who gave a great sum of money toward the building of a waterworks. Another monument, **the Cenotaph,** commemorates the 124 Singaporeans who died in World War I; it was dedicated by the Prince of Wales. On the reverse side, the names of those who died in World War II have been inscribed. The third prominent memorial is dedicated to **Maj. Gen. Lim Bo Seng,** a member of the Singaporean underground resistance in World War II who was captured and killed by the Japanese. His memorial was unveiled in 1954 on the 10th anniversary of his death. At the far end of the park, the Esplanade–Theatres on the Bay opened in October 2002. Fashioned after the Sydney Opera House, the unique double-domed structure is known locally as the Durians, because the spiky domes resemble halves of durian shells (the building itself is actually smooth—the "spikes" are sun shields).

Connaught Dr., on the marina, running from the mouth of the Singapore River along the Padang to the Esplanade–Theatres on the Bay. Free admission. Daily until midnight. 10-min. walk from City Hall MRT.

Merlion Park The Merlion is Singapore's half-lion, half fish national symbol, the lion representing Singapore's roots as the "Lion City" and the fish representing the nation's close ties to the sea. Such a magical and awe-inspiring beast has likely been around in tales for hundreds of years, right? No such luck. Rather, he was the creation of some scheming marketers at the Singapore Tourism Board in the early 1970s. Despite the Merlion's commercial beginnings, he's been adopted as the national symbol and spouts continuously every day at the mouth of the Singapore River.

South bank, at the mouth of the Singapore River, adjacent to One Fullerton. Free admission. Daily 7am–10pm. 15-min. walk from either City Hall or Raffles Place MRT.

Sri Thandayuthapani Temple One of the richest and grandest of its kind in Southeast Asia, the Sri Thandayuthapani Temple is most famous for a *thoonganai maadam,* a statue of an elephant's backside in a seated position. It's said that there are only four others of the kind, located in four temples in India.

The original temple was completed in 1860, restored in 1962, and practically rebuilt in 1984. The many sculptures of Hindu deities and the carved Kamalam-patterned rosewood doors, arches, and columns were executed by architect-sculptors imported from Madras, India, specifically for the job. The Hindu child god, Lord Muruga, rules over the temple and is visible in one form or another wherever you look. Also notice the statues of the god Shiva and his wife, Kali, captured in their lively dance competition. The story goes that Kali was winning the competition, so Shiva lifted his leg above his head, something a woman wasn't thought capable of doing. He won and quit dancing—good thing, too, because every time Shiva did a little jig, he destroyed part of the world. Outside in the courtyard are statues of the wedding of Lord Muruga; his brother, Ganesh; another brother, Vishnu; and their father, Shiva; along with Brahma, the creator of all.

Used daily for worship, the temple is also the culmination point of Thaipusam, a celebration of thanks. You may also hear this temple called Chettiar's Hindu Temple or the Tank Road Temple.

15 Tank Rd., close to the intersection of Clemenceau Ave. and River Valley Rd. ℂ **65/6737-9393.** Free admission. Daily 8am–noon and 5:30–8pm. 20-min. walk from Clarke Quay MRT.

Chinatown & Tanjong Pagar

Al-Abrar Mosque This mosque, also called Masjid Chulia after the Chulias, the group of Indian moneylender immigrants who funded its construction (*masjid* is Malay for mosque), was originally erected as a thatched building in 1827, thus its Tamil name Kuchu Palli, which means "hut mosque." The building that stands today was built in the 1850s, and even though it faces Mecca, the complex conforms with the grid of the neighborhood's city streets. It was designated a national monument in 1974, and in the late 1980s, the mosque underwent major renovations that enlarged the mihrab and stripped away some of the ornamental qualities of the columns in the building. The one-story prayer hall was extended upward into a two-story gallery. Little touches like the timber window panels and fanlight windows have been carried over into the new renovations.

192 Telok Ayer St., near the corner of Telok Ayer St. and Amoy St., near Thian Hock Keng Temple. ℂ **65/6220-6306.** Free admission. 15-min. walk from either Raffles Place or Tanjong Pagar MRT.

Chinatown Heritage Centre ★★ This block of three old shophouses in the center of the Chinatown heritage district has been converted into a display that tells the story of the Chinese immigrants who came to Singapore to find work in the early days of the colony. Walk through rooms filled with period antiques replicating coolie living quarters, shops, clan association houses, and other places that were prominent in daily life. It reminded me of the museum on Ellis Island in New York City that walks visitors through the immigrant experience of the early 1900s. Like Ellis Island, this display also has detailed descriptions to explain each element of the immigrant experience. The tiny cubicles where large families and groups scratched out a meager existence are an affecting picture of the hardships they faced.

48 Pagoda St. ℂ **65/6325-2878.** www.chinatownheritagecentre.sg. Admission S$10 adults, S$6 children. Daily 9am–8pm. 5-min. walk from Chinatown MRT.

Jamae Mosque   Jamae Mosque was built by the Chulias, Tamil Muslims who were some of the earlier immigrants to Singapore and who had a very influential hold over Indian Muslim life centered in the Chinatown area. The Chulias built not only this mosque, but the Al-Abrar Mosque and the Nagore Durgha Shrine as well. Jamae Mosque dates from 1827 but wasn't completed until the early 1830s. The mosque stands today almost exactly as it did then.

Although the front gate is typical of mosques you'd see in southern India, inside, most of the buildings reflect the neoclassical style of architecture introduced in administrative buildings and homes designed by George Coleman and favored by the Europeans. There are also some Malay touches in the timberwork. A small shrine inside, which may be the oldest part of the mosque, was erected to memorialize a local religious leader, Muhammad Salih Valinva.

218 South Bridge Rd., at the corner of South Bridge Rd. and Mosque St. ℂ **65/6221-4165.** Free admission. Chinatown MRT. 10-min. walk from Chinatown MRT.

Lau Pa Sat Festival Pavilion   Though it used to be well beloved, the locals think this place has become quite touristy—though lunchtime finds it still packed with financial district workers. Once the happy little hawker center known as Telok Ayer Market, it began life as a wet market, selling fruits, vegetables, and other foodstuffs. Now it's part hawker center, part Western fast-food outlets.

It all began on Market Street in 1823, in a structure that was later torn down, redesigned, and rebuilt by G. D. Coleman. Close to the water, seafood could be unloaded fresh off the pier. After the land in Telok Ayer Basin was reclaimed in 1879, the market was moved to its present home. A new design by James MacRitchie kept the original octagonal shape and was constructed of 3,000 prefab cast-iron elements brought in from Europe.

In the 1970s, as the financial district began to develop, the pavilion was dominated by hawkers who fed the lunchtime business crowd. In the mid-1980s, the structure was torn down to make way for the MRT construction and then meticulously put back together, puzzle piece by puzzle piece. By 1989, the market was once again an urban landmark, but it sat vacant until Scotts Holdings successfully tendered to convert it into a festival market. At this time, numerous changes were made to the building, which was renamed Lau Pa Sat (Old Market) in acknowledgment of the name by which the market had been known by generations of Singaporeans. Lau Pa Sat is one of the few hawker centers that's open 24 hours, in case you need a coffee or snack before retiring.

18 Raffles Quay, located in the entire block flanked by Robinson Rd., Cross St., Shenton Way, and Boon Tat St. Free admission. Daily 24 hr. 10-min. walk from Raffles Place MRT.

Nagore Durgha Shrine   Although this is a Muslim place of worship, it is not a mosque, but a shrine, built to commemorate a visit to the island by a Muslim holy man of the Chulia people (Muslim merchants and moneylenders from India's Coromandel Coast) who was traveling around Southeast Asia spreading the word of Indian Islam. The most interesting visual feature is its facade: Two arched windows flank an arched doorway, with columns in between. Above these is a "miniature palace"—a massive replica of the facade of a palace, with tiny cutout windows and a small arched doorway in the middle. The cutouts in white plaster make it look like lace. From the corners of the facade, two 14-level minarets rise, with three little domed cutouts on each level and onion domes on top. Inside, the prayer halls and two shrines are painted and decorated in shockingly tacky colors.

Controversy surrounds the dates on which the shrine was built. The government, upon naming the Nagore Durgha a national monument, claimed it was built sometime in the 1820s; however, Nagoreallauddeen, who is the 15th descendant of the holy man for whom the shrine is named, claims it was built many years before. According to Nagoreallauddeen, the shrine was first built out of wood and *attap* (a thatch roof made from a type of palm), and later, in 1815, was rebuilt from limestone, 4 years before the arrival of Sir Stamford Raffles. In 1818, rebuilding materials were imported from India to construct the present shrine.

140 Telok Ayer St., at the corner of Telok Ayer St. and Boon Tat St. 15-min. walk from either Raffles Place or Tanjong Pagar MRT.

Sacred Buddha Tooth Temple ★★

Allow at least an hour and a half to appreciate this huge temple, which was founded in 2002. Built in the Tang Dynasty style, this is actually a Chinese cultural center, encompassing, among other things, a temple, a museum and reference library, a theater, a dining hall providing free meals, and, of course, the magnificent reliquary that gives the temple its name. The best place to start is in the huge 100 Dragons Hall on the first floor, where services dedicated to the Maitreya Buddha take place, with a further hall behind celebrating the Avalokitesvara Bodhisattva. I'd then take the elevator (lined with gold-embroidered fabric) to the third story, where a nicely laid-out museum examines the life of the Buddha and explains the role of the future Maitreya Buddha and the Bodhisattva Avalokitesvara, the representation of Kindness and Compassion. The sacred tooth itself is on the fourth floor, encased in a magnificent golden stupa, which itself sits on a (presumably reinforced) floor of pure gold tiles. The stupa depicts the 35 Buddhas who have achieved enlightenment and nirvana, surrounding the serene figure of the Maitreya Buddha, guarded by four lions. The stupa is unveiled from 9am to noon and 3 to 6pm daily. A staircase leads to the lovely roof garden (there is a stair lift, if required) where the world's largest enameled prayer wheel turns slowly in the Ten Thousand Buddhas Pavilion. Still not enough Buddhas for you? There are another 12,000 in the galleries outside the pavilion. These are dedicated to the Buddha of Longevity. For S$68 a year, you can light up one of these tiny figures and help to negate all the bad karma created since the beginning of time. Free vegetarian meals are served in the basement.

288 South Bridge Rd. ✆ **65/6220-0220.** www.btrts.org.sg. Free admission. Daily 7am–7pm. 5-min. walk from Chinatown MRT.

Singapore City Gallery

This expansive display is perhaps of real interest only to Singaporeans and civil planners, but if you're in the neighborhood, it's worth a pop inside to see the giant wooden plan of the city in miniature that sits on the right side of the lobby. If you have time, sift through 48 permanent exhibits and 25 interactive displays that paint a historical picture of the development of urban Singapore.

URA Centre, 45 Maxwell Rd. ✆ **65/6321-8321.** www.ura.gov.sg. Free admission. Mon–Sat 9am–5pm. 10-min. walk from Tanjong Pagar MRT.

Sri Mariamman Hindu Temple As the oldest Hindu temple in Singapore, Sri Mariamman has been the central point of Hindu tradition and culture. In its early years, the temple housed new immigrants while they established themselves and also served as social center for the community. Today the main celebration here is the Thimithi Festival in October or November. The shrine is dedicated to the goddess Sri Mariamman, who is known for curing disease (a very important goddess to have around in those days), but as is the case at all other Hindu temples, the entire pantheon of Hindu gods are present to be worshiped as well. On either side of the *gopuram* are statues of Shiva and Vishnu, while inside are two smaller shrines to Vinayagar and Sri Ararvan. Also note the sacred cows that lounge along the top of the temple walls.

The temple originated as a small wood-and-thatch shrine founded by Naraina Pillai, an Indian merchant who came to Singapore with Raffles's first expedition and found his fortune in trade. In the main hall of the temple is the small god that Pillai originally placed here.

244 South Bridge Rd., at the corner of South Bridge Rd. and Pagoda St. ℂ **65/6223-4064.** Free admission. 10-min. walk from Chinatown MRT.

Thian Hock Keng Temple ★★★ Thian Hock Keng, the "Temple of Heavenly Bliss," is one of the oldest Chinese temples in Singapore. Before land reclamation, when the shoreline came right up to Telok Ayer Road, the first Chinese sailors landed here and immediately built a shrine, a small wood-and-thatch structure, to pray to the goddess Ma Cho Po for allowing their voyage to be safely completed. For each subsequent boatload of Chinese sailors, the shrine was always the first stop upon landing. Ma Cho Po, the Mother of the Heavenly Sages, was the patron goddess of sailors, and every Chinese junk of the day had an altar dedicated to her.

The temple that stands today was built in 1841 over the shrine with funds from the Hokkien community, led by the efforts of two Melaka-born philanthropists, Tan Tock Seng and Tan Kim Seng. All of the building materials were imported from China, except for the gates, which came from Glasgow, Scotland, and the tiles on the facade, which are from Holland. The doorway is flanked by two lions, a male with a ball to symbolize strength and a female with a lion cub to symbolize fertility. On the door are door gods, mythical beasts made from the combined body parts of many animals. Note the wooden bar that sits at the foot of the temple entrance (as do similar bars in so many Chinese temples). This serves a couple of purposes: First, it keeps out wandering ghosts, who cannot cross over the barrier. Second, it forces anyone entering the temple to look down as they cross, bowing their head in humility. Just inside the door are granite tablets that record the temple's history.

Ahead at the main altar is Ma Cho Po, and on either side are statues of the Protector of Life and the God of War. To the side of the main hall is a Gambler Brother statue, prayed to for luck and riches. From here you can see the temple's construction of brackets and beams, fitting snugly together and carved with war heroes, saints, flowers, and animals, all in red and black lacquer and gilded in gold. Behind the main hall is an altar to Kuan Yin, the Goddess of Mercy. Beside her are the sun and moon gods.

To the left of the courtyard are the ancestral tablets. In keeping with Confucian filial piety, each represents a soul. The tablets with red paper are for souls still alive. Also in the temple complex are a pagoda and a number of outer buildings that at one time housed a school and community associations. The right wing of the temple is shared with The Faculty, a center for creative arts, holding classes for dance, acting, and vocals. Even if you don't have a burning desire to learn to tango, the elaborate pagoda is an incredible spot for a cool drink, tucked away behind the ornate temple gate.

158 Telok Ayer St., ½ block beyond Nagore Durgha Shrine. ☏ **65/6423-4616.** Free admission. 15-min. walk from Tanjong Pagar MRT.

Wak Hai Cheng Bio Temple ★★   One of the oldest Taoist temples in Singapore, this is also known as Yueh Hai Ching Temple. Like most of Singapore's Chinese temples, Wak Hai Cheng Bio had its start as a simple wood-and-thatch shrine where sailors, when they got off their ships, would go to express their gratitude for sailing safely to their destination. Before the major land-reclamation projects shifted the shoreline outward, the temple was close to the water's edge, and so it was named "Temple of the Calm Sea Built by the Guangzhou People." It's a Teochew temple, located in a part of Chinatown originally populated by this dialect group.

Inside the Taoist temple walls are two blocks, the one on the left devoted to Ma Cho Po, the Mother of Heavenly Sages, who protects travelers and ensures a safe journey. The one on the right is devoted to Siong Tek Kong, the god of business. Both are as important to the Chinese community today as they were way back when. Look for the statue of the Gambler Brother, with coins around his neck. The Chinese pray to him for wealth and luck; in olden days, they would put opium on his lips. This custom is still practiced today, only now they use a black herbal paste called *kuyo,* which is conveniently legal.

Inside the temple, you can buy joss sticks and paper for S$2.50. Three joss sticks are for heaven, your parents, and yourself, to be burned before the altar. Three corresponding packets of elaborately decorated paper and gold leaf are to be burned outside in the gourd-shaped kilns (gourd being a symbol of health). The joss, or "wishing paper," four thin sheets stamped with black and red characters, has many meanings. The red sheet is for luck (red being particularly auspicious), and the other three are to wash away your sins, for a long life, and for your wishes to be carried to heaven. Even if you are not Taoist, you're more than welcome to burn the joss.

The temple itself is quite a visual treat, with ceramic figurines and pagodas adorning the roof, and every nook and cranny of the structure adorned with tiny three-dimensional reliefs that depict scenes from Chinese operas. The spiral joss hanging in the courtyard adds an additional picturesque effect.

30-B Phillip St., at the corner of Phillip St. and Church St. Free admission. 5-min. walk from Raffles Place MRT.

Little India

Little India did not develop as a community planned by the colonial authorities like Kampong Glam or Chinatown, but came into being because immigrants to India were drawn to business developments here. In the late 1920s, the government established a brick kiln and lime pits here that attracted Indian workers, and the abundance of grass and water made the area attractive to Indian cattle traders.

*A **word of advice:*** If you visit Little India on a Sunday, be prepared for a mob scene the likes of Calcutta! Sunday is the only day off for Singapore's many immigrant Indian and Bangladeshi laborers, so Serangoon Road gets pretty lively.

Abdul Gafoor Mosque   This charming little mosque is resplendent, thanks to a loving restoration completed in 2008. Nestled behind a row of shophouses, it really can't be seen until you arrive at the gate. Inside the compound, the bright yellow and green facade and minarets reflect an Indian Muslim architectural preference, most likely imported with the mosque's builder, Sheik Abdul Gafoor. The original mosque on this site, called Al-Abrar Mosque, was constructed of wood in 1859 and is commemorated on a granite plaque within the compound above what could have been either an entrance gate or part of the mosque itself. The newer mosque on the site was built in 1907 and includes some unusual features, including ornate European-style columns and the sunburst above the main entrance. This "sundial" has 25 rays in Arabic calligraphy relief said to represent the 25 prophets in the Koran.

Inside the courtyard, an information office provides robes for those in shorts and sleeveless tops. As in every mosque, the main prayer hall is off-limits to non-Muslims.

41 Dunlop St., btw. Perak Rd. and Jalan Besar. ✆ **65/6295-4209.** Free admission. 15-min. walk from Little India MRT.

Sakya Muni Buddha Gaya (Temple of a Thousand Lights)   Thai elements influence this temple, from the *chedi* (stupa) roofline to the huge Thai-style Buddha image inside. Often this temple is brushed off as strange and tacky, but all sorts of surprises are inside, making the place a veritable Buddha theme park. On the right side of the altar, statues of baby bodhisattvas receive toys and sweets from devotees. Around the base of the altar, murals depict scenes from the life of Prince Siddhartha (the Buddha) as he searches for enlightenment. Follow them around to the back of the hall, and you'll find a small doorway to a chamber under the altar. Another Buddha image reclines inside, this one shown at the end of his life, beneath the Yellow Seraka tree. On the left side of the main part of the hall is a replica of a footprint left by the Buddha in Ceylon. Next to that is a wheel of fortune; one spin for S50¢!

336 Race Course Rd., 1 block past Perumal Rd. ✆ **65/6294-0714.** Free admission, daily 8am–4:45pm. 5-min. walk from Farrer Park MRT.

Sri Perumal Temple   Sri Perumal Temple, built in 1855, is devoted to the worship of Vishnu. As part of the Hindu trinity, Vishnu is the sustainer, balancing out Brahma the creator and Shiva the destroyer. When the world is out of whack, he rushes to its aid, reincarnating himself to show mankind that there are always new directions for development.

On the first tier to the left of the front entrance on the *gopuram*, statues depict Vishnu's nine reincarnations. Rama, the sixth incarnation, is with Hanuman, the monkey god, who helped him in the fierce battle to free his wife from kidnapping. Krishna, shown reclining amid devotees, is the eighth incarnation and a hero of many Hindu legends, most notably the Bhagavad-Gita. Also up there is the half-human and half-bird Garuda, Vishnu's steed. Inside the temple are altars to Vishnu, his two wives, and Garuda.

During Thaipusam, the main festival celebrated here, male devotees who have made vows over the year carry *kavadi*—huge steel racks decorated with flowers and fruits and held onto their bodies by skewers and hooks—to show their thanks and devotion, while women carry milk pots, in a parade from Sri Perumal Temple to Chettiar's Temple on Tank Road.

397 Serangoon Rd., ½ block past Perumal Rd. Free admission. Best times to visit are daily 6am–noon or 6-9pm. 5-min. walk from Farrer Park MRT.

Sri Veerama Kaliamman Temple ★★   This Hindu temple is primarily for the worship of Shiva's wife, Kali, who destroys ignorance, maintains world order, and blesses those who strive for knowledge of God. The box on the walkway to the front entrance is for smashing coconuts, a symbolic smashing of the ego, asking the gods to show "the humble way." The coconuts have two small "eyes" at one end so they can "see" the personal obstacles to humility they are being asked to smash.

Inside the temple in the main hall are three altars, the center one for Kali (depicted with 16 arms and wearing a necklace of human skulls) and two altars on either side for her two sons—Ganesh, the elephant god, and Murugan, the four-headed child god. To the right is an altar with nine statues representing the nine planets. Circle the altar and pray to your planet for help with a specific trouble.

Around the left side of the main hall, the first tier of the *gopuram* tells the story of how Ganesh got his elephant head. A small dais in the rear-left corner of the temple compound is an altar to Sri Periyachi, a very mean-looking woman with a heart of gold. She punishes women who say and do things to make others feel bad. She also punishes men—under her feet is an exploiter of ladies.

Here's a bit of trivia: Red ash, as opposed to white, is applied to the forehead after prayers are offered in a temple devoted to a female god.

141 Serangoon Rd. at Veerasamy Rd. ℂ **65/6298-5771.** Free admission. Daily 8am–noon and 5:30–8:30pm. 10-min. walk from Little India MRT.

Arab Street & Kampong Glam

Alsagoff Arab School   Built in 1912, the school was named for Syed Ahmad Alsagoff, a wealthy Arab merchant and philanthropist who was very influential in Singapore's early colonial days and who died in 1906. It is the oldest girls' school in Singapore and was the island's first Muslim school.

121 Jalan Sultan, across from Sultan Plaza. ℂ **65/6295-4807.** 15-min. walk from Bugis MRT.

Hajjah Fatimah Mosque ★★   Hajjah Fatimah was a wealthy businesswoman from Melaka and something of a local socialite. She married a Bugis prince from Celebes, and their only child, a daughter, married Syed Ahmed Alsagoff, son of Arab trader and philanthropist Syed Abdul Rahman Alsagoff. Hajjah Fatimah had originally built a home on this site, but after it had been robbed a couple of times and later set fire to, she decided to find a safer home and built a mosque here instead.

Inside the high walls of the compound are the prayer hall, an ablution area, gardens and mausoleums, and a few other buildings. You can walk around the main prayer halls to the garden cemeteries, where flat square headstones mark the graves of women and round ones mark the graves of men. Hajjah Fatimah is buried in a private room to the side of the main prayer hall, along with her daughter and son-in-law.

The minaret tower in the front was designed by an unknown European architect and could be a copy of the original spire of St. Andrew's Cathedral. The tower leans a little, a fact that's much more noticeable from the inside. On the outside of the tower is a bleeding heart—an unexpected place to find such a downright Christian symbol. It's a great example of what makes this mosque so charming—all the combined influences of Moorish, Chinese, and European architectural styles.

4001 Beach Rd., past Jalan Sultan. ℂ **65/6297-2774.** Free admission. Daily 9am–9pm. 20-min. walk from Bugis MRT.

Malay Heritage Centre (Istana Kampong Glam) ★★   When the Malay Heritage Centre opened its doors in 2004, it became the first museum dedicated to the history, culture, and arts of this often-marginalized ethnic group. The Centre has lovingly displayed exhibits that offer a glimpse into Singapore's early Malay settlements, the sultan's royal family, Malay arts, and 20th-century Malay life.

There's a bit of irony here. The museum is housed in the Istana Kampong Glam, the former royal palace that housed the descendants of the original sultan that oversaw Singapore. In 1819, Sultan Hussein signed away his rights over the island in exchange for the land at Kampong Glam plus an annual stipend for his family. After the Sultan's death, the family fortunes began to dwindle and disputes broke out among his descendants. In the late 1890s, they went to court, where it was decided that because no one in the family had the rights as the successor to the sultanate, the land should be reverted to the state. The family was allowed to remain in the house, but because they didn't own the property, they lost the authority to improve the buildings. Over the years, the compound fell into a very sad state of dilapidation. Eventually, Sultan Hussein's family was given the boot by the government to make way for this museum heralding the value of the Malay, and the Sultan's, cultural contribution to Singapore. Hmm.

Galleries on the first floor relate the story of the immigration of Muslim Malays to Singapore and their central role in the island's trading culture. Upstairs there are displays that deal with the modern history of the Malay community, and a re-creation of a traditional kampong (village) house and an early HDB apartment.

The house to the left before the main gate of the Istana compound is called **Gedong Kuning,** or Yellow Mansion. It was the home of Tenkgu Mahmoud, the heir to Kampong Glam. When he died, it was purchased by local Javanese businessman Haji Yusof, the belt merchant. Today it houses a Malay restaurant, **Tepak Sireh** (*©* 65/6393-4373; daily 11:30am–2:30pm and 6:30–9:30pm).

85 Sultan Gate. *©* **65/6391-0450.** Admission S$4 adults, S$3 children; free admission to Istana compound. Daily 8am–9pm. 15-min. walk from Bugis MRT.

Sultan Mosque ★   Though more than 80 mosques exist on the island of Singapore, Sultan Mosque is the real center of the Muslim community. The mosque that stands today is the second Sultan Mosque to be built on this site. The first was built in 1826, partially funded by the East India Company as part of their agreement to leave Kampong Glam to Sultan Hussein and his family in return for sovereign rights to Singapore. The present mosque was built in 1928 and was funded by donations from the Muslim community. The Saracenic flavor of the onion domes, topped with crescent moons and stars, is complemented by Mogul cupolas. Funny thing, though: The mosque was designed by an Irish guy named Denis Santry, who was working for the architectural firm Swan and McLaren.

Other interesting facts about the mosque: Its dome base is a ring of black bottles; the carpeting was donated by a prince of Saudi Arabia and bears his emblem; and at the back of the compound, North Bridge Road has a kink in it, showing where the mosque invaded the nicely planned urban grid pattern. Also, if you make your way through the chink where the back of the building almost touches the compound wall, peer inside the *makam* to see the royal graves. Sultan Mosque, like all the others, does not permit shorts, miniskirts, low necklines, or other revealing clothing to be worn inside. However, they do realize that non-Muslim travelers like to be comfortable as they tour around and provide cloaks free of charge. They hang just to the right as you walk up the stairs.

3 Muscat St. *©* **65/6293-4405.** Free admission. Daily 9am–1pm and 2–4pm. No visiting is allowed during Mass congregation Fri 11:30am–2:30pm. 15-min. walk from Bugis MRT.

Orchard Road Area

ION Sky   At the top of Orchard Road's most fashionable shopping mall and luxury condominium complex is ION Sky, the 55th-level observatory that's open to the public. Buy tickets from the concierge counter on level 4 of the ION Orchard Shopping Mall, and enter the express lift inside the ION Art Gallery. The panoramic view of Singapore is aided by the use of a Behold telescope similar to that found in Dubai's Burj Khalifa, the world's tallest tower. The Behold is a high-definition camera that projects images onto a screen for easier viewing. Viewing is permitted in 2-hour slots, at 10am, 2pm, 4pm, and 6pm.

ION Orchard, 2 Orchard Turn. © **65/6835-8750.** www.ionorchard.com Admission S$16 adults, S$8 children. See above for daily viewing times. Orchard MRT.

The Istana and Sri Temasek   In 1859, the construction of Fort Canning necessitated the demolition of the original governors' residence, and the autocratic and unpopular governor-general Sir Harry St. George Ord proposed this structure be built as the new residence. Though the construction of such a large and expensive edifice was unpopular, Ord had his way, and design and construction went through, with the building mainly performed by convicts under the supervision of Maj. J. F. A. McNair, the colonial engineer and superintendent of convicts.

In its picturesque landscaped setting, Government House echoed Anglo-Indian architecture, but its symmetrical and cross-shaped plan also echoed the form of the traditional Malay *istana* (palace). During the occupation, the house was occupied by Field Marshal Count Terauchi, commander of the Japanese Southern Army, and Major General Kawamura, commander of the Singapore Defense Forces. With independence, the building was renamed the Istana and today is used mainly for state and ceremonial occasions. The grounds are open to every citizen on selected public holidays, though they're not generally open for visits. The house's domain includes several other houses of senior colonial civil servants. The colonial secretary's residence, a typical 19th-century bungalow, is also registered as a national monument and is now called Sri Temasek.

Orchard Rd., btw. Claymore and Scotts roads. Admission S$1. 5-min. walk from Dhoby Ghaut MRT.

Peranakan Place ★   Emerald Hill was once nothing more than a wide treeless street along whose sides quiet families lived in typical terrace houses¾residential units similar to shophouses, with a walled courtyard in the front instead of the usual "five-foot way." Toward Orchard Road, the terrace houses turned into shophouses, with their first floors occupied by small provisioners, seamstresses, and dry goods stores.

As Orchard Road developed, so did Emerald Hill—the buildings were all renovated. The shophouses close to Orchard Road became restaurants and bars, and the street was closed off to vehicular traffic. Now it's an alfresco cafe, landscaped with a veritable jungle of potted foliage and peopled by colorful tourists—much different from its humble beginnings.

But as you pass Emerald Hill, don't just blow it off as a tourist trap. Walk through the cafe area and out the back onto Emerald Hill. All of the terrace houses have been redone, and magnificently. The facades have been freshly painted and the tiles polished, and the dark-wood details add a contrast that is truly elegant. When these places were renovated, they could be purchased for a song, but as Singaporeans began grasping at their heritage in recent years, their value shot up, and now these homes fetch huge sums.

For a peek inside some of these wonderful places, browse *Living Legacy: Singapore's Architectural Heritage Renewed,* by Robert Powell, at local bookstores. Gorgeous photographs take you inside a few of these homes and some other terrace houses and bungalows around the island, showing off the traditional interior details of these buildings.

Intersection of Emerald Hill and Orchard Rd. Free admission. 5-min. walk from Somerset MRT.

Western Singapore

Bukit Timah Nature Reserve ★★   Bukit Timah Nature Reserve is pure primary rainforest. Believed to be as old as 1 million years, it's the only place on the island with vegetation that exists exactly as it was before the British settled here. The park is more than 160 hectares (400 acres) of soaring canopy teeming with mammals and birds and a lush undergrowth with more bugs, butterflies, and reptiles than you can shake a vine at. Here you can see more than 700 plant species, many of which are exotic ferns, plus mammals like long-tailed macaques, squirrels, and lemurs. There's a visitor center and four well marked paths, one of which leads to Singapore's highest point. At 163m (535 ft.) above sea level, don't expect a nosebleed, but some of the scenic views of the island are really nice. Also at Bukit Timah is Hindhede Quarry, which filled up with water at some point, so you can take a dip and cool off during your hike. The National Parks Board gives free guided tours on the third Saturday of the month at around 9:25am; call *C* **65/6554-5127** to register.

177 Hindhede Dr. *C* **65/6468-5736.** www.nparks.gov.sg. Free admission. Daily 9:30am–6:30pm. Newton MRT, then bus 171 to park entrance.

Chinese and Japanese Gardens   Situated on two islands in Jurong Lake, the gardens are reached by an overpass and joined by the Bridge of Double Beauty. The **Chinese Garden** dedicates most of its area to "northern style" landscape architecture, the style of Imperial gardens, integrating brightly colored buildings with the surroundings. The Stoneboat is a replica of the stone boat at the Summer Palace in Beijing. Inside the Pure Air of the Universe building are courtyards and a pond, and there is a seven-story pagoda, the odd number of floors symbolizing continuity.

I like the Garden of Beauty, in Suzhou style, representing the southern style of landscape architecture. Southern gardens were built predominantly by scholars, poets, and men of wealth. Sometimes called Black-and-White gardens, these smaller gardens had more fine detail, featuring subdued colors, as the plants and elements of the rich natural landscape gave them plenty to work with. Inside the Suzhou garden are 2,000 pots of *penjiang* (bonsai) and displays of small rocks.

While the Chinese garden is more visually stimulating, the **Japanese Garden** is intended to evoke feeling. And though it can't compete with the attention with which its native counterparts are lavished, it is successful in capturing the themes at the heart of Japanese garden design. Marble-chip paths let you hear your own footsteps and meditate on the sound. They also serve to slow the journey for better gazing. The Keisein, or "Dry Garden," uses white pebbles to create images of streams. Ten stone lanterns, a small traditional house, and a rest house are nestled between two ponds with smaller islands joined by bridges. The pond area is regularly patrolled by huge monitor lizards! There is also a live turtle and tortoise museum, with a famous two-headed specimen; adults S$5, children S$3.

Toilets are situated at stops along the way, as well as benches to have a rest or to just take in the sights. Paddle boats can be rented for S$5 per hour just outside the main entrance.

1 Chinese Garden Rd. ©℅ **65/6261-3632.** Free admission; admission to garden of abundance S$2 adults, S$1 children. Main Garden daily 6am–11pm. Bonsai Garden & Garden of Abundance 9am–6pm. Chinese Garden MRT.

Haw Par Villa (Tiger Balm Gardens) ★

In 1935, brothers Haw Boon Haw and Haw Boon Par—creators of Tiger Balm, the camphor and menthol rub that comes in those cool little pots—took their fortune and opened Tiger Balm Gardens as a venue for teaching traditional Chinese values. They made more than 1,000 statues and life-size dioramas depicting Chinese legends and historical tales, and illustrating morality and Confucian beliefs. Many of these were gruesome and bloody, and some of them were really entertaining. But Tiger Balm Gardens suffered a horrible fate. In 1985, it was converted into an amusement park and reopened as Haw Par Villa. Most of the statues and scenes were taken away and replaced with rides. Well, business did not exactly boom. In fact, the park lost money fast. But recently, in an attempt to regain some of the original Tiger Balm Garden edge, they replaced many of the old statues, some of which are a great backdrop for really kitschy vacation photos, and ditched the rides. They also decided to open the gates free of charge.

262 Pasir Panjang Rd. ©℅ **65/6872-2780.** Free admission. Daily 9am–7pm. Buona Vista MRT and transfer to bus 200.

Jurong BirdPark ★ ☺

Jurong BirdPark, with a collection of 9,000 birds from more than 600 species, showcases Southeast Asian breeds plus other colorful tropical beauties, some of which are endangered. The more than 20 hectares (49 acres) can be easily walked or, for S$5 extra, you can ride the panorail for a bird's-eye view (so to speak) of the grounds. I enjoy the Waterfall Aviary, the world's largest walk-in aviary. It's an up-close-and-personal experience with African and South American birds, plus a pretty stroll through landscaped tropical forest. This is where you'll also see the world's tallest man-made waterfall, but the true feat of engineering here is the panorail station, built inside the aviary. Another smaller walk-in aviary is for Southeast Asian endangered bird species; at noon every day, this aviary experiences a man-made thunderstorm, and in the Lory Loft, a couple of dollars on bird feed buys you a swooping entourage of colorful friends. The daily guided tours and regularly scheduled feeding times are enlightening. Other bird exhibits are the flamingo pools, the World of Darkness (featuring nocturnal birds), and the penguin parade, a favorite for Singaporeans, who adore all things arctic.

The **World of Hawks** show at 10am and **Kings of the Skies** at 4pm feature birds of prey either acting out their natural instincts or performing falconry tricks. The **Birds n' Buddies** show takes place at 11am and 3pm, with trained parrots that race bikes and birds that perform all sorts of silliness, including staged birdie misbehaviors. There's also a **Children's Parrot Show** at 1pm.

2 Jurong Hill. ©℅ **65/6265-0022.** www.birdpark.com.sg. Admission S$18 adults, S$12 children 3–12. Park Hopper Ticket for Zoo, Night Safari, and BirdPark S$45 adults, S$28 children. Daily 8:30am–6pm. Boon Lay MRT and transfer to bus 194 or 251.

Singapore Botanic Gardens ★★

In 1822, Singapore's first botanic garden was started at Fort Canning by Sir Stamford Raffles. After it lost funding, the present Botanic Garden came into being in 1859, thanks to the efforts of a horticulture society; it was later turned over to the government for upkeep. More than just a garden, this space occupied an important place in the region's economic development when "Mad" Henry Ridley, one of the garden's directors, imported Brazilian rubber-tree seedlings from Great Britain. He devised improved latex-trapping methods and led the campaign to convince reluctant coffee growers to switch plantation crops. The garden also pioneered orchid hybridization, breeding a number of internationally acclaimed varieties.

Carved out within the tropical setting lies a marshgarden awash with waterlilies and papyrus plants, the sundial garden with pruned hedges, and a ginger garden filled with 300 related specimens of a family that includes lilies, turmeric, and even bananas. Who knew? Sculptures by international artists dot throughout. As you wander, look for the Cannonball tree (named for its cannonball-shaped fruit), Para rubber trees, teak trees, bamboos, and a huge array of palms, including the sealing wax palm—distinguished by its bright scarlet stalks—and the rumbia palm, which bears the pearl sago. The fruit of the silk-cotton tree is a pod filled with silky stuffing that was once used for stuffing pillows. Flowers like bougainvilleas and heliconias add beautiful color.

The **National Orchid Garden** is 3 hectares (7½ acres) of gorgeous orchids growing along landscaped walks. The English Garden features hybrids developed here and named after famous visitors to the garden—there's the beautifully twisted Margaret Thatcher, the Benazir Bhutto, the Vaclav Havel, and more. The gift shops sell live hydroponic orchids in test tubes for unique souvenirs.

At the Bukit Timah edge of the Botanic Gardens is Asia's first dedicated children's garden. The **Jacob Ballas Children's Garden** is a lovely place for under-12s to play and explore, while developing an appreciation for plants and nature. Children can do outdoor puzzles, learn about food and drinks that come from plants, explore the maze, or become happily soaked in a fountain play area (bring swimming gear). Admission is free and it's open Tuesday to Sunday from 8am to 7pm (© **65/6465-0196**).

The gardens have three lakes. Symphony Lake surrounds an island band shell for "Concert in the Park" performances by the local symphony and international entertainers. Call visitor services at the number below for performance schedules.

Volunteers run free guided tours of different areas of the park every Saturday at 9am and 10am, often with additional tours at 11am and 4pm. Register 15 minutes before the walk at the Visitor Centre near Nassim Gate.

Main entrance at corner of Cluny Rd. and Holland Rd. © **65/6471-7361**. www.nparks.gov.sg. Free admission. Daily 5am–midnight. The National Orchid Garden S$5 adults. Daily 8am–7pm. Orchard MRT, then bus 7, 105, 106, or 174 from Orchard Blvd.

Southern Ridges ★★ This 9km (5⅔-mile) chain of park area starts at Mount Faber Park (where you can catch the cable car to HarbourFront and Sentosa island) and ends at the West Coast Park. It incorporates two new pedestrian bridges, the Alexandra Arch and, my favorite, The Henderson Waves bridge, which connects Mount Faber Park to Telok Blangah Hill; this is the highest pedestrian bridge in Singapore, offering pretty views of the sea. It's also a beautiful piece of design in its own right, weaving like a ribbon over the treetops and featuring a curved wooden deck that rises in places to resemble a breaking wave, creating sheltered areas with seating. The Henderson Waves lead to a forest walk with an elevated pedestrian walkway and cycling trails through the Telok Blangah Hill Park. You can take bus nos. 131, 145, 176, or 648 to Henderson Road and walk up the hill, but it's more fun to take the MRT to HarbourFront and then the cable car to Mount Faber, and walk from there.

Mount Faber Park entrance is from Telok Blangah Rd. or Henderson Rd., or via HarbourFront MRT/cable car. © **800/471-7300**. www.nparks.gov.sg. Free admission. Daily 24 hr. Bus 131, 145, 176, or 648 to Henderson Rd., or MRT to HarbourFront and then cable car to Mount Faber.

Central & Northern Singapore

The northern part of Singapore contains most of the island's nature reserves and parks. Here's where you'll find the Singapore Zoo, in addition to some sights with historical and religious significance. Despite the presence of the **MRT** in the area, there is not any simple way to get from attraction to attraction with ease. Bus transfers to and from MRT stops are the way to go—or you could stick to taxicabs.

Kong Meng San Phor Kark See Temple   The largest religious complex on the island, this place, called Phor Kark See for short, is composed of prayer and meditation halls, a hospice, gardens, and a vegetarian restaurant. The largest building is the Chinese-style Hall of Great Compassion. There is also the octagonal Hall of Great Virtue and a towering pagoda. For S50¢, you can buy flower petals to place in a dish at the Buddha's feet. Compared to other temples on the island, Phor Kark See seems shiny, having been built only in 1981. As a result, the religious images inside carry a strange, almost artificial, cartoonlike air about them.

88 Bright Hill Dr., located in the center of the island to the east of Bukit Panjang Nature Preserve (Bright Hill Dr. is off Ang Mo Kio Ave.). ✆ **65/6849-5300.** Daily 6am–9:30pm. Take MRT to Bishan, then take bus 410.

Kranji War Memorial   Kranji Cemetery commemorates the Allied men and women who fought and died in World War II. Prisoners of war in a camp nearby began a burial ground here, and after the war it was enlarged to provide space for all the casualties. The Kranji War Cemetery is the site of 4,000 graves of servicemen, while the Singapore State Cemetery memorializes the names of more than 20,000 who died and have no known graves. Stones are laid geometrically on a slope with a view of the Strait of Johor. The memorial itself is designed to represent the three arms of the services.

Woodlands Rd., located in the very northern part of the island. Daily 7am–6pm. Kranji MRT.

Lian Shan Shuang Lin Temple   This temple, in English "the Twin Groves of the Lotus Mountain Temple," has a great story behind its founding. One night in 1898, Hokkien businessman Low Kim Pong and his son had the same dream¾of a golden light shining from the west. The following day, the two went to the western shore and waited until, moments before sundown, a ship appeared carrying a group of Hokkien Buddhist monks and nuns on their way to China after a pilgrimage to India. Low Kim Pong vowed to build a monastery if they would stay in Singapore. They did.

Laid out according to feng shui principles, the buildings include the Dharma Hall, a main prayer hall, and drum and bell towers. They are arranged in *cong lin* style, a rare type of monastery design with a universal layout so that no matter how vast the grounds are, any monk can find his way around. The entrance hall has granite wall panels carved with scenes from Chinese history. The main prayer hall has fantastic details in the ceiling, wood panels, and other woodcarvings. In the back is a shrine to Kuan Yin, goddess of mercy.

Originally built amid farmland, the temple became surrounded by suburban highrise apartments in the 1950s and 1960s, with the Toa Payoh Housing Development Board New Town project and the Pan-Island Expressway creeping close by.

184-E Jalan Toa Payoh. ✆ **65/6259-6924.** Free admission. Daily 8:30am–5pm. Located in Toa Payoh New Town. Toa Payoh MRT to bus 232, 237, or 238.

MacRitchie Nature Trail   Of all the nature reserves in Singapore, the Central Catchment Nature Reserve is the largest, at 2,000 hectares (4,940 acres). Located in the center of the island, it's home to four of Singapore's reservoirs: MacRitchie, Seletar, Pierce, and Upper Pierce. The rainforest here is secondary forest, but the animals don't care; they're just as happy with the place. There's one path for walking and jogging (no bicycles allowed) that stretches 3km (1.75 miles) from its start in the southeast corner of the reserve, turning to the edge of MacRitchie Reservoir, then letting you out at the Singapore Island Country Club. The TreeTop Walk is a 250m-long (820-ft.) suspension walkway that rises 25m (82 ft.) from the forest floor. The views are great, but it is a hike from the parking lots.

Central Catchment Nature Reserve. © **65/6468-5736.** www.nparks.gov.sg. Free admission. From Orchard Rd., take bus 132 from the Orchard Parade Hotel. From Raffles City, take bus 130. Get off at the bus stop near Little Sisters of the Poor. Next to Little Sisters of the Poor, follow the paved walkway, which turns into the trail.

Mandai Orchid Gardens   John Laycock, the British founder of the Orchid Society of Southeast Asia, began the Mandai garden in 1951 to house his own collection. Now owned and operated by Singapore Orchids Pte. Ltd, Mandai breeds and cultivates hybrids for international export, and the gardens double as an STB tourist attraction. Some of Mr. Laycock's original collection survives, though many were lost in World War II. Arranged in English garden style, orchid varieties are separated in beds that are surrounded by grassy lawn. Tree-growing varieties prefer the shade of the covered canopy. On display is Singapore's national flower, the Vanda Miss Joaquim, a natural hybrid in shades of light purple. Behind the gift shop is the Water Garden, where a stroll will reveal many houseplants common to the West, as you would find them in the wild.

The Vanilla Pod restaurant gets many of its ingredients from its own herb and spice gardens, and the specialty crabmeat salad uses the garden's orchid as an ingredient (daily noon–10pm; © **65/6368-0672**).

Mandai Lake Rd., on the route to the Singapore Zoo. © **65/6269-1036.** Admission S$3.50 adults, S$1 children 12 and under. Mon 8am–6pm; Tues–Sun 8am–7pm. Ang Mo Kio MRT bus 138.

Night Safari ★★★ ☺   Singapore takes advantage of its unchanging tropical climate and static ratio of daylight to night to bring you the world's first open-concept zoo for nocturnal animals. Here, as in the zoological gardens, animals live in landscaped areas, their barriers virtually unseen by visitors. These areas are dimly lit to create a moonlit effect, and a guided tram leads you through "regions" designed to resemble the Himalayan foothills, the jungles of Africa, and, naturally, Southeast Asia. Some of the free-range prairie animals come very close to the tram. The 45-minute ride covers almost 3.5km (2¼ miles) and has a stop half way to get off and have a rest or stroll along trails for closer views of smaller creatures. It costs S$10 extra, but it's worth it since it reaches areas of the zoo that don't have paths.

Staff, placed at regular intervals along each of the three trails, help you find your way, though it's almost impossible to get lost along the trails; however, it is nighttime, you are in the forest, and it can be spooky. The guides are there to add peace of mind (and all speak English). Flash photography is strictly prohibited, and be sure to bring plenty of insect repellent. Check out the bathrooms; they're all open-air, Bali style.

Singapore Zoo, 80 Mandai Lake Rd., at the western edge of the Bukit Panjang Nature Reserve, on the Seletar Reservoir. © **65/6269-3411.** www.zoo.com.sg. Admission S$22 adults, S$15 children 12 and under. Combination Zoo and Night Safari ticket (without tram) S$32 adults, S$20 children. Park Hopper Ticket for Zoo, Night Safari, and BirdPark S$45 adults, S$28 children. Daily 7:30pm–midnight. Ticket sales close at 11pm. Entrance Plaza, restaurant, and fast-food outlet 6–11:30pm. Ang Mo Kio MRT to bus 138.

Sasanaramsi Buddhist Temple   Known simply as the Burmese Buddhist Temple, it was founded by a Burmese expatriate to serve the overseas Burmese Buddhist community. His partner, an herbal doctor also from Burma, traveled home to buy a 10-ton block of marble from which was carved the 3.3m-tall (11-ft.) Buddha image that sits in the main hall, surrounded by an aura of brightly colored lights. The original temple was off Serangoon Road in Little India and was moved here in 1991 at the request of the Housing Development Board. On the third story is a standing Buddha image in gold and murals of events in the Buddha's life.

14 Tai Gin Rd., located next to the Sun Yat-sen Villa near Toa Payoh New Town. Daily 6:30am–9pm. Chanting Sun 9:30am and Sat 6:30pm. Take MRT to Toa Payoh, then take a taxi.

Singapore Zoo ★★ ☺   They call themselves the Open Zoo because, rather than coop the animals in jailed enclosures, they let them roam freely in landscaped areas. Beasts of the world are kept where they are supposed to be using psychological restraints and physical barriers that are disguised behind waterfalls, vegetation, and moats. Some animals are grouped with other species to show them coexisting as they would in nature. For instance, the white rhinoceros is neighborly with the wildebeest and ostrich—not that wildebeests and ostriches make the best company, but certainly contempt is better than boredom. Guinea and pea fowl, Emperor tamarinds, and other creatures are free-roaming and not shy; however, if you spot a water monitor or long-tailed macaque, know that they're not zoo residents—just locals looking for a free meal. Major zoo features are the Primate Kingdom, Wild Africa, the Reptile Garden, and underwater views of polar bears, sea lions, and penguins. Daily shows are themed around ecological issues and include "The Rainforest Fights Back," featuring 15 species, including orangutans, lemurs, otters, and birds at 10:30am and 1:30pm; sea lions, penguins, and pelicans at 11:30am, 2:30pm, and 5pm; and the elephants at 11:30am and 3:30pm. Witness the bond between animals and trainers at the Animal Friends show at 12:30pm and 4:30pm. You can take your photograph with an orangutan, a chimpanzee, or a snake, and there are elephant and camel rides too. The new Rainforest Kidzworld area is phenomenal: part water park, part adventure playground, and part petting zoo.

Zoo literature includes half-day and full-day agendas to help make the most of your visit. The best time to arrive, however, is at 9am, to have breakfast with an orangutan, which feasts on fruits and puts on a hilarious and very memorable show. If you miss that, you can also have tea with it at 4pm. Another good time to go is just after a rain, when the animals cool off and get frisky. See also the Night Safari listing, above.

80 Mandai Lake Rd., at the western edge of the Bukit Panjang Nature Reserve, on the Seletar Reservoir. ℂ **65/6269-3411.** www.zoo.com.sg. Admission S$18 adults, S$12 children 3–12. Combination Zoo and Night Safari ticket S$32 adults, S$20 children. Park Hopper Ticket for Zoo, Night Safari, and BirdPark S$45 adults, S$28 children. Daily 8:30am–6pm. Ang Mo Kio MRT to bus 138.

Sungei Buloh Wetland Reserve ★   Located to the very north of the island and devoted to the wetland habitat and mangrove forests that are so common to the region, 130-hectare (321-acre) Sungei Buloh (pronounced "Soong-eye Bull-low") is out-of-the-way, and not the easiest place to get to; but it's a beautiful park, with constructed paths and boardwalks taking you through tangles of mangroves, soupy marshes, grassy spots, and coconut groves. More than 75% of Singapore's wildlife species are represented here, but of the flora and fauna, the most spectacular sights here are the birds, of which there are somewhere between 140 and 170 species in residence or just passing through for the winter. Of the migratory birds, some have traveled from as far as Siberia to escape the cold months from September to March. Bird observatories are set up at different spots along the paths. Also, even though you're in the middle of nowhere, Sungei Buloh has a visitor center, a cafeteria, and souvenirs. Go early to beat the heat, and douse yourself well in mosquito repellent. The National Parks Board gives free guided tours every Saturday at 9 and 10am, and 3 and 4pm; call for registration.

301 Neo Tiew Crescent. ☏ **65/6794-1401.** Free admission weekdays; weekends S$1 adults, S50¢ children and seniors. Mon–Sat 7:30am–7pm; Sun 7am–7pm. Audiovisual show Mon–Sat 9am, 11am, 1pm, 3pm, and 5pm; hourly Sun and public holidays. Kranji MRT to bus 925. Stop at Kranji Reservoir Dam and cross causeway to park entrance.

Sun Yat-sen Nanyang Memorial Hall ★ Dr. Sun Yat-sen visited Singapore eight times to raise funds for his revolution in China and made Singapore his headquarters for gaining the support of overseas Chinese in Southeast Asia. A wealthy Chinese merchant built the villa around 1880 for his mistress, and a later owner permitted Dr. Sun Yat-sen to use it. The house reflects the classic bungalow style, which is becoming endangered in modern Singapore. Renovated in 2008, its typical bungalow features include a projecting carport with a sitting room overhead, verandas with striped blinds, second-story cast-iron railings, and first-story masonry balustrades. A covered walkway leads to the kitchen and servants' quarters in the back.

Inside, the life of Dr. Yat-sen is traced in photos and watercolors, from his birth in southern China through his creation of a revolutionary organization.

12 Tai Gin Rd., near Toa Payoh New Town. ☏ **65/6256-7377.** Admission S$4 adults, S$3 children and seniors. Tues–Sun 9am–5pm. Toa Payoh MRT to bus 45.

Eastern Singapore Attractions

The east coast leads from the edge of Singapore's urban area to the tip of the eastern part, at Changi Point. Eastern Singapore is home to Changi International Airport, nearby Changi Prison, and the long stretch of East Coast Park along the shoreline. The **MRT** heads east in this region, but swerves northward at the end of the line. A new MRT track, the circle line, will extend the network wider in the east and west from 2010. A popular **bus line** for east-coast attractions not reached by MRT is bus no. 2, which takes you to Changi Prison, Changi Point, and East Coast Park.

Changi Museum ★ Upon successful occupation of Singapore, the Japanese marched all British, Australian, and Allied European prisoners to Changi by foot, where they lived in a prison camp for 3 years, suffering overcrowding, disease, and malnutrition. Prisoners were cut off from the outside world except to leave the camp for labor duties. The hospital conditions were terrible; some prisoners suffered public beatings, and many died. In an effort to keep hope alive, they built a small chapel from wood and attap. Years later, at the request of former POWs and their families and friends, the government built this replica.

The museum displays sketches by W. R. M. Haxworth, replicas of the murals painted by Bombardier Stanley Warren in St Luke's Chapel and secret photos taken by George Aspinall—all POWs who were imprisoned here. Displayed with descriptions, the pictures, along with writings and other objects from the camp, bring this period to life, depicting the day-to-day horror with a touch of high morale.

1000 Upper Changi Rd., in the same general area as the airport. ☏ **65/6214-2451.** www.changimuseum.com. Free admission. Guided tour or audio-tour headset rental S$8 adults, S$4 children. Daily 9:30am–5pm. Tanah Merah MRT to bus 2.

East Coast Park   East Coast Park is a narrow strip of reclaimed land, 8.5km (5¼ miles) long, tucked in between the shoreline and East Coast Parkway, that serves as a hangout for Singaporean families on the weekends. Moms and dads barbecue under the trees while the kids swim at the beach, which is nothing more than a narrow lump of grainy sand sloping into yellow-green water that has more seaweed than a sushi bar. Paths for bicycling, in-line skating, walking, or jogging run the length of the park and are crowded on weekends and public and school holidays. On Sundays, you'll find kite flyers in the open grassy parts. The lagoon is the best place to go for bicycle rentals, canoeing, and windsurfing. If you go to the McDonald's Carpark C entrance, you'll find beach cafes, some sea-kayak rentals, plus in-line skates and bicycle rentals as well. A couple of outfits, listed in "Outdoor Activities," later in this chapter, offer equipment rentals and instruction. The park is also home to **UDMC Seafood Centre** (see earlier in this chapter), located not far from the lagoon.

East Coast Pkwy. Free admission. Bus 36 or 16 to Marine Parade and use the underpass to cross the highway.

Sentosa Island

In the 1880s, Sentosa was a hub of British military activity, with hilltop forts built to protect the harbor from sea invasion from all sides. Today it has become a weekend getaway spot and Singapore's answer to Disneyland. It's also home to one of Singapore's two massive "integrated resorts," Resorts World Sentosa.

If you're spending the day, there are restaurants in abundance and a couple of affordable food courts. For a unique dining option, consider **Sky Dining,** aboard the **Jewel Cable Car,** where you can spend a couple hours eating a three- or four-course Western meal (set menus S$168 or S$248 for two; children's set menu S$24). It's especially popular on Valentine's Day or for birthdays and wedding proposals. Meals are pretty tasty, provided by the Jewel Box restaurant. For more information, call ② 65/6377-9688, or visit www.mountfaber.com.sg.

For overnights, the **Shangri-La's Rasa Sentosa Resort and Spa,** the **Sentosa Resort & Spa,** and the **Hard Rock Hotel Singapore** at Resorts World Sentosa are popular options. For all general Sentosa inquiries, call ② 1800/736-8672 or see www.sentosa.com.sg.

GETTING THERE

Island admission is S$2 each for adults and children, payable at the causeway upon entry or factored into the cost of transport to the island.

The most entertaining way to get there is to take the cable car. From the Cable Car Towers (② 65/6270-8855), they make the trip daily from 8:30am to 10pm at a cost of S$26 round-trip adults and S$15 children. The one-way ticket is only one Singapore dollar less for children and two Singapore dollars less for adults. The view is okay (but too far from the city to see skyline) and the ride is especially fun for kids. The cable cars also extend up Mt. Faber on the Singapore side. If you choose to take a cable car up to the top, you can take it back down again. Otherwise, if you choose to alight at this stop, you can take a taxi back to civilization.

The Sentosa Express light-rail train operates between VivoCity shopping mall at the HarbourFront MRT station and Sentosa, with stops at the beach, major attractions, and Resorts World Sentosa. Pick up the train to Sentosa at VivoCity, third level, where you can purchase tickets for S$3, which include all-day rides, plus Sentosa admission. The train operates daily from 7am to midnight.

The orange Sentosa bus operates from the HarbourFront Interchange (near HarbourFront MRT) daily from 7am to 10pm, with extended hours until midnight on Friday, Saturday, and the eve of public holidays; it costs S$2 per person payable at the HarbourFront ticketing counter. Stops include Resorts World Sentosa and Beach Station.

The Sentosa Rider bus plies routes along Orchard Road, along Marina Bay, and through Chinatown daily from 9am to 10:30pm. The cost is S$8 per person, and if you go this route you can also choose a number of packages for Sentosa attractions—tickets and packages are available from hotel tour desks.

The SIA Hop-On-Hop-Off bus also stops on Sentosa.

A city taxi can take you there; just pay the entrance fee after you cross the causeway, and the driver can drop you anywhere you'd like to go within the island. Alternatively, you can walk across the boardwalk on foot from the causeway entrance at VivoCity shopping mall.

GETTING AROUND

Once on Sentosa, a free bus system with three color-coded routes snakes around the island from 7am to 11pm from Sunday to Thursday and 12:30am on Fridays and Saturdays. There's a free map that's available everywhere, which is necessary to navigate all that's here.

SEEING THE SIGHTS

The most notable attractions that you get free with your Sentosa admission are the **Animal and Bird Encounters,** a range of displays featuring reptiles, macaques, parrots, and birds of prey that runs from noon to 5:30pm at the amphitheater at Palawan Beach; the Nature Trail that starts from the bottom of the Merlion statue and the **Dragon Trail Nature Walk,** a 1.5km (1-mile) stroll through secondary rainforest to see dragon sculptures and local flora and fauna; and the **beaches.**

Sentosa has three beaches, but be advised, the water here is murky with some floating litter due to heavy shipping traffic in surrounding waters. At **Siloso Beach,** deck chairs, beach umbrellas, and a variety of **watersports equipment** like pedal boats, aqua bikes, fun bugs, canoes, surfboards, and banana boats are available for hire at nominal charges. This is where the beautiful young things hang out and play beach volleyball, and where nighttime beach parties are often held. Bicycles are also available for hire. Shower and changing facilities, food kiosks, and snack bars are at rest stations. **Palawan Beach** ☺ is recommended for families, as it has a longer stretch of beach, a fountain playground, a cheap local-food-hawker center and showering/locker facilities just behind. **Tanjong Beach** is the quietest and most remote of the three, with few facilities.

Most attractions on Sentosa charge separate entrance fees. They include the **Songs of the Sea** laser fountain show (S$10 per person for ages 3 and over; daily 7:40 and 8:40pm); **Skyline Luge Sentosa** (S$12 per ride; daily 10am–7:30pm, extended to 9:30pm on weekends); **MegaZip Adventure Park,** a ride on a 450m (1,476-ft.) zip cable (S$29 per ride, S$24 for the aerial obstacle course, and S$12 for the ParaJump ride, or S$59 for all three; Mon–Fri 2–7pm, Sat–Sun 11am–7pm); **Wave House Sentosa,** with artificial waves for body-boarding and surfing (S$30–S$40 per hour weekdays and S$35–S$45 weekends; Sun–Thurs 11am–11pm, Fri–Sat 11am–2am); **Sentosa 4D Magix** motion cinema (S$18 adults, S$11 children; daily 10am–9pm); and the **TigerSky Tower** (S$12 adults, S$8 children; daily 9am–9pm). The best attractions, in my opinion, are as follows:

Sentosa Island Attractions

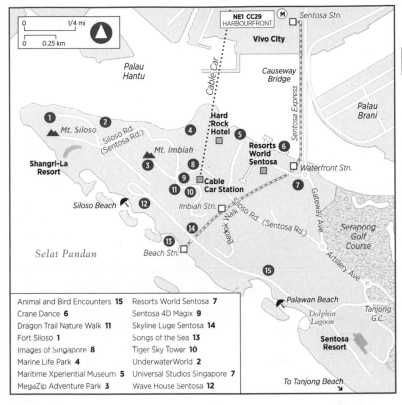

Animal and Bird Encounters **15**	Resorts World Sentosa **7**
Crane Dance **6**	Sentosa 4D Magix **9**
Dragon Trail Nature Walk **11**	Skyline Luge Sentosa **14**
Fort Siloso **1**	Songs of the Sea **13**
Images of Singapore **8**	Tiger Sky Tower **10**
Marine Life Park **4**	UnderwaterWorld **2**
Maritime Xperiential Museum **5**	Universal Studios Singapore **7**
MegaZip Adventure Park **3**	Wave House Sentosa **12**

Fort Siloso Fort Siloso guarded Keppel Harbour from invasion in the 1880s. It's one of three forts built on Sentosa, and it later became a military camp in World War II. The buildings have been outfitted to resemble a barracks, kitchen, laundry, and military offices as they looked back in the day. In places, you can explore the underground tunnels and ammunition holds, but they're not as extensive as you would hope they'd be. The **Surrender Chambers** lead you through authentic footage, photos, maps, and recordings of survivors to chronologically tell the story of the Pacific theater activity of World War II and how the Japanese conquered Singapore. The grand finale is a wax museum depicting, first, a scene of the British surrender and, last, another of the Japanese surrender.

✆ **65/6275-0388.** Admission S$8 adults, S$5 children. Daily 10am–6pm.

Images of Singapore ★★ Images of Singapore is a highlight of a visit to Sentosa. "Pioneers of Singapore" is an exhibit of beautifully constructed life-size dioramas that place figures like Sultan Hussein, Sir Stamford Raffles, Tan Tock Seng, and Naraina Pillai, to name just a few, in the context of Singapore's timeline and note their contributions to its development. Also interesting are the dioramas depicting scenes from the daily routines of the different cultures as they lived during colonial times. It's a great stroll that brings history to life and gives a good introduction to the cultural influences that continue to shape modern Singapore.

The newest addition, **Festivals of Singapore,** is another life-size diorama exhibit depicting a few of the major festivals and traditions of the Chinese, Malay, Indian, and Peranakan cultures in Singapore.

© **65/6275-0388.** S$10 adults, S$7 children. Daily 9am–7pm.

Resorts World Sentosa ★★ Singapore's second "integrated resort," Resorts World is more of a leisure destination compared to its urban counterpart, Marina Bay Sands. A S$6.59 billion project, the resort covers 49 hectares (121 acres) on Sentosa, Singapore's fun island getaway. The resort's six different hotels (which offer a total 1,200 rooms and suites) accommodate mainly leisure travelers and families, as do the attractions here, the highlight of which is Universal Studios Singapore. The shopping arcade is packed with gift shops and candy stores, plus shops selling luxury fashion and accessories. Look for the **Chihuly Studio** (Hotel Michael; © **65/6577-6990**) to see the world-renowned artist's eye-popping glass sculptures, all for sale. More than 60 dining choices offer everything from inexpensive local treats to outstanding dining experiences from possibly the world's greatest chef, Joël Robuchon. The resort also hosts meetings and conventions, and at night there's the Voyage de la Vie show and a few nightlife options.

The **Casino** has 530 gaming tables with more than 19 different games, plus 1,300 electronic game machines set amid glass sculptures by artist Dale Chihuly and a garden court with natural sunlight, fresh air, and water features. A resident band plays nightly, and you'll find food promotions and drink trolleys throughout. You must be 21 years or older to enter; the main entrance is on the basement level just beneath the Crockfords Tower hotel. Foreigners can enter for free (bring your passport), while Singapore citizens and residents must pay a fee. There's also a dress code prohibiting beachwear, flip-flops, casual shorts, and sleeveless T-shirts.

Universal Studios Singapore ★★★ ☺ (8 Sentosa Gateway; © **65/6577-8899**) opened in 2010, but at press time not all rides and attractions were up and running. The theme park is divided into seven zones that include Jurassic Park, Shrek, Sci-Fi City, New York, Hollywood, Madagascar, and Ancient Egypt, with 24 themed rides for all ages. Inside the park you'll also find restaurants, snack bars, and gift shops. *Before you go, here are some critical tips:* Book in advance—if this is a big part of your holiday plan, buy tickets online when you plan your trip. Limited tickets are available each day on a first-come-first-served basis, but they run out fast—especially on weekends and holidays. Otherwise, you can line up on the day itself and hope there are tickets left. I also recommend getting to the park at opening. The crowds pour in by 11am, so if you're early you can try to beat some of the long lines for rides. Also, you may want to bring a change of clothes if you plan to get wet on the water rides.

The park is open daily from 10am to 7pm, but hours can vary, so it's a good idea to call in advance. On Fridays and Saturdays the park hosts Hollywood After Hours from 7 to 10pm, with discounted dining and shopping, plus a pyrotechnic show (rides are closed, though). Ticket prices are as follows: Weekday 1-day pass S$66 adults, S$48 children (ages 4–12), and S$32 seniors. Weekend and public holiday 1-day pass S$72 adults, S$52 children, and S$36 seniors. Two-day passes are S$118 adults, S$88 children, and S$58 for seniors. The ticket includes free passage on all rides, except for the Amber Rock Climb, which is an extra S$10 per person. *Note:* The park also sells a Universal Express feature that lets you jump to the head of the queue for an extra S$30 per person on weekdays and S$48 per person on weekends and public holidays. Access to Hollywood After Hours is S$5 per person and includes 15% discount on all meals at park restaurants. Tickets can be purchased online from www.rwsentosa.com or by making a reservation at ☎ 65/6577-8899. The Universal Studios Singapore ticket booth, located at the main entrance, is open Sunday to Thursday 9am to 8pm and Friday to Saturday 9am to 9pm.

At press time, additional attractions are slated to open starting in 2011. The **Marine Life Park,** opening schedule for late 2011, promises to be the world's largest oceanarium, with more than 700,000 creatures on display in 20 million gallons of water, plus special entertainment and educational programs, all built around a conservation theme (which ironically has drawn criticism from local and international conservationists about the ethics of keeping wild marine life in a leisure attraction in the first place). Also on the books for a 2011 summer launch is the **Maritime Xperiential Museum,** a waterfront display dedicated to the history and global importance of sea trade, with a multimedia, interactive theater-in-the-round. Finally, the resort is building a water and light show, the **Crane Dance,** at its waterfront promenade, that will open by the end of 2011 and is free of charge.

There are six hotels here, including the Hard Rock Hotel (p. 446). Two hotels, Equarius Hotel and Spa Villas, are scheduled to open in 2011–2012. The ESPA spa will also open in 2011.

A final tip: The complex has a kids club that is open to everyone, whether you're staying at the resort's hotels or not. It's located in the Hard Rock Hotel, with excellent staff and planned activities and games for children 3 years and older. The cost is S$12 per hour, extra if you want them to serve meals.

You can get to the resort by following any of the routes mentioned above that will take you to Sentosa. The public bus that leaves from VivoCity shopping mall drops you in the basement just near the casino. The light rail train's first stop on Sentosa lets you off at the resort's main promenade.

Sentosa Island. ☎ **65/6577-8888.** www.rwsentosa.com.

Underwater World ★ ☺ Underwater World is without a doubt one of the most-visited attractions on Sentosa. Everybody comes for the tunnel: 83m (272 ft.) of transparent acrylic tube through which you glide on a conveyor belt, gaping at sharks, stingrays, eels, and other creatures of the sea drifting by, above and on both sides. If you're lucky, you might see the scuba diver who hops in several times a day and feeds them by hand. In smaller tanks, you can view other unusual sea life, like the puffer fish and the mysteriously weedy and leafy sea dragons. The price also includes admission to the Dolphin Lagoon, with pink-dolphin shows daily at 1:30, 3:30, and 5:30pm, with an additional show at 11am on weekends.

☎ **65/6275-0030.** www.underwaterworld.com.sg. S$23 adults, S$15 children. Daily 9am–9pm.

OUTDOOR ACTIVITIES

Beaches

Besides the beach at East Coast Park and those on Sentosa Island (see above), you can try the smaller beach at Changi Village, called Changi Point. From the shore, you have a panoramic view of Malaysia, Indonesia, and several smaller islands that belong to Singapore. The beach is calm and frequented mostly by locals who set up camps and barbecues to hang out all day. There are kayak rentals along the beach, and in Changi Village you'll find, in addition to a huge hawker center, quite a few international restaurants and pubs to hang out in and have a fresh seafood lunch when you get hungry. To get there, take SBS bus no. 2 from either the Tanah Merah or Bedok MRT station.

On Kusu and St. John's Islands, there are quiet swimming lagoons, a couple of which have quite nice views of the city.

Bicycle Rental

Bicycles are not for rent within the city limits, and traffic does not really allow for cycling on city streets, so sightseeing by bicycle is not recommended for city touring. If you plan a trip out to **Sentosa,** cycling provides a great alternative to that island's tram system and gets you closer to the parks and nature there. For a little light cycling, most people head out to **East Coast Park,** where rentals are inexpensive, the scenery is nice on cooler days, and there are plenty of great stops for eating along the way. One favorite place where the locals go for mountain biking sorts of adventures (and to cycle amid the old kampong villages) is **Pulau Ubin,** off the northeast coast of Singapore.

AT EAST COAST PARK   There are several rental shops for bicycles and inline skates along the East Coast Park; couples and families often hire tandems too. Try **SDK Recreation** (② 65/6445-2969), near McDonald's at Carpark C; open 7 days from about 11am to 8 or 9pm. Rentals are S$4 to S$8 per hour, depending on the type and quality of bike you're looking for. Identification may be requested, or leave a S$50 deposit.

ON SENTOSA ISLAND   There are several rental places near Siloso Beach off Siloso Road, a short walk from Underwater World (see "Sentosa Island," earlier in this chapter). There's a kiosk at Sakae Sushi (② 65/6271-6385) and another at Costa Sands (② 65/6275-2471). Both are open 7 days from around 10am to 6:30 or 7pm. Rental for a standard bicycle is S$5 per hour. A mountain bike goes for S$8 per hour. Identification is required.

IN PULAU UBIN   When you get off the ferry, there are a number of places to rent bikes. The shops are generally open between 8am and 6pm and will charge between S$8 and S$14 per day, depending on which bike you choose. Most rental agents will have a map of the island for you—take it. Even though it doesn't look too impressive, it'll be a great help.

Golf

Golf is big in Singapore, and although there are quite a few clubs, many are exclusively for members only. However, many places are open for limited play by nonmembers. All will require you to bring an international par certificate. Most hotel concierges will be glad to make arrangements for you, and this may be the best way to go. Also, it's really popular for Singaporeans to go on day trips to Malaysia for the best courses.

Changi Golf Club   This 9-hole walking course is par 34, and nonmembers may play at this private club only on weekdays (walk-ins okay, but advance booking recommended). They may even be able to set you up with other players. The course opens at 7:30am. Last tee is 4:30pm.

20 Netheravon Rd. ② **65/6545-5133.** Greens fees S$45; caddy fees S$10. Mon–Fri 7:30am–4:30pm. Closed for maintenance Mon mornings.

Marina Bay Golf Course This 18-hole golf course opened in 2006 and comes with a great view of the city skyline. It's designed to resemble a Scottish links–style course, with 91 challenging pot bunkers. Marina Bay even offers night golfing from Wednesday to Friday, with the course entirely floodlit. The attached driving range is open daily from 7am to 10:15pm.

80 Rhu Cross, #01-01. ℂ **65/6345-7788.** Greens fees Mon–Fri S$83 or S$115 (9 or 18 holes), Sat–Sun S$103 or S$200. Sat–Tues 7am–5pm; Wed–Fri 7am–8:20pm.

Sentosa Golf Club The best idea if you're traveling with your family and want to get in a game, Sentosa's many activities will keep the kids happy while you practice your swing guilt free at one of the club's two 18-hole 72-par courses, the Tanjong and the Serapong (the home of the Singapore Open). This private club charges much more for nonmembers than other courses (and weekend play for nonmembers is restricted to Sun afternoon), but both are beautiful championship courses and a relaxing time away from the city. Advance phone bookings are required.

27 Bukit Manis Rd., Sentosa Island. ℂ **65/6275-0022.** Greens fees Mon–Fri S$305–S$355, Sun S$425–S$475. Daily 7am–7pm.

Scuba Diving

The locals are crazy about scuba diving but are more likely to travel to Malaysia and other Southeast Asian destinations for good underwater adventures. The most common complaint is that the water surrounding Singapore is really silty—sometimes to the point where you can barely see your hand before your face.

Sea Canoeing

Rubber sea canoes and one- or two-person kayaks can be rented at Siloso Beach on Sentosa, the beach at East Coast Park (near McDonald's Carpark C), and the beach at Changi Point. Prices range from S$14 to S$35 per hour, depending on the type of craft you rent. Life jackets are provided. These places don't have phones, so just go to the beach and scout out the rental places on the sand.

Tennis

Quite a few hotels in the city provide tennis courts for guests, many floodlit for night play (which allows you to avoid the daytime heat), and even a few that can arrange lessons, so be sure to check out the hotel listings earlier in this chapter. If your hotel doesn't have tennis facilities, ask your concierge for help to arrange a game at a facility outside the hotel. Many hotels have signing agreements with sister hotel properties or special rates with independent fitness centers within the city.

Water-Skiing & Wakeboarding

The new hot spot for water-skiing and wakeboarding is **Ski 360°** at the East Coast Park (ℂ **65/6442-7318;** www.ski360degree.com). Rather than a boat, skiers are pulled by an overhead cable like a snow ski lift around the perimeter of the lake. Ski passes range from S$32 per hour on weekdays to S$42 on weekends and public holidays. Boat-based skiing is run by various clubs on Seletar Island—contact the Singapore Waterski and Wakeboard Federation (ℂ **65/6348-9943;** www.swwf.org.sg) for information on courses and contacts.

Windsurfing & Sailing

You'll find both windsurfing boards and sailboats for rent at the lagoon in East Coast Park, which is where these activities primarily take place. Many require membership, but the Mana Mana Beach Club rents out to visitors at 1212 E. Coast Pkwy. (© **65/6339-8878**). For S$55 an hour, you can rent a Laser, or for S$55 an hour, you can rent windsurf gear.

SHOPPING

In Singapore, shopping is a sport, and from the practiced glide through haute couture boutiques to skillful back-alley bargaining, it's always exciting, with something to satiate every shopper's appetite. The focal point of shopping in Singapore is **Orchard Road,** a very long stretch of glitzy shopping malls packed with Western clothing stores, from designer apparel to cheap chic, and many other mostly imported finds.

HOURS   Shopping malls are generally open from 10am to 9pm Monday through Saturday, with some stores keeping shorter Sunday hours. The malls sometimes remain open until 10pm on holidays. Smaller shops are open from around 10am to 5pm Monday through Saturday but are almost always closed on Sunday. Hours will vary from shop to shop. Arab Street is closed on Sunday.

PRICES   Almost all of the larger stores in shopping malls have fixed prices. Sometimes these stores will have seasonal sales, especially from June into July, during the month-long **Great Singapore Sale,** when prices are discounted 50% or 70%. In the smaller shops and at street vendors, prices are sometimes not marked, and vendors will quote you higher prices than the going rate in anticipation of the bargaining ritual. These are the places to find good prices, if you negotiate well.

BARGAINING   In Singapore, not all shops fix prices on merchandise, and even many that display price tags are open to negotiation. For outsiders who are unaccustomed to this tradition, bargaining can be embarrassing and frustrating at first—especially for those who are used to accepting fixed prices without an argument. The most important tip for successful bargaining is to first have an idea of the value of what you're buying—a little comparison shopping goes a long way.

GLOBAL REFUND SCHEME   When you shop in stores that display the blue "Tax Free Shopping" logo, the government will refund the 7% goods and services tax (GST) you pay on purchases totaling S$100 or more, if you are leaving Singapore via air travel. At the point of purchase, the sales clerk will fill out a Tax Free Shopping Cheque, which you retain with your receipt.

When you leave Singapore, present your checks at Customs along with your passport and let them see the goods you've purchased to show that you're taking them out of the country with you. Customs will stamp the forms, which you then present at any of the Global Refund Counters in the airport for an on-the-spot cash refund (in Singapore dollars), a check, a direct transfer of the amount to your credit card account, or an airport shopping voucher. For complete details, call the Global Refund Scheme hot line at © **65/6225-6238;** www.globalrefund.com.

Another company, Premier Tax Free (www.premiertaxfree.com), also offers GST refunds with kiosks at the airport.

Orchard Road Area

The malls on Orchard Road are a tourist attraction in their own right, with smaller boutiques and specialty shops intermingled with huge department stores. Takashimaya and Isetan have been imported from Japan. **John Little** is the oldest department store in Singapore, followed by **Robinson's. Tangs** is significant, having grown from a cartful of merchandise nurtured by the business savvy of local entrepreneur C. K. Tang. Boutiques range from the younger styles of Topshop and Miss Selfridge to the sophisticated fashions of Chanel and Salvatore Ferragamo. You'll also find antiques, oriental carpets, art galleries and curio shops, HMV music stores, Kinokuniya and Borders bookstores, video arcades, and scores of restaurants, local food courts, fast-food joints, and coffeehouses—even a few bars, which open in the evenings (see "Singapore After Dark" later in this chapter). It's hard to say when Orchard Road is not crowded, but it's definitely a mob scene on weekends, when folks have the free time to come and hang around, looking for fun.

Centrepoint Centrepoint is home to Robinson's department store, which first opened in Singapore in 1858. Here you'll find about 150 other shops, plus fast-food outlets and a Times bookstore. 176 Orchard Rd. © **65/6737-9000.** www.fraserscentrepointmalls. com.

Far East Plaza At this crowded mall, a jumble of little shops sells everything from CDs to counterculture fashions, luggage to camera equipment, eyewear to souvenirs. Mind yourself here: Some of these shops do not display prices, but rather gauge the price depending on how wealthy the customer appears. If you must shop here, use your shrewdest bargaining powers. It may pay off to wear an outfit that has seen better days. 14 Scotts Rd. No phone. www.fareast-plaza.com.

The Heeren Three levels of The Heeren are taken up by trendy aLT, which carries hip labels from Japan, Korea, and around the region. Most of the shops here carry young fashion, street wear, and active wear. 260 Orchard Rd. © **65/6733-4725.** www.heeren. com.sg.

Hilton Shopping Gallery This shopping arcade is the most exclusive in Singapore. Gucci, Donna Karan, Missoni, and Louis Vuitton are just a few of the international design houses that have made this their Singapore home. 581 Orchard Rd. © **65/6733-4725.**

ION Orchard Futuristic and fantastical, ION Orchard was designed by the same architects behind the Bullring in Birmingham, U.K. It has attracted the most luxurious names in haute couture as tenants, including Christian Dior, Cartier, Dolce & Gabbana, and Giorgio Armani. Restaurants and food courts are plenty, and on the 56th floor there's an observatory. 2 Orchard Turn. © **65/6238-8228.** www.ionorchard.com.

Lucky Plaza The map of this place will take hours to decipher, as more than 400 stores are here. It's basically known for sportswear, camera equipment, watches, and luggage. If you buy electronics, please make sure you get an international warranty with your purchase. Also, like Far East Plaza, Lucky Plaza is a notorious rip-off problem for travelers. Make sure you come here prepared to fend off slick sales techniques. It may also help to take the government's advice and avoid touts and offers that sound too good to be true. 304 Orchard Rd. © **65/6235-3294.** www.luckyplaza.com.sg.

Ngee Ann City/Takashimaya Shopping Centre Takashimaya, a major Japanese department store import, anchors Ngee Ann City's many smaller boutiques.

Alfred Dunhill, Chanel, Coach, Tiffany & Co., Royal Copenhagen, Waterford, and Wedgwood boutiques are found here, along with many other local and international fashion shops. 391 Orchard Rd. ✆ **65/6506-0458.** www.ngeeanncity.com.sg.

Palais Renaissance   Shops here include upmarket boutiques like Prada, Versus, and DKNY. 390 Orchard Rd. ✆ **65/6737-6993.** www.palais.sg.

Paragon   Another upmarket shopping mall, with tenants including Diesel, Emanuel Ungaro, Escada, and Ferragamo. 290 Orchard Rd. ✆ **65/6738-5535.** www.paragon.com.sg.

Shaw House   The main floors of Shaw House are taken up by Isetan, a large Japanese department store with designer boutiques for men's and women's fashions, accessories, and cosmetics. On the fifth level, the Lido Theatre screens new releases from Hollywood and around the world. 350 Orchard Rd. ✆ **65/6735-4225.**

Tanglin Mall ★   A mecca for expatriates, this mall has charming boutiques filled with regional handicrafts for the home and interesting Southeast Asian ethnic-inspired fashions. 163 Tanglin Rd. ✆ **65/6736-4922.**

Tanglin Shopping Centre ★★   Tanglin Shopping Centre is unique and fun. You won't find many clothing stores here, but you'll find shop after shop selling antiques, art, and collectibles—from curios to carpets. 19 Tanglin Rd. ✆ **65/6373-0849.** www.tanglinsc.com.

Tangs   Once upon a time, C. K. Tang peddled goods from an old cart in the streets of Singapore. An industrious fellow, he parlayed his business into a small department store. A hit from the start, Tangs has grown exponentially over the decades and now competes with the other international megastores that have moved in. But Tangs is truly Singaporean, and its history is a local legend. 320 Orchard Rd. ✆ **65/6737-5500.** www.tangs.com.sg.

313@Somerset   A new addition to Orchard Road's walk of shopping fame, this funky mall is named for the nearest MRT station, Somerset, and anchored by a large Forever 21, with smaller shops catering to a younger, midmarket audience. 313 Orchard Rd. ✆ **65/6496-9313.** www.313somerset.com.sg.

Wisma Atria   Wisma Atria caters to midmarket shoppers. Here you'll find everything from Gap to Nine West mixed in with numerous eyewear, cosmetics, and high- and low-fashion boutiques. 435 Orchard Rd. ✆ **65/6235-8177.** www.wismaonline.com.

Marina Bay

The Marina Bay area arose from a plot of reclaimed land and now boasts the giant **Suntec Singapore convention center** and all the hotels, restaurants, and shopping malls that support it. Shopping here is convenient, with the major malls and hotels interconnected by covered walkways and pedestrian bridges, making it easy to get around with minimal exposure to the elements. It's also connected to **Raffles City Shopping Centre** by an underground shopping mall, the **City Link Mall** (✆ **65/6339-9913**). Across the reservoir, the mall at the new **Marina Bay Sands** is accessible by the scenic Helix pedestrian bridge.

Marina Square   Marina Square is a midsized complex that, in addition to a wide variety of shops, has a cinema, fast-food outlets and cafes, pharmacies, and convenience stores. 6 Raffles Blvd. ✆ **65/6339-8787.** www.marinasquare.com.sg.

Millenia Walk   Smaller than Marina Square, Millenia Walk has more upmarket boutiques, like Fendi, Guess?, and Liz Claiborne, to name a few. 9 Raffles Blvd. ✆ **65/6883-1122.** www.milleniawalk.com.

The Shoppes at Marina Bay Sands This opulent, airy mall is resplendent, no doubt from the scent of money wafting from the complex's 24-hour casino, and from the high-end boutiques, like Manolo Blahnik and Hermès. Shoppers glide past window displays in sampan boats along the mall's indoor canal (adults S$10, children S$6 per ride). Louis Vuitton's Asian home base commands a huge crystal pavilion that juts out into the bay. 2 Bayfront Ave. ✆ **65/6688-8868.** www.marinabaysands.com/shopping.

Suntec City Mall Tons of shops selling fashion, sports equipment, books, CDs, plus restaurants and food courts, and a cinema adjacent to the Suntec convention center. 3 Temasek Blvd. ✆ **65/6825-2669.** www.sunteccity.com.sg.

Around the City Center

Although the Historic District doesn't have as many malls as the Orchard Road area, it still has some good shopping. Raffles City Shopping Centre can be overwhelming in its size but is convenient because it sits right atop the City Hall MRT stop. One of my favorite places to go, however, is the very upmarket Raffles Hotel Shopping Arcade, where you can enhance your post-shopping high with a Singapore Sling.

Parco Bugis Junction Here you'll find a few restaurants—fast food and fine dining—mixed in with clothing retailers, most of which sell fun fashions for younger tastes. 230 Victoria St. ✆ **65/6557-6557.**

Raffles City Shopping Centre Raffles City sits right on top of the City Hall MRT station, which makes it a very well visited mall, anchored by Robinson's department store. Men's and women's fashions, books, cosmetics, and accessories are sold in shops here, along with gifts. 252 North Bridge Rd. ✆ **65/6338-7766.** www.rafflescity.com.sg.

Raffles Hotel Shopping Arcade These shops are mostly haute couture; however, there is the Raffles Hotel gift shop for interesting souvenirs. For golfers, there's a Jack Nicklaus signature store. 328 North Bridge Rd. ✆ **65/6337-1886.**

VivoCity Singapore's largest shopping mall, Vivo is near the causeway to Sentosa, where you'll find the light rail service and buses to the island. VivoCity is anchored by Tang's department store, and has a fair amount of dining choices within many price ranges, an outdoor playground, and a rooftop splash pool for kids. 1 HarbourFront Walk. ✆ **65/6377-6860.** www.vivocity.com.sg.

Chinatown

For Chinese goods, nothing beats **Yue Hwa ★★**, 70 Eu Tong Sen St. (✆ **65/6538-4222**), a five-story Chinese emporium that's an attraction in its own right. The superb inventory includes all manner of silk wear (robes, underwear, blouses), embroidery and house linens, bolt silks, tailoring services (for perfect mandarin dresses), cloisonné (enamel work) jewelry and gifts, pottery, musical instruments, traditional Chinese clothing for men and women (from scholars' robes to coolie duds), jade and gold, cashmere, art supplies, herbs—I could go on and on. Prices are terrific. Plan to spend some time here.

For one-stop souvenir shopping, you can tick off half your list at **Chinatown Point,** aka the **Singapore Handicraft Center,** 133 New Bridge Rd. (✆ **65/6534-0102**), with dozens of small shops that sell mainly Chinese handicraft items from carved jade to imported Chinese classical instruments and lacquerware. The best gifts there include hand-carved chops (Chinese seals), with a few shops offering good selections of carved stone, wood, bone, glass, and ivory chops ready to be carved to your specifications. Simple designs are affordable, although some of the more elaborate chops and carvings fetch a handsome sum. You can also commission a personalized Chinese scroll painting or calligraphy piece.

In the heart of Chinatown, Pagoda and Trengganu streets are closed to vehicular traffic and host a vibrant **Chinatown Street Market** (open daily about 11am–11pm), where you can find a wide variety of Chinese silk robes, Indonesian batik souvenirs, Vietnamese lacquerware, Thai silk home linens, and Singaporean souvenirs—the list goes on. I've found the prices here to be inflated. If you're on a shoestring budget, find similar items at the market at the corner of Trengganu and Sago streets, called **Chinatown Complex,** where you may find it easier to bargain.

My all-time favorite gift idea? Spend an afternoon learning the traditional Chinese tea ceremony at the **Tea Chapter,** 9–11 Neil Rd. (✆ 65/6225-3026), and pick up a tea set—they have a lovely selection of tea pots, cups, and accessories, as well as quality teas for sale. When you return home, you'll be ready to give a fabulous gift—not just a tea set, but your own cultural performance as well. Another neat place to visit is **Kwong Chen Beverage Trading,** 16 Smith St. (✆ 65/6223-6927), for some Chinese teas in handsome tins. Although the teas are really inexpensive, they're packed in lovely tins—great to buy lots to bring back as smaller gifts. For serious tea aficionados or those curious about Traditional Chinese Medicine (TCM), stop by **Eu Yan Sang,** 269 South Bridge Rd. (✆ 65/6749-8830; www.euyansang.com.sg), where they have stocks of very fine (and expensive) teas, plus herbal remedies for health. For something a little more unusual, check out **Siong Moh Paper Products,** 39 Mosque St. (✆ 65/6861-1819), which carries a full line of ceremonial items. Pick up some joss sticks (temple incense) or joss paper (books of thin sheets of paper, stamped in reds and yellows with bits of gold and silver leaf). Definitely a conversation piece, as is the "hell money," stacks of false paper notes that believers burn at the temple for their ancestors to use for cash in the afterlife. Perfect for that friend who has everything. Also, if you duck over to **Sago Lane** while you're in the neighborhood, there are a few souvenir shops that sell Chinese kites and Cantonese Opera masks—cool for kids.

Arab Street

On Arab Street, shop for handicrafts from Malaysia and Indonesia. I go to **Hadjee Textiles,** 75 Arab St. (✆ 65/6298-1943), for their stacks of folded sarongs in beautiful colors and traditional patterns. They're perfect for traveling, as they're lightweight, but can serve you well as a dressy skirt, bedsheet, beach blanket, window shade, bath towel, or whatever you need—when I'm on the road, I can't live without mine. Buy a few here and the prices really drop. For modern styles of batik, check out **Basharahil Brothers,** 101 Arab St. (✆ 65/6296-0432), for their very interesting designs, but don't forget to see their collection of fine silk batiks in the back. For batik household linens, you can't beat **Maruti Textiles,** 93 Arab St. (✆ 65/6392-0253), where you'll find high-quality place mats and napkins, tablecloths, pillow covers, and quilts from India. The buyer for this shop has a good eye for style.

I've also found a few shops in the area that carry **handicrafts** from Southeast Asia. For antiques and curios, try **Gim Joo Trading,** 16 Baghdad St. (✆ 65/6293-5638), a jumble of the unusual, some of it old. A lovely antiques shop, **Melor's Curios,** 39 Bussorah St. (✆ 65/6292-3934), is almost a minimuseum of furnishings, home fixtures, and objets d'art that will fill any Singaporean with nostalgia.

Other unique treasures include the large assortment of fragrance oils at **Jamal Kazura Aromatics,** 21 Bussorah St. (✆ 65/6293-3320). Muslims are forbidden from consuming alcohol in any form (a proscription that includes the wearing of alcohol-based perfumes as well), so these oil-based perfumes re-create designer scents plus other floral and heady creations. Check out their delicate cut-glass bottles and atomizers as well. Finally, for the crafter in your life, **Kin Lee & Co.,** 109 Arab St. (© **65/6291-1411**), carries a complete line of patterns and accessories to make local Peranakan beaded slippers. In vivid colors and floral designs, these traditional slippers were always made by hand, to be attached later to a wooden sole. The finished versions are exquisite, plus they're fun to make.

Little India

I have a ball shopping the crowded streets of Little India. The best shopping is on Serangoon Road, where Singapore's Indian community heads for Indian imports and cultural items. The absolute best place to start is **Mustafa Centre ★★**, 320 Serangoon Rd./145 Syed Alwi Rd., at the corner of Serangoon and Syed Alwi roads (© **65/6295-5855**), but be warned, you can spend the whole day there—and night too, because Mustafa's is open 24 hours every day. This maze of a department store fills 2 city blocks full of imported items from India. Granted, much of it is everyday stuff, but the real finds are rows of saris and silk fabrics; two floors of jaw-dropping gold jewelry in Indian designs; an entire supermarket packed with spices and packets of instant curries; ready-made Indian-style tie-dye and embroidered casual wear; incense and perfume oils; cotton tapestries and textiles for the home—the list goes on. And prices can't be beat, seriously.

Little India offers all sorts of small finds, especially throughout **Little India Arcade** (48 Serangoon Rd.) and just across the street on Campbell Lane at **Kuna's,** 3 Campbell Lane (© **65/6294-2700**). Here you can buy inexpensive Indian costume jewelry like bangles, earrings, and necklaces in exotic designs and a wide assortment of decorative dots (called *pottu* in Tamil) to grace your forehead. Indian handicrafts include brass work, woodcarvings, dyed tapestries, woven cotton household linens, small curio items, very inexpensive incense, colorful pictures of Hindu gods, and other ceremonial items. Look here also for Indian cooking pots and household items.

Across the street from Little India Arcade, **Tekka Centre** is being renovated. This popular market carried stall after stall of inexpensive *salwar kameez,* or Punjabi suits, the three-piece outfits—long tunic over pants, with matching shawl—worn by northern Indian ladies, plus lots of cheap Indian-made *prêt-a-port.* They've all put up in a temporary location along Race Course Road, not far from Tekka Centre.

Punjab Bazaar, #01–07 Little India Arcade, 48 Serangoon Rd. (© **65/6296-0067**), carries a more upmarket choice of *salwar kameez,* in many styles and fabrics. If nothing strikes your fancy at Punjab Bazaar, try **Roopalee Fashions,** a little farther down at 88 Serangoon Rd. (© **65/6298-0558**). Both shops carry sandals, bags, and other accessories to complement your new outfit.

SINGAPORE AFTER DARK

Major cultural festivals are publicized by the **Singapore Tourism Board (STB),** who will give you complete details at their Visitors Centres (see p. 415 for locations) or on their website (www.visitsingapore.com). I highly recommend browsing the SISTIC site at www.sistic.com.sg for a complete schedule of upcoming ticketed performances, from rock concerts to children's productions, local dramas to touring ballet companies. Another good resource is the Life! section of Friday's *The Straits Times* newspaper, which lists weekend and upcoming events. *Where Singapore,* a free magazine with local events listings, is available at STB kiosks as well. Another freebie, *I-S Magazine,* promotes Singapore's clubbing lifestyle.

TICKETS Sistic (© 65/6348-5555; www.sistic.com.sg) handles bookings for almost all theater performances, concert dates, and special events. Their website offers a comprehensive events schedule, with online booking and ticket payment. (Tickets can be picked up at the venue prior to the performance.) Visit them online or at one of their centrally located kiosks at The Centrepoint, Esplanade–Theatres on the Bay, ION Orchard, Millenia Walk, Plaza Singapura, Raffles City Shopping Centre, VivoCity, or Wisma Atria.

HOURS Theater and dance performances can begin anywhere between 7:30 and 9pm. Don't be late—at Esplanade, they turn latecomers away. Many bars open in the late afternoon, a few as early as lunchtime. Disco and entertainment clubs usually open around 6pm but generally don't get lively until 10 or 11pm. Closing time for bars and clubs is at 1 or 2am on weekdays, 3 or 4am on weekends. A few have extended hours until 6am.

DRINK PRICES Because of the government's added tariff, alcoholic beverage prices are high everywhere, whether in a hotel bar or a neighborhood pub. "House pour" drinks (made with inexpensive brands of alcohol) are between S$12 and S$18—this is considered cheap. A glass of house wine will cost between S$14 and S$18, depending on whether it's a red or a white. A pint of local draft beer (Tiger, brewed in Singapore) is around S$14. Hotel establishments are, on average, the most expensive venues, while standalone pubs and cafes are better value. Almost every bar and club has a happy hour in the early evenings, and discounts can be up to 50% off for house pours and drafts. Most of the dance and entertainment clubs charge covers, but they will usually include one or more drinks. Many places offer ladies' nights— usually Wednesdays—when those of the feminine persuasion get in for free and sometimes even drink for free, too.

DRESS CODE Many clubs will require smart casual attire. Feel free to be trendy, but avoid dressing too casual or you may be turned away. Local clubbers dress up for a night on the town, usually in fashionista threads.

SAFETY You'll be fairly safe out during the wee hours in most parts of the city, and even a single woman alone has little to worry about. You can always get home safely in a taxi, which, fortunately, isn't too hard to find even late at night, with a couple of exceptions: When clubs close, there's usually a mob of revelers scrambling for cabs. Also, after midnight, a 50% surcharge is added to the fare, so it's become common for drivers to disappear from 11pm to midnight, when they can return to work and earn more in fares.

Bars

Brix In the basement of the Grand Hyatt Regency, Brix hosts a good house band and international visiting music groups as well. A pickup joint of sorts, it's a bit more sophisticated than others. The Music Bar features live jazz and R & B, while the Wine & Whiskey Bar serves up a fine selection of wine, Scotch, and cognac. Hours are Sunday to Wednesday 9pm to 2am, Thursday to Saturday 9pm to 3am. Happy hour nightly, from 7 to 9pm. Basement, Grand Hyatt Singapore, 10 Scotts Rd. © **65/6732-1234.** Cover charge after 10pm S$25.

Café del Mar Singapore ★★★ Savor cooling cocktails while you sink your toes in the sand and gaze at the tropical sunset. Café del Mar, based on the successful Ibiza formula, is pure tropical island paradise, with a soundtrack of chill-out grooves, just minutes from Singapore's urban center. Friday and Saturday beach parties are a welcome change from urban life—have dinner here from a Mediterranean tapas menu and take a dip in their pool or Jacuzzis. Singapore's sun sets from about 7 to 7:30pm, so be sure to come early for the Sundowner Special happy hour from 5 to 7pm, with two-for-one cocktails, so you can get lit before it gets dark. Hours are Monday to Thursday 11am to 11pm, Friday and Saturday 11am to 2am. 40 Siloso Beach Walk, Sentosa Island. © **65/6235-1296.** www.cafedelmar.com.sg.

The Crazy Elephant   Crazy Elephant is the city's home for blues and rock music. Have a drink alfresco beside the Singapore River and listen to classic rock and blues performed by resident bands. This place has hosted, in addition to some excellent local and regional guitarists, international greats such as Rick Derringer, Eric Burdon, and Walter Trout. It's an unpretentious place to chill out and have a cold one. Beer is reasonably priced as well. Hours are Sunday to Thursday 5pm to 2am, and Friday and Saturday 5pm to 3am, with daily happy hour 5 to 9pm. 3E River Valley Rd., #01-03/04 Traders Market, Clarke Quay. © **65/6337-7859.** www.crazyelephant.com.

The Dubliner Singapore   Located in a restored colonial building, Dubliner's got great atmosphere, with vaulted ceilings, tiled floors and pretty plasterwork, and outdoor seating on the veranda. It's also a pretty decent Irish pub, with a friendly staff and a cast of regulars from local and expat drinking crowds. Sports matches are broadcast regularly (mainly football, erm, sorry . . . soccer), and there's a variety of cold beer on tap. Hours are Sunday to Thursday 11:30am to 2am, and Friday and Saturday 11:30am to 3am; daily happy hour runs all day until 9pm and later on weekends. Winsland Conservation House, 165 Penang Rd. © **65/6735-2220.** www.dublinersingapore.com.

Home Club   The "home" of Singapore's arty underground clubbing scene, this small down-to-earth club hosts local DJs who specialize in alternative and retro grooves and indie band parties. True to its name, expect a homey atmosphere, furnished with mismatched cozy chairs and sofas. The crowd is equally funky, with a fun mix of young art-school music heads and people employed in creative industries here. Open Tuesday to Thursday 9pm to 3am, Friday and Saturday 10pm to 6am. The Riverwalk, #B1-01/06, 20 Upper Circular Rd. © **65/6538-2928.** www.homeclub.com.sg. Cover charges are sometimes levied but include a complimentary drink.

KU DÉ TA ★   Atop the SkyPark at Marina Bay Sands, KU DÉ TA is the newest addition to Singapore's nightlife, but be warned: With a S$50 cover charge (which includes one drink), prices match its high-altitude location. Sister property of Bali's famous beachside KU DÉ TA, this place is equally unforgettable, with an alfresco rooftop bar where only a glass barrier separates patrons from the gorgeous 360° view of the city and the sea. Later in the evening, DJs spin dance music in an air-conditioned space with floor-to-ceiling windows sporting the same spectacular views. SkyPark at Marina Bay Sands North Tower, 1 Bayfront Ave. © **65/6688-7688.** www.kudeta.com.sg. Cover charge S$50 (includes 1 drink).

The Long Bar ★   Touristy and expensive, the Long Bar is still a cultural institution. With tiled mosaic floors, large shuttered windows, and punkah fans waving above, this Raffles Hotel bar has tried to retain much of the charm of yesteryear so you can enjoy a Singapore Sling in its birthplace. And truly, the thrill at the Long Bar is tossing back one of these sweet, juicy drinks while pondering the Singapore adventures of all the famous actors, writers, and artists who came through here in the first decades of the 20th century. To be honest, they make the Slings in batches behind the bar, as opposed to drink by drink. After a couple, who cares? Hours are Sunday to Thursday 11am to 12:30am, Friday and Saturday 11am to 1:30am. Happy hour nightly 6 to 9pm, with special deals on pitchers of beer and some mixed drinks. A

Singapore Sling is S$25, and a Sling with souvenir glass costs an extra S$20. Raffles Hotel Arcade, Raffles Hotel, 1 Beach Rd. ℂ **65/6412-1816.** www.raffles.com.

No. 5   Down Peranakan Place are a few bars, one of which is No. 5, a cool, dark place just dripping with Southeast Asian ambience, from its 1910 shophouse exterior to its partially crumbling interior walls hung with rich woodcarvings. The hardwood floors and beamed ceilings are complemented by seating areas cozied with oriental carpets and kilim throw pillows. Upstairs is more conventional table-and-chair seating. The glow of the skylighted air shaft and the whirring fans above make this an ideal place to stop for a cool drink on a hot afternoon. In the evenings, be prepared for a lively mix of people. Open Monday to Thursday noon to 2am, Friday and Saturday noon to 3am, Sunday 5pm to 2am. Happy hour daily noon to 9pm. 5 Emerald Hill Rd. ℂ **65/6732-0818.** www.emeraldhillgroup.com.

Orgo   If KU DÉ TA has the best view gazing down at the city, then Orgo has the best view gazing up at it. On the fourth-story roof of the Esplanade–Theatres on the Bay, this alfresco lounge has outstanding views. Cocktails are interesting, with some organic selections, and some that incorporate unusual ingredients like chili and rose. In my opinion, Orgo's Singapore Sling, made entirely from fresh ingredients, save the gin, is better than The Long Bar's, and at S$20 it's cheaper too. Orgo also has a dinner menu featuring mainly French food with some tapas selections. Open daily 5pm to 2am. Happy hour daily 5 to 8pm. 8 Raffles Ave., #04–01, Esplanade-Theatres on the Bay. ℂ **65/6336-9366.**

Microbreweries

Brewerkz   Brewerkz, with outside seating along the river and an airy contemporary vibe inside—like a giant warehouse built around brewing kettles and copper pipes—brews the best house beer in Singapore. The bar menu features 13 tasty brew selections from recipes created by their English brew master, including Nut Brown Ale, Red Ale, Wiesen, Bitter, and India Pale Ale. Their American-cuisine lunch, dinner, and snack menu is also very good—I recommend planning a meal here as well. Open Sunday to Thursday noon to midnight, Friday and Saturday noon to 1am. Happy hour is held daily noon to 3pm, with two-for-one beers. #01-05 Riverside Point, 30 Merchant Rd. ℂ **65/6438-7438.** www.brewerkz.com.

Jazz Bars

Harry's Bar ★   The official after-work drink stop for finance professionals from nearby Shenton Way, Harry's biggest claim to fame is that it was bank-buster Nick Leeson's favorite bar. But don't let the power ties put you off. Harry's is a cool place, from airy riverside seating to cozy tables next to the stage. Of all the choices along Boat Quay, Harry's remains the classiest; even though it's also the most popular, you can usually get a seat. Upstairs, the wine bar is very laid-back, with plush sofas and dimly lit seating areas. Harry's is known for its live music, which is always good, but at the time of writing only two outlets had live music: **Harry's @ Dempsey Hill,** Blk. 11 Dempsey Rd., #01–17A (ℂ **65/6471-9018**) and **Harry's @ Orchard,** Orchard Towers, #01–05 and #02–08/09, 1 Claymore Dr. (ℂ **65/6736-7330**). There's also **Harry's @ Esplanade,** Esplanade Mall #01–05/07, 8 Raffles Ave. (ℂ **65/6334-0132**). Open Sunday to Thursday 11:30am to 1am, Friday and Saturday 11:30am to 2am. Happy hour daily 11am to 9pm. 28 Boat Quay. ℂ **65/6538-3029.** www.harrys.com.sg.

Raffles Bar & Billiards   Rich with the kind of elegance only history can provide, Raffles Bar & Billiards began as a bar in 1896 and over the decades has been transformed to perform various functions as the hotel's needs dictated. In its early days, legend has it that a patron shot the last tiger in Singapore under a billiards table here. Whether or not the tiger part is true, one of its two billiards tables is an original piece, still in use after 100 years. In fact, many of the fixtures and furniture here are original Raffles antiques, including the lights above the billiards tables and the scoreboards, and are marked with small brass placards. In the evenings, a jazzy little trio shakes the ghosts out of the rafters, while the well heeled lounge around enjoying single malts, cognacs, coffee, port, champagne, chocolates, and imported cigars. Expect to drop a small fortune. Open daily 11:30am to 12:30am. Raffles Hotel, 1 Beach Rd. ☎ **65/6331-1746.** www.raffles.com.

Clubs

The Cannery   Clarke Quay houses a number of dining and nightclub venues, many of which are operated under one management: The Cannery. Venues include **Zirca,** a mega dance club with a Cirque du Soleil feel; **Rebel,** a hip-hop club with a street graffiti attitude; and **Yello Jello Retrobar,** spinning nostalgic dance tunes; plus a few more lounges and cafes that serve a variety of styles for discriminating clubbers. Hours vary from club to club. Clarke Quay, 3B River Valley Rd. ☎ **65/6887-3733.** www.the-cannery.com. Cover charges vary from club to club.

dbl O   This cavernous place with a light-up wall and dance floor is very popular with those who want to hang out without the pretenses of some of the newer fashion-victim clubs. Two smaller dance floors within the club play hip hop and house grooves, and the club has a rooftop terrace garden for alfresco cocktails. Open Tuesday to Friday 8pm to 3am and Saturday 8pm to 4am. 11 Unity St., #01-24 Robertson Walk. ☎ **65/6735-2008.** www.emeraldhillgroup.com. Cover charges vary.

Insomnia   Modeled after three popular sister clubs in Hong Kong, Insomnia is named for its hours: 24/7. It's the first club in Singapore to have a license to operate 24 hours a day every day. A stable of bands revolve from club to club, playing dance rock, Top-40 hits, and pop to a packed dance floor. It has plenty of outside seating and also serves meals. It shares a central location at CHIJMES with a number of other bars and restaurants, so you can come here and check out several nightlife options in one place. Open daily 24 hours. 30 Victoria St., CHIJMES. ☎ **65/6338-6883.** www.liverockmusic247.com. No cover charge.

St James Power Station   An old 1927 coal-fired power station has been given a new lease on life as a mecca for clubbing. Its 60,000 square feet of space have been divided between nine independent clubs, each in a different flavor, including a jazzy show lounge, a karaoke bar, and a sports bar. For a cultural experience, try **Dragonfly,** with nightly Mandarin pop music shows featuring live performers and dancers on stage. Or **Movida,** a dance club that specializes in world beats. Hours vary from club to club. 3 Sentosa Gateway, #01-01. ☎ **65/6270-7676.** www.stjamespowerstation.com. Cover charges vary from club to club.

Zouk ★   Singapore's first innovative danceteria, Zouk introduced the city to house music, which throbs nightly in its cavernous disco, comprising three warehouses joined together. They play the best in modern music, so even if you're not much of a groover, you can still have fun watching the party from the many levels that tower above the dance floor. If you need a bit more intimacy in your nightlife, **Velvet Underground (VU),** within the Zouk complex, drips in red velvet and soft lighting—a good complement to the more soulful sounds spinning here. The newer addition to Zouk, **Phuture,** draws a young, hip-hop-loving crowd. Including the outdoor wine bar, Zouk is your one-stop shop for a party; in Singapore this place is legendary. All clubs are open daily 6pm to 3am. 17 Jiak Kim St. ☎ **65/6738-2988.** www.zoukclub.com. Cover charges vary.

Gay Nightspots

Singapore's gay clubbing scene is alive and well but still very underground. Bars come and go, so to get the absolute latest happenings, you'll have to go beyond mainstream media. The Web has listings at **www.utopia-asia.com**, where you'll find the best updated information about the most recent parties and hangouts. For the latest info, I'd recommend one of the chat rooms suggested at the address above, and talk to the experts. **Velvet Underground,** part of the Zouk complex (see above), welcomes a mixed clientele of gay, lesbian, and straight folk.

Wine Bars

Beaujolais 🍷 This little gem, in a shophouse built on a hill, is tiny, but its charm makes it a favorite for loyal regulars. Two tables outside (on the Five-Foot-Way, which serves more as a patio than a sidewalk) and two tables inside don't seem like much room, but there's more seating upstairs. They believe that wine should be affordable, and so their many labels tend to be more moderately priced per glass and bottle. Hours are Monday to Thursday 11am to midnight, Friday 11:30am to 2am, and Saturday 6pm to midnight; happy hour runs from opening to 9pm. 1 Ann Siang Hill. ℭ **65/6224-2227.**

Que Pasa One of the more mellow stops along Peranakan Place, this little wine bar serves up a collection of some 70 to 100 labels with plenty of atmosphere and a nice central location. It's another bar in a shophouse, but this one has as its centerpiece a very unusual winding stairway up the air shaft to the level above. Wine bottles and artwork line the walls. In the front, you can order tapas and cigars. The upstairs VIP club looks and feels like a formal living room, complete with wing chairs and board games. Hours are Monday to Thursday noon to 2am, Friday and Saturday noon to 3am, and Sunday 5pm to 2am. 7 Emerald Hill Rd. ℭ **65/6235-6626.** www.emeraldhillgroup.com.

The Performing Arts

Professional and amateur theater companies, dance troupes, opera companies, and musical groups offer a wide variety of not only Asian-focused performances, but Western as well. Many Broadway and West End road shows stop by Singapore along their world tour itineraries, and international stars the likes of Placido Domingo, Yo Yo Ma, The Red Hot Chili Peppers, and Elvis Costello have come to town, and you may be surprised to find lesser-known greats like Allan Holdsworth, Laurie Anderson, and The Flaming Lips. International stars make up only a portion of the performance scene, though. Singapore theater comprises four distinct language groups—English, Chinese, Malay, and Tamil—and each maintains its own voice and culture through theater, dance, music, and traditional performances.

CLASSICAL PERFORMANCES

The **Singapore Symphony Orchestra** performs at the Esplanade–Theatres on the Bay, with regular special guest appearances by international celebrities. For information about the orchestra, check out www.sso.org.sg, or for performance dates, see www.esplanade.com. Purchase tickets through **Sistic** (www.sistic.com.sg).

The **Singapore Lyric Opera** collaborates with renowned opera companies from around the world to stage such Western operas as *Turandot* and *Madame Butterfly* at the Esplanade. Check their website at www.singaporeopera.com.sg for what's on. Sistic handles ticket sales.

The **Singapore Chinese Orchestra,** the only professional Chinese orchestra in Singapore, has won several awards for its classic interpretations. They perform every 2 weeks, mainly at the Singapore Conference Hall, 7 Shenton Way (© **65/6440-3839**). See performance schedules at www.sco.com.sg, and buy tickets through Sistic.

THEATER

Most international companies will perform at either the **Esplanade–Theatres on the Bay,** 1 Esplanade Dr., a 10-minute walk from City Hall MRT (© **65/6828-8222;** www.esplanade.com), or at **Marina Bay Sands,** 2 Bayfront Ave., a 5-minute walk from Marina Bay MRT (© **65/6688-8868;** www.marinabaysands.com). Smaller shows are sometimes staged at the **Victoria Concert Hall,** 2nd Floor Victoria Memorial Hall, 11 Empress Place (© **65/6338-6125**). **SISTIC** (© **65/6348-5555;** www.sistic.com.sg) handles bookings for all venues.

Singapore's original rock circus, **Voyage de la Vie,** embodies the spirit of Cirque du Soleil. Voyage features internationally acclaimed circus artists who perform amazing stunts alongside Singapore Idol 2006 runner-up Jonathan Leong. The show is at **Resorts World Sentosa** on Sentosa Island; performances are Wednesday to Friday at 8:30pm, and Saturday and Sunday at 5 and 8:30pm. For information, call © **65/6577-8899.** Tickets cost S$68 to S$128, and can be purchased from **SISTIC** (© **65/6348-5555;** www.sistic.com.sg) or at the Universal Studios ticket counter.

A few local companies are quite noteworthy and manage their own performance spaces. **The Necessary Stage,** 278 Marine Parade Rd., #B1–02 Marine Parade Community Building (© **65/6440-8115;** www.necessary.org), blazed trails for the local performing arts scene after staging productions that touched tender nerves for the community, including a startlingly frank monologue by the first Singaporean to publicly declare his struggle with AIDS. The **Singapore Repertory Theatre,** DBS Arts Centre, 20 Merbau Rd., Robertson Quay (© **65/6733-0005;** www.srt.com.sg), is another company to watch; in recent years, they've staged local productions of perennial favorites like *The Glass Menagerie* and *Little Shop of Horrors.*

ARTS PROGRAMS

A number of venues have nightly programs of performance art pieces, fringe music productions, art talks, demonstrations, readings, and other specialized arts events.

The Arts House, 1 Old Parliament Lane (© **65/6332-6900;** www.theartshouse.com.sg), is a popular venue located in the former Parliament House, whose government rooms, in grand colonial style, have been converted into intimate spaces for use as an alternative arts venue. The building also hosts an intimate music club and small cafe, plus a theater that screens avant-garde films.

Also check out the many events at the **Substation,** 45 Armenian St. (© **65/6337-7535;** www.substation.org), which offers its space to smaller theater troupes, cinema groups, fine arts exhibitors, and performance artists.

CULTURAL SHOWS

Once upon a time, **Cantonese opera** could be seen under tents on street corners throughout the city. These days, local and visiting companies still perform, but very sporadically. For a performance you can count on, the **Chinese Theatre Circle,** 5 Smith St. (© **65/6323-4862;** www.ctcopera.com.sg), has a show on Fridays and Saturdays, with excerpts from the most famous and beloved tales, with explanations of the craft. Come at 7pm for the preshow "dinner" (chicken nuggets, really; tickets are S$35), or, better yet, have dinner elsewhere and drop in at 8pm to catch the show with tea and pay only S$20.

MALAYSIA

by Jennifer Eveland

8

Malaysia's wow factor is its diversity. Malay Muslims, Chinese Taoists and Buddhists, Indian Hindus, a large number of indigenous people, plus an assortment of Peranakans, Eurasians, and other races and religions all call themselves Malaysian, and each contributes to the fabric of this surprisingly colorful nation. Its long history is the story of how original Malays have accepted newcomers from Arabia, India, China, Thailand, Indonesia, and Europe, and fused their cultures into a hodgepodge of a national identity. Malaysia has survived colonial rule of the Portuguese, Dutch, and English, plus the Japanese Occupation. Today the country manages to hold it together, albeit sometimes by a hair.

Diversity is also present in the landscape of Malaysia's cities and towns, where colonial heritage mixes with modern development and an underlying attitude of *kampung* (village) friendliness. Many visitors delight in the chaos of Kuala Lumpur. Its twisty narrow roads, sweltering traffic jams, haphazard development, and back-alley shops and food stalls represent an Asia that is still a little bit untamed, even as the marvelous futuristic-Moorish Petronas Twin Towers loom overhead. Meanwhile, in places like Georgetown, Melaka, and Kuching, the past is everywhere you turn.

Not far from Malaysia's cities and towns, you'll find rainforests and mountains, beaches and idyllic tropical islands, blue seas and coral reefs, and an abundance of peculiar flora and fauna, all so accessible it's a wonder these places aren't overwhelmed by tourists.

Accessibility is perhaps the best thing about Malaysia. Infrastructure is of good quality, communications are up-to-date, travel operators are very organized, and accommodations and airports are some of the best in Southeast Asia. Better still, many Malaysians are comfortable speaking English, which opens up enormous possibilities for visitors to connect with local people in a very meaningful way.

GETTING TO KNOW MALAYSIA
The Lay of the Land

Malaysia's territory covers peninsular Malaysia—bordering Thailand in the north and across a strait from Singapore in the south—and two states on the island of Borneo, Sabah and Sarawak, approximately 240km (149 miles) east across the South China Sea. All of its 13 states and three federal territories total 329,749 sq. km (127,317 sq. miles) of land.

Peninsular Malaysia makes up about 132,149 sq. km (51,023 sq. miles) and contains 11 of Malaysia's 13 states: Kedah, Perlis, Penang, and Perak are in the northwest; Kelantan and Terengganu are in the northeast; Selangor, Negeri Sembilan, and Melaka are about midway down the peninsula on the western side; Pahang, along the east coast, sprawls inward to cover most of the central area (which is mostly forest preserve); and Johor covers the entire southern tip from east to west, with two vehicular causeways linking it to Singapore, just over the Straits of Johor. Surrounded by the Straits of Malacca to the west and the South China Sea to the east, the peninsula is edged by coastal plains and mangrove swamps. The interior of the peninsula is mainly forested, with a number of mountain ranges that run from north to south.

Malaysia's People & Culture

The Malaysia of today is a peaceful nation of many races and ethnicities. Currently, the population is estimated at 28.3 million inhabitants. Of this number, Bumiputeras are the most numerous ethnic group (broadly speaking) and are defined as those with cultural affinities indigenous to the region and to one another. Technically, this group includes people of the aboriginal groups and ethnic Malays. A smaller segment of the population is non-Bumiputera groups such as the Chinese, Indians, Arabs, and Eurasians, most of whom descended from settlers to the region in the past 150 years. It is important to know the difference between the Bumiputera and non-Bumiputera groups to understand Malaysian politics, which favors the first group in every policy. It is equally important to understand that, despite ethnic divisions, each group is considered no less Malaysian.

The state religion is Islam. The Muslim way of life is reflected in almost every element of Malaysian life. The strict adherence to Islam will most likely affect your vacation plans in some way. If you're traveling to Malaysia for an extended period of time or are planning to work here, consider *Malaysian Customs & Etiquette: A Practical Handbook,* by Datin Noor Aini Syed Amir (Times Books, 2003), for its great advice on how to negotiate any situation.

Language

The national language is Malay, or Bahasa Malaysia, although English is widely spoken. Chinese dialects and Tamil are also spoken.

THE BEST OF MALAYSIA IN 1 WEEK

This route brings you to Peninsular Malaysia's most historically significant destinations: Kuala Lumpur, Penang, and Melaka. You'll learn about the earliest trading ports and colonial history, and have time to shop and savor local treats.

Days 1 & 2: Arrive in Kuala Lumpur

After arriving in Malaysia's capital city, allow yourself a full day to recover and just spend your time wandering through the city's streets. Start at **Merdeka Square,** the focal point of colonial KL (Kuala Lumpur). Just behind the Moorish Sultan Abdul Samad Building, in the streets surrounding the Jame Mosque, you'll find KL's Little India of sorts. Continue your walk to the **Central Market ★,** where nearby coffee shops can provide a place to rest. After exploring stall after stall of Malaysian handicrafts at the Central Market, if you still have time and energy, cross the street to **Chinatown,** where you'll find more shopping, a street bazaar, and the **Sri Mahamariaman Hindu Temple.** See p. 521.

Day 3: Melaka (Malacca) ★★

Take an early morning bus to Melaka and spend the day exploring the town's historic heart. The most important things to see here are the **Stadthuys ★** (p. 543), the history museum, located in the hard-to-miss red colonial building; the **Cultural Museum ★** (p. 543), in a replica of a Malay-style palace; and the **Baba Nyonya Heritage Museum ★** (p. 542), located inside an old millionaire's mansion. From the Baba Nyonya Museum, head to **Jonker Walk** to wander through temples and antiques shops. See p. 539.

Day 4: Penang

Take an early morning bus back to KL, then board a flight to Penang. Allow 1 day for the journey. Check into your resort at **Batu Feringgi** so that when you arrive, you can unwind with a cocktail as you watch the setting sun from the beach. See p. 545.

Day 5: Georgetown ★★★

Here's what I have to say about Georgetown: Don't plan your time too closely. Start off at the **Penang Museum and Art Gallery ★★** (p. 553), where you'll get a brilliant overview of the island's history and cultures, then just spend your time walking through the streets. Attractions are all situated within walking distance, but don't rush: Take time to peek in the shop doors and snack on the local treats you'll find along the way. Just make sure you're at the **Cheong Fatt Tze Mansion ★★★** (p. 548) in time for the 11am or 3pm tour—consider it a must! Afterward, mosey over to the **E&O Hotel ★★** (p. 548) for either lunch or high tea in the old colonial dame.

Day 6: Penang Hill

The funicular train up the side of Penang Hill was originally built in 1923 to take British colonials up to the cooler climate of the hill, where they built lovely country homes and gardens. The new funicular railway will open in 2011. Get there before 9am to beat the long queue. At the top of the hill, you'll find restaurants, temples, and trails, one of which will lead you down to the botanical gardens. See p. 554.

Days 7 & 8: Back to KL

Hop a flight back to KL to prepare for your return home. If you have time, you can stock up on gifts at the **KLCC;** you'll find something for everyone on your list, in all price ranges, at this handicrafts showroom. See p. 537.

PLANNING YOUR TRIP TO MALAYSIA

Visitor Information

Tourism Malaysia (www.tourismmalaysia.gov.my) provides excellent information, including websites, brochures, pamphlets, and other information that is regularly

Peninsular Malaysia

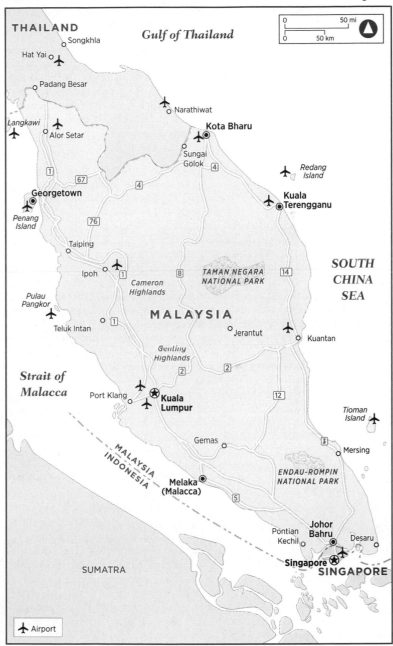

THAILAND

Gulf of Thailand

Songkhla

Hat Yai

Padang Besar

Narathiwat

Kota Bharu

Langkawi

Alor Setar

Sungai
Golok

Redang
Island

Georgetown

Kuala
Terengganu

*Penang
Island*

Taiping

*Cameron
Highlands*

*TAMAN NEGARA
NATIONAL PARK*

**SOUTH
CHINA
SEA**

Ipoh

*Pulau
Pangkor*

MALAYSIA

Teluk Intan

Jerantut

Kuantan

*Genting
Highlands*

*Strait of
Malacca*

Port Klang

Kuala
Lumpur

*Tioman
Island*

Gemas

*ENDAU-ROMPIN
NATIONAL PARK*

Mersing

MALAYSIA
INDONESIA

Melaka
(Malacca)

Johor
Bahru

Pontian
Kechil

Desaru

Singapore

SINGAPORE

SUMATRA

✈ Airport

0   50 mi
0   50 km

updated. Within Malaysia, each state or tourist destination has its own tourism board that operates a website and local offices for tourist information. These are also good sources for information, as they have on-the-ground knowledge that's more current. For each destination, I have provided websites, telephone contacts, and locations of information offices.

Malaysia Hotel News (www.malaysiahotelnews.blogspot.com) is a blog that covers all aspects of tourism in Malaysia, from government policy to hotel openings to special events. It is a very comprehensive source for what's happening in the industry, with valuable information for tourism professionals and travelers alike.

Entry Requirements

To enter Malaysia you must have a passport that is valid for at least 6 months beyond your date of entry. To obtain a passport, contact one of the following passport offices:

- **Australia** Australian Passport Information Service (⟨© **131-232,** or visit www. passports.gov.au).
- **Canada Passport Office,** Department of Foreign Affairs and International Trade, Ottawa, ON K1A 0G3 (© **800/567-6868;** www.ppt.gc.ca).
- **Ireland Passport Office,** Setanta Centre, Molesworth Street, Dublin 2 (© **01671-1633;** www.foreignaffairs.gov.ie).
- **New Zealand Passports Office,** Department of Internal Affairs, 47 Boulcott St., Wellington, 6011 (© **0800/225-050** in New Zealand or 04/474-8100; www. passports.govt.nz).
- **United Kingdom** Visit your nearest passport office, major post office, or travel agency or contact the **Identity and Passport Service (IPS),** 89 Eccleston Sq., London, SW1V 1PN (© **0300/222-0000;** www.ips.gov.uk).
- **United States** To find your regional passport office, check the U.S. State Department website (travel.state.gov/passport) or call the **National Passport Information Center** (© **877/487-2778**) for automated information.

Customs Regulations

With regard to currency, you can bring into the country as many foreign currency notes or traveler's checks as you please, but amounts exceeding RM10,000 or its equivalent in foreign currency need to be declared. Social visitors can enter Malaysia with 1 liter of alcohol and 1 carton of cigarettes without paying duty—anything over that amount is subject to local taxes. Prohibited items include firearms and ammunition, daggers and knives, and pornographic materials. Be advised that, similar to Singapore, Malaysia enforces a very strict drug-abuse policy that includes the death sentence for convicted drug traffickers. For more information, visit www.customs.gov.my.

Money

Malaysia's currency is the **Malaysian ringgit.** Prices are marked as RM (a designation I've used throughout this book). Notes are issued in denominations of RM1, RM2, RM5, RM10, RM20, RM50, and RM100. One ringgit is equal to 100 sen. Coins come in denominations of 5, 10, 20, and 50 sen. In 2005, Malaysia ended a 7-year peg of the ringgit at RM3.80 to US$1. Now, the country uses a managed float system that measures the currency against a basket of several major currencies. The exchange rate used throughout this chapter is approximately **RM3.59 = $1.**

Currency can be changed at banks and hotels, but you'll get a more favorable rate if you go to one of the money-changers who seem to be everywhere—in shopping

centers, in lanes, and in small stores—just look for signs. They are often men in tiny booths with a display on the wall behind them showing the exchange rate. All major currencies are accepted, and there is never a problem with the U.S. dollar, except for dirty or old notes.

Automated teller machines (**ATMs**) are found throughout the country, especially where tourists frequent. They will be hard to find on smaller islands and remote beach areas. In addition, some ATMs may not accept credit cards or debit cards from your home bank. I have found that debit cards on the MasterCard/Cirrus or Visa/Plus networks are almost always accepted at **Maybank,** with at least one location in every major town. Cash is dispensed in ringgit deducted from your account at the day's rate.

Credit cards are widely accepted at hotels and restaurants, and at many shops as well. Most popular are American Express, MasterCard, and Visa. Some banks may also be willing to advance cash against your credit card, but you have to ask around because this service is not available everywhere.

Health & Safety

HEALTH   Malaysia does not require visitors to obtain specific vaccinations to enter, with the exception of travelers arriving from areas where yellow fever is present, mainly Africa and South America. Sun exposure and insect bites will be your main worry in Malaysia, whether you are in a city, jungle trekking, or lying on a beach. Drink plenty of fluids and avoid the outdoors during the middle of the day, if possible, and wear sunscreen with an SPF of at least 30. Day or night, mosquito repellent is a must, and for certain heavily forested areas I've found only products containing DEET will work. In general, the quality of healthcare in Malaysia is very good, with most doctors educated overseas and many hospitals awarded international accreditation. Over-the-counter medications are easy to find at well stocked pharmacies in major towns. Note that some drugs have different names, for example, Tylenol (acetaminophen) is sold under the brand name Panadol (paracetamol) in Malaysia.

o **DIETARY RED FLAGS**   The **tap water** in KL is supposedly potable, but I don't recommend drinking it—in fact, I don't recommend drinking tap water anywhere in Malaysia. Bottled water is inexpensive enough and readily available at convenience stores and food stalls. Food prepared in hawker centers is generally safe—I have yet to experience trouble, and I'll eat almost anywhere. If you buy fresh fruit, wash it well with bottled water, and carefully peel the skin if you are really concerned. Vegetarians will find variety in southern Indian vegetarian curries, known locally as "banana leaf," and a smattering of Chinese Buddhist vegetarian restaurants.

o **TROPICAL ILLNESSES**   **Malaria** has not been a continual threat in most parts of Malaysia, even Malaysian Borneo. **Dengue fever,** on the other hand, which is also carried by mosquitoes, remains a constant threat in most areas, especially rural parts. Dengue, if left untreated, may cause fatal internal hemorrhaging, so if you come down with a sudden fever or skin rash, consult a physician immediately. There are no prophylactic treatments for dengue; the best protection is to wear plenty of insect repellent—the *aedes* mosquito that carries dengue bites during the day, as opposed to malaria-carrying varieties that bite at dusk. Choose a product that contains DEET or is specifically formulated to be effective in the tropics.

SAFETY   Malaysia has an unfortunate problem with thievery, though the crime rate in the country has been decreasing. "Snatch thieves" have been known to ride on motorcycles through heavily populated areas in KL, Johor Bahru, and other cities, snatching handbags from women's shoulders. When you're out, don't wear your handbag on your side that's facing the street, or better yet, don't carry a handbag.

The first thing to do at the hotel is put passport, international tickets, extra cash, and traveler's checks, plus any credit or unneeded ATM cards, straight into the safe, either in the room or behind the hotel's front desk.

Be careful when traveling on overnight trains and buses where there are opportunities for theft. Keep your valuables close to you as you sleep.

Getting There

BY PLANE   Malaysia has five international airports—at Kuala Lumpur, Penang, Langkawi, Kota Kinabalu, and Kuching, although international flights come into some domestic airports—and 15 domestic airports, including Kota Bharu, Kuantan, and Kuala Terengganu. Specific airport information is listed for each city.

A passenger service charge, or **airport departure tax,** is incorporated into all ticket prices and depends upon the airport from which you depart: RM6–RM20 for domestic flights and RM25–RM51 for international flights.

Malaysia Airlines (www.malaysiaairlines.com) flies to six continents. I have found Malaysia Airlines service to be of a very good standard. From within Malaysia you can contact them at ✆ **1300/883-000.**

AirAsia (www.airasia.com; in KL ✆ **03/2171-9333**) is a low-cost carrier that flies long-haul flights to KL from Australia and the U.K., plus shorter flights from countries throughout the region, some with direct flights to Penang, Kota Kinabalu, or Kuching. Another regional low-cost carrier to consider is **Tiger Airways** (www. tigerairways.com.sg; in KL ✆ **03/7849-4608,** in Singapore ✆ **65/680-TIGER** [6808-4437]), which connects Singapore to KL, Penang, and Sarawak.

To find out which airlines travel to Malaysia, please see "Airline Websites," p. 645.

BY TRAIN From Singapore: In mid-2010, Singapore and Malaysia announced that the Singapore railway station for **Keretapi Tanah Melayu Berhad (KTM)** rail services to Malaysia will move to the Woodlands rail checkpoint, in the north of Singapore, commencing July 1, 2011. At press time, there were no details available, except that a bus connection will be offered from the nearest MRT station to the Woodlands station. KTM operates trains that connect cities along the west coast of Malaysia with Singapore to the south and Thailand to the north. Trains to Kuala Lumpur depart daily for fares from S$34 to S$68. The trip takes around 7 hours on an *ekspres* train (avoid the 10pm mail train if you want to reach there before your next birthday). Kuala Lumpur's KL Sentral railway station (✆ **03/2267-1200**) is a 10-minute taxi ride from the center of town and is connected to the Putra LRT, KL Monorail city public transportation trains, and the Express Rail Link (ERL) to Kuala Lumpur International Airport (KLIA).

From Thailand: KTM's international service departs from the **Hua Lamphong Railway Station** (✆ **662/220-4444**) in Bangkok, in partnership with the State Railway of Thailand, with operations to Hua Hin, Surat Thani, Nakhon Si Thammarat, and Hat Yai in Thailand's southern peninsula. The final stop in Malaysia is at Butterworth, near Penang, so passage to KL will require you to catch a connecting train onward. The daily service departs at 2:45pm and takes approximately 20 hours from Bangkok to Butterworth. There is no first- or third-class service on this train, only air-conditioned second class; an upper berth goes for about $37, and a lower is $40. The latter is roomier.

For a romantic journey from Thailand, the **Eastern & Orient Express** (**E&O;** www.orient-express.com) operates a route between Chiang Mai and Bangkok, Kuala Lumpur, or Singapore. Traveling in the luxurious style for which the Orient Express is renowned, you'll finish the journey in about 42 hours. A double-occupancy Pullman cabin is priced at S$3,500 per person, with State and Presidential Suites also available. Fares include meals on the train plus tours along the way. Overseas reservations for the E&O Express can be made through travel agents or by booking online at www.orient-express.com. From Singapore, Malaysia, and Thailand, contact the E&O office in Singapore at ✆ **65/6395-0678.**

BY BUS From Singapore, there are many bus routes to Malaysia. If you want to travel on land, I personally prefer the bus over the train from Singapore to Kuala Lumpur. Executive coaches operated by **Aeroline** (in Singapore, ✆ **65/6258-8800**) have huge seats that recline, serve a box lunch onboard, and show movies. Seven buses depart daily from HarbourFront Centre at 1 Maritime Sq. for the 5-hour trip (adults: S$49 one-way, S$98 round-trip; children: S$38 one-way, S$76 round-trip).

Buses to Johor Bahru can be picked up at the Ban Sen terminal at the corner of Queen and Arab streets (✆ **65/6292-8149;** S$2.40 one-way). **Grassland Express**

(5001 Beach Rd., Golden Mile Complex; © **65/6293-1166**) has daily morning buses to Melaka for S$22 one-way on weekdays and S$30 one-way on weekends.

From Thailand, you can find buses from Bangkok or Hat Yai (in the southern part of the country) heading for Malaysia. I don't recommend the bus trip from Bangkok, which is very far—take the train. From Hat Yai, many buses leave regularly to northern Malaysian destinations, particularly Butterworth (Penang). Also be warned, the U.S. Department of State does not recommend U.S. citizens travel in certain parts of southern Thailand due to terrorist violence near Pattani and Narathiwat.

BY TAXI (From Singapore) From the Johor-Singapore bus terminal at Queen and Arab streets, the **Singapore Johor Taxi Operators Association** (© **65/6296-7054**) can drive you to Johor Bahru for S$40.

BY CAR Major international car-rental agencies operating in Singapore will rent cars that you can take over the causeway to Malaysia, but be prepared to pay a small fortune. They're much cheaper if you rent within the country. At Kuala Lumpur International Airport, find **Avis** at Counter B-16 at the arrival hall in the main terminal (© **03/8776-4540**). There's another branch at the international airport in Penang (**04/643-9633**), or make a booking through www.avis.com.

Getting Around

Within Malaysia, infrastructure is of good quality with regard to domestic travel—depending on your budget and the amount of time you have, you'll have a variety of choices that include air carriers, regular train service, a wide web of intercity buses, and well maintained roads.

BY PLANE **Malaysia Airlines** (© **1300/883-000;** www.malaysiaairlines.com) links from its hub in Kuala Lumpur the cities of Johor Bahru, Kota Bharu, Kota Kinabalu, Kuala Terengganu, Kuantan, Kuching, Langkawi, Penang, and other smaller cities not covered in this volume. Individual airport information is provided in sections for each city that follows. One-way domestic fares can average RM100 to RM400.

AirAsia (© **03/8775-4000;** www.airasia.com) competes with Malaysia Airlines with incredibly affordable rates. It links all the country's major cities with fares that, on average, run from RM40 and up—seriously.

Berjaya Air (© **03/2141-0088;** www.berjaya-air.com) operates a small fleet of aircraft that services KL to Pangkor, Tioman, Redang, and Langkawi islands, with flights from Koh Samui in Thailand and Singapore as well.

Firefly (© **03/7845-4543;** www.fireflyz.com) has a small fleet that services some peninsular and East Malaysian destinations.

BY TRAIN The **Keretapi Tanah Melayu Berhad (KTM)** provides train service throughout peninsular Malaysia. Trains run from north to south between the Thai border and Singapore, with stops including Butterworth (Penang), Kuala Lumpur, and Johor Bahru. There is a second line that branches off at Gemas, midway between Johor Bahru and KL, and heads northeast to Tempas near Kota Bharu. Fares range from RM64 for first-class between Johor Bahru and KL, to RM30 for first-class passage between KL and Butterworth. Train station information is provided for each city under individual city headings throughout this chapter.

BY BUS Malaysia's intercity coach system is extensive and inexpensive, but I don't really recommend it. With the exception of executive coach services between KL, Penang, Singapore, and Melaka, which are excellent, standard coaches get dirtier and

telephone dialing AT A GLANCE

○ **To place a call from your home country to Malaysia:** Dial the international access code (011 in the U.S. and Canada; 0011 in Australia; or 00 in the U.K., Ireland, and New Zealand), plus the country code (60), plus the Malaysia area code (Cameron Highlands 5, Desaru 7, Genting Highlands 9, Johor Bahru 7, Kuala Lumpur 3, Kuala Terengganu 9, Kota Bharu 9, Kota Kinabalu 88, Kuantan 9, Kuching 82, Langkawi 4, Melaka 6, Mersing 7, Penang 4, Tioman 9), followed by the six-, seven-, or eight-digit phone number (for example, from the U.S. to Kuala Lumpur, you'd dial 011-60-3/0000-0000).

The nation's fixed telephone provider, Telekom Malaysia, also provides International Direct Dialing (IDD) services from most hotels.

○ **To place a direct international call from Malaysia:** Dial the international access code (00), plus the country code of the place you are dialing (U.S. and Canada 1, Australia 61, Republic of Ireland 353, New Zealand 64, U.K. 44), plus the area/city code and the residential number.

○ **To reach the international operator:** Dial ✆ 108.

Prepaid international calling cards are available from a number of companies and can be purchased at most convenience stores. Be warned that not all phones accept all cards—most likely card-operated phones are located next to the shops that sell corresponding cards.

With widespread mobile phone usage, coin-operated phones are becoming a scarcity. If you find one, local calls are charged at 10 sen for 3 minutes.

dirtier each year, maintenance issues are a question mark, and road safety is a roll of the dice. Still, if you must, for each city covered, I've listed bus terminal locations, but scheduling information must be obtained from the bus company itself.

BY TAXI You can take special hired cars, called **outstation taxis,** between every city and state on the peninsula. Rates depend on the distance you plan to travel. They are fixed and stated at the beginning of the trip but many times can be bargained down. Cars are not of the best quality (usually older sedans), and this is probably the most expensive way to travel between cities, with most trips running between RM250 and RM500. In Kuala Lumpur, the outstation taxi stand has been temporarily relocated from its former base at the Puduraya Bus Terminal, so I recommend contacting them through MTC at ✆ **03/9235-4800.**

Also, within each of the smaller cities, feel free to negotiate with unmetered taxis for hourly, half-day, or daily rates. It's an excellent way to get around for sightseeing and shopping without transportation hassles. Hourly rates are usually up to RM60 per hour.

BY CAR The cities along the west coast of the peninsula are linked by the North–South Highway. There are rest areas with toilets, food outlets, and emergency telephones at intervals along the way. There is also a toll that varies depending on the distance you're traveling.

Driving along the east coast of Malaysia is actually much more pleasant than driving along the west coast. The highway is narrower and older, but it takes you through oil palm and rubber plantations, and the essence of *kampung* Malaysia permeates throughout. As you near villages, you'll often have to slow down and swerve past cows and goats, which are really quite oblivious to oncoming traffic. You have to get very close to honk at them before they move.

The speed limit on highways is 110kmph (68 mph). On the minor highways, the limit ranges from 70 to 90kmph (43–56 mph). Do not speed, as there are traffic police strategically situated around certain bends.

Distances between major towns are as follows: from KL to Johor Bahru, 368km (229 miles); from KL to Melaka, 144km (89 miles); from KL to Kuantan, 259km (161 miles); from KL to Butterworth, 369km (229 miles); from Johor Bahru to Melaka, 224km (139 miles); from Johor Bahru to Kuantan, 325km (202 miles); from Johor Bahru to Mersing, 134km (83 miles); from Johor Bahru to Butterworth, 737km (458 miles).

To rent a car in Malaysia, you must produce a driver's license from your home country that shows you have been driving at least 2 years. There are desks for major car-rental services at the international airports in Kuala Lumpur and Penang, and additional outlets throughout the country (see individual city sections for this information).

Tips on Accommodations

Major hotel chains represented in Malaysia include Four Seasons, Hilton, Hyatt, Holiday Inn, Le Meridien, Mandarin Oriental, Marriott, Melia, Mercure, Renaissance, Ritz Carlton, Shangri-La, Sheraton, and Westin. KL has the highest concentration of international business hotels, but a few operate luxurious resorts in other parts of the country as well, most notably on Penang and Langkawi.

Peak months of the year for hotels in western peninsular Malaysia are December through February and July through September. For the east coast, the busy times are July through September. You will need to make reservations well in advance to secure your room during these months.

TAXES & SERVICE CHARGES   All nonbudget hotels levy a 10% service charge and 5% government tax. As such, there is no need to tip. But bellhops could be tipped at least RM2 per bag; I give RM5 per bag in very expensive hotels and resorts.

Homestays

There are now over 100 operators offering homestays in virtually every Malaysian state, including Sabah and Sarawak. Through a homestay experience, travelers immerse themselves in local culture in meaningful ways, exchanging stories with local people and exploring their unique lifestyles in ways that a typical tour or holiday would never afford. In a homestay, a traveler will sleep with a local family in a village home, interact with the community to prepare and share local food, and engage in traditional cultural activities, including farming or fishing. The **Sabah Tourism Board** promotes homestays through its website, www.sabahtourism.com, listing reputable homestays across the state. **Sarawak's Ministry of Urban Development & Tourism** helps to organize homestays with indigenous communities, promoting packages on their website at www.right.sarawak.gov.my/Homestay.

Tips on Dining

A Malay meal always revolves around rice, accompanied with curries, fried chicken or fish, vegetable dishes, and small portions of condiments, called *sambal.* Some of these condiments can be harsh to foreign noses, particularly *sambal belacan,* which is made with extremely pungent fermented shrimp paste. Malays also favor seafood, especially fish, prawns, and squid. As all Malays are Muslim, you won't find pork on the menu and most restaurants are *halal.* Where you see mutton, most times it's goat, which is preferred over lamb for its milder, less musty taste and smell.

A good example of a local favorite is *nasi lemak,* rice cooked in coconut milk and served with fried chicken, prawn crackers, dried anchovies, a bit of egg, and a dark, sweet chili sauce. Other favorites are curry-based dishes like *kari ayam,* a mellow, almost creamy, golden curry with chunks of chicken meat and potatoes; and *rendang,* stewing beef with a dry curry that's as sweet as it is savory.

Probably the most famous Malay dish is *satay,* barbecued skewers of marinated chicken, beef, or mutton that are dipped in a chili peanut sauce. Another great dish is *ikan bakar,* which is fish smothered in chili sauce and grilled in foil over an open flame.

An interesting local variation to try is Malay food influenced by Indian Muslim cooking. *Mamak,* or Indian Muslim, stalls specialize in a dish called *roti canai,* fried bread to be dipped in curry or *dhal cha* (vegetarian curry); as well as *murtabak,* which is bread fried with egg, onion, and meat, which is also dipped in curry. These dishes are best enjoyed with a cup of *teh tarik,* frothy tea made with sweetened condensed milk.

Regional variations are also notable, particularly when it comes to Penang, which is famous for its food. A perfect example of how region affects a dish can be found in *laksa,* a seafood noodle soup created by the Peranakans. In Singapore, *laksa* has a rich, spicy coconut-based broth, almost like gravy. Alternately, Penang *laksa* is not coconut based, but is a fish broth with a tangy and fiery flavor from sour tamarind and spicy bird's-eye chili. Yet another variation, Sarawak *laksa* also forgoes coconut milk and instead focuses on a base of *sambal belacan,* or fermented shrimp paste. There are as many variations of *laksa* as there are towns.

Sarawak and Sabah also have their own unique cuisines, but mostly visitors will find typical Malay, Chinese, and Indian dishes, but with local twists. One of my favorite purely indigenous dishes is *umai,* raw mackerel seasoned with onion, chili, and salt, "cooked" in lime juice. It can be found primarily in Sarawak, but sometimes also in Sabah.

Tips on Shopping

Shopping is a huge attraction for tourists in Malaysia. In addition to modern fashions and electronics, there are great local handicrafts. Prices can vary considerably: There are many handicraft centers such as Karyaneka, with outlets all over the country, where goods can be a bit more expensive, but where you are assured of top quality. Alternatively, you can hunt out bargains in markets and at roadside stores in little towns, which can be much more fun.

Batik is one of the most popular arts in Malaysia, and the fabric can be purchased just about anywhere in the country. It can be fashioned into outfits and scarves or just purchased as sarongs. Another beautiful textile craft is *sogket* weaving. The beautiful cloths are woven with metallic threads and are usually sold as sarongs.

Traditional woodcarvings have become popular collectors' items. Carvings by *orang asli* groups in peninsular Malaysia and by the indigenous tribes of Sabah and Sarawak have traditional uses in households or are employed for ceremonial purposes. Malaysia's pewter products are also famous; Selangor Pewter is the brand that seems to have the most outlets, with anything from picture frames to dinner sets. Silver designs are very refined, and jewelry and fine home items are still made by local artisans, especially in the northern parts of the peninsula. In addition, crafts such as *wayang kulit* (shadow puppets) and *wau* (colorful Malay kits) make great gifts.

[FastFACTS] MALAYSIA

Area Codes Malaysia's country code is 60. Area codes for destinations covered in this book are as follows: 03 for Kuala Lumpur; 06 for Melaka; 07 for Johor Bahru; 04 for Penang and Langkawi; 09 for Tioman, Kuantan, Cherating, Kuala Terengganu, and Kota Bharu; 082 for Sarawak; and 088 for Sabah.

Business Hours Banks are open from 9:30am to 3pm Monday through Friday. Government offices are open from 8am to 12:45pm and 2 to 4:15pm Monday through Friday. Smaller shops like provision stores may open as early as 6 or 6:30am and close as late as 9pm, especially those near the wet markets. Many such stores are closed on Saturday evenings and Sunday afternoons and are busiest before lunch. Other shops are open 9:30am to 7pm. Department stores and shops in malls tend to open later, about 10:30 or 11am until 8:30 or 9pm throughout the week. Note that in the states of Kelantan, Terengganu, and Kedah, the working week runs from Saturday to Wednesday, with weekends on Thursday and Friday.

Doctors All hotels and resorts have qualified physicians on call who speak English. These doctors will come directly to your room for treatment. If your condition is serious, they can help you check into a local hospital.

Drinking Laws Liquor is sold in pubs and supermarkets in all big cities, or in provision stores. If you're going to a smaller island, your resort may have limited alcohol selections, so you may wish to bring your own. In Terengganu and Kelantan, liquor is strictly limited to a handful of Chinese restaurants. Pubs and other nightspots should officially close by 1am nationwide, but there are places in KL that stay open later. The legal age for alcohol purchase and consumption is 18, but foreigners are rarely checked.

Drug Laws As in Singapore, the death sentence is mandatory for drug trafficking (defined as being in possession of more than 15g of heroin or morphine, 200g of marijuana or hashish, or 40g of cocaine). For lesser quantities, you'll be thrown in jail for a very long time and flogged with a cane.

Electricity The voltage used in Malaysia is 220 to 240 volts AC (50 cycles). Three-point square plugs are used, so buy an adapter if you plan to bring any appliances, although most larger hotels can provide adapters upon request.

Embassies & Consulates Most embassies are located in Kuala Lumpur. Contacts for major embassies in Malaysia are as follows: **Australian High Commission,** 6 Jalan Yap Kwan Seng, Kuala Lumpur (☎ **03/2146-5555;** www.australia.org.my); **British High Commission,** 185 Jalan Ampang, Kuala Lumpur (☎ **03/2170-2200;** www.ukinmalaysia.fco.gov.uk); **Canadian High Commission,** 17th Floor, Menara Tan & Tan, 207 Jalan Tun Razak, Kuala Lumpur (☎ **03/2718-3333;** www.canadainternational.gc.ca); **New Zealand High Commission,** Level 21, Menara IMC, 8 Jalan Sultan Ismail, Kuala Lumpur (☎ **03/2078-2533;** www.nzembassy.com/malaysia); and the **United States Embassy,** 376 Jalan Tun Razak, Kuala Lumpur (☎ **03/2168-5000;** http://malaysia.usembassy.gov).

Emergencies Call ☎ **999** for all emergencies.

Internet & Wi-Fi Most hotels in Malaysia offer Internet connectivity; in hotels, most often you'll find broadband Internet in-room and Wi-Fi (wireless Internet) access in the public areas of the hotel, but recently some hotels have added Wi-Fi access in-room. Airports and coffee shops (like Starbucks) often have Wi-Fi hotspots as well. In general, Internet is available to most of the nation, and I have found Internet cafes in the most surprisingly remote places. However, with more people carrying laptops and smartphones, Internet cafes are going out of style, but they can still be found in areas frequented by travelers.

Internet cafes tend to open, close, or move frequently, so wherever you are, your best bet is to ask your concierge or the local tourism information office for the best places close by. Usage costs only about RM5 to RM10 per hour.

Mail Post office locations in each city covered are provided in each section. Overseas airmail postage rates are as follows: RM.50 for postcards and from RM1.40 for a 100g letter.

Newspapers & Magazines Local English-language papers include the *New Straits Times, The Star, The Sun,* and *The Edge* and are sold in hotel lobbies and magazine stands. International newspapers such as the *International Herald Tribune* and the *Asian Wall Street Journal* are also widely available. Of the local KL magazines, *Time Out* has good listings and local "what's happening" information.

Police For all emergencies, call **999**. By and large, law-enforcement agents in Malaysia's cities and major towns can speak English. While tourist police do exist, they are not as ubiquitous as tourist police in other countries such as Thailand.

Taxes Hotels, with the exception of those on

Langkawi, add a 5% government tax to all rates, plus an additional 10% service charge. Larger restaurants also figure the same 5% tax into your bill, plus a 10% service charge, whereas small coffee shops and hawker stalls don't charge anything above the cost of the meal. Although most tourist goods (such as crafts, camera equipment, sports equipment, cosmetics, and select small electronic items) are tax-free, a small, scaled tax is issued on various other goods such as clothing, shoes, and accessories that you'd buy in the larger shopping malls and department stores.

Telephones The international country code for Malaysia is **60**. To reach the international operator, dial tel **108**. See "Telephone Dialing at a Glance" above for details on how to make calls to, from, and within the country.

Time Malaysia is 8 hours ahead of Greenwich Mean Time, 16 hours ahead of U.S. Pacific Standard Time, 13 hours ahead of Eastern Standard Time, and 2 hours behind Sydney. It is in the same zone as Singapore. There is no daylight saving time.

Tipping Tipping is not expected, but most will leave coins behind. For

bellhops, I give at least RM2 per bag; RM5 in a very expensive hotel or resort.

Toilets To find a public toilet, ask for the *tandas*. In Malay, *lelaki* is male and *perempuan* is female. Be prepared for pay toilets. Coin collectors sit outside almost every public facility, taking RM.20 per person, RM.30 if you want tissue. Once inside, you'll find that your money doesn't go for cleaning crews. Public toilets are pure filth. They smell horrible and the floors are always an inch deep with stagnant water. While most toilets are of the "squatty-potty" variety (a porcelain bowl set into the floor), even if you find a seat-style toilet bowl, locals typically place their feet on the seat to squat. The nicer toilets are in hotels, upmarket shopping malls, and restaurants.

Water Water in Kuala Lumpur is supposed to be potable, but most locals boil the water before drinking it. I advise against drinking the tap water anywhere in Malaysia. Hotels will supply bottled water in your room. If they charge you for it, expect inflated prices, especially for premium imported water. A 1.5-liter bottle goes for RM7 in a hotel minibar, but RM2 at 7-Eleven.

KUALA LUMPUR ★★

Kuala Lumpur (or KL, as it is commonly known) is, more often than not, a traveler's point of entry to Malaysia. As the capital, it is the most modern and developed city in the country, with contemporary high-rises and world-class hotels, glitzy shopping malls, and local and international cuisine.

Kuala Lumpur

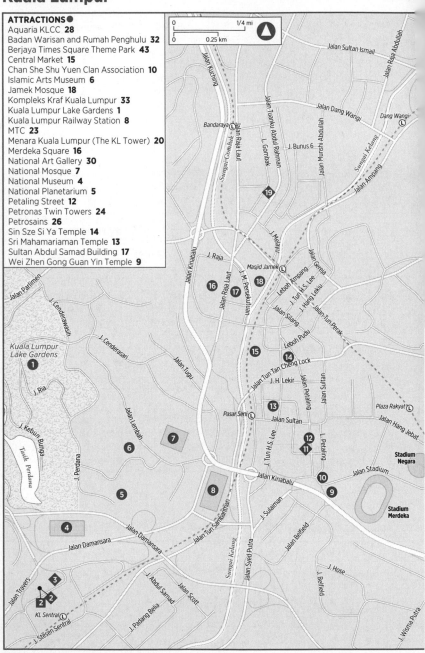

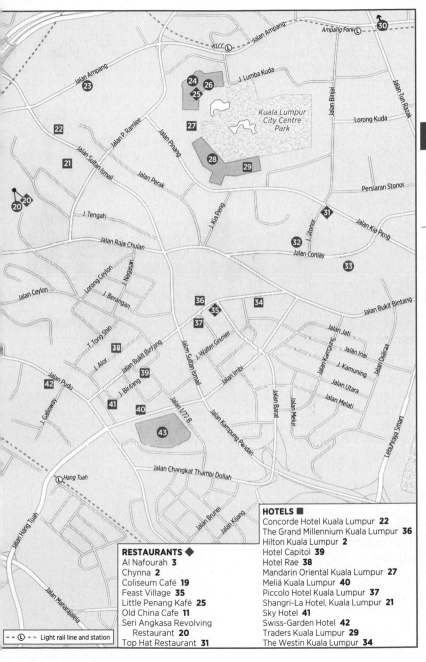

RESTAURANTS ◆
Al Nafourah **3**
Chynna **2**
Coliseum Café **19**
Feast Village **35**
Little Penang Kafé **25**
Old China Cafe **11**
Seri Angkasa Revolving
  Restaurant **20**
Top Hat Restaurant **31**

HOTELS ■
Concorde Hotel Kuala Lumpur **22**
The Grand Millennium Kuala Lumpur **36**
Hilton Kuala Lumpur **2**
Hotel Capitol **39**
Hotel Rae **38**
Mandarin Oriental Kuala Lumpur **27**
Meliá Kuala Lumpur **40**
Piccolo Hotel Kuala Lumpur **37**
Shangri-La Hotel, Kuala Lumpur **21**
Sky Hotel **41**
Swiss-Garden Hotel **42**
Traders Kuala Lumpur **29**
The Westin Kuala Lumpur **34**

- - ⓛ - - Light rail line and station

Today the original city center at **Merdeka Square** is the core of KL's history. Buildings like the Sultan Abdul Samad Building, the Royal Selangor Club, and the Old Kuala Lumpur Railway Station are excellent examples of British architectural sensibilities peppered with Moorish spice. South of this area is KL's **Chinatown.** Along Jalan Petaling and surrounding areas are markets, shops, food stalls, and the bustling life of the Chinese community. There's also a **Little India** in KL, around the area occupied by Masjid Jame, where you'll find flower stalls, Indian Muslim and Malay costumes, and traditional items. Across the river you'll find **Lake Gardens,** a large sanctuary that houses Kuala Lumpur's bird park, butterfly park, and other attractions and gardens. Modern Kuala Lumpur is rooted in the city's **"Golden Triangle,"** bounded by Jalan Ampang, Jalan Tun Razak, and Jalan Imbi. This section is home to most of KL's hotels, office complexes, shopping malls, and sights like the KL Tower and the Petronas Twin Towers, the tallest buildings in the world from 1998 to 2004, when Taipei 101 stole the title. They are now officially the world's tallest twin towers.

Getting There

BY TRAIN KL's train station, **KL Sentral,** provides a clean, safe, and orderly base for arrivals from Keretapi Tanah Melayu Berhad (KTM) rail services, linking cities up and down the Malaysian peninsula. It's also the city's base for express train services to and from KL International Airport, as well as a hub for local mass transit commuter train services around the city; it's got tons of facilities, money-changers, ATMs, fast food, and shops; and it's got an easy taxi coupon system (about RM10 or RM16 to central parts of the city)—it's located not far from the city's main tourist areas. For KTM train information, call ✆ **03/2267-1200.**

BY BUS If you're arriving via executive coach, your drop-off location will vary depending on the coach company. For example, **Nice buses** (✆ 03/4047-7878) arrive at KL Sentral (see above) and **Aeroline** buses (✆ 03/6258-8800) arrive at the Corus Hotel on Jalan Ampang; taxis are readily available from both points. Domestic companies offering standard bus services, such as **Transnasional** (✆ 03/2272-3634), will arrive in one of the city's three main terminals: the **Putra Terminal** on Jalan Tun Ismail, **Pekililing Terminal** on Jalan Ipoh, or the **Puduraya Bus Terminal,** which is located temporarily at the Bukit Jalil Stadium until the permanent terminal in Jalan Pudu is renovated (slated for completion in 2011). From each of these terminals, you can find taxis to your hotel.

BY PLANE The **Kuala Lumpur International Airport (KLIA)** (✆ 03/8776-4386; www.klia.com.my), located in Sepang, 53km (33 miles) outside the city, opened in 1998. KLIA is a huge complex, with business centers, dining facilities, a fitness center, medical services, shopping, post offices, and a nearby luxurious airport hotel operated by **Pan Pacific** (✆ 03/8787-3333; www.panpacific.com/KL airport).

The **Low Cost Carrier Terminal (LCCT)** (✆ 03/8777-6777; www.lcct.com. my), which services budget airlines like AirAsia, is 20km (12 miles) away from the KLIA main terminal, with transfer buses that will take you back and forth between terminals every 15 to 20 minutes with service from 5:30am to 12:30am for RM 1.50. The LCCT also has ATMs and money-changers, luggage lockers, dining facilities and some shops. ATM queues can be long at both airports.

Getting Around

Kuala Lumpur is a prime example of a city that was not planned, per se, from a master graph of streets. Rather, because of its beginnings as an outpost, it grew as it needed to, expanding outward and swallowing up rural surroundings. The result is a tangled web of streets too narrow to support the traffic of a capital city. Cars and buses weave through one-way lanes, with countless motorbikes snaking in and out, sometimes in the opposite direction of traffic or up on the sidewalks. Taxis are a convenient way of getting around, but expect agonizing traffic jams in the morning rush between 8 and 10am, and again between 5 and 8pm—during these times the commuter rail system might be a better bet, if it's going in your direction. There's also an easy Hop-on Hop-off tourist bus that hits virtually every major attraction. Walking is the best way to see the city, but be warned of the heat and horribly buckled sidewalks and gaping gutters. Areas within the colonial heart of the city, Chinatown, Little India, and central parts of the Golden Triangle are within walking distance of each other.

BY TAXI   There are two kinds of taxi service in KL, standard and executive. Standard taxis can be flagged down from roadsides or at taxi stands and charge a metered fare of RM3 for the first 2km (1¼ miles) and an additional RM.20 for each 200m (656 ft.) after that. Between midnight and 6am, you'll be charged an extra 50% of the total fare. Most drivers don't like to use the meter, and will tout a flat rate of between RM10 and RM20. Most (non-rush-hour) rides in the city are about RM6 to RM10, so for RM10 I usually don't fuss. I usually don't argue over meter usage, because I've found it to be an exercise in futility. KL taxi drivers will drive you mad if you let them. Sometimes it can be difficult to even find a taxi that will stop for you, especially if it's raining. There are a number of booking hot lines to call, but I have yet to find one with an operator who is helpful and can speak English well. Try **Public Cab** (✆ 03/6259-2020), which is reliable but charges an extra RM2 for booking.

If you're lucky, you can flag down an executive taxi. They cost a bit more but are cleaner and more comfortable. Most can be found outside major hotels and shopping malls, and use a metered charge of RM6 for the first 2km (1¼ miles) and an additional RM.20 for each 200m (656 ft.) after that. Between midnight and 6am, you'll be charged an extra 50% of the total fare.

BY HIRED CAR   A car and driver can be booked for around RM60 per hour or RM500 for a 10-hour whole-day booking from most tour operators. Try **Red Fury Tours & Travel** (✆ 03/2162-2693).

BY BUS   The **KL Hop On Hop Off** bus (✆ 03/2141-0927; www.myhoponhopoff.com) cruises most of the major attractions and neighborhoods of interest around KL, with stops near almost all leading hotels. Purchase tickets from travel agents, participating hotels, or the driver; a 24-hour ticket costs RM38 for adults and RM17 for children, while a 48-hour ticket costs RM65 for adults and RM29 for children. Your ticket gives you unlimited access to the bus during the period for which you paid. Buses operate from 8:30am to 8:30pm daily.

BY RAIL   KL has a network of mass transit commuter trains that weave through the city and out to the suburbs, and it'll be worth your time to become familiar with them, because taxis are sometimes unreliable and traffic jams can be unbearable. Trouble is, there are five train routes and sometimes the lines don't seem to connect in any logical way.

The four lines that are most useful to visitors are the **Kelana Jaya Line** (which is still commonly referred to by its old name, the Putra LRT), the **Ampang & Sri Petaling Line** (which is also still commonly referred to by its former name, the Star LRT), the **KL Monorail,** and the **KLIA Ekspres** to the airport.

The Kelana Jaya Line has stops at Bangsar (featured in the section "Kuala Lumpur After Dark," later in this chapter), KL Sentral (train station), Pasar Seni (Chinatown), Masjid Jamek, Dang Wangi, and KLCC shopping center. The Ampang & Sri Petaling Line is convenient if you need to get to the Putra World Trade Centre. It also stops at Masjid Jamek and Plaza Rayat. Average trips on both lines will cost around RM2.

The **KL Monorail** provides good access through the main hotel and shopping areas of the city, including stops at KL Sentral, Imbi, Bukit Bintang (the main shopping strip), and Raja Chulan (along Jalan Sultan Ismail, where many hotels are). Fares run between RM1.20 and RM2.50.

As a rough guide, all lines operate between 5 or 6am to around midnight, with trains coming every 10 minutes or so. Tickets can be purchased at any station either from the stationmaster or from single-fare electronic ticket booths.

ON FOOT   The heat and humidity can make walking between attractions pretty uncomfortable. However, sometimes the traffic is so unbearable that you'll get where you're going much faster by strapping on your tennis shoes and hiking it.

Visitor Information

In Kuala Lumpur, Tourism Malaysia has several offices. The largest is at the **MTC,** the **Malaysia Tourist Centre** (see "What to See & Do," later in this chapter), located on 109 Jalan Ampang (✆ **03/9235-4800**) and open daily from 8am to 10pm. In addition to a tourist information desk, MTC has a moneychanger; ATM; tourist police post; travel agent booking for Taman Negara trips, city tours, and limited hotel bookings; souvenir shops; an amphitheater; and Transnasional bus ticket bookings.

The monthly *Time Out* magazine has listings for events in KL and Malaysia. At newsstands, it costs RM6.90.

[Fast FACTS] KUALA LUMPUR

Area Code   The area code for Kuala Lumpur is 03, and the city's phone numbers have an eight-digit format. Numbers in the rest of the country have seven digits.

Banks   Branches for local and many international banks can be found along Jalan Sultan Ismail. ATMs as well as money-changers are located at virtually every shopping mall and entertainment or transportation hub.

Business Hours   Shopping centers and shops generally open daily at 10am and stay open until 9 or 10pm. Banks are open Monday through Friday 9:30am to 3pm and on Saturdays from 9:30 to 11:30am.

Emergencies   The emergency number for **police** and **ambulance** is ✆ **999**. For **fire** emergencies, call ✆ **994.**

Hospitals   In the event of an accident or emergency, the best facility in Kuala Lumpur is **Hospital Kuala Lumpur** on Jalan Pahang (✆ **03/2615-5555**). English is spoken there.

Internet Access   Internet service in KL will run about RM3 to RM6 per hour for usage. Internet cafes come and go, popping up in backpacker areas like Chinatown and the streets around BB Plaza off Jalan Bukit Bintang. **Yoshi Connection**

(C21-F Concourse Level, Suria KLCC; ✆ **03/2161-5000**) is a business center that is located just next to a Pos Malaysia post office branch; it offers Internet access for RM8 per hour, plus photocopying, fax, and executive PC services in a quiet and professional environment. It's open 10am to 10pm daily.

Mail   KL's General Post Office is on Jalan Sultan Hishamuddin in the enormous Pos Malaysia Komplex Dayabumi (✆ **1300/300-300**), but there are more convenient branches at Suria KLCC, Lot C21-G/H/I, Concourse Level (✆ **03/2161-8069**), and along Jalan Bukit Bintang at KL Plaza, Lot C12 & C13, Blok C (✆ **03/2142-9273**).

Where to Stay
VERY EXPENSIVE

Hilton Kuala Lumpur ★★★   This is the hottest hotel in KL. From the airy, art-filled public spaces to the compact rooftop lagoon pool, everything in this hotel feels innovative and hip. Large rooms have sleek contemporary decor, with a desk area wired for work, mood lighting, and a 42-inch plasma TV. A "magic button" handles all service requests, and three "lifestyle boxes" provide little extras like desk accessories, bath treats, and games. The marble bathrooms are sleek and contemporary, with deep tubs and a mini LCD-screen TV built into the shaving mirror. The hotel is just across the street from KL Sentral train station, the city's main transportation hub and terminal for the KLIA Ekspres train.

3 Jalan Stesen Sentral, 50470 Kuala Lumpur. ✆ **03/2264-2264,** 800/HILTONS (445-8667) in the U.S. and Canada, 800/445-8667 in Australia, 800/448-002 in New Zealand, or 08705/909090 in the U.K. Fax 03/2264-2266. www.hilton.com. 510 units. RM504 double; from RM820 suite. AE, DC, MC, V. Opposite KL Sentral station. **Amenities:** 6 restaurants; cafe; wine bar; 2 lounges; airport transfers; babysitting; concierge; health club and spa operated by Clark Hatch Fitness; rooftop lagoon-style outdoor pool; room service; smoke-free rooms. *In room:* A/C, TV w/satellite programming, in-house movies, and home theater systems with DVD players, hair dryer, high-speed Internet, minibar.

Mandarin Oriental Kuala Lumpur ★★★   The iconic Mandarin Oriental is part of the KL City Centre, Suria KLCC shopping mall, Petronas Twin Towers and the KL Convention Centre cluster. Setting the benchmark for hospitality standards in the city, the hotel is *the address* for corporate travelers, who seek the finest treatment on club floors and arguably the best club lounge in KL. The black marble lobby exudes sophistication which is carried over into guest rooms, which are luxe, in exotic oriental-inspired hues and local decor touches—though some of the rooms do feel worn. First-class restaurants fill up with weekday power lunchers—if you have time, you can book a cooking class with one of the hotel's celebrated chefs. The spa offers an array of treatments, including a traditional Malay massage. Sultan Lounge, located in the hotel, is a nighttime hot spot jumping with locals and expats.

Kuala Lumpur City Center (KLCC), 50088 Kuala Lumpur. ✆ **03/2380-8888,** 866/526-6566 in the U.S. and Canada, 800/123-693 in Australia, 800/2828-3838 in New Zealand, or 800/2828-3838 in the U.K. Fax 03/2380-8833. www.mandarinoriental.com. 643 units. RM559 double; from RM2,199 suite. AE, DC, MC, V. 2-min walk to KLCC and the Convention Center. **Amenities:** 6 restaurants; 3 lounges; airport transfers; babysitting; concierge; health club w/Jacuzzi, steam room, and sauna; rooftop infinity pool; room service; signature spa; 2 outdoor tennis courts; cooking school; 2 air-conditioned squash courts. *In room:* A/C, TV w/satellite and DVD player, hair dryer, minibar, MP3 docking station, Wi-Fi.

The Westin Kuala Lumpur ★★ ☺   The Westin is no ordinary hotel. Its sensory approach to hospitality is obvious the minute you enter from busy Bintang Walk and notice the aromatherapy candles, the fruit-flavored welcome drinks, and the mood of the music. The staff looks more like smart shop assistants from the nearby Louis Vuitton store than those of a chain hotel. There is a trendy vibe to everything from restaurants to bars, and the rooms are contemporary, functional, and welcoming. The fitness center here is tops, with competent trainers, state-of-the-art equipment, good exercise programs, and terrific views. The buffet breakfast is easily the region's best. EEST serves up a wide array of Asian cuisines, and Qba features live salsa bands almost every night. The Westin has an excellent kids' club, which is fully staffed and offers plenty of activities.

199 Jalan Bukit Bintang, 55100 Kuala Lumpur. ℂ **03/2731-8333,** 888/625-5144 in the U.S. and Canada, 800/656-535 in Australia, 800/490-375 in New Zealand, 800/325-95959 in the U.K. Fax 03/2731-8000. www.starwoodhotels.com. 443 units. RM520 double; from RM970 suite. AE, DC, MC, V. 5-min walk to monorail station and on the doorstep to the restaurants, bars, and entertainment of Bintang Walk. **Amenities:** 4 restaurants; 2 bars; airport transfers; babysitting; children's club; concierge; executive-level rooms; health club; outdoor pool; room service; spa. *In room:* A/C, TV w/satellite and in-house movies, hair dryer, minibar, Wi-Fi (RM50 per day).

EXPENSIVE

The Grand Millennium Kuala Lumpur ★   One of the best five-star properties in Kuala Lumpur, this landmark along KL's fashionable Jalan Bukit Bintang shopping strip has an ever-bustling lobby to match the excitement along the sidewalks outside. Surprisingly, the staff is always polite and professional, despite the barrage. The guest rooms are spacious, quiet, and cool, with huge plush beds covered in soft cozy cotton sheets and down comforters. Bathrooms are large marble affairs with plenty of counter space. The outdoor pool is a palm-lined free-form escape, and the fitness center is state-of-the-art, with sauna, steam, spa, and Jacuzzi. Pavilion Kuala Lumpur, a smart shopping mall, adjoins the hotel. The hotel's Pulse bar and nightclub is a darling with KL's happening clubbers.

160 Jalan Bukit Bintang, 55100 Kuala Lumpur. ℂ **03/2117-4888,** 866/866-8066 in the U.S. and Canada, 800/124-420 in Australia, 800/808-228 in New Zealand, or 800/414-741 in the U.K. Fax 03/2117-1441. www.millenniumhotels.com. 468 units. RM425 double; from RM625 suite. AE, DC, MC, V. 5-min. walk to Bukit Bintang Monorail station. **Amenities:** 2 restaurants; nightclub and lobby lounge/cafe; airport transfers; babysitting; concierge; executive-level rooms; health club w/Jacuzzi, sauna, steam, and massage; rooftop pool; room service; smoke-free rooms; Wi-Fi; air-conditioned squash court. *In room:* A/C, TV w/satellite programming and in-house movies, hair dryer, minibar.

Shangri-La Hotel, Kuala Lumpur ★★   The Shang is one of the most beloved hotels in KL. Well heeled locals meet up in its grand lobby, with floor-to-ceiling views of verdant foliage, while VIP guests wine and dine in its award-winning restaurants. Because it's an older property in the city, it has space for a ground-level outdoor lagoon swimming pool, which is nestled in lush tropical gardens. Guest rooms are nice and large, and are priced according to view, with the Petronas Twin Towers view commanding top prices, followed by city and gardenview rooms. The hotel lives up to its reputation for excellent service and world-class facilities.

11 Jalan Sultan Ismail, 50250 Kuala Lumpur. ℂ **03/2032-2388,** 886/565-5050 in the U.S. and Canada, 800/222-448 in Australia, 800/442-179 in New Zealand, or 800/028-3337 in the U.K. Fax 03/2070-1514. www.shangri-la.com. 662 units. RM380 double; from RM975 suite. AE, DC, MC, V. 10-min. walk to Raja Chulan LRT station. **Amenities:** 5 restaurants; 3 cafes; lobby lounge; airport transfers; babysitting; concierge; health club; large landscaped outdoor pool; room service; spa w/Jacuzzi, steam, and sauna; outdoor tennis court. *In room:* A/C, TV w/satellite programming and in-house movies, hair dryer, high-speed Internet (free), minibar.

Traders Kuala Lumpur ★   Sister hotel to the Shangri-La, this business hotel advertises itself as a "value" choice for accommodations, but room rates can be pricey.

Still, it is an excellent hotel for the money, with facilities you'd expect from a high-end hotel. In the evenings, the rooftop swimming pool and spa, located on the 33rd floor, are converted into SkyBar, a semi-alfresco lounge with unsurpassed views of the city skyline, including the Twin Towers—having a drink at this hot spot is a must whether you're staying in the hotel or not. This hotel has a fresh, contemporary feel in decor and attitude and is equipped with everything business travelers need. Its location, next to the KL City Centre, Suria KLCC shopping mall, and KL Convention Centre, makes it popular with conference delegates and leisure travelers.

Kuala Lumpur City Center (KLCC), 50088 Kuala Lumpur. ✆ **03/2332-9888,** 886/565-5050 in the U.S. and Canada, 800/222-448 in Australia, 800/442-179 in New Zealand, or 800/028-3337 in the U.K. Fax 03/2332-2666. www.shangri-la.com. 571 units. RM375 double; from RM675 suite. AE, DC, MC, V. 10-min. walk to the Twin Towers and 15-min. walk to Bintang Walk. **Amenities:** 2 restaurants; rooftop bar; airport transfers; babysitting; concierge; health club; rooftop pool; room service; spa w/Jacuzzi, sauna, and steam bath. *In room:* A/C, TV w/satellite and in-house movies, hair dryer, high-speed Internet (free), minibar.

MODERATE

Concorde Hotel Kuala Lumpur ★

Concorde is one of my favorites in this price category for its central location and quality accommodations at a price that's fair for leisure travelers. A recent renovation has outfitted Tower Wing rooms with plush new furnishings and decor. Rooms vary in size from category to category, so be sure to ask at the time of booking if this is important to you. Concorde has a small outdoor pool with a charming cafe and a small fitness center. The lobby lounge is noisy at night because it's popular. Hard Rock Cafe is also on the premises.

2 Jalan Sultan Ismail, 50250 Kuala Lumpur. ✆ **03/2144-2200.** Fax 03/2144-1628. www.concorde.net/kl. 570 units. RM260 double; from RM820 suite. AE, DC, MC, V. 5-min. walk to Bukit Nanas Monorail station and 10-min. walk to Dang Wangi LRT station. **Amenities:** 3 restaurants; Hard Rock Cafe; lobby lounge; airport transfers; babysitting; concierge; health club w/sauna, steam room, and massage; small outdoor pool; room service. *In room:* A/C, TV w/satellite programming, in-house movies, and DVD players, hair dryer, high speed Internet, minibar.

Meliá Kuala Lumpur

This hotel is located next to a KL Monorail station and across the street from the mind-bogglingly enormous Berjaya Times Square shopping and entertainment complex, making it an appealing option for visitors who need convenience. The small lobby is functional, with space for tour groups. Guest rooms have light-wood furnishings, contemporary fixtures, wall desks with a swivel arm for extra space, and big-screen TVs. Bathrooms, although small, are well maintained, with good counter space. Mealtimes in the hotel's coffee shop can be a little crowded.

16 Jalan Imbi, 55100 Kuala Lumpur. ✆ **03/2785-2828,** 888/95MELIA (956-3542) in the U.S. and Canada, 800/221-176 in Australia, 800/933-123 or 808/234-1953 in the U.K. Fax 03/2785-2818. www.solmelia.com. 300 units. RM275 double; from RM650 suite. AE, DC, MC, V. Imbi Monorail station. **Amenities:** Restaurant; lounge; airport transfer; babysitting; concierge; health club w/massage; small outdoor pool; room service; Wi-Fi. *In room:* A/C, TV w/satellite programming and in-house movies, hair dryer, high-speed Internet (free); minibar.

Piccolo Hotel Kuala Lumpur ★★ 🗡

This hotel can afford such low rates because it has few facilities to support—only a small spa and an Italian restaurant. No matter—the location, along Jalan Bukit Bintang, is excellent; just outside the hotel's front door, you'll find restaurants, nightclubs, shops, and more. Though rooms are basic, they are cool contemporary affairs, decorated with colorful marine photography. You really can't find a better deal in the city, but book in advance.

101 Jalan Bukit Bintang, 55100 Kuala Lumpur. ✆ **03/2146-5000.** Fax 03/2146-5001. www.piccolohotel.com.my. 168 units. RM305 double; from RM690 suite. AE, MC, V. 5-min. walk to Bukit Bintang Monorail

station. **Amenities:** Restaurant; smoke-free rooms; spa. *In room:* A/C, TV w/satellite programming and in-house movies, hair dryer, high-speed Internet, minibar.

Swiss-Garden Hotel   For midrange prices, Swiss-Garden offers reliable comfort, okay location, and affordability that attracts many leisure travelers to its doors. It also knows how to make you feel right at home, with a friendly staff (the concierge is on the ball) and a hotel lobby bar that fills up with travelers having cool cocktails at the end of a busy day of sightseeing. The guest rooms are basic, but tidy. Swiss-Garden is within walking distance from KL's Chinatown district and close to the Puduraya bus station, which was undergoing massive renovation at the time of writing.

117 Jalan Pudu, 55100 Kuala Lumpur. ✆ **03/2141-3333.** Fax 03/2141-5555. www.swissgarden.com. 310 units. RM310 double; from RM600 suite. AE, DC, MC, V. **Amenities:** 2 restaurants; lobby lounge; airport transfers; babysitting; concierge; small health club; small outdoor pool; room service; spa w/massage and sauna. *In room:* A/C, TV w/satellite programming and in-house movies, hair dryer, minibar, Wi-Fi (free).

INEXPENSIVE

Hotel Capitol ★ 🏷   A top pick for a budget hotel, Capitol is located in a lively part of the city's popular Golden Triangle district, close to the junction of Jalan Sultan Ismail and Jalan Bukit Bintang. In the surrounding lanes, you'll find small eateries and shops for necessities, and shopping malls are close by. The place has a minimalist lobby that's function over frills. Inside the guest rooms, the wooden furniture seems like it's been around a while, but the upholstery, bedding, carpeting, and drapes all seem fresh. The big tiled bathroom also has a long bathtub. There are no leisure facilities to speak of, but if you've come to KL to sightsee, you won't miss them.

Jalan Bulan, off Jalan Bukit Bintang, 55100 Kuala Lumpur. ✆ **03/2143-7000,** 800/448-8355 in the U.S. and Canada, 800/221-176 in Australia, 800/933-123 in New Zealand, or 800/660-066 in the U.K. Fax 03/2143-0000. www.fhihotels.com. 235 units. RM180 double. AE, DC, MC, V. 5-min. walk to either Imbi or Bintang Monorail stations. **Amenities:** Restaurant; room service. *In room:* A/C, TV w/satellite pro-gramming and in-house movies, hair dryer, high-speed Internet access, minibar.

Hotel Rae   Located near the popular restaurants and bars at Changkat Bukit Bin-tang, Hotel Rae offers clean, new rooms in a good location. Beware that the lowest-priced standard rooms don't have windows—be sure to request a room with windows when you book if this is important to you. Superior rooms have basic amenities, including small closets, minifridges, and luggage racks. As you climb the price ladder, rooms become more stylish.

No. 42–46 Tengkat Tong Shin, off Jalan Bukit Bintang, 50200 Kuala Lumpur. ✆ **03/2148-1770.** Fax 03/2148-1760. www.hotelrae.com. 48 units. RM140 double. MC, V. **Amenities:** Restaurant; room service. *In room:* A/C, TV w/in-house movies, minifridge, Wi-Fi (free).

Sky Hotel ★ 🏷   Located down an alleyway midway between the trendy cafes and shops of Bukit Bintang and the cultural attractions in Chinatown, this smallish hotel offers a welcome change from the musty and shoddy rooms offered by most of the city's cheaper hotels. Opened in mid-2010, Sky Hotel is my favorite for simple, tidy rooms that feel fresh thanks to clean tile floors and new soft furnishings, and with a few comforts like writing desks, wall-mounted flatscreen TVs, and luggage space. Rooms are not large, but the bathrooms are spotless. Staff is helpful, but friendliness can be hit-or-miss.

No. 1A Jalan Bukit Bintang, 55100 Kuala Lumpur. ✆ **03/2148-6777.** Fax 03/2148-5777. www.skyhotel. com.my. 50 units. RM168 double. MC, V. **Amenities:** Restaurant; room service. *In room:* A/C, TV with in-house movies, high-speed Internet (RM10 per hour), minifridge.

Where to Dine

In KL, diners have a wide range of choices. Local food abounds, from Malay to Chinese to Indian cuisine, and can be found everywhere, from humble street stalls and shopping mall food courts to fine-dining restaurants.

Al Nafourah ★★★ LEBANESE   Dripping with the magical allure of a desert oasis, Al Nafourah is pure Arabian Nights. With Moorish arches, twinkling lanterns, carved screens, silken hangings, mosaic tiles, and woven carpets throughout, the restaurant also has booths in private nooks for extra romance. The Lebanese cuisine is some of the best around, with lamb, chicken, and fish dishes in tangy herbs and warm flatbreads straight from a wood-fire oven. Outside on the terrace, sit back and drink a heady coffee and smoke from a hookah while taking in belly-dance performances. A truly memorable evening.

Le Meridien Kuala Lumpur, 2 Jalan Stesen Sentral. ✆ **03/2263-7888.** Reservations recommended. Main courses RM48-RM128. AE, DC, MC, V. Daily noon-2:30pm and 6:30-10:30pm.

Chynna ★★ CANTONESE   Chynna is pure dinner theater: From the Madam Wong–style red lanterns to the Old China antique replica furnishings, you'll think you're in a highly stylized Shanghai of yesteryear. For fun, there's a show kitchen where you can watch delectable dim sum morsels being prepared, or you can just sit at your table and watch the tea master refill your cup with long-stem tea pourers and acrobatic moves. The delicious dim sum menu (served only at lunch) is extensive, with most dishes between RM8 and RM12. Dinner is standard Cantonese fare, but expensive, with a vast menu of soups and rice and noodle dishes.

Hilton Kuala Lumpur, 3 Jalan Stesen Sentral. ✆ **03/2264-2264.** Reservations recommended. Small dishes RM28-RM56. AE, DC, MC, V. Daily noon-2:30pm and 6:30-10:30pm.

Coliseum Cafe 🍴 WESTERN   What can I say about Coliseum? Okay, the place is 90 years old, and so is the staff (seriously, some have worked here forever). Located in the grottiest hotel I've ever seen, with stained white walls, worn tile floors, and threadbare linens, this is KL's authentic "greasy spoon." It sounds dreadful, but the place is legendary, and someday it will be gone and there will never be anything else like it. It used to be *the place* for the starched-shirt colonial types to get real Western food back in the day. Now it's a favorite with the locals, who come for enormous sizzling steaks (which fill the place with greasy smoke), baked crabmeat served in the shell, and the house-favorite caramel custard pudding. Actually, the food is quite nice, and the prices are terrific for the steaks, which I highly recommend ordering. You either get this place or you don't.

98-100 Jalan Tuanku Abdul Rahman. ✆ **03/2692-6270.** Reservations not accepted. Main courses RM20-RM60. MC. Daily 8am-10pm.

Feast Village ★★ INTERNATIONAL   I'm one of those people who can never decide what to eat, so this is the place for me. Located in the basement of Starhill Gallery, an exclusive shopping mall, Feast Village isn't a single restaurant, but a cluster of 13 restaurants arranged like a small Malay village. As you stroll along stone and timber pathways, you'll pass cafes that serve seafood, steaks, Malay, Chinese, Thai, Korean, Indian, and more. Within each cafe, the menu is unique and so is the decor. Shook! stands out for its Japanese, Chinese, and Western offerings. Wander, smell the smells, read the menus, check out the sights, and find the perfect food for your mood.

Basement, Starhill Gallery, 181 Jalan Bukit Bintang. ✆ **03/2782-3800.** Reservations not required. Main courses vary from outlet to outlet. AE, DC, MC, V. Most outlets daily noon-2:30pm and 6:30-10:30pm.

Little Penang Cafe ★ MALAYSIAN/CHINESE   This cafe serves authentic Penang-style Malay and Chinese cuisine, including *char kway teow* (fried Chinese flat noodles), *nasi lemak* (Malay coconut rice with condiments), and Penang-style *laksa* (fragrant and tangy noodle soup). For dessert, try *cendol* (shaved ice with sweet jelly and beans). Arrive early at lunch, as the queue gets long—it's very popular.

Lot 409-411, 4th Floor, Suria KLCC shopping mall. © **03/2163-1215.** Reservations recommended. Main courses around RM9.80. AE, DC, MC, V. Daily noon-10:30pm.

Old China Cafe ★★ PERANAKAN   This humble cafe, located in a semidecrepit shophouse on the edge of Chinatown, has surprisingly good food. The restaurant has strived to maintain the feel of a vintage Chinese shophouse cafe, which is evident in its authentic—albeit dingy—furnishings and decor. The restaurant offers a full menu of Malay and Chinese favorites in a local fusion style known as Nyonya, or Peranakan, cuisine. Here you'll find a wide array of flavorful choices at reasonable prices. Upstairs, there is a small, welcoming teahouse.

11 Jalan Balai Polis. © **03/2072-5915.** www.oldchina.com.my. Reservations not necessary. Main courses RM9.80-RM29. MC, V. Daily 11am-11pm.

Seri Angkasa Revolving Restaurant MALAYSIAN/WESTERN   Located at the top of the KL Tower, 282m (925 ft.) above the city, this revolving restaurant's views are the main attraction here. A large buffet spread of local Malay favorites also includes some familiar Western choices as well. It's not cheap, but it's an enjoyable evening.

Jalan Punchak (off Jalan P. Ramlee). © **03/2020-5055.** Reservations recommended. Buffet service only: lunch RM60 adults, RM35 children; tea RM35; dinner RM135 adults, RM75 children. AE, MC, V. Mon-Fri noon-11pm; Sat-Sun 11:30am-11pm.

Top Hat Restaurant ★★★ 🎒 ASIAN FUSION   Top Hat has a unique atmosphere. In a 1930s bungalow that was once a school, the place winds through room after room, its walls painted in bright hues and furnished with an assortment of mix-and-matched teak tables, chairs, and antiques. The menu is fabulous. While a la carte is available, Top Hat puts together set meals featuring Nyonya, Melaka (Malacca) Portuguese, traditional Malay, Thai, Western, and even vegetarian recipes. They're all brilliant. Desserts are huge and sinful. There's a sampler dish for those who can't decide.

No. 7 Jalan Kia Peng. © **03/2142-8611.** www.top-hat-restaurants.com. Reservations recommended. Main courses RM30-RM75. Set meals RM30-RM100. AE, DC, MC, V. Lunch Mon-Fri noon-2:30pm; dinner daily 6-10:30pm.

What to See & Do

Most of Kuala Lumpur's historic sights are located in and around the Merdeka Square/Jalan Hishamuddin area, while many of the gardens, parks, and museums are out at Lake Gardens. Taxi fare between the two locations should run you about RM8.

KL Hop-on Hop-off City Tours (© **1800/885-546;** www.myhoponhopoff. com) is a recommended way to sightsee. Double-decker buses circle the city daily, passing near most major attractions and hotels, and operating from 8:30am to 8:30pm at 30-minute intervals. Buy your ticket from the nearest Hop-On Hop-Off bus stop, from your hotel's front desk, or from the bus driver directly. A 24-hour ticket costs RM38 adults and RM17 children, and once you purchase your ticket, you can hop on and off the bus as many times as you like within this period.

Aquaria KLCC ☺   Inside the KL Convention Centre, this surprisingly large aquarium is home to more than 5,000 creatures representing more than 300 species. Feedings occur throughout the day. There's a large gift shop, plus the Aquazone Fish

Therapy Centre where *garra rufa* fish nibble dead skin off your toes while you soak them in a pool (RM38 adults, RM22 children)—though it seems strange for a child to try fish therapy, the staff assured me that it is safe for children under adult supervision.

Concourse Level, Kuala Lumpur Convention Centre. ✆ **03/2333-1888.** www.aquariaklcc.com. Admission RM45 adults, RM35 children. Daily 11am–8pm.

Badan Warisan and Rumah Penghulu ★★★   Tour an early-20th-century traditional Malay wooden house that was found in the overgrown jungles of Perak, painstakingly disassembled and removed, and lovingly rebuilt and restored in KL. Badan Warisan is the nonprofit organization behind the project, and they accept donations in exchange for excellent guided tours of the house. Give yourself at least an hour and a half to tour the house—longer if you'd like to view the video of how they did it.

2 Jalan Stonor. ✆ **03/2144-9273.** www.badanwarisan.org.my. RM10 suggested donation. Mon–Sat 9am–5pm. Guided tours at 11am and 3pm.

Berjaya Times Square Theme Park ☺   This place rocks! Formerly called Cosmo's World Themepark, it's an indoor amusement park that is literally built into the walls of Berjaya Times Square, a 900-outlet shopping mall. You don't even need to ride the looping roller coaster to feel that thrill in the pit of your stomach. In all, there are 14 rides—recommended for families with active kids.

Berjaya Times Square Shopping Mall, No. 1 Jalan Imbi. ✆ **03/2117-3118.** www.timessquarekl.com/themepark. Admission Mon–Fri RM38 adults, RM28 children; Sat–Sun RM43 adults, RM33 children. Mon–Fri noon–10pm; Sat–Sun 11am–10pm.

Central Market ★   The original Central Market, built in 1936, used to be a wet market, but the place is now a cultural center (air-conditioned!) for local artists and craftspeople selling antiques, crafts, and curios. It's fantastic for buying Malaysian and Asian crafts and souvenirs, with two floors of shops from which to choose.

Jalan Benteng. ✆ **03/2031-0399.** Daily 10am–10pm. Shops open until 9–9:30pm.

Chan She Shu Yuen Clan Association   Completed in 1906, this building served as a community base for Chinese with a shared Chan ancestry. The elaborate roof sculptures are made from glimmering shards of pottery, typical of many Chinese temples and shrines.

172 Jalan Petaling. ✆ **03/2070-6511.** Free admission. Daily 9am–5pm.

Islamic Arts Museum ★★   The seat of Islamic learning in Kuala Lumpur, the center has more than 7,000 displays of Islamic texts, artifacts, porcelain, textiles, and weaponry in local and visiting exhibits. The architecture of blue and white domes is reason enough to visit. There is a fine Middle Eastern restaurant and an excellent book and souvenir shop here.

Jalan Lembah Perdana. ✆ **03/2274-2020.** www.iamm.org.my. Admission RM12 adults, RM6 children. Daily 10am–6pm.

Jamek Mosque (Masjid Jamek) ★★   The first settlers landed in Kuala Lumpur at the spot where the Gombak and Klang rivers meet, and in 1909 a mosque was built here. Styled after an Indian Muslim design, it is one of the oldest mosques in the city. Interestingly, the mosque was designed by an Englishman, A. B. Hubbock, who was responsible for several other fine buildings in the city. Avoid prayer times, especially on Fridays at midday. For women, cloaks and head scarves are on loan for free at the entrance gate.

Jalan Tun Perak. Free admission. Daily 9am–5pm, but avoid prayer times on Fri 12:15–2:45pm.

Kuala Lumpur Lake Gardens (Taman Tasik Perdana)   Built around an artificial lake, the 92-hectare (227-acre) park is popular with joggers and families. Inside the Lake Gardens, a number of attractions are within walking distance of each other—bring a parasol and insect repellent to protect yourself from the elements.

The **Kuala Lumpur Bird Park ★ ☺** (Jalan Perdana; ✆ **03/2272-1010;** www.klbirdpark.com; RM45 adults, RM35 children; daily 9am–7pm) is nestled in nicely landscaped gardens, with more than 3,000 birds within a huge walk-in aviary where they stage daily feedings and bird shows. Stop in for refreshments at the **Hornbill Café** (✆ **03/2693-8086;** main dishes RM16–RM42; daily 9am–8pm), next to the Bird Park's main entrance, which serves sandwiches, soups, and pasta, as well as a kids' menu.

Across the street from the Bird Park, the **Kuala Lumpur Orchid Garden** (Jalan Perdana; ✆ **03/2693-5399;** weekend and public holiday admission RM1 adults, free for children; free weekday admission for all; daily 9am–6pm) has a collection of more than 800 orchid species from Malaysia and thousands of international varieties.

The **Kuala Lumpur Butterfly Park** (Jalan Cenderasari; ✆ **03/2693-4799;** RM18 adults, RM8 children; daily 9am–6pm) has more than 6,000 butterflies belonging to 120 species that make their home in this park, which has been landscaped with more than 15,000 plants to simulate the butterflies' natural rainforest environment. There is also a large insect museum. Pay an extra RM1 to bring in a camera and RM4 for a video camera.

Enter through Jalan Parliament. Free admission to the park. Daily 9am–6pm.

Kuala Lumpur Railway Station   Built in 1911, the KL Railway Station exemplifies the Moorish architecture that was popular with British colonials at the time. Nearby KL Sentral is now the main rail hub.

Jalan Sultan Hishamuddin.

Malaysia Tourist Centre (MTC)   At MTC you'll find an exhibit hall, tourist information services for Kuala Lumpur and Malaysia, and other travel-planning services. Saloma Café, within the complex, serves Malay food, and in the evening there are cultural dances and preformances.

109 julan Ampang. ✆ **03/9235-4900.** Free admission. Daily 7am–10pm.

Menara Kuala Lumpur (KL Tower)   Standing 421m (1,381 ft.) tall, this concrete structure is the 18th-tallest tower in the world, and the views from the top reach to the far corners of the city and beyond. The tower rises up from a tropical forest in the center of the city, where visitors can sign up for guided tours through forest trails, visit an exotic animal farm, and ride ponies or Formula One Grand Prix simulators. There's a free shuttle to the tower from the main entrance at Jalan Puncak next to the Pacific Regency Hotel. The ticket price includes entrance to all of the attractions. Seri Angkasa Revolving Restaurant is located near the summit (see review, p. 532).

No. 2 Jalan Puncak, off Jalan P. Ramlee. ✆ **03/2020-5444.** www.menarakl.com.my. Admission RM38 adults, RM28 children. Daily 9am–10pm.

Merdeka Square   Surrounded by colonial architecture with exotic Moorish flair, the square was once the site of British social and sporting events. These days, Malaysia holds its spectacular Independence Day celebrations on the field, which is home to the world's tallest flagpole, standing at 100m (328 ft.).

Jalan Sultan. Free admission.

National Art Gallery   In a tranquil complex that combines traditional Malay architectural elements with modern lines, the nation's most prominent art gallery claims a permanent collection of more than 2,500 works, most by Malaysia's most celebrated contemporary artists. The museum has six galleries, plus outdoor exhibitions and a cafe.

2 Jalan Temerloh off Jalan Tun Razak.✆ **03/4025-4990.** www.artgallery.gov.my. Free admission. Daily 10am–6pm.

National Mosque (Masjid Negara)   This mosque was built in 1965—the year that Malaysia and Singapore split—and its architectural style reflects that era. The most distinguishing features of the mosque are its 73m (240-ft.) minaret and the umbrella-shaped roof, which is said to symbolize a newly independent Malaysia's aspirations for the future. Visitors must dress respectfully, and cloaks and head scarves are available for women.

Jalan Sultan Hishamuddin (near the KL Railway Station). Free admission. Daily 9am–6pm.

National Museum (Muzim Negara) ★★   Built in the style of a grand Malay palace, the National Museum traces the nation's history from prehistoric times through today, with exhibits on ancient Malay kingdoms and the Colonial era, among others. This museum offers a good overview of Malaysian history and culture. There are free guided tours Monday to Thursday and Saturday at 10am.

Jalan Damansara. ✆ **03/2267-1000.** www.muziumnegara.gov.my. Admission RM2 adults, free for children 11 and under. Daily 9am–6pm.

National Planetarium ☺   The National Planetarium has a Space Hall with touch-screen interactive computers and hands-on experiments, a Viewing Gallery with binoculars for city views, and an Observatory Park with models of Chinese and Indian astronomy systems. Educational shows are screened throughout the day (Sat–Thurs), and cost an extra RM3 for adults and RM2 for children.

53 Jalan Perdana.✆ **03/2273-5484.** Admission to exhibition hall RM1 adults, free for children 11 and under. Daily 9:30am–4:15pm.

Petronas Twin Towers ★   Standing at an awesome 452m (1,483 ft.) above street level, with 88 stories, the towers were the tallest buildings in the world from 1998 to 2004 (when Taipei 101 snatched the title). From the outside, the structures are designed with the kind of geometric patterns common to Islamic architecture, and on levels 41 and 42 the two towers are linked by a bridge. Visitors are permitted on the viewing deck on the bridge from 9am to 7pm every day except Monday and public holidays. Also note that the viewing deck closes every Friday from 1 to 2:30pm. Otherwise, the building is accessible only if you are conducting business inside. Limited free tickets go fast, so line up early—the ticket counter is on the lower ground (concourse) level of the Twin Towers.

Kuala Lumpur City Centre.✆ **03/2051-7770.** www.petronastwintowers.com.my. Free admission, but tickets are limited.

Petrosains ☺   Pronounced "Petro-science," this hands-on discovery center occupies two levels within the Petronas Twin Towers and provides a solid morning of fun for kids. The center is very focused on geological science, which is natural given its sponsor, oil company Petronas. Joining galleries focused on energy and refinery are galleries that explore space travel, physics, and paleontology.

Level 4, Suiria KLCC, Petronas Twin Towers. ✆ **03/2331-8181.** www.petrosains.com.my. Admission RM12 adults, RM7 youth 13–17, RM4 children 5–12, free for children 4 and under. Tues–Fri 9:30am–4pm; Sat–Sun 9:30am–5pm. Closed Mon.

Sin Sze Si Ya Temple   Squeezed between buildings in a way that created favorable feng shui, this temple was founded in 1864 by Kapitan Yap Ah Loy to honor two prophets, Sin Sze Ya and Si Sze Ya, who guided him during the Selangor Civil War of 1870–1873.

Jalan Tun HS Lee. Free admission. Daily 9am–5pm.

Sri Mahamariaman Temple   This bright temple, tucked along a lively street in Chinatown, was built in 1873 by Thambusamy Pillai, a pillar of old KL's Indian community. It was originally a private temple to Hindu deities, who are depicted in colorful dioramas inside and up the tall *gopuram* at the main entrance. For RM.20 (20 sen), keep your shoes at the counter on the side wall before you enter. Across the street, the 121-year-old Guan Di Temple is dedicated to the Chinese God of War, who also represents loyalty and righteousness.

Jalan Bandar. Free admission. Daily 9am–5pm.

Sultan Abdul Samad Building   In 1897, this exotic building was designed by two colonial architects, A. C. Norman and A. B. Hubbock, in a style called Muhammadan or neo-Saracenic, which combines Indian Muslim architecture with Gothic and other Western elements. Built to house government administrative offices, today it is the home of Malaysia's Supreme Court and High Court. At night, the building is lit up.

Jalan Raja. No entry allowed.

Wei Zhen Gong Guan Yin Temple   This small Hokkien temple is believed to date back to 1898. Inside the main hall, there are three altars with gold-plated statues devoted to the Buddha, bodhisattva Guan Yin, and the deity Huat Chu Kong.

10 Jalan Maharajalela. ✆ **03/2070-8650.** Free admission. Daily 9am–5pm.

GOLF

Malaysia has an abundance of golf courses, many of which are high-standard courses designed by pros. You can hire a car from any tour operator (try **Red Fury Tours;** Suite 2.18, Wisma Central, Jalan Ampang; ✆ **03/2162-2693**) for about RM90 each way to either of the country clubs listed below. Each club is located 30 or so minutes outside of KL in ideal traffic conditions. During early morning rush hour, you should double this time.

The **Kuala Lumpur Golf & Country Club,** 10 Jalan 1/70D off Jalan Bukit Kiara (✆ **03/2093-9999;** www.klgcc.com), has two courses, 18 holes each, par 71 and 72, designed by R. Nelson and R. Wright. Greens fees are RM400 weekdays and RM600 weekends (only the East Course is open to nonmembers).

Saujana Golf & Country Club, Km 3, Jalan Lapangan Terbang Sultan Abdul Aziz Shah, 46783 Subang Selangor (✆ **03/7846-1466;** www.saujana.com.my), has two 18-hole courses, each par 72, designed by Ronald Fream, with greens fees from RM280 weekdays and RM400 weekends and holidays.

Shopping

MARKETS   The huge **Central Market** on Jalan Benteng (✆ **03/2274-6542**) offers a wide array of Malaysian handicrafts, but the market has become more gentrified in recent years, and as a result, it offers fewer bargains.

Pasar malam **(night markets)** are very popular evening activities in KL. Whole blocks are taken up with these brightly lit and bustling markets packed with stalls selling almost everything you can dream of. Two good bets for catching one: On

Saturday nights, head for Jalan Tuanku Abdul Rahman, while the Bangsar Night Market starts at dusk and is popular with trendy residents.

Another shopping haunt in KL is **Chinatown,** along Petaling Street, but for me this place is more circus than anything else. Day or night, it's an interesting wander past stalls of knockoff designer clothing and accessories, sunglasses, T-shirts, souvenirs, fake watches, and pirated CDs and DVDs. Hawkers can be quite forward.

SHOPPING MALLS Most of the major shopping malls are located in the area around Jalan Bukit Bintang.

Suria KLCC (✆ **03/2333-1888;** www.suriaklcc.com.my), just beneath the Petronas Twin Towers, has a number of shops worthy of individual mention: **Aseana Fashion** (✆ **03/2382-9988**), located on the ground level, has gorgeous Asian-inspired haute couture; on level one, **Royal Selangor** (✆ **03/2382-0240**) sells an array of pewter gift items; on level two, you'll find **iKartini** (✆ **03/2382-2833**), which sells locally inspired high-quality batik clothing; and on level three, **Pucuk Rebung** (✆ **03/382-0769**) offers a small but interesting collection of Peranakan antiques and clothing.

Pavilion KL (✆ **03/2188-8833;** www.pavilion-kl.com), at the corner of Jalan Bukit Bintang and Jalan Raja Chulan, is without a doubt the city's most upmarket mall, with stores including Burburry, Furla, and Gucci. **Berjaya Times Square** (✆ **03/2117-3111;** www.timessquarekl.com) in Jalan Imbi wins the prize for excess, with 900 shops, food and entertainment outlets, plus one of the world's largest indoor amusement parks.

TRADITIONAL CRAFTS For Malaysian handicrafts, visit **Kompleks Kraf Kuala Lumpur,** Section 63 Jalan Conlay (✆ **03/2162-7533**), with its warehouse selection of assorted goods from around the country, all of it very good quality. Make time for the artists' village located behind the complex. This cluster of bungalows houses painters, batik artists, woodcarvers, potters, and other artisans who create their works and display them for sale.

You can also try the Central Market on Jalan Benteng (see review in "Markets," above), where you'll find local artists and craftspeople selling their wares.

Kuala Lumpur After Dark

There's nightlife to spare in KL, from fashionable lounges to cavernous discos to casual pubs. There are several hot areas for nightlife in the city. Along **Jalan P. Ramlee,** near the corner of Jalan Sultan Ismail, you'll find mostly tiki bars with Polynesian thatched roofs and live music. **Changkat Bukit Bintang** has a good selection of restaurants and bars for almost any taste and budget. In recent years, **Jalan Bukit Bintang** has become a trendy spot for clubs, bars, and late-night cafes—it's also a great people-watching spot. **Bangsar,** just outside the city limits, is 2 or 3 blocks of bars, cafes, and restaurants that cater to a variety of tastes (in fact, so many expatriates hang out there, they call it Kwei-loh Lumpur, "Foreigner Lumpur" in Mandarin). Every taxi driver knows where it is. Get in and ask to go to Jalan Telawi Tiga in Bangsar—fare should be in the neighborhood of RM10—and once there, it's very easy to catch a cab back to town.

Side Trips from Kuala Lumpur

BATU CAVES ★★

Located 13km (8 miles) north of Kuala Lumpur, **Batu Caves** have become one of the most significant Hindu religious sites outside of India. Built within a series of caves inside a limestone hill, three main caves make up a temple complex devoted to the Lord Murugan. During the Hindu Thaipusam festival, held each year in either January or February, devotees bathe in the nearby Batu River before donning *kevadis,* stainless-steel racks decorated with flowers and fruits and held to the body with pins and skewers. A procession leads from the river to the hill and up the 272 steps to the main cave. The festival draws more than 800,000 each year, but the caves are a nice side trip any time. The most convenient way to visit is by booking a taxi in advance from any tour operator. A round-trip tour, with a 2-hour wait, will cost about RM150. If you can get a regular metered taxi to take you, the trip from KL will take about 25 to 30 minutes and cost approximately RM20. During Thaipusam, regular shuttles depart from the Central Market to the cave site, and it is an absolute madhouse—but a memorable and fun experience. The Malaysia Tourism Centre will have complete instructions on how to catch one of the shuttles.

TAMAN NEGARA NATIONAL PARK ★★★

Malaysia's most famous national park, **Taman Negara,** covers 434,350 hectares (1.1 million acres) of primary rainforest estimated to be as old as 130 million years, and encompasses within its border **Gunung Tahan,** peninsular Malaysia's highest peak, at 2,187m (7,175 ft.) above sea level.

Prepare to see lush vegetation and rare orchids, some 675 bird species, and maybe, if you're lucky, some barking deer, tapir, elephants, tigers, leopards, and wild cattle or gaur. As for primates, there are long-tailed macaques, leaf monkeys, gibbons, and more. Taman Negara showcases efforts to keep this land in as pristine a state as possible, despite extensive logging in many parts of the country.

There are outdoor activities for any level of adventurer. Short **jungle walks** to observe nature are lovely, but then so are the hard-core 9-day treks or climbs up Gunung Tahan. There are also overnight trips to night hides where you can observe animals up close. The jungle canopy walk is one of the longest in the world, and at 25m (82 ft.) above ground, the view is spectacular. There are also rivers for rafting and swimming, fishing spots, and a couple of caves. Fishing permits must be obtained beforehand from the Ranger Headquarters.

If you plan your trip through one of the main resort operators, they can arrange, in addition to accommodations, all meals, treks, and a coach transfer to and from Kuala Lumpur. Prices vary, depending on the season and your level of comfort desired. The best time to visit is between the months of April and September; other times, it will be a tad wet (that's why it's called a rainforest).

Mutiara Taman Negara Resort ★, well established in the business of hosting visitors to the park, is the best accommodation in terms of comfort. It organizes package trips for as few as 3 days and 2 nights or up to 7 days and 6 nights, as well as an a la carte deal where you pay for lodging and activities separately. Accommodations come in many styles: a bungalow suite for families; chalet and chalet suite, both good for couples; standard guesthouse rooms; and dormitory hostels for budget travelers. To get an idea of pricing, a 3-day, 2-night package runs about RM1,040 per person, double occupancy in a chalet, with air-conditioning with attached bathroom, plus full board, meals, and activities. What it doesn't include is bus transfer from KL (RM140 per person round-trip) and the boat upriver from the park entrance (RM100 per person round-trip). A la carte activities include a 3-hour jungle trek, a 1½-hour night jungle walk, the half-day Lata Berkoh river trip with swimming, a 2-hour cave exploration, and a trip down the rapids in a rubber raft (Kuala Tahan, Jerantut, 27000

Pahang; ℭ **09/266-3500,** Kuala Lumpur Sales Office 03/2782-2222; www.mutiara hotels.com).

GENTING HIGHLANDS

Genting calls itself the "City of Entertainment," serving as Malaysia's answer to Las Vegas, complete with bright lights (which can be seen from Kuala Lumpur) and gambling. And although most people come here for the casino, there's a wide range of other activities, although most of them seem to serve the purpose of entertaining the kids while you bet your college funds at the roulette wheel. While it lacks the sophistication of other casino destinations, it is very popular with local punters and families seeking a one-stop destination in the cooler mountain air.

CAMERON HIGHLANDS

Located in the hills, between 1,070 and 1,830m (3,510–6,000 ft.) above sea level, this Colonial-era resort town has a cool, crisp climate, which makes it a popular retreat for Malaysians and Singaporeans who want to escape the heat. If you've been in the region awhile, you might also appreciate the respite. Temperatures in the highlands average 70°F (21°C) during the day and 50°F (10°C) at night.

The climate is also conducive to agriculture. After the area's discovery by British surveyor William Cameron in 1885, the major crop here became tea, which is still grown today. The area's lovely gardens supply cities throughout the region with vegetables, flowers, and fruit year-round. Among the favorites here are the strawberries, which can be eaten fresh or transformed into yummy desserts in the local restaurants. At the many commercial flower nurseries, you can see chrysanthemums, fuchsias, and roses growing on terraces cut into the hills. Rose gardens are prominent.

The three main towns here are **Ringlet, Tanah Rata,** and **Brinchang.** Tanah Rata has the most facilities for travelers, including the bus terminal, a taxi stand, banks (with ATMs), tour operators, a post office, convenience shops, and restaurants. Most of the area's major accommodations are located in Brinchang, which also hosts a *pasar malam* (night market) Friday and Saturday evenings.

MELAKA ★

Melaka's attraction is in its cultural heritage, around which a substantial tourism industry has grown. In 2008, Melaka was awarded UNESCO World Heritage status.

The historic heart of town is distinctive, with narrow one-way lanes hugged by old colonial-style shophouses built by the Dutch and British and later inhabited by wealthy Chinese and Peranakan (Straits-born Chinese) families. The most striking of the town's old buildings are the bright red structures—an old church and administrative buildings built by the Dutch during their rule. Just steps away are the remains of a Portuguese fort and church, and also close by you'll find English churches as well.

Getting There

BY TRAIN Melaka doesn't have a proper train station, but certain **KTM** trains stop at Tampin station (ℭ **06/441-1034**), 38km (24 miles) north of the city, though it's not the most convenient way in and out of Melaka. From the station you can catch a taxi to town for about RM50.

BY BUS The recently built **Melaka Sentral** bus terminal is north of the city center. From here, a taxi anywhere within town will cost about RM15.

To reach Melaka from Singapore, contact **Grassland Express** at 5001 Beach Rd., #01–25, Golden Mile Complex (✆ **65/6293-1166;** www.grassland.com.sg); a Super VIP coach departs at around 8am daily for the 4½-hour trip (S$45 weekdays, S$54 weekends). From KL, contact **NICE** at the Mezzanine Floor of the KTMB Building, Jalan Sultan Hishamuddin (✆ **03/2272-3634**). They operate executive coach services to Melaka six times a day for RM19 to RM22 for the 2½-hour trip.

BY COACH TOUR Several tour companies offer day trips from KL, with early morning pickups for a daylong whoosh around the major sights in Melaka that will have you back in KL in time for bed. In my opinion these tours don't leave enough time to explore and get a true sense of the town, but if you're short on time you can try **Red Fury Tours** (✆ **03/2162-2693;** RM260 for a day trip).

Getting Around

Most of the historic sights around the town square are well within walking distance. For other trips, **taxis** are the most convenient way around but are at times difficult to find. They're also not as clearly marked as in KL or Johor Bahru. They are not metered, and the going rate for trips within town seems to be RM15.

Visitor Information

The **Melaka Tourism Information Centre** (✆ **06/281-4803**) is on Jalan Kota at the Town Square next to the bridge. They're open daily from 9am to 6pm, but close at midday for lunch. **Tourism Malaysia** (✆ **06/283-6220**) also operates an office in Melaka at the Menara Taming Sari on Jalan Merdeka, open daily from 10am to 10pm.

[FastFACTS] MELAKA

Melaka's **area code** is 06. Major **banks** are located in the historic center of town, with a couple along Jalan Putra; ATMs are in every shopping mall. **Internet** places come and go. Your best bet is to ask your hotel's concierge or the Melaka Tourism Information Centre (see above) for the nearest cafes.

Where to Stay

Heeren House ★★ Started by a local family, this small guesthouse is in a renovated 100-year-old building furnished in traditional Peranakan and colonial style and located right in the heart of Chinatown. Small rooms have very basic amenities, but all have views of the Melaka River. The rooms on the second floor are somewhat larger. This is a friendly establishment run by a family who is very knowledgeable on local events. Reserve well in advance.·

1 Jalan Tun Tan Cheng Lock, 75200 Melaka. ✆ **06/281-4241.** Fax 06/281-4239. www.heerenhouse.com. 6 units. RM129–RM149 double; RM259 family room. No credit cards. **Amenities:** Cafe. *In room:* A/C, TV.

Hotel Equatorial Melaka ★ A solid choice for business and leisure travelers, Equatorial is located in the center of town. The 22-story hotel has some very good views of Melaka's downtown area—be sure to request a view when booking. Clean rooms have comfortable beds, small desks, and small balconies. This large property also has a good selection of restaurants.

Melaka

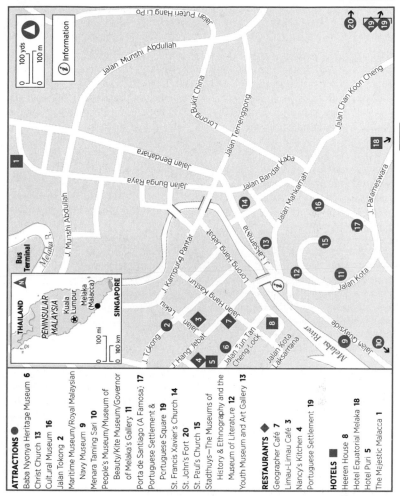

ATTRACTIONS ●
Baba Nyonya Heritage Museum **6**
Christ Church **13**
Cultural Museum **16**
Jalan Tokong **2**
Maritime Museum/Royal Malaysian
Navy Museum **9**
Menara Taming Sari **10**
People's Museum/Museum of
Beauty/Kite Museum/Governor
of Melaka's Gallery **11**
Porta de Santiago (A Famosa) **17**
Portuguese Settlement &
Portuguese Square **14**
St. Francis Xavier's Church **14**
St. John's Fort **20**
St. Paul's Church **15**
Stadthuys—The Museums of
History & Ethnography and the
Museum of Literature **12**
Youth Museum and Art Gallery **13**

RESTAURANTS ◆
Geographer Café **7**
Limau-Limau Café **3**
Nancy's Kitchen **4**
Portuguese Settlement **19**

HOTELS ■
Heeren House **8**
Hotel Equatorial Melaka **18**
Hotel Puri **5**
The Majestic Malacca **1**

Bandahar Hilil, 75000 Melaka. © **06/282-8333.** Fax 06/282-9333. www.equatorial.com/mel. 496 units. RM315 double; from RM680 suite. AE, MC, V. **Amenities:** 4 restaurants; cafe; lounge; airport transfers; babysitting; concierge; health club w/sauna, steam, and massage; large outdoor pool; room service; tennis courts. *In room:* A/C, TV w/satellite programming and in-house movies, hair dryer, high-speed Internet, minibar.

Hotel Puri 🔥   In the olden days, Jalan Tun Tan Cheng Lock was known as "Millionaire Row" for the wealthy families who lived here. This old "mansion" has been converted into a guesthouse, its tiled parlor has become a lobby, and the courtyard is where breakfast is served each morning. Although Hotel Puri isn't big on space, it is big on value (discount rates can be pretty low). Rooms are very clean and, while not overly stylish, are comfortable enough for any traveler. A friendly and responsive staff adds to the appeal.

118 Jalan Tun Tan Cheng Lock, 75200 Melaka. ℂ **06/282-5588.** Fax 06/281-5588. www.hotelpuri.com. 82 units. RM184 double; RM265 triple; from RM403 suite. AE, MC, V. **Amenities:** Restaurant; babysitting; room service; Wi-Fi. *In room:* A/C, TV w/satellite programming, fridge, hair dryer.

The Majestic Malacca ★★   Built from a restored 1920s mansion, this is Melaka's most luxurious property. The Majestic is celebrated for its colonial-era decor; large guest rooms feature teak beds, rich Asian silks, and claw-foot bathtubs. Even the guest-room annex remains faithful to the bungalow's original architectural heritage. The Spa Village here is the world's only spa to incorporate Peranakan, or Straits Chinese, beauty and wellness concepts into its offerings, and is considered one of the country's best. This boutique property is highly recommended for travelers who enjoy the allure of old grand hotels.

188 Jalan Bunga Raya, 75100 Melaka. ℂ **06/289-8000,** or 800/9899-9999 in the U.S., Canada, Australia, and the U.K. Fax 06/289-8080. www.majesticmalacca.com. 54 units. RM800 double; from RM2,000 suite. AE, DC, MC, V. **Amenities:** Restaurant; bar; airport transfers; concierge; health club; library; outdoor pool; room service; spa. *In room:* A/C, TV w/satellite programming and in-house movies, hair dryer, high-speed Internet, minibar.

Where to Dine

Geographer Café INTERNATIONAL   This place is very accommodating to travelers. They know which buttons to push to make travelers happy, so expect icy-cold beer, international comfort food, local dishes, souvenirs, Wi-Fi, and evening entertainment (from 8:30pm onward). The East-meets-West menu features only white meat—the tandoori chicken is recommended. Vegetarians are well catered to.

83 Jalan Hang Jebat. ℂ **06/281-6813.** www.geographer.com.my. Main courses from RM10. AE, DC, MC, V. Sun–Thurs 10am–1am; Fri–Sat 10am–2:30am.

Limau-Limau Café LIGHT FARE   If you're exploring Chinatown and Jonker Walk, Limau-Limau Café is a good stop for a cool fruit smoothie and a light meal, like a sandwich or pasta. Expect funky decor and a very nice staff.

9 Jalan Hang Lekiu. ℂ **06/698-4917.** Main courses RM4.90–RM16. No credit cards. Mon–Tues and Thurs 9am–7pm; Fri and Sun 9am–9pm; Sat 9am–1pm; closed Wed.

Nancy's Kitchen ★ PERANAKAN   This charming shophouse establishment has excellent traditional Straits Chinese dishes including *otak-otak,* pounded fish grilled in a banana leaf; *laksa,* spicy noodle soup with seafood; and *popiah,* a Nyonya take on spring rolls. The shop also carries cookies and cakes. Nancy also teaches cooking classes upon request for RM100 per person, advance booking required.

7 Jalan Hang Lekir. ℂ **06/283-6099.** Reservations recommended. Main courses from RM10; seafood sold at market prices. AE, MC, V. Mon–Thurs 11am–5:30pm; Fri–Sun 11am–9:30pm.

What to See & Do

Most of the preserved historical sites are on both sides of the Melaka River. Start at **Stadthuys** (the old town hall, pronounced "stat-highs"), and you'll see most of Melaka pretty quickly.

MUSEUMS

Baba Nyonya Heritage Museum ★   Called "Millionaire's Row," Jalan Tun Tan Cheng Lock is lined with row houses that were built by the Dutch and later bought by wealthy Peranakans; the architectural style reflects their East-meets-West lifestyle.

The house dates from 1896, when three houses were combined into one. The entrance fee includes a guided tour.

48–50 Jalan Tun Tan Cheng Lock. 📞 **06/283-1273.** Admission RM8 adults, RM4 children. Daily 10am–12:30pm and 2–4:30pm.

Cultural Museum (Muzium Budaya) ★ A replica of the former palace of Sultan Mansur Syah (1456–77), this museum was rebuilt according to historical descriptions to house a fine collection of cultural artifacts such as clothing, weaponry, and royal items. The gardens are quite nice.

Kota Rd., next to Porta de Santiago. 📞 **06/282-6526.** Admission RM2 adults, RM.50 children. Daily 9am–5pm.

Maritime Museum and the Royal Malaysian Navy Museum These two museums are located across the street from one another but share admission fees. The Maritime Museum is in a restored 16th-century Portuguese ship, with exhibits dedicated to Melaka's history with the sea. The Navy Museum is a modern display of Malaysia's less pleasant relationship with the sea.

Quayside Rd. 📞 **06/282-6526.** Admission RM2 adults, RM1 children. Mon–Thurs 9am–5pm; Fri–Sun 9am–8:30pm.

The People's Museum, the Museum of Beauty, the Kite Museum, and the Governor of Melaka's Gallery This strange collection of displays is housed under one roof. The People's Museum is the story of development in Melaka. The Museum of Beauty is a look at cultural differences of beauty throughout time and around the world. The Kite Museum features the traditions of making and flying *wau* (kites) in Malaysia, and the governor's personal collection is on exhibit at the Governor's Gallery.

Kota Rd. 📞 **06/282-6526.** Admission RM2 adults, RM.50 children. Daily 9am–5pm.

Stadthuys—The Museums of History & Ethnography and the Museum of Literature ★ The Stadthuys Town Hall was built by the Dutch in 1650, and it's now home to the Melaka Ethnographical and Historical Museum, which displays customs and traditions of all the peoples of Melaka, and takes you through the rich history of this city. Behind Stadthuys, the Museum of Literature includes old historical accounts and local legends. Admission price is for both exhibits.

Located at the circle intersection of Jalan Quayside, Jalan Laksamana, and Jalan Chan Koon Cheng. 📞 **06/282-6526.** Admission RM5 adults, RM2 children. Mon–Thurs 9am–5pm; Fri–Sun 9am–8:30pm.

Youth Museum and Art Gallery In the old General Post office are displays dedicated to Malaysia's youth organizations and to the nation's finest artists. An unusual combination.

Laksamana Rd. 📞 **06/282-6526.** Admission RM2 adults, RM1 children. Tues–Sun 9am–5pm.

HISTORICAL SITES

Christ Church The Dutch built this place in 1753 as a Dutch Reform Church, and its architectural details include such wonders as ceiling beams cut from a single tree and a Last Supper glazed-tile motif above the altar. It was later consecrated as an Anglican church, and mass is still performed today in English, Chinese, and Tamil.

Located on Jalan Laksamana. Free admission.

Jalan Tokong ★ Not far from Jalan Tun Tan Cheng Lock is Jalan Tokong, called the "Street of Harmony" by the locals because it has three coexisting places of worship:

the Kampung Kling Mosque, the Cheng Hoon Teng Temple, and the Sri Poyyatha Vinayagar Moorthi Temple.

Located on Jalan Tokong. Free admission

Melaka River Cruise ★   The Melaka River was once in a pretty nasty state, but the authorities realized its tourism potential and cleaned it up. A flotilla of small boats transports sightseers up and down past historic buildings, old warehouses (godowns), interesting mangrove stands, churches, and villages. The 1998 Sean Connery movie *Entrapment* was partially filmed here. Tours last about 45 minutes in boats ranging from 20- to 40-seaters, and normally a minimum of eight passengers is required before departure. Take a taxi to the jetty at Taman Rempah, about 20 minutes from Melaka town (about RM20). You can request beforehand to be dropped at the jetty beside the Maritime Museum instead of traveling back upriver, but it's not advisable to take the boat from that jetty as it's not a normal stop.

Departs Taman Rempah near Jalan Mata Kuching. © **06/281-4322.** Admission RM10 adults, RM5 children. Daily 9am–11pm.

Porta de Santiago (A Famosa) ★   Once the site of a Portuguese fortress called A Famosa, all that remains today of the fortress is the entrance gate, which was saved from demolition by Sir Stamford Raffles. When the British East India Company demolished the place, Raffles realized the arch's historical value and saved it. The fort was built in 1512, but the inscription above the arch, ANNO 1607, marks the date when the Dutch overthrew the Portuguese.

Located on Jalan Kota, at the intersection of Jalan Parameswara. Free admission.

Portuguese Settlement and Portuguese Square   The Portuguese Settlement is an enclave once designated for Portuguese settlers after they conquered Melaka in 1511. Some elements of their presence remain in the Lisbon-style architecture. Later, in 1920, the area was a Eurasian neighborhood. In the center of the settlement, Portuguese Square is a modern attraction with Portuguese restaurants, handicrafts, souvenirs, and cultural shows. It was built in 1985 in an architectural style to reflect the surrounding flavor of Portugal.

Located down Jalan d'Albuquerque off of Jalan Ujon Pasir in the southern part of the city. Free admission.

St. Francis Xavier's Church   This church was built in 1849 and dedicated to St. Francis Xavier, a Jesuit who brought Catholicism to Melaka and other parts of Southeast Asia.

Jalan Laksamana. Free admission.

St. John's Fort   The fort, built by the Dutch in the late 18th century, sits on top of St. John's Hill. Funny how the cannons point inland, huh? At the time, threats to the city came from land. It was named after a Portuguese church to St. John the Baptist, which originally occupied the site.

Located off Lorong Bukit Senjuang. Free admission.

St. Paul's Church   The church was built by the Portuguese in 1521, but when the Dutch came in, they made it part of A Famosa, converting the altar into a cannon mount. The open tomb inside was once the resting place of St. Francis Xavier, a missionary who spread Catholicism throughout Southeast Asia and whose remains were later moved to Goa.

Located behind Porta de Santiago. Free admission.

ANOTHER ATTRACTION

Menara Taming Sari   View the Straits of Malacca, the town of Melaka, and beyond from an air-conditioned, revolving cabin that rises 80m (262 ft.) on a tower in the center of Melaka's historic town, near the mouth of the Melaka River. The entire ride is about 7 minutes. The cabin can take more than 60 people; on weekends with good weather, queues can be long.

Jalan Merdeka, Banda Hilir (near the Maritime Museum). ✆ **06/288-1100.** www.menaratamingsari. com. Admission RM20 adults, RM10 children. Daily 10am–10pm.

Shopping

Antiques hunting has been a major draw to Melaka for decades. Distinct Peranakan and teak furniture, porcelain, and household items fetch quite a price these days, due to a steady increase in demand for these rare treasures. The area down and around Jalan Hang Jebat and Jalan Tun Tan Cheng Lok called **Jonker Walk** sports many little antiques shops that are filled with as many gorgeous items as any local museum. You'll also find handmade crafts, ready-made batik clothing, and other souvenirs. Whether you're buying or just looking, it's a fun way to spend an afternoon. On weekend evenings, Jonker Walk turns into a *pasar malam,* or night market, with souvenir shopping and street food.

For crafts and souvenirs, you'll also find a row of shops along the lane beside Stadthuys. Most prices seem fair, but you may need to do a little bargaining.

PENANG ★★★

Penang is made up of the island and a small strip of land on the Malaysian mainland. Georgetown is the seat of government for the state. Penang Island is 285 sq. km (110 sq. miles) and has a population of a little more than one million. The population is mostly Chinese (59%), followed by Malays (32%) and Indians (7%).

Georgetown's narrow streets are lined with shophouses that bustle with activity. Historic churches, temples, and mosques mingle with the city's newer architecture. The town's preserved buildings and its broad and harmonious mix of cultures earned it UNESCO World Heritage Site status in 2007, a title it shares with Melaka.

Getting There

BY PLANE   **Penang International Airport** (✆ **04/643-4411;** airport code PEN) is 20km (12 miles) south of the city, but in rush-hour traffic the airport transfer can take over an hour to Batu Feringgi. Taxi coupons at fixed rates are purchased in the Arrival Hall: RM45 to Georgetown, RM75 to Batu Feringgi.

Malaysia Airlines (✆ **1300/883-000;** www.malaysiaairlines.com) has about 20 flights to Penang each day from KL, plus connecting flights from all over the country and region. Other full-service airlines that service Penang are SilkAir, Thai Airways, and Cathay Pacific. Low-cost carriers also fly to Penang, including AirAsia, Firefly, and Tiger Airways. For more information on these airlines, see chapter 10.

BY TRAIN   Trains arrive at the **Butterworth Railway Station** (✆ **04/323-7962**), on Jalan Bagan Dalam (near the ferry terminal) in Butterworth, on the Malaysian mainland. Most times there will be taxis waiting, but if you arrive late at night, sometimes not. The station staff can help call a taxi for you. If you're in the mood for adventure, follow the signs and walk from the train station to the ferry terminal and take a boat across to Penang Island (see below).

By rail, the afternoon train from KL arrives around 11pm, or you can take an overnight trip from KL to Butterworth, which takes around 10 hours. Tickets cost RM85 first-class passage, or as low as RM17 for economy class. The prices vary greatly depending on whether you choose upper or lower berth (for overnight trains) and what class of passage you take. Call **KL Sentral** (✆ **03/2267-1200**) for schedule information.

BY BUS   There are a few VIP bus services to Butterworth or Georgetown. The trip from KL is about 5 hours, and most buses arrive at the **Sungai Nibong Bus Terminal** south of Georgetown near the airport. There's a taxi stand at the bus terminal; fares are about RM40 to Georgetown and RM60 to RM70 to Batu Feringgi.

Aeroline (In KL ✆ **03/6258-8800,** in Penang ✆ 04/657-2122; www.aeroline. com.my) buses depart daily at 9:30am and 3:30pm from Corus Hotel on Jalan Ampang in KL; round-trip fares are RM120 for adults and RM60 for children.

BY FERRY   The ferry to Penang is nestled between the Butterworth Railway Station and the Butterworth bus terminal. It operates from 6am to 12:30am daily and takes 20 minutes from pier to pier. Ferries leave every 10 minutes. Purchase your passage by dropping RM1.40 exact change in the turnstile (there's a change booth if you don't have it). Fare is paid only on the trip to Penang. The return is free. The ferry lets you off at Weld Quay.

Getting Around

BY TAXI   Taxis are abundant, but be warned they do not use meters, so you must agree on the price before you ride. Most trips within the city are between RM20 and RM25. If you're staying out at the Batu Feringgi beach resort area, expect taxis to town to run RM50. The ride is about 15 or 20 minutes but can take 30 minutes during rush hour.

BY BUS   Buses run all over the island and are well used by travelers who don't want to drop cash on taxis. **Rapid Penang** (✆ **04/238-1212**) operates a handy service from Georgetown to Batu Feringgi for only RM4. Bus 101 has stops at Weld Quay, KOMTAR, Chulia Street, and on Batu Feringgi Road outside Rasa Sayang Resort, Holiday Inn, and all the way out to the Butterfly Farm. It operates every 5 minutes from 5:20am to 10:30pm. Get exact change from your hotel's cashier before you set off.

BY CAR   Self-driving is not a bad idea in Penang, and cars can be rented through **Avis** at the Penang International Airport (✆ **04/643-9633;** www.avis.com.my); rates start from about RM200 per day for a small sedan, but you can often find good promotional rates. There's no need to have an international drivers license.

BY BICYCLE & MOTORCYCLE   Along Batu Feringgi, there are bicycles and motorcycles (little 100cc scooters, really) available for rent. I don't recommend renting the scooters. You can never be certain of their maintenance record, and Penang's drivers are careless about watching your back. A sad number of visitors are injured or worse because of scooter accidents. I also am not a fan of bicycle rentals here, for the same reasons.

BY TRISHAW   In Georgetown, it's possible to find some trishaw action for about RM30 for an hour. It's kitschy and touristy, and I completely recommend it for traveling between in-town sights, at least for a few trips.

ON FOOT   Georgetown is really about exploring the sights between the sights—back alleys where elderly haircutters set up alfresco shops, streets where you'll see bicycle repairmen fixing tires in front of their stores, and more—and the best way to get a feel for everyday life is by traversing the city on foot. Start wandering early in

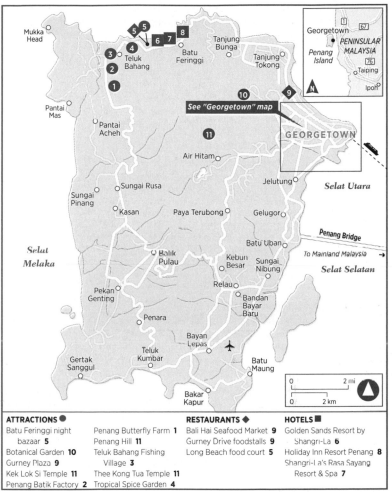

ATTRACTIONS ●		RESTAURANTS ◆	HOTELS ■
Batu Feringgi night bazaar **5**	Penang Butterfly Farm **1**	Bali Hai Seafood Market **9**	Golden Sands Resort by Shangri-La **6**
Botanical Garden **10**	Penang Hill **11**	Gurney Drive foodstalls **9**	Holiday Inn Resort Penang **8**
Gurney Plaza **9**	Teluk Bahang Fishing Village **3**	Long Beach food court **5**	Shangri-La's Rasa Sayang Resort & Spa **7**
Kek Lok Si Temple **11**	Thee Kong Tua Temple **11**		
Penang Batik Factory **2**	Tropical Spice Garden **4**		

the morning, by the waterfront, down the back alleys, before the heat of the sun takes hold—the lighting is perfect for photography and you will find fantastic subjects here.

Visitor Information

The main **Tourism Malaysia** office is located at Level 56, KOMTAR Building (Kompleks Tun Abdul Razak) on Jalan Penang (② **04/264-3494**), but for walk-in enquiries the tourism information office is opposite the Clock Tower in downtown Georgetown near the port (② **04/262-2093**; Mon–Fri 8am–5pm). There's another Tourism Malaysia information center at **Penang International Airport** (② **04/ 642-6981;** daily 8am–9pm).

[FastFACTS] PENANG

Penang's **area code** is 04. The **banking center** of Georgetown is in the downtown area (close to Ft. Cornwallis) on Leboh Pantai, Leboh Union, and Leboh Downing, but you'll find ATMs in KOMTAR and other smaller shopping plazas as well. **Internet** cafes come and go, so it's best to ask your hotel's concierge for the closest place to your hotel, or use the hotel's. If you're in town, Chulia Street, the main drag for backpacker tourists, has Internet access in a number of places.

Where to Stay

Although Georgetown has many city hotels, leisure travelers often choose to stay at one of the beach resorts 30 minutes away at Batu Feringgi.

Bayview Hotel Georgetown   This city hotel is a good choice for those who want to stay in town, close to the history, but need a hotel that is of a reliable standard. Bayview provides good value-for-money, with rooms that are plain but clean. In 2010, guest rooms underwent refurbishment. Some of the more expensive rooms have excellent views of the city.

25-A Farquhar St., Georgetown, 10200 Penang. ✆ **04/263-3161.** Fax 04/263-4124. www.bayview hotels.com. 333 units. RM208 double; from RM696 suite. AE, DC, MC, V. **Amenities:** 3 restaurants, including a revolving restaurant; club w/live entertainment; lobby lounge; airport transfers; babysitting; concierge; fitness center; outdoor pool and Jacuzzi; room service. *In room:* A/C, TV w/satellite programming, hair dryer, high-speed Internet, minibar.

Cheong Fatt Tze Mansion ★★ 🎁   This is definitely one of the most unique and memorable hotel experiences in Malaysia—to sleep inside the walls of one of Asia's most carefully restored heritage homes, the huge and opulent mansion of 19th-century millionaire Cheong Fatt Tze. The lobby is a simple desk in the front hall; inside, the only facilities to speak of are a courtyard breakfast area, a library, and a TV room (guest rooms do not have TVs). Guest rooms are each distinctive in shape and decor, all with terra-cotta or teak floors, charming architectural detail, and antiques and replicas of the period. Double rooms have either twin beds or one king-size bed. All are air-conditioned and have private bathrooms, though they are pretty small and bare. The experience is described by the management as an "owner-hosted home-stay," which is quite accurate.

14 Leith St., 10200 Penang. ✆ **04/262-0006.** Fax 04/262-5289. www.cheongfatttzemansion.com. 16 units. RM350 double; from RM450 suite. AE, MC, V. **Amenities:** Breakfast area w/tea and beverage service; TV room. *In room:* A/C.

Eastern & Oriental Hotel (E&O) ★★   E&O first opened in 1885, established by the same Sarkies brothers who were behind Raffles Hotel in Singapore. It is without a doubt the most atmospheric hotel in Penang, with manicured lawns and tropical gardens flanking a white colonial-style mansion, a lacelike facade, and Moorish minarets. Accommodations are all suites, with cozy sitting nooks and sleeping quarters separated by pocket sliding doors. You can expect molding details around every door and paned window, oriental carpets over polished teak floorboards, and Egyptian cotton linens dressing each poster bed. Some suites have pretty sea views. Dining along the hotel's many verandas is gorgeous. *One caveat:* No beach, but the pool in the seafront garden is very pretty.

10 Farquhar St., 10200 Penang. ✆ **04/222-2000.** Fax 04/261-6333. www.e-o-hotel.com. 101 units. RM630–RM4,880. AE, DC, MC, V. **Amenities:** 2 restaurants; English-style pub; airport transfers;

Georgetown map showing Penang Island, Selat Utara, Selat Selatan, Sungai Pinang, and street layout.

ATTRACTIONS ●

Cheong Fatt Tze Mansion **3**
Fort Cornwallis **11**
Goddess of Mercy Temple **8**
Han Jiang Ancestral Temple of the Penang Teochew Association **15**
Kapitan Kling Mosque **7**
Khoo Kongsi **17**
KOMTAR shopping complex **18**
Penang Islamic Museum **16**
Penang Museum and Art Gallery **10**
Pinang Peranakan Mansion **13**
Sri Mariamman Temple **14**
St. George's Church **9**

RESTAURANTS ◆

The 1885 **5**
Bali Hai Seafood Market **1**
Chin's Stylish Chinese Cuisine **12**
Mama's Nyonya Restaurant **2**
Gurney Drive foodstalls **1**

HOTELS ■

Bayview Hotel Georgetown **4**
Cheong Fatt Tze Mansion **3**
Eastern & Oriental Hotel **5**
Yeng Keng Hotel **6**

concierge; small health club w/sauna; room service. *In room:* A/C, TV w/satellite programming, hair dryer, high-speed Internet, minibar.

Golden Sands Resort by Shangri-La ★ ☺ Shangri-La has been operating resorts on Penang longer than anyone else, and claimed the best stretch of beach on Batu Feringgi. Shangri-La has two neighboring properties on this site, Golden Sands and its more exclusive sister, Rasa Sayang. Rooms are large and newly refurbished in relaxing tropical Zen style, and the higher-priced categories have views of the pool and sea. A four-star resort, Golden Sands is priced lower than the Rasa Sayang, attracting more families. The beach, lush landscaped pool area, and restaurants fill up fast, and folks are occupied all day with beach sports like parasailing and jet-skiing, and pool games. For the younger set, a large indoor playground is popular with kids under 12.

Batu Feringgi Beach, 11100 Penang. ℂ **04/886-1911,** 886/565-5050 in the U.S. and Canada, 800/222-448 in Australia, 800/442-179 in New Zealand, or 800/028-3337 in the U.K. Fax 04/881-1880. www. shangri-la.com. 387 units. RM564 double; RM1,483 suite. AE, DC, MC, V. **Amenities:** 3 restaurants; lobby lounge; airport transfers; babysitting; children's center; concierge; executive golf course; 2 outdoor lagoon-style pools; room service; outdoor lighted tennis courts; watersports equipment and activities. *In room:* A/C, TV w/satellite programming and in-house movies, fridge, hair dryer, Wi-Fi.

Holiday Inn Resort Penang ☺   This is a recommended choice for families, but be warned this resort has little appeal for vacationing couples or singles sans children. For families it has everything—special Kidsuites have a separate room for the wee ones with TV, video, and PlayStation, some with bunk beds. Holiday Inn also has a Kids Club, fully supervised day care with activities and games and a lifeguard. Older kids can join in beach volleyball, water polo, bike tours, and an assortment of water-sports arranged by the staff. Guest rooms are in two blocks: a low-rise structure near the beach and a high-rise tower along the hillside, connected by a second-story walk-way. Naturally, the beachside rooms command the greater rate. Beachside rooms also have better ambience and slightly larger space, with wood floors and details, while tower rooms have less charm. The lack of dining options gets tiring.

72 Batu Feringgi, 11100 Penang. ℂ **04/881-1601,** 800/465-4329 in U.S. and Canada, 800/138-388 in Australia, 800/801-111 in New Zealand, or 800/405060 in the U.K. Fax 04/881-1389. www.holidayinn penang.com. 358 units. RM300–RM370 hillview double; RM350–RM420 seaview double; RM540–RM630 Kidsuite; from RM1,000 suite. AE, DC, MC, V. **Amenities:** Restaurant; lobby lounge; airport transfers; babysitting; children's club; concierge; health club with massage; outdoor pool and children's pool; room service; outdoor lighted tennis courts; watersports equipment rentals. *In room:* A/C, TV w/ satellite programming and in-house movies, hair dryer, high-speed Internet, minibar.

Shangri-La's Rasa Sayang Resort & Spa ★★★   Rasa Sayang has 12 hectares (30 acres) of grounds along Penang's best beach—enough for a par-3 executive golf course, two pools, extensive gardens, two wings of guest rooms (Rasa and Garden), and an award-winning spa. Standard rooms are gorgeous; most have sea views, and are decorated in contemporary style, with natural tones, large bathrooms, and big fluffy beds. In the more luxurious Rasa Wing, guest rooms have private verandas and gardens or balconies with tubs outside. Guests who stay in the Rasa Wing also have access to a private lounge and swimming pool. Rasa Sayang is home to the Shangri-La's new spa brand, CHI; this luxurious and peaceful spa offers treatments based on Chinese principles of yin and yang and the five elements: metal, wood, water, fire, and earth. The hotel has several restaurants, but the Ferringi Grill attracts well-to-do locals with its lavish menu, including items like wood-plank-roasted cod and smoked lamb with sautéed crab.

Batu Feringgi Beach, 11100 Penang. ℂ **04/888-8888,** 886/565-5050 in the U.S. and Canada, 800/222-448 in Australia, 800/442-179 in New Zealand, or 800/028-3337 in the U.K. Fax 04/881-1880. www. shangri-la.com. 304 units. RM828 double; from RM1,242 suite. AE, DC, MC, V. **Amenities:** 4 restaurants; 2 bars; airport transfers; babysitting; concierge; health club; 2 outdoor lagoon-style pools; room service; spa; outdoor lighted tennis courts; watersports equipment and activities. *In room:* A/C, TV w/satellite programming and in-house movies, hair dryer, high-speed Internet (free), minibar.

Yeng Keng Hotel   Opened in 2010, Yeng Keng is a terrific addition to the George-town hotel scene. Located on Chulia Street, in the heart of the city, it is close to the best attractions, shopping, restaurants, and nightlife here. Once a private residence, the hotel is a 19th-century masterpiece that has been lovingly restored to preserve its charming local heritage while still offering modern conveniences. Rooms are cheerful and decorated in vibrant colors, antique furniture, and local crafts. Facilities are few, but the staff here is eager to please.

362 Chulia St., Georgetown, 10200 Penang. ✆ **04/262-2177.** Fax 04/262-3177. www.yengkenghotel.com. 20 units. RM380 double; from RM440 suite. **Amenities:** Small restaurant; outdoor pool. *In room:* A/C, TV w/satellite programming, Wi-Fi (free).

Where to Dine

Bali Hai Seafood Market ★★ SEAFOOD   Under garish neon lights that illuminate tired tiki-hut decor, you'll find mind-boggling quantities of live seafood in aquariums: gigantic lobsters and crabs from all over the world, huge prawns, and all kinds of fresh fish—select what you'd like and the chefs will prepare it for you while you watch through glass windows. Most dishes are prepared in a variety of Asian styles. Dining is alfresco along Penang's famous Gurney Drive, and the place gets packed and noisy. Check the prices of everything before you commit.

90 Gurney Dr. ✆ **04/228-8272.** www.balihaiseafood.com. Reservations recommended. Seafood priced according to market value. DC, MC, V. Daily 5–11:30pm.

Chin's Stylish Chinese Cuisine ★★★ CHINESE   After earning a number of prestigious awards in London, Restaurateur Dave Chin has brought his own style of chic Chinese to the Georgetown waterfront with a cluster of dining and nightlife venues under his Sol To group. Chin's Stylish Chinese Cuisine's specialties are to die for: Try crispy aromatic duck, fiery Szechuan poached fish, lobster noodles, or crispy chili beef. The setting is quirky, with sparkly chandeliers, colorful mismatched table settings, and even mismatched chairs.

Also in the complex, **QE II** serves wood-fire pizzas and Mediterranean cuisine with a panoramic view of the waterfront and marina, and after hours on weekends turns into a disco. **Chin-Chin Bar** is a sophisticated spot for cocktails.

Tanjong City Marina, Church St. Pier, 8A Pengkalan Weld. ✆ **04/261-2611.** Reservations recommended. Main courses RM20–RM50. AE, MC, V. Daily 6:30–10:30pm.

The 1885 ★★ CONTINENTAL   If you're celebrating a special occasion while in Penang, The 1885 will make the experience beyond memorable. The nostalgic romance of the E&O Hotel, its colonial architecture, interiors, and manicured lawns evoking times when tigers probably roamed the grounds after dark, provides the most incredible backdrop for a perfect meal. From an ever-changing menu, poultry, special cuts of meats, and fresh seafood are prepared in delicate contemporary Western style. Candlelight, starched linens, silver service, and extremely attentive staff create a magical experience. The wine list is extensive. By Malaysian standards, this is an expensive meal, but if you compare the quality of the service, cuisine, and surroundings, really, you will never find such elegance for this price in Europe or the States. English afternoon teas are also superb. Men are asked to kindly wear a shirt with a collar.

Eastern & Oriental Hotel (E&O), 10 Lebuh Farquhar. ✆ **04/222-2000.** Reservations recommended. Main courses RM78–RM180. AE, DC, MC, V. Daily tea 2:30–5pm, dinner 6:30–11pm.

Mama's Nyonya Restaurant ★ 🍴 PERANAKAN   Those who crave Penang's most famous culinary style of Nyonya food (or Peranakan) have to visit this cozy family-run restaurant in Abu Siti Lane. Ruby, one of the four sisters who run the place, learned her cooking from her Mama, hence the name. It's authentic, as Mama keeps a watchful eye on her protégés, although she no longer cooks. You'll see her there every day though, lending a helping hand with all the painstaking detail required for this kind of food. You might encounter some of her famous clients, including Malaysia's own international shoemaker, Datuk Jimmy Choo, or Hong Kong director Ang Lee. All the favorite Nyonya dishes are on the menu—try *tau eu* *bak, purut ikan,* Nyonya fish-head curry, and *otak otak.* Look like a tourist, and some-one will help you negotiate the menu.

31-D, Abu Siti Lane, Georgetown. ✆ **04/229-1318.** Main courses RM10–RM25. No credit cards. Tues–Sun 11:30am–2:30pm and 6:30–9:30pm.

FOOD STALL DINING

No discussion of Penang dining would be complete without coverage of the local food stall scene, which is famous. Penang hawkers can make any dish you've had in Malay-sia, Singapore, or even southern Thailand—only better. Penang may be attractive for many things—history, culture, nature—but it is loved for its food.

Gurney Drive Food Stalls, toward the water just down from the intersection with Jalan Kelawai, is the biggest and most popular hawker center. It has all kinds of food, including local dishes with every influence: Chinese, Malay, and Indian. Find *char kway teow* (fried flat noodles with seafood), *char bee hoon* (a fried thin rice noodle), *laksa* (noodles and seafood in a tangy and spicy broth), *murtabak* (mutton, egg, and onion fried inside Indian bread and dipped in *dhal*), *oh chien* (oyster omelet with chili dip), and *rojak* (a spicy fruit-and-seafood salad). After you've eaten your way through Gurney Drive, you can try the stalls on Jalan Burmah near the Lai Lai Super-market or the stalls at **Long Beach** food court in Batu Ferringi.

What to See & Do

IN GEORGETOWN

Cheong Fatt Tze Mansion ★★★
Cheong Fatt Tze (1840–1917), once dubbed "China's Rockefeller" by the *New York Times,* built a vast commercial empire in South-east Asia, first in Indonesia, then in Singapore. He came to Penang in 1890 and con-tinued his success, giving some of his spoils to build schools throughout the region. His mansion, where he lived with his eight wives, was built between 1896 and 1904.

The mansion is a sight to behold. Cheong spent lavishly for Chinese detail that reflects the spirit of his heritage and the fashion of the day, as well as the rules of traditional feng shui. Every corner is dripping with ambience, equipped throughout with stained glass, carved moldings, gilded wood-carved doors, ceramic ornaments, lovely courtyard and gardens, plus seven staircases.

In 2000, the mansion won UNESCO's Asia-Pacific Heritage Award for Conserva-tion, so lovingly has this historic treasure been preserved. Guided tours explain the history, personalities, and culture behind the home, plus the details of the conserva-tion efforts. If you're really hooked, accommodation is available.

14 Lebuh Leith. ✆ **04/262-0006.** www.cheongfatttzemansion.com. Admission RM12. Daily guided tours at 9:30am, 11am, and 3pm.

Fort Cornwallis
Fort Cornwallis is built on the site where Capt. Francis Light, founder of Penang, first landed in 1786. The fort was first built in 1793, but this site was an unlikely spot to defend the city from invasion. In 1810, it was rebuilt in an attempt to make up for initial strategic planning errors. In the shape of a star, the only actual buildings still standing are the outer walls, a gunpowder magazine, and a small Christian chapel. The magazine houses an exhibit of old photos and historical accounts of the old fort. Nearby, the yellow Town Hall is the oldest municipal build-ing in Penang, built in 1880. City Hall was built in 1903 and still serves the govern-ment administration today. The Cenotaph was erected in 1922 in memorial to those who lost their lives here during World War I.

Lebuh Light. No phone. Admission RM1 adults, RM.50 children. Daily 8am–7pm.

Goddess of Mercy Temple   Dedicated jointly to Kuan Yin, the goddess of mercy, and Ma Po Cho, the patron saint of sea travelers, this is the oldest Chinese temple in Penang. On the 19th of each second, sixth, and ninth month of the lunar calendar (the months that fall between Feb/Mar, June/July, and Sept/Oct, respectively), Kuan Yin is celebrated with Chinese operas and puppet shows.

Leboh Pitt. Free admission.

Han Jiang Ancestral Temple of the Penang Teochew Association   Penang's Teochew community lovingly restored its ancestral temple (circa 1870), earning it a UNESCO Asia-Pacific Heritage Award for Culture Heritage Conservation in 2006. The project was funded by the local Teochew community, who has seen a recent drive to preserve its heritage in Penang, with work carried out by traditional craftsmen brought in from China. Donations are welcome.

127 Chulia St. ℂ **04/261-5629.** Daily 9am–5pm.

Kapitan Kling Mosque   Captain Light donated a large parcel of land on this spot for the settlement's sizable Indian Muslim community to build a mosque and grave-yard. The leader of the community, known as Kapitan Kling (or Keling, which, ironically, was once a racial slur against Indians in the region), built a brick mosque here. Later, in 1801, he imported builders and materials from India for a new, brilliant mosque. Expansions in the 1900s topped the mosque with stunning domes and turrets, adding extensions and new roofs.

Jalan Masjid Kapitan Kling (Leboh Pitt). Free admission.

Khoo Kongsi ★   The Chinese who migrated to Southeast Asia created clan associations in their new homes. Based on common heritage, these social groups formed the core of Chinese life in the new homelands. The Khoo clan, who immigrated from Hokkien province in China, acquired this spot in 1851 and set to work building row houses, administrative buildings, and a clan temple around a large square. The temple here now was actually built in 1906 after a fire destroyed its predecessor. It was believed the original was too ornate, provoking the wrath of the gods. One look at the current temple, a Chinese baroque masterpiece, and you'll wonder how that could possibly be. Come here in August for Chinese operas.

18 Cannon Sq. ℂ **04/261-4609.** Admission RM10 adults, RM1 children. Daily 9am–5pm.

Penang Islamic Museum   This historical display traces the development of Islam in Penang, with information on important public figures and their cultural influence on the island. It's housed in the former mansion of Arab pepper trader Syed Mohammed Al-Attas.

128 Armenian St. ℂ **04/262-0172.** Admission RM3 adults, RM1 children. Wed–Mon 9:30am–6pm.

Penang Museum and Art Gallery ★★   The historical society has put together this marvelous collection of ethnological and historical findings from Penang, tracing the port's history and diverse cultures through time. It's filled with paintings, photos, costumes, and antiques, among much more, all presented with fascinating facts and trivia. Upstairs is an art gallery. Originally the Penang Free School, the building was built in two phases, the first half in 1896 and the second in 1906. Only half of the building remains; the other was bombed to the ground in World War II. Its recent renovation has added life, at least to the exterior. It's a favorite stop on a sightseeing itinerary because it's air-conditioned.

Lebuh Farquhar. ℂ **04/263-1942.** Admission RM1 adults, RM.50 children. Sat–Thurs 9am–5pm.

Pinang Peranakan Mansion   Another peek into a restored private home, this mansion is decorated with 1,000 antiques and collectibles from the Peranakan tradition, including ornately carved and inlaid furniture and colorful pottery; these wares and furniture meld Chinese and Malay aesthetic tastes. The mansion itself belonged to a Chinese towkay, or big boss, Kapitan Cina Chung Keng Kwee. Tours are offered at 11:30am and 3:30pm.

29 Church St. ✆ **04/264-2929**. www.pinangperanakanmansion.com.my. Admission RM10 adults, RM5 children. Daily 9:30am–5pm.

St. George's Church   Built by Rev. R. S. Hutchins (who was also responsible for the Free School next door, home of the Penang Museum) and Capt. Robert N. Smith, whose paintings hang in the museum, this church was completed in 1818. Although the outside is almost as it was then, the contents were completely looted during World War II. All that remains are the font and the bishop's chair.

Lebuh Farquhar. Free admission.

Sri Mariamman Temple   This Hindu temple was built in 1833 by a Chettiar, a group of southern Indian Muslims, and it received a major face-lift in 1978 with the help of Madras sculptors. The Hindu Navarithri festival is held here, whereby devotees parade Sri Mariamman, a Hindu goddess worshiped for her powers to cure disease, through the streets in a night procession. It is also the starting point of the Thaipusam Festival, which leads to a temple on Jalan Waterfall.

Jalan Masjid Kapitan Kling. Free admission.

BEYOND GEORGETOWN

Botanical Garden   Covering 30 hectares (74 acres) of landscaped grounds, this botanical garden was established by the British in 1884, with grounds that are perfect for a shady walk. Monkeys crawl all over these gardens, and they are *not* shy: They won't hesitate to approach visitors for food (ironically, you can buy peanuts for the monkeys right beneath the DO NOT FEED THE MONKEYS sign). Also in the gardens is a jogging track and kiddie park. The gardens are important for tropical research.

About a 5- or 10-min. drive west of Georgetown. ✆ **04/227-0428**. Free admission. Daily 7am–7pm.

Kek Lok Si Temple   The "Temple of Supreme Bliss" is the largest Buddha temple complex in Malaysia. Built on terraces into the side of Penang Hill, the oldest parts date back to the temple's 1893 founding. The seven-story Pagoda of Ten Thousand Buddhas can be climbed for a donation of RM2. The grand 30m (98-ft.) statue of Kuan Yin, the Chinese Goddess of Mercy, is a newer addition to the complex, as is a huge pavilion that was completed in 2009; these are located in the higher part of the complex, which can be accessed by the Sky Lift, a tram that costs RM2. The massive complex also has gardens and ponds with live tortoises. To get here, see "Penang Hill," below.

Air Hitam. ✆ **04/828-3317**. Free admission. Daily 7am–9pm.

Penang Hill   Malaysia's first hill resort, Penang Hill is only 833m (2,733 ft.) above sea level, but it is noticeably cooler than the rest of the island. At the top you will find the **Kek Lok Si Temple** (see above) and **Thee Kong Tua** (Temple of the Jade Emperor; Air Hitam; no phone; free admission; daily 9am–5pm), a Taoist temple dedicated to the supreme ruler of heaven. The hills are covered with jungle and 20 nature trails with great trekking.

Penang Hill was formerly reached by an old funicular railway that started from the base station at Air Hitam and traversed to the top of the hill. It's been closed for renovations that will remove all traces of the old railway and install new cars and track, but no official authorities have been able to give a clear estimate of when the new railway will be opened. When you visit, do contact the tourism board to find out if it's reopened, because it's a nice ride up the hill, even if the old wooden cars have been replaced. You can also trek up to the top of Penang Hill starting from the "Moon Gate" at the entrance to the Botanical Garden for a 5.5km (3.5-mile), 3-hour hike to the summit.

A 20- to 30-min. drive southwest from Georgetown. The funicular station is on Jalan Stesen Keretapi Bukit.

Teluk Bahang Fishing Village   Almost every family in this humble fishing village, located on the northwest tip of the island past the resorts of Batu Feringgi, survives by fishing the waters around Penang. There's not much to see here, except the fishing jetty, which is busiest in the early mornings when the fishing boats return with their catch. Most visitors come only for the nearby attractions, which are listed below.

Here you'll find the **Penang Butterfly Farm** (830 Jalan Teluk Bahang; ✆ 04/885-1253; adults RM20, children RM10, free for children 4 and under; daily 9am–5pm), a .8-hectare (2-acre) landscaped area that is home to more than 4,000 flying butterflies from 120 species. At 10am and 3pm, there are informative butterfly shows. Don't forget the insect exhibit—there are about 2,000 or so bugs.

Nearby is the organic **Tropical Spice Garden** (Lot 595 Mukim 2, Jalan Teluk Bahang; ✆ 04/881-1797; www.tropicalspicegarden.com; adults RM14, children RM8; daily 9am–6pm). Once an abandoned rubber plantation, this garden features native species in their natural landscape, while incorporating found and recycled materials. There are trails to explore the gardens, along with indoor displays, a visitor's center with a spice museum, a gift shop, and a cafe overlooking the sea.

Also in the area is the touristy but interesting **Penang Batik Factory** (669 Mk. 2, Teluk Bahang; ✆ 04/885-1284; www.penangbatik.com.my; free admission; daily 9am–5:30pm), where you'll see a batik printing demonstration followed by a trip to the factory store.

Teluk Bahang.

Shopping

The first place anyone here will recommend for shopping is **KOMTAR.** Short for "Kompleks Tun Abdul Razak," it is the largest shopping complex in Penang, four stories of clothing shops, restaurants, and large department stores. For those staying in Batu Ferringi resorts, **Gurney Plaza** (✆ 04/228-1111) is close by.

Good shopping finds in Penang are batik, pewter products, locally produced curios, paintings, antiques, pottery, and jewelry. If you care to walk around in search of finds, there are a few streets in Georgetown that are the hub of shopping activity. In the city center, the area around Jalan Penang, Lebuhraya Campbell, Lebuhraya Kapitan Keling, Lebuhraya Chulia, and Lebuhraya Pantai is near the Sri Mariamman Temple, the Penang Museum, the Kapitan Kling Mosque, and other sites of historic interest. Here you'll find everything from local crafts to souvenirs and fashion, and maybe even a bargain or two. Most of these shops are open from 10am to 10pm daily.

Out at Batu Feringgi, the main road turns into a fun **night bazaar** every evening just at dark. During the day, there are also some good shops for batik and souvenirs.

Penang After Dark

I highly recommend a cocktail at **Farquhar's Bar** (✆ **04/222-2000**; daily 11am–11pm), located within the old E&O Hotel, from where you can tour the areas of the hotel that are open to the public. Across the street from the E&O, Upper Penang Road has an entire strip of shophouses dedicated to nightlife. Here you'll find pubs and discos, beer gardens and live music, good beer on tap, and patrons from Penang's local, expatriate, and tourism populations. Possibly the most notorious bar in Penang is the **Hong Kong Bar,** 371 Lebuh Chulia (✆ **04/261-9796**), which opened in 1920 and was a regular hangout for military personnel based in Butterworth. It has an extraordinary archive of photos of the servicemen who have patronized the place throughout the years, plus a collection of medals, plaques, and buoys from ships. Be warned, it's a real dive bar.

LANGKAWI ★★

Where the beautiful Andaman Sea meets the Straits of Malacca, Langkawi Island positions itself as one of the region's best island paradise destinations. Since 1990, Tourism Malaysia has dedicated itself to promoting the island and developing it as an ideal travel spot. Now, after 2 decades of work, the island has proven itself as one of this country's best holiday gems.

One final note: Malaysia has declared Langkawi a duty-free zone, so take a peek at some of the shopping in town, and enjoy RM1.50 beers!

Getting There

BY PLANE   The **Langkawi International Airport** (✆ **04/955-1311**; airport code: LGK) is located on the southwest side of the island. The best way to reach town from the airport is to prearrange a shuttle pickup from your resort; otherwise, there's a taxi counter where you can buy coupons for RM30 to most resorts.

Malaysia Airlines, AirAsia, Silk Air, and **Firefly** make Langkawi very convenient from Kuala Lumpur, Penang, or Singapore.

BY TRAIN   Taking the train can be a bit of a hassle because the nearest stop (in Alor Star) is quite far from the jetty to the island, requiring a cab transfer. Still, if you prefer rail, hop on the overnight train from KL (the only train), which will put you in Alor Star at around 7am. Just outside the train station, you can find the taxi stand, with cabs to take you to the Kuala Kedah jetty for the ferry ride to Kuah.

BY BUS   To be honest, I don't really recommend taking a bus to Langkawi. If you're coming from KL, the bus ride is long and uncomfortable, catching the taxi transfer to the jetty can be problematic, and by the time you reach the island, you'll need a vacation from your vacation. Fly or use the train. If you're coming from Penang, the direct ferry is wonderfully convenient, as are a few flights per day.

BY FERRY   From the jetty at Kuala Kedah, on the mainland, there are about five companies that provide ferry service to the island (trip time: about 1 hr. and 45 min.; cost: RM25). Ferries let you off at the main ferry terminal in Kuah, where you can hop a taxi to your resort for RM20 to RM50, depending on where you're staying.

Ferries also ply between Penang and Langkawi, with operators clustered around the tourism office at the Clock Tower in downtown Georgetown. **Langkawi Ferry** (Ground Floor, PPC Building, Pesara King Edward; ✆ **04/264-2008** or 04/966-3779) has two early morning ferries for RM60 one-way and RM115 round-trip.

Langkawi

THAILAND

PENINSULAR MALAYSIA

Kuala Lumpur

SINGAPORE

Langkawi Island

100 mi
100 km

Straits of Chinchin

Straits of Malacca

Tk. Chira Mati

Pulau Dendang

Tk. Mempelam

Pulau Langgun

Selat P. Peluru

Tk. Belangkas

Straits of Panchor

Pulau Chorong

Pulau Timun

Kuala Perlis

Waterfall

Kisap

Kuah

Kuala Kedah

Kuala Kedah

Tanjung Rhu

Padang Lalang

Langkawi Craft and Cultural Complex

Pasir Hitam

Mt. Raya

Views from Fishing Village

Pulau Dayang Bunting

Makam Mahsuri Tomb

Hospital

Ibrahim Hussein Museum and Cultural Foundation

Ulu Melaka

Lookout Point

Kecawang

Tempyang

Datai Bay Golf Course

Market

Padang Matsirat

Pantai Tengah

Datai Bay

Kuala Teriang

Pantai Cenang

Pantai Kok

Pulau Rebak Besar

Telaga Tujuh Waterfall

Mt. Machincang

S. Data

S. Tama Besar

S. Peranjin

112

112

120

108

115

117

113

Beach

Ferry routes

The Andaman **1**
Casa del Mar Langkawi **3**
Four Seasons Langkawi **7**
Frangipani Langkawi Resort & Spa **4**
Nam Restaurant **2**
Tanjung Rhu Resort **6**
The Westin Langkawi Resort & Spa **5**

3 mi
3 km

557

Getting Around

BY TAXI   Taxis generally hang around at the airport, the main jetty, the taxi stand in Kuah, and some major hotels. From anywhere in between, your best bet is to ask your hotel's concierge to call a taxi for you. Keep in mind, if you're going as far as one side of the island to the other, your fare can go as high as RM50.

CAR & MOTORCYCLE RENTAL   Car and motorcycle rentals are very cheap and easy on Langkawi, which is good and bad. I'm wary of maintenance issues, as well as safety implications of how lax rental agencies are with regard to driving experience and insurance matters. Locally operated car-rental desks can be found at Langkawi Airport, and if you're at the beach areas at Cenang or Tengah, a few places rent jeeps and motorcycles from RM80 and RM30 per day, respectively. Pick a good helmet. *Note:* If you have an accident, you could be responsible for all repairs.

BY FOOT   The main beaches at Cenang and Tengah can be walked quite nicely; however, don't expect to be able to walk around to other parts of the island.

Visitor Information

There's no Tourism Malaysia representation on Langkawi, but the local tourism board provides information at two service counters, one at the ferry terminal in Kuah (℅ **04/966-0494**; daily 9am–5pm) and one at the airport (℅ **04/955-7155**; daily 9am–11pm) where you can find brochures and answers to queries.

[Fast FACTS] LANGKAWI

The only major **bank** branches are located far from the beach areas, in Kuah, mostly around the blocks across the street from the Night Hawker Center (off Jalan Persiaran Putra); there is an ATM at the airport. Money-changers keep long hours out at Pantai Cenang and Pantai Tengah, but for other resorts you'll have to change your money at the resort. Along the Pantai Cenang and Pantai Tengah main road, you'll find at least a half dozen small **Internet** places.

Where to Stay

The Andaman ★★ ☺   You will be surprised how large this resort is, its buildings blend so perfectly with the jungle surrounding them. Andaman has a sprawl of lush grounds hugging a beautiful white beach. The temptation to clear the coastal forests has been avoided, and rooms quite pleasantly look into these forests and their native fauna, but with glimpses of the sea. The Andaman welcomes families with special facilities and a safe, shallow beach. The entrance and main lobby are overpowering in size but visually quite stunning in open-air local-style architecture with vaulted roofs built from polished hardwoods. Guest rooms, in two wings that span out to either side of the main building, are big, with wall-to-wall carpeting and Western-style decor, save for a few local textiles for effect. Ground-floor lanai rooms have a private sun deck with umbrella stand. The pool is huge, with lots of shady spots, and the excellent spa features traditional Malay herbal beauty and health treatments.

Jalan Teluk Datai, P.O. Box 94, 07000 Langkawi, Kedah. ℅ **04/959-1088.** Fax 04/959-1168. www.the andaman.com. RM790 double; from RM2,790 suite. Prices jump Dec–Jan. AE, DC, MC, V. **Amenities:** 3 restaurants; 2 bars; airport transfers; babysitting; mountain bike rental; concierge; golf course; health club; kids' club; outdoor pools surrounded by gardens; room service; spa w/Jacuzzi, sauna, steam, and massage; 2 outdoor lighted tennis courts; nonmotorized watersports equipment. *In room:* A/C, TV w/ satellite programming and DVD player, hair dryer, high-speed Internet, minibar.

Casa del Mar Langkawi   This small boutique resort is located at the north tip of Pantai Cenang, within walking distance of the area's restaurants, bars, beach, and conveniences. It's a smaller property with very personalized service. Built in a picturesque Mediterranean style, all rooms face the sea. Deluxe rooms are located on the ground level with floor-to-ceiling glass sliding doors that lead to garden terraces. Inside, rooms are furnished with cozy oriental carpets over cool marble floors, ceiling fans, and large, clean tiled bathrooms. The resort's two restaurants are romantic beachside affairs, with glorious evening views of the setting sun.

Jalan Pantai Cenang, Mukim Kedawang 07000 Langkawi, Malaysia. *©* **04/955-2388.** Fax 04/955-2228. www.casadelmar-langkawi.com. 34 units. RM880 double; from RM1,400 suite. AE, MC, V. **Amenities:** 2 restaurants; mountain bike rental; fitness center; Jacuzzi; outdoor lagoon pool; spa; nonmotorized watersports equipment (sea kayaks); Wi-Fi (free); movie library. *In room:* A/C, TV w/satellite programming and DVD player, hair dryer, minibar.

Four Seasons Langkawi ★★★   Every detail of this resort is perfectly exotic, influenced by contemporary Moorish style. Pavilion rooms are surrounded by floor-to-ceiling windows and wraparound verandas. Under soaring ceilings, huge bedrooms have wood floors, ceiling fans, carved wood detailing, and plush furnishings. Through double doors, huge bathrooms are majestic, with oversize terrazzo tubs built into arched nooks, separate closets for rain shower and toilet, a huge clothes closet, and a center island with double sinks. Throughout the rooms you'll find touches such as lanterns, hammered bronze work, lovely toiletries on marble pedestals, and cozy throw pillows that add an intimate Middle Eastern flavor. The resort has two infinity pools that look like they're spilling onto the beach, which is a long, wide stretch of perfect sand. Every dining venue fronts the beach. At Rhu Bar, cocktails are served with Turkish water pipes, amid Indian Moghul hanging swings, glowing lanterns, and Moorish carved latticework arches that frame the sea view gorgeously. The spa has private villas with tubs for four, space for floor and table massages, private indoor/outdoor showers, and changing rooms all encased in glass with lovely garden views.

Jalan Tanjung Rhu, 07000 Langkawi, Kedah. *©* **04/950-8888,** 800/332-3442 in the U.S., 800/268-6282 in Canada. Fax 04/950-8899. www.fourseasons.com. RM1,850 pavilion; from RM5,800 villa. Prices jump Dec-Jan. AE, DC, MC, V. **Amenities:** 3 restaurants; 2 bars; airport transfers; children's center; concierge; health club; 2 outdoor pools; room service; spa w/yoga and juice bar; tennis; nonmotorized watersports equipment (free). *In room:* A/C, TV w/satellite programming and in-house movies, hair dryer, minibar, MP3 docking station, Wi-Fi.

Frangipani Langkawi Resort & Spa ★   This green resort has won several awards for its efforts in preserving the environment. Environmentally friendly practices—like solar paneling, recycling, chemical-free gardening, and more—are incorporated into the everyday operations of this resort. It's got a great location, along a 400m-long (1,312-ft.) beachfront and within walking distance of restaurants, shops, and bars. There are rooms in two-story blocks, but the best choices are the sea-facing villas with rooftop showers. All are tastefully furnished, and the Coco Beach Bar is the best place to view spectacular sunsets. A new spa is set to open in 2011.

Jalan Teluk Baru, Pantai Tengah, 07100 Langkawi, Kedah. *©* **04/952-0000.** Fax 04/952-0001. www.frangipanilangkawi.com. 118 units. RM560 double; from RM1,300 suite. **Amenities:** Restaurant; bar; babysitting; concierge; 2 outdoor pools; room service; watersports equipment. *In room:* A/C, TV w/satellite programming and in-house movies, hair dryer, high-speed Internet access (free), minibar.

Tanjung Rhu Resort   The beach at Tanjung Rhu is a wide crescent of dazzlingly pure sand wrapped around a perfect crystal azure bay. Tree-lined karst islets jut up from the sea, dotting the horizon. Just gorgeous. This resort claims 440 hectares

(1,087 acres) of jungle in this part of the island, monopolizing the scene for extra privacy, but it has its pros and cons. The pros? Guest rooms are enormous and decorated with sensitivity to the environment, from natural materials to organic recycled-paper-wrapped toiletries. A second pool and spa facility add value. The cons? The resort is a little isolated, so guests will be locked into using the resort restaurants. This isn't all bad, as the food is good and they offer all-inclusive packages.

Tanjung Rhu, Mukim Ayer Hangat, 07000 Langkawi, Kedah. ☎ **04/959-1033.** Fax 04/959-1899. www.tanjungrhu.com.my. 136 units. RM1,400 double; RM2,800 suite. AE, DC, MC, V. **Amenities:** 3 restaurants; bar; airport transfers; babysitting; concierge; health club; 2 outdoor pools, 1 saltwater and 1 freshwater; room service; spa w/Jacuzzi, sauna, steam, and massage; outdoor lighted tennis courts; watersports equipment (nonmotorized). *In room:* A/C, TV w/satellite programming and in-room video w/movie library, hair dryer, minibar.

The Westin Langkawi Resort & Spa ★★★ ☺ This ultraluxurious five-star hotel, the first Westin-branded resort in Southeast Asia, is located close to the township of Kuah. The resort is located along a reasonable beach, but it is the swimming pools that will appeal to most guests. It has majestic views of the Andaman Sea and several of the islands in the archipelago. It doesn't get much better than having a cocktail in Breeze Lounge around sunset. All rooms and villas are contemporarily designed, with the villas being my pick, as they are spacious and include a private plunge pool. All rooms feature the Westin's signature Heavenly Bed. This is a great resort for kids, who will love the pools and kids' club.

Jalan Pantai Dato Syed Omar, 07000 Langkawi, Kedah. ☎ **04/960-8888,** 800/937-8461 in the U.S. and Canada, 800/656-535 in Australia, 800/490-375 in New Zealand, or 800/325-95959 in the U.K. Fax 04/966-3097. www.westin.com/langkawi. 222 units. RM933 double; from RM1,893 suite. AE, DC, MC, V. The resort is a 30-min. drive from the airport and 5 min. from Kuah. **Amenities:** 2 restaurants; lounge; pool bar; airport transfers; babysitting; bikes; concierge; health club w/Jacuzzi; 4 outdoor pools; room service; sauna; spa w/bar; 2 outdoor lighted tennis courts; watersports. *In room:* A/C, 42-in. plasma TV w/satellite programming, DVD player and in-house movies, hair dryer, high-speed Internet (RM50 per day), minibar.

Where to Dine

If you're out at one of the more secluded resorts, chances are, you'll stay there for most of your meals. However, it is worth venturing out of your hotel to try **Nam Restaurant** in the Bon Ton Resort, Pantai Cenang (☎ **04/955-6787;** main courses RM48–RM78; daily 11am–11pm; reservations highly recommended), the best restaurant on Langkawi—and perhaps in all of Malaysia. Located within the small and charming Bon Ton Resort, Nam serves "West meets spice" dishes along with an excellent selection of wines and desserts in a dreamy Balinese-inspired setting. If you're in Kuah town, the best local dining experience can be found at the evening **hawker stalls** just along the waterfront near the taxi stand. A long row of hawkers cooks up every kind of local favorite, including seafood dishes. You can't get any cheaper or more laid-back.

What to See & Do

Fifteen years ago, Langkawi was just a backwater island supporting small fishing communities. When the government came in with big money to develop the place for tourism, they thought they needed a catch, so they dug up some old moldy "legends" about the island and have tried to market them as bona fide cultural attractions. Basically, these attractions appeal more to local tourists. However, the main attractions here are the beautiful beaches and clear waters that are home to vibrant marine life.

Snorkeling enthusiasts may want to visit the **Pulau Payar Marine Park,** 19 nautical miles south of Langkawi. The marine park is teeming with coral and marine life, and in the middle of the marine park, a giant platform floats above a coral reef, providing an excellent base for snorkeling. **Langkawi Coral (℘ 04/899-8822;** www.langkawicoral.com) conducts day trips to the platform, which include a ride in a glass-bottomed boat, snorkeling, and lunch on the platform; the full-day trip costs RM300 per person. Langkawi Coral also conducts dive trips in the marine park; a day trip that includes hotel transfer, a boat to the marine park, equipment for two dives, and lunch will cost RM400 per person.

Dev's Adventure Tours, Pantai Cenang (℘ **019/494-9193;** www.langkawi-nature.com) is a well known nature tour operator on Langkawi, and is quite respected in the field of conservation tours; it offers jungle trekking, cycling tours, bird-watching, and more. Dev's conducts round-island boat trips to explore mangroves, seaside villages, and wildlife for RM180 per person, and sea-kayaking trips for RM220.

For a sweeping view of the island, visitors may be interested to take the **cable car** that extends to the summit of Mount Macinchang. It's a dramatic, near-vertical lift high above the rainforest canopy to the 706m-high (2,316-ft.) rocky summit. From here visitors can see most of the island's attractions and the distant islands of southern Thailand. The departure point for the ride is Oriental Village at Burau Bay. There is a carnival-like atmosphere here, with restaurants and souvenir shops that all seem to sell basically the same items. The 14-minute ride to the summit is one of the world's steepest, at 42 degrees, and it has the longest free-span single-rope cable in the world. At the top, there is a 125m (410-ft.) curved platform across a deep chasm. Open daily from 9:30am to 7pm. Prices are RM30 adults, RM20 children. Call ℘ **04/959-4225** for more information.

Langkawi has four marinas. The international charter company **Sunsail** (℘ **04/966-5869;** www.sunsailmalaysia.com) operates from Royal Langkawi Yacht Club on Jalan Dato Syed Omar, where they maintain a fleet of yachts and catamarans from 10 to 15m (33–50 ft.) for trips around the islands or to Phuket in neighboring Thailand.

The **Ibrahim Hussein Museum and Cultural Foundation** (Pasir Tengkorak, Jalan Datai; ℘ **04/959-4669;** www.ihmcf.org), is a lovely museum. The artistic devotion of the foundation's namesake fueled the creation of this enchanting modern space designed to showcase Malaysia's contribution to the international fine-arts scene. Mr. Hussein has created a museum worthy of international attention. It's open daily from 10am to 6pm; adults pay RM12, children visit free.

Shopping

Langkawi's designated Duty Free Port status makes shopping here cheap and very popular. In Kuah town, two shopping malls, **Langkawi Parade** (Jalan Kelibang; ℘ **04/966-6372**) and **Langkawi Fair** (Persiaran Putra; ℘ **04/969-8100**), are filled with duty-free shopping. For local handicrafts, the **Langkawi Craft and Cultural Complex** (Jalan Teluk Yu; ℘ **04/959-1913;** daily 10am–6pm) sells an assortment of batik, baskets, ceramic, silver jewelry, brass ware, and more, and also has daily crafts demonstrations and cultural shows.

EAST MALAYSIA: BORNEO

For the past 2 centuries Borneo has been the epitome of adventure travel. While bustling ports like Penang, Melaka, and Singapore attracted early travelers with dollars in their eyes, Borneo attracted those with adventure in their hearts. Today the island still draws visitors who seek new and unusual experiences, and few leave disappointed. Rivers meander through dense tropical rainforests, beaches stretch for miles, and caves tunnel farther than any in the world. All sorts of creatures you'd never imagine live in the rainforest: deer the size of house cats, owls only 15cm (6 in.) tall, the odd proboscis monkey, and the endangered orangutan, whose only other natural home is Sumatra. It's also home to the largest flower in the world, the Rafflesia, spanning up to a meter (3¼ ft.) wide. Small wonder this place has special interest for scientists and researchers the world around.

The people of Borneo can be credited for most of the alluring tales of early travels. The exotically adorned tribes of warring headhunters and pirates of yesteryear, some of whom still live lifestyles little changed (though both headhunting and piracy are now illegal), today share their mysterious cultures and colorful traditions openly with outsiders.

Add to all of this the romantic adventure of the White Raja of Sarawak, Sir James Brooke, whose family ruled the state for just over 100 years, and you have a land filled with mystery and allure unlike any other.

Malaysia, Brunei Darussalam, and Indonesia have divided the island of Borneo. Indonesia claims Kalimantan to the south and east, and the Malaysian states of **Sarawak** and **Sabah** lie to the north and northwest. The small sultanate of Brunei is situated between the two Malaysian states on the western coast.

Sarawak ★★★ & Kuching

Tropical rainforest once accounted for more than 70% of Sarawak's total landmass, providing homes for not only exotic species of plants and animals, but also the myriad ethnic groups who are indigenous to the area. With more than 15 national parks and wildlife preserves, Malaysia shows its commitment to conserving the delicate balance of life here, despite extensive logging that has cleared many other natural areas. The national parks located around the state's capital **Kuching** provide quick access to forest life, while longer, more detailed trips to northern Sarawak lead you deeper into the jungle, to explore remote forests and extensive ancient cave networks. A number of rivers connect the inland areas to the main towns, and a boat trip from Kuching to visit tribal communities and trek into the surrounding forests is the most memorable attraction going.

The perfect introduction to Sarawak begins in its capital. Kuching's museums, cultural exhibits, and historical attractions will help you form an overview of the history, people, and natural wonders of the state. In Kuching, your introduction to Sarawak will be comfortable and fun; culture by day and good food and fun by night. Kuching, meaning "cat" in Malay, also has a wonderful sense of humor, featuring monuments and exhibits to its feline mascot on almost every corner.

GETTING THERE   Most travelers to Sarawak enter through **Kuching International Airport** (© **082/454-242;** airport code KCH), which is 11km (6¾ miles) south of the city proper, about a 25-minute drive. The airport has ATMs, moneychangers, restaurants, and tourist information (see above). Taxis from the airport use coupons that you purchase outside the arrival hall. Priced according to zones, most trips to the central parts of town will be about RM26.

Malaysia Airlines has international flights from Singapore, with domestic service from KL, Johor Bahru, and Kota Kinabalu. **AirAsia** flies direct between Kuching and Singapore, KL, Penang, Johor Bahru, Kota Kinabalu, Miri, Bintulu, and Sibu. Both **SilkAir** and **Tiger Airways** connect Kuching with Singapore.

East Malaysia's National Parks

GETTING AROUND Centered around a *padang,* or large ceremonial field, Kuching resembles many other Malaysian cities. Buildings of beautiful colonial style rise on the edges of the field; many of these today house Sarawak's museums. The main sights, as well as the Chinatown area and the riverfront, are easily accessible on foot. Taxis are also available and do not use meters; most rides around town are quoted between RM10 and RM15. Taxis can be waved down from the side of the road, or if you're in the Chinatown area, the main taxi stand is on Gambier Road near the end of the India Street Pedestrian Mall.

[FastFACTS] SARAWAK & KUCHING

Sarawak's area code is 082. Major **banks** have branches on Tunku Abdul Rahman Road near the river or in the downtown area around Khoo Hun Yeang Road. There are a few **Internet** cafes around town; it's best to ask your hotel's concierge for the nearest one before you start wandering around—or use your hotel's facilities.

WHERE TO STAY

Damai Puri Resort & Spa Opposite Sarawak Cultural Village, 30km (19 miles) from Kuching and not far from Bako National Park, this is the only five-star beach resort you'll find in the state of Sarawak. The welcoming entrance pavilion is open to the lush tropical surrounds—the resort is nestled in a cove of pretty sandy beach. Recently refurbished rooms are inspired by local themes, with wood used generously throughout, private balconies with either sea or garden views, and bathrooms with rain showers and spa amenities. The hotel is about a 45-minute drive from Kuching, but it offers shuttle service to and from the city from 9am to 5pm.

Teluk Penyuk Santubong, P.O. Box 3058, 93762 Kuching, Sarawak, Malaysia. ⓒ **082/846-900.** Fax 082/846-901. www.damaipuriresort.com. 207 units. RM255 double; from RM450 suites. AE, MC, V. **Amenities:** 3 restaurants; 2 lounges; children's club; fitness center; 2 outdoor lagoon-style pools; room service; spa; outdoor tennis court; watersports equipment rentals. *In room:* A/C, TV w/satellite programming, hair dryer, minibar, Wi-Fi.

Grand Margherita Hotel The Grand Margherita is located along the riverfront, about 5 minutes' walk from the Main Bazaar. At this former Holiday Inn, rooms are midsized and are appointed with all of the conveniences you would expect of a standard international hotel. The owners of the Grand Margherita also operate the adjacent Sarawak Plaza, which has some fast food, ATMs, a money-changer, a cinema, and a supermarket. The hotel also has a shuttle to Damai beach.

Jalan Tunku Abdul Rahman, P.O. Box 2362, 93100 Kuching, Sarawak, Malaysia. ⓒ **082/423-111.** Fax 082/426-169. www.grandmargherita.com. 288 units. RM244 double; from RM460 suites. AE, MC, V. **Amenities:** 2 restaurants; lounge; babysitting; children's pool and playground; concierge; basic fitness center; outdoor pool; room service; smoke-free rooms. *In room:* A/C, TV w/satellite programming, hair dryer, high-speed Internet, minibar.

Hilton Kuching Located in the center of Kuching along the riverfront, the Hilton is one of the best hotels here, with international standard service and facilities, and panoramic views of the Sarawak River and the historic Fort Margherita on the other side. While the hotel is a little dated, it is well maintained and is especially recommended for business travelers. The premier views are those facing the river and then from the 10th floor upward.

Jalan Tunku Abdul Rahman, Kuching, 93000 Sarawak. ⓒ **82/248-200,** 800/HILTONS (445-8667) in the U.S. and Canada, 800/445-8667 in Australia, 800/448-002 in New Zealand, or 08705/909090 in the U.K. Fax 82/428-984. www.hilton.com. 315 units. RM299 double; from RM769 suite. AE, DC, MC, V. **Amenities:** 4 restaurants; bar and lobby lounge; health club w/sauna and steam; outdoor pool; room service; outdoor floodlit tennis courts. *In room:* A/C, TV w/satellite programming, hair dryer, high-speed Internet, minibar.

The LimeTree Hotel ★ 🗲 Located about a 15-minute walk from the Main Bazaar, this newer boutique hotel is an excellent budget choice. Built from a converted office building, it has smallish guest rooms with comfortable beds, good showers, and cozy sheets and towels. Note that the lowest-priced rooms have no windows. Although there aren't many amenities, there is a nice rooftop lounge. This is a top pick for leisure travelers.

Lot 317 Abell Rd., 93100 Kuching, Sarawak, Malaysia. ⓒ **082/414-600.** Fax 082/424-600. www.lime treehotel.com.my. 50 units. RM160 double; from RM310 suites. Rates include breakfast. AE, MC, V. **Amenities:** Restaurant; rooftop lounge; airport transfer; concierge; smoke-free rooms. *In room:* A/C, TV w/satellite programming, hair dryer, Wi-Fi (free).

Pullman Kuching Stylish and vibrant, Pullman has designer decor throughout, giving it a very urban feel in this quiet city. Located beside a small shopping mall and

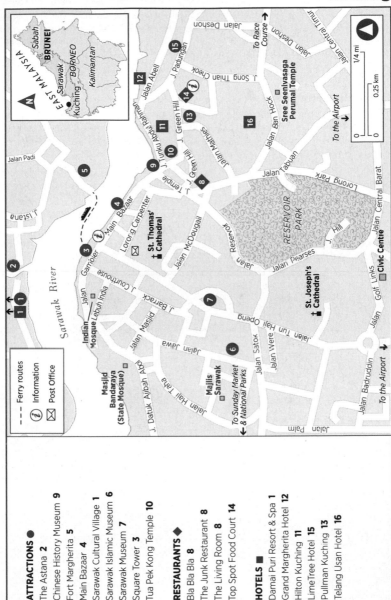

ATTRACTIONS ●

The Astana **2**
Chinese History Museum **9**
Fort Margherita **5**
Main Bazaar **4**
Sarawak Cultural Village **1**
Sarawak Islamic Museum **6**
Sarawak Museum **7**
Square Tower **3**
Tua Pek Kong Temple **10**

RESTAURANTS ◆

Bla Bla Bla **8**
The Junk Restaurant **8**
The Living Room **8**
Top Spot Food Court **14**

HOTELS ■

Damai Puri Resort & Spa **1**
Grand Margherita Hotel **12**
Hilton Kuching **11**
LimeTree Hotel **15**
Pullman Kuching **13**
Telang Usan Hotel **16**

within walking distance of attractions and the main business center of Kuching, it's popular with both business and leisure travelers. Even the lowest category rooms here are very comfortable, with spacious interiors, wood floors, big windows, and plush beds.

1A Jalan Mathies, 93100 Kuching, Sarawak, Malaysia. © **082/222-888.** Fax 082/222-999. www. pullmankuching.com. 389 units. RM310 double; from RM820 suite. AE, MC, V. **Amenities:** 2 restaurants; lounge and cafe; airport transfer; babysitting; children's playground; concierge; fitness center; outdoor pool; room service; spa. *In room:* A/C, TV w/satellite programming, hair dryer, high-speed Internet, minibar.

Telang Usan Hotel ★★ 🗡️ Telang Usan is not as flashy as the higher-priced places, but it's a decent bargain. Most guests are leisure travelers, many of whom are repeat visitors. The small public areas sport murals in local Iban and Orang Ulu styles, revealing the origin of the hotel's owner and operator. While rooms are small and decor is not completely up-to-date, they're spotless. Some rooms have only standing showers, so be sure to specify when making your reservation if a bathtub is important to you. The coffee shop is a fine place to try local food, but they have Western selections as well. There is an excellent tour agency under the same ownership here.

Persiaran Ban Hock, P.O. Box 1579, 93732 Kuching, Sarawak, Malaysia. © **082/415-588.** Fax 082/245-316. www.telangusan.com. 66 units. RM120 double. AE, DC, MC, V. **Amenities:** Restaurant; room service. *In room:* A/C, TV, hair dryer, minibar (some rooms).

WHERE TO DINE

Everyone ends up at the **Top Spot Food Court,** a huge hawker center on Jalan Bukit Mata off Jalan Tunku Abdul Rahman just near the Pullman Hotel. Various stalls cook Chinese, Malay, and Western food, but it's especially known for its seafood. Located on the roof of a multistory parking garage, this place doesn't offer anything but "local charm" for decor. *Be warned:* You will be accosted by touts, but once you pick your stall, the staff is very good about helping select seafood and dishes. Check prices before you commit.

The Living Room (23 Tabuan Rd.; © **082/426-608;** Wed–Mon 6–11pm; AE, MC, V) is a groovy place for drinks either indoors or in an alfresco garden that's dripping with romantic ambience.

WHAT TO SEE & DO

The Astana and Fort Margherita   At the waterfront by the Square Tower, you'll find *perahu tambang,* or water taxis, to take you across the river (for about RM.40) to see these two reminders of the White Rajas of Sarawak. The Astana, built in 1870 by Raja Charles Brooke, the second raja of Sarawak, is now the official residence of the governor. It is not open to the public, but visitors may still walk in the gardens. The best view of the Astana, however, is from the water.

Raja Charles Brooke's wife, Ranee Margaret, gave her name to Fort Margherita, which was erected in 1879 to protect the city of Kuching. Inside the great castlelike building is a police museum, the most interesting sights of which are the depictions of criminal punishment.

Across the Sarawak River from town. Fort: © **082/244-232.** Free admission. Daily 9am-4:30pm.

Chinese History Museum   Built in 1911, this old Chinese Chamber of Commerce building is a picturesque venue for a museum that traces the history of Chinese communities in Sarawak. Though small, it's been very recently renovated to upgrade displays and facilities.

Corner of Main Bazaar and Jalan Tunku Abdul Rahman. © **082/231-520.** Free admission. Daily 9am-5pm.

Main Bazaar   Main Bazaar, the major thoroughfare along the river, is home to Kuching's antiques and handicraft shops. If you're walking along the river, a little time in these shops is like a walk through a traditional handicrafts art gallery. You'll also find souvenir shops, tour operators, and a few restaurants.

Along the river. Free admission.

Sarawak Cultural Village ★   What appears to be a contrived theme park turns out to be a really fun place to learn about Sarawak's indigenous people. Built around a lagoon, the park re-creates the various styles of longhouse dwellings of each of the major tribes. Inside each house are representative members of each tribe displaying cultural artifacts and performing music, teaching dart blowing, and showing off carving talents. Give yourself plenty of time to stick around and talk with the people, who are recruited from villages inland and love to tell stories about their homes and traditions. Performers dance and display costumes at 11:30am and 4:30pm daily. A shuttle bus leaves at regular intervals from the Grand Margherita on Jalan Tunku Abdul Rahman.

Kampung Budaya Sarawak, Pantai Damai, Santubong. ✆ **082/846-411.** Admission RM60 adults, RM30 children. Daily 9am–5pm.

Sarawak Islamic Museum   A splendid array of Muslim artifacts at this quiet and serene museum depicts the history of Islam and its spread to Southeast Asia. Local customs and history are also highlighted. Although women are not required to cover their heads, respectable attire that covers the legs and arms is requested.

Jalan P. Ramlee. ✆ **082/244-232.** Free admission. Sat–Thurs 9am–4:30pm; Fri 9am–12:45pm and 3–5pm.

Sarawak Museum ★   Two branches, one old and one new, display exhibits of the natural history, indigenous peoples, and culture of Sarawak, plus the state's colonial and modern history. The two branches are connected by an overhead walkway above Jalan Tun Haji Openg. The wildlife exhibit is a bit musty, but the arts and artifacts in the other sections are well tended. A tiny aquarium sits neglected behind the old branch, but the gardens here are lovely.

Jalan Tun Haji Openg. ✆ **082/244-232.** Free admission. Sat–Thurs 9am–4:30pm; Fri 9am–12:45pm and 3–4:30pm.

Square Tower   The tower, built in 1879, served as a prison camp, but today the waterfront real estate is better served by an information center for travel agents. The Square Tower is also a prime starting place for a stroll along the riverside and is where you'll also find out about cultural performances and exhibitions held at the waterfront, or call the number below for performance schedules.

Jalan Gambier near the riverfront. ✆ **082/426-093.** Free admission.

Tua Pek Kong Temple   At a main crossroads near the river stands the oldest Chinese temple in Sarawak. Although officially it is dated at 1876, most locals acknowledge the true date of its beginnings as 1843. It's still lively in form and spirit, with colorful dragons tumbling along the walls and incense filling the air.

Junction of Jalan Tunku Abdul Rahman and Jalan Padungan. Free admission.

TOURING LOCAL CULTURE ★★★

One of the highlights of a trip to Sarawak is a visit to a longhouse community. Trips can last from simple overnight stays to 2-week intensive discovery tours. It goes without saying that shorter trips venture only as far as those longhouse villages closest to

Kuching. The benefit is that these communities are at ease with foreigners and so are better able to demonstrate their culture. The drawback is that these villages are the ones most trampled by coach loads of tourists looking to gawk at "primitive tribes." Basically, the more time you have, the deeper you will venture into the interior and the more time you will have to spend with different ethnic groups, allowing greater insight into these cultures.

A typical longhouse trip starts with a van ride from Kuching followed by a longtail boat ride upriver, through gorgeous forests. If you are stopping in only for the night, you'll be welcomed, fed, and entertained—the food is generally edible and always prepared under sanitary conditions. Fruits are delicious. Your guide, through translations, will help you chat with villagers and ask questions about their lifestyle and customs. At night you will sleep in a longhouse provided especially for guests. It's basic but cool, with mosquito nets (very necessary) provided. The following day includes a very brief jungle trek, plus hunting and fishing demonstrations before your departure back whence you came. If your trip is longer, you will probably avoid the closer villages and head straight for more remote communities, depending on how much time (and money) you have.

For budgeting longhouse tours, plan to spend about RM800 per person for each night you spend on the tour. Good tour operators making longhouse tours are **Borneo Adventure,** 55 Main Bazaar (© **082/245-175;** www.borneoadventure.com), and **Telang Usan Travel & Tours,** Ban Hock Road (© **082/236-945;** fax 082/236-589). These agencies can also arrange trips into Sarawak's national parks.

Touring Sarawak's National Parks

The Sarawak National Parks & Wildlife Centre has opened access to all of Sarawak's national parks to DIY (do-it-yourself) travelers. From their booking center in Kuching, you can apply for parks permits and book reservations in state-run lodging within each park. They can also advise how to travel to and from each park: Those closer to Kuching will involve only local road and river transportation, while more remote parks will require commercial flights to either Sibu or Miri, plus transfers to ground and river transportation and even chartered flights. If you have the time to plan your travel this way, you will be rewarded with the thrill of "getting there," experiencing local life a little closer to the ground.

Most people do not have the luxury of time, which is why I recommend booking trips that interest you through a tour operator who will arrange all transportation, parks permits, lodging, meals, and guides for you, freeing your time to experience the attractions themselves.

NATIONAL PARKS A LITTLE FARTHER OUT

Borneo Adventure, 55 Main Bazaar (© **082/245-175;** www.borneoadventure. com), and **Asian Overland Services,** Lot 112, First Floor, Lorong Datuk Abang Abdul Rahim 5A, behind 360 Hotel (© **082/330-398;** www.asianoverland.com. my), also book trips to national parks in other parts of the state. You'll have to fly to Miri or Sibu, as these two towns are the hop-off points for these excursions. Malaysia Airlines and AirAsia both service these two towns from KL and Kuching.

Gunung Mulu National Park provides an amazing adventure, with its astounding underground network of caves. The park claims the world's largest cave passage (Deer Cave), the world's largest natural chamber (Sarawak Chamber), and Southeast Asia's longest cave (Clearwater Cave). No fewer than 18 caves offer explorers trips of varying degrees of difficulty, from simple treks with minimal gear to technically difficult caves that require specialized equipment and skills. Aboveground are 544 sq. km (214 sq. miles) of primary rainforest, peat swamps, and mountainous forests teeming with mammals, birds, and unusual insects. Located in the north of Sarawak, Mulu is very close to the Brunei border. Borneo Adventure has a 2-day/1-night package for around RM240 per person (minimum two people). The trip includes accommodations; ground transportation; longboat rides; nature guides to see Deer Cave, Sarawak Chamber, and Clearwater Cave; plus some rainforest trekking (wear a hat in the caves to protect yourself from bat droppings). They can book your flights from Kuching, but you'll have to pay extra.

Sabah ★★★ & Kota Kinabalu

Sabah presents a wonderland of natural scenery, lush primary rainforest, vibrant coral reefs, and mysterious indigenous cultures. It is, in my opinion, Southeast Asia's hidden treasure. A playground for adventure seekers, extreme sportsters, and bums in search of the ultimate beach, Sabah rewards those who venture here with a holiday in an unspoiled paradise.

Covering 73,711 sq. km (28,747 sq. miles) of the northern part of Borneo, the world's third-largest island, Sabah stretches from the South China Sea in the west to the Sulu Sea in the east, both seas containing an abundance of uninhabited islands, postcard-perfect beaches, and pristine coral reefs bubbling with marine life. In between, more than half of the state is covered in ancient primary rainforest that's protected in national parks and forest reserves. In these forests, some rare species of mammals like the Sumatran rhino and Asian pygmy elephant (herds of them) take effort to witness, but other animals, such as the orangutan, proboscis monkey, gibbon, lemur, civet, Malaysian sun bear, and a host of others can be seen on jungle treks if you search them out. Of the hundreds of bird species here, the hornbills and herons steal the show.

Sabah's tallest peak is one of the highest mountains between the Himalayas and Irian Jaya. At 4,095m (13,432 ft.), it's the tallest in Malaysia, and a challenge to trek or climb. The state's interior has endless opportunities for jungle trekking, river rafting, mountain biking and 4×4 exploration for every level of excitement, from soft adventure to extreme sports.

This state holds not only mysterious wildlife and geography, but people as well. Sabahans count among their many ethnic groups some 32 different peoples whose cultures and traditions are vastly different from the Malay majority that makes up the rest of the country. In fact, ethnic Malays are a minority in Sabah.

About one-third of the population is Kadazandusun, a group that inhabits mainly the west coast and parts of the interior of Sabah. They are one of the first groups travelers come into contact with, especially during the Pesta Kaamatan, or harvest festival, held during May, where the high priest or priestess presides over a ceremony performed to appease the rice spirit. Although it's a Kadazandusun tradition, it has come to be celebrated by all cultures in the state. Although this group produces the majority of Sabah's agricultural products, most members live in towns and hold everyday jobs. The exception is the Runggus, the last group of Kadazandusun to live in traditional longhouse communities, where they produce exquisite basket weaving, fabric weaving, and beadwork in traditional designs.

The Bajau are a group of seafarers who migrated from the Philippines only a couple hundred years ago. The Bajau on the eastern coast of Sabah carry on their traditional connection to the water, living as sea gypsies and coming to shore only for burials. On the west coast, however, many Bajau have settled on dry land as farmers and cattle raisers.

Known locally as the "cowboys of the east," Bajau men are very skilled equestrians. During festivals, their brilliant costumes and decorated ponies almost always take center stage.

Kota Belud, 76km (47 miles) north of Kota Kinabalu, is a town inhabited mostly by Bajau people. In the background is Mount Kinabalu, which dominates the landscape in most of Western Sabah. The town comes alive every Sunday morning with the weekly *tamu*, or market.

The third-most-prominent indigenous group, the Murut, shares the southwest corner of Sabah with the Bajau, expanding inland along the border with Sarawak and Kalimantan (Indonesia). Skilled hunters, they use spears, blowpipes, poisoned darts, and trained dogs. In past days, these skills were used for headhunting, which thankfully is not practiced today (although many skulls can still be seen during visits to longhouse settlements). One nonlethal Murut tradition involves a trampoline competition. The *lansaran* (the trampoline), situated in the community longhouse, is made of split bamboo. During Murut ceremonies, contestants drink rice wine and jump on the trampoline to see who can reach the highest. A prize is hung above for the winner to grab.

Sabah also has a small community of Chinese families that settled during colonial days, and newer Filipino immigrants, many of whom are illegal plantation workers. The best place to begin exploring Sabah's marine wonders, wildlife and forests, adventure opportunities, and indigenous peoples is from its capital, Kota Kinabalu, also known as KK. Located on the west coast, it's where you'll find the headquarters for all of Sabah's adventure-tour operators and package-excursion planners.

GETTING THERE   Because of Sabah's remote location, just about everybody will arrive by air through the **Kota Kinabalu International Airport** in the capital city (*©* **088/235-555;** airport code: BKI), about a 20-minute drive south of the central part of the city. A surprising number of direct international flights connect Sabah to the region. **Malaysia Airlines** flies from Hong Kong, Manila, Osaka, Seoul, Singapore, and Tokyo, among others, and **AirAsia** flies from Bangkok. Both airlines also have direct domestic flights to Kota Kinabalu from KL, Johor Bahru, Kuching, Sibu, and Miri, with in-state service to Sandakan and other towns.

The most efficient way to get into town from the airport is by taxi using a coupon system. You'll pay about RM30 for a trip to town. Ignore the drivers that try to lure you away from the coupon counter; they will always overcharge you.

GETTING AROUND   In the downtown area, you can get around quite easily on foot. For longer trips, a taxi will be necessary; in town, trips cost about RM15. Taxis are flagged down on the street or by your hotel's bellhop.

VISITOR INFORMATION   The **Sabah Tourism Board** (51 Jalan Gaya; *©* **088/212-121;** www.sabahtourism.com) provides the most comprehensive information about the state. It's open daily: weekdays 8am–5pm and weekends 9am–4pm. **Tourism Malaysia** has a small office at Api-Api Centre, Blok 1 Lorong Api-Api 1 (*©* **088/248-698**), but almost all of their information promotes travel in other parts of the country.

[FastFACTS] SABAH & KOTA KINABALU

The **area code** for Sabah is **088.** While on the same time as KL, the sun rises and sets earlier than the peninsula. You'll find **banks** with ATMs conveniently located in

Kota Kinabalu

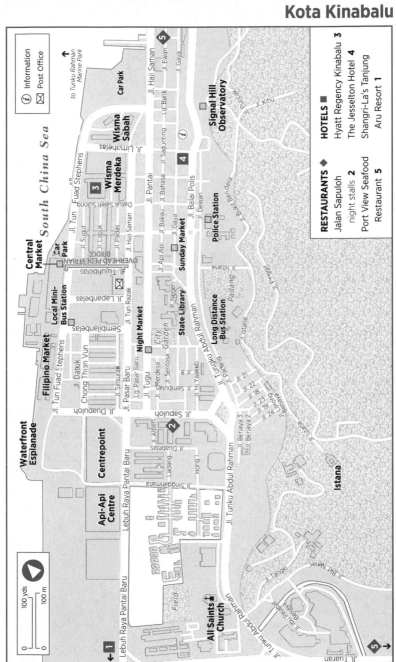

South China Sea

Central Market

Car Park

Waterfront Esplanade

Filipino Market

Local Mini-Bus Station

Centrepoint

Api-Api Centre

Night Market

City Garden

State Library

Sunday Market

Long Distance Bus Station

Police Station

Wisma Sabah

Wisma Merdeka

Signal Hill Observatory

Istana

All Saints Church

Car Park

to Tunku Rahman Marine Park

ⓘ Information
✉ Post Office

100 yds
100 m

HOTELS ■
Hyatt Regency Kinabalu **3**
The Jesselton Hotel **4**
Shangri-La's Tanjung Aru Resort **1**

RESTAURANTS ◆
Jalan Sapuloh
night stalls **2**
Port View Seafood Restaurant **5**

the downtown area around Jalan Limabelas, Jalan Gaya, and Jalan Pantai, and ATMs in shopping malls throughout the town. While there are no large **Internet** cafes, you'll find access in small shopfronts around the main parts of town.

WHERE TO STAY

Gayana Eco Resort ★★   A 25-minute speedboat ride from Kota Kinabalu, in the heart of the Tunku Abdul Rahman Marine Park (see below), this gorgeous tropical resort is a treat. Villas built on stilts over the water are peaceful with the sound of the sea lapping all around. With views of the surrounding lush jungle, lagoon, or sea (with Mt Kinabalu visible on the distant horizon), some villas have private terraces with stairs that lead down to the sea. The resort offers diving, snorkeling, sea kayaking, and jungle trekking tours, plus a Marine Ecology Research Centre. Two restaurants feature the freshest seafood.

Malohom Bay, Gaya Island, Tunku Abdul Rahman Park, Kota Kinabalu, Sabah. ✆ **088/247-611.** Fax 088/475-714. www.gayana-eco-resort.com. 44 units. RM950 jungle or lagoon view villa; RM1,350 mangrove villa; RM1,550 ocean-view villa. AE, MC, V. **Amenities:** 2 restaurants; lounge; airport and ferry transfers; outdoor pool; spa; watersports equipment rental. *In room*: A/C, TV with DVD players, minibar, Wi-Fi (free).

Hyatt Regency Kinabalu ★   One of the best international business-class hotels in town, the Hyatt is located close to the waterfront, near major stores, restaurants, and travel operators. Rooms here are large, modern, and are decorated in a way that nods to the local culture. There is a good selection of restaurants here, but one of the high points is Shenanigan's, a lively bar with live entertainment. Local tour and car-rental booking in the lobby makes the place convenient for leisure travelers.

Jalan Datuk Salleh Sulong, 88994 Kota Kinabalu, Sabah. ✆ **088/221-234,** or 800/233-1234 in the U.S. and Canada, 800/131-234 in Australia, or 800/441-234 in New Zealand. Fax 088/218-909. www.kinabalu. regency.hyatt.com. 288 units. RM320 double; from RM570 suite. AE, DC, MC, V. **Amenities:** 3 restaurants; bar; airport transfers; babysitting; concierge; health club; outdoor pool; room service. *In room:* A/C, TV w/ satellite programming and in-house movies, hair dryer, high-speed Internet, minibar.

The Jesselton Hotel ★★   A quaint boutique hotel in the center of Kota Kinabalu, Jesselton is one of the few reminders in this city of a colonial presence. Personalized service is excellent. Guest rooms are completely modern, yet they retain their charm with lovely Audubon-style inks and attractive wallpapers and fabrics— sort of a cross between a cozy guesthouse and a top-class hotel. Due to lack of space in the building, there's no pool, fitness center, or business center, but the staff at the front desk can help you with tour information and transportation. The coffeeshop serves local and Western food, which is quite good. Bella Italia Pizzeria Ristorante Café serves Italian and local favorites.

69 Jalan Gaya, 88000 Kota Kinabalu, Sabah. ✆ **088/223-333.** Fax 088/240-401. www.jesseltonhotel. com. 32 units. RM247 double; RM518 suite. AE, DC, MC, V. **Amenities:** Restaurant; bar and lounge; coffee shop; airport transfers; babysitting; room service; smoke-free rooms. *In room:* A/C, TV (movies available), hair dryer, high-speed Internet, minibar.

Shangri-La's Tanjung Aru Resort & Spa ★★★ ☺   A short ride southwest of Kota Kinabalu and you're at Tanjung Aru, a pleasant beachside district. The Shangri-La here is located in a most impressive setting, surrounded on three sides by water. It serves the finest local Sabahan cuisine and freshest seafood you can get in the region. Book a room in the Tanjung Wing, which is nestled amid Shangri-La's signature lush garden setting, or the Kinabalu Wing, which has panoramic views of the South China Sea. Every room has a stunning view of either the sea or Mount

Kinabalu, with a balcony for full appreciation. Tropical touches include furnishings in cool colors and local fabrics with wood details. Their tour desk can arrange everything from scuba to trekking and rafting. Special activities for kids make this place a good choice for families.

Locked Bag 174, 88744 Kota Kinabalu, Sabah. ⓒ **088/225-800,** 800/942-5050 in the U.S. and Canada, 800/222-448 in Australia, 800/442-179 in New Zealand. Fax 088/217-155. www.shangri-la.com. 499 units. RM855 double; from RM1,060 suite. AE, DC, MC, V. **Amenities:** 3 restaurants; beach bar and lounge; airport transfers; concierge; health club w/Jacuzzi, sauna, steam, and massage; 2 outdoor lagoon-style pools; room service; 4 outdoor lighted tennis courts. *In room:* A/C, TV w/satellite programming and in-house movies, hair dryer, high-speed Internet, minibar.

WHERE TO DINE

One of the best local specialties, *hinava,* is a mouthwatering delicacy of raw fish marinated in lime juice, ginger, shallots, herbs, and chilies—definitely try something from food stalls in any of the markets.

Kota Kinabalu is known for its fresh seafood, and there are a lot of places to choose from, but the locals and expatriates all agree that **Port View Seafood Restaurant,** Lot 18, Ground floor, Anjung Samudera, Jalan Tun Fuad Stephens, along the waterfront (ⓒ **088/252-813;** daily noon–11:30pm; MC, V), is best. It's a very typical Chinese seafood joint, not much for ambience, with walls of aquariums and a very long menu. Dishes are prepared primarily in Chinese and Malay styles, are moderately priced (sold by weight), and are always succulent, but do double check the weight and price of the seafood dishes before you place your order.

Hands down, the city's most romantic dining spot is **@tmosphere,** on the 18th floor of Menara Tun Mustapha (ⓒ **088/425-100;** www.atmosphererestaurant.com; Tues–Sun 11am–11pm; MC, V), about 20 minutes south of the city center—take a taxi there for about RM40. The menu is contemporary Pacific Rim cuisine, a mix of local and Western, with seafood dishes highlighted. Expect to pay about RM50 or so per person. Plan to arrive in time for a sunset cocktail.

WHAT TO SEE & DO

There's a bit of nice sightseeing in Kota Kinabalu. The **Waterfront Esplanade**, aka Anjung Samudera, is a long boardwalk where you'll find some handicraft shopping, cafes, restaurants and bars. At the northeast end you'll find the Handicraft Market, which is open daily from 7:30am until 7:30pm. Another popular market is the **Gaya Street Sunday Market,** every Sunday from early morning til about lunchtime.

Most travelers use KK as a jumping-off point to adventures elsewhere in Sabah. If you want to stay close to the town, I recommend visiting the **Tunku Abdul Rahman Marine Park** (aka TAR Marine Park), a group of five islands located about 8km (5 miles) off the coast of Kota Kinabalu which have been protected since the mid-1970s. very close to the coast. Islands like Manukan and Sapi have restaurants, toilets, some convenience facilities, snorkel gear and watersports equipment for rent along their pretty white sand beaches, but the snorkeling isn't the best here as these islands are the most accessible, so corals have been trampled by tourism. **Snorkel** rentals here go for around RM15, and parasailing charges start from RM100. There's also the novel **seawalking**—donning an enormous helmet connected to the surface with a tube, which allows you to breathe underwater without tanks. This costs RM250 per person for around 20 to 30 minutes underwater (ⓒ **088/249-115;** www. borneoseawalking.com). *Tip for snorkelers:* Bring cotton socks to wear under your rental fins to prevent blisters.

Gaya, the largest and most secluded island, has two luxury resorts (Gayana Eco Resort is reviewed above), with another two on the way. Tiny Mamutik Island is the park base for Borneo Divers who arrange day trips for scuba diving in the park as well as PADI courses. Their office in KK is at the 9th floor, Menara Jubili, 53 Jalan Gaya (℃ **088/222-226;** www.borneodivers.info; RM329 day trip includes full equipment). Finally Sulug Island has virtually no development, but is the best site for dive trips.

Getting to the park is an easy, 15-minute speedboat ride from KK's shiny new **Jesselton Point Ferry Terminal** (℃ **088/243-708**, which is located to the north of the town. Ferries depart from around 8:30 in the morning with the last ferry leaving the park at around 4pm (sometimes later, but always double check!). Round trip fare is RM24, which includes a RM6 terminal fee, then upon arrival you'll be asked for an additional RM10 Environmental Conservation Fee. If you want to hop between islands, top up an additional RM10 for each trip.

Sabah has many other dive sites, including sites such as Pulau Tiga, of *Survivor* TV fame. A couple of sites also offer wreck diving, so if you're interested, inquire when you make your booking.

Of special interest to divers is **Sipadan,** an island resort off the east coast of the state which has been ranked as one of the top-10 dive sites in the world. The site is a tall limestone "tower" rising from the bed of the Celebes Sea, supporting vast numbers of marine species, some of which may still be unidentified. Since 2004, the Malaysian government revoked the licenses of the five dive operators that managed resorts on the tiny island, in an effort to prevent environmental degradation. The dive operators have since moved their base camps to surrounding islands, offering day trips to the area or running live-aboard trips.

Borneo Divers (9th floor, Menara Jubili, 53 Jalan Gaya; ℃ **088/222-226;** www. borneodivers.info) was the first full-service dive operator in Borneo and the pioneering operator to Sipadan. They house divers at their resort on Mabul island, along a gorgeous sandy beach with easy access to dive sites around Mabul and Sipadan. For RM580 per night per person, you'll get accommodation, meals, and airport transfers (for Sipadan diving the minimum stay is 5 days and 4 nights). Sipadan dive trips are RM40 per day, which includes weight belts and tanks. You'll have to pay extra for a round-trip flight into Tawau, which costs about RM455 on Malaysia Airlines, and cheaper if you take AirAsia. Sipadan has good diving year-round, but March through October has the best weather.

A newer spot, **Layang Layang,** located off the coast of northwest Borneo in the South China Sea, is also making a splash as an underwater bounty of marine life amid pristine deep-water corals. **Layang Layang Island Resort** (head office in KL at Blk. A, ground floor, A-0-3, Megan Ave. II, 12 Jalan Yap Kwan Seng; ℃ **03/2170-2185;** www.layanglayang.com) pioneered this area for divers. Their standard package of 6 days/5 nights runs at RM1,250 per person, which includes accommodations, meals, and three dives a day with equipment. The chartered flight from Kota Kinabalu airport is an extra RM320 round-trip (booked through the resort when you make your reservation). Layang Layang closes during the monsoon season (early Sept to Feb).

Sabah's rugged terrain makes for terrific hiking, camping, biking, and white-water rafting for any level, from soft adventure or extreme sports. **TYK Adventure** (Borneo Travel; Lot 48-2F, 2nd floor, Beverly Hill Plaza; ℃ **088/727-825;** www.tykadventure tours.com) was founded by a local award-winning tour guide Tham Yau Kong, who also happens to hold records for the longest cultural walk (1998) and for leading the first group to circum-cycle Mt. Kinabalu (1999). They specialize in educational trips (good history tours), a range of homestays, and adventure travel; they can also organize tailor-made excursions around your plans and adventure level. Their mountain biking half day trips from KK tour villages, jungles and farms in nearby Papar and Penampang for RM250 per person; the rate includes hotel transfer, mountain bike, helmet, cycling guide and lunch.

Many come to Sabah to climb **Mt. Kinabalu.** It's an exhilarating trip if you are prepared and if you hit it just right, in terms of weather and timing. It can be done only on an overnight trip, which includes a 4- or 5-hour hike from the park headquarters uphill to a ranger station, where you stay the night. Groups awake at 2:30am to begin the 3-hour hike to the summit. This is not light trekking, as some parts are steep, altitude sickness can cause headaches and nausea, and remember—you're tooling along in the pitch darkness, the whole point being to arrive at the summit in time for the spectacular sunrise. Come prepared with cold weather wear, or at the very least a wool sweater or fleece, long pants, windbreaker, rain poncho, and hiking boots. Bring a good, strong flashlight and pack plenty of trail mix and sports drinks for rejuvenation. And finally, there's no guarantee that the weather will cooperate with your itinerary. You might hit rain or find the summit covered in clouds. There's pretty much nothing any tour operator can do to guarantee you'll get a clear view. **TYK Adventure** is an excellent outfit for this tour; a 3-day/2-night trip costs RM1,840 per person. Make sure you book early, because they need to make sure there's space available at park accommodations. The price includes transfer, lodging (in a heated dormitory), and your guide to the summit.

Monsopiad Cultural Village, a Kadazandusun heritage center with its creepy House of Skulls, is located in Penampang, not far from Kota Kinabalu. During the 3-hour visit to the village, you'll tour the place and be treated to a cultural performance. It's about the height of "touristy" Sabah but can be a fun half-day trip if you want to peep at a bit of local culture. Call them at © 088/774-337 to make a booking; RM100 includes transportation to and from your hotel, the tour and show, plus a welcome drink. The tour leaves daily at 9:30am and again at 2:30pm.

In 2000, the **North Borneo Railway** (Tanjung Aru Railway Station; © **088/263-933**) revived the tradition of steam train travel with the launch of a 1954 fully renovated British Vulcan steam locomotive pulling six restored carriages. Traversing a 58km (36-mile) route from Tanjung Aru, near Kota Kinabalu, to the town of Papar, the train passes water and mangrove views, past fishermen and local sea crafts, through a mountain tunnel, and out the other side into a vast scenery of paddy fields. Carriages are open-air but comfortable, with soft seats and wood and brass accents. A swanky bar car and observation deck round out facilities that also include toilets. The railway, recently closed for repairs, reopened in early 2011.

BALI (INDONESIA)

by Jen Lin-Liu

9

Though Bali is known to the world as an island resort destination, one could argue that its beaches are the least spectacular of its draws. If you're looking for pristine, quiet beaches, go elsewhere, but if you're looking for a balanced combination of culture, nightlife, good waves, beautiful rice paddies, mountain scenery, fantastic year-round weather, pampering spa treatments, and the world's best-rated resorts at reasonable prices, Bali is the place to go.

A Hindu haven in the Muslim-majority Indonesian archipelago, Bali has for decades attracted artists, honeymooners, spiritual seekers, surfers, and those otherwise looking for the "good life." The Balinese have always been accommodating hosts, and their acceptance of different lifestyles has drawn an assortment of "misfit" residents. During your trip to Bali, you're destined to meet some characters, whether they be of the "Kuta cowboy" variety—young Indonesian bachelors trolling the beach for foreign girl-friends—or the cult of New Age, yoga-obsessed foreigners who have settled in the rice paddies of Ubud.

The Balinese practice a unique amalgam of Indian Hindu traditions, Buddhism, ancient Javanese practices, and indigenous animistic beliefs. The beauty of their faiths colors every aspect of life, from fresh flowers strewn everywhere in obeisance to the calm of morning prayer at temple. During your visit, you're sure to catch the distinctive tones of the gamelan, a xylophone-like instrument, and the gathering of sarong-clad worshipers at the island's ubiquitous temples.

After a decade of ups and downs, Bali's tourism industry is on the upswing. With terrorism fears dwindling and the worldwide economy recovering from the 2008 financial crisis, Bali is becoming crowded with more tourists than ever. The movie *Eat, Pray, Love*—disparagingly called *Eat, Pay, Leave* by some locals—has added to Bali's tourism surge. The rise in tourism has led to overcongested roads that have doubled travel times around the island and rampant overdevelopment of cookie-cutter villas in the south. Property prices have more than tripled over the past 5 years. Russian and Chinese tourists are coming in ever-increasing numbers as well. But the glut of new villas and developments means that good deals are still able to be had on the island.

You'll likely hear complaints from longtime residents that much of Bali's charm has been lost with its growing villas, strip malls, Western outposts of Starbucks and Dunkin' Donuts, and its sometimes rowdy nightlife. But get out of south Bali, the center of the island's development, and you'll be rewarded in every direction with quiet villages, pristine scenery, and plenty of time to restore your "inner balance."

GETTING TO KNOW BALI

The Lay of the Land

Tiny Bali has great topographical variety. Located in the center of Indonesia's vast archipelago, the island has an area of 5,620 sq. km (roughly 2,170 sq. miles), only the size of a large metropolis. The land is divided in half, east to west, by a volcanic mountain chain and is scored lengthwise by deep river gorges. White-sand beaches line the coast to the east, as well as near Kuta in the most populated area of wider lowlands to the south. Dotting the island are active volcanoes, including Gunung Agung, a dynamic peak and a power point of Balinese culture and belief. Central Ubud is one of the more beautiful spots, with mountainous scenery, lush vegetation, and Bali's famed terraced rice farms. The far west is the least developed area of the island, with mountainous terrain mostly given over to national parkland.

A Look at the Past

As distinct as Balinese life is, its people and culture originated elsewhere. Evidence of settlement goes back to the Neolithic period of around 3000 B.C., but the culture flourished under Chinese and Indian influences, including the introduction of Buddhism and Hinduism beginning in 800 B.C. Bali was ruled periodically by the Javanese. With the rise of Islam on the mainland, the last Javanese Majapahit king fled Jakarta for Bali in 1515, cementing the island's Javanese influence and affecting a renaissance in art and culture that would survive years of Muslim incursion.

The first real Western presence was established in 1601, when a Dutch contingent came to set up formal relations and establish trade. Attempts to expand relations were largely rebuffed—even as the **Dutch East India Company** expanded throughout the area—but Balinese slaves were shipped to Dutch and French merchants nonetheless. In the era of Napoleon, Holland's East Indian holdings passed first to the French and then to the British, who returned them to the Dutch in the peace agreement following Napoleon's Waterloo defeat in 1815. After protracted struggle, the Dutch fully secured control in 1909.

A steady stream of European settlers and visitors followed—doctors and teachers at first, then the first tourists, artists, and cultural explorers. By the 1930s, Bali's reputation as a magical paradise was spreading rapidly, and such figures as anthropologist Margaret Mead and artist Walter Spies frequented the island.

World War II saw an exodus of foreigners with the arrival of Japanese troops. For Indonesians, it was a time of both strain under the brief Japanese occupation and revelation in light of the withdrawal of Dutch control. Shortly after the end of the war in 1945, Nationalist Party founder **Sukarno,** a thorn in the side of the Dutch since the 1920s, announced a declaration of Indonesian independence and was named president. The Dutch withdrew under international pressure in 1949, allowing the creation of the Republic of Indonesia, a tentative federation.

Hindu Bali was suspect under the rule of Muslim Jakarta, and the island was hit very hard by economic collapse. In 1965, **Suharto** seized control in response to a staged communist coup, and bloody conflicts continued for several years. As many as 100,000 Balinese were killed as suspected communists or as ethnic Chinese.

Under Suharto, the military gained a far-reaching influence over national affairs. For the next 3 decades, until the major economic crisis of 1997, Indonesia enjoyed a period of prosperity in spite of Suharto's embezzling autocracy. During this time, and with government attention, Bali rose to prominence as a top tourist destination in the region.

In just the past half-century, Bali has undergone remarkable change and weathered turmoil on the Indonesian mainland. The riots and protests that erupted in Indonesia in 1998 were the result of 3 decades of military rule and struggles to bring the world's fourth-most-populous country into the modern global economy. Chafing under the yoke of Suharto, the Indonesians finally revolted, and demonstrations turned into riots that made headlines around the world. In June 1999, Indonesians witnessed their first free parliamentary election since 1955, ousting Suharto. But riots, bombings, and separatist protests continued to plague the country, specifically in Aceh and Irian Jaya. On May 20, 2002, East Timor was internationally recognized as an independent state after a protracted struggle. Indonesia achieved a tentative peace under a provisional government headed by **President Megawati,** the daughter of Sukarno (predecessor to Suharto). Megawati inherited political instability and an economic crisis, but addressed corruption and the military's human rights record.

The former military general **Susilo Bambang Yudhoyono**—known as "SBY"— defeated Megawati in 2004 and was reelection in 2009. He has ruled under a period of relative peace and stability, and, with the help of Australian and American forces, many alleged terror cells have been broken under his watch. But recent efforts by politicians to impose Sharia law and antipornographic measures seem to indicate that support for an Islamic state is still strong.

Bali Today

Huge foreign investments in new luxury resorts—such as the Karma Kandara, where palatial villas can go for as much as $7,000 per night—indicate that many see a hopeful future for Balinese tourism. An increase in guards, bomb-sniffing dogs, and regular vehicle checks nearly everywhere in Bali also shows that the tourism industry and the government are taking security seriously. Ironically, the areas hardest hit by the drop in tourists are the more far-flung, remote parts of Bali where terrorists are least likely to strike. Rather than skipping out on one of the world's best beach holidays, travelers can alleviate their terrorism concerns by visiting Bali's more remote destinations, asking their hotels what security measures are in place, and staying alert when visiting crowded areas.

As with any undiscovered paradise that isn't so undiscovered anymore, Bali buffs mourn the loss of the island's innocence. You're sure to meet one or two scruffy old expats who'll be more than happy to tell you about "how it once was." Where there were no hotels or even electricity only a few decades ago, the island is now spotted with cybercafes, upscale lodging, and pesky touts. Don't be dissuaded. The "real Bali" is wherever you look for it.

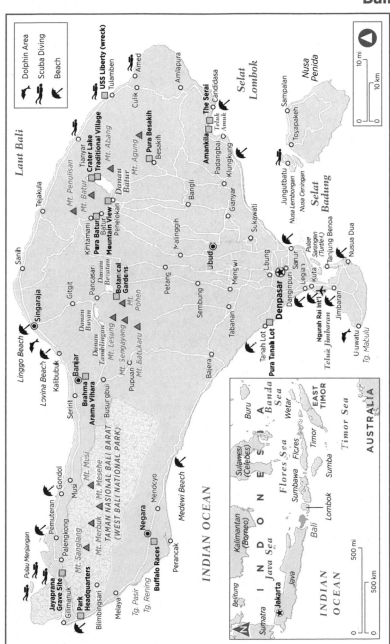

Bali's People & Culture

RELIGION   More than 90% of the population is Hindu, with the minority made up of Muslims, Buddhists, and Christians. Religious ritual plays into every facet of life. Balinese Hindus believe in the pantheon of Hindu gods, as well as dharma and adharma, order and disorder, and the need for balance between the two. The importance of karma, or the consequence of individual actions, plays into the peaceful daily rhythms, and forms of "making merit" are as many as the people who practice them. Whether placing daily offerings of flowers on someone's car or undertaking rigorous mountain pilgrimages, Balinese believe that to achieve harmony the forces of good must be saluted with offerings, while the forces of evil must be appeased. With an estimated 20,000 temples and shrines, Bali is known as the "Island of the Gods," and every village has at least one temple with buildings dedicated to Vishnu, Brahma, and Shiva (the Creator, the Preserver, and the Destroyer).

CELEBRATIONS   **Tooth filing** is a rite of maturation, wherein the sharp front teeth, especially the canines, are filed down smooth (the idea being to differentiate humans from the animals). This can happen at any age, even after death, but is most often done to adolescents.

Weddings in Bali are unique, colorful affairs not to be missed, and **cremations** are surprisingly festive as well. Burning the body is the only way a soul can be freed of its earthly self and travel to its next incarnation (or to enlightenment), and death is a joyous occasion in Bali, full of floats and fanfare. Complicated towers (the higher the caste, the higher the tower) hold the body, carried aloft by cheering men who turn the tower in circles to send the spirit to heaven as they carry it to the burning ground. It's an extraordinary and wonderful event; there are even tours that will take you, or you can ask at any *losmen* (hostel) or at your hotel front desk. Cremations in Ubud are particularly noteworthy.

Compared to Western churchgoing, celebrations in Bali are very casual: Women gossip, children play, and dogs wander temple grounds freely, snacking on offerings. A priest chants, people pray and then get up, and others take their places. Ask before taking photos, and stay on your best behavior. Balinese are generally most welcoming and might even invite you for food or drinks.

MUSIC & DANCE   The tones of the **gamelan**—the bright-sounding metal percussion ensembles that accompany just about every celebration and ceremony here—will turn your head. Music is everywhere in Bali, from the raucous *dangdut,* or Indonesian pop, pouring from restaurants and shops, to folk music and the refined classical music that accompanies the many staged dance performances and temple worship.

If you have a chance, don't miss a performance of traditional dance. **Legong** and **Barong dances** are intricate ballets depicting scenes from the epic *Ramayana.* **Kecak dance** is a circle of up to 100 men chanting rhythmically and telling the saga of a monkey king and his warriors. It's a colorful, fun experience. Many hotels hold shows; the Royal Palace in Ubud is a good choice. If you're lucky, you'll find a real, nontourist performance in an outlying village.

Wayang Kulit, or **shadow-puppet plays,** feature intricately cut leather figures that puppeteers use to project images against a screen. *Wayang Kulit* shows also depict tales from the Hindu epics and are accompanied by a gamelan ensemble and the voices of puppeteers (often injecting news, gossip, and bawdy jokes).

ARTS & CRAFTS Decoration and craft are as seamlessly woven into the fabric of life in Bali as are dance, music, and ritual. Fine carving and craft work can be found adorning the most humble dwelling. Craftsmen are highly revered, and skilled wood and stone carvers turn out authentic works in streetside studios all over the island (concentrated in Ubud). Visitors are sure to walk away with some beautiful, original finds in wood and stone.

Masks used in traditional performance, many of the bug-eyed demoness Rangda, make fine souvenirs. (***Beware:*** Tradition has it that even tourist copies can be inhabited by spirits.) There's a lot of mass-produced clutter, and lots of these works have been "aged" by an artful banging around on the sidewalk; authentic antiques are rare, so be cynical of claims of authenticity—though the copies can be quite good.

Ancient stylized **paintings of deities** and the delicately carved "lontar" **palm-frond books** are both still produced on the island. Expatriates have had as much influence on modern Balinese art as the ancients. As guiding patrons, men such as **Rudolf Bonnet,** a Dutchman, and **Walter Spies,** whose home on the site of the Tjampuhan Hotel in Ubud became central to the arts in Ubud, influenced local painters, opened societies, and brought the glory of Bali to the world at large. With a little searching, you can find some real masterpieces.

Etiquette

Since the Balinese have been hosting foreign tourists for decades, they are fairly laid-back and accepting of Western habits—but even the Balinese have their traditions that should be respected. The most important rule is to cover up your legs and shoulders when entering a temple; most hotels supply sarongs for temple visits. The Balinese also ban menstruating women from temples. When speaking with locals, avoid pointing with your index finger. If you must point, stick out your thumb and make a fist with the rest of your fingers. As in India, pick up things with your right hand, not your left, which is perceived as being unclean.

Language

The Balinese speak both Indonesian and Balinese—the former when out in public, the latter at home. Aside from the tendency toward seemingly jaw-breaking polysyllabic phrases, Indonesian is not that hard to learn; pronunciation is pretty straightforward, and spelling is phonetic. Balinese is much more complicated, not least because there are three levels—high, middle, and low—depending on the class and authority of the person to whom you are speaking.

English is spoken widely, and if you've learned a few words of Malay, you can give them a try here as the languages are quite similar.

THE BEST OF BALI IN 2 WEEKS

A visit to Bali is, as always, replete with kingly comforts, beautiful resorts, fine dining, and immersion in an ancient culture amid an island dreamscape. The following 2-week plan starts you off in Seminyak and then takes you to Ubud, Gunung Bakur, Menjangan, Jimbaran Bay, and Tanjung Banoa. The last stop is Nusa Dua, where you can treat yourself to a luxury spa.

Days 1-2: Seminyak ★

This hip, yuppie beachside enclave is a great alternative to the overrun Kuta just south of here. Lounge at the oceanfront pool at the luxurious **Legian,** followed by a sunset visit to the temple Tanah Lot. The next day, take a surf lesson at the **Rip Curl School of Surf,** followed by a sunset cocktail and dinner at **Ku De Ta** or **Sarong.** Dance late into the night at **Hu'u Bar.**

Days 3-4: Ubud ★★

The 1-hour drive to Ubud takes you from the shore to the lush rice paddies and jungles of Bali. The stellar **COMO Shambhala** (a wellness resort and spa that dubs itself "The Estate") and the **Chedi Club** (a collection of boutique private villas with personal butlers) are worth every rupiah. Take a morning trek through the rice paddies and get a back scrub and rub at **Ubud Body Works Center** or the **Alila Ubud,** both great-value spas. Tuck into a gourmet French meal at **Mosaic,** run by chef Chris Salans. The next day, peruse the numerous house-wares shops on Monkey Forest Road and take a break at **Monkey Forest,** where you can feed the monkeys a few bananas. Late in the afternoon, take the 1-hour drive to Penelokan, a town that sits on the outer crater's edge of **Gunung Batur.** The digs aren't fancy here, but the best of the lot is the **Lakeview Hotel.**

Day 5: Gunung Batur

Make the 2-hour ascent of Gunung Batur, an active volcano. At the top, you can boil eggs in pockets of erupting steam and walk along one of the volcano's ridges. In the afternoon, hire a car for the 2-hour trip to **Candi Dasa,** on Bali's east shore. The boutique **Alila Manggis** has good-value accommodations, beach-side massage pavilions, and one of the area's best restaurants, Sea Salt.

Days 6-7: Temples & Diving in the East ★★

Take a day trip to **Besakih,** Bali's most important temple, and spend the after-noon wandering around the village of **Tenganan,** followed by dinner at **Vincent's** on Candi Dasa's sleepy commercial strip. The next day, go diving or snorkeling at the **Blue Lagoon.** If you're an advanced diver, sign up for the famed wreck dive at **Tulamben.**

Days 8-9: Total Relaxation in the North or on Lombok ★★

To truly get away from it all, head to either Bali's northern beaches by car or the neighboring island of Lombok via plane or boat. In the north, stay at **The Damai** or the brand-new **Menjangan,** all away from the hubbub of the south. On Lombok, the most luxurious choices are the funky **Hotel Tugu** and the **Oberoi,** with a gorgeous swimming pool and a secluded beach.

Days 10-11: Jimbaran Bay

Hire a car to the romantic yet local area of Jimbaran Bay, home to a number of the world's top resorts. The cream of the crop are the **Karma Kandara** and the **Four Seasons Resort at Jimbaran Bay.** Visit the cliffside temple **Uluwatu** at sunset, followed by a grilled lobster and shrimp dinner at **Menega Cafe,** the best seafood hut on Jimbaran beach.

Days 12–14: Nusa Dua ★

End your holiday by winding down beachside or poolside at any number of the resorts in this five-star enclave. If you're seeking a peaceful and quiet alternative to the brand-name resorts, head to the pristine **Balé,** a series of minimalist villas with ocean views. The **St. Regis** offers fantastic restaurants and a top-notch spa. Visit **Bumbu Bali,** one of the island's top restaurants, which offers authentic Balinese cuisine and cooking classes.

PLANNING YOUR TRIP TO BALI

Visitor Information

The Bali Department of Tourism operates visitor information centers at a number of locations: at **Ngurah Rai International Airport** (✆ **361/751011,** ext. 5123); in **Ubud** at the crossroad of Monkey Forest Road and Jalan Raya Ubud; and in **Kuta** at Jalan Benesari 36B, Legian (✆ **361/754090** or 081/2392-8098). Or try the **Bali Tourism Board** (✆ **361/235600;** www.bali-tourism-board.com).

Some good online sources include **Bali Paradise Online** (www.bali-paradise. com), **Bali & Indonesia on the Net** (www.indo.com), and **Bali Guide** (www. baliguide.com). **Bali Echo** (www.baliecho.com) is an informative arts-and-culture magazine.

There are lots of free pamphlets with listings, information, and maps: *Hello Bali* and *Bali Plus* have general info; *The Beat* (www.beatmag.com) is a free guide to nightlife, dining, and activities. *The Yak* and *The Bud* are local glossies focusing on restaurants and nightlife in Seminyak and Ubud. For information about surfing, check www.indosurf.com.au, or pick up a copy of *Indo Surf Guide,* published by the same folks.

Entry Requirements

Visitors from the U.S., Canada, Australia, New Zealand, and most of Europe can get visas on arrival through Ngurah Rai International Airport or the seaports of Padang Bai and Benoa. For stays of 7 days or less, the charge is $10; for stays of up to 30 days, the charge is $25. For stays of longer than 30 days, a tourist or business visa must be arranged *before* coming to Indonesia. A service called **Bali Concierge** (✆ **361/766880;** www.thebaliconcierge.com) can speed you through immigration and Customs once you land for a fee of $50 per person, plus visa charges.

Customs Regulations

Customs allows you to bring in, duty-free, 200 cigarettes, 50 cigars, or 100 grams of tobacco; cameras and film; 1 liter of alcohol; and perfume clearly intended for personal use. Forbidden are guns, weapons, narcotics, pornography (leave it at home if you're unsure how it's defined), televisions, fresh fruit, Chinese medicine, and printed matter with Chinese characters. Plants might also be confiscated. The export of tortoiseshell, crocodile skin, and ivory is prohibited.

Money

The currency of Indonesia is the **rupiah,** from the Sanskrit word for wrought silver, *rupya.* Coins come in denominations of Rp25, 50, 100, and 500. Notes are Rp100, 500, 1,000, 5,000, 10,000, 20,000, 50,000, and 100,000; the largest denomination is worth about $8.90. The rate of exchange is relatively stable. At press time, it was about **Rp8,810 = $1.**

ATMS   In Bali, ATMs are common in all major tourist areas and trade at good rates.

CURRENCY EXCHANGE   Most major hotels will change currency, but offer less than favorable rates. Storefront exchange services line most streets and offer the best rates, but it's important to be careful of scams such as counterfeit bills and damaged currency that won't be accepted anywhere. Ask first about commission, and be sure to count your bills before walking away. State-sponsored **Wartel Telecommunications Service** offices are the best bet.

CREDIT CARDS   Credit cards are accepted at Bali's higher-end restaurants and hotels. For transactions elsewhere, be prepared to use cash. To report a lost or stolen credit card, you can call **American Express** (counter at Danamon Bank, Jalan Legian 87) at ✆ **361/757510,** or **MasterCard** and **Visa** internationally at ✆ **(+1)303-967-1090.**

When to Go

The high seasons are July and August and the weeks surrounding Christmas and New Year's, when prices are higher and tourist traffic is considerably increased. Try to avoid these times as well as February and March (given the heat and humidity).

CLIMATE   Bali is just below the equator—so days are a consistent 12 hours long—and the temperatures always hover in the 80s (upper 20s to low 30s Celsius). The rainy season lasts from October to April; rain usually comes in short, violent bursts that last an hour or so, and the humidity is at its crushing worst during this period. The hottest months are February, March, and April. Remember that it gets a bit nippy at night up in the mountains, but a light sweater will certainly be enough.

PUBLIC HOLIDAYS & EVENTS   Public holidays and events include **New Year's Day** (Jan 1); **Idul Fitri** (celebration of the end of Ramadan); **Nyepi** (a major purification ritual and a time when Balinese are supposed to sit at home, silent, in late Mar); **Good Friday** and **Easter Sunday** (late Mar/early Apr); **Muslim New Year; Indonesia Independence Day** (Aug 17); **Ascension Day of Mohammed** (early Dec); and **Christmas** (Dec 25).

Health & Safety

HEALTH CONCERNS   See "Health & Safety" in chapter 10 (p. 632) for information on health concerns, vaccinations, and general issues that affect the region. No inoculations are required for Bali, but it's always a good idea to get shots for hepatitis A, tetanus, polio, and typhoid (likely you've already had some of these). It's also a good idea to check the most recent information at the **Centers for Disease Control** (click "Travelers' Health" at **www.cdc.gov**).

The CDC has declared Bali malaria free, though it is not uncommon on other islands in the Indonesian archipelago. Of concern, though, are the many stray dogs (and monkeys) on Bali and therefore rabies, so beware of strays.

You can't drink the water on Bali, but bottled water is cheap and readily available. Just about every hotel will supply you with a couple bottles or a jug of boiled water—to be extra cautious, use it to brush your teeth as well. Restaurants in tourist areas supply safe water and ice, but to be sure, ask for *air minum* (bottled drinking water) and no ice. Avoid "Bali belly" (the Indonesian version of Montezuma's revenge) by sticking to foods that have been peeled or cooked.

SAFETY CONCERNS To alleviate any terrorism concerns you may have, consider visiting Bali's more remote destinations, asking hotels what security measures are in place, and staying alert when visiting crowded areas. It is recommended that you check with your home country's overseas travel bureau or with the **U.S. State Department** (for a complete up-to-date listing click "more" under "Travel Warnings" at **www.travel.state.gov**) to keep abreast of travel advisories and current affairs that could affect your trip.

Getting There

BY PLANE **Ngurah Rai International Airport** (✆ **361/751011**) is 13km (8 miles) southwest of Denpasar. For airport information and connection to airline reservations counters, call ✆ **361/751011,** ext. 1454. When you leave Bali, there will be an airport departure tax of Rp150,000.

Most visitors from the U.S. and Canada fly here via connection in Taipei on **China Airlines** or **EVA Air,** Bangkok on **Thai Airways,** Jakarta on **Garuda Indonesia,** Singapore on **Singapore Airlines,** Tokyo on **Japan Airlines** and **Northwest Airlines,** Hong Kong on **Cathay Pacific,** or Seoul on **Korean Air.** Check with travel agents for deals and package rates, some with affordable overnight connections via Bangkok. Bali is served from Europe by **Cathay Pacific** via Hong Kong; tickets can be purchased from **British Airways, Singapore Airlines,** or **Air France.** Flights from Australia and New Zealand can be booked through **Qantas** and **Australian Airlines.**

Few travelers stop in the city; most connect directly with their resort area of choice. To get to your destination from the airport, it is a good idea to prearrange pickup through your hotel (the rate is comparable to the official rates at the airport); otherwise, you can buy a ticket at the official taxi counter just outside Customs and arrange a fixed-rate ride to your hotel. Avoid the temptation to go with unofficial cabs; you might get caught in a taxi scam that will leave you frustrated, overcharged, or in the wrong place.

Getting Around

BY PRIVATE CAR Given how cheap and easy it is to hire someone to drive, many folks just avoid the headache of driving themselves. **Private taxis** are the most common choice of transport and can get you to any destination for a reasonable price. A driver and car should be around $35, plus gas charges, for an 8-hour day. A reputable agency is **Amertha Dana** (✆ **361/735406**), which can arrange transport in most of southern Bali. Otherwise, guys offering "transport" and pantomime-steering a car will be at your heels wherever you go and, depending on your luck, can be pretty helpful. Be specific about destination and price (and check for seat belts) before setting out.

We don't recommend that you drive, but if you feel the urge to play chicken with the locals, cars can be rented cheaply and some agencies require only a driver's license from your home country. Try **Bali Car Hire** (Denpasar Ngurah Rai Airport, Denpensar; ✆ **361/411499**). For agencies that require an international driver's license or a locally issued tourist driving license, 1-month licenses are issued on the spot for Rp150,000 at the **Foreign License Service** (Jalan Gunung Sanghiang, Denpasar; ✆ **361/422323**). Traffic is on the left side, and "third-world rules" apply: The more aggressively honking, larger vehicle goes first. Traffic police are just bribe collectors.

BY PUBLIC TRANSPORTATION   Blue and brown vans called *bemos* operate as buses in Bali. They have regular routes, but these aren't really written down. Most tourists save the headache and go for private transport. *Bemos* are better for short hops (around town, for example) than long distances. **Metered taxis,** if you can find them, are your best bet. Be sure that the driver turns on his meter (you might have to insist more than once). One other option is to ask at your hotel or a travel agent about the **tourist shuttles** that connect the main destinations on the island.

A Note on Addresses

Street addresses in Bali can be as vague as "on the main street." In some areas, that's all that passes for an address. Don't worry—most are easy to find. Some addresses include an X to denote a new spot that has been wedged between two older addresses.

BY MOTORBIKE   Riding a motorbike on Bali is a dangerous proposition; on even the briefest visit to the island, you will see your share of crashes. Renting a scooter or motorbike, however, is a cheap (from $3 per day) and fun way to see the island. Keep in mind that riding is safer and more beautiful in remote areas. The same driver's license requirements for cars apply to motorbikes and scooters.

BY BOAT   Several companies offer diving and snorkeling day trips, sunset or dinner cruises, and connection to the nearby islands of Nusa Penida and Nusa Lembongan. Both **Bounty Cruises** (© 361/726666; www.balibountycruises.com) and **Bali Hai Cruises** (© 361/720331; www.balihaicruises.com) run regular high-end tours from Bali's Benoa Harbor. **Sail Sensations** (© 361/725864; www.bali-sailsensations.com) offers day and overnight sails. The *Wakalouka* (© 085/237083731), a luxury catamaran, transports you in style to its exclusive property on Nusa Lembongan.

Tips on Accommodations

Bali accommodations range from bungalows that cost Rp40,000 to luxury villas serviced by a retinue of servants and priced at more than $1,000. Another increasingly popular trend for families and groups of friends is to rent a villa for the duration of the trip; villas range from $1,000 to $4,000 per week and often include a cook, cleaning staff, and a driver (p. 594). On the lower end, and for a more authentic experience, visitors can stay in *losmen* (traditional homestay, a bastardization of the Dutch word *logement*) or rustic bungalows. Bali's resorts and fine Western hotels cost a fraction of what luxury accommodations would elsewhere, and many come to enjoy the upgrade.

Promotional and Internet rates are available at all hotels in Bali. Paying the rack rates, or published rates (which are listed in this guide), even in high season, is almost unheard of. Especially in the off season, it pays to shop around; you can show up at the front desk of even the largest hotels and ask for the best rate.

Almost all hotels charge a 21% government tax and service charge on top of the quoted rates. Some hotels tack on a charge of $30 per night in high season—the 2 or 3 weeks around Christmas and New Year's, plus the months of July and August.

Tips on Dining

The choices in Bali are many, but it's rare to find authentic Balinese or Indonesian food on a menu for foreigners; for that, you'll have to go to a *warung*, a local cafe, and

telephone dialing AT A GLANCE

○ **To place a call from your home country to Bali:** Dial the international access code (011 in the U.S. and Canada, 0011 in Australia, 0170 in New Zealand, 00 in the U.K.), plus Indonesia's country code **(62),** the city or local area code (**361** for Kuta, Jimbaran, Nusa Dua, Sanur, and Ubud; **362** for Lovina; **363** for Candi Dasa; **370** for Lombok), and the six-digit phone number (for example, 011 62 362 000000). Mobile phone numbers do not have a city or local area code, and rather begin with an 8 followed by a long string of numbers. Dial Indonesia's country code (62) followed by the number.

○ **To place a call within Indonesia:** You must use the area code if calling between states. For calls within the country, area codes are all preceded by a **0** (for example,

0361 for Ubud, 0362 for Lovina, 0363 for Candi Dasa, 0370 for Lombok, and so on). Dial the city or area code preceded by a **0,** and then the local number (for example, 0362 000000). For mobile phones, add a 0 to the number.

○ **To place a direct international call from Indonesia:** Dial the international access code **(00),** plus the country code, the area or city code, and the number (for example, to call the U.S., you'd dial 00 1 000/000-0000).

○ **To reach the international operator:** Dial 102.

○ **International country codes are as follows:** Australia, 61; Cambodia, 855; Canada, 1; Hong Kong, 852; Laos, 856; Malaysia, 60; Myanmar, 95; New Zealand, 64; the Philippines, 63; Singapore, 65; Thailand, 66; U.K., 44; U.S., 1; Vietnam, 84.

many visitors are dissuaded by the typical *warung's* appearance (some are pretty grungy). If you're not put off by a bit of grime, the food at *warungs* is authentic, delicious, and cheap. Most visitors, however, surrender to the call of high-quality international dining options, which are affordable and varied, with great options for vegetarians.

Indonesian dishes that you are most likely to encounter include *nasi goreng* (fried rice, usually topped with an egg), *mie goreng* (fried noodles), *nasi campur* (a plate of boiled rice with sides of meat and veggies, a house specialty), *ayam goreng* (fried chicken), *gado gado* (salad with peanut sauce, served hot or cold), and satay (small chunks of meat on skewers served with peanut sauce). *Padang* food (sold in little cafes called *rumah makan*) is spicy tidbits of fried fish, chicken, or veggies on a buffet; you pick what you want. A truly authentic Balinese dish found in roadside cafes is *babi guling,* delicious roast suckling pork prepared with spices over a spit. Just look for the ubiquitous signs with a picture of a pig. Visit www.baliguide.com/restaurants_guide.html for more information on Bali restaurants.

Tips on Shopping

The quantity of Balinese arts and crafts available on the island is overwhelming. Woodcarvers, jewelers, and craftspeople of all types line the streets around all tourist areas, particularly in and around Ubud and on the streets of Kuta. There's something for all budgets, from tourist trinkets to fine art and antiques. It's a shopper's paradise of fabrics, clothing, wood and stone carvings, paintings, and doodads of varying quality. Generally, you get what you pay for—but with a bit of haggling, you can get a lot more for what you pay. Shop around; the same item gets cheaper the more you look at it, and it's really the same stuff everywhere. Ask the price, offer half, smile, and go from there. Even at inflated prices, you'll still come out ahead of the game.

[Fast FACTS] BALI

American Express The American Express office is at Banamon Bank at Jalan Legian 87 (✆ **361/ 757510**).

Business Hours Most places keep "daylight hours," which on the equator pretty much means 6am to 6pm (or a little later).

Drug Laws Though you might be offered marijuana, Indonesia takes drug offenses very seriously. American and Australian forces have teamed up with Indonesian police to fight drugs, along with terrorism, and penalties for mere possession include long jail sentences and large fines.

Electricity Currents can be either 110 volts (50 AC) or 220 to 240 volts (50 AC).

Embassies & Consulates **U.S.:** Jalan Hayam Wuruk 310, Denpasar (✆ **361/233605**). **Great Britain:** Tirtra Nadi 20, Sanur (✆ **361/270601**). **Australia:** Jalan Tantular 32, Renon, Denpasar (✆ **361/ 241118**). The Australian consulate also assists nationals of Canada and New Zealand.

Emergencies Bali has a new emergency response center that coordinates all governmental bureaus and services: Just dial ✆ **112.**

Otherwise, you can call ✆ **110** for the police, ✆ **118** for an ambulance, ✆ **113** in case of fire, and ✆ **111/115/ 151** for search and rescue. The Red Cross can be reached at ✆ **26465.**

Hospitals If you need a doctor or dentist, ask your hotel for a referral—many have one on call. In Kuta, try the **Bali International Medical Centre,** Jalan Bypass Ngurah Rai 100X (✆ **361/761263**); it's open daily from 8am to midnight and sometimes will send someone to your hotel. Another option in Kuta is the **International SOS Bali,** Jalan Bypass Ngurah Rai (✆ **361/710505**). There is a city hospital in Denpasar, but for any serious ailment, you should evacuate to Hong Kong, Singapore, Kuala Lumpur, or Bangkok.

Internet Access Internet cafes, some with wireless laptop access, are springing up all over Bali. Expect to pay about $1.50 per hour.

Language The Balinese speak both Indonesian and Balinese—the former when out in public, the latter at home. English is widely spoken throughout Bali, particularly in the major tourist areas. While not

everyone is fluent, most of the people you will be dealing with will speak enough English that you can communicate with them. See "Language," p. 581, for more information.

Liquor Laws You won't find liquor in *halal* restaurants catering to Muslims, but there are no restrictions elsewhere. The legal drinking age is 17, but the police rarely enforce this law.

Mail Your hotel can send mail for you, or you can go to the post office in Denpasar, at Jalan Raya Puputan Renon (✆ **361/ 223566**). Other branches are in Kuta (Jalan Raya Kuta; ✆ **361/754012**), Ubud, and Sanur. For big items, there are packing and shipping services in all major tourist areas, but the cost can be exorbitant.

Police Dial ✆ **110** for the police.

Safety Bali is by and large a safe place, even after dark. Violent crime is rare. However, pickpockets are not, so you should exercise considerable caution by using a money belt, particularly in crowded tourist areas, and being careful not to flash large wads of cash. If you need assistance, contact the **Guardian Angels**

Tourist Police (📞 361/ **763753**), available 24 hours a day.

Many hotels offer safety deposit boxes, the best place to keep your extra cash and other valuables. If nothing else, make sure your suitcase has a good lock on it. Even the best hotel can't always guarantee security for valuables left lying in plain sight.

Telephones   The international country code for Indonesia is **62.** Because many hotels charge a great deal even for using your calling card, you're better off using the Wartel network of privately owned pay phones. There's one in every tourist center, though some work better than others. Some also have Internet access. See "Telephone Dialing at a Glance," p. 587, for details.

Time Zone   Bali is 8 hours ahead of Greenwich Mean Time, except during daylight saving time, which it does not observe. That's 13 hours ahead of Eastern Standard Time in the U.S.

Tipping   Tipping is optional, though of course appreciated by hotel staff. Most restaurants include a service charge. Leave a small tip if you feel the need, and round up taxi bills to the nearest thousand.

Toilets   Western-style toilets with seats are becoming more common than the Asian squat variety, though cheap *losmen* (homestays) and some less touristy public places still have the latter. Always carry toilet paper with you, or you might have to use your hand (the left one only, please) and the dip bucket.

Water   Avoid tap water in Bali unless properly boiled. Bottled water is available everywhere, and restaurants in tourist areas seem to use it as a matter of course, but you should always ask to be sure.

KUTA

Just a 10-minute drive from the airport, Kuta is a popular destination for budget travelers and Aussies who hop over for long weekends or holidays. Some might say that Kuta is a den of iniquity, with all the bars, drag queen shows, and Kuta cowboys waiting to find a foreign woman who will give them a taste of the good life. Over the years, Kuta has fallen victim to rampant commercialization, which has drastically changed the environment from a small fishing village lining a pristine beach to a hopping city with blaring disco music. Kuta is really more for a younger crowd looking for action. If that describes you, then by all means stay awhile.

Kuta is made up of narrow streets and alleys, and pedestrians share space with honking, mufflerless cars and motorbikes. You'll be harried by some of the most aggressive touts on the island, and the beaches are crowded with imploring sellers and masseurs; the tourist rush, however, means some of the best nightlife and dining on the island. Unfortunately, the current makes swimming difficult and dangerous.

Getting There

Kuta is near the airport, and most hotels offer free airport pickup. If you're hiring a cab, it's best to go to the airport's official taxi counter, where you'll pay a set fare.

Getting Around

Kuta is a big rectangle. The two main north-south streets are oceanside Jalan Pantai Kuta and Jalan Legian. They're connected east-west by Jalan Benesari, Poppies Gang I, and many quaint alleys. You can easily walk all of this area or take the reasonably priced blue-and-yellow metered taxis.

[FastFACTS] KUTA

Currency Exchange There are a number of ATMs in Kuta. **Wartel** outlets are found all around the main streets.

Internet Access Restaurants, cafes, and even some mini-marts provide free Wi-Fi for customers. Internet cafes generally charge between Rp10,000 and Rp37,000 per hour and are easily spotted on streets.

Mail There is a main post office on Jalan Raya Tuban, but it's far from the town center. There are also some postal agents around town, or your hotel can send mail for you.

Telephones The area code in Kuta is **361.**

Where to Stay

Kuta Beach, while still a booming resort, is quite noisy and busy. We've listed the better choices in town and at nearby Legian and Seminyak to the north.

KUTA & LEGIAN BEACH
Expensive

Villa de daun ★★ 📖 Among the chaos of high-octane Kuta sits this new exclusive retreat of 12 luxuriously appointed villas. Owners Michelle and Jimmy have captured the vibe of the island with stylish live-in pads with indulgent bathrooms, and private swimming pools and gazebos. Add 40-inch plasma TVs with knockout Bose sound systems, gourmet kitchens complete with fridges that stock the iciest drinks on the planet, and lavish king-size beds perfect after a day out bargaining with the locals. You're breaths away from the bevy of shops, restaurants, and local nightlife but a good 500m (1,640 ft.) walk to the beach. Get in if you can.

Jl. Raya Legian, Kuta. ☎ **0361/756276.** Fax 0361/750643. www.villadedaun.com. 12 villas. High season $350–$450 1-bedroom, $550 2-bedroom, $650 3-bedroom; low season $300–$400 1-bedroom, $500 2-bedroom, $600 3-bedroom. AE, MC, V. **Amenities:** Restaurant; babysitting; room service; spa; Wi-Fi (restaurant and lobby only). *In room:* A/C, TV/DVD, stereo or CD, hair dryer, minibar.

Moderate

Padma Hotel ★ ☺ You've got all you need at the Padma, a self-contained compound just the right distance from the fray for peace and quiet, but close enough to go play and shop. There's something for the whole family here, including a good kids' club, daily activities, a roster of day trips, the fine Mandara Spa, and cultural classes such as egg painting and musical demonstrations. Garden rooms have parquet floors and Balinese furnishings. Standard rooms all have balconies and great views. Family rooms open onto a patio and central garden. There is a quiet, tout-free grassy spot between the pool and the beach where the kids can frolic.

Jl. Padma 1, Legian. ☎ **0361/752111.** Fax 0361/752140. www.padmahotels.com. 406 units. High season $165–$390 standard, $1,225 villa; low season $140–$365 standard, $1,200 villa. AE, DC, MC, V. **Amenities:** 7 restaurants; 2 bars; babysitting; kids' club; concierge; gym; outdoor pool; room service; spa; tennis; watersports; Wi-Fi. *In room:* A/C, TV/DVD, movie library, hair dryer, minibar.

Ramada Bintang Bali Resort & Spa ★ ☺ This resort is set on more than 6 hectares (15 acres) of tropical gardens extending down to the beachfront of South Kuta. The "Romantic" rooms are ideal for honeymooners or any couple seeking something out of the ordinary. The cozy rooms have elegant netting over the bed, parquet floors, and ethnic accents throughout. Bathrooms feature marble floors and a nice bathtub. The excellent activity program includes yoga, aqua aerobics, beach volleyball, and water-pillow fights. Kids have their own special program to keep them busy so moms and dads can have a relaxing holiday in paradise.

Jl. Kartika Plaza, Kuta. ℭ **0361/753292.** Fax 0361/752015. www.bintang-bali-hotel.com. 402 units. High season $155-$685 standard, $1,435 suite; low season $120-$650 standard, $1,400 suite; extra bed $35. AE, DC, MC, V. **Amenities:** 2 restaurants; coffee shop; 2 bars; lounge; babysitting; kids' club and children's play group; concierge; gym; health club; Jacuzzi; outdoor pool; room service; sauna; spa; tennis court; Wi-Fi (for a fee). *In room:* A/C, TV, hair dryer, minibar.

Inexpensive
Poppies Cottages ★★   This is by far the best midrange hotel in Kuta, with atmospheric thatched cottages set among gorgeous gardens abloom with a riot of bougainvillea. Located at the town center, the property has a small central pool designed to look like a natural pond, surrounded by lush garden nooks perfect for lounging. The rooms are a bit compact for the price, but the open-air bathrooms are done in marble, complete with sunken tubs, and everything is very clean and cozy.

Poppies Lane I, Kuta. ℭ **361/751059.** Fax 361/752364. www.poppiesbali.com. 20 units. $79-$93 double (seasonal rates available) plus 21% service fee. AE, DC, MC, V. **Amenities:** Restaurant; bar; Internet access (in business center); outdoor pool; room service. *In room:* A/C, TV, IDD phone.

SEMINYAK & THE SOUTHWEST COAST
Very Expensive
Alila Villas Soori ★★★   It's a 1-hour drive from the restaurant-and-bar scene but what you get is definitely worth the ride: pristine Art Deco villas set on a black-sand beach framed by palm trees. The cozy units come with plenty of indoor and outdoor lounging spaces, not to mention a plunge pool that snakes around your room, a spacious bathtub, and an Apple TV unit stocked with movies and music. A beautiful restaurant serving modern "comfort food" by former Jean-Georges chef Ashton Hall, a large common pool, yoga classes, horseback riding, and even Segway tours give you plenty of recreational options, but you might never leave the comfort of your superb villa.

Banjar Dukuh, Desa Kelating, Kerambitan, Tabanan. ℭ **361/8946388.** Fax 361/8946377. www.alila hotels.com. 49 units. $600 beach villa; $650 rice terrace villa; $750 ocean villa; $1,200-$1,500 1- to 4-bedroom villas; $10,000 10-bedroom residence. AE, MC, V. **Amenities:** 2 restaurants; bikes; pool; spa. *In room:* A/C, 2 satellite TVs w/Apple TV, fridge, hair dryer, minibar, free Wi-Fi.

Legian ★★   Set right on the coast with spacious, well-outfitted rooms, the Legian is the perfect beach resort for those who want to be right in the heart of the action in Seminyak. Balconies, some directly facing the ocean, offer a great place to chill out, as does the simple rectangular pool that abuts the beach. Across the street at the **Club,** you sacrifice the ocean views but get the privacy of your own contemporary villa. The **Beach House,** a two-story home with panoramic ocean views, is big enough to host 60-person events. Service is very professional and the location is rivaled only by the Oberoi (see below).

Jalan Laksmana, Seminyak, Kuta, Bali. ℭ **361/730622.** Fax 361/730623. www.ghmhotels.com. 79 units. $550-$900 suite; $2,700-$3,000 beach house; $900-$1,300 bedroom villa. AE, DC, MC, V. **Amenities:** Restaurant; 2 bars; airport shuttle service; babysitting; 2-tiered pool; spa; watersports facilities. *In room:* A/C, satellite TV w/in-house movies, fridge, hair dryer, minibar, Wi-Fi.

Oberoi ★★   The first hotel in Seminyak and one of the earliest luxury hotels on Bali, the Oberoi has long attracted celebrities, from Henry Kissinger to Julia Roberts. The property is composed of individual lanais—native bungalows of coral stone with wood beams and thatch roofs. Rooms are cozy and strike a great balance between high-end comforts and local style. Amenities are first class: raised futon beds, and marble bathrooms with sunken tubs facing private gardens. Private pool villas are luxurious beyond belief. The beach here is great, with a nice expanse of sand and few touts to harass you. An outdoor amphitheater hosts traditional dance performances. Service is genuinely warm and helpful without fawning, and you can feel at ease here without forgetting that you're in Bali. The fine spa is managed by Banyan Tree.

Jalan Laksmana, Seminyak, Kuta, Bali. (C) **361/730361.** Fax 361/730791. www.oberoihotels.com. 74 units. $355 lanai; $525–$1,075 villa. AE, DC, MC, V. **Amenities:** Restaurant; bar; babysitting; fitness center; outdoor pool; room service; sauna; spa; tennis court. *In room:* A/C, satellite TV w/in-house movies, DVD player, fridge, hair dryer, minibar, IDD phone.

The Samaya ★★   Close to half of all Samaya's guests are repeat clientele—which comes as no surprise. Smack dab in the middle of prime beachfront Seminyak, here you pay practically half of what you pay at other hotels in this übertrendy area. Choose from one-, two-, or three-bedroom villas, which, although a bit tired, are within spitting distance of the beach. The Samaya also offers a new 24-villa Royal Courtyard Complex, a 90-second buggy ride from the main hotel and across the street. The new villas offer all the modern conveniences of the moment, like flatscreen TVs in the marble tubs. Sublime sunsets show nightly and an evening at Breeze restaurant overlooking the beach is perfect. Recently named "Best for Romance" by Trip Advisor, each villa comes with wooden gazebos housing daybeds that make an ideal perch for private dining or a double daybed for a massage for two.

Jl. Laksmana, Seminyak Beach. (C) **0361/731149.** Fax 0361/731203. www.thesamayabali.com. 46 units. High season $575 and up; low season $475 and up. AE, DC, MC, V. **Amenities:** 2 restaurants; 2 bars; babysitting; bikes; concierge; gym; outdoor pool; room service; spa; Wi-Fi. *In room:* A/C, TV/DVD, movie library, stereo or CD player, hair dryer, minibar, MP3 docking station.

Expensive

The Amala ★   The Amala has done a good job of creating a relaxing atmosphere in the middle of Seminyak's bustle. You'll hear the occasional hum of motorcycles but no noise from children, since kids 12 and under aren't allowed. A sister resort to the pristine Bale in Nusa Dua, the Amala's emphasis is on its professional spa and central location—a stone's throw from the restaurant-and-bar scene and a 15-minute walk to the beach. Each spa villa features its own steam shower room and an outdoor bathtub and Jacuzzi, while the more opulent and cozy pool villas feature an open-air living room and kitchen set around a plunge pool.

Jalan Kunti, Seminyak, Bali. (C) **361/738866.** Fax 361/734299. www.theamala.com. 12 units. $325 spa villa; $430 pool villa; $610 Amala residence. AE, DC, MC, V. **Amenities:** Restaurant; fitness center; outdoor pool; room service; spa; library. *In room:* A/C, satellite flatscreen TV, DVD player, fridge, hair dryer, minibar, MP3 docking station, IDD phone, free Wi-Fi.

Anantara ★   These oversize suites overlooking Seminyak's beach are pretty much the closest you can sleep to the ocean without having to camp on the beach. This luxurious four-story hotel (one of the tallest buildings around) resembles something plunked down from Miami's South Beach with a hip, urban vibe rather than a traditional Balinese resort. Decadent touches such as an outdoor bathtub on the balcony of each of the rooms (in addition to an extravagantly roomy tub in the bathroom), an espresso machine, and an iPod with Bose speakers make this a hit among a young, wealthy, globe-trotting crowd. The rooftop bar, SOS (Sunset on Six), and the swimming pool on the ground level are perfect spots for lounging and watching sunsets. Guests will find themselves right in the center of all of Seminyak's action.

Jalan Dhyana Pura, Seminyak, Bali. ✆ **361/737773.** Fax 361/737772. www.anantara.com. 60 units. $450–$570 garden suite; $550–$670 ocean suite; $2,900–$4,900 penthouse. AE, DC, MC, V. **Amenities:** 2 restaurants; rooftop bar; babysitting; fitness center; outdoor pool; room service; sauna; spa; library. *In room:* A/C, satellite flatscreen TV w/in-house movies, DVD player, fridge, hair dryer, minibar, MP3 docking station, IDD phone, free Wi-Fi.

Hotel Tugu ★   The darkened, high-ceilinged lobby decorated with long, flowing curtains and a huge Hindu sculpture immediately sets the tone for this resort, which offers plenty of peace and quiet, in addition to a romantic ambience and a perfect surfer's beach. Rooms are decorated with an eclectic mix of Art Deco and Balinese antique furniture, Chinese porcelain vases, and four-poster beds. Two large villas, the Walter Spies Pavillion and the Puri Le Mayeur, have private plunge pools and outdoor bathrooms. Woerung Tugu, a rustic dining room decorated with picnic-style tables and chairs and Hindu stone sculptures, serves authentic Balinese cuisine. Located in between the bustling Seminyak area and the Tanah Lot temple, this resort strikes the right balance for those who want accessible restaurants and nightlife without having to be in the fray.

Jalan Pantai Batu Bolong, Canggu, Bali. ✆ **361/731701.** Fax 361/731708. www.tuguhotels.com. 20 units. $360–$600 suite; $490 Walter Spies Pavillion; $600 villa. AE, DC, MC, V. **Amenities:** Restaurant; bar; free airport transfer; bike rental; golf (nearby); fitness center; outdoor pool; room service; sauna; spa; tennis court. *In room:* A/C, satellite TV w/in-house movies, DVD player, fridge, hair dryer, minibar, IDD phone, Wi-Fi.

Moderate

Desa Seni ★   Set up by a Canadian pair, this eco-resort just north of Seminyak has a Wizard-of-Oz-meets-Balinese-countryside feel. Whimsical cottages with curvy eaves and brightly colored umbrellas decorate the grounds, along with several friendly dogs. The individually designed wood bungalows with rustic touches are more luxurious at second glance, with amenities such as air-conditioning, rain-shower heads, and DVD players and stereos hidden away in the cabinetry. Yoga sessions are held twice daily in an open-air studio, while a saltwater lap pool is the perfect lounging spot. A good surfing beach is just a short walk away, and you won't be more than a 15-minute drive away from Seminyak.

Jalan Kayu Putih 13, Pantai Berawa, Canggu, Bali. ✆ **361/8446392.** www.desaseni.com. 10 units. $150–$385 1- and 2-bedroom bungalows. Rates include breakfast. AE, MC, V. **Amenities:** Restaurant; bar; pool bar; airport transfer; Internet access; outdoor pool; room service. *In room:* A/C, TV, DVD player, fridge, IDD phone.

Villa Ixora ✦   Hidden away down a dirt road is this small cluster of villas and hotel rooms with a homey French countryside feel. The six hotel rooms are decorated with hardwood floors and Balinese furniture, and nearby is a large swimming pool next to a shaded patio, where breakfast is served. The two villas, featuring two- and three-bedroom accommodations, are rented to families and, given their size and the large garden areas surrounding them, are also a good value. A small footpath leads to an uncrowded beach with good waves. Though it feels like it's in the middle of nowhere, set next to rice paddies and private homes, the property is just a short drive away from Seminyak.

Jalan Petitenget, Gang Cendrawasih, Kerobokan, Bali. ✆ **361/739390.** Fax 361/739394. www.ixorabali.com. 8 units. $77–$99 double; $210–$275 2-bedroom villa; $275–$360 3-bedroom villa. MC, V. **Amenities:** Restaurant; pool bar; airport transfer; Internet access; outdoor pool; room service; library. *In room:* A/C, TV, DVD player, kitchen, minibar, IDD phone, free Wi-Fi.

renting your own VILLA

The real-estate boom in Bali has created a market of more than 1,000 privately owned villas, ranging from one-bedroom bungalows to palatial mansions with more than 10 bedrooms, which are available as vacation rentals. Prices range from around $150 per night for the smallest villas to several thousand dollars for the largest. It's an ideal arrangement for large families or groups of friends traveling together. Most villas come with at least several staff who attend to your every need, including cooking, cleaning, and driving, just as in a hotel. There are dozens of rental agencies on the island. Two reputable agencies are **Elite Havens** (✆ **0361/731-074;** www.elitehavens.com) and **Bali Villa Worldwide** (✆ **361/732-013;** www.balivillaworldwide.com).

Vivalavi ★ 🍷 ☺ Just a few minutes' drive away from Seminyak is this French-owned villa hotel perfect for families or groups of friends seeking an alternative from the usual hotel and resort scene. Each of the private villas comes with its own private yard, daybed pavilion, and Jacuzzi. The villas' two bedrooms, both the same size and decorated with modern furniture, connect to their own bathrooms decorated with greenery and a skylight. In between the bedrooms is a partially outdoor kitchen and living area that opens up to the yard. The common area includes a restaurant, a large swimming pool, and a game area with billiards and a small driving range, and the beach is a short drive away. Another draw is that the hotel is set in a typical Balinese neighborhood with *warungs,* away from anything remotely touristy.

Jalan Mertasari, Puri Prisklia 31x, Kerobokan, Bali. ✆ **361/8476028.** Fax 361/8476039. www.vivalavivillas.com. 6 units. $225–$286 2-bedroom villas. AE, MC, V. **Amenities:** Restaurant; bar; babysitting; fitness center; outdoor pool; room service; sauna; spa. *In room:* A/C, satellite TV, fridge, hair dryer, minibar, IDD phone, Wi-Fi.

Where to Dine

The international variety in Kuta is a result of homesick tourists; unfortunately, this translates into mediocre copies of Western fare. There are a couple of standouts, listed below.

KUTA

Golden Lotus Chinese Restaurant ★ 🏮 CHINESE Kuta's best-kept secret. Inside the Bali Dynasty Hotel, this elegant restaurant serves some of the finest Cantonese and Szechuan cuisine in Bali. Many guests also frequently stop in for all-you-can-eat dim sum, which include 60 varieties for only Rp85,000 (Sun 10am–2:30pm). The stir-fried beef and the fried prawns with yellow bean curd sauce are absolutely scrumptious.

In the Bali Dynasty Hotel, Jl. Kartika Plaza. ✆ **0361/752403.** Reservations recommended. Main courses Rp85,000–Rp105,000; set menu Rp105,000 and up for 6 dishes. AE, MC, V. Daily 11:30am–2:30pm and 6–10pm.

Kori Restaurant and Bar ★ INTERNATIONAL/STEAKHOUSE Valet parking in the narrow and chaotic Poppies Gang II? Finery uncharacteristic of Bali abounds at this chic venue. Sit in the dining room, replete with linen and silver, or on one of the more romantic cushioned bamboo platforms that bridge the narrow garden oasis.

The lunch menu is light, featuring dishes such as *malai köfte,* spicy vegetarian fritters in a curry sauce, or the mouth-burning Bali chile burger (if you dare). The dinner menu has all the bells and whistles of a Western steakhouse. Try the mixed grill of U.S. beef loin, spareribs, pork cutlet, and Nuerberger sausages; or order the Singapore chile crab, savory and spicy fresh black Bali crabs served with a big ol' bib. At the high end of the menu is the giant seafood grill, cooked and served on a hot lava stone. To finish off your meal, there's a respectable stock of brandy and cognac.

Poppies Gang II, Kuta. *©* **361/758605.** www.korirestaurant.co.id. Main courses Rp80,000–Rp150,000. AE, DC, MC, V. Daily noon–11pm.

Poppies Restaurant ★★ INDONESIAN/EUROPEAN   Poppies has a 30-year tradition of serving Indonesian and international specials on the busy beach. It's the place for your Western fix and is certainly the prettiest restaurant in the Kuta area: a garden setting with crawling vines overhead that keep the hot sun at bay, accompanied by babbling pools and waterfalls. Indonesian dishes include an outstanding *ikan pepes*—mashed fish cooked in a banana leaf with fine spices and very spicy local "pickles" (beware). The *mie goreng,* loaded with shrimp and vegetables, is also good. Service is slow, but this is a good place to dawdle.

Poppies Cottages, Poppies Lane I, Kuta. *©* **361/751059.** www.poppiesbali.com. Reservations recommended. Men must wear shirts. Main courses (Indonesian) Rp47,000–Rp66,000. AE, MC, V. Daily 8am–11pm.

TJ's Restaurant ★★ MEXICAN   Set up more like a typical Asian bistro, TJ's is a real Bali original. Stop in, if only for one of the famous frozen margaritas and to listen to some good tunes in this laid-back, open-air spot. Meals start with homemade corn chips, delicious dips, and an extensive menu of specials. TJ's advertises the "best burgers in town," and though the jury is still out on that one, most everything from the quesadillas to the fish Veracruz is delicious. Order up, kick back, and enjoy the vibe in this popular spot.

Poppies Lane 1/24, Kuta. *©* **361/751093.** www.tjsbali.com. Main courses Rp35,000–Rp100,000. MC, V. Daily 8:30am–11pm.

SEMINYAK

This northern stretch of the Kuta Beach area is *the* place for fine dining and hip nightlife. The restaurants listed below are only a few of the many bistros popping up. Check out Jalan Laksmana, called "Eat Street," crammed with a growing number of international cafes and restaurants. Highlights include modern Indonesian cuisine at **Chandi** (*©* **361/731060;** www.chandibali.com); Moroccan delights at **Khaima** (*©* **361/7423925;** www.khaimabali.com); and home-style Italian pizza and pastas at **Trattoria** (*©* **361/737082;** www.trattoriabali.com).

Ku De Ta ★★ BISTRO   This is Kuta's "Europe meets Asia" international bistro, aimed at an upscale clientele. It's also one of the town's hippest catwalks. The best time to go is at sunset, for the ocean views and lounge-worthy patio. Though the daytime ambience is dominated by the nearby beach, at night it's all about romantic lighting in the restaurant's open-air, minimalist rotunda. Add an elegant bar and a cigar lounge—complete with putting green—and you've got an all-purpose evening out. Happily, what comes out of the kitchen makes you want to stay: Try the signature dish of slow-roasted, yellow-curry duck or the chile-and-sea-salted squid with a mango/papaya marmalade. The cigar lounge is open from 6pm to late. The place roars with the carefree laughter of the ridiculously rich.

Jalan Oberoi 9, Seminyak. ✆ **361/736969.** www.kudeta.net. Reservations recommended. Main courses Rp300,000–Rp600,000. AE, MC, V. Daily 8am–midnight. Bar open later.

La Lucciola ★ ITALIAN   If there's a see-and-be-seen spot among the Kuta crowd, it's La Lucciola. Even breakfast draws the beautiful people, and why not, with its prime beachfront location on this deserted stretch of Legian. Morning eyepoppers include tasty ricotta hot cakes and smoked-salmon scrambled eggs on toasted focaccia. The dinner menu is equally enticing, with choice offerings such as lemon-grass bok choy risotto with sesame ginger, or oven-baked snapper with braised shallots and oregano. The seafood specials, calamari, and a unique prawn-and-snapper pie are tops, in addition to a complement of good pasta and traditional Italian fare. End with a bracing espresso and tiramisu.

Jalan Laksmana (Oberoi), Temple Petitenget, Kerobokan. ✆ **361/730838.** Main courses Rp80,000–Rp250,000. AE, MC, V. Daily 9am–11pm last order.

Made's Warung ★★ 🏠 INDONESIAN   This is a longtime Bali favorite, and for good reason. The original location is an open-air place at streetside in Kuta, but the new space in Seminyak is a big improvement—it's protected from the road and bustling with people, not beeping motorbikes. If it's busy, and it often is, don't be surprised if you end up sharing a table. *Gado gado,* satay, and curries are all recommended, and the price is right. Fun surprises on the menu include a bagel with smoked marlin, tofu burgers, and Caesar salad. Don't pass up the daily specials, particularly the fresh fish. Beverage choices range from iced coffee and juices to some very potent booze concoctions (be warned).

Br. Pando Mas, Kuta. ✆ **361/732130.** There's another location at Jalan Raya Seminyak, Seminyak (✆ **316/732130**). www.madeswarung.com. Main courses Rp30,000–Rp300,000. AE, MC, V. Daily 10am–11:30pm.

Metis ★ FRENCH/MEDITERRANEAN   This open-air 350-seat emporium houses a patisserie, bars, event space, an arts and interior shop, a jewelry boutique, and a women's fashion boutique. The French cuisine focuses on fois gras and seasonal truffles, white asparagus, and mushrooms. Vegetarians also have plenty of options.

Jl. Petitenget 6. ✆ **0361/737888.** www.metisbali.com. Reservations recommended. Lunch Rp90,000–Rp155,000; pasta Rp175,000–Rp205,000; seafood Rp185,000–Rp305,000; meat Rp170,000–Rp250,000. AE, MC, V. Daily noon–11pm.

Sardine ★★ SEAFOOD   Strikingly housed in a sprawling bamboo structure overlooking rice paddies, Sardines is equally inviting for a drink or a meal. A comfortable lounge area sits next to a pond, home to a school of very rare white koi carp—the chef assures us they will not end up on your table. The menu is made of predominately fish and organic greens. The owners have taken a tip from the locals and serve surprisingly delicious *arak* cocktails—no mean feat. Sardines of course are the house specialty on the daily changing menu.

Jl. Petitenget. ✆ **0361/738202.** www.sardinebali.com. Main courses Rp90,000–Rp180,000. MC, V. Tues–Sun noon–1am.

Sarong ★★ PAN-ASIAN   Chef Will Meyrick cooked and traveled throughout Asia, searching for the best street food and home cooking, and has brought his experiences—and some of the chefs—to a sophisticated dining room just north of Seminyak. The charm of Sarong is that Meyrick makes food fun—unlike most chefs, he doesn't take himself too seriously and gives plenty of credit to his Thai, Indian, and Indonesian chefs in the kitchen. The kitchen serves delicious lamb and fish curries, oysters, and Thai salads. Sarong also has an excellent bar worthy of a visit on its own accord. Keep an eye on the cool crowd via the huge overhanging gilt mirror.

Jl. Petitenget 19X. ✆ **0361/737809.** www.sarongbali.com. Reservations recommended. Main courses $15; set menu $30. AE, MC, V. Daily 7pm–1am.

Outdoor Activities

Surfers from all over are drawn to Kuta's stupendous breakers, which are at their best between March and July. Surf shops line the main drags and can help with rentals or tide information. Any hotel can arrange a private or group lesson, or you can contact **Rip Curl School of Surf** (✆ 361/735858; www.ripcurlschoolofsurf.com). Beginners start off at Kuta or Legian (with soft-sand beaches), but the legendary surf is at the low reef breaks and "barrels" of **Kuta Reef** at the southern end.

Unfortunately, the same surf makes recreational swimming virtually impossible. Even past the breakers, the current can be too strong. Pay close attention to swimming warnings and restrictions, and be very careful if you do swim. Tanning and splashing to cool off are about all that are left to do.

You can book adventure tours to destinations across the island using Kuta as a hub. For day trips to Ubud, the volcanoes, or the temples of central Bali, contact **Sobek Tours** (✆ 361/768050; www.balisobek.com), **Bali Adventure Tours** (✆ 361/721480; www.baliadventuretours.com), or **Bali Discovery Tours** (✆ 361/286283; www.balidiscovery.com). If money is no obstacle, take a ride on a helicopter to remote stretches of the island and pass over volcanoes and jungle scenery. Contact **Air Bali** (✆ 361/766582; www.airbali.com) for details.

And if the kids aren't getting enough of a kick out of the busy beach at Kuta, take 'em to the **Waterbom Park,** in the south end of Kuta on Jalan Kartika Plaza (✆ 361/755676; www.waterbom.com).

Shopping

Shopping in Kuta is inevitable. Even if you aren't interested in buying anything, the touts are quick to steer you none-too-subtly to their merchandise (usually by waving it in your face). The streets (particularly **Poppies Gang II**) are lined with stalls offering tie-dyed sarongs, shorts, swimsuits, knockoff brand-name cologne, hats, and wristwatches. Given the hard sell, this might be the best place to hone your bargaining skills.

Spa Treatments

There are some fine spas in the area, and most large hotels and resorts offer at least basic spa services. The newest spa in Kuta is **Theta Spa,** Jalan Kartika Plaza, on the beach, within the Ramada Bintang Bali Resort (✆ 361/755726; www.thetaspa.com); it is a pristine, white, two-level sanctuary overlooking the ocean. Equally luxurious are the Anantara Spa, on the top floor of the hotel, and the Spa at the Legian. For a good-value massage, head to the expat-friendly **Jari Menari** (✆ 361/736740; Jalan Raya Basangkasa; www.jarimenari.com) in Seminyak. For a bikini wax (which is hard to come by in Bali, strangely enough), head to **Glo** (Jalan Kunti; ✆ 361/766762).

The eastern side of Jalan Laksmana (aka "eat street") is full of fledgling clothing designers, many of them foreigners living in Bali. Some of the better women's boutiques include Franklin Lee at No. 34A, Magali Pascal at No. 65B, and Paul Ropp at No. 39 with his wild Betsey-Johnson-meets-South-Asian styles. Uluwatu Lace, with locations around the island, sells elegant styles. These labels aren't cheap—dresses and shirts start around $100.

For the more budget-minded, a nice chain of beachwear and clubby outfits can be found at Body & Soul, with several outlets in Kuta and around the island. Surfer Girl, on Jalan Legian (© **361/752693**), has a good collection of women's swimwear and active clothing.

Kuta Square has many international brands including Nike, Polo, and Armani, plus fast-food outlets such as McDonald's and KFC. The Discovery Mall contains the British department store Marks & Spencer, along with a Starbucks and Coffee Bean & Tea Leaf. The **Galleria Bali** (© **361/761945;** www.dfsgalleria.com)—a new luxury shopping mall with duty-free goods by Chanel, Coach, and other big brands—offers shuttles from many hotels.

For books, stop by **Periplus,** with locations in Kuta Square (© **361/763988**), in Seminyak near Made's Warung (© **361/734843**), and even at the airport.

Kuta & Seminyak After Dark

Kuta is party central, going full-on from 11pm to dawn every night. Clubs and bars abound, each with its own flavor, though they're mostly "same-same but different." Thankfully, it is all pretty family-friendly and not the go-go bar scene you'd find in parts of Thailand and other Southeast Asian destinations.

Start your evening at **SOS,** the rooftop bar at the Anantara (p. 592), which features lounge-worthy padded beds that offer prime views of ocean sunsets. Or make your way to the much-hyped bistro and bar **Ku De Ta ★** (p. 595), which has been going strong for years, particularly for cocktails at sunset. **Sea Circus** (Jalan Laksmana 22; © **361/738667**), a cozy newcomer located near The Oberoi and The Legian, serves delicious seafood and cocktails well into the evening. For a classy, romantic ambience, head to the sophisticated **Living Room** (© **361/735735;** www.thelivingroom-bali.com). For the club crowd, the hottest beachside spots at the moment include **Hu'u Bar ★** (Jalan Dhyana Pura, Seminyak; © **361/736443;** www.huubali.com) and the new **Cocoon Beach Club** (Jalan Double Six 66; © **361/731266;** www.cocoon-beach.com), with poolside dining and drinks. **Kama Sutra** (© **361/761999**), chock-full of local teenagers, is a busy club on the north end of Kuta; it has nightly shows and features local bands. Vibrant **Q Bar,** Jl. Dhyana Pura (© **0361/730927**), throbs with DJ music, live drag shows, and an enthusiastic patronage of trendy gay men.

Side Trips from Kuta

Uluwatu ★★ is a spectacular pinnacle of land at the far south of Bali. A visit at dusk reveals a sunset panorama framed by frolicking monkeys. At the right times of year, it has some of the best surfing in the world. Arrange trips to Uluwatu, Tanah Lot (see below), or sights listed later in this chapter under "Side Trips from Ubud" (p. 617) by contacting any hotel concierge or tour desk. Daily car rental (with driver) starts as low as $20.

Tanah Lot ★ Founded by a Brahmin priest in the 16th century, the temple at Tanah Lot is notable less for its construction than for its spectacular setting, high on craggy bluffs overlooking the Java Sea. This is a truly magnificent example of how well temples in Bali are wedded to their locations, be they lakeside, mountainside, or seaside. Legend has it that a Brahmin priest had a rivalry with the local, established priest that nearly led to his expulsion from the order; instead, he meditated so hard he pushed Tanah Lot "out to sea," where it rests on an inlet that actually becomes an island at high tide. The walk from the parking lot is not as long or as steep as at many other sites, and there are no stairs. Non-Hindus cannot enter the temple, but may access the other parts of the complex strung out across the rocks. Many of these afford stunning views. Try to come at sunset, when Tanah Lot is truly glorious.

15km (9⅓ miles) west of Denpasar. Admission Rp3,000. Daily during daylight hours.

JIMBARAN BAY ★★

Jimbaran has some of the best sandy beaches in South Bali, and the clear, calm water is great for swimming. Developers were quick to realize this; thus, Jimbaran now hosts some of the finest high-end resorts on the island. Despite development, the town still looks like a fishing village, with small mom-and-pop seafood shacks serving up some of the best fish dishes on the island. It's a worthy day trip from Kuta for good eats alone, and the many resorts make it a comfy place to stay.

Getting There

Jimbaran is on the road to Nusa Dua, south of Kuta. Cabs are plentiful.

Where to Stay

The area around Uluwatu temple is being developed by a number of luxury resorts.

VERY EXPENSIVE

Alila Villas Uluwatu ★★ This brand-new, top-of-the-line eco-resort has Green Globe's stamp of approval, meaning all of the materials are sustainable or recycled and the use of water and energy meets their stringent requirements. Perched on a plateau of wild savanna landscape, every villa has a spectacular ocean view and its own pool. The hotel also offer "Alila Journeys," half-day wellness programs that include yoga and meditation classes and self-care recommendations, Bali arts and crafts, culinary experiences, and excursions. While staying here, slip into the cliff-top Sunset Cabana for dinner at dusk and simply get inebriated on the sea air and stars.

Jl. Belimbing Sari, Banjar Tambiyak, Desa Pecatu. © **0361/8482166.** Fax 0361/8482188. www.alila hotels.com. 85 units. High season $800 and up; low season $725 and up. AE, MC, V. **Amenities:** 3 restaurants; babysitting; gym; outdoor pool; spa. *In room:* A/C, TV/DVD, hair dryer, minibar, MP3 docking station, Wi-Fi.

Four Seasons Resort at Jimbaran Bay ★★★ The very picture of luxury, the exquisitely landscaped grounds of the Four Seasons are on a stunning hillside overlooking the bay. The layout is meant to suggest a series of Balinese villages, each thatched villa consisting of a large bedroom, generous dressing area, and marble bathroom with oversize tub. The resort's horizon pool blends seamlessly with the ocean blue, and there are other small pools and lots of private corners where you can

relax and escape from it all. Walk or be driven in a golf cart down to the beach, passing *bales* (open-air pavilions) and viewing spots along the way. The luxe beach club has all the same amenities as the pool, plus plenty of watersports activities including surfing, kayaking, and sailing on catamarans. Though the other Four Seasons Bali property, at Sayan, is equally luxurious, Jimbaran is preferable for its romantic vibe, convenient location, and superb service.

Jimbaran, Bali. ✆ **361/701010.** Fax 361/701020. www.fourseasons.com. 147 units. $680–$920 1-bedroom villa; $1,700–$3,100 2-bedroom villa and Royal Villa. AE, DC, MC, V. **Amenities:** 3 restaurants; 2 bars; babysitting; concierge; health club; Internet access (in business center); Jacuzzi; 2 outdoor pools; room service; sauna; spa; tennis courts; watersports equipment rental. *In room:* A/C, satellite TV, DVD player, stereo w/CD player, fridge, minibar, IDD phone, Wi-Fi.

Karma Kandara ★★ ☺ This unique and luxurious set of villas, which sits on a stunning cliff near the Uluwatu temple, is the brainchild of John Spence, a music entrepreneur who has worked with singers such as Boy George. He models his resorts after ultraluxury resorts including the Aman, but amenities like a complimentary kids' club give the place a family-oriented feel. The small and unassuming lobby leads down a path lined with high stone walls, giving each villa optimum privacy. The villas are decorated with modern teak furnishing and earth tones, but the real draw is the vantage points each of the villas offers: Each private infinity pool leads the eye to a horizon of unobstructed views of the Indian Ocean. Try Mediterranean restaurant di Mare for fine dining, or take the funicular down to the Nammos Beach Club bar and restaurant with its own secluded beach.

Jalan Villa Kandara, Banjar Wijaya Kusuma, Ungasan, Bali. ✆ **361/8482200.** Fax 361/8482201. www.karmakandara.com. 40 villas. $865–$8,000 villa. AE, MC, V. **Amenities:** 2 restaurants; bar; kids' club; golf (nearby); fitness center; Internet access (in business center); outdoor pool; complimentary room service; spa; cooking classes. *In room:* A/C, satellite TV, DVD player, hair dryer, fully equipped kitchen, minibar, IDD phone, Wi-Fi.

EXPENSIVE

Ayana Resort & Spa ★★ The doormen still greet guests occasionally with "Welcome to the Ritz-Carlton." The Ayana, as it is now known, hasn't strayed from its former management, since the resort is run by an ex-Ritz-Carlton executive. You can still expect the same anticipatory service chasing you around the 77 hectares (190 acres) overlooking Jimbaran Bay. Each room is decorated in muted colors with a touch of sea blue to match. The resort has its own private beach. Facilities include five swimming pools, six wedding venues, renowned restaurants, private villas, and more. Do not miss treating yourself to a rejuvenating water-treatment session at the **Thallaso Spa**. The new **Rock Bar** has to be one of the best beach bars on the island.

Jl. Karang Mas Sejahtera Jimbaran. ✆ **0361/702222.** Fax 0361/701555. www.ayanaresort.com. 368 units. $350–$450 double; $500–$600 suite; $700–$1,000 villa. AE, MC, V. **Amenities:** 3 restaurants, Kisik, Dava, and Honzen 97; bar; babysitting; kids' club; gym; Jacuzzi; outdoor pool; room service; spa; tennis court. *In room:* A/C, TV/DVD, hair dryer, minibar, MP3 docking station, Wi-Fi.

MODERATE

Jimbaran Puri Bali ★★ The pioneer resort on Jimbaran beach, the Puri Bali, originally the Pansea, has stylish, self-contained garden cottages scattered among lily ponds, coconut trees, and statuary, set back from the beautiful beach. Despite its top location, this is not a big resort and you won't have to fight for sun loungers or crawl your way through the crowd to get to the breakfast area. All cottages have terraces, shaded by umbrellas, with privacy-providing screens and outdoor deck showers. Rooms are done in carved teak under thatched roofing, with mosquito netting and natural linen touches. Bathrooms have sunken tubs and all the goodies. The resort is a haven of privacy and calm, a good choice for getting away from it all.

Jl. Uluwatu, Jimbaran. © **0361/701605.** Fax 0361/701320. www.jimbaranpuribali.com. 41 units. Peak season $270–$580 cottage, $680–$950 pool villa; high season $220–$520 cottage, $610–$860 pool villa; low season $200–$500 cottage, $530–$700 pool villa. AE, MC, V. **Amenities:** 2 restaurants; bar; babysitting; outdoor pool; room service. In room: A/C, satellite TV, DVD player, fridge, hair dryer, minibar.

INEXPENSIVE

Puri Bambu 🎁 Although Puri Bambu has no beachfront, it is in Kedonganan, a peaceful traditional village near Jimbaran, and the beach is only 5 minutes' walk away. The large rooms frame lovely garden courtyards, one of which holds a decent-size pool. Be sure to take an early-morning or early-evening walk around the village to get a feel for the age-old traditions that make Bali so beautiful.

Jl. Pengeracikan, Kedonganan. © **0361/701468.** www.puribambu.com. 48 units. High season $65–$95; low season $50–$80; extra bed $12. MC, V. **Amenities:** Cafe; bar; babysitting; concierge; Internet; outdoor pool; room service. In room: A/C, TV, hair dryer, minibar.

Where to Dine

For lunch or an early-evening dinner (or just a drink), the best place to head is **Nammos Beach Club** at Karma Kandara (see above). You'll descend in a funicular down a steep cliff to a small strip of protected beach, where an alternative scene of hip young families (think parents who haven't given up the Ibiza lifestyle, with kids in tow) and 20-somethings chow on pizza and tapas and drink martinis. Try **PJ's** at the Four Seasons for a beachside Sunday brunch. But remember, folks come from far and wide for the good, fresh seafood barbecue, priced by the pound, served at beachside. Look for **Menega Cafe** (© **361/705888;** www.menega.com/cafe.html), which stands out for its more unique grilling approach, among the row of restaurants that basically offer the same thing. Lobster and snapper are served with dipping sauces, rice, cucumber salad, and spinach cooked in sweet chile. Follow it up with some fresh fruit. It's romantic at sunset and afterward by candlelight—and it's inexpensive too.

NUSA DUA ★

In the 1970s, a French firm, commissioned by the Indonesian government, came up with the idea for a self-contained resort complex to "minimize the impact of tourism on the Balinese culture." It chose this 300-hectare (741-acre) tract of undeveloped land, devoid of any infrastructure, and basically transformed it into a theme park. Nusa Dua is now a roster of five-star, all-inclusive properties, all secluded and finely manicured. The beaches are clean and blissfully tout free, but it can all seem a bit sterile. Still, it's suitable for families and business conventions.

Getting There

Most hotels in Nusa Dua offer airport pickup, but you can find shuttles and cheap taxis at the airport and in Kuta. (Be sure to take only the official blue-and-yellow metered taxis in Kuta.) *Bemos* from Denpasar go to Nusa Dua by way of Kuta and Jimbaran.

Getting Around

These big resorts make it so comfortable, you won't have to leave the grounds—but even the most starry-eyed honeymooners might want a break from expensive hotel meals. Most hotel taxis are rentable at an exorbitant $11 per hour; it's smarter to hire a car and driver for a day from a private company such as **Amertha Dana** (✆ 361/735406). A new swanky mall in Nusa Dua, the **Bali Collection** (✆ 361/771662;** www.bali-collection.com), has an hourly shuttle that makes the rounds to most of the hotels.

Where to Stay
NUSA DUA

Nusa Dua is like a Disneyland of high-end hotels and resorts. Most of the properties have their own private beaches, and many offer babysitting (some include it in the price of the room), making it a good option for families (unless otherwise noted). A good share of honeymooners come here as well. The atmosphere is a bit sterile, but you'll at least avoid the touts and tacky tourists in places such as Kuta.

Very Expensive

Amanusa ★★ Typical of the refined Aman resorts in Ubud and Candi (among others), the Amanusa boasts a magnificent setting on a high hilltop overlooking a golf course and the beaches of Nusa Dua beyond. Rooms are crafted in rich redwood with four-poster beds, sunken tubs, and outdoor and indoor showers. Each suite has a small *bale,* or covered sitting area, with a stylish daybed for lounging. Cozy nooks, such as the library, abound; the central 24m (79-ft.) pool is stunning; and in-house dining at the Terrace is an experience in itself, with great views and delicious local cuisine. The beach club is just a short drive down the hill; it's a collection of private *bales* that front the Bali Golf and Country Club property.

Nusa Dua, Bali. ✆ **361/772333.** Fax 361/772335. www.amanresorts.com. 35 units. $850–$1,500 suite; $1,250–$1,650 pool suite. AE, MC, V. **Amenities:** 2 restaurants; bar; babysitting; bike rental; concierge; golf course; Internet access (in library); outdoor pool; room service; smoke-free rooms; 2 tennis courts; watersports equipment rental. *In room:* A/C, TV w/DVD and stereo, fridge, minibar, IDD phone.

Balé ★★ *Balé* means "bungalow" in Balinese, but the moniker is rather modest—this is a beautiful collection of villas set on a hill overlooking the ocean. After being ushered into a high-ceilinged, open-air lobby, you'll climb a set of steps that lead to the villas, all of which are walled off for privacy. Each has its own plunge pool and a daybed in the courtyard for lounging. The interiors are elegantly simple, with large bathrooms and outdoor showers. Rivers of water flow around the property; the scent of the tropical flower ylang-ylang wafts throughout. While not set right on the beach, the Balé has a shuttle that whisks you to the water in 2 minutes. The resort is popular with yuppies and a fair number of gay couples as well. For adults seeking peace, an added bonus is that no children 14 and under are allowed.

If the private-villa-no-children-allowed concept appeals to you but the Balé seems too expensive, try the slightly cheaper **Kayumanis** (✆ 361/770777), a property nearby that features 20 private villas, though it doesn't have the view and the beach access that Balé provides.

Jalan Raya Nusa Dua Selatan, P.O. Box 76, Nusa Dua, Bali. ✆**361/775111.** Fax 361/775222. www.thebale. com. 20 units. $600–$800 double; $900–$1,000 suite. AE, DC, MC, V. No children 14 and under accepted. **Amenities:** Restaurant; bar; nearby golf; fitness center; outdoor pool; room service; spa; Wi-Fi (free in library). *In room:* A/C, satellite TV, DVD player, fridge, minibar, IDD phone.

St. Regis Bali ★★ From the private concierge who whisks you through airport immigration and baggage claim to the personal butler who is assigned to each room or villa, the emphasis at the St. Regis is on service. A number of the private villas have private access to a 3,408-sq.-m (36,680-sq.-ft.) swimmable lagoon that sits at the center of the resort, while other villas sit directly beachfront. Rooms and villas are tastefully decorated with Balinese and colonial-style furniture. The resort also pays special attention to food, with top-notch quality at all the outlets featuring a beachside continental restaurant, buffet, and gourmet deli—the only hazard is overindulging yourself with all the choices.

Kawasan Pariwisata Nusa Dua Lot S6, Nusa Dua, Bali.(ⓒ **361/8478111.** Fax 361/8478099. www.stregis. com/bali. 123 units, including suites, villas, and residences. $750–$4,500 suite; $1,350–$3,000 villa. AE, DC, MC, V. **Amenities:** 3 restaurants; bar; nearby golf; fitness center; 2 very large outdoor pools; room service; spa; watersports equipment rental. *In room:* A/C, satellite TV, fridge, minibar, IDD phone.

Expensive

Laguna Resort & Spa Nusa Dua ★ A former Sheraton, the rooms, once flower-fussy, have turned modern. The main draws remain the beachfront and the meandering lagoonlike pool, which can be accessed directly by ladders from some of the ground-floor rooms. Bathrooms are large and done in marble. The amenities, such as the classy restaurants and spa, have also undergone dramatic face-lifts.

P.O. Box 77, Nusa Dua, Bali.(ⓒ **361/771327.** Fax 361/771326. www.luxurycollection.com/bali. 270 units. $350–$380 double; $575–$3,050 suite. AE, DC, MC, V. **Amenities:** 3 restaurants; 3 bars; nearby golf; fitness center; Jacuzzi; motorbike rental; 7 outdoor pools; room service; spa; tennis court; watersports equipment rental; Wi-Fi (in business center). *In room:* A/C, satellite TV w/in-house movies, fridge, hair dryer, minibar, IDD phone.

Westin Resort Nusa Dua 🏄 ☺ Catering to conventioneers and business travelers, this resort is nicely outfitted for those who want to combine a few hours of telecommuting with their vacation. The hotel is also a good choice for families, with little touches for the kids including a separate check-in area, special buffet counter at breakfast, and, most important, a kids' club with complimentary babysitting all day long. With these amenities and rates as low as $150 for a double during the low season, the Westin is a bargain for families. Beachside daybeds, where you can get spa treatments, are the perfect place to unwind. It's a high-quality version of the McDonald's experience—that is, you know what you're going to get: great service, fantastic dining options, and beds so comfortable they're branded the "Heavenly Beds."

P.O. Box 36, Nusa Dua, Bali. ⓒ **361/771906.** Fax 361/771908. www.starwood.com. 334 units. $340–$410 double; $655–$955 suite. AE, DC, MC, V. **Amenities:** 3 restaurants; 4 bars; nearby golf; fitness center; Jacuzzi; motorbike rental; 3 outdoor pools (and kids' pool); room service; spa; tennis court; watersports equipment rental. *In room:* A/C, satellite TV w/in-house movies, fridge, hair dryer, Internet access, minibar, IDD phone.

TANJUNG BENOA

Just north of Nusa Dua along the coast is the fishing village of Benoa. The labyrinth of streets in this town makes for a good stroll, certainly more interesting than sterile Nusa Dua.

Expensive

The Conrad ★★★ ☺ The most family-friendly of Bali's resorts, the Conrad has over 300m (1,000 ft.) of pristine beach fronting a calm, child-safe lagoon—and a plethora of activities. Friendly, switched-on staffers guide older kids and parents in watersports like kayaking, parasailing, sailing, and wakeboarding; they also run the

Kura Kura Kid's Club, where younger kids participate in Balinese arts and crafts, kite making, and sand-castle building. The rooms are spacious and contemporary. There is even a children's hair salon. The rooms have a refreshing contemporary feel with natural linen covers, dark woods, and impressive original Indonesian tribal art pieces. The Deluxe Lagoon rooms have full ocean views, and you can dive off your terrace into the lagoon.

Jl. Pratama 168, Tanjung Benoa. © **0361/778788.** Fax 0361/778780. www.conradhotels.com. 360 units. High season $310–$650; low season $210–$450. AE, MC, V. **Amenities:** 3 restaurants; bar; babysitting; bikes; kids' club; gym; Jacuzzi; outdoor pool; room service; spa; tennis court; watersports; Wi-Fi. *In room:* A/C, TV/DVD, hair dryer, minibar.

Moderate

Novotel Coralia Benoa Bali ★ This hotel is slightly more upscale than your typical Novotel. Public spaces are grand, and the design throughout reflects Bali. Opt for the "beach cabanas," even bigger suites in semiprivate bungalows (two per pavilion), complete with outdoor stone tubs—most of them honeymoon worthy. Rooms throughout are big, bright, and airy, decorated in a minimalist Asian style with coconut wood. Each of the three pools has its own flair, though none is very big. Lots of activities, including aerobics, soccer, a kids' club, and dance and cooking lessons, will keep you on the run if you like. The free shuttle to Nusa Dua is convenient for touring, but given that this is the best of both worlds—a terrific resort and authentic Bali—it's hard to see that you would need it.

Jalan Pratama Tanjung Benoa, P.O. Box 39, Nusa Dua, Bali. © **361/772239.** Fax 361/772237. www.novotelbali.com. 190 units. $149–$184 double; $218–$253 beach cabana. AE, DC, MC, V. **Amenities:** 2 restaurants; 2 bars; airport shuttle service; babysitting; kids' club; fitness center; Internet access; 3 outdoor pools; room service; spa; tennis court; library. *In room:* A/C, satellite TV, fridge, minibar, IDD phone.

Rumah Bali ★★ ♦ This bed-and-breakfast is one of the best values in Bali. The bungalows feature outdoor kitchens and generous bathrooms (with outdoor shower); deluxe bungalows get their own plunge pool. The people who run this hotel also own Bumbu Bali, the restaurant and cooking school, and they'll send a chef over to cook all your meals if you wish. The peaceful pool area is set in a garden, while the beach is just a 5-minute walk away. If you're on a budget, you can stay here and use the beachside pool at the restaurant Tao for something close to a five-star experience.

Jalan Pratama Tanjung Benoa, P.O. Box 132, Nusa Dua, Bali. © **361/771256.** Fax 361/771258. www.balifoods.com. 10 units. $73–$93 bungalow. AE, MC, V. **Amenities:** 2 restaurants; outdoor pool; tennis court; cooking school. *In room:* A/C, satellite TV, kitchen, minibar, IDD phone.

Where to Dine

Most of Nusa Dua's dining takes place in pricey hotels. **Kayuputi** at the St. Regis (p. 603) serves delicious Continental and Mediterranean cuisine in a stand-alone modern white bungalow on the beach. The outdoor tables, covered with trellises, are particularly romantic. **Bumbu Bali** (Jalan Pratama; © **361/774502;** www.balifoods.com), run by former Grand Hyatt chef Heinz von Holzen, serves authentic Balinese food in a well appointed environment. The restaurant also offers entertaining **cooking classes ★★** on Mondays, Wednesdays, and Fridays. Across from the Ramada Resort is the fusion restaurant **Tao** (Jalan Pratama 96; © **361/772902;** www.taobali.com), decorated with Buddhist statues and featuring a lagoon pool, lounge chairs, and beachside tables where diners are free to laze about all day. **The**

Conrad (Jalan Pratama 168; ✆ **0361/778788**) is home to two outstanding restaurants, **Rin,** featuring Japanese cuisine, and **Eight Degrees South,** an outdoor barbecue joint.

Outdoor Activities

Unlike Kuta, the surf here is a considerable distance offshore, making swimming in the clear blue-green water most pleasant at high tide (at low tide, it's only ankle-high). It's a popular surf, windsurf, and jet-ski spot. Dive excursions, all arranged by the hotels, will probably take you to areas closer to Sanur or to Amed and Tambulen in the northeast.

The **Bali Golf and Country Club** (✆ **361/771791;** www.baligolfandcountry club.com) sits at the southern tip of the island and has sweeping views of the beaches and clear waters off Nusa Dua. It has a fine course, worth the whopping $165 outlay to the serious enthusiast.

Shopping

A mall called the **Bali Collection** (✆ **361/771662;** www.bali-collection.com) offers some of the same shopping you'll find in Kuta (without the crowded streets and the touts), as well as a Starbucks and the Japanese department store Sogo, which has great cosmetic counters and name-brand clothing labels.

UBUD ★★

For a thorough exploration of Balinese culture and tradition, Ubud is the place. Unfortunately, since the release of the movie *Eat, Pray, Love,* the once-quiet area has become congested with tour buses. Though unabashedly touristic, the town is the cultural pulse of the island, the richest region in Bali for art production, and the very reason why so many expat artists and collectors have made Bali their home. Ubud has a royal legacy and hosts the **Royal Palace,** a center for cultural performances and dance. In and among the smaller streets of town, you'll find refined boutiques, chic galleries, and cool trinket shops, alongside open-air cafes that swallow passersby on lazy days. Outside the busy town labyrinth, the phosphorescent rice paddies, virgin jungle, gorges, and river valleys of this hilly Shangri-La are ripe for exploration. Ubud's central location makes the whole island accessible as a day trip. About the only thing it doesn't have is a beach, but they're all a short drive away.

Getting There

Many hotels in the area offer pickup service, and taxis connect from the airport, about an hour away. *Bemos* drop you in the center of town, while the tourist shuttles have their own stops, usually on one of the two main drags.

Getting Around

Central Ubud is small enough to see on foot, and hotels away from the main action generally provide regular shuttles into town. The main street is Jalan Raya, which runs east-west; Monkey Forest Road runs perpendicular. Transport touts in town are quite aggressive; **minivans** are for hire on every corner for either day trips or the short jaunt across town. A superb private driver is **Gusti Ngurah Nariasa** (✆ **081/ 23928171**), who often works for the Chedi Club.

Ubud is a good a place to rent a motorbike (Rp50,000 per day) if you're an experienced rider. Bicycles are available for hire at two or three streetside locations along Monkey Forest Road for about Rp10,000.

Visitor Information & Tours

The **information kiosk,** on Jalan Raya (☏ 361/973285), on the south side of the main street near the intersection with Monkey Forest Road, is a good place to start. There are also travel agencies all over town, each offering competitive prices for day trips and shuttles to other tourist areas.

[FastFACTS] UBUD

Currency Exchange There are plenty of ATMs on the main road and along Monkey Forest Road. The best money-changer is **Central Kuta** (☏ 0361/974381), on Jalan Raya Ubud in front of Museum Puri Lukisan, and in between Permata Bank and Animale shop.

Internet Access Ubud has several Internet cafes, including **Pizza Bagus** (☏ 361/978520). The cheapest and the fastest-speed connection are **Netvice Internet,** Jl. Hanoman 35A, Padang Tegal; on Jalan Raya Ubud, **Bali 3000 Internet Cafe** (☏ 0361/978538) and **Highway Internet Cafe** (☏ 0361/972107); **Fairway Café & Internet,** Jl. Dewi Sita (☏ 0361/978810); and **Triscom.net,** Jl. Kajeng 4 (☏ 0361/971898).

Mail The post office is on the main road, but very far to the east. Major hotels offer postal service.

Telephones The area code in Ubud is **361.**

Where to Stay

No matter what your budget is, Ubud has it all, from sublime honeymoon compounds to the humblest cottage. Below is an assortment of options, both in central Ubud and outside of town. Staying at the more rural properties might mean a long walk or ride, but the scenery is breathtaking.

VERY EXPENSIVE

Amandari ★★★ If you have serious disposable income, a stay at the Amandari ensures the kind of luxurious seclusion and unrivaled service afforded celebrities (it's where Mick Jagger and Jerry Hall got married). Laid out like a fanciful Balinese village, the plush rooms are housed within huge stone cottages roofed in thatch. Each suite is enclosed in its own walled compound and appointed with every kingly comfort (some even have a private pool). Amandari is over-the-top without sacrificing local charm: There are outdoor tubs and indoor showers, Balinese decor, and a unique connection to the surrounding villages. The resort looks out over a beautiful jungle gorge; the Amandari's emerald-green infinity-edge pool mimics the color, to blend seamlessly with the green beyond. There is a free shuttle to Ubud, but it's hard to imagine wanting to leave very often. The terrific restaurant has a bar and serves local and European favorites.

Kedewatan, Ubud, Bali. ☏ **361/975333.** Fax 361/975335. www.amandari.com. 30 units. $800–$1,000 double; $3,700 villa. AE, DC, MC, V. **Amenities:** Restaurant; bar; babysitting; free bikes; concierge; golf course; health club; Jacuzzi; outdoor pool; room service; spa; tennis courts. *In room:* A/C, fridge, hair dryer, minibar, IDD phone, Wi-Fi.

Chedi Club at Tanah Gajah ★★★ One of the best resorts in all of Bali, the Chedi Club offers a small number of luxurious yet cozy villas set in rice fields and accompanied by highly tailored personal service. The freebies offered here—including breakfast brought to your villa, butler service, afternoon tea, evening drinks, yoga lessons, escorted treks, and airport transfers—make other hotels seem stingy. Your private courtyard offers shaded daybeds, plunge pools with rice-paddy views, a huge outdoor tub, and Bose speakers that link with an indoor stereo system that you can hook up to your iPod. The bedrooms, decorated in wood tones and Balinese art, are just as luxe. After a stay at the Chedi Club, it's likely that you'll compare every other resort to the experience and discover that they simply don't match up.

Jalan Goa Gajah, Tengkulak Kaja, Ubud, Bali. © **361/975685.** Fax 361/975686. www.ghmhotels.com. 20 units. $360–$410 1-bedroom villa; $920–$970 2-bedroom villa. Rates include breakfast, afternoon tea, and evening drinks. AE, DC, MC, V. **Amenities:** Restaurant; bar; airport shuttle service; health club; outdoor pool; spa; tennis court. *In room:* A/C, TV, DVD player, Bose stereo w/CD player, fridge, free high-speed Internet access, free minibar, IDD phone.

COMO Shambhala ★★★ This resort and wellness spa dubs itself "The Estate," assigns P.A.s (personal assistants, that is) to its guests, and runs a raw-food restaurant, Glow, on its beautiful 40-hectare (99-acre) property set right on the steep Ayung River gorge. The Estate satisfies guests of all sensibilities, from the ultra-high-maintenance to those who are simply seeking to completely unwind. Each private, stand-alone villa comes decorated with elegant antiquelike furniture, a four-poster bed flanked with curtains, and beautiful semioutdoor bathrooms with classy fixtures. Balconies, which overlook lush jungle with chirping cicadas and lively squirrels, are outfitted with lounge chairs that make an ideal place to read and rest, while a nearby semiprivate infinity pool is available for lap swimming. The resort also encourages guests to experience its wellness programs. With half a dozen foreign staff members including an Ayurvedic doctor, a psychologist, and a Pilates instructor, custom detox or therapy programs can be arranged for guests. Even if you don't stay here, it's worth a visit to try the delicious food at Glow and to do the 1-hour walk around the grounds.

Begawan Giri, P.O. Box 54, Ubud, Gianyar, Bali. © **361/978888.** Fax 361/978889. www.cse.como.bz. 20 units. $720–$1,720 1-bedroom villa; $3,385–$3,570 2-bedroom villa. AE, DC, MC, V. **Amenities:** 2 restaurants; bar; free airport transfer; health club; 9 outdoor pools; aqua therapy pool; room service; spa; tennis court; library. *In room:* A/C, TV, DVD player, CD player, fridge, minibar, IDD phone, free Wi-Fi and broadband.

Four Seasons Resort at Sayan ★★ The Four Seasons here is a masterpiece of planning that takes full advantage of its extraordinary setting right on the River Ayung. It's incredibly posh, though not intimidatingly so. You enter across a long bridge leading to a lily pond that, almost unbelievably, rests atop the lobby, all in an immense crater of rice terraces. The design throughout is ultramodern, but with references to Balinese tradition. Guests stay in two-story suites (bedroom below the sitting area), deluxe suites, or high-end villas with private plunge pools. Interiors are done in gleaming woods and natural fabrics, highlighted by precious local art and artifacts. Every room has views of the deep-green gorge and/or the river. Expect luxurious bathrooms with huge tubs, showers, and dressing areas, and more plush towels than a linen shop. The two-level horizon pool follows the serpentine shape of the river below. Pampering, of course, is at a maximum and includes "seamless" transfer between here and the Four Seasons at Jimbaran Bay; the staff takes care of everything—including, if you wish, your packing. There is also regular shuttle service to Ubud.

Sayan, Ubud, Bali. © 361/977577. Reservations line is © 361/701010. Fax 361/977588. www.four seasons.com. 60 units. $680–$880 1-bedroom villa; $2,100–$2,400 2-bedroom villa; $3,100–$3,500 3-bedroom villa. AE, DC, MC, V. **Amenities:** 2 restaurants; bar; bike rentals; health club; outdoor pool; room service; spa; watersports rentals; library w/games. *In room:* A/C, TV, stereo w/CD player, fridge, free high-speed Internet access, minibar, IDD phone.

EXPENSIVE

Alila Ubud ★ A good value, the Alila Ubud overlooks a stunning northern portion of the Ayung Gorge, one of the most scenic stretches of the popular rafting trips that go through here. The infinity-edge swimming pool was voted one of the "50 Most Spectacular Pools in the World" by *Travel + Leisure;* it's like a cube of water in otherworldly (or at least unlikely) suspension over the spectacular gorge. Accommodations are large and luxe, with top amenities (though no bathtubs), and the Mandara Spa complex offers deluxe spa treatments for reasonable prices. The resort is far from town, but it's perfectly self-contained and offers regular shuttle service.

Desa Melinggih Kelod, Payangan, Gianyar, Bali. © 361/975963. Fax 361/975968. www.alilahotels.com. 64 units. $260–$560 double; $570–$670 villa. AE, MC, V. **Amenities:** Restaurant; bar; airport transfer; babysitting; bike rental; concierge; Internet access (in library and TV room); Jacuzzi; outdoor pool; room service; sauna; spa. *In room:* A/C, TV, fridge, hair dryer, minibar, IDD phone.

Bambu Indah ★★ Savvy travelers with an environmental bent will think they have died and gone to heaven. Bambu Indah ("Beautiful Bamboo") is the creation of the multitalented team of the Green School. The four antique teak *joglo* have the most fantastic view of the Sayan ridge and the Ayung. Just past the swimming pool that could be mistaken for a natural pond and past the working rice fields is the temple Pura Dalem Gede Bongkasa. (The temple is not easily accessible as it requires a trek through small back roads. If you make it there, bring your own sarong and sash.) There is no cafe or restaurant on-site but home-cooked organic meals are delivered to your porch at any time of day.

Br. Baung, Sayan-Ubud. © 0361/977922. Fax 0361/974404. www.bambuindah.com. 7 villas. Peak season $180–$280; high season $175–$275; low season $160–$260. Rates include breakfast. MC, V. **Amenities:** Lounge; babysitting; bikes; outdoor pool; room service; Wi-Fi. *In villa:* A/C, hair dryer, minibar.

Komaneka Resort ★ Located on Monkey Forest Road right in the center of town, the Komaneka is clean, modern, and chic. Tracing a long, narrow corridor ending in a small pool with an elegant vanishing edge, guest buildings are well away from street noise and have views of gardens and rice paddies. Accommodations are done in a cool, contemporary style with shiny marble tiles and spartan wooden furnishings. The decor employs lots of natural woods and fabrics, and the beds are hung with netting suspended from the thatched ceiling. Deluxe units have unique bathrooms: Some feature outdoor-type showers and tubs, while others have sunken marble tubs. The owners also run a high-end resort north of town called **Komaneka Tanggayuda,** a more deluxe compound of suites and pool villas from $220.

Monkey Forest Rd., Ubud, Bali. © 361/976090. Fax 361/977140. www.komaneka.com. 20 units. $193–$250 double; $330 garden or pool villa. AE, DC, MC, V. **Amenities:** Restaurant; outdoor pool; room service; full spa; library. *In room:* A/C, TV, DVD player, CD player, fridge, minibar, IDD phone.

Maya Ubud Resort & Spa ★★ This fine resort is a short hop outside of Ubud proper (just to the east) and is set in a quiet, mountainous area surrounded by rice fields. The hotel's design makes elegant use of local materials, blended in an immaculate, contemporary style. Rooms reflect that refined simplicity, with cool white and yellow tones set against the dark wood of Art Deco furnishings. Floors are made of river stone and ceilings of thatch. The double-height lobby rotunda echoes the shape of a Dongsan Drum, a relic of an ancient culture and an important regional motif. The property stretches in a line of low-profile buildings all the way down to the river. An elevator transports you down the steep valley to the riverside, where the fine spa rooms literally hang over the rushing water; there's also a small restaurant and a riverside pool with a vanishing edge. Fine dining, spa facilities, and plenty of activities—including onsite meditation, Pilates, and yoga sessions—make the Maya quite self-sufficient, but regular shuttle service to town keeps you connected.

Jalan Gunung Sari, Peliatan, Ubud, Bali. ✆ **361/977888.** Fax 361/977555. www.mayaubud.com. 108 units. $295–$325 double; $395–$1,400 villa. AE, DC, MC, V. **Amenities:** 2 restaurants; bar; airport transfer; bike rental; Internet access (in library); Jacuzzi; 2 outdoor pools; comprehensive spa; tennis courts; meditation; Pilates; yoga. *In room:* A/C, satellite TV, fridge, hair dryer, minibar, IDD phone.

Uma Ubud ★★   A sister resort to the luxurious COMO Shambhala, this set of boutique villas decorated in a minimalist white style are aimed at a hip, young, jet-setting audience who prefer to be close to central Ubud. White gauzy curtains cover four-poster beds and stand-alone bathtubs, and some rooms have nice views of the surrounding rice paddies. Though the property is significantly smaller than the COMO Shambhala, it does its best with its landscaping to create a relaxing environment, with a large central pool and pond. In addition to the usual amenities, Uma Ubud offers meditation, Pilates, and yoga sessions on site.

Jalan Raya Sanggingan, Banjar Lungsiakan, Kedewatan, Ubud, Bali. ✆ **361/972448.** Fax 361/972449. www.uma.ubud.como.bz. 29 units. $260–$285 terrace double; $374–$525 villa double. $30 surcharge during high season villa suite. AE, DC, MC, V. **Amenities:** Restaurant; bar; airport transfer; bike rental; outdoor pool; comprehensive spa; library w/free Wi-Fi. *In room:* A/C, satellite TV, fridge, hair dryer, minibar, IDD phone, free Wi-Fi.

MODERATE

Alam Sari ★ ☺   This hotel offers an excellent combination of comfort, social responsibility, setting, and low price—and is a delightful find for families, eco-warriors, and those who want to immerse themselves in Balinese culture. Everything the Alam Sari does is with a thought toward the local economy, ecology, and culture. The hotel almost exclusively employs villagers from neighboring Keliki. Environmentally friendly touches are everywhere, from solar water heaters to the use of recycled paper Rooms are lovely, with views of the gorge and looming volcano. Traditional music is featured at night. Book on the Internet for cheaper rates.

Keliki, Tromoi Pos 03, Kantor Pos Tegallalang (9km/5⅔ miles north of Ubud), Ubud, Bali. ✆ **361/981420.** Fax 361/981421. www.alamsari.com. 12 units. $98 double; $112 suite; $120–$180 family unit. AE, MC, V. **Amenities:** Restaurant; bar; bike rental; Internet access; library. *In room:* A/C, fridge, minibar, IDD phone.

Bali Spirit Hotel and Spa ★   Located a fair jaunt from central Ubud in the village of Nyuh Kuning, this is a reasonable alternative to the really high-end luxury hotels in the north of Ubud. At Bali Spirit, you get a great setting and comfortable rooms at a good price, without all the bells, whistles, and fees. The stunning hillside setting overlooks a river gorge. Large, well appointed rooms come with small kitchen nooks and decks, with local fabrics and materials employed throughout. The pool is just right, a cozy perch with lounges overlooking the gorge, and there are traditional Balinese bathing pools in the holy river below. A fine spa offers a full range of services.

There are regular shuttles to town, in addition to a car available to take you wherever you want to go "at a moment's notice." The lack of in-room TVs keeps your eyes on the beautiful hills.

P.O. Box 189, Nyuh Kuning Village, Ubud, Bali. © **361/974013.** Fax 361/974012. www.balispirithotel.com. 25 units. $95 double; $145 villa. Rates include breakfast. AE, MC, V. **Amenities:** Restaurant; bar; airport transfer; mountain-bike rental; Internet access; outdoor pool; room service; full spa; cooking school. *In room:* A/C, TV, fridge, minibar, IDD phone.

Hotel Tjampuhan ★★ This hotel is a tropical sanctuary with terraces that lead to a beautiful gorge, the Tjampuhan River, and the 900-year-old Gunung Lebah Temple. The hotel was built in 1928 for guests of the prince of Ubud and was chosen by Western artists Walter Spies and Rudolf Bonnet as headquarters for their art association, Pita Maha. All units have Balinese thatched roofs. Air-conditioned rooms are larger and have better views than fan rooms. Splurge for a Raja Room (or even Spies's own villa), with verandas overlooking the gorge. The grounds are done in beautiful stonework, and immaculate gardens line the path down to the river. There are two very pretty pondlike pools and another with cold spring water, perfect for hot days. A shuttle goes into town every hour.

Jalan Raya Campuhan, Ubud, Bali. © **361/975368.** Fax 316/975137. www.tjampuhan-bali.com. 67 units. $95 double with fan; $135 double with A/C; $175 Walter Spies villa. Rates include breakfast. AE, MC, V. **Amenities:** 2 restaurants; 4 bars; babysitting; 2 outdoor pools; full spa; library. *In room:* A/C (in some units), fridge, minibar, IDD phone.

INEXPENSIVE

Other budget choices line Monkey Forest Road and the Jalan Hanoman; better still, turn down any little alley or side street that cuts across them.

Ananda Cottages ★ Just north of Ubud proper, Ananda Cottages is atmospheric enough for the Balinese experience you're hoping for, yet situated far enough from the town center to discourage the tourist hordes. The rice fields and thatched cottages of this bungalow campus are almost more "Balinese" than real villages you might visit (where you'll find TVs instead of shrines, and roaring machines instead of hand tools). Cozy rooms are connected by paths along terraced retaining walls, which are lit at night with miniature coal-fed, torchlike flames. The cottages are bi-level brick huts with bamboo pavilion roofs. Downstairs rooms are the better choice, with outdoor tubs and patio living rooms. Upstairs rooms have modern bathrooms and small verandas. The pool is small, but set on an interesting raised rice terrace. The three new deluxe bungalows are very cozy and well worth the outlay.

Campuhan, Ubud, Bali. © **361/975376.** Fax 361/975375. www.anandaubud.com. 60 units. $95 single; $125 double; $250 suite villa. AE, MC, V. **Amenities:** Restaurant; bar; outdoor pool; room service. *In room:* A/C (in some units), fridge, minibar, IDD phone.

Ubud Sari Health Resort ★ This was the first health retreat in Ubud. It is a good value with small cottages with real rustic charm, though it could do with a face-lift. The rushing water of the river below will sing you to sleep. Breakfast is served on your balcony and the staff is attentive without fawning. A garden path leads to the spa with a cold plunge pool, herbal steam bath, and sauna. Colonic fasting sessions are popular among the expat crowd that frequents this place.

35 Jalan Kajeng, Ubud, Bali. © **361/974393.** Fax 361/976305. www.ubudsari.com. 17 units. $50–$75 double. AE, MC, V. **Amenities:** Restaurant; babysitting; Jacuzzi; outdoor pool; limited room service; sauna; extensive spa. *In room:* A/C, no phone.

Where to Dine

Ubud has many eateries, mostly international restaurants in the busy town center, though you'll also find small *warungs* or stands selling *babi guling* (suckling pig). Much of Ubud's fine dining comes with a Western price tag.

Ary's Warung ★ MODERN INDONESIAN   Ary's gourmet European and Indonesian specialties have fans from around the world. Stop in for at least one of the honey-ginger-lime drinks (with or without the booze), and kick back on a couch streetside for a bit of people-watching. The metallic, angular construction of this open-air bistro would look great in a big-city gallery district, but is a bit at odds with ancient Hindu temples and the adjacent Royal Palace. It is the place to see and be seen, however, and Ary's is quite pleasant at night, when tranquil trance music plays and candles light every corner. Second-floor dining gives you a good view of the busy street below or the bats swooping to catch bugs at dusk. The food is good—overpriced, but good. Try the gazpacho, perfect on a hot day, or the grilled goat-cheese salad. The grilled tuna and lamb cutlets are done to perfection, and the ponzu-grilled snapper is delicious. The tasting menu (Rp320,000; Rp480,000 with wine) includes two glasses of house wine. Ary's also makes for a good meeting place or for reconnoitering when the kids are trekking and Mom is off shopping.

Main road. ☏ **361/975053.** www.dekco.com. Main courses Rp95,000–Rp130,000. MC, V. Daily 10:30am–10pm (last order).

Batan's Waru ★★ INDONESIAN/EUROPEAN   Tucked away on a pleasant side street, Batan's Waru is particularly atmospheric at night, when the entrance is lit with candles. The ambitious menu has traditional dishes beyond the usual suspects, and plenty of vegetarian options. For an appetizer, try *urap pakis*, wild fern tips with roasted coconut and spices, or *lemper ayam*, chicken dumplings simmered in a banana leaf. Uncle Karaman's Hummus is spicy and comes with grilled-pepper flatbread and tomato-mint relish. Everything is served with a dish of spicy condiments. Finish off with a perfect cup of decaf Illy-brand espresso. The restaurant also does smoked duck and a *babi guleng* feast, with a day's advance order, and there is a full menu of pasta, sandwiches, and light fare as well.

Jalan Dewi Sita. ☏ **361/977528.** www.baligoodfood.com. Main courses Rp42,000–Rp84,000. AE, MC, V. Daily 8am–10:30pm last order.

Bebek Bengil (Dirty Duck) ★★ INDONESIAN/EUROPEAN   The Dirty Duck is the best place to try Ubud's famous dish. First stewed in local spices, then deep-fried, the duck here is finger-lickin' good, but not quite as oily as in other restaurants. Another way to go is the stuffed chicken with shiitake, sprouts, and spinach. The menu also features salads, overstuffed crunchy sandwiches, and good veggie options. The atmosphere is romantic; book a table toward the back of the open-air restaurant, which looks out onto the paddy fields.

Padang Tegel (at end of street as it hooks into Monkey Forest Rd.). ☏ **361/975489.** www.agungraka.com/bebekbengil. Main courses Rp12,500–Rp35,000. AE, DC, MC, V. Daily 10am–10pm.

Cafe Lotus ★ MODERN INDONESIAN/INTERNATIONAL   The food here isn't half bad, but the real reason to come to Cafe Lotus is for the chance to dine in the shadow of the Pura Saraswati temple (p. 613). It's cozy in the shaded dining area or on bamboo platforms overlooking the temple. The menu features good Western options, pastas and such, some modified into fiery dishes with hot chiles, black olives, and hearts of palm. Try the Balinese Satay Lilit, a mixed-fish kabob with a hint of coconut, served on skewers and presented on a plate the size of a boat. The fresh health drinks are a delight. This is a good place to kick back when touring the town. Note that no beef is served due to the restaurant's proximity to the temple.

Main road. ✆ **361/975660.** www.lotus-restaurants.com/cafe-lotus-ubud. Main courses Rp50,000–Rp100,000. AE, MC, V. Daily 8:30am–9:45pm (last order).

Mozaic ★★ 💣 INTERNATIONAL   Chef Chris Salans's constant upgrades and refinements to food and decor since his restaurant opened in 2001 has turned Mozaic into one of Asia's top fine-dining destinations. Salans employs traditional French ingredients and methods but pays respect to his surroundings with Indonesian flavors such as spicy sambal sauce, turmeric, and cardamom. A recent renovation added a classy bar and lounge in the front and a private kitchen and chef's table in the back, where cooking classes are taught several times a week. Guests chose from several six-course, constantly changing tasting menus (which can be paired with wines), and excellent service ensures the right pacing throughout the meal. Highlights from a recent meal include curry butter roasted yabbies (Australian crayfish), which came with a delectable truffle sauce, and a crispy seared foie gras served with mango purée. The restaurant offers excellent value for the money. Salans, who has worked with New York chef David Bouley and Napa Valley chef Thomas Keller of the French Laundry fame, has finally come into his own.

Jalan Raya Sanggingan. ✆ **361/975768.** www.mozaic-bali.com. Reservations required. Tasting menu Rp550,000–Rp1,500,000. AE, DC, MC, V. Daily 6–10pm.

Naughty Nuri's Warung and Grill ★★ BARBECUE/BALINESE   This old expat hangout has the best barbecue in town, with ribs so tender the meat falls right off the bone. On Thursday, a regular shipment of fresh tuna arrives and the place fills right up. The burgers, dogs, and local curries and satay are also good. Free-flowing drinks (try the honkin' martinis) add to the laid-back, picnic-table atmosphere at streetside. Bring your appetite, a high booze tolerance, and a good sense of humor.

Tromol Pos 219 (just across from the Neka Art Museum on the road leading north of town). ✆ **361/977547.** Main courses Rp25,000–Rp175,000. No credit cards. Daily 10am–10pm.

Sari Organic (Bodag Maliah) ★ 🎁 ORGANIC   It is somehow reassuring to know that places like Sari Organic exist and that there are people behind them who believe in "making the world a better place"—their exact words. The project supports local farmers, uses organic produce, and spreads virtue, as the only way to get here is on foot, taking a pleasant 15-minute trek from Jalan Raya Ubud near the aqueduct down a small pathway through the farms and rice fields. When you arrive, you will be pleasantly surprised by this quirky restaurant with 360-degree views of the paddy fields and wildlife. Call to reserve a table as this place is packed and popular.

Subak Sok Wayah. ✆ **0361/972087.** Reservations recommended. Main courses Rp35,000–Rp65,000. No credit cards. 8am–8pm.

TeraZo ★ MEDITERRANEAN   The spacious interior of this hip bistro is simple yet welcoming, with terraces set behind a nice garden with decorative fountains. The menu is extensive. Cool tomato gazpacho is a welcome starter in the tropical heat, while the spring rolls are light and delicious. The eight-layer pie is a delicious pastry crust filled with smoked blue marlin, spinach, ricotta, and mushrooms. There's also a host of grilled items, fine pasta, and gourmet Asian-influenced dishes, such as the *nasi kuning,* yellow coconut rice with raisins, cashews, and strips of egg; or the *kue tiaun,* stir-fried rice noodles, chicken, and local greens. A tempting breakfast menu features surprises including ricotta blintzes topped with honey and fresh yogurt.

Jalan Suweta. ℭ **361/978941.** www.baligoodfood.com. Main courses Rp170,000–Rp195,000. AE, MC, V. Daily 10am–11:30pm.

SNACKS & CAFES

Casa Luna, on the main road (ℭ **361/977409**), is a longtime favorite with expats for its local and international cuisine, coffee, and desserts. (It also has cooking classes.) For desserts and ice cream, **Mumbul's Cafe,** also on the main road (ℭ **361/975364**), is a tasty choice with a serene garden terrace. The town's best coffee shop is **Tutmak Warung Kopi,** on Jalan Dewi Sita, near Batan's Waru (ℭ **361/975754**), with great desserts and a whole range of healthy treats, from salads to light lunches. There's also a good menu for kids.

    Kafe, on Jalan Hanoman (ℭ **361/970992;** www.balispirit.com), offers fantastic vegetarian mains, California-style burritos, coffee, and desserts. It also contains a yoga and massage center and a gift shop featuring crafts from nonprofit organizations.

    Bali Buddha Cafe, Jalan Jembawan 1, in front of the post office to the east of town (ℭ **361/976324;** www.balibuddha.com), is a happening little expat spot with a small grocery store that sells good fresh bread, organic vegetables, healthy snacks, and supplements. Upstairs is a popular juice bar—a good place to meet long-staying folks or get info off the bulletin board. It's New Age central here, more or less.

What to See & Do

Botanic Garden Ubud ★ ☺   Created by a former German journalist who has retired in Ubud, the gardens are spread over 4.9 hectares (12 acres) and provide an excellent look at the variety of lush plant life that exists on the island. Highlights include the orchid greenhouse, a Muslim garden with a symmetrical tiled path, and the fruit tree area, where visitors can see how passion fruits ripen on the vine and dragon fruits grow on crazy-looking cacti. A labyrinth, purportedly the first in Bali, is a surefire hit with the kids.

Kutuh Kaja. ℭ **361/970951.** www.botanicgardenbali.com. Admission Rp50,000. Daily 8am–6pm.

Pura Saraswati ★★   The royal family commissioned this temple and water garden, dedicated to the Hindu goddess of art and learning, at the end of the 19th century. The main shrine is covered in fine carvings, and the *bale* houses (small pavilions) and giant *barong* masks are interesting. The restaurant **Cafe Lotus** (see above) is situated at the front, on the main street, so that diners can look out over the lovely grounds.

Jalan Raya Ubud. Free admission. Daily during daylight hours.

Puri Saren Agung (Royal Palace) ★   From the late 19th century to the mid-1940s, this was the seat for the local ruler. It's a series of elegant and well preserved pavilions, many of them decorated incongruously with colonial-era European furniture. Visitors are welcome to stroll around, though there are no signs indicating what you are looking at. Evening dance performances are held in the courtyard, by far the best and most dramatic setting for these in Ubud.

Jalan Raya Ubud. Free admission. Daily during daylight hours.

MUSEUMS

Ubud has enjoyed a long relationship with foreign artists. As a result, the town has good museums and many galleries. All give you a crash course in authentic Balinese art, not to mention welcome respite from souvenir stalls. Of the many small museums in town, those listed below are the best choices, but don't pass up the free galleries around town, especially on Jalan Raya Sangginan going north toward the more high-end resorts. In addition to the following, stop by the free **Seniwati Gallery of Art by Women** (Jalan Sriwedari 2B, Banjar Taman; ℰ **361/975485;** www.seniwati gallery.com) and the **Agung Rai Museum and Gallery** (Jalan Pengosekan; ℰ **361/ 975742;** www.armamuseum.com), another popular local collection.

Antonio Blanco Museum   The museum is an homage to Bali's famous Catalan expat. Born in the Philippines, Blanco arrived here penniless, but eventually befriended the king, married, had children, and lived the life of Riley all his days. He was a favorite at court and the confidant of many powerful people on Bali and in Indonesia. This grand gallery houses a collection of his work that is as much a romp through Blanco's sexual dalliances as anything, a collection of homespun, baroque pornography. Some paintings feature Blanco's raunchy prose poetry. Don't miss touring his studio space. The consummate egomaniacal artist, Blanco envisioned this monument to himself and participated fully in its creation before shuffling off this mortal coil in 1999. The museum grounds are a trip, with Blanco's menagerie of dachshunds, monkeys, and exotic birds still ruling the roost.

Jalan Campuhan, just past the bridge heading north of Ubud. ℰ **361/975502.** www.blancobali.com. Suggested admission Rp50,000 for international visitors; Rp30,000 for locals. Daily 9am–5pm.

Neka Art Museum ★★   Founded in 1982 by Suteja Neka, a former school-teacher and patron of the arts, this museum is a good introduction to the Balinese school. Housed in several pavilions, works are labeled in English and provide informed access to rural traditions and modern movements on the island and locally in Ubud. The collection features the work of the Dutch-born Indonesian artist Arie Smit, as well as contemporary works both local and from abroad. Don't miss the view of the Campuhan Gorge from the Smit Pavilion—you can see what inspires local artists (or get inspired yourself).

Jalan Raya Campuhan (about 10 min. north of central Ubud, near Ananda Cottages). ℰ**361/975074.** www.museumneka.com. Admission Rp40,000. Daily 9am–5pm.

Puri Lukisan Museum ★   A major renovation has turned this formerly dilapidated display into something nearly on par with the Neka Art Museum (see above). The gorgeous gardens of lily ponds and rice paddies are worth a visit on their own. Founded in 1956 by a prince of Ubud and a Dutch artist, the collection of painting and sculpture here traces the evolution of Balinese art. One space is dedicated to a revolving exhibit of up-and-coming local artists.

Jalan Raya Ubud. ℰ **361/975136.** www.mpl-ubud.com. Admission Rp30,000 adults, free for children 15 and under. Daily 9am–5pm.

Outdoor Activities

Just west of Ubud, the Ayung River has some good white-water rafting and kayaking. The rapids aren't too impressive for experienced rafters, but the scenery along the way is, with rice paddies, deep gorges, and photo-op waterfalls. Two-hour trips include all equipment, hotel pickup, and lunch; most hotels can make the reservations. You can also contact **Bali Adventure Tours** (☎ 361/721480; www.baliadventuretours.com) or **Sobek** (☎ 361/287059).

Ubud is surrounded by fascinating villages, scenic rice paddies, gorges, and rivers, and roads and paths lead to all of them. You can just wander, but I strongly urge you to buy a copy of the *Ubud Surroundings* map, available in all shops. Then head for the picturesque village of **Penestanan** or go on the rigorous **Campuhan Ridge** walk. Hiring a local guide is also a good option.

Ever seen a scarlet-headed flowerpecker? For an interesting day, meet up with famed author and naturalist **Victor Mason** (☎ 361/975009 in the daytime, or 812/29313801 in the evening; su_birdwalk@yahoo.com) for his popular **bird-watching tour ★** of Ubud with his company Bali Birdwalk (www.balibirdwalk.com). Tours cost $33 and leave Tuesday, Friday, Saturday, and Sunday from the bridge at Tjampuhan in the northeastern end of town. You're bound to see a good many of Bali's 100 species of birds. The scenic walk includes lunch, water, and binocular use.

Elephant Safari Park ★★ ☺ The Elephant Safari Park, run by **Bali Adventure Tours,** is less safari and more elephant ride and it's great for the kids. These native Sumatra elephants are well cared for and live in large, lush enclosures. The owners have worked carefully with locals from Taro Village, previously one of Bali's most remote and untouched villages, to make sure they leave little more than elephant tracks. A safari starts with Pachyderm 101, as knowledgeable guides tell about the animals' care and feeding, local ecology, threats to the native population, and preservation efforts. Then, along with a *mahout* (guide), you'll have a galumphing trip through the jungle. An elephant show is staged three times daily at 11am, 1pm, and 3:30pm. The park has recently begun offering a night safari from 6 to 9:30pm every night that includes an elephant talent show and a four-course dinner for $99 adults and $69 children. Stay overnight at the new Elephant Safari Lodge, which features beautiful suites starting at $250 a night.

Jalan Bypass Ngurah Rai, Pesanggaran. ☎ **361/721480.** Fax 361/721481. www.baliadventuretours.com. Reservations recommended. Admission (including transport, buffet lunch, and show) $64 adults, $86 with elephant ride; $41 children, $58 with elephant ride; family rates and Internet rates available.

Monkey Forest ★ ☺ Yes, there is a monkey forest at the southern end of Monkey Forest Road, and this is a popular day trip. The towering tree clusters here are home to a troop of bad-tempered but photogenic primates that swing from branches, cannonball into pools of water, and do everything short of putting on suits and paying taxes, all to the general delight of photo-snapping visitors. Signs warn you not to feed the monkeys, but locals stand under those very signs selling you bananas and nuts for precisely that purpose. Do so if you must, but do not tease the critters, which are grumpy enough as it is—just hand them the food. Make sure you have no other food on you—they will smell it. They're also known to snatch at dangling or glittering objects and to gnaw on sandals. There's a small temple in the forest, and the track also leads to Nyuhkuning, a woodcarving village.

Monkey Forest Rd. ☎ **361/971304.** www.monkeyforestubud.com. Admission Rp20,000 adults, Rp10,000 children. Daily 8:30am–6pm.

Shopping

Ubud is the shopper's paradise of Bali, with everything from tacky plastic doohickeys to priceless works that will have you thinking of selling the SUV.

spa treatments FOR ALL BUDGETS

Some of the best massages on the island can be found at the new **Fivelements Healing Center** ★★★ (Banjar Baturning; 🕾 **0361/469206;** www.fivelements.org; treatments $80–$155), where the owners, an American and Italian couple, have sought traditional healers from around the island for invigorating massages in a pristine riverside setting.

The Mother Earth of spas, **COMO Shambhala's wellness retreat** (p. 607; single treatment $80–$150; AE, DC, MC, V; 10am–7pm) has tailor-made programs prescribed after consultation with a team of professionals, including Ayurvedic doctors, nutritionists, and psychologists. Colonic hydrotherapy and herbal cleansers are popular here. The award-winning spa in the **Maya Ubud Resort** ★★★ (p. 608; single treatment $60–$75, package $121–$175; AE, DC, MC, V; 8am–8pm) is suspended down a gravity-defying cliff. Blending effortlessly with the colors of nature, the spa pavilions all are made with local materials and include outdoor bathtubs filled with the waters of the Petanu River. **Spa Alila** ★, in Alila Ubud (p. 608; single

treatment $45–$65, package $78–$170; AE, DC, MC, V; 9am–9pm), has excellent therapists who warm up with a daily yoga session for themselves to get in the right frame of mind for working on you. The local treatments made from green tea, bamboo, and virgin coconut oil proved so popular that they have started to sell them to guests. The Alila Recovery signature massage includes techniques from Thai, Swedish, and Balinese massage. At **Spa Hati,** Jl. Raya Andong 14 (🕾 **0361/977578;** www.spahati.com; single treatment Rp70,000–Rp185,000, package Rp530,000; MC, V; 9am–9pm), you can feel good as well as do good since all of the proceeds go to support the expansion and upkeep of the Bali Hati School for children in Mas. Repeat visitors to Ubud are escapists, spiritual seekers, and relaxation junkies. The **Ubud Body Works Center** ★ (25 Hanuman Rd.; 🕾 **361/975720;** www.ubudbodyworkscentre.com) focuses on Balinese healing techniques; while the atmosphere isn't luxe, the massages and body scrubs are fantastic and inexpensive.

Start at **Ubud Market,** at the southeast corner of Monkey Forest Road and Jalan Raya Ubud. Open during daylight hours only, it's a real market—great noisy fun, with dozens of stalls selling produce and livestock along with tourist kitsch.

All along **Monkey Forest Road, Jalan Raya Ubud,** and **Jalan Hanoman,** shop after shop is filled with gorgeous sarongs, woodcarvings, mobiles, jewelry, incense, pottery, and gaily colored shirts. It's all geared to tourists, but the quality isn't bad. Elsewhere in town, you can find jewelry, housewares, and textiles.

Treasures, Toko, and **Toko East** are fine boutiques owned by the folks at Ary's Warung; find them on the main road in the center of Ubud or online at www.dekco.com. Other boutiques and galleries line the road running north of central Ubud toward the high-end resort area. The lace shop **Toko Uluwatu** has outlets all over Bali. You can find its popular storefront on Monkey Forest Road in the center of Ubud. **Okrakartini,** east of the palace on the main road (🕾 361/975624), is an upmarket boutique with fine cloth, jewelry, and antiques. **Threads of Life,** Jalan Kajeng 24 (🕾 **361/972187;** www.threadsoflife.com), a foundation that supports groups of weavers on the eastern islands of Indonesia, sells unique local patterns. For books, stop by **Periplus,** on Monkey Forest Road (✆ **361/975178**).

Ubud After Dark

Ubud's nightlife scene is growing, but it's still rather sedate. **Jazz Café** (Jalan Sukma 2, east of Monkey Forest Rd.; ✆ **361/976594**) has good live jazz. There are lots of little laid-back places along Monkey Forest Road that are more than happy to stay open late. Upscale **Lamak** (✆ **361/974668;** www.lamakbali.com) stays up, but its scene is mostly calm. For a night of drinking and fun, hit **Naughty Nuri's** (p. 612; ✆ **361/977547**), where most dinners turn into a romp. For an evening of culture, there are usually several dance, music, and shadow-puppet performances to choose from every night in Ubud, both at the **Royal Palace** (p. 613) and on other nearby stages. A *barong* performance at the Royal Palace is the best and most stimulating choice; even the kids will like it. Touts selling tickets are ubiquitous; ask at any front desk for a recommendation.

Side Trips from Ubud

Day hiking in and around Bali is the real attraction, with rice fields set among low hills and small towns as far as the eye can see. Ask at any tour desk about day trips to the **Sayan Rice Terraces** ★, just north of Ubud. This deep-green valley, striated in stunning tiers and hanging with palms, is a photographer's dream.

Bali Safari & Marine Park ★★ Set on 40 hectares (99 acres) of splendid natural habitat, the Bali Safari & Marine Park has 400 animals from regions including Indonesia, India, and Africa. The many sensational highlights include a traditional Balinese purifying sacred bath, the story of man-eating lions in Tsavo of Kenya, and the majestic white tigers of India. This park is the latest establishment of the world-renowned Taman Safari Indonesia, a name made famous for more than 20 years of efforts in nature conversation and recreational business. Bali Safari & Marine Park is tremendously active in protecting endemic and endangered species, as well as orchestrating educational campaigns to save the animals. While having lunch, you can watch white tigers at play in their natural habitat. You can also stay overnight in the park for more animal viewing time. The Park recently launched a new theater showing Balinese puppet performances three to four times per week—for more details, visit www.balitheatre.com.

Jl. Bypass Prof. Dr. Ida Bagus Mantra, Km 19.8. ✆ **0361/950000.** www.balisafarimarinepark.com. Admission $35–$59. Mon–Fri 9am–5pm; Sat–Sun 8:30am–5pm. Pickup can be arranged.

Besakih Temple ★ Called the "Mother Temple," Besakih is Bali's premier Hindu site. Even if you come with your own guide, you'll have to hire a local to take you around the temple site; meet one out in front (he'll find you). The compound is a collection of 22 multitiered temples that look like Chinese pagodas. They're more interesting for their significance to Balinese culture than for their architectural qualities. The temples were destroyed in eruptions in 1917, and damaged in another incident in 1963. This is a working temple complex, with each compound attended by families. There are no signs for tourists, and ceremonies are often in progress—but the compulsory guides help prevent visitors from treading where they're not welcome. Be respectful and certainly ask before taking pictures, though usually foreign visitors

SCALING THE HEIGHTS: bali's volcanoes

Gunung Agung, the tallest peak on the island at 3,014m (9,886 ft.), is quite a spectacle, visible from as far away as the island of Lombok and from high buildings in busy Kuta. It is a grueling 5-hour climb to the top. Easier is nearby **Gunung Batur,** Agung's little brother, just a few hours' hike. Both Batur and Agung are still active volcanoes, with eruptions as recent as 1997. Start before first light to catch the dawn. From the top, you can see the geothermally active surrounding crater, the volcanoes of nearby Lombok, and the looming peak of Agung. You'll need a guide. It's not just the rules; it's a good idea. We recommend **Gung Bawa Trekking** (✆ 08/123878168), a reliable guide who has been trekking this mountain for years; **M&G Trekking** (✆ 036/341464 or 08/133153991) in Candidasa, can offer alternative routes; or **Ketut Uriada** (✆ 0812/3646426), based in Muncan, who is very knowledgeable about the area. Be sure to be fastidious and specific about details: Is it a private tour? Is breakfast included? What route will you follow?

There are a few different routes up both peaks. Most follow the trail to the main viewing point near the top of Batur (there's a little lean-to where folks have breakfast and wait for the sunrise). From there, you can follow a short loop to the various craters. You can arrange for a basic tour and then offer the guide a little extra for an upgrade. It makes for a fun morning, which you can follow with a visit to the small hot springs near the lake.

Stay nearby in Bangli, which has very basic accommodations. **Artha Sastra Inn,** Jl. Merdeka 5 (no phone; year-round Rp35,000–Rp50,000; cold water showers), is situated opposite the *bemo* terminal and close to the market in an old palace (the building was once the royal place of Bangli), though the grandeur is somewhat faded. The nine rooms vary enormously, so look at a few. The **Bangli Inn,** Jl. Rambutan (✆ 0366/91419; year-round Rp120,000; cold water only; no shower), is the more conventional, with clean rooms built around a small courtyard.

are made welcome. This is a possible day trip from Ubud or Kuta; most visitors include a detour to the nearby volcanoes.

40km (25 miles) north of Klungkung. Admission Rp8,000, plus about $2 for a guide.

CANDI DASA

The best reason to camp out in Candi Dasa is to take advantage of the peace, relaxation, and historic riches of the eastern corner of the island. The beaches are eroded and it's overdeveloped, but you can find some of the island's finest accommodations here. Many choose to stay in nearby **Padangbai,** an atmospheric little fishing village with some basic accommodations.

Getting There

There are shuttles from all major tourist areas to Candi Dasa. Most of the hotels offer airport pickup for a fee.

Getting Around

There isn't much to the town of Candi Dasa itself—just one road, parallel to the beach—so your feet will do you just fine. Hotels just outside the center generally offer regular shuttles into town. Most businesses catering to tourists will offer free pickup and drop-off. Motorbike rental and *bemos* are available, too.

[FastFACTS] CANDI DASA

Car & Motorbike Rental **Safari,** on the main road (☏ **363/41707**), is a reliable and friendly tourist agency with a selection of cars, jeeps, and motorbikes.

Currency Exchange Money-changers can be found up and down the main road, offering competitive prices.

Internet Access Internet storefronts line the main street.

Mail **Asri Shop,** on the main street, offers postal services.

Telephones Candi Dasa's area code is **363.**

Where to Stay
VERY EXPENSIVE

Amankila ★★ The name of this ultraluxe resort means "beautiful hill," and it is just that. Private villas, luxurious beyond compare, open to the most stunning views of surrounding hills and ocean below. There is nothing typical about an Aman resort, and this breathtaking perch is no exception. Accommodations have it right in every detail. A solid-wood four-poster canopy bed dominates each spacious unit, which also comes with an enormous dressing area, lavish bathroom with sunken tub, and cushioned window seats. The high-end suites have better views and private pools. The Amankila has the only beach in Candi Dasa with sand. Its most striking feature is the giant tiered pool at the center, with water that matches the color of the ocean it seems to spill into. Amankila has every amenity, of course, and rooms and restaurants beyond compare, but what really sets this place apart is its meticulous service. Everyone is a rock star here.

Manggis, Bali. ☏ **363/41333.** Fax 363/41555. www.amanresorts.com/amankila/home.aspx. 34 units. $800–$1,500 suite; $1,250–$2,950 pool suite. AE, DC, MC, V. **Amenities:** 2 restaurants; bar; Internet access (in library); motorbike rental; outdoor pool; room service; spa; tennis court; watersports equipment rental. *In room:* A/C, satellite TV, fridge, minibar, IDD phone, Wi-Fi.

EXPENSIVE

Alila Manggis ★★ 🖋 From the outside, this comfortable, contemporary place looks more like a boxy, concrete apartment complex, but inside it's all stark luxury. Chic rooms have clean lines, and everything is new and tidy. The staff is very friendly, and there are nice little touches such as afternoon tea and treats on your patio. The lush central lawn and pool area is surrounded by teak lounges and leads to a large pebble beach. Getting to town is a bit of a haul, but regular shuttles make it convenient. The hotel features its own line of special soaps that have spawned a local cottage industry. The hotel's restaurant, Sea Salt, takes its name from nearby salt-producing villages. Days at their popular cooking school include a visit to these areas.

Buitan, Manggis, Bali. ℂ **363/41011.** Fax 363/41015. www.alilahotels.com/manggis. 58 units. $225–$350 double; $500–$650 suite. AE, MC, V. **Amenities:** Restaurant; bar; shuttle bus; babysitting; bike rental; Internet access; room service; watersports equipment rental; cooking lessons. *In room:* A/C, satellite TV, fridge, minibar, IDD phone.

MODERATE

Alam Asmara Dive Resort
This set of bungalows with an on-site dive shop are packed in tightly but are made private and intimate by the greenery and ponds surrounding each of the units. The rooms, while dark, are nicely furnished and come with luxurious partially outdoor bathrooms. A small swimming pool next to the ocean and an outdoor restaurant patio look out to the sea, and the sunsets from here are particularly nice. The reception area is decorated with a goldfish pond, and stone Buddhist sculptures dot the grounds. It's one of the best options on the sleepy Candi Dasa strip. Guests receive a complimentary 50-minute massage upon arrival.

Jalan Raya, Candi Dasa, Bali. ℂ **363/41929.** Fax 363/42101. www.alamasmara.com. 12 units. $115 bungalow. MC, V. **Amenities:** Restaurant; bar; airport transfer; concierge; outdoor pool; room service; spa; watersports; cooking classes. *In room:* A/C, TV, hair dryer, minibar, IDD phone.

Bloo Lagoon Resort ★
Sitting on top of a hill with panoramic views, the resort consists of self-contained villas surrounding a central pool and dining area overlooking the perfect, yet small, Bloo Lagoon Beach. The resort has an eco-friendly approach and strives to integrate new energy-saving technologies; they compost, grow their own food, and recycle water. Their amphitheater occasionally hosts Balinese and Western performances. Spa Biroo overlooks the sea at the top of the hill and offers a selection of treatments from manicures and pedicures and aromatherapy massages using high-quality essential oils, to the Shama-Shama massage, a four-hand massage.

Jl. Silayukti, Padangbai. ℂ **0363/41211.** www.bloolagoon.com. 17 units. High season $140 1-bedroom, $170 2-bedroom, $190 3-bedroom; low season $120 1-bedroom, $150 2-bedroom, $170 3-bedroom. Discount available when booking online. AE, MC, V. **Amenities:** Restaurant; babysitting; kids' club; concierge; outdoor pool; room service; spa; watersports. *In room:* A/C, fan.

Watergarden ★★
The simple thatched bungalows of the Watergarden may not be spectacular, but they're very comfortable. Each has a wide veranda overlooking the many lily ponds that give the hotel its name. The best and most private rooms are at the back. In-house dining at the Watergarden Kafé (see "Where to Dine," below) is some of the best in town. The place has a good laid-back feel that draws lots of return guests.

Main road, Candi Dasa. ℂ **363/41540.** Fax 363/41164. www.watergardenhotel.com. 14 units. $125 double; $325 2-bedroom suite. AE, MC, V. **Amenities:** Restaurant; popular bar (TJ's); airport transfer; small outdoor pool; library. *In room:* A/C (in some units), TV, minibar, IDD phone, Wi-Fi.

INEXPENSIVE

Puri Bagus ★ 🏊
The Puri Bagus is a short ride from the town center and a good value compared to Candi Dasa's more expensive options. It's set on land jutting into the ocean, with steps leading right down to the beach. Good-size bungalows are airy and light, thanks to many large windows, and each has a small sitting area. Cool outdoor bathrooms have hand-held showers. The U-shaped pool has a deep section

for scuba practice and a shallow area for kids. Dance programs and movies are offered at night, plus there's a full range of free daily activities and good dining at seaside. You'll also find a beautiful new spa area.

P.O. Box 129, Manggis, Bali. © **363/41304.** Fax 363/41290. www.manggis.puribagus.net. 26 units. $78 double. AE, DC, MC, V. **Amenities:** 2 restaurants; 2 bars; bike and scooter rental; concierge; outdoor pool; room service; nearby tennis court; watersports equipment rental. *In room:* A/C, fridge, minibar, IDD phone.

Where to Dine

The Alila's **Sea Salt** (p. 619) features interesting Balinese dishes and cooking class offered several times a week for $85 per student. On Candidasa's sleepy strip, **Vincent's** (Jalan Raya; © **363/41368;** www.vincentsbali.com) Continental and Balinese dishes keep its foreign crowd satisfied. The restaurant features a nice garden, a vibrant bar, and jazz tunes from the likes of Frank Sinatra and Diana Krall. The **Watergarden Kafé** (© **363/41540;** www.watergardenhotel.com) has decent local and Western fare (see "Where to Stay," above).

Outdoor Activities

Big, healthy reefs teeming with marine life are just a short trip from the shores of Candi Dasa. There are lots of storefront outfitters in town able to arrange snorkeling and diving trips. Some spots are fit only for advanced divers; the wreck of the World War II USS *Liberty* is offshore at Tulamben. Hotels can arrange trips with operators along the main road, or you can try **Geko Divers,** out of Padangbai to the south (© **363/41516;** www.gekodive.com).

Side Trips from Candi Dasa

Tracing the coast north from Candi Dasa, travelers have the chance to see volcanoes to the left and stunning coast to the right. In the mornings, a visit to **Klung Klung market** (30 min. away from Candi Dasa), where locals shop for everything from live ducks to hand-woven baskets, gives visitors a real insight into daily life. **Tenganan,** just up the road from Candi Dasa, was set up as a tourist attraction by the government to show visitors the basic layout of a village. It feels a bit gimmicky but retains a sleepy enough feel that it's still worthwhile. At the village's gate, a guard asks for an entry donation; usually Rp10,000 to Rp20,000 is sufficient. The fishing village of **Amed,** about 2 hours north of Candi Dasa, is popular for snorkeling and diving. You can come on a day trip from Candi Dasa or even Ubud (it's easy to arrange land transport), though you might want to spend the night. The **Anda Amed Resort** (© **363/23498;** www.andaamedresort.com) is a property perched atop a cliff with bargain rates ranging from $66 to $114 for one- to two-bedroom villas. A good beachside budget choice is **Amed Café** (© **363/23473;** www.amedcafe.com), with rooms as low as $10.

THE NORTH AND LOMBOK ★★

Some 4 hours of driving north and west along the coast brings you to **Lovina.** Famous for the schools of dolphins swimming just offshore, Lovina hosts a number of bungalows and hotels on a quiet stretch of beach, far from the madding crowd of southern

Bali. The **Damai** ★★ (Jalan Damai, Kayuputih; ℂ **362/41008;** www.damai.com) features a set of newly built villas suspended on a cliffside overlooking the ocean starting at $250 and a classy restaurant featuring healthy tasting menus. **Puri Bagus Lovina** (ℂ **362/21430;** www.puri-bagus.com) offers less pricey luxury, with beach-side rooms starting at $135. Budget accommodations are wall-to-wall along the beaches in Lovina. All accept cash only and cost between Rp80,000 and Rp150,000. Check out **Angsoka,** Jalan Bina Ria, Lovina Beach (ℂ **362/41841;** www.angoska. com), a clean, comfortable choice with a pool; some rooms have air-conditioning. An hour to the east of Lovina, a new luxury resort worthy of note is the **Spa Village Resort** ★★ (Jalan Singaraja-Amlapura 100; ℂ **362/32033;** www.spavillage.com). Featuring deluxe suites and villas, the resort specializes in several spa programs that guests can chose from, focusing on harnessing "balance, creativity, and vigor" through a range of treatments and classes.

Farther west of Lovina is the small village of **Pemuteran,** a quiet spot with a small cluster of beachside resorts. Pemuteran is a great base for diving and snorkeling trips to **Menjangan,** a small island bordering northwestern Bali. The newest resort, and the highlight of any trip to Bali, is **The Menjangan** ★★ (Jalan Raya Gilimanuk; ℂ **362/94708;** www.themenjangan.com), a resort in the middle of the Bali Barat National Park that features a huge range of activities, including trekking, bird-watching, kayaking, and diving. For diving and snorkeling, a reputable agency is **Reef Seen Aquatics** (ℂ **362/93001;** www.reefseen.com). The dive center has a turtle hatchery and reef gardening project, plus basic but nicely appointed rooms around $40. The best of Pemuteran's resorts is the **Matahari Beach Resort & Spa** ★ (ℂ **362/ 92312;** www.matahari-beach-resort.com), with rooms ranging between $205 and $514. Owned by a German butcher, the property features fantastic service, a world-class beachside restaurant, and a beautiful full-service spa. Just west of Matahari is the good-value **Taman Selini Resort** (ℂ **362/94746;** www.tamanselini.com), with a good Greek restaurant.

Lombok, a smaller island off the east coast of Bali, is a flight into the rugged landscape of unspoiled Indonesia. With a dry climate that's dominated by central volcanic peaks, Lombok is a predominantly Muslim island that attracts travelers hoping to get off the beaten track. Tourism infrastructure is limited, but beaches are unspoiled; this is also a popular base for trips to the outlying Gili Islands, known for their diving and snorkeling and Mount Rinjani, an active volcano ringed by a lake.

From Bali, we recommend flying to Lombok—the safest of the dodgy Indonesian carriers is Garuda Airlines (ℂ **08/041807807,** or 0370/646846 at the Bali airport; www.garuda-indonesia.com), which connects the two islands with an evening flight on a Boeing 737. If you prefer a bouncy ride by sea, **Blue Water Safari** (ℂ **361/ 8951082** or 813/38418988; www.bwsbali.com) and **Gili Cat** (ℂ **361/271680;** www.gilicat.com) both have daily service to Lombok, leaving from Tanjung Benoa and Padangbai, respectively. Be prepared for a bumpy ride, especially in the wet season.

The top choice for accommodations is the self-contained, luxurious **Oberoi Lombok** ★★★, cousin of the popular Seminyak resort (Medana Beach, Tanjung, West Lombok; ℂ **370/6138444;** www.oberoihotels.com), located on the far north of the island. The thatched-roof rooms and villas overlook a beautiful strip of beach and the Gili Islands beyond; the restaurants serve delicious Continental and Indonesian fare, and most guests enjoy the setting so much they don't set foot away from the resort.

The hotel can arrange dive trips with a private Divemaster for a bargain $45 per dive, and the resort also offers surfing, snorkeling, and trips to the Gili Islands.

Also nearby is the **Hotel Tugu Lombok** (© **370/6120111;** www.tuguhotels. com), a funky, bohemian cluster of villas and rooms decorated with antiques on a palm plantation near an 18-hole golf course. In contrast to Oberoi's luxurious feel, the Hotel Tugu is more for the offbeat traveler with a variety of rates. A main strip of hotels and inexpensive accommodations are available in the beach town of Senggigi farther south but are not particularly recommended.

PLANNING YOUR TRIP TO SOUTHEAST ASIA

The previous chapters in this guide provide specific information on traveling to and getting around Southeast Asia's individual countries, but in this chapter we give you some regionwide tips and information that will help you plan your trip.

10

GETTING THERE
By Plane

If you're flying to Southeast Asia, you will more than likely arrive via one of the region's three main hubs: Bangkok, Singapore, or Hong Kong, from where you can pick up flights to any other destination in Southeast Asia. Your home country's national carriers will almost certainly connect with all three of these airports. In addition, check with Southeast Asian–based airlines for fare deals: Cathay Pacific, Thai Airways, Malaysian Airlines, and Singapore Airlines. United also has direct flights between the U.S. West Coast and Vietnam.

GETTING AROUND SOUTHEAST ASIA

Regional flights in Southeast Asia are affordable and convenient—a great way to get around if your time is short. That said, half the fun of traveling is getting there—many walk away from land travel in this part of the world saying, "I'll never do it again, but what a trip!" When the massive Soviet 4×4 nearly lays on its side in the deep ruts of a washed-out road in Laos, or that rattletrap motorbike you rented in hill-tribe country in the north of Vietnam catches a flat and leaves you stranded, you might curse yourself or the very road you're on, but you'll have lots of stories to tell when you get back.

By Plane

Myriad routes into the region are served by international carriers, including Silk Air (the regional arm of Singapore Airlines), Malaysia Airlines, Thai Airways, Cathay Pacific, Vietnam Airlines, and Garuda Indonesia. Domestic carriers include Pelangi Air, AirAsia, and Berjaya Air in Malaysia; Lao Airlines in Laos; and Bangkok Airways and P.B. Air in Thailand and Cambodia.

Remember that international airports are not restricted to capital cities. In addition to Bangkok, Thailand has international access via Chiang Mai and Chiang Rai (to China and Laos), U-Tapao and Phuket (to Cambodia), and Phuket and Ko Samui (to Singapore and Kuala Lumpur). You can fly into Malaysia at Penang, Langkawi, and Tioman Island, and to Borneo destinations direct from Singapore. Laos has international access at both Luang Prabang and Pakse, in addition to the capital, Vientiane. Vietnam has international flights to both Ho Chi Minh City (Saigon) and Hanoi. And in Cambodia, you can fly directly to Siem Reap, the access city to Angkor Wat, from Bangkok, Chiang Mai, U-Tapao (near Pattaya), Phuket, Vientiane, Vietnam, and Singapore.

Check out the UNESCO World Heritage routes, a new schedule of flights offered by Bangkok Airways. Originating in Bangkok, this tour connects Sukhothai (Thailand) with Luang Prabang (Laos), Hue (Vietnam), and Angkor Wat (Cambodia).

Ask any travel agent for information, and be sure to research all flight options for the most direct routes and best fares. Each chapter gives specific details for booking.

By Train

With a few exceptions, trains that operate throughout Southeast Asia are poorly maintained, overcrowded, and slow. While trains used to be a good option for long distances, the recent increase in budget airlines offering rock-bottom prices has made train travel a less appealing option. The most popular rail route—and the only one with interconnecting service among countries in all of Southeast Asia—runs from Singapore to Bangkok (and vice versa) through the heart of the Malaysian peninsula, with stops along the way at the cities of Johor Bahru, Malacca, Kuala Lumpur, and Butterworth (for Penang). It takes 6 hours from Singapore to Kuala Lumpur, and another 35 hours from Kuala Lumpur to Bangkok. You can board the train at the Singapore Railway Station in Tanjong Pagar, at the Kuala Lumpur Central Railway Station on Jalan Hishamuddin, and in Bangkok at the Hua Lamphong Railway Station on Rama IV Road.

Upscale travelers with unlimited budgets can book passage on one of the world's foremost luxury trains, the *Eastern & Oriental Express,* which covers the distance between Singapore and Bangkok in 42 hours. Find more details in the Thailand chapter.

Reliable rail service also runs north to south along coastal Vietnam, with interesting new luxury cars that connect Hanoi, the capital, with the northern hill country and make a further connection to the vast rail networks of China.

By Bus

Buses are good on the budget and often the best way into the back of beyond. Bus trips in the region range from VIP tours with air-conditioning and video monitors to rattletrap, overcrowded, broken-down mobiles. Thai and Malay buses are quite reliable and a good option, connecting the far north of Thailand with the far southern tip of Malaysia and on to Singapore. In Laos and Cambodia, local buses, with the exception of a few interior routes, are rough. Check specific "Getting There" sections in individual chapters before embarking on long hauls. Also, check each country's individual visa requirements, as you often need to prearrange visas for land crossings.

By Boat

There are lots of boat adventures in the region. More and more travelers are heading down the Mekong, starting from the town of Chiang Khong in northern Thailand and ending in Luang Prabang in Laos. Luxury riverboats run the same trip, as well as trips in the far south of Laos between Pakse and Si Phan Don (look for Luang Say Cruises under the relevant sections). Boat trips in Vietnam's Halong Bay, just east of Hanoi, are very popular; outfitters such as Handspan and Buffalo Tours run great excursions. Don't miss the new boat connections along the Mekong tributaries between Vietnam's Mekong Delta and Phnom Penh, Cambodia's capital. Boats also connect Cambodia's capital, Phnom Penh, with Siem Reap, the town that supports Angkor Wat, along the Mekong as it flows through Tonle Sap Lake.

By Car

Car rental is affordable in Southeast Asia. In the developing countries—Vietnam, Laos, Cambodia—it is a good idea (and costs not much more) to hire a car with driver. Insurance is often unavailable. Road rules vary, and in some places seem nonexistent—though there is always a method to the madness—so it's not a bad idea to spring for a driver where affordable. Be sure to research details and invest in good maps before heading out.

ENTRY REQUIREMENTS & CUSTOMS

Entry Requirements

Many countries covered in this guide require only a **valid passport** for citizens of the U.S., U.K., Canada, Australia, and New Zealand. For an up-to-date listing of passport requirements around the world, go to the "Foreign Entry Requirement" page of the U.S. State Department at **www.travel.state.gov**.

Note that Vietnam, Laos, and Cambodia require all visitors to have entry **visas.** Though most international airports offer visas upon arrival, and there are more overland points where you can apply with passport photos and money when you arrive, if you plan to enter Vietnam, Laos, or Cambodia from rural overland points, you often need to obtain a visa beforehand (you may even need to specify which entry point). See individual country chapters for specific information.

BALI (INDONESIA)   Visitors from the U.S., Canada, most of Europe, Australia, and New Zealand are given a visa upon arrival for a fee of $25 for stays of up to 30 days. The only official gateways to Bali are Ngurah Rai Airport or the seaports of Padang Bai and Benoa. If you want to stay longer than 30 days, you must get a tourist or business visa before coming to Indonesia. Tourist visas cannot be extended, while business visas can be extended for 6 months at Indonesian immigration offices.

CAMBODIA   All visitors are required to carry a passport and visa. A 1-month visa can be obtained upon entry at the Phnom Penh or Siem Reap international airports for $20. Visa on arrival is also available at all land crossings. Applying online (www. mfaic.gov.kh) for a 1-month e-visa costs $25 and it can be used on arrival by air or by land (only via Bavet from Vietnam and Poipet and Koh Kong from Thailand). The procedure is simple and straightforward, and will save you time and energy. Bring one 4×6-inch passport photo for your application.

LAOS Visitors need a valid passport and visa to visit Laos. There are a number of entry sites where visas are granted upon arrival: by air to Vientiane or Luang Prabang, and when crossing by land from Thailand over the Friendship Bridge between Vientiane and Nong Khai, or between Chiang Khong and Houay Xai in the far north, and Mukdahan and Savannakhet or Chong Mek and Vung Tao (near Pakse) in the far south. A 30-day visa at these arrival points costs $30. You will also need a passport-size photo. When coming from Vietnam, be sure to have a prearranged visa. At an embassy outside of Laos, the going rate for a 30-day visa is $35; you'll have to wait up to 5 days. For a fee, travel agents in Thailand and other countries in the region can help you jump over the bureaucratic hurdles and get a visa in 1 day.

MALAYSIA To enter Malaysia, you must have a valid passport. Citizens of the U.S. do not need visas for tourism and business visits. Citizens of Canada, Australia, New Zealand, and the U.K. do not require a visa for tourism or business visits not exceeding 1 month.

SINGAPORE To enter Singapore, you'll need a valid passport. Visas are not necessary for citizens of the U.S., Canada, the U.K., Australia, and New Zealand. Upon entry, visitors from these countries will be issued a 30-day pass for a social visit only, except for Americans, who get a 90-day pass.

THAILAND All visitors to Thailand must carry a passport valid for at least 6 months. Technically, you need proof of onward passage (either a return or through ticket), though this is rarely requested. Visas are not required for stays of up to 30 days for citizens of the U.S., Australia, Canada, New Zealand, or the U.K., but 3-month tourist visas can be arranged before arrival.

VIETNAM Residents of the U.S., Canada, Australia, New Zealand, and the U.K. need both a passport and a valid visa to enter Vietnam. A tourist visa usually lasts 30 days and costs $65. Though there's no official policy, tourist visas can commonly be extended with little hassle. Multiple-entry business visas are available that are valid for up to 3 months; however, you must have a sponsoring agency in Vietnam, and it can take much longer to process. For short business trips, it's less complicated simply to enter as a tourist.

Customs

WHAT YOU CAN BRING INTO SOUTHEAST ASIA

Allowable amounts of tobacco, alcohol, and currency are comparable in all countries: usually two cartons of cigarettes, up to two bottles of liquor, and between $3,000 and $10,000. Check individual chapters for exact amounts. Plant material and animals fall under restrictions across the board. For Singapore, there are no duty-free allowances for cigarettes.

WHAT YOU CAN TAKE HOME FROM SOUTHEAST ASIA

Restrictions on what you can take out of the various nations of Southeast Asia are loose at best. Expect a red flag if you have any kind of plant materials or animals, but the most notable restriction has to do with antiques. To prevent the kind of wholesale looting of the region's treasures in the recent colonial past, you might be stopped if you are carrying any Buddhist statuary or authentic antiques or religious artifacts. This does not apply to tourist trinkets, however aged and interesting. In fact, despite any salesman's claim of authenticity, you'll be hard-pressed to find authentic antiques.

U.S. CITIZENS   For specifics on what you can bring back and the corresponding fees, download the invaluable free pamphlet *Know Before You Go* online at **www.cbp. gov.** (Click on "Travel" and then "Know Before You Go.") Or contact **U.S. Customs & Border Protection (CBP),** 1300 Pennsylvania Ave. NW, Washington, DC 20229 (✆ **877/287-8667**), and request the pamphlet.

CANADIAN CITIZENS   For a clear summary of Canadian rules, write for the booklet *I Declare,* issued by the **Canada Border Services Agency** (✆ **800/461-9999** in Canada, or 204/983-3500; www.cbsa-asfc.gc.ca).

U.K. CITIZENS   For information, contact **HM Customs & Excise** (✆ **0845/010-9000,** or 020/8929-0152 from outside the U.K.; www.hmce.gov.uk).

AUSTRALIAN CITIZENS   A helpful brochure available from Australian consulates or Customs offices is *Know Before You Go.* For more information, contact the **Australian Customs Service** (✆ **1300/363-263;** www.customs.gov.au).

NEW ZEALAND CITIZENS   Most questions are answered in a free pamphlet available at New Zealand consulates and Customs offices: *New Zealand Customs Guide for Travellers, Notice no. 4.* For more information, contact **New Zealand Customs,** The Customhouse, 17–21 Whitmore St., Box 2218, Wellington (✆ **04/473-6099** or 0800/428-786; www.customs.govt.nz).

MONEY

The East Asian financial crisis is now a distant memory, and the countries of Southeast Asia are generally gaining economic clout in the world; but the rate of exchange, not to mention the price of most goods and services, means that travel in the region is very budget-friendly. In places such as Laos or Cambodia, you'll find that you can live quite well on very little, and the region's resort destinations and luxury accommodations in general come at a fraction of what you might pay in your home country. **ATM** service is good in the larger cities but can be scant, at best, in some of the region's backwaters. **Traveler's checks,** an anachronism elsewhere in the world, are still not a bad idea, especially in the developing countries of the region. Note that the **U.S. dollar** is the de facto currency for many Southeast Asian countries, particularly in Laos, Vietnam, and Cambodia. Hotels in particular prefer doing business in U.S. dollars to dealing in local currency, a practice that helps them stay afloat amid fluctuating currency values. In some parts, everybody down to the smallest shop vendor quotes prices in U.S. dollars, and particularly the big-ticket items are best handled with greenbacks instead of large stacks of local currency.

While dealing in U.S. dollars can make things less complicated, always keep in mind local currency values so you know if you're being charged the correct amount. In this book, we've listed **hotel, restaurant, and attraction rates** in whatever form the establishments quoted them—in U.S. dollars where those were quoted, and in local currencies where those were used.

Note that with the exception of the Singapore dollar, Malaysian ringgit, and Hong Kong dollar (which have remained stable), all other Southeast Asian national currencies are still in a state of flux. Before you budget your trip based on rates we give in this book, be sure to check the currency's current status. You can find a comprehensive currency converter at **www.oanda.com/convert/classic**.

Currency

You will have to rely on local currency when traveling in many rural areas where neither traveler's checks nor credit cards are accepted. The U.S. dollar is the most readily accepted foreign currency throughout Southeast Asia, and it's a good idea to carry some greenbacks as backup.

It's not a bad idea to try to exchange at least some money—just enough to cover airport incidentals and transportation to your hotel—before you leave home (though don't expect the exchange rate to be ideal) so that you can avoid lines at airport ATMs; most international arrival points in the region, however, have 24-hour exchange counters. You can exchange money at your bank or local American Express or Thomas Cook office. If you're far away from a bank with currency-exchange services, American Express offers traveler's checks and foreign currency, though with a $15 order fee and additional shipping costs, through www.americanexpress.com or ℰ **800/807-6233.**

Listed below are the currencies of all destinations in this guide.

BALI (INDONESIA) Indonesia's main currency is the **rupiah (Rp),** with bills of Rp100, 500, 1,000, 5,000, 10,000, 20,000, 50,000, and 100,000. Coins come in denominations of Rp25, 50, 100, and 500. After wild fluctuations in the 1990s, the rupiah has stabilized in recent years to **Rp8,810 = $1.**

CAMBODIA Cambodia's monetary unit is the **riel,** which is available in 100, 200, 500, 1,000, 5,000, 10,000, 20,000, 50,000, and 100,000 riel notes. Cambodia's volatile exchange rate typically fluctuates, but is currently at **4,000 riel = $1.** It's a good idea to bring a supply of U.S. dollars, as the dollar is considered Cambodia's second currency and is accepted—even preferred—by many hotels, guesthouses, and restaurants. If paying in dollars, you'll get the small change in riel.

LAOS The primary unit of currency is the **kip** (pronounced *keep*), which comes in denominations of 500, 1,000, 2,000, 5,000, 10,000, 20,000 and 50,000 notes. The exchange rate is approximately **8,000 kip = $1.** As in Cambodia, many tourist establishments prefer payment in U.S. dollars. In many areas of Laos, both U.S. dollars and Thai baht are preferred over the local currency.

MALAYSIA The **ringgit (RM),** which is also referred to as the Malaysian dollar, is the unit of currency. One ringgit equals 100 sen, and notes come in RM1, 2, 5, 10, 20, 50, 100, 500, and 1,000. Coins come in denominations of 1, 2, 5, 10, and 50 sen, as well as RM1. The exchange rate is approximately **RM3.59 = $1.**

SINGAPORE The **Singapore dollar (S$),** commonly referred to as the Sing dollar, is the local unit of currency, with notes issued in denominations of S$2, 5, 10, 50, 100, 500, and 1,000; coins come in denominations of 1, 5, 10, 20, and 50 cents and the gold-colored S$1. The exchange rate is approximately **S$1.49 = $1.**

THAILAND The Thai **baht (B)** is made up of 100 satang. It comes in colored notes of 20 (green), 50 (blue), 100 (red), 500 (purple), and 1,000 (khaki) baht. Coins come in denominations of 1, 2, 5, and 10 baht, as well as 25 and 50 satang. The exchange rate is approximately **35B = $1.**

VIETNAM The main unit of Vietnamese currency is the **dong (VND),** which comes in denominations of 500,000, 200,000, 100,000, 50,000, 10,000, 5,000,

1,000, 500, and 200 notes. There are no coins. Most tourist venues accept dollars, and even in small towns you will at least be able to exchange greenbacks, if not use dollars directly. The exchange rate is approximately **19,495VND = $1.**

ATMs

The easiest and best way to get cash away from home is from an ATM. The **Cirrus** (© **800/424-7787;** www.mastercard.com) and **PLUS** (© **800/843-7587;** www. visa.com) networks span the globe; look at the back of your bank card to see which network you're on, then call or check online for ATM locations at your destination. Be sure you know your personal identification number (PIN) and daily withdrawal limit before you depart. *Note:* Many banks impose a fee every time you use a card at another bank's ATM, and that fee can be higher for international transactions (up to $5 or more) than for domestic ones (where they're rarely more than $2). In addition, the bank from which you withdraw cash may charge its own fee. For international withdrawal fees, ask your bank.

Credit Cards

Credit cards are another safe way to carry money. They provide a convenient record of all your expenses, and they generally offer relatively good exchange rates. You can get cash advances from your credit cards at banks or ATMs, provided you know your PIN. Keep in mind that you'll pay interest from the moment of your withdrawal, even if you pay your monthly bills on time. Also, note that many banks now assess a 1% to 3% "transaction fee" on *all* charges you incur abroad (whether you're using the local currency or your native currency). Before you leave home, call your credit card company to find out if there's a daily limit on cash advances.

Traveler's Checks

In most parts of the world, traveler's checks are an anachronism from the days before ATMs made cash accessible at any time. But be forewarned that the developing countries in Southeast Asia have scant ATM service, especially in rural areas. Traveler's checks are a sound alternative to traveling with dangerously large amounts of cash, and they can be replaced if lost or stolen.

You can buy traveler's checks at most banks. They are offered in denominations of $20, $50, $100, $500, and sometimes $1,000. Generally, you'll pay a service charge ranging from 1% to 4%.

The most popular traveler's checks are offered by **American Express** (© **800/807-6233,** or 800/221-7282 for cardholders—this number accepts collect calls, offers service in several foreign languages, and exempts Amex gold and platinum cardholders from the 1% fee); **Visa** (© **800/732-1322,** or AAA members can call © **866/339-3378** to get checks up to $1,500 for a $9.95 fee); and **MasterCard** (© **800/223-9920**).

American Express, Thomas Cook, Visa, and MasterCard all offer **foreign-currency traveler's checks,** which are useful if you're traveling to one country; they're accepted at locations where dollar checks may not be.

If you carry traveler's checks, keep a record of their serial numbers separate from your checks in the event that they are stolen or lost. You'll get a refund faster if you know the numbers.

WHEN TO GO

With a few exceptions, wherever and whenever you travel in Southeast Asia, you are likely to encounter hot and humid weather. All of Southeast Asia lies within the Tropics, and the countries closest to the Equator—Singapore, Malaysia, Indonesia, and southern Thailand—have the hottest annual temperatures. See the individual destination chapters for weather information in each country.

HOLIDAYS & FESTIVALS   Some of the holidays celebrated in Southeast Asia might affect your vacation plans, either positively or negatively. See the individual destination chapters for listings of the major holidays celebrated in each country.

TRAVEL INSURANCE

Check your existing insurance policies and credit card coverage before you buy travel insurance. You may already be covered for lost luggage, canceled tickets, or medical expenses.

The cost of travel insurance varies widely, depending on the cost and length of your trip, your age and health, and the type of trip you're taking, but expect to pay between 5% and 8% of the vacation itself. You can get estimates from various providers through **InsureMyTrip.com.**

TRIP-CANCELLATION INSURANCE   Trip-cancellation insurance will help you retrieve your money if you have to back out of a trip or depart early, or if your travel supplier goes bankrupt. Permissible reasons for trip cancellation can range from sickness to natural disasters to the State Department declaring a destination unsafe for travel.

For more information, contact one of the following recommended insurers: **Access America** (© 866/807-3982; www.accessamerica.com), **Travelex Insurance Services** (© 888/457-4602; www.travelex-insurance.com), **Travel Guard International** (© 800/826-4919; www.travelguard.com), **Travel Insured International** (© 800/243-3174; www.travelinsured.com).

MEDICAL INSURANCE   For travel overseas, most U.S. health plans (including Medicare and Medicaid) do not provide coverage, and the ones that do often require you to pay for services upfront and reimburse you only after you return home. As a safety net, you may want to buy travel medical insurance, particularly if you're heading to a remote or high-risk area where emergency evacuation might be necessary. If you require additional medical insurance, try **MEDEX Assistance** (© **410/453-6300;** www.medexassist.com) or **Travel Assistance International** (© **800/821-2828;** www.travelassistance.com; for general information on services, call the company's Worldwide Assistance Services, Inc., at © 800/777-8710).

LOST-LUGGAGE INSURANCE   On flights within the U.S., checked baggage is covered up to $2,500 per ticketed passenger. On international flights (including U.S. portions of international trips), baggage coverage is limited to approximately $9.07 per pound, up to approximately $635 per checked bag. If you plan to check items more valuable than what's covered by the standard liability, see if your homeowner's policy covers your valuables, get baggage insurance as part of your comprehensive travel-insurance package, or buy Travel Guard's "BagTrak" product.

If your luggage is lost, immediately file a lost-luggage claim at the airport, detailing the luggage contents. Most airlines require that you report delayed, damaged, or lost baggage within 4 hours of arrival. The airlines are required to deliver luggage, once found, directly to your house or destination free of charge.

HEALTH & SAFETY
Staying Healthy

Health concerns should comprise much of your preparation for a trip to Southeast Asia, and staying healthy on the road takes vigilance. Tropical heat and mosquitoes are the biggest dangers. Travelers should also exercise caution over dietary change and cleanliness. Just a few pretrip precautions and general prudence, though, are all that you need for a safe and healthy trip.

GENERAL AVAILABILITY OF HEALTHCARE

The best hospitals and healthcare facilities are located in the large cities of countries that have the greatest number of Western visitors—Singapore, Hong Kong, Kuala Lumpur (Malaysia), and Bangkok (Thailand). In rural areas of these countries and throughout the lesser-developed countries of Vietnam, Cambodia, and Laos, there are limited healthcare facilities: Hospitals are few and far between and are generally of poor quality. Even in heavily touristed Bali, you're better off evacuating to one of the more developed countries if faced with a serious medical situation. Over-the-counter medications are available anywhere, but it's a good idea to bring antidiarrheal medication and rehydration salts, among others.

Contact the **International Association for Medical Assistance to Travelers** (**IAMAT;** ✆ **716/754-4883,** or 416/652-0137 in Canada; www.iamat.org) for tips on health concerns and lists of local, English-speaking doctors in the countries you're visiting. The U.S. **Centers for Disease Control and Prevention** (✆ **800/311-3435;** www.cdc.gov) provides up-to-date information on health hazards by region or country and offers tips on food safety. You can find listings of reliable clinics overseas at the **International Society of Travel Medicine** (www.istm.org). The website **www.tripprep.com**, sponsored by a consortium of travel medicine practitioners, may also offer helpful advice on traveling abroad.

COMMON AILMENTS

TROPICAL ILLNESSES Among Southeast Asia's tropical diseases carried by mosquitoes are **malaria, dengue fever, chikungunya,** and **Japanese encephalitis.** Reports about malaria prophylactics vary. While most local health agencies tell you not to waste your time with antimalarial drugs, the CDC still advises people to take tablets, most of which cause uncomfortable side effects. In truth, your only sure way to avoid mosquito-borne diseases is to avoid being bitten. Repellents that contain **DEET** are the most effective, but gentler alternatives (see baby-care products in any pharmacy) provide DEET-free mosquito protection without the chemicals. Also be aware that malaria mosquitoes bite between the hours of 5 and 7 in the morning and in the evening, so it's important to exercise caution at those times (wearing long sleeves and long trousers is a good idea, as is burning mosquito coils). Dengue-fever mosquitoes bite during the day.

Hepatitis A can be contracted from water or food, and **cholera** epidemics sometimes occur in remote areas. **Bilharzia, schistosomiasis,** and **giardia** are parasitic diseases that can be contracted from swimming in or drinking from stagnant or untreated water in lakes or streams.

Anyone contemplating sexual activity should be aware that **HIV** is rampant in many Southeast Asian countries, along with other STDs such as gonorrhea, syphilis, herpes, and hepatitis B.

DIETARY RED FLAGS   Unless you intend to confine your travels to the big cities and dine only at restaurants that serve Western-style food, you will likely be sampling some new cuisine. This could lead initially to upset stomach or diarrhea, which usually lasts just a few days as your body adapts to the change in your diet.

Except for Singapore, where tap water is safe to drink, **always drink bottled water,** and **never use tap water for drinking or even brushing teeth.** Peel all fruits and vegetables, and avoid raw shellfish and seafood. Also beware of ice unless it is made from purified water. (Any suspicious water can be purified by boiling for 10 min. or treating with purifying tablets.)

If you're a vegetarian, you will find that Southeast Asia is a great place to travel; vegetarian dishes abound throughout the region. In terms of hygiene, restaurants are generally better options than street stalls, but don't forgo good local cuisine just because it's served from a cart. Be sure to carry diarrhea medication as well as any prescription medications you might need. It's acceptable to wipe down utensils in restaurants, and in some places locals even ask for a glass of hot water for just that purpose (some travelers even carry their own plastic chopsticks or cutlery). Bringing antiseptic hand-washing gel is a good idea for when you're out in the sticks.

So how can you tell if something will upset your stomach before you eat it? Trust your instincts. Avoid buffet-style places, especially on the street, and be sure all food is cooked thoroughly and made to order. If your gut tells you not to eat that gelatinous chicken foot, don't eat it. If your hosts insist but you're still afraid, explain about your "foreign stomach" with a regretful smile and accept a cup of tea instead. Be careful of raw ingredients, common in most Asian cuisines, but realize that questions such as, "Are these vegetables washed in clean water?" are inappropriate anywhere. Use your best judgment or simply decline.

BUGS, BITES & OTHER WILDLIFE CONCERNS   There are all kinds of creepy critters to be aware of in any tropical climate. In rural accommodations, mosquito nets are often required and, if so, are always provided by hoteliers. Check your shoes in the morning (or wear sandals) just in case some ugly little thing is taking a nap in your Nikes. Keep an eye out for snakes and poisonous spiders when in jungle terrain or when doing any trekking. Having a guide doesn't preclude exercising caution. **Rabies** is rampant, especially in rural areas of the less-developed nations, and extreme care should be taken when walking, particularly at night. In places such as Thailand, dogs are simply fed and left to roam free, and you are likely to run into some ornery mutts. A walking stick or umbrella is a suitable deterrent when out in the countryside. It's also important to know that all dogs have been hit with hurled stones sometime in their life, and, a nod to Pavlov here, the very act of reaching to the ground for a handful of stones is often enough to send an angry dog on the run, for fear of being pelted. If you are bitten, wash the wound immediately and, even if you suffer just the slightest puncture or scrape, seek medical attention and a series of rabies shots (now quite a simple affair of injections in the arm in a few installments over several weeks).

RESPIRATORY ILLNESSES   **SARS** hit the region hard in the winter and spring of 2003. Singapore reported some cases and essentially closed to tourism, and though most other countries in the region reported no cases of the disease, places such as

Thailand suffered the fallout of the regionwide scare. There have been no reported cases of SARS since 2004. **Tuberculosis** is a concern in more remote areas where testing is still uncommon.

The **avian influenza,** also called the **bird flu,** is another public-relations nightmare in Southeast Asia. A number of cases have been reported in Thailand and Vietnam, and millions of chickens suspected of carrying the illness have been slaughtered. The victims of the bird flu have been few in number (statistically insignificant, really) and are mostly isolated to people working in the poultry industry. The countries affected have been unusually forthright about reporting new cases, and the disease is yet limited in scope. It is important to note that you cannot contract bird flu from consuming cooked chicken.

Air quality is not good in the larger cities such as Bangkok or Ho Chi Minh City; with no emissions standards, buses, trucks, and cars belch some toxic stuff, so visitors with respiratory concerns or sensitivity should take caution.

SUN/ELEMENTS/EXTREME WEATHER EXPOSURE Sun and heatstroke are a major concern anywhere in Southeast Asia. Limit your exposure to the sun, especially during the first few days of your trip and, thereafter, from 11am to 2pm. Use a sunscreen with a high protection factor, and apply it liberally. Asians are still big fans of parasols, so don't be shy about using an umbrella to shade yourself (all the Buddhist monks do). Remember that children need more protection than adults.

Always be sure to drink plenty of bottled water, which is the best defense against heat exhaustion and the more serious, life-threatening heatstroke. Also remember that coffee, tea, soft drinks, and alcoholic beverages should not be substituted for water because they are diuretics that dehydrate the body. In extremely hot and humid weather, try to stay out of the midday heat, and confine most of your daytime traveling to early morning and late afternoon. If you ever feel weak, fatigued, dizzy, or disoriented, get out of the sun immediately and go to a shady, cool place. To prevent sunburn, always wear a hat and apply sunscreen to all exposed areas of skin.

Be aware of major weather patterns; many island destinations are prone to typhoons or severe storms.

WHAT TO DO IF YOU GET SICK AWAY FROM HOME

Hospitals and **emergency numbers** are listed under "Fast Facts" in each destination chapter. Any foreign embassy or consulate can provide a list of area doctors who speak English. If you get sick, consider asking your hotel concierge to recommend a local doctor—even his or her own. You can also try the emergency room at a local hospital. Many hospitals also have walk-in clinics for cases that are not life-threatening; you may not get immediate attention, but you won't pay the high price of an emergency-room visit. In the larger cities of Southeast Asia, healthcare at hospitals and private clinics is of an international caliber and quite affordable.

You will need to pay in advance for any medical treatment and be reimbursed later. See "Medical Insurance," under "Travel Insurance," above, for details.

If you suffer from a chronic illness, consult your doctor before your departure. Pack **prescription medications** in your carry-on luggage, and keep them in their original containers, with pharmacy labels—otherwise they won't make it through airport security. Also bring the generic name of prescription medicines, in case a local pharmacist is unfamiliar with the brand name. Prescription medication is readily available, often over the counter.

Staying Safe

The good news is that anonymous, violent crime is not an issue in most countries in the region, but petty theft, pickpocketing, and purse snatching are common. It is a good idea to carry a hidden travel wallet with your passport and documents, and keep an eye on valuables in public.

Road conditions vary throughout the region, but most large cities, from Bangkok to Ho Chi Minh, are busy and chaotic. Even for intrepid travelers who push their limits out in the wilds, crossing big-city streets, even at prescribed crossings, can be the greatest risk on your trip; move slowly and exercise caution. Rural roads in places such as Laos and Cambodia are often no more than dirt tracks. And even where the roads are good, Western visitors are often shocked at the seeming lack of rules and the fact that, on most roads, might is right: The biggest, fastest, and most aggressive vehicle takes precedence, and belligerent horn blowing is the rule. It is best to rent a car with a hired driver instead of trying to drive yourself. On some bus rides, you might want to keep your eyes just on the scenery and not on the road ahead.

In places such as the beach towns of Thailand, motorbike accidents are all too common, and you're sure to meet one or two road-rashed victims. Exercise extreme caution on rented bikes, especially if you're inexperienced, and always wear a helmet.

Dicey political situations arise and pass with frequency; it's important to check travel warnings with the U.S. State Department (www.travel.state.gov) or the most up-to-date sources on the region. Places such as Laos, Cambodia, Indonesia, and southern Thailand are known to flare with separatist movements and terrorism, while the ongoing unrest in Thailand shows that even supposedly stable countries are susceptible to political turmoil. Stay abreast of any and all news before traveling.

When it comes to drugs: "Just say no." Grown, produced, and shipped through the region, drugs such as heroin, opium, and marijuana are readily available. There are island spots and mountain retreats where it might seem like the thing to do, but in all cases here, national laws are strict. Many visitors find themselves in an intensive language school of another variety (in other words, jail) in short order if they can't bribe their way out of it. It's certainly not worth it anywhere.

SPECIALIZED TRAVEL RESOURCES

Travelers with Disabilities

Most disabilities shouldn't stop anyone from traveling. There are more options and resources out there than ever before. Larger hotels in the major cities of the region have adequate facilities for visitors with disabilities, though in rural destinations, specialized amenities are scant at best.

Many travel agencies offer customized tours and itineraries for those with disabilities. Among them are **Flying Wheels Travel** (℗ **507/451-5005;** www.flyingwheels travel.com), **Access-Able Travel Source** (℗ **303/232-2979;** www.access-able.com), and **Accessible Journeys** (℗ **800/846-4537** or 610/521-0339; www.disability travel.com). **Avis Rent a Car** has an "Avis Access" program that offers such services as a dedicated 24-hour toll-free number (℗ **888/879-4273**) for customers with special travel needs; special car features such as swivel seats, spinner knobs, and hand controls; and accessible bus service.

Organizations that offer assistance to travelers with disabilities include **MossRehab** (www.mossresourcenet.org), the **American Foundation for the Blind** (**AFB;** ✆ **800/232-5463;** www.afb.org), and **SATH** (Society for Accessible Travel & Hospitality; ✆ **212/447-7284;** www.sath.org). **AirAmbulanceCard.com** is now partnered with SATH and allows you to preselect top-notch hospitals in case of an emergency.

For more information specifically targeted to travelers with disabilities, the online magazine **Gimp on the Go** (www.gimponthego.com) has destination reviews, travel tips, bulletin boards, and links to other sites. Also check out the magazines *Emerging Horizons* (www.emerginghorizons.com), published quarterly, and *Open World,* published by SATH.

Gay & Lesbian Travelers

Acceptance of alternative lifestyles in Southeast Asia, like anywhere, runs the gamut. One thing to remember is that many of the societies and cultures of the region are, by tradition, very modest, and public displays of affection of any kind are not acceptable. Gay nightlife choices are many and varied in larger cities such as Bangkok, Singapore, and Hong Kong, but in rural areas, provincial attitudes vary and intolerance is not uncommon.

The **International Gay and Lesbian Travel Association** (**IGLTA;** ✆ **800/448-8550** or 954/776-2626; www.iglta.org) is the trade association for the gay and lesbian travel industry. It offers an online directory of gay- and lesbian-friendly travel businesses; go to its website and click on "Members."

Many agencies offer tours and travel itineraries specifically for gay and lesbian travelers. Among them are **Above and Beyond Tours** (✆ **800/397-2681;** www.abovebeyondtours.com), **Now, Voyager** (✆ **800/255-6951;** www.nowvoyager.com), and **Olivia Cruises & Resorts** (✆ **800/631-6277;** www.olivia.com).

Gay.com Travel (✆ **800/929-2268** or 415/644-8044; www.gay.com/travel or www.outandabout.com) is an excellent online successor to the popular *Out & About* print magazine. It provides updated information about gay-owned, gay-oriented, and gay-friendly lodging, dining, sightseeing, nightlife, and shopping establishments in destinations worldwide.

The following travel guides are available at many bookstores, or you can order them from any online bookseller: *Spartacus International Gay Guide* (Bruno Gmünder Verlag; www.spartacusworld.com/gayguide), *Odysseus: The International Gay Travel Planner* (Odysseus Enterprises Ltd.), and the *Damron* guides (www.damron.com), with separate, annual books for gay men and lesbians.

Senior Travel

Seniors traveling in the region can bask in the glow of filial piety and the region's notorious Confucian respect for elders, but they are less likely to enjoy the major discounts found in the West. Mention the fact that you're a senior when you make your travel reservations, though. In some cases, people over 60 qualify for reduced admission to theaters, museums, and other attractions, as well as discounted fares on public transportation.

Members of **AARP** (formerly known as the American Association of Retired Persons), 601 E St. NW, Washington, DC 20049 (✆ **888/687-2277;** www.aarp.org), often get discounts on hotels, airfares, and car rentals. AARP offers members a wide

PLANNING YOUR TRIP TO SOUTHEAST ASIA | Specialized Resources range of benefits, including *AARP The Magazine* and a monthly newsletter. Anyone 50 and older can join.

Many reliable agencies and organizations target the 50-plus market. **Elderhostel** (*©* **877/426-8056;** www.elderhostel.org) arranges study programs for those 55 and over. **ElderTreks** (*©* **800/741-7956;** www.eldertreks.com) offers small-group tours to off-the-beaten-path or adventure-travel locations, restricted to travelers 50 and older. **INTRAV** (*©* **800/456-8100;** www.intrav.com) is a high-end tour operator that caters to the mature, discerning traveler (not specifically seniors), with trips around the world that include guided safaris, polar expeditions, private-jet adventures, and small-boat cruises down jungle rivers.

Recommended publications offering travel resources and discounts for seniors include the quarterly magazine *Travel 50 & Beyond* (www.travel50andbeyond.com); *Travel Unlimited: Uncommon Adventures for the Mature Traveler* (Avalon); *101 Tips for Mature Travelers,* available from Grand Circle Travel (*©* **800/221-2610** or 617/350-7500; www.gct.com); and *Unbelievably Good Deals and Great Adventures That You Absolutely Can't Get Unless You're Over 50* (McGraw-Hill), by Joann Rattner Heilman.

More and more seniors are considering Southeast Asia as a retirement destination. If you fall into this category, take a look at *Retire to Asia* (www.retiretoasia.com), an e-book by Ken Silver, or **www.retire-asia.com,** a highly informative website by a British expat living in Vientiane. Although it is geared toward those considering a move to the region, it also has some of the most up-to-date nuts-and-bolts travel information available online.

Family Travel

If you have enough trouble getting your kids out of the house in the morning, dragging them thousands of miles away might seem like an insurmountable challenge. The rough roads of Southeast Asia can be difficult, and concerns about communicable disease in rural areas should certainly be weighed. However, more accessible destinations and larger cities offer a glimpse into ancient civilizations and varied cultures that delight the kid in all of us. Most hotels can arrange extra beds at little additional cost, and connecting-room capability is common. To locate those accommodations, restaurants, and attractions that are particularly kid-friendly, refer to the "Kids" icon throughout this guide.

Recommended family travel websites include **Family Travel Forum** (www.familytravelforum.com), **Family Travel Network** (www.familytravelnetwork.com), **Traveling Internationally with Your Kids** (www.travelwithyourkids.com), and **Family Travel Files** (www.thefamilytravelfiles.com).

Women Travelers

Women traveling together or alone will find exploring this region particularly pleasant and easy. The Buddhist and Islamic codes of conduct and ethics followed by many mean that you will be treated with respect and courtesy.

Although you will almost never find local women dining or touring alone, as a visitor, your behavior will be accepted. You will rarely, if ever, be approached or hassled by strangers. At the same time, you can feel free to start a conversation with a stranger without fear of misinterpretation. *Note:* If you are traveling with a man, public displays of affection are not welcome, and it's you, the female, who will be scorned. Also, you will have to take even more care than your male counterpart to dress modestly, meaning no cleavage- or midriff-baring tops, miniskirts, or short shorts. Otherwise, you risk offending people on the grounds of either religious or local moral standards. Though wearing revealing clothing or sunbathing topless might appear to be tolerated, that's only because your hosts wish to avoid confrontation. Deep inside, it is very embarrassing.

It's still not advisable to take risks that you wouldn't normally take at home. Don't hitchhike, accept rides, or walk around late at night, particularly in dimly lit areas or in unfamiliar places. Be acutely aware of purse or jewelry snatchers in large cities. When meeting strangers in nightclubs, for example, buy your own drinks and keep an eye on them. In Cambodia, where a system of impunity prevails, precautions are highly recommended—and that includes within the temple complex of Angkor.

Check out the award-winning website **Journeywoman** (www.journeywoman. com), a "real-life" women's travel network where you can sign up for a free e-mail newsletter and get advice on everything from etiquette and dress to safety; or the travel guide *Safety and Security for Women Who Travel,* by Sheila Swan and Peter Laufer (Travelers' Tales, Inc.), offering common-sense tips on safe travel.

African-American Travelers

Agencies and organizations that provide resources for black travelers include **Rodgers Travel** (© 800/825-1775; www.rodgerstravel.com) and **Henderson Travel & Tours** (© 800/327-2309 or 301/650-5700; www.hendersontravel.com), which has specialized in trips to Africa since 1957.

For more information, check out the following collections and guides: *Go Girl: The Black Woman's Guide to Travel & Adventure* (Eighth Mountain Press), a compilation of travel essays by writers including Jill Nelson and Audre Lorde; *Travel and Enjoy Magazine* (© 866/266-6211; www.travelandenjoy.com); and *Pathfinders Magazine* (© 877/977-PATH [977-7284]; www.pathfinderstravel.com), which includes articles on everything from Rio de Janeiro to Ghana, as well as information on upcoming ski, diving, golf, and tennis trips.

Student Travel

This region has become a hot destination for budget-minded students, who often hit the shores in Southeast Asia and travel for extended periods of time. From bases such as Bangkok's Khao San Road, backpackers roam the rugged highways and byways, paving the way for high-end tourism. Places such as southern Thailand are attracting a young, spring-break crowd.

Any discounts to be found in Southeast Asia come from hard bargaining or tolerance for the most basic accommodations, but it's not a bad idea to have an **International Student Identity Card (ISIC),** which offers substantial savings on plane tickets and some entrance fees. It also provides you with basic health and life insurance and a 24-hour help line. The card is available from **STA Travel** (© 800/781-4040 in North America; www.statravel.com, or www.statravel.co.uk in the U.K.), the biggest student travel agency in the world. If you're no longer a student but are still 25 or under, you can get an **International Youth Travel Card (IYTC)** from the same people, and it entitles you to some discounts (but not on museum admissions). **Travel CUTS** (© 800/667-2887 or 416/614-2887; www.travelcuts.com) offers similar services for both Canadians and U.S. residents. Irish students may prefer to turn to **USIT** (✆ 01/602-1600; www.usitnow.ie), an Ireland-based specialist in student, youth, and independent travel.

Single Travelers

By and large, travelers in Southeast Asia are seekers of some kind, so many prefer to go it alone. For independent travelers, solo journeys are opportunities to make friends and meet locals. There is also a certain camaraderie that develops on long bus rides or in the uncertainty and wonder shared with fellow travelers. A trip that starts out solo often ends in friendships that last a lifetime.

For advice about hopping off the track and finding your own path, check out **Vagabonding** (www.vagabonding.net), which has information both practical and spiritual about the ways of the wanderer. Another inspiration is *The Art of Travel,* by Alain de Botton (Penguin Press). For more practical information, check out Eleanor Berman's latest edition of *Traveling Solo: Advice and Ideas for More Than 250 Great Vacations* (Globe Pequot), which has advice on traveling alone, either solo or as part of a group tour.

If you're going by tour, it is important to know that single travelers are often hit with a "single supplement" to the base price. To avoid it, you can agree to room with other single travelers or find a compatible roommate before you go, from one of the many roommate-locator agencies.

Travel Buddies Singles Travel Club (✆ 800/998-9099; www.travelbuddies worldwide.com), based in Canada, runs small, intimate, single-friendly group trips and will match you with a roommate free of charge. **TravelChums** (✆ 212/787-2621; www.travelchums.com) is an Internet-only travel-companion matching service with elements of a personals-type site, hosted by the respected New York–based Shaw Guides travel service.

Many reputable tour companies offer singles-only trips. **Singles Travel International** (✆ 877/765-6874; www.singlestravelintl.com) offers singles-only trips to places such as London, Fiji, and the Greek Islands. **Backroads** (✆ 800/462-2848; www.backroads.com) offers more than 160 active-travel trips to 30 destinations worldwide, including Bali, Morocco, and Costa Rica.

STAYING CONNECTED

Internet Access Away from Home

Internet cafes in Southeast Asia are many and affordable, preferable to expensive hotel business centers (you'll also meet lots of fellow travelers at Internet cafes). Of course, using your own laptop or PDA gives you the most flexibility, but connections in hotels are expensive and wireless hotspots are, as yet, few.

WITHOUT YOUR OWN COMPUTER

In most parts of Southeast Asia, you'll find **Internet cafes** on every street corner. Backpacker ghettos are always a good bet for finding cheap and reliable service. Avoid **hotel business centers** unless you're willing to pay exorbitant rates.

Most major airports now have **Internet kiosks** scattered throughout their gates. These give you basic Web access for a per-minute fee that's usually higher than cybercafe prices.

WITH YOUR OWN COMPUTER

More and more hotels, cafes, and retailers are signing on as Wi-Fi (wireless fidelity) "hotspots." Some places provide **free wireless networks.** With your own wireless-capable computer, connection is a snap.

If Wi-Fi is not available, most business-class hotels offer dataports for laptop modems, some using an Ethernet network cable. You can bring your own cables, but most hotels offer them as well. In addition, major Internet service providers (ISPs) have **local access numbers** around the world, allowing you to go online by placing a local call. Check your ISP's website or call its toll-free number and ask how you can use your current account away from home, and how much it will cost.

Wherever you go, bring a **connection kit** of the right power and phone adapters, a spare phone cord, and a spare Ethernet network cable—or find out whether your hotel supplies them to guests.

Most Southeast Asian countries run on **220-volt electrical currents.** Some hotels have 110-volt service. Plugs are two-pronged, with either round or flat prongs. If you're coming from the U.S. and you must bring electrical appliances, bring your own converter and adapter (a surge protector is a good idea for a laptop, too). Check the "Fast Facts" section of individual country chapters for more details.

Cellphone Use

If your cellphone is on a GSM system, and you have a world-capable multiband phone, you can make and receive calls across civilized areas around much of the globe. Just call your wireless operator and ask for "international roaming" to be activated on your account. Unfortunately, per-minute charges can be high.

For many, **renting a phone** is a good idea. We suggest renting the phone before you leave home. North Americans can rent one before leaving home from **InTouch USA** (© 800/872-7626; www.intouchglobal.com) or **RoadPost** (© 888/290-1606 or 905/272-5665; www.roadpost.com). InTouch will also, for free, advise you on whether your existing phone will work overseas; simply call © 703/222-7161 between 9am and 4pm EST, or go to www.intouchglobal.com/travel.htm.

For trips of more than a few weeks spent in one country, **buying a phone** can be economically attractive, as many nations have cheap prepaid phone systems. Once you arrive at your destination, stop by a local cellphone shop and get the cheapest package.

True wilderness adventurers, or those heading to less-developed countries, should consider renting a **satellite phone ("satphone").** It's different from a cellphone in that it connects to satellites and works where there's no cellular signal or ground-based tower. Satphones are much more expensive to buy or rent than cellphones, however, and this cost, combined with the improved cellphone coverage throughout Southeast Asia, makes cellphones the much more sensible option.

ESCORTED GENERAL-INTEREST TOURS

Among the most experienced and knowledgeable tour operators specializing in Southeast Asia are **Absolute Asia** and **Asia Transpacific Journeys.** In-country tour providers **Diethelm** and **Exotissimo** can do anything from arranging deluxe tours to just helping out with small details or bookings. Most companies allow clients to design their own trip or deviate from exact schedules (often at a small cost).

Companies such as **Intrepid,** among others, offer unique itineraries for solo travelers. See individual destination chapters for other in-country tour operators.

Here are the top outfitters:

- **Abercrombie & Kent** (1520 Kensington Rd., Ste. 212, Oakbrook, IL 60523; ℂ **800/554-7016;** fax 630/954-3324; www.abercrombieandkent.com) offers Southeast Asia programs with numerous comprehensive itineraries. This well known luxury-tour operator can take you to Thailand (on spa tours too), Cambodia, Vietnam, Indonesia, and Laos, with stays at the finest hotels in Southeast Asia, such as the Oriental in Bangkok and the Sofitel Metropole in Hanoi.

- **Absolute Asia** (180 Varick St., 16th Floor, New York, NY 10014; ℂ **800/736-8187;** fax 212/627-4090; www.absoluteasia.com), founded in 1989, offers an array of innovative itineraries, specializing in individual or small-group tours customized to your interests, with experienced local guides and excellent accommodations. Talk to these folks about tours that feature art, cuisine, religion, antiques, photography, wildlife study, archaeology, and soft adventure—they can plan a specialized trip to see just about anything you can dream up for any length of time. They can also book you on excellent coach programs in Indochina.

- **Asia Transpacific Journeys** (2995 Center Green Court, Boulder, CO 80301; ℂ **800/642-2742** or 303/443-6789; fax 303/443-7078; www.asiatranspacific. com) coordinates tours to every corner of South and Southeast Asia and the Pacific. It deals with small groups and custom programs that include luxury accommodations. The flagship package, the 23-day "Passage to Indochina" tour, takes you through the major attractions of Laos, Vietnam, and Cambodia with a well planned itinerary, and it is but one of many fun tours that promote cultural understanding. It's a model of sustainable tourism and a highly recommended choice.

- **Backroads** (801 Cedar St., Berkeley, CA 94710; ℂ **800/462-2848** or 510/527-1555; fax 510/527-1444; www.backroads.com), the cycling and hiking specialist, has an 11-day bike tour of Vietnam and Angkor Wat, an 8-day Thailand Golden Triangle tour, and others. Check out the website; Backroads is always coming up with innovative itineraries in the region.

- **Diethelm Travel** (Kian Gwan Building II, 140/1 Wireless Rd., Bangkok 10330, Thailand; ℂ **662/660-7000;** fax 662/660-7020; www.diethelmtravel.com), a Swiss-based tour company, has offices throughout the region (it's a popular choice for European tour groups). The folks here are friendly and helpful; they also operate as de facto tourist information centers in places such as Laos. Diethelm has full tour programs and, like Exotissimo (see below), can help with any details for travelers in-country, arrange car rental or vans for small groups, and offer discount options to all locations.

- **Exotissimo Travel** (40 bis, Rue du fg Poissonnière, 75010 Paris, France, ℂ **149/490-360,** fax 149/490-369; or Saigon Trade Center, 37 Ton Duc Thang, District 1, Ho Chi Minh City, Vietnam, ℂ **08/825-1723,** fax 08/829-5800; www.exotissimo. com), a French outfit and outbound (in-country) agency with offices in every major city in the region, has excellent guides on-site. Agents not only can arrange all-inclusive tours, but also are helpful with all travel details, from ticketing to visas. See the office locations in each chapter.

- **Imaginative Traveler** (1 Betts Ave., Martlesham Heath, Suffolk IP5 7RH, U.K.; ℂ **0800/316-2717;** fax 0280/742-3045; www.imaginative-traveler.com), a U.K.-based firm, gets rave reviews for organizing all sorts of bicycling, trekking, and motorcycling adventures throughout Southeast Asia, particularly Indochina.

- **Intrepid Travel** (11 Spring St., Fitzroy, Victoria, 3065 Australia; ℭ **613/9473-2626,** or 877/488-1616 in the U.S.; fax 613/9419-4426; www.intrepidtravel.com), a popular Australian operator, is probably the best choice for an off-the-beaten-track tour of Asia. Intrepid caters trips for the culturally discerning, those with humanitarian goals, those in search of comfort and adventure, those on a budget, or those looking for a looser structure and lots of options. Its name is its motto, and with some of the best guides in Asia, these folks will take you to the back of beyond safely, in style, and with lots of laughs.

SPECIAL-INTEREST TRIPS

For cultural tours and museum tours, contact any of the smaller local travel agents listed in each chapter. For the amateur ethnographer, contact any of the ecotour outfitters below or those listed in specific sections (particularly in the north of Thailand, Laos, Vietnam, or western Cambodia).

OUTDOOR ADVENTURES & ECOTOURS   Adventure-seekers can find any number of small outfitters in many parts of Southeast Asia. Consider first what kind of terrain you'd like to explore—the choices are anything from jungle to dry plains, coastal estuaries to inland rivers. The best areas to get out and get your boots wet are in the farthest reaches of Thailand, Laos, and Vietnam.

In the north of Thailand, go with **Contact Travel** (420/3 Changklan Rd., Chiang Mai; ℭ **05320-4664;** fax 05327-9505; www.activethailand.com) for cycling, off-road, and other eco-adventures. In the far south of Thailand, **Paddle Asia** (9/71 Thanon Rasdanusorn, Phuket; ℭ **07624-0952;** fax 07621-6145; www.paddleasia. com) has some of the best nature kayaking trips—you're guaranteed to see some exciting wildlife.

In Laos, **Green Discovery** (P.O. Box 9811, Hang Boun Rd., Ban Hay Sook, Vientaine; ℭ **021/264528;** www.greendiscoverylaos.com) runs great rafting and kayaking adventures anywhere in the country and has some unique village and cultural tours as well.

In the north of Vietnam, the folks at **Handspan** (80 Ma May St., Hanoi; ℭ **04/04-926-2828;** fax 04/926-2383; www.handspan.com) as well as **Buffalo Tours** (94 Ma May St., Hanoi; ℭ **04/828-0702;** www.buffalotours.com) put together exciting kayaking adventures in Halong Bay, hiking trips to Sapa, and jeep trips up to Dien Bien Phu. In central Vietnam, the old French colonial hill station of Dalat plays host to a great outfitter, **Phat Tire Ventures** (73 Truong Cong Dinh, Dalat; ℭ **063/829-422;** fax 063/820-331; www.phattireventures.com), which can help you rock climb, mountain bike, or trek with the most professional guides and experienced technicians.

In Malaysia, **Asian Overland Services** (ℭ **03/4252-9100;** fax 03/4257-1133; www.asianoverland.com.my) offers homestays in Taman Negara national park, Lemanak longhouse stays (Sarawak), diving off Sipadan Island, and a number of diverse tours planned with sensitivity to the environment and local cultures.

In Bali, **Sobek Tours** (ℭ **361/287059**), **Bali Discovery Tours** (ℭ **361/286283;** www.balidiscovery.com), and **Bali Adventure Tours** (ℭ **361/721480;** www.bali adventuretours.com) can both arrange fun day and overnight itineraries to volcanoes, the jungle, and rural villages.

The folks at **Exotissimo Travel** have offices throughout Southeast Asia and are the best for arranging all kinds of rural adventures. See individual chapters for office locations.

DIVING TRIPS   There are more dive outfits in Southeast Asia than we could possibly list. Be sure to choose a PADI-accredited dive company and ask lots of questions before any trip: What is the ratio of diver to instructor? Does the company have its own boat?

For details, check specific chapters of this book. In Thailand, look under **Phuket** or **Ko Tao;** in Vietnam, try **Nha Trang;** in Cambodia, **Sihanoukville;** in Malaysia, **Langkawi.**

COOKING SCHOOLS   The varied cuisine of the countries of Southeast Asia is a veritable banquet for the gourmet or the fearless eater, and there's no better way to learn about and participate in a culture than to take a cooking class. Opportunities abound.

In Thailand, a favorite option is the upscale **Blue Elephant Restaurant and Cooking School** (233 S. Sathorn Rd., Bangkok; ✆ **02673-9353;** www.blue elephant.com), set in an old mansion in the heart of the city. The restaurant is a popular luxury chain from Europe that has returned to its roots and set up shop in the Thai capital. It's not to be missed. In the north of Thailand, try the **Chiang Mai Cookery School** (47/2 Moonmuang Rd., Chiang Mai; ✆ **05320-6388;** www.thai cookeryschool.com). In the far south, there are lots of small resorts with cooking schools attached.

In northern Laos, enjoy a fun and informative day at **Tamnak Lao Restaurant and Cooking School** (Sakhalin Rd., Ban Wat Sene, Luang Prabang; ✆ **071/252-525**), where you'll not only get the dish on Lao specialties and some unique derivations, but also learn a good bit about local culture, history, and language.

In central Vietnam, Ms. Vy, who runs the **Mermaid (Nhu Y) Restaurant** (02 Tran Phu St., Hoi An; ✆ **0510/861-527;** www.hoianhospitality.com) and several other establishments in town, offers great cooking programs of varying length.

Gourmands in Singapore shouldn't miss a chance to take a quick course at the **Raffles Culinary Academy** (✆ **65/6412-1256;** www.raffles.com). Whole-day courses on Asian and Western haute cuisine are led by chefs from the grand hotel's acclaimed restaurants.

In Bali, try **Bumbu Bali** (✆ **361/774502**) in the south for Heinz von Holzen's informative cooking classes. The **Seasalt** restaurant (✆ **363/41011**), located in the Alila Manggis hotel (see p. 619), holds cooking classes. Executive chef Chris Salans gives gourmet French-Indonesian cooking classes at his restaurant **Mosaic** (✆ **361/975768**), which is also well worth a trip for a meal.

TIPS ON ACCOMMODATIONS

Affordable luxury is the name of the game in the countries of Southeast Asia. For what you might pay for a cracker-box room in big cities in the U.S. and Europe, you can go in style in Indochina and the countries on the Malay Peninsula. Pay more than $100, and you'll live like royalty. Budget travelers and young backpackers flock to the region, and a big part of the charm is spending $2 to $5 per night; it makes the budget go on and on. If your trip is short, live it up. Go for a luxury room and take advantage of affordable spa treatments (at a fraction of what you'd pay elsewhere). Midrange boutique hotels and rustic eco-friendly rural resorts are also a new trend as developers discover that *refurbished* is cool, and that location—whether overlooking the Mekong or set in a tropical rainforest—is everything.

You'll find many of the major chains represented in the region. **Sheraton** has hotels throughout Thailand, in Singapore, and in the major stops in Vietnam. **Inter-Continental** has high-end business properties in Hanoi, Bangkok, Phnom Penh, and Singapore. **Hilton** has fine properties in Hanoi (Vietnam), Bangkok and Phuket (Thailand), throughout Malaysia and Singapore, and on Bali. The French hoteliers at **Accor** host a number of **Sofitel** and **Novotel** hotels in the region; many of the big-city properties are aimed at the business market, but in Vietnam Sofitel takes the cake with some of the most unique refurbished hotels going, and in Cambodia it has a top resort as well. **Four Seasons** has fine properties in Bangkok, Singapore, Kuala Lumpur, and outside of Chiang Mai. **JW Marriott** has a hotel in Bangkok and a luxury resort on Phuket. **Le Meridien** boasts top resorts and golf in Thailand and Bali (Indonesia).

There are also a few good local chains. The **Amari** group is a Swiss-managed hotel chain with semiluxurious properties in all of the major stops in Thailand; service is conscientious and there is a good consistency among its many hotels (and good rates). In Vietnam, and now Cambodia, the **Victoria** hotels are a charming blend of atmosphere and connection to place, without sacrificing all of the comforts of home. **Pansea** hotels, now individually branded under the management of the luxury **Orient Express** group, host some of the most luxurious sanctuaries that take you away from it all but remind you of local culture—find them in Laos, Thailand, and Cambodia. **Aman Resorts** are in a class all their own, with their sprawling villa properties in Indonesia, Cambodia, and soon in Laos, all at rock-star prices.

Villa rental is a popular choice in island destinations. Balinese villas are a particular steal, best over a longer period of time and with hired staff. In places such as Thailand's Phuket, you'll find timeshares and long-term rates for private, serviced, beachside places that are quite enticing (beware the hard sell, though).

Each of the countries in Southeast Asia sets its own star standards for hotels, usually one through five. Note that a five-star might only be rated so because of the quantity, not quality, of services offered.

SUGGESTED ITINERARIES

Routes through the region are as varied as the ragtag bunch that travels them. With the many convenient air connections, you can choose your destinations and connect them as you like, but here are a few suggestions to get you started.

TOURING INDOCHINA Clockwise or counterclockwise routes starting in Bangkok and including northern Thailand, Laos, Vietnam, and Cambodia are popular and avoid boring backtracking. Connecting northern Thailand with Laos by boat is appealing, and flying from Vientiane, the Lao capital, to Hanoi or Ho Chi Minh City is a better choice than the rough overland route (which also leaves you in the middle of the north-south route, whereas a flight will get you to a terminus). After a sweep down the coast of Vietnam, connect with Cambodia overland (or by boat from the Mekong Delta) and continue on to Angkor Wat by bus, boat, or plane. There is frequent air service between Angkor Wat and Bangkok.

This itinerary can take anywhere from a few weeks to 6 months, depending on your inclinations. Highlights include the historic temple towns of Thailand, hill-tribe treks throughout the region, sleepy Luang Prabang, busy Hanoi and Ho Chi Minh City (Saigon), all of the stops along coastal Vietnam (historical and recreational), and, of course, Angkor Wat. After a trip like this, you'll have earned your time on the beaches of Thailand, Malaysia, or Bali.

HEADING DOWN THE MALAY PENINSULA   Starting in Bangkok and heading south, you can connect the major resort destinations of southern Thailand with a tour down the length of Malaysia to Singapore and end up in Bali.

You can do this trip in a fly-by-night week or stretch it out over a few months. Highlights include pristine beaches (maybe even *The Beach*) in Thailand; great food, affordable cosmopolitan comforts, and cultural stops in Malaysia; shop-'til-you-drop spending in Singapore; and the tranquil beaches of Bali.

BASING YOURSELF IN A HUB   From Bangkok, Singapore, or other major urban centers, travelers can make short forays into the countryside or to the resort of their choice from a comfortable, familiar base in a big city with all the comforts of home. Many visitors aim for the cultural and historic sights recommended by UNESCO—places such as Luang Prabang (Laos); Hoi An, Hue, and Halong Bay (Vietnam); Sukhothai and Ayuthaya (Thailand); and the temples of Angkor Wat (Cambodia)—all reachable via larger cities. Or start in a comfy hub and connect with local outfitters for short adventure trips before coming back to hot showers and room service.

AIRLINE WEBSITES

MAJOR AIRLINES

Aeroméxico
www.aeromexico.com

Air France
www.airfrance.com

Air India
www.airindia.com

Air Jamaica
www.airjamaica.com

Air New Zealand
www.airnewzealand.com

Air Tahiti Nui
www.airtahitinui-usa.com

Alitalia
www.alitalia.com

Alaska Airlines/ Horizon Air
www.alaskaair.com

American Airlines
www.aa.com

Aviacsa (Mexico & Southern US)
www.aviacsa.com.mx

Bahamasair
www.bahamasair.com

British Airways
www.british-airways.com

Cape Air
www.flycapeair.com

Caribbean Airlines (formerly BWIA)
www.caribbean-airlines.com

China Airlines
www.china-airlines.com

Continental Airlines
www.continental.com

Cubana
www.cubana.cu

Delta Air Lines
www.delta.com

EgyptAir
www.egyptair.com

El Al Airlines
www.elal.co.il

Emirates Airlines
www.emirates.com

Finnair
www.finnair.com

Frontier Airlines
www.frontierairlines.com

Hawaiian Airlines
www.hawaiianair.com

Iberia Airlines
www.iberia.com

Icelandair
www.icelandair.com

Israir Airlines
www.israirairlines.com

Japan Airlines
www.jal.co.jp

JetBlue Airways
www.jetblue.com

Korean Air
www.koreanair.com

Lan Airlines
www.lan.com

Lufthansa
www.lufthansa.com

Midwest Airlines
www.midwestairlines.com

Nantucket Airlines
www.nantucketairlines.com

North American Airlines
www.flynaa.com

Olympic Airlines
www.olympicairlines.com

Qantas Airways
www.qantas.com

Pan Am Clipper Connection
www.flypanam.com

PenAir (The Spirit of Alaska)
www.penair.com

Philippine Airlines
www.philippineairlines.com

South African Airways
www.flysaa.com

Swiss Air
www.swiss.com

TACA
www.taca.com

Thai Airways International
www.thaiair.com

Turkish Airlines
www.thy.com

United Airlines
www.united.com

US Airways
www.usairways.com

Virgin America
www.virginamerica.com

Virgin Atlantic Airways
www.virgin-atlantic.com

BUDGET AIRLINES

Aegean Airlines
www.aegeanair.com

Aer Lingus
www.aerlingus.com

AirTran Airways
www.airtran.com

Air Berlin
www.airberlin.com

BMI Baby
www.bmibaby.com

Click Mexicana
www.clickmx.com

easyJet
www.easyjet.com

Frontier Airlines
www.frontierairlines.com

go! (Hawaii based)
www.iflygo.com

Interjet
www.interjet.com.mx

JetBlue Airways
www.jetblue.com

Jetstar (Australia)
www.jetstar.com

Ryanair
www.ryanair.com

Southwest Airlines
www.southwest.com

Spirit Airlines
www.spiritair.com

Volaris
www.volaris.com.mx

WestJet
www.westjet.com

Index

A

Abdul Gafoor Mosque
(Singapore), 477–478
Abercrombie & Kent, 365, 641
Absolute Asia, 641
Accommodations, 643–644
best, 7–9
Laos, 192
Thailand, 41
Adventure Divers (Thailand), 87
Aeroline, 515, 524, 546
A Famosa (Porta de Santiago;
Melaka), 544
African-American travelers, 638
Agung Rai Museum and Gallery
(Ubud), 614
Air Asia, 40, 99, 122, 142, 150,
171, 515, 516
Airport Express (Bangkok), 45
Airport Information (Bangkok), 45
The Airport (Sihanoukville), 407
Air travel, 624, 625
airline websites, 645–646
Bali, 585
Cambodia, 368, 369
Laos, 189, 190
Malaysia, 514–516
Singapore, 421–422
Thailand, 39, 40, 45
Vietnam, 245
Al-Abrar Mosque (Singapore),
473
Alcazar (Pattaya), 88
Alexandre Yersin Museum
(Nha Trang), 317
Allez Boo (Ho Chi Minh City),
355
All Lao Services (Luang
Prabang), 213
Alsagoff Arab School
(Singapore), 479
Amarinda Vinichai Hall
(Bangkok), 70
Amazon Bar (Hanoi), 275
Amber Room (Ho Chi Minh City),
355
Amed (Bali), 621
American Express
Bali, 588
Cambodia, 371
Laos, 192
Thailand, 42, 49
traveler's checks, 630
Vietnam, 248
Hanoi, 255
Ho Chi Minh City, 338
AM Minimart (Vientiane), 207
Amulet market (Bangkok), 71
The Angkor What? (Siem
Reap), 401
Angkor Thom (Angkor Wat),
399–400
Angkor Village (Siem Reap), 401

Angkor Wat (Cambodia),
387, 398–399
Animal and Bird Encounters
(Singapore), 490
Ann Tours (Vietnam),
254, 278, 335, 357
Antonio Blanco Museum (Ubud),
614
Ao Kiew (Ko Samet), 89
Ao Prao (Ko Samet), 90
Apricot Gallery
Hanoi, 274
Ho Chi Minh City, 354
Apsara Dance (Siem Reap), 401
Aquaria KLCC (Kuala Lumpur),
532–533
Arab Street (Singapore)
restaurants, 455–456
shopping, 500
sights and attractions,
479–480
Ark Bar (Ko Samui), 114
Armenian Church (Singapore),
460–461
Army Museum (Hanoi), 267
The ArtScience Museum
(Singapore), 467
The Arts House (Singapore), 507
Asasax Art Gallery (Phnom
Penh), 386
Aseana Fashion (Kuala Lumpur),
537
Asia Books (Bangkok), 49
Asian Civilisations Museum
(Singapore), 461
Asian Overland Services
(Malaysia), 568, 642
Asia Transpacific Journeys,
365, 641
The Astana (Sarawak), 566
ATMs (automated-teller
machines), 630
Authentique Interiors (Ho Chi
Minh City), 354
Ayutthaya Historical Study
Center (Thailand), 80
Ayutthaya (Thailand), 79–80

B

Baan Celadon (Chiang Mai), 168
Baan Khily Gallery (Luang
Prabang), 225
Baba Nyonya Heritage Museum
(Melaka), 542–543
Bac Ha Market (Vietnam), 281
Backroads, 641
Badan Warisan (Kuala Lumpur),
533
Ba Dinh District (Hanoi),
267–270
Bajau people, 569–570
Bakeng Hill (Phnom Bakeng;
near Angkor Wat), 399
Balcony (Bangkok), 77
Bali Adventure Tours, 597, 615,
642
Bali Collection (Nusa Dua), 605

Bali Discovery Tours, 597, 642
Bali Golf and Country Club, 605
Bali (Indonesia), 17, 576–623
accommodations, 586
American Express, 588
business hours, 588
currency and currency
exchange, 583–584, 629
customs regulations, 583
drug laws, 588
electricity, 588
embassies and consulates,
588
emergencies, 588
entry requirements, 583, 626
geography and topology, 577
getting around, 585–586
health and safety, 584–585,
588–589
history of, 577–578
holidays and events, 584
hospitals, 588
language, 588
liquor laws, 588
mail. 588
money matters, 583–584
people and culture, 580–581
people and culture of, 20–21
planning your trip to,
583–588
police, 588
restaurants, 586–587
shopping, 587–588
suggested itinerary, 581–583
telephones, 587, 589
time zone, 589
tipping, 589
toilets, 589
traveling to, 585
visitor information, 583
water, 589
when to go, 584
Bali Safari & Marine Park, 617
Bamboo Bar (Bangkok), 76
Bamboo Island (Thailand), 87
Bamboo train (Battambang),
404
Bambou Company
Hoi An, 307
Hue, 290
Bangkok Airways, 40, 90, 101,
122, 142, 148
Bangkok Golf Club, 74
Bangkok Mass Transit System
(BTS skytrain), 46–47
Bangkok (Thailand), 44–80
accommodations, 51–60
American Express, 49
banks and currency
exchange, 49
bookstores, 49
buses, 45, 48
cultural pursuits, 73–74
embassies, 49–50
emergencies, 50
getting around, 46–49
hospitals, 50
Internet access, 50
layout of, 46